A treatise on the law of torts in obligations arising from civil wrongs in the common law.

Frederick Pollock

A treatise on the law of torts in obligations arising from civil wrongs in the common law.
Pollock, Frederick, Sir
collection ID ocm20278282
Reproduction from Harvard Law School Library
Includes index.
St. Louis : F.H. Thomas Law Book Co, 1894.
xxvi, 803 p. ; 23 cm.

The Making of Modern Law collection of legal archives constitutes a genuine revolution in historical legal research because it opens up a wealth of rare and previously inaccessible sources in legal, constitutional, administrative, political, cultural, intellectual, and social history. This unique collection consists of three extensive archives that provide insight into more than 300 years of American and British history. These collections include:

Legal Treatises, 1800-1926: over 20,000 legal treatises provide a comprehensive collection in legal history, business and economics, politics and government.

Trials, 1600-1926: nearly 10,000 titles reveal the drama of famous, infamous, and obscure courtroom cases in America and the British Empire across three centuries.

Primary Sources, 1620-1926: includes reports, statutes and regulations in American history, including early state codes, municipal ordinances, constitutional conventions and compilations, and law dictionaries.

These archives provide a unique research tool for tracking the development of our modern legal system and how it has affected our culture, government, business – nearly every aspect of our everyday life. For the first time, these high-quality digital scans of original works are available via print-on-demand, making them readily accessible to libraries, students, independent scholars, and readers of all ages.

The BiblioLife Network

This project was made possible in part by the BiblioLife Network (BLN), a project aimed at addressing some of the huge challenges facing book preservationists around the world. The BLN includes libraries, library networks, archives, subject matter experts, online communities and library service providers. We believe every book ever published should be available as a high-quality print reproduction; printed on-demand anywhere in the world. This insures the ongoing accessibility of the content and helps generate sustainable revenue for the libraries and organizations that work to preserve these important materials.

The following book is in the "public domain" and represents an authentic reproduction of the text as printed by the original publisher. While we have attempted to accurately maintain the integrity of the original work, there are sometimes problems with the original work or the micro-film from which the books were digitized. This can result in minor errors in reproduction. Possible imperfections include missing and blurred pages, poor pictures, markings and other reproduction issues beyond our control. Because this work is culturally important, we have made it available as part of our commitment to protecting, preserving, and promoting the world's literature.

GUIDE TO FOLD-OUTS MAPS and OVERSIZED IMAGES

The book you are reading was digitized from microfilm captured over the past thirty to forty years. Years after the creation of the original microfilm, the book was converted to digital files and made available in an online database.

In an online database, page images do not need to conform to the size restrictions found in a printed book. When converting these images back into a printed bound book, the page sizes are standardized in ways that maintain the detail of the original. For large images, such as fold-out maps, the original page image is split into two or more pages

Guidelines used to determine how to split the page image follows:

- Some images are split vertically; large images require vertical and horizontal splits.
- For horizontal splits, the content is split left to right.
- For vertical splits, the content is split from top to bottom.
- For both vertical and horizontal splits, the image is processed from top left to bottom right.

A TREATISE

ON THE

LAW OF TORTS

IN OBLIGATIONS ARISING FROM CIVIL
WRONGS IN THE COMMON LAW.

BY

SIR FREDERICK POLLOCK, BART.

OF LINCOLN'S INN, BARRISTER AT LAW,
CORPUS PROFESSOR OF JURISPRUDENCE IN THE UNIVERSITY OF OXFORD,
LATE FELLOW OF TRINITY COLLEGE, CAMBRIDGE, AND
HONORARY DOCTOR OF LAWS IN THE UNIVERSITIES OF EDINBURGH AND DUBLIN

Author of "Principles of Contract," "A Digest of the Law of Partnership," &c

NEW AMERICAN—FROM THIRD ENGLISH EDITION.

ELABORATED WITH NOTES AND REFERENCES TO AMERICAN CASES.

By JAMES AVERY WEBB,

Of the Memphis Bar.

ST. LOUIS:
THE F. H. THOMAS LAW BOOK CO.
1894.

Entered according to Act of Congress in the year 1894, by
THE F. H. THOMAS LAW BOOK CO.,
In the office of the Librarian of Congress, at Washington.

OCT 4 1919

St Louis, Mo
Press of Nixon Jones Printing Co

TO HONORABLE

HENRY C. CALDWELL,

JUDGE OF THE UNITED STATES CIRCUIT COURT OF APPEALS OF THE EIGHTH JUDICIAL CIRCUIT.

Recognizing our indebtedness to you for the suggestion that the text of POLLOCK ON TORTS was the foundation of the greatest book ever published on this important branch of the law, we take the liberty to dedicate this American edition to you. In doing so, permit us to express the hope that the notes which have been prepared by our editor may tend to strengthen your exalted opinion of the practical value of this book, which you have so aptly styled "A Legal Classic."

THE PUBLISHERS.

PREFACE TO THE NEW AMERICAN EDITION.

The fact that the English edition of this book was acknowledged by distinguished members of the American Bar, to be a scholarly treatment of the law of torts, replete with learning, founded on research, and clear in the exposition of the fundamental principles and explicit in their application to special cases, led the publishers to believe that an American edition would fill a want long felt by students and practitioners in this country. In annotating this book the editor has not altered the text and notes of the author but has added such notes and references as seemed pertinent. The editor's notes are usually arranged under headings, either the same or very near the same as those used in the text, so that no difficulty will be met in identifying by the paragraph headings the connection between the text and the notes. Occasionally American cases upon single phrases or sentences in the text are cited among the English notes. These are inclosed in brackets [   ].

Generally, practically all the American cases are cited, but upon a few subjects like "Damages," it was found impracticable to refer to more than the late cases and the leading cases. The agreement or disagreement of the English and American authorities is usually mentioned in the editor's notes and where they are not in harmony the points of difference are specified and briefly discussed.

J. A. WEBB.

MEMPHIS, TENN.
April, 1894.

TO THE HONOURABLE

OLIVER WENDELL HOLMES, JUNR.,

A JUSTICE OF THE SUPREME JUDICIAL COURT OF THE
COMMONWEALTH OF MASSACHUSETTS

My Dear Holmes,

A preface is a formal and a tedious thing at best; it is at its worst when the author, as has been common in law-books, writes of himself in the third person. Yet there are one or two things I wish to say on this occasion, and cannot well say in the book itself; by your leave, therefore, I will so far trespass on your friendship as to send the book to you with an open letter of introduction. It may seem a mere artifice, but the assurance of your sympathy will enable me to speak more freely and naturally, even in print, than if my words were directly addressed to the profession at large. Nay more, I would fain sum up in this slight token the brotherhood that subsists, and we trust ever shall between all true followers of the Common Law here and on your side of the water; and give it to be understood, for my own part, how much my work owes to you and to others in America, mostly citizens of your own Commonwealth, of whom some are known to me only by their published writing, some by commerce of letters; there are some also, fewer than I could wish, whom I have had the happiness of meeting face to face.

When I came into your jurisdiction, it was from the Province of Quebec, a part of Her Majesty's dominions which is governed, as you know, by its old French law, lately repaired and beautified in a sort of Revised Version of the Code Napoleon. This, I doubt not, is an excellent thing in its place. And it is indubitable that, in a political sense, the English lawyer who travels from Montreal to Boston exchanges the rights of a natural-born subject for the comity accorded by the United States to friendly aliens. But when his eye is caught, in the every-day advertisements of the first Boston newspaper he takes up, by those words — "Commonwealth of Massachusetts: Suffolk to wit" — no amount of political geography will convince him that he has gone into foreign parts and has not rather come home. Of Harvard and its Law School I will say only this, that I have endeavored to turn into practical account the lessons of what I saw and heard there, and that this present book is in some measure the outcome of that endeavor. It contains the substance of between two and three years' lectures in the Inns of Court, and nearly everything advanced in it has been put into shape after, or concurrently with, free oral exposition and discussion of the leading cases.

My claim to your good will, however, does not rest on these grounds alone. I claim it because the purpose of this book is to show that there really is a Law of Torts, not merely a number of rules of law about various kinds of torts — that this is a true living branch of the Common Law, not a collection of heterogeneous instances. In such a cause I make bold to count on your sympathy, though I will not presume on your final opinion. The contention is certainly not superfluous, for it seems opposed to the weight of recent opinion among those who have fairly faced the problem. You will recognize in my armoury some weapons of your own forging, and if they are ineffective, I must have handled them worse than I am willing, in any reasonable terms of humility, to suppose.

It is not surprising, in any case, that a complete theory of Torts is yet to seek, for the subject is altogether mod-

on. The earliest text-book I have been able to find is a meagre and unthinking digest of "The Law of Actions on the Case for Torts and Wrongs," published in 1720, remarkable chiefly for the depths of historical ignorance which it occasionally reveals. The really scientific treatment of principles begins only with the decisions of the last fifty years; their development belongs to that classical period of our jurisprudence which in England came between the Common Law Procedure Act and the Judicature Act. Lord Blackburn and Lord Bramwell, who then rejoiced in their strength, are still with us.* It were impertinent to weigh too nicely the fame of living masters; but I think we may securely anticipate posterity in ranking the names of these (and I am sure we cannot more greatly honor them) with the name of their colleague Willes, a consummate lawyer too early cut off, who did not live to see the full fruit of his labor.

Those who know Mr. Justice Willes will need no explanation of this book being dedicated to his memory. But for others I will say that he was not only a man of profound learning in the law, joined with extraordinary and varied knowledge of other kinds, but one of those whose knowledge is radiant, and kindles answering fire. To set down all I owe to him is beyond my means, and might be beyond your patience; but to you at least I shall say much in saying that from Willes I learnt to taste the Year Books, and to pursue the history of the law in authorities which not so long ago were collectively and compendiously despised as "black letter." It is strange to think that Manning was as one crying in the wilderness, and that even Kent dismissed the Year Books as of doubtful value for any purpose, and certainly not worth reprinting. You have had a noble revenge in editing Kent, and perhaps the laugh is on our side by this time.

---

* We have now (1892) to lament the loss of Lord Bramwell.

But if any man still finds offence, you and I are incorrigible offenders, and like to maintain one another therein as long as we have breath; and when you have cast your eye on the historical note added to this book by my friend Mr. F. W. Maitland, I think you will say that we shall not want for good suit.

One more thing I must mention concerning Willes, that once and again he spoke or wrote to me to the effect of desiring to see the Law of Obligations methodically treated in English. This is an additional reason for calling him to mind on the completion of a work which aims at being a contribution of materials towards that end; of materials only, for a book on Torts added to a book on Contracts does not make a treatise on Obligations. Nevertheless this is a book of principles if it is anything. Details are used, not in the manner of a digest, but so far as they seem called for to develop and illustrate the principles; and I shall be more than content if in that regard you find nothing worse than omission to complain of. But the toils and temptations of the craft are known to you at first hand; I will not add the burden of apology to faults which you will be ready to forgive without it. As to other readers, I will hope that some students may be thankful for brevity where the conclusions are brief, and that, where a favourite topic has invited expatiation or digression, some practitioner may some day be helped to his case by it. The work is out of my hands, and will fare as it may deserve: in your hands, at any rate, it is sure of both justice and mercy.

I remain, yours very truly,

FREDERICK POLLOCK.

LINCOLNS INN,
Christmas Vacation, 1886.

TABLE OF CONTENTS.

Book I.
GENERAL PART.

CHAPTER I.
THE NATURE OF TORT IN GENERAL.

PAGE 1. Absence of authoritative definition.
    2 Historical distinctions.
    7. Personal wrongs.
    7. Wrongs to property.
    7. Wrongs affecting person and property
    8. Wilful wrongs.
    9. Wrongs unconnected with moral blame.
    11. Wrongs of imprudence and omission.
    13 Historical anomaly of law of trespass and conversion.
    13. Early forms of action.
    16. Rationalized version of law of trespass
    17. Analogies of Roman law.
    18. *Dolus* and *Culpa*.
    18. Liability *quasi ex delicto*.
    19. Summary of results.

CHAPTER II.
PRINCIPLES OF LIABILITY.

    22. Want of generality in early law.
    23. General duty not to do harm in modern law.
    24 Breach of specific legal duty.
    25. Duty of respecting property.
    25 Duties of diligence.
    26 Assumption of skill
    28 Exception of action under necessity

PAGE 29. Liability in relation to consequences of act or default.
31. Measure of damages.
32. "Immediate cause."
33. Liability for consequences of wilful act
35. "Natural consequences"
36. "Natural and probable" consequence.
40 Liability for consequences of trespass.
41 Consequences too remote.
42 Liability for negligence
43. Contrasted cases of non-liability and liability: Cox v. Burbidge; Lee v. Riley.
49. Metropolitan Rail. Co. v Jackson
50. Non-liability for consequences of unusual state of things Blyth v. Birmingham Waterworks Co.
51. Sharp v Powell.
52. Whether same rule holds for consequences of wilful wrong. Clark v Chambers.
54. Consequences natural in kind though not in circumstance
54 Damages for "nervous or mental shock"

CHAPTER III

PERSONS AFFECTED BY TORTS.

1. *Limitations of Personal Capacity.*

58. Personal status immaterial in law of tort but capacity material.
59. Exceptions: Convicts and aliens.
60. Infants
63 Married women the common law.
65 Married Women's Property Act, 1882
66. Common law liability of infants and married women
66. Corporations.
69. Responsibility of public bodies for management of works under their control.

2. *Effect of a Party's Death.*

71. *Actio personalis moritur cum persona*
74 Qu. of the extension of the rule in Osborn v. Gillett
75. Exceptions: Statutes of Edw. III. giving executors right of suit for trespasses.
76 Of Will. IV. as to injuries to property
76. No right of action for damage to personal estate consequential on personal injury.
77 Lord Campbell's Act: rights created by it

PAGE
78. Construction.
79. Interests of survivors distinct
80 Statutory cause of action is in substitution not cumulative.
80 Scottish and American laws
81 Right to follow property wrongfully taken or converted
83 Rule limited to recovery of specific property or its value· Phillips v Homfray

3 Liability for the Torts of Agents and Servants

84 Command of principal does not excuse agent's wrong
85 Cases of special duty, absolute or in nature of warranty, distinguished
86. Modes of liability for wrongful acts of others
87. Command and ratification.
88 Master and servant
89. Reason of master's liability.
90. Who is a servant.
94 Specific assumption of control
95 Temporary transfer of service
96 "Power of controlling the work" explained
97. What is in course of employment
98   (a) Execution of specific orders
98   (b) Negligence in conduct of master's business.
100   Departure or deviation from master's business
103   (c) Excess or mistake in execution of authority
104   Interference with passengers by guards, etc
106   Arrest of supposed offenders.
107.   Act wholly outside authority· master not liable
109.   (d) Wilful trespasses, etc , for master's purposes.
112   Fraud of agent or servant.
114.   Liability of firm for fraud of a partner
115 Injuries to servants by fault of fellow-servants
115 Common law rule of master's immunity.
116 Reason given in the later cases
118. Servants need not be about same kind of work.
119. Provided there is a general common object
121. Relative rank of servants immaterial.
126 Servants of sub-contractor.
126 Volunteer assistant on same footing as servant.
127 Exception where master interferes in person
127. Employers' Liability Act, 1880
128. Resulting complication of the law

CHAPTER IV.

GENERAL EXCEPTIONS.

PAGE 130 Conditions excluding liability for act *prima facie* wrongful
131 General and particular exceptions.

1. *Acts of State*

132. Acts of state.
133. General ground of exemption.
135. Local actions against viceroy or governor.
135 Power to exclude aliens
136. Acts of foreign powers
137. Summary.

2. *Judicial Acts.*

138. Judicial acts.
140. Liability by statute in special cases
140. Judicial acts of persons not judges.

3. *Executive Acts.*

141. Executive acts.
143. Acts of naval and military officers.
144. Of other public authorities
145 Indian Act XVIII. of 1850

4. *Quasi-judicial Acts.*

145. Acts of quasi-judicial discretion
146. Rules to be observed.
148. Absolute discretionary powers.
148. Whether duty judicial or ministerial Ashby v. White.

5. *Parental and Quasi-parental Authority.*

149 Authority of parents
150. Of custodians of lunatics

6. *Authorities of Necessity.*

151. Of the master of a ship.

7. *Damage Incident to Authorized Acts.*

152. Damage incidentally resulting from lawful act.
154. Damage from execution of authorized works.
155 No action for unavoidable damage
157. Care and caution required in exercise of discretionary powers

8. *Inevitable Accident.*

PAGE 160. Inevitable accident resulting from lawful act.
161. On principle such act excludes liability.
163. Apparent conflict of authorities
164. American decisions The Nitro-Glycerine Case (Sup Ct. U S)
166 Brown *v* Kendall (Mass.)
167. Other American cases.
168. English authorities. cases of trespass and shooting
171 Cases where exception allowed.

9. *Exercise of Common Rights*

174. Immunity in exercise of common rights.
177. Digging wells, etc., in a man's own land.
179 Chasemore *v.* Richards.
179 Other applications of same principle
182 Whether malice material in these cases.
183 Roman doctrine of "animus vicino nocendi."
184. No exclusive right to names

10. *Leave and Licence · Volenti non fit iniuria.*

185 Consent or acceptance of risk.
186. Express licence
186 Limits of consent.
190. Licence obtained by fraud.
190. Extended meaning of *volenti non fit iniuria.*
191. Relation of these cases to inevitable accident.
192 Knowledge of risk opposed to duty of warning
195 Cases between employers and workmen · Smith *v.* Baker.
197. Distinction where no negligence at all.
197 Distinction from cases where negligence is ground of action.

11 *Works of Necessity.*

199.

12. *Private Defence.*

201. Self-defence.
202. Killing of animals in defence of property.
203. Assertion of rights distinguished from self-defence.
204. Injury to third person in self-defence

13. *Plaintiff a Wrong-doer.*

205 Harm suffered by a wrong-doer.
208. Sunday travelling · conflict of opinion in U. S.
208 Cause of action connected with unlawful agreement

CHAPTER V

OF REMEDIES FOR TORTS

PAGE 209 Diversity of remedies.
- 210 Self-help
- 211. Judicial remedies. damages.
- 212. Nominal damages.
- 214. Nominal damages possible only when an absolute right is infringed.
- 215. Cases where the damage is the gist of the action
- 217 Peculiarity of law of defamation
- 217. Ordinary damages
- 219 Exemplary damages
- 222. Analogy of breach of promise of marriage to torts in this respect
- 222. Mitigation of damages
- 223. Concurrent but severable causes of action
- 224. Injunctions
- 226. On what principle granted
- 227. Former concurrent jurisdiction of common law and equity to give compensation for fraud
- 228 Special statutory remedies when exclusive
- 230 Joint wrong-doers
- 231. Rules as to contribution and indemnity
- 233. Supposed rule of trespass being " merged in felony "
- 236 No known means of enforcing the rule if it exists
- 237. Locality of wrongful act as affecting remedy in English Court.
- 237. Acts not wrongful by English law
- 238. Acts justified by local law
- 238. Act wrongful by both laws
- 239 Phillips v Eyre
- 242 Limitation of actions.
- 243. Suspension of the statute by disabilities
- 244. From what time action runs.
- 245. Special protection of justices, constables, etc
- 245 Exception of concealed fraud.
- 246 Conclusion of General Part

Book II

SPECIFIC WRONGS

CHAPTER VI

PERSONAL WRONGS

I Assault and Battery.

PAGE 217. What is a battery
219. What an assault
252 Excusable acts.
255. Self-defence
256. Menace distinguished from assault
258 Summary proceedings when a bar to civil action

II. False Imprisonment

259 What is false imprisonment.
262. Justification of arrest and imprisonment
264 Who is answerable.
267 Reasonable and probable cause.

III Injuries in Family Relations

269 Protection in personal relations
270 Historical accidents of the common law herein.
270. Trespass for taking away wife, etc , and *per quod servitium amisit*.
273. "Criminal conversation."
275. Enticing away servants.
276. Actions for seduction in modern practice.
280. Damages
282 Services of young child.
282. Capricious operation of the law
283. Constructive service in early cases
283 Intimidation of servants and tenants

CHAPTER VII.

DEFAMATION.

286. Civil and criminal jurisdiction
286 Slander and libel

1. Slander

PAGE 289. When slander is actionable.
290. Meaning of "*prima facie* libellous."
290. Special damage
292. Repetition of spoken words
292. Special damage involves definite temporal loss
294. Imputation of criminal offence
298. Charges of mere immorality not actionable
298. Slander of Women Act.
299. Imputation of contagious disease.
300. Evil-speaking of a man in the way of his business
303. Words indirectly causing damage to a man in his business

2. Defamation in General.

304. Defamation
305. "Implied malice"
306. What is publication.
309. Vicarious publication
311. Construction of words — Innuendo
314. Libellous tendency must be probable in law and proved in fact
315. Repetition and reports may be libellous

3. Exceptions

317. Exceptions — fair comment
320. What is open to comment, matter of law
322. Whether comment is fair, matter of fact
323. Justification on ground of truth
325. Must be substantially complete.
326. Defendant's belief immaterial.
326. Parliamentary and judicial immunity.
330. Other persons in judicial proceedings
331. Report of officers, etc.
331. Qualified immunity of "privileged communications."
332. Conditions of the privilege.
333. "Express malice"
335. What are privileged occasions
335. Moral or social duty
337. Self-protection.
338. Information for public good
340. Fair reports.
340. Parliamentary papers
340. Parliamentary debates and judicial proceedings
342. Volunteered reports
344. Excess of privilege.

PAGE
344. Honest belief is not necessarily reasonable belief
345. Power of jury in assessing damages
346. Statutory defences
346. Limits of interrogatories in action for libel.
346. Bad reputation of plaintiff
347. Injunctions.

CHAPTER VIII.

WRONGS OF FRAUD AND MALICE.

I. *Deceit*

348. Nature of the wrong
348. Concurrent jurisdiction of common law and equity.
349. Difficulties of the subject. complication with contract.
353. Questions of fraudulent intent
355. Fraud of agents
355 General conditions of right of action
356.   (a) Falsehood in fact.
360   Misrepresentations of law.
362   Falsehood by garbled statements.
362   (b) Knowledge or belief of defendant.
365.   Representations subsequently discovered to be untrue.
367   Reckless assertions
368   Breach of special duty to give correct information.
371   Estoppel. *Burrowes* v. *Lock:* former supposed rule of equity.
372.   (c) Intention of the statement.
373   Representations to class. Polhill *v* Walter
373   Denton *v* G. N. R Co.
374   Peek *v.* Gurney
375   (d) Reliance on the representation
377   Means of knowledge immaterial without independent inquiry
379   Perfunctory inquiry will not do
380.   Ambiguous statements.
380   (e) Lord Tenterden's Act.
382   *Quaere* as to law under Judicature Acts.
383   Misrepresentation by agents
386   Liability of corporations herein
387   Reason of an apparently hard law.

II *Slander of Title*

388. Slander of title.
389. Recent extensions of the principle.
391 Trade marks and trade names.

III. *Malicious Prosecution and Abuse of Process*

PAGE 392. Malicious prosecution.
397. Malicious civil proceedings.

IV. *Other Malicious Wrongs.*

401. Conspiracy.
406. Malicious interference with one's occupation
409.   Contract.
410.   Or franchise.
411.   Maintenance

CHAPTER IX.

WRONGS TO POSSESSION AND PROPERTY

I. *Duties Regarding Property Generally.*

412. Absolute duty to respect other's property
413. Title, justification, excuse
414. Title dependent on contract
415. Exceptional protection of certain dealings in good faith
416. Common law rights and remedies.
417. Possession and detention
419. Trespass and conversion.
420. Alternative remedies

II. *Trespass*

421. What shall be said a trespass.
423. *Quaere* concerning balloons.
424. Trespass to goods

III. *Injuries to Reversion.*

426. Wrongs to an owner not in possession

IV. *Waste*

427. What is waste.
429. Modern law of waste — tenants for life.
431. Landlord and tenant.

V. *Conversion.*

432. Relation of trover to trespass.
433. What amounts to conversion.

PAGE 437. Acts not amounting to conversion
439. Dealings under authority of apparent owner
441. Acts of servants.
442. Redelivery by bailees
443. Abuse of limited interest
446. Conversion by estoppel

VI. *Injuries between Tenants in Common*

447. Trespasses between tenants in common

VII. *Extended Protection of Possession*

449. Rights of *de facto* possessor against strangers
452. Rights of owner entitled to resume possession
453. Rights of derivative possessors
454. Possession derived through trespasser

VIII. *Wrongs to Easements, &c.*

456. Violation of incorporeal rights

IX. *Grounds of Justification and Excuse.*

457. Licence
459. Revocation of licence.
464. Distinction from grant as regards strangers.
465. Justification by law.
465. Re-entry herein of forcible entry
468. Fresh re-entry on trespasser
469. Recaption of goods.
471. Process of law: breaking doors
472. Distress
473. Damage feasant
474. Entry of distrainor.
475. Trespasses justified by necessity
477. Foxhunting not privileged
477. Trespass *ab initio*

X. *Remedies.*

480. Taking or retaking goods.
480. Costs where damages nominal
482. Injunctions.
483. Effect of changes in procedure.

CHAPTER X

NUISANCE

PAGE
- 484 Nuisance, public or private.
- 487 Special right of action for public nuisance.
- 488 Special damage must be shown.
- 491. Private nuisance, what
  Kinds of nuisance affecting —
  - 492. 1 Ownership.
  - 494 2. *Iuria in re aliena*.
  - 494 3 Convenience and enjoyment
- 496. Measure of nuisance
- 496 Injury to health need not be shown.
- 497. Plaintiff not disentitled by having come to the nuisance
- 499. Innocent or necessary character of offensive occupation, or convenience of place, no answer.
- 502. Modes of annoyance.
- 508. Injury common to the plaintiff with others
- 508. Injury caused by independent acts of different persons
- 508. Obstruction of lights
- 509. Nature of the right to light
- 510 Any substantial diminution is a wrong
- 511. Supposed rule as to angle of forty-five degrees.
- 511. Enlargement or alteration of lights.
- 512 "Nuisance" to market or ferry.
- 512. Remedies for nuisance.
- 513. Abatement.
- 514. Notice to wrong-doer.
- 515. Nuisances of omission.
- 517. Old writs
- 518 Damages.
- 520. Injunctions.
- 526 Difficulty or expense of abatement no answer.
- 527. Parties entitled to sue for nuisance.
- 529. Parties liable

CHAPTER XI.

NEGLIGENCE

I *The General Conception.*

- 532. Omission contrasted with action as ground of liability.
- 533 General duty of caution in acts.

PAGE 531. Overlapping of contract and tort
537. Definition of negligence
540. Standard of duty is external
542. Diligence includes competence.

II. *Evidence of Negligence*

543. Negligence a question of mixed fact and law
545. Burden of proof.
548. Where there is a contract or undertaking.
550. Things within defendant's control
551. Common course of affairs judicially noticed
553. On evidence sufficient in law, question is for jury.
554. Metropolitan R. Co. *v.* Jackson
555. Cases of level crossings.
559. "Invitation to alight"
560. Complications with contributory negligence.
560. "Evidence of negligence" Smith *v.* L. & S. W. R Co.
563. No precise general rule.
563. Due care varies as *apparent* risk application of this to accidents through personal infirmity
565. Distinction where person acting has notice of special danger to infirm or helpless person

III. *Contributory Negligence.*

566. Actionable negligence must be proximate cause of harm where plaintiff's own negligence proximate cause, no remedy.
571. Tuff *v* Warman.
571. Radley *v* L. & N. W R W. R Co
572. "Proximate" or "decisive" cause
575. Self-created disability to avoid consequences of another's negligence.
576. Earlier illustrations: Davies *v.* Mann
577. Butterfield *v* Forrester
580. The exploded doctrine of "identification"
582. Accidents to children in custody of adult.
584. Children, &c., unattended.
587. Child *v.* Hearn.
588. Admiralty rule of dividing loss.

IV. *Auxiliary Rules and Presumptions.*

589. Action under difficulty caused by another's negligence.
591. No duty to anticipate negligence of others
592. Choice of risks under stress of another's negligence.

xxiv TABLE OF CONTENTS

PAGE 593. Clayards v Dethick.
594. Doctrine of New York Courts.
595. Separation of law and fact in United States.

CHAPTER XII

DUTIES OF INSURING SAFETY.

598. Exceptions to general limits of duties of caution.
599. Rylands v. Fletcher.
605. Exception of act of God
607 Act of stranger, &c.
608. Authorized works.
609. G W R Co. of Canada v Braid
610 Other cases of insurance liability
610 Duty of keeping in cattle
613 Dangerous or vicious animals
615. Fire, fire-arms, &c
616. Duty of keeping in fire.
617. Carrying fire in locomotives
618 Fire-arms Dixon v. Bell
619 Explosives and other dangerous goods.
620. Gas escapes
621 Poisonous drugs: Thomas v. Winchester
622. Difficulties felt in England George v. Skivington
624. Duties of occupiers of buildings in respect of safe repair.
625. Modern date of the settled rule
625 Indermaur v. Dames.
627 Persons entitled to safety
629. Duty in respect of carriages, ships, &c
631. Limits of the duty.
632 *Volenti non fit injuria*.
633. Duty towards passers-by
635 Presumption of negligence (*res ipsa loquitur*).
638. Distinctions
639 Position of licensees.
641. Host and guest
642. Liability of licensor for "ordinary negligence."
643. Owner not in occupation

CHAPTER XIII

SPECIAL RELATIONS OF CONTRACT AND TORT.

PAGE 644 Original theory of forms of action
 645. Actions on the case.
 646. Causes of action: modern classification as founded on contract or tort.
 647 Classes of questions arising.

1. *Alternative Forms of Remedy on the same Cause of Action*

 647. One cause of action and alternative remedies
 647 Common law doctrine of misfeasance
 650. Special duty of carriers and innkeepers by "custom of the realm"
 652 Alternative of form does not affect substance of duty or liability.
 654. In modern law obligation wholly in contract
 655. Limits of the rule.

2. *Concurrent Causes of Action.*

 656 Cases of tort, whether contract or no contract between same parties.
 658 Contract "implied in law" and waiver of tort
 659. Implied warranty of agent's authority.
 660. Concurrent causes of action against different parties
 661 Dalyell v. Tyrer.
 661. Foulkes v Metropolitan Dist R Co.
 662 Causes of action in contract and tort at suit of different plaintiffs
 663 Alton v Midland R. Co. qu. whether good law
 666 Winterbottom v Wright, &c
 667 Concurrence of breach of contract with delict in Roman law

3 *Causes of Action in Tort Dependent on a Contract not Between the Same Parties*

 668. Causes of action dependent on a collateral contract.
 668 What did Lumley v. Gye decide?
 669. Special damage.
 669 Malice.
 670 Question of remoteness of damage.
 671. Motive as an ingredient in the wrong

PAGE 672. American doctrine
   673. Wilful interference with contract.
   673 Damage to stranger by breach of contract.
   674. Position of receiver of erroneous telegram: different view in England and United States
   677 The conflict considered on principle
   679 Uncertainty still remaining in English doctrine
   680 Character of morally innocent acts affected by extraneous contract

4 *Measure of Damages and Other Incidents of the Remedy*

   682 Measure of damages
   684 Rule as to consequential damage
   685 Penal character of action for breach of promise of marriage
   686 Contracts on which executors cannot sue.

THE LAW OF TORTS.

Book I.—GENERAL PART.

CHAPTER I.

THE NATURE OF TORT IN GENERAL.

What is a tort? Our first difficulty in dealing with the law of torts is to fix the contents and boundaries of the subject. If we are asked, What are torts? nothing seems easier than to answer by giving examples. Assault, libel, and deceit are torts. Trespass to land and wrongful dealing with goods by trespass, "conversion," or otherwise are torts. The creation of a nuisance to the special prejudice of any person is a tort. Causing harm by negligence is a tort. So is, in certain cases, the mere failure to prevent accidental harm arising from a state of things which one has brought about for one's own purposes. Default or miscarriage in certain occupations of a public nature is likewise a tort, although the same facts may constitute a breach of contract, and may, at the option of the aggrieved party, be treated as such. But we shall have no such easy task if we are required to answer the question, What is a tort?—in other words, what principle or element is common to all the classes of cases we have enumerated, or might enumerate, and also distinguishes them as a whole from other classes of facts giving rise to legal duties and liabilities? It is far from a simple matter to define a contract. But we have this much to start from, that there are two parties, of whom one agrees to terms offered by the other. There are variant and abnormal forms to be dealt with, but this is the normal one. In the law of torts we have no such starting-point, nothing (as it appears at first sight) but a heap of miscellaneous instances. The word itself will plainly not help us. *Tort* is nothing but the French equivalent of our English word *wrong*, and was freely used by Spenser as a poetical synonym for it. In common speech everything is a wrong, or wrongful, which is thought to do violence to any right. Manslaying, false witness, breach of covenant, are wrongs in this case. But thus we should include all breaches of all duties, and therefore should not even be on the road to any distinction that could serve as the base of a legal classification.

History and limits of English classification. In the history of our law, and in its existing authorities, we may find some little help, but, considering the magnitude of the subject, singularly little. The ancient common law knew nothing of large classifications. There were forms of action with their appropriate writs and process, and authorities and traditions whence it was known, or in theory was capable of being known, whether any given set of facts would fit into any and which of these forms. No doubt the forms of action fell, in a manner, into natural classes or groups. But no attempt was made to discover or apply any general principle of arrangement. In modern times, that is to say, since the Restoration, we find a certain rough classification tending to prevail (*a*). It is assumed, rather than distinctly asserted or established, that actions maintainable in a court of common law must be either actions of contract or actions of tort. This divi-

(*a*) Appendix A.

sion is exclusive of the real actions for the recovery of land, already becoming obsolete in the seventeenth century, and finally abolished by the Common Law Procedure Act, with which we need not concern ourselves; in the old technical terms, it is, or was, a division of personal actions only. Thus torts are distinguished from one important class of causes of action. Upon the other hand, they are distinguished in the modern law from criminal offences. In the medieval period the procedure whereby redress was obtained for many of the injuries now classified as torts bore plain traces of a criminal or quasi-criminal character, the defendant against whom judgment passed being liable not only to compensate the plaintiff, but to pay a fine to the king. Public and private law were, in truth, but imperfectly distinguished. In the modern law, however, it is settled that a tort, as such, is not a criminal offence. There are various acts which may give rise both to a civil action of tort and to a criminal prosecution, or to the one or the other, at the injured party's option; but the civil suit and the criminal prosecution belong to different jurisdictions, and are guided by different rules of procedure. Torts belong to the subject-matter of Common Pleas as distinguished from Pleas of the Crown. Again, the term and its usage are derived wholly from the Superior Courts of Westminster as they existed before the Judicature Acts. Therefore, the law of torts is necessarily confined by the limits within which those Courts exercised their jurisdiction. Divers and weighty affairs of mankind have been dealt with by other Courts in their own fashion of procedure and with their own terminology. These lie wholly outside the common law forms of action and all classifications founded upon them. According to the common understanding of words, breach of trust is a wrong, adultery is a wrong, refusal to pay just compensation for saving a vessel in distress is a wrong. An order may be made compelling restitution from the defaulting trustee; a decree of judicial separation may be pronounced against the unfaithful wife or husband, and payment of reasonable salvage may be enforced against the ship-owner. But that which is remedied in each case is not a tort. The administration of trusts belongs to the law formerly peculiar to the Chancellor's Court, the settlement of matrimonial causes between husband and wife to the law formerly peculiar to the King's Ecclesiastical Courts; and the adjustment of salvage claims to the law formerly peculiar to the Admiral's Court. These things being unknown to the old common law, there can be no question of tort in the technical sense.

Exclusive limits of "tort." Taking into account the fact that in this country the separation of courts and of forms of action has disappeared, though marks of the separate origin and history of every branch of jurisdiction remain, we may now say this much. A tort is an act or omission, giving rise, in virtue of the common law jurisdiction of the Court, to a civil remedy which is not an action of contract. To that extent we know what a tort is not. We are secured against a certain number of obvious errors. We shall not imagine (for example) that the Married Women's Property Act of 1882, by providing that husbands and wives cannot sue one another for a tort, has thrown doubt on the possibility of a judicial separation. But whether any definition can be given of a tort beyond the restrictive and negative one that it is a cause of action (that

---

Exclusive limits of "tort." In Bishop on Non-Contract Law, the author presents a division of the grounds of legal liability into those based upon contract and those based upon relations not of contract

"The word 'tort' means nearly the same thing as the expression 'civil wrong.' It denotes an injury inflicted otherwise than by a mere breach of contract; or, to be more nicely accurate, a tort is one's disturbance of another in rights which the law has created either in the absence of contract, or in consequence of a relation which a contract has established between the parties. Of course the wrong must be of a sort which the law redresses, not a mere infraction of good morals." Bishop on Non-Contract Law, § 4.

is, of a "personal" action as above noted) which can be sued on in a court of common law without alleging a real or supposed contract, and what, if any, are the common positive characters of the causes of action that can be so sued upon:—these are matters on which our books, ransack them as we will, refuse to utter any certain sound whatever. If the collection of rules which we call the law of torts is founded on any general principles of duty and liability, those principles have nowhere been stated with authority. And, what is yet more remarkable, the want of authoritative principles appears to have been felt as a want by hardly any one (*b*).

Are any general principles discoverable? We have no right, perhaps, to assume that by fair means we shall discover any general principles at all. The history of English usage holds out, in itself, no great encouragement. In the earlier period we find a current distinction between wrongs accompanied with violence and wrongs which are not violent; a distinction important for a state of society where open violence is common, but of little use for the arrangement of modern law, though it is still prominent in Blackstone's exposition (*c*). Later we find a more consciously and carefully made distinction between contracts and causes of action which are not contracts. This is very significant in so far as it marks the ever gaining importance of contract in men's affairs. That which is of contract has come to fill so vast a bulk in the whole frame of modern law that it may, with a fair appearance of equality, be set over against everything which is independent of contract. But this unanalyzed remainder is no more accounted for by the dichotomy of the Common Law Procedure Act than it was before. It may have elements of coherence within

---

(*b*) The first, or almost the first, writer who has clearly called attention to it is Sir William Markby. See the chapter on Liability in his "Elements of Law."

(*c*) Comm. III. 118.

itself, or it may not. If it has, the law of torts is a body of law capable of being expressed in a systematic form and under appropriate general principles, whether any particular attempt so to express it be successful or not. If not, then there is no such thing as the law of torts in the sense in which there is a law of contracts, or of real property, or of trusts, and when we make use of the name we mean nothing but a collection of miscellaneous topics which, through historical accidents, have never been brought into any real classification.

The genera of torts in English law. The only way to satisfy ourselves on this matter is to examine what are the leading heads of the English law of torts as commonly received. If these point to any sort of common principle, and seem to furnish acceptable lines of construction, we may proceed in the directions indicated, well knowing, indeed, that excrescences, defects, and anomalies will occur, but having some guide for our judgment of what is normal and what is exceptional. Now the civil wrongs for which remedies are provided by the common law of England, or by statutes creating new rights of action under the same jurisdiction, are capable of a threefold division according to their scope and effects. There are wrongs affecting a man in the safety and freedom of his own person, in honor and reputation (which, as men esteem of things near and dear to them, come next after the person, if after it at all), or in his estate, condition, and convenience of life generally: the word *estate* being here understood in its widest sense, as when we speak of those who are " afflicted or distressed in mind, body, or estate." There are other wrongs which affect specific property, or specific rights in the nature of property: property, again, being taken in so large a sense as to cover possessory rights of every kind. There are yet others which may affect, as the case happens, person or property, either or both. We may exhibit this division by arranging the familiar and typical species of torts in groups, omitting for the present such as are obsolete or of little practical moment.

Group A.

Personal Wrongs.

1. Wrongs affecting safety and freedom of the person:
    Assault, battery, false imprisonment.
2. Wrongs affecting personal relations in the family:
    Seduction, enticing away of servants.
3. Wrongs affecting reputation:
    Slander and libel.
4. Wrongs affecting estate generally:
    Deceit, slander of title.
    Malicious prosecution, conspiracy.

Group B.

Wrongs to Property.

1. Trespass: (a) to land.
              (b) to goods.
    Conversion and unnamed wrongs *ejusdem generis*.
    Disturbance of easements, etc.
2. Interference with rights analogous to property, such as private franchises, patents, copyrights.

Group C.

Wrongs to Person, Estate, and Property generally.

1. Nuisance.
2. Negligence.
3. Breach of absolute duties specially attached to the occupation of fixed property, to the ownership and custody of dangerous things, and to the exercise of certain public callings. This kind of liability results, as will be seen hereafter, partly from ancient rules

of the common law of which the origin is still doubtful, partly from the modern development of the law of negligence.

All the acts and omissions here specified are undoubtedly torts, or wrongs in the technical sense of English law. They are the subject of legal redress, and under our old judicial system the primary means of redress would be an action brought in a common law court, and governed by the rules of common law pleading (*d*).

We put aside for the moment the various grounds of justification or excuse which may be present, and if present must be allowed for. It will be seen by the student of Roman law that our list includes approximately the same matters (*e*) as in the Roman system are dealt with (though much less fully than in our own) under the title of obligations *ex delicto* and *quasi ex delicto*. To pursue the comparison at this stage, however, would only be to add the difficulties of the Roman classification, which are considerable, to those already on our hands.

Character of wrongful acts, etc., under the several classes. Wilful wrongs. The groups above shown have been formed simply with reference to the effects of the wrongful act or omission. But they appear, on further examination, to have certain distinctive characters with reference to the nature of the act or omission itself. In Group A., generally speaking, the wrong is wilful or wanton. Either the act is intended to do harm, or, being an act evidently likely to cause harm, it is done with reckless indifference to what may befall by reason of it. Either

---

(*d*) In some cases the really effectual remedies were administered by the Court of Chancery, but only as auxiliary to the legal right, which it was often necessary to establish in an action at law before the Court of Chancery would interfere.

(*e*) Trespass to land may or may not be an exception, according to the view we take of the nature of the liabilities enforced by the possessory remedies of the Roman law. Some modern authorities, though not most, regard these as *ex delicto*

there is deliberate injury, or there is something like the self-seeking indulgence of passion, in contempt of other men's rights and dignity, which the Greeks called ὕβρις. Thus the legal wrongs are such as to be also the object of strong moral condemnation. It is needless to show by instances that violence, evil-speaking, and deceit, have been denounced by righteous men in all ages. If anyone desires to be satisfied of this, he may open Homer or the Psalter at random. What is more, we have here to do with acts of the sort that are next door to crimes. Many of them, in fact, are criminal offences as well as civil wrongs. It is a common border land of criminal and civil, public and private law.

Wrongs apparently unconnected with moral blame. In Group B. this element is at first sight absent, or at any

---

Wrongs apparently unconnected with moral blame Agreeing with the text It is established in the United States that to sustain an action, where there is a clear violation of a right, it is not necessary to show actual damage, for the reason that every violation imports damage and the plaintiff is entitled to nominal damages, if no other be proved. Webb v. Portland Mfg Co., 3 Sumn 189, Dixon v Clow, 24 Wend. 188; Hastings v Livermore, 7 Gray, 194; Chaffee v. Pease, 10 Allen, 537; Blodgett v. Stone, 60 N. H. 167.

This rule, however, is subject to exceptions. See Upton v Vail, 6 Johns. 181, Ming v. Woolfolk, 116 U. S 599, 6 Sup Ct Rep 489, Taylor v Guest, 58 N Y 262, Tryon v. Whitmarsh, 1 Metc 1; Benton v. Pratt, 2 Wend 385.

The fact that an unlawful act of a defendant was done in good faith does not relieve him of liability. Dexter v. Cole, 6 Wis 319, Reynolds v Shuler, 5 Cow 232; Gibbs v. Chase, 10 Mass 125; Guille v. Swan, 19 Johns 381, Kamerick v. Castleman, 29 Mo. App 658; Higginson v. York, 5 Mass. 34, Caldwell v. Farrell, 28 Ill. 438; Allison v Little, 85 Ala. 512, 5 So. Rep. 221, Wintringham v Lafoy, 7 Cow. 735, Miller v. Baker, 1 Met. 27, Morgan v Varick, 8 Wend 587, Jordan v. Wyatt, 4 Grat. 151; Burch v Carter, 32 N J L. 554, Drew v Peer, 93 Pa St. 234, Parker v Mise, 27 Ala. 480; Woolf v Chalker, 31 Conn. 121; Lowenburg v. Rosenthal, 18 Oreg. 178, 22 Pac. Rep. 601; Jefferies v Hargus, 50 Ark 65, Conway v Russell, 151 Mass. 581; 24 N E. Rep. 1026, Formwalt v Hylton, 66 Tex. 288, 1 S W Rep 376, Amick v O'Hara, 6 Blackf 258; Cate v. Cate, 44 N H 211, Hazelton v Week, 49 Wis 661, Tobin v. Deal,

rate indifferent. Whatever may or might be the case in other legal systems, the intention to violate another's rights, or even the knowledge that one is violating them, is not in English law necessary to constitute the wrong of trespass as regards either land or goods, or of conversion as regards goods. On the contrary, an action of trespass — or of ejectment, which is a special form of trespass — has for centuries been a common and convenient method of trying an honestly disputed claim of right. Again, it matters not whether actual harm is done. "By the laws of England, every invasion of private property, be it ever so minute, is a trespass. No man can set his foot upon my ground without my license, but he is liable to an action, though the damage be nothing, which is proved by every declaration in trespass, where the defendant is called upon to answer for bruising the grass and even treading upon the soil" (*f*). Nor is this all; for dealing with another man's goods without lawful authority, but under the honest and even reasonable belief that the dealing is lawful, may be an actionable wrong notwithstanding the innocence of the mistake (*g*). Still less will good intentions afford an excuse. I find a watch lying in the road; intending to do the owner a good turn, I take it to a watchmaker, who to the best of my knowledge is competent, and leave it with him to be cleaned. The task is beyond him, or an incompetent hand is employed on it, and the watch is spoilt in the attempt to restore it. Without question the owner may hold me liable. In one word, the duty which the law of England enforces is an absolute duty not to meddle without lawful authority with land or goods that belong to others. And the same principle applies to rights which, though

(*f*) Per Cur. *Entick* v *Carrington*, 19 St. Tr. 1066.

(*g*) See *Hollins* v *Fowler*, L R 7 H L. 757, 44 L J Q B 169.

60 Wis. 87, Cubit *v.* O'Dett, 51 Mich 347, Hatch *v* Donnell, 74 Me. 163. Newkirk *v.* Sabler, 9 Barb 652

not exactly property, are analogous to it. There are exceptions, but the burden of proof lies on those who claim their benefit. The law, therefore, is stricter, on the face of things, than morality. There may, in particular circumstances, be doubt what is mine and what is my neighbour's; but the law expects me at my peril to know what is my neighbour's in every case. Reserving the explanation of this, to be attempted afterwards, we pass on.

Wrongs of imprudence and omission. In Group C. the acts or omissions complained of have a kind of intermediate character. They are not as a rule wilfully or wantonly harmful, but neither are they morally indifferent, save in a few extreme cases under the third head. The party has for his own purposes, done acts, or brought about a state of things, or brought other people into a situation, or taken on himself the conduct of an operation, which a prudent man in his place would know to be attended with certain risks. A man who fails to take order, in things within his control, against risk to others which he actually foresees, or which a man of common sense and competence would in his place foresee, will scarcely be held blameless by the moral judgment of his fellows. Legal liability for negligence and similar wrongs corresponds approximately to the moral censure on this kind of default. The commission of something in itself forbidden by the law, or the omission of a positive and specific legal duty, though without any intention to cause harm, can be and is, at best, not more favourably considered than imprudence if harm happens to come of it; and here, too, morality will not dissent. In some conditions, indeed, and for special reasons which must be considered later, the legal duty goes beyond the moral one.

Wrongs of imprudence and omission For the authorities supporting the doctrine stated in the text, see *post*, pp. 533, 537

There are cases of this class in which liability cannot be avoided, even by proof that the utmost diligence in the way of precaution has in fact been used, and yet the party liable has done nothing which the law condemns (*h*).

Except in these cases, the liability springs from some shortcoming in the care and caution to which, taking human affairs according to the common knowledge and experience of mankind, we deem ourselves entitled at the hands of our fellow-men. There is a point, though not an easily defined one, where such shortcoming gives rise even to criminal liability, as in the case of manslaughter by negligence.

Relation of the law of torts to the semi-ethical precept alterum non laedere. We have, then, three main divisions of the law of torts. In one of them, which may be said to have a quasi-criminal character, there is a very strong ethical element. In another no such element is apparent. In the third such an element is present, though less manifestly so. Can we find any category of human duties that will approximately cover them all, and bring them into relation with any single principle? Let us turn to one of the best-known sentences in the introductory chapter of the Institutes, copied from a lost work of Ulpian. "Iuris praecepta sunt haec: honeste vivere, alterum non laedere, suum cuique tribuere." *Honeste vivere* is a vague phrase enough; it may mean refraining from criminal offences, or possibly general good behaviour in social and family rela-

---

(*h*) How far such a doctrine can be theoretically or historically justified is not an open question for English courts of justice, for it has been explicitly affirmed by the House of Lords *Rylands v Fletcher* (1868), L. R. 3 H. L. 330, 37 L. J. Ex 161

Precepts. *Honeste vivere* (to live honorably), *alterum non laedere* (not to injure others), and *suum cuique tribuere* (to render to every man his due), were the three general precepts to which Justinian reduced the whole doctrine of the law Black's Law Dic., p. 579

tions. *Suum cuique tribuere* seems to fit pretty well with the law of property and contract. And what of *alterum non laedere?* "Thou shalt do no hurt to thy neighbor." Our law of torts, with all its irregularities, has for its main purpose nothing else than the development of this precept (*i*). This exhibits it, no doubt, as the technical working out of a moral idea by positive law, rather than the systematic application of any distinctly legal conception. But all positive law must pre-suppose a moral standard, and at times more or less openly refer to it; and the more so in proportion as it has or approaches to having a penal character.

Historical anomaly of law of trespass and conversion. The real difficulty of ascribing any rational unity to our law of torts is made by the wide extent of the liabilities mentioned under Group B., and their want of intelligible relation to any moral conception.

A right of property is interfered with "at the peril of the person interfering with it, and whether his interference be for his own use or that of anybody else" (*k*).

And whether the interference be wilful, or reckless, or innocent but imprudent, or innocent without imprudence, the legal consequences and the form of the remedy are for English justice the same.

Early division of forms of action. The truth is that we have here one of the historical anomalies that abound in English law. Formerly we had a clear distinction in the forms of procedure (the only evidence we have for much of the older theory of the law) between the simple assertion or vindication of title and claims for redress against

---

(*i*) Compare the statement of "duty towards my neighbor," in the Church Catechism, probably from the hand of Goodrich, Bishop of Ely, who was a learned civilian "To hurt nobody by word nor deed· To be true and just in all my dealing "

(*k*) Lord O'Hagan, L. R, 7 H L. at p. 799.

specific injuries. Of course the same facts would often, at the choice of the party wronged, afford ground for one or the other kind of claim, and the choice would be made for reasons of practical convenience, apart from any scientific or moral ideas. But the distinction was in itself none the less marked.

Writs of right and writs of trespass: restitution or punishment. For assertion of title to land there was the writ of right, and the writ of debt, with its somewhat later variety, the writ of detinue, asserted a plaintiff's title to money or goods in a closely corresponding form (*l*). Injuries to person or property, on the other hand, were matter for the writ of trespass and certain other analogous writs, and (from the 13th century onwards) the later and more comprehensive writ of trespass on the case (*m*). In the former kind of process, restitution is the object sought; in the latter, some redress or compensation which, there is great reason to believe, was originally understood to be a substitute for private vengeance (*n*). Now the writs of restitution, as we may collectively call them, were associated with many cumbrous and archaic points of procedure, exposing a plaintiff to incalculable and irrational risk, while the operation of the writs of penal redress was by

(*l*) The writ of right (Glanvill, Bk. 1 c. 6) runs thus: "Rex vicecomiti salutem. Praecipe A. quod sine dilatione reddat B. unam hidam terrae in villa illa, unde idem B. queritur quod praedictus A. ei deforceat et nisi fecerit, summone eum," etc. The writ of debt (Bk. x. c. 2) thus: "Rex vicecomiti salutem. Praecipe N. quod iuste et sine dilatione reddat R. centum marcas quas ei debet, ut dicit, et unde queritur quod ipse ei iniuste deforceat. Et nisi fecerit, summone eum," etc. The writs of covenant and account, which were developed later, also contain the characteristic words *iuste et sine dilatione*.

(*m*) Blackstone, III. 122, 1 N. B. 92. The mark of this class of actions is the conclusion of the writ *contra pacem*. Writs of assize, including the assize of nuisance, did not so conclude, but show analogies of form to the writ of trespass in other respects. Actions on the case might be founded on other writs besides that of trespass, *e.g.*, deceit, which contributed largely to the formation of the action of assumpsit. The writ of trespass itself is by no means one of the most ancient: see F. W. Maitland in Harv. Law Rev. III 217-219.

(*n*) Not retaliation. Early Germanic law shows no trace of retaliation in the strict sense. A passage in the introduction to Alfred's laws, copied from the Book of Exodus, is no real exception

comparison simple and expeditious. Thus the interest of suitors led to a steady encroachment of the writ of trespass and its kind upon the writ of right and its kind. Not only was the writ of right first thrust into the background by the various writs of assize—forms of possessory real action which are a sort of link between the writ of right and the writ of trespass—and then superseded by the action of ejectment, in form a pure action of trespass, but in like manner the action of detinue was largely supplanted by trover, and debt by assumpsit, both of these new-fashioned remedies being varieties of action on the case (o) In this way the distinction between proceedings taken on a disputed claim of right, and those taken for the redress of injuries where the right was assumed not to be in dispute, became quite obliterated. The forms of action were the sole embodiment of such legal theory as existed, and therefore, as the distinction of remedies was lost, the distinction between the rights which they protected was lost also. By a series of shifts and devices introduced into legal practice for the ease of litigants a great bulk of what really belonged to the law of property was transferred, in forensic usage and thence in the traditional habit of mind of English lawyers, to the law of torts. In a rude state of society the desire of vengeance is measured by the harm actually suffered and not by any consideration of the actor's intention; hence the archaic law of injuries is a law of absolute liability for the direct consequences of a man's acts, tempered only by partial exceptions in the hardest cases. These archaic ideas of absolute liability made it easy to use the law of wrongful injuries for trying what were really questions of absolute right; and that practice again tended to the preservation

---

(o) For the advantages of suing in case over the older forms of actions, see Blackstone, iii 153, 155 The reason given at p 152 for the wager of law (as to which see Co Litt 295 a) being allowed in debt and detinue is some one's idle guess, due to mere ignorance of the earlier history

of these same archaic ideas in other departments of the law. It will be observed that in our early forms of action contract, as such, has no place at all (p): an additional proof of the relatively modern character both of the importance of contract in practical life, and of the growth of the corresponding general notion

Rationalized version of law of trespass. We are now independent of forms of action. Trespass and trover have become historical landmarks, and the question whether detinue is, or was, an action founded on contract or on tort (if the foregoing statement of the history be correct, it was really neither) survives only to raise difficulties in applying certain provisions of the County Courts Act as to the scale of costs in the Superior Courts (q) It would seem, therefore, that a rational exposition of the law of torts is free to get rid of the extraneous matter brought in, as we have shown, by the practical exigency of conditions that no longer exist. At the same time a certain amount of excuse may be made on rational grounds for the place and function of the law of trespass to property in the English system. It appears morally unreasonable, at first sight, to require a man at his peril to know what land and goods are his neighbour's. But it is not so evidently unreasonable to expect him to know what is his own, which is only the statement of the same rule from the other side. A man can but seldom go by pure unwitting misadventure beyond the limits of his own dominion Either he knows he is not within his legal right, or he takes no heed, or he knows there is a doubt as to his right, but for causes deemed by him sufficient, he is content to abide (or perhaps intends to provoke) a legal contest by which the doubt may be resolved. In none of these cases can he complain with

(p) Except what may be implied from the technical rule that the word *debet* was proper only in an action for a sum of money between the original parties to the contract F N B 119, Blackstone, iii 156

(q) *Bryant* v *Herbert* (1875), 3 C P. Div 389 17 L J C P 670.

moral justice of being held to answer for his act. If not wilfully or wan, only injurious, it is done with some want of due circumspection, or else it involves the conscious acceptance of a risk. A form of procedure which attempted to distinguish between these possible cases in detail would for practical purposes hardly be tolerable. Exceptional cases do occur, and may be of real hardship. One can only say that they are thought too exceptional to count in determining the general rule of law. From this point of view we can accept, though we may not actively approve, the inclusion of the morally innocent with the morally guilty trespasses in legal classification.

Analogy of the Roman obligations ex delicto. We may now turn with profit to the comparison of the Roman system with our own. There we find strongly marked the distinction between restitution and penalty, which was apparent in our old forms of action, but became obsolete in the manner above shown. Mr. Moyle (r) thus describes the specific character of obligations *ex delicto*.

"Such wrongs as the withholding of possession by a defendant who *bona fide* believes in his own title are not delicts, at any rate in the specific sense in which the term is used in the Institutes; they give rise, it is true, to a right of action, but a right of action is a different thing from an *obligatio ex delicto*; they are redressed by mere reparation, by the wrong-doer being compelled to put the other in the position in which he would have been had the wrong never been committed. But delicts, as contrasted with them and with contracts, possess three peculiarities. The obligations which arise from them are independent, and do not merely modify obligations already subsisting; *they always involve dolus or culpa; and the remedies by which they are redressed are penal.*"

(r) In his edition of the Institutes, note to Bk. iv. tit 1, p. 497

Dolus and culpa. The Latin *dolus*, as a technical term, is not properly rendered by "fraud" in English; its meaning is much wider, and answers to what we generally signify by "unlawful intention." *Culpa* is exactly what we mean by "negligence," the falling short of that care and circumspection which is due from one man to another. The rules specially dealing with this branch have to define the measure of care which the law prescribes as due in the case in hand. The Roman conception of such rules, as worked out by the lawyers of the classical period, is excellently illustrated by the title of the Digest "ad legem Aquiliam," a storehouse of good sense and good law (for the principles are substantially the same as ours) deserving much more attention at the hands of English lawyers than it has received. It is to be observed that the Roman theory was built up on a foundation of archaic materials by no means unlike our own; the compensation of the civilized law stands instead of a primitive retaliation which was still recognized by the law of the Twelve Tables. If then we put aside the English treatment of rights of property as being accounted for by historical accidents, we find that the Roman conception of delict altogether supports (and by a perfectly independent analogy) the conception that appears really to underlie the English law of tort. Liability for delict, or civil wrong in the strict sense, is the result either of wilful injury to others, or wanton disregard of what is due to them (*dolus*), or of a failure to observe due care and caution which has similar though not intended or expected consequences (*culpa*).

Liability quasi ex delicto. We have, moreover, apart from the law of trespass, an exceptionally stringent rule in certain cases where liability is attached to the befalling of harm without proof of either intention or negligence, as was mentioned under Group C of our provisional scheme. Such is the case of the landowner who keeps on his land an artificial reservoir of water, if the reservoir bursts and floods the lands of his neighbours. Not that it was wrong of him to have a reservoir there, but the law says he must do so at his own risk (*s*). This kind of liability has its parallel in Roman law, and the obligation is said to be not *ex delicto*, since true delict involves either *dolus* or *culpa*, but *quasi ex delicto* (*t*). Whether to avoid the difficulty of proving negligence, or in order to sharpen men's precaution in hazardous matters by not even allowing them, when harm is once done, to prove that they have been diligent, the mere fact of the mischief happening gives birth to the obligation. In the cases of carriers and innkeepers a similar liability is a very ancient part of our law. Whatever the original reason of it may have been as matter of history, we may be sure that it was something quite unlike the reasons of policy governing the modern class of cases of which *Rylands* v. *Fletcher* (*u*) is the type and leading authority; by such reasons, nevertheless, the rules must be defended as part of the modern law, if they can be defended at all.

Summary. On the whole, the result seems to be partly negative, but also not to be barren. It is hardly possible to frame a definition of a tort that will satisfy all the meanings in which the term has been used by persons and in documents of more or less authority in our law, and will at the same time not be wider than any of the authorities warrant. But it appears that this difficulty or impossibility is due to particular anomalies, and not to a total want of general principles. Disregarding those anomalies, we may

(*s*) *Rylands* v. *Fletcher*, L. R. 3 H. L. 330, 371 J. v. 161

(*t*) Austin's perverse and unintelligent criticism of this perfectly rational terminology has been treated with far more respect than it deserves It is true, however, that the application of the term in the Institutes is not quite consistent or complete See Mr Moyle's notes on I. iv 5

(*u*) L. R. 3 H. L. 330 See Ch XII. below.

try to sum up the normal idea of tort somewhat as follows:—

Tort is an act or omission (not being merely the breach of a duty arising out of a personal relation, or undertaken by contract) which is related to harm suffered by a determinate person in one of the following ways:—

- (a) It may be an act which, without lawful justification or excuse, is intended by the agent to cause harm, and does cause the harm complained of.
- (b) It may be an act in itself contrary to law, or an omission of specific legal duty, which causes harm not intended by the person so acting or omitting.
- (c) It may be an act or omission causing harm which the person so acting or omitting did not intend to cause, but might and should with due diligence have foreseen and prevented.
- (d) It may, in special cases, consist merely in not avoiding or preventing harm which the party was bound, absolutely or within limits, to avoid or prevent.

A special duty of this last kind may be (i) absolute, (ii) limited to answering for harm which is assignable to negligence.

In some positions a man becomes, so to speak, an insurer to the public against a certain risk, in others he warrants only that all has been done for safety that reasonable care can do.

Connected in principle with these special liabilities, but running through the whole subject, and of constant occurrence in almost every division of it, is the rule that a master is answerable for the acts and defaults of his servants in the course of their employment.

This is indication rather than definition: but to have guiding principles indicated is something. We are entitled, and in a manner bound, not to rush forthwith into a detailed enumeration of the several classes of torts, but to seek first the common principles of liability, and then the common principles of immunity which are known as matter of justification and excuse. There are also special conditions and exceptions belonging only to particular branches, and to be considered, therefore, in the places appropriate to those branches.

CHAPTER II.

PRINCIPLES OF LIABILITY.

Want of generality in early law. There is no express authority that I know of for stating as a general proposition of English law that it is a wrong to do wilful harm to one's neighbour without lawful justification or excuse. Neither is there any express authority for the general proposition that men must perform their contracts. Both principles are, in this generality of form or conception, modern, and there was a time when neither was true. Law begins not with authentic general principles, but with enumeration of particular remedies. There is no law of contracts in the modern lawyer's sense, only a list of certain kinds of agreements which may be enforced. Neither is there any law of delicts, but only a list of certain kinds of injury which have certain penalties assigned to them. Thus in the Anglo-Saxon and other early Germanic laws we find minute assessments of the compensation due for hurts to every member of the human body, but there is no general prohibition of personal violence; and a like state of things appears in the fragments of the Twelve Tables (*a*). Whatever agreements are outside the specified forms of obligation and modes of proof are incapable of enforcement; whatever injuries are not in the table of compensation must go without legal redress. The phrase

---

(*a*) In Gaius iii. 223, 224, the contrast between the ancient law of fixed penalties and the modern law of damages assessed by judicial authority is clearly shown. The student will remember that, as regards the stage of development attained, the law of Justinian, and often that of Gaius, is far more modern than the English law of the Year Books.

damnum sine injuria, which for the modern law is at best insignificant, has meaning and substance enough in such a system. Only that harm which falls within one of the specified categories of wrong-doing entitles the person aggrieved to a legal remedy.

General duty not to do harm in modern law. Such is not the modern way of regarding legal duties or remedies. It is not only certain favoured kinds of agreement that are protected, but all agreements that satisfy certain general conditions are valid and binding, subject to exceptions which are themselves assignable to general principles of justice and policy. So we can be no longer satisfied in the region of tort with a mere enumeration of actionable injuries. The whole modern law of negligence, with its many developments, enforces the duty of fellow-citizens to observe in varying circumstances an appropriate measure of prudence to avoid causing harm to one another. The situations in which we are under no such duty appear at this day not as normal but as exceptional. A man cannot keep shop or walk into the street without being entitled to expect and bound to practice observance in this kind, as we shall more fully see hereafter. If there exists, then, a positive duty to avoid harm, much more must there exist the negative duty of not doing wilful harm; subject, as all general duties must be subject, to the necessary exceptions The three main heads of duty with which the law of torts is concerned — namely, to abstain from wilful injury, to respect the property of others, and to use due diligence to avoid causing harm to others — are all alike of a comprehensive nature As our laws of contract has been generalized by the doctrine of consideration and the action of *assumpsit*, so has our laws of civil wrongs by the wide and various application of actions on the case (*b*).

(*b*) The developed Roman law has either attained or was on the point of attaining a like generality of application "Denique aliis pluribus modis admitti injuriam manifestum est". I. iv 4, 1.

Acts in breach of specific legal duty. The commission of an act specifically forbidden by law, or the omission or failure to perform any duty specifically imposed by law, is generally equivalent to an act done with intent to cause wrongful injury. Where the harm that ensues from the unlawful act or omission is the very kind of harm which it was the aim of the law to prevent (and this is the commonest case), the justice and necessity of this rule are manifest without further comment. Where a statute, for example, expressly lays upon a railway company the duty of fencing and watching a level crossing, this is a legislative declaration of the diligence to be required of the company in providing against harm to passengers using the road. Even if the mischief to be prevented is not such as an ordinary man would foresee as the probable consequence of disobedience, there is some default in the mere fact that the law is disobeyed; at any rate a court of law cannot admit discussion on that point; and the defaulter must take

---

Acts in breach of specific legal duty. Supporting the doctrine of the text *vide*, Miller *v* Woodhead, 104 N. Y. 471, 11 N E Rep 57, Guest *v* Reynolds, 68 Ill. 478, Gramlich *v*. Wurst, 86 Pa. St. 74, Railroad Co. *v*. Schwindling, 101 Pa. St 258, Galligan *v*. Manufacturing Co., 143 Mass 527; 10 N E. Rep. 171, Gillespie *v*. McGowan, 100 Pa. St 144, Lamb *v*. Stone, 11 Pick 526, Rice *v* Coolidge, 121 Mass 393, Randlette *v*. Judkins, 77 Me 114; Adams *v* Marshall, 138 Mass 228, Wilson *v*. Dubois, 35 Minn. 471, 29 N. W. Rep 68, Lilly *v* Boyd, 72 Ga 83.

Illustrating the creating of legal duty by statute, *vide*, Willy *v* Mulledy, 78 N. Y. 310, Commissioners *v* Duckett, 20 Md. 468, Hover *v*. Barkhoof, 44 N Y 113, Heeney *v* Sprague, 11 R I. 454, Baxter *v*. Doe, 142 Mass. 558; 8 N E Rep 115, Dudley *v* Mayhew, 3 N. Y 9, Grant *v* Power Co , 14 R I. 380, Boot *v* Pratt, 33 Minn 323

There are numerous statutes enacting legal duties the violation of which is a tort Among such statutes are those requiring railroad companies to fence their tracks, to use the best approved appliances for the protection of life and property, etc See Keyer *v*. Chicago, etc , Co , 56 Mich. 559; 33 N W Rep 867, Hayes *v* Michigan Cent. R R Co , 111 U. S. 228, Wilson *v*. Rochester, etc., R R Co., 16 Barb. 167, Patterson *v*. Detroit, etc., R R Co., 56 Mich 172, Houston, etc R R Co *v* Terry, 42 Tex 451, Reynolds *v* Hindman, 32 Ia 146; Bartlett, etc , Co. *v* Roach, 68 Ill 174, Titcomb *v* Fitchburg R R. Co., 12 Allen, 254.

the consequences. The old-fashioned distinction between *mala prohibita* and *mala in se* is long since exploded. The simple omission, after notice, to perform a legal duty, may be a wilful offense within the meaning of a penal statute (c). As a matter of general policy, there are so many temptations to neglect public duties of all kinds for the sake of private interest that the addition of this quasi-penal sanction as a motive to their observance appears to be no bad thing. Many public duties, however, are wholly created by special statutes. In such cases it is not an universal proposition that a breach of the duty confers a private right of action on any and every person who suffers particular damage from it. The extent of the liabilities incident to a statutory duty must be ascertained from the scope and terms of the statute itself. Acts of Parliament often contain special provisions for enforcing the duties declared by them, and those provisions may be so framed as to exclude expressly, or by implication, any right of private suit (d). Also there is no cause of action where the damage complained of " is something totally apart from the object of the Act of Parliament," as being evidently outside the mischiefs which it was intended to prevent. What the legislature has declared to be wrongful for a definite purpose cannot be therefore treated as wrongful for another and different purpose (e).

Duty of respecting property. As to the duty of respecting proprietary rights, we have already mentioned that it is an absolute one. Further illustration is reserved for the special treatment of that division of the subject.

Duties of diligence. Then we have the general duty of using due care and caution. What is due care and caution

---

(c) *Gully* v *Smith* (1883) 12 Q B D 121, 53 L J M C 35.
(d) *Atkinson* v *Newcastle Waterworks Co.* (1877) 2 Ex Div 441, 46 L J Ex 775

(e) *Gorris* v *Scott* (1874) L R 9 Ex. 125, 43 L J Ex 92, *Ward* v *Hobbs* (1878) 4 App Ca 13, 23, 48 L J Q B 281

under given circumstances has to be worked out in the special treatment of negligence. Here we may say that, generally speaking, the standard of duty is fixed by reference to what we should expect in the like case from a man of ordinary sense, knowledge, and prudence.

Assumption of skill. Moreover, if the party has taken in hand the conduct of anything requiring special skill and

---

Assumption of skill. In the United States the rule is somewhat stricter than in England, that persons who hold themselves out to the world as possessing skill and qualifications in their respective trades or professions are bound to reasonable skill and diligence in the performance of their duties. Citizens Loan F. & S. Assn. v. Friedly, 123 Ind. 115, following Waugh v. Shunk, 20 Pa. St. 130, citing Watson v. Muirhead, 57 Pa. St. 161; United States Mortgage Co. v. Henderson, 111 Ind. 84. See McCandless v. McWha, 22 Pa. St. 261.

A majority of the authorities upon this subject relating to special classes of persons are collated as follows: —

Agents. Varnum v. Martin, 15 Pick. 440; Williams v. Higgins, 30 Md. 404; Harriman v. Stowe, 57 Mo. 93; Myles v. Myles, 6 Bush. 237; Evans v. Watrous, 2 Port. 205; Holliday v. Kennard, 12 Wall. 254; Howard v. Grover, 28 Me. 97, 48 Am. Dec. 478; Leighton v. Sargent, 7 Fost. 460; 59 Am. Dec. 388; Milwaukee Bank v. City Bank, 103 U. S. 668; Webster v. Whitworth, 49 Ala. 201; Long v. Morrison, 14 Ind. 595; Wood v. Clapp, 4 Sneed (Tenn.), 65; Patten v. Wiggin, 51 Me. 594; Matthews v. Fuller, 123 Mass. 446; Gilson v. Collins, 66 Ill. 136; Fay v. Strawn, 32 Ill. 295; Gettins v. Scudder, 71 Ill. 86; Whitney v. Martine, 88 N. Y. 535; First Nat. Bank of Meadville v. Fourth Nat. Bank of N. Y., 77 N. Y. 320; Heineman v. Heard, 50 N. Y. 27; Gleason v. Clark, 9 Cow. 57; Leverick v. Meigs, 1 Cow. 645; Bigelow v. Walker, 24 Vt. 149; 58 Am. Dec. 156; Wilmot v. Howard, 39 Vt. 447; Gheen v. Johnson, 90 Pa. St. 38; Fowler v. Sergeant, 1 Grant Cas. 355.

Apothecaries. Hansford v. Payne, 11 Bush. 380; Walton v. Booth, 34 La. An. 913; Ray v. Burbank, 61 Ga. 505; Beckwith v. Oatman, 43 Hun, 265; McCubbin v. Hastings, 27 La. An. 713; Fleet v. Hollenkemp, 13 B. Mon. 219; Gwynn v. Duffield, 66 Iowa, 708; Davidson v. Nichols, 11 Allen, 514.

Attorneys. Citizens Loan F. & S. Assn. v. Friedly, *supra*; Pennington v. Yell, 11 Ark. 212; Cox v. Sullivan, 7 Ga. 144; Varnum v. Martin, 15 Pick. 450; Oldham v. Sparks, 28 Tex. 425; Roots v. Stone, 2 Leigh, 650; Reilley v. Cavanaugh, 29 Ind. 435; Cox v. Sullivan, 7 Ga. 148; Fenaille v. Coudest, 44 N. J. L. 286; Stevens v. Walker, 55 Ill. 151; Dearborn v. Dearborn, 15 Mass. 316; Fox v. Jones, 14 S. W. Rep. 1007; Thomas v.

knowledge, we require of him a competent measure of the skill and knowledge usually found in persons who undertake such matters. And this is hardly an addition to the general rule; for a man of common sense knows wherein he is competent and wherein not, and does not take on himself things in which he is incompetent. If a man will drive a carriage, he is bound to have the ordinary competence of a coachman; if he will handle a ship, of a seaman; if he will treat a wound, of a surgeon; if he will lay bricks, of a bricklayer; and so in every case that can be put. Whoever takes on himself to exercise a craft holds himself out as possessing at least the common skill of that craft, and is answerable accordingly. If he fails, it is no excuse that he did the best he, being unskilled, actually could. He

---

Schee, 80 In 237, Walpole v. Carlisle, 82 Ind 415, Caverly v McOwen, 123 Mass 571, Bowman v. Tallman, 27 How. Pr. 212

Caterer Bishop v Weber, 139 Mass 411

Engineer. McCarty v. Bauer, 3 Kan. 237

Physicians and Surgeons Rowe v Lent, 62 Hun, 62; 17 N. Y. S. Rep 131; Barney v Pinkham, 29 Neb. 350, Becker v Janinski, 15 N Y S. Rep. 675; 27 Abb N C 15, Hitchcock v Burget, 38 Mich. 501, Hesse v. Knippel, 1 Mich N P 109, Getchell v. Hill, 21 Minn 464; Getchell v Lindley, 24 Minn. 265; Reynolds v Graves, 3 Wis 416; Gates v Fleischer, 67 Wis 504, Briggs v Taylor, 28 Vt. 180, Wood v Clapp, 4 Sneed (Tenn.), 65, Alder v. Buckley, 1 Swan, 69; Graham v. Gautier, 21 Tex. 111, Hathorn v. Richmond, 48 Vt. 557; Potter v Warner, 91 Pa St 362, Haire v. Reese, 7 Phila. Rep. 138, Fowler v Sergeant, 1 Grant Cas 355; Small v Howard, 128 Mass 131, Branner v. Stormont, 9 Kan 51; Utley v Burns, 70 Ill 162; Fischer v Niccolls, 2 Ill. App 484, Quinn v Donovan, 85 Ill. 194, Long v. Morrison, 14 Ind. 595; Jones v Angell, 95 Ind 376, Tefft v Wilcox, 6 Kan. 46, Peck v Martin, 17 Ind 115, Gramm v Boener, 56 Ind. 497, Holtzman v. Hoy, 19 Ill. App. 459, Landon v Humphrey, 9 Conn 209; Ritchey v West, 23 Ill. 385, McNevins v Lowe, 40 Ill. 209, Kendall v Brown, 74 Ill. 232, Barnes v. Means, 82 Ill 379.

There is an exception to the general rule requiring skill in favor of persons who act during an emergency or who volunteer to act without professing special qualifications. Higgins v. McCabe, 126 Mass 13; Beardslee v Richardson, 11 Wend 25; Gladwell v. Steggall, 5 Bing. (N C.) 733

On the subject of competence see *post*, p 542

must be reasonably skilled at his peril. As the Romans put it, *imperitia culpae adnumeratur* (*f*). A good rider who goes out with a horse he had no cause to think ungovernable, and notwithstanding all he can do to keep his horse in hand, is run away with by the horse, is not liable for what mischief the horse may do before it is brought under control again (*g*), but if a bad rider is run away with by a horse which a fairly good rider could have kept in order, he will be liable.

Exception of Necessity. An exception to this principle appears to be admissible in one uncommon but possible kind of circumstances, namely, where in emergency, and to avoid imminent risk, the conduct of something generally entrusted to skilled persons is taken by an unskilled person; as if the crew of a steamer were so disabled by tempest or sickness that the whole conduct of the vessel fell upon an engineer without knowledge of navigation, or a sailor without knowledge of steam-engines. So if the driver and stoker of a train were both disabled, say by sunstroke or lightning, the guard, who is presumably unskilled as concerns driving a locomotive, is evidently not bound to perform the driver's duties. So again, a person who is present at an accident requiring immediate "first aid," no skilled aid being on the spot, must act reasonably according to common knowledge if he acts at all; but he cannot be answerable to the same extent that a surgeon would be. There does not seem to be any distinct authority for such cases, but we may assume it to be law that no more is required of a person in this kind of situation than to make a prudent and reasonable use of such skill, be it much or little, as he actually has.

(*f*) D. 50. 17, de div. reg. iuris antiqui, 132, cf. D. 9. 2, ad legem Aquiliam, 8. Both passages are from Gaius.

(*g*) *Hammack* v *White* (1862), 11 C. B. N. S. 588, 31 L. J. C. P. 129; *Holmes* v *Mather* (1875), L. R. 10 Ex. 261, 44 L. J. Ex. 176.

Liability in relation to consequences of act or default.
We shall now consider for what consequences of his acts

Liability in relation to consequences of act or default. A comprehensive statement of the law of this subject is that contained in the opinion of the court in the leading case of McDonald v Snelling (1' Allen, 90) "Where a right or duty is created wholly by contract, it can only be enforced between the contracting parties; but where the defendant has violated a duty imposed upon him by the common law, it seems just and reasonable that he should be held liable to every person injured, whose injury is the natural and probable consequence of the misconduct. In our opinion this is the well-established and ancient doctrine of the common law, and such a liability extends to consequential injuries, by whomsoever sustained, so long as they are of a character likely to follow, and which might reasonably have been anticipated as the natural and probable result, under ordinary circumstances, of the wrongful act." See Pennsylvania R Co. v Kerr, 62 Pa. St. 353, 1 Am. Rep 431, Ætna Ins. Co v. Boone, 95 U. S. 130, Hoag v Lake Shore, etc , R Co., 85 Pa St 293; 27 Am Rep. 653; Salem Bank v. Gloucester Bank, 17 Mass. 1, Dunlap v. Wagner, 85 Ind. 529, Henry v Dennis, 93 Ind. 452, Ryan v Miller, 12 Daly, 77, Brown v. Howard Ins Co., 42 Ind 384, 20 Am. Rep. 90, Scott v Hunter, 46 Pa St 192, Baltimore & P R. R Co v Reaney, 42 Md 117, Marble v Worcester, 4 Gray, 395, Campbell v Stillwater, 32 Minn. 308.

In McGrew v Stone (53 Pa. St 436), the maxim *In jure causa proxima non remota spectatur* is said by the court to mean · "When one is engaged in an act which the circumstances indicate may be dangerous to others, and the event whose occurrence is necessary to make the act injurious, can be readily seen as likely to occur under the circumstances, the defendant is liable if he does not take all the care which prudence would suggest to avoid the injury " But the consequence may not flow naturally and directly from the alleged cause, as some other force may intervene and then the cause is said to be "remote" and insufficient to warrant a recovery.

Thus where a train was forty-five minutes late when a gust of wind threw it from the track and injured a passenger, it was held that though the train would have escaped the gust of wind had it been on time, yet the accident was neither the natural nor probable consequence of the delay, and only an independent force took advantage of it and the road was not liable to the passenger McClary v. Sioux City, etc , R R., 3 Neb 44,

"A party who by contract is entitled to all the articles manufactured by a certain company, he furnishing the raw materials, cannot maintain an action against a wrong-doer who by trespass, stops the machinery of the company and obstructs its operations in performing the contract " Cooley on Torts, 75, Dale v. Grant, 34 N J L. 142,

and defaults a man is liable. When complaint is made that one person has caused harm to another, the first question is whether his act (h) was really the cause of that harm in a sense upon which the law can take action. The harm or loss may be traceable to his act, but the connexion may be, in the accustomed phrase, too remote. The maxim "In jure non remota causa sed proxima spectatur" is Englished in Bacon's constantly cited gloss: "It were infinite for the law to judge the causes of causes, and their impulsions one of another therefore it contenteth itself

---

(h) For shortness' sake I shall often use the word "act" alone as equivalent to "act or default."

---

citing Connecticut Ins Co v New York, etc., R I Co, 25 Conn 265, Anthony v Slaid, 11 Met. 290, Rockingham Ins Co. v Boscher, 39 Me. 253. See Zler v. Hofflin, 33 Minn 66, Austin v Barrows, 31 Conn 287, Brooke v Tradesman's Nat Bank, 69 Hun, 202, 23 N. Y S. Rep. 802; Swift v. Eastern Warehouse Co., 86 Ala 294, 5 So Rep 505, Jex v Strauss, 55 N Y Superior Ct. 52, Malone v. Pittsburgh & L E. R Co, 152 Pa St 390, 25 At. Rep 638, 31 W. N. C 407, Kahl v Love, 37 N J L. 5, McClelland v. Louisville, etc., Ry Co, 94 Ind 276

A city is not liable for an accident caused by a horse's taking fright at the sound caused by the wheel of the vehicle, which plaintiff is driving, scraping against a stone in the road, although such stone is an obstacle over which a vehicle could not pass in safety. Bowes v City of Boston, 155 Mass. 344; 29 N. E. Rep. 633.

By reason of a collision of railway trains a passenger was injured, and becoming thereby disordered in mind and body he, some eight months thereafter, committed suicide. *Held*, in a suit by his personal representatives against the railway company, that as his own act was the proximate cause of his death, they are not entitled to damages. Scheffer v. Railroad Co, 105 U S. 249.

If there is a defect in a hitching post, and the horse hitched to it is frightened by the running away of another horse, and breaks the post and runs over a person in the street, the latter cannot maintain an action for the defect in the post as the cause of his injury. Rockford v Tripp, 83 Ill 347.

A woman's illness caused by fright from the shooting of a dog in her presence is not such a consequence as would be supposed to naturally follow the act. Renner v Canfield, 36 Minn. 90.

Nor is a woman's premature delivery caused by a quarrel near her house. Phillips v Dickerson, 85 Ill 11.

with the immediate cause; and judgeth of acts by that, without looking to any further degree" (i). Liability must be founded on an act which is the "immediate cause" of harm or of injury to a right. Again, there may have been an undoubted wrong, but it may be doubted how much of the harm that ensues is related to the wrongful act as its "immediate cause," and therefore is to be counted in estimating the wrong-doer's liability. The distinction of proximate from remote consequences is needful first to ascertain whether there is any liability at all, and then, if it is established that wrong has been committed, to settle the footing on which compensation for the wrong is to be awarded.

Measure of damages. The normal form of compensation for wrongs, as for breaches of contract, in the procedure of our Superior Courts of common law has been the fixing of damages in money by a jury under the direction of a judge. It is the duty of the judge (k) to explain to the jurors, as a matter of law, the footing upon which they should calculate the damages if their verdict is for the plaintiff. This footing or scheme is called the "measure of damages." Thus, in the common case of a breach of contract for the sale of goods, the measure of damages is the difference between the price named in the contract and the market value of the like goods at the time when the contract was broken. In cases of contract there is no trouble in separating the question whether a contract has been made and broken from the question what is the proper measure of damages (l). But in cases of tort the primary question

(i) Maxims of the Law Reg 1 It is remarkable that not one of the examples adduced by Bacon belongs to the law of torts, or raises a question of the measure of damages. There could be no stronger illustration of the extremely modern character of the whole subject as now understood.

(k) *Hadley* v *Baxendale* (1854), 9 Ex 341, 23 L J Ex 179

(l) Whether it is practically worth while to sue on a contract must, indeed, often turn on the measure of damages. But this need not concern us here.

of liability may itself depend, and it often does, on the nearness or remoteness of the harm complained of. Except where we have an absolute duty and an act which manifestly violates it, no clear line can be drawn between the rule of liability and the rule of compensation. The measure of damages, a matter appearing at first sight to belong to the law of remedies more than of "antecedent rights," constantly involves, in the field of torts, points that are in truth of the very substance of the law. It is under the head of "measure of damages" that these for the most part occur in practice, and are familiar to lawyers; but their real connexion with the leading principles of the subject must not be overlooked here.

Meaning of "immediate cause." The meaning of the term "immediate cause" is not capable of perfect or general definition. Even if it had an ascertainable logical meaning, which is more than doubtful, it would not follow that the legal meaning is the same. In fact, our maxim only points out that some consequences are held too remote to be counted. What is the test of remoteness we still have to inquire. The view which I shall endeavour to justify is that, for the purpose of civil liability, those consequences, and those only, are deemed "immediate," "proximate," or, to anticipate a little, "natural and probable," which a person of average competence and knowledge, being in the like case with the person whose conduct is complained of, and having the like opportunities of observation, might be expected to foresee as likely to follow upon such conduct. This is only where the particular consequence is not known to have been intended or foreseen by the actor. If proof of that be forthcoming, whether the consequence was "immediate" or not does not matter. That which a man

---

Meaning of "Immediate Cause." See American notes to Proximate Cause, *post*, p 573

actually foreseen is to him, at all events, natural and probable.

Liability for consequences of wilful act. In the case of wilful wrong-doing we have an act intended to do harm, and harm done by it. The inference of liability from such an act (given the general rule, and assuming no just cause of exception to be present) may seem a plain matter. But even in this first case it is not so plain as it seems. We have to consider the relation of that which the wrong-doer intends to the events which in fact are brought to pass by his deed; a relation which is not constant, nor always evident. A man strikes at another with his fist or a stick, and the blow takes effect as he meant it to do. Here the connexion of act and consequence is plain enough, and the wrongful actor is liable for the resulting hurt.

It extends to some consequences not intended. But the consequences may be more than was intended, or different. And it may be different either in respect of the event, or of the person affected. Nym quarrels with Pistol and knocks him down. The blow is not serious in itself,

---

Liability for consequences of wilful act. Malicious motives, alone, can never constitute a cause of action, but where the allegations are sufficient to sustain the action, independent of malice, it may be alleged and proved in enhancement of damages. Jenkins v. Fowler, 24 Pa. St. 308, Fowler v. Jenkins, 28 Id. 176; Mahan v. Brown, 13 Wend. 261, Stevens v. Kelley, 78 Me. 445, Jones v. Jones, 77 Ill. 562, Burke v. Smith, 69 Mich. 380, Hutch v. Pendergast, 15 Md. 251, 37 N. W. Rep. 838; Harwood v. Tompkins, 24 N. J. L. 425, Thornton v. Thornton, 63 N. C. 211, Jenks v. Williams, 115 Mass. 217, Heywood v. Tilson, 75 Me. 225, Bangor, etc., R. R. v. Smith, 49 Me. 9; Morris v. Scott, 21 Wend. 281, Jacksonville, T. & K. W. Ry. Co. v. Peninsular Land, etc., Co., 27 Fla. 157; 9 So. Rep. 679, Auburn, etc., R. Co. v. Douglass, 9 N. Y. 444, Stearns v. Sampson, 59 Me. 568, White v. Carroll, 42 N. Y. 161, Johnson v. Bouton, 55 Neb. 898, 53 N. W. Rep. 995; Johnson v. Chicago, etc., R. Co., 51 Ia. 25, 50 N. W. Rep. 543, Glendon Iron Co. v. Uhler, 75 Pa. St. 467, South Royalton Bank v. Suffolk Bank, 27 Vt. 505, West v. Forrest, 22 Mo. 344, Smith v. Goodman, 75 Ga. 198, Hawes v. Knowles, 114 Mass. 519.

but Pistol falls on a heap of stones which cut and bruise him. Or they are on the bank of a deep ditch; Nym does not mean to put Pistol into the ditch, but his blow throws Pistol off his balance, whereby Pistol does fall into the ditch, and his clothes are spoilt. These are simple cases where a different consequence from that which was intended happens as an incident of the same action. Again, one of Jack Cade's men throws a stone at an alderman. The stone misses the alderman, but strikes and breaks a jug of beer which another citizen is carrying. Or Nym and Bardolph agree to waylay and beat Pistol after dark. Poins comes along the road at the time and place where they expect Pistol; and, taking him for Pistol, Bardolph and Nym seize and beat Poins. Clearly, just as much wrong is done to Poins, and he has the same claim to redress, as if Bardolph and Nym meant to beat Poins, and not Pistol (*m*). Or, to take an actual and well-known case in our books (*n*), Shepherd throws a lighted squib into a building full of people, doubtless intending it to do mischief of some kind. It falls near a person who, by an instant and natural act of self-protection, casts it from him. A third person again does the same. In this third flight the squib meets with Scott, strikes him in the face, and explodes, destroying the sight of one eye. Shepherd neither threw the squib at Scott, nor intended such grave

---

(*m*) In criminal law there is some difficulty in the case of attempted personal offences. There is no doubt that if A shoots and kills or wounds X, under the belief that the man he shoots at is Z, he is in no way excused by the mistake, and cannot be heard to say that he had no unlawful intention as to X. *R. v. Smith* (1855), Dears. 559. But if he misses, it seems doubtful whether he can be said to have attempted to kill either X or Z. Cf. *R. v. Latimer* (1886), 17 Q. B. D. 359, 55 L. J. M. C. 135. In Germany there is a whole literature of modern controversy on the subject. See Dr. R. Franz, "Vorstellung und Wille in der modernen Dolusiehre," Ztsch. für die gesamte Strafrechtswissenschaft, x. 169.

(*n*) *Scott v. Shepherd*, 2 W. Bl. 892, and in 1 Sm. L. C. No doubt was entertained of Shepherd's liability, the only question being in what form of action he was liable. The inference of wrongful intention is in this case about as obvious as it can be. It was, however, not necessary, squib throwing as Nares J. pointed out, having been declared a nuisance by statute.

harm to any one, but he is none the less liable to Scott. And so in the other cases put, it is clear law that the wrong-doer is liable to make good the consequences, and it is likewise obvious to common sense that he ought to be. He went about to do harm, and having begun an act of wrongful mischief, he cannot stop the risk at his pleasure, nor confine it to the precise objects he laid out, but must abide it fully and to the end.

"Natural consequences:" relation of the rule to the actor's intention. This principle is commonly expressed in the maxim that "a man is presumed to intend the natural consequences of his acts:" a proposition, which, with due explanation and within due limits, is acceptable, but which in itself is ambiguous. To start from the simplest case, we may know that the man intended to produce a certain consequence, and did produce it. And we may have independent proof of the intention; as if he announced it beforehand by threats or boasting of what he would do. But oftentimes the act itself is the chief or sole proof of the intention with which it is done. If we see Nym walk up to Pistol and knock him down, we infer that Pistol's fall was intended by Nym as the consequence of the blow. We may be mistaken in this judgment. Possibly Nym is walking in his sleep, and has no real intention at all, at any rate none which can be imputed to Nym awake. But we do naturally infer inten-

---

"Natural Consequences." relation of the rule to the actor's intention. The maxim that "a man is presumed to intend the natural consequences of his acts" is accepted as true. See authorities establishing and illustrating its application, *ante*, p. 26, *post*, pp 37, 42. The foundation of the maxim lies in the fact that when it said that from certain acts the law presumes an intent, what is meant is that the intention with which the act is done is immaterial. Thus, one who in sport intentionally threw a piece of mortar at another without meaning to harm him, and injured a third person, is liable to the person struck. Peterson *v.* Haffner, 59 Ind. 130.

tion, and the chances are greatly in favour of our being right. So nobody could doubt that when Shepherd threw a lighted squib into a crowded place he expected and meant mischief of some kind to be done by it. Thus far it is a real inference, not a presumption properly so called. Now take the case of Nym knocking Pistol over a bank into the ditch. We will suppose there is nothing (as there well may be nothing but Nym's own worthless assertion) to show whether Nym knew the ditch was there; or, if he did know, whether he meant Pistol to fall into it. These questions are like enough to be insoluble. How shall we deal with them? We shall disregard them. From Nym's point of view his purpose may have been simply to knock Pistol down, or to knock him into the ditch also; from Pistol's point of view the grievance is the same. The wrong-doer cannot call on us to perform a nice discrimination of that which is willed by him from that which is only consequential on the strictly wilful wrong. We say that intention is presumed, meaning that it does not matter whether intention can be proved or not; nay, more, it would in the majority of cases make no difference if the wrong-doer could disprove it. Such an explanation as this — "I did mean to knock you down, but I meant you not to fall into the ditch" — would, even if believed, be the lamest of apologies, and it would no less be a vain excuse in law

Meaning of "natural and probable" consequence. The habit by which we speak of presumption comes

---

Meaning of "Natural and Probable" consequences. A "natural and probable consequence" flows from a "natural and probable" or "proximate" cause. Natural consequences are always proximate. The leading American case on this subject is Milwaukee & St. P. Ry. Co. v. Kellogg (94 U. S. 474), in which the court said: "The primary cause may be the proximate cause of a disaster though it may operate through successive instruments, as an article at the end of a chain may be moved by a force applied at the other end, that force being the proximate cause of the movement; or, as in the oft-

probably from the time when, inasmuch as parties could not give evidence, intention could hardly ever be matter of direct proof. Under the old system of pleading and

---

cited case of the squib in the market place. Scott v Shepherd, 2 Black. W 892. The question always is, was there an unbroken connection between the wrongful act and the injury, a continuous operation? Did the facts constitute a continuous succession of events so linked together as to make a natural whole, or was there some new and independent cause intervening between the wrong and injury?"

Consequences which follow in unbroken sequence, without an intervening sufficient cause, from the original wrong, are natural; and for such consequences the original wrong-doer is responsible, even though he could not have foreseen the particular results, provided that by the exercise of ordinary care he might have foreseen that some injury would result from his act. Baltimore, etc., R Co. v Kemp, 61 Md. 71, 18 Am & Eng R Cas 220, Terre Haute, etc., R. Co. v. Buck, 69 Ind 316, 19 Am & Eng. R. Cas 234, 49 Am. Rep 168, Ricker v. Freeman, 50 N. H 420, 9 Am Rep 267, Jeffersonville, etc., R Co v. Riley, 39 Ind. 568, Louisiana Mut Ins Co v. Tweed, 7 Wall. 44, Binford v. Johnson, 9 Ind 126, 12 Am Rep 508, Billman v Indianapolis, etc., R. Co., 76 Ind 166, 6 Am. & Eng R Cas 41, 40 Am Rep 230, Beauchamp v. Saginaw Mining Co., 50 Mich 163, 15 Am. Rep 30, Liming v. Illinois Cent R Co., 81 Ia 246, 47 N W Rep 67, Lowery v Manhattan R Co., 99 N Y 158, 23 Am & Eng. R. Cas. 276, Brown v Chicago, etc., R Co., 54 Wis. 312, 3 Am. & Eng R. Cas. 444, Hill v Windsor, 118 Mass. 251, Louisville, etc., R Co. v Krinning, 87 Ind. 351, Pittsb. S Ry Co v. Taylor, 104 Pa St. 306, Holmes v. Harrington, 30 Mo. Ap 661, Allen v. Truesdell, 135 Mass 75, Jacksonville, T. & K W Ry. Co v Peninsular Land, etc., Co, 27 Fla. 157, 9 So. Rep. 678, Childress v. Yourie, Meigs, 561, Topeka v. Tuttle, 5 Kan. 312

This doctrine is followed in the case of Lowery v Manhattan Ry. Co (99 N. Y. 158, 1 N. E Rep 608), in which the facts were, in substance, that fire from defendant's locomotive engine on its elevated tracks fell upon a horse attached to a wagon in the street below, and upon the hand of the driver, causing the horse to run away. The driver, after failing in an attempt to stop the horse by driving against a post, intentionally turned him against the curb stone to arrest his progress, but the wagon passed over the curbstone, threw out the driver, and ran over and injured plaintiff. It was held by the court, that the defendant was liable, even though plaintiff would not have been injured but for the driver's diversion of the horse from the natural course it might have taken, for though there might have been an error of judgement on the driver's part he had been placed by defendant's negligence in a position of sudden pain and surprise, excusing him from ordinary prudence.

procedure, Brain C. J. might well say, "the thought of man is not triable" (o). Still there is more in our maxim than this. For although we do not care whether the man intended the particular consequence or not, we have in mind such consequences as he might have intended, or without exactly intending them, contemplated as possible; so that it would not be absurd to infer as a fact that he either did mean them to ensue, or recklessly put aside the risk of some such consequences ensuing. This is the limit introduced by such terms as "natural"—or more fully, "natural and probable"—consequence (p). What is natural and probable in this sense is commonly, but not always, obvious. There are consequences which no man could, with common sense and observation, help foreseeing. There are others which no human prudence could have foreseen. Between these extremes is a middle region of various probabilities divided by an ideal boundary which will be differently fixed by different opinions, and as we approach this boundary the difficulties increase. There is a point where subsequent events are, according to common understanding, the consequence not of the first wrongful act at all, but of something else that has happened in the meanwhile, though, but for the first act, the event might or could not have been what it was (q). But that point cannot be defined by science or philosophy (r), and even if it could, the definition would not be of much use for the guidance of juries. If English law seems vague on these

---

(o) Year Book, 17 Edw. IV. 1, translated in Blackburn on Sale, at p. 193 in 1st ed., 261 in 2nd ed. by Graham.

(p) "Normal, or likely or probable of occurrence in the ordinary course of things, would perhaps be the better expression." Grove J. in *Smith v. Green*, 1 C. P. D. at p. 96. But what is normal or likely to a specialist may not be normal or likely to a plain man's knowledge and experience.

(q) Thus Quain J. said (*Sneesby v. L.*

& Y. Rail. Co., L. R. 9 Q. B. at p. 268) "In tort the defendant is liable for all the consequences of his illegal act, when they are not so remote as to have no direct connexion with the act, as by the lapse of time for instance."

(r) "The doctrine of causation," said Fry L. J., "involves much difficulty in philosophy as in law." *Seton v. Lafone* (1887), 19 Q. B. Div. at p. 74, 56 L. J. Q. B. 415.

questions, it is because, in the analysis made necessary by the separation of findings of fact from conclusions of law, it has grappled more closely with the inherent vagueness of facts than any other system. We may now take some illustrations of the rule of "natural and probable consequences" as it is generally accepted. In whatever form we state it, we must remember that it is not a logical definition, but only a guide to the exercise of common sense. The lawyer cannot afford to adventure himself with philosophers in the logical and metaphysical controversies that beset the idea of cause

Vandenburgh v. Truax. In *Vandenburgh v Truax* (s), decided by the Supreme Court of New York in 1817, the plaintiff's servant and the defendant quarrelled in the street. The defendant took hold of the servant, who broke loose from him and ran away; "the defendant took up a pick-axe and followed the boy, who fled into the plaintiff's store, and the defendant pursued him there, with the pick-axe in his hand." In running behind the counter for shelter the servant knocked out the faucet from a cask of wine, whereby the wine ran out and was lost. Here the defendant (whatever the merits of the original quarrel) was clearly a wrong-doer in pursuing the boy; the plaintiff's house was a natural place for his servant to take refuge in, and it was also natural that the servant, "fleeing for his life from a man in hot pursuit armed with a deadly weapon," should, in his hasty movements, do some damage to the plaintiff's property in the shop.

Guille v. Swan. There was a curious earlier case in the same State (*t*), where one Guille, after going up in a balloon, came down in Swan's garden. A crowd of people, attracted by the balloon, broke into the garden and trod down the

(s) 4 Denio, 464 The decision seems to be generally accepted as good law

(*t*) *Guille v Swan* (1822), 19 Johns 381

vegetables and flowers. Guille's descent was in itself plainly a trespass; and he was held liable not only for the damage done by the balloon itself but for that which was done by the crowd. "If his descent under such circumstances would, ordinarily and naturally, draw a crowd of people about him, either from curiosity, or for the purpose of rescuing him from a perilous situation, all this he ought to have foreseen, and must be responsible for" (*u*). In both these cases the squib case was commented and relied on. Similarly it has many times been said, and it is undoubted law, that if a man lets loose a dangerous animal in an inhabited place he is liable for all the mischief it may do.

Liability for consequences of trespass. The balloon case illustrates what was observed in the first chapter on the place of trespass in the law of torts. The trespass was not in the common sense wilful, Guille certainly did not mean to come down into Swan's garden, which he did, in fact, with some danger to himself. But a man who goes up in a balloon must know that he has to come down somewhere, and that he cannot be sure of coming down in a place which he is entitled to use for that purpose, or where his descent will cause no damage and excite no objection. Guille's liability was accordingly the same as if the balloon had been under

---

(*u*) Per Spencer C. J. It appeared that the defendant (plaintiff in error) had called for help, but this was treated as immaterial. The recent Scottish case of *Scott's Trustees v. Moss* (1889), 17 Ct. of Sess. C. 4th S. 32, is hardly so strong for there a parachute descent was not only contemplated but advertised as a public entertainment.

Liability for consequences of trespass. If the act of trespass shows a wanton disregard of the rights of others, actual malice need not be shown. Baltimore, etc., R. Co. *v.* Boone, 45 Md. 344; Drohn *v.* Brewer, 77 Ill. 280; Raynor *v.* Nims, 37 Mich. 34, 26 Am. Rep. 493; Cheeney *v.* Nebraska, etc., Stone Co., 41 Fed. Rep. 170; Wilson *v.* Gunning, 80 Ia. 331, 45 N. W. Rep. 920; Dexter *v.* Cole, 6 Wis. 319; Amick *v.* O'Hara, 6 Blackf. 258; Cate *v.* Cate, 44 N. H. 211; Burch *v.* Carter, 32 N. J. L. 554. See Savage *v.* Fullar, Brayt. 223.

his control, and he had guided it into Swan's garden. If balloons were as manageable as a vessel at sea, and by some accident which could not be ascribed to any fault of the traveller the steering apparatus got out of order, and so the balloon drifted into a neighbour's garden, the result might be different. So, if a landslip carries away my land and house from a hillside on which the house is built, and myself in the house, and leaves all overlying a neighbour's field in the valley, it cannot be said that I am liable for the damage to my neighbor's land; indeed, there is not even a technical trespass, for there is no voluntary act at all. But where trespass to property is committed by a voluntary act, known or not known to be an infringement of another's right, there the trespasser, as regards liability for consequences, is on the same footing as a wilful wrong-doer.

Consequence too remote: Glover v L. & S. W Rail Co. A simple example of a consequence too remote to be ground for liability, though it was part of the incidents following on a wrongful act, is afforded by *Glover* v. *London and South Western Railway Company* (v). The plaintiff, being a passenger on the railway, was charged by the company's ticket collector, wrongly as it turned out, with not having a ticket, and was removed from the train by the company's servants with no more force than was necessary for the purpose. He left a pair of race-glasses in the carriage, which were lost; and he sought to hold the company liable not only for the personal assault committed by taking him out of the train, but for the value of these glasses. The Court held without difficulty that the loss was not the " necessary consequence " or " immediate result " of the wrongful act: for there was nothing to show that the plaintiff was prevented from taking his glasses with him, or that he would not have got them if after leaving the carriage he had asked for them.

(v) (1867) L R 3 Q B 25, 37 L J Q B 57

Question of what is killing in criminal law. In criminal law the question not unfrequently occurs, on a charge of murder or manslaughter, whether a certain act or neglect was the "immediate cause" of the death of the deceased person. We shall not enter here upon the cases on this head, but the comparison of them will be found interesting. They are collected by Sir James Stephen (a).

Liability for negligence depends on probability of consequence, i. e., its capability of being foreseen by a reasonable man. The doctrine of "natural and probable consequence" is most clearly illustrated, however, in the

(a) Digest of the Criminal Law, Arts 219, 220

Liability for negligence depends on probability of consequence The doctrine of the text has been generally accepted and applied by the courts of the United States Thus, in a leading case it was said "The true rule is that the injury must be the natural and probable consequence of the (defendant's) negligence — such a consequence, as, under the surrounding circumstances of the case, might and ought to have been foreseen by the wrong-doer as likely to flow from his act This is not a limitation of the maxim *causa proxima non remota spectatur*, it only affects its application" Hoag v Lake Shore, etc, R Co, 85 Pa St 293, 27 Am Rep 653.

In Henry v Southern Pacific R. Co. (50 Cal 183), McKinstry, J., said. "A long series of judicial decisions has defined proximate or immediate and direct damages to be ordinary and natural results of the negligence, such as are usual, and therefore might have been expected" See Goshen Turnpike Co v. Sears, 7 Conn. 86, Pennsylvania R Co v Hope, 80 Pa St 373, 21 Am. Rep 100, Pennsylvania R Co v Kerr, 62 Pa St 353, 1 Am Rep 431, Phillips v Dickerson, 85 Ill 11, 28 Am Rep 607, McGrew v. Stone, 53 Pa St. 436, Doggett v. Richmond, etc., R. Co., 78 N. C 305, Chicago v Starr, 42 Ill 174, 89 Am Dec 422, Bellefontaine, etc, R Co v Snyder, 18 Ohio St. 399, 98 Am Dec. 181, Harrison v Berkley, 1 Strobh 525, 17 Am Dec. 578, McDonald v Snelling, 14 Allen, 290; Campbell v. Stillwater, 32 Minn 308, 50 Am Rep. 567, McClary v. Sioux City, etc., R Co, 3 Neb. 44, Township of West Mahoney v Watson, 112 Pa St 574; Louisville, etc, R. Co v. Guthrie, 10 Lea, 432, 11 Am & Eng. R. Cas 478, Lane v Atlantic Works, 111 Mass 136, Hill v Windsor, 118 Mass. 251; Wabash, etc, R Co v. Locke, 112 Ind 404, Atchison v Goodrich Transp Co, 60 Wis 141, Toledo, etc, R Co v Muthersbaugh, 71 Ill 572, Tutein v. Harley, 98 Mass. 211.

Where a railway company, through negligence by the escape of fire

law of negligence. For there the substance of the wrong itself is failure to act with due foresight. It has been

from its locomotive engine, sets fire to a depot, from which a hotel in the vicinity is destroyed, to make the company liable to the owner of the hotel, "It was not at all necessary that the burning of the hotel should be so certain to result from the burning of the depot that a reasonable person could have foreseen that the hotel *would* burn, or that it would probably burn. It is enough if it be a consequence so natural and direct that a reasonable person might, and naturally would, see that it was liable to result from the burning of the depot, — that is, that it might follow." C. & A. R. R. Co. v. Pennell, 110 Ill. 446.

Where plaintiff was injured, while walking by the side of a railroad track, by a cow which was thrown from the track by the engine, and which fell against plaintiff after striking the ground, the injury is the proximate consequence of the engine striking the cow. "The direct cause was put in operation by the force of the engine, which continued until the injury, and injuries directly produced by instrumentalities thus put in operation and continued, are proximate consequences of the primary act, though they may not have been contemplated or foreseen. The relation of cause and effect between the primary cause and the injury is established by the connection and succession of the intervening circumstances." Ala. G. S. R. Co. v. Chapman, 80 Ala. 615.

Where the horses of a traveler, being frightened by an overturn of their load caused by a defect in the highway, escape from him, run ninety rods, and collide with another traveler, the injury of the latter may be a natural and probable consequence of the defect, for which the town is liable. Merriel v. Claremont, 58 N. H. 468. See Aldrich v. Gorham, 77 Me. 287, Hampson v. Taylor, 15 R. I. 283, 23 At. Rep. 732, Smalley v. City of Appleton, 75 Wis. 18; Dickson v. Hollister, 123 Pa. St. 421, 16 At. Rep. 484, 23 W. N. C. 128.

With regard to the spreading of negligent fires the decisions in the different States upon analogous statements of fact are not uniform, but the weight of the authorities, and the true doctrine is, that proximity of cause has no necessary connection with contiguity of space or nearness of time. Thus, in the case of Chicago, St. L. & P. R. Co. v. Williams (131 Ind. 30, 30 N. E. Rep. 696), it was held, that where a fire originated on the defendant's right of way, and was carried by the wind to plaintiff's property, though other lands intervened over which the fire burned several days, and was several times partially subdued before reaching his land, defendant is not relieved from the liability on the ground that its negligence was not the proximate cause of the injury. See Tyler v. Ricsmore, 87 Va. 466, 12 S. E. Rep. 799, Marvin v. Chicago, M. & St. P. Ry Co., 79 Wis. 140, 47 N. W. Rep. 1123; St. Louis, A. & T. Ry. Co. v. McKinsey, 78 Tex. 298; 14 S. W. Rep. 645, Frace v. New York L. E. & W. R. Co., 68 Hun, 325; 22 N. Y. S. Rep. 958, Adams v. Young, 44 Ohio

defined as "the omission to do something which a reasonable man, guided upon those considerations which ordinarily

St. 80, Pennsylvania R. Co., v. Kerr, 62 Pa. St. 353, Atchison T. & S. F. R. Co. v. Stafford, 12 Kan. 354, Del L. & W. R. Co. v. Salmon, 39 N. J. L. 300, Hoyt v. Jeffers, 30 Mich. 181, Poeppers v. M. K. & P. Ry. Co., 67 Mo. 715, Perley v. Eastern R. Co., 98 Mass. 414, Fent v. Toledo, etc., R. R. Co., 59 Ill. 349, 11 Am. Rep. 13, Atchison, etc., R. Co. v. Stafford, 12 Kan. 354, 15 Am. Rep. 362, Krippner v. Biebl, 28 Minn. 139, Burlington R. Co. v. Westover, 4 Neb. 268, Salmon v. Delaware, etc., R. Co., 11 Am. Law Reg. 560, Pittsburg, etc., R. Co. v. Noel, 77 Ind. 110; 7 Am. & Eng. R. Cas. 571, Butcher v. Vaca V. etc., R. Co., 67 Cal. 518, 22 Am. & Eng. R. Cas. 644, Poeppers v. Missouri, etc., R. Co., 67 Mo. 715, Simmonds v. New York, etc. R. Co., 52 Conn. 264, 23 Am. & Eng. R. Cas. 369.

Non-liability examples. Where defendants, knowing a county treasurer to be a defaulter, loaned him money and certificates to enable him to have his accounts audited, and to conceal his embezzlement from the board of county commissioners, after which he embezzled a further sum, and fled from the territory, it was held, that the damage that the county sustained by reason of such act of defendants was too contingent, remote, and indefinite to constitute a cause of action. County of Nelson v. Northcote, 6 Dak. 378, 43 N. W. Rep. 897, citing Morgan v. Bliss, 2 Mass. 111, Randall v. Hazelton, 12 Allen, 412.

The obstruction of a public crossing by a railroad train, thereby preventing plaintiff from driving across for more than half an hour, does not render the company liable for injuries to him caused by the fact that at the end of that time his horse became frightened and ran away at the approach of a second engine and train. "The damages resulting from the fright of the horse were too remote, as a consequence of the obstruction of the public road." Stanton v. Louisville & N. R. Co., 91 Ala. 382, 8 So. Rep. 798.

Another case, involving the connection of defective highways with injury to travellers, is that of Schaeffer v. Township of Jackson (150 Pa. St. 145; 24 At. Rep. 629), in which the facts were that plaintiff had been driven safely past a hole in the road and a pile of stones negligently placed by the town supervisors on a highway. When about 120 feet beyond this obstruction plaintiff's horse became frightened by a donkey, turned short around, breaking a wheel of the buggy, and ran back, one axle dragging on the ground. The dragging axle caused the buggy to be drawn to the side of the road, where it caught in the hole. The buggy was upset and the plaintiff was thrown out upon the stone pile and injured. It was held, that the township was not liable, the occurrence being extraordinary, and not the natural and probable result of the negligence, but of an independent, primary, efficient, proximate cause.

Upon remoteness of cause of injury arising out of negligence, see

regulate the conduct of human affairs, would do, or doing something which a prudent and reasonable man would not do" (*y*). Now a reasonable man can be guided only by a reasonable estimate of probabilities. If men went about to guard themselves against every risk to themselves or others which might by ingenious conjecture be conceived as possible, human affairs could not be carried on at all. The reasonable man, then, to whose ideal behaviour we are to look as the standard of duty, will neither neglect what he can forecast as probable, nor waste his anxiety on events that are barely possible. He will order his precaution by the measure of what appears likely in the known course of things. This being the standard, it follows that if in a particular case (not being within certain special and more stringent rules) the harm complained of is not such as a reasonable man in the defendant's place should have foreseen as likely to happen, there is no wrong and no liability. And the statement proposed, though not positively laid down, in *Greenland* v. *Chaplin* (*z*), namely, "that a person is expected to anticipate and guard against all reasonable consequences, but that he is not, by the law of England, expected to anticipate and guard against that which no

---

(*y*) Alderson B. In *Blythe* v. *Birmingham Waterworks Co.* (1856), 11 Ex. 781, 25 L.J. Ex. 212. This is not a complete definition, since a man is not liable for even wilful omission without some antecedent ground of duty. But of that hereafter.

( ) Per Pollock C. B. (1850), 5 Ex. at p. 248.

Seale v. G. C. & S. F. Ry. Co., 65 Tex. 274; Reiper v. Nichols, 31 Hun, 491; Benson v. Cent. Pac. Ry. Co., 98 Cal. 45, 32 Pac. Rep. 809, Id. 33 Pac. Rep. 206; Western Ry. v. Mutch (Ala.), 11 So. Rep. 894; Barton v. Pepin Co. Ag. Soc., 83 Wis. 19, 52 N. W. Rep. 1129; Texas & P. Ry. v. Doherty (Tex. App.) 15 S. W. Rep. 44; Louisville & N. R. Co., v. Kelsey, 89 Ala. 287, 7 So. Rep. 648; Lowry v. St. Louis & H. Ry. Co., 40 Mo. Ap. 554; Childrey v. Huntington, 34 W. Va. 457, 12 S. E. Rep. 536; South Side, etc., Co. v. Fitch (Pa.), 11 At. Rep. 627; People v. Rockwell, 39 Mich. 503; Nelson v. Chicago, etc., Ry. Co., 30 Minn. 74; Railroad Co. v. Guthrie, 10 Lea, 432; Poland v. Earhart, 70 Ia. 285; Swiffin v. Lowry, 37 Minn. 345, 34 N. W. Rep. 22.

reasonable man would expect to occur," appears to contain the only rule tenable on principle where the liability is founded solely on negligence. "Mischief which could by no possibility have been foreseen, and which no reasonable person would have anticipated," may be the ground of legal compensation under some rule of exceptional severity, and such rules, for various reasons, exist, but under an ordinary rule of due care and caution it cannot be taken into account.

Examples. We shall now give examples on either side of the line.

Hill v. New River Co. In *Hill* v. *New River Company* (a), the defendant company had in the course of their works caused a stream of water to spout up in the middle of a public road, without making any provision, such as fencing or watching it, for the safety of persons using the highway. As the plaintiff's horses and carriage were being driven along the road, the horses shied at the water, dashed across the road, and fell into an open excavation by the roadside which had been made by persons and for purposes unconnected with the water company. It was argued that the immediate cause of the injuries to man, horses, and carriage ensuing upon this fall was not the unlawful act of the water company, but the neglect of the contractors who had made the cutting in leaving it open and unfenced. But the court held that the "proximate cause" was "the first negligent act which drove the carriage and horses into the excavation." In fact, it was a natural consequence that frightened horses should bolt off the road; it could not be foreseen exactly where they would go off, or what they might run against or fall into. But some such harm as did happen was probable enough, and it was immaterial for the

---

(a) 9 B. & S. 303 (1868), cp. *Harris* v. *Mobbs* (Denman J. 1878), 3 Ex. D. 268, which, perhaps, goes a step farther.

purpose in hand whether the actual state of the ground was temporary or permanent, the work of nature or of man. If the carriage had gone into a river, or over an embankment, or down a precipice, it would scarcely have been possible to raise the doubt.

Williams v. G. W. Rail Co. *Williams v. Great Western Railway Company* (b) is a stronger case, if not an extreme one. There were on a portion of the company's line in Denbighshire two level crossings near one another, the railway meeting a carriage-road in one place and a footpath (which branched off from the road) in the other. It was the duty of the company under certain Acts to have gates and a watchman at the road crossing, and a gate or stile at the footpath crossing; but none of these things had been done.

"On the 22d December, 1871, the plaintiff, a child of four and a-half years old, was found lying on the rails by the footpath, with one foot severed from his body. There was no evidence to show how the child had come there, beyond this, that he had been sent on an errand a few minutes before from the cottage where he lived, which lay by the roadside, at about 300 yards distance from the railway, and farther from it than the point where the footpath diverged from the road. It was suggested on the part of the defendants that he had gone along the road, and then, reaching the railway, had strayed down the line; and on the part of the plaintiff, that he had gone along the open footpath, and was crossing the line when he was knocked down and injured by the passing train."

On these facts it was held that there was evidence proper to go to a jury, and on which they might reasonably find that the accident to the child was caused by the railway company's omission to provide a gate or stile. "One at

(b) L R 9 Ex 157, 43 L J Ex 105 (1874). Cp *Hayes v Michigan Central Rail Co* (1883), 111 U S 228

least of the objects for which a gate or stile is required is to warn people of what is before them, and to make them pause before reaching a dangerous place like a railroad" (c)

Bailiffs of Romney Marsh v. Trinity House. In *Bailiffs of Romney Marsh v. Trinity House* (d), a Trinity House cutter had by negligent navigation struck on a shoal about three-quarters of a mile outside the plaintiffs' seawall. Becoming unmanageable, the vessel was inevitably driven by strong wind and tide against the sea-wall, and did much damage to the wall. It was held without difficulty that the Corporation of the Trinity House was liable (under the ordinary rule of a master's responsibility for his servants, of which hereafter) for this damage, as being the direct consequence of the first default which rendered the vessel unmanageable.

Lynch v. Nurdin. Something like this, but not so simple, was *Lynch v. Nurdin* (e), where the owner of a horse and cart left them unwatched in the street; some children came up and began playing about the cart, and as one of them, the plaintiff in the cause, was climbing into the cart another pulled the horse's bridle, the horse moved on, and the plaintiff fell down under the wheel of the cart and was hurt. The owner who had left the cart and horse unattended was held liable for this injury. The Court thought it strictly within the province of a jury " to pronounce on all the circumstances, whether the defendant's conduct was wanting in ordinary care, and the harm to the

(c) Amphlett B at p 162
(d) L R 5 Ex 204, 39 L J Ex 163 (1870), in Ex Ch L R 7 Ex 247 (1872) This comes near the case of letting loose a dangerous animal, a drifting vessel is in itself a dangerous thing In *The George and Richard*, L R 3 A & E 466, a brig by negligent navigation ran into a bark, and disabled her, the bark was driven on shore, held that the owners of the brig were liable for injury ensuing from the wreck of the bark to persons on board her

(e) 1 Q B 29, 10 L J Q B 73 (1841), cp *Clark v Chambers*, 3 Q B D at p. 331

plaintiff such a result of it as might have been expected" (*f*).

Contrasted cases of non-liability and liability. It will be seen that on the whole the disposition of the Courts has been to extend rather than to narrow the range of "natural and probable consequences." A pair of cases at first sight pretty much alike in their facts, but in one of which the claim succeeded, while in the other it failed, will show where the line is drawn.

Cox v. Burbidge, Lee v. Riley. If a horse escapes into a public road and kicks a person who is lawfully on the road, its owner is not liable unless he knew the horse to be vicious (*g*). He was bound indeed to keep his horse from straying, but it is not an ordinary consequence of a horse being loose on a road that it should kick human beings without provocation. The rule is different however if a horse by reason of a defective gate strays not into the road but into an adjoining field where there are other horses, and kicks one of those horses. In that case the person whose duty it was to maintain the gate is liable to the owner of the injured horse (*h*).

Metropolitan Rail. Co. v. Jackson. The leading case of *Metropolitan Rail. Co. v. Jackson*, (*i*) is in truth of

---

(*f*) This case was relied on in Massachusetts in *Powell v. Deveney* (1819), 3 Cush. 300, where the defendant's truck had, contrary to local regulations, been left out in the street for the night, the shafts being shored up and projecting into the road; a second truck was similarly placed on the opposite side of the road; the driver of a third truck, endeavouring with due caution, as it was found, to drive past through the narrowed fairway thus left, struck the shafts of the defendant's truck, which whirled round and struck and injured the plaintiff, who was on the sidewalk. Held, the defendant was liable. If the case had been that the shafts of the truck remained on the sidewalk, and the plaintiff afterwards stumbled on them in the dark, it would be an almost exact parallel to *Clark v. Chambers* (3 Q. B. D. 327, 47 L. J. Q. B. 427, see below).

(*g*) *Cox v. Burbidge* (1863), 13 C. B. N. S. 430, 32 L. J. C. P. 89.

(*h*) *Lee v. Riley* (1865), 18 C. B. N. S. 722, 34 L. J. C. P. 212. Both decisions were unanimous, and two judges (Erle C. J. and Keating J.) took part in both. Cp. *Ellis v. Loftus Iron Co.*, L. R. 10 C. P. 10, 44 L. J. C. P. 24.

(*i*) 3 App. Ca. 193, 47 L. J. C. P. 303 (1877).

this class, though the problem arose and was considered, in form, upon the question whether there was any evidence of negligence. The plaintiff was a passenger in a carriage already over-full. As the train was stopping at a station, he stood up to resist yet other persons who had opened the door and tried to press in. While he was thus standing, and the door was open, the train moved on. He laid his hand on the door-lintel for support, and at the same moment a porter came up, turned off the intruders, and quickly shut the door in the usual manner. The plaintiff's thumb was caught by the door and crushed. After much difference of opinion in the courts below, mainly due to a too literal following of certain previous authorities, the House of Lords unanimously held that, assuming the failure to prevent overcrowding to be negligence on the company's part, the hurt suffered by the plaintiff was not nearly or certainly enough connected with it to give him a cause of action. It was an accident which might no less have happened if the carriage had not been overcrowded at all.

Non-liability for consequences of unusual state of things. Blyth v. Birmingham Water-works Co. Unusual conditions brought about by severe frost have more than

---

Non-liability for consequences of unusual state of things. In the case of Hoag v. Lake Shore, etc., R. Co. (85 Pa. St. 293, 27 Am. Rep. 653), the facts were, that owing to a sudden rain, an embankment was detached and slid down upon the track. An oil train of defendant's coming along a few minutes after the slide was thrown from the track by this detached earth upon the track, the oil cars thrown off and the oil spilled and set on fire, and thus running down into a creek below swollen by the rain, was carried by the current several hundred feet to the buildings of plaintiff which were thereby set on fire and consumed. The court decided as a matter of law that the cause was too remote from its consequence and refused to submit the question to the jury.

It has been held that a city is not liable for the injury resulting to a person from the breaking, in a violent wind, of a sound and properly secured liberty pole. Allegheny v. Zimmerman, 95 Pa. St. 287.

Where a bridge having become impassable, one who desired to carry wood across piled it on the levee to await opportunity, and a flood car-

once been the occasion of accidents on which untenable claims for compensation have been founded, the Courts holding that the mishap was not such as the party charged with causing it by his negligence could reasonably be expected to provide against. In the memorable "Crimean winter" of 1854–5 a fire-plug attached to one of the mains of the Birmingham Waterworks Company was deranged by the frost, the expansion of superficial ice forcing out the plug, as it afterwards seemed, and the water from the main being dammed by incrusted ice and snow above. The escaping water found its way through the ground into the cellar of a private house, and the occupier sought to recover from the company for the damage. The Court held that the accident was manifestly an extraordinary one, and beyond any such foresight as could be reasonably required(*k*). Here nothing was alleged as constituting a wrong on the company's part beyond the mere fact that they did not take extraordinary precautions.

Sharp v Powell The later case of *Sharp* v *Powell* (*l*) goes farther, as the story begins with an act on the defendant's part which was a clear breach of the law. He caused his van to be washed in a public street, contrary to the Metropolitan Police Act. The

---

(*k*) *Blyth* v *Birmingham Waterworks Co* (1856), 11 Ex 781, 25 L J Ex 212. The question was not really of remoteness of damage, but whether there was any evidence of negligence at all, nevertheless the case is instructive for comparison with the others here cited Cp Mayne on Damages, Preface to the first edition

(*l*) L R 7 C P 253, 41 L J C P 95 (1872)

"—d it off, it was held, that a suit for the loss, as being occasioned by the non-repair of the bridge, could not be maintained Dubuque Wood, etc., Ass'n v Dubuque, 30 Ia. 176. See Morrison v Davis, 20 Pa St 171, Hoadley v Nor Transp. Co, 115 Mass 304, Scott v. Hunter, 46 Pa. St 191

The burning of a lot of cotton in a high wind by sparks from a burning building was held to be not the proximate result of failing to forward it promptly from the cotton yard. Wharfboat Ass'n v Wood, 64 Miss 661

water ran down a gutter, and would in fact (*m*) (but for a hard frost which had then set in for some time) have run harmlessly down a grating into the sewer, at a corner some twenty-five yards from where the van was washed. As it happened, the grating was frozen over, the water spread out and froze into a sheet of ice, and a led horse of the plaintiff's slipped thereon and broke its knee. It did not appear that the defendant or his servants knew of the stoppage of the grating. The Court thought the damage was not "within the ordinary consequences" (*n*) of such an act as the defendant's, not "one which the defendant could fairly be expected to anticipate as likely to ensue from his act" (*o*): he "could not reasonably be expected to foresee that the water would accumulate and freeze at the spot where the accident happened" (*p*)

Question, if the same rule holds for consequences of wilful wrong. Clark v. Chambers. Some doubt appears to be cast on the rule thus laid down — which, it is submitted, is the right one — by what was said a few years later in *Clark* v. *Chambers* (*q*), though not by the decision itself. This case raises the question whether the liability of a wrong-doer may not extend even to remote and unlikely consequences where the original wrong is a wilful trespass, or consists in the unlawful or careless use of a dangerous instrument. The main facts were as follows —

1 The defendant without authority set a barrier, partly armed with spikes (chevaux-de-frise), across a road subject to other persons' rights of way. An opening was at most times left in the middle of the barrier, and was there at the time when the mischief happened

---

(*m*) So the Court found, having power to draw inferences of fact
(*n*) Grove J.
(*o*) Keating J
(*p*) Bovill C J
(*q*) 3 Q B D 327, 47 L. J. Q. B. 427 (1878)

2. The plaintiff went after dark along this road and through the opening, by the invitation of the occupier of one of the houses to which the right of using the road belonged, and in order to go to that house.

3. Some one, not the defendant or any one authorized by him, had removed one of the chevaux-de-frise barriers, and set it on end on the footpath. It was suggested, but not proved, that this was done by a person entitled to use the road, in exercise of his right to remove the unlawful obstruction.

4. Returning later in the evening from his friend's house, the plaintiff, after safely passing through the central opening above mentioned, turned on to the footpath. He there came against the chevaux-de-frise thus displaced (which he could not see, the night being very dark), and one of the spikes put out his eye.

After a verdict for the plaintiff the case was reserved for further consideration, and the Court (*r*) held that the damage was nearly enough connected with the defendant's first wrongful act — namely, obstructing the road with instruments dangerous to people lawfully using it — for the plaintiff to be entitled to judgment. It is not obvious why and how, if the consequence in *Clark* v. *Chambers*, was natural and probable enough to justify a verdict for the plaintiff, that in *Sharp* v. *Powell* was too remote to be submitted to a jury at all. The Court did not dispute the correctness of the judgments in *Sharp* v. *Powell* " as applicable to the circumstances of the particular case;" but their final observations (*s*) certainly tend to the opinion that in a case of active wrong-doing the rule is different. Such an opinion, it is submitted, is against the general weight of authority, and against the principles underlying the author-

---

(*r*) Cockburn C J and Manisty J The point chiefly argued for the defendant seems to have been that the intervention of a third person's act prevented him from being liable, a position which is clearly untenable (see *Scott* v *Shepherd*), but the judgment is of wider scope

(*s*) 3 Q B. D. at p. 338.

ities(*l*). However, their conclusion may be supported, and may have been to some extent determined, by the special rule imposing the duty of what has been called "consummate caution" on persons dealing with dangerous instruments

Consequences natural in kind though not in circumstance. Perhaps the real solution is that here, as in *Hill v. New River Co.*, the kind of harm which in fact happened might have been expected, though the precise manner in which it happened was determined by an extraneous accident. If in this case the spikes had not been disturbed, and the plaintiff had in the dark missed the free space left in the barrier, and run against the spiked part of it, the defendant's liability could not have been disputed. As it was, the obstruction was not exactly where the defendant had put it, but still it was an obstruction to that road which had been wrongfully brought there by him. He had put it in the plaintiff's way no less than Shepherd put his squib in the way of striking Scott, whereas in *Sharp* v *Powell* the mischief was not of a kind which the defendant had any reason to foresee.

The turn taken by the discussion in *Clark* v. *Chambers*, was, in this view, unnecessary, and it is to be regretted that a considered judgment was delivered in a form tending to unsettle an accepted rule without putting anything definite in its place. On the whole, I submit that, whether *Clark v. Chambers* can stand with it or not, both principle and the current of authority concur to maintain the law as declared in *Sharp* v. *Powell*

Damages for "nervous or mental shock" whether too remote. Where a wrongful or negligent act of A, threat-

---

(*l*) Compare the cases on slander collected in the notes to *Vicars* v *Wilcocks*, 2 Sm L C Compare also, as to consequential liability for disregard of statutory provisions, *Gorris* v *Scott* (1874), L R 9 Ex 125, 43 L J Ex 92

Damages for "nervous or mental shock" whether too remote It is a rule based upon the very best of reason that damages for fright,

oning Z. with immediate bodily hurt, but not causing such hurt, produces in Z a sudden terror or "nervous shock"

---

anguish, remorse, or any other abnormal mental condition, unaccompanied by an injury to the person, cannot be estimated, and are too remote to warrant a recovery. Wilcox v. Richmond & D R Co., 52 Fed Rep 264, 3 C C A. 73, 8 U. S Ap 118, Yoakum v. Dunn, 1 Tex Ch Ap 521, 21 N W Rep 111, Indianapolis, etc., R Co. v Stables, 62 Ill 313, Oliver v La Valle, 36 Wis 593, Wyman v Leavitt, 71 Me 227, 36 Am Rep 303, Renner v Canfield, 36 Minn 90, 30 N W Rep 15, Ewing v Pittsburg, etc., Ry Co., 117 Pa St 10, 23 Atl Rep 340, 29 W N C 218, Canning v Williamston, 1 Cush. 451, Covington Street Ry Co. v. Packer, 9 Bush 455, Tex. Mex. Ry Co v Douglas, 69 Tex 694, 7 S W Rep. 77, Keyes v. Minneapolis & St. L Ry Co., 36 Minn 290, 30 N W Rep 888, Quigley v Central Pac R Co, 11 Nev 350, Illinois Cent R Co v Sutton, 53 Ill. 397, Dorrah v Railroad Co, 65 Miss 14, 3 So Rep 36.

In Boyce v Danville (53 Vt. 190), in which a woman was caused by the injury to give premature birth to twins, it was held that any injured "feelings" following the miscarriage, not part of the pain naturally attending it, are too remote to be considered an element of damage. The court said "If like Rachel, she wept for her children, and would not be comforted, a question of continuing damage is presented too delicate to be weighed by any scales which the law has yet invented." While every well-considered decision supports this rule, the lack of uniformity of the decisions upon the subject of liability of telegraph companies for delinquency in delivering messages to addresses is so significant as to justify special notice. In a few of the States the courts have essayed to compensate in money the grief or regret of the addressee of a telegraphic message negligently delivered too late to permit him to attend on the bedside of the ill or the obsequies of the dead; although he has suffered no pecuniary loss or bodily injury. Young v Tel. Co., 107 N. C. 370, 11 S E Rep. 1044, Thompson v. W. U Tel Co., 107 N C 449, 12 S. E Rep. 427, Gulf, C. & S. F. Tel Co. v Richardson, 79 Tex 649, 15 S W. Rep. 689; W. U. Tel Co v. Berdue (Tex. Civ App), 21 S W Rep 982, Reese v Telegraph Co, 123 Ind. 294, 24 N. E Rep 163, W U Tel. Co v Stratemeier (Ind. App), 32 N E. Rep 871, W U. Tel Co v Newhouse (Ind. App.), 33 N. E. Rep 800, W U Tel Co v Carter (Tex Civ. App) 21 S W. Rep. 688, W U Tel. Co v. Stephens (Tex Civ. App), 21 S W Rep 148; W. U. Tel. Co v. Beringer, 84 Tex 38, 19 S W Rep. 336, Potts v. W. U Tel Co., 82 Tex. 545, 18 S W Rep 604, Stuart v W U Tel Co, 66 Tex 580, 18 S W. Rep. 351, Wadsworth v W U Tel Co, 86 Tenn. 695, 6 Am. St. Rep 864, Loper v W. U Tel Co, 70 Tex 689, Chapman v W U Tel Co (Ky. App.), 13 S. W. Rep 880, Reese v W U. Tel Co, 123 Ind 294, Stuart v. W U. Tel Co., 66

from which bodily illness afterwards ensues, is this damage too remote to enter into the measure of damages if A.'s act was an absolute wrong, or to give Z. a cause of action if actual damage is the gist of the action? The Judicial Committee decided in 1888 (*u*) that such consequences are too remote, but it is submitted that the decision is not satisfactory. A husband and wife were driving in a buggy across a level railway crossing, and, through the obvious and admitted negligence of the gatekeeper, the buggy was nearly but not quite run down by a train; the husband "got the buggy across the line, so that the train, which was going at a rapid speed, passed close to the back of it and did not touch it." The wife then and there fainted, and it was proved to the satisfaction of the Court below "that she received a severe nervous shock from the fright, and that the illness from which she afterwards suffered was the consequence of the fright." It may be conceded that the passion of fear, or any other emotion of the mind, however painful and distressing it be, and however reasonable the apprehension which causes it, cannot in itself be regarded as measurable temporal damage, and that the judgment appealed from, if and so far as it purported to allow any distinct damages for " mental injuries " (*v*), was

(*u*) *Victorian Railway Commissioners v Coultas*, 13 App. Ca. 222, 57 L. J. P. C. 69

(*x*) It is by no means clear that such was the intention or effect. See the report, 12 V. L. R. 895 The physical injuries were substantial enough, for they included a miscarriage (*ibid*) Whether

Tex. 580, 59 Am. Rep. 623, 13 Am. & Eng Corp. Cas. 590, W U. Tel. Co *v* Rosentreter, 80 Tex 406

The contrary is the sounder doctrine. In the opinion of the court in Chapman *v* Western Union Telegraph Co (88 Ga 763, 15 S. W. Rep. 901) and in Telegraph Co. *v*. Rogers (68 Miss. 748; 9 So. Rep. 823), the authorities on both sides of the question are reviewed and the right of recovery denied. See Judge Thompson's article on this subject in 33 Cent Law Jl 5, and Chase *v* W U. Tel Co., 44 Fed. Rep. 554; W U. Tel. Co. *v* Carter, 85 Tex 580, 22 S W. Rep. 961, Ester *v*. W U Tel Co, 55 Fed Rep 603, Connell *v*. W. U. Tel. Co, 22 S W Rep 345, Tyler *v* W. U Tel Co, 54 Fed Rep 634, Crawson *v*. W U Tel. Co, 47 Fed Rep 544

erroneous. But their Lordships seem to have treated this as obviously involving the further proposition that physical illness caused by reasonable fear is on the same footing. This does not follow. The true question would seem to be whether the fear in which the plaintiff was put by the defendant's wrongful or negligent conduct was such as, in the circumstances, would naturally be suffered by a person of ordinary courage and temper, and such as might thereupon naturally and probably lead, in the plaintiff's case (*y*) to the physical effects complained of. Fear taken alone falls short of being actual damage, not because it is a remote or unlikely consequence, but because it can be proved and measured only by physical effects. The opinion of the Judicial Committee, outside the colony of Victoria, is as extra-judicial as the contrary and (it is submitted) better opinion expressed in two places (*z*) by Sir James Stephen as to the possible commission of murder or manslaughter by the wilful or reckless infliction of "nervous shock." And if the reasoning of the Judicial Committee be correct, it becomes rather difficult to see on what principle assault without battery is an actionable wrong (*a*).

that was really due to the fright was eminently a question of fact, and this was not disputed or discussed.

(*y*) This must be so unless we go back to the old Germanic method of a fixed scale of compensation. So, as regards the measure of damages when liability is not denied, the defendant has to take his chance of the person disabled being a workman, or a tradesman in a small way, or a physician with a large practice.

(*z*) Dig Cr Law, note to art 221, Hist Cr Law, iii. 5

(*a*) Cp Mr Beven's criticism of this case, Principles of the Law of Negligence, 66—71. As he justly points out, it has never been questioned that an action may lie for damage done by an animal which has been frightened by the defendant's negligent act. *Manchester South Jn R Co* v *Fullerton* (1863), 14 C B N S 54, *Simkin* v *L & N W R Co* (1888), 21 Q B Div 453, 59 L T 797, *Brown* v *Eastern and Midlands R Co* (1889), 22 Q B Div. 391, 58 L. J. Q. B. 212

CHAPTER III

PERSONS AFFECTED BY TORTS.

1.— *Limitations of Personal Capacity*

Personal status, as a rule, immaterial in law of tort: but capacity in fact may be material. In the law of contract various grounds of personal disability have to be considered with some care. Infants, married women, lunatics, are in different degrees and for different reasons incapable of the duties and rights arising out of contracts. In the law of tort it is otherwise. Generally speaking, there is no limit to personal capacity either in becoming liable for civil injuries, or in the power of obtaining redress for them. It seems on principle that where a particular intention, knowledge, or state of mind in the person charged as a wrong-doer is an element, as it sometimes is, in constituting the alleged wrong, the age and mental capacity of the person may and should be taken into account (along with other relevant circumstances) in order to ascertain as a fact whether that intention, knowledge, or state of mind was present. But in every case it would be a question of fact, and no exception to the general rule would be established or propounded (*a*). An idiot would scarcely be held answerable for incoherent words of vituperation, though, if uttered by a sane man, they

---

(*a*) Ulpian, in D. 9, 2, ad leg. Aquil. 5, § 2. Quaerimus, si furiosus damnum dederit, an legis Aquiliae actio sit? Et Pegasus negavit: quae enim in eo culpa sit, cum suae mentis non sit? Et hoc est verissimum. Quod si impubes id fecerit, Labeo ait, quia furti tenetur, teneri et Aquilia eum, et hoc puto verum, si sit iam injuriae capax.

might be slander. But this would not help a monomaniac who should write libellous post-cards to all the people who had refused or neglected, say to supply him with funds to recover the Crown of England. The amount of damages recovered might be reduced by reason of the evident insignificance of such libels; but that would be all. Again, a mere child could not be held accountable for not using the discretion of a man, but an infant is certainly liable for all wrongs of omission as well as of commission in matters where he was, in the common phrase, old enough to know better. It is a matter of common sense, just as we do not expect of a blind man the same actions or readiness to act as of a seeing man.

Partial or apparent exceptions. There exist partial exceptions, however, in the case of convicts and alien enemies, and apparent exceptions as to infants and married women.

Partial or apparent exceptions. *Convict* The doctrine of the common law, that a convict is *civiliter mortuus*, is not wholly accepted in the United States.

In Dade Coal Co. v. Haslett (83 Ga. 549; 10 S. E. Rep. 435), it is held, that an action for personal injuries received while a felon, in confinement, is maintainable. See Willingham v. King, 23 Fla. 478; Cannon v. Windsor, 1 Houst. 143.

Alien enemy Upon the right of an alien enemy to sue and be sued in the United States see McVeigh v. United States, 11 Wall. 259, McNair v. Toler, 21 Minn. 175, Burnside v. Matthews, 54 N. Y. 78.

Lunatic "By the common law, as generally stated in the books, a lunatic is civilly liable to make compensation in person to persons injured by his acts" Morain v. Devlin, 132 Mass. 87, citing Moise v. Crawford, 17 Vt. 499, Cross v. Kent, 32 Md. 581, Bullock v. Babcock, 3 Wend. 391, Behrens v. McKenzie, 23 Ia. 333, Lancaster Bank v. Moore, 78 Pa. St. 407, Dickinson v. Barber, 9 Mass. 225, Brown v. Howe, 9 Gray, 84, Harding v. Larned, 4 Allen, 426, Harding v. Weld, 128 Mass. 587. See McIntyre v. Sholty, 24 Ill. App. 605, affirmed 121 Ill. 660; 13 N. E Rep. 239.

But vindictive damages, in such a case, cannot be recovered Ward v. Conatser, 4 Baxt. 64; Krom v. Schoonmaker, 3 Barb. 647, Jewell v. Colby (N. H.), 24 At. Rep. 902.

Drunkenness Drunkenness as a defense to a tort may be properly

Convicts and alien enemies. A convicted felon whose sentence is in force and unexpired, and who is not "lawfully at large under any licence," cannot sue "for the recovery of any property, debt, or damage whatsoever" (*b*). An alien enemy cannot sue in his own right in any English court. Nor is the operation of the Statute of Limitations suspended, it seems, by the personal disability (*c*).

Infants. contract not to be indirectly enforced by suing in tort. With regard to infants, there were certain cases under the old system of pleading in which there was an option to sue for breach of contract or for a tort. In such a case an infant could not be made liable for what was in truth a breach of contract by framing the action *ex delicto*. "You cannot convert a contract into a tort to

---

(*b*) 33 & 34 Vict. c 23, ss 8, 30. Can he sue for an injunction? Or for a dissolution of marriage or judicial separation?

(*c*) See *De Wahl v Braune* (1856), 1 H. & N. 178, 25 L. J. Ex. 343 (alien enemy; the law must be the same of a convict)

---

mentioned here. The fact that a tort-feasor was intoxicated is not a general defense; but, it seems, that his condition may be proved in mitigation of damages, however, this right has not yet been conceded. See Mix *v* McCoy, 22 Mo App 488; McKee *v* Ingalls, 5 Ill. 30, Reed *v* Harper, 25 Ia 87

Infants. Contract not to be indirectly enforced by suing in tort Agreeing with the text, *vide* Gibson *v* Spear, 38 Vt. 311, Merriam *v.* Cunningham, 11 Cush 40, Tucker *v* Moreland, 10 Pet 59, Wilt *v* Welsh, 6 Watts 9; Livingston *v* Cox, 6 Pa St. 360; Kean *v* Coleman, 39 Id 299; Curtin *v.* Patton, 11 Serg & R 309; Kilgore *v* Jordan, 17 Tex. 341, Carpenter *v.* Carpenter, 45 Ind 142, Burns *v* Hill, 19 Ga. 22.

But there is a tendency in equity to establish a contrary rule, especially when the personal appearances of the infant indicates the truth of his assertions of full age. Schmitheimer *v* Elseman, 7 Bush 298, Fitz *v.* Hall, 9 N. H. 441, Norris *v.* Vance, 2 Rich 164, Rice *v* Boyer, 108 Ind. 472, Hayes *v.* Parker, 41 N. J Eq. 630, Ferguson *v* Bobo, 54 Miss 121, Brantley *v* Wolf, 60 Miss. 420, Baker *v.* Stone, 136 Mass. 405; Davidson *v* Young, 38 Ill 145, Dibble *v* Jones, 5 Jones Eq 389, Yeager *v.* Knight, 60 Miss 730

enable you to sue an infant: *Jennings* v *Randall*"(d). And the principle goes to this extent, that no action lies against an infant for a fraud whereby he has induced a person to contract with him, such as a false statement that he is of full age (e).

Limits of rule: independent wrongs. But where an infant commits a wrong of which a contract, or the obtain-

(d) 8 T R 335, 1 R R 689, thus cited by Parke B, *Fairhurst Liverpool Adelphi Loan Association* (1854), 9 Ex. 422, 23 L J Ex 163.

(e) *Johnson* v *Pie*, 1 Sid 258, etc. See the report fully cited by Knight Bruce V C (1847) in *Stikeman* v *Dawson*, 1 De G & Sm at p 113, cp. the remarks at p. 110.

Limits of the rule: independent wrongs. An infant is liable for injuries to property or person wrongfully committed by him. To be excused from liability he must show his incapacity to know what would be the natural consequences of his act Shaw v. Coffin, 58 Me 254, 4 Am. Rep 290, Elwell v Martin, 32 Vt. 217, Huchting v Engel, 17 Wis. 230, Marshall v Wing, 50 Me. 62, School Dist v. Bragdon, 23 N H 507, McCoon v Smith, 3 Hill, 147; Beckley v. Newcomb, 24 N H 363, Conway v Reed, 66 Mo. 346, 27 Am Rep 354, Peigne v. Sutcliffe, 4 McCord, 387, 17 Am. Dec 756, Oliver v McClellan, 21 Ala 675, Peterson v Haffner, 59 Ind 130, 26 Am Rep. 81, Burham v. Turbeville, 1 Swan, 437, Conklin v. Thompson, 29 Barb 218, Matthews v Cowan, 29 Ill 311, Hartfield v. Roper, 21 Wend 620, Schaefer v. Osterbrink, 67 Wis 495, Baxter v Bush, 29 Vt 465, Green v. Sperry, 16 Vt 392, Lewis v Littlefield, 15 Me 233, Neal v Gillett, 23 Conn 437, Fry v. Leslie, 87 Va 269, 12 S. E Rep. 671

An examination of the cases just cited will show that the intent of the wrong doer is immaterial, except in same cases as to the *quantum* of damages An infant who procures a tort to be committed is liable for the result. Sikes v Thompson, 16 Mass 389, Tifft v Tifft, 4 Denio, 175.

An infant is, also, responsible for a tort committed at the command of any one having lawful authority over him Humphrey v Douglass, 10 Vt 71, 33 Am Dec 177, Scott v Watson, 46 Me 362, Kirkpatrick v Hall, 67 Me 513, Smith v. Kron, 96 N C 392, Hutching v. Engel, 17 Wis 230, School Dist v Bragdon, 23 N. H 507

An infant is not liable for his breach of contract however tortious the case may be Doran v Smith, 49 Vt 533, 17 Am. Law Reg (N. S) 42, Moore v Eastman, 1 Hun, 578, Munger v. Hess, 28 Barb 75, Studwell v. Shafter, 54 N Y 249, West v Moore, 14 Vt. 447, Prescott v Norris, 32 N. H. 101, Campbell v Perkins, 8 N Y 430; Morrill v. Aden, 19 Vt 505, Nolan v Jones, 53 Ia. 387.

But this protection of the law is accorded him only within the limits of the contract and when he goes beyond the scope of the agreement

ing of something under a contract is the occasion, but only the occasion, he is liable. In *Burnard* v. *Haggis* (*f*), the defendant in the County Court, an infant undergraduate, hired a horse for riding on the express condition that it was not to be used for jumping; he went out with a friend who rode this horse by his desire, and making a cut across country, they jumped divers hedges and ditches, and the horse staked itself on a fence and was fatally injured. Having thus caused the horse to be used in a manner wholly unauthorized by its owner, the defendant was held to have committed a mere trespass or "independent tort" (*g*),

(*f*) 14 C. B. N. S. 45, 32 L. J. C. P. 189 (1863).

(*g*) See per Willes J. If the bailment had been at will, the defendant's act would have wholly determined the bailment, and under the old forms of pleading he would have been liable at the owner's election in case or in trespass *vi et armis*. See Litt. s. 71.

---

and does a wrong he is responsible. The wrongful act, not being contemplated by the contract, is independent of it, though concerned with the subject of the contract, and of such a nature that, but for the opportunity created by the contract, it could not have been committed.

Thus in Eaton *v.* Hill (50 N. H. 235, 9 Am. Rep. 189) the court said: "We think then that the doctrine is well established, that an infant bailee of a horse is liable for any positive and wilful tort done to the animal distinct from a mere breach of contract, as by driving to a place other than the one from which he is hired, refusing to return upon demand after the time has expired, wilfully beating him to death, and the like, so if he wilfully and intentionally drive him at such an immoderate rate of speed as to seriously endanger his life, knowing that it will do so * * * But when * * * the infant wholly departs from his character of bailee, and by some positive act wilfully destroys or injures the thing bailed, the act is, in its nature, essentially a tort, the same as if there had been no bailment, even if assumpsit might be maintained in case of an adult, on a promise to return the thing safely." See Ray *v.* Tubbs, 50 Vt. 688, 28 Am. Rep. 519, Towne *v.* Wiley, 23 Vt. 355, Hall *v.* Corcoran, 107 Mass. 251; Homer *v.* Thwing, 3 Pick. 492, Freeman *v.* Boland, 14 R. I. 39, 51 Am. Rep. 340, Schenk *v.* Strong, 4 N. J. L. 87, Campbell *v.* Stakes, 2 Wend. 137, 19 Am. Dec. 561, Woodman *v.* Hubbard, 25 N. H. 73, Green *v.* Sperry, 16 Vt. 390, 42 Am. Dec. 519, Fish *v.* Ferris, 5 Duer, 49.

This doctrine is, however, not free from criticism. See Livingston *v.* Cox, 6 Pa. St. 360, Wilt *v.* Welsh, 6 Watts, 9, Penrose *v.* Curren, 3 Rawle, 351, 24 Am. Dec. 356, Root *v.* Stevenson, 24 Ind. 115; 1 Am. Lead. Cas. 262.

for which he was liable to the owner apart from any question of contract, just as if he had mounted and ridden the horse without hiring or leave.

Infant shall not take advantage of his own fraud. Also it has been established by various decisions in the Court of Chancery that "an infant cannot take advantage of his own fraud"; that is, he may be compelled to specific restitution where that is possible, of anything he has obtained by deceit, nor can he hold other persons liable for acts done on the faith of his false statement, which would have been duly done if the statement had been true (h). Thus, where an infant had obtained a lease of a furnished house by representing himself as a responsible person and of full age, the lease was declared void, and the lessor to be entitled to delivery of possession, and to an injunction to restrain the lessee from dealing with the furniture and effects, but not to damages for use and occupation (h).

Married women: the common law. As to married women, a married woman was by the common law inca-

---

(h) *Lempriere v. Lange* (1879), 12 Ch. D. 675, and see other cases in the writer's "Principles of Contract," p. 75, 5th ed.

Married women: the common law. A married woman is not liable for her wrongs of the nature of violation of contract. Keen v. Coleman, 39 Pa. St. 299, Woodward v. Barnes, 46 Vt. 332, 14 A. n. Rep. 626, Owens v. Snodgrass, 6 Dana, 229, Keen v. Hartman, 48 Pa. St. 497, Patterson v. Frazer, 5 La. An. 586, Andrews v. Orsbee, 11 Mo. 400, Carleton v. Haywood, 49 N. H. 314, Barnes v. Harris, Busb. L. 15, Weathersbee v. Farrar, 97 N. C. 106, Cross v. Everts, 29 Tex. 523, Ferguson v. Brooks, 67 Me. 251. But see, Anderson v. Line, 14 Fed. Rep. 700.

Generally, a husband is liable for all torts committed by his wife during coverture. They may sue and be sued jointly for torts committed upon or by the wife. Baker v. Young, 44 Ill. 42, Austin v. Bacon, 49 Hun, 386, 3 N. Y. S. Rep. 587, Thatcher v. Phinney, 7 Allen, 146, Ferguson v. Collins, 8 Ark. 241, Dailey v. Houston, 58 Mo. 361, Jackson v. Kirby, 37 Vt. 448, Bobe v. Frowner, 18 Ala. 89, Hubble v. Fogartie, 3 Rich. 413, Ball v. Bennett, 21 Ind. 427, Solomon v. Waas, 2 Hill 179, Quilty v. Battle, 135 N. Y. 201, 32 N. E. Rep. 47, Fowler v. Chichester, 26 Ohio St. 9, 10 Am. Dec. 698, Smith v. Smith, 45 Pa. St. 403, Genenzo v. De Forest,

pable of binding herself by contract, and therefore, like an infant, she could not be made liable as for a wrong in an action for deceit or the like, when this would have in substance amounted to making her liable on a contract (*i*). In other cases of wrong she was not under any disability, nor had she any immunity; but she had to sue and be sued jointly with her husband, inasmuch as her property was the husband's; and the husband got the benefit of a favorable judgment and was liable to the consequences of an adverse one

---

2 N. Y S Rep 152, Dalley v Houston, 58 Mo 361, Marshall v Oakes, 51 Me 308, Starbird v Frankfort, 35 Me. 89, Hinds v Jones, 48 Me. 148, Bellous v. McGinnis, 17 Ind 164, McKeown v Johnson, 1 McCord, 578, Brazil v Moran, 8 Minn. 236, Allen v. McCullough, 2 Heisk. 117, 5 Am Rep. 27, Enders v Beck, 18 Ia 86, McQueen v Fulgham, 27 Tex 463, Anderson v. Hill, 53 Barb. 238, Horton v. Payne, 27 How Pr 374, Clark v Bayer, 32 Ohio St 299, Illinois R Co v. Grabbe, 46 Ill 115

Also, a man may "marry a tort" when he marries a woman against whom a valid cause of action for tort exists Ferguson v Collins, 8 Ark 241, Phillips v Richardson, 4 A. K Marsh. 212; Gibson v Gibson, 43 Wis 23, Hawk v Harman, 5 Binn 43.

For her torts committed in person a married woman is liable as if a *feme sole*. Dalley v. Houston, 58 Mo. 361, Matthews v Fiestel, 2 E D Smith, 90, Carter v. Jackson, 56 N H 364, Ball v Bennett, 21 Ind. 427 Vanneman v Powers, 56 N Y. 39, Baum v. Mullen, 47 N. Y 577, Kowing v Manley, 49 N Y 192, Heckle v Lurvey, 101 Mass 344, Davidson v Smith, 20 Ia 166

But one spouse cannot recover against the other for tort Peters v Peters, 42 Ia 183, Libby v. Berry, 74 Me. 286, Schultz v Schultz, 89 N Y. 684, Abbott v Abbott, 67 Me 304

Since the husband and wife are, in legal contemplation, but one person, the wife's torts committed in the presence of the husband are presumed to be impelled by his marital power and she is not liable at all Nolan v Traber, 49 Md. 460, Ball v. Bennett, 21 Ind 427, Kosminsky v Goldberg, 44 Ark 401, Baker v Young, 44 Ill 42, Quick v Miller, 103 Pa St 67, Brazil v Moran, 8 Minn 236, Park v Hopkins, 2 Bailey, 411, Sisco v. Cheeney, Wright (Ohio), 19, Phillips v. Phillips, 7 B Mon 268

But the presumption may be overthrown by evidence. Carleton v Haywood, 49 N H 314; Miller v. Switzer, 22 Mich. 391, Cassin v Delaney, 38 N Y 178, Chanviere v Fliege, 6 La. An. 56; Clement v. Wafer, 12 Id. 599, Handy v Foley, 121 Mass 259, Wagner v Bill, 19 Barb. 321, Crawford v Doggett, 82 Tex 139, 17 S W Rep 929

Married Women's Property Act, 1882. Since the Married Woman's Property Act, 1882, a married woman can acquire and hold separate property in her own name, and sue and be sued without joining her husband. If she is sued alone, damages and costs recovered against her are payable out of her separate property (*k*). If a husband and wife sue jointly for personal injuries to the wife, the damages recovered are the wife's separate property (*l*). She may sue her own husband, if necessary, "for the protection and security of her own separate property;" but otherwise actions for a tort between husband and wife cannot be entertained (*m*). That is, a wife may sue her husband in an action which under the old forms of pleading would have been trover for the recovery of her goods, or for a trespass or nuisance to land held by her as her separate property; but she may not sue him in a civil action for a personal wrong, such as assault, libel, or injury by negligence. Divorce does not enable the divorced wife to sue her husband for a personal tort committed during the coverture (*n*). There is not anything in the Act to prevent a husband and wife from suing or being sued jointly according to the old practice; the husband is not relieved from liability for wrongs committed by the wife during

---

(*i*) *Fairhurst* v *Liverpool Adelphi Loan Association* (1854), 9 Ex. 422, 23 L J Ex 163

(*k*) 45 & 46 Vict. c 75, s 1. The right of action given by the statute applies to a cause of action which arose before it came into operation *Weldon* v *Winslow*, (1884) 13 Q B Div 784, 53 L J Q B 528. In such case the Statute of Limitation runs not from the committing of the wrong, but from the commencement of the Act *Lowe* v *Fox* (1885), 15 Q B Div 667, 54 L J Q B 561

(*l*) *Beasley* v *Roney*, '91, 1 Q B 509, 60 L J Q B 408

(*m*) Sect 12. A trespasser on the wife's separate property cannot justify under the husband's authority. Whether the husband himself could justify entering a house, his wife's separate property, acquired as such before or since the Act, in which she is living apart, *quære*. *Weldon* v *De Bathe* (1884), 14 Q B Div 339, 54 L J Q B 113

(*n*) *Phillips* v *Barnet* (1876), 1 Q B Div 436, 45 L J Q B 277

Married women's property acts. In several of the United States married women have been authorized by special legislative enactments, to hold property, make contracts, sue and be sued as though unmarried.

coverture, and may still be joined as a defendant at need. If it were not so, a married woman having no separate property might commit wrongs with impunity (o). If husband and wife are now jointly sued for the wife's wrongs, and execution issues against the husband's property, a question may possibly be raised whether the husband is entitled to indemnity from the wife's separate property, if in fact she has any (p).

Common law liability of infants and married women limited, according to some, to wrongs contra pacem. There is some authority for the doctrine that by the common law both infants (q) and married women (r) are liable only for "actual torts" such as trespass, which were formerly laid in pleading as *contra pacem*, and are not in any case liable for torts in the nature of deceit, or, in the old phrase, in actions which "sound in deceit." But this does not seem acceptable on principle.

Corporations. As to corporations, it is evident that personal injuries, in the sense of bodily harm or offence,

---

(o) *Scrola v. Kattenburg* (1886), 17 Q. B Div 177, 55 L J. Q B 375

(p) Sect 13, which expressly provides for ante nuptial liabilities, is rather against the existence of such a right.

(q) *Johnson v Pie*, p 50, *supra* (a dictum wider than the decision).

(r) *Wright v Leonard* (1861), 11 C B N. S. 258, 30 L. J C P 365, by Erle C. J and Byles J , against Willes J. and Williams J. The judgment of Willes J. seems to me conclusive

---

Corporations Corporations may sue for libel affecting their property, if special damage is alleged and proved. Shoe & Leather Bank *v.* Thompson, 18 Abb. Pr. 413, Aldrich *v.* Press Printing Co , 9 Minn. 133, Trenton Ins. Co. *v.* Perrine, 23 N J. L. 402, Knickerbocker Ins. Co *v.* Eclesine, 11 Abb. Pr (N. S.) 385, 42 How. Pr 201; Buffalo Lubricating Oil Co *v.* Standard Oil Co , 42 Hun, 153, Nat. Reserve Fund Life Assn. *v.* Spectatur Co , 50 N. Y Super Ct 460, Boogher *v.* Life Assn., 75 Mo 321 , Wilson *v.* Fitch, 41 Cal 364

Also, a corporation may be sued for a libel published by its authority: in some cases it has been held, that the malice of the officials may be imputed to the corporation. Maynard *v.* Fireman's Fund Ins. Co., 34 Cal. 48, Fogg *v.* Boston & L R Co , 148 Mass 513; Aldrich *v.* Press

cannot be inflicted upon them. Neither can a corporation be injured in respect of merely personal reputation. It can

Printing Co , 9 Minn. 133, Johnson v St. Louis Dispatch Co., 65 Mo. 539; 2 Mo App 565, Bacon v Mich. Cent R Co., 55 Mich. 224, 20 Am. & Eng R Cas 633; Hewitt v Pioneer Press Co , 23 Minn. 178; Vinas v Merchants, etc , Ins. Co., 27 La. An. 367; Phila. R. Co v Quigley, 21 How 202; Howe Machine Co v Sowder, 58 Ga. 64, Samuels v Evening Mail Ass'n , 75 N. Y 601, Evening Journal Ass'n. v. McDermott, 44 N J L 430, Cleghorn v N Y Cent, etc , R. Co., 56 N. Y. 44; Merrills v Tariff, etc , Co , 10 Conn. 384; Goddard v Grand Trunk R , 57 Me 223, Ætna Life Ins Co v Paul, 37 Ill. App 439

The old doctrine that corporations, having no souls, could not be liable in tort, is now obsolete, and it is well settled that they are responsible for every wrong committed by their servants in the line of employment Johnson v. St. Louis Dispatch Co., 2 Mo. App. 570, Peebles v Patapsco Guano Co , 77 N C. 233, New York, etc., R Co v Schuyler, 34 N. Y 49, Nat Bank v Graham, 100 U S. 699, Brokaw v N J R., etc , Co , 82 N J L 329, Weightman v. Washington, 1 Black, 39; Philadelphia, W. & B. R C v Quigley, 21 How 202, Orleans v. Platt, 99 U S. 676, Salt Lake City v Hollister, 118 U S .766, Denver & R. G. R Co v. Harris, 7 Sup Ct Rep 1286, Merchants' Nat Bank v. State Nat. Bank, 10 Wall 604, Hood v N Y & N. H R. Co , 22 Conn. 502, Hussey v. King, 98 N C 34, 3 S. E Rep. 923, Craker v. Chicago & N W R Co., 36 Wis. 657, Miller v Burlington & C. R , 8 Neb 219, Goodspeed v. East Haddam Bank, 22 Conn. 541, Marion v. C., R I & P R Co , 59 Ia 428, Peck v Cooper, 112 Ill 192, 54 Am Rep 231, Goodyear v. Phelps, 3 Blatchf. 91, Riddle v Proprietors, 7 Mass 169.

Corporations have been held liable for particular torts in the following cases. —

Assault and battery Denver & R G R v. Harris, 122 U S. 597, Brokaw v Railroad Co , 32 N. J. L. 328, Ramsden v. Boston & A. R. Co., 104 Mass. 117, Monument Bank v. Globe Works, 101 Mass. 57; Higgins v Watervliet T R R. Co v Dalby, 19 Ill. 353.

Conspiracy Reed v. Home Savings Bank, 130 Mass 443, Buffalo Lubricating Oil Co v Standard Oil Co., 17 Am. & Eng. Corp. Cas. 61, Jordan v. Alabama, etc , R Co , 74 Ala. 85, Morton v Met. Life Ins. Co , 34 Hun, 366, affirmed, 180 N Y 645, Krulevitz v. Eastern R Co., 140 Mass. 575; 26 Am. & Eng. R. R. Cas 118, Western News Co. v. Dilmarth, 33 Kan. 510

Contempt of Court United States v. Memphis, etc , R Co., 6 Fed. Rep 237, People v. Albany, etc , R Co., 12 Abb. Pr. 171; Mayor, etc , v Ferry Co., 64 N. Y. 624; First Cong. Ch. v. Muscatine, 2 Clarke (Ia), 69

Conversion. Fishkill Saving Inst. v. Bostwick, 19 Hun, 354; Beach v Fulton Bank, 7 Cow. (N. Y.) 485

Deceit. Peebles v Patapsco Guano Co , 77 N C 233, Cragie v Had-

sue for a libel affecting property, but not for a libel purporting to charge the corporation as a whole with corruption, for example. The individual officers or members of the corporation whose action is reflected on are the only proper plaintiffs in such a case (s). It would seem at first sight, and it was long supposed, that a corporation also cannot be liable for personal wrongs (t). But this is really part of the larger question of the liability of principals and employers for the conduct of persons employed by them; for a corporation can act and become liable only

---

(s) *Mayor of Manchester v. Williams*, '91, 1 Q B 94, 60 L. J Q B 23.

(t) The difficulty felt in earlier times was one purely of process, not that a corporation was metaphysically incapable of doing wrong, but that it was not physically amenable to *capias* or *exigent* 22 Ass 100, pl 67, and other authorities collected by Serjeant Manning in the notes to *Maund v. Monmouthshire Canal Co*, 1 M. & G 452 But it was decided in the case just cited (1842) that trespass, as earlier in *Yarborough v Bank of England* (1812),16 East 6, that trover, would lie against a corporation aggregate. In Massachusetts a corporation has been held liable for the publication of a libel *Fogg v Boston and Lowell R Co* (1869), 118 Mass 513 And see per Lord Bramwell, 11 App Ca at p 254

---

ley, 99 N Y. 131, Zabriskie *v* Cleveland, etc., R. Co., 23 How. 381, Planters' Rice Mill Co *v* Olmstead, 78 Ga. 586, 3 S. E. Rep 647; Moran *v* Miami County, 2 Black, 722, Kennedy *v* McKay, 43 N. J. L 288, White *v* Sawyer, 16 Gray, 586.

False imprisonment Lynch v. Metropolitan Elevated R. Co, 90 N.Y. 77, 12 Am. & Eng R Cas 119, 18 Am. Rep. 141, Standish v. Naragansett S. S Co., 111 Mass. 512, 15 Am. Rep 66 Krulevitz v. Eastern R. Co., 140 Mass. 575, 28 Am. & Eng. R Cas. 138, American Express Co. v. Patterson, 73 Ind 430, Owsley *v* Montgomery, etc., R R Co , 37 Ala. 560; Murdock v. Boston & A. R. R. Co., 133 Mass 15, Frost v. Domestic, etc., Co., 133 Mass. 563; Wheeler v. Boyce, 36 Kan 350, 13 Pac. Rep. 609.

Malicious prosecution Godspeed *v* East Haddam Bank, 22 Conn. 530; Denver, etc , R Co *v* Harris, 122 U S 597, Hussey *v* Norfolk So. R. Co., 98 N C. 34, 2 Am St. Rep. 312, Vance v. Erie R. Co., 32 N. J. L 334, 90 Am. Dec 665, National Bank v. Graham, 100 U. S 699; Iron Mountain Bank *v* Mercantile Bank, 40 Mo. App. 505, Williams v. Planter's Ins. Co., 57 Miss 759, Copley v. G & B Sewing Machine Co., 2 Woods, 494; Ricord *v* Central Pac R Co , 15 Nev 167, Carter *v* Howe Machine Co , 51 Md 290, Fenton v. Wilson S. M. Co., 9 Phila. Rep. 189; Reed *v.* Home Savings Bank, 130 Mass. 443, Morton *v* Metropolitan Ins. Co , 34 Hun, 366, affirmed 103 N Y. 645; Wheless v. Second Nat. Bank, 1 Baxt. 469, 25 Am Rep 783, Booger v. Life Assn., 75 Mo 319, Woodward *v* St Louis, etc., R Co., 85 Mo 142 See *post*, p 284.

through its agents or servants. In that connexion we recur to the matter further on.

The greatest difficulty has been (and by some good authorities still is) felt in those kinds of cases where "malice in fact" — actual ill-will or evil motive — has to be proved.

Responsibility of public bodies for management of works, etc., under their control. Whole bodies of persons, incorporated or not, are intrusted with the manage-

---

Responsibility of public bodies for management of works, etc., under their control. The American cases illustrating the application of this doctrine are principally those against municipal corporations. When the act of a municipal corporation is not protected by its charter or the law, it is responsible therefor, as an individual. Galesburg v. Higley, 61 Ill. 287; Butchers' Ice, etc., Coal Co. v. City of Philadelphia, 156 Pa. St. 54, 27 At. Rep. 376, Drummond v. City of Eau Clair (Wis.), 55 N. W. Rep. 1028, Allentown v. Kramer, 73 Pa. St. 406, Schattner v. City of Kansas, 53 Mo. 162, Mayor of Savannah v. Waldner, 49 Ga. 316; Chicago v. Ioney, 40 Ill. 383, Chicago v. Dermody, 61 Ill. 431, Kobs v. Minneapolis, 22 Minn. 159; Neuert v. Boston, 120 Mass. 338, Rowell v. Williams, 29 Ia. 210, Clarissy v. Metropolitan Fire Dept., 7 Abb. Pr. (N. S.) 352, Sheldon v. Kalamazoo, 24 Mich. 383, Lansing v. Toolan, 27 Mich. 152, Mulcahiny v. Janesville, 67 Wis. 24, Indianapolis v. Emmelmann, 108 Ind. 530; 58 Am. Rep. 65, Hart v. Red Cedar, 63 Wis. 634, Lincoln v. Walker, 18 Neb. 244, Lehn v. San Francisco, 66 Cal. 76, North Vernon v. Voegler, 103 Ind. 314, Susquehanna Depot v. Simmons, 112 Pa. St. 384, 56 Am. Rep. 317, Denver v. Rhodes, 9 Col. 554; Springfield v. Scheevers, 21 Ill. App. 203, City of Birmingham v. McCreary, 84 Ala. 469; 4 So. Rep. 630, Hitchins v. Frostburg, 68 Md. 100, 11 At. Rep. 826, City of Boulder v. Fowler, 11 Col. 396; 18 Pac. Rep. 337, Jefferson v. Chapman, 27 Ill. App. 43, 127 Ill. 438; 20 N. E. Rep. 33, Maguire v. Cartersville, 76 Ga. 84, Omaha v. Jensen, 35 Neb. 68, 52 N. E. Rep. 833; Savannah v. Donnelly, 71 Ga. 258, Morse v. Worcester, 139 Mass. 389, Levy v. Salt Lake City, 3 Utah, 63, Deane v. Randolph, 132 Mass. 475; Lemon v. Newton, 134 Mass. 476; Broadwell v. Kansas, 75 Mo. 213, 42 Am. Rep. 395, Cumberland v. Wilson, 50 Md. 138, O'Brien v. St. Paul, 25 Minn. 331, Elgin v. Kimball, 90 Ill. 356, Logansport v. Dick, 70 Ind. 65; 36 Am. Rep. 166; Joliet v. Harwood, 86 Ill. 110, Murphy v. Lowell, 124 Mass. 564.

The following are some of the wrongs for which municipalities are ordinarily liable: —

Defective streets and sidewalks. Winbigler v. City of Los Angeles, 45 Cal. 36, Sterling v. Thomas, 60 Ill. 264, Rockford v. Hildebrand, 61 Ill.

ment and maintenance of works, or the performance of other duties of a public nature, they are in their corporate or *quasi*-corporate capacity responsible for the proper con-

---

155, Craig v Sedalia, 63 Mo. 117, McDonough v. Virginia City, 6 Nov 90, Alton v. Hope, 68 Ill. 167; Mayor of Rome v Dodd, 58 Ga. 238; Hutchinson v Olympia, 2 Wash. St 314, Waldron v. Haverhill, 143 Mass 582, Flanders v. Norwood, 141 Mass. 17, Saulsbury v. Ithica, 94 N Y 27, 46 Am Rep 122, Kellogg v. Janesville, 34 Minn 132, Shippy v. Au Sable, 85 Mich 280, 48 N. W. Rep. 584, Higgins v Glens Falls, 57 Hun, 594; 11 N. Y. S. Rep 289, Flora v Maney, 31 Ill. App 193, 26 N. E Rep 615; McDonald v. Ashland, 78 Wis. 251, 47 N. W. Rep 131; Kinney v Tekamah, 30 Neb. 605, 46 N. W. Rep. 835; Denver v. Dunsmore, 7 Colo 328; Bleazan v. Mason City, 58 Ia. 283, Hand v. Brookline, 126 Mass. 324; Clark v. Epworth, 56 Ia 462

Lights, excavations. Seneca Falls v. Zulinski, 15 N. Y. Supreme Ct 571, Randall v Eastern R. Co., 106 Mass. 276; Groves v Rochester, 39 Hun, 5; Gaskins v Atlanta, 73 Ga 716; Monongahela City v. Fischer, 111 Pa St. 9, 56 Am Rep. 317, Lyon v Cambridge, 136 Mass. 419, Alexander v Big Rapids, 76 Mich 282, 42 N. W. Rep 1071; Dooley v. Sullivan, 112 Ind 451, 14 N E Rep 566, McAllister v Albany, 18 Oreg. 426; 23 Pac. Rep. 945, McCoull v Manchester, 85 Va 579; 8 S. E Rep. 379; Birmingham v Lewis, 92 Ala 352; 9 So. Rep 243, Powers v. Boston, 154 Mass 60, 27 N E. Rep 995, South Omaha v Cunningham, 31 Neb. 816; 47 N. W. Rep 930, Hamford v. Kansas City, 103 Mo. 72; 15 S. W Rep. 753, Keating v Cincinnati, 38 Ohio St 141, 43 Am Rep. 421; Wilson v. Wheeling, 19 W Va. 323; 42 Am. Rep. 780.

Sewers. Wendell v Mayor of Troy, 4 Abb. App Dec 563, Van Pelt v. Davenport, 42 Ia. 308, Ashley v. Port Huron, 35 Mich. 296; Smith v. Mayor of New York, 66 N. Y 295; Spelman v. Portage, 41 Wis. 144, Springfield v LeClaire, 49 Ill. 476; Leavenworth v Casey, McCahon, 124; Smith v. Mayor, 6 Thomp. & C. 685, 4 Hun, 637, Summer v. St Paul, 23 Minn. 408, Forte Wayne v. Coombs, 107 Ind. 75; 57 Am Rep. 82; Leeds v Richmond, 102 Ind 372; Krauz v. Baltimore, 64 Md. 491, Rozell v. Anderson, 91 Ind 591; Rice v Evansville, 108 Ind. 7; Terre Haute v Hudnut, 112 Ind 542; Young v. Kansas City, 27 Mo App. 101, Chope v Eureka, 78 Cal. 588, 21 Pac Rep. 364, Kanakee v. Linden, 38 Ill. App. 657, Arn v Kansas, 14 Fed 236, Bloomington v Murvin, 36 Ill. App 647.

Street grades and grading. Ilmer v. City of Springfield, 56 Mo. 119, Littlefield v Norwich, 40 Conn. 406; Clemence v Auburn, 66 N Y. 334, Lee v City of Minneapolis, 22 Minn. 18; City of Detroit v. Beckman, 34 Mich. 125, Cheever v Ladd, 13 Blatchf. 258; Tate v. Missouri R Co., 64 Mo 149; Russell v Burlington, 30 Ia. 262, Dixon v. Baker, 65 Ill. 518; Dore v Milwaukee, 42 Wis. 108; Shawneetown v. Mason, 82 Ill. 337, Hendershott v. Ottumwa, 46 Ia 658, Mayor of Nashville v. Nichol, 59

duct of their undertakings no less than if they were private owners: and this whether they derive any profit from the undertaking or not (*u*).

The same principle has been applied to the management of a public harbour by the executive government of a British colony (*x*). The rule is subject, of course, to the special statutory provisions as to liability and remedies that may exist in any particular case (*y*).

2. — *Effect of a Party's Death.*

Effect of death of either party Actio personalis moritur cum persona. We have next to consider the effect produced on liability for a wrong by the death of either the person wronged or the wrong-doer. This is one of the least rational parts of our law. The common law maxim is *actio personalis moritur cum persona*, or the right of action for tort is put an end to by the death of either party, even if an action has been commenced in his lifetime. This maxim " is one of some antiquity, but its origin is obscure and post-classical " (*z*). Causes of action on a contract are quite as much " personal " in the technical sense, but, with the exception of promises of marriage, and (it seems) injuries to the person by negligent performance of a contract, the maxim does not apply to these. In cases of tort not falling within statutory exceptions, to be

---

(*u*) *Mersey Docks Trustees* v. *Gibbs* (1864-5), L. R. 1 H. L. 93, 35 L. J. Ex. 225 see the very full and careful opinion of the judges delivered by Blackburn J., L. R. 1 H. L. pp. 102 *sqq*., in which the previous authorities are reviewed.

(*x*) *Reg* v. *Williams* (appeal from New Zealand), 9 App. Ca. 418.
(*y*) L. R. 1 H. L. 107, 110.
(*z*) Bowen and Fry L. JJ., *Finlay* v. *Chirney* (1888), 20 Q. B. Div. 494, 502, 57 L. J. Q. B. 247 see this judgment on the history of the maxim generally.

Tenn. 338; Ross *v.* City of Clinton, 46 Ia. 606, West Orange *v.* Field, 37 N. J. Eq. 600, 45 Am. Rep. 670, Noonan *v.* Albany, 79 N. Y. 470, 35 Am. Rep. 540, Smith *v.* Alexandria, 33 Gratt. 208, 36 Am. Rep. 788; Gillison *v.* Charleston, 16 W. Va. 282, 37 Am. Rep. 763

presently mentioned, the estate of the person wronged has no claim, and that of the wrong-doer is not liable. Where an action on a tort is referred to arbitration, and one of the parties dies after the hearing but before the making of the award, the cause of action is extinguished notwithstanding a clause in the order of reference providing for delivery of the award to the personal representatives of a party dying before the award is made. Such a clause is insensible with regard to a cause of action in tort; the agreement for reference being directed merely to the mode of trial, and not extending to alter the rights of the parties (a). A very similar rule existed in Roman law, with the modification that the inheritance of a man who had increased his estate by *dolus* was bound to restore the profit so gained, and that in some cases heirs might sue but could not be sued (b) Whether derived from a hasty following of the Roman rule or otherwise, the common law knew no such variations; the maxim was absolute At one time it may have been justified by the vindictive and *quasi*-criminal character of suits for civil injuries. A process which is still felt to be a substitute for private war may seem incapable of being continued on behalf of or against a dead man's estate, an impersonal abstraction represented no doubt by one or more living persons, but by persons who need not be of kin to the deceased. Some such feeling seems to be implied in the dictum, "If one doth a trespass to me, and dieth, the action is dead also, because it should be inconvenient to recover against one who was not party to the wrong" (c). Indeed, the survival of a cause of action was the exception in the earliest English law (d).

(a) *Bowker* v *Evans* (1885), 15 Q B Div 565, 54 L J Q B 421

(b) I iv. 12, de perpetuis et temporalibus actionibus, 1 Another difference in favour of the Roman law is that death of a party after *litis contestatio* did not abate the action in any case It has been conjectured that *personalis* in the English maxim is nothing but a misreading of *poenalis*.

(c) Newton C J in Year Book 19 Hen VI 66, pl 10 (A D. 1440–41)

(d) 20 Q B Div 503

A barbarous rule. But when once the notion of vengeance has been put aside, and that of compensation substituted, the rule *actio personalis moritur cum persona* seems to be without plausible ground. First, as to the liability, it is impossible to see why a wrong-doer's estate should ever be exempted from making satisfaction for his wrongs. It is better that the residuary legatee should be to some extent cut short than that the person wronged should be deprived of redress. The legatee can in any case take only what prior claims leave for him, and there would be no hardship in his taking subject to all obligations, *ex delicto*, as well as *ex contractu*, to which his testator was liable. Still less could the reversal of the rule be a just cause of complaint in the case of intestate succession. Then as to the right: it is supposed that personal injuries cause no damage to a man's estate, and therefore after his death the wrong-doer has nothing to account for. But this is oftentimes not so in fact. And, in any case, why should the law, contrary to its own principles and maxims in other departments, presume it, in favour of the wrong-doer so to be? Here one may almost say that *omnia praesumuntur pro spoliatore* Personal wrongs, it is allowed, may "operate to the temporal injury" of the personal estate, but without express allegation the Court will not intend it (e), though in the case of a wrong not strictly personal it is enough if such damage appears by necessary implication (f). The burden should rather be on the wrong-doer to show that the estate has not suffered appreciable damage. But it is needless to pursue the argument of principle against a rule which has been made at all tolerable for a civilized country only by a series of exceptions (g); of which presently.

(e) *Chamberlain* v *Williamson*, 2 M & S at p 414

(f) *Twycross* v *Grant* (1878), 4 C P Div 40, 48 L. J C P 1

(g) Cp Bentham, Traités de Législation, vol ii pt 2, c 10

Extension of the rule in Osborn v. Gillett. The rule has even been pushed to this extent, that the death of a human being cannot be a cause of action in a civil Court for a person not claiming through or representing the person killed, who in the case of an injury short of death would have been entitled to sue. A master can sue for injuries done to his servant by a wrongful act or neglect, whereby the service of the servant is lost to the master. But if the injury causes the servant's death, it is held that the master's right to compensation is gone (*h*). We must say it is so held, as the decision has not been overruled, or, that I know of, judicially questioned. But the dissent of Lord Bramwell is enough to throw doubt upon it. The previous authorities are inconclusive, and the reasoning of Lord Bramwell's (then Baron Bramwell's) judgment is, I submit, unanswerable on principle. At all events "actio personalis moritur cum persona" will not serve in this case. Here the person who dies is the servant; his own cause of action dies with him, according to the maxim, and his executors cannot sue for the benefit of his estate (*i*). But the master's cause of action is altogether a different one. He does not represent or claim through the servant; he sues in his own right, for another injury, on another estimation of damage; the two actions are independent, and recovery in the one action is no bar to recovery in the other. Nothing but the want of positive authority can be shown against the action being maintainable. And if want of authority were fatal, more than one modern addition to the resources of the Common Law must have been rejected (*k*). It is

---

(*h*) *Osborn v. Gillett* (1873), L. R. 8 Ex. 88, 42 L. J. Ex. 53, diss. Bramwell B.

(*i*) Under Lord Campbell's Act (*infra*) they may have a right of suit for the benefit of certain persons, not the estate as such.

(*k*) *E. q. Collen v. Wright*, Ex. Ch. 8 E. & B. 647, 27 L. J. Q. B. 215 (agent's implied warranty of authority—a doctrine introduced, by the way, for the very purpose of escaping the iniquitous effect of the maxim now in question, by getting a cause of action in contract which could be maintained against executors); *Lumley v. Gye* (1853), 2 E. & B. 216, 22 L. J. Q. B. 463, which we shall have to consider hereafter.

alleged, indeed, that "the policy of the law refuses to recognize the interest of one person in the death of another" (*l*)—a reason which would make life insurance and leases for lives illegal. Another and equally absurd reason sometimes given for the rule is that the value of human life is too great to be estimated in money; in other words, because the compensation cannot be adequate there shall be no compensation at all (*m*). It is true that the action by a master for loss of service consequential on a wrong done to his servant belongs to a somewhat archaic head of the law which has now become almost anomalous; perhaps it is not too much to say that in our own time the courts have discouraged it. This we shall see in its due place. But that is no sufficient reason for discouraging the action in a particular case by straining the application of a rule in itself absurd. *Osborn* v. *Gillett* stands in the book, and we cannot actually say it is not law; but one would like to see the point reconsidered by the Court of Appeal (*n*).

Exceptions. Statutes of Ed. III. giving executors right of suit for trespasses. We now proceed to the exceptions. The first amendment was made as long ago as 1330, by the statute 4 Ed. III. c. 7, of which the English version runs thus: Item, whereas in times past executors have not had actions for a trespass done to their testators, as of the goods and chattels of the same testators carried away in their life, and so such trespasses have hitherto remained unpunished; it is enacted that the executors in such cases shall have an action against the trespassers to recover damages in like manner as they, whose executors they be, should have had if they were in life.

The right was expressly extended to executors of execu-

(*l*) L. R. 8 Ex. at p. 90, *Arg.*

(*m*) The Roman lawyers, however, seem to have held a like view "Liberum corpus nullam recipit aestimationem" D. 9. 3, de his qui effud., 1, § 5, cf. h. t. 7,
and D. 9. 1, si quadrupes, 3. See Grueber on the Lex Aquilia, p. 17

(*n*) Cp. Mr. Horace Smith's remarks on this case (Smith on Negligence, 2d ed. 256).

tors by 25 Ed. III. st. 5, c. 5, and was construed to extend to administrators (*o*). It was held not to include injuries to the person or to the testator's freehold, and it does not include personal defamation, but it seems to extend to all other wrongs where special damage to the personal estate is shown (*p*).

Of Will. IV. as to injuries to property. Then by 3 and 4 Will IV. c. 42 (A. D 1833) actionable injuries to the real estate of any person committed within six calendar months before his death may be sued upon by his personal representatives, for the benefit of his personal estate, within one year after his death; and a man's estate can be made liable, through his personal representatives, for wrongs done by him within the six calendar months before his death " to another in respect of his property, real or personal." In this latter case the action must be brought against the wrong-doer's representatives within six months after they have entered on their office. Under this statute the executor of a tenant for life has been held liable to the remainderman for waste committed during the tenancy (*q*).

No right of action for damage to personal estate consequential on personal injury. Nothing in these statutes affects the case of a personal injury causing death, for which according to the maxim there is no remedy at all. It has been attempted to maintain that damage to the personal estate by reason of a personal injury, such as expenses of medical attendance, and loss of income through inability to work or attend to business, will bring the case within the statute of Edward III. But it is held that

---

(*o*) See note to *Pinchon's* case, 9 Co Rep. 89 a, vol v p 161 in ed 1826.

(*p*) *Twycross* v *Grant* (1878), 4 C P. Div 40, 45, 48 L J C P 1, *Hatchard* v *Mège* (1887), 18 Q B D 771, 56 L J Q B 397, *Oakey* v *Dalton* (1887), 35 Ch D 700, 56 L J Ch 823.

(*q*) *Woodhouse* v. *Walker* (1880), 5 Q.B Div 404, 49 L J Q B 609

"where the cause of action is in substance an injury to the person," an action by personal representatives cannot be admitted on this ground: the original wrong itself, not only its consequences, must be an injury to property (*r*).

Lord Campbell's act: peculiar rights created by it. Railway accidents, towards the middle of the present century, brought the hardship of the common law rule into prominence. A man who was maimed or reduced to imbecility by the negligence of a railway company's servants might recover heavy damages. If he died of his injuries, or was killed on the spot, his family might be ruined, but there was no remedy. This state of things brought about the passing of Lord Campbell's Act (9 & 10 Vict. c. 93, A.D. 1846), a statute extremely characteristic of English legislation (*s*). Instead of abolishing the barbarous rule which was the root of the mischief complained of, it created a new and anomalous kind of right and remedy by way of exception. It is entitled "An Act for compensating the Families of Persons killed by Accidents:" it confers a right of action on the personal representatives of a person whose death has been caused by a wrongful act, neglect, or default such that if death had not ensued that person might have maintained an action; but the right conferred is not for the benefit of the personal estate, but "for the benefit of the wife, husband, parent, and child (*t*) of the

---

(*r*) *Pulling* v *G E R Co* (1882), 9 Q. B. D 110, 51 L J Q B 453, cp *Leggott* v *G N R Co* (1876), 1 Q B. D. 599, 45 L. J Q B 557, the earlier case of *Bradshaw* v *Lancashire and Yorkshire R Co* (1875), L R 10 C P 189, 44 L J C P 148, is doubted, but distinguished as being on an action of contract.

(*s*) It appears to have been suggested by the law of Scotland, which already gave a remedy see Campbell on Negligence, 20 (2nd edit.), and *Blake* v *Midland R Co* (1852), 18 Q B 93, 21 L J Q B 233 (in argument for plaintiff)

(*t*) "Parent" includes father and mother, grandfather and grandmother, stepfather and stepmother. "Child" includes son and daughter, grandson and granddaughter, stepson and stepdaughter sect 5 It does not include illegitimate children *Dickinson* v *N E R Co* (1863), 2 H & C. 735, 33 L. J. Ex 91 There is no reason to doubt that it includes an unborn child. See *The George and Richard* (1871), L. R 3 A & E 466, which, however, is not of judicial authority on this point, for a few months later (*Smith* v *Brown* (1871), L R 6 Q B

person whose death shall have been so caused." Damages have to be assessed according to the injury resulting to the parties for whose benefit the action is brought, and apportioned between them by the jury (u). The nominal plaintiff must deliver to the defendant particulars of those parties and of the nature of the claim made on their behalf.

By an amending Act of 1864, 27 & 28 Vict. c. 95, if there is no personal representative of the person whose death has been caused, or if no action is brought by personal representatives within six months, all or any of the persons for whose benefit the right of action is given by Lord Campbell's Act may sue in their own names (x).

Construction of Lord Campbell's act. The principal Act is inaccurately entitled to begin with (for to a lay reader "accidents" might seem to include inevitable accidents, and again, "accident" does not include wilful wrongs, to which the Act does apply); nor is this promise much bettered by the performance of its enacting part It is certain that the right of action, or at any rate the right to compensation, given by the statute is not the same which the person killed would have had if he had lived to sue for his injuries. It is no answer to a claim under Lord Campbell's Act to show that the deceased would not himself have sustained pecuniary loss "The statute . . . gives to the personal representative a cause of action beyond that which the deceased would have had if he had survived, and based on a different principle" (y).

---

720), the Court of Queen's Bench held in prohibition that the Court of Admiralty had no jurisdiction to entertain claims under Lord Campbell's Act, and after some doubt this opinion has been confirmed by the House of Lords *Seward* v. *The Vera Cruz* (1884), 10 App Ca 59, overruling *The Franconia* (1877), 2 P D 163.

(u) Where a claim of this kind is satisfied by payment to executors without an action being brought, the Court will apportion the fund, in proceedings taken for that purpose in the Chancery Division, in like manner as a jury would have done *Bulmer* v *Bulmer* (1883), 25 Ch D 409

(x) Also, by sect. 2, " money paid into Court may be paid in one sum, without regard to its division into shares" (marginal note).

(y) Erle C J, *Pym* v *G N R. Co.* (1863), Ex Ch 4 B & S at p 406

But "the statute does not in terms say on what principle the action it gives is to be maintainable, nor on what principle the damages are to be assessed; and the only way to ascertain what it does, is to show what it does not mean" (z). It has been decided that some appreciable pecuniary loss to the beneficiaries (so we may conveniently call the parties for whose benefit the right is created) must be shown; they cannot maintain an action for nominal damages (a); nor recover what is called *solatium* in respect of the bodily hurt and suffering of the deceased, or their own affliction (b); they must show "a reasonable expectation of pecuniary benefit, as of right or otherwise," had the deceased remained alive. But a legal right to receive benefit from him need not be shown (c). Thus, the fact that a grown-up son has been in the constant habit of making presents of money and other things to his parents, or even has occasionally helped them in bad times (d), is a ground of expectation to be taken into account in assessing the loss sustained. Funeral and mourning expenses, however, not being the loss of any benefit that could have been had by the deceased person's continuing in life, are not admissible (e)

Interests of survivors distinct The interests conferred by the Act on the several beneficiaries are distinct. It is no answer to a claim on behalf of some of a man's children who are left poorer that all his children, taken as an undivided class, have got the whole of his property (f).

(z) Pollock C B in *Franklin* v *S E. R Co* (1858), 3 H & N at p 213
(a) *Duckworth* v *Johnson* (1859), 4 H & N 653, 29 L. J Ex 25
(b) *Blake* v *Midland R Co* (1852), 18 Q B 93, 21 L J Q B 233. In Scotland it is otherwise 1 Macq 752, n
(c) *Franklin* v *S E R Co* (1858), 3 H & N 211
(d) *Hetherington* v *N E R Co*, 9 Q B D 160, 51 L J Q B 495
(e) *Dalton* v *S J R Co* (1858), 4 C B N. S 296, 27 L J C P. 227, closely following *Franklin* v *S E R Co*
(f) *Pym* v *G. N R Co* (1863), 4 B. & S 396, 32 L. J Q B 377. The deceased had settled real estate on his eldest son, to whom other estates also passed as heir at law. As to the measure of damages where the deceased has insured his own life for the direct benefit of the plaintiff, see *Grand Trunk R of Canada* v *Jennings* (1888), 13 App Ca 800, 58 L J P C 1

The statutory cause of action is in substitution, not cumulative. It is said that the Act does not transfer to representatives the right of action which the person killed would have had, "but gives to the representative a totally new right of action on different principles" (*g*). Nevertheless the cause of action is so far the same that if a person who ultimately dies of injuries caused by wrongful act or neglect has accepted satisfaction for them in his life-time, an action under Lord Campbell's Act is not afterwards maintainable (*h*). For the injury sued on must, in the words of the Act, be "such as would, if death had not ensued, have entitled the party injured to maintain an action, and recover damages in respect thereof": and this must mean that he might immediately before his death have maintained an action, which if he had already recovered or accepted compensation, he could not do

Scottish and American laws. In Scotland, as we have incidentally seen, the surviving kindred are entitled by the common law to compensation in these cases, not only to the extent of actual damage, but by way of *solatium*. In the United States there exist almost everywhere statutes generally similar to Lord Campbell's Act; but they differ considerably in details from that Act and from one another (*i*). The tendency seems to be to confer on the survivors, both in legislation and in judicial construction, larger rights than in England.

(*g*) 18 Q B at p 110
(*h*) *Read* v. *G E R Co* (1868), L. R 3 Q. B 555, 37 L J Q B 278
(*i*) Cooley on Torts (Chicago, 1880), 262 *sqq* , Shearman & Redfield on Negligence, ss 263 *sqq* In Arkansas the doctrine of *actio personalis*, &c., appears to have been wholly abrogated by statute *ib* s 895

Effect of death of either party. In the absence of special statutes the decisions in America follow the common law rule, that in a civil court, the death of a human being cannot be complained of as an injury. Carey *v* Berkshire R. Co , 1 Cush 475; Kearney *v* Boston & W R Corp, 9 Cush 109, Conn. Mut Life Ins. Co *v* New York & N H R Co 25,

Right to follow property wrongfully taken or converted as against wrong-doer's estate.

In one class of cases there is a right to recover against a wrong-doer's estate, notwith-

Conn 265, Whitford v Panama R Co, 25 N. Y. 465, Kramer v Market Street R Co, 25 Cal. 434, Hyatt v. Adams, 16 Mich, Robert v. Lisenbee, 86 N. C 136, 11 Am. Rep 450, Peoria, etc., Ins. Co. v Frost, 37 Ill. 333, Hugh v New Orleans, etc., R Co, 6 La. Am 495, Insurance Co. v. Brame, 95 U S 754, Woodward v. Michigan, etc, R Co., 10 Ohio St 121, Boldings v Black Hills & Ft. P R. Co. (S D), 58 N W. Rep. 750, Illinois Cent R. Co. v. Pendergrass, 69 Miss. 425; 12 So. Rep. 951, Wyatt v. Williams, 13 N H. 102; Schuffler v. Minneapolis, etc, Ry, 32 Minn 125; Sherman v. Johnson, 58 Vt 40, Pitts v. Hale, 8 Mass 821; Stetson v. Kempton, 13 Mass 272, Moe v Smiley, 125 Pa St. 136; 17 At. Rep 228; 2 W. N. C. 461, Browner v. Sterdevant, 9 Ga. 69, Newsom v. Jackson, 29 Ga. 61; Schreiber v Sharpless, 17 Fed. Rep 589, Coker v Crozier, 5 Ala. 369, McClure v. Miller, 4 Hawks. 133.

Contra Ford v Monroe, 20 Wend. 210, Cross v. Guthery, 2 Root, 90; Green v Hudson River R. Co., 2 Keyes, 294.

This rule applies to every cause of action not satisfied by final judgment, thus it has been held, that if the plaintiff die after an appeal by the defendant from an award in favor of the plaintiff, for an assault and battery, his representatives cannot be substituted and the award is at an end Miller v Umbehower, 10 Serg & R 31. See Gibbs v Belcher, 30 Tex 79; Long v. Hitchcock, 3 Ohio, 274, Faith v Carpenter, 33 Ga. 79; Harrison v. Mosley, 31 Tex 608; Kelsey v Jewett, 34 Hun, 11; Kimbrough v Mitchell, 1 Head, 539, Baltimore R Co. v. Richie, 31 Md. 191; In re First Nat Bank, 49 Fed. Rep. 120

In most or all the United States, statutes containing provisions substantially similar to those of Lord Campbell's Act are in force. When the right of action is thus given it is ordinarily limited to those cases wherein the deceased person could have maintained a suit for the injury had he survived. The decisions construing these statutes are numerous and often peculiar to certain provisions, and it is not deemed consistent or practicable to undertake to cite them here. It is, however, important to note that the term "personal representative" employed in these statutes, means the executor or administrator of the deceased, and not his next of kin Chicago v Mayor, 18 Ill 349; Haley v Mobile & O R. Co., 7 Baxt 239, 8 Am & Eng R. Cas 344; Kramer v Market St. R. Co., 24 Cal 434, Boutiller v Milwaukee, 8 Minn 97, Whiton v Chicago, etc., R Co, 21 Wis. 305, Needham v. Grand Tr R. Co., 38 Vt. 294, Woodward v Chicago, etc., R. Co, 23 Wis. 400; Schmidt v Degan, 69 Wis. 300, 34 N. W. Rep 83 The constitutionality of such a statute was sustained in Georgia R. Co. v Pittman, 73 Ga 325; 26 Am & Eng. R. Cas. 474 See Carroll v Mo Pac. R Co, 26 Am & Eng R Cas 268

Under these statutes the measure of damages for the wrongful killing

standing the maxim of *actio personalis*, yet not so as to constitute a formal exception. When it comes to the point of direct conflict, the maxim has to prevail.

As Lord Mansfield stated the rule, "where property is acquired which benefits the testator, there an action for the value of the property shall survive against the executor" (*h*). Or, as Bowen L. J. has more fully expressed it, the cases under this head are those "in which property, or the proceeds or value of property, belonging to another, have been appropriated by the deceased person and added to his own estate or moneys." In such cases, inasmuch as the action brought by the true owner, in whatever form, is in

---

(*h*) *Hambly* v *Trott*, 1 Cowp 375.

---

of a person is the estimate of compensation for the pecuniary loss to the survivors. Demarest *v.* Little, 47 N. J. L. 28, Chicago, etc., R Co *v* Morris, 26 Ill. 400, Kessler *v* Smith, 66 N C 154; Atlanta, etc., R. Co *v.* Ayres, 53 Ga. 12, Atchison *v.* Twine, 9 Kan 350, Tilly *v.* N. Y., etc. R. Co., 24 N Y 471, Stoker *v.* St Louis, etc., R Co, 91 Mo. 511, Annas *v.* Milwaukee, etc., R. Co., 67 Wis. 46, Railroad Co *v* Barron, 5 Wall. 90; Chicago, etc., R. Co. *v* Swett, 45 Ill. 197, Paulmier *v* Erie R. Co 31 N J. L. 151, Rockford, etc., R. Co. *v.* Delaney, 82 Ill. 198, Chicago *v* Hesing, 83 Ill. 205, Houston, etc., R. Co. *v.* Cowser, 57 Tex. 293.

In several of the States it is held, that the action can only be brought in those States where the statute gives the right and where the killing occurred Woodward *v.* Mich., etc., R. Co, 10 Ohio St. 121; Illinois Central, etc., Co. *v.* Cragin, 71 Ill. 177; Limekiller *v.* Hannibal, etc., Co., 33 Kan 83; Chicago, etc., Co. *v* Schroder, 18 Ill. App. 328; Needham *v.* Grand Frank, etc., R. Co., 38 Vt. 294; Davis *v.* New York, etc., Co., 143 Mass. 301, Vawter *v.* Miss., etc., Co, 84 Mo 679.

But, ordinarily, a foreign administrator may maintain the action when the laws are substantially the same, and the action is not opposed to the general policy of the State in which the suit is brought. Leonard *v.* Columbia S. N. Co, 84 N. Y 48, Kansas Pac. R. Co *v* Cutter, 16 Kan 568, Taylor's Admr *v* Penna. Co, 7 Am. & Eng. Cas 23, South Carolina R Co *v* Nix, 68 Ga 572; Wabash, etc., Co. *v.* Shackett, 105 Ill 364; 12 Am. & Eng. R. Cas. 166, Jeffersonville, etc., R. Co. *v.* Hendricks, 41 Ind 49; Illinois Cent., etc, Co *v* Crudup, 63 Miss. 291, Burns *v.* Grand Rapids, etc., Co., 113 Ind. 169; 15 N. E. Rep. 230, Dennick *v.* Railroad Co., 103 U. S. 11, Knight *v.* West Jersey R. P Co., 108 Pa. St. 250, Luke *v.* Calhoun Co, 52 Ala. 115, Missouri Pac. Ry. Co. *v.* Lewis, 28 Neb. 848, 40 N W Rep 401.

substance to recover property, the action does not die with the person, but "the property or the proceeds or value which, in the lifetime of the wrong-doer, could have been recovered from him, can be traced after his death to his assets" (by suing the personal representatives) "and recaptured by the rightful owner there." But this rule is limited to the recovery of specific acquisitions or their value. It does not include the recovery of damages, as such, for a wrong, though the wrong may have increased the wrong-doer's estate in the sense of being useful to him or saving him expense (*l*).

The rule limited to recovery of specific property or its value: Phillips v. Homfray. If A. wrongfully gets and carries away coal from a mine under B.'s land, and B. sues for the value of the coal and damages, and inquiries are directed, pending which A. dies, B. is entitled as against A.'s estate to the value of the coal wrongfully taken, but not to damages for the use of the passages through which the coal was carried out, nor for the injury to the mines or the surface of the ground consequent on A.'s workings (*h*).

Again, A., a manufacturer, fouls a stream with refuse to the damage of B., a lower riparian owner; B. sues A., and pending the action, and more than six months after its commencement (*i*), A. dies. B. has no cause of action against A.'s representatives, for there has been no specific benefit to A.'s estate, only a wrong for which B. might in A.'s lifetime have recovered unliquidated damages (*k*).

The like law holds of a director of a company who has committed himself to false representations in the prospectus, whereby persons have been induced to take shares,

---

(*l*) The technical rule was that executors could not be sued in respect of an act of their testator in his lifetime in any form of action in which the plea was not guilty. *Hambly* v *Trott*, 1 Cowp. 375

(*h*) *Phillips* v *Homfray* (1883), 24 Ch. D. 439, 454, 52 L. J. Ch. 833. The authorities are fully examined in the judgment of Bowen and Cotton L.JJ. As to allowing interest in such cases, see *Phillips* v *Homfray*, '92, 1 Ch. 465, C. A.

(*i*) 3 & 4 Will. IV c. 42, p. 60, above

(*k*) *Kirk* v *Todd* (1882), 21 Ch. Div. 484, 52 L. J. Ch. 224

and have acquired a right of suit against the issuers. If he dies before or pending such a suit, his estate is not liable (*l*). In short, this right against the executors or administrators of a wrong-doer can be maintained only if there is "some beneficial property or value capable of being measured, followed, and recovered" (*m*). For the rest, the dicta of the late Sir George Jessel and of the Lords Justices are such as to make it evident that the maxim which they felt bound to enforce was far from commanding their approval.

3. *Liability for the Torts of Agents and Servants.*

Command of principal does not excuse agent's wrong. Whoever commits a wrong is liable for it himself. It is no excuse that he was acting, as an agent or servant, on

(*l*) *Peek v. Gurney* (1873), L. R. 6 H. L. at p. 392.   (*m*) 21 Ch. D. at p. 163.

Command of principal does not excuse agent's wrong. If a servant commit a tort out of his course of employment, he alone is responsible to the person injured thereby. If he commit a tort while acting within the course of his employment, he and his master are each liable for the resulting damages. Mitchell v. Harmony, 14 How. 115; Brown v. Lent, 20 Vt. 529, Wright v. Wilcox, 19 Wend. 343, Richardson v. Kimball, 28 Me. 463, Suydam v. Moore, 8 Barb. 458; Althorf v. Wolfe, 22 N. Y. 355, Phelps v. Waite, 30 N. Y. 78; Hewitt v. Swift, 3 Allen, 420, Grand Trunk R. Co. v. Latham, 63 Me. 177, McClanathan v. Oswego, etc., R. Co., 1 Thomp. & C. 501, Mitchell v. Harmony, 13 How. 115, Harriman v. Stowe, 57 Mo. 93, Hawksworth v. Thompson, 98 Mass. 77, Johnson v. Barber, 5 Gilm. 425, Bennett v. Joes, 30 Conn. 329, Wright v. Crompton, 53 Ind. 337, Evansville, etc., R. Co. v. Baum, 26 Ind. 70; Peck v. Cooper, 112 Ill. 192, Reynolds v. Hanrahan, 100 Mass. 313, The State v. Walker, 16 Me. 241; Porter v. Thomas, 23 Ga. 467, Sagers v. Nuckolls (Colo. App.), 32 Pac. Rep. 187.

So, one servant may recover damages from a co-servant for injuries suffered through the latter's negligence. Griffiths v. Wolfram, 22 Minn. 185; Osborne v. Morgan, 130 Mass. 102; overruling Albro v. Jaquith, 4 Gray, 99, Hinds v. Harbon, 58 Ind. 21, Hinds v. Duenacker, 66 Ind. 547.

behalf and for the benefit of another (*n*). But that other may well be also liable, and in many cases a man is held answerable for wrongs not committed by himself. The rules of general application in this kind are those concerning the liability of a principal for his agent, and of a master for his servant. Under certain conditions responsibility goes farther, and a man may have to answer for wrongs which, as regards the immediate cause of the damage, are not those of either his agents or his servants.

Cases of absolute positive duty distinguished. Thus we have cases where a man is subject to a positive duty, and is held liable for failure to perform it. Here, the absolute character of the duty being once established, the question is not by whose hand an unsuccessful attempt was made, whether that of the party himself, of his servant, or of an "independent contractor" (*o*), but whether the duty has been adequately performed or not. If it has, there is nothing more to be considered, and liability, if any, must be sought in some other quarter (*p*). If not, the non-performance in itself, not the causes or conditions of non-performance, is the ground of liability. Special duties created by statute, as conditions attached to the grant of exceptional rights or otherwise, afford the chief examples of this kind. Here the liability attaches, irrespective of any question of agency or personal negligence, if and when the conditions imposed by the legislature are not satisfied (*q*)

(*n*) *Cullen* v *Thomson's Trustees and Kerr*, 4 Macq 424, 433. "For the contract of agency or service cannot impose any obligation on the agent or servant to commit or assist in the committing of fraud," or any other wrong.

(*o*) The distinction will be explained below

(*p*) See *Hyams* v *Webster* (1868), Ex Ch L R 4 Q B 138, 38 L J Q B 21

(*q*) See *Gray* v *Pullen* (1864), Ex Ch. 5 B & S 970, 34 L J Q B 265

Cases of absolute positive duty. warranty These cases are discussed under separate headings on other pages.

Upon duties imposed by statute, see *ante*, p 24 Upon the general subject, see *post*, chap XII.

Also duties in nature of warranty. There occur likewise, though as an exception, duties of this kind imposed by the common law. Such are the duties of common carriers, of owners of dangerous animals or other things involving, by their nature or position, special risk of harm to their neighbours; and such, to a limited extent, is the duty of occupiers of fixed property to have it in reasonably safe condition and repair, so far as that end can be assured by the due care on the part not only of themselves and their servants, but of all concerned.

The degrees of responsibility may be thus arranged, beginning with the mildest:

(i) For oneself and specifically authorized agents (this holds always).

(ii) For servants or agents generally (limited to course of employment).

(iii) For both servants and independent contractors (duties as to safe repair, etc.).

(iv) For everything but *vis major* (exceptional: some cases of special risk, and anomalously, certain public occupations).

Modes of liability for wrongful acts, etc., of others. Apart from the cases of exceptional duty where the responsibility is in the nature of insurance or warranty, a man may be liable for another's wrong —

(1) As having authorized or ratified that particular wrong:

(2) As standing to the other person in a relation making him answerable for wrongs committed by that person in virtue of their relation, though not specifically authorized.

The former head presents little or no difficulty. The latter includes considerable difficulties of principle, and is often complicated with troublesome questions of *fact*.

Command and ratification. It scarce needs authority to show that a man is liable for wrongful acts which have been done according to his express command or request, or which, having been done on his account and for his benefit, he has adopted as his own. "A trespasser may be not only he who does the act, but who commands or procures it to be done . . . who aids or assists in it . . . or who assents afterwards" (r). This is not the less so because the person employed to do an unlawful act may be employed as an "independent contractor," so that, supposing it lawful, the employer would not be liable for his negligence about doing it. A gas company employed a firm of contractors to break open a public street, having therefor no lawful authority or excuse, the thing contracted to be

---

(r) De Grey C J, in *Barker v Braham* (1773), 2 W Bl 866, Bigelow, L C 235

Command and ratification. The doctrine of the text is sustained by all well considered authorities. Congreve v. Morgan, 5 Duer, 195, Clark v Fry, 8 Ohio St. 358, Elder v. Bemis, 2 Metc. 599, Armstrong v. Cooley, 10 Ill. 509, McCullough v. Shoneman, 105 Pa. St 169, 51 Am. Rep 194, Schmidt v Adams, 18 Mo. App 432, Craker v. Chicago & N. W. Ry Co, 36 Wis 669, McClung v. Dearborne, 134 Pa. St 396; 19 At Rep. 698; 26 W N. C. 42, Tucker v. Jenis, 75 Me. 188; Corner v. Mackintosh, 48 Md. 347, Byne v. Hatcher, 75 Ga. 289; Nashville & C. R Co. v Starnes, 9 Heisk. 52; Barden v. Felch, 109 Mass. 154, Williams v Palace Car Co., 40 La An 87, 33 Am. & Eng. R. Cas. 414, Dempsey v Chambers, 154 Mass. 330; 28 N. E Rep. 279; Harrison v. Mitchell, 13 La. An 260, Bass v Chicago & N W Ry. Co, 42 Wis. 654, Milwaukee & M. R. R. Co. v. Finney, 10 Wis 388, Allred v. Bray, 41 Mo. 484, Brainard v. Dunning, 30 N. Y 211, Hewitt v. Swift, 8 Allen, 420; Knight v. Nelson, 117 Mass. 457

And so if the wrongful act be done by an "independent contractor" Ware v St Paul Water Co., 2 Abb. U. S. 261; Leber v Minneapolis & N W. R Co, 29 Minn 256, Ketcham v Cohn, 22 N. Y. S. Rep. 181; Hawver v Whalen, 49 Ohio St. 69, 29 N. E. Rep. 1049, Engel v. Eureka Club, 59 Hun, 593, 14 N Y. S. Rep 184.

Subsequent approval of a tort will not affect a third person, unless the act were originally done in his name or for his use. Grand v. Van Vleck, 69 Ill. 481, Coomes v Houghton, 102 Mass. 211, New England Dredging Co. v. Rockport Granite Co., 149 Mass. 381 See Dempsey v. Chambers, 154 Mass 330, 28 N. E. Rep. 279, reviewing the cases

done being in itself a public nuisance, the gas company was held liable for injury caused to a foot-passenger by falling over some of the earth and stones excavated and heaped up by the contractors (s). A point of importance to be noted in this connexion is that only such acts bind a principal by subsequent ratification as were done at the time on the principal's behalf. What is done by the immediate actor on his own account cannot be effectually adopted by another, neither can an act done in the name and on behalf of Peter be ratified either for gain or for loss by John. "Ratum quis habere non potest, quod ipsius nomine non est gestum" (t).

Master and servant The more general rule governing the other and more difficult branch of the subject was expressed by Willes J. in a judgment which may now be regarded as a classical authority "The master is answerable for every such wrong of the servant or agent as is committed in the course of the service and for the master's benefit, though no express command or privity of the master be proved" (u).

(s) *Ellis* v *Shefield Gas Consumers Co* (1853), 2 E & B 767, 23 L J Q B 42

(t) *Wilson* v *Tumman* (1843), 6 M & G 236, and Serjeant Manning's note, ib 239

(u) *Barwick* v *English Joint Stock Bank* (1867), Ex Ch L R 2 Ex 259, 265, 36 L J Ex 147 The point of the decision is that fraud is herein on the same footing as other wrongs of which in due course

---

Master and servant. The general statement in the text is that also of the law in the United States.

It is accepted that the master's liability for the torts of the servant springs out of the relation itself, and does not depend upon the stipulations of their contract. Within the scope of his authority, the servant may be said to be the medium through which the master acts, it follows, as a general rule, that for the tortious acts of the servant the master is liable. Ward *v.* Young, 42 Ark. 542, Northern Pac. R. Co, *v.* Herbert, 116 U. S. 624; 24 Am. & Eng. R Cas. 407; The Eleanor, 2 Wheat. 345; Robinson *v* Webb, 11 Bush, 465, Sawyer *v* Martins, 25 Ill. Ap. 521. The cases subsequently cited in this chapter sustain and show the special application of these general principles.

Reason of the master's liability. No reason for the rule, at any rate no satisfying one, is commonly given in our books. Its importance belongs altogether to the modern law, and it does not seem to be illustrated by any early authority (*x*). Blackstone (1 417) is short in his statement, and has no other reason to give than the fiction of an "implied command." It is currently said, *Respondeat superior;* which is a dogmatic statement, not an explanation. It is also said *Qui facit per alium facit per se;* but this is in terms applicable only to authorized acts, not to acts that, although done by the agent or servant "in the course of the service," are specifically unauthorized or even forbidden. Again, it is said that a master ought to be careful in choosing fit servants; but if this were the reason, a master could discharge himself by showing that the servant for whose wrong he is sued was chosen by him with due care, and was in fact generally well conducted and competent: which is certainly not the law.

A better account was given by Chief Justice Shaw of Massachusetts. "This rule," he said, "is obviously founded on the great principle of social duty, that every man in the management of his own affairs, whether by himself or by his agents or servants, shall so conduct them as not to injure another; and if he does not, and another thereby sustains damage, he shall answer for it" (*y*). This is, indeed, somewhat too widely expressed, for it does not in terms limit the responsibility to cases where at least negligence is proved. But no reader is likely to suppose that, as a general rule, either the servant or the

---

(*x*) Joseph Brown Q C in evidence before Select Committee on Employers' Liability, 1876, p. 38, Brett L J, 1877, p. 11(

(*y*) Farwell v. *Boston and Worcester Railroad Corporation* (1842), 4 Met 49, and Bigelow L C 688 The judgment is also reprinted in 3 Macq 316 So, too, M. Sainctelette, a recent Continental writer on the subject, well says "La responsabilité du fait d'autrui n'est pas une fiction inventée par la loi positive C'est une exigence de l'ordre social" De la Responsabilité et de la Garantie, p 124 Paley (Mor. Phil bk 3, c 11) found it difficult to refer the rule to any principle of natural justice.

master can be liable where there is no default at all. And the true principle is otherwise clearly enounced. I am answerable for the wrongs of my servant or agent, not because he is authorized by me or personally represents me, but because he is about my affairs, and I am bound to see that my affairs are conducted with due regard to the safety of others.

Some time later the rule was put by Lord Cranworth in a not dissimilar form: the master "is considered as bound to guarantee third persons against all hurt arising from the carelessness of himself or of those acting under his orders in the course of his business" (z).

The statement of Willes J. that the master "has put the agent in his place to do that class of acts" is also to be noted and remembered as a guide in many of the questions that arise. A just view seems to be taken, though artificially and obscurely expressed, in one of the earliest reported cases on this branch of the law: "It shall be intended that the servant had authority from his master, it being for his master's benefit" (a).

Questions to be considered herein. The rule, then (on whatever reason founded), being that a master is liable for the acts, neglects, and defaults of his servants in the course of the service, we have to define further —

1. Who is a servant.
2. What acts are deemed to be in the course of service.
3. How the rule is affected when the person injured is himself a servant of the same master.

Who is a servant: responsibility goes with order and control. 1. As to the first point, it is quite possible to do

---

(z) *Bartonshill Coal Co* v. *Reid* (1858), 3 Macq. 266, 283.

(a) *Tuberville* v. *Stampe* (end of 17th century), 1 Ld. Raym. 264.

Who is a servant. Responsibility. "A servant is one who is engaged not merely in doing work or services for another, but who is in

work for a man, in the popular sense, and even to be his agent for some purposes, without being his servant. The relation of master and servant exists only between persons

---

his service, usually upon or about the premises or property of his employer, and subject to his direction and control therein, and who is, generally, liable to be dismissed." Heygood v. The State, 59 Ala 51.

It is a uniform rule that, where one has the right to direct or control the action of another, the relation of master and servant exists. The chief difficulty in applying this rule is in determining what state of facts amounts to a release of control by the person possessing the right to retain it, as an employer, and what amounts to a retention of control. These questions are usually for the jury, under proper instructions from the court See Mumby v. Bowden, 25 Fla 154; Andrews v. Boedecker, 17 Ill App 213; Bennett v. Truebody, 66 Cal 509; 56 Am Rep. 117, Mullan v. Steamship Co, 78 Pa. St. 25, 21 Am Rep. 2, Riley v. State Line Steamship Co, 29 La An 791; 29 Am Rep. 349; St. Louis, etc., R. Co v Willis, 38 Kan 330; 16 Pac Rep 728, Rankin v Merchants' & M. T Co., 73 Ga 229, 54 Am. Rep 874, Toledo v Cone, 41 Ohio St 149, Rummell v Dilworth, 11 Pa St 343, Lean v Burbank, 11 Minn. 277, Lowell v. Boston & L R. Co., 23 Pick 24, Earle v. Hall, 2 Metc. 353, Brackett v. Lubke, 4 Allen, 138; Ballow v. Farnum, 9 Allen, 47, Schwartz v Gilmore, 45 Ill 455, Larock v Ogdensburg & L C R. Co, 26 Hun, 382, Forsyth v. Hooper, 11 Allen, 419, Cincinnati v. Stone, 5 Ohio St. 38, Clark v Fitch, 2 Wend 459, Lipe v. Eisenlerd, 32 N. Y 229, Hartwig v. Bay State S & L Co, 43 Hun, 425, Schrubbe v. Connell, 69 Wis 476; 84 N W. Rep 503, Stone v Codman, 15 Pick 297, Morgan v. Bowman, 22 Mo. 538, Linnehan v Rollins, 137 Mass 123; 50 Am Rep. 287, New Orleans, etc., R. R Co v. Norwood, 62 Minn. 565, 52 Am Rep 191 Ward v. Young, 42 Ark 542, Burton v. Galveston & H. R. Co, 61 Tex 526, 21 Am & Eng. R R Cas 218, Clapp v. Kemp, 122 Mass 481; Huff v. Ford, 126 Mass. 24, Baxter v. Warner, 13 N Y Supreme Ct. 585, Eaton v European R Co, 59 Me. 520; Darmstuetter v. Moynahan, 27 Mich. 188; Larson v Metropolitan S. R Co, 110 Mo. 234; 19 S. W. Rep. 46, Spisak v Baltimore & O R Co., 152 Pa. St 281, 25 At. Rep. 497; Bernauer v Hartman Steel Co, 33 Ill. App. 491; Southern Express Co v. Brown, 67 Miss 260. 7 So Rep. 318; 8 So. Rep 425, Hickey v Merchants' & M. T Co, 152 Mass. 39; 24 N. E. Rep 860; Singer Mfg. Co. v. Rahn, 132 U S 518, Brown v Smith, 86 Ga. 274, 12 S. E. Rep. 411; Douglass v Stephens, 18 Mo. 362, Wilkins v Gilmore, 2 Humph 140.

An extreme case is that of Fay v Davidson (113 Minn. 523), in which it was held, that although the owner of an interest in a vessel, by contract, renounce his right to control, right to hire, discharge, etc., yet, if the boat is run *for* him and his interest, he is liable as master. But see Sproul v Hemmingway, 14 Pick 1

of whom the one has the order and control of the work done by the other. A master is one who not only prescribes to the workman the end of his work, but directs, or at any

---

Where one contracts with another, exercising an independent calling, to do certain work for him, not subject to his orders or control as to manner of performance, but only as to results to be obtained, the latter is said to be an "independent contractor," for whose torts and those of his servants the employer is not liable. Hittle v. Republican Valley R. Co., 19 Neb. 620; McDonnell v Rifle Broom Co, 71 Mich. 61, 38 N. W. Rep. 681; Chicago City R. Co v Hennessey, 16 Ill. Ap 153; Hexamer v. Weber, 101 N. Y 377, 54 Am Rep. 703, Matthes v Kerrigan, 58 N. Y. Superior Ct. 431, Blake v. Ferris, 5 N Y 48; Boswell v. Laird, 8 Cal. 469, Kellogg v Payne, 21 Ia. 575, Hass v. Philadelphia, etc., Steamship Co, 88 Pa St 269; Am. Rep. 462; McCarthy v Second Parish, 71 Me. 318, 36 Am Rep. 320, Wabash, etc., R Co v. Farver, 111 Ind. 195; 31 Am. & Eng. R. Cas 134; Edmundson v Pittsburg, etc., R Co., 111 Pa. St 316, 23 Am & Eng. R. Cas 423; Wray v. Evans, 80 Pa. St. 102; Callahan v Burlington R Co, 23 Ia. 562, Sweeny v. Murphy, 32 Ia. An. 628, Hilliard v. Richardson, 3 Gray, 349; Vanderpool v Husson, 28 Barb 196, Gilbert v. Beach, 4 Duer, 423, Annen v. Willard, 57 Pa St 374, Fink v. Missouri Furnace Co., 82 Mo. 276, 52 Am Rep. 376, Martin v Tribune Assn., 30 Hun, 391, Smith v. Simmons, 103 Pa. St 32 New Orleans & N. E R Co v Reese, 61 Miss 581; Aston v Nolan, 63 Cal 269, Bailey v. Troy & B. R Co, 57 Vt. 252, 52 Am Rep. 129, Harrison v Collins, 86 Pa St 153, Tiffin v McCormack, 34 Ohio St 638, Hale v. Johnson, 80 Ill. 185; Deford v State, 30 Md. 179; Schular v Hudson River R. Co, 38 Barb 653, O'Rourke v Hart, 7 Bosw. 511, Clarke v. Vermont & C. R. Co., 28 Vt. 103, Du Pratt v Lick, 38 Cal 691, Harris v McNamar (Ala.), 12 So Rep 103; Geer v. Darrow, 61 Conn. 230, 23 At. Rep 1087, Charlebois v Gogebic & M R. Co., 91 Mich. 59; 51 N W. Rep. 812; Fulton County S R Co. v McConnell, 87 Ga 756; 13 S E Rep 828; Long v Moon, 107 Mo 334; 15 S. W. Rep 810; Scarborough v. Alabama Midland R. Co, 94 Ala. 497, 10 So. Rep 816, Wiener v Hammel, 14 N Y. S. Rep. 365; McCann v Kings Co. E. R Co., 19 N. Y S Rep 668, Atlanta & F. R Co. v. Kimberly, 87 Ga. 161, 13 S E Rep. 277; St. L A & T. R Co. v. Knott, 54 Ark 424, 16 S W. Rep 9; Charlock v. Freed, 125 N Y. 357, 26 N. E. Rep. 262, Larow v Clute, 14 N. Y. 616; Vincennes Water Supply Co v. White, 124 Ind. 376, 24 N. E. Rep. 747; Rome & D R. Co v. Chasteen, 88 Ala 591, 7 So Rep. 94; St. L. I. M. & S. R Co. v. Yonley, 53 Ark. 503; 12 S W. Rep. 333

And the same rule obtains as between a contractor and a sub-contractor. Hart v. Ryan, 6 N. Y. S. Rep. 921; Gourdier v. Cormack, 2 E. D. Smith, 254, Gately v Kniss, 64 Ia 537, McCleary v. Kent, 3 Duer, 27, Devlin v. Smith, 89 N. Y. 470; Hilliard v. Richardson, 3 Gray, 349.

But where work causing injury is done by an independent contractor

moment may direct the means also, or, as it has been put, "retains the power of controlling the work" (b); and he who does work on those terms is in law a servant for whose acts, neglects, and defaults, to the extent to be specified, the master is liable. An independent contractor is one who undertakes to produce a given result, but so that in the actual execution of the work he is not under the order or control of the person for whom he does it, and may use his own discretion in things not specified beforehand. For the acts or omissions of such a one about the performance of his undertaking his employer is not liable to strangers, no more than the buyer of goods is liable to a person who may be injured by the careless handling of them by the seller or his men in the course of delivery. If the contract, for example, is to build a wall, and the builder " has a right to say to the employer, 'I will agree to do it, but I shall do it after my own fashion; I shall begin the wall at this end, and not at the other;' there the relation of master and servant does not exist, and the employer is not liable" (c). " In ascertaining who is liable for the act of a wrong-doer, you must look to the wrong-doer himself or to the first person in the ascending line who is the employer and has control over the work. You cannot go further back and make the employer of that person liable" (d). He who controls the work is answerable for the workman; the remoter employer who does not control it is not answerable. This distinction is thoroughly settled in our law; the difficulties that may arise in apply-

(b) Crompton J, *Sadler v. Henlock* (1855), 4 E. & B. 570, 578, 24 L. J. Q. B. 138, 141

(c) Bramwell L J, Emp. L. 1877, p 53. An extra judicial statement, but made on an occasion of importance by a great master of the common law

(d) Willes J, *Murray v Currie* (1870), L. R. 6 C. P. 24, 27, 40 L J C P 26,

the employer is liable if the particular work was directly authorized. Palmer v London, 5 Neb 136, Waller v. Lasher, 37 Ill. App. 609, Beaity v. Thileman, 8 N Y. Rep. 645, Stone v Cheshire R. Co., 19 N. H 427; Robbins v Chicago, 4 Wall 679, Chicago v Robbins, 2 Blackf. 418.

ing it are difficulties of ascertaining the facts (e). It may be a nice question whether a man has let out the whole of a given work to an "independent contractor," or reserved so much power of control as to leave him answerable for what is done (f)

Specific assumption of control. It must be remembered that the remoter employer, if at any point he does interfere and assume specific control, renders himself answerable, not as master, but as principal. He makes himself "dominus pro tempore." Thus the hirer of a carriage, driven by a coachman who is not the hirer's ser-

---

(e) One comparatively early case, *Bush v. Steinman*, 1 B. & P. 404, disregards the rule, but that case has been repeatedly commented on with disapproval, and is not now law. See the modern authorities well reviewed in *Hilliard v. Richardson* (Sup. Court Mass 1855), 3 Gray, 349, and in Bigelow L C. Exactly the same distinction appears to be taken under the Code Napoleon in fixing the limits within which the very wide language of Art. 1384 is to be applied Sainctelette, op cit. 127

(f) *Pendleburgh v Greenhalgh* (1876), 1 Q. B Div 36, 45 L. J Q B 3, differing from the view of the same facts taken by the Court of Queen's Bench in *Taylor v Greenhalgh* (1874), L R 9 Q. B. 487, 43 L. J. Q B 168.

Specific assumption of control Following the general rule that the employer who retains direction and control of the work is responsible for the wrongful acts of the contractor and his servants, it is reasonable, that where the employer interferes during the progress of the work let to another and assumes control, he should, at that moment, assume the responsibilities as master, and this is the rule Hefferman v. Benkard, 1 Robt 432; Savannah & W. R Co. v. Phillips, 90 Ga 829; 17 S E Rep 82.

A coachman, hired with the coach, does not become the bailee's servant. New York, etc., R. Co v. Steinbrenner, 47 N. J L 161, 54 Am Rep. 126; S. P., Crockett v Calvert, 8 Ind. 127; Quinn v. Complete Electric Co , 46 Fed Rep 506, Muse v. Stern, 82 Va. 33.

So, it has been held, that where a passenger in a carriage, driven by a servant of the carrier, upon being assured by the driver that a vehicle in front can be passed, gives an order to that effect to the driver, the passenger is not liable for the resulting accident. Richardson v Van Ness, 53 Hun, 267; 6 N. Y. S. Rep. 618; Michael v. Stanton, 3 Hun, 463; 5 Thomp. & C. 634 See Joslin v. Grand Rapids Ice Co., 50 Mich. 520; 45 Am Rep. 54, Brophy v. Bartlett, 108 N Y. 632, 15 N. E Rep. 368, Chicago R Co v. Volk, 45 Ill. 175, Morrell v Pheinfrank, 24 Fed Rep. 94. *Contra*, Boniface v Relyea, 6 Robt 897; 5 Abb Pr. (N. S) 259.

vant but the latter's, is not, generally speaking, liable for harm done by the driver's negligence (g). But if he orders, or by words or conduct at the time sanctions, a specific act of rash or careless driving, he may well be liable (h). Rather slight evidence of personal interference has been allowed as sufficient in this class of cases (i).

Temporary transfer of service. One material result of this principle is that a person who is habitually the servant of A. may become, for a certain time and for the purpose of certain work, the servant of B.; and this although the hand to pay him is still A.'s. The owner of a vessel employs a stevedore to unload the cargo. The stevedore employs his own labourers; among other men, some of the ship's crew work for him by arrangement with the master, being like the others paid by the stevedore and under his orders. In the work of unloading these men are the servants of the stevedore, not of the owner (j).

(g) Even if the driver was selected by himself *Quarman* v *Burnett* (1840), 6 M & W 499. So where a vessel is hired with its crew *Dalyell* v *Tyrer* (1858), E. B & E. 899, 28 L J Q B 52. So where a contractor finds horses and drivers to draw watering carts for a municipal corporation, the driver of such a cart is not the servant of the corporation *Jones* v *Corporation of Liverpool* (1885), 14 Q B D 890, 54 L J Q B. 345, cp *Little* v. *Hackett* (1886), 116 U S at pp. 371-3, 377

(h) *McLaughlin* v *Pryor* (1842), 4 M. & G 48

(i) Ib., *Burgess* v *Gray* (1845), 1 C B 578, 14 L J C P, 184 It is difficult in either case to see proof of more than adoption or acquiescence. Cp *Jones* v *Corporation of Liverpool* (1885), 14 Q. B. D at pp. 893-4, 54 L. J Q B. 345

(j) *Murray* v *Currie* (1870), L R 6 C P. 24, 40 L J C P 26 Cp *Wild* v *Waygood*, '92, 1 Q. B. 783, 61 L J Q B 391, C A

Temporary transfer of service. A person availing himself of the services of another's servant becomes, for the time, his master. Wood v. Cobb, 8 Allen. 58; Burke v. Norwich R Co , 34 Conn. 874; Stevens v. Armstrong, 6 N Y 435, Young v. New York, R. Co., 30 Barb. 229; Stone v Western Transportation Co , 38 N. Y. 240.

Where A. told his servant to drive to B's, then to return by a certain route. On the servant's arrival, B. persuaded him to go on an errand for him; it was held, that for the space of time used on the errand the servant was not A's, but B's Stone v Hill, 45 Conn. 44. See Sheridan v Charlick, 4 Daly, 338; Cavanaugh v. Dinsmore, 19 N Y Supreme Ct. 465, Wyllie v. Palmer, 63 Hun, 33, 17 N Y S. Rep 424

Owners of a colliery, after partly sinking a shaft, agree with a contractor to finish the work for them, on the terms, among others, that engine power and engineers to work the engine are to be provided by the owners. The engine that has been used in excavating the shaft is handed over accordingly to the contractor; the same engineer remains in charge of it, and is still paid by the owners, but is under the orders of the contractor. During the continuance of the work on those terms the engineer is the servant not of the colliery owners but of the contractor (*k*).

But where iron founders execute specific work about the structure of a new building under a contract with the architect, and without any contract with the builder, their workmen do not become servants of the builder (*l*).

"**Power of controlling the work**" explained. It is proper to add that the "power of controlling the work" which is the legal criterion of the relation of a master to a servant does not necessarily mean a present and physical ability. Shipowners are answerable for the acts of the master, though done under circumstances in which it is impossible to communicate with the owners (*m*). It is enough that the servant is bound to obey the master's

---

(*k*) *Rourke* v *White Moss Colliery Co.* (1877), 2 C P Div 205, 46 L J C P 283
(*l*) *Johnson* v *Lindsay* (1891), A C 371

(*m*) See Maude and Pollock, Merchant Shipping, 1 158, 4th ed

---

"Power of controlling the work," explained. Upon this subject see cases cited in American notes, *ante*, p 91.

Shipowners are liable for the torts of the officers in charge Spencer *v.* Kelley, 32 Fed Rep 838, Yates *v.* Brown, 8 Pick. 23, The E M Norton, 15 Fed Rep 686, Korah *v* Ottawa, 82 Ill 121 St. John *v* Paine, 10 How. 557, Germania Ins Co *v.* The Lady Pike, 21 Wall 1, Chamberlain *v* Ward, 21 How 548, Ward *v* Chamberlain, 21 How 572

But the shipowners are not liable for the personal tort of the master, that being beyond the scope of his authority North American D. & I. Co *v* The River Mersey, 46 Fed. Rep 686.

In Geer *v.* Darrow (61 Conn. 230, 23 At Rep 1087), it is held, that a contractor is liable for an injury resulting from improper use of construction apparatus, although not present.

directions if and when communicated to him. The legal power of control is to actual supervision what in the doctrine of possession the intent to possess is to physical detention. But this much is needful; therefore a compulsory pilot, who is in charge of the vessel independently of the owner's will, and, so far from being bound to obey the owner's or master's orders, supersedes the master for the time being, is not the owner's servant, and the statutory exemption of the owner from liability for such a pilot's acts is but in affirmance of the common law (*n*).

What is in course of employment. 2. Next, we have to see what is meant by the course of service or employment. The injury in respect of which a master becomes subject to this kind of vicarious liability may be caused in the following ways:—

(a) It may be the natural consequence of something being done by a servant with ordinary care in execution of the master's specific orders.

(b) It may be due to the servant's want of care in carrying on the work or business in which he is employed. This is the commonest case.

(*n*) Merchant Shipping Act, 1854, s. 388, *The Halley* (1868), L. R. 2 P. C. at p. 201. And see Marsden on Collisions at per, ch 5 On the other hand there may be a statutory relation which does resemble that of master and servant for the purpose of creating a duty to the public *King v London Improved Cab Co* (1889), 23 Q B Div 281.

What is in course of employment There are a few cases defining what is meant by "course of employment," and many illustrating the application of the term as a limitation of the liability of the master for the torts of the servant. See Gregory's Admr. *v.* Ohio River R. Co., 37 W. Va 606; 16 S E Rep. 819, Moore *v.* Columbia & G. R. Co (S. C), 16 S. E. Rep. 781, Illinois Cent R. Co. *v.* Ross, 31 Ill. App 170, Donaldson *v.* Miss. & Mo R. Co., 18 Ia. 281, Consolidated Ice M Co *v* Keifer, 134 Ill. 481, 25 N. E Rep. 799; Jones *v* St Louis N & P. Packet Co., 43 Mo. App. 398, Courtney *v.* Baker, 37 N. Y. Superior Ct 249, and see cases cited *infra*, pp. 91–105

"An act though not ordered is in the scope of employment if of such a nature as might be justified without such order, and the master is liable for its unskillful execution" Gilmartin *v* New York, 55 Barb 239.

(c) The servant's wrong may consist in excess or mistaken execution of a lawful authority.

(d) Or it may even be a wilful wrong, such as assault, provided the act is done on the master's behalf and with the intention of serving his purposes

Let us take these heads in order.

Execution of specific orders. (a) Here the servant is the master's agent in a proper sense, and the master is liable for that which he has truly, not by the fiction of a legal maxim, commanded to be done. He is also liable for the natural consequences of his orders, even though he wished to avoid them, and desired his servant to avoid them. Thus, in *Gregory* v. *Piper* (o) a right of way was disputed between adjacent occupiers, and the one who resisted the claim ordered a labourer to lay down rubbish to obstruct the way, but so as not to touch the other's wall. The labourer executed the orders as nearly as he could, and laid the rubbish some distance from the wall, but it soon "shingled down" and ran against the wall, and in fact could not by any ordinary care have been prevented from doing so. For this the employer was held to answer as for a trespass which he had authorized. This is a matter of general principle, not of any special kind of liability. No man can authorize a thing and at the same time affect to disavow its natural consequences; no more than he can disclaim responsibility for the natural consequences of what he does himself.

Negligence in conduct of master's business (b) Then comes the case of the servant's negligence in the perform-

(o) 9 B & C 591 (1829).

Negligence in conduct of master's business The American authorities agree with the statement of the text, a few of the numerous cases are Williams v Pullman Palace Car Co., 40 La. An. 417, 33 Am. & Eng R Cas. 414, Atchison, etc., R. Co v. Galins, 36 Kan. 749; Coulon v Eastern R Co, 135 Mass 195; 15 Am & Eng. R Cas. 99; McIntire R. Co. v.

ance of his duty, or rather while he is about his master's business. What constitutes negligence does not just now concern us; but it must be established that the servant is a wrong-doer, and liable to the plaintiff, before any question of the master's liability can be entertained. Assuming this to be made out, the question may occur whether the servant was in truth on his master's business at the time, or engaged on some pursuit of his own. In the latter case the master is not liable. "If the servant, instead of doing that which he is employed to do, does something which he is not employed to do at all, the master cannot be said to do it by his servant, and therefore is not responsible for the negligence of his servant in doing it" (*p*). For example: "If a servant driving a carriage, in order to effect some purpose of his own, wantonly strike the horses of another person, . . . the master will not be liable. But if, in order to perform his master's orders, he strikes but injudiciously, and in order to extricate himself from a difficulty, that will be negligent and careless conduct, for which the master will be liable, being an act done in pursuance of the servant's employment" (*q*).

(*p*) Maule J., *Mitchell* v *Crassweller* (1853), 13 C B 237, 22 L J C. P 100.

(*q*) *Croft* v *Alison* (1821), 4 B & A. 590

Bolton, 43 Ohio St 224, 21 Am & Eng. R Cas 501, Northern Pc. R. Co. v Herbert, 116 U S 642, 24 Am. & Eng. R. Cas 407, Osborne v. McMasters, 40 Minn 103; Cincinnati, etc., R Co. v. Smith, 22 Ohio (N. S), 227, 10 Am. Rep 729; Luttrell v. Hazen, 3 Sneed (Tenn.), 20, Tuel v. Weston, 47 Vt 634; Quinn v Power, 87 N. Y. 535, Hays v Miller, 77 Pa. St. 238; 18 Am. Rep. 445; Pickens v Diecker, 21 Ohio (N. S), 212, 8 Am. Rep. 55, Martin v Richards, 155 Mass. 381; 29 N. E. Rep. 591; Brazil v. Peterson, 44 Minn. 212; 46 N. W. Rep. 331, Ellegard v Acklund, 43 Minn. 352, 45 N. W. Rep. 715, Oil Creek, etc , R. Co. v. Keighron, 74 Pa. St. 316, Thayer v. City of Boston, 19 Pick. 511; Hays v. Gainesville St. R. Co , 70 Tex. 602, 34 Am. & Eng R. Cas 97, Philadelphia, W & B. R Co v Philadelphia, etc., Towboat Co., 23 How 209; Mobile & M. Ry. Co. v. Smith, 59 Ala. 245, Denver, S. P & P R. Co v Conway, 8 Colo. 1; Banister v Pennsylvania Co., 98 Ind 220, Leavenworth etc., Ry. Co v. Forbes, 37 Kan. 445, Colvin v Peabody, 155 Mass. 104; 29 N. E. Rep. 59; Singer Mfg. Co v. Rahn, 132 Mass. 518, 10 S. Ct. Rep. 175.

Departure or deviation from master's business. Whether the servant is really bent on his master's affairs

Departure or deviation from master's business. The American authorities are in substantial accord with those of England. Thus, it was said by the court in the case of Howe v Newmarch (12 Allen, 49), that "If the servant, wholly for a purpose of his own, disregarding the object for which he is employed, and not intending by his act to execute it, does an injury to another not within the scope of his employment, the master is not liable." See Way v. Powers, 57 Vt 135, Sheridan v. Charlick, 4 Daly, 338; Chicago, B. & Q R Co v Casey, 9 Ill. App 632, Cavanaugh v. Dinsmore, 19 N. Y Supreme Ct. 165, Bard v. John, 26 Pa. St. 182, Baker v Kinsey, 38 Cal 631; Wright v Wilcox, 19 Wend. 343; Parsons v Winchell, 5 Cush 592; Boulard v. Calhoun, 13 La. An 445; Brown v. Purtrance, 2 Har. & G. 316, Adams v Cost, 62 Md. 264, 50 Am. Rep. 211; Dawkins v Gulf C & S F R Co., 77 Tex 232; 13 S W. Rep. 984; Thorp v Minot, 109 N. C. 152, 13 S E. Rep. 702; Stephenson v. South Pac. R. Co., 93 Cal 558, 29 Pac Rep 234, Louisville, etc , R Co. v Douglass, 69 Miss 723, 11 So Rep. 933, Southern Express Co v. Fitzner, 59 Miss 581, Dolls v. Stollenwerk 78 Wis. 330, 47 N W. Rep 431.

Where a master of a ferry boat left the wharf without the requisite consent of the owners of the boat and took a burning barge in tow, which set fire to other boats, it was held, that the owners of the boat were not responsible for the conduct of the master. Aycrigg v. New York, etc., R. Co., 30 N. J. L 460.

A bill-poster who wantonly throws a heap of bills into the road fifteen miles from where they should have been posted, does not charge his employer with liability for a runaway caused by two of the bills being blown against the horse of plaintiff's intestate. Smith v. Spitz, 156 Mass. 319; 31 N E Rep. 5.

The nice discrimination sometimes observed by the courts in the application of these principles is illustrated in the case of Cobb v. Columbia & G. R Co (37 S C. 194; 15 S. E. Rep. 878), in which a railroad company is held liable for the misconduct of an engineer in unnecessarily and wilfully sounding the whistle and blowing off steam, so as to frighten a horse, and cause him to run away, but not for the misconduct of the trainmen in yelling and shouting at the horse.

In the case of Mielvehill v. Bates (31 Minn. 364), where the owner of an express wagon employed a driver, and intrusted the wagon to him, generally, to be used, at his discretion, in securing and doing business, thus employed, the driver, having delivered a trunk, on his return got "a load of poles for himself," and, while taking them home, negligently drove over and injured the plaintiff's child; it was held, that the master was liable for the injury

In another case, where the pilot in charge of a ferry boat took on a boatman, agreeing without compensation, to put him on board his boat,

or not is a question of fact, but a question which may be troublesome. Distinctions are suggested by some of the reported cases which are almost too fine to be acceptable. The principle, however, is intelligible and rational. Not every deviation of the servant from the strict execution of duty, nor every disregard of particular instructions, will be such an interruption of the course of employment as to determine or suspend the master's responsibility. But where there is not merely deviation, but a total departure from the course of the master's business, so that the servant may be said to be "on a frolic of his own" (r), the master is no longer answerable for the servant's conduct. Two modern cases of the same class and period, one on either side of the line, will illustrate this distinction.

Whatman v. Pearson. In *Whatman* v. *Pearson* (s), a carter who was employed by a contractor, having the allowance of an hour's time for dinner in his day's work, but also having orders not to leave his horse and cart, or the place where he was employed, happened to live hard

(r) Parke B., *Joel* v. *Morison* (1834), 6 C. & P. 503 a nisi prius case, but often cited with approval, see *Burns* v. *Poul-*

som (1873), L. R. 8 C. P. at p. 567, 42 L. J. C. P. 302.

(s) L. R. 3 C. P. 422 (1868).

---

which was part of a tow passing up the river. The ferry boat diverged from its course to reach the tow, and through the negligence of those in charge, collided with a canal boat attached thereto, upon which was plaintiff's intestate, who was thrown by the collision into the river and drowned. The defendant (the owner of the ferry boat), was held responsible for the accident. Quinn v. Power, 87 N. Y. 535, 41 Am. Rep. 392, reversing 17 Hun. 102. See Smith v. Webster, 23 Mich. 298; Tuel v. Weston, 47 Vt. 624; Leviness v. Post, 6 Daly, 321; Wolfe v. Mersereau, 4 Duer 473, Chapman v. New York, etc., R. Co., 33 N. Y. 369; Simons v. Monier, 29 Barb. 219, Chicago, M. & St. P. R. Co. v. West, 125 Ill. 320, 17 N. E. Rep. 788; Simonin v. New York, etc., R. Co., 36 Hun, 214, Bonner v. Bryant (Tex.), 21 S. W. Rep. 549, Baxter v. Chicago, etc., R. Co. (Ia.), 54 N. W. Rep. 350, Garretzen v. Duenchkel, 50 Mo. 104, Northwestern R. Co. v. Hack, 66 Ill. 238; Schaefer v. Osterbrink, 67 Wis. 495; 58 Am. Rep. 875.

by. Contrary to his instructions, he went home to dinner, and left the horse and cart unattended at his door; the horse ran away and did damage to the plaintiff's railings. A jury was held warranted in finding that the carman was throughout in the course of his employment as the contractor's servant "acting within the general scope of his authority to conduct the horse and cart during the day" (*t*).

Storey v. Ashton. In *Storey* v *Ashton* (*u*), a carman was returning to his employer's office with returned empties. A clerk of the same employer's who was with him induced him, when he was near home, to turn off in another direction to call at a house and pick up something for the clerk. While the carman was driving in this direction he ran over the plaintiff. The Court held that if the carman "had been merely going a roundabout way home, the master would have been liable; but he had started on an entirely new journey on his own or his fellow-servant's account, and could not in any way be said to be carrying out his master's employment" (*x*). More lately it has been held that if the servant begins using his master's property for purposes of his own, the fact that by way of afterthought he does something for his master's purposes also is not necessarily such a "re-entering upon his ordinary duties" as to make the master answerable for him. A journey undertaken on the servant's own account "cannot by the mere fact of the man making a pretence of duty by stopping on his way be converted into a journey made in the course of his employment" (*y*)

(*t*) Byles J , at p 425.
(*u*) (1869) L. R 4 Q B. 476, 38 L J Q B 223 *Mitchell* v *Crassweller*, cited on p 77, was a very similar case
(*x*) Lush J at p 480 It was "an entirely new and independent journey, which had nothing at all to do with his employment " Cockburn C J "Every step he drove was away from his duty " Mellor J , ibid. But it could have made no difference if the accident had happened as he was coming back See the next case
(*y*) *Rayner* v *Mitchell* (1877), 2 C. P D 357

Williams v. *Jones.* The following is a curious example. A carpenter was employed by A. with B.'s permission to work for him in a shed belonging to B. This carpenter set fire to the shed in lighting his pipe with a shaving. His act, though negligent, having nothing to do with the purpose of his employment, A. was not liable to B. (z). It does not seem difficult to pronounce that lighting a pipe is not in the course of a carpenter's employment; but the case was one of difficulty as being complicated by the argument that A., having obtained a gratuitous loan of the shed for his own purposes, was answerable, without regard to the relation of master and servant, for the conduct of persons using it. This failed for want of anything to show that A. had acquired the exclusive use or control of the shed. Apart from this, the facts come very near to the case which has been suggested, but not dealt with by the Courts in any reported decision, of a miner opening his safety-lamp to get a light for his pipe, and thereby causing an explosion; where "it seems clear that the employer would not be held liable" (a).

Excess or mistake in execution of authority. (c) Another kind of wrong which may be done by a servant in his

(z) *Williams* v *Jones* (1865), Ex Ch 3 H & C 256, 602, 33 L J Ex 297, diss Mellor and Blackburn JJ

(a) R S (now Mr Justice) Wright, Emp L 1876, p 47

Excess or mistake in execution of authority The master is liable for the wrongful act of the servant to the injury of a third person, when the servant is engaged at the time in doing his master's business and was acting in the scope of his general authority, although, the servant departed from the private instructions of the master, abused his authority, was reckless in the performance of his duty, and inflicted unnecessary injury Rounds *v.* Del L & W. R. Co., 64 N. Y. 129, 5 Thomp & C 475, 4 Hun, 329.

Thus, where a gate-keeper, authorized to keep order, ejects plaintiff for fanciful objections to his demeanor and assaults him, the employer is liable. Oakland City A & I Soc. *v* Bingham (Ind. App), 31 N E Rep. 383. See New Orleans, etc , R Co *v.* Hanning, 15 Wall. 649, Ochsenbein

master's business, and so as to make the master liable, is the excessive or erroneous execution of a lawful authority. To establish a right of action against the master in such a case it must be shown that (α) the servant intended to do on behalf of his master something of a kind which he was in fact authorized to do, (β) the act, if done in a proper manner, or under the circumstances erroneously supposed by the servant to exist, would have been lawful.

The master is chargeable only for acts of an authorized class which in the particular instance are wrongful by reason of excess or mistake on the servant's part. For acts which he has neither authorized in kind nor sanctioned in particular he is not chargeable.

Interference with passengers by guards, etc. Most of the cases on this head have arisen out of acts of railway servants on behalf of the companies. A porter whose duty

---

v. Shapley, 85 N Y 214, Heenrich v Pullman, etc, Co., 20 Fed. Rep 100, 18 Am. & Eng. R Cas. 379, Molloy v New York, etc. R. Co., 10 Daly, 453, Gulf & S F R. Co. v. Kirkland, 79 Tex 457, 15 S. W. Rep 495, Chicago, R I & P. R. Co v. Conklin, 82 Kan. 55, Isaacson v. New York, etc., R Co., 94 N Y 278, Pittsburg, etc, R. Co. v. Kirk, 102 Ind. 399.

So, a railroad conductor or brakeman has implied authority to remove trespassers, but if he recklessly ejects one from a train, the company is liable. Hoffman v. New York, etc, R. Co, 87 N. Y. 25, Carter v. Louisville, etc., Ry. Co, 98 Ind. 552, Atchison, etc., R. Co v. Thul, 32 Kan. 255, Kansas City, etc, R. Co. v Kelley, 86 Kan 655; 14 Pac. Rep. 172; Lovett v Salem & S D. R. Co., 9 Allen, 557, Holmes v. Wakefield, 12 Allen, 580; Jeffersonville R. Co v. Rogers, 38 Ind 116; Kline v. C P R Co., 37 Cal. 400, Shea v Sixth Ave. R Co., 62 N Y 180, Higgins v Watervliet Turnpike Co, 46 N Y 23; Chicago, M. & St. P. R. Co. v West, 24 Ill App 44, affirmed 125 Ill. 320; 17 N E Rep 788.

For the servant's mistakes the master is liable. Marshall v. St. Louis, K. C & N Ry. Co, 78 Mo 610, White v. Bank, 1 Brews. 234; See McKinley v. C & N. W R Co, 44 Ia 314.

Interference with passengers by guards, etc. Where a street car conductor threw a boy from the car, whom he erroneously supposed was stealing a ride, it was held, that though the conductor acted without malice and with a sole view to further the master's business, as he viewed

is, among other things, to see that passengers do not get into wrong trains or carriages (but not to remove them from a wrong carriage), asks a passenger who has just taken his seat where he is going. The passenger answers, "To Macclesfield." The porter, thinking the passenger is in the wrong train, pulls him out, but the train was in fact going to Macclesfield, and the passenger was right. On these facts a jury may well find that the porter was acting within his general authority so as to make the company liable (b). Here are both error and excess in the servant's action: error in supposing facts to exist which make it proper to use his authority (namely, that the passenger has got into the wrong train); excess in the manner of executing his authority, even had the facts been as he supposed. But they do not exclude the master's liability.

"A person who puts another in his place to do a class of acts in his absence necessarily leaves him to determine,

(b) *Bayley v. Manchester, Sheffield and Lincolnshire R. Co.* (1872-3), L. R. 7 C. P. 415, 11 L. J. C. P. 278, in Ex. Ch. 8 C. P. 148, 12 L. J. C. P. 78.

it, defendant company was liable. Schulz v. Third Ave. R. Co, 46 N. Y Super. Ct. 211

In Pennsylvania R. C. v Toomey (91 Pa. St. 256), it was held, that a railroad company is responsible for an ejectment from a car, by the conductor, when the act was wrongful or reckless, but not when it was malicious See New York, etc., Ry. Co v Haring, 47 N J L 137, Higgins v Watervliet, etc., Co., 46 N. Y. 23, 7 Am Rep. 293, Coleman v. New York, etc, R. Co, 106 Mass. 160, Hoffman v New York, etc, R. Co, 87 N. Y. 25, 41 Am Rep 337; Pennsylvania R. Co v Vandiver, 42 Pa. St. 365 New York L. E. & H. R Co. v Harring, 47 N. J L 137, Randolph v. Hannibal & St J. R Co, 18 Mo App. 609, Kansas City, etc., R Co. v Kelly, 36 Kan 655, Wabash R. Co. v. Savage, 110 Ind. 156; Savannah St. R. Co. v Bryan, 86 Ga. 312, 12 S. E. Rep 307, Meyer v Second Ave. R. Co., 8 Bosw 305, Chicago & E. R Co. v. Flexman, 103 Ill 846; 8 Am. & Eng R Cas 354, 42 Am Rep. 83, Stewart v. Brooklyn, etc., R. Co., 90 N. Y 588, 43 Am Rep. 185, Terre Haute & I R Co v. Jackson, 81 Ind. 19, Campbell v. Pullman Palace Car Co, 42 Fed Rep. 484, Illinois Cent. R. Co. v Sheehan, 29 Ill. App. 90; Same v Smith, Id. 94; Croaker v. Chicago & N W. R Co., 39 Wis 657; 17 Am. Rep 504; Jardine v. Cornell, 50 N. J L 485, 14 At Rep 590, Sanford v Eighth Ave. R. Co., 23 N. Y. 343; Goddard v Grand Trunk Ry, 57 Mo. 202

according to the circumstances that arise, when an act of that class is to be done, and trusts him for the manner in which it is done; and consequently he is held responsible for the wrong of the person so intrusted either in the manner of doing such an act, or in doing such an act under circumstances in which it ought not to have been done; provided that what was done was done, not from any caprice of the servant, but in the course of the employment" (c).

Seymour v. *Greenwood* (d) is another illustrative case of this class. The guard of an omnibus removed a passenger whom he thought it proper to remove as being drunken and offensive to the other passengers, and in so doing used excessive violence. Even if he were altogether mistaken as to the conduct and condition of the passenger thus removed, the owner of the omnibus was answerable. "The master, by giving the guard authority to remove offensive passengers necessarily gave him authority to determine whether any passenger had misconducted himself."

Arrest of supposed offenders. Another kind of case under this head is where a servant takes on ' .self to arrest a supposed offender on his employer's behalf.

(c) Per Willes J., *Bayley* v. *Manchester, Sheffield, and Lincolnshire R. Co.*, L. R. 7 C. P. 415, 41 L. J. C. P. 278.

(d) 7 H. & N. 355, 30 L. J. Ex. 189, 327, Ex. Ch. (1861).

Arrest of supposed offenders. The apparently severe rule of holding the master responsible for the servant's wrongful arrest is generally upheld where the conduct of the servant is within the scope of his employment and authority. The courts are rightly disposed to vigilantly guard the natural right to liberty against infraction, even by an erring servant. Accordingly it is held that a railroad is liable for the false arrest, by its ticket agent, of a passenger on charge of paying for a ticket with counterfeit money. *Mulligan* v. *New York & R. R. R. Co.*, 14 N. Y. S. Rep. 456; S. P., *Palmer* v. *Manhattan R. Co.*, 14 N. Y. S. Rep. 468. See *Rown* v. *Christopher & T. R. Co.*, 34 Hun, 471; G. H. & S. A. Ry. Co. v. *Donaho*, 56 Tex. 165; *Fortune* v. *Trainor*, 19 N. Y. S. Rep. 598; *Galveston, etc., R. Co.* v. *Donaho*, 56 Tex. 162; 9 Am. & Eng. R. Cas. 287;

Here it must be shown, both that the arrest would have been justified if the offence had really been committed by the party arrested, and that to make such an arrest was within the employment of the servant who made it. As to the latter point, however, "where this is a necessity to have a person on the spot to act on an emergency, and to determine whether certain things shall or shall not be done, the fact that there is a person on the spot who is acting as if he had express authority is *prima facie* evidence that he had authority" (*e*). Railway companies have accordingly been held liable for wrongful arrests made by their inspectors or other officers as for attempted frauds on the company punishable under statutes or authorized by-laws, and the like (*f*).

Act wholly outside authority, master not liable. But the master is not answerable if the servant takes on him-

---

(*e*) Blackburn J., Moore v. Metrop. R. Co. (1872), L. R. 8 Q. B. 36, 39, 42 L. J. Q. B. 21.

(*f*) Ib., following Goff v. G. N. R. Co., (1861), 3 E. & E. 672, 30 L. J. Q. B. 148

Lynch v. Metropolitan, etc., R. Co., 90 N. Y. 77, 12 Am. & Eng. R. Cas. 119.

But it has been held, that an arrest by a servant is a departure from the course of employment, and that the master is not liable: as where employes in a store called a policeman and directed him to arrest and examine the person of a lady suspected of stealing goods, which was done without the authority of the proprietor. The court said: "It cannot be presumed, that a master, by intrusting his servant with his property, and conferring power upon him to transact his business, thereby authorizes him to do any act for its protection that he could not lawfully do himself if present." Mali v. Lord, 39 N. Y. 381. See Mallach v. Ridley, 43 Hun, 336, Porter v. The C. R. J. & P. R. Co., 41 Ia. 358.

Act wholly outside authority, master not liable. Sustaining this proposition are numerous cases. Thus, in Golden v. Newbrand (52 Ia. 59), it was held, that where an armed watchman, employed to guard a brewery, shot a person who was retreating from the brewery, the act of shooting was not within the line of the watchman's duty. See Cardiff v. Louisville, etc., R. Co., 42 La. An. 477; 7 So. Rep. 601.

A railroad company is not liable for fire caused by section hands cook-

self, though in good faith and meaning to further the master's interest, that which the master has no right to do even if the facts were as the servant thinks them to be; as where a station-master arrested a passenger for refusing to pay for the carriage of a horse, a thing outside the company's powers (g). The same rule holds if the particular servant's act is plainly beyond his authority, as where the

(g) Poulton v. L. & S. W. R. Co (1866), L. R. 2 Q. B. 534, 36 L. J. Q. B. 294

ing dinner on railroad embankment. Morier v. Minneapolis, etc., R. Co., 31 Minn. 351, 17 Am. Rep. 793.

Servants of house-mover, who, after their day's work is done, build steps for plaintiff, do not charge the house-mover with their negligence. Dells v. Stollenwerk, 78 Wis. 330, 17 N. W. Rep. 431.

A corporation, owning a parlor car in use on a railroad, is not liable for an injury to a person not a passenger, caused by the porter of the car, throwing from the car a bundle containing his personal effects, solely for his own convenience. Walton v. New York, etc., R. Co., 139 Mass. 556.

In the case of Gilliam v. South & N. A. R. Co (70 Ala. 268), the facts were, in substance, that the conductor of a passenger train stopped his train, pursued a boy on foot, into the house of the boy's father, with a pistol in his hand, and seized and carried him off on the train; it was held, that these wrongful acts were not within the range of his employment and the company not liable. See Tharp v. Minor, 109 N. C. 152, 13 S. E. Rep. 152, Texas P. Ry Co v. Moody (Tex. App.), 23 S. W. Rep. 41, Yates v. Squires, 19 Ia. 26, Weldon v. Harlem R. Co., 5 Bosw. 576, McClenaghan v. Brock, 5 Rich. 17, Wilste v. State Board Bridge Co., 63 Mich. 639; 30 N Y Rep. 370, Walton v. New York, etc., Co., 139 Mass. 556, Noblesville, etc., Co. v. Gause, 76 Ind. 142, 40 Am. Rep. 224; Laflille v. New Orleans & L. R. Co., 43 La. An. 34; Marion v. Chicago, etc., R. Co., 59 Ia. 428, Thames Steamboat Co. v. Housatonic R. Co., 24 Conn. 40, Church v. Mansfield, 20 Conn. 284, Evansville, etc., R. Co. v. Baum, 26 Ind. 70, McCoy v. McKowen, 26 Miss. 487, Yerger v. Warren, 31 Pa. St. 319, Harris v. Nicholas, 2 Munf. 583, Little Miami R. Co. v. Wetmore, 19 Ohio St. 110, Chicago B. and S. R. Co v. Epperson, 26 Ill. App. 72, Nashville & C. R. Co v. Starnes, 9 Heisk. 66, Campbell v. Northern Pac. R. Co (Minn.), 53 N W Rep. 768, McCarthy v. Boston, 135 Mass. 197, Southern Exp. Co v. Fitzner, 59 Miss. 581; Foster v. Essex Bank, 17 Mass. 479, Crocker v. New London, etc., R. Co., 24 Conn. 249; Sheridan v. Charlick, 4 Daly, 338; Burke v. Shaw, 59 Miss. 445, 42 Am Rep. 390, Cawthorn v. Deas, 2 Port. 275, Baker v. Kinsey, 38 Cal. 631; Long v. Chicago, etc., R. Co., 48 Kan. 28, 28 Pac. Rep. 977, Wilste v. State Board Bridge Co., 63 Mich. 639, 30 N W. Rep. 370.

officer in charge of a railway station arrests a man on suspicion of stealing the company's goods, an act which is not part of the company's general business, nor for their apparent benefit (*h*). In a case not clear on the face of it, as where a bank manager commences a prosecution, which turns out to be groundless, for a supposed theft of the bank's property — a matter not within the ordinary routine of banking business, but which might in the particular case be within the manager's authority — the extent of the servant's authority is a question of fact (*i*). Much must depend on the nature of the matter in which the authority is given. Thus an agent entrusted with general and ample powers for the management of a farm has been held to be clearly outside the scope of his authority in entering on the adjacent owner's land on the other side of a boundary ditch in order to cut underwood which was choking the ditch and hindering the drainage from the farm. If he had done something on his employer's own land which was an actionable injury to adjacent land, the employer might have been liable. But it was thought unwarrantable to say "that an agent entrusted with authority to be exercised over a particular piece of land has authority to commit a trespass on other land" (*j*). More generally, an authority cannot be implied for acts not necessary to protect the employer's property, such as arresting a customer for a supposed attempt to pass bad money (*k*).

Wilful trespasses, etc., for master's purposes. (d) Lastly, a master may be liable even for wilful and deliberate

---

(*h*) *Edwards* v *L & N. W. R. Co* (1870), L. R. 5 C. P. 445, 39 L. J. C. P. 241, cp. *Allen* v *L & S. W. R. Co* (1870), L. R. 6 Q B 65, 40 L. J. Q. B. 55

(*i*) *Bank of New South Wales* v *Owston* (1879) (J. C.), 4 App. Ca. 270, 48 L. J. P. C. 25.

(*j*) *Bolingbroke* v *Swindon Local Board* (1874), L. R. 9 C. P. 575, 43 L. J. C. P. 575

(*k*) *Abrahams* v *Deakin*, '91, 1 Q B 516 (C. A.), 60 L. J. Q. B. 238.

Wilful trespasses, etc., for master's purposes. The American authorities substantially agree with the text. Thus, in the case of *Rogahn* v

wrongs committed by the servant, provided they be done on the master's account and for his purposes; and this, no

Moore Mfg. & F. Co. (79 Wis. 573, 48 N. W. Rep. 669), where the material facts were, that the plaintiff, who had been discharged by the defendant's foreman, was assaulted for not leaving the premises quickly enough to suit the foreman; the defendant was held liable. See Ramsden v. Boston & A. R. Co., 104 Mass 117

Where a servant in driving a strange cow from his master's field, killed the cow by striking her with a stone, the master was held liable. Evans v Davidson, 53 Md 245, 36 Am Rep 100 See Fraser v Freeman, 56 Barb 234, Cohen v Dry Dock, etc, R Co, 69 N. Y 170, Gere v Stern, 30 Hun, 426, Dillingham v. Anthony, 73 Tex. 47, 11 S. W. Rep 139, Weed v. Panama R Co, 17 N Y 362, Pittsburgh, etc., R. Co. v. Shields, 47 Ohio St 387, 24 N E Rep 658, McKay v Irvine, 11 Biss. 168, Marion v Chicago, etc, Ry. Co, 59 Ia 128, Birmingham Water Works Co v Hubbard, 85 Ala 179, 4 So Rep. 607, Johnson v Barber, 10 Ill. 425, Hartman v Railway Co, 45 Ohio St. 11, 32 Am & Eng R Cas 37, Tuller v Voght, 13 Ill 277, Terre Haute & S R Co. v. Jackson, 81 Ind 19, Bess v. Chesapeake & O. Ry Co, 35 W. Va 492, 14 S E. Rep. 234

But the master is not liable for a wrong designedly inflicted by the servant, where the act is neither authorized nor ratified by the master. Steele v Smith, 3 E D Smith, 321, Garvey v. Dung, 30 How. Pr 315, Cox v. Keahey, 36 Ala 340. Snodgrass v Bradley, 2 Grant Cas. 43; Campbell v Stairt, 2 Murph 389, Deibl v Ottenville, 14 Lea, 191; McCann v. Tielinghast, 140 Mass 327; Farber v Mo. Pac R Co, 32 Mo App 378; Murphy v Central Park R. Co, 48 N. Y. Superior Ct. 96; Baylis v Schwalbach Cycle Co., 14 N. Y. S Rep 933; Central R. Co. v Peacock, 69 Md. 257, 14 At. Rep. 709, Mott v. Consumer's Ice Co, 73 N Y. 517; Wallace v. Finberg, 46 Texas, 35, Lindsay v Griffin, 22 Ala. 629.

It is a rule that disobedience by the servant of the master's general orders does not excuse the master from liability for resulting damages. Schmidt v Adams, 18 Mo App. 432, Powell v. Deveney, 3 Cush. 300, Philadelphia, etc, R. R Co. v Derby, 14 How 468, Atchison, etc., R. Co. v. Randall, 14 Kan 421, Duggins v. Watson, 15 Ark. 118; Toledo, etc Ry. Co. v. Harman, 47 Ill. 298, Southwick v. Estes, 7 Cush 385; Garretzen v Duenckel, 50 Mo 104; 11 Am Rep 405, Robinson v. Webb, 11 Bush, 482, French v. Creswell, 13 Oreg. 418, 11 Pac Rep 63, Keedy v. Howe, 72 Ill 136

But there are cases holding the contrary, where the master's orders are specific. Haack v. Fearing, 5 Robt. 528; Oxford v. Peter, 28 Ill. 434, Deibl v Ottenville, 14 Lea, 191, Wood v Detroit St Ry, 52 Mich. 402, Attaway v. Cartersville, 68 Ga. 740, Wright v. Wilcox, 19 Wend. 343, Andrews v Green, 62 N H 436

less than in other cases, although the servant's conduct is of a kind actually forbidden by the master. Sometimes it has been said that a master is not liable for the "wilful and malicious" wrong of his servant. If "malicious" means "committed exclusively for the servant's private ends," or "malice" means "private spite" (*l*), this is a correct statement; otherwise it is contrary to modern authority. The question is not what was the nature of the act in itself, but *whether the servant intended to act in the master's interest*.

This was decided by the Exchequer Chamber in *Limpus* v. *London General Omnibus Company* (*m*), where the defendant company's driver had obstructed the plaintiff's omnibus by pulling across the road in front of it, and caused it to upset. He had printed instructions not to race with or obstruct other omnibuses. Martin B. directed the jury, in effect, that if the driver acted in the way of his employment and in the supposed interest of his employers as against a rival in their business, the employers were answerable for his conduct, but they were not answerable if he acted only for some purpose of his own: and this was approved by the Court (*n*) above. The driver "was employed not only to drive the omnibus, but also to get as much money as he could for his master, and to do it in rivalry with other omnibuses on the road. The act of driving as he did is not inconsistent with his employment, when explained by his desire to get before the other omnibus." As to the company's instructions, "the law is not so futile as to allow a master, by giving secret instructions to his servant, to discharge himself from liability" (*o*).

(*l*) See per Blackburn J., 1 H. & C. 541.

(*m*) 1 H. & C. 526, 32 L. J. Ex. 34 (1862) This and *Seymour* v. *Greenwood* (above) overrule anything to the contrary in *M'Manus* v. *Crickett*, 1 East, 106.

(*n*) Williams, Crompton, Willes, Byles, Blackburn JJ., diss. Wightman, J.

(*o*) Willes J., 1 H. & C. at p. 539.

Fraud of Agent or Servant. That an employer is liable for frauds of his servant committed without authority, but in the course of the service and for the employer's purposes, was established with more difficulty, for it seemed harsh to impute deceit to a man personally innocent of it, or (as in the decisive cases) to a corporation, which, not being a natural person, is incapable of personal wrong doing (*p*). But when it was fully realized that in all these cases the master's liability is imposed by the policy of the law without regard to personal default on his part, so that his express command or privity need not be shown, it was a necessary consequence that fraud should be on the same footing as any other wrong (*q*). So the matter is handled in our leading authority, the judgment of the Exchequer Chamber delivered by Willes J., in *Barwick* v. *English Joint Stock Bank*

"With respect to the question, whether a principal is answerable for the act of his agent in the course of his

---

(*p*) This particular difficulty is fallacious. It is in truth neither more nor less easy to think of a corporation as deceiving (or being deceived) than as having a consenting mind. In no case can a corporation be invested with either rights or duties except through natural persons who are its agents Cp *British Mutual Banking Co* v *Charnwood Forest R Co* (1887), 18 Q. B. Div 714, 56 L J Q B 449

(*q*) It makes no difference if the fraud includes a forgery *Shaw* v *Port Philip Gold Mining Co* (1884), 13 Q B D 103.

Fraud of agent or servant. Supporting the statement in the text *vide*, Moir *v*. Hopkins, 16 Ill. 315, Frankfort Bank *v* Johnson, 24 Me. 491, Calvin *v* Holbrook, 2 N. Y. 126, McKay *v*. Irwine, 11 Biss. 168, McDongald *v*. Bellamy, 18 Ga 411, Adams *v* Cole, 1 Daly, 147; Leavitt *v*. Sizer, 35 Neb. 80, 52 N W Rep 832; Locke *v* Stearns, 1 Metc 560, Johnson *v* Barber, 10 Ill. 425, Armstrong *v*. Cooley, Id. 509, Sanford *v*. Handy, 23 Wend. 259; Lynch *v* Mercantile Trust Co , 18 Fed Rep 486, Reynolds *v* Witte, 13 S. C 5, 36 Am Rep. 678, Mundorff *v* Wickersham, 63 Pa. St. 87, Upton *v* Tribilcock, 91 U. S 45, Taggs *v*. Tenn. Nat. Bank, 9 Heisk, 479, Crans *v* Hunter, 28 N Y 389, Brokaw *v*. N. J. R Co., 32 N J. L 328, Rhoda *v* Annis, 75 Me. 17, 46 Am Rep. 354; Concord Bank *v*. Gregg, 14 N H 331, Ellenberger *v*. Prot Mut. F. Ins Co., 89 Pa. St 464, Wilson *v*. Peverly, 2 N H. 584; Galena R. Co. *v*. Rae, 18 Ill 488, 68 Am. Dec 574, Vance *v*. Erie R. Co., 32 N. J. L. 334.

master's business, and for his master's benefit, no sensible distinction can be drawn between the case of fraud and the case of any other wrong" (r).

This has been more than once fully approved in the Privy Council (s), and may now be taken, notwithstanding certain appearances of conflict (t), to have the approval of the House of Lords also (u). What has been said to the contrary was either extra-judicial, as going beyond the *ratio decidendi* of the House, or is to be accepted as limited to the particular case where a member of an incorporated company, not having ceased to be a member, seeks to charge the company with the fraud of its directors or other agents in inducing him to join it (x).

But conversely a false and fraudulent statement of a servant made for ends of his own, though in answer to a question of a kind he was authorized to answer on his master's behalf, will not render the master liable in an action for deceit (y).

The leading case of *Mersey Docks Trustees* v. *Gibbs* (z) may also be referred to in this connexion, as illustrating the general principles according to which liabilities are imposed on corporations and public bodies.

(r) (1867) L R 2 Ex at p 265

(s) *Mackay* v *Commercial Bank of New Brunswick* (1874), L R 5 P C 412, 43 L J P C 31, *Swire* v *Francis* (1877), 3 App Ca. 106, 47 L J P C 18

(t) *Addie* v *Western Bank of Scotland* (1867), L R 1 Sc & D 145, dicta at pp 158, 166, 167

(u) *Houldsworth* v *City of Glasgow Bank* (1880), 5 App Ca 317

(x) Ib, Lord Selborne at p 326, Lord Hatherley at p 331, Lord Blackburn's language at p. 339 is more cautious, perhaps for the very reason that he was a party to the decision of *Barwick* v *English Joint Stock Bank*. Shortly, the shareholder is in this dilemma while he is a member of the company, he is damnified by the alleged deceit, if at all, solely in that he is liable as a shareholder to contribute to the company's debts this liability being of the essence of a shareholder's position, claiming compensation from the company for it involves him in a new liability to contribute to that compensation itself, which is an absurd circuity. But if his liability as a shareholder has ceased, he is no longer damnified Therefore restitution only (by rescission of his contract), not compensation, is the shareholder's remedy as against the company though the fraudulent agent remains personally liable

(y) *British Mutual Banking Co* v *Charnwood Forest R Co* (1887), 18 Q B Div 714, 56 L J Q B 449

(z) L R 1 H L 93 (1864-6)

Liability of firm for fraud of a partner There is abundant authority in partnership law to show that a firm is answerable for fraudulent misappropriation of funds, and the like, committed by one of the partners in the course of the firm's business and within the scope of his usual authority, though no benefit be derived therefrom by the other partners. But, agreeably to the principles above stated, the firm is not liable if the transaction undertaken by the defaulting partner is outside the course of partnership business. Where, for example, one of a firm of solicitors receives money to be placed in a specified investment, the firm must answer for his application of it, but not, as a rule, if he receives it with general instructions to invest it for the client at his own discretion (*a*). Again, the firm is not liable if the facts show that exclusive credit was given to the actual wrongdoer (*b*). In all these cases

(*a*) Partnership Act, 1890, ss 10—12 Cp *Blair v Bromley*, 2 Ph 354, and *Cleather v Twisden* (1883), 24 Ch D 731, with *Harman v Johnson*, 2 E & B 61, 22 L J Q B 297

(*b*) *Ex parte Eyre*, 1 Ph 227 See more illustrations in my "Digest of the Law of Partnership," 5th ed pp 13—16

Liability of firm for fraud of a partner The rule as to liability of a firm for the torts of a partner, as stated and limited in the text, holds true in America The firm's liability has been said to be based upon the principle, that as every member is responsible for the tortious acts committed by an agent of the firm in matters connected with the business so when a partner acts in the same capacity he, in like manner, binds the firm Hall *v* Younts, 87 N C 285 See Lockwood *v* Bartlett, 130 N Y 310, 7 N Y S Rep 481, 29 N E Rep. 257, Rocky Mountain Nat Bank *v* McCaskill, 15 Col 408, 26 Pac Rep 821, Warner *v* Winters 38 Ill. App. 149, Stanhope *v.* Swafford, 80 Ia 45, 45 N W Rep 403, Baldy *v.* Brackenridge, 39 La An 660, Fletcher *v* Ingram, 46 Wis 191, Helm *v.* McCaugham, 32 Miss 17, 56 Am. Dec. 589, Chapman *v* Bostwick, 18 Wend. 174, 31 Am Dec. 376, Tucker *v* Cole, 54 Wis. 540, Morehead *v* Gilmore, 77 Pa. St 118, 18 Am Rep 435, Myers *v* Gilbert, 18 Ala 467, Witcher *v* Brewer, 49 Ala 119, Doremus *v* McCormick, 7 Gill 49; Pierce *v.* Wood, 23 N H 519, Church *v* Sparrow, 5 Wend. 223, Chester *v* Dickinson, 52 Barb 349, Wolf *v* Mills, 56 Ill. 360 But a firm is not liable for the act of a partner outside the general course of the business Brent *v* Davis, 9 Md 217 Selden *v* Bank of Commerce, 3 Minn 166; Newman *v* Richardson, 4 Woods, 81

the wrong is evidently wilful. In all or most of them, however, it is at the same time a breach of contract or trust. And it seems to be on this ground that the firm is held liable even when the defaulting partner, though professing to act on behalf of the firm, misapplies funds or securities merely for his own separate gain. The reasons given are not always free from admixture of the Protean doctrine of "making representations good," which is now, I venture to think, exploded (c).

Injuries to servants by fault of fellow-servants 3. There remains to be considered the modification of a master's liability for the wrongful act, neglect, or default of his servant when the person injured is himself in and about the same master's service. It is a topic far from clear in principle; the Employers' Liability Act, 1880, has obscurely indicated a sort of counter principle, and introduced a number of minute and empirical exceptions, or rather limitations of the exceptional rule in question.

Common law rule of master's immunity. That rule, as it stood before the Act of 1880, is that a master is not liable to his servant for injury received from any ordinary risk of or incident to the service, including acts or defaults of any other person employed in the same service. Our law can show no more curious instance of a rapid modern development. The first evidence of any such rule is in *Priestley* v. *Fowler* (d), decided in 1837, which proceeds on the theory (if on any definite theory) that the master "cannot be bound to take more care of the servant than he may reasonably be expected to do of himself;" that a servant has better opportunities than his master of watch-

(c) I have discussed it in Appendix E to "Principles of Contract," 5th ed p 707 See now *Maddison* v *Alderson* (1883), 8 App Ca at p 473, 51 L J Q B 737

(d) 3 M & W 1 All the case actually decided was that a master does not warrant to his servant the sufficiency and safety of a carriage in which he sends him out

ing and controlling the conduct of his fellow-servants; and that a contrary doctrine would lead to intolerable inconvenience, and encourage servants to be negligent. According to this there would be a sort of presumption that the servant suffered to some extent by want of diligence on his own part. But it is needless to pursue this reasoning, for the like result was a few years afterwards arrived at by *Chief Justice Shaw* of *Massachusetts* by another way, and in a judgment which is the fountain-head of all the later decisions (c)

Reason given in the later cases. The accepted doctrine is to this effect. Strangers can hold the master liable for the negligence of a servant about his business. But in the case where the person injured is himself a servant in the same business he is not in the same position as a stranger. He has of his free will entered into the business and made it his own. He cannot say to the master,

---

(c) *Farwell v. Boston and Worcester Railroad Corporation*, 4 Met. 49.

Injuries to servants by fault of fellow-servants. In those States of the Union where the common law is unaffected by special legislation on this subject, the rule and reasons stated in the text are generally accepted. Thus, in the case of Cooper v. Mullins (30 Ga. 151) the court said. "The reason of the exception is to make each employé a help to the carefulness of the rest, and where that object cannot be accomplished the exception ought to cease, * * *."

In Chicago & Alton R. Co. v. Murphy (53 Ill. 339) it is said by the court "When the ordinary duties and occupations of the servants of a common master are such that one is necessarily exposed to hazard by the carelessness of another, they must be supposed to have voluntarily taken the risks of such possible carelessness when they entered the service, and must be regarded as fellow servants, within the meaning of this rule." S. P., Murray v. South Carolina R. Co., 1 McMull. 385, Lalor v. Chicago, etc., R. Co. 52 Ill. 401, Haskins v. N. N. & H. R. R. Co., 65 Barb. 129, affirmed, 56 N. Y. 608.

Sustaining the exception to the master's liability are numerous cases, a few are Renfro v. Chicago, etc., R. Co., 86 Mo. 302; Benn v. Null, 65 Ia. 407; Luce v. Chicago, etc., R. Co., 67 Ia. 75, Beaulieu v. Portland Co., 48 Me. 291; McDermott v. Pacific R. Co., 30 Mo. 115; Henderson v. New

You shall so conduct your business as not to injure me by want of due care and caution therein. For he has agreed with the master to serve in that business, and his claims on the master depend on the contract of service. Why should it be an implied term of that contract, not being an express one, that the master shall indemnify him against the negligence of a fellow-servant, or any other current risk? It is rather to be implied that he contracted with the risk before his eyes, and that the dangers of the service, taken all round, were considered in fixing the rate of payment. This is, I believe, a fair summary of the reasoning which has prevailed in the authorities. With its soundness we are not here concerned. It was not only adopted by the House of Lords for England, but forced by them upon the reluctant Courts of Scotland to make the jurisprudence of the two countries uniform (*f*). No such doctrine appears to exist in the law of any other country in Europe. The following is a clear judicial statement of it in its settled form: "A servant, when he engages to serve a master, undertakes, as between himself and his master, to run all the ordinary risks of the service, including the risk of

---

(*f*) See *Wilson v. Merry* (1868), L. R. 1 Sc. & D. 326.

Jersey, etc., R Co., 7 Robt. 611, Ponton v. Wilmington, etc., R. Co., 6 Jones L. 245, Illinois, etc., R Co. v. Cox, 21 Ill. 20, Hough v. Railroad Co., 100 U S. 213, Sullivan v. Mississippi R Co., 11 Ia 121, Caldwell v Brown, 53 Pa St. 453, McDonald v Hazeltine, 53 Cal. 35, Walker v Bolling, 22 Ala 294, Homer v Illinois, etc., R Co., 15 Ill 550, Carle v. Bangor, etc., R Co., 43 Me 269, Mosley v. Chamberlain, 18 Wis. 700, Filch v Allen, 98 Mass 572, Benzing v Steinway, 101 N Y. 547, 5 N. E Rep. 449, Hefferen v. Northern P R Co., 45 Minn 471, 48 N W Rep. 1, Webber v Piper 109 N Y. 496, 17 N. E Rep 216, Pantzar v Tilly Foster Min. Co., 99 N Y 368, 2 N E Rep. 24, Rogers v Manufacturing Co., 144 Mass. 198, 11 N E Rep 77, Stringham v Hilton, 111 N Y 188, 18 N. E. Rep 870, Buzzell v Manufacturing Co., 48 Me. 113, Tuttle v Railway, 122 U S 189, 7 Sup Ct Rep 1166, Hayden v. Manufacturing Co., 29 Conn. 548, Yeaton v Railroad Corp., 135 Mass. 418; Memphis R Co v. Thomas, 51 Mass. 637, Hasty v Sears, 157 Mass 123, 31 N. E. Rep 759, Fitzgerald v. Honkomp, 44 Ill App 365.

negligence upon the part of a fellow-servant when he is acting in the discharge of his duty as servant of him who is the common master of both" (g).

The servants need not be about the same kind of work. The phrase "common employment" is frequent in this class of cases. But it is misleading in that it suggests a limitation of the rule to circumstances where the injured servant had in fact some opportunity of observing and guarding against the conduct of the negligent one; a limitation rejected by the Massachusetts Court in Farwell's case, where an engine-driver was injured by the negligence of a switchman (pointsman as we say on English railways) in the same company's service, and afterwards constantly rejected by the English Courts.

"When the object to be accomplished is one and the same, when the employers are the same, and the several persons employed derive their authority and their compensation from the same source, it would be extremely difficult to distinguish what constitutes one department and what a distinct department of duty. It would vary with the circumstances of every case. If it were made to depend upon the nearness or distance of the persons from each other, the question would immediately arise, how near or how distant must they be to be in the same or different departments. In a blacksmith's shop, persons working in the same building, at different fires, may be quite independent of each other, though only a few feet distant. In a ropewalk several may be at work on the same piece of cordage, at the same time, at many hundred feet distant from each other, and beyond the reach of sight or voice, and yet acting together.

"Besides, it appears to us that the argument rests upon

(g) Erle C J in *Tunney* v *Midland R Co* (1866), L R 1 C P at p 296, Archibald J, used very similar language in *Lovell* v *Howell* (1876), 1 C P. D at p. 167, 45 L J C P 387.

an assumed principle of responsibility which does not exist. The master, in the case supposed, is not exempt from liability because the servant has better means of providing for his safety when he is employed in immediate connexion with those from whose negligence he might suffer, but because the *implied contract* of the master does not extend to indemnify the servant against the negligence of any one but himself; and he is not liable in tort, as for the negligence of his servant, because the person suffering does not stand towards him in the relation of a stranger, but is one whose rights are regulated by contract, express or implied" (*h*)

Provided there is a general common object. So it has been said that " we must not over-refine, but look at the common object, and not at the common immediate object" (*i*) All persons engaged under the same em

(*h*) Shaw C J , *Farwell* v. *Boston, &c Corporation*, 4 Met 49 M Sainctelette of Brussels, and M Sauzet of Lyons, whom he quotes (*op cit* p 110), differ from the current view among French-speaking lawyers, and agree with Shaw C J and our Courts, in referring the whole matter to the contract between the master and servant, but they arrive at the widely different result of holding the master bound, as an implied term of the contract, to insure the servant against all accidents in the course of the service, and not due to the servant's own fault or *vis major*

(*i*) Pollock C B , *Morgan* v. *Vale of Neath R Co* (1865), Ex Ch L R. 1 Q B 149, 155, 35 L. J Q B 23

The servants need not be about the same kind of work. provided there is a general common object. Subject to the limitation specified under the next heading the doctrine announced in the text is uniformly accepted in America where many of the courts have broadly stated similar rules It is practicable only to refer to a few of the late cases, an examination of which will illustrate the meaning of the foregoing propositions of law as applied to special statements of facts.

In the following cases the persons injured and the one injuring were held to be fellow-servants and the master not liable. Haley *v* Keim, 151 Pa. St 117, 25 At Rep. 98, 31 W N. C 18, Texas & P. R. Co. *v.* Harrington, 62 Tex. 597, 21 Am & Eng. R Cas. 571; Van Den Heuvel *v.* National Furnace Co., 84 Wis 636; 54 N. W. Rep. 1016; Indianapolis, etc., R.Cas Co. *v* Morgenstein, 106 Ill 216; 12 Am & Eng. R R Cas. 228, Holden *v*. Fitchburg R Co , 129 Mass. 268, 2 Am. & Eng. R. Cas. 94, Malone *v*. Hathaway, 64 N Y. 5; McBride *v*. Indianapolis Frog & Switch

ployer for the purposes of the same business, however different in detail those purposes may be, are follow-

Co. (Ind App.), 32 N E. Rep. 579, Roux v Blodgett & Davis Lbr. Co, 94 Mich. 607; 51 N W Rep. 492, Baltimore & O R Co v Baugh, 149 U. S. 368, 13 S Ct Rep. 914; Hughes v. Fagin, 46 Mo App. 87, Coal Creek M. Co. v. Davis, 90 Tenn. 711; 18 S. W Rep. 387, Snyder v. Viola Mining & S. Co., 2 Idaho, 771, 26 Pac. Rep. 127, Bergstron v Staples, 82 Mich 651, 46 N W Rep 1035, Ocean Steamship Co. v. Cheyney, 86 Ga 278, 12 S. E Rep 851; Fraser v Red River Lbr. Co, 45 Minn 235; 47 N. W. Rep. 785, Butler v Townsend, 126 N. Y 105, 26 N. E Rep 1017; Gumsley v. Hankins, 46 Fed. Rep. 400; Kehoe v. Allen, 92 Mich 464; 52 N. W Rep 740, Thyng v Fitchburg R Co, 156 Mass 13, 30 N. E Rep. 169; Baltimore & O R. Co v Andrews, 50 Fed Rep. 728; 1 C C. A. Rep 636, Cincinnati, etc., R. Co. v Mealer, 50 Fed Rep. 725; 1 C. C. A. Rep. 633, Dwyer v Hickler, 16 N. Y S. Rep. 814, McDonald v. New York, etc., R. Co, 63 Hun, 587, 18 N. Y S. Rep 609, Spencer v. Ohio & M. R Co., 130 Ind 181, 29 N E. Rep. 915; International & G N. R Co. v. Ryan, 82 Tex. 565; 18 S. W Rep. 219, Corona v Galveston, etc, R Co. (Tex), 17 S. W Rep 384, Parrish v Pensacola & A R Co, 28 Fla. 251, 9 So. Rep 696, Lasky v Canadian P. R Co., 83 Me. 461, 22 At Rep 367, Miller v. Southern P R Co, 20 Oreg 285, 26 Pac Rep 70, Bier v Jeffersonville M & I. R Co., 138 Ind 78, 31 N E Rep 471, Warmington v Atchison, etc., R. Co, 46 Mo App 159, Kerlin v Chicago, etc, R. Co, 50 Fed Rep. 185; Mele v. Delaware & H C. Co, 14 N Y S Rep. 630, Knathla v Oregon, etc, R Co, 21 Oreg 136, 27 Pac. Rep 91, Ohio & M R. Co v Robb, 36 Ill App 627, McKay v Northern P R Co, 42 Fed. Rep 288, Abend v Terre Haute & I R. Co., 11 Ill. 202; Kilroy v Delaware & H C Co., 121 N. Y. 22, 24 N E. Rep. 192, Adams v Iron Cliffs Co, 78 Mich. 271, 44 N W Rep 270, Hoar v Merritt, 62 Mich. 386; 29 N W Rep. 15, Julbec S S Co v Merchant, 133 U S. 375, 10 S Ct Rep 397, Bergquist v City of Minneapolis, 42 Minn. 471, 44 N W Rep. 530, Niantic C & M. Co v. Leonhard, 25 Ill. App 95, affirmed 126 Ill 216, 19 N E Rep 294; St Louis, A & T R. Co v Welch, 72 Tex. 298, 10 S W Rep 529, Fagundes v Central P. R Co., 79 Cal 97, 21 Pac Rep. 437, Carr v. North River Const Co, 48 Hun, 266, Stringham v Stewart, 11 N Y 188, 18 N E. Rep 870, Blazinski v Perkins, 77 Wis 9, 15 N W. Rep 547, McCoy v Empire Warehouse Co, 10 N. Y. S Rep 99, Hankins v New York, etc., R Co, 55 Hun, 51, 8 N Y S Rep. 272, McMasters v. Illinois Central R Co, 65 Miss. 264, 4 So. Rep 59, Byrnes v. New York, etc, R. Co, 113 N. Y 251, 21 N E. Rep 50; Evans v. Lippincott, 47 N J. L 192, 34 Am. Rep. 148

In the following cases it was held, that the master was by the rule excepted from liability. Jacques v Great Falls Mfg. Co, (N H) 22 At Rep. 552, Evans v Carbon Hill Coal Co, 47 Fed Rep 437; Marshall v. Herman, 47 Minn. 537, 50 N W. Rep 611, Sadowski v Michigan Car

servants in a common employment within the meaning of this rule: for example, a carpenter doing work on the roof of an engine-shed and porters moving an engine on a turntable (j). "Where there is one common general object, in attaining which a servant is exposed to risk, he is not entitled to sue the master if he is injured by the negligence of another servant whilst engaged in furthering the same object" (k).

Relative rank of the servants immaterial. It makes no difference if the servant by whose negligence another is

---

(j) See last note.   (k) Thesiger L. J., *Charles v. Taylor* (1878), 3 C. P. Div. 492, 498.

Co., 84 Mich 100, 17 N W. Rep. 498, Daniel v Chesapeake & O R Co., 36 W Va 397, 15 S E Rep 162, Noonan v New York etc. R. Co., 131 N York. 594, 62 Hun 618; 16 N Y S. Rep. 678, 30 N. E. Rep. 67; Gross v Pennsylvania P & B R. Co., 62 Hun 619, 16 N. Y. S Rep. 616, Miller v. Missouri P. R. Co., 109 Mo 350, 19 S W Rep. 58, Columbus & T R. Co v. O'Brien, 4 Ohio Cir. Ct. Rep. 515, North Chicago R. M Co. v. Johnson, 114 Ill. 57, 29 N E. Rep. 186, Dixon v. Chicago & A R Co, 109 Mo. 413, 19 S W Rep. 413, Tudor Iron Works v. Weber, 31 Ill App 306; affirmed 129 Ill. 535, 21 N E Rep 1078, Ohio & M. R Co v Pearcy, 128 Ind 197, 27 N E Rep 479, Pool v. Southern P. R Co, 7 Utah 303, 26 Pac Rep 654, Webb v Denver & R G R. Co, 7 Utah, 363, 26 Pac Rep 981, St Louis & S F R Co v Weaver, 35 Kan 412, 11 Pac. Rep 408, Hobson v. New Mexico & A R Co, (Ariz) 11 Pac Rep 545, Louisville & N R Co v Sheets, (Ky) 13 S. W Rep 248, Morton v Detroit etc R Co, 81 Mich 423, 46 N. W. Rep 111, Daniels v Union P R Co, 6 Utah 357, 23 Pac. Rep 762; Cincinnati, H & D R Co v McMullen, 117 Ind 439, 20 N E Rep 287, Ragsdale v Northern P R Co., 42 Fed Rep 383; Sanford v Standard Oil Co., 118 N Y. 571, 24 N E Rep 313, Evans v. American Iron & Tube Co., 42 Fed Rep. 519, Harvard v Delaware & H C Co, 40 Fed Rep. 195; Sullivan v Missouri P R Co, 97 Mo 113, 10 S. W. Rep 852, Northern P R Co v O'Brien, 1 Wash St. 599, 21 Pac Rep 32, Pike v Chicago & A R Co, 41 Fed Rep 95, Central Trust Co v Wabash, St L & P R Co, 34 Fed. Rep 616, Hall v Galveston, etc R Co, 39 Fed. Rep 18, Sullivan v Tioga R. Co., 112 N Y 643, 20 N E Rep 569, Kelley v Erie Tel. & T. Co., 34 Minn 321, James v. Emmet Minning Co., 55 Mich 335.

Relative rank of the servants immaterial. This general proposition is sustained by numerous authorities, *vide* Brick v Rochester, etc., R Co., 98 N Y 511, 21 Am & Eng R Cas 605, Zeigler v. Day, 123 Mass.

injured is a foreman, manager, or other superior in the same employment, whose orders the other was by the terms of his service bound to obey. The foreman or man-

152; Richmond & D. R Co. v Jones, 92 Ala. 218, 9 So. Rep. 276; McGinty v Athol Reservoir Co., 155 Mass 183, 29 N. E. Rep 510, O'Brien v. American Dredging Co., 53 N J L 291, 21 At Rep. 324, Dube v City of Lewiston, 83 Me. 211, 22 At. Rep. 112, Jenkins v Mahopac Iron Ore Co., 10 N Y S Rep 451, Sayward v Carlson, 1 Wash St 29, 23 Pac Rep 830, Kenny v Cunard S S Co., 55 N Y. Superior Ct 558, Kinney v Corbin, 132 Pa St. 311, 19 At Rep 141, Lagrone v Mobile & O R Co., 67 Miss 592, 7 So. Rep 132, Duffy v Oliver, 131 Pa St 203, 18 At Rep 872, Yates v McCulloch Iron Co, 69 Md. 370, 16 At Rep 280; Rogers L & M Works v Hand, 50 N J L. 464, 14 At Rep 766, Galveston etc R Co v. Farmer, 73 Tex 637, 11 S W. Rep. 156, Louisville & N R Co. v Martin, 87 Tenn. 398, 10 S. W Rep 772, McBride v. Union P R Co, 3 Wyo 247, 21 Pac Rep. 687; Wilson v Dunreath etc Co, 77 Ia 429, 42 N W Rep. 360, Conley v Portland, 78 Me. 217, Loughlin v. State, 105 N. Y 159, Willis v Oregon R & N Co. 11 Oreg. 257, Reese v. Biddle, 112 Pa St 72, Waddell, v Simonson, 112 Pa St. 567, Kirk v Atlanta & C A R Co, 94 N C 625, 55 Am. Rep 621; Chicago & L. I. R v Geary, 110 Ill 383, Lincoln Coal M Co v McNally, 15 Ill App. 181, Matthews v Case, 61 Wis 49, 50 Am Rep 151; Peschel v. Chicago etc R Co., 62 Wis 338, Fraker v. St. Paul etc R. Co, 32 Minn, 54, Doughty v Penobscot Log Driving Co, 76 Md. 143, Scott v. Sweeny, 34 Hun, 292, Heine v. Chicago & N W. R Co., 58 Wis. 525, Olson v Clyde, 32 Hun, 425; Yager v Atlantic etc R Co, 44 Hughes, 192; Flynn v. Salem, 134 Mass. 351; Keystone Bridge Co. v Newberry, 96 Pa St 246, 42 Am. Rep. 543, Thompson v Chicago etc. R Co., 18 Fed Rep 239; Peterson v. Whitebreast C. & M Co, 50 Ia 673, Lehigh Valley Co v Jones, 86 Pa St. 432, Hofnagle v New York, C & H. R R Co., 55 N Y. 608, Shank v Northern etc. R Co, 25 Md. 462, O'Connell v Baltimore etc R Co., 20 Md 212, McLean v. Blue Point Min. G. Co, 51 Cal. 255, Johnson v Netherland, A. S. N. Co, 132 N Y 576, 30 N. E Rep. 505, affirming 10 N Y. S. Rep. 927, Hart v New York F. D C Co., 48 N Y Superior Ct 460, McDonald v Eagle & Phoenix Mfg. Co., 67 Ga 761; 68 Ga. 839, Hoth v Peters, 55 Wis. 405, Lawler v Androscoggin R. Co, 62 Me 463

Vice-Principal. The rule just stated is declared by the courts of several of the States to be subject to a limitation, in what is called the doctrine of vice-principal. "At common law, whatever the master delegates to any officer, servant, agent, or employe, high or low, the performance of any of the duties * * * which really devolves upon the master himself, then such officer, servant, agent or employe stands in the place of the master and becomes a substitute for the master, a vice-principal, and the master is liable for his acts or his negligence to the same extent as

ior is only a servant having greater authority; foremen and workmen, of whatever rank, and however authority and duty may be distributed among them, are " all links in

---

though the master himself had performed the acts or was guilty of negligence."

Atchison etc R Co v Moore, 29 Kan 644, 11 Am. & Eng. R. Cas. 91; S. P., Zintek v. Stimson Mill Co., (Wash St.) 32 Pac. Rep 997, Palmer v Mich Cent. R Co, 93 Mich. 363; 53 N W Rep 397; Mullan v Phila & S M S. S. Co., 78 Pa. St 25; Stockmeyer v. Reed, 55 Fed Rep 263, Bloyd v. St. Louis & S F Ry. Co, (Ark.) 22 S W Rep 1089. Upon the soundness of the doctrine of vice-principal the courts of the United States are nearly equally divided Supporting the doctrine see the cases last above cited and Kansas City, M & B. R Co. v Burton, (Ala) 13 So Rep 88, Missouri P. Ry. Co v Basse, (Tex. Civ. App) 22 S W. Rep 187, Dayharsh v Hannibal & St J. R. Co., 103 Mo. 570; 15 S W Rep. 554, Nall v Louisville, etc. R Co, 129 Ind. 260; 28 N E Rep 123, Cullen v. Norton, 126 N Y 1, 26 N. E. Rep. 905, reversing 9 N.Y. S Rep 174, Colorado M. R Co v. O'Brien, 16 Colo 219; 27 Pac. Rep. 701, Fink v Des Moines Ice Co., 84 Ia 321, 51 N. W. Rep. 155, Kelley v Ryus, 48 Kan 120, 29 Pac. Rep 144, Schroeder v. Chicago & A R Co, 108 Mo. 322, 18 S. W. Rep. 1094, Anderson v. Ogden, 8 Utah, 128; 30 Pac. Rep. 305, McElligott v. Randolph, 61 Conn 157, 22 At Rep. 1094, Woods v Lindvall, 48 Fed Rep. 62; 4 U. S App. 49, 1 C. C. A Rep 37, affirming 47 Fed Rep. 195, Wooden v Western etc. R Co, 18 N Y. S Rep 768; Nix v. Texas & P. R. Co., 82 Tex. 423; 18 S W. Rep 571, Fisher v Oregon etc R Co., 22 Oreg 533, 30 Pac. Rep 425, Sweeney v Gulf etc. R Co., 84 Tex. 433; 19 S. W. Rep 555; Newport News & M V. R. Co. v. Old Colony R Co., 153 Mass. 356, 26 N. E Rep 868; Lyttle v Chicago & W. M. R. Co., 84 Mich. 289, 47 N. W. Rep. 571, Lindvall v. Woods, 41 Fed. Rep. 855, Consolidated Coal Co v. Wombacher, 31 Ill. App. 288, 134 Ill 57; 24 N. E Rep. 627; Cox v. Syenite Granite Co., 39 Mo App 424, Chicago etc. R. Co. v. Ross, 112 U. S. 377; 17 Am. & Eng. R. Cas. 501, Malcolm v Fuller, 152 Mass. 160; 25 N. E. Rep 83, Chicago v Anderson Pressed Brick Co, 34 Ill. App. 312, Missouri P. R Co. v. Williams, 75 Tex. 4; 12 S. W. Rep. 835; Coleman v. Wilmington, C & A R Co., 25 S. C 446, Taylor v Evansville & T H. R. Co., 121 Ind. 124, 22 N E Rep 876, Borgman v. Omaha & St L R. Co. 41 Fed. Rep. 667, Chicago D & D. Co. v McMahon, 30 Ill. App. 358; Lund v Hersey L'b'r Co, 41 Fed Rep. 202; Boatwright v. Northeastern R. Co., 25 S. C 128, Louisville etc. R. Co. v. Graham, 124 Ind 89; 24 N. E Rep 668, Baldwin v St Louis etc. R. Co., 75 Ia. 547; 39 N W. Rep. 507; Sioux City & P. R Co. v. Smith, 22 Neb, 775; 36 N W. Rep. 285, Carpenter v Mexican Nat R. Co, 39 Fed Rep. 315; Brown v Sennett, 68 Cal. 225, Missouri P. R. Co v Peregoy, 36 Kan 424, Hussey v. Coger, 39 Hun,

the same chain" (*l*). So the captain employed by a ship-owner is a fellow-servant of the crew, and a sailor injured by the captain's negligence has no cause of action against

(*l*) *Feltham v. England* (1866), L. R. 2 Q. B. 33, 36 L. J. Q. B. 14, *Wilson v. Merry* (1868), L. R. 1 Sc. & D. 326 see per Lord Cairns at p. 331, and per Lord Colonsay at p. 345. The French word *collaborateur*, which does not mean "fellow workman" at all, was at one time absurdly introduced into these cases. It is believed by Lord Brougham, and occurs as late as *Wilson v. Merry*.

639, St. Louis etc. R. Co. v. Harper, 41 Ark. 524, Chicago etc. R. Co. v. Lundstrom, 16 Neb. 254, 19 Am. Rep. 719, Buick v. Rochester etc. R. Co. 98 N. Y. 211, Miller v. Union P. R. Co. 17 Fed. Rep. 67, Gravelle v. Minneapolis & St. L. R. Co., 3 McCrary, 352, Ryan v. Bagaley, 50 Mich. 179, 45 Am. Rep. 35, Dowling v. Allen, 74 Mo. 13, 41 Am. Rep. 298, Mitchell v. Robinson, 80 Ind. 281, 41 Am. Rep. 812, Gormly v. Vulcan Iron Works, 61 Mo. 492, Berea Stone Co. v. Kraft, 31 Ohio St. 287.

Different departments. Another proposed limitation of the general rule is that having its origin in the fact that in the operation of the large industrial enterprises of this country it has been found necessary to divide the labor into separate departments, and where this is the case the servants of one department are not the fellow-servants of those of another department. This doctrine is accepted by only a few of the courts. See Colorado M. R. Co. v. Naylon, 17 Colo. 501; 30 Pac. Rep. 249; Cooper v. Mullins, 30 Ga. 150, Chicago etc. R. Co. v. Moranda, 108 Ill. 576, 17 Am. & Eng. R. Cas. 564, Nashville etc. R. Co. v. Jones, 9 Heisk. 37, Ryan v. Chicago & N. W. R. Co., 60 Ill. 171, Nashville etc. R. Co. v. Carroll, 6 Heisk. 347.

And in several cases the doctrine is denied. See Farwell v. Boston & W. R. Co., 4 Metc. 49, Johnson v. City of Boston, 118 Mass. 114, Texas & P. R. Co. v. Harrington, 62 Tex. 597, 21 Am. & Eng. R. Cas. 571; Kirk v. Atlanta etc. R. Co., 94 N. C. 625, 25 Am. & Eng. R. Cas. 507, New York etc. R. Co. v. Bell, 112 Pa. St. 400, 28 Am. & Eng. R. R. Cas. 348.

Means and resources. The master must make a reasonable effort to furnish suitable machinery and appliances, and keep the same in safe and serviceable condition. Hough v. Texas & P. R. Co., 100 U. S. 213, Northern Pac. R. Co. v. Herbert, 116 U. S. 642, 24 Am. & Eng. R. Cas. 407; Cunningham v. Union Pac. R. Co., 4 Utah 206, 7 Pac. Rep. 795, Murphy v. Boston & A. R. Co., 88 N. Y. 146; 8 Am. & Eng. R. Cas. 610; Solomon R. Co. v. Jones, 30 Kan. 601, 15 Am. & Eng. R. Cas. 201; Moynihan v. Hills Co., 146 Mass. 586, Sioux City, etc. R. Co. v. Finlayson, 26 Neb. 272, 18 Am. & Eng. R. Cas. 77, Smith v. Oxford Iron Co., 42 N. J. L. 467; 36 Am. Rep. 535, Houston, etc. R. Co. v. Marcelles, 59 Tex. 334, 12 Am. & Eng. R. Cas. 231; Cowles v. Richmond, etc. R. Co., 84 N. C. 309, 2 Am. & Eng. R. Cas. 90, 37 Am. Rep. 620, Penn Co. v. Lynch, 90 Ill. 333, Mulvey v. Rhode Island Locomotive Works, 14 R. I.

the owner (*m*). The master is bound, as between himself and his servants, to exercise due care in selecting proper and competent persons for the work (whether as fellow-workmen in the ordinary sense, or as superintendents or foremen), and to furnish suitable means and resources to accomplish the work (*n*), and he is not answerable further (*o*).

(*m*) *Hedley* v. *Pinkney and Sons' S. S. Co.*, 9⁰ 1 Q. B. 58, 61 L. J. Q. B. 179, C. A.

(*n*) According to some decisions, which seem on principle doubtful, he is bound only not to furnish means or resources which are to his own knowledge defective. *Gallagher* v. *Piper* (1864), 16 C. B. N. S. 669, 33 L. J. C. P. 329. And quite lately it has been decided in the Court of Appeal that where a servant seeks to hold his master liable for injuries caused by the dangerous condition of a building where he is employed, he must allege distinctly both that the master knew of the danger and that he, the servant, was ignorant of it. *Griffiths* v. *London and St. Katharine Docks Co.* (1884), 13 Q. B. Div. 259. Cp. *Thomas* v. *Quartermaine* (1887), 18 Q. B. Div. 685, 56 L. J. Q. B. 340.

(*o*) Lord Cairns, as above; to same effect Lord Wensleydale, *Weems* v.

[...] Romont Oolitic Stone Co. v Johnson, (Ind. App.) 33 N. E. Rep. 1000, Consolidated Coal Co. v. Bonner, 43 Ill. App. 17, Cowan v. Chicago etc. R Co., 80 Wis. 284; 50 N. W. Rep. 180, Propsom v. Leathem, 80 Wis. 608, 50 N. W. Rep. 586.

The master must furnish a reasonably safe place for the servant to work. Heckman v. Mackey, 35 Fed. Rep. 353, Hannibal etc. R. Co. v. Fox, 31 Kan. 586, 15 Am. & Eng. R. Cas. 325, Hullehan v. Green Bay etc. R. Co., 68 Wis. 520, 31 Am. & Eng. R. Cas. 332, Kelly v. Erie Tel. etc. Co. 34 Minn. 321, Green v. Banta, 18 N. Y. Superior Ct. 156, Porter v. Silver Creek & M. C. Co., 84 Wis. 418, 54 N. W. Rep. 1019, Davies v. Griffith, 27 Wkly. Law Bul. 180; Stuber v. McEntee, 19 N. Y. S. Rep. 900.

Competent servants. Supporting the text, vide Alabama etc. R. Co. v. Waller, 48 Ala. 459, New Orleans etc. R. Co. v. Hughes, 49 Minn. 258, Moss v. Pacific R. Co., 49 Mo. 167, Chicago etc. R. Co. v. Doyle, 18 Kan. 58, Jordan v. Wells, 3 Woods, 527; Blake v. Maine Cent. R. Co., 70 Me. 60, Tyson v. South & N. A. R. Co., 61 Ala. 554, Indiana Mfg. Co. v. Millen, 87 Ind. 87, Huffman v. Chicago etc. R. Co., 78 Mo. 50, Hilts v. Chicago & G. T. R. Co., 55 Mich. 437, Brennan v. Gordon, 13 Daly, 208, Bonner v. Whitcomb, 80 Tex. 178, 15 S. W. Rep. 899, Copping v. New York & H. R. R. Co., 122 N. Y. 557, 25 E. Rep. 915, affirming 48 Hun, 292, Harper v. Indianapolis & St. L. R. Co., 44 Mo. 567, Flike v. Boston & A. R. Co., 53 N. Y. 549, Kersey v. Kansas City etc. R. Co., 79 Mo. 362, 17 Am. & Eng. R. Cas. 638, East Tenn. etc. R. Co. v. Gurley, 12 Lea, 46; Mentzer v. Armour, 19 Fed. Rep. 373, Huffman v. Chicago etc. R. Co., 78 Mo. 50, 17 Am. & Eng. R. Cas. 625, Satterly v. Morgan, 35 La. An. 1116; Sutton v. New York, etc. R. Co., 66 Hun, 632, 21 N. Y. S. Rep. 312.

Servants of sub-contractor. Attempts have been made to hold that the servants of sub-contractors for portions of a general undertaking were for this purpose fellow-servants with the servants directly employed by the principal contractors, even without evidence that the sub-contractors' work was under the direction or control of the chief contractors. This artificial and unjust extension of a highly artificial rule has fortunately been stopped by the House of Lords (*p*).

Volunteer assistant is on same footing as servant. Moreover, a stranger who gives his help without reward to a man's servants engaged in any work is held to put himself, as regards the master's liability towards him, in the same position as if he were a servant. Having of his free will (though not under a contract of service) exposed himself to the ordinary risks of the work and made himself a partaker in them, he is not entitled to be indemnified against them by the master any more than if he were in his regular employment (*q*). This is really a branch of the doctrine "volenti non fit injuria," discussed below under the title of General Exceptions.

Mathieson (1861), 4 Macq. at p. 227. "All that the master is bound to do is to provide machinery fit and proper for the work, and to take care to have it superintended by himself or his workmen in a fit and proper manner." In *Skipp* v. *E C R Co* (1853), 9 Ex. 223, 23 L. J. Ex. 23, it was said that this duty does not extend to having a sufficient number of servants for the work. *sed qu.* The decision was partly on the ground that the plaintiff was in fact well acquainted with the risk and had never made any complaint.

(*p*) *Johnson* v. *Lindsey*, '91, A. C. 371, overruling *Biggett* v. *Fox*, 11 Ex. 832, 25 L. J. Ex. 188.

(*q*) *Potter* v. *Faulkner* (1861), Ex. Ch. 1 B. & S. 800, 31 L. J. Q. B. 30, approving *Degg* v. *Midland R. Co.* (1857), 1 H. & N. 773, 26 L. J. Ex. 174.

Volunteer assistant is on same footing as servant. Supporting the text, *vide* Johnson v Ashland Water Works Co. 71 Wis 553, 37 N W Rep 825, Eason v S. & E. T. Ry. Co , 65 Tex 577, Mayton v T & P. Ry Co , 63 Tex 77, Barstow v Old Colony R Co , 143 Mass 535; Osborne v. Knox, 68 Me 49. Flower v Pennsylvania R Co , 69 Pa. St. 210, Chicago etc R Co v. West, 125 Ill 320 17 N E Rep 788.

Exception where the master interferes in person. On the other hand, a master who takes an active part in his own work is not only himself liable to a servant injured by his negligence, but, if he has partners in the business, makes them liable also. For he is the agent of the firm, but not a servant (*r*). The partners are generally answerable for his conduct, yet cannot say he was a fellow-servant of the injured man.

Employers' Liability Act, 1880. Such were the results arrived at by a number of modern authorities, which it seems useless to cite in more detail (*s*): the rule, though not abrogated, being greatly limited in application by the statute of 1880. This Act (43 & 44 Vict. c. 42) is on the face of it an experimental and empirical compromise between conflicting interests. It was temporary, being enacted only for seven years and the next session of Parliament, and since continued from time to time (*t*), it is confined in its operation to certain specified causes of injury; and only certain kinds of servants are entitled to the benefit of it, and then upon restrictive conditions as to notice of action, mode of trial, and amount of compensation, which are unknown to the common law. The effect is that a "workman" within the meaning of the Act is put as against his employer in approximately (not altogether, I think) the same position as an outsider as regards the safe and fit condition of the material instruments, fixed or movable, of the master's business. He is also entitled to compensation for harm incurred through the negligence of another servant exercising superintendence, or by the effect of specific orders or rules issued by the master or some one representing him; and there is a

---

(*r*) *Ashworth* v. *Stanwix* (1861), 3 E. & E. 701, 30 L. J. Q. B. 183.

(*s*) They are well collected by Mr Horace Smith (Law of Negligence, pp. 73-76, 2nd ed.).

(*t*) Further legislation has been expected almost every year, but nothing has been done yet.

special wider provision for the benefit of railway servants, which virtually abolishes the master's immunity as to railway accidents in the ordinary sense of that term. So far as the Act has any principle, it is that of holding the employer answerable for the conduct of those who are in delegated authority under him. It is noticeable that almost all the litigation upon the Act has been caused either by its minute provisions as to notice of action, or by desperate attempts to evade those parts of its language which are plain enough to common sense.

Resulting complication of the law. On the whole we have, in a matter of general public importance and affecting large classes of persons who are neither learned in the law nor well able to procure learned advice, the following singularly intricate and clumsy state of things.

First, there is the general rule of a master's liability for his servants (itself in some sense an exceptional rule to begin with).

Secondly, the immunity of the master where the person injured is also his servant.

Thirdly, in the words of the marginal notes of the Employers' Liability Act, "amendment of law" by a series of elaborate exceptions to that immunity.

Fourthly, "exceptions to amendment of law" by provisoes which are mostly but not wholly re-statements of the common law.

Fifthly, minute and vexatious regulations as to procedure in the cases within the first set of exceptions.

It is incredible that such a state of things should nowadays be permanently accepted either in substance or in form. This, however, is not the place to discuss the principles of the controversy, which I have attempted to do elsewhere (*u*). In the United States the doctrine laid down

---

(*u*) Essays in Jurisprudence and Ethics (1882) ch. 5. See for very full information and discussion on the whole matter the evidence taken by the Select

by the Supreme Court of Massachusetts in Farwell's case has been very generally followed. Except in Massachusetts, however, an employer does not so easily avoid responsibility by delegating his authority, as to choice of servants or otherwise, to an intermediate superintendent (x). There has been a good deal of State legislation, but mostly for the protection of railway servants only. Massachusetts has a more recent and more comprehensive statute based on the English Act of 1880 (y). A collection of more or less detailed reports " on the laws regulating the liability of employers in foreign countries" has been published by the Foreign Office (z).

Committees of the House of Commons in 1876 and 1877 (Parl. Papers, H. C. 372, 5°, 1877, 285.) And see the report of a Select Committee of the House of Commons on amending Bills, 1886, 192.

(x) Cooley on Torts, 560, Shearman and Redfield, §§ 86, 88, 102. And see *Chicago M. & S. R. Co. v. Ross* (1884), 112 U. S. 377. Also a stricter view than ours is taken of a master's duty to disclose to his servant any non-apparent risks of the employment which are within his own knowledge. *Wheeler v. Mason Manufacturing Co.* (1883), 135 Mass. 294.

(y) See Mr. McKinney's Article in L. Q. R. vi. 189, April 1890, at p. 197.

(z) Parl. Papers, Commercial, No. 21, 1886.

CHAPTER IV.

GENERAL EXCEPTIONS

Conditions excluding liability for act prima facie wrongful We have considered the general principles of liability for civil wrongs. It now becomes needful to consider the general exceptions to which these principles are subject, or in other words the rules of immunity which limit the rules of liability. There are various conditions which, when present, will prevent an act from being wrongful which in their absence would be a wrong. Under such conditions the act is said to be justified or excused. And when an act is said in general terms to be wrongful, it is assumed that no such qualifying condition exists. It is an actionable wrong, generally speaking, to lay hands on a man in the way of force or restraint. But it is the right of every man to defend himself against unlawful force, and it is the duty of officers of justice to apply force and restraint in various degrees, from simple arrest to the infliction of death itself, in execution of the process and sentences of the law. Here the harm done, and wilfully done, is justified. There are incidents, again, in every football match which an uninstructed observer might easily take for a confused fight of savages, and grave hurt sometimes ensues to one or more of the players. Yet, so long as the play is fairly conducted according to the rules agreed upon, there is no wrong and no cause of action. For the players have joined in the game of their own free will, and accepted its risks. Not that a man is bound to play football or any other rough game, but if he does he must abide its ordinary chances. Here the harm done, if not justified (for, though in a manner unavoidable, it was not in a legal sense necessary), is nevertheless excused (a). Again, defamation is a wrong, but there are certain occasions on which a man may with impunity make and publish untrue statements to the prejudice of another. Again, "sic utere tuo ut alienum non laedas" is said to be a precept of law; yet there are divers things a man may freely do for his own ends, though he well knows that his neighbour will in some way be the worse for them.

General and particular exceptions. Some of the principles by which liability is excluded are applicable indifferently to all or most kinds of injury, while others are confined to some one species. The rule as to "privileged communications" belongs only to the law of libel and slander, and must be dealt with under that particular branch of the subject. So the rule as to "contributory negligence" qualifies liability for negligence, and can be understood only in connection with the special rules determining such liability. Exceptions like those of consent and inevitable accident, on the other hand, are of such wide application that they cannot be conveniently dealt with under any one special head. This class is aptly denoted in the Indian Penal Code (for the same or similar principles apply to the law of criminal liability) by the name of General Exceptions. And these are the exceptions which now concern us. The following seem to be their chief categories. An action is within certain limits not maintainable in respect of the acts of political power called "acts of state," nor of judicial acts. Executive acts of lawful authority form another similar class. Then a class of acts has to be considered which may be called quasi-judicial, and which, also within limits, are protected. Also, there are

---

(a) Justification seems to be the proper word when the harm suffered is inseparably incident to the performance of a legal duty or the exercise of a common right, excuse, when it is but an accident, but I do not know that the precise distinction is always possible to observe, or that anything turns on it.

various cases in which unqualified or qualified immunity is conferred upon private persons exercising an authority or power specially conferred by law. We may regard all these as cases of privilege in respect of the person or the occasion. After these come exceptions which are more an affair of common right; inevitable accident (a point, strange to say, not clearly free from doubt), harm inevitably incident to the ordinary exercise of rights, harm suffered by consent or under conditions amounting to acceptance of the risk, and harm inflicted in self-defence or (in some cases) otherwise by necessity. These grounds of exemption from civil liability for wrongs have to be severally examined and defined. And first of "Acts of State."

1.—*Acts of State.*

Acts of state. It is by no means easy to say what an act of state is, though the term is not of unfrequent occurrence. On the whole, it appears to signify—(1) An act done or adopted by the prince or rulers of a foreign independent State in their political and sovereign capacity, and within the limits of their *de facto* political sovereignty; (2) more particularly (in the words of Sir James Stephen (b)), "an act injurious to the person or to the property of some person who is not at the time of that act a subject (c) of her Majesty; which act is done by any representative of her Majesty's authority, civil or military, and is either previously sanctioned, or subsequently ratified by her Majesty" (such sanction or ratification being, of course, expressed in the proper manner through responsible ministers).

(b) History of the Criminal Law, ii. 61.

(c) This includes a friendly alien living in "temporary allegiance" under the protection of English law; therefore an act of state in this sense cannot take place in England in time of peace.

General ground of exemption. Our courts of justice profess themselves not competent to discuss acts of these kinds for reasons thus expressed by the Judicial Committee of the Privy Council:— "The transactions of independent States between each other" (and with subjects of other States), "are governed by other laws than those which municipal courts administer; such courts have neither the means of deciding what is right, nor the power of enforcing any decision which they may make" (*d*).

A series of decisions of the Indian Supreme Courts and

(*d*) *Secretary of State in Council of India v. Kamachee Boye Sahaba* (1859), 13 Moo. P. C. 22, 75.

General ground of exemption. The language of the text is based on conditions peculiar to the system of the British government. The American doctrine may be stated thus: An act of state is the commission by the executive branch of the government, for reasons of polity, of an act affecting a person not a citizen. When such an act is made the subject of complaint, the mere avowal, by the executive department of responsibility therefor, will move the court to dismiss the matter from its consideration.

If the act has affected a citizen and the executive department acknowledge responsibility therefor, it must show that the act was within its authority under the Constitution and laws. The government of this republic is a system of powers delegated by the people and as long as the government acts within the limits of those powers the people cannot complain. The guarding of these limits is one of the chief duties and sacred rights of the judiciary, but the judiciary possesses neither rule for determination nor power to enforce its decisions regarding acts of the executive department towards a person not a citizen. The relations of Great Britain to her Indian dependencies has a close parallel in our relations to the Indian nations. The question arose in the case of Cherokee Nation *v.* State of Georgia (5 Pet. 1), in which the plaintiff sought the aid of the Supreme Court of the United States to restrain the State of Georgia from enforcing certain of its laws directed against the Cherokee Nation. It was held that the court had no power to interfere. "In such a case," said Johnson, J., "the appeal is to the sword and Almighty Justice, not to courts of law or equity."

In Ruan *v.* Perry (3 Caines, 120) it was held, that orders from the President of the United States and the Secretary of Navy protected a naval officer who stopped a neutral vessel, the property of a foreigner, though the delay caused its subsequent capture by the enemy. See Durand *v.* Hollins, 4 Blatchf. 451.

the Privy Council have applied this rule to the dealings of the East India Company with native States and with the property of native princes (e). In these cases the line between public and private property, between acts of regular administration and acts of war or of annexation, is not always easy to draw. Most of them turn on acts of political annexation. Persons who by such an act become British subjects do not thereby become entitled to complain in municipal courts deriving their authority from the British Government of the act of annexation itself or anything incident to it. In such a case the only remedy is by petition of right to the Crown. And the effect is the same if the act is originally an excess of authority, but is afterwards ratified by the Crown.

"The leading case on this subject is *Buron v Denman* (*f*). This was an action against Captain Denman, a captain in the navy, for burning certain baracoons on the West Coast of Africa, and releasing the slaves contained in them. His conduct in so doing was approved by a letter written by Mr. Stephen, then Under Secretary of State for the Colonies, by the direction of Lord John Russell, then Secretary of State. It was held that the owner of the slaves [a Spanish subject] could recover no damages for his loss, as the effect of the ratification of Captain Denman's act was to convert what he had done into an act of state, for which no action would lie."

So far Mr Justice Stephen, in his History of the Criminal Law (*g*). It is only necessary to add, as he does on the next page, that "as between the sovereign and his subjects there can be no such thing as an act of state. Courts of law are established for the express purpose of limiting public authority in its conduct towards individuals. If one British subject puts another to death or

---

(e) See *Doss* v *Secretary of State for India in Council* (1875), 19 Eq 509, and the case last cited

(*f*) (1847) 2 Ex 167

(*g*) Vol ii p 64

destroys his property by the express command of the King, that command is no protection to the person who executes it unless it is in itself lawful, and it is the duty of the proper courts of justice to determine whether it is lawful or not" as, for example, when the Court of King's Bench decided that a Secretary of State had no power to issue general warrants to search for and seize papers and the like (*h*).

Local actions against viceroy or governor. Another question which has been raised in the colonies and Ireland, but which by its nature cannot come before an English court for direct decision, is how far an action is maintainable against an officer in the nature of a viceroy during his term of office, and in the local courts of the territory in which he represents the Crown. It has been held by the Judicial Committee that the Lieutenant-Governor of a colony is not exempt from suit in the courts of that colony for a debt or other merely private cause of action (*i*); and by the Irish courts, on the other hand, that the Lord-Lieutenant is exempt from being sued in Ireland for an act done in his official or "politic" capacity (*j*).

Power to exclude aliens. An alien not already admitted to the enjoyment of civil rights in England (or any British possession) seems to have no remedy in our law if prevented by the local executive authority from entering

---

(*h*) *Entick* v. *Carrington*, 19 St. Tr. 1043.

(*i*) *Hill* v. *Bigge* (1841), 3 Moo. P. C. 465, dissenting from Lord Mansfield's dictum in *Mostyn* v. *Fabrigas*, Cowp. 172, that "locally during his government no civil or criminal action will lie against him," though it may be that he is privileged from personal arrest where arrest would, by the local law, be part of the ordinary process.

(*j*) *Luby* v. *Wodehouse*, 17 Ir. C. L. R. 618, *Sullivan* v. *Spencer*, Ir. R. 6 C. L. 173, following *Tandy* v. *Westmoreland*, 27 St. Tr. 1246. These cases go very far, for the Lord-Lieutenant was not even called on to plead his privilege, but the Court stayed proceedings against him on motion. As to the effect of a local Act of Indemnity, see *Phillips* v. *Ayre* (1870), Ex. Ch. L. R. 6 Q. B. 1.

British territory (k). It seems doubtful whether admission to temporary allegiance in one part of the British Empire would confer any right to be admitted to another part.

Acts of foreign powers. There is another quite distinct point of jurisdiction in connection with which the term "act of state" is used. A sovereign prince or other person representing an independent power is not liable to be sued in the courts of this country for acts done in a sovereign capacity; and this even if in some other capacity he is a British subject, as was the case with the King of Hanover, who remained an English peer after the personal union between the Crowns of England and Hanover was dissolved (l). This rule is included in a wider one which not only extends beyond the subject of this work, but belongs to international as much as to municipal law. It has been thus expressed by the Court of Appeal: "As a consequence of the absolute independence of every sovereign authority, and of the international comity which induces

(k) *Musgrave v. Chung Teeong Toy*, '91, A. C. 272, 60 L. J. P. C. 28.

(l) *Duke of Brunswick v. King of Hanover* (1843-4), 6 Beav. 1, 57, affirmed in the House of Lords, 2 H. L. C. 1.

Acts of foreign powers. A sovereign power cannot be sued in the federal or state courts of the United States, but it may exercise its option to appear. Therefore, a complaint in which a sovereign power is made a co-defendant is not demurrable until the time has elapsed for the exercise of this option. Manning v. State of Nicaragua, 14 How. Pr. 517.

A state of the Union cannot be sued in the courts of a sister state without its express consent. People v. Talmage, 6 Cal. 256, Treasurer v. Cleary, 3 Rich. 372, Hosmer v. De Young, 1 Tex. 764, Patterson v. Shaw, 6 Ind. 377, Williamsport etc. R. Co. v. Commonwealth, 33 Pa. St. 288, Beers v. Arkansas, 20 How. 527.

In Chisholm v. Georgia, (2 Dall. 419) it was held, that a state was suable in the federal courts. This decision led to the adoption of the eleventh Amendment in negation of that construction of the constitution. See North Carolina v. Temple, 134 N. S. 22, Hans v. Louisiana, 134 U. S. 1.

every sovereign state to respect the independence of every other sovereign state, each and every one declines to exercise by means of any of its Courts, any of its territorial jurisdiction over the person of any sovereign or ambassador of any other state, or over the public property of any state which is destined to its public use, or over the property of any ambassador (*m*), though such sovereign, ambassador, or property be within its territory, and therefore, but for the common agreement, subject to its jurisdiction" (*n*)

Summary. If we may generalize from the doctrine of our own courts, the result seems to be that an act done by the authority, previous or subsequent, of the government of a sovereign state in the exercise of *de facto* sovereignty (*o*), is not examinable at all in the courts of justice of any other state. So far forth as it affects persons not subject to the government in question, it is not examinable in the ordinary courts of that state itself. If and so far as it affects a subject of the same state, it may be, and in England, it is, examinable by the courts in their ordinary jurisdiction. In most Continental countries, however, if not in all, the remedy for such acts must be sought before a special tribunal (in France the Conseil d'Etat: the preliminary question whether the ordinary court or the Conseil d'Etat has jurisdiction is decided by the Tribunal des Conflits, a peculiar and composite court) (*p*).

(*m*) What if cattle belonging to a foreign ambassador were distrained damage feasant? It would seem he could not get them back without submitting to the jurisdiction.

(*n*) *The Parliament Belge* (1880), 5 P. D. 197, 214.

(*o*) I have not met with a distinct statement of this qualification in existing authorities, but it is evidently assumed by them, and is necessary for the preservation of every state's sovereign rights within its own jurisdiction. Plainly the command of a foreign government would be no answer to an action for trespass to land, or for the arrest of an alleged offender against a foreign law, within the body of an English county.

(*p*) Law of May 24, 1872. But the principle is ancient, and the old law is still cited on various points.

2.—*Judicial Acts*

Judicial acts. Next as to judicial acts. The rule is that "no action will lie against a judge for any acts done or words spoken in his judicial capacity in a court of justice" (q). And the exemption is not confined to judges of superior courts. It is founded on the necessity of judges being independent in the exercise of their office, a reason which applies equally to all judicial proceedings

---

(q) *Scott v. Stanfield* (1868), L. R. 3 Ex. 220, 37 L. J. Ex. 155, which confirms and sums up the effect of many previous decisions.

Judicial acts. It is an accepted rule that judicial acts are excepted from liability. Brodie v Rutledge, 2 Bay, 69, Ambler v. Church, 1 Root, 211, Phelps v Sill, 1 Day, 315, Moor v Ames, 3 Caines, 170, Young v Herbert, 2 Nott. & M. 168, Yates v Lansing, 5 Johns 282, 9 Id. 395, Vanderheyden v. Young, 11 Id 150, Ely v Thomson, 3 A. K. Marsh. 70, Little v Moore, 4 N. J. L 74, Tracy v Williams, 2 Conn. 113, Thompkins v Sands, 8 Wend. 408, Lining v Bertham, 2 Bay, 1, Burnham v Stevens, 33 N. H. 247, Ross v. Rittenhouse, 2 Dall 160, Hamilton v Williams, 26 Ala 527, Henley v Wiggins, 5 Harr (Del) 162, Carter v Dow, 16 Wis. 298, Maguire v Hughes, 13 La An 281, Way v Townsend, 4 Allen, 114, Wood v Ruland, 10 Mo 143, Hatfield v. Towsley, 3 Ia 584, Lancaster v Lane, 19 Ill 242, Deal v Harris, 8 Md. 40, Walker v. Hallock, 32 Ind 239, Busteed v. Parsons, 54 Ala 393, Lange v Benedict, 73 N. Y 12, Bevard v Hoffman, 18 Md. 379.

The text substantially states the American law upon the responsibility of judicial officers acting without jurisdiction or in excess thereof. See Grove v Van Duyn, 44 N J L 654, Clark v. Holmes, 1 Dough (Mich) 390, Blood v Sayre, 17 Vt 609, Wright v. Rouse, 18 Neb. 234, Piper v. Pearson, 2 Gray, 120, Borden v Fitch, 15 Johns 121, Estopinal v. Peyroux, 37 La An. 477, Pitzack v Van Gerichten, 10 Mo. App 424, Case v Shepherd, 2 Johns Cas 27, Allen v Gray, 11 Conn 95, Barkdoor v Randall, 4 Blackf 476, Connelly v Wood, 31 Kan 359, Olmstead v Brewer, 91 Ala. 124, 8 So. Rep. 345, Bradley v Fisher, 13 Wall 348, Stewart v. Cooley, 23 Minn 347

There are *dicta* to the effect that a judicial officer is liable for malicious and corrupt acts committed in his judicial capacity. Randall v. Brigham, 7 Wall 253; Garfield v Douglass, 22 Ill. 100.

But the proper remedy in such cases lies in the removal of the official by impeachment and not in an attack upon that protection which public policy bestows upon the office. Kress v. State, 65 Ind 106, Pratt v. Gardner, 2 Cush 98, State v. Hastings (Neb), 55 N W Rep 774

But in order to establish the exemption as regards proceedings in an inferior court, the judge must show that at the time of the alleged wrong-doing some matter was before him in which he had jurisdiction (whereas in the case of a superior court it is for the plaintiff to prove want of jurisdiction); and the act complained of must be of a kind which he had power to do as judge in that matter.

Thus a revising barrister has power by statute (r) "to order any person to be removed from his court who shall interrupt the business of the court or refuse to obey his lawful orders in respect of the same" but it is an actionable trespass if under colour of this power he causes a person to be removed from the court, not because that person is then and there making a disturbance, but because in the revising barrister's opinion he improperly suppressed facts within his knowledge at the holding of a former court (s). The like law holds if a county court judge commits a party without jurisdiction, and being informed of the facts which show that he has no jurisdiction (t), though an inferior judge is not liable for an act which on the facts apparent to him at the time was within his jurisdiction, but by reason of facts not then shown was in truth outside it (u).

A judge is not liable in trespass for want of jurisdiction, unless he knew or ought to have known of the defect; and it lies on the plaintiff, in every such case, to prove that fact (x). And the conclusion formed by a judge, acting judicially and in good faith, on a matter of fact which it is within his jurisdiction to determine, cannot be disputed in an action against him for anything judicially done by him in the same cause upon the footing of that conclusion (y)

(r) 28 & 29 Vict c 36, s 16.

(s) Willis v Maclachlan (1876), 1 Ex. D 376, 45 L J Q B 689

(t) Houlden v Smith (1850), 14 Q B 841, 19 L J Q B 170

(u) Lowther v Earl of Radnor (1806), 8 East, 113, 115

(x) Calder v Halket (1839), 3 Moo P C. 28, 78

(y) Kemp v Neville (1861), 10 C B N S 523, 31 L J C P 158 (an action against the Vice Chancellor of the University of Cambridge), and authorities there cited

Allegations that the act complained of was done "maliciously and corruptly," that words were spoken "falsely and maliciously," or the like, will not serve to make an action of this kind maintainable against a judge either of a superior (z) or of an inferior (a) court.

Liability by statute in special cases. There are two cases in which by statute an action does or did lie against a judge for misconduct in his office, namely, if he refuses to grant a writ of *habeas corpus* in vacation time (b), and if he refused to seal a bill of exceptions (c).

Judicial acts of persons not judges. The rule of immunity for judicial acts is applied not only to judges of the ordinary civil tribunals, but to members of naval and military courts-martial or courts of inquiry constituted in accordance with military law and usage (d). It is also applied to a limited extent to arbitrators, and to any person who is in a position like an arbitrator's, as having been chosen by the agreement of parties to decide a matter that is or may be in difference between them. Such a person, if he acts honestly, is not liable for errors in judgment (e). He would be liable for a corrupt or partisan exercise of his office; but if he really does not use a judicial discretion,

---

(z) *Fray* v *Blackburn* (1862), 3 B & S. 576.

(a) *Scott* v *Stansfield* (1868), L R 3 Ex 220, 37 L J Ex 155.

(b) 31 Car II c 2, s 9.

(c) 13 Edw I (Stat Westm 2) c 31, cf. Blackstone, III, 372, [See *Horne v. Pudil* (Ia), 55 N W Rep 485.]

(d) This may be collected from such authorities as *Dawkins* v *Lord Rokeby* (1875), L R 7 H L 744, 45 L J Q B 8, *Dawkins* v *Prince Edward of Saxe Weimar* (1876), 1 Q B D 499, 45 L J Q B 567, which however go to some extent on the doctrine of "privileged communications," a doctrine wider in one sense,

and more special in another sense, than the rule now in question. Partly, also, they deal with acts of authority not of a judicial kind, which will be mentioned presently.

(e) *Pappa* v *Rose* (1872), Ex Ch L R 7 C P 525, 41 L J C P 187 (broker authorized by sale note to decide on quality of goods), *Tharsis Sulphur Co* v *Loftus* (1872), L R 8 C P 1, 42 L J C P 6 (average adjuster nominated to ascertain proportion of loss as between ship and cargo), *Stevenson* v *Watson* (1879), 4 C P D 148, 48 L J C P 318 (architect nominated to certify what was due to contractor).

the rightness or competence of his judgment cannot be brought into question for the purpose of making him personally liable.

The doctrine of our courts on this subject appears to be fully and uniformly accepted in the United States (*f*).

3 — *Executive Acts*

Executive acts. As to executive acts of public officers, no legal wrong can be done by the regular enforcement of any sentence or process of law, nor by the necessary use of force for preserving the peace. It will be observed that private persons are in many cases entitled, and in some bound, to give aid and assistance, or to act by themselves, in executing the law, and in so doing they are similarly protected (*g*). Were not this the rule, it is evident that

---

(*f*) Cooley on Torts, Ch 11 See Acts of quasi Judicial Discretion, post p 110

(*g*) The details of this subject belong to criminal law [Payne v Green, 15 Miss 507, Kilpatrick v Frost, 2 Grant Cas 168, Elder v Morrison, 10 Wend 128, Hooper v Smith, 19 Vt 151]

Executive acts. The general doctrine stated in the text prevails in the United States Thus, it has been held in numerous cases that, trespass does not lie for acts done by a ministerial officer under process regular on its face and issuing from a court of competent jurisdiction Ludington v. Peck, 2 Conn. 700, Waterburg v Lockwood, 4 Day, 257, W me v Shed, 10 Johns. 138, Taylor v. Alexandria, 6 Ohio, 144, McHugh v. Pundt, 11 Bailey, 141 Norcross v Nunan, 61 Cal 640, Beatty v Perkins, 6 Wend 382, Camp v. Mosley, 2 Fla 171, Tefft v Ashbaugh, 13 Ill 602, State v. McNally, 34 Me 210, Milburn v Gilman, 10 Mo 64, Woods v Davis, 34 N H 328, Gray v. Kimball, 42 Me 299, Mason v Vance, 1 Sneed (Tenn), 178, Ortman v. Greenman, 4 Mich. 291, McLean v Cook, 23 Wis 364, Hicks v. Dorn, 1 Lans. 81; 54 Barb. 172, Shaw v. Davis, 55 Barb. 389, Dunn v Gilman, 34 Mich 256, Breckwoldt v. Morris, 149 Pa 291; 24 At. Rep. 300, Van Kewren v. Switzer, 58 Hun, 602, 11 N Y. S Rep. 263, Trowbridge v. Ballard, 81 Mich 451.

the law could not be enforced at all. But a public officer may err by going beyond his authority in various ways. When this happens (and such cases are not uncommon), there are distinctions to be observed. The principle which runs through both common law and legislation in the matter is that an officer is not protected from the ordinary consequence of unwarranted acts which it rested with himself to avoid, such as using needless violence to secure a prisoner; but he is protected if he has only acted in a manner in itself reasonable, and in execution of an apparently regular warrant or order which on the face of it he was

---

If the process is merely voidable it will be a defense to the officer acting under it. Cogborn v Spence, 15 Ala. 549, Sheldon v Stryker, 54 Barb 116, Wilton Mfg. Co v. Butler, 34 Me. 431, Averett v Thompson, 15 Ala 678, Mower v Stickney, 5 Minn 397, Billings v Russell, 23 Pa. St 189. But not where the process is void. Keir v Mount, 28 N Y. 659; Stephens v Wilkins, 6 Pa St 260; Lincoln v. Cross, 10 Wis 91. Nor where the process shows its irregularity upon its face. Clark v. Bond, 7 Blxf. 288, Elsmore v. Longfellow, 76 Me 128.

Where an officer exceeds the original lawful authority of his warrant he becomes a trespasser *ab initio* Mussey v Cummings, 34 Me 74, Burton v. Calloway, 20 Ind 169; Bradley v. Davis, 14 Me. 44, Jarrett v. Gwathmey, 5 Blackf. 237, Taylor v Jones, 42 N H. 25; Camp v. Ganley, 6 Ill. App 499, Parmelee v. Leonard, 9 Ia. 131

There are late authorities holding that an officer is not liable for exceeding his lawful authority unless it appears that the original lawful act was done with an unlawful purpose. Grafton v Carmichael, 48 Wis 660, Davis v Webster, 59 N. H. 471; State v Martin, 77 Mo. 670, Wentworth v. Sawyer, 76 Mo 434, Page v. Du Puy, 40 Ill 506, Gates v. Lonsburg, 20 Johns. 427, Acton v Cooper, 29 Vt. 44, Stoughton v. Mott, 25 Vt 668.

A sheriff or constable is responsible for his mistakes in making a levy or an arrest. Atkinson v Gatcher, 23 Ark 101, Sims v Reed, 12 B Mon 51; Fosso v. Stewart, 14 Me. 312, Bean v. Hubbard, 4 Cush. 85, Caldwell v. Arnold, 8 Minn. 265, Meadow v Wise, 41 Ark. 285, Oliver v White, 18 S. C 235; Sullivan v. Failey, 63 How Pr 238; Bailey v Tipton, 29 Mo 206; Markley v. Rand, 12 Cal 275, Atkinson v. Atkinson, 15 La An 491, Lathrop v Arnold, 25 Me. 136, Brownell v. Carnley, 3 Duer, 9, Rafferty v. People, 69 Ill 111, 72 Ill 37, 18 Am. Rep 601; Savacool v Boughton, 5 Wend. 170, State v. Weed, 21 N. H. 262, 3 Am Dec. 188, Hubbard v. Lord, 59 Tex. 384, O'Shaughnessy v. Baxter, 121 Mass 515, McGuire v. Galligan, 57 Mich. 38

bound to obey (*h*). This applies only to irregularity in the process of a court having jurisdiction over the alleged cause. Where an order is issued by a court which has no jurisdiction at all in the subject-matter, so that the proceedings are, as it is said, "coram non judice," the exemption ceases (*i*). A constable or officer acting under a justice's warrant is, however, specially protected by statute, notwithstanding any defect of jurisdiction, if he produces the warrant on demand (*k*). Many particular statutes contain provisions which give a qualified protection to persons acting under the statute, by requiring notice of action to be given, or the action to be brought within a limited time, or both. It would serve no useful purpose to attempt a collection of such provisions, which are important, and sometimes intelligible, only in connexion with the special branches of public law in which they occur (*l*).

As to a mere mistake of fact, such as arresting the body or taking the goods of the wrong person, an officer of the law is not excused in such a case. He must lay hands on the right person or property at his peril, the only exception being on the principle of estoppel, where he is misled by the party's own act (*m*).

Acts of naval and military officers. Acts done by naval and military officers in the execution or intended

---

(*h*) *Mayor of London* v *Cox* (1867), L. R. 2 H L. at p 269 (in opinion of judges, per Willes J) The law seems to be understood in the same way in the United States Cooley on Torts, 459-462.

(*i*) The case of *The Marshalsea*, 10 Co Rep 76 a, *Clark* v *Woods* (1848), 2 Ex. 395, 17 L. J M C 189

(*k*) 24 Geo II c 44, s 6 (Action lies only if a demand in writing for perusal and copy of the warrant is refused or neglected for six days)

(*l*) Cf Dicey on Parties, 430 Sect 170 of the Army Act, 1881, will serve as a recent specimen Cf the Indian Code of Civil Procedure (Act XIV. 1882), s 424

(*m*) See *Glasspoole* v *Young* (1829), 9 B & C 696, *Balme* v *Hutton*, Ex Ch (1833), 9 Bing 471, *Dunston* v *Paterson* (1857), 2 C B. N. S 495, 26 L J C P 267, and other authorities collected in Fisher's Digest, ed Mews, sub tit Sheriff

---

Acts of naval and military officers Where the military duty of obedience amounts to duress it is a defense to trespass Witherspoon *v.* Woody, 4 Coldw 605; Barrow *v.* Page, 5 Hayw (Tenn.) 197, Pollard *v*

execution of their duty, for the enforcement of the rules of the service and preservation of discipline, fall to some extent under this head. The justification of a superior officer as regards a subordinate partly depends on the consent implied (or indeed expressed) in the act of a man's joining the service that he will abide by its regulations and usages, partly on the sanction expressly given to military law by statutes. There is very great weight of opinion, but no absolute decision, that an action does not lie in a civil court for bringing an alleged offender against military law (being a person subject to that law) before a court-martial without probable cause (n). How far the orders of a superior officer justify a subordinate who obeys them as against third persons has never been fully settled. But the better opinion appears to be that the subordinate is in the like position with an officer executing an apparently regular civil process, namely, that he is protected if he acts under orders given by a person whom he is generally bound by the rules of the service to obey, and of a kind which that person is generally authorized to give, and if the particular order is not necessarily or manifestly unlawful (o)

Of other public authorities. The same principles apply to the exemption of a person acting under the orders of any public body competent in the matter in hand. An

---

(n) *Johnstone v Sutton* (1786-7), Ex Ch 1 T R 510, 548, affirmed in H L Ibid 784, 1 Bro P C 76, 1 R R 257 The Ex Ch thought the action did not lie, but the defendant was entitled to judgment even if it did No reasons appear to have been given in the House of Lords

(o) See per Willes J in *Keighly v Bell* (1866), 4 F & F at p 790 In time of war the protection may perhaps be more extensive As to criminal responsibility in such cases, cf Stephen, Dig Cr Law, art 202, Hist Cr Law, 1 200-206

Baldwin, 22 Ia. 328, Hess v Johnson, 3 W Va. 645, Kammell v Bassett, 24 Ark. 499 But there are decisions holding that no authority can justify an unlawful act. Hogue v Penn, 3 Bush, 663, Wilson v Franklin, 63 N C 259, Smith v Tsenhour, 3 Coldw 214, Mitchell v. Harmony, 13 How 115, Brown v Howard, 14 Johns 119.

action does not lie against the Serjeant-at-arms of the House of Commons for excluding a member from the House in obedience to a resolution of the House itself; this being a matter of internal discipline in which the House is supreme (p).

Indian Act, XVIII. of 1850. The principles of English law relating to the protection of judicial officers and persons acting under their orders have in British India been declared by express enactment (Act XVIII. of 1850).

1 — *Quasi-judicial Acts.*

Acts of quasi-judicial discretion. Divers persons and bodies are called upon, in the management of public institutions or government of voluntary associations, to exercise

---

(p) *Bradlaugh* v *Gossett* (1884), 12 Q B D 271, 53 L. J Q B 209 As to the limits of the privilege, see per Stephen J at p 283 As to the power of a colonial legislative assembly over its own members, see *Barton* v *Taylor* (J C 1886), 11 App Ca 197, 55 L. J P C 1

Acts of quasi-judicial discretion. In the United States the doctrine of the text has a very general application, being recognized in decisions covering various employments, such as military and naval officers, arbitrators, tax-assessors, grand and petit jurors, collectors of customs, school commissioners, etc. See Jones v Brown, 54 Ia 74, Hunter v. Mathis, 40 Ind 356, Gould v. Hammond, 1 McAll. 235, Van Steenbergh v Bigelow, 3 Wend. 42; Turpen v Booth, 56 Cal. 65, Harrington v. Commissioners, 2 McCord, 400, Hoggott v Bigley, 6 Humph. 236; Weaver v. Devendorf, 3 Denio, 117; Freeman v Cornwall, 10 Johns. 470; Auditor v Atchison etc. R. Co., 6 Kan. 500; Lilienthal v. Campbell, 22 La An 600, McDaniel v. Tebbetts, 60 N H. 497; Gregory v. Brooks, 37 Conn. 365, Edwards v Ferguson, 73 Mo 686, Billings v. Lafferty, 31 Ill. 318, Donahoe v. Richards, 38 Me. 379; Shoemaker v. Nesbit, 2 Rawle, 201, Bennett v. Fulmer, 49 Pa. St. 157, Wall v. Trumbull, 16 Mich. 228, Wasson v. Mitchell, 18 Ia. 153, Pike v. Megoun, 44 Mo. 291; Walker v. Halleck, 32 Ind. 293; Downing v McFadden, 18 Pa St 334, State v. Hastings (Neb), 55 N. W. Rep. 774, Johnson v. Dist. of Columbia, 118 U S 19, Seifert v. Brooklyn, 101 N Y 136

a sort of conventional jurisdiction analogous to that of inferior courts of justice. These quasi-judicial functions are in many cases created or confirmed by Parliament. Such are the powers of the universities over their officers and graduates, and of colleges in the universities over their fellows and scholars, and of the General Council of Medical Education over registered medical practitioners (*q*). Often the authority of the quasi-judicial body depends on an instrument of foundation, the provisions of which are binding on all persons who accept benefits under it. Such are the cases of endowed schools and religious congregations. And the same principle appears in the constitution of modern incorporated companies, and even of private partnerships. Further, a quasi-judicial authority may exist by the mere convention of a number of persons who have associated themselves for any lawful purpose, and have entrusted powers of management and discipline to select members. The committees of most clubs have by the rules of the club some such authority, or at any rate an initiative in presenting matters of discipline before the whole body. The Inns of Court exhibit a curious and unique example of great power and authority exercised by voluntary unincorporated societies in a legally anomalous manner. Their powers are for some purposes quasi-judicial, and yet they are not subject to any ordinary jurisdiction (*r*).

Rules of natural justice and special rules, if any, must be observed. The general rule as to quasi-judicial powers

---

(*q*) See *Allbutt* v. *General Council, &c.* (1889), 23 Q. B. Div. 400; *Leeson* v. *General Council, &c.* (1889), 43 Ch. Div. 366; *Partridge* v. *General Council, &c.* (1890), 25 Q. B. Div. 90; 59 L. J. Q. B. 475.

(*r*) See *Neate* v. *Denman* (1874), 18 Eq. 127.

Rules of natural justice and special rules, if any, must be observed. In *Farnsworth* v. *Staris* (3 Cush. 412) it is held that members of a church council who have by the constitution of the church a right to investigate the moral conduct of members are as fully protected, if acting in the

of this class is that persons exercising them are protected from civil liability if they observe the rules of natural justice, and also the particular statutory or conventional rules, if any, which may prescribe their course of action. The rules of natural justice appear to mean, for this purpose, that a man is not to be removed from office or membership, or otherwise dealt with to his disadvantage, without having fair and sufficient notice of what is alleged against him, and an opportunity of making his defence, and that the decision, whatever it is, must be arrived at in good faith with a view to the common interest of the society or institution concerned. If these conditions be satisfied, a court of justice will not interfere, not even if it thinks the decision was in fact wrong (*s*). If not, the act complained of will be declared void, and the person affected by it maintained in his rights until the matter has been properly and regularly dealt with (*t*). These principles apply to the expulsion of a partner from a private firm where a power of expulsion is conferred by the partnership contract (*u*).

(*s*) *Inderwick* v. *Snell* (1850), 2 Mac & G 216 (removal of a director of a company), *Dawkins* v *Antrobus* (1881), 17 Ch. Div 615 (expulsion of a member from a club), cf 13 Ch D 352, *Partridge* v *General Council*, &c, note (*q*) last page, although no notice was given, the council honestly thinking they had no option. In the case of a club an injunction will be granted only in respect of the member's right of property, therefore where the club is proprietary the only remedy is in damages. *Baird* v *Wells* (1890), 44 Ch D 661 59 L J Ch 673

(*t*) *Fisher* v *Keane* (1878), 11 Ch D 353, 49 L J Ch 11 (a club case, no notice to the member), *Labouchere* v. *Wharncliffe* (1879), 13 Ch D 346 (the like, no sufficient inquiry or notice to the member, calling and proceedings of general meeting irregular), *Dean* v *Bennett* (1870), 6 Ch 489, 40 L J Ch 452 (minister of Baptist chapel under deed of settlement, no sufficient notice of specific charges either to the minister or in calling special meeting)

(*u*) *Blisset* v *Daniel* (1853), 10 Ha 493, *Wood* v *Wood* (1874), L R 9 Ex 190, 43 L J Ex 190. Without an express power in the articles a partner cannot be expelled at all

---

scope of that authority and in good faith, as secular judges. See *Lucas v Case*, 9 Bush, 297. But in *State v Williams* (75 N C 134) it is held, that members of a society are liable for subjecting a fellow member to a "ceremony of expulsion" which involves personal violence, though the ceremony was known to the plaintiff at the time of joining. See 24 Am. Law Rev 537

Absolute discretionary powers. It may be, however, that by the authority of Parliament (or, it would seem, by the previous agreement of the party to be affected) a governing or administrative body, or the majority of an association, has power to remove a man from office or the like without anything in the nature of judicial proceedings, and without showing any cause at all. Whether a particular authority is judicial or absolute must be determined by the terms of the particular instrument creating it (*v*).

Questions whether duty judicial or ministerial. Ashby v. White, &c. On the other hand there may be question whether the duties of a particular office be quasi-judicial, or merely ministerial, or judicial for some purposes and ministerial for others. It seems that at common law the returning or presiding officer at a parliamentary or other

---

(*v*) *E g Dean v Bennett supra, Fisher v Jackson '91, 5 Ch 84, 60 L J Ch 482 (power judicial), Hayman v Governors of Rugby School* (1874), 18 L q 28, 43 L J Ch 834 (power absolute).

Questions, whether duty judicial or ministerial. In America the law is not settled that officers having charge of elections and the registration of voters are protected like judges from the injurious consequences of their conduct in the performance of their functions. However, the tendency of the late decisions is towards uniformity in exempting such officers from liability where they act in good faith. Rail v Potts, 8 Humph 225, Hannon v Grizzard, 99 N C. 161, 6 S. E Rep 92, Jenkins v Waldron, 11 Johns. 114, Griffin v Rising, 11 Metc. 339, Faussler v. Parsons, 6 W Va 186, 20 Am. Rep 431, Goetcheus v Mathewson, 61 N Y. 420, Patterson v D'Auterive, 6 La An 467; State v McDonald, 4 Harr (Del) 555, Turnpike Co. v Champney, 2 N H 199, Weckerly v Geyer, 11 Serg. & R. 35, Keenan v Cook, 12 R I 5', Morgan v Dudley, 18 B Mon. 693, Caulfield v Bullock, Id 495, Gordon v Farm, 2 Dough (Mich) 411; Murphy v. Ramsey, 114 U S. 15, Wheeler v Patterson, 1 N H 88, Larned v Wheeler, 140 Mass 390, Butler v Kent, 19 Johns 223, Jenkins v Waldron, 11 Id 114. But there are decisions holding such officers to the strict rule of liability for erroneously excluding a person entitled to vote, although they act in good faith. Lincoln v Hapgood, 11 Mass. 350, Capen v. Foster, 12 Pick 312, Jeffries v. Ankenny, 11 Ohio, 372, Long v Long, 57 Ia. 497.

election has a judicial discretion, and does not commit a wrong if by an honest error of judgment he refuses to receive a vote (x); but now in most cases it will be found that such officers are under absolute statutory duties (y), which they must perform at their peril

5.—*Parental and quasi-parental Authority*

Authority of parents and persons in loco parentis. Thus much of private quasi-judicial authority. There are also several kinds of authority in the way of summary

(x) *To— v Child* (1857) 1 N Ch 7 F 5 B 15, 26 L J Q B 151, explaining *Ashby v White* Ld Raym 938, and In 1 Sm L C and see the special report of Holt's judgment published in 1837 and referred to in *To— v Child*. There is some difference of opinion in America, see Cooley on Torts, 113, 114

(y) 6 & 7 Vict c 18, s 52 As to presiding officers under The Ballot Act, 1872, *Pickering v James* (1873), L R 8 C P 489, 42 L J C P 217, *Ackers v Howard* (1886), 16 Q B D 739, 55 L J Q B 273

Authority of parents and persons in loco parentis A parent has the right to correct his child by corporal punishment in a reasonable and humane manner for the purpose of family discipline State v Jones, 95 N C 588, Johnson v State, 2 Humph 283, State v Alford, 68 N. C. 322, People v Cooper, 8 How Pr 288

But it is not lawful for the parent to inflict unreasonable punishment or permanent injury upon the child. Fletcher v People, 52 Ill. 395, Hinkle v State, 127 Ind 490, 26 N E Rep. 777, Commonwealth v. Coffey, 121 Mass 66, Neal v State, 54 Ga 281

A step father is *in loco parentis* Gorman v State, 42 Tex 221 See Snowden v State, 12 Tex App 105, 41 Am Rep 667

School teachers may inflict a reasonable measure of corporal punishment if the right is exercised in good faith for the purpose of enforcing discipline Heritage v Dodge, 64 N H 297, 9 At Rep 722, Dowlen v State, 16 Tex App 61; Anderson v State, 3 Head, 455, Cooper v McJunkin, 4 Ind 290, Sheehan v Sturgis, 53 Conn 481, State v Mizner, 45 Ia 248, 24 Am Rep 769, Deskins v Gore, 85 Mo 485, 55 Am Rep 387, Danenhofer v State, 69 Ind 295, 395 Am Rep 216; Hathaway v Rice, 19 Vt 102, Fertich v Micherner, 111 Ind 472

But the teacher is responsible for any abuse of his authority State v. Vanderbilt, 116 Ind 11, 18 N E Rep 266, Lander v Seaver, 32 Vt

force or restraint which the necessities of society require to be exercised by private persons. And such persons are protected in exercise thereof, if they act with good faith and in a reasonable and moderate manner. Parental authority (whether in the hands of a father or guardian, or of a person to whom it is delegated, such as a schoolmaster) is the most obvious and universal instance (z). It is needless to say more of this here, except that modern civilization has considerably diminished the latitude of what judges or juries are likely to think reasonable and moderate correction (a).

Of custodians of lunatics, etc. Persons having the lawful custody of a lunatic, and those acting by their direction, are justified in using such reasonable and moderate restraint as is necessary to prevent the lunatic from doing mischief to himself or others, or required, according to competent opinion, as part of his treatment. This may be regarded as a quasi-paternal power; but I conceive the

---

(z) Blackstone, 1 452. See modern examples collected in Addison on Torts, 5th ed p 115

(a) The ancient right of a husband to beat his wife moderately (F N B 80 F 239 A) was discredited by Blackstone (1 445) and is not recognized at this day, but as a husband and wife cannot in any case sue one another for assault in a civil court, this does not concern us. As to imprisonment of a wife by a husband, *Reg v Jackson*, '91. 1 Q B, 671, 60 L J Q B 346, C A

114, 76 Am. Dec 156, Patterson v. Nutter, 78 Mo. 50; 8 Eastern Rep 662, 57 Am Rep 818, Morrow v. Wood, 35 Wis. 59

The hirer of convicts is not *in loco parentis*. Cornell v State, 6 Lea, 624, Prewitt v State, 51 Ala 33.

Nor is the keeper of an almshouse. State v. Hull, 34 Conn. 132 Unless to preserve present order. State v Neff, 58 Ind 516.

Although the supreme court of North Carolina declared in State v. Rhodes, (Phill L 453), that a husband has a right to whip his wife with "a stick as large as his finger but not larger than his thumb," this decision was in recognition of a barbarous custom which modern authorities condemn. Fulgham v State, 46 Ala. 143, State v Oliver, 70 N C. 60, Shackett v Shackett, 49 Vt 195, Gholston v Gholston, 31 Ga. 625, Edmond's App 57 Pa St. 232, Commonwealth v. McAfee, 108 Mass. 458, 11 Am App 383

person entrusted with it is bound to use more diligence in informing himself what treatment is proper than a parent is bound (I mean, can be held bound in a court of law) to use in studying the best method of education. The standard must be more strict as medical science improves. A century ago lunatics were beaten, confined in dark rooms, and the like. Such treatment could not be justified now, though then it would have been unjust to hold the keeper criminally or civilly liable for not having more than the current wisdom of experts. In the case of a drunken man, or one deprived of self-control by a fit or other accident, the use of moderate restraint, as well for his own benefit as to prevent him from doing mischief to others, may in the same way be justified.

6.— *Authorities of Necessity*

Of the master of a ship. The master of a merchant ship has by reason of necessity the right of using force to preserve order and discipline for the safety of the vessel and the persons and property on board. Thus, if he has

---

Of the master of a ship. The authority of the master of a vessel to punish those on board is limited to the preservation of discipline and the ship's safety, and it must not be excessive. It is not co-extensive with the authority of a parent or schoolmaster. Bangs v. Little, 1 Ware, 506, United States v. Alden, 1 Sprague, 95, Cushman v. Ryan, 1 Story, 91, Turner's Case, 1 Ware, 83, Wilson v The Mary, Gilp. 31, Michaelson v Dennison, 3 Day, 294, Brown v Howard, 14 Johns. 119, Sampson v. Smith, 15 Mass 365, Henning v Ball, 1 Bay, 3; Mathews v Torrey, 10 Conn. 455, Allen v Hallet, 1 Abb Adm 573; Payne v. Allen, 2 Sprague, 84, Schelter v York, Crabbe, 499, Jay v Almy, 1 Woodb & M. 262, Butler v McLellan, 1 Ware, 219, Padmore v. Pietz, 44 Fed. Rep 104, Addington v Smith, 13 Conn 334

Many of the foregoing cases contain extremes in the conduct of masters and the opinions of courts which would hardly be sanctioned in this time by a changed sentiment

Upon the theory of "homicide by necessity" see Arp v State (Ala.), 11 So. Rep. 301, where the authorities are collated and reviewed.

reasonable cause to believe that any sailor or passenger is about to raise a mutiny, he may arrest and confine him. The master may even be justified in a case of extreme danger in inflicting punishment without any form of inquiry. But "in all cases which will admit of the delay proper for inquiry, due inquiry should precede the act of punishment; and . . . the party charged should have the benefit of that rule of universal justice, of being heard in his own defence" (*b*). In fact, when the immediate emergency of providing for the safety and discipline of the ship is past, the master's authority becomes a quasi-judicial one. There are conceivable circumstances in which the leader of a party on land, such as an Alpine expedition, might be justified on the same principle in exercising compulsion to assure the common safety of the party. But such a case, though not impossible, is not likely to occur for decision.

7.—*Damage incident to authorized Acts.*

Damage incidentally resulting from act not unlawful. Thus far we have dealt with cases where some special relation of the parties justifies or excuses the intentional doing

---

(*b*) Lord Stowell, *The Agincourt* (1824) 1 Hagg. 271, 274. This judgment is the classical authority on the subject. For further references see Maude and Pollock's Merchant Shipping, 4th ed. 1. 127.

Damage incidentally resulting from an act not unlawful. Upon this subject it is said by the court in Losee *v*. Buchanan (51 N. Y. 484, 10 Am. Rep. 623): "By becoming a member of civilized society, I am compelled to give up many of my natural rights, but I receive more than a compensation from the surrender of every other man of the same right, and the security, advantage and protection which the laws give me. So, too, the general rules that I may have the exclusive and undisturbed use and possession of my real estate, and that I must so use my real estate as not to injure my neighbor, are much modified by the exigencies of the social state."

For injuries from lawful acts done in a lawful manner the law gives no redress. There must be a concurrence of wrong and damage. Accord-

of things which otherwise would be actionable wrongs. We now come to another and in some respects a more interesting and difficult category. Damage suffered in consequence of an act done by another person, not for that intent, but for some other purpose of his own, and not in itself unlawful, may for various reasons be no ground of action. The general precept of law is commonly stated to be "Sic utere tuo ut alienum non laedas." If this were literally and universally applicable, a man would act at his peril whenever and wherever he acted otherwise than as the servant of the law. Such a state of things would be intolerable. It would be impossible, for example, to build or repair a wall, unless in the middle of an uninhabited plain. But the precept is understood to be subject to large exceptions. Its real use is to warn us against the abuse of the more popular adage that "a man has a right to do as he likes with his own" (c), which cuts much more dangerously on the other side.

(c) Cf. Gaius (D 50, 17, de div. reg.) 'Nullus videtur dolo facere, qui suo iure utitur.'

ingly it is said in Phelps v. Nowlen (72 N. Y. 16.) "The maxim sic utere tuo est alienum non laedas applies only to cases where the act complained of violates some right, and an act legal in itself violating no right cannot be made actionable upon the ground of the motive which induced it." See National Copper Co. v. The Minnesota Mining Co., 57 Mich. 83, Lord v. Carbon Iron Mfg. Co., 12 N. J. Eq. 147, Lachat v. Lutz (Ky.), 22 S. W. Rep. 218, Victory v. Baker, 67 N. Y. 366; Chatfield v. Wilson, 28 Vt. 49, Kiff v. Youmans, 86 N. Y. 325, Burroughs v. Housatonic R. Co., 15 Id. 124, Paxton v. Boyer, 67 Ill. 132, 16 Am. Rep. 615, Flint etc. R. Co. v. Detroit etc. R. Co., 64 Mich. 350, 31 N. W. Rep. 281; Larmore v. Crown Point Iron Co., 101 N. Y. 391, 4 N. E. Rep. 752, Bizzell v. Brooker, 16 Ark. 308, Heywood v. Tillson, 75 Me. 225, De Bawn v. Bean, 29 Hun, 2.6, Pennsylvania Coal Co. v. Sanderson, 113 Pa. St. 126; Bullard v. Saratoga Victory Mfg. Co., 77 N. Y. 525, Williams v. Pomeroy Coal Co., 37 Ohio St. 583, Grand Rapids Street Ry. Case, 48 Mich. 433, Watson v. City of Kingston, 114 N. Y. 88; 21 N. E. Rep. 102, Griffin v. Ohio & M. Ry. Co., 124 Ind. 326, 24 N. E. Rep. 888.

A builder in a large city is responsible for greater care in construction than would be required in the same work in the country. Gigg v. Vetter, 41 Ind. 228, Hoyt v. Jeffers, 30 Mich. 381.

There are limits to what a man may do with his own; and if he does that which may be harmful to his neighbour, it is his business to keep within those limits. Neither the Latin nor the vernacular maxim will help us much, however, to know where the line is drawn. The problems raised by the apparent opposition of the two principles must be dealt with each on its own footing. We say apparent; for the law has not two objects, but one, that is, to secure men in the enjoyment of their rights and of their due freedom of action. In its most general form, therefore, the question is, where does the sphere of a man's proper action end, and aggression on the sphere of his neighbour's action begin?

Damage from execution of authorized works. The solution is least difficult for the lawyer when the question has been decided in principle by a sovereign legislature. Parliament has constantly thought fit to direct or authorize the doing of things which but for that direction and authority might be actionable wrongs. Now a man cannot be held a wrong-doer in a court of law for acting in conformity with the direction or allowance of the supreme

---

Damage from execution of authorized works. The fifth amendment to the constitution of the United States forbids that "private property be taken for public use without just compensation." In the constitutions of probably all the States similar provisions are incorporated. In construing these provisions the courts have generally held, that damages not direct but merely *incidental* to the establishment of public works under the power of eminent domain constituted *damnum absque injuria*. To remove this hardship upon the property owners many of the states have provided in their several constitutions that private property shall not be "taken, damaged or destroyed" without compensation. See Constitutions of Ala., Ariz., Cal., Colo., Ga., Ill., La., Me., Mass., Mich., Minn., Mo., Neb., Nev., N Y., N J., R. S., Tex., Va., Vt., W Va.

Under these provisions, a property owner may recover for the diminution in value of his property caused by the noise, smoke and vibration incident to the operation of a railroad. Gainesville etc R. Co. v Hall, 78 Tex 169, 14 S. W. Rep 259, Moses v Manhattan R. Co., 58 Hun, 611, 13 N. Y. S. Rep. 46, Omaha etc R Co v Janecek, 30 Neb 276, 46 N W Rep. 478, Fox v. Baltimore R Co., 34 W Va 466, 12 S E Rep. 757.

legal power in the State. In other words "no action will lie for doing that which the Legislature has authorized, if it be done without negligence, although it does occasion damage to any one." The meaning of the qualification will appear immediately. Subject thereto, "the remedy of the party who suffers the loss is confined to recovering such compensation" (if any) "as the Legislature has thought fit to give him" (d). Instead of the ordinary question whether a wrong has been done, there can only be a question whether the special power which has been exercised is coupled, by the same authority that created it, with a special duty to make compensation for incidental damage. The authorities on this subject are voluminous and discursive, and exhibit notable differences of opinion. Those differences, however, turn chiefly on the application of admitted principles to particular facts, and on the construction of particular enactments. Thus it has been disputed whether the compensation given by statute to persons who are "injuriously affected" by authorized railway works, and by the same statutes deprived of their common-law rights of action, was or was not co-extensive with the rights of action expressly or by implication taken away, and it has been decided, though not without doubts and weighty dissent, that in some cases a party who has suffered material loss is left without either ordinary or special remedy (e).

No action for unavoidable damage. Apart from the question of statutory compensation, it is settled that no

(d) Lord Blackburn, *Geddis v Proprietors of Bann Reservoir* (1878), 3 App. Ca. at p 455, *Caledonian R. Co. v. Walker's Trustees*, (1882), 7 App Ca at p 293, *Mersey Docks Trustees v Gibbs* (1864-6), L R. 1 H L at p 112
(e) *Hammersmith R Co v Brand* (1869), L R 4 H L 171, 38 L J Q B 265

No action for unavoidable damage. There are numerous American railroad cases agreeing with the text. See *Pennsylvania Co etc v Pennsylvania S. V R. Co*, 151 Pa St 334, 25 At. Rep 107, 31 W N. C 30, *Abbott v Kansas City etc. R Co.*, 83 Mo 271, *Dooley Block v. Salt Lake*

action can be maintained for loss or inconvenience which is the necessary consequence of an authorized thing being done in an authorized manner. A person dwelling near a railway constructed under the authority of Parliament for the purpose of being worked by locomotive engines cannot complain of the noise and vibration caused by trains passing and repassing in the ordinary course of traffic, however unpleasant he may find it (*f*); nor of damage caused by the escape of sparks from the engines, if the company has used due caution to prevent such escape so far as practicable (*g*). So, where a corporation is empowered to make a river navigable, it does not thereby become bound to keep the bed of the river clear beyond what is required for navigation, though an incidental result of the navigation works may be the growth of weeds and accumulation of silt to the prejudice of riparian owners (*h*).

(*f*) *Hammersmith R. Co. v. Brand*, last note, confirming and extending *Rex v. Pease* (1832), 4 B. & Ad. 30, where certain members and servants of the Stockton and Darlington Railway Company were indicted for a nuisance to persons using a high road near and parallel to the railway. Lord Bramwell must have forgotten his authority when he said in the Court of Appeal that *Rex v. Pease* was wrongly decided (5 Q. B. D. 601).

(*g*) *Vaughan v. Taff Vale R. Co.* (1860), L. R. 5 H. & N. 679, 29 L. J. Ex. 247. See below in Ch. VII. So of noise made by pumps in the authorized sinking of a shaft near a man's land or house. *Harrison v. Southwark and Vauxhall Water Co.*, '91, 2 Ch. 409, 60 L. J. Ch. 630.

(*h*) *Cracknell v. Corporation of Thetford* (1869), L. R. 4 C. P. 629, 38 L. J. C. P. 353, decided partly on the ground that the corporation were not even entitled

---

Rapids Transit Co. (Utah), 33 Pac. Rep. 229, Dean v. Ann Arbor St. Ry. Co., 93 Mich. 330, 53 N. W. Rep. 396, Jones v. Erie & W. V. R. Co., 151 Pa. St. 30, 25 At. Rep. 134, 31 W. C. 1, Kansas N. & D. Ry. Co. v. Mahler, 45 Kan. 565, 26 Pac. Rep. 22, Finch v. Riverside & A. Ry. Co., 87 Cal. 597, 25 Pac. Rep. 765, Ransom v. Citizens' Ry. Co., 104 Mo. 375, 16 S. W. Rep. 416.

In Hamilton v. Vicksburg etc. R. Co. (119 U. S. 280, affirming Escanaba v. Chicago, 107 U. S. 678) it was held, that where the building of a bridge authorized by law was delayed by unusual rains and the work thus unavoidably prolonged, plaintiff, whose vessel was thereby prevented from passing beyond the bridge, suffered *damnum absque injuria*. See Cardwell v. American Bridge Co., 113 U. S. 205, Losee v. Buchanan, 51 N. Y. 484, 10 Am. Rep. 623, Mills v. United States, 46 Fed. Rep. 738, Kansas City, etc. R. Co. v. St. Joseph Terminal R. Co., 97 Mo. 457, 10 S. W. Rep. 826.

Care and caution required in exercise of discretionary powers. But in order to secure this immunity the powers conferred by the Legislature must be exercised without

to enter on land which did not belong to them to remove weeds, &c., for any purposes beyond those of the navigation. A rather similar case, but decided the other way in the last resort on the construction of the particular statute there in question, is *Geddis v. Proprietors of Bann Reservoir*, 3 App. Ca. 430. *Cracknell's case* seems just on the line, *cp. Biscoe v. G. J. R. Co* below.

Care and caution required in exercise of discretionary powers. It is a settled principle that in the exercise of authority granted by law due care must be used, and that negligence or excess therein invokes responsibility for the results. King v Burrough of Mary, 152 Pa. St. 30; 25 At. Rep. 161, Id. 152 Pa. St. 37, 25 At. Rep. 162, Martin v Chicago, etc., 47 Mo. App. 452, Leavenworth, N. & S. Ry. Co. v. Curton (Kan.), 33 Pac. Rep. 297, McNulta v. Ralston, 5 Ohio Cir. Ct. Rep. 330; Griffin v. Shreveport & A. R. Co., 41 La. An. 808, 6 So. Rep. 624; Pennsylvania S. V. R. Co. v. Walsh, 124 Pa. St. 544, 17 At. Rep. 23 W. N. C. 121; City of Durango v. Luttrell (Col.), 31 Pac. Rep. 853, City of Bloomington v. Chicago & A. R. Co., 134 Ill. 151, 26 N. E. Rep. 366, Rockwood v. Wilson, 11 Cush. 221, Burely v. Town of Lake, 30 Ill. App. 23, Georgetown etc. R. Co. v. Doyle, 9 Col. 549, 30 Am. & Eng. R. Cas. 231, Brewer v. Boston etc. R. Co., 113 Mass. 52; Gudger v. Western etc. R. Co., 87 N. C. 325, 19 Am. & Eng. R. Cas. 144; Hazen v. Boston etc. Co., 2 Gray, 574, Memphis etc. R. Co. v. Hicks, 5 Sneed (Tenn.), 427, Lake Shore etc. R. Co. v. Hutchins, 37 Ohio St. 282, 4 Am. & Eng. R. Cas. 219, Cairo etc. R. Co. v. Worsley, 85 Ill. 370, Brown v. Cayuga etc. R. Co., 12 N. Y. 486, Shaw v. New York etc. R. Co., 159 Mass. 182, 41 Am. & Eng. R. Cas. 517.

A municipality is liable for the removal of lateral support when the result is apparent and could have been prevented. Parke v. City of Seattle, 5 Wash. St. 1; 31 Pac. Rep. 310, Stearns v. City of Richmond, 88 Va. 992, 14 S. E. Rep. 847, Nichols v. City of Duluth, 40 Minn. 389, 42 N. W. Rep. 84, McCullough v. St. Paul, M. & M. Ry. Co. (Minn.), 53 N. W. Rep. 802.

For damage resulting from the proper execution of lawful authority no action lies. Sedalia Gaslight Co. v. Mercer, 48 Mo. App. 644, Beseman v. Pennsylvania R. Co., 42 N. J. L. 221; 20 At. Rep. 169; Durand v. Borough of Ansonia, 57 Conn. 70, 17 At. Rep. 283, Iron Mountain R. Co. v. Bingham, 3 Pick. (Tenn.) 522, 11 S. W. Rep. 705, Bell v. Norfolk S. R. Co., 110 N. C. 21, 7 S. E. Rep. 767, Jones v. St. Louis etc. Ry. Co., 84 Mo. 151, Slattern v. Des Moines etc. R. Co., 29 Ia. 154, 4 Am. Rep. 205, Richardson v. Vermont etc. R. Co. 25 Vt. 465, 60 Am. Dec. 283, Ellis v Iowa City, 29 Ia. 229; Hatch v Vermont Cent. R. Co., 29 Vt. 49, Dodge v. Essex Co., 3 Metc. 380.

negligence, or, as it is perhaps better expressed, with judgment and caution (*i*). For damage which could not have been avoided by any reasonably practicable care on the part of those who are authorized to exercise the power, there is no right of action. But they must not do needless harm, and if they do, it is a wrong against which the ordinary remedies are available. If an authorized railway comes near my house, and disturbs me by the noise and vibration of the trains, it may be a hardship to me, but it is no wrong. For the railway was authorized and made in order that trains might be run upon it, and without noise and vibration trains cannot be run at all. But if the company makes a cutting, for example, so as to put my house in danger of falling, I shall have my action, for they need not bring down my house to make their cutting. They can provide support for the house, or otherwise conduct their works more carefully. "When the company can construct its works without injury to private rights, it is in general bound to do so" (*k*). Hence there is a material distinction between cases where the Legislature "directs that a thing shall at all events be done" (*l*), and those where it only gives a discretionary power with choice of times and places. Where a discretion is given, it must be exercised with regard to the common rights of others. A public body which is by statute empowered to set up hospitals within a certain area, but not empowered to set up a hospital on any specified site, or required to set up any hospital at all, is not protected from liability if a hospital established under this power is a nuisance to the neighbors (*m*). And even where a particular thing is required to be done, the burden of proof is on the person who has to do it to show that it cannot be done without

(*i*) Per Lord Truro, *L. & N. W. R. Co. v. Bradley* (1851), 3 Mac. & G. at p. 341.
(*k*) *Biscoe v. G. E. R. Co.* (1873), 16 Eq. 636.
(*l*) 6 App. Ca. 203.
(*m*) *Metropolitan Asylum District v. Hill* (1881), 6 App. Ca. 193.

creating a nuisance (n). A railway company is authorized to acquire land within specified limits, and on any part of that land to erect workshops. This does not justify the company, as against a particular householder, in building workshops so situated (though within the authorized limits) that the smoke from them is a nuisance to him in the occupation of his house (o). But a statutory power to carry cattle by railway, and provide station yards and other buildings for the reception of cattle and other things to be carried (without specification of particular places or times) is incidental to the general purposes for which the railway was authorized, and the use of a piece of land as a cattle yard under this power, though such as would be a nuisance at common law, does not give any right of action to adjoining occupiers (p). Such a case falls within the principle not of *Metropolitan Asylum District* v. *Hill*, but of *Rea* v. *Pease*.

A gas company was authorized by statute to have its pipes laid under certain streets, and was required to supply gas to the inhabitants. The vestry, being charged by statute with the repair of the streets, but not required or authorized to use any special means, used steam rollers of such weight that the company's pipes were often broken or injured by the resulting pressure through the soil. It was held that, even if the use of such rollers was in itself the best way of repairing the streets in the interest of the ratepayers and the public, the act of the vestry was wrongful as against the gas company, and was properly restrained by injunction (q).

(n) *Attorney General* v. *Gaslight and Coke Co* (1877), 7 Ch. D 217, 221, 47 L J Ch 534.

(o) *Ramohun Bose* v *East India R Co* (High Court, Calcutta), 10 Ben L R 241. Qu whether this be consistent with the case next cited.

(p) *London and Brighton R Co* v *Truman* (1885), 11 App Ca 45, 55 L J Ch 354, reversing the decision of the Court of Appeal, 29 Ch. Div 89.

(q) *Gas Light and Coke Co* v *Vestry of St Mary Abbott's* (1885), 15 Q B Div 1, 54 L J Q B 414. The Court also relied, but only by way of confirmation, on certain special Acts dealing with the relations between the vestry and the company. See 15 Q B D at p 6.

"An Act of Parliament may authorize a nuisance, and if it does so, then the nuisance which it authorizes may be lawfully committed. But the authority given by the Act may be an authority which falls short of authorizing a nuisance. It may be an authority to do certain works provided that they can be done without causing a nuisance, and whether the authority falls within that category is again a question of construction. Again the authority given by Parliament may be to carry out the works without a nuisance, if they can be so carried out, but in the last resort to authorize a nuisance if it is necessary for the construction of the works" (r).

An authority accompanied by compulsory powers, or to be exercised concurrently with authorities *ejusdem generis* which are so accompanied, will, it seems, be generally treated as absolute; but no single test can be assigned as decisive (s).

---

8. — *Inevitable Accident.*

Inevitable accident resulting from lawful act. In the cases we have just been considering the act by which the damage is caused has been specially authorized. Let us now turn to the class of cases which differ from these in that the act is not specially authorized, but is simply an act which, in itself, a man may lawfully do then and there; or (it is perhaps better to say) which he may do without breaking any positive law. We shall assume from the first that there is no want of reasonable care on the actor's part. For it is undoubted that if by failure in due care I cause harm to another, however innocent my intention, I am liable. This has already been noted in a general way (t). No less is it certain, on the other hand, that I am not

---

(r) Bowen L. J., 29 Ch. D. at p. 108
(s) See especially Lord Blackburn's opinion in *London and Brighton R. Co. v. Truman.*
(t) P. 35, above.

answerable for mere omission to do anything which it was not my specific duty to do.

It is true that the very fact of an accident happening is commonly some evidence, and may be cogent evidence, of want of due care. But that is a question of fact, and there remain many cases in which accidents do happen notwithstanding that all reasonable and practicable care is used. Even the "consummate care" of an expert using special precaution in a matter of special risk or importance is not always successful. Slight negligence may be divided by a very fine line from unsuccessful diligence. But the distinction is real, and we have here to do only with the class of cases where the facts are so given or determined as to exclude any negligence whatever.

Conditions of the inquiry. The question, then, is reduced to this, whether an action lies against me for harm resulting by inevitable accident from an act lawful in itself, and done by me in a reasonable and careful manner. Inevitable accident is not a verbally accurate term, but can hardly mislead; it does not mean absolutely inevitable (for, by the supposition, I was not bound to act at all), but it means not avoidable by any such precaution as a reasonable man, doing such an act then and there, could be expected to take. In the words of Chief Justice Shaw of Massachusetts, it is an accident such as the defendant could not have avoided by use of the kind and degree of care necessary to the exigency, and in the circumstances, in which he was placed.

On principle such action excludes liability. It may seem to modern readers that only one solution of the problem thus stated is possible, or rather that there is no problem at all (*u*). No reason is apparent for not accept-

(*u*) This, at any rate, is the view of modern juries; see *Nichols* v *Marsland* (1875), L. R. 10 Ex. at p. 256, 46 L. J. Ex. 174, *Holmes* v *Mather*, L. R. 10 Ex. at p. 262.

ing inevitable accident as an excuse. It is true that we may suppose the point not to have been considered at all in an archaic stage of law, when legal redress was but a mitigation of the first impulse of private revenge. But private revenge has disappeared from our modern law; moreover we do not nowadays expect a reasonable man to be angry without inquiry. He will not assume, in a case admitting of doubt, that his neighbour harmed him by design or negligence. And one cannot see why a man is to be made an insurer of his neighbour against harm which (by our hypothesis) is no fault of his own. For the doing of a thing lawful in itself with due care and caution cannot be deemed any fault. If the stick which I hold in my hand, and am using in a reasonable manner and with reasonable care, hurts my neighbour by pure accident, it is not apparent why I should be liable more than if the stick had been in another man's hand (*v*). If we go far back enough, indeed, we shall find a time and an order of ideas in which the thing itself that does damage is primarily liable, so to speak, and through the thing its owner is made answerable. That order of ideas was preserved in the noxal actions of Roman law, and in our own criminal law by the forfeiture of the offending object which had moved, as it was said, to a man's death, under the name of deodand. But this is matter of history, not of modern legal policy. So much we may concede, that when a man's act is the apparent cause of mischief, the burden of proof is on him to show that the consequence was not one which by due diligence he could have prevented (*x*). But

(*v*) Trespass for assault by striking the plaintiff with a stick thrown by the defendant. Plea, not guilty. The jury were directed that, in the absence of evidence for what purpose the defendant threw the stick, they might conclude it was for a proper purpose, and the striking the plaintiff was a mere accident for which the defendant was not answerable. *Alderson* v. *Waistell* (1844), 1 C. & K. 358 (before Rolfe B.) This, if it could be accepted, would prove more than is here contended for. But it is evidently a rough and ready summing-up given without reference to the books.

(*x*) Shaw C. J. would not concede even this in the leading Massachusetts case of *Brown* v. *Kendall*, 6 Cush. at p. 297.

so does (and must) the burden of proving matter of justification or excuse fall in every case on the person taking advantage of it. If he were not, on the first impression of the facts, a wrong-doer, the justification or excuse would not be needed.

Apparent conflict of authorities. We believe that our modern law supports the view now indicated as the rational one, that inevitable accident is not a ground of liability. But there is a good deal of appearance of authority in the older books for the contrary proposition that a man must answer for all direct consequences of his voluntary acts at any rate, or as Judge O. W. Holmes (*y*) has put it " acts at his peril." Such seems to have been the early Germanic law (*z*), and such was the current opinion of English lawyers until the beginning of this century, if not later. On the other hand, it will be seen on careful examination that no actual decision goes the length of the dicta which embody this opinion. In almost every case the real question turns out to be of the form of action or pleading. Moreover, there is no such doctrine in Roman or modern Continental jurisprudence (*a*); and this, although for us not conclusive or even authoritative, is worth considering whenever our own authorities admit of doubt on a point of general principle. And, what is more important for our purpose, the point has been decided in the sense here contended for by Courts of the highest authority in the

(*y*) See on the whole of this matter Mr Justice Holmes's chapter on "Trespass and Negligence"

(*z*) Heusler, Inst des deutschen Privatrechts, ii 263, Ll Hen Primi, c. 88 § 6, 90 § 11, see p 129, below.

(*a*) "Inpunitus est qui sine culpa et dolo malo casu quodam damnum committit." Gai 3. 211. Paulus indeed says (D. 9 2, ad legem Aquiliam, 45, § 4), " Si defendendi mei causa lapidem in adversarium misero, sed non eum sed praetereuntem percussero, tenebor lege Aquilia, illum enim solum qui vim infert ferire con-

ceditur." But various explanations of this are possible Perhaps it shows what kind of cases are referred to by the otherwise unexplained dictum of Ulpian in the preceding fragment, " in lege Aquilia et levissima culpa venit " Paulus himself says there is no *iniuria* if the master of a slave, meaning to strike the slave, accidentally strikes a free man D. 47. 10, de iniuriis, 4. According to the current English theory of the 16th-18th centuries an action on the case would not lie on such facts, but trespass *vi et armis* would.

United States. To these decisions we shall first call attention.

American decisions; The Nitro-glycerine Case. In *The Nitro-glycerine Case* (b) the defendants, a firm of

(b) 15 Wall 524 (1872)

Inevitable accident resulting from lawful act. An unexpected injury caused by operation of nature or by a person without intention or negligence is an accident

In the case of Morris v Platt (32 Conn. 75, post, p 201), accidents are classified by the court, as follows "In the first class are all those which are *inevitable* or absolutely unavoidable, because effected or influenced by uncontrollable operations of nature, In the second class are those which result from human agency alone, but were unavoidable *under the circumstances;* and the third class, those which were *avoidable,* because the act was not called for by any duty or necessity and the injury resulted from the want of extraordinary care which the law reasonably requires from one doing such a lawful act, or because the accident was the result of actual folly, and might with reasonable care adapted to the exigency have been avoided" It is well established law that for damage caused by a lawful accident no recovery can be had. Strouse v. Whitlesy, 41 Conn. 559, DeFrancis v Spencer, 2 Greene (Iowa), 46°, Schneider v Provident etc Co, 24 Wis. 28, Gault v. Humes, 20 Md 304, Worheide v. Missouri C & T Co, 32 Mo App. 367, Brown v. Collins, 53 N. H. 442, Schroeder v Michigan Car Co, 56 Mich 132, Lewis v. Flint & P. M Ry Co, 54 Mich. 55, Richards v Rough, 53 Mich 212, Gould v. Stater Woolen Co., 147 Mass 315; 17 N. E Rep 531; Allison Mfg. Co. v McCormick, 118 Pa St 519, 12 At. Rep 273; McCauley v. Logan, 152 Pa. St. 202, 25 At Rep. 490; 31 W N C 437, Chicago etc Ry Co. v. Becker, 38 Ill. App 523, Grant v Union Pac Ry. Co, 45 Fed. Rep. 673, Klupp v United Ice Lines, 15 N Y. S Rep 597; McCaffrey v. Twenty-third St R. Co, 47 Hun, 404, Haskins v. Stewart, 57 Hun, 380, 10 N. Y S Rep 833, Brown v Boom Co, 109 Pa. St 57, 1 At Rep 156; Lansing v. Stone, 37 Barb 15, Wabash etc. Ry. Co. v. Locke, 112 Ind 404, 14 N. E Rep. 391, Frost v. Grand Trunk R Co., 10 Allen, 387, Kohn v. Lovett, 44 Ga 251; Cahils v Layton, 57 Wis. 600, Burton v. Davis, 15 La An 448, Sikes v. Sheldon, 58 Ia 744, Wright v Clark, 50 Vt 130, 28 Am. Rep 496, Nelson v Chicago etc Ry Co, 30 Minn. 47

In Standard Oil Co. v. Tierney (Ky — 17 S. W Rep 1025), a shipper of a quantity of naptha was held to be bound to so mark the barrels that the employés of the carrier, in the exercise of ordinary prudence, would ascertain the explosive nature of the goods, and whether the brand mentioned was sufficient for its purpose was a question for the jury.

carriers, received a wooden case at New York to be carried to California. "There was nothing in its appearance calculated to awaken any suspicion as to its contents," and in fact nothing was said or asked on that score. On arrival at San Francisco it was found that the contents (which "had the appearance of sweet oil") were leaking. The case was then, according to the regular course of business, taken to the defendants' offices (which they rented from the plaintiff) for examination. A servant of the defendants proceeded to open the case with a mallet and chisel. The contents, being in fact nitro-glycerine, exploded. All the persons present were killed, and much property destroyed and the building damaged. The action was brought by the landlord for this last-mentioned damage, including that suffered by parts of the building let to other tenants as well as by the offices of the defendants. Nitro-glycerine had not then (namely, in 1866) become a generally known article of commerce, nor were its properties well known. It was found as a fact that the defendants had not, nor had any of the persons concerned in handling the case, knowledge or means of knowledge of its dangerous character, and that the case had been dealt with "in the same way that other cases of similar appearance were usually received and handled, and in the mode that men of prudence engaged in the same business would have handled cases having a similar appearance in the ordinary course of business when ignorant of their contents." The defendants admitted their liability as for waste as to the premises occupied by them (which in fact they repaired as soon as possible after the accident), but disputed it as to the rest of the building.

Doctrine of Supreme Court; no liability for accidental result of lawful act without negligence. The Circuit Court held the defendants were not further liable than they had admitted, and the Supreme Court of the United States affirmed the judgment. It was held that in the first place the defendants were not bound to know, in the absence of reasonable grounds of suspicion, the contents of packages offered them for carriage; and next, that without such knowledge in fact and without negligence they were not liable for damage caused by the accident (c). "No one is responsible for injuries resulting from unavoidable accident, whilst engaged in a lawful business. . . . . The measure of care against accident which one must take to avoid responsibility is that which a person of ordinary prudence and caution would use if his own interests were to be affected and the whole risk were his own."

Brown v. Kendall (Massachusetts). The Court proceeded to cite with approval the case of *Brown v. Kendall* in the Supreme Court of Massachusetts (d). There the plaintiff's and the defendant's dogs were fighting; the defendant was beating them in order to separate them, and the plaintiff looking on. "The defendant retreated backwards from before the dogs, striking them as he retreated; and as he approached the plaintiff, with his back towards him, in raising his stick over his shoulder in order to strike the dogs, he accidentally hit the plaintiff in the eye, inflicting upon him a severe injury." The action was trespass for assault and battery. It was held that the act of the defendant in itself "was a lawful and proper act which he might do by proper and safe means;" and that if "in doing this act, using due care and all proper precautions necessary to the exigency of the case to avoid hurt to others, in raising his stick for that purpose, he accidentally hit the plaintiff in the eye and wounded him, this was the result of pure accident, or was involuntary and unavoidable (e), and therefore the action

---

(c) The plaintiff's proper remedy would have been against the consignor who despatched the explosive without informing the carriers of its nature See *Lyell v. Ganga Dai* (1875), Indian Law Rep 1 All 60

(d) 6 Cush. 292 (1850)

(e) The consequence was involuntary or rather unintended, though the act itself was voluntary, and it was also unavoidable. *i. e.* not preventable by reasonable diligence

would not lie." All that could be required of the defendant was "the exercise of due care adapted to the exigency of the case." The rule in its general form was thus expressed: "If, in the prosecution of a lawful act, a casualty purely accidental arises, no action can be supported for an injury arising therefrom."

Other American cases: contrary opinion in Castle v. Duryee (N. Y.). There have been like decisions in the Supreme Courts of New York (*f*) and Connecticut. And these rulings appear to be accepted as good law throughout the United States (*g*). The general agreement of American authority and opinion is disturbed, indeed, by one modern case in the Court of Appeal of New York, that of *Castle v. Duryee* (*h*). But the conflicting element is not in the decision itself, nor in anything necessary to it. The defendant was the colonel of a regiment of New York militia, who at the time of the cause of action were firing blank cartridge under his immediate orders in the course of a review. The plaintiff was one of a crowd of spectators who stood in front of the firing line and about 350 feet from it. Upon one of the discharges the plaintiff was wounded by a bullet, which could be accounted for only by one of the men's pieces having by some misadventure been loaded with ball cartridge. It appeared that one company had been at target practice an hour or two before, and that at the end of the practice arms had been examined in the usual way (*i*), and surplus ammunition collected. Moreover, arms had again been inspected by the commanding officers of companies, in pursuance of the colonel's orders, before the line was formed for the regimental parade. The plaintiff sued the defendant in an action "in the

---

(*f*) *Harvey v. Dunn*, Lalor 193, cited 15 Wall. 539, *Morris v. Platt*, 32 Conn. 75.
(*g*) Cooley on Torts, 80.
(*h*) 2 Keyes, 169 (1865)
(*i*) It will be remembered that this was in the days of muzzle loaders. A like accident, however, happened not many years ago at an Aldershot field day, fortunately without hurt to any one.

nature of trespass for an assault." A verdict for the plaintiff was ultimately affirmed on appeal, the Court being of opinion that there was evidence of negligence. Knowing that some of the men had within a short time been in possession of ball ammunition, the defendant might well have done more. He might have cleared the front of the line before giving orders to fire. The Court might further have supported its decision, though it did not, by the cases which show that more than ordinary care, nay "consummate caution" (j), is required of persons dealing with dangerous weapons. The Chief Judge added that, as the injury was the result of an act done by the defendant's express command, the question of negligence was immaterial. But this was only the learned judge's individual opinion. It was not necessary to the decision, and there is nothing to show that the rest of the Court agreed to it (k).

English authorities: cases of trespass and shooting. We may now see what the English authorities amount to They have certainly been supposed to show that inevitable accident is no excuse when the immediate result of an act is complained of. Erskine said a century ago in his argument in the celebrated case of *The Dean of St. Asaph* (l) (and he said it by way of a familiar illustration of the difference between criminal and civil liability) that "if a man rising in his sleep walks into a china shop and breaks everything about him, his being asleep is a complete answer to an *indictment* for trespass (m), but he must answer in an *action* for everything he has broken." And Bacon had said earlier to the same purpose, that "if a man be killed by misad-

(j) Erle C. J obiter, in *Potter* v *Faulkner*, 1 B. & S at p 800, 31 L J Q B. 30, *Dixon* v *Bell*, 5 M. & S 198

(k) The reporter adds this significant note: "The Court did not pass upon the first branch of the case, discussed by the Chief Judge, as to the question of the general liability of the commanding officer"

(l) 21 St Tr 1022 (A D 1783)

(m) Would an indictment ever lie for simple trespass? I know not of any authority that it would, though the action of trespass originally had, and retained in form down to modern times, a public and penal character

venture, as by an arrow at butts, this hath a pardon of course: but if a man be hurt or maimed only, an action of trespass lieth, though it be done against the party's mind and will" (n). Stronger examples could not well be propounded. For walking in one's sleep is not a voluntary act at all, though possibly an act that might have been prevented: and the practice of archery was, when Bacon wrote, a positive legal duty under statutes as recent as Henry VIII.'s time, though on the other hand shooting is an extra-hazardous act (o). We find the same statement about accidents in shooting at a mark in the so-called laws of Henry I. (p), and in the arguments of counsel in a case in the Year-Book of Edward IV. where the general question was more or less discussed (q). Brian (then at the bar) gave in illustration a view of the law exactly contrary to that which was taken in *Brown* v. *Kendall*. But the decision was only that if A. cuts his hedge so that the cuttings *ipso invito* fall on B.'s land, this does not justify A. in entering on B.'s land to carry them off. And by Choke C. J. it is said, not that (as Brian's view would require) A. must keep his thorns from falling on B.'s land at all events, but that "he ought to show that he could not do it in any other way, or that he did all that was in his power to keep them out."

Weaver v. Ward. Another case usually cited is *Weaver* v. *Ward* (r). The plaintiff and the defendant were both members of a train-band exercising with powder, and the plaintiff was hurt by the accidental discharge of the defendant's piece. It is a very odd case to quote for the doctrine

(n) Maxims of the Law, Reg. 7, following the dictum of Rede J. in 21 Hen. VII. 28. We cite Bacon, not as a writer of authority, but as showing, like Erskine, the average legal mind of his time.

(o) O. W. Holmes, 103.

(p) C. 88 § 6 "Si quis in ludo sagittandi vel alicuius exercitii iaculo vel huiusmodi casu aliquem occidat, reddat eum, legis enim est, qui insclenter peccat, sclenter emendet." C. 90 § 11 adds an English form of the maxim "et qui brecht ungewealdes, bete gewealdes."

(q) 6 Edw. IV. 7, pl. 18, O. W. Holmes, 85, cf. 21 Hen. VII. 27, pl. 5, a case of trespass to goods which does not really raise the question.

(r) Hob. 134, A. D. 1616.

of absolute liability, for what was there holden was that in trespass no man shall be excused, "except it may be judged utterly without his fault;" and the defendant's plea was held bad because it only denied intention, and did not properly bring before the Court the question whether the accident was inevitable. A later case (s), which professes to follow *Weaver* v. *Ward*, really departs from it in holding that "unavoidable *necessity*" must be shown to make a valid excuse. This in turn was apparently followed in the next century, but the report is too meagre to be of any value (t).

All these, again, are shooting cases, and if they occurred at this day the duty of using extraordinary care with dangerous things would put them on a special footing. In the celebrated squib case they are cited and more or less relied upon (u). It is not clear to what extent the judges intended to press them. According to Wilson's report, inevitable accident was allowed by all the judges to be an excuse. But Blackstone's judgment, according to his own report, says that nothing but "inevitable necessity" will serve, and adopts the argument of Brian in the case of the cut thorns, mistaking it for a judicial opinion; and the other judgments are stated as taking the same line, though less explicitly. For the decision itself the question is hardly material, though Blackstone may be supposed to represent the view which he thought the more favourable to his own dissenting judgment. His theory was that

(s) *Dickeson* v *Watson*, Sir T Jones, 205, A D 1682 *Lambert* v *Bessey*, T Raym 421, a case of false imprisonment in the same period, cites the foregoing authorities, and Raymond's opinion certainly assumes the view that inevitable accident is no excuse even when the act is one of lawful self defence But then Raymond's opinion is a dissenting one S. C nom *Bessey* v *Olliott*, T. Raym 467, being given in the former place alone and without explanation, it has apparently been sometimes taken for the judgment of the Court. At most, therefore, his illustrations are evidence of the notions current at the time

(t) *Underwood* v. *Hewson*, 1 Strange, 596, A D. 1723 (defendant was uncocking a gun, plaintiff looking on) It looks very like contributory negligence, or at any rate voluntary exposure to the risk, on the plaintiff's part But the law of negligence was then quite undeveloped

(u) *Scott* v *Shepherd* (1773), 2 W. 892, 3 Wils 403.

liability in trespass (as distinguished from an action on the case) is unqualified as regards the immediate consequences of a man's act, but also is limited to such consequences.

Leame v. Bray. Then comes *Leame* v. *Bray* (x), a comparatively modern case, in which the defendant's chaise had run into the plaintiff's curricle on a dark night. The defendant was driving on the wrong side of the road; which of itself is want of due care, as every judge would now tell a jury as a matter of course. The decision was that the proper form of action was trespass and not case. Grose J. seems to have thought inevitable accident was no excuse, but this was extra-judicial. Two generations later, in *Rylands* v. *Fletcher*, Lord Cranworth inclined, or more than inclined, to the same opinion (y). Such is the authority for the doctrine of strict liability. Very possibly more dicta to the same purpose might be collected, but I do not think anything of importance has been left out (z). Although far from decisive, the weight of opinion conveyed by these various utterances is certainly respectable.

Cases where exception allowed. On the other hand we have a series of cases which appear even more strongly to imply, if not to assert, the contrary doctrine. A. and B. both set out in their vessels to look for an abandoned raft laden with goods. A. first gets hold of the raft, then B., and A's vessel is damaged by the wind and sea driving B.'s against it. On such facts the Court of King's Bench held in 1770 that A. could not maintain trespass, " being of opinion that the original act of the

---

(x) 3 East, 593 (A D 1803).
(y) (1868) L R 3 H L at p. 341.
(z) Sometimes the case of *James* v. *Campbell* (1832), 5 C & P. 372, is cited in this connexion But not only is it a Nisi Prius case with nothing particular to recommend it, but it is irrelevant. The facts there alleged were that A in a quarrel with B. struck C Nothing shows that A would have been justified or excused in striking B And if the blow he intended was not lawful, it was clearly no excuse that he struck the wrong man (p 29 above, and see *R* v *Latimer* (1886), 17 Q B D 359, 55 L J. M C 135).

defendants was not unlawful" (a). Quite early in the century it had been held that if a man's horse runs away with him, and runs over another man, he is not even *prima facie* a trespasser, so that under the old rules of pleading it was wrong to plead specially in justification (b). Here however it may be said there was no voluntary act at all on the defendant's part. In *Wakeman* v. *Robinson*, a modern running-down case (c), the Court conceded that "if the accident happened entirely without default on the part of the defendant, or blame imputable to him, the action does not lie;" thinking, however, that on the facts there was proof of negligence, they refused a new trial, which was asked for on the ground of misdirection in not putting it to the jury whether the accident was the result of negligence or not. In 1842 this declaration of the general rule was accepted by the Court of Queen's Bench, though the decision again was on the form of pleading (d).

Holmes v Mather. Lastly, we have two decisions well within our own time which are all but conclusive In *Holmes* v. *Mather* (e) the defendant was out with a pair of horses driven by his groom. The horses ran away, and the groom, being unable to stop them, guided them as best he could; at last he failed to get them clear round a corner, and they knocked down the plaintiff. If the driver had not attempted to turn the corner, they would have run straight into a shop-front, and (it was suggested) would not have touched the plaintiff at all. The jury found there was no negligence. Here the driver was certainly acting, for he was trying to turn the horses. And it was

---

(a) *Davis* v *Saunders*, 2 Chitty, 639
(b) *Gibbons* v *Pepper*, 1 Lord Raym 38
(c) 1 Bing 213 (1823). The argument for the defendant seems to have been very well reasoned
(d) *Hall* v *Fearnley* (1842), 3 Q B 919, 12 L. J Q B 22 The line between this and *Gibbons* v *Pepper* is rather fine
(e) L R 10 Ex 261, 44 L. J Ex. 176 (1875)

argued, on the authority of the old cases and dicta, that a trespass had been committed. The Court refused to take this view, but said nothing about inevitable accident in general. "For the convenience of mankind in carrying on the affairs of life, people as they go along roads must expect, or put up with, such mischief as reasonable care on the part of others cannot avoid" (f). Thus it seems to be made a question not only of the defendant being free from blame, but of the accident being such as is incident to the ordinary use of public roads. The same idea is expressed in the judgment of the Exchequer Chamber in *Rylands* v. *Fletcher*, where it is even said that all the cases in which inevitable accident has been held an excuse can be explained on the principle " that the circumstances were such as to show that the plaintiff had taken that risk upon himself " (g)

Stanley v. Powell. More lately, in *Stanley* v. *Powell* (h), Denman J. came, on the English authorities alone, to the conclusion above maintained, namely that, where negligence is negatived, an action does not lie for injury resulting by accident from another's lawful act.

Conclusion. These decisions seem good warrant for saying that the principle of *The Nitro-glycerine Case* and *Brown* v. *Kendall* is now part of the common law in England as well as in America. All this injury may be thought to belong not so much to the head of exceptions from liability as to the fixing of the principles of liability in the first instance. But such an inquiry must in practice always present itself under the form of determining whether the particular circumstances exclude liability for

(f) Bramwell B at p 267.
(g) L. R 1 Ex at pp 286, 287 But see per Lord Halsbury in *Smith* v *Baker*, '91, A C 325, 337, 60 L J Q B 683.
(h) '91, 1 Q B 86, 60 L. J. Q B 52. This was a shooting case (a pellet glanced from a bough and wounded the plaintiff's eye) A point might have been made for the plaintiff, but apparently was not, on the "extra hazardous" character of fire-arms

an act or consequence which is at first sight wrongful. The same remark applies, to some extent, to the class of cases which we take next in order.

---

9. — *Exercise of common Rights.*

Immunity in exercise of common rights. We have just left a topic not so much obscure in itself as obscured by the indirect and vacillating treatment of it in our authorities. That which we now take up is a well settled one in principle, and the difficulties have been only in fixing the limits of application. It is impossible to carry on the common affairs of life without doing various things which are more or less likely to cause loss or inconvenience to others, or even which obviously tend that way; and this in such a manner that their tendency cannot be remedied by any means short of not acting at all. Competition in business is the most obvious example. If John and Peter are booksellers in the same street, each of them must to some extent diminish the custom and profits of the other. So if they are shipowners employing ships in the same trade, or brokers in the same market. So if, instead of John and Peter, we take the three or four railway companies whose lines offer a choice of routes from London to the north. But it is needless to pursue examples. The relation of profits to competition is matter of common knowledge. To say that a man shall not seek profit in business at the expense of others is to say that he shall not do business at all, or that the whole constitution of society shall be altered. Like reasons apply to a man's use of his own land in the common way of husbandry, or otherwise for ordinary and lawful purposes. In short, life

---

Immunity in exercise of common rights. Closely analogous to this subject in their application are the cases cited under Damage Incidentally Resulting from an Act not Unlawful, *ante*, p. 152.

could not go on if we did not, as the price of our own free action, abide some measure of inconvenience from the equal freedom of our neighbours. In these matters *veniam primusque damusque vicissim*. Hence the rule of law that the exercise of ordinary rights for a lawful purpose and in a lawful manner is no wrong even if it causes damage (*i*). It is chiefly in this class of cases that we meet with the phrase or formula *damnum sine iniuria*, a form of words which, like many other Latin phrases and maxims, is too often thought to serve for an explanation, when in truth it is only an abridgment or *memoria technica* of the things to be explained. It is also of doubtful elegance as a technical phrase, though in general Latin literature *iniuria* no doubt had a sufficiently wide meaning (*k*). In English usage, however, it is of long standing (*l*).

The case of Gloucester Grammar School. A classical illustration of the rule is given by a case in the Year-Book of Henry IV., which has often been cited in modern books, and which is still perfectly good authority (*m*). The

---

(*i*) *A. G. v. Tomline* (1880), 14 Ch. Div. 58, 49 L. J. Ch. 377, is a curious case, but does not make any real exception to this. It shows that (1) the Crown as owner of foreshore has duties for the protection of the land, though not enforceable duties, (2) those duties, where the Crown rights have become vested in a subject, are laid upon and may be enforced against that subject.

(*k*) Ulpian wrote (D. 9. 1, si quadrupes, 1, § 3) "Pauperies est damnum sine iniuria facientis datum, nec enim potest animal iniuria fecisse, quod sensu caret." This is a very special context, and is far from warranting the use of "damnum sine iniuria" as a common formula. Being, however, adopted in the Institutes, 4, 9, pr. (with the unidiomatic variant "*iniuriam* fecisse"), it probably became, through Azo, the origin of the phrase now current. In Gaius 3. 211 (on the lex Aquilia) we read "Iniuria autem occidere intellegitur

cuius dolo aut culpa id acciderit, nec ulla alia lege damnum quod sine iniuria datur reprehenditur." This shows that "damnum sine iniuria dare" was a correct if not a common phrase though it could never have for Gaius or Ulpian the wide meaning "of harm [of any kind] which gives no cause of action." "Damnum sine iniuria" standing alone as a kind of compound noun, according to the modern use, is hardly good Latin.

(*l*) Bracton says, fo. 221 a. "Si quis in fundo proprio construat aliquod molendinum, et sectam suam et aliorum vicinorum subtrahat vicino, facit vicino damnum et non iniuriam." "Dampnum sine iniuria" occurs in 7 Ed. III. 65, pl. 67, "damnum absque iniuria" in 11 Hen. IV. 47, pl. 21 (see below).

(*m*) Hil. 11 Hen. IV. 47, pl. 21 (A.D. 1410–11). In the course of argument the opinion is thrown out that the education of children is a spiritual matter, and therefore the right of appointing a

action was trespass by two masters of the Grammar School of Gloucester against one who had set up a school in the same town, whereby the plaintiffs, having been wont to take forty pence a quarter for a child's schooling, now got only twelve pence. It was held that such an action could not be maintained. "*Damnum*," said Hankford J., "may be *absque injuria*, as, if I have a mill, and my neighbour build another mill, whereby the profit of my mill is diminished, I shall have no action against him, though it is damage to me . . . . but if a miller disturbs the water from flowing to my mill, or doth any nuisance of the like sort, I shall have such action as the law gives." If the plaintiffs here had shown a franchise in themselves, such as that claimed by the Universities, it might have been otherwise.

Case of mills. A case very like that of the mills suggested by Hankford actually came before the Court of Common Pleas a generation later (*n*), and Newton C. J. stated the law in much the same terms. Even if the owner of the ancient mill is entitled to sue those who of right ought to grind at his mill, and grind at the new one, he has not any remedy against the owner of the new mill. "He who hath a freehold in the vill may build a mill on his own ground, and this is wrong to no man." And the rule has ever since been treated as beyond question. Competition is in itself no ground of action, whatever damage it may cause. A trader can complain of his rival only if a definite exclusive right, such as a patent right, or the right to a trade-mark, is infringed, or if there is a wilful attempt to damage his business by injurious falsehood ("slander of title") or acts otherwise unlawful in themselves. Underselling is not a wrong, though the seller may purposely sell

school-master cannot be tried by a temporal court. The plaintiff tried to set up a *quasi* franchise as holding an ancient office in the gift of the Prior of Lantone, near Gloucester (*sic* probably Llanthony is meant).

(*n*) 22 Hen VI 14, pl 23 (A D 1443). The school case is cited

some article at unremunerative prices to attract custom for other articles; nor is it a wrong even to offer advantages to customers who deal with oneself to the exclusion of a rival (*o*).

"To say that a man is to trade freely, but that he is to stop short at any act which is calculated to harm other tradesmen, and which is designed to attract their business to his own shop, would be a strange and impossible counsel of perfection" (*p*). "To draw a line between fair and unfair competition, between what is reasonable and unreasonable, passes the power of the Courts. Competition exists where two or more persons seek to possess or to enjoy the same thing, it follows that the success of one must be the failure of another, and no principle of law enables us to interfere with or to moderate that success or that failure so long as it is due to mere competition" (*q*). There is "no restriction imposed by law on competition by one trader with another with the sole object of benefiting himself" (*r*).

Digging wells, &c., in a man's own land. Another group of authorities of the same class is that which establishes "that the disturbance or removal of the soil in a man's own land, though it is the means (by process of natural percolation) of drying up his neighbour's spring or well, does not constitute the invasion of a legal right, and will not sustain an action. And further, that it makes no difference whether the damage arise by the water percolating away, so that it ceases to flow along channels through which it previously found its way to the spring or well; or whether, having found its way to the spring or well, it ceases to be retained there" (*s*). The leading

---

(*o*) *Mogul Steamship Co* v *McGregor* (1889-91), 23 Q B Div 598, affirmed in H L, '92, A C 25

(*p*) Bowen L J, 23 Q B Div at p 613

(*q*) Fry L J, ibid at pp 625, 626

(*r*) Lord Hannen, S. C in H L '92, A C, at p 59

(*s*) Per Cur, *Ballacorkish Mining Co.* v *Harrison* (1873), L R 5 P C at p 61, 43 L J P C 19

cases are *Acton* v *Blundell* (*t*) and *Chasemore* v *Richards* (*u*). In the former it was expressly laid down as the governing principle "that the person who owns the surface may dig therein, and apply all that is there found to his own purposes, at his free will and pleasure, and that if in the exercise of such right he intercepts or drains off the water collected from underground springs in his neighbour's well, this inconvenience to his neighbour falls within the description of *damnum absque injuria* which cannot become the ground of an action." In this case the defendant had sunk a deep pit on his own land for mining purposes, and kept it dry by pumping in the usual way,

(*t*) 12 M. & W. 324, 13 L. J. Ex. 289 (1843)   (*u*) 7 H. L. C. 319, 29 L. J. Ex. 81 (1859)

Digging wells, etc. in a man's own land. The courts of the United States, were in advance of those of England in establishing, as settled law, the rights pertaining to subterranean waters. In both countries it is now a uniform rule, that if, in digging into his own land, a man cuts off the source which by percolation supplies his neighbor's well, the latter is without remedy, if the digging is not negligently or maliciously done. Ocean Grove Camp Meeting Assoc. v. Asbury Park Comm'rs, 40 N. J. Eq 447; Southern P. R. Co v Dufour, 95 Cal. 615; 30 P. Rep 783; Elster v City of Springfield, 49 Ohio St. 82; 30 N. E. Rep. 274; Luther v. Winnisimmet Co., 9 Cush. 171; Greenleaf v. Francis, 18 Pick. 117; Bloodgood v Ayres, 108 N. Y. 400, 15 N. E. Rep. 433; Goodale v. Tuttle, 29 N. Y. 459, Chatfield v Wilson, 27 Vt. 670, 28 Vt. 49; Chase v. Silverton, 62 Me. 175; New Albany etc. R. Co. v Peterson, 14 Ind. 112; Ellis v Duncan, 21 Barb. 230; Burroughs v. Saterlee, 67 Ia. 396, 56 Am. Rep. 350; Bliss v Greeley, 45 N. Y. 671; Haldeman v Bruckhart, 45 Pa St. 514; Lybe's Appeal, 106 Pa. St. 626, 51 Am. Rep. 542.

A novel question was that presented in Peoples' Gas Co. v Tyner (13 Ind. 277, 31 N. E. Rep. 59), where it was held, that an owner of a natural gas well may explode nitro-glycerine in it, though the natural effect is to draw gas from another's land.

But the owner of the land has no right to direct or draw away a natural and well defined underground stream of water to the injury of another. Trustees etc v Youmans, 45 N. Y. 362; McClellan v. Hurdle (Col App.), 33 Pac Rep. 280; Wheatley v. Baugh, 25 Pa St. 528; Smith v Adams, 6 Paige, 435. The special nature of the right precludes its vesting by prescription. See Hanson v. McCue, 42 Cal. 303; Greenleaf v. Francis, 18 Pick. 117, *supra*; Roath v Driscoll, 20 Conn. 533; Frazier v. Brown, 12 Ohio St. 294.

with the result of drying up a well which belonged to the plaintiff, and was used by him to supply his cotton mill.

Chasemore v. Richards. *Chasemore* v. *Richards* carried the rule a step further in two directions. It is settled that it makes no difference if the well or watercourse whose supply is cut off or diminished is ancient, and also (notwithstanding considerable doubt expressed by Lord Wensleydale) that it matters not whether the operations carried on by the owner of the surface are or are not for any purpose connected with the use of the land itself. The defendants in the cause were virtually the Local Board of Health of Croydon, who had sunk a deep well on their own land to obtain a water supply for the town. The making of this well, and the pumping of great quantities of water from it for the use of the town, intercepted water that had formerly found its way into the river Wandle by underground channels, and the supply of water to the plaintiff's ancient mill, situated on that river, was diminished. Here the defendants, though using their land in an ordinary way, were not using it for an ordinary purpose. But the House of Lords refused to make any distinction on that score, and held the doctrine of *Acton* v. *Blundell* applicable (*x*). The right claimed by the plaintiff was declared to be too large and indefinite to have any foundation in law. No reasonable limits could be set to its exercise, and it could not be reconciled with the natural and ordinary rights of land-owners. These decisions have been generally followed in the United States (*y*).

Other applications of same principle. There are many other ways in which a man may use his own property to the prejudice of his neighbour, and yet no action lies. I

(*x*) Cp., as to the distinction between the "natural user" of land and the maintenance of artificial works, *Hurdman* v. *N. E. R. Co.* (1878), 3 C. P. Div. at p. 174, 47 L. J. C. P. 368, and further as to the limits of "natural user," *Ballard* v. *Tomlinson* (1885), 29 Ch. Div. 115, 54 L. J. Ch. 454.

(*y*) Cooley on Torts, 580.

have no remedy against a neighbour who opens a new window so as to overlook my garden: on the other hand, he has none against me if, at any time before he has gained a prescriptive right to the light, I build a wall or put up a screen so as to shut out his view from that window. But the principle in question is not confined to the use of property. It extends to every exercise of lawful discretion in a man's own affairs. A tradesman may depend in great measure on one large customer. This person, for some cause of dissatisfaction, good or bad, or without any assignable cause at all, suddenly withdraws his custom. His conduct may be unreasonable and ill-conditioned, and the manifest cause of great loss to the tradesman. Yet no legal wrong is done. And such matters could not be otherwise ordered. It is more tolerable that some tradesmen should suffer from the caprice of customers than that the law should dictate to customers what reasons are or are not sufficient for ceasing to deal with a tradesman.

Rogers v. Rajendro Dutt. But there are cases of this class which are not so obvious. A curious one arose at Calcutta at the time of the Indian Mutiny, and was taken up to the Privy Council. Rajendro Dutt and others, the plaintiffs below, were the owners of the *Underwriter*, a tug employed in the navigation of the Hoogly. A troopship with English troops arrived at the time when they were most urgently needed. For towing up this ship the captain of the tug asked an extraordinary price. Failing to agree with him, and thinking his demand extortionate, Captain Rogers, the Superintendent of Marine (who was defendant in the suit), issued a general order to officers of the Government pilot service that the *Underwriter* was not to be allowed to take in tow any vessel in their charge. Thus

---

Other applications of same principle. This principle is applied to light and prospect in several American cases, see *post*, p. 509.

the owners not only failed to make a profit of the necessities of the Government of India, but lost the ordinary gains of their business so far as they were derived from towing ships in the charge of Government pilots. The Supreme Court of Calcutta held that these facts gave a cause of action against Captain Rogers, but the Judicial Committee reversed the decision on appeal (z). The plaintiffs had not been prejudiced in any definite legal right. No one was bound to employ their tug, any more than they were bound to take a fixed sum for its services. If the Government of India, rightly or wrongly, thought the terms unreasonable, they might decline to deal with the plaintiffs both on the present and on other occasions, and restrain public servants from dealing with them.

"The Government certainly, as any other master, may lawfully restrict its own servants as to those whom they shall employ under them, or co-operate with in performing the services for the due performance of which they are taken into its service. Supposing it had been believed that the *Underwriter* was an ill-found vessel, or in any way unfit for the service, might not the pilots have been lawfully forbidden to employ her until these objections were removed? Would it not indeed have been the duty of the Government to do so? And is it not equally lawful and right when it is honestly believed that her owners will only render their services on exorbitant terms?" (x).

It must be taken that the Court thought the order complained of did not, as a matter of fact, amount to an obstruction of the tug-owners' common right of offering their vessel to the non-official public for employment. Conduct might easily be imagined, on the part of an officer in the defendant's position, which would amount to this. And if it did, it would probably be a cause of action (y)

(z) *Rogers* v *Rajendro Dutt*, 8 Moo I. A. 103

(x) 8 Moo I. A. at p 134.

(y) See per Holt C J in *Keeble* v *Hickeringill*, 11 East at pp 575, 576

Whether malice material in these cases. In this last case the harm suffered by the plaintiff in the Court below was not only the natural, but apparently the intended consequence of the act complained of. The defendant however acted from no reason of private hostility, but in the interest (real or supposed) of the public service. Whether the averment and proof of malice, in other words that the act complained of was done with the sole or chief intention of causing harm to the plaintiff as a private enemy (*z*), would make any difference in cases of this class, does not appear to be decided by any authority in our law. In *Rogers* v. *Rajendro Dutt* the Judicial Committee expressly declined to say what the decision would be if this element were present. In *Chasemore* v. *Richards* the statement of facts (by an arbitrator) on which the case proceeded expressly negatived any intention to harm the plaintiff. Lord Wensleydale thought (apparently with reluctance) that the principle of regarding the presence or absence of such an intention had found no place in our law (*a*); and partly for that reason he would have liked to

---

(*z*) It is very difficult to say what 'malice,' as a term of art, really means in any one of its generally similar but not identical uses; but I think the gloss here given is sufficiently correct for the matter in hand. At all events, the intention of causing disadvantage to the plaintiff as a competitor in business by acts in themselves lawful, and done in the course of that business, does not make such acts wrongful. *Mogul Steamship Co.* v. *McGregor* (1889), 23 Q. B. Div. 598, H. L., '92, A. C. 25, 61 L. J. Q. B. 295.

(*a*) 7 H. L. C. at p. 388. But see per Fry L. J., 23 Q. B. Div. at p. 625, on the hypothetical case of "competition used as a mere engine of malice."

Whether malice material in these cases. The American authorities upon this subject seem to have gone further than the English. In numerous American cases the courts have held that a legal act cannot be made illegal by the motive with which it is done. Occum Co. *v.* Sprague etc. Co., 34 Conn. 529; Chatfield *v.* Wilson, 28 Vt. 49; Auburn etc. Co. *v.* Douglass, 9 N. Y. 444; Fahin *v.* Reichard, 8 Wis. 255; Macey *v.* Childress, 2 Tenn. Ch. 438; South Royalston Bank *v.* Saffolk Bank, 27 Vt. 105; Ramsey *v.* Gould, 57 Barb. 398; Hunt *v.* Somonds, 19 Mo. 583; Orr *v.* Home Mutual Ins. Co., 12 La. An. 255; Paine *v.* Chandler, 134 N. Y. 385, 32 N. E. Rep. 18; Gallagher *v.* Dodge, 48 Conn. 387, 40 Am. Rep. 180; Glendon Iron Co. *v.* Uhler, 75 Pa. St. 467.

draw the line of unquestionable freedom of use at purposes connected with the improvement of the land itself; but he gave no authority for his statement. At the same time it must be allowed that he expressed the general sense of English lawyers (b).

Roman doctrine of " animus vicino nocendi." The Roman lawyers on the other hand allowed that " animus vicino nocendi" did or might make a difference. In a passage cited and to some extent relied on (in the scantiness, at that time, of native authority) in *Acton* v. *Blundell*, we read. " Denique Marcellus scribit, cum eo qui in suo fodiens vicini fontem avertit, nihil posse agi, nec de dolo actionem. et sane non debet habere, si non animo vicino nocendi, sed suum agrum meliorem faciendi id fecit" (c). And this view is followed by recognized authorities in the law of Scotland, who say that an owner using his own land must act " not in mere spite or malice, *in aemulationem vicini*" (d). There seems on principle to be much to recommend it. Certainly it would be no answer to say, as one is inclined to do at first sight, that the law can regard only intentions and not motives. For in some cases the law does already regard motive as distinct from purpose or intention, as in actions for malicious prosecution, and in the question of privileged communications in actions for libel. And also this is really a matter of intention. The motives for a man wishing ill to his neighbour in the supposed case may be infinite the purpose, the contemplated and desired result, is to do such and such ill to him, to dry up his well, or what else it may be. If our law is to be taken as Lord Wensleydale assumed it to be, its policy must be rested simply on a balance of expediency. *Animus vicino nocendi* would be very difficult of proof, at

(b) See Sir W. Markby's "Elements of Law," s. 239.
(c) D 30, 3, de aqua, 1, § 12 (Ulpian).
(d) Bell's Principles, 966 (referred to by Lord Wensleydale).

all events if proof that mischief was the only purpose were required (and it would hardly do to take less), and the evil of letting a certain kind of churlish and unneighbourly conduct, and even deliberate mischief, go without redress (there being no reason to suppose the kind a common one), may well be thought less on the whole than that of encouraging vexatious claims. In Roman law there is nothing to show whether, and how far, the doctrine of Ulpian and Marcellus was found capable of practical application. I cannot learn that it has much effect in the law of Scotland. It seems proper, however, to point out that there is really no positive English authority on the matter.

Cases of similar names. Again our law does not in general recognize any exclusive right to the use of a name, personal or local. I may use a name similar to that which my neighbour uses — and that whether I inherited or found

---

Cases of similar names. The name of a person or locality cannot become the exclusive trade name of a single person or combination of persons in that place. Fish Bros. Wagon Co v La Belle Wagon Co., 82 Wis. 546, 52 N. W. Rep 595, Meneely v Meneely, 62 N Y. 427; 20 Am. Rep 489, Rogers v. Taintor, 97 Mass. 291, Candee v. Deere, 54 Ill 439, 5 Am Rep 125, Glendon Iron Co v Uhler, 75 Pa St. 467, 15 Am Rep 599, supra, p 182, Del & H C Co. v Clark, 13 Wall. 311.

But a person living in a different place may appropriate such a trade name La Republique Francaise v. Schultz, 57 Fed Rep 37, Sanders v Jacob, 20 Mo App. 96, Newman v Alvord, 51 N. Y. 189, 10 Am Rep 588

Persons having the same names and using their names as trade-marks must act in good faith towards each other and not use the trade-mark to deceive the public Gilman v Hunnewell, 122 Mass. 139, Holmes v Holmes, etc Co , 37 Conn 278, 9 Am. Rep 324, Shaver v. Shaver, 54 Ia 208; Landreth v. Landreth, 22 Fed Rep 41.

Words purely descriptive, as "Liver Medicine," cannot be appropriated as a trade-mark Simmons Medicine Co v Mansfield Drug Co. (Tenn), 23 S. W. Rep. 165 See Amoskeag Mfg. Co. v Trainer, 101 U. S 51, Gilman v. Hunnewell, 121 Mass 139, Royal etc Co v. Sherrel, 93 N. Y. 331, Lorrillard v Pride, 28 Fed. Rep 434; Fleischmann v Starkey, 25 Id. 127

it, or have assumed it of my own motion, so long as I do not use it to pass off my wares or business as being his. The fact that inconvenience arises from the similarity will not of itself constitute a legal injury (e), and allegations of pecuniary damage will not add any legal effect. "You must have in our law injury as well as damage" (f).

10.—*Leave and Licence. Volenti non fit iniuria*

Consent or acceptance of risk (leave and licence). Harm suffered by consent is, within limits to be mentioned, not a cause of civil action. The same is true where it is met with under conditions manifesting acceptance, on the part of the person suffering it, of the risk of that kind of harm. The maxim by which the rule is commonly brought to mind is "Volenti non fit iniuria." "Leave and licence" is the current English phrase for the defence raised in this class of cases. On the one hand, however, *volenti non fit iniuria* is not universally true. On the other hand, neither the Latin nor the English formula provides in terms for the state of things in which there is not specific will or assent to suffer something which, if inflicted against the party's will, would be a wrong, but only conduct showing that, for one reason or another, he is content to abide the chance of it (g)

(e) See *Burgess* v *Burgess* (1853), 3 D M G 896, 22 L J Ch 675, a classical case, *Du Boulay* v *Du Boulay* (1869), L. R. 2 P C 430, 38 L J P C 35, *Day* v *Brownrigg* (1878), 10 Ch Div 294, 48 L J Ch 173, *Street* v *Union Bank, &c* (1885), 30 Ch D 156, 55 L J Ch. 31 Cp *Montgomery* v *Thompson*, '91, A C 217, 60 L J Ch 757

(f) Jessel M R, 10 Ch Div 304.

(g) Unless we said that *leave* points to specific consent to an act, *licence* to general assent to the consequences of acts consented to but such a distinction seems too fanciful

Consent or acceptance of risk Supporting the text *vide*, State v Beck, 1 Hill (S. C) 363, Harrison v Marshall, 6 Port 65, Illinois Cent R. Co v Allen, 39 Ill. 205, Walker v. Fitts, 24 Pick 191; Commonwealth v Parker, 9 Metc. 263; Stout v Wren, 1 Hawks, 420; 9 Am. Dec. 653. See post, p 253

Express licence. The case of express consent is comparatively rare in our books, except in the form of a licence to enter upon land. It is indeed in this last connexion that we most often hear of "leave and licence," and the authorities mostly turn on questions of the kind and extent of permission to be inferred from particular language or acts (*h*)

Limits of consent Force to the person is rendered lawful by consent in such matters as surgical operations. The fact is common enough; indeed authorities are silent

---

(*h*) See Addison on Torts, p 384, 6th ed , Cooley on Torts, 303, *seq*

Limits of consent One consenting to receive lawful force cannot recover damages for an injury resulting therefrom where the force was exercised in a reasonable manner and for a justifiable purpose In the case of McClallen *v.* Adams (19 Pick 333), defendant's wife, being afflicted with a dangerous disease was carried by him to a distance and left under the care of plaintiff as a surgeon, plaintiff performed an operation on her for the cure of the disease, soon after which she died Plaintiff sued defendant to recover compensation for his services It was held, that the consent of defendant's wife was presumed, that no notice to defendant of the operation was necessary, and that plaintiff could recover. See Caldwell *v* Ferrell, 28 Ill 438.

In America, although there are authorities to the contrary, it may now be announced as established law, that where persons voluntarily engage in a fight, any one of them may recover damages for the injuries he may receive The fact that the fight was voluntary is admissible in evidence to keep down punitive damages, but not to reduce or defeat actual damages Dole *v* Erskine, 35 N. H. 503, Grotton *v* Glidden, 84 Me. 589, 24 At Rep. 1008; Shay *v* Thomson, 59 Wis 540; 18 N. W. Rep 473, Adams *v* Waggoner, 33 Ind. 531; Logan *v.* Austin, 1 Stew 476, Bell *v* Hansley, 3 Jones L 131, Evans *v.* Waite, 83 Wis. 286, 53 N W Rep. 445, Jones *v* Gale, 22 Mo. App 637, Smith *v.* Simon, 69 Mich 481, 37 N. E. Rep. 548

One is liable for an injury to another caused by intentional excess in mutual sport Peterson *v* Haffner, 59 Ind. 130.

But "The common law recognizes as not necessarily unlawful certain manly sports calculated to give bodily strength, skill and activity and to fit people for defence, public as well as personal, in time of need Playing at cudgels or foils, or wrestling by consent, there being no motive to do bodily harm on either side, are said to be exercises of this description * * * But prize-fighting, boxing matches and encoun-

or nearly so, because it is common and obvious. Taking out a man's tooth without his consent would be an aggravated assault and battery. With consent it is lawfully done every day. In the case of a person under the age of discretion, the consent of that person's parent or guardian is generally necessary and sufficient (*i*). But consent alone is not enough to justify what is on the face of it bodily harm. There must be some kind of just cause, as the cure or extirpation of disease in the case of surgery. Wilful hurt is not excused by consent or assent if it has no reasonable object. Thus if a man licenses another to beat him, not only does this not prevent the assault from being a punishable offense, but the better opinion is that it does not deprive the party beaten of his right of action. On this principle prize-fights and the like · are unlawful even when entered into by agreement and without anger or mutual ill-will" (*k*). "Whenever two persons go out to strike each other, and do so, each is guilty of an assault" (*l*). The reason is said to be that such acts are against the peace, or tend to breaches of the peace. But, inasmuch as even the slightest direct application of force, if not justified, was in the language of pleading *vi et armis* and *contra pacem*, something more than usual must be meant by this expression. The distinction seems to be that agreement will not justify the wilful causing or endeavouring to cause appreciable bodily harm for the mere pleasure of the parties

---

(*i*) Cp Stephen, Digest of the Criminal Law, art 204
(*k*) *Commonwealth* v *Collberg* (1876), 119 Mass 350, and 20 Am Rep 328, where authorities are collected See also *Reg* v *Coney* (1882), 8 Q B D 534, 538, 546, 549, 567, and *infra*

(*l*) Coleridge J. in *Reg* v *Lewis* (1844), 1 C & K at p 421, cp. Buller N P 16 The passage there and elsewhere cited from Comberbach, a part from the slender authority of that reporter, is only a dictum. Buller's own authority is really better

---

ters of that kind, serve no useful purpose, tend to breaches of the peace, and are unlawful even when entered into by agreement and without anger or mutual ill will If one party licenses another to beat him, such license is void, because it is against the law." Commonwealth v. Collberg, 119 Mass. 353; 20 Am. Rep 828

or others. Boxing with properly padded gloves is lawful, because in the usual course of things harmless. Fighting with the bare fist is not. Football is a lawful pastime, though many kicks are given and taken in it; a kicking match is not. "As to playing at foils, I cannot say, nor was it ever said that I know of, that it is not lawful for a gentleman to learn the use of the small sword, and yet that cannot be learned without practising with foils" (*m*). Fencing, single-stick, or playing with blunt sabres in the accustomed manner, is lawful, because the players mean no hurt to one another, and take such order by the use of masks and pads that no hurt worth speaking of is likely. A duel with sharp swords after the manner of German students is not lawful, though there be no personal enmity between the men, and though the conditions be such as to exclude danger to life or limb. Here it cannot be said that "bodily harm was not the motive on either side" (*n*). It seems to be what is called a question of mixed law and fact whether a particular action or contest involves such intention to do real hurt that consent or assent will not justify it (*o*). Neglect of usual precautions in any pastime known to involve danger would be evidence of wrongful intention, but not conclusive evidence.

Reg. v. Coney. This question was incidentally considered by several of the judges in the recent case of *Reg* v. *Coney* (*p*), where the majority of the Court held that mere voluntary presence at an unlawful fight is not necessarily punishable as taking part in an assault, but there was no

(*m*) Foster's Crown Law, 260.
(*n*) Foster, *l. c.* "Motive" is hardly the correct word, but the meaning is plain enough.
(*o*) Cp. Pulton, De Pace Regis, 17 b. It might be a nice point whether the old English backswording (see "Tom Brown") was lawful or not. And *quaere* of the old rules of Rugby football, which allowed deliberate kicking in some circumstances. *Quaere*, also, whether one monk might have lawfully licensed another to beat him by way of spiritual discipline. But anyhow he could not have sued, being civilly dead by his entering into religion.
(*p*) 8 Q. B. D. 534, 51 L. J. M. C. 66 (1882). For fuller collection and consideration of authorities, cp. Mr. Edward Manson's note in L. Q. R. vi. 110.

difference of opinion as to a prize-fight being unlawful, or all persons actually aiding and abetting therein being guilty of assault notwithstanding that the principals fight by mutual consent. The Court had not, of course, to decide anything as to civil liability, but some passages in the judgments are material. Cave J. said: "The true view is, I think, that a blow struck in anger, or which is likely or is intended to do corporal hurt, is an assault, but that a blow struck in sport, and not likely nor intended to cause bodily harm, is not an assault, and that, an assault being a breach of the peace and unlawful, the consent of the person struck is immaterial. If this view is correct a blow struck in a prize-fight is clearly an assault; but playing with singlesticks or wrestling do not involve an assault, nor does boxing with gloves in the ordinary way" (q) Stephen J. said: "When one person is indicted for inflicting personal injury upon another, the consent of the person who sustains the injury is no defence to the person who inflicts the injury, if the injury is of such a nature, or is inflicted under such circumstances, that its infliction is injurious to the public as well as to the person injured. . . . In cases where life and limb are exposed to no serious danger in the common course of things, I think that consent is a defence to a charge of assault, even when considerable force is used, as for instance in cases of wrestling, singlestick, sparring with gloves, football, and the like; but in all cases the question whether consent does or does not take from the application of force to another its illegal character is a question of degree depending upon circumstances" (r) These opinions seem equally applicable to the rule of civil responsibility (s).

(q) 8 Q B D at p 539 As to the limits of lawful boxing, see *Reg.* v *Orton* (1878), 39 L T 293.

(r) 8 Q B D at p 549 Compare arts 206, 208 of the learned judge's "Digest of the Criminal Law" The language of art 208 follows the authorities, but I am not sure that it exactly hits the distinction

(s) Notwithstanding the doubt expressed by Hawkins, J, 8 Q B D at pp 553, 554

Licence gotten by fraud. A licence obtained by fraud is of no effect. This is too obvious on the general principles of the law to need dwelling upon (*t*).

Extended meaning of volenti non fit iniuria. Trials of strength and skill in such pastimes as those above mentioned afford, when carried on within lawful bounds, the best illustration of the principle by which the maxim *volenti non fit iniuria* is enlarged beyond its literal meaning. A man cannot complain of harm (within the limits we have mentioned) to the chances of which he has exposed himself with knowledge and of his free will. Thus in the case of two men fencing or playing at singlestick, *volenti non fit iniuria* would be assigned by most lawyers as the governing rule, yet the words must be forced. It is not the will of one player that the other should hit him; his object is to be hit as seldom as possible. But he is content that the other shall hit him as much as by fair play he can; and in that sense the striking is not against his will. Therefore the "assault" of the school of arms is no assault in law. Still less is there an actual consent if the fact is an accident, not a necessary incident, of what is being done; as where in the course of a cricket match a player or spectator is struck by the ball. I suppose it has never occurred to any one that legal wrong is done by such an accident even to a spectator who is taking no part in the game. So if two men are fencing, and one of the foils breaks, and the broken end, being thrown off with some force, hits a bystander, no wrong is done to him. Such too is the case put in the

---

(*t*) A rather curious illustration may be found in *Davies* v *Marshall* (1861), 10 C B N S 697, 31 L J C P 61, where the so called equitable plea and replication seems to have amounted to a common law plea of leave and licence and joinder of issue, or perhaps new assignment thereon

---

Extending the meaning of volenti non fit iniuria. Where one is injured in a mutual play, the maxim applies, unless there was an intention to injure. Fitzgerald v Cavin, 110 Mass. 153.

Indian Penal Code (*u*) of a man who stands near another cutting wood with a hatchet, and is struck by the head flying off. It may be said that these examples are trivial. They are so, and for that reason appropriate. They show that the principle is constantly at work, and that we find little about it in our books just because it is unquestioned in common sense as well as in law.

Relation of these cases to inevitable accident. Many cases of this kind seem to fall as naturally under the exception of inevitable accident. But there is, we conceive, this distinction, that where the plaintiff has voluntarily put himself in the way of risk the defendant is not bound to disprove negligence. If I choose to stand near a man using an axe, he may be a good woodman or not; but I cannot (it is submitted) complain of an accident because a more skilled woodman might have avoided it. A man dealing with explosives is bound, as regards his neighbour's property, to diligence and more than diligence. But if I go and watch a firework-maker for my own amusement, and the shop is blown up, it seems I shall have no cause of action, even if he was handling his materials unskilfully. This, or even more, is implied in the decision in *Ilott* v. *Wilkes* (*x*), where it was held that one who trespassed in a wood, having notice that spring-guns were set there, and was shot by a spring-gun, could not recover. The maxim "volenti non fit injuria" was expressly held applicable: "he voluntarily exposes himself to the mischief which has

---

(*u*) Illust to s 80 On the point of actual consent, cf ss 87 and 88

(*x*) 3 B & Ald 304 (1820), cp and dist the later case of *Bird* v. *Holbrook*, 4 Bing 628 The argument that since the defendant could not have justified shooting a trespasser with his own hand, even after warning, he could not justify shooting him with a spring gun, is weighed and found wanting, though perhaps it ought to have prevailed

---

Relation of these cases to inevitable accident. With reference to spring guns it should be noted that where the trespasser is *without notice* the rule above stated is reserved. See *post*, p 206

happened" (y). The case gave rise to much public excitement, and led to an alteration of the law (z), but it has not been doubted in subsequent authorities that on the law as it stood, and the facts as they came before the Court, it was well decided. As the point of negligence was expressly raised by the pleadings, the decision is an authority that if a man goes out of his way to a dangerous action or state of things, he must take the risk as he finds it. And this appears to be material with regard to the attempt made by respectable authorities, and noticed above, to bring under this principle the head of excuse by reason of inevitable accident (a).

Knowledge of risk opposed to duty of warning. It was held by a majority of the Court of Appeal that if a man undertakes to work in a railway tunnel where he

---

(y) Per Bayley J 3 B & Ald at p 311, and Holroyd J at p 314

(z) Edin. Rev xxxv 123, 410 (reprinted in Sydney Smith's works) Setting spring guns, except by night in a dwelling house for the protection thereof, was made a criminal offense by 7 & 8 Geo IV. c 18, now repealed and substantially re-enacted (24 & 25 Vict c 95, s. 1, and c 100, s 31)

(a) *Holmes* v *Mather* (1875), L R 10 Ex at p 267, *Rylands* v *Fletcher* (1866), L R 1 Ex. at p 287

Knowledge of risk opposed to duty of warning: employers and employes An employé who knows or has been fully cautioned as to the risks of his situation, however dangerous they may be, and accepts them, cannot recover for any injuries received in the course of his employment Hoosier Stone Co. *v* McCain, 133 Ind. 231, 31 N. E Rep 956; Prentice *v* Village of Wellsville, 66 Hun, 634, 21 N Y S Rep. 820, Paland *v* Chicago etc R Co , 44 La An 1003, Swanson *v* City of La Fayette (Ind) 33 N E Rep. 1033, Knight *v*. Cooper, 36 W Va 232, 14 S E Rep 999, Foley *v*. Jersey City etc. Co (N J), 24 At. Rep 487, Cook *v* St. Paul, etc R Co., 34 Minn. 45, Bengston *v* Chicago, etc Ry Co , 47 Minn 486, 50 N W Rep 531, Titus *v*. Bradford, etc. R Co , 136 Pa. St 618, 20 At Rep 517; 26 W. N C 472, Little Rock, etc R Co. *v* Duffy, 35 Ark. 602, 4 Am & Eng. R Cas 638, Little Rock, etc. R Co *v*. Townsend, 41 Ark 382, 21 Am. & Eng R Cas 619, McGlynn *v* Brodie, 31 Cal 377, Baxter *v* Roberts, 44 Cal 187, Malone *v* Hawley, 46 Cal. 409, Palmer *v*. Denver, etc. R Co (Colo.), 12 Fed. Rep. 392, Indianapolis etc. R. Co. *v*. Flanagan, 77 Ill 365, Pennsylvania Co. *v*. Lynch, 90 Ill. 334; Missouri Furnace Co. *v* Abend, 107 Ill. 44, Abend *v* T. H & G R Co , 111 Ill

knows that trains are constantly passing, he cannot complain of the railway company for not taking measures to warn the workmen of the approach of trains, and this though he is the servant not of the company but of the

202, Houser v Chicago, etc. R. Co., 60 Ia 230, 8 Am. & Eng. R Cas 600, Money v. Lower Vein Coal Co, 55 Ia 671, Kelly v. Silver Spring Bleaching Co, 12 R I 112, Nashville, etc. R. Co. v. Elliott, 1 Coldw. 612, Houston, etc. R Co v. Fowler, 56 Tex. 452, 8 Am & Eng. R Cas. 604, Baltimore, etc. R Co. v. McKenzie, 81 Va. 71; 24 Am & Eng. R. Cas. 395, Smith v. Sellers, 40 La An 527, Chicago, etc R. Co v Mahoney, 4 Ill App 262, Camp Point Mfg. Co. v Ballou, 71 Ill 417, Leary v. Boston, etc. R. Co, 139 Mass. 580, Russell v. Tillotson, 140 Mass 201, Woods v St Paul, etc R Co, 39 Minn 135, Porter v Hannibal R Co, 71 Mo 66, 2 Am. & Eng. R Cas. 11, St. Louis, etc Ry. Co v. Kelton, 55 Ark 483, 18 S W Rep 933

So, where the employé discovers risks after entering the employment but continues his service without complaint He must quit work or it will be presumed that he assumes the risks Davis v Detroit, etc. R. Co, 20 Mich 105; Rains v St. L etc R. Co., 71 Mo 164, 5 Am & Eng. R Cas 610, Sweeney v Central Pac R Co, 57 Cal 15, 8 Am & Eng R Cas 151, Umback v. Lake Shore, etc R Co., 83 Ind. 191, 8 Am & Eng R Cas 98, Louisville, etc R Co. v. Orr, 84 Ind 50, 8 Am. & Eng. R Cas 91, Houston, etc R Co v. Meyers, 55 Tex 110; 8 Am & Eng. R. Cas 114, Covey v Hannibal, etc R. Co., 86 Mo 635, 28 Am & Eng R Cas 382, Norfolk & W. R Co v Jackson, 85 Va 189, 8 S E Rep 870; New York, etc, R Co. v Lyons, 119 Pa. St 324, Sowden v Idaho Quartz Mining Co, 55 Cal. 443, Welgreffe v. Daw, 49 Ill. App 53, Ryan v Porter Mfg. Co, 57 Hun, 253, 589, 10 N Y. S Rep 774, Missouri P R. Co v Somers, 78 Tex. 439, 14 S. W. Rep. 779; Davidson v Southern P Co, 44 Fed Rep 474 But see Mahoney v Dore, 155 Mass. 513; 30 N. E. Rep 366

But the employé does not assume unexplained risks, which are not known to him nor apparent to a reasonably prudent man, or the risk of latent defects which are known or should be known to his employer. Conlon v Oregon, etc R Co, 21 Oreg 462, 32 Pac. Rep. 397, Ballou v Chicago, etc. R. Co., 54 Wis 257, 5 Am & Eng R Cas 480, Warner v. Erie, etc R. Co, 39 N Y 468, DeGraff v New York, etc R. Co, 76 N. Y. 125, East St L Packing Co v Hightower, 92 Ill. 139, Indianapolis, etc R Co. v. Toy, 91 Ill. 174, Steffen v. Chicago, etc R. Co., 46 Wis 265, Morrison v Phillips etc Cons Co, 42 Wis 405, Wedgwood v Chicago, etc. R Co, 41 Wis. 478, McCampbell v. Cunard S S. Co, 69 Hun, 131, 23 N Y. S. Rep. 477, Evansville & R. R Co. v Maddux (Ind), 33 N. E Rep 345; Taylor etc R Co. v Taylor, 79 Tex 104, 14 S. W Rep 918, Lofrano v New York, etc. Co, 55 Hun, 453, 8 N Y. S Rep. 717.

contractor (b). The minority held that the railway company, as carrying on a dangerous business, were bound not to expose persons coming by invitation upon their property to any undue risk, and at all events the burden of proof was on them to show that the risk was in fact understood and accepted by the plaintiff (c). "If I invite a man who has no knowledge of the locality to walk along a dangerous cliff which is my property, I owe him a duty different to that which I owe to a man who has all his life birdnested on my rocks" (d).

But where a man goes on doing work under a risk which

(b) *Woodley v. Metr. Dist. R. Co.* (1877), 2 Ex. Div. 384, 46 L. J. Ex. 521, Mellish and Baggallay L. JJ. diss.

(c) Cp. *Thomas v. Quartermaine* (1887), 18 Q. B. Div. 685, 56 L. J. Q. B. 340, and Lord Herschell's judgment in *Membery v. G. W. R. Co.* (1889), 14 App. Ca. 179, 190.

(d) Fry L. J. 18 Q. B. Div. at p. 701. And see *Yarmouth v. France* (1887), 19 Q. B. D. 647, 57 L. J. Q. B. 7.

Nor does the employé lose his right of action for injuries if the risk assumed is such that a prudent man would not refuse it and discontinue work, as where the employer promises to repair defective appliances used by the employe.

Dwyer v. St. Louis, etc. R. Co., 52 Fed. Rep. 82; Thorpe v. Missouri P. R. Co., 89 Mo. 650, Southern P. R. Co. v. Lasch (Tex.), 21 N. W. Rep. 563, Chicago & G. W. R. Co. v. Travis, 14 Ill. App. 466, Stephenson v. Duncan, 73 Wis. 404, Conroy v. Vulcan Iron Works, 62 Mo. 85, Patterson v. Pittsburgh, etc. R. Co., 76 Pa. St. 389, Le Clair v. First Div. St. P. & P. R. Co., 20 Minn. 9, Brabbits v. Chicago, etc. R. Co., 38 Wis. 289, Little Rock, etc. R. Co. v. Duffey, 35 Ark. 602, 4 Am. & Eng. R. Cas. 637, Greenleaf v. Illinois etc. R. Co., 29 Ia. 14, Kroy v. Chicago, etc. R. Co., 32 Ia. 357, Greenleaf v. Dubuque R. Co., 33 Ia. 52, Way v. Illinois, etc. R. Co., 40 Ia. 341, Lumley v. Caswell, 47 Ia. 159, Atchison etc. R. Co. v. McKee, 37 Kan. 592; St. Clair Nail Co. v. Smith, 43 Ill. App. 105, Breckenridge Co. v. Hicks (Ky.), 22 S. W. Rep. 554, Harrison v. Denver etc. Ry. Co., 7 Utah, 523, 27 Pac. Rep. 728, Colorado M. Ry. Co. v. O'Brien, 16 Colo. 219, 27 Pac. Rep. 701, Hough v. Texas etc., R. Co., 100 U. S. 102, Jones v. Lake Shore, etc., R. Co., 49 Mich. 573.

But if such repair is not made within a reasonable time the employé must quit the service or assume the consequent risk. Davis v. Graham, 2 Colo. App. 210, 29 Pac. Rep. 1007, Weber Wagon Co. v. Kehl, 139 Ill. 644, 29 N. E. Rep. 714, Lyttle v. Chicago & W. M. Ry. Co., 84 Mich. 289, 47 N. W. Rep. 571. Contra, see New Jersey etc. R. Co. v. Young, 49 Fed. Rep. 723, 1 U. S. App. 96; 1 C. C. A. 428.

is known to him, and which does not depend on any one else's acts, or on the condition of the place where the work is done, but is incident to the work itself, he cannot be heard to say that his exposure of himself to such risk was not voluntary (e).

Cases between employers and their workmen: Smith v. Baker. The principle expressed by *volenti non fit iniuria* is different from that of contributory negligence (f), as it is in itself independent of the contract of service or any other contract (g). It does not follow that a man is negligent or imprudent because he chooses to encounter a risk which he knows and appreciates; but if he does voluntarily run the risk, he cannot complain afterwards (h). At the same time knowledge is not of itself conclusive. The maxim is *volenti* — not *scienti* — *non fit iniuria*, "the question whether in any particular case a plaintiff was *volens* or *nolens* is a question of fact and not of law" (i). A workman is not bound, for example, to throw up his employment rather than go on working with appliances which he knows or suspects to be dangerous, and continuing to use such appliances if the employer cannot or will not give him better is not conclusive to show that he voluntarily takes the attendant risk (k). As between an employer and his own workmen, it is hardly possible to separate the question of knowledge and acceptance of a particular risk from the question whether it was a term in the contract of service (though it is seldom, if ever, an

---

(e) *Membery* v *G W R Co* note (c), last page. Lord Bramwell's extra judicial remarks cannot be supported, see per Lord Herschell, 14 App. Ca. at pp 192, 193, and *Smith* v *Baker*, note (i), p 185.

(f) Bowen L J in *Thomas* v *Quartermaine* (1887), 18 Q B Div 685, 694, 697, 56 L. J Q B 340.

(g) 18 Q B Div at p 698.

(h) Bowen L J. 18 Q B Div. at p 695.

(i) *Ibid* at p 696, Lindley L J in *Yarmouth* v *France* (1887), 19 Q B D 647, 659, before judges of the C A sitting as a divisional Court.

(k) *Yarmouth* v *France*, last note, *Thrussell* v *Handyside* (1888), 20 Q B D 359, 57 L J Q. B 347, *Smith* v. *Baker*, '91, A C 325, 60 L. J. Q. B. 683.

express form) that the workman should accept that risk. Since the Employers' Liability Act has deprived the master, as we have already seen, of defence of "common employment" in a considerable number of cases, the defence of *volenti non fit injuria* has several times been resorted to, with the effect of raising complicated discussion on tolerably simple facts. By treating the maxim as if it were of literal authority (which no maxim is), and then construing it largely, something very like the old doctrine of "common employment" might have been indirectly restored. For some time there was appreciable danger of this result. But the tendency has been effectually checked by the decision of the House of Lords in *Smith* v. *Baker* (e). Except where there is an obvious and necessary danger in the work itself, it must be a question of fact in every case whether there was an agreement or at any rate consent to take the risk. "Where a person undertakes to do work which is intrinsically dangerous, notwithstanding that reasonable care has been taken to render it as little dangerous as possible, he no doubt voluntarily subjects himself to the risks inevitably accompanying it, and cannot, if he suffers, be permitted to complain that a wrong has been done him, even though the cause from which he suffers might give to others a right of action": as in the case of works unavoidably producing noxious fumes. But where "a risk to the employed, which may or may not result in injury, has been created or enhanced by the negligence of the employer," there "the mere continuance in service, with knowledge of the risk," does not "preclude the employed, if he suffer from such negligence, from recovering in respect of his employer's breach of duty" (f). And it seems that (apart from contracts to take a class of risks) there must be consent to the particular act or operation which is

(e) '91, A C 325   (f) Lord Herschell, '91, A C at pp. 360, 362 hazardous, not a mere general assent inferred from knowledge that risk of a certain kind is possible (g).

Distinction where no negligence at all. Cases of *volenti non fit iniuria* are of course to be distinguished from cases of pure unexpected accident where there is no proof of any negligence at all on the defendant's part (h) It seems that *Thomas* v. *Quartermaine*, though not so dealt with, was really a case of this latter kind (i).

In the construction of a policy of insurance against death or injury by accident, an exception of harm "happening by exposure of the insured to obvious risk of injury" includes accidents due to a risk which would have been obvious to a person using common care and attention (k)

Distinction from cases where negligence is ground of action We now see that the whole law of negligence assumes the principle of *volenti non fit iniuria* not to be

---

(g) Lord Halsbury, '91, A. C. at pp 338-339

(h) *Walsh* v *Whiteley* (1888), 21 Q B Div 371, 57 L J Q B 586

(i) See Lord Morris's remarks in *Smith* v *Baker*, '91, A C at p 369 In *Smith* v *Baker* itself, an appeal from a County Court, this point, not having been raised at the trial below, was not open on the appeal It was nevertheless extra judicially discussed with considerable variety of opinion

(k) *Cornish* v *Accident Insurance Co* (1889), 23 Q B Div 453

Distinction from cases where negligence is ground of action Illustrating this distinction reference is made to the case of Pittsburg, etc R Co *v.* Noel (77 Ind 110), in which it was held, that the piling of wood by the plaintiff, with the consent of the defendant, along the line of defendant's railroad, where it was liable to and did take fire, did not constitute contributory negligence on the part of the plaintiff.

Again, it has been held in another case, that persons who have authorized the use of a locomotive on their premises have no right of action for damage done to their property by fire set by sparks from such locomotive Spear *v* Marquette, etc R Co , 49 Wis 246.

Upon the distinction between lawful risk and negligence, by footmen in crossing streets the Supreme Court of Indiana says "We agree that it is the duty of a person crossing, or about to cross, a public street on foot, to look and take precautions according to the character of the

applicable It was suggested in *Holmes v. Mather* (*l*) that when a competent driver is run away with by his horses, and in spite of all he can do they run over a foot-passenger, the foot-passenger is disabled from suing, not simply because the driver has done no wrong, but because people who walk along a road must take the ordinary risks of traffic. But if this were so, why stop at misadventure without negligence? It is common knowledge that not all drivers are careful. It is known, or capable of being known, that a certain percentage are not careful. "No one (at all events some years ago, before the admirable police regulations of later years) could have crossed London streets without knowing that there was a risk of being run over" (*m*). The actual risk to which a man crossing the street is exposed (apart from any carelessness on his own part) is that of pure misadventure, and also that of careless driving, the latter element being probably the greater. If he really took the whole risk, a driver would not be liable to him for running over him by negligence; which is absurd. Are we to say, then, that he takes on himself the one part of the risk and does not take the other? A reason thus artificially limited is no reason at all, but a mere fiction. It is simpler and better to say plainly that the driver's duty is to use proper and reason-

(*l*) L. R. 10 Ex. at p. 267.   (*m*) Lord Halsbury, '91, A. C. at p. 35.

thoroughfare, so as to avoid collision with approaching horsemen or vehicles; but it is obviously not necessary that the same high degree of vigilance should be demanded of a footman about to cross a public street, in order to avoid contact with a horseman who is likewise under a duty to be on the lookout, and to have his horse under careful control, as is required at railroad crossings over which engines and trains of cars are necessarily run at a rate of speed not readily governable." Stringer *v.* Frost, 116 Ind. 480; 19 N. E. Rep. 332, citing Wendell *v.* Railway Co., 91 N. Y. 420, Baker *v.* Savage, 45 N. Y. 191; Williams *v* Grealy, 112 Mass. 79; Simmons *v.* Gaynor, 89 Ind. 165, Danils *v* Clegg, 28 Mich. 32; Shapleigh *v* Wyman, 134 Mass. 118, Coombs *v.* Purrington, 42 Me. 332. See *post*, p. 553.

able care, and beyond that he is not answerable. The true view, we submit, is that the doctrine of voluntary exposure to risk has no application as between parties on an equal footing of right, of whom one does not go out of his way more than the other. A man is not bound at his peril to fly from a risk from which it is another's duty to protect him, merely because the risk is known (*n*). Much the same principle has in late years been applied, and its limits discussed, in the special branch of the law which deals with contributory negligence. This we shall have to consider in its place (*o*).

11 — *Works of necessity*

Works of necessity. A class of exceptions as to which there is not much authority, but which certainly exists in every system of law, is that of acts done of necessity to avoid a greater harm, and on that ground justified. Pull-

---

(*n*) *Smith* v *Baker*, '91, A. C 325, 60 L J Q B 683, *Thrussell* v *Handyside* (1885), 20 Q B D 359, 57 L J Q B 317.

(*o*) See *Gee* v *Metropolitan R Co* (1873), L R 8 Q B 161, 42 L J Q B 105, *Robson* v *N L R Co* (1876),
L R 10 Q B at p 274, 44 L J Q B 112, and per Bramwell L J (not referring to these authorities, and taking a somewhat different view), *Lax* v *Corporation of Darlington* (1879), 5 Ex D at p 35, 49 L. J Ex 105

Works of necessity. Agreeing with the text, *vide* Beach *v* Trudgain, 2 Gratt. 219, Sorrucco *v.* Geary, 3 Cal 69, American Print. Works *v* Lawrence, 23 N J. L J , Hale *v.* Lawrence, Id 590, Miller *v* Craig, 11 N J Eq 175, Taylor *v.* Plymouth, 8 Metc. 462; Fisher *v.* McGirr, 1 Gray, 11, McDonald *v.* Redburg, 13 Mass. 48, Penrice *v.* Wallace, 17 Mass 172, Russell *v* Major, 2 Denio, 561; Rentz *v.* Etna Ins Co., 3 Edw Ch. 341, Coe *v.* Schultz, 47 Barb 64, Republican *v* Sparhawk, 1 Dall 357; Parkham *v* Decatur, 9 Ga. 341. Proctor *v.* Adams, 113 Mass 376, Burton *v* McClellan, 3 Ill 434, Bowditch *v.* Boston, 101 U. S. 16.

But "public interest" does not justify the commission of a wrong. Henderson *v.* Railroad Co , 17 Tex. 650; Boyle *v* Case, 18 Fed Rep 880 See Harrison *v.* Wisdom, 7 Heisk, 99, Glenn *v* Kays, 11 Ill. App 479, Vossen *v* Dantel (Mo), 22 S. W. Rep 734.

Self-defence may be termed a work of necessity, and as such is justifiable, see *post*, p. 201

ing down houses to stop a fire (*p*), and casting goods overboard, or otherwise sacrificing property, to save a ship or the lives of those on board, are the regular examples. The maritime law of general average assumes, as its very foundation, that the destruction of property under such conditions of danger is justifiable (*q*). It is said also that "in time of war one shall justify entry on another's land to make a bulwark in defence of the king and the kingdom." In these cases the apparent wrong "sounds for the public good" (*r*). There are also circumstances in which a man's property or person may have to be dealt with promptly for his own obvious good, but his consent, or the consent of any one having lawful authority over him, cannot be obtained in time. Here it is evidently justifiable to do, in a proper and reasonable manner, what needs to be done. It has never been supposed to be even technically a trespass if I throw water on my neighbour's goods to save them from fire, or seeing his house on fire, enter on his land to help in putting it out (*s*). Nor is it an assault for the first passer-by to pick up a man rendered insensible by an accident, or for a competent surgeon, if he perceives that an operation ought forthwith to be performed to save the man's life, to perform it without waiting for him to recover consciousness and give his consent. These works of charity and necessity must be lawful as well as right. Our books have only slight and scattered hints on the subject, probably because no question has ever been made (*t*).

(*p*) Dyer, 36 *b*.

(*q*) *Mouse's case*, 12 Co. Rep. 63, is only just worth citing as an illustration that no action lies.

(*r*) Kingsmill J. 21 Hen. VII. 27, pl. 5, cp. Dyer, *ubi supra*. In 8 Ed. IV. 23, pl. 41, it is thought doubtful whether the justification should be by common law or by special custom.

(*s*) Good will without real necessity would not do, there must be danger of total loss, and, it is said, without remedy for the owner against any person, per Rede C. J. 21 Hen. VII. 28, pl. 5, but if this be law, it must be limited to remedies against a trespasser, for it cannot be a trespass or a lawful act to save a man's goods according as they are or are not insured. Cp. Y. B. 12 Hen. VIII. 2, where there is some curious discussion on the theory of trespass generally.

(*t*) Cf. the Indian Penal Code, s. 92, and the powers given to the London Fire Brigade by 28 & 29 Vict. c. 90, s. 12, which seem rather to assume a pre-existing right at common law.

12. — *Private defence.*

Self-defence. Self-defence (or rather private defence (*u*), for defence of one's self is not the only case) is another ground of immunity well known to the law. To repel force by force is the common instinct of every creature that has means of defence. And when the original force is unlawful, this natural right or power of man is allowed, nay approved, by the law. Sudden and strong resistance to unrighteous attack is not merely a thing to be tolerated, in many cases it is a moral duty. Therefore it would be a grave mistake to regard self-defence as a necessary evil suffered by the law because of the hardness of men's hearts. The right is a just and perfect one. It extends not only to the defence of a man's own person, but to the defence of his property or possession. And what may be lawfully done for oneself in this regard may likewise be done for a wife or husband, a parent or child, a master or servant (*x*). At the same time no right is to be

---

(*u*) This is a term adopted in the Indian Penal Co.

(*x*) Blackstone iii 3, and see the opinion of all the Justices of K B, 21 Hen VII 39, pl 50 There has been some doubt whether a master could justify on the ground of the defence of his servant But the practice and the better opinion have always been otherwise Before the Conquest it was understood that a lord might fight in defence of his men as well as they in his Ll Alf c 42, § 5

Self-defence Agreeing with the text, *vide* Murray v Boyne, 42 Mo. 472, Commonwealth v Elleger, 1 Brews. 352, Morris v Platt, 32 Conn 75, 47 Am Dec 265; Scribner v. Beach, 4 Denio, 448, Elliott v. Brown, 2 Wend 497, 20 Am Dec 644; Dole v. Erskine, 35 N H 503; Philbrick v. Foster, 1 Ind 442, Hazel v Clark, 3 Harr (Del) 22, Fortune v Jones, 128 Ill 518, 21 N E Rep 523, Russell v. Barrow, 7 Port. 106; Stoneman v Commonwealth, 86 Va. 523, Barnards v. State, 88 Tenn. 183, Howland v Day, 56 Vt 318, Close v Cooper, 34 Ohio St. 98; Gyre v. Culver, 4 Barb 593, Davis v Whitridge, 2 Strobh. 232; Thompson v Berry, 1 Cranch C. Ct. 45, McIlvoy v. Cockran, 2 A K Marsh. 270, Robinson v Hawkins, 4 T. B Mon 136, Baldwin v Hayden, 6 Conn. 453, Hill v Rogers, 2 Ia 67, McCarty v Fremont, 23 Cal 196; Pitford v. Armstrong, Wright, 94; Woodman v Howell, 45 Ill. 367, Newkirk v Sabler, 9 Barb 652, Jones v Gale, 22 Mo App 637, Bliss v. Johnson, 73 N Y 529, Simmonds v Holmes, 61 Conn 1 See *post*, p 235

abused or made the cloak of wrong, and this right is one easily abused. The law sets bounds to it by the rule that the force employed must not be out of proportion to the apparent urgency of the occasion. We say apparent, for a man cannot be held to form a precise judgment under such conditions. The person acting on the defensive is entitled to use as much force as he reasonably believes to be necessary. Thus it is not justifiable to use a deadly weapon to repel a push or a blow with the hand. It is even said that a man attacked with a deadly weapon must retreat as far as he safely can before he is justified in defending himself by like means. But this probably applies (so far as it is the law) only to criminal liability (y). On the other hand if a man presents a pistol at my head and threatens to shoot me, peradventure the pistol is not loaded or is not in working order, but I shall do no wrong before the law by acting on the supposition that it is really loaded and capable of shooting

Killing of animals in defence of property. Cases have arisen on the killing of animals in defence of one's property. Here, as elsewhere, the test is whether the party's act was such as he might reasonably, in the circumstances,

---

(y) See Stephen, Digest of Criminal Law, art. 200. Most of the authority on this subject is in the early treatises on Pleas of the Crown.

Killing of animals in defence of property. It may be stated as a general rule that the killing of a trespassing animal is not justifiable. Johnson v. Patterson, 14 Conn 1; Ford v. Taggart, 4 Tex. 492; Tyner v. Cory, 5 Ind 216; Holson v. Perry, 1 Hill (S C.), 277; Clark v. Keliher, 107 Mass. 406; Livermore v. Batchelder, 141 Mass 179; Sosat v. State, 2 Ind App 586, 28 N. E Rep 1017.

But where the owner of property has reasonable cause to suppose that his property is about to be substantially or irreparably injured by an animal and that the killing of the animal is the only available method of preventing such injury, he may slay the animal. Parrott v Hartsfield, 4 Dev. & B 110; Hinckley v Emerson, 4 Cow. 351; Boescher v Lutz, 13 Daly, 28; Dunning v Bird, 24 Ill App 270; Lipe v. Blackwelder, 25 Ill. App 123.

think necessary for the prevention of harm which he was not bound to suffer. Not very long ago the subject was elaborately discussed in New Hampshire, and all or nearly all the authorities, English and American, reviewed (z). Some of these, such as *Deane* v. *Clayton* (a), turn less on what amount of force is reasonable in itself than on the question whether a man is bound, as against the owners of animals which come on his land otherwise than as of right, to abstain from making the land dangerous for them to come on. And in this point of view it is immaterial whether a man keeps up a certain state of things on his own land for the purpose of defending his property or for any other purpose which is not actually unlawful.

As to injuries received by an innocent third person from an act done in self-defence, they must be dealt with on the same principle as accidental harm proceeding from any other act lawful in itself. It has to be considered, however, that a man repelling imminent danger cannot be expected to use as much care as he would if he had time to act deliberately.

Assertion of rights distinguished from self-defence.
Self-defence does not include the active assertion of a dis-

(z) *Aldrich* v. *Wright* (1873), 53 N. H. 398, 16 Am. Rep. 339. The decision was that the penalty of a statute ordaining a close time for minks did not apply to a man who shot on his own land, in the close season, minks which he reasonably thought were in pursuit of his geese. Compare *Taylor* app. *Newman* resp. (1863), 4 B. & S. 89, 32 L. J. M. C. 186.

(a) 7 Taunt. 489, the case of dog spears, where the Court was equally divided (1817), *Jordin* v. *Crump* (1841), 8 M. & W. 782, where the Court took the view of Gibbs C. J. in the last case, on the ground that setting dog spears was not in itself illegal. Notice, however, was pleaded.

Assertion of rights distinguished from self-defence. In an attempt by the owner, to recapture property from the possession of a trespasser, the law does not justify the owner in a resort to the use of a deadly weapon in such manner as to be reasonably calculated to endanger human life, although, because of the superior physical power of the trespasser, such object cannot be otherwise accomplished, but leaves him to his legal remedy. Kimple v. State, 32 Ind. 220, McCarty t

puted right against an attempt to obstruct its exercise. I am not justified in shooting, or offering to shoot, one who obstructs my right of way, though I may not be able to pass him otherwise, and though I am justified in resisting, within due bounds, any active force used on his part. It seems the better opinion "that the use of force which inflicts or may inflict grievous bodily harm or death — or what in short may be called extreme force — is justifiable only for the purpose of strict self-defence" (*b*). I may be justified in pushing past the obstructor, but this is not an act of self-defence at all; it is the pure and simple exercise of my right itself (*c*).

Many interesting questions, in part not yet settled, may be raised in this connexion, but their interest belongs for most practical intents to public and not to private law. It must not be assumed, of course, that whatever is a sufficient justification or excuse in a criminal prosecution will equally suffice in a civil action.

Injury to third persons from acts of self-defence. Some of the dicta in the well-known case of *Scott* v. *Shepherd* (*d*) go the length of suggesting that a man acting on

(*b*) Dicey, Law of the Constitution, 3rd ed. 1889, app. 410, which see for fuller discussion.

(*c*) Dicey, *op. cit.* 411.

(*d*) 2 W. Bl. 892.

Fremont, 23 Cal 196, Kiff v Youmans, 86 N Y 324, Woodman v Howell, 45 Ill 267, State v. Burke, 82 N C 551, Brothers v Morris, 49 Vt. 460, Abt v Burghein, 80 Ill 92, Bliss v Johnson, 73 N Y 529, Johnson v Perry, 56 Vt 703; 48 Am Rep 826, Higgins v Minaghan, 76 Wis 298, 17 N W. Rep 941, McIntire v Plaisted, 57 N H 606, Anderson v Smith, 7 Ill App 354, Marshall v Blackshire, 44 Ia 475, Parsons v Brown, 15 Barb. 590 See the cases cited on the preceding pages of this subject

Injuries to third persons from acts of self-defence In the case of Morris v. Platt (32 Conn. 75, *supra*, p. 164) it was held, that where a person in lawful self-defence and without negligence, fires a pistol at an assailant, and missing him wounds an innocent bystander, he is not liable for the injury.

the spur of the moment under "compulsive necessity" (the expression of De Grey C. J.) is excusable as not being a voluntary agent, and is therefore not bound to take any care at all. But this appears very doubtful. In that case it is hard to believe that Willis or Ryal, if he had been worth suing and had been sued, could have successfully made such a defence. They "had a right to protect themselves by removing the squib, but should have taken care"—at any rate such care as was practicable under the circumstances—"to do it in such a manner as not to endamage others" (e). The Roman lawyers held that a man who throws a stone in self-defence is not excused if the stone by misadventure strikes a person other than the assailant (f). Perhaps this is a harsh opinion, but it seems better, if the choice must be made, than holding that one may with impunity throw a lighted squib across a market-house full of people in order to save a stall of gingerbread. At all events a man cannot justify doing for the protection of his own property a deliberate act whose evident tendency is to cause, and which does cause, damage to the property of an innocent neighbour. Thus if flood water has come on my land by no fault of my own, this does not entitle me to let it off by means which in the natural order of things cause it to flood an adjoining owner's land (g).

13.—*Plaintiff a wrong-doer.*

Harm suffered by a wrong-doer: doubtful whether any special disability. Language is to be met with in some books to the effect that a man cannot sue for any injury suffered by him at a time when he is himself a

---

(e) Blackstone J. in his dissenting judgment.

(f) D. 9, ad l. Aquil. 15, § 4, *supra*, pp. 123, 124.

(g) Whalley v. Lanc. and Yorkshire R. Co. (1884), 13 Q. B. Div. 131, 53 L. J. Q. B. 285, distinguishing the case of acts lawful in themselves which are done by way of precaution against an impending common danger.

wrong-doer. But there is no such general rule of law. If there were, one consequence would be that an occupier of land (or even a fellow trespasser) might beat or wound a trespasser without being liable to an action, whereas the right of using force to repel trespass to land is strictly limited; or if a man is riding or driving at an incautiously fast pace, anybody might throw stones at him with impunity. In *Bird* v. *Holbrook* (*h*) a trespasser who was wounded by a spring-gun set without notice was held entitled to maintain his action. And generally, "a trespasser is liable to an action for the injury which he does; but he does not forfeit his right of action for an injury sustained" (*i*). It does not appear on the whole that a plaintiff is disabled from recovering by reason of being himself a wrong-doer, unless some unlawful act or conduct on his own part is connected with the harm suffered by him as part of the same transaction: and even then it is difficult to find a case where it is necessary to assume any special rule of this kind. It would be no answer to an action for killing a dog to show that the

---

(*h*) 4 Bing 628 Cp p 151 above The cause of action arose, and the trial took place, before the passing of the Act which made the setting of spring guns unlawful

(*i*) *Barnes* v *Ward* (1850), 9 C B 392, 19 L J C P 195

Harm suffered by a wrong-doer The authorities in both England and America agree that humanity requires that the person of a trespasser be not exposed to bodily injury or death on the mere ground that he is at the time acting in violation of the law In the case of Hooker v Miller (37 Ia 613), plaintiff, having no knowledge of a spring gun set in defendant's vineyard, entered therein for the purpose of taking grapes without permission, and coming in contact with the gun received a severe wound The defendant was held responsible for the injury, citing Loomis v Terry, 17 Wend 496, Shufey v. Bartley, 4 Sneed, 58 See Aldrich v Wright, 53 N H. 396, 16 Am Rep 339; Churchill v Hulbert, 110 Mass 42, 14 Am. Rep. 578.

The mere fact that a person is a tort-feasor does not prevent him from recovering for a subsequent wrong done him. Fletcher v. Cole, 26 Vt 170. See Gray v Ayres, 7 Dana, 375; Love v. Moynehan, 16 Ill. 277, Ogden v. Claycomb, 52 Ill 365, Getzler v. Witzee, 82 Ill. 392. But see Jones v Gale, 22 Mo. App 637, Phillips v. Kelly, 29 Ala. 628.

owner was liable to a penalty for not having taken out a dog licence in due time. If, again, A. receives a letter containing defamatory statements concerning B., and reads the letter aloud in the presence of several persons, he may be doing wrong to B. But this will not justify or excuse B. if he seizes and tears up the letter. A. is unlawfully possessed of explosives which he is carrying in his pocket. B., walking or running in a hurried and careless manner, jostles A. and so causes an explosion. Certainly A. cannot recover against B. for any hurt he takes by this, or can at most recover nominal damages, as if he had received a harmless push. But would it make any difference if A.'s possession were lawful? Suppose there were no statutory regulation at all: still a man going about with sensitive explosives in his pocket would be exposing himself to an unusual risk obvious to him and not obvious to other people, and on the principles already discussed would have no cause of action. And on the other hand it seems a strong thing to say that if another person does know of the special danger, he does not become bound to take answerable care, even as regards one who has brought himself into a position of danger by a wrongful act. Cases of this kind have sometimes been thought to belong to the head of contributory negligence. But this, it is submitted, is an unwarrantable extension of the term, founded on a misapprehension of the true meaning and reasons of the doctrine as if contributory negligence were a sort of positive wrong for which a man is to be punished. This, however, we shall have to consider hereafter. On the whole it may be doubted whether a mere civil wrong-doing, such as trespass to land, ever has in itself the effect now under consideration. Almost every case that can be put seems to fall just as well, if not better, under the principle that a plaintiff who has voluntarily exposed himself to a known risk cannot recover, or the still broader rule that a defendant is liable only for those consequences of his acts which are, in the sense explained in a former chapter (*k*), natural and probable.

Conflict of opinion in United States in cases of Sunday travelling. In America there has been a great question, upon which there have been many contradictory decisions, whether the violation of statutes against Sunday travelling is in itself a bar to actions for injuries received in the course of such travelling through defective condition of roads, negligence of railway companies, and the like. In Massachusetts it has been held that a plaintiff in such circumstances cannot recover, although the accident might just as well have happened on a journey lawful for all purposes. These decisions must be supported, if at all, by a strict view of the policy of the local statutes for securing the observance of Sunday. They are not generally considered good law, and have been expressly dissented from in some other States (*l*)

Cause of action connected with unlawful agreement. It is a rule not confined to actions on contracts that "the plaintiff cannot recover where in order to maintain his supposed claim he must set up an illegal agreement to which he himself has been a party" (*m*): but its application to actions of tort is not frequent or normal. The case from which the foregoing statement is cited is the only clear example known to the writer, and its facts were very peculiar.

(*k*) P. 35 above
(*l*) *Sutton v. Town of Wauwatosa* (Wisconsin, 1871), Bigelow L. C. 711, and notes thereto, pp. 721-2, Cooley on Torts, 156. And see *White v. Lang*, 128 Mass. 598
(*m*) Maule J., *Fivaz v. Nicholls* (1846), 2 C. B. 501, 512

CHAPTER V.

OF REMEDIES FOR TORTS

Diversity of remedies. At common law there were only two kinds of redress for an actionable wrong. One was in those cases — exceptional cases according to modern law and practice — where it was and is lawful for the aggrieved party, as the common phrase goes, to take the law into his own hands. The other way was an action for damages (*a*). Not that a suitor might not obtain in a proper case, other and more effectual redress than money compensation; but he could not have it from a court of common law. Specific orders and prohibitions in the form of injunctions or otherwise were (with few exceptions, if any) (*b*) in the hand of the Chancellor alone, and the principles according to which they were granted or withheld were counted among the mysteries of Equity. But no such distinctions exist under the system of the Judicature Acts, and every branch of the Court has power to administer every remedy. Therefore we have at this day, in considering one and the same jurisdiction, to bear in mind the manifold forms of legal redress which for our predecessors were separate and unconnected incidents in the procedure of different courts.

(*a*) Possession could not be recovered, of course, in an action of ejectment. But this was an action of trespass in form only. In substance it took the place of the old real actions, and it is sometimes called a real action. Detinue was not only not a substantial exception, but hardly even a formal one, for the action was not really in tort.

(*b*) I do not think any of the powers of the superior courts of common law to issue specific commands (*e.g.* mandamus) were applicable to the redress of purely private wrongs, though they might be available for a private person wronged by a breach of public duty. Under the Common Law Procedure Acts the superior courts of common law had limited powers of granting injunctions and administering equitable relief. These were found of little importance in practice, and there is now no reason for dwelling on them.

Self-help. Remedies available to a party by his own act alone may be included, after the example of the long established German usage, in the expressive name of *self help*. The right of private defence appears at first sight to be an obvious example of this. But it is not so, for there is no question of remedy in such a case. We are allowed to repel force by force " not for the redress of injuries, but for their prevention" (c); not in order to undo a wrong done or to get compensation for it, but to cut wrong short before it is done; and the right goes only to the extent necessary for this purpose. Hence there is no more to be said of self-defense, in the strict sense, in this connexion. It is only when the party's lawful act restores to him something which he ought to have, or puts an end to a state of things whereby he is wronged, or at least puts pressure on the wrong-doer to do him right, that self-help is a true remedy. And then it is not necessarily a complete or exclusive remedy. The acts of this nature which we meet with in the law of torts are expulsion of a trespasser, retaking of goods by the rightful possessor, distress damage feasant, and abatement of nuisances. Peaceable re-entry upon land where there has been a wrongful change of possession is possible, but hardly occurs in modern experience. Analogous to the right of retaking goods is the right of appropriating or retaining debts under certain conditions; and various forms of lien are more or less analogous to distress. These, however, belong to the domain of contract, and we are not now concerned with them. Such are the species of remedial self-help recognized in the law of England. In every case alike the right

(c) This is well noted in Cooley on Torts, 50

Self-help. The above doctrine is accepted by the courts of the United States and its application and enlargement is illustrated by the cases cited in the American notes upon SELF-DEFENCE, *ante*, p. 201; ASSERTION OF RIGHTS DISTINGUISHED FROM SELF-DEFENCE, *ante*, p. 203 and ABATEMENT, *post*, p. 515.

of the party is subject to the rule that no greater force must be used, or damage done to property, than is necessary for the purpose in hand. In some cases the mode of exercising the right has been specially modified or regulated. Details will best be considered hereafter in relation to the several kinds of wrong to which these kinds of redress are applicable (*d*).

Judicial remedies damages. We pass, then, from extra-judicial to judicial redress, from remedies by the act of the party to remedies by the act of the law. The most frequent and familiar of these is the awarding of damages (*e*). Whenever an actionable wrong has been done, the party wronged is entitled to recover damages; though, as we shall immediately see, this right is not necessarily a valuable one. His title to recover is a conclusion of law from the facts determined in the cause. How much he shall recover is a matter of judicial discretion, a discretion

---

(*d*) Cp. Blackstone, Bk. III. c. 1.
(*e*) It is hardly needful to refer the reader for fuller illustration of the subject to so well known a work as "Mayne on Damages."

Judicial remedies damages. In the case of Dwyer *v* St Louis & S. F. R. Co. (52 Fed. Rep. 89), the court in following Schumacher *v* Railroad Co. (39 Fed. Rep. 174), said: "At common law, if damages given by a jury were so extravagant as to make it probable that the jury was actuated by passion or prejudice, a verdict might, upon this ground, be set aside." See Tennessee C. & R. Co. *v* Roddy, 85 Tenn. 400; Kelly *v* McDonald, 39 Ark. 387; Toledo, etc. R. Co. *v* Arnold, 43 Ill. 418; Jones *v* Jennings, 10 Humph. 428; Delphi *v* Lowery, 71 Ind. 520; Goodall *v* Shurman, 1 Head, 209; P., C. & St. L. R. Co. *v* Sponier, 85 Ind. 165, 5 Am. & Eng. R. Cas. 453; Graham *v* Pacific R. Co., 66 Mo. 536; W. U. Tel Co. *v* Simpson, 73 Tex. 422; 11 S. W. Rep. 385; Berry *v* Vreeland, 21 N. J. L. 183. So, where the damages were clearly insufficient McDonald *v* Walker, 40 N. Y. 551; Chesapeake etc. R. Co. *v* Higgins, 85 Tenn. 621; Nicholson *v* New York, etc. R Co., 22 Conn. 74; Donovan *v* Gay, 97 Mo. 440, 11 S. W. Rep. 44; Matthews *v* Missouri P. Ry Co., 26 Mo. App. 75.

In the notes to this and subsequent paragraphs upon the subject of damages it is impracticable to cite more than a few of the late cases and the leading cases.

exercised, if a jury tries the cause, by the jury under the guidance of the judge. As we have had occasion to point out in a former chapter (*f*), the rule as to "measure of damages" is laid down by the Court and applied by the jury, whose application of it is, to a certain extent, subject to review. The grounds on which the verdict of a jury may be set aside are all reducible to this principle: the Court, namely, must be satisfied not only that its own finding would have been different (for there is a wide field within which opinions and estimates may fairly differ) (*g*), but that the jury did not exercise a due judicial discretion at all (*h*). Among these grounds are the awarding of manifestly excessive or manifestly inadequate damages, such as to imply that the jury disregarded, either by excess or by defect, the law laid down to them as to the elements of damage to be considered (*i*), or, it may be, that the verdict represents a compromise between jurymen who were really not agreed on the main facts in issue (*j*).

Nominal damages. Damages may be nominal, ordinary, or exemplary. Nominal damages are a sum of so little value as compared with the cost and trouble of suing that it may be said to have "no existence in point of quantity" (*k*), such as a shilling or a penny, which sum is awarded with the purpose of not giving any real compensation. Such a verdict means one of two things. According to the nature of the case it may be honourable or contumelious to the plaintiff. Either the purpose of the action is merely to establish a right, no substantial harm or loss having been suffered, or else the jury, while unable to

---

(*f*) P. 31, above.

(*g*) The principle is familiar. See it stated, *e.g.* 5 Q. B. Div. 85.

(*h*) See *Metropolitan R. Co. v. Wright* (1886), 11 App. Ca. 152.

(*i*) *Phillips v. L. & S. W. R. Co.* (1879), 5 Q. B. Div. 78, 49 L. J. Q. B. 233, where-on the facts shown, a verdict for 7000*l*. was set aside on the ground of the damages being insufficient.

(*j*) *Falvey v. Stanford* (1874), L. R. 10 Q. B. 54, 44 L. J. Q. B. 7.

(*k*) Maule J. 2 C. B. 499.

deny that some legal wrong has been done to the plaintiff, have formed a very low opinion of the general merits of his case. This again may be on the ground that the harm he suffered was not worth suing for, or that his own conduct had been such that whatever he did suffer at the defendant's hands was morally deserved. The former state of things, where the verdict really operates as a simple declaration of rights between the parties, is most commonly exemplified in actions of trespass brought to settle disputed claims to rights of way, rights of common, and other easements and profits. It is not uncommon to give forty shillings damages in these cases if the plaintiff establishes his right, and if it is not intended to express any disapproval of his conduct (*l*). The other kind of award of nominal damages,

---

(*l*) Under the various statutes as to costs which were in force before the Judicature Acts, 40s. was, subject to a few exceptions, the least amount of damages which carried costs without a special certificate from the judge. Frequently juries asked before giving their verdict what was the least sum that would carry costs; the general practice of the judges was to refuse this information.

Nominal damages. In practice, nominal damages is defined as: "A trifling sum awarded to a plaintiff in an action, where there is no substantial loss or injury to be compensated, but still the law recognizes a technical invasion of his rights or a breach of the defendant's duty." Black's Law Dic. 818. Illustrating this definition, see the following cases: Dixon v. Clow, 24 Wend. 191; Hatch v. Donnell, 74 Me. 163; Champion v. Vincent, 20 Tex. 811; Smith v. Whiting, 100 Mass. 122; Lake Erie & W. R. Co. v. Christison, 39 Ill. App. 495; Gifford v. Weber, 33 Mo. App. 595; McDonnell v. Cambridge R. Co., Mass. 159, 23 N. E. Rep. 841; Becker v. Janinski, 27 Abb. N. C. 45, 15 N. Y. S. Rep. 675; Drum v. Harrison, 83 Ala. 384, 3 So. Rep. 715; Little v. Stauback, 63 N. C. 285; Cory v. Silcox, 6 Ind. 39; Wright v. Stowe, 4 Jones L. 516; Owen v. O'Reilly, 30 Mo. 603; Southern R. Co. v. Kendrick, 40 Miss. 374; Brown v. Emerson, 18 Mo. 103; Custard v. Burdett, 15 Tex. 456.

A cause will not be reversed for failure to award nominal damages. Ellithorpe v. Reidesel (Ia.), 55 N. W. Rep. 313; Machine Co. v. Haven, 65 Ia. 359; Eaton v. Lyman, 30 Wis. 41; Watson v. Moeller, 63 Ia. 161.

In an action for damage for trespass to try the title, nominal damages will establish the plaintiff's title. Bassett v. Salisbury, 8 Fost. 438; Ronsee v. Hammond, 39 Barb. 89; Devendorf v. Wert, 42 Barb. 227; Delaware & H. C. Co. v. Torrey, 33 Pa. St. 143.

where the plaintiff's demerits earn him an illusory sum such as one farthing, is illustrated chiefly by cases of defamation, where the words spoken or written by the defendant cannot be fully justified, and yet the plaintiff has done so much to provoke them, or is a person of such generally worthless character, as not to deserve, in the opinion of the jury, any substantial compensation (m) This has happened more than once in actions against the publishers of newspapers which were famous at the time, but have not found a place in the regular reports

Nominal damages possible only when an absolute right is infringed The enlarged power of the Court over costs since the Judicature Acts has made the question of nominal damages, which, under the old procedure, were described as

---

(m) *Kelly v. Sherlock* (1866), L R 1 Q B 686, 35 L J Q B 209, is a case of this kind where, notwithstanding that the libels sued for were very gross, the jury gave a farthing damages, and the Court, though not satisfied with the verdict, refused to disturb it

---

Nominal damages possible only when an absolute right is infringed. Some damage is presumed to flow from the violation of a right. Fitzpatrick v Boston & M R R, 84 Me 33, 24 At Rep 432, Webb v Portland Mfg Co, 3 Summ. 189, Mitchell v Mayor of Rome, etc, 49 Ga 19, Monroe v Stickney, 48 Me 462, Cowley v. Davidson, 10 Minn 392 Smith v Whiting, 100 Mass. 122, Fullam v Stearns, 30 Vt. 443, Bagby v Harris, 9 Ala 173, Seat v Moreland, 7 Humph. 575, Paul v. Slason, 22 Vt 231; Devendorf v Werf, 42 Barb. 227, Bassett v Salisbury Mfg Co, 28 N H. 438, Stowell v Lincoln, 11 Gray, 434, Seneca Road Co v Auburn, etc R Co, 5 Hill, 175; Allaire v Whitney, 1 Hill, 484, Townsend v Bell, 62 Hun, 306, 17 N Y S Rep. 210

In America, contrary to the rule in England, public officers are liable in nominal damages for breach of their duty to individuals, although no actual damage results. Moore v. Floyd, 4 Oreg 101, Patterson v. Westervelt, 17 Wend 543, Hamilton v Ward, 4 Tex 356, Palmer v Gallup, 16 Conn. 555. Laflin v Willard, 16 Pick 64, Bondurant v Lane, 9 Port 484, Doggett v Adams, 1 Me 198; Rich v Bell, 16 Mass 294

Nominal damages are recoverable for the violation of a right although the injury results in an actual benefit to the complainant. Bond v. Hilton, 2 Jones L 149, Stowell v Lincoln, 11 Gray, 434; Jewett v Whitney, 43 Me. 242, Hibbard v W U Tel. Co, 33 Wis 558, Francis v Schoellkopf, 53 N Y 152

"a mere peg on which to hang costs" (n), much less important than it formerly was. But the possibility of recovering nominal damages is still a test, to a certain extent, of the nature of the right claimed. Infringements of absolute rights like those of personal security and property give a cause of action without regard to the amount of harm done, or to there being harm estimable at any substantial sum at all. As Holt C. J. said in a celebrated passage of his judgment in *Ashby* v. *White* (o), "*a damage is not merely pecuniary, but an injury imports a damage, when a man is thereby hindered of his right.* As in an action for slanderous words, though a man does not lose a penny by reason of the speaking them, yet he shall have an action. So if a man gives another a cuff on the ear, though it cost him nothing, no not so much as a little *diachylon*, yet he shall have his action, for it is a personal injury. So a man shall have an action against another for riding over his ground, though it do him no damage, for it is an invasion of his property, and the other has no right to come there."

Cases where damage is the gist of the action. On the other hand, there are cases even in the law of property where, as it is said, damage is the gist of the action, and there is not an absolute duty to forbear from doing a certain thing, but only not to do it so as to cause actual damage. The right to the support of land as between adjacent owners, or as between the owner of the surface and the owner of the mine beneath, is an example. Here there is not an easement, that is, a positive right to restrain the neighbour's use of his land, but a right to the un-

---

(n) By Maule J. (1846), in *Beaumont* v *Greathead*, 2 C. B. 499. Under the present procedure costs are in the discretion of the Court, the costs of a cause tried by jury follow the event (without regard to amount of damages) unless the judge or the Court otherwise orders. Order LXV. r. 1, &c. The effect of the Judicature Acts and Rules of Court in abrogating the older statutes was settled in 1878 by *Garnett* v *Bradley*, 3 App. Ca. 944, 48 L. J. Ex. 186. A sketch of the history of the subject is given in Lord Blackburn's judgment, pp. 962, *sqq*.

(o) 2 Lord Raym. at p. 955.

disturbed enjoyment of one's own. My neighbour may excavate in his own land as much as he pleases, unless and until there is actual damage to mine: then, and not till then, a cause of action arises for me (p). Negligence, again, is a cause of action only for a person who suffers actual harm by reason of it. A man who rides furiously in the street of a town may thereby render himself liable to penalties under a local statute or by-laws, but he does no wrong to any man in particular, and is not liable to a civil action, so long as his reckless behaviour is not the cause of specific injury to person or property. The same rule holds of nuisances. So, in an action of deceit, the cause of action is the plaintiff's having suffered damage by acting on the false statement made to him by the defendant (q). In all these cases there can be no question of nominal damages, the proof of real damage being the foundation of the plaintiff's right. It may happen, of course, that though there is real damage there is not much of it, and that the verdict is accordingly for a small amount. But the smallness of the amount will not make such damages nominal if they are arrived at by a real estimate of the harm suffered. In a railway accident due

---

Cases where damage is the gist of the action. A property owner is liable for injuries to the adjoining property from the wrongful removal of lateral support. Freeman v. Sayre, 18 N. J. L. 37; Stevenson v. Wallace, 27 Gratt. 77; Farrand v. Marshall, 19 Barb. 380; Coleman v. Chadwick, 80 Pa. St. 81; Foley v. Wyeth, 2 Allen, 131; Charless v. Rankin, 22 Mo. 566; Guest v. Reynolds, 68 Ill. 478; Phillips v. Bordman, 4 Allen, 147.

But a man may use his land as he pleases so long as his use of it does not damage his neighbor. Penn Coal Co. v. Sanderson, 113 Pa. St. 116; Mitchell v. Mayor of Rome, etc., 49 Ga. 19; Gilmore v. Driscoll, 122 Mass. 199; Livingston v. Moingena Coal Co., 49 Ia. 369; Lasala v. Holbrook, 4 Paige, 169.

to the negligence of the railway company's servants one man may be crippled for life, while another is disabled for a few days, and a third only has his clothes damaged to the value of five shillings. Every one of them is entitled, neither more nor less than the others, to have amends according to his loss.

Peculiarity of law of defamation. In the law of slander we have a curiously fine line between absolute and conditional title to a legal remedy; some kinds of spoken defamation being actionable without any allegation or proof of special damage (in which case the plaintiff is entitled to nominal damages at least), and others not, while as to written words no such distinction is made. The attempts of text-books to give a rational theory of this are not satisfactory. Probably the existing condition of the law is the result of some obscure historical accident (r).

Ordinary damages. Ordinary damages are a sum awarded as a fair measure of compensation to the plaintiff, the amount being, as near as can be estimated, that by

(r) See more in Ch. VII below.

Ordinary damages. The American cases sustain the statement of the text. In Baker v. Drake (53 N. Y. 210), the court said: "An amount sufficient to indemnify the party injured for the loss, which is the natural, reasonable and proximate result of the wrongful act complained of, and which a proper degree of prudence on the part of the complainant would not have averted, is the measure of damages which juries are usually instructed to award, except in cases, which punitive damages are allowable."

The measure of damages is the actual damage done. See Brewster v. Van Liew, 119 Ill. 562; Burkett v. Lanata, 15 La. An. 337; Township of Martic, 152 Pa. St. 68, 25 At. Rep. 178, 31 W. N. C. 180; South Covington etc. Ry. Co. v. Gest, 34 Fed. Rep. 628; Hartshorn v. Chaddock 135 N. Y. 116, 31 N. E. Rep. 997; Kansas City, etc. R. Co. v. Cook (Ark.) 21 S. W. Rep. 1066; Young v. Gentis (Ind.), 32 N. E. Rep. 796; Perrin v. Wells, 155 Pa. St. 299, 26 At. Rep. 543; Stoner v. Texas & P. Ry. Co., 45 La. An. 115, 11 So. Rep. 875; St. Louis, etc. Ry. Co. v. Lyman (Ark.), 22 S. W. Rep. 170; Reynolds v. Franklin, 44 Minn. 30, 46 N. W. Rep. 139; Easter-

which he is the worse for the defendant's wrong-doing, but in no case exceeding the amount claimed by the plaintiff himself (s). Such amount is not necessarily that which it would cost to restore the plaintiff to his former condition. Where a tenant for years carried away a large quantity of valuable soil from his holding, it was decided that the reversioner could recover not what it would cost to replace

(s) A jury has been known to find a verdict for a greater sum than was claimed, and the judge to amend the statement of claim to enable himself to give judgment for that greater sum. But this is an extreme use of the power of the Court, justifiable only in an extra ordinary case. "It will not do for Mr. Justice Kay, or for this Court, to exercise that unknown equity which is sometimes exercised by juries." Cotton L. J., *Dreyfus v. Peruvian Guano Co.* (1889), 43 Ch. Div. 316, 327.

---

brook v. Erie R. Co., 51 Barb. 91, Vermilya v. Chicago, etc. R. Co., 66 Ia. 606, Willey v. Hunter, 57 Vt. 179, Sabine etc. R. Co. v. Joachimi, 58 Tex. 456, Van Deusen v. Young, 29 Barb. 9, Herdic v. Young, 55 Pa. St. 176, Georgia Pac. R. Co. v. Fullerton, 79 Ala. 298, Farrell v. Calwell, 30 N. J. L. 123, Cressey v. Parks, 76 Me. 532, Hine v. Cushing, 53 Hun. 519, 6 N. Y. S. Rep. 850. The measure of damage for injury to a schooner is the cost of repairs, and not the difference between her value before and her value after the injury. Union Ice Co. v. Crowell, 55 Fed. Rep. 87.

The same rule applies to injuries to vehicles by collision in the street. Travis v. Pierson, 43 Ill. App. 579.

A special value to the owner, such as family portraits possesses, is to be considered. Spicer v. Waters, 65 Barb. 227, Houston, etc. R. Co. v. Burke, 55 Tex. 523; 40 Am. Rep. 808, Green v. Boston, etc. R. Co., 128 Mass. 221.

The elements of damage to be considered in cases of personal injury are the plaintiff's loss of capacity, loss of time, loss of position, and the expenses, pain and insult resulting from the injury. City of Joliet v. Conway, 119 Ill. 489, George v. Haverhill, 110 Mass. 506, Wade v. Leroy, 20 How. 34, Hall v. Fond du Lac, 42 Wis. 274, Rockwell v. Third Av. R. Co., 53 N. Y. 625, Tomlinson v. Derby, 43 Conn. 562, Houston, etc. R. Co. v. Boehm, 57 Tex. 152, 9 Am. & Eng. R. Cas. 366, Eighott v. Mayor etc. 96 N. Y. 264, Luck v. Ripon, 52 Wis. 196, Cracker v. Chicago, etc. R. Co., 36 Wis. 657, 9 Am. Ry. Rep. 118, Chicago etc. R. Co. v. Wilson, 63 Ill. 167, Hammond v. Mukwa, 40 Wis. 35, Chicago v. Elzeman, 71 Ill. 131, Scott v. Montgomery, 95 Pa. St. 444, Wabash W. Ry. Co v. Morgan, 132 Ind. 430, 21 N. L. Rep. 661, 32 Id. 85, Howard Oil Co. v. Davis, 76 Tex. 630, 13 S. W. Rep. 665, Whelan v. New York, etc. R. Co., 38 Fed. Rep. 15, Ohio & M. Ry. Co. v. Hecht, 115 Ind. 443, 17 N. E. Rep. 297, Stuckum v. Wabash, etc. Ry. Co., 93 Mo. 400, 4 S. W. Rep. 701, Conner v. Pioneer Fire-proof Const. Co., 29 Fed. Rep. 629.

the soil, but only the amount by which the value of the reversion was diminished (*t*). In other words compensation, not restitution, is the proper test. Beyond this it is hardly possible to lay down any universal rule for ascertaining the amount, the causes and circumstances of actionable damage being infinitely various. And in particular classes of cases only approximate generalization is possible. In proceedings for the recovery of specific property or its value there is not so much difficulty in assigning a measure of damages, though here too there are unsettled points (*u*). But in cases of personal injury and consequential damage by loss of gains in a business or profession it is not possible either completely to separate the elements of damage, or to found the estimate of the whole on anything like an exact calculation (*x*). There is little doubt that in fact the process is often in cases of this class even a rougher one than it appears to be, and that legally irrelevant circumstances, such as the wealth and condition in life of the parties, have much influence on the verdicts of juries: a state of things which the law does not recognize, but practically tolerates within large bounds.

Exemplary damages. One step more, and we come to cases where there is great injury without the possibility of measuring compensation by any numerical rule, and juries have been not only allowed but encouraged to give damages that express indignation at the defendant's wrong rather than a value set upon the plaintiff's loss. Damages awarded on this principle are called exemplary or vindictive. The kind of wrongs to which they are applicable are those which, besides the violation of a right or the actual damage, import insult or outrage, and so are not merely injuries

---

(*t*) *Whitham* v. *Kershaw* (1885–6), 16 Q B Div 613, cp *Rust* v. *Victoria Graving Dock Co* (1887), 36 Ch Div 113, *Chifferiel* v. *Watson* (1888), 40 Ch D 45, 58 L J Ch 137 (compensation under conditions of sale)

(*u*) See Mayne on Damages, c 13

(*x*) See the summing up of Field J in *Phillips* v. *L & S W R Co* (1879), 5 Q B Div 78, 49 L J Q B 233, which was in the main approved by the Court of Appeal

but *iniuriae* in the strictest Roman sense of the term. The Greek ὕβρις perhaps denotes with still greater exactness the quality of the acts which are thus treated. An assault and false imprisonment under colour of a pretended right in breach of the general law, and against the liberty of the subject (y), a wanton trespass on land, persisted in with violent and intemperate behaviour (z), the seduction of a

---

(y) *Huckle v. Money* (1763) 2 Wils. 205, one of the branches of the great case of general warrants; the plaintiff was detained about six hours and civilly treated, "entertained with beef steaks and beer," but the jury was upheld in giving 300l. damages, because "it was a most daring public attack made upon the liberty of the subject."

(z) *Merest v. Harvey* (1814), 5 Taunt. 442; the defendant was drunk, and passing by the plaintiff's land on which the plaintiff was shooting, insisted, with oaths and threats, on joining in the sport; a verdict passed for 500l., the full amount claimed, and it was laid down that juries ought to be allowed to punish insult by exemplary damages.

Exemplary damages. It is an established rule of law that, "exemplary," "punitive," or "vindictive" damages may be awarded by juries by way of punishment in an amount not exceeding the sum sued for, and this is true although the damage is purely nominal. "The true theory of exemplary damages is that of punishment, involving the ideas of retribution for wilful misconduct, and an example to deter its repetitions." *Alabama G. S. R. Co. v. Sellers*, 93 Ala. 9, 9 So. Rep. 377; *Alabama G. S. R. Co. v. Frazier*, 93 Ala. 45, 9 So. Rep. 303; *Kemmitt v. Adamson*, 44 Minn. 121, 46 N. W. Rep. 327; *Samuels v. Richmond & D. R. Co.*, 35 C. 493, 14 S. L. Rep. 943; *Voltz v. Blackman*, 64 N. Y. 440; *Shook v. Hobson*, 64 Ia. 146; *Parker v. Lanier*, 82 Ga. 216, 8 S. E. Rep. 57; *Chiles v. Drake*, 2 Metc. (Ky.) 146; *Graham v. Roder*, 5 Tex. 141; *McWilliams v. Bragg*, 3 Wis. 424; *Millison v. Hoch*, 17 Ind. 227.

To warrant a verdict for exemplary damages it is necessary to prove either actual malice, wanton negligence, reckless conduct, or fraud. *Chicago K. & W. R. Co. v. O'Connell*, 46 Kan. 581, 26 Pac. Rep. 947; *Citizens' St. R. Co. v. Willoeby* (Ind.), 33 N. E. Rep. 627; *Patterson v. South & N. A. R. Co.*, 89 Ala. 318, 7 So. Rep. 437; *Cady v. Case*, 45 Kan. 733; *Phila., etc. R. Co. v. Hoeflich*, 62 Md. 301, 50 Am. Rep. 223; *Drohn v. Brewer*, 77 Ill. 280; *Raynor v. Nims*, 37 Mich. 34, 26 Am. Rep. 493; *Fillebrown v. Hoar*, 124 Mass. 580; *Marin v. Satterfield*, 44 La. An. 742, 6 So. Rep. 553; *Alabama G. S. R. Co. v. Arnold*, 84 Ala. 159, 4 So. Rep. 359; *Green v. Pennsylvania R. Co.*, 36 Fed. Rep. 66; *McCullough v. Walton*, 11 Ala. 492; *Philadelphia, etc. R. Co. v. Quigley*, 21 How. 202.

Exemplary damages may be awarded in an action for conversion of personal property as well as in an action for the recovery of the property itself. *Arzaga v. Villalba*, 81 Cal. 191, 24 Pac. Rep. 656. See *Morris v. S*——, —— Kan. ——; *Smiley v. Waco T. R. Co.* (Tex.) ——, 10 S. W. Rep. 543; *Mowry v. Wood*, 12 Wis. 413.

man's daughter with deliberate fraud, or otherwise under circumstances of aggravation (a), such are the acts which, with the open approval of the Courts, juries have been in the habit of visiting with exemplary damages. Gross defamation should perhaps be added, but there it is rather that no definite principle of compensation can be laid down than that damages can be given which are distinctly not compensation. It is not found practicable to interfere with juries either way (b), unless their verdict shows manifest mistake or improper motive. There are other miscellaneous examples of an estimate of damages coloured, so to speak, by disapproval of the defendant's conduct (and in the opinion of the Court legitimately so), though it be not a case for vindictive or exemplary damages in the proper sense. In an action for trespass to land or goods substantial damages may be recovered though no loss or diminution in value of property may have occurred (c). In an action for negligently pulling down buildings to an adjacent owner's damage, evidence has been admitted that the defendant wanted to disturb the plaintiff in his occupation, and purposely caused the work to be done in a reckless manner; and it was held that the judge might properly authorize a jury to take into consideration the words and conduct of the defendant " showing a contempt of the plaintiff's rights and of his convenience " (d). Substantial damages have been allowed for writing disparaging words on a paper belonging to the plaintiff, although there was no publication of the libel (e).

"It is universally felt by all persons who have had occasion to consider the question of compensation, that there is a difference between an injury which is the mere result of such negligence as amounts to little more than accident, and an injury, wilful or negligent, which is accompanied with expressions of insolence. I do not say that in actions of negligence there should be vindictive damages such as are sometimes given in actions of trespass, but the measure of damage should be different, according to the nature of the injury and the circumstances with which it is accompanied." (*f*)

The case now cited was soon afterwards referred to by Willes J., as an authority that a jury might give exemplary damages, though the action was not in trespass, from the character of the wrong and the way in which it was done (*g*).

Analogy of breach of promise of marriage to torts in this respect. The action for breach of promise of marriage, being an action of contract, is not within the scope of this work, but it has curious points of affinity with actions of tort in its treatment and incidents; one of which is that a very large discretion is given to the jury as to damages (*h*)

Mitigation of damages. As damages may be aggravated by the defendant's ill-behaviour or motives, so they

---

(*f*) Pollock C B 6 H & N. 58, 30 L J Ex 72 Cp per Bowen L J in *Whatham v Kershaw* (1886), 16 Q B Div at p 618
(*g*) *Bell v Midland R Co* (1861), 10 C B N S 287, 307, 30 L J C P 273, 281

(*h*) See, e g , *Berry v Da Costa* (1866), L R 1 C P 331, 35 L J C P 191, and the last chapter of the present work, *ad fin*

Analogy of breach of promise of marriage to torts in this respect The action for breach of promise of marriage is an action *ex contractu* The damages recoverable therefor are not limited to the rules governing actions upon ordinary contracts but rest with the sound discretion of the jury Southard *v* Rexford, 6 Cow 254, Malone *v* Ryan, 14 R I 614, Reid *v* Clark, 47 Cal 149, Daggett *v* Wallace, 75 Tex 352, 13 S W. Rep. 49, Coil *v* Wallace, 34 N J L 291, Shreckengast *v* Ealey, 16 Neb 510, Grant *v* Willey, 101 Mass 356; Coolidge *v* Neat, 129 Mass 146, Collins *v* Mack, 31 Ark 684, Coryell *v* Cobaugh, 1 N J L 77, Wolters *v* Schult, 21 N Y S Rep 768; Chellis *v* Chapman, 125 N. Y 214, 26 N E Rep 308

may be reduced by proof of provocation, or of his having acted in good faith: and many kinds of circumstances which will not amount to justification or excuse are for this purpose admissible and material. "In all cases where motive may be ground of aggravation, evidence on this score will also be admissible in reduction of damages" (*i*). For the rest, this is an affair of common knowledge and practice rather than of reported authority.

Concurrent but severable causes of action "Damages resulting from one and the same cause of action must be assessed and recovered once for all;" but where the same facts give rise to two distinct causes of action, though between the same parties, action and judgment for one of these causes will be no bar to a subsequent action on the other. A man who has had a verdict for personal injuries cannot bring a fresh action if he afterwards finds that his hurt was graver than he supposed. On the other hand, trespass to goods is not the same cause of action as trespass to the person, and the same principle holds of injuries caused not by voluntary trespass, but by negligence; therefore where the plaintiff, driving a cab, was run down by a van negligently driven by the defendant's servant, and the cab was damaged and the plaintiff suffered bodily harm, it was held that after suing and recovering for the damage to

---

(*i*) Mayne on Damages, 160 (3rd ed.)

Mitigation of damages. Supporting the text, vide Norfolk & W. R. Co. v Lipscomb (Va.), 17 S. E. Rep 811, Wannamaker v. Bowes, 36 Md 42, Kolb v O'Brien, 86 Ill. 210; Chicago, etc. R Co v McKean, 40 Ill 218, Goetz v Ambs, 27 Mo. 28, Hell v Glauding, 42 Pa St. 493, Hamilton v Third Ave R. Co, 53 N Y 25, Snow v. Grace, 25 Ark 570, Morse v Duncan, 14 Fed Rep 396, Dow v Julian, 32 Kan 576, Wilkinson v Searcy, 76 Ala 176, Ross v Scott, 15 Lea, 479, Greenfield Bank v Leavit, 17 Pick 1, Chicago, etc. R Co. v. Flagg, 43 Ill 364, Plummer v Harbut, 5 Ia. 308, Rippey v Miller, 11 Ired. 347; Varril v. Heald, 2 Me 91, Brooks v. Hoyt, 6 Pick 468, Mabin v Webster, 129 Ind 430, 28 N E Rep 863, Pacific Ins Co v Conard, Bald 137, affirmed, 6 Pet 262, Paine v Fail, 118 Mass 75

the cab the plaintiff was free to bring a separate action for the personal injury (*k*). Apart from questions of form, the right to personal security certainly seems distinct in kind from the right to safe enjoyment of one's goods, and such was the view of the Roman lawyers (*l*).

Injunctions Another remedy which is not, like that of damages, universally applicable, but which is applied to many kinds of wrongs where the remedy of damages would

(*k*) *Lumsden* v *Humphrey* (1884), 11 Q B Div 111 53 L J Q B 176, by Brett M R and Bowen L J , *diss* Lord Coleridge C J Cp per Lord Bramwell, 11 App Ca at p 114

(*l*) Liber homo suo nomine utilem Aquiliae habet actionem directam enim non habet, quoniam dominus membrorum suorum nemo videtur Ulpian, D 9 2, ad 1 Aquil 13 pr

Injunctions The granting of injunctions rests in the sound discretion of the court of equity jurisdiction and should be exercised only in a clear case of right to prevent irreparable mischief. Where the injury threatened is such as would not be susceptible of compensation in damages it is deemed irreparable; but each case must depend on its own circumstances. There is no characteristic variance between the English and American authorities upon this subject, but the mandatory injunction seems to have been granted more freely by the courts of England than those of this country. See Rogers L. & M Works *v*. Erie Ry Co , 20 N J Eq 387, Longwood Valley R Co *v*. Baker, 27 Id 171, Corning *v* Troy, I. & N Factory, 40 N Y. 191, Auburn & C P R. Co *v*. Douglass, 12 Barb. 553, Appeal of Brown, 62 Pa St 17, Webb *v* Portland Mfg. Co , 3 Sumn 189, Reddall *v*. Bryan, 14 Md. 444, 71 Am. Dec 550, Nesbet *v* Sawyer, 66 Ga 256, Troy etc. R Co *v* Boston etc R Co , 86 N Y 107, Haskell *v* Shurston, 80 Me 129, 13 At Rep 273, Putnam *v* Valentine, 5 Ohio, 187, Wakeman *v* New York etc R Co , 35 N J Eq 496, Trowbridge *v* True, 52 Conn 190, 52 Am Rep 579, Livingston *v* Livingston, 6 Johns Ch 501 , 10 Am Dec 353, Boston W P Co *v* Boston etc. Co., 16 Pick 525, Cox *v* Douglass, 20 W Va 175, Indianapolis Nat Gas Co. *v* Kibby (Ind), 35 N E Rep 392, Citizens Natural Gas Co *v* Shenango Natural Gas Co , 138 Pa St 22, 20 At Rep 947, Shafer *v* Stull, 32 Neb. 94 , 48 N W. Rep 882.

A few cases illustrating the circumstances upon which injunctions are ordinarily granted are as follows —

Copyrights. Matsell *v* Flanagan, 2 Abb. Pr. (N S.) 459, Greene *v* Bishop, 1 Cliff 186, Folsom *v* Marsh, 2 Story, 100, Keene *v*. Kimball, 16 Gray, 545, Denis *v* Leclerc, 1 Mart. (La) 297, 5 Am. Dec 712, Fishel *v*. Lueckel, 53 Fed. Rep 499

Libel and slander See INJUNCTIONS, *post*, p 347

INJUNCTIONS.

be inadequate or practically worthless, is the granting of an injunction to restrain the commission of wrongful acts threatened, or the continuance of a wrongful course of

---

Lights   See OBSTRUCTION OF LIGHTS, *post*, p 509

Nuisances   See INJUNCTIONS, *post*, p 520

Patents   Brooks *v* Norcross, 2 Fish. Pat Cas 251, Furbish *v*. Bradford, 1 Id 315, Potter *v* Muller, 2 Id 465, Buchanan *v*. Howland, 5 Blatchf 151, Goodyear *v* Day, 2 Wall. Jr 283, Orr *v*. Littlefield, 1 Woodb & M 13, New York B. & P Co *v* Gutta Percha & R. Mfg. Co, 4 Fed Rep 264, Sawyer Spindle Co *v* Turner, 55 Fed. Rep 979, Stanton Mfg Co *v* McFarland (N. J. Ch.), 27 Atl. Rep 828, Campbell etc. Co *v* Manhattan etc. Ry. Co., 49 Fed Rep 930.

Trade marks   California Fig Syrup Co. *v* Improved Fig Syrup Co., 54 Fed Rep 296, Electro Silicon Co *v*. Levy, 59 How Pr 469, Avery *v*. Meikle, 81 Ky 73, Anheuser-Busch Brewing Assn. *v* Clarke, 26 Fed Rep. 410, Colman *v* Hunnewell, 122 Mass. 139, Pierce *v* Guittard, 68 Cal. 68, Alexandre *v*. Morse, 14 R I 153, 51 Am Rep 359, Morgan *v* Schwachofer, 55 How. Pr 37, Godillot *v*. Harris, 81 N Y 263, Estes *v* Worthington, 31 Fed Rep. 154, Coffeen *v* Brunton, 4 McLean, 516, City of Carlsbad *v* Tibbetts, 51 Fed. 852, Cuervo *v* Jacob Henkel Co., 50 Fed Rep 171, G G White Co *v* Miller, 50 Fed Rep 277.

Trespass   Cattle *v*. Harold, 72 Ga 830, Stetson *v* Stevens, 64 Vt 649, 25 Atl Rep 429, Mooney *v*. Coolidge, 30 Ark 640, Schoonover *v*. Bright, 24 W Va 698, Carney *v* Hadley (Fla.), 14 So Rep. 4, Musselman *v* Marquis, 1 Bush, 463, Thorn *v* Sweeney, 12 Nev. 256, New York etc. R Co *v* Schuyler, 17 N. Y 592, 34 N. Y 30, Althen *v* Kelley, 32 Minn 280, Nichols *v*. Jones, 19 Fed. Rep 857, Switzer *v*. McCulloch, 76 Vt 777, West etc Co *v* Regmeit, 45 N Y 703, Lockwood *v* Lunsford, 56 Mo 68, Smith *v*. Rock, 59 Vt 232, Moore *v* Massini, 32 Cal 590, Sisson *v* Johnson (Cal), 34 Pac. Rep 617, Richards *v* Dower, 64 Cal. 62, 28 Pac Rep. 113.

Waste   Sapp *v* Roberts, 18 Neb 299, Lanier *v*. Allison, 31 Fed. Rep. 299, Natoma etc Co *v*. Clarkin, 14 Cal 544, Thurston *v* Mustin, 3 Cranch C Ct 335, Hawley *v*. Clowes, 2 Johns Ch. 122, Marshall *v*. Turnbull, 32 Fed Rep 124, Kankakee *v* Kankakee etc R Co, 115 Ill 88, Silva *v* Garcia, 65 Cal 591, Rossman *v* Adams, 91 Mich. 69, Basore *v* Henkel, 82 Vt 174

Water rights   Daniel *v* Town of Princeton (Ky), 22 S W. Rep 324, Graham *v* Dahlonega G M Co, 71 Ga 296, Pettigrew *v* Evansville, 25 Wis 223, Willcox *v* Wheeler, 17 N H 188, Arthur *v* Case, 1 Paige, 447; Patten *v* Marden, 14 Wis 473, Hulme *v* Shreve, 3 Green Ch. 116, Fuller *v* Daniels, 63 N H 395, Cole S. M Co *v* Virginia etc. Co, 1 Sawyer, 470, Swett *v* Cutts, 50 N H 439, 9 Am Rep 276, Ferris *v* Welborn, 64 Miss 29, 8 So Rep 165, Conkling *v*. Pacific Imp. Co., 87 Cal 296, 25 Pac Rep 399

action already begun. There is now no positive limit to the jurisdiction of the Court to issue injunctions, beyond the Court's own view (a judicial view, that is) of what is just and convenient (*m*). Practically, however, the lines of the old equity jurisdiction have thus far been in the main preserved. The kinds of tort against which this remedy is commonly sought are nuisances, violations of specific rights of property in the nature of nuisance, such as obstruction of light and disturbance of easements, continuing trespasses, and infringements of copyright and trade-marks. In one direction the High Court has, since the Judicature Acts, distinctly accepted and exercised an increased jurisdiction. It will now restrain, whether by final (*n*) or interlocutory (*o*) injunction, the publication of a libel or, in a clear case, the oral uttering of slander (*p*) calculated to injure the plaintiff in his business. In interlocutory proceedings, however, this jurisdiction is exercised with caution (*o*), and only in a very clear case (*q*), and not where the libel, however unjustifiable, does not threaten immediate injury to person or property (*r*).

On what principle granted. The special rules and principles by which the court is guided in administering this remedy can be profitably discussed only in connexion with the particular causes of action upon which it is sought. All of them, however, are developments of the one general principle that an injunction is granted only where damages would not be an adequate remedy, and an interim injunction only where delay would make it impossible or

---

(*m*) Judicature Act, 1873, s. 25 sub s. 8. Per Jessel M. R., *Beddow v. Beddow* (1878), 9 Ch. D. 89, 91, 47 L. J. Ch. 588, *Quartz Hill etc. Co. v. Beall* (1882), 20 Ch. Div. at p. 507.

(*n*) *Thorley's Cattle Food Co. v. Massam* (1880), 14 Ch. Div. 763, *Thomas v. Williams* ib. 864.

(*o*) *Quartz Hill Consolidated Gold Mining Co. v. Beall* (1882) 20 Ch. Div. 501, 51 L. J. Ch. 874, *Collard v. Marshall*, '92 1 Ch. 571.

(*p*) *Hermann Loog v. Bean* (1884), 26 Ch. Div. 306, 53 L. J. Ch. 1128.

(*q*) *Bonnard v. Perryman*, '91 2 Ch. 269, 60 L. J. Ch. 617, C. A.

(*r*) *Salomons v. Knight*, '91, 2 Ch. 294, 60 L. J. Ch. 743, C. A.

highly difficult to do complete justice at a later stage (s). In practice very many causes were in the Court of Chancery, and still are, really disposed of on an application for an injunction which is in form interlocutory: the proceedings being treated as final by consent, when it appears that the decision of the interlocutory question goes to the merits of the whole case

Former concurrent jurisdiction of common law and equity to give compensation for fraud. In certain cases of fraud (that is, willfully or recklessly false representation of fact) the Court of Chancery had before the Judicature Acts concurrent jurisdiction with the courts of common law, and would award pecuniary compensation, not in the name of damages, indeed, but by way of restitution or "making the representation good" (t). In substance, however, the relief came to giving damages under another name, and with more nicety of calculation than a jury would have used. Since the Judicature Acts it does not appear to be material whether the relief administered in such a case be called damages or restitution; unless indeed it were contended in such a case that (according to the rule of damages as regards injuries to property) (s) the plaintiff was entitled not to be restored to his former position or have his just expectation fulfilled, but only to recover the

---

(s) In *Mogul Steamship Co. v. M'Gregor, Gow & Co.* (1888), 15 Q. B. D. 476, 54 L. J. Q. B. 540, the Court refused to grant an interlocutory injunction to restrain a course of conduct alleged to amount to a conspiracy of rival ship owners to drive the plaintiffs' ships out of the China trade. The decision of the case on the merits is dealt with elsewhere.

(t) *Burrowes v. Lock* (1805), 10 Ves. 470, *Slim v. Croucher* (1860), 1 D. F. J. 518, 29 L. J. Ch. 273 (these cases are now cited only as historical illustration), *Peek v. Gurney* (1871-3), L. R. 13 Eq. 79, 6 H. L. 377, 43 L. J. Ch. 19. See under the head of Deceit, Ch. VIII below.

(s) *Jones v. Gooday* (1841), 8 M. & W. 146, 10 L. J. Ex. 275, *Wigsell v. School for Indigent Blind* (1882), 8 Q. B. D. 57, 51 L. J. Q. B. 330, *Whitham v. Kershaw* (1885-6), 16 Q. B. Div. 613. In an action for inducing the plaintiff by false statements to take shares in a company, it is said that the measure of damages is the difference between the sum paid for the shares and their real value (the market value may, of course, have been fictitious) at the date of allotment. *Peek v. Derry* (1887), 37 Ch. Div. 591, 57 L. J. Ch. 347.

amount by which he is actually the worse for the defendant's wrong-doing. Any contention of that kind would no doubt be effectually excluded by the authorities in equity, but even without them it would scarcely be a hopeful one.

Special statutory remedies, when exclusive. Duties of a public nature are constantly defined or created by statute, and generally, though not invariably, special modes of enforcing them are provided by the same statute. Questions have arisen as to the rights and remedies of persons who suffer special damage by the breach or non-performance of such duties. Here it is material (though not necessarily decisive) to observe to whom and in what form the specific statutory remedy is given. If the Legislature, at the same time that it creates a new duty, points out a special course of private remedy for the person aggrieved (for example, an action for penalties to be recovered, wholly or in part, for the use of such person), then it is generally presumed that the remedy so provided was intended to be, and is, the only remedy. The provision of a public remedy without any special means of private compensation is in itself consistent with a person specially aggrieved having an independent right of action

---

Special statutory remedies, when exclusive. In the case of Cole v. City of Muscatine (14 Ia 296), the court, agreeing with the doctrine of the text, said: "that where a statute gives a right and creates a liability which did not exist at common law, and the statute at the same time provides a specific mode in which such right shall be asserted and liability ascertained, that mode and that alone must be observed." This is a substantial statement of the general rule. See Moore v. White, 45 Mo 206; Commissioners v. Bank, 32 Ohio St 193; Andover v. Gould, 6 Mass 1; Victory v. Fitzpatrick, 8 Ind 281; Bissell v. Larned, 16 Mass 65; Kroop v. Forman, 31 Mich 144; Bennett v. Drain Commissioner, 56 Mich 634; Johnston v. Louisville, 11 Bush, 527; Becler v. Turnpike Co., 14 Pa St 162; Grant v. Slater, etc. Co., 14 R I 380; Almy v. Harris, 5 Johns. 175; Holloran v. Bray, 29 Ga 422; Thurston v. Prentiss, 1 Mich 193; Pittsburg etc. R Co v. Hine, 25 Ohio St 629; Jackson v. St Louis, etc R Co, 87 Mo 422; 56 Am Rep 460.

for injury caused by a breach of the statutory duty (*t*). And it has been thought to be a general rule that where the statutory remedy is not applicable to the compensation of a person injured, that person has a right of action (*u*). But the Court of Appeal has repudiated any such fixed rule, and it is laid down that the possibility or otherwise of a private right of action for the breach of a public statutory duty must depend on the scope and language of the statute taken as a whole. A waterworks company was bound by the Waterworks Clauses Act, 1847, incorporated in the company's special Act, to maintain a proper pressure in its pipes, under certain public penalties. It was held that an inhabitant of the district served by the company under the Act had no cause of action against the company for damage done to his property by fire by reason of the pipes being insufficiently charged. The Court thought it unreasonable to suppose that Parliament intended to make the company insurers of all property that might be burnt within their limits by reason of deficient supply or pressure of water (*x*).

No private redress unless the harm suffered is within the mischief aimed at by the statute. Also the harm in respect of which an action is brought for the breach of a statutory duty must be of the kind which the statute was intended to prevent. If cattle being carried on a ship are washed overboard for want of appliances prescribed by an Act of Parliament for purely sanitary purposes, the shipowner is not liable to the owner of the cattle by reason of the breach of the statute (x), though he will be liable if his conduct amounts to negligence apart from the statute and with regard to the duty of safe carriage which he has undertaken (y), and in an action not founded on a statutory duty the disregard of such a duty, if likely to cause harm of the kind that has been suffered, may be a material fact (z).

Joint wrongdoers may be sued jointly or severally. Where more than one person is concerned in the commis-

---

(x) Gorris v. Scott (1874), L. R. 9 Ex. 125; 43 L. J. Ex. 92.
(y) See per Pollock, B., at p. 131.
(z) Blamires v. Lancashire and Yorkshire Ry. Co. (1873), L. R. 8 Ex. 283; 42 L. J. Ex. 182.

Joint wrongdoers.—Agreeing with the text it is an established rule in America, that where torts are committed by several persons the action may be brought against all who participate or against any number of them. Thus, in the case of Ayer v. Ashmead, 31 Conn. 447, 83 Am. Dec. 154), the court said: "It is true, undoubtedly, that for a joint trespass they may all be sued jointly or separate suits may be brought against each, because trespasses committed by several, while they are in fact the joint acts of all, are also the separate acts of each individual, each being liable in law for whatever was done by all or any of them, and if suits are separately brought against each they may all be pursued to final judgment, and the plaintiff may elect which of the separate he will enforce and collect. But having received damages recovered against any one, and his costs recovered against all, he must be content with that, as otherwise he would receive more than one satisfaction for his injury." See Wisconsin Cent. R. Co. v. Ross, 142 Ill. 9, 31 N. E. Rep. 412; Oliver v. Perkins, 92 Mich. 304, 52 N. W. Rep. 609; City of Chicago v. Babcock, 143 Ill. 358, 32 N. E. Rep. 271; Bonnell v. Dunn, 29 N. J. L. 153; Williams v. Sheldon, 10 Wend. 654; Bell v. Loomis, 29 N. Y. 112; Wheeler v. Worcester, 10 Allen, 591; Moore v. Appleton, 26 Ala. 633; Page v. Freeman, 19 Mo. 421; Klauder v. McGrath, 35 Pa. St. 128; Murphy v. Wilson, 44 Mo. 313; Cook v. Hopper, 23 Mich. 511; Colegrove v. New York etc. R. Co., 20 N. Y. 492; Stewart v. Wells, 6 Barb. 81; Knickerbocker v. Colver, 8 Cow. 111; Currier v. Brown, 63 Mo. 323; Burden v. Fitch, 101 Mass. 154; McManus v. Lee, 43 Mo. 206; Little Schuylkill etc. Co. v. Richards, 57 Pa. St. 142; Westbrook v. Mize, 35 Kan. 299; Gould v. Gould, 4 N. H. 174; Mitchell v. Allen, 25 Hun, 543; Sharpe v. Williams, 41 Kan. 57; Aldrich v. Parnell, 147 Mass. 409; Irwin v. Scribner, 15 La. An. 583; Sheldon v. Kibbe, 3 Conn. 214; Printup v. Patton (Ga.), 18 S. E. Rep. 311.

sion of a wrong, the person wronged has his remedy against all or any one or more of them at his choice. Every wrong-doer is liable for the whole damage, and it does not matter (as we saw above) (a), whether they acted, as between themselves, as equals, or one of them as agent or servant of another. There are no degrees of responsibility, nothing answering to the distinction in criminal law between principals and accessories. But when the plaintiff in such a case has made his choice, he is concluded by it.

But judgment against any is bar to further action. After recovering judgment against some or one of the joint authors of a wrong, he cannot sue the other or others for the same matter, even if the judgment in the first action remains unsatisfied. By that judgment the cause of action "transit in rem judicatam," and is no longer available (b). The reason of the rule is stated to be that otherwise a vexatious multiplicity of action would be encouraged.

Rules as to contribution and indemnity. As between joint wrong-doers themselves, one who has been sued alone and compelled to pay the whole damages has no right to

(a) Page 89
(b) Brinsmead v. Harrison (1872), L.R. Ch. 1 R 7 C P 547 41 L J C P 190, finally settled the point. It was formerly doubtful whether judgment without satisfaction was a bar. And in the United States it seems to be generally held that it is not. Cooley on Torts, 138, and see L R 7 C P 549

Contribution between joint wrong-doers No right of contribution exists between joint wrong-doers where there has been an intentional violation of law or where the wrong-doer is presumed to have known that the act was unlawful. Boyer v. Bolender, 129 Pa St 324, 18 Atl Rep 127, 24 W N C 300, Johnson v. Torpy, 35 Neb 604, 53 N W Rep 575, Kend v Chicago, etc Ry Co, 8 Bradwell, 517, Atkins v Johnson, 43 Vt 78, Bailey v Bussing, 28 Conn. 455, Jacobs v Pollard, 10 Cush 287, 57 Am Dec. 105, Moore v Appleton, 26 Ala 633, Miller v Fenton, 11 Paige, 18, Campbell v. Phelps, 1 Pick. 65, Acheson v Miller, 2 Ohio St 203, Dent v King, 1 Ga 200, Andrews v Murray, 33 Barb 354 Shermer v Spear, 92 N C 148, Cumpston v. Lambert, 18 Ohio, 81,

indemnity or contribution from the other (c), if the nature of the case is such that he "must be presumed to have known that he was doing an unlawful act" (d). Otherwise, "where the matter is indifferent in itself," and the wrongful act is not clearly illegal (e), but may have been done in honest ignorance, or in good faith to determine a claim of right, there is no objection to contribution or indemnity being claimed. "Every man who employs another to do an act which the employer appears to have a right to authorize him to do undertakes to indemnify him for all such acts as would be lawful if the employer had the authority he pretends to have." Therefore an auctioneer who in good faith sells goods in the way of his business on behalf of a person who turns out to have no right to dispose of them is entitled to be indemnified by that person against the resulting liability to the true owner (f). And persons intrusted with goods as wharfingers or the like who stop delivery in pursuance of their principal's instructions may claim indemnity if the stoppage turns out to be wrongful, but was not obviously so at the time (g). In short, the proposition that there is no contribution between wrongdoers must be understood to affect only those who are

---

(c) *Merryweather v. Nixan* (1799), 8 T. R. 186, where the doctrine is too widely laid down.

(d) *Adamson v. Jarvis* 4 Bing. at p. 73

(e) *Betts v. Gibbins*, 2 A. & E. 57

(f) *Adamson v. Jarvis* (1827), 4 Bing. 66, 72. The ground of the action for indemnity may be either deceit or warranty see at p. 73

(g) *Betts v. Gibbins* (1834), 2 A. & E. 57 See too *Collins v. Evans* (1844) (Ex. Ch.), 5 Q. B. at p. 820, 13 L. J. Q. B. 180

---

51 Am. Dec. 442, Selz v. Unna, 6 Wall. 327, Spalding v. Oakes, 343 But where joint tort feasors honestly do what is apparently lawful, and the wrong inflicted upon another arises out of their conduct by construction or inference of law, and is not the foreseen result of the wrongful act, the law will allow contribution between them. Armstrong Co v. Clarion Co., 66 Pa. St. 218, Nichols v. Nowling, 82 Ind. 488, Churchill v. Holt, 131 Mass. 67, Farwell v. Becker, 129 Ill. 261, 21 N. E. Rep. 792, Vandiver v. Pollak (Ala.), 12 So. Rep. 173, Lowell v. Boston &c. R. Co., 23 Pick. 24, 34 Am. Dec. 33, Gray v. Boston Gas Light Co., 114 Mass. 149, Peirce v. Cluss, 32 Md. 215, Horbach v. Elder, 18 Pa. St. 33, Westfield v. Mayo, 122 Mass. 100.

wrong-doers in the common sense of the word as well as in law. The wrong must be so manifest that the person doing it could not at the time reasonably suppose that he was acting under lawful authority. Or, to put it summarily, a wrong-doer by misadventure is entitled to indemnity from any person under whose apparent authority he acted in good faith, a wilful or negligent (*h*) wrong-doer has no claim to contribution or indemnity. There does not appear any reason why contribution should not be due in some cases without any relation of agency and authority between the parties. If several persons undertake in concert to abate an obstruction to a supposed highway, having a reasonable claim of right and acting in good faith for the purpose of trying the right, and it turns out that their claim cannot be maintained, it seems contrary to principle that one of them should be compellable to pay the whole damages and costs without any recourse over to the others. I cannot find, however, that any decision has been given on facts of this kind; nor is the question very likely to arise, as the parties would generally provide for expenses by a subscription fund or guaranty.

Supposed rule of trespass being " merged in felony." It has been currently said, sometimes laid down, and once or twice acted on as established law, that when the facts affording a cause of action in tort are such as to

---

(*h*) I am not sure that authority covers this. But I do not think an agent could claim indemnity for acts which a reasonable man in his place would know to be beyond the lawful power of the principal. See Indian Contract Act, s. 223.

Supposed rule of trespass being "merged in felony." In England, where the party injured is relied upon to take the place of a public prosecutor and where formerly the estate of a felon was forfeited to the crown, redress for a private grievance resulting from a criminal act is postponed until after criminal prosecution. "But in this country this doctrine of the suspension of the civil remedy in cases of felony has been repudiated by the great weight of American authorities. Under the

amount to a felony, there is no civil remedy against the felon (i) for the wrong, at all events, before the crime has been prosecuted to conviction. And as, before 1870 (j), a convicted felon's property was forfeited, there would at common law be no effectual remedy afterwards. So that the compendious form in which the rule was often stated, that "the trespass was merged in the felony," was sub-

(i) It is settled that there is no rule to prevent the suing of a person who was not party or privy to the felony. Stolen goods, or their value, e.g. can be recovered from an innocent possessor who has not bought in market overt, whether the thief has been prosecuted or not. *Marsh v. Keating* (1834), 1 Bing. N. C. 198, 217; *White v. Spettigue* (1845), 1 M. & W. 603, 14 L. J. Ex. 99. In these cases indeed the cause of action is not the offence itself, but something else which is wrongful because an offence has been committed.

(j) 33 & 34 Vict. c. 23.

system of laws prevailing in the United States the reasons for this rule are entirely absent. Here we have a public officer whose duty it is to prosecute all offenders against the State without reliance upon the injured individual, and here we have no forfeiture of the felon's goods. The civil and the criminal prosecution may, therefore, go on *pari passu* or the one may precede or succeed the other, or if the criminal prosecution is never commenced at all, the failure to seek public justice is no bar to the private remedy. Neither is an acquittal or conviction upon the criminal charge any bar to the civil action." Williams v. Dickinson, 28 Fla. 96, 9 So. Rep. 847, citing Pettingill v. Rideout, 6 N. H. 454, Blassingame v. Glaves, 6 B. Mon. 38, Boston & W. R. Co. v. Dana, 1 Gray, 83, Howk v. Minnick, 19 Ohio St. 462, Newell v. Cowan, 30 Miss. 492, See Austin v. Carswell, 67 Hun, 579, 22 N. Y. S. Rep. 478, Heller v. City of Alvarado, 1 Tex. Civ. App. 409, 20 S. W. Rep. 700.

The American courts are not in harmony upon the question whether punitive damages should be allowed where the tort is punishable as a crime.

The Supreme Court of Colorado, in the case of Howlett v. Tuttle (24 Pac. Rep. 921, following Murphy v. Hobbs, 7 Colo. 541, 5 Pac. Rep. 119), said: "Perhaps the most impressive objection to allowing damages as a punishment in cases like the one at bar, is that which relates to dual prosecutions for a single tort. Our State constitution declares that no one shall be twice put in jeopardy for the same offence. * * * Yet, under the rule allowing exemplary damages, not only may two prosecutions, but also two convictions and punishments, be had. * * * A second weighty objection to the rule under discussion relates to the procedure. It is doubtful if another instance can be found within the whole range of English and American jurisprudence where the distinctions between civil and criminal procedure are so completely ignored.

stantially if not technically correct. But so much doubt has been thrown upon the supposed rule in several recent cases, that it seems, if not altogether exploded, to be only awaiting a decisive abrogation. The result of the cases in question is that, although it is difficult to deny that some such rule exists, the precise extent of the rule, and the reasons of policy on which it is founded, are uncertain, and it is not known what is the proper mode of applying it. As to the rule, the best-supported version of it appears to be to this effect. Where the same facts amount to a felony and are such as in themselves would constitute a civil wrong, a cause of action for the civil wrong does arise. But the remedy is not available for a person who might have prosecuted the wrong-doer for the felony, and has failed to do so. The plaintiff ought to show that the felon has actually been prosecuted to conviction (by whom it does not matter, nor whether it was for the same specific offence), or that prosecution is impossible (as by the death of the felon or his immediate escape beyond the jurisdiction), or that he

---

plaintiff sues for damages arising from the injury done to himself, his complaint or declaration is framed with a view to compensation for a purely private wrong." See Meidel v. Anthis, 76 Ill. 241, Storall v. Smith, 4 B. Mon. 378, Lucas v. Flinn, 35 Ia. 9, Stowe v. Heywood, 7 Allen, 118.

But the weight of authority is otherwise and, as said by the court in Hendrickson v. Kingsbury (21 Ia. 391), is "that the damages allowed in civil case, by way of punishment, have no necessary relation to the *penalty* incurred for the *wrong done* to the *public*, but are called punitive damages by way of distinction from pecuniary damages, and to characterize them as a punishment for the *wrong done to the individual.* In this view, the awarding of punitive damages can in no sense be said to be in conflict with the constitutional or common law inhibition against inflicting two punishments for the same offense." See Brown v. Swineford, 44 Wis. 282, Cook v. Ellis, 6 Hill, 466, Edwards v. Leavitt, 46 Vt. 126, Hoadley v. Watson, 45 Vt. 289, Rhodes v. Rogers, 151 Pa. St. 634, 24 At. Rep. 1044, Roach v. Caldbeck, 64 Vt. 593; 24 At. Rep. 989, Kimball v. Holmes, 60 N. H. 163, Chicago v. Martin, 49 Ill. 241, Corwin v. Walter, 18 Mo. 71, Wilson v. Vaughn, 23 Fed. Rep. 229, Phillips v. Kelly, 29 Ala. 628, Boetcher v. Staples, 27 Minn. 308, 38 Am. Rep. 295.

has endeavoured to bring the offender to justice, and has failed without any fault of his own (*k*).

No known means of enforcing the rule if indeed it exists. It is admitted that when any of these conditions is satisfied there is both a cause of action and a presently available remedy. But if not, what then? It is said to be the duty of the person wronged to prosecute for the felony before he brings a civil action; "but by what means that duty is to be enforced, we are nowhere informed" (*l*). Its non-performance is not a defence which can be set up by pleading (*m*), nor is a statement of claim bad for showing on the face of it that the wrongful act was felonious (*n*). Neither can the judge nonsuit the plaintiff if this does not appear on the pleadings, but comes out in evidence at the trial (*o*). It has been suggested that the Court might in a proper case, on the application of the Crown or otherwise, exercise its summary jurisdiction to stay proceedings in the civil action (*p*); but there is no example of this. Whatever may be the true nature and incidents of the duty of the wronged party to prosecute, it is a personal one and does not extend to a trustee in bankruptcy (*q*), nor, it is conceived to executors in the cases where executors can sue. On the whole there is apparent in quarters of high authority a strong though not unanimous disposition to discredit the rule as a mere

---

(*k*) See the judgment of Baggallay L. J. in *Ex parte Ball* (1879), 10 Ch. Div. at p. 672. For the difficulties see per Bramwell L.J., *ib* at p. 674.

(*l*) Lush J., *Wells* v. *Abrahams* (1872), L. R. 7 Q. B. at p. 563.

(*m*) Blackburn J. *ibid.*

(*n*) *Roope* v. *D'Avigdor* (1883), 10 Q. B. D. 412, cp. *Midland Insurance Co.* v. *Smith* (1881), 6 Q. B. D. 561, 50 L. J. Q. B. 329.

(*o*) *Wells* v. *Abrahams* (1872), L. R. 7 Q. B. 554, 41 L. J. Q. B. 306 dissenting from *Wellock* v. *Constantine* (1863), 2 H. & C. 146, 32 L. J. Ex. 285, a very indecisive case, but the nearest approach to an authority for the enforcement of the supposed rule in a court of common law.

(*p*) Blackburn J., L. R. 7 Q. B. at p. 559. In a late Irish case, S. v. S. (1882), 16 Cox, 566, it was said that, in a proper case, the Court might stay the action of its own motion, and one member thought the case before them a proper one, but the majority did not.

(*q*) *Ex parte Ball* (1879), 10 Ch. D. 667, 48 L. J. Bk. 57.

semblant of text-writers founded on ambiguous or misapprehended cases, or on dicta which themselves were open to the same objections (r). At the same time it is certain that the judges consulted by the House of Lords in *Marsh v. Keating* (s) thought such a rule existed, though it was not applicable to the case in hand; and that in *Ex parte Elliott* (t) it was effectually applied to exclude a proof in bankruptcy.

Locality of wrongful act as affecting remedy in English court. Lastly we have to see under what conditions there may be a remedy in an English court for an act in the nature of a tort committed in a place outside the territorial jurisdiction of the court. It is needless to state formally that no action can be maintained in respect of an act which is justified or excused according to both English and local law. Besides this obvious case, the following states of things are possible.

Acts not wrongful by English law. 1. The act may be such that, although it may be wrongful by the local law, it would not be a wrong if done in England. In this case no action lies in an English court. The court will not carry respect for a foreign municipal law so far as to "give a remedy in the shape of damages in respect of an act which, according to its own principles, imposes no liability on the person from whom the damages are claimed" (u).

(r) See the historical discussion in the judgment of Blackburn J. in *Wells v. Prentice*, L. R. 7 Q. B. 60 sqq. And see per Martin J. in *Ward v. Lloyd* (1843), 7 Scott N. R. 10, 507, a case of alleged compounding of felony. "It would be a strong thing to say that every man is bound to prosecute all the felonies that come to his knowledge, and I do not know why it is the duty of the party who suffers by the felony to prosecute the felon; rather than that of any other person; on the contrary, it is a Christian duty to forgive one's enemies, and I think he does a very humane and charitable and Christian like thing in abstaining from prosecuting."

(s) 1 Bing. N. C. 198, 217 (1834).

(t) 3 Mont. & A. 110 (1837).

(u) *The Halley* (1868), L. R. 2 P. C. 193, 204, 37 L. J. Adm. 33; *The M. Moxham* (1876), 1 P. Div. 107.

Acts justified by local law. 2. The act, though in itself it would be a trespass by the law of England, may be justified or excused by the local law. Here also there is no remedy in an English court (x). And it makes no difference whether the act was from the first justifiable by the local law, or, not being at the time justifiable, was afterwards ratified or excused by a declaration of indemnity proceeding from the local sovereign power. In the well-known case of *Phillips* v. *Eyre* (y), where the defendant was governor of Jamaica at the time of the trespasses complained of, an Act of indemnity subsequently passed by the colonial Legislature was held effectual to prevent the defendant from being liable in an action for assault and false imprisonment brought in England. But nothing less than the justification by the local law will do. Conditions of the *lex fori* suspending or delaying the remedy in the local courts will not be a bar to the remedy in an English court in an otherwise proper case (z). And our courts would possibly make an exception to the rule if it appeared that by the local law there was no remedy at all for a manifest wrong, such as assault and battery committed without any special justification or excuse (a).

Act wrongful by both laws. 3. The act may be wrongful by both the law of England and the law of the place where it was done. In such a case an action lies in England, without regard to the nationality of the parties (b), provided the cause of action is not of a purely

---

(x) *Blad's Case*, Blad v. Bamfield (1673-4), in P. C. and Ch., 3 Swanst. 603-4 from Lord Nottingham's MSS.; *The M. Moxham*, 1 P. Div. 107.
(y) Ex. Ch. L. R. 6 Q. B. 1, 40 L. J. Q. B. 28 (1870).
(z) *Scott* v. *Seymour* (1862), 1 N. Ch. 1 H. & C. 219, 32 L. J. Ex. 61.
(a) Ib. per Wightman and Willes JJ.
(b) Per Cur., *The Halley*, L. R. 2 P. C. at p. 202.

Acts justified by local law. Agreeing with the text, vide American U. T. Co. v. Middleton, 80 N. Y. 408, Livingston v. Jefferson, 1 Brocken. 203, Niles v. How, 57 Vt. 385, Chapman v. Morgan, 2 Greene (Ia), 374, Carter v. Good, 50 Ark. 155, 6 S. W. Rep. 719.

local kind, such as trespass to land. This last qualification was formerly enforced by the technical rules of venue, with the distinction thereby made between *local* and *transitory* actions: but it seems to involve matter of real principle, though since the Judicature Acts abolished the technical forms an occasion of re-stating the principle has not yet arisen (c). It cannot well have been the intention of the Judicature Acts to throw upon our courts the duty of trying (for example) an action for disturbing a right to use a stream in Bengal for irrigation, or to float timber down a particular river in Canada; the result of which would be that the most complicated questions of local law might have to be dealt with here as matters of fact, not incidentally (as must now and then unavoidably happen in various cases), but as the very substance of the issues (d).

Judgment of Ex. Ch. in Phillips v. Eyre. We have stated the law for convenience in a series of distinct

(c) See per Lord Cairns, *Whitaker v. Forbes* (1875), 1 C. P. Div. at p. 52, and the notes to *Mostyn v. Fabrigas* in Smith's Leading Cases.

(d) It was doubted by James L. J. (since the Judicature Acts) whether the Court could entertain proceedings in respect of an injury done to foreign soil *The M. Moxham* (1876), 1 P. Div. at p. 109. The other members of the Court said nothing on this point.

Act wrongful by both laws. Agreeing with the doctrine of the text, in the United States where two States have similar statutes upon the same subject, a suit may be maintained under one statute for a right which accrued under the like statute of the other State, the rule being that the remedy is governed by the *lex fori* and the right by the *lex loci*. Leonard v. Columbia S. N. Co., 84 N. Y. 48; McLeod v. Railroad Co., 58 Vt. 727; Herrick v. Minn. etc., R. Co., 31 Minn. 11; Mannville Co. v. Worcester, 138 Mass. 89; Knight v. Railroad Co., 108 Pa. St. 250; Boyce v. Railroad Co., 63 Ia. 70, 10 N. W. Rep. 673; Anderson v. Milwaukee, etc., Ry., 37 Wis. 321; Stoeckman v. Terre Haute etc., R. Co., 15 Mo. App. 503; Morris v. Chicago, etc., R. Co., 65 Ill. 727, 54 Am. Rep. 39; Chicago & N. W. Ry. Co. v. Tuite, 44 Ill. App. 535; Wintuska v. Louisville & N. R. Co. (Ky.), 20 S. W. Rep. 819; Hanna v. Grand Trunk Ry. Co., 41 Ill. App. 116; Texas & P. Ry. Co. v. Cox, 145 U. S. 593, 12 S. Ct. Rep. 905; Wooden v. Western N. Y. & P. R. Co., 126 N. Y. 10, 26 N. E. Rep. 1050.

propositions. But, considering the importance of the subject, it seems desirable also to reproduce the continuous view of it given in the judgment of the Exchequer Chamber delivered by Willes J. in *Phillips* v. *Eyre*:—

"Our courts are said to be more open to admit actions founded upon foreign transactions than those of any other European country, but there are restrictions in respect of locality which exclude some foreign causes of action altogether, namely, those which would be local if they arose in England, such as trespass to land: *Doulson* v *Matthews* (*e*), and even with respect to those not falling within that description our courts do not undertake universal jurisdiction. As a general rule, in order to found a suit in England for a wrong alleged to have been committed abroad, two conditions must be fulfilled. First, the wrong must be of such a character that it would have been actionable if committed in England: therefore, in *The Halley* (*f*) the Judicial Committee pronounced against a suit in the Admiralty founded upon a liability by the law of Belgium for collision caused by the act of a pilot whom the shipowner was compelled by that law to employ, and for whom, therefore, as not being his agent, he was not responsible by English law. Secondly, the act must not have been justifiable by the law of the place where it was done. Therefore in *Blad's Case* (*g*), and *Blad* v. *Bamfield* (*h*), Lord Nottingham held that a seizure in Iceland, authorized by the Danish Government and valid by the law of the place, could not be questioned by civil action in England, although the plaintiff, an Englishman, insisted that the seizure was in violation of a treaty between this country and Denmark—a matter proper for remonstrance, not litigation. And in *Dobree* v *Napier* (*i*), Admiral Napier, having, when in the

(*e*) 4 T. R. 503 (1792: no action here for trespass to land in Canada). The student will bear in mind that *Phillips* v *Eyre* (1870), was before the Judicature Acts.

(*f*) L. R. 2 P. C. 193, 37 L. J. Adm. 33 (1868).
(*g*) 3 Swanst. 603.
(*h*) 3 Swanst. 604.
(*i*) 2 Bing. N. C. 781 (1836).

service of the Queen of Portugal, captured in Portuguese water an English ship breaking blockade, was held by the Court of Common Pleas to be justified by the law of Portugal and of nations, though his serving under a foreign prince was contrary to English law, and subjected him to penalties under the Foreign Enlistment Act. And in *Reg* v. *Lesley* (*k*), an imprisonment in Chili on board a British ship, lawful there, was held by Erle C. J., and the Court for Crown Cases Reserved, to be no ground for an indictment here, there being no independent law of this country making the act wrongful or criminal. As to foreign laws affecting the liability of parties in respect of bygone transactions, the law is clear that, if the foreign law touches only the remedy or procedure for enforcing the obligation, as in the case of an ordinary statute of limitations, such law is no bar to an action in this country; but if the foreign law extinguishes the right it is a bar in this country equally as if the extinguishment had been by a release of the party, or an act of our own Legislature. This distinction is well illustrated on the one hand by *Huber* v. *Steiner* (*l*), where the French law of five years' prescription was held by the Court of Common Pleas to be no answer in this country to an action upon a French promissory note, because that law dealt only with procedure, and the time and manner of suit (*tempus et modum actionis instituendae*), and did not affect to destroy the obligation of the contract (*valorem contractus*); and on the other hand by *Potter* v. *Brown* (*m*), where the drawer of a bill at Baltimore upon England was held discharged from his liability for the non-acceptance of the bill here by a certificate in bankruptcy, under the law of the United States of America, the Court of Queen's Bench adopting the general rule laid down by Lord Mansfield in *Ballantine* v. *Golding* (*n*), and ever since recognized, that, ' what is a

(*k*) Bell C. C. 220; 29 L. J. M. C. 97
(*l*)
(*l*) 2 Bing. N. C. 202
(*m*) 5 East, 124
(*n*) Cooke's Bankrupt Law, 487

discharge of a debt in the country where it is contracted is a discharge of it everywhere.' So that where an obligation by contract to pay a debt or damages is discharged and avoided by the law of the place where it was made, the accessory right of action in every court open to the creditor unquestionably falls to the ground. And by strict parity of reasoning, where an obligation *ex delicto* to pay damages is discharged and avoided by the law of the country where it was made, the accessory right of action is in like manner discharged and avoided. Cases may possibly arise in which distinct and independent rights or liabilities or defences are created by positive and specific laws of this country in respect of foreign transactions, but there is no such law (unless it be the Governors Act already discussed and disposed of) applicable to the present case."

Limitation of actions. The times in which actions of tort must be brought are fixed by the Statute of Limitation of James I. (21 Jac. 1, c. 16) as modified by later enactments (*n*). No general principle is laid down, but actionable wrongs are in effect divided into three classes, with a different term of limitation for each. These terms, and the causes of action to which they apply, are as follows, the result being stated, without regard to the actual words of the statute, according to the modern construction and practice:—

Six years.

Trespass to land and goods, conversion, and all other common law wrongs (including libel) except slander by words actionable *per se* (*o*) and injuries to the person

---

(*n*) See the text of the statutes, Appendix C. (*o*) See Blake Odgers, Digest of Law of Libel, 2nd ed. 520.

Limitation of actions. In the United States the several States have varying statutes regulating the time in which actions for torts must be begun.

Four years

Injuries to the person (including imprisonment).

Two years

Slander by words actionable *per se*

Suspension of the statute by disabilities. Persons who at the time of their acquiring a cause of action are infants, married women, or lunatics (*p*), have the period of limitation reckoned against them only from the time of the disability ceasing, and if a defendant is beyond seas at the time of the right of action arising, the time runs against the plaintiff only from his return. No part of the United

---

Plaintiffs imprisoned or being beyond the seas had the same right by the statute of James I, but this was repealed by 19 & 20 Vict. c. 97 (the Mercantile Law Amendment Act, 1856), s. 10. The existing law as to defendants beyond seas is the result of 4 & 5 Anne, c. [rd 16] s. 19, as explained by 19 & 20 Vict. c. 97, s. 12. As to the retrospective effect of s. 10 see *Pardo v. Bingham* (1869), 4 Ch. 735, 38 L J Ch 170.

Suspension of the statute by disabilities. The running of the statute is suspended by civil disability, as *insanity*, Smith v. Bayright, 31 N J Eq 124, Little v. Downing, 37 N H 355, Wright v. West, 2 Lea, 78, Fults v. Hines, 57 Miss. 735, Moore v. City of Waco, 85 Tex 206, 20 S W Rep 61, Clark v. Trail, 1 Metc. (Ky.) 35, Sasser v. Davis, 27 Tex. , Rutherford v. Folger, 50 N J L 299, Oliver v. Berry, 53 Me 206; , Baumin v. Grubbs, 26 Ind 419, Norwood v. Gonzales County, 79 Tex 218, 14 S W Rep 1057, Ragsdale v. Barnes, 68 Tex 504; 5 S W Rep 68, Buley v. Reed, 14 Phila Rep 167, Sledge v. Clopton, 6 Ala , Mickle v. Wyatt, 21 Ala 813, Fearn v. Shiley, 31 Miss. 301; McLean v. Jackson, 12 Ired L 149, Wilson v. Wilson, 36 Cal 447, *infancy*, Smith v. Coombs, 13 La An 932, 9 So Rep 907, Vance v. Vance, 108 U S , Harris v. Ross, 86 Mo 89, Moore v. Willis, 18 Ala 458, Ross v. Morrow, 85 Tex 172, 19 S W. Rep 1090, Grimsby v. Hudnell, 76 Ga. , Henley v. Robb, 2 Pick (Tenn.) 171; 7 S W Rep 190, Watson v. Watson, 53 Mich 168; Fewell v. Collins, 3 Brev. 286, Treadw Const 202, Piposet v. Trowell, 3 Rich 231, "*beyond the seas*," Umbler v. Whipple, 1 Ill 311, 28 N E Rep 841, Murray v. Baker, 3 Wheat 541, Harris v. Harris, 71 N C 174, Darle v. Briggs, 97 U S 628, Culp v. Culp (Kan.), 32 Pac Rep 1118, Pells v. Snell, 130 Ill. 379, 23 N E Rep 117, Rhodes v. Faish, 16 Mo App 130, State v. Furlong, 60 Miss 839, Alexander v. Dyer, 11 Pet 141, *imprisonment*, State v. Calhoun, 50 Kan 523, 33 Pac. Rep 38, Downs v. Allen, 10 Lea, 652.

Kingdom or of the Channel Islands is deemed to be beyond seas for this purpose (q). If one cause of disability supervenes on another unexpired one (as where a woman marries under age), the period of limitation probably runs only from the expiration of the latter disability (r).

From what time action runs. Where damage is the gist of the action, the time runs only from the actual happening of the damage (s).

In trover the statute runs from demand on and refusal by the defendant, whether the defendant were the first converter of the plaintiff's goods or not (t).

(q) See last note.
(r) Cp. Borrows v. Ellison (1871), L. R. 6 Ex. 128, 40 L. J. Ex. 131 (on the Real Property Limitation Act, 3 & 4 Wm. IV. c. 27), but the language of the two statutes might be distinguished.
(s) Backhouse v. Bonomi (1861), 9 H. L. C. 503, 34 L. J. Q. B. 181; Darley Main Colliery Co. v. Mitchell (1886), 11 App. Ca. 127, 55 L. J. Q. B. 529, affirming S. C. 14 Q. B. Div. 125. The same principle applies, of course, to special periods of limitation of actions against public bodies or officers, see Crumbie v. Wood Local Board, 91, 1 Q. B. 503, 60 L. J. Q. B. 92.
(t) Miller v. Dell, 91, 1 Q. B. 468, 60 L. J. Q. B. 404, C. A.

From what time action runs. In the case of Hogin v. Wolf (57 Hun, 588, 26 Abb. N. C. 1, 10 N. Y. S. Rep. 896) it was held, that the statute of limitation begins to run against a cause of action for enticing away of plaintiff's husband from the time of the enticement. The general rule agrees with the text. See Strickler v. McCland Ry. Co., 125 Ind. 412, 25 N. E. Rep. 455; Hempstead v. Cargill, 46 Minn. 188, 48 N. W. Rep. 578, 686; Harbich v. Des Moines & K. C. Ry. Co., 80 Ia. 593, 45 N. W. Rep. 548; Berson v. Ewing, 84 Cal. 89, 23 Pac. Rep. 1112; Murphy v. Chicago etc. R. Co., 80 Ia. 26, 45 N. W. Rep. 592; Omaha & R. V. Co. v. Brown, 29 Neb. 492, 46 N. W. Rep. 39; Culver v. Chicago, etc., R. Co., 38 Mo. App. 130; Wright v. Syracuse, etc., R. Co., 49 Hun, 445, 2 N. Y. S. Rep. 480; St. Louis, etc., Ry. Co. v. Biggs, 52 Ark. 240, 12 S. W. Rep. 331; Garrett v. Bickler, 78 Ill. 115, 42 N. W. Rep. 621; Houston Water Works Co. v. Kennedy, 70 Tex. 233, 8 S. W. Rep. 36; Fordyce v. Stone, 50 Ark. 230, 7 S. W. Rep. 129; Sullens v. Chicago, etc., Ry. Co., 74 Ia. 659, 38 N. W. Rep. 545; Athens Mfg. Co. v. Rucker, 80 Ga. 291, 4 S. E. Rep. 885; Gale v. McDaniel, 72 Cal. 334, 13 Pac. Rep. 871; Colrick v. Swinburne, 105 N. Y. 503; Printup v. Smith, 74 Ga. 157; Miller v. Keokuk etc., Ry. Co., 63 Ia. 680; Kinsley v. Stein, 52 Mich. 380; Deer v. Hyland, 3 Utah, 308; Werges v. St. Louis, etc., R. Co., 35 La. An. 641; Van Otsdal v. Burlington, etc., Ry. Co., 56 Ia. 470; Sharp v. Miller, 57 Cal. 431.

Protection of justices, constables, &c. Justices of the peace (u) and constables (v) are protected by general enactments that actions against them for anything done in the execution of their office must be brought within six months of the act complained of.

The enforcement of statutory duties is often made subject by the same Acts which create the duties to a short period of limitation. These provisions do not really belong to our subject, but to various particular branches of public law.

Exception of concealed fraud. The operation of the Statute of Limitation is further subject to the exception of concealed fraud, derived from the doctrine and practice of the Court of Chancery, which, whether it thought itself bound by the terms of the statute, or only acted in analogy to it (x), considerably modified its literal application. Where a wrong-doer fraudulently conceals his own wrong the period of limitation runs only from the time when the plaintiff discovers the truth, or with reasonable diligence would discover it. Such is now the rule of the Supreme Court in every branch of it and in all causes (y).

(u) 11 & 12 Vict. c. 44, s. 8.
(v) 24 Geo. II. c. 44, s. 8.
(x) … … Div. Cs., per Brett L. J. … … Gould (1884), 9 Q. B. Div. … … … which makes the

equitable doctrine of general application without regard to the question whether before the Judicature Acts the Court of Chancery would or would not have had jurisdiction in the case.

Exception of concealed fraud. The American authorities agree with … … Hickman v. Hickman, 46 Mo. App. 496, Bailey v. Glover, 21 Wall. 342, Johnson v. Roe, 1 Fed. Rep. 692, Amy v. Watertown No. 2, 130 U. S. 320, Michoud v. Girod, 4 How. 503, Piper v. Hoard, 107 N. Y. 67, Copper v. Lee, 1 Tex. Civ. App. 9, 21 S. W. Rep. 998, Reynolds v. Hennessy 17 R. I. 169, 20 At. Rep. 307, 23 At. Rep. 639, Cook v. Chicago, etc. Ry. Co., 81 Ia. 551, 46 N. W. Rep. 1080, Peck v. Bank of America, 16 R. I. 710, 19 At. Rep. 369, Jones v. Van Doren, 130 U. S. 684, 9 S. Ct. Rep. 685, Tomkins v. Hollister, 60 Mich. 470, 27 N. W. Rep. 651, South Covington & C. S. Ry. Co. v. Gest, 34 Fed. Rep. 628, Quimby v. Blackey, 63 N. H. 77, Clews v. Traer, 57 Ia. 459, Pendergrast v. Foley, 8 Ga. 1, Williams v. Cule, 10 N. J. Eq. 543, Bricker v. Lightner, 40 Pa. St. 199, Smith v. Talbot, 18 Tex. 774, Coolidge v. Alcock, 30 N. H. 329, Cole v. McGlathry, 9 Me. 131, Farnam v. Brooks, 9 Pick. 212.

A plaintiff may not set up by way of amendment claims in respect of causes of action which are barred by the statute at the date of amendment, though they were not so at the date of the original writ (z).

It has often been remarked that, as matter of policy, the periods of limitation fixed by the statute of James are unreasonably long for modern usage; but modern legislation has done nothing beyond removing some of the privileged disabilities.

Conclusion of General Part. We have now reviewed the general principles which are common to the whole law of Torts as to liability, as to exceptions from liability, and as to remedies. In the following part of this work we have to do with the several distinct kinds of actionable wrongs, and the law peculiarly applicable to each of them.

(z) *Weldon v. Neal* (1887), 19 Q. B. Div. 394, 56 L. J. Q. B. 621.

Book II.

SPECIFIC WRONGS.

CHAPTER VI.

PERSONAL WRONGS

1.—Assault and Battery.

Preliminary. Security for the person is among the first conditions of civilized life. The law therefore protects us, not only against actual hurt and violence, but against every kind of bodily interference and restraint not justified or excused by allowed cause, and against the present apprehension of any of these things. The application of unlawful force to another constitutes the wrong called battery: an action which puts another in instant fear of unlawful force, though no force be actually applied, is the wrong called assault. These wrongs are likewise indictable offences, and under modern statutes can be dealt with by magistrates in the way of summary jurisdiction, which is the kind of redress most in use. Most of the learning of assault and battery, considered as civil injuries, turns on the determination of the occasions and purposes by which the use of force is justified. The elementary notions are so well settled as to require little illustration.

What shall be said a battery. " The least touching of another in anger is a battery" (*a*); " for the law cannot

(*a*) Holt C. J., Cole v. Turner (1705), 6 Mod. 149 and Bigelow L. C. 218

draw the line between different degrees of violence, and therefore totally prohibits the first and lowest stage of it.

What shall be called a battery? There are various definitions in the authorities of what constitutes a battery, all agreeing in substance with the text. Thus in a Texas case it is said by the court: "The use of any lawful violence upon the person of another, with intent to injure him, whatever be the means or degree of violence used, is an assault and battery. This definition makes it necessary that two things should concur—one physical the other mental." McKay v. State, 44 Tex. 43.

From a reckless disregard for the safety of others the law presumes an intent to injure. Peterson v. Hoffner, 59 Ind. 13, 26 Am. Rep. 81; Cowley v. State, 10 Lea, 282; Walker v. State, 8 Ind. 290; Markley v. Whitman (Mich.), 51 N. W. Rep. 768.

The result of a successful assault is a battery, and, therefore, every battery includes an assault. The quantity of physical force to be used by an assailant in order that his attack may amount to a battery will depend upon the circumstances. Such questions may be affected by the method adopted in applying the force, by the positions in society that the parties occupy, etc. Fitzgerald v. Fitzgerald, 51 Vt. 420; State v. Wright, 52 Ind. 307; Cooper v. McKenna, 124 Mass. 284, 26 Am. Rep. 667; State v. Smith, 80 Mo. 518; 1 Abbott's Law Dic. 134; Boyle's Case, 18 Fed. Rep. 880; Ricker v. Freeman, 50 N. H. 420, 9 Am. Rep. 267; Johnson v. State, 17 Tex. 515; Frederickson v. Singer Mfg. Co., 8 Minn. 356, 37 N. W. Rep. 453; Chipman v. State, 78 Ala. 463; Lawson v. State, 30 Ala. 44; Kirkland v. State, 43 Ind. 146, 13 Am. Rep. 386; Hinman v. Gloss, 5 Wash. St. 703, 32 Pac. Rep. 787; Napp v. Wischeart (Ind. App.), 34 N. E. Rep. 1066.

The mere taking hold of the coat, or laying the hand gently on the person of another, if done in anger, or in a rude and insolent manner or with hostility, is a battery. United States v. Ortega, 4 Wash. 534.

So is a blow on the skirt of one's coat, when upon his person, or striking one's cane, while in his hand. Respublica v. De Longchamps, 1 Dall. 111. See State v. Davis, 1 Sneed (Tenn.), 66.

"One is guilty of an assault and battery who delivers to another a thing to be eaten, knowing that it contains a foreign substance and concealing the fact, if the other, in ignorance of the fact, eats it and is injured in health." Commonwealth v. Stratton, 114 Mass. 303. See Carr v. State (Ind.), 34 N. E. Rep. 533.

One who rides a bicycle against another, who is racing the other way, where there is ample room for passing and nothing to obstruct the view, is liable in assault and battery. Mercer v. Corbin, 117 Ind. 450, 20 N. E. Rep. 132.

For cases on the liability of corporations for assault and battery, see, *ante*, p. 67.

every man's person being sacred, and no other having a right to meddle with it in any the slightest manner." (b) It is immaterial not only whether the force applied be sufficient in degree to cause actual hurt, but whether it be of such a kind as is likely to cause it. Some interferences with the person which cause no bodily harm are beyond comparison more insulting and annoying than others which do cause it. Spitting in a man's face is more offensive than a blow, and is as much a battery in law (c). Again, it does not matter whether the force used is applied directly or indirectly, to the human body itself or to anything in contact with it, nor whether with the hand or anything held in it, or with a missile (d).

What is assault. Battery includes assault, and though assault strictly means an inchoate battery, the word is in modern usage constantly made to include battery. No reason appears for maintaining the distinction of terms in our modern practice; and in the draft Criminal Code of 1879 "assault" is deliberately used in the larger popular sense. "An assault" (so runs the proposed definition) "is the act of intentionally applying force to the person of another directly or indirectly, or attempting or threatening by any act or gesture to apply such force to the person of another, if the person making the threat causes the other to believe (e) upon reasonable grounds that he has present ability to effect his purpose." (f)

(b) Chief st Co. Litt. 161. 120.

(c) *Cole's case*, 6 Mod. 172.

(d) *Pursell v. Horn* (1838) 8 N. & P. [throwing water at a person is assault, if the water falls on him as intended it is battery also). But there is older authority, see Reg. Brev. 108 b, a writ for throwing "quendam liquor calidum" on the plaintiff. "Casus istius huiusmodi praecedentis brevis pro tam multis prolocit super aliam in eorum viro illum quod an. llce . . . scilicet quod erat minis calidum."

(e) One might expect "believes or causes," etc., but this would be an extension of the law. No assault is committed by presenting a gun at a man who cannot see it, any more than by forming an intention to shoot at him.

(f) Criminal Code (Indictable Offences) Bill, s. 203. Mr. Justice Stephen's definition in his Digest (art. 241) is more elaborate, and the Indian Penal Code has an extremely minute definition of "using force to another" (s. 349). As Mr. Justice Stephen remarks, if legis

Examples of acts which amount to assaulting a man are the following. "Striking at him with or without a weapon, or presenting a gun at him at a distance to which the gun will carry, or pointing a pitchfork at him, standing within the reach of it, or holding up one's fist at him, or drawing a sword and waving it in a menacing manner." (q) The

latter begin defining in this way it is hard to see what they can assume to be known

(q) Bacon Abr "Assault and Battery," A, Hawkins P C I 110

What an assault The numerous American authorities upon this subject are in substantial accord with the text. Thus, in the case of Tarver v State (43 Ala 356), the court said —

"An assault is any attempt or offer, with force or violence, to do a corporal hurt to another, whether from malice or wantonness, with such circumstances as denote, at the time, an intention to do it, coupled with a present ability to carry such intention into effect See State v Baker, 65 N C 332, State v Neely, 74 N C 426, State v Myerfield, Phil L 109, People v Campbell, 30 Cal 312, People v Bransby, 32 N Y 525, Johnson v. State, 43 Tex 576, Cooper v State, 8, Lawson v State, 30 Ala 15, State v Davis, 1 Ired 125, 35 Am Dec 735, State v Morgan, 3 Ired 186, State v Vannoy, 65 N C. 532, State v Chipman, 81 N C. 513, State v. Marsteller, 84 Id 726, State v Martin, 85 Id 508, 39 Am Rep 711, Simpson v. State, 59 Ala 18, 31 Am Rep 1, Commonwealth v. Hurley, 99 Mass 433, Bonner v State (Ala), 12 So Rep 108, Richmond v Fiske (Mass), 35 N E Rep 103.

The offense is complete if there is an act done, indicating an intention coupled with ability. Higginbotham v. State, 23 Texas, 574, State v Epperson, 27 Mo 255, State v. Church, 63 N C 15, Barnes v Martin, Wis 240, Tarver v. State, 43 Ala 354, Commonwealth v White, 110 Mass 407, Crow v State, 41 Texas, 468, State v Taylor, 20 Kas 643, Birbee v Reese, 60 Miss 906, Englehardt v State, 88 Ala 100, 7 So Rep 154, State v Myers, 19 Ia 517.

Where the act is done with intent to do corporal hurt, an assault may be committed by striking at a person with the hand, or with a stick, or by shaking the fist at him, or by presenting any weapon within such distance that hurt might be inflicted United States v Hand, 2 Wash 435, United States v Richardson, 5 Cranch C Ct. 348. See State v Martin, 85 N. C 508, 39 Am Rep 711, State v Vannoy, 65 N C 532, Bishop v. Ranney, 59 Vt. 316, 7 At. Rep 820. See Mitchell v Mitchell, 45 Minn. 50, 47 N W Rep. 308, State v Rawles, 65 N. C. 334, Morgan v State, 33 Ala. 413, State v Taylor, 20 Kan. 643; United States v Kierman, 8 Cranch C Ct 435, State v Shepherd, 10 Ia. 126; Beach v

ASSAULT. 251

essence of the wrong i. putting a man in present fear of violence, so that any act fitted to have that effect on a reasonable man may be an assault, though there is no real present ability to do the harm threatened. Thus it may be an assault to present an unloaded fire-arm (*h*), or even, it is apprehended, anything that looks like a fire-arm. So if a man is advancing upon another with apparent intent to strike him, and is stopped by a third person before he is

(*h*) *r* v *James* (1844), 1 C. & K. 530, is apparently to the contrary. Tindal C. J. held that a man could not be convicted of an attempt to discharge a loaded fire-arm under a criminal statute nor even of an assault, if the arm is (*e.g.* by defective priming) not in a state capable of being discharged; but this opinion (also held by Lord Abinger, *Blake* v *Barnard*, 9 C. & P. at p. 626) is against that of Parke B. in *R* v *St. George* (1840), 9 C. & P. 483, 493, which on this point would almost certainly be followed at this day. The case is overruled on another point purely on the words of the statute, and not here material, in *R* v *Duckworth*, '92, 2 Q. B. 83.

Hancock, 27 N. H. 223; State v Cherry, 11 Ired. 475; Commonwealth v McLaughlin, 5 Allen, 507.

Malice is not an ingredient of an assault with a dangerous weapon United States v. Lunt, 1 Sprague, 311; United States v. Small, 2 Curtis, 241.

To violently strike a horse before a carriage in which a person is riding is an assault on the person. De Marentile v. Oliver, 2 N. J. L. 380; Kirkland v State, 43 Ind. 146; Clark v Downing, 55 Vt. 259, 45 Am. Rep. 612. So is riding a horse so near to one as to endanger his person, to his alarm. State v Sims, 3 Strobh. 137; 1 Sneed (Tenn.), 606; Commonwealth v McLaughlin, 5 Allen, 507; Tarver v State, 43 Ala. 356; State v Blackwell, 9 Ala. 79.

What is not an assault. But a person does not commit an assault by merely holding a cocked pistol by his side, without any attempt to use it, and saying to his antagonist, "I am ready for you." Warren v State, 33 Texas, 517. See Mitchell v State, 41 Ga. 537; Lawson v State, 30 Ala. 14.

A pointed a gun at B who was armed with a knife and threatened to assault A, but A did not intend to shoot, unless in self-defense. held, not an assault by A. State v Blackwell, 9 Ala. 79. See White v State, 29 Tex. App 530, 16 S W Rep 340.

A held out his arms to take hold of B, a female who ran away. held, not an assault to commit rape. House v. State, 9 Tex. App 53.

Where a person raised a whip and shook it at another within striking distance and said, "Were you not an old man, I would knock you down," the act did not constitute an assault. State v Crow, 1 Ired 375

actually within striking distance, he has committed an assault (*i*). Acts capable in themselves of being an assault may on the other hand be explained or qualified by words or circumstances contradicting what might otherwise be inferred from them: A man put his hand on his sword and said, "If it were not assize-time, I would not take such language from you;" this was no assault, because the words excluded an intention of actually striking (*k*).

Excusable acts. Hostile or unlawful intention is necessary to constitute an indictable assault, and such touching,

---

(*i*) *Stephens v. Myers*, 4 C. & P. 349; Bigelow L. C. 217. A large proportion of the authorities on this subject are Nisi Prius cases (cp. however *Read v. Coker* (1853), 13 C. B. 850, 22 L. J. C. P. 201) see the sub titles of Assault under Criminal Law and Trespass in Fisher's Digest. Some of the dicta, as might be expected, are in conflict.

(*k*) *Tuberville v. Savage* (1669), 1 Mod. 3.

Excusable acts. A civil action lies for an unwarranted assault and battery although not committed in anger. *Johnson v. McConnell*, 15 Hun, 293. See *People v. Lilley*, 43 Mich. 521, citing *Wilson v. People*, 24 Id. 410, *Woodruff v. Woodruff*, 22 Ga. 237, *Palmer v. Chicago* etc. R. R. Co., 112 Ind. 250, *Mercer v. Corbin*, 117 Id. 453, *Ricker v. Freeman*, 50 N. H. 420, *Prall v. Lull*, 19 Wis. 183, *Carmichael v. Dolen*, 25 Neb. 335, 41 N. W. Rep. 178, *Vandenburgh v. Truax*, 4 Denio, 464, *Welch v. Duran*, 36 Conn. 182, *Richels v. State*, 1 Sneed (Tenn.), 606.

In the case of *Vosburg v. Putney* (80 Wis. 523, 50 N. W. Rep. 403, 50 N. W. Rep. 480), where the ground of action was that the defendant had kicked the plaintiff, the court said: "The jury have found that the defendant, in touching the plaintiff with his foot, did not intend to do him any harm; counsel for defendant maintain that the plaintiff has no cause of action, and that the defendant's motion for judgement on the special verdict should have been granted. In support of this proposition counsel quote from 2 Greenl. Ev. §83, the rule that 'the intention to do harm is of the essence of the assault.' Such is the rule, no doubt, in actions or prosecutions for mere assaults. In such a case the rule is correctly stated, in many of the authorities cited by counsel, that plaintiff must show either that the intention was unlawful, or that the defendant is in fault. If the intended act is unlawful, the intention to commit it must necessarily be unlawful. Hence as applied to this case, if the kicking of the plaintiff by the defendant was an unlawful act, the intention of the defendant to kick him was also unlawful."

Words not an assault. The law abhors the use of force either for

pushing, or the like as belongs to the ordinary conduct of life, and if free from the use of unnecessary force, is

attack or defense and never permits its use unnecessarily. And it is for this reason that the courts accord in holding that words in themselves never amount to an assault. "No words, whether spoken or printed or written, however insulting and opprobrious they may be, will justify an assault and battery or even an assault." Fatnall v. Courtney, 6 Houst. 147. See People v. Lilley, 43 Mich. 525, supra; Burns v. State, 80 Ga. 544, 7 S. E. Rep. 88; Scott v. Fleming, 16 Ill. Ap. 539; Smith v. State, 39 Miss. 521; State v. Mooney, Phill. L. 134; State v. Workman (S. C.), 17 S. E. Rep. 694; State v. Briggs (Tex. Cr. App.), 21 S. W. Rep. 46.

Upon the question whether violent words may be proved in mitigation of damages the English cases are unanimous in holding that they may, but in the United States, this rule has been adopted by the majority of the courts with the qualification that the assault and battery in resentment of insulting words must be committed immediately upon the provocation being offered and before the hot blood of indignation has had time to cool. "In Thrall v. Knapp (17 Iowa, 468) the court said: "The clear distinction is that contemporaneous provocation of words or acts are admissible, but previous provocation are not, and the test is whether the blood has had time to cool." In Goldsmith v. Joy (61 Vt. 449) an interesting question was proposed and discussed by the court, as follows: "If provoking words may mitigate, it follows that they may reduce the damages to a mere nominal sum and thus practically justify an assault and battery. But why under this rule may they not fully justify? If in one case, the provocation is so great the jury may award only nominal damages, why, in another, in which the provocation is far greater, should they not be permitted to acquit the defendant and thus overturn the well settled rule of the law, that words cannot justify an assault? On the other hand, if words cannot justify they should not be heard to say that the plaintiff was first in the wrong by abusing him with insulting words and therefore though he struck and injured the plaintiff, he was only partly in the wrong and should pay only part of the actual damages." In this case the authorities are collated and discussed and it is followed in Walker v. Carpenter, 61 Vt. 212.

Consent. It is a recognized rule that a person cannot recover a recompense for an injury received by his own consent, provided the act from which the injury results be lawful. *Volenti non fit injuria.* See Stout v. Wren, 1 Hawks, 420, 9 Am. Dec. 653; Champer v. State, 14 Ohio St. 437; Duncan v. Commonwealth, 6 Dana, 295; State v. Beck, 1 Hill (S. C.), 363, 26 Am. Dec. 190; Fitzgerald v. Valvin, 110 Mass. 153; Bell v. Hansley, 3 Jones L. 131. A majority of the decisions hold that consent to the commission of an unlawful act resulting in an injury, may be proved in mitigation of damages, but this is the full extent of the compassion which has been shown by the courts for vanquished

neither an offence nor wrong. "If two or more meet in a narrow passage, and without any violence or design of harm the one touches the other gently, it will be no battery" (l). The same rule holds of a crowd of people going into a theatre or the like (m). Such accidents are treated as inevitable, and create no right of action even for nominal damages. In other cases an intentional touching is justified by the common usage of civil intercourse, as when a man gently lays his hand on another to attract attention. But the use of needless force for this purpose, though it does not seem to entail criminal liability where no actual hurt is done, probably makes the act civilly wrongful (n).

Mere passive obstruction is not an assault, as where a man by standing in a doorway prevents another from coming in (o).

Words cannot of themselves amount to an assault under any circumstances, though it is said that a contrary opinion formerly prevailed:

> "For Meade's case proves, or my Report's in fault,
> That singing can't be reckoned an assault" (p).

There is little direct authority on the point, but no doubt is possible.

Consent, or in the common phrase "leave and licence," will justify many acts which would otherwise be assaults

---

(l) Holt C. J., Cole v. Turner, 6 Mod. 149.

(m) Steph. Dig. Cr. Law, art. 241, illustrations.

(n) Coward v. Baddeley (1859), 4 H. & N. 478, 28 L. J. Ex. 260.

(o) Innes v. Wyhe (1834), 1 C. & K. 257. But it seems the other, if he is going where he has a right to go, is justified in pushing him aside, though not in striking or other violence outside the actual exercise of his right see p. 253 above.

(p) The Circuiteers, by John Leycester Adolphus (the supposed speaker is Sir Gregory Lewin), L. Q. R. 1. 232, Meade's and Belt's ca., 1 Lewin C. C. 184 "no words or singing are equivalent to an assault," per Holroyd J. Cp. Hawkins P. C. 1. 110 But it was formerly held otherwise see 27 Ass. 134, pl. 11, 17 Ed. IV. 3, pl. 2, 36 Hen. VI. 20 b, pl. 8

pugilists. Barholt v. Wright, 45 Ohio St. 179; 12 N. E. Rep. 185, reviewing the cases. See Limits of Consent, ante, p. 186.

(*q*), striking in sport for example; or even, if coupled with reasonable cause, wounding and other acts of a dangerous kind, as in the practice of surgery. But consent will not make acts lawful which are a breach of the peace, or otherwise criminal in themselves, or unwarrantably dangerous. To the authorities already cited (*r*) under the head of General Exceptions we may add Hawkins' paragraph on the matter.

"It seems to be the better opinion that a man is in no danger of such a forfeiture [of recognizances for keeping the peace] from any hurt done to another by playing at cudgels, or such like sport, by consent, because the intent of the parties seems no way unlawful, but rather commendable, and tending mutually to promote activity and courage. Yet it is said that he who wounds another in fighting with naked swords does in strictness forfeit such a recognizance, because no consent can make so dangerous a diversion lawful" (*s*).

It has been repeatedly held in criminal cases of assault that an unintelligent assent, or a consent obtained by fraud, is of no effect (*t*). The same principles would no doubt be applied by courts of civil jurisdiction if necessary.

Self-defence. When one is wrongfully assaulted it is lawful to repel force by force (as also to use force in the

---

(*q*) Under the old system of pleading this was not a matter of special justification, but evidence under the general issue, an assault by consent being a contradiction in terms. *Christopherson v. Bare* (1848), 11 Q. B. 473, 17 L. J. Q. B. 109. But this has long ceased to be of any importance in England.

(*r*) P. 185, above.

(*s*) Hawkins, P. C. 1. 484. The Roman law went even farther in encouraging contests "gloriae causa et virtutis," D. 9. 2, ad. 1. Aquil. 7, § 4.

(*t*) Cases collected in Fisher's Dig ed Mews, 2081-2. Similarly where consent is given to an unreasonably dangerous operation or treatment by one who relies on the prisoner's skill, it does not excuse him from the guilt of manslaughter if death ensues. *Commonwealth v. Pierce*, 138 Mass. 165, 180.

Self Defence. Agreeing with the text, *vide* Shorter *v.* People, 2 N. Y 193, Patton *v.* People, 114 Ill. 505, 2 N. E. Rep 541; Marts *v* State, 26 Ohio St. 162, People *v.* Dann, 53 Mich. 490; 19 N W. Rep. 159; Miller *v.*

defence of those whom one is bound to protect, or for keeping the peace), provided that no unnecessary violence

State, 74 Ind. 1, followed in Presser v. State, 77 Ind. 278, Long v. State, 52 Miss 23, Keep v. Quallman, 68 Wis 451; 32 N. W Rep. 238; Drew v. Comstock, 57 Mich 176; Commonwealth v. Kennard, 8 Pick. 133, Pond v People, 8 Mich. 150; People v. Lennon, 71 Mich. 300; 38 N W. Rep. 871, Harrison v Harrison, 19 Vt 117; Jamison v. Mosely, 68 Miss. 336; 10 So Rep. 582, Ogden v. Claycomb, 52 Ill. 365, Commonwealth v. Mann, 116 Mass. 58; State v. Nash, 88 N. C 118; Commonwealth v White, 110 Mass 409. See cases cited, ante, p. 201.

The authorities are not uniform as to the obligation of one violently assaulted to retreat but the better doctrine seems to be that where a person has used every reasonable precaution to prevent an encounter and has, without any fault of his own, had a fight thrust upon him, it is not his legal duty (undoubtedly not his moral duty), to cowardly retire as his assailant approaches See Haynes v. State, 17 Ga 465, Tweedy v. State, 5 Ia. 433, State v. Dixon, 75 N C. 275, Steinmetz v Kelly, 72 Ind 442; Morris v. Casel, 90 Id 148. Contra Howland v. Day, 56 Vt 318.

It is a general rule in law that one should not use an unreasonable and a disproportionate degree of violence towards the person of another in self-defense. Thus in the case of Dole v. Erskine (35 N H 511), the court said " But if the person assaulted uses excessive force, beyond what is necessary for self defense he is liable for the excess, and the facts may be shown under the replication of de injuria. Up to the time that the excess is used, the party assaulted is in the right. Until he exceeds the bounds of self-defense he has committed no breach of the peace and done no act for which he is liable, while his assailant, up to that time, is in the wrong, and is liable for his illegal acts See State v Brooks, 99 Mo. 141.

It is apparent that in such a case there have, in effect, been two trespasses committed; the one by the assailant in commencing the assault, and the other by the assailed party in using excessive force.

The only difference would seem to consist in the length of time that has elapsed between the two trespasses. In a case where excessive force is used, the party using it is innocent up to the time that he exceeds the bounds of self-defense. When he uses excessive force, he then for the first time becomes a trespasser. In such a case each party may have an action against the other; the one for the original assault and the other for the assault which begins with the employment of excessive force. Curtis v Carson, 2 N H. 539, Hannen v. Edes, 15 Mass. 349; Scribner v Beach, 4 Denio, 448, Thompson v. Berry, 1 Cranch C. Ct. 45; McIlhoy v Cockran, 2 A. K. Marsh. 274; Robinson v. Hawkins, 4 T. B Mon. 136; Philbrick v Foster, 4 Ind 442; Hazel v. Clark, 3 Harr. (Del.) 222; Close v. Cooper, 34 Ohio St 98, Breitenbach v Trowbridge, 64 Mich. 393, 31

be used. How much force, and of what kind, it is reasonable and proper to use in the circumstances must always be a question of fact, and as it is incapable of being concluded beforehand by authority, so we do not find any decisions which attempt a definition. We must be content to say that the resistance must "not exceed the bounds of mere defence and prevention" (*u*), or that the force used in defence must be not more than "commensurate" with that which provoked it (*v*). It is obvious, however, that the matter is of much graver importance in criminal than in civil law (*w*).

(*u*) Blackst. Comm. III. 4.
(*v*) Reece v. Taylor, 1 N. & M. 479.
(*w*) See Stephen's Digest of the Criminal Law, art. 200, and cp. Criminal Code Bill, ss. 55—57, and for full discussion Dicey, Law of the Constitution, 3rd ed. appx. note 3. There are many modern American decisions, chiefly in the Southern and Western States. See Cooley on Torts, 165.

N. W. Rep. 102; Marsh v. Bristol, 65 Mich. 378, 32 N. W. Rep. 645, Tucker v. Walters, 78 Ga. 232, 2 S. E. Rep. 689, Drinkhorn v. Dubel, 85 Mich. 532, 18 N. W. Rep. 719, Baldwin v. Hayden, 6 Conn. 157, Gallagher v. State, 3 Minn. 270, Floyd v. State, 36 Ga. 91.

Still it seems that where the excess of violence used in defense is inconsiderable in amount the law gives no right of action therefor. "The law has enough regard for the weakness of human nature to regard a violent attack as a sufficient excuse for going beyond the mere necessities of self-defense and chastising the aggressor within such bounds as did not exceed the natural limits of the provocation." People v. Pearl, 16 Mich. 210.

Defence of dwelling. A man may defend his dwelling or "castle" to the last extremity. Pitford v. Armstrong, Wright (Ohio), 94, McPherson v. State, 22 Ga. 478; Thompson v. State, 55 Id. 47, State v. Burwell, 62 N. C. 661, State v. Abbott, 8 W. Va. 741, Wall v. State, 51 Ind. 453, State v. Stockton, 61 Mo. 382; State v. Peacock, 40 Ohio St. 333, State v. Middleham, 62 Ia. 150; 17 N. W. Rep. 446.

Defence of family. It is, also, an established rule that a person may defend any member of his family against an assault as he could himself. Staten v. State, 30 Miss. 619; Patten v. People, 18 Mich. 314, Commonwealth v. Malone, 114 Mass. 295; Stoneman v. Commonwealth, 25 Gratt. 887, Smith v. Slocum, 62 Ill. 354; State v. Greer, 22 W. Va. 800.

But no one has a right to revenge wrongs done to any member of his family after the danger is repelled and the violence not impending. State v. Gibson, 10 Ired. 214.

Menace distinguished from assault. Menace without assault is in some cases actionable. But this is on the ground of its causing a certain special kind of damage, and then the person menaced need not be the person who suffers damage. In fact the old authorities are all, or nearly all, on intimidation of a man's servants or tenants whereby he loses their service or dues. Therefore, though under the old forms of action this wrong was of the same genus with assault and battery, we shall find it more convenient to consider it under another head. Verbal threats of personal violence are not, as such, a ground of civil action at all. If a man is thereby put in reasonable bodily fear he has his remedy, but not a civil one, namely by security of the peace.

Summary proceedings when a bar to civil action. Where an assault is complained of before justices under 24 & 25 Vict. c. 100, and the complaint has been dismissed (after an actual hearing on the merits) (x), either for want of proof, or on the ground that the assault or battery was "justified or so trifling as not to merit any punishment," or the defendant has been convicted and paid the fine or suffered the sentence, as the case may be, no further proceedings either civil or criminal can be taken in respect of the same assault (y).

(x) *Reed* v *Nutt* (1890), 24 Q. B. D. 669, 59 L. J Q B 311.

(y) 24 & 25 Vict c. 100, ss 42—45 *Masper* v *Brown* (1876), 1 C P D 97, decides that the Act is not confined to suits strictly for the same cause of action, but extends to bar actions by a husband or master for consequential damage the words of the Act are "same cause," but they are equivalent to "same assault" in the earlier Act, 16 & 17 Vict c 30, s 1, repealed by 24 & 25 Vict c 95

Menace distinguished from assault Where menace without assault results in special damages it appears that it should be a ground of action but it seems that this question has never arisen in the courts of the United States except in so far as it relates to the menacing of tenants and employes, and in this class of cases the English decisions have been followed See Dickson *v.* Dickson, 33 La An. 1261, Carew *v.* Rutherford, 106 Mass. 1; and see *post*, p. 216. It is certain that a menace is not an assault. Johnson *v.* State, 35 Ala. 365; People *v.* Yslas, 27 Cal. 633.

II.— *False Imprisonment.*

False imprisonment. Freedom of the person includes immunity not only from the actual application of force, but from every kind of detention and restraint not authorized by law. The infliction of such restraint is the wrong of false imprisonment; which, though generally coupled with assault, is nevertheless a distinct wrong. Laying on of hands or other actual constraint of the body is not a necessary element; and, if "stone walls do not a prison make" for the hero or the poet, the law none the less takes notice that there may be an effectual imprisonment without walls of any kind. "Every confinement of the person is an imprisonment, whether it be in a common prison, or in a private house, or in the stocks, or even by forcibly detaining one in the public streets" (*z*). And when a man is lawfully in a house it is imprisonment to prevent him from leaving the room in which he is (*a*). The de-

---

(*z*) Blackst. Comm. iii. 127.
(*a*) *Warner v. Riddiford*, 4 C. B. N. S. 180, even if he is disabled by sickness from moving at all; the assumption of control is the main thing. *Grainger v. Hill* (1838), 4 Bing. N. C. 212.

False imprisonment. Several of the courts of the United States have defined the meaning of false imprisonment substantially as the text. A very comprehensive statement of what constitutes this wrong is that of the court in *Come v. Knowles*, (17 Kan. 440), as follows: "False imprisonment is necessarily a wrongful interference with the personal liberty of an individual. The wrong may be committed by words alone, or by acts alone, or by both, and by merely operating on the will of the individual or by personal violence, or by both. It is not necessary that the individual be confined within a prison, or within walls; or that he be assaulted or even touched. It is not necessary that there should be any injury done to the individual's person, or to his character, or reputation. Nor is it necessary that the the wrongful act be committed with malice, or ill-will, or with the slightest wrongful intention. Nor is it necessary that the act be under the color of any legal or judicial proceedings. All that is necessary is, that the individual be restrained of his liberty without any sufficient legal cause thereof, and by words or acts which he fears to disregard." See *State v. Lunsford*, 81 N. C. 530; *Floyd v. State*, 7 Eng. (Ark.) 44; *Moses v. Dubois*, Dudley (S. C.), 210; *Brushaber v.*

tainer, however, must be such as to limit the party's freedom of motion in all directions. It is not an imprisonment to obstruct a man's passage in one direction only.

Stegeman, 22 Mich 269, Alorn v Collins, 39 Mo 151, Soreson v Dundas, 50 Wis 335, McNay v Stratton, 9 Ill. Ap 215; Herring v. State, 3 Tex. App 108, Fuller v. Bowker, 11 Mich 201, Pike v Hanson, 9 N. H 491, Mowry v. Chase, 100 Mass. 79, How v Ridgway, 33 Ill 173, Maloney v Doane, 15 La. 278, 35 Am Dec. 201, Payson v Macomber, 3 Allen, 69; Marshall v Heller, 55 Wis. 192; French v. Bancroft, 1 Met 502, Bonesteel v Bonesteel, 28 Wis 245, Hill v Taylor, 50 Mich. 549, Doyle v Doyle, 19 Kan. 168, Brock v Stimpson, 108 Mass. 520, 11 Am. Rep. 390, State v Parker, 75 N C 219, 22 Am Rep 669, Smith v St 7 Humph 11, Gold v Bissell, 1 Wend 210, 19 Am. Dec. 480, Mauer v State, 8 Tex App 361 Manning v Mitchell, 73 Ga. 664, Johnson v. Thompson, 1 Baldw 571; Moore v. Thompson, 92 Mich 498, 52 N W Rep 1000 The detention need not confine him in any particular spot Hawkins v State, 6 Tex. App. 452 An action for false imprisonment will lie for the misuse or abuse of legal process after it has issued. Wood v Graves, 114 Mass 365, Crowell v. Gleason, 10 Me 325, Francisco v State, 24 N. J. L. 30; Sleight v Leavenworth, 5 Duer, 122; Lange v Benedict, 73 N Y 12.

Where a person was for about two weeks constantly guarded by the detectives of an express company without any warrant and all his movements were under their control, and he was repeatedly urged to confess a robbery, showing that he was regarded as a criminal and that force would be used if necessary to detain him, it was held that he could maintain against the express company for false imprisonment. Fotheringham v. Adams Express Co., 36 Fed. Rep. 252.

So, where a person went to a bank on business, and remained after the usual time of closing, which he knew, and the teller locked the door and thereby detained him Woodard v. Washburn, 3 Denio, 369 See Hildebrande v. McCrum, 101 Ind. 61

Where one was arrested without a warrant and detained five days before being taken before a magistrate, although there was nothing to prevent its being done, and at the end of five days was discharged and released without any legal proceedings whatever having been taken, it was held that the time of detention was clearly unreasonable Cochran v. Toher, 14 Minn. 385 See Lavinia v. State, 63 Ga 513

So where a sheriff kept a prisoner lawfully arrested in jail for thirty days before bringing him before a magistrate. Anderson v. Beck, 64 Miss. 113 A sheriff has no right to imprison a party arrested without an order from a judicial officer unless on account of the lateness of the hour or that such officer be inaccessible or for other cause it be necessary Hayes v Mitchell, 69 Ala. 452. It was held not improper to confine a

FALSE IMPRISONMENT.   261

"A prison may have its boundary large or narrow, invisible or tangible, actual or real, or indeed in conception only; it may in itself be moveable or fixed; but a boundary it must have, and from that boundary the party imprisoned must be prevented from escaping; he must be prevented from leaving that place within the limit of which the party imprisoned could be confined." Otherwise every obstruction of the exercise of a right of way may be treated as an imprisonment (*b*). A man is not imprisoned who has an escape open to him (*c*), that is, we apprehend,

---

(*b*) *Bird v. Jones* (1845), 7 Q. B. 742; 15 L. J. Q. B. 82, per Coleridge J.
(*c*) Williams J., *ib.* To the same effect Patteson J. "Imprisonment is a total restraint of liberty of person." Lord Denman C. J. dissented.

---

person in a room adjoining the court room until the magistrates disposed of a case of trial and the complaint was prepared. Hopner *v.* McDowan, 116 N. Y. 405, 22 N. E. Rep. 558.

By recognizing, submitting to examination, and taking the pauper's oath, an illegal arrest is not waived. Carleton *v.* Akron Sewer Pipe Co., 125 Mass. 10. But an irregularity in process is waived by giving bail, Nemitz *v.* Conrad, 22 Oreg. 164, 29 Pac. Rep. 548.

Where a person suing in an action for false imprisonment shows that only a portion of the time of imprisonment was wrongful he may recover. Bauer *v.* Clay, 8 Kan. 580. One who is arrested without reason, and kept in defiance of offers to give bail and sue out a writ of *habeas corpus* may maintain an action against all concerned. Manning *v.* Mitchell, 73 Ga. 660. See Cargill *v.* State, 8 Tex. App. 431; Gibbs *v.* Randlett, 58 N. H. 407.

It is also established that one who participates in or instigates or encourages an unlawful arrest, is liable, however pure his motives may have been. Chisman *v.* Carney, 33 Ark. 316. Ruffner *v.* Williams, 3 W. Va. 245; Frazier *v.* Turner, 76 Wis. 562; 45 N. W. Rep. 411. But it is not false imprisonment to remand a prisoner brought on *habeas corpus* issued by a judge who has no jurisdiction of such case. State *v.* Guest, 6 Ala. 778. Nor for an officer to retake an escaped prisoner after his writ has been returned. Strong *v.* Ives, 1 Root, 388. Nor for the arrest of a person who commits a breach of the peace in the exercise of a common right. Taafe *v.* Kyne, 9 Mo. App. 15. Nor for the arrest of a person for violating a void town ordinance. Trammell *v.* Russellville, 34 Ark. 105; 36 Am. Rep. 1. See Wheeler *v.* Gavin, 5 Ohio Cir. Ct. Rep. 240; Brooks *v.* Mangan, Mich. 576, 49 N. W. Rep. 633. Nor where a person under lawful arrest, is at his own request confined in a jail other than that specified by law. Ellis *v.* Cleveland, 54 Vt. 437.

a means of escape which a man of ordinary ability can use without peril of life or limb. The verge of a cliff, or the foot of an apparently impracticable wall of rock, would in law be a sufficient boundary, though peradventure not sufficient in fact to restrain an expert diver or mountaineer. So much as to what amounts to an imprisonment.

Justification of arrest and imprisonment. When an action for false imprisonment is brought and defended, the real question in dispute is mostly, though not always,

---

Justification of arrest and imprisonment. It is a doctrine sustained by a long line of cases, that a ministerial officer, acting under process fair upon its face and issuing from a tribunal or person with apparent jurisdiction to issue such process, is protected thereby in its execution against all irregularities and illegalities except his own. Clay v Caperton, 1 T B. Mon 10, 15 Am. Dec 77, Clinton v Nelson, 2 Utah, 284, Savacool v. Boughton, 5 Wend 170, 21 Am Dec. 181, Davis v. Wilson, 65 Ill 525, Wilmarth v. Burt, 7 Metc 257, Herzog v Graham, 9 Lea, 152, Chase v Fish, 16 Me 132; Repler v Pents, 86 Ill 275, Trammell v. Russelville, 34 Ark 105; 36 Am Rep 1, Lindt v Hilts, 19 Barb 283, Allison v. Rheam, 3 Serg & R 139, 8 Am Dec 644, Neth v Crofat, 30 Conn 580, Cleveland v. Rogers, 6 Wend. 138, Erskine v. Hohnback, 14 Wall. 613, Bergin v. Hayward, 102 Mass. 414, Keniston v. Little, 30 N H 318, Hill v Haynes, 54 N Y 153, Newbury v Munshower, 29 Ohio St 617, 23 Am Rep. 769, Nowell v Tripp, 61 Me 426, Sturbridge v Winslow, 21 Pick. 83, Floyd v State, 12 Ark. 43. See Coupal v Ward, 106 Mass. 289, Joiner v. Ocean Steam Ship Co , 86 Ga 238, 12 S. E. Rep 361

Any peace officer is justified in arresting without process one who is committing a breach of the peace in his presence, or he may, upon reasonable suspicion, arrest a person charged with commission of a felony, although the felony was not in fact committed. Rohan v Sawin, 5 Cush. 281, Eanes v. State, 6 Humph 53, 44 Am Dec 289, Bryan v Bates, 15 Ill. 87; Taylor v. Strong, 3 Wend. 384, Quinn v Heisel, 40 Mich. 576. In re Powers, 25 Vt. 261, McCarthy v. De Armit, 99 Pa St 63; Scircle v Neeves, 47 Ind 289; Doering v. State, 49 Id 56, 19 Am Rep 669, Neal v Joyner, 89 N C 287, Malcolmson v Scott, 56 Mich 459. But see Shanley v. Wells, 71 Ill 78, Newton v. Locklin, 77 Ill. 103, Paw v Beckner, 3 Ind 475, Schneider v. McLane, 36 Barb 495, Philips v Fadden, 125 Mass 198, Moore v. Durgin, 68 Me 148, Kennedy v. Favor, 14 Gray, 200, McLennon v Richards, 15 Id. 74.

To justify the arrest by a private person without process of one suspected of a felony, the proof must show that the felony had actually

whether the imprisonment was justified. One could not account for all possible justifications except by a full enumeration of all the causes for which one man may lawfully put constraint on the person of another, an undertaking not within our purpose in this work. We have considered, under the head of General Exceptions (d), the principles on which persons acting in the exercise of special duties and authorities are entitled to absolute or qualified immunity. With regard to the lawfulness of arrest and imprisonment in particular, there are divers and somewhat minute distinctions between the powers of a peace-officer and those of a private citizen (e): of which the chief is that an officer may without a warrant arrest on reasonable suspicion of felony, even though a felony has not in fact

(d) Ch IV p 130, above
(e) Stephen, Dig Crim Proc c 12, 1 Hist. Cr Law, 193 and see *Hogg v Ward* (1858), 3 H & N 417, 27 L J Ex 443

been committed, and that the one causing the arrest had reasonable ground for believing the one arrested guilty. As is said in the case of Burns *v* Erben (40 N Y 466), "but if an innocent person be arrested upon suspicion by a private individual, such individual is not excused unless such offence has, in fact, been committed, and there was reasonable ground to suspect the person arrested" See Wakely *v.* Hart, 6 Binn 316, Commonwealth *v.* Deacon, 8 Serg & R. 49, Renck *v.* McGregor, 32 N J L. 70; Allen *v* Lonard, 28 Ia 529, Morley *v.* Chase, 143 Mass 396, Holley *v* Mix, 3 Wend 350, 20 Am. Dec 703, Mandeville *v* Guernsey, 51 Id 99; 50 N. Y. 669, Guernsey *v.* Lowell, 9 Wend 320

Threats made by a person under arrest justify an officer in putting him in irons. Cochran *v* Toher, 14 Minn 385

An evidence of threats was held admissible as bearing on the question of the propriety of the force used by the officer. Fulton *v* Statts, 41 N. Y 498. Same point on arrest by private citizen. Lander *v* Miles, 3 Oreg 35 But see Hackett *v* Lawrence, 7 Abb. Pr (N. S.) 403. See *ante,* pp. 180, 182

Advice by counsel, though followed in good faith and under and by virtue of which an alleged false imprisonment took place will not be a justification. Josselyn *v* McAllister, 22 Mich. 300 See Fire Assn *v* Fleming, 78 Ga. 733; 3 S E. Rep. 420 And the inexperience of the attorney giving such advice will not justify the arrest, but may be shown in mitigation of damages. Mortimer *v* Thomas, 23 La. Ann. 165. As to how far the attorney is liable, see Tenney *v.* Harvey, 63 Vt. 520, 22 At. Rep. 659.

been committed, whereas a private person so arresting, or causing to be arrested, an alleged offender, must show not only that he had reasonable grounds of suspicion but that a felony had actually been committed (*f*). The modern policeman is a statutory constable having all the powers which a constable has by the common law (*g*), and special statutory powers for dealing with various particular offences (*h*).

Who is answerable Every one is answerable for specifically directing the arrest or imprisonment of another, as for any other act that he specifically commands or ratifies, and a superior officer who finds a

---

(*f*) This applies only to felony "the law [i e, common law] does not excuse constables for arresting persons on the reasonable belief that they have committed a misdemeanor" see *Griffin* v *Coleman* (1859), 4 H & N 265, 28 L J Ex 134

(*g*) Stephen, 1 Hist Cr. Law, 197, 199

As to the common law powers of constables and others to arrest for preservation of the peace, which seem not free from doubt, see *Timothy* v *Simpson* (1835), 1 C M. & R. 757, Bigelow L C 257, per Parke B

(*h*) Bigelow L. C. 200.

Who is answerable. Supporting the statement of the text, *vide* McQueen *v.* Heck, 1 Coldw 212; Chrisman *v* Carney, 33 Ark. 33; Bailey *v.* Wiggins, 1 Houst. 29; Hays *v.* Creary, 60 Tex 445, Rafferty *v* Peoples, 69 Ill. 111; 18 Am. Rep 601, Pierce *v* Hubbard, 10 Johns. 405; Frazier *v* Turner, 76 Wis 562, 45 N W. Rep 411, Gelzenlenchter *v* Neimeyer, 64 Wis. 316; 54 Am. Rep. 616, Peoples *v* Smith, 20 Johns. 63, Lewis *v.* Avery, 8 Vt. 287, Grumon *v.* Raymond, 1 Conn. 39, Grace *v.* Teague, 81 Me 559, 18 At Rep 89; De Courcy *v* Cox, 94 Cal. 665, 30 Pac. Rep 95, Gillingham *v.* Ohio River R Co , 35 N C 588; 14 S E. Rep 243, Touhey *v.* Ring, 9 Lea, 422, Tracy *v* Williams, 4 Conn 107; Wilson *v* Robinson, 6 How. Pr. 110; Curry *v* Pringle, 11 Johns 444, Green *v.* Rumsey, 2 Wend. 611; Dietrichs *v* Schaw, 43 Ind. 175, Hauss *v.* Kohlar, 25 Kan. 640, Gorton *v* Frizzell, 20 Ill 292; Von Kettler *v.* Johnson, 57 Id. 109; Johnson *v* Von Kettler, 66 Id. 63, Barhydt *v* Valk, 12 Wend. 145, 27 Am. Dec 124, Abbott *v.* Booth, 51 Barb 546; Harwood *v.* Siphers, 70 Me 464; Stoyel *v* Lawrence, 3 Day, 1; Peck *v* Rooks, 22 Ark 221; Grumon *v.* Raymond, 1 Conn 40, Sheldon *v* Hill, 33 Mich 171; Fisher *v* Langbein, 62 How. Pr. 238, Gold *v* Bissell, 1 Wend. 210; 19 Am Dec 480, Langford *v.* Boston & A R Co., 144 Mass 431; 11 N. E Rep 697.

"A person who procures an illegal arrest to be made is liable in trespass for false imprisonment, though not aiding and abetting." Clifton

FALSE IMPRISONMENT.

person taken into custody by a constable under his orders, and then continues the custody, is liable to an action if the original arrest was unlawful (*i*). Nor does it matter

(*i*) Griffin v. Coleman, note (*f*) last page

---

r Grayson, 2 Stew. 412, Stovel v Lawrence, 3 Day, 1, Stoddard v Bird, Kirby, 65, Burlinghand v Wyloo, 2 Root, 151, Pierson v Gale, 8 Vt 509, Gilbert v Emmons, 12 Ill. 113, Taylor v. Trask, 7 Cow. 219; Snydacker v Brosse, 51 Ill 357, Poulk v Slocum, 3 Blackf 421; Miller v. Adams, 52 N Y 409; Harwood v. Siphers, 70 Me. 464; Gelzeulenchter v. Neimeyer, 64 Miss 316, 51 Am Rep 616, Hackett v. King, 6 Allen, 58, Chapman v. Dyett, 11 Wend 31, 25 Am. Dec. 598, Vredenburgh v. Hendricks, 17 Barb. 179, Emery v Hapgood, 7 Gray, 55, Letzler v Huntington, 24 La An. 330, Thorpe v Wray, 68 Ga. 359, Luddington v. Peck, 2 Conn. 700

A person who by acts approves a wrongful arrest is liable therefor Webber v Kenny, 1 A K Marsh (Ky.) 345. See Pollock v. Dominey, 7 Hun, 52, Clifton v Grayson, 2 Stew. 412. Where the facts have been passed upon by the judge making an order for arrest the plaintiff cannot be held responsible. Finley v. St Louis Refrigerator Co, 99 Mo 559; 13 S. W. Rep 87, Dusy v. Helm, 59 Cal 188.

Nor can one who merely directs the attention of a policeman to another who is thereupon arrested Veneman v Jones, 118 Ind. 41, 20 N E Rep 644. But see McCarrahan v. Lavers, 15 R. I. 302, 3 At. Rep 592; Mallniemi v. Groulund, 92 Mich 22; 52 N. W Rep. 627.

A mere observer where a person is forced to sign a "lie bill" held not liable. Walker v State, 25 Tex. App 443, 8 S W. Rep. 547.

For cases on the liability of corporations for false imprisonment and malicious prosecution, see *ante*, p. 68.

False imprisonment and malicious prosecution distinguished In an action for false imprisonment, the gist of the action is an unlawful detention, while in an action for malicious prosecution more is necessary. In Turpin v Remy (3 Black. 210), it was said by Stevens J, in delivering the opinion of the court: "An action for a malicious prosecution can only be supported for the malicious prosecution of some legal proceeding, before some judicial officer or tribunal. If the proceedings commenced are extra-judicial, the remedy is trespass, and not an action on the case for malicious prosecution. No proof of malice or want of probable cause is necessary to make out a case for false imprisonment" Coulter v Lower, 35 Ind. 287; 9 Am Rep. 735 See Painter v. Ives, 4 Neb 122, Baird v Householder, 32 Pa St 168; Murphy v Martin, 58 Wis. 278; Brown v. Chadsey, 39 Barb. 263; Atkins v. Newell, 32 Ark 607; Bauer v Clay, 8 Kan. 584, Hewitt v Newburger, 66 Hun, 230, 20 N. Y. S Rep 913, Johnson v Bouton, 35 Neb. 898, 53 N. W. Rep 913; Hobbs v Ray (R. I), 25 At Rep 694.

whether he acts in his own interest or another's (*j*). But one is not answerable for acts done upon his information or suggestion by an officer of the law, if they are done not as merely ministerial acts, but in the exercise of the officer's proper authority or discretion. Rather troublesome doubts may arise in particular cases as to the quality of the act complained of, whether in this sense discretionary, or ministerial only. The distinction between a servant and an "independent contractor" (*k*) with regard to the employer's responsibility is in some measure analogous. A party who sets the law in motion without making its act his own is not necessarily free from liability. He may be liable for malicious prosecution (of which hereafter) (*l*), but he cannot be sued for false imprisonment, or in a court which has not jurisdiction over cases of malicious prosecution. "The distinction between false imprisonment and malicious prosecution is well illustrated by the case where, parties being before a magistrate, one makes a charge against another, whereupon the magistrate orders the person charged to be taken into custody and detained until the matter can be investigated. The party making the charge is not liable to an action for false imprisonment, because he does not set a ministerial officer in motion, but a judicial officer. The opinion and the judgment of a judicial officer are interposed between the charge and the imprisonment" (*m*). Where an officer has taken a supposed offender into custody of his own motion, a person who at his request signs the charge-sheet does not thereby make the act his own (*n*), any more than one who certifies

---

(*j*) *Baker* v. *Braham* (1773), 2 W. Bl. 866 (attorney suing out and procuring execution of void process).

(*k*) Pp. 92, 93, above.

(*l*) See *Fitzjohn* v. *Mackinder* (1861), Ex. Ch. 1861, 9 C. B. N. S. 505, 30 L. J. C. P. 257.

(*m*) Willes J., *Austin* v. *Dowling* (1870), L. R. 5 C. P. at p. 540, *West* v. *Smallwood* (1838), 3 M. & W. 418, Bigelow L. C. 237, nor does an action for malicious prosecution lie where the judicial officer has held on a true statement of the facts that there is reasonable cause. *Hope* v. *Evered* (1886), 17 Q. B. D. 338, 55 L. J. M. C. 146, *Lea* v. *Charrington* (1889), 23 Q. B. Div. 45, 272, 58 L. J. Q. B. 461.

(*n*) *Grinham* v. *Willey* (1859), 4 H. & N. 496, 28 L. J. Ex. 242.

work done under a contract thereby makes the contractor his servant. But where an officer consents to take a person into custody only upon a charge being distinctly made by the complainant, and the charge-sheet signed by him, there the person signing the charge-sheet must answer for the imprisonment as well as the officer (*o*)

Again, where a man is given into custody on a mistaken charge, and then brought before a magistrate who remands him, damages can be given against the prosecutor in an action for false imprisonment only for the trespass in arresting, not for the remand, which is the act of the magistrate (*p*).

Reasonable and probable cause. What is reasonable cause of suspicion to justify arrest may be said, paradoxical as the statement looks, to be neither a question of law nor of fact, at any rate in the common sense of the terms. Not of fact, because it is for the judge and not for the

---

(*o*) *Austin v. Dowling* (1870), L. R. 5 C. P. 534, 39 L. J. C. P. 260. Other illustrations may be found in Addison on Torts, 5th ed. 130, 131. As to the protection of parties issuing an execution in regular course, though the judgment is afterwards set aside on other grounds, see *Smith v. Sydney* (1870), L. R. 5 Q. B. 203,

39 L. J. Q. B. 144. One case often cited, *Flewster v. Royle* (1808, Lord Ellenborough), 1 Camp. 187, is of doubtful authority, see *Gosden v. Elphick* (1849), 4 Ex. 445, 19 L. J. Ex. 9, and *Grinham v. Willey*, above.

(*p*) *Lock v. Ashton* (1848), 12 Q. B. 871, 18 L. J. Q. B. 76.

Reasonable and probable cause. It is a general rule that in an action for false imprisonment, the plaintiff need prove neither malice nor want of probable cause. Boaz v. Tate, 43 Ind. 60, Adkin v. Newell, 32 Ark. 605, Boeger v. Langberg, 97 Mo. 390; 11 S. W. Rep. 223, Rosen v. Stein, 7 N. Y. S. 368. See Clow v. Wright, Brayt. 118, Krebs v. Thomas, 12 Ill App 266, Neal v. Hart, 115 Pa. St. 347, 8 At. Rep. 628, Firestone v. Rice, 71 Mich 377, 38 N W Rep. 885; Olmstead v Doland, 6 N. Y. S. 130, Mitchell v Malone, 77 Ga, 301.

Evidence that the defendant acted without malice, or want of probable cause, may always be admitted to mitigate exemplary damages, but not to diminish actual damages. Livingston v. Burroughs, 33 Mich. 511; Comer v Knowles, 17 Kan. 436, Sleight v. Ogle, 4 E. D. Smith, 445, Miller v Grice, 2 Rich. L. 27; 44 Am. Dec. 271, McDaniel v Needham, 61 Tex. 269, Bogers v. Wilson, Minor, 407, Hill v Taylor, 50 Mich. 549, Roth v Smith, 41 Ill. 314.

jury (q); not of law, because "no definite rule can be laid down for the exercise of the judge's judgment" (r). It is a matter of judicial discretion such as is familiar enough in the classes of cases which are disposed of by a judge sitting alone; but this sort of discretion does not find a natural place in a system which assigns the decision of facts to the jury and the determination of the law to the judge. The anomalous character of the rule has been more than once pointed out and regretted by the highest judicial authority (s). The truth seems to be that the question was formerly held to be one of law and has for some time been tending to become one of fact, but the change has never been formally recognized. The only thing which can be certainly affirmed in general terms about the meaning of "reasonable cause" in this connexion is that on the one hand a belief honestly entertained is not of itself enough (t); on the other hand, a man is not bound to wait until he is in possession of such evidence as would be admissible and sufficient for prosecuting the offence to conviction, or even of the best evidence which he might obtain by further inquiry "It does not follow that because it would be very reasonable to make further inquiry, it is not reasonable to act without doing so" (u). It is obvious, also, that the existence or non-existence of reasonable cause must be judged, not by the event, but by the party's means of knowledge at the time.

Although the judge ought not to leave the whole ques-

(q) *Hailes* v *Marks* (1861), 7 H. & N 56, 30 L J Ex 389.

(r) *Lister* v. *Perryman* (1870), L R 4 H L 521, 535, per Lord Chelmsford So per Lord Colonsay at p 540

(s) Lord Campbell in *Broughton* v *Jackson* (1852), 18 Q B 378, 383, 21 L J Q B 266, Lord Hatherley, Lord Westbury, and Lord Colonsay (all familiar with procedure in which there was no jury at all) in *Lister* v *Perryman*, L R 4 H L 531, 538, 539

(t) *Broughton* v *Jackson* (1852), 18 Q B. 378, 21 L J Q B 266 the defendant must show "facts which would create a reasonable suspicion in the mind of a reasonable man," per Lord Campbell C J

(u) Bramwell B, *Perryman* v *Lister* (1868), L R 3 Ex at p. 202, approved by Lord Hatherley, S. C nom *Lister* v *Perryman*, L R 4 H L at p. 533.

tion of reasonable cause to the jury, there seems to be no objection to his asking the jury, as separate questions, whether the defendant acted on an honest belief, and whether he used reasonable care to inform himself of the facts (a).

III.— *Injuries in Family Relations*

Protection of personal relations Next to the sanctity of the person comes that of the personal relations constituting the family. Depriving a husband of the society of his wife, a parent of the companionship and confidence of his children, is not less a personal injury, though a less tangible one, than beating or imprisonment. The same may to some extent be said of the relation of master and servant, which in modern law is created by contract, but is still regarded for some purposes as belonging to the permanent organism of the family, and having the nature of status. It seems natural enough that an action should lie at the suit of the head of a household for enticing away a person who is under his lawful authority, be it wife, child or servant; there may be difficulty in fixing the boundary where the sphere of domestic relations ends and that of pure contract begins, but that is a difficulty of degree. That the same rule should extend to any wrong done to a wife, child, or servant, and followed as a proximate consequence by loss of their society or service, is equally to be expected. Then, if seduction in its ordinary sense of physical and moral corruption is part of the wrong-doer's conduct, it is quite in accordance with principles admitted in other parts of the law that this should be a recognized ground for awarding exemplary damages. It is equally plain that on general principle a daughter or servant can herself have no civil remedy against the seducer, though the parent or master may; no civil remedy, we say, for other remedies

(a) II Stephen on Malicious Prosecution, ch.

have existed and exist. She cannot complain of that which took place by her own consent. Any different rule would be an anomaly. Positive legislation might introduce it on grounds of moral expediency; the courts, which have the power and the duty of applying known principles to new cases, but cannot abrogate or modify the principles themselves, are unable to take any such step.

Historical accidents of the common law herein. There seems, in short, no reason why this class of wrongs should not be treated by the common law in a fairly simple and rational manner, and with results generally not much unlike those we actually find, only free from the anomalies and injustice which flow from disguising real analogies under transparent but cumbrous fictions. But as matter of history (and pretty modern history) the development of the law has been strangely halting and one-sided. Starting from the particular case of a hired servant, the authorities have dealt with other relations, not by openly treating them as analogous in principle, but by importing into them the fiction of actual service; with the result that in the class of cases most prominent in modern practice, namely, actions brought by a parent (or person *in loco parentis*) for the seduction of a daughter, the test of the plaintiff's right has come to be, not whether he has been injured as the head of a family, but whether he can make out a constructive "loss of service" (*y*).

Trespass for taking away wife, etc., and per quod servitium amisit. The common law provided a remedy by writ of trespass for the actual taking away of a wife, servant, or heir, and perhaps younger child also (*z*). An

---

(*y*) Christian's note on Blackstone iii. 142 is still not amiss, though the amendments of this century in the law of evidence have removed some of the grievances mentioned.

(*z*) F. N. B. 89 O, 90 H, 91 I, Blackst. Comm. iii. 139. The writ was *de uxore abducta cum bonis viri sui*, or an ordinary writ of trespass (F. N. B. 52 K), a case as late as the Restoration is mentioned in Bac. Abr. v. 328 (Ed. 1832).

action of trespass also lay for wrongs done to the plaintiff's wife or servant (not to a child as such), whereby he lost the society of the former or the services of the latter.

Injuries to wife or servant. A master has a right of action for an assault or an assault and battery, upon his servant, where some loss of service or capacity to serve results therefrom Plunker v. Georgia Railroad & Banking Co , 81 Ga. 161, 8 S. E. Rep 529, Knight v Wilcox, 14 N Y 113. See Schouler's Dom. Rel. pp , 631, 692

A master may sue for an injury to his apprentice causing disability, *per quod servitium amisit*, although the act was in violation of a contract made with the apprentice. Ames v Union R. Co , 117 Mass. 541

A father may maintain an action for harboring and secreting his minor daughter, and persuading her to remain absent from his family and service without his consent. Stowe v. Heywood, 7 Allen, 118.

The services and earnings of a married woman belong to her husband Nat Bk. of Metropolis v Sprague, 20 N J. Eq. 18, Bowden v. Grey, 49 Mass 517, Yopst v. Yopst, 51 Ind. 61; Reynold v Robinson, 64 N Y 589, Shaefer v Sheppard, 54 Ala. 214, Bolman v. Overall, 80 Ala 451, 2 So Rep 624, Uransky v. Drydock, E. B. & B. R. Co., 118 N. Y. 304, 23 N. E. Rep. 451, Porter v. Dunn, 131 N Y 311; 30 N. E Rep 122 So, therefore, for an injury to his wife, resulting in the loss of her services, the husband may recover damages Kavanaugh v Janesville, 24 Wis 618, Barnes v. Allen, 1 Abb. App. Dec. 111, Philippi v. Wolf, 14 Abb Pr (N S), 196, Sloan v New York Central R. Co , 4 Thomp. & Co. 135, Hun, 540; McWhirter v. Hatten, 42 Ia. 288, Meese v. Fond du Lac, 48 Wis. 323, City of Wyandotte v. Agan, 37 Kan. 528, 15 Pac Rep 529, Maine v. City of Rich Hill, 28 Mo App. 497; Blair v. Chicago & A. Ry Co , 89 Mo 334, 1 S W. Rep. 367; Scogland v. Minneapolis St. Ry. Co , 45 Minn. 530; 47 N. W. Rep 1071.

A distinction is drawn in the case of Brooks v. Schuverin, (54 N. Y. 343), between where the wife performs household services and where she works for another, the court holding that in the latter case she alone can recover for an injury disabling her from performing such service. See Tuttles v Chicago, R. I etc. R. Co., 42 Ia. 518; Newmeister v. Dubuque, 47 Ia 465, Carr v. Easton, 7 Penn. Co. Rep 403.

Taking away of wife. "It is a common law rule, that a husband may maintain an action for enticing away his wife and separating her from him, whereby he loses her services and society." Hutcheson v. Peck, 5 Johns 196, followed in Wood v Mathews, 47 Ia. 410; Turner v. Estes, 3 Mass. 316, Barbee v Armistead, 10 Ired 530, 51 Am. Dec. 404; Tasker v Stanley (Mass), 26 N E Rep. 617; White v. Ross, 47 Mich 172

"It is well settled that a husband may maintain an action for enticing away his wife, or enticing her to live apart from him, and this, whether the wrong-doer be the father of the wife or any other person. But merely

The language of pleading was *per quod consortium*, or *servitium amisit*. Such a cause of action was quite distinct from that which the husband might acquire in right of the wife, or the servant in his own right. The trespass is one, but the remedies are "diversis respectibus" (a). "If my servant is beat, the master shall not have an action for the battery, unless the battery is so great that by reason thereof he loses the service of his servant, but the servant himself for every small battery shall have an action, and the reason of this difference is that the master has not any damage by the personal beating of his servant, but by rea-

---

(a) Y B 19 Hen VI 45, pl 94

---

allowing the wife to come and remain in his house, by a stranger, and much less, her father, from good motives, will not give the husband a right of action Something further tending to prevent or dissuade the wife from living with her husband is necessary" Bennett v Smith, 21 Barb. 439.

Where one voluntarily interferes with the relations of husband and wife, even though the relations have been so violent that a divorce would be granted if sued for, he does so at his peril "The wife may have a just cause for separation or divorce, but she may elect to abide by her situation, and remain with her husband nevertheless If she chooses to do so, no stranger has a right to intermeddle with the domestic and marital relation of the husband and wife and if he voluntarily does so he is amenable for the consequences" Mosisett v. McPide, 47 Mo 646 See Schouler's Dom Rel, pp 57, 58, Rulbe v Hanna, 5 Ohio, 530, Campbell v Carter, 8 Daly, 165, Smith v Lyke, 20 N. Y. Supreme Ct 204, Perry v. Lovejoy, 49 Mich 529.

Taking away of husband At common law a wife could not maintain an action for the enticing away and harboring of her husband, but in some of the States statutes have conferred upon her this right. See Van Arnam v Ayres, 67 Barb 544, Reeder v. Purdy, 41 Ill 279, 282, Michigan v Coleman, 28 Mich 440, Duffies v. Duffies, 76 Wis 374, 45 N. Y. Rep 522 However, the authorities are not uniform on this point, and the common law doctrine is criticized in Westlake v. Westlake, 34 Ohio St 621. See Bennett v Bennett, 116 N. Y. 584, 23 N. E. Rep 117, Wolf v Wolf, 130 Ind 599; 30 N. E Rep 308, Haynes v. Nowlin, 129 Ind. 581, 9 N E Rep 289, annulling Logan v Logan, 77 Ind 588, Warren v Warren, 89 Mich 123; 50 N W Rep. 842; Waldron v. Waldron, 45 Fed Rep. 315; Huling v Huling, 32 Ill App 519, and cases collected in 31 Cent Law J. 29 n.

son of a *per quod*, viz., *per quod servitium, etc., amisit*, so that the original act is not the cause of his action, but the consequent upon it, viz., the loss of his service, is the cause of his action, for be the battery greater or less, if the master doth not lose the service of his servant, he shall not have an action" (b). The same rule applies to the beating or maltreatment of a man's wife, provided it be "very enormous, so that thereby the husband is deprived for any time of the company and assistance of his wife" (c).

"Criminal conversation." Against an adulterer the husband had an action at common law, commonly known as an action of criminal conversation. In form it was

(b) *Robert Marys's case*, 9 Co. Rep 113a It is held in *Osborn v. Gillett* (1873), L R 8 Ex 88, 12 L J Ex 53, that a master shall not have an action for a trespass whereby his servant is killed (diss Bramwell B) It is submitted that the decision is wrong, and Lord Bramwell's dissenting judgment right See pp 71–76, above

(c) Blackst. Comm iii 140.

Criminal conversation. A husband has a right of action, either in trespass or on the case, against any one who commits adultery with his wife. Peters v Lake, 66 Ill. 206, Coleman v White, 59 Ind. 548, Hadlock v. Heywood, 121 Mass. 236, Johnston v. Disbrow, 47 Mich. 59; Van Vacter v McKillip, 7 Blackf 578, Barnes v. Allen, 30 Barb 663.

"The action of trespass and case are concurrent remedies for this injury. And Chitty, in his work on pleadings, says that though it had been usual to sue in case, it is considered preferable to declare in trespass But in either form of action, loss of services may be averred in aggravation of damages. And being averred, a failure to prove actual loss of services would not defeat a right of recovery." Yundt v. Hartrunft 41 Ill 17 In the same case the court said "This action does not proceed upon the theory of the loss of services of the wife. It is for the injury the husband sustains by the dishonor of his bed; the alienation of his wife's affections; the destruction of his domestic comfort, and the suspicion cast upon the legitimacy of her offspring. * * * When loss of service is claimed, damages would not be given therefor unless it is proved." With reference to this action the husband's interest is expressed by the word *consortium*, "the right to the conjugal fellowship of the wife, to her company, co-operation and in every conjugal relation * * * The loss of the *consortium* is presumed, although the wife may have herself been the seducer, or may not have been living

generally trespass *vi et armis*, on the theory that " a wife is not, as regards her husband, a free agent or separate person " (d), and therefore her consent was immaterial, and the husband might sue the adulterer as he might have sued any mere trespasser who beat, imprisoned, or carried away his wife against her will. Actions for criminal conversation were abolished in England on the establishment of the Divorce Court in 1857, but damages can be claimed on the same principles in proceedings for a dissolution of marriage or judicial separation (e)

In practice these actions were always or almost always

(d) Coleridge J in *Lumley v Gye* (1853), 22 L. J Q B at p 178 Case would also lie, and the common form of declaration was for some time considered to be rather case than trespass *Macfadzen v Olivant* (1805), 6 East, 387 See note (f) next page

(e) 20 & 21 Vict c. 85, ss. 33, 59

---

with the husband. A husband who is living apart from his wife, if he has not removed his marital rights, can maintain an action, and it is not necessary for him to prove alienation of the wife's affection, or actual loss of her society and assistance." Bigaouette v Paulet, 134 Mass. 123. See Phillipi v. Wolf, 14 Abb. Pr. (N. S) 196, Adams v. Main, 3 Ind App. 232, 29 N E. Rep. 792

A husband may sue for criminal intercourse with his wife though he is separated from her, and before the commencement of the action she had obtained a divorce Michel v Dunkle, 84 Ind 544. See Wood v Mathews, 47 Ia 409, Sherwood v Titman, 55 Pa St 77.

And the action is not defeated by the death of the wife before the suit is brought Cox v. Whitfield, 18 Ala. 738, Garrison v. Burden, 40 Ala 515

But the husband cannot maintain an action for adultery with his wife where he voluntarily agrees to it and does separate from her Fry v Derstler, 2 Yeates, 278. See Schorn v. Berry, 63 Hun, 110; 17 N. Y S Rep. 572; Cook v. Wood, 30 Ga 891; Sherwood v Titman, 55 Pa. St 77

Negligence of the husband in preventing criminal conversation with his wife, not amounting to a consent, may be shown in reduction of damages Bunnell v Greathead, 49 Barb 106.

The fact that a husband cohabits with his wife, after knowledge of her adultery, is not a bar to the action of criminal conversation by him against her paramour Verholf v. Van Houwenlengen, 21 Ia 429. See Clouser v. Clapper, 59 Ind 548

Punitive damages may be recovered Williams and Green, JJ, dissenting, Cornelius v Hambey, 50 Pa. 359, 24 At Rep 515, Sturam v. Hummel, 39 Ia 478, Peters v. Lake, 66 Ill 206.

instituted with a view to obtaining a divorce by private Act of Parliament; the rules of the House of Lords (in which alone such Bills were brought in) requiring the applicant to have obtained both the verdict of a jury in an action, and a sentence of separation *a mensa et toro* in the Ecclesiastical Court.

Enticing away servants. An action also lay for enticing away a servant (that is, procuring him or her to depart voluntarily from the master's service), and also for knowingly harbouring a servant during breach of service; whether by the common law, or only after and by virtue of the Statute of Labourers (*f*), is doubtful. Quite modern examples are not wanting (*g*).

Much later the experiment was tried with success of a husband bringing a like action " against such as persuade

---

(*f*) 23 Edw III (A D 1349) this statute, passed in consequence of the Black Death, marks a great crisis in the history of English agriculture and land tenure As to its bearing on the matter in hand, see the dissenting judgment of Coleridge J in *Lumley* v *Gye* (1853), 2 E & B 216, 22 L J Q B 163, 480 The action was generally on the case, but it might be trespass e g, *Tullidge* v *Wade* (1769), 3 Wils 18, an action for seducing the plaintiff's daughter, where the declaration was in trespass *vi et armis* How this can be accounted for on principle I know not, short of regarding the servant as a *quasi* chattel, the difficulty was felt by Sir James Mansfield, *Woodward* v *Walton* (1807), 2 B & P N R 476, 482 For a time it seemed the better opinion, however, that trespass was the only proper form. Ibid, *Ditcham* v *Bond* (1811), 2 M & S 436 It was formally decided as late as 1839 (without giving any other reason than the constant practice) that trespass or case might be used at the pleader's option *Chamberlain* v *Hazelwood* (1839), 5 M. & W 515, 9 L J Ex 87. The only conclusion which can or need at this day be drawn from such fluctuations is that the old system of pleading did not succeed in its professed object of maintaining clear logical distinctions between different causes of action

(*g* (*Hartley* v. *Cummings* (1847), 5 C B. 247, 17 L J. C P 84

Enticing away servants. It is an actionable wrong to wilfully entice from the service of another one who is in his employment under a contract not fully executed Haight *v* Badgeley, 15 Barb. 499; Milburne *v.* Byrne, 1 Cranch C. Ct. 239; Butterfield *v.* Ashley, 2 Gray, 254, Scidmore *v.* Smith, 13 Johns. 322; Bixby *v* Dunlap, 56 N. H. 556; Huff *v.* Watkins, 15 S C. 82, 40 Am. Rep 680, Sherwood *v.* Hall, 3 Sumn. 127, Plummer *v* Webb, 4 Mason, 380, Peter *v.* Blocker, 43 Ga 331, Carew *v.* Rutherford, 106 Mass. 1, Noice *v* Brown, 39 N J L 569; Hudson *v.* State, 46 Ga. 624; Lee *v.* West, 47 Ga 311; Walker *v.* Cronin, 107 Mass. 555;

and entice the wife to live separate from him without a sufficient cause" (h).

Still later the action for enticing away a servant, *per quod servitium amisit*, was turned to the purpose for which alone it may now be said to survive, that of punishing seducers; for the latitude allowed in estimating damages makes the proceeding in substance almost a penal one.

Actions for seduction in modern practice: proof or presumption of service. In this kind of action it is not necessary to prove the existence of a binding contract of service between the plaintiff and the person seduced or

---

(h) Blackst Comm III 139, Ins- moro v Greenbank (1745), Willes 577. Bigelow L C 328 It was objected that there was no precedent of any such action

---

Ames v. Union R Co, 117 Id 541; Turner v State, 43 Ala 549, Roseberry v State, 50 Id. 160, Salter v. Howard, 43 Ga. 601, Caughey v. Smith, 47 N. Y. 250; Sargent v. Mathewson, 38 N. H 54.

This principle is consistent and "it extends impartially to every grade of service, from the most brilliant and best paid to the most homely, and it shelters our nearest and tenderest domestic relations from the interference of malicious intermeddlers" Haskins v. Royster, 70 N. C 605 See Daniel v Swearengen, 6 S. C 303, Morgan v. Smith, 77 N. C. 37, following Haskins v Royster, 70 Id. 601.

One is liable to an employer if he harbors such employer's servants so as to deprive him of their services Campbell v. Cooper, 34 N. H 49, Dubois v. Allen, Anthon, 94.

But knowledge that the servant has absconded is necessary to attach liability. Huntoon v. Hazleton, 20 N. H. 388; Gale v. Parrott, 1 Id. 33, Coughey v. Smith, 46 N Y 244

One who detains a servant after demand made by the master is liable therefor Ferrell v Boykin, Phil L 9.

Seduction. Seduction is "The act of a man in enticing a woman to commit unlawful sexual intercourse with him, by means of persuasion, solicitation, promises, bribes, or other means without the employment of force." Black's Law Dic., p 1074 See Reed v. Williams, 5 Sneed (Tenn), 580; 73 Am. Dec 157, Comer v Taylor, 82 Mo. 341, Delvee v. Boardman, 20 Id. 446, Hopkins v. Mathias, 66 Ia. 833; Broughton v. Smart, 59 Ill. 440; Simpson v Grayson, 54 Ark. 404, Eagan v Murray, 80 Ia 180; Hawn v Baughart, 76 Id. 683; Brown v. Kingsley, 38 Id. 220.

"The common law gave the father an action for the seduction of his

SEDUCTION.

enticed away. The presence or absence of seduction in the common sense (whether the defendant "debauched the plaintiff's daughter," in the forensic phrase) makes no

daughter, but regarded it as an action for trespass for assaulting his servant, whereby he lost her services, later, an action on the case was allowed, and it is now well settled that the action may be brought in either form

The action was based upon the relation of master and servant, and not upon that of parent and child, and the measure of damages was such only as a master would recover for a disabling injury to his servant. The extent of the recovery has been enlarged by the courts from the necessity of the case, rather than from the principles which govern the action, until compensation is awarded to the parents as such, for the shame and mortification which that wrong brings upon him and his family. No action could be maintained by the father for the injury in his parental capacity, but in the struggle between substantial justice to the parent and the precedents in actions for seduction, the courts have clung to the latter and striven to attain the former, until the anomaly has been produced of requiring the action to be prosecuted by the father for an injury inflicted upon him in his relation as master, and permitting a recovery in his relation as parent." 21 Am. & Eng. Enc. of Law, 1009

To the same point, "Both the alleged relation of master and servant and the loss of service have long been considered as innocent fictions, which only served to bring the real grievance before the court where damages were allowed, not for the loss of services only, but principally for the humiliation and disgrace brought upon the plaintiff's family, and for the mental anguish suffered on account of the ruin of his daughter and the dishonor of his household." Hudkins v. Haskins, 22 W Va 645 See Barbour v Stephenson, 32 Fed. Rep. 66; Simpson v Grayson, 45 Ark. 401, Coon v Maflitt, 3 N. J. L 169, 4 Am Dec 392, Dain v. Wyckoff, 7 N Y 191, Lawyer v Fritcher, 54 Hun, 586, Stoudt v. Shepherd, 73 Mich 588.

In making out the constructive relation of master and servant and determining what constitutes sufficient service the English rule requires actual service or actual residence with the father at the time of the seduction, but the American courts have been more liberal and have established the rule that it is only necessary to show that the parent has the legal right, at the time, to command the services of the child which may be employed by a third person. Boyd v Byrd, 8 Black 113; 44 Am. Dec. 740, Bartley v Richtmeyer, 4 N. Y 38, 53 Am. Dec. 338, White v. Murtland, 71 Ill 250, 22 Am. Rep. 100. Ellington v. Ellington, 47 Miss. 329; Emery v Gowen, 4 Me. 33, 16 Am. Dec 223; Clinton v. York, 26 Me. 167, Kennedy v Shea, 110 Mass. 147, 14 Am. Rep. 584, Nickleson v Stryker, 10 Johns 115, 6 Am Dec 318, Furman v. Van Sise, 56 N Y. 435, 15 Am.

difference in this respect; it is not a necessary part of the cause of action, but only a circumstance of aggravation (i) Whether that element be present or absent, proof of

(i) *Evans v Walton* (1867), L. R. 2 C. P 615, 36 L. J. C. P. 307, where it was unsuccessfully contended that the action for seducing a daughter with loss of service as the consequence, and for enticing away a servant, were distinct species, and that to sustain an action for "enticing away" alone, a binding contract of service must be proved

Rep 411, Clark v Fitch, 2 Wend 459, 20 Am. Dec 669, Mulvehall v. Millward, 11 N Y. 343, Mercer v Walmsley, 4 Har. & J 27, 9 Am Dec 486, Hornketh v. Barr, 8 Serg & R. 36, 11 Am. Dec 568, Riddle v McGinnis, 22 W. Va 253, Molny v. Hoffman, 86 Pa St. 358, Benson v Remington, 2 Mass. 113, Lavery v. Crooke, 52 Wis 612, 38 Am. Rep 768, Roberts v Connolly, 11 Ala 235; Thompson v Patterson, 23 Ark 159, Greenwood v Greenwood, 28 Md. 369, Bolton v. Mille, 6 Ind 262, Hays v. Borders, 6 Ill 46, Anderson v. Ryan, 8 Id 583, White v. Murtland, 71 Id 252, Franklin v. McCorkle, 16 Lea, 609, 1 S. W. Rep 250, Lipe v. Eisenlord, 32 N Y 229, Hewitt v Prime, 21 Wend 79, Doyle v Jessup, 29 Ill 460, Damon v Moore, 5 Lans 459, South v Denniston, 2 Watts, 474, Davidson v. Abbott, 52 Vt. 570, 36 Am Rep. 767, Abrahams v Kidney, 104 Mass. 222; 6 Am. Rep 220; Knight v. Wilcox, 14 N Y. 413; Blagge v. Ilsley, 127 Mass. 191, 34 Am Rep. 361, Russell v Chambers, 31 Minn. 54.

Where the daughter was more than twenty-one years of age, the American courts agree with the English courts in holding that there must exist some kind of service; "but the slightest acts have been held to constitute the relation of master and servant in such a case." Martin v. Payne, 9 Johns 387; 6 Am. Dec 288, Kelly v. Donnelly, 5 Md. 211, Kendrich v. McCrary, 11 Ga. 603, Vossel v Cole, 10 Mo. 634, Mulvehall v Millward, 11 N.Y 342, Briggs v Evans, 5 Ired. 16, Whitney v. Elmer, 6 Barb. 256; Wert v. Strause, 38 N J. L 184, Lamb v. Taylor, 67 Md 85, 8 A. Rep. 760, Lee v Hodges, 13 Gratt 726, Patterson v. Thompson, 24 Ark. 55.

Any one entitled to the services of a female may sue for her seduction. Hamilton v Lomax, 26 Barb 615; Pence v. Dozier, 7 Bush 133, Ellington v. Ellington, 47 Miss. 329, White v. Nellis, 31 N Y 405, 88 Am. Dec. 282; and authorities cited *supra*.

Any person who stands *in loco parentis*, as a step-father, or grandfather or guardian, where the facts prove the relation of master and servant, can maintain such suit Davidson v. Goodall, 18 N H. 423; Ingersoll v. Jones, 5 Barb. 661, Bracy v Kibbe, 31 Id 273, Maginnay v Sandek, 5 Sneed (Tenn.), 146; Certwell v Hoyt, 13 N. Y. Supreme Ct. 575, 6 Hun, 575, Kinney v Langhenour, 89 N C 365, Morgan v. Dawls, 4 Cow. 412, Bartley v. Richtmyer, 4 N Y. 38, 53 Am. Dec. 338; Ball v Bruce, 21 Ill. 161, Keller v. Donnelly, 5 Md. 211; Moritz v. Ganhart, 7 Watts 302,

a *de facto* relation of service is enough; and any fraud whereby the servant is induced to absent himself or herself affords a ground of action, "when once the relation of master and servant at the time of the acts complained of is established" (*h*).

This applies even to an actual contract of hiring made by the defendant with a female servant whom he has seduced, if it is found as a fact that the hiring was a merely colourable one, undertaken with a view to the seduction which followed (*l*). And a *de facto* service is not the less recognized because a third party may have a paramount claim. A married woman living apart from her husband in her father's house may be her father's servant, even though that relation might be determined at the will of the husband (*m*). Some evidence of such a relation there must be, but very little will serve. A grown-up daughter

(*l*) Willes J., L. R. 2 C. P. 622.
(*l*) *Speight* v. *Oliviera* (1819), 2 Stark. 493, cited with approved by Montague Smith J., L. R. 2 C. P. 624.

(*m*) *Harper* v. *Luffkin* (1827), 7 B. & C. 387. This was long before courts of law did or could recognize any capacity of contracting in a married woman.

---

semble, 32 Am. Dec. 762, Blanchard *v* Ilsley, 120 Mass. 487, 26 Am Rep. 535, Butler Co. *v* McCann, 23 Ala. 599. But see Fernslee *v* Moyer, 3 Watts & S. 416, 39 Am. Dec 33.

Or, the mother, when she becomes the head of the family by the death of the father. Logan *v.* Murray, 6 Serg & R. 175, 9 Am. Dec. 422, Heinrichs *v* Kenchner, 85 Mo. 378, Vossel *v.* Cole, 10 Mo. 634, 47 Am. Dec 136, Felkner *v* Scarlet, 29 Ind. 154; Gray *v.* Durland, 50 Barb 100, Gray *v* Durland, 51 N. Y. 424; Ryan *v.* Fralick, 50 Mich. 483; George *v.* Van Horn, 9 Barb. 523; Hobson *v.* Fullerton, 4 Ill. App 282; Villepique *v* Shuler 3 Strobh. 462, Davidson *v.* Abbott, 52 Vt 570; 36 Am. Rep 767, Parker *v* Meek, 3 Sneed (Tenn), 29.

Where one entitled to the services of a female consents to her seduction such consent is a complete bar to recovery of damages therefor. Tarvis *v* Barger, 24 Barb 614, Parker *v.* Elliott, 6 Munf. 587; Seager *v* Sligerland, 2 Caines, 219, Smith *v.* Martin, 15 Wend. 270; Vossel *v* Cole, 10 Mo 634, 47 Am. Dec. 136.

The negligence or careless indifference of the plaintiff in respect to his daughter may be proved in mitigation of damages. Zerbing *v.* Mourer, 2 Greene (Iowa), 520; Hollis *v* Wells, 3 Penn Law Jour Rep 169, Graham *v* Smith, 1 Edm. Sel Cas 267, and authorities cited *supra*.

keeping a separate establishment cannot be deemed her father's servant (*n*); nor can a daughter, whether of full age or not, who at the time of the seduction is actually another person's servant, so that no part of her services is at her parents' disposal (*o*). On the other hand, the fact of a child living with a parent, or any other person *in loco parentis*, as a member of the family of which that person is the head, is deemed enough to support the inference "that the relation of master and servant, determinable at the will of either party, exists between them" (*p*). And a daughter under age, returning home from service with another person which has been determined, may be deemed to have re-entered the service of her father (*q*). "The right to the service is sufficient" (*r*).

Partial attendance in the parents' house is enough to constitute service, as where a daughter employed elsewhere in the daytime is without consulting her employer free to assist, and does assist, in the household when she comes home in the evening (*s*).

Damages. Some loss of service, or possibility of service, must be shown as consequent on the seduction, since that is, in theory, the ground of action (*t*), but when that condition is once satisfied, the damages that may be given are by no means limited to an amount commensurate with

(*n*) *Manley* v *Field* (1859), 7 C B N S. 96, 29 L J C P 79

(*o*) *Dean* v *Peel* (1804), 5 East, 45, even if by the master's licence she gives occasional help in her parents' work, *Thompson* v *Ross* (1859), 5 H & N 16, 29 L J. Ex 1, *Hedges* v *Tagg* (1872), L R 7 Ex 283, 41 L J Ex 169 In the United States it is generally held that actual service with a third person is no bar to the action, unless there is a binding contract which excludes the parents' right of reclaiming the child's services—i e that service either *de facto* or *de jure* will do *Martin* v *Payne* (Sup Court N Y 1812), Bigelow L C 286, and notes

(*p*) Bramwell B in *Thompson* v *Ross*, last note

(*q*) *Terry* v *Hutchinson* (1868), L R 3 Q B 599, 37 L J Q B 257.

(*r*) Littledale J. cited with approval by Blackburn J , L R 3 Q B 602.

(*s*) *Rist* v *Faux* (1863), Ex Ch 4 B & S 409, 32 L J Q B 386

(*t*) *Grinnell* v *Wells* (1844), 7 M & G 1033, 14 L J C P 19, *Eager* v *Grimwood* (1847), 1 Ex 61, 16 L J Ex 236, where the declaration was framed in trespass, it would seem purposely on the chance of the court holding that the *per quod servitium amisit* could be dispensed with

the actual loss of service proved or inferred. The awarding of exemplary damages is indeed rather encouraged than otherwise (u). It is immaterial whether the plaintiff be a

(u) See *Terry v. Hutchinson*, note (q) last page.

Damages. In computing the damages suffered by the plaintiff in a suit for seduction the jury will consider "not only the loss of services which he suffered, and the expenses incurred by him by reason of the seduction, pregnancy, confinement and other illness," but also the anxiety and the suffering of mind caused by the loss of virtue of his daughter, the corrupting influence upon his other children, and the disgrace of his family. Phillips v. Hoyle, 4 Gray, 568, Rollins v. Chalmers, 51 Vt. 592, Taylor v. Shelkett, 66 Ind. 297; Wandell v Edwards, 25 Hun, 498, Barbour v Stephenson, 32 Fed. Rep. 66, Akerly v Haines, 2 Caines, 292, Hogan v. Cregan, 6 Robt. 138; Stiles v Tilford, 10 Wend. 338, Wilds v Bogan, 57 Ind. 453, Hatch v. Fuller, 131 Mass. 574, Rollins v Chalmers, 51 Vt 592, Hornketh v. Barr, 8 Serg. & R 36; 11 Am. Dec 568, Kendrick v McCrary, 11 Ga 603, Clem v Holmes, 33 Gratt. 722; 36 Am Rep. 793, Luecker v Stellen, 89 Ill. 545, 31 Am. Rep 104; Grable v. Margrave, 3 Ill 372, 38 Am Dec 88, Phelin v Kenderline, 20 Pa. St 354.

Exemplary or vindictive damages may be awarded, in the discretion of the jury, for the double purpose of setting an example and of punishing the wrongdoer. Lavery v Crook, 52 Wis 612, 38 Am. Rep. 768, Badgley v. Decker, 44 Barb 577, Torre v. Summers, 2 Nott & M. 267, 10 Am Dec. 597, Fox v. Stevens, 13 Minn 272, Morgan v Rose, 74 Mo. 318, Davidson v. Abbott, 52 Vt 570; 36 Am. Rep. 767, Johnston v Disbrow, 47 Mich. 59, Geise v Schultz, 69 Wis. 521, 34 N. W Rep. 913; Franklin v McCorkle, 16 Lea, 609, 1 S. W Rep. 250; Ingersol v Jones, 5 Barb. 661.

In forming their verdict the jury should consider both the merits of the plaintiff and the demerits of the defendant, and all the circumstances which diminish one or enhance the other. The moral reputation of the parties may be put in issue and their social position, and pecuniary condition may be shown either in aggravation or mitigation of damages, as the case may be. Cochran v. Ammon, 16 Ill 316, Peters v. Lake, 66 Id 209, Shattuck v Hammond, 2 Rowell, 496, Hoffman v. Kemerer, 44 Pa. St 452, Love v Masoner, 6 Baxt 24, 32 Am. Rep. 522, Carder v. Forehand, 1 Mo. 704, 14 Am. Dec 317; White v Murtland, 71 Ill 250, 22 Am Rep. 100, Patterson v Hayden, 17 Oreg. 238, 11 Am. St. Rep. 822, Wallace v. Clark, 2 Overt. 93, 5 Am Dec. 654, Drish v Davenport, 2 Stew, 266, Hawn v Baughart, 76 Ia 683; Fry v. Leslie. 87 Va. 269, Leckey v Bloser, 24 Pa. St. 401, Stoudt v. Shepherd, 73 Mich. 588; Aulay v. Birkhead, 13 Ired 28, 55 Am Dec. 427; Tillotson v. Cheetham, 3 Johns. 56, 3 Am Dec 459, Shewalter v. Bergman, 123 Ind. 155, Grable v. Margrave, 4 Ill 372, 38 Am Dec 90, Rea v Tucker, 51 Ill. 110, 99 Am Dec. 539, Thompson v Clendening, 1 Head, 287; Hays v Sinclair, 23 Vt. 108.

parent or kinsman, or a stranger in blood who has adopted the person seduced (x).

Services of young child. On the same principle or fiction of law a parent can sue in his own name for any injury done to a child living under his care and control, provided the child is old enough to be capable of rendering service; otherwise not, for "the gist of the action depends upon the capacity of the child to perform acts of service" (y).

Capricious operation of the law. The capricious working of the action for seduction in modern practice has often been the subject of censure. Thus, Serjeant Manning wrote more than forty years ago: "the *quasi* fiction of *servitium amisit* affords protection to the rich man whose daughter occasionally makes his tea, but leaves without redress the poor man whose child is sent unprotected to earn her bread amongst strangers" (z). All devices for obtaining what is virtually a new remedy by straining old forms and ideas beyond their original intention are liable to this kind of inconvenience. It has been truly said (a) that the enforcement of a substantially just claim "ought not to depend upon a mere fiction over which the courts possess no control." We have already pointed out the bolder course which might have been taken without doing violence to any legal principle. Now it is too late to go back upon the cases, and legislation would also be difficult and troublesome, not so much from the nature of the subject in itself as from the variety of irrelevant matters that would probably be imported into any discussion of it at large.

(x) *Irwin* v *Dearman* (1809), 11 East, 23

(y) *Hall* v *Hollander* (1825), 4 B & C 660 But this case does not show that, if a jury chose to find that a very young child was capable of service, their verdict would be disturbed

(z) Note to *Grinnell* v *Wells*, 7 M & G 1044

(a) Starkie's note to *Speight* v *Oliviera* (1819), 2 Stark 496

Constructive service in early cases. It would be merely curious, and hardly profitable in any just proportion to the labour, to inquire how far the fiction of constructive service is borne out by the old law of the action for beating or carrying away a servant. Early in the 15th century we find a dictum that if a man serves me, and stays with me at his own will, I shall have an action for beating him, on the ground of the loss of his service (*b*); but this is reported with a *quaere*. A generation later (*c*) we find Newton C. J. saying that a relation of service between father and son cannot be presumed "for he may serve where it pleaseth him, and I cannot constrain him to serve without his good will:" this must apply only to a son of full age, but as to that case Newton's opinion is express that some positive evidence of service, beyond living with the parent as a member of the household, is required to support an action. Unless the case of a daughter can be distinguished, the modern authorities do not agree with this. But the same Year Book bears them out (as noted by Willes J.) (*d*) in holding that a binding contract of service need not be shown. Indeed, it was better merely to allege the service as a fact (*in servitio suo existentem cepit*), for an action under the Statute of Labourers would not lie where there was a special contract varying from the retainer contemplated by the statute, and amounting to matter of covenant (*e*).

Intimidation of servants and tenants. A similar cause of action, but not quite the same, was recognized by the medieval common law where a man's servants or tenants at will (*f*) were compelled by force or menace to depart from

---

(*b*) 11 Hen. IV. fo. 1-2, pl. 2, per Huls J. (A.D. 1410)

(*c*) 22 Hen. VI. 31 (A.D. 1443)

(*d*) L. R. 2 C. P. 621-2

(*e*) 22 Hen. VI. 32 b, per Cur. (Newton C. J., Fulthorpe, Ascue or Ayscoghe, Portington JJ.), F. N. B. 168 F.

(*f*) If the tenancy were not at will, the departure would be a breach of contract; this introduces a new element of difficulty, never expressly faced by our courts before *Lumley* v. *Gye*, of which more elsewhere.

their service or tenure. "There is another writ of trespass," writes Fitzherbert, "against those who lie near the plaintiff's house, and will not suffer his servants to go into the house, nor the servants who are in the house to come out thereof" (g). Examples of this kind are not uncommon down to the sixteenth century or even later; we find in the pleadings considerable variety of circumstance, which may be taken as expansion or specification of the *alia enormia* regularly mentioned in the conclusion of the writ (h).

In the early years of the eighteenth century the genius of Holt found the way to use this, together with other special classes of authorities, as a foundation for the

---

(g) F N B. 87 N., and see the form of the writ there. It seems therefore, that "picketing," so soon as it exceeds the bounds of persuasion and becomes physical intimidation, is a trespass at common law against the employer.

(h) 11 Edw IV. 7, pl 11, a writ "quare tenentes suos verberavit per quod a tenura sua recesserunt", 9 Hen. VII 7, pl 4, action for menacing plaintiff's tenants at will "de vita et mutilatione membrorum, ita quod recesserunt de tenura", Rastell, Entries 661, 662, similar forms of declaration, one (pl 9) is for menacing the king's tenants, so that "negotia sua palam incedere non audebant", *Garret v Taylor*, Cro Jac 567, action on the case for threatening the plaintiff's workmen *and customers*, " to mayhem and vex them with suits if they bought any stones ", 21 Hen VI 26, pl 9, "manassavit vulneravit et verberavit", note that in this action the "vulneravit" is not justifiable and therefore must be traversed, otherwise under a plea of *son assault demesne*, 22 Ass 102, pl 76, is for actual beating, aggravated by carrying away timber of the plaintiff's (*mer imentum=materiamen*, see Du Cange, s v. *materia*, in Anglo French *mercsme* In A. D. 1200 an action is recorded against one John de Mewle for deforcing the plaintiff of land which she had already recovered against him by judgment, " so that no one dare till that land, because of him, nor could she deal with it in any way because of him " Select Civil Pleas, Selden Soc. 1890, ed Baildon, vol 1, pl. 7. Op Reg. Brev (1595), 104a, " quando tenentes non audent morari super tenuris suis," and *Tarleton v McGawley* (1794), 1 Peake, 270, 3 R R 689, action for deterring negroes on the coast of Africa from trading with plaintiff's ship

---

Intimidation of servants and tenants. A person is liable, who for the purpose of injuring another and of inducing him to abandon a lease, persuaded and threatened his laborers so that they left him. Dickerson v. Dickson, 33 La Ann 1261. See, *ante*, p. 201. It is recognized as unlawful for strikers or others to interfere by threats, intimidation or coercion with the free will of workmen inducing them to leave the service of their employers. Rogers v. Evarts, 17 N Y. S. 264, Perkins v Rogg (Sup. Ct. Cin.), 28 Wkly. Law Bul. 32, see notes on CONSPIRACY. p. 287

broader principle that "he that hinders another in his trade or livelihood is liable to an action for so hindering him" (*i*), subject, of course, to the exception that no wrong is done by pursuing one's own trade or livelihood in the accustomed manner though loss to another may be the result (*k*) and even the intended result (*l*). Historically both this principle and that of *Lumley* v. *Gye* (*m*) are developments of the old "per quod servitium amisit;" but in the modern law they depend on different and much wider reasons, and raise questions which are not technical but fundamental. We shall therefore deal with them not here but under another head.

(*i*) *Keeble* v *Hickeringill* (1705), 11 East, 574 n Op. Select Civil Pleas, vol 1, pl 106

(*k*) 11 East, 576, *supra*, p 174

(*l*) *Mogul Steamship Co* v. *McGregor* (1889), 23 Q B. Div 598, 58 I J. Q B 465, H. L. Dec 1891

(*m*) 2 E. & B 216, 22 L J. Q B. 463 (1853)

CHAPTER VII.

DEFAMATION.

Civil and criminal jurisdiction distinguished. Reputation and honour are no less precious to good men than bodily safety and freedom. In some cases they may be dearer than life itself. Thus it is needful for the peace and well-being of a civilized commonwealth that the law should protect the reputation as well as the person of the citizen. In our law some kinds of defamation are the subject of criminal proceedings, as endangering public order, or being offensive to public decency or morality. We are not here concerned with libel as a criminal offence, but only with the civil wrong and the right to redress in a civil action; and we may therefore leave aside all questions exclusively proper to the criminal law and procedure, some of which are of great difficulty (*a*).

Slander and libel distinguished. The wrong of defamation may be committed either by way of speech, or

---

(*a*) Such as the definition of blasphemous libel, and the grounds on which it is punishable

---

Slander. Slander is "oral defamation, the speaking of false and malicious words concerning another, whereby injury results to his reputation" Black's Law Dic., p 1101 See Achorn v Piper, 66 Ia 694, McKee v. Wilson, 87 N C 300. Kedrolivansky v. Niebaum, 70 Cal. 216, Williams v Karnes, 4 Humph 11, Dawson v. Holt, 11 Lea, 583, 47 Am. Rep. 312; Widrig v. Oyer, 13 Johns 124, Goodrich v Hooper, 97 Miss. 1, Wonson v Sayward, 13 Pick 402; Georgia v Kifford, 45 Ia 48, and authorities cited *post*.

Libel Several American cases define libel concisely and in substantial conformity to the text. The following are examples —

" Any publication is a libel which tends to degrade, injure or bring

by way of writing or its equivalent. For this purpose it may be taken that significant gestures (as the finger-language of the deaf and dumb) are in the same case with audible words; and there is no doubt that drawing, printing, engraving, and every other use of permanent visible symbols to convey distinct idea, are in the same case with writing. The term slander is appropriated to the former kind of utterances, libel to the latter. Using the terms " written " and " spoken " in an extended sense, to include the analogous cases just mentioned, we may say that slander is a spoken and libel is a written defamation.

---

a person into contempt and ridicule, or accuse him of a crime or other act odious and disgraceful." Smart v. Blanchard, 42 N H 151

"A malicious defamation of any person, made by either printing, writing, signs or pictures, in order to provoke wrath, or expose him to public hatred, contempt or ridicule." Root v King, 7 Cow 620

"Any malicious publication, written, printed or painted, which by words or signs, tends to expose a person to contempt, ridicule, hatred or degradation of character is a libel." Neeb v Hope, 111 Pa St. 115 See Huse v Inter-Ocean Co., 12 Ill. App 627, Bergman v. Jones, 94 N Y 51, Dexter v. Spear, 4 Mass. 115, Torrance v Hurst, 1 Miss. 403, Armentrout v Moranda, 8 Blackf. 426, Obaugh v Finn, 4 Ark. 110; Fonville v McNease, Dudley (S C), 303; 31 Am Dec. 556, Wiel v. Israel, 42 La An 955, 8 So. Rep 826; Republican Pub Co. v Miner (Colo. App), 31 Pac Rep 485, Buckstaff v. Viall (Wis.), 54 N. W. Rep. 111; Winchell v Argus Co., 69 Hun, 354; 23 N. Y. S Rep. 650, Hart v Evening News Assoc., 94 Mich. 114; 53 N W Rep. 952, Id. 94 Mich. 119; 54 N. W Rep 266; Keemle v. Sass, 54 Mo 99; Legg v Dunleavy, 80 Id. 563, Nelson v Musgroove, 10 Id 648, Hillhouse v. Dunning, 6 Conn. 107, Adams v Lawson, 17 Gratt. 250; 94 Am. Dec. 456, Tillson v Robbins, 68 Me. 295 See also, the authorities cited under the special divisions of the subject in the American notes to this chapter.

Slander and libel, distinguished. False defamatory words, if written and published, constitute a libel; if spoken a slander. Steele v. Southwick, 9 Johns 214, 1 Am Lead Cas 106, Lansing v. Carpenter, 9 Wis. 540, 76 Am Dec. 281, Layton v. Harris, 3 Harr (Del) 406.

The American authorities concur with the English in holding that the distinction between verbal and written slander is well defined and established In the case of Hillhouse v Dunning (6 Conn. 408), the court said, "the law of libel makes a material difference between words *spoken* and words *written*. To be actionable the former must tend to

The law has made a great difference between the two. Libel is an offence as well as a wrong, but slander is a civil wrong only (b). Written utterances are, in the absence of special ground of justification or excuse, wrongful as against any person whom they tend to bring into hatred, contempt, or ridicule. Spoken words are actionable only when special damage can be proved to have been their proximate consequence, or when they convey imputations of certain kinds.

No branch of the law has been more fertile of litigation than this (whether plaintiffs be more moved by a keen sense of honour, or by the delight of carrying on personal controversies under the protection and with the solemnities

---

(b) *Scandalum magnatum* was, and in strictness of law still might be, an exception to this Blake Odgers, Digest of the Law of Libel and Slander, 131—137 Mr Odgers has not found any case after 1710

---

bring a man into danger of punishment, exclude him from society, or injure him in his reputation, but it is enough, if the latter induce an ill opinion to be had of the party, or make him contemptible and ridiculous "

In the case of Colby v. Reynolds (6 Vt. 493, 27 Am. Dec. 576), the doctrine was announced as follows. " A distinction has long been known and recognized between verbal and written slander. Words, when committed to writing and published, are considered as libelous, which if only spoken, would not subject the person speaking to any action. Perhaps it is to be regretted that a distinction was ever made between oral and written slander, and if it was a new question, no distinction would now be made. The reasons which have been given for the distinction, have been questioned both by writers and judges of eminence. It has been made, however, and become a part of the law, and as such we must receive it. There can be no question, but that a slander written and published, evinces a more deliberate intention to injure, is calculated more extensively to circulate the accusation, and to provoke the person accused, to take the means of redress in his own hands, and thus commit a breach of the peace, than mere oral slander which is spoken and soon forgotten " See Tillson v Robbins, 68 Me. 299, Stow v. Converse, 3 Conn 325, Hake v Brames, 95 Ind 162, Cary v. Allen, 39 Wis. 487; Armentrout v. Moranda, 8 Blackf 426, Allen v. News Pub Co., 81 Wis. 120, 50 N. W. Rep 1093; Manner v Simpson, 13 Daly, 156, Shelton v. Nance, 7 B Mon 128, White v. Nichols, 3 How. 266; Dexter v. Spear, 4 Mason, 115.

of civil justice), nor has any been more perplexed with minute and barren distinctions. This latter remark applies especially to the law of slander; for the law of libel, as a civil cause of action, is indeed overgrown with a great mass of detail, but is in the main sufficiently rational. In a work like the present it is not possible to give more than an outline of the subject. Those who desire full information will find it in Mr Blake Odgers' excellent and exhaustive monograph (c). We shall, as a rule, confine our authorities and illustrations to recent cases.

1 — *Slander*

When slander is actionable. Slander is an actionable wrong when special damage can be shown to have followed from the utterance of the words complained of, and also in the following cases:—

Where the words impute a criminal offence.

Where they impute having a contagious disease which would cause the person having it to be excluded from society.

Where they convey a charge of unfitness, dishonesty, or incompetence in an office of profit, profession, or trade, in short, where they manifestly tend to prejudice a man in his calling.

Spoken words which afford a cause of action without proof of special damage are said to be actionable *per se:* the theory being that their tendency to injure the plain-

---

(c) A Digest of the Law of Libel and Slander, etc. By W. Blake Odgers, London, 2nd ed. 1887. Part IV of Mr Shortt's "Law relating to Works of Literature and Art" (2nd ed. London, 1884), may also be usefully consulted but this does not cover the whole ground.

What slander is actionable. In the case of Pollard *v.* Lyon (91 U S. 226), the court makes substantially the same classification of actionable slander as that of the text.

tiff's reputation is so manifest that the law does not require evidence of their having actually injured it. There is much cause however to deem this and other like reasons given in our modern books mere afterthoughts, devised to justify the results of historical accident: a thing so common in current expositions of English law that we need not dwell upon this example of it (*d*).

Meaning of "prima facie libellous." No such distinctions exist in the case of libel: it is enough to make a written statement *prima facie* libellous that it is injurious to the character or credit (domestic, public, or professional) of the person concerning whom it is uttered, or in any way tends to cause men to shun his society, or bring him into hatred, contempt, or ridicule. When we call a statement *prima facie* libellous, we do not mean that the person making it is necessarily a wrong-doer, but that he will be so held unless the statement is found to be within some recognized ground of justification or excuse.

Such are the rules as to the actionable quality of words, if that be a correct expression. The authorities by which they are illustrated, and on which they ultimately rest, are to a great extent antiquated or trivial (*e*); the rules themselves are well settled in modern practice.

Special damage. Where "special damage" is the ground of action, we have to do with principles already considered in a former chapter (*f*): namely, the damage

---

(*d*) See Blake Odgers, pp 2—4, and 6 Amer Law Rev 593 It seems odd that the law should presume damage to a man from printed matter in a newspaper which, it may be, none of his acquaintances are likely to read, and refuse to presume it from the direct oral communication of the same matter to the persons most likely to act upon it

(*e*) The old abridgments, e g Rolle, sub tit Action sur Case, Pur Parolls, abound in examples, many of them sufficiently grotesque A select group of cases is reported by Coke, 4 Rep. 12 *b*—20 *b*

(*f*) P 85, above

Special damage By *special damage* is meant such as the law will not infer from the nature of the act, but must be alleged in the pleadings

must be in a legal sense the natural and probable result of the words complained of. It has been said that it must also be " the legal and natural consequence of the words spoken" in this sense, that if A. speaks words in disparagement of B. which are not actionable *per se*, by reason of which speech C. does something to B.'s disadvantage that is itself wrongful as against B. (such as dismissing B. from his service in breach of a subsisting contract), B. has no remedy against A., but only against C. (*g*) But this doctrine is contrary to principle: the question is not whether C.'s act was lawful or unlawful, but whether it might have been in fact reasonably expected to result from the original act of A. And, though not directly overruled, it has been disapproved by so much and such weighty authority that we may say it is not law (*h*). There is authority for the proposition that where spoken words, defamatory but not actionable in themselves, are followed by special damage, the cause of action is not the original speaking, but the damage itself (*i*) This does not seem

(*g*) Vicars v Wilcocks (1806), 8 East. 1.
(*h*) Lynch v Knight (1861), 9 H L C 577 See notes to Vicars v Wilcocks, in 2 Sm L C
(*i*) Maule J *ex relat* Bramwell L J., 7 Q B D. 437

and proved at the trial. Wilson v Runyon, Wright, 651, Tobias v. Harland, 4 Wend. 539. The American cases cited under the several paragraphs of this chapter illustrate, in many instances, the application of the doctrine of the text to particular statements of facts And see Herrick v. Lapham, 10 Johns. 281; Malloy v. Bennett, 15 Fed Rep 871, Barnes v. Trundy, 31 Me. 321, Bassil v. Elmore, 65 Barb 627, Stauss v. Meyer, 48 Ill. 385, Achorn v Piper, 66 Ia. 694, Bailey v. Dean, 5 Barb. 297, Walker v. Tribune Co , 29 Fed. Rep. 827, Williams v. Hill, 19 Wend 305, Democrat Pub. Co. v Jones, 83 Tex 302; 18 S W. Rep. 652, Oakley v. Farrington, 1 Johns Cas. 129, Cook v. Cook, 100 Mass. 194; Birch v. Benton, 26 Mo 154, Flatow v Von Bremsen, 11 N. Y. 680; 19 Civil Proc. R. 125, 131, Morasse v. Brochu, 151 Mass. 567; 25 N. E. Rep. 74, Bostwick v Nickelson, Kirby, 65, Harcourt v. Harrison, 1 Hall, 474, Shipman v. Burrows, Id. 399, Kelly v Huffington, 3 Cranch C. Ct 81, Melvin v Weiant, 36 Ohio St 184, Reenholts v. Becker, 3 Denio, 346; Moore v. Stevenson, 27 Conn. 14; Burford v Wible, 32 Pa. St. 95.

to affect the general test of liability. Either way the speaker will be liable if the damage is an intended or natural consequence of his words, otherwise not.

Repetition of spoken words. It is settled however that no cause of action is afforded by special damage arising merely from the voluntary repetition of spoken words by some hearer who was not under a legal or moral duty to repeat them. Such a consequence is deemed too remote (*j*). But if the first speaker authorized the repetition of what he said, or (it seems) spoke to or in the hearing of some one who in the performance of a legal, official, or moral duty ought to repeat it, he will be liable for the consequences (*k*).

Special damage involves a definite temporal loss. Losing the general good opinion of one's neighbours, con-

---

(*j*) *Parkins v Scott* (1862), 1 H & C 153, 31 L J Ex 331 (wife repeated to her husband gross language used to herself, wherefore the husband was so much hurt that he left her).

(*l*) Blake Odgers 331. *Riding v Smith*, (1876), 1 Ex D 91, 45 L J. Ex 281, must be taken not to interfere with this distinction, as the majority of the court disclaimed any intention of so doing but see thereon Mayne on Damages, 4th ed 72

Repetition of spoken words Supporting the text are several American cases.

Thus, in Hastings *v* Stetson (126 Mass. 331), the court said "A person who utters slander is not responsible for its voluntary and unjustifiable repetition, without his authority or request, by other over whom he has no control, and who thereby render themselves liable to the person slandered. Such repetition cannot be considered in law the necessary, natural and probable consequence of the original slander Followed in Shurtleff *v*. Parker, 130 Mass. 295. See Marker *v* Dunn, 68 Ia. 720, Moberly *v*. Preston, 8 Me 462; Cade *v* Redditt, 15 La. An. 492, Knight *v*. Foster, 39 N H 576, Clarkson *v*. McCarty, 5 Blackf. 574

Special damage involves a definite temporal loss Among the decisions determining what losses constitute special damages are the following· Defamation of a female's reputation resulting in her dejection of mind, and loss of health and consequent inability to attend to her ordinary business McQueen *v* Fulgham, 27 Tex 463 But an allegation that by means of the words spoken the plaintiff has fallen in disgrace, contempt and infamy and has lost her credit, reputation and

sortium virorum as the phrase goes, is not of itself special damage. A loss of some material advantage must be shown. Defamatory words not actionable *per se* were spoken of a member of a religious society who by reason thereof was excluded from membership, there was not any allegation or proof that such membership carried with it as of right any definite temporal advantage. It was held that no loss appeared beyond that of *consortium virorum*, and therefore there was no ground of action (*l*). Yet the loss of *consortium* as between husband and wife is a special damage of which the law will take notice (*m*), and so is the loss of the voluntary hospitality of friends, this last on the ground that a dinner in a friend's house and at his expense is a thing of some temporal value (*n*). Actual membership of a club is perhaps a thing of temporal value for this purpose, but the mere chance of being elected is not: so that an action will not lie for speaking disparaging words of a candidate for a club, by means whereof the majority of the club decline to alter the rules in a manner which would be favourable to his election. "The risk of temporal loss is not the same as temporal loss" (*o*). Trouble of mind caused by defamatory words is not sufficient special damage, and illness consequent upon such trouble is too remote. "Bodily pain or

---

(*l*) *Roberts v. Roberts* (1864), 5 B. & S. 384, 33 L J Q B 249
(*m*) *Lynch v. Knight*, 9 H L C 577
(*n*) *Davies v. Solomon* (1871), L R 7 Q B 112, 41 L. J Q B 10

(*o*) *Chamberlain v. Boyd* (1883), 11 Q B Div 407, per Bowen L J at p 416, 52 L. J Q B 277 The damage was also held too remote

---

peace of mind, is not the laying of special damages. Woodbury *v* Thompson, 3 N H. 194 Refusal of civil entertainment at a public house. Olmsted *v* Miller, 1 Wend. 506 So, the loss of a contracted marriage Moody v. Baker, 5 Cow. 351 So, the refusal to provide food and clothing for the plaintiff, by the persons who were in the habit of so doing Beach *v* Ranny, 2 Hill, 309 So, where the plaintiff was turned away from the house of her uncle, where she had been a welcome visitor Williams *v* Hill, 19 Wend 622, 48 N. Y 563 See Geisler *v.* Brown, 6 Neb 254, Pettibone *v* Simpson, 66 Barb 492.

suffering cannot be said to be the natural result in all persons" (p).

Imputations of criminal offence. As to the several classes of spoken words that may be actionable without special damage, words sued on as imputing crime must

(p) Alisop v. Alisop (1860), 5 H. & N. 534, 29 L. J. Ex. 315.

Imputations of criminal offence. Generally words which impute a crime punishable with imprisonment are actionable without proof of special damage. Ranger v. Goodrich, 17 Wis. 80; Filber v. Dautermann, 26 Wis. 518; Hillhouse v. Peck, 2 Stew. & P. 395; Hollingsworth v. Shaw, 19 Ohio St. 430, 2 Am. Rep. 411; Davis v. Brown, 27 Ohio St. 326; Smith v. Stewart, 5 Pa. St. 372; Parker v. Lewis, 2 Greene (Ia.), 311; Murry v. McAllister, 38 Vt. 167; Distler v. Walther, 1 N. Y. S. Rep. 385; Widrig v. Oyer, 13 Johns. 124; Van Ness v. Hamilton, 19 Johns. 349; Demarest v. Haring, 6 Cow. 76, 88; Quinn v. O'Gara, 2 E. D. Smith, 388; Case v. Buckley, 15 Wend. 327; Crawford v. Wilson, 4 Barb. 504; Andrews v. Hoppenheifer, 3 Serg. & R. 255; Gorham v. Ives, 2 Wend. 534; Alexander v. Alexander, 9 Id. 141; Van Ankin v. Westfall, 14 Johns. 233; Todd v. Rough, 10 Serg. & R. 18; Johnson v. Morrow, 9 Port. 525; Kieb v. Oliver, 12 Gray, 239; Burlingham v. Burlingham, 8 Cow. 141; Coburn v. Harwood, Minor, 93; Vickers v. Stoneman, 73 Mich. 419, 41 N. W. Rep. 495; Giddens v. Mirk, 4 Ga. 364; Giger v. Shelton, 3 Rich. 249; Young v. Kuhn, 71 Tex. 645, 511; Ellsworth v. Hayes, 71 Wis. 427; Kinney v. Hosea, 3 Harr. (N. J.) 77; Bell v. Fernald, 71 Mich. 267, 38 N. W. Rep. 910; Thomas v. Beasdale, 117 Mass. 438; Harris v. Terry, 98 N. C. 131; Rosewater v. Hoffman, 24 Neb. 222; Prosser v. Callis, 117 Ind. 105; Halley v. Gregg, 74 Ia. 563; Blumhardt v. Rohr, 70 Md. 278; 17 At. Rep. 266.

But such words, to be in themselves actionable, must impute a crime involving moral turpitude, and which is punishable by indictment at common law or by statute. St. Martin v. Desnoyer, 1 Minn. 156; Demarest v. Haring, 6 Cow. 76; Lewis v. McDaniel, 82 Mo. 577; Lukehart v. Beverly, 53 Pa. St. 418; Wright v. Paige, 36 Barb. 438; Crawford v. Wilson, 4 Barb. 504; Hoag v. Hatch, 23 Conn. 590; Young v. Miller, 3 Hill, 22; Smith v. Smith, 2 Sneed (Tenn.), 473; Hendrickson v. Sullivan, 44 N. W. Rep. 448, 28 Neb. 329; Davis v. Brown, 27 Ohio St. 326; Gibbs v. Dewey, 5 Cow. 503; Davis v. Sladden, 17 Oreg. 259, 21 Pac. Rep. 140; State v. Burroughs, 2 Halst. 426, 1 Am. Lead. Cas. 113, 3rd ed.; Dial v. Holter, 6 Ohio St. 228; Taylor v. Kneeland, 1 Dougl. (Mich.) 67; Olfele v. Wright, 17 Ohio St. 238; Montgomery v. Dooley, 3 Wis. 709; Billings v. Wing, 7 Vt. 439; Filber v. Dautermann, 26 Wis. 520; Downing v. Wilson, 36 Ala. 717; Sidgreaves v. Myatt, 22 Ala. 617; Iron Age Pub. Co. v.

amount to a charge of some offence which, if proved against the party to whom it is imputed, would expose him

Gudup, 85 Ala 519; McKinney v Roberts, 68 Cal. 192, Johnson v. Shields, 1 Dutch 118, Redway v Gray, 31 Vt. 292; Coleman v Playstead, 36 Barb 26, Carroll v White, 33 Barb 615, Guard v Risk, 11 Ind. 156, Robinson v Keyser, 2 Fost 323, Ranger v Goodrich, 17 Wis 78, Rodgers v. Lacey, 23 Ind 507; Adams v Rankin, 1 Duv 58, Proctor v. Owens, 18 Ind 21, State v Spear, 13 R I 324, Miller v Butler, 6 Cush 72, Bradley v Cramer, 59 Wis. 309, 48 Am. Rep 511, Bergmann v Jones, 94 N Y 51, Carter v Andrews, 16 Pick 1, Rea v Harrington, 58 Vt 181, Massuere v Dickens, 70 Wis 83, Burnett v Ward, 36 Ohio St, 107, Klewin v Bauman, 53 Wis 244, West v Hanrahan, 28 Minn 325, Hermann v Bradstreet Co, 19 Mo App 227, Shattuc v McArthur, 25 Fed Rep 133, Quigley v McKee, 12 Oreg 22, 53 Am Rep 520, Shelby v Sun Printing & Pub Co Ass, 109 N Y 611, Stumer v Pitchman, 124 Ill 250, In re MacDonald (Wyo), 3 Pac Rep. 18, Post Pub Co. v Moloney (Ohio), 33 N E Rep 921

It is sufficient if the words spoken charge an offense which is made criminal by statute Stallings v Whittaker, 55 Ark 494, 18 S W Rep 829, Noyes v Hall, 62 N H 594, Bissel v Cornell, 24 Wend 354, Spencer v McMasters, 16 Ill 405, Sterling v Juggenheimer, 69 Ia 210, Moberly v Preston, 8 Mo 462, Symonds v Carter, 32 N. H 458, Burford v Wible, 32 Pa St 95, Stroebel v Whitney, 31 Minn 384, Vanderslip v Roe, 23 Pa St 82, Mayer v Schleichter, 29 Wis 646, Ranger v Goodrich, 17 Wis. 78, Montgomery v Deeley, 3 Wis 709, Gibson v Gibson, 43 Wis 22, Truman v Taylor, 4 Ia 125, Wilson v Beighler, 4 Ia. 129, Healey v Gregg, 74 Ia 563.

In the leading case of Brooker v Coffin (5 Johns 188, s c Bigelow Lead Cas on Torts, 77), the following test of the sufficiency of the charge was established —

"In case the charge, if true, will subject the party charged to an indictment for a crime involving moral turpitude, or subject him to infamous punishment, then the words are themselves actionable." See Wilson v. McCrory, 86 Ind 170, Rundell v Butler, 7 Barb. 260, Zeliff v Jennings, 61 Tex 458, Garrett v Dickerson, 19 Md 418, Carmichael v. Shiel, 21 Ind 66, Cass v Anderson, 33 Vt 182, Dorland v Patterson, 23 Wend. 422, Walton v. Singleton, 7 Serg & R 449, Stroebel v. Whitney, 31 Minn 384, Lewis v Hudson, 44 Ga 568, Proctor v Owens, 18 Ind 21

Even an allusion to some extrinsic fact may become actionable. Hays v Mitchell, 7 Blackf 117 See McDonald v Press Pub Co , 55 Fed. Rep 264

So, where words are spoken by way of interrogation Hotchkiss v Oliphant, 2 Hill, 510, Sawyer v Eifert, 2 Nott & M 511

Or by innuendo Sewell v Catlin, 3 Wend 291, Gorham v Ives, 2 Id. 534, Gibson v Williams, 4 Id 320, Rundel v Butler, 7 Barb. 260 May-

to imprisonment or other corporal penalty (not merely to a fine in the first instance, with possible imprisonment in

son v Sheppard, 12 Rich 254, McKennon v. Greer, 2 Watts 352, Dottover v Bushey, 16 Pa. St. 204.

It is not essential that the words charge a felony. Lemons v Wells, 78 Ky. 117.

For words merely disclosing a suspicion in the mind of the speaker that a person is guilty of a felony no action lies without proof of special damages. Dickson v Phillips, 51 N Y Superior Ct 162, Dickey v. Andros, 32 Vt 55, Smith v Gaffard, 31 Ala 45, Campbell v. Bannister, 79 Ky 205

Words which only impute a criminal intent are not actionable but those charging an attempt to commit a crime are actionable McKee v Ingalls, 5 Ill. 30, Seaton v Cordry, Wright, 101, Wilson v Tatum, 8 Jones L 300

No action lies for spoken words imputing a crime which it is not possible for the person charged to commit. Carter v Andrews, 16 Pick 1, Ogden v Riley, 14 N. J 186, Underhill v Welton, 32 Vt 40, Dexter v Taber, 12 Johns 239, McCaleb v. Smith, 22 Ia , 242, Trabue v May 3, 3 Dana, 138, Edgerly v Swain, 32 N H 178, Ayres v. Grider, 15 Ill 37.

The words need not necessarily bear a criminal import. Stroebel v Whitney, 31 Minn. 381, Campbell v Campbell, 54 Wis 90 Nor need the judicial proceedings in which imputed perjury occurred have really existed. Bricker v Potts, 12 Pa St 200, Holt v Turpin, 78 Ky 433

Charges Actionable per se. The following examples of spoken words imputing crime which are actionable *per se* may prove of value as illustrative of the application of the foregoing general rules —

"I know enough that he has done to send him to the penitentiary" Johnson v Shields, 1 Dutch 116

"You have altered the marks of four of my hogs" Perdue v Burnett, Minor (Ala), 138

"He tried to steal a dog but could not." Berdeaux v Davis, 58 Ala 611.

"He is the best hand at stealing sheep I ever saw He stole P.'s sheep" Herman v Cundiff, 82 Va. 239

"You thief! &c" Frolich v McKierman, 84 Cal 177, 24 Pac. Rep 114. See Savoie v Scanlan, 43 La. An. 963, 9 So. Rep 916, Roberts v. Ramsey, 86 Ga. 432, 12 S. E Rep 644. So, to say of a woman to her employer, "what are you doing with that nine dollar blackmailer here." Hess v Sparks, 44 Kan 465, 24 Pac Rep. 779 So, to charge one with having committed perjury Gudger v. Penland, 108 N. C 593, 13 S. E Rep 168, Ward v Clark, 2 Johns 10, Schmidt v Witherick, 29 Minn. 156; Crone v. Angell, 14 Mich 340, Spooner v Keeler, 51 N Y 527, Coons v Robinson, 3 Barb 625, Gilman v. Lowell, 8 Wend 573, Sherwood v Chace, 11 Wend 38

So, to charge one with burning his own property to defraud the insur-

default of payment) (q). The offence need not be specified with legal precision, indeed it need not be specified at all if the words impute felony generally. But if particulars are given they must be legally consistent with the offence imputed. It is not actionable *per se* to say of a man that he stole the parish bell-ropes, when he was churchwarden, for the legal property is vested in him *ex officio* (r), it might be otherwise to say that he fradulently converted them to his own use. The practical inference seems to be that minute and copious vituperation is safer than terms of general reproach, such as "thief," inasmuch as a layman who enters on details will probably make some impossible combination.

It is not a libel as against a corporation (though it may be as against individual members or officers) to charge the body as a whole with an offence which a corparate body cannot commit (s)

(r) This is the true distinction It matters not whether the offence be indictable or punishable by a court of summary jurisdiction. *Webb v Beavan* (1883), 11 Q. L. D. 609, 52 L J Q B 544 In the United States the received opinion is that such words are actionable only if on the charge, if true, will subject the party charged to an indictment for a crime involving moral turpitude, or subject him to an infamous punishment." *Brooker v Coffin* (1809), 5 Johns 188, Bigelow L C 77, 80, later authorities *ap* Cooley on Torts, 197

(r) *Jackson v Adams* (1835), 2 Bing N C 402. The words were "who stole the parish bell ropes, you scamping rascal?" If spoken while the plaintiff held the office, they would probably have been actionable, as tending to his prejudice therein

(s) *Mayor of Manchester v Williams*, '91, 1 Q B 94, 60 L J Q B 23

ance company Davis v Carey, 8 Pa Co Ct Rep 578, 21 Ap. Rep. 363, 28 W N C 10, House v. House, 5 Har & J. 125

Charges not actionable per se. Among examples of slanderous charges which are not actionable *per se*, are such as to say "You will steal" Bays v Hunt, 60 Ia 251 Or "you have took my pocket book and have it in your pocket." Chrstal v Craig, 80 Mo. 367. Or, of a woman, that she is a "bitch" or "slut." Roby v. Murphy, 24 Ill. App. 394.

Words which do not amount to an imputation of a crime are not actionable *per se* Dorsey v Whipps, 8 Gill, 355, 154, Brace v. Brink, 33 Mich 91, Winter v Sumwalt, 3 Har. & J 38, Parmer v Anderson, 33 Ala 78, Casselman v Winship, 3 Dako. 292, Melvin v Weiant, 36 Ohio St 184, 38 Am Rep 572 Curry v Collins, 37 Mo 324, Ford v. Johnson, 21 Ga 399, Bays v Hunt, 60 Ia 251, Adams v Stone, 131 Mass 433, Rock v McClucon, 95 Ind 415

Other charges of mere immorality not actionable. Slander of Women Act. False accusation of immorality or disreputable conduct not punishable by a temporal court is at common law not actionable *per se*, however gross. The Slander of Women Act, 1891 (54 & 55 Vict. c. 51), has abolished the need of showing special damage in the case of "words . . . which impute unchastity or adultery to any woman or girl." The courts might without violence have presumed that a man's reputation for courage, honour, and truthfulness, a woman's for chastity and modest conduct, was something of which the loss would naturally lead to damage in any lawful walk of life. But the rule was otherwise (*l*), and remains so as regards all slander of this kind against men, and against women also as regards all charges of improper conduct short of unchastity, which yet

---

(*l*) The technical reason was that charges of incontinence, heresy, etc., were "spiritual defamation," and the matter determinable in the Ecclesiastical Court, *tlnq pro salute animae*. See *Davis v. Gardiner*, 4 Co. Rep. 16 b; *Palmer v. Thorpe*, ib. 20 a.

Imputing unchastity to a female. It is a rule of the common law that to charge a female with unchastity, even with being a common prostitute, is not actionable without proof of special damages. Brooker *v.* Coffin, 5 Johns. 188, *supra*; Kenler *v.* Lessford, 2 Cranch, 190; McQueen *v.* Fulgham, 27 Tex. 463; Linney *v.* Maton, 13 Id. 449; Pollard *v.* Lyon, 91 U.S. 225; Terwilliger *v.* Wands, 17 N.Y. 54; Wilson *v.* Goit, 17 Id. 442; Woodbury *v.* Thompson, 3 N.H. 119; Stanfield *v.* Boyer, Har. & J. 248; Simpson *v.* Pettibone, 66 Barb. 492.

But in those States where fornication is made indictable and punishable, by statute, the decisions are uniform in holding charges of unchastity to be slanderous for the reason that such imputations thus become, by statute, a charge of a crime. Klewin *v.* Bauman, 53 Wis. 244; Rodgers *v.* Lacey, 23 Ind. 508; Linney *v.* Maton, 32 Vt. 40; Bradt *v.* Towsley, 13 Wend. 253; Ranger *v.* Goodrich, 17 Wis. 80; Snediker *v.* Poorbaugh, 29 Ia. 488; Pledger *v.* Hathcock, 1 Ga. 550; Kelly *v.* Flaherty, 16 R.I. 234, 14 Atl. Rep. 876; Smith *v.* Silence, 4 Ia. 321; Pink *v.* Catnick, 51 Cal. 420; Adover *v.* Hall, 67 Cal. 80; Freeman *v.* Saunderson, 123 Ind. 264, 24 N.E. Rep. 239; Henderson *v.* Sullivan, 28 Neb. 329, 44 N.W. Rep. 448; Noyes *v.* Hall, 62 N.H. 594; Indianapolis Journal Nwp. Co. *v.* Pugh (Ind. App.), 33 N.E. Rep. 991.

may sometimes be quite as vexatious, and more mischievous because more plausible. The law went wrong from the beginning in making the damage and not the insult the cause of action; and thus seems the stranger when we have seen that with regard to assault a sounder principle is well established (u).

A person who has committed a felony and been convicted may not be called a felon after he has undergone the sentence, and been discharged, for he is then no longer a felon in law (v).

Imputations of contagious disease. Little need be said concerning imputations of contagious disease unfitting a person for society, that is, in the modern law, venereal disease (x). The only notable point is that "charging another with having had a contagious disorder is not

(u) P. 249, above.
(v) *Leyman v. Latimer* (1877), 3 Ex. Div. 352, 47 L. J. Ex. 470.

(x) Leprosy and, it is said, the plague, were in the same category. Small pox is not. See Blake Odgers 64.

Imputations of contagious disease. Spoken words charging one with having a loathsome disease, which imputation if believed would exclude such one from society, are actionable *per se*. Williams v Holdridge, 22 Barb. 396, Golderman v Stearns, 7 Gray, 181, Chaddock v Briggs, 13 Mass. 248, Joannes v Burt, 6 Allen, 236, 83 Am Dec. 625, Irons v Fields, 9 R. I. 216, Kauch v Blinn, 29 Ohio St. 62, 23 Am Rep. 757, Bruce v Soule, 69 Me. 562, Bloss v. Tobey, 2 Pick. 320, Hewit v. Mason, 24 How Pr. 366

The only diseases that have been adjudged loathsome, in this sense of the term, are of the plague, leprosy and venereal disorders. Upton v Upton, N. Y. Supreme Ct. 936, Watson v. McCarthy, 2 Ga. 57, 47 Am Dec. 380, and authorities cited *supra*

Judge Cooley in his treatise on the Law of Torts (2nd ed., p 235), says "What diseases would be embraced within this rule is not certain but it is probable that at the present day only those which are contagious or infectious, and which are usually brought upon one by disreputable practices, and the list would perhaps be limited to venereal diseases"

To be actionable within themselves the words must impute a continuance of the disorder at the time of speaking. Pike v. Van Wormer, 5 How Pr. 171, and authorities cited *supra*

actionable; for unless the words spoken impute a continuance of the disorder at the time of speaking them, the gist of the action fails; for such a charge cannot produce the effect which makes it the subject of an action, namely, his being avoided by society" (y). There does not seem to be more than one reported English case of the kind within the present century (z)

Evil speaking of a man in the way of his business Concerning words spoken of a man to his disparagement

(y) *Carslake v. Mapledoram* (1788), 2 T. R. 473, Bigelow L. C. 54, per Ashhurst J.

(z) *Bloodworth v. Gray* (1844), 7 M. & G. 334. The whole of the judgment runs thus "This case falls within the principle of the old authorities"

Evil speaking of a man in the way of his business. Defamatory words spoken of a person in relation to his trade, profession or office are actionable *per se*, provided, they are spoken while he is following such trade or profession or holding such office. McKenzie v. Denver Times Pub Co. (Colo. App.), 31 Pac Rep 577, Kinner v Grant, 12 Vt 456, Davis v Davis, 1 Nott & M 290, Ostrom v. Calkins, 5 Wend 263, Williams v Davenport, 42 Minn 393, 44 N W Rep. 311, Lotto v Sime, 42 Minn 395, 44 N W. Rep. 31, Morasse v Brochu, 151 Mass 567, 25 N. E. Rep 74, McKee v Wilson, 87 N C 300, Brown v. Mims, 2 Mill Const 235, Beck v. Stitzel, 21 Pa. St 522; Fitzgerald v Redfield, 51 Barb 484, Rammell v Otis, 60 Me 365, Craig v Brown, 5 Blackf 44, Seely v. Blair, Wright, 358; Buck v Hersey, 31 Me 558; Decker v Shepherd, 22 Md 299, Windsor v Oliver, 41 Ga. 538, Harris v. Bailey, 8 N H. 216, Allen v Hillman, 12 Pick. 101, Brown v. Vannaman (Wis), 55 N. W. Rep 183, Lapham v Noble, 54 Fed Rep. 108.

Attorney To say of an attorney at the time he is engaged in the trial of a case, "You are the dirty sewer through which all the slums of this embezzlement have flowed," is actionable without proof of special damages Mains v Whiting, 87 Mich 172, 49 N W. Rep. 559

So, to call an attorney "a cheat" Rush v Cavanaugh, 2 Pa. St. 187 Or, to say that an attorney "will take fees on both sides of a case." Chipman v Cook, 2 Tyler, 456, or, that an attorney is particularly incompetent Mattice v. Wilcox, 59 Hun, 626, 13 N. Y S Rep 330; or, to call an attorney "shyster" Gribble v Pioneer Press Co., 34 Minn. 342 Or, to charge that an attorney will betray his clients' secrets and overthrow their cause Garr v Selden, 6 Barb 416, Foot v. Brown, 8 Johns 64, Riggs v Denniston, 3 Johns Cas. 198

Clerk. To impute incompetency, dishonesty or special unfitness to a

in his office, profession, or other business: they are actionable on the following conditions: — They must be spoken of

clerk is actionable per se. Wilson v. Cottman, 65 Md. 190, Fowles v. Bowen, 30 N. Y. 20, Ware v Clowney, 24 Ala. 707.

Clergyman. Calling a preacher "a drunkard" is slanderous per se. McMillan v. Birch, 1 Blnn 178. See Hayner v. Cowden, 27 Ohio St. 292, 22 Am Rep 303, Chaddock v. Briggs, 13 Mass. 248; Buck v. Hersey, 31 Me 558, O'Hanlon v. Myers, 10 Rich 129.

Physician. To say of a physician, that "he has killed six children in one year" is slander per se. Carroll v. White, 33 Barb. 615, 42 N Y 161. Or, "he is no good, only a butcher, I would not have him for a dog!" Cruikshank v. Gordon, 118 N. Y. 178, 23 N. E. Rep. 457. Or, that a physician caused the death of a patient through his ignorance or culpable negligence. Foster v. Scripps, 39 Mich 376. Secor v. Harris, 18 Barb 425. See Sumner v. Utley, 7 Conn. 258, Camp v. Martin, 23 Conn 86, Foster v. Small, 3 Whart 138, Lynde v. Johnston, 39 Hun, 12, Rodgers v. Kline, 56 Miss. 808, Hargan v. Purdy (Ky), 20 S. W. Rep. 432.

But it is not actionable to say that a physician destroyed the life of a patient by mistake, but legal and well meant efforts to save his life. March v. Davison, 9 Paige, 580. Or, to give as an opinion that a physician gave medicine to another which caused the death of the latter. Jones v. Diver, 22 Ired. 184.

Public Officer. Spoken words which impute to a person a want of capacity or integrity in office or which are calculated to diminish public confidence in him are actionable *per se*. Russell v. Anthony, 21 K n 150, State v. Schmidt, 49 N. J. L 579, Kinney v. Nash, 3 N Y 177, Spiering v. Andrews, 45 Wis 332, Knight v. Blackford, 3 Mackey, 117, Am Rep 772; Maises v. Thornton, 8 Tenn Rep 303, Lansing v. Carpenter, 9 Wis 540, Truth Pub Co v Reed, 13 Ky Law R. 323. As to charge a sheriff with malpractice in office. Dole v. Van Rensselaer, 1 Johns Cas 330. Or, a town clerk with destroying votes at an election. Doddy v Henry, 9 Mass. 262.

Spoken words are not actionable without proof of special damages, if relative to the discharge of official duties, where the office has ceased at the time of the speaking of the words. Forward v. Adams, 7 Wend 204. Nor, are words spoken of a magistrate unless he is described as a magistrate. McGuire v Blair.

To say of a legislator who has changed his opinion, that "sometimes the change of heart comes from the pocket," is not actionable *per se*. Sillars v. Collier, 151 Mass. 50, 23 N E Rep. 723.

So are words spoken of a candidate which cause others to not vote for him at an election. Brewer v Weakley, 2 Overt 99. See Seely v Blair, Wright, 358, 683, Burke v Mascarich, 81 Cal 302, 22 Pac. Rep 673, Ludd v Colson (Ky), 20 S W Rep 264. But it is not actionable, with-

him in relation to or " in the way of " a position which he holds, or a business he carries on, at the time of speaking. Whether they have reference to his office or business is, in case of doubt, a question of fact. And they must either amount to a direct charge of incompetence or unfitness, or impute something so inconsistent with competence or fitness that, if believed, it would tend to the loss of the party's employment or business. To call a stonemason a "ringleader of the nine hours system" is not on the face of it against his competence or conduct as a workman, or a natural and probable cause why he should not get work; such words therefore, in default of anything showing more distinctly how they were connected with the plaintiff's occupation, were held not to be actionable (a). Spoken charges of habitual immoral conduct against a clergyman or a domestic servant are actionable, as naturally tending, if believed, to the party's deprivation or other ecclesiastical censure in the one case, and dismissal in the other. Of a clerk or messenger, and even

---

(a) *Miller v. David* (1874), L. R. 9 C. P. 118, 43 L. J. C. P. 84.

out proof of special damages, to impute weakness of understanding to a candidate for Congress. Mayrant v. Richardson, 1 Nott & M. 347. Or to call such a candidate "a corrupted old tory." Hogg v Dorrah, 2 Port 212.

Trader. To say of a drover, who buys and sells cattle, that "he is a bankrupt, and not able to pay his just debts" is actionable without alleging special damages. Lewis v Hawley, 2 Day, 495. Or, that a merchant cannot pay his debts and does not deserve credit. Sewell v. Catlin, 3 Wend 291, Mott v Comstock, 7 Cow 654. See 5 Lawy Rep. Ann 643, note, Mitchell v Bradstreet Co (Mo), 22 S. W Rep 358

Other instances. To say of a man in reference to his business that he is a notorious liar and dishonest, is actionable *per se*. Fowles v Bowen, 30 N Y 20. So it is to say of a blacksmith that "he keeps false books," of his business. Burtch v Nickerson, 17 Johns 217. But not to charge a person with keeping false books of account unless a credit business is done. Rathburn v Emigh, 6 Wend 407. Or, to say that a plaintiff is a "loafer" and a "pimp" and "don't understand his business" that his wife is not virtuous, and to threaten to ruin him. Flatow v Von Bremsen, 19 Civil Proc R 125, 131, 11 N. Y S. Rep 680.

of a medical man, it is otherwise, unless the imputation is in some way specifically connected with his occupation. It is actionable to charge a barrister with being a dunce, or being ignorant of the law; but not a justice of the peace, for he need not be learned. It is actionable to charge a solicitor with cheating his clients, but not with cheating other people on occasions unconnected with his business (b).

It makes no difference whether the office or profession carries with it any legal right to temporal profit, or in point of law is wholly or to some extent honorary, as in the case of a barrister or a fellow of the College of Physicians, but where there is no profit in fact, an oral charge of unfitness is not actionable unless, if true, it would be a ground for removal (bb). Nor does it matter what the nature of the employment is, provided it be lawful (c); or whether the conduct imputed is such as in itself the law will blame or not, provided it is inconsistent with the due fulfilment of what the party, in virtue of his employment or office, has undertaken. A gamekeeper may have an action against one who says of him, as gamekeeper, that he trapped foxes (d) As regards the reputation of traders the law has taken a broader view than elsewhere. To impute insolvency to a tradesman, in any form whatever, is actionable. Substantial damages have been given by a jury, and allowed by the court, for a mere clerical error by which an advertisement of a dissolution of partnership was printed among a list of meetings under the Bankruptcy Act (e)

Words indirectly causing damage to a man in his business. There are cases, though not common in our

---

(b) *Doyley* v *Roberts* (1837), 3 Bing. N C 835, and authorities there cited

(bb) *Alexander* v *Jenkins*, '92, 1 Q B 797, C A

(c) L R 2 Ex at p 330 *Vide*, Johnson v Simonton, 43 Cal 242.

(d) *Foulger* v *Newcomb* (1867), L. R. 2 Ex 327, 36 L J Ex 169

(e) Blake Odgers 80, *Shepheard* v. *Whitaker* (1875), L R 10 C P 502

books, in which a man suffers loss in his business as the intended or "natural and probable result" of words spoken in relation to that business, but not against the man's own character or conduct: as where a wife or servant dwelling at his place of business is charged with misbehaviour, and the credit of the business is thereby impaired. In such a case an action lies, but is not, it seems, properly an action of slander, but rather a special action (on the case in the old system of pleading) analogous to those which have been allowed for disturbing a man in his calling, or in the exercise of a right in other ways. It is doubtful how far the rule that a man is not liable for unauthorized repetition of his spoken words applies to an action of this kind (*f*). On principle the conditions of liability would seem to be that the defendant made the original statement without belief in its truth (for the cause of action is more akin to deceit than to defamation), and that he expected, or had reasonable cause to expect, that it would be repeated in such a manner as in fact it was, and would lead to such damage as in fact ensued.

2 — *Defamation in general.*

Rules as to defamation generally. We now pass to the general law of defamation, which applies to both slander and libel, subject, as to slander, to the conditions

(*f*) *Riding* v. *Smith* (1876), 1 Ex. D. 91, 45 L. J. Ex. 281, see Mr. Blake Odgers and Mr. J. D. Mayne thereon.

Slander of property used in business. One may be as seriously injured by the disparagement of his property connected with the business in which he is engaged as by the slander of himself in respect to his business. Snow v. Judson, 38 Barb. 210, *supra*, S. P., Gott v. Pulsifer, 122 Mass. 235, 23 Am. Rep. 322, Swan v. Tappan, 5 Cush. 104, Boynton v. Shaw Stocking Co., 146 Mass. 219, Weir v. Allen, 51 N. H. 171, Watson v. Trask, 6 Ohio, 531, 27 Am. Dec. 271, Paul v. Halferty, 63 Pa. St. 46.

and distinctions we have just gone through. Considerations of the same kind may affect the measure of damages for written defamation, though not the right of action itself.

"Implied malice." It is commonly said that defamation to be actionable must be malicious, and the old form

---

Implied malice. In the leading libel case of King v. Root (4 Wend. 114, 21 Am. Dec. 102) it was held, that the term *maliciously*, means *intentionally* and wrongfully, without legal excuse. See Haley v. State, 63 Ala. 83.

Malice in uttering false statements may consist either in direct intention to injure another, or in a reckless disregard of his rights and the consequences that may result to him. Gott v. Pulsifer, 122 Mass. 239; Commonwealth v. Bonner, 9 Metc. 410; Broughton v. McGrew, 39 Fed. Rep. 672. See Commonwealth v. Snelling, 15 Pick. 340; Lewis v. Chapman, 16 N. Y. 372; Wilson v. Noonan, 35 Wis. 353; Liles v. Gaster, 12 Ohio St. 646.

Implied malice is inferred from the falsity of the charge, or when the words are actionable *per se*. It is not necessary to prove express malice. Yeates v. Read, 4 Blackf. 463, 32 Am. Dec. 463; Byrket v. Monohan, 7 Blackf. 83, 41 Am. Dec. 212; Trabue v. Mays, 3 Dana, 138, 28 Am. Dec. 61; Smart v. Blanchard, 42 N. H. 37; Estes v. Antrobus, 1 Mo. 110, 13 Am. Dec. 496; True v. Plumley, 36 Me. 466; Humphries v. Parker, 52 Me. 506; Zuckerman v. Sonnenschein, 62 Ill. 115; McKee v. Ingals, 4 Scam. 30; Usher v. Severence, 20 Mo. 19; Dixon v. Allen, 69 Cal. 528; Mitchell v. Milholland, 106 Ill. 179; Hagan v. Hendry, 18 Md. 177; Fry v. Bennett, 5 Sandf. 54; Boullemet v. Phillips, 2 Rob. (La.) 365; Gilbert v. Palmer, 8 La. An. 130; Croausdale v. Bright, 6 Houst. 52; Harris v. Zanone, 93 Cal. 59, 28 Pac. Rep. 845; Brueshaber v. Hertling, 78 Wis. 198, 47 N. W. Rep. 725; Smith v. Rodecap, 31 N. E. Rep. 479; Kent v. Bougartz, 15 R. I. 72; Weil v. Schmidt, 28 Wis. 139; Curtis v. Mussey, 8 Gray, 261; McKinley v. Rob, 20 Johns. 351; Massuere v. Dickens, 70 Wis. 83; Wynne v. Parsons, 57 Conn. 73; Mosier v. Stole, 119 Ind. 244; Hudson v. Garner, 22 Mo. 433; Gaul v. Fleming, 10 Ind. 253; Parker v. Lewis, 2 Greene (Ia.), 311; Hatch v. Potter, 7 Ill. 725; Indianapolis Sun v. Horrell, 53 Ind. 527; Bergman v. Jones, 94 N. W. 51. And belief in the truth of the charge, and the absence of ill-will toward the defendant, cannot be shown as a defence to an action for defamation. Wozelka v. Hettrick, 93 N. C. 10; Lick v. Owen, 47 Cal. 252.

It is a rule that the right to damages follows consequentially the utterance of the words actionable in themselves, because it is the inevitable tendency of such words to injure the person of whom they are spoken. To constitute malice in law it is not necessary to show by

of pleading added " maliciously " to " falsely " Whatever may have been the origin or the original meaning of
this language (g), malice in the modern law signifies
neither more nor less, in this connexion, than the absence
of just cause or excuse (h), and to say that the law implies
malice from the publication of matter calculated to convey
an actionable imputation is only to say is an artificial form
that the person who so publishes is responsible for the
natural consequences of his act (i). " Express malice "
means something different, of which hereafter.

What is publication Evil-speaking, of whatever
kind, is not actionable if communicated only to the person
spoken of The cause of action is not insult, but proved

(g) See Bigelow L C 117
(h) Bayley J Bromage v Prosser (1825), 4 B & C at p 255, Bigelow L C 137 " Malice in common acceptation means ill will against a person, but in its legal sense it means a wrongful act done intentionally without just cause or excuse " so Littledale J in McPherson v Daniels (1829), 10 B & C 272
(i) Lord Blackburn in Capital and Counties Bank v Henty (1882), 7 App Ca 787, 52 L J Q B 232

direct proof an intention to injure the plaintiff Rodgers v Kline, 56 Miss 808, Burt v McBain, 29 Mich 260, Bodwell v Osgood, 3 Pick. 381, Eviston v Cramer, 54 Wis 220, Johnson v Robertson, 8 Port. 189, Hatch v Patten, 2 Gilm 728

What is publication Publication is the communication of defamatory words to some third person or persons Defamation is punishable for the reason that it is injurious to one's reputation. But no such injury is done when the words are uttered only to the person concerning whom they are spoken, no one else being present or within hearing. Or when any written or printed communication addressed to one person is put in the possession of that person without its contents being made known to any other person before delivering to the one to whom it is addressed. See Black's Law Dic., p. 965, Delaware etc Ins Co. v. Croasdale, 6 Houst. 181, Davis v Werden, 13 Gray, 305

It is sufficient if the defamation is made known to a single person. Adams v Lawson, 17 Gratt. 257.

It is not necessary that there be a visible presence of another or others at the time slanderous words are spoken to render such words actionable, but it is sufficient if such words were heard and understood by another or others Desmond v. Brown, 33 Ia 15.

So, on the other hand, it would not constitute slander if defamatory

or presumed injury to reputation. Therefore there must be a communication by the speaker or writer to at least one third person, and this necessary element of the wrong-

---

words were spoken in the visible presence of a person who could not hear the words, because of the distance between him and the person speaking. And this is true although such words be spoken in a public place. Sheffill v. Van Deusen, 13 Gray, 1037. Compare Giles v. State, 6 Ga. 276.

To allege merely that one "printed" a libel is not a sufficient allegation of publication. Sproul v. Pillsbury, 72 Me. 20, S. P., Prescott v. Tousey, 50 N. Y. Superior Ct. 12.

The distribution of pamphlets was held to constitute publication in Woods v. Wiman, 122 N. Y. 445, 25 N. E. Rep. 919. See Warnock v. Mitchell, 43 Fed. Rep. 428.

A civil action lies against the seller for every sale or delivery of a libellous publication, and the *onus* is on him to prove that he was ignorant of its contents. Every such sale is a fresh publication. Thorn v. Moses, 1 Denio, 488, Staub v. Van Benthuysen, 36 La. An. 467, Commonwealth v. Blanding, 3 Pick. 304, Belo v. Wren, 63 Tex. 723.

A letter is not a publication until it is read by or in the presence of a third person or persons. The mere sending of a sealed letter containing libellous matter to the party defamed, will not support a civil action. Spaits v. Poundstone, 87 Ind. 522, Lyle v. Clason, 1 Caines, 581. *Compare* Rolland v. Batchelder, 84 Va. 664, 5 S. E. Rep. 695.

Where two persons having participated in the composition of a libellous letter written by one of them, which was afterwards put in the post-office, and sent by mail to the person to whom it was addressed; such participation was held to be competent and sufficient evidence to prove the publication by both. Miller v. Butler, 6 Cush. 72.

Where a letter was written by one person to another containing libellous statements relative to a third person the libel was published. Young v. Clegg, 93 Ind. 371, Gough v. Goldsmith, 44 Wis. 262, 28 Am. Rep. 579, Fowles v. Bowen, 30 N. Y. 20.

In the case of Snyder v. Andrews (6 Barb. 43), it was held that where a writer of a letter, containing libellous matter, reads the same aloud to a stranger, it was a publication. S. P., McCombs v. Tuttle, 5 Blackf. 432.

The responsibility of the writer of a private letter, for the publication of libel contained therein, is not limited to the consequences of a communication of it to the person to whom the letter is addressed, but extends to the probable consequences of thus putting it in circulation. Miller v. Butler, 6 Cush. 72.

To prove the publication of a libel written in a foreign language it must be shown that it was read by some one, other than the plaintiff, who understood such language. K—— v. H——, 20 Wis. 239. See Mic-

ful act is technically called publication. It need not amount to anything like publication in the common usage of the word. That an open message passes through the hands of a telegraph clerk (*j*), or a manuscript through those of a compositor in a printing-office (*k*), or a letter dictated by a principal is taken down in shorthand and type-written by a clerk (*l*), is enough to constitute a publication to those persons if they are capable of understanding the matters so delivered to them. The opening of a letter addressed to a firm by a clerk of that firm authorized to open letters, is a publication to him (*l*). Every repetition of defamatory words is a new publication, and a distinct cause of action. The sale of a copy of a newspaper, published (in the popular sense) many years ago, to a person sent to the newspaper office by the plaintiff on purpose to buy it, is a fresh publication (*m*). It appears on the whole that if the defendant has placed defamatory matter within a person's reach, whether it is likely or not that he will attend to the meaning of it, this throws on the defendant the burden of proving that the paper was not read, or the words heard by that person, but if it is proved that the matter did not

---

(*j*) See *Williamson v. Freer* (1874), L. R. 9 C. P. 393, 43 L. J. C. P. 161.

(*k*) Printing is for this reason *prima facie* a publication *Baldwin v. Elphinston*, 2 W. Bl. 1037. There are obvious exceptions, as if the text to be printed is Arabic or Chinese, or the message in cipher.

(*l*) *Pullman v. Hill & Co.*, '91, 1 Q. B. 524, 60 L. J. Q. B. 299, C. A.

(*m*) *Duke of Brunswick v. Harmer* (1849), 14 Q. B. 185, 19 L. J. Q. B. 20

Ienz v. Qusdorf, 68 Ia. 727, Kiene v. Ruff, 1 Clark (Ia.), 452, Palmer v. Harris, 60 Pa. St. 156

The printing in a Dutch paper circulated in the United States of a libellous article is a publication. Steketee v. Kinsm, 48 Mich. 322

Words spoken by a husband to a wife, not in the presence of any other person, are confidential in law and cannot constitute a publication within the meaning of the law of slander. Scher v. Montgomery (Cal.), 21 Pac. Rep. 185, reversing 19 Pac. Rep. 686. See People v. Richards, 67 Cal. 412. See Wilcox v. Moon, 17 Vt. 484, 17 At. Rep. 742, 24 At. Rep. 244

But a sealed letter addressed and delivered to the wife containing a libel on her husband is a publication. Schenck v. Schenck, 1 Spencer (N. J.), 208

come to his knowledge, there is no publication (n). A person who is an unconscious instrument in circulating libellous matter, not knowing or having reason to believe that the document he circulates contains any such matter, is free from liability if he proves his ignorance. Such is the case of a newsvendor, as distinguished from the publishers, printers, and owners of newspapers. "A newspaper is not like a fire; a man may carry it about without being bound to suppose that it is likely to do an injury" (o). If A is justified in making a disparaging communication about B's character to C (as, under certain conditions, we shall see that he may be), it would seem upon the tendency and analogy of the authorities now before us that there will be no excuse if, exchanging the envelopes of two letters by inadvertence, or the like, he does in fact communicate the matter to D. It has been held otherwise (p), but we do not think the decision is generally accepted as good law; if it is right on principle, the earlier authorities on "publication" can hardly be right also.

Sending a defamatory letter to a wife about her husband is a publication: "man and wife are in the eye of the law, for many purposes, one person, and for many purposes" — of which this is one — "different persons" (q).

Vicarious publication. On the general principles of liability, a man is deemed to publish that which is published

---

(n) Blake Odgers 154.

(o) *Emmens v. Pottle* (1885), 16 Q. B. D. 354, per Lowen L.J. at p. 58, 55 L. J. Q. B. 51. But it seems the vendor would be liable if he had reason to know that the publication contained, or was likely to contain, libellous matter.

(p) *Tompson v. Dashwood* (1883), 11 Q. B. D. 43, 52 L. J. Q. B. 425. Qu. whether this case be consistent with *Pullman v. Hill & Co.*, '91, 1 Q. B. 524, C. A., 60 L. J. Q. B. 299, though not expressly commented on by the Court.

(q) *Wenman v. Ash* (1853), 13 C. B. 836, 22 L. J. C. P. 190, per Maule J. But communication by the defendant to his wife is not a publication: *Wennhak v. Morgan* (1888), 20 Q. B. D. 635, 57 L. J. Q. B. 241.

Vicarious publications. As a rule the publisher of a newspaper is liable for everything appearing in its columns. Scripps v. Reilly, 38 Mich. 10; Buckley v. Knapp, 48 Mo. 152; Storey v. Wallace, 11 Ill. 51; Inv v. Bennett, 28 N. Y. 324; Clay v. State, 86 Ill. 147.

And this is true, though he was ignorant of or forbade the publication.

by his authority. And the authority need not be to publish a particular form of words. A general request, or words intended and acted on as such, to take public notice of a matter, may make the speaker answerable for what is published in conformity to the general "sense and substance" of his request. (r)

(r) *Parke v. Prescott* (L 69), L R 4 Ex 169, 38 L J Ex 105, L C h r ether the particular publication be within the authority I a question of fact All the court decide is that verbal dictation or approval by the principal need not be shown

---

Andrews v Wells, 7 Johns 260 5 Am Dec 266, Curtis v Mussey, 6 Gray, 260, Dunn v Hall, 1 Ind 344, Perret v Times Newspaper, 25 La. An 170, Commonwealth v Morgan, 107 Mass. 199 *Contra*, Wheaton v. Beecher, 79 Mich 443, 44 N W Rep 927, Smith v Ashley, 11 Metc 367 A journalist cannot protect himself from the consequences of publishing a libellous article by assurances of its truthfulness, and by a contract of indemnity from the writer. The parties being joint wrong-doers, the law will not interfere in aid of either. "The freedom of the press does not consist in lawlessness, or in freedom from wholesome legal restraint. The publisher of a newspaper has no more right to publish a libel upon an individual, than he or any other man has to make a slanderous proclamation by word of mouth" Atkins v Johnson, 43 Vt 82 See Negley v Farrow, 60 Md 176

One to whom a printing press and a newspaper establishment were assigned has not such a property as will render him liable as proprietor for a libellous publication McCabe v Jones, 10 Daly, 222, Andres v Wells, 7 Johns. 260 But a receiver appointed to take charge of a newspaper was held liable for libellous publications in Martin v Van Schaick, 4 Paige, 479. See Dayton v Wilkes, 17 How. Pr. 510

The proprietor of a newspaper as well as the advertiser is responsible for the publication of a libellous advertisement. Boynton v Remington, 3 Allen, 397 See Robertson v Bennett, 11 N. Y Superior Ct 66, Tier v Hofflin, 33 Minn 66, 53 Am Rep. 9

He who by words causes another to write or print the thing conveying the libellous matter, may be guilty, as if his own hand traced the lines But the speaker of words out of which another, of his own motion, composes and publishes a libel cannot be charged as the author of the libel. Cochran v Butterfield, 18 N H. 117.

But "one who adopts or recognizes the publication of a libellous article purporting to emanate from him may be liable therefor, though the publication was made by another without his authority." Crousdale v Bright, 6 Houst 52 See Allen v Wortham, 89 Ky. 485, Simmons v. Holster, 13 Minn 259

A person who is generally responsible for publication (such as an editor), and who has admitted publication, is not as a rule bound to disclose the name of the actual author(s).

Construction of words innuendo. Supposing the authorship of the words complained of to be proved or admitted, many questions may remain.

The construction of words alleged to be libellous (we

_{v. Gibson v. Evans (1889) 23 Q. B. D. 384, 58 L. J. Q. B. 612}

Construction of words. It is now well settled, "that words are to be understood in their plain and natural import, according to the ideas they are calculated to convey to those to whom they are addressed. In ascertaining the meaning of the speaker, reference must be had to the words used and the circumstances under which they were uttered, and the author is presumed to have used them in the sense which their use is calculated to convey to the minds of the hearers." Roe v Chitwood, 36 Ark. 215, citing Harrison v Findley, 23 Ind. 265, Rogers v Lacey, Id. 507, O'Conner v O'Conner, 21 Id. 218. See Castleberry v Kelly, 26 Ga. 606, Wagaman v Byers, 17 Md. 187, Stieber v Wensell, 19 Mo. 513, Hudson v Garner, 22 Mo. 423, Worth v. Butler, 7 Id. 251, Guard v Risk, 11 Ind. 156, Drummond v Leslie, 5 Blackf. 453, Blickenstaff v. Perrin, 27 Ind. 527, Edwards v. San Jose P & P Co (Cal.) 84 Pac Rep 128, Buckstaff v Vial (Wis.), 54 N. W. Rep 111, Campbell v Campbell, 54 Wis. 94.

"Where words are susceptible of a twofold meaning, it is the province of the jury to determine, from the circumstances, in what sense they were uttered and understood. This is the rational and legal rule as now well established by authority." Deday v Powell, 4 Bush, 78. See Van Victor v. Walkup, 46 Cal. 133, Rankine v. Elliott, 16 N. Y. 376; Thompson v Powning, 15 Nev. 212; Snyder v. Andrews, 6 Barb. 43, Sanderson v Caldwell, 45 N Y 398, Clarke v. Fitch, 41 Cal. 480, Mosier v Stoll, 119 Ind. 244, 20 N E Rep 752, Ex parte Bailey, 2 Cow. 479; Patch v The Tribune Assoc., 38 Hun, 368, McKinly v Rob, 20 Johns 356, Boyle v State, 6 Ohio Cir Ct R 163, Barnard v. Press Pub Co., 63 Hun, 626, 17 N Y S Rep 573, Simmons v. Morse, 6 Jones L 6, Powers v. Price, 12 Wend 500, Bullock v Koon, 9 Cow 33, Green v. Telfair, 20 Barb. 20, Gregory v Atkins, 42 Vt 250, Davies v Johnston, 2 Bailey, 579, Reeves v Bowden, 97 N C 29, Turrill v. Dolloway, 17 Wend. 428, 429; Dorland v Patterson, 23 Wend 422; State v. Jeandell, 5 Harr (Del.) 475, Hays v Hays, 1 Humph. 402; McLaughlin v. Bascom, 38 Ia 660, Hess v. Fockler, 25 Ia 252, Garrett v Dickerson, 19 Md. 418

Words or signs will, after verdict for plaintiff be construed by the

shall now use this term as equivalent to " defamatory," unless the context requires us to advert to any distinction

court to have been used in the worst sense. Bloom v. Bloom, 5 Serg. & R. 391, Walton v. Singleton, 7 Id. 451, Butterfield v. Buffum, 9 N. H. 156, Northern Cent. R Co v. Canton Co., 21 Md. 492, Brown v. Lamberton, 2 Binn. 36, Wilson v. Cottman, 65 Md. 190, Hancock v. Stephens, 11 Humph. 509, Goodrich v. Woolcott, 3 Cow. 231, Tuttle v. Bishop, 30 Conn. 80, Kennedy v. Gifford, 19 Wend. 296.

It is the duty of the court to define what is libel in point of law, and leave it to the jury to say whether the publication in question falls within that definition. State v. Goold, 62 Me. 511, Shattuck v. Allen, 4 Gray, 540, In re Noyes' Will, 61 Vt. 14, 17 At. Rep. 743, Dunnell v. Fiske, 11 Metc. 553, Jackson v. Wood, 12 Johns. 242, Bourreslau v. Detroit Evening Journal, 63 Mich. 425, 30 N. W. Rep. 379, Filber v. Dautermann, 28 Wis. 134, Gottbehuet v. Hubachek, 36 Wis. 518, Haight v. Cornell, 15 Conn. 74, Thompson v. Grimes, 5 Ind. 385, Calkins v. Wheaton, 1 Edm. Sel. Cas. 226, Pittock v. O'Neill, 63 Pa. St. 253, Matthews v. Beach, 5 Sandf. 256, Waugh v. Waugh, 47 Ind. 580, Snyder v. Andrews, 6 Barb. 43, Pugh v. McCarty, 44 Ga. 383, 40 Id. 114, Gabe v. McGinnis, 68 Ind. 538, Estaban v. Curd, 15 B. Mon. 102.

It is the duty of the jury to construe words and phrases, and as long as the words are not absolutely unintelligible the jury will judge of the meaning as other readers or hearers. Mix v. Woodward, 12 Conn. 262, Gibson v. Cincinnati Inquirer, 2 Flip. (U S) 121, Laughlin v. Bascom, 38 Iowa, 660, Ryckman v. Delavan, 25 Wend. 186, Stanley v. Webb, 4 Sandf. 21, Arnott v. Standard Assn., 57 Conn. 86, True v. Plumley, 36 Me. 466, Dorland v. Patterson, 23 Wend. 422, Andrews v. Woodmansee, 15 Id. 232, Foval v. Hellett, 10 Bradw. (Ill.) 265, Aldrich v. Brown, 11 Wend. 596, Emery v. Miller, 1 Denio, 208, Perry v. Mann, 1 R. I. 263; Tribue v. Mays, 3 Dana, 133, Haines v. Campbell, 74 Md. 58, 21 At. Rep. 703

As where the phrase is grammatically incorrect, and where cant or slang terms or ironical, figurative or allegorical language is employed. Cornelius v. Van Slyke, 21 Wend. 70, Goodrich v. Woolcott, 3 Cow. 231, Hickley v. Grosjean, 6 Blackf. 351, Mielenz v. Quasdorf, 68 Ia. 726; Saunderlin v. Bradstreet, 46 N. Y. 188; Commonwealth v. Kneeland, 20 Pick. 206, Elam v. Badger, 23 Ill. 498, Vanderlip v. Roe, 23 Pa. St. 82

If words are spoken in jest or of a doubtful meaning defamatory of another the speaker is responsible to that other for the hearing of the bystanders. Maybee v. Fisk, 42 Barb. 336, Maynard v. Firemans' Fund Ins Co., 34 Cal. 48, 47 Cal. 207, Binford v. Young, 115 Ind. 174, Foval v. Hallett, 10 Ill. App. 265, Weed v. Bibbins, 32 Barb. 315, Jacksonville Journal Co v. Beymer, 42 Ill. App. 443 See Shecut v. McDowell, 3 Brev. 38.

Foreign language. In cases of alleged defamation in a foreign language, the impression upon the minds of the hearers goes to the gist of the

between libel and slander) is often a matter of doubt. In the first place the Court has to be satisfied that they are capable of the defamatory meaning ascribed to them. Whether they are so is a question of law (*l*). If they are, and if there is some other meaning which they are also capable of, it is a question of fact which meaning they did convey under all the circumstances of the publication in question. An averment by the plaintiff that words not libellous in their ordinary meaning or without a special

---

(*l*) *Capital and Counties Bank v. Henty* (1882), 7 App. Ca. 741, 52 L. J. Q. B. 232, where the law is elaborately discussed; for a shorter example of word held, upon consideration, not to be capable of such a meaning, see *Mulligan v. Cole* (1875), L. R. 10 Q. B. 549, 44 L. J. Q. B. 153; for one on the other side of the line, *Hart v. Hall* (1877), 2 C. P. D. 146, 46 L. J. C. P. 227.

---

action, and a slander not understood by the bystander is not actionable. Nelson v. Borchenius, 52 Ill. 239. See Delaney v. Kaetel, 81 Wis. 353, 51 N. W. Rep 559; Blakeman v. Blakeman, 31 Minn. 396, 18 N. W. Rep 103; Schild v. Legler, 82 Wis 73; 51 N W Rep 1098.

Innuendo. The office of innuendo is to explain doubtful words and phrases, and annex to them their proper meaning. "It is, however, well settled that an innuendo cannot extend the sense of the words used beyond their natural meaning, unless something is put upon the record by way of introducing matter, with which they can be connected, in which case, words which are equivocal, or ambiguous, or fall short in their natural sense of stating a slanderous charge, may fix to them a meaning extending beyond their ordinary import, which renders them certain or defamatory by means of a proper innuendo." Vickers v Stoneman, 73 Mich 421. See Boyce v Aubuchon, 34 Mo. App. 323; Hays v. Brierly, 1 Watts, 393; Black's Law Dic, p 626; Crystal v. Craig, 80 Mo. 367; Weir v Hoss, 6 Ala. 880; Dicken v Shepherd, 22 Md. 418.

"Words that are not actionable *ex vi termini* cannot be made so by innuendo but must be aided by a proper averment and colloquium, which will warrant the explanatory meaning given them by innuendo." Peterson v. Sentman, 39 Md 153.

But if the words are capable of the meaning attributed to them in the innuendo as explanatory of the previous part of the declaration it must be left to the jury to find whether they were in fact so understood by the persons who heard them. Haines v. Campbell, 74 Md. 58, 21 At. Rep 703.

Where the meaning is plain no innuendo is required. Randall v Evening News Assoc 79 Mich 266, 44 N W Rep 783. See Boyce v. Aubuchon, 34 Mo. App 315; Bain v Myrick, 88 Ind. 137.

application were used with a specified libellous meaning or application is called an *innuendo*, from the old form of pleading. The old cases contain much minute, not to say frivolous, technicality, but the substance of the doctrine is now reduced to something like what is expressed above. The requirement of an innuendo, where the words are not on the face of them libellous, is not affected by the abolition of forms of pleading. It is a matter of substance, for a plaintiff who sues on words not in themselves libellous, and does not allege in his claim that they conveyed a libellous meaning, and show what that meaning was, has failed to show any cause of action (*u*). Again, explanation is required if the words have not, for judicial purposes, any received ordinary meaning at all, as being foreign, provincial or the like (*v*). This however is not quite the same thing as an innuendo. A libel in a foreign language might need both a translation to show the ordinary meaning of the words, and a distinct further innuendo to show that they bore a special injurious meaning.

Libellous tendency must be probable in law and proved in fact. The actionable or innocent character of words depends not on the intention with which they were published, but on their actual meaning and tendency when published (*w*). A man is bound to know the natural effect of the language he uses. But where the plaintiff seeks to put an actionable meaning on words by which it is not obviously conveyed, he must make out that the words are capable of that meaning (which is matter of law) and that they did convey it (which is matter of fact). So that he has to convince both the Court and the jury, and will lose his cause if he fail with either (*x*). Words are not deemed capable of a particular meaning merely because it might by possibility

---

(*u*) See 7 App. C. 748 (Lord Selborne).
(*v*) Blake Odgers 109—112.

(*w*) 7 App. Ca. 768, 782, 790, cf. p. 787.
(*x*) Lord Blackburn, 7 App. Ca. 776.

be attached to them: there must be something in either the context or the circumstances that would suggest the alleged meaning to a reasonable mind (*y*). In scholastic language, it is not enough that the terms should be " patent " of the injurious construction, they must not only suffer it, but be fairly capable of it

Repetition and reports may be libellous The publication is no less the speaker's or writer's own act, and none the less makes him answerable, because he only repeats

---

(*y*) Lord Selborne, 7 App Ca 741, Lord Blackburn, *ib* 778, Lord Bramwell, *ib* 790 "I think that the defamer is he who, of many inferences chooses a defamatory one "

Repetition and reports may be libellous The speaker is liable for the repetition of slanderous words although such words were a current report and generally believed by the speaker and others, to be true of the plaintiff Knight *v.* Foster, 39 N. H 576, Cado *v* Redditt, 15 La An 492, Moberly *v* Preston, 8 Mo 462, State *v* Burtman, 15 La. An. 166, Hayes *v* Leland, 29 Me. 233, Stacy *v.* Portland Pub Co., 68 Me 279, Huson *v* Dah, 19 Mich 17, Clark *v* Munsell, 6 Metc 373, 389, Jones *v* Chapham, 1 Blackf 88, Mapes *v* Weeks, 1 Wend 659, Skinner *v* Grant, 12 Vt. 456 See Hinkle *v* Davenport, 38 Ia. 356, Thompson *v* Bowers, 1 Dougl 321, Mason *v* Mason, 4 N H 110, Wheeler *v* Shields, 8 Ill. 348, State *v* Burtman, 15 La An 166, Beardsley *v* Bridgmen, 17 Ia 290, Haskins *v* Lumsden, 10 Wis 359, Skinner *v* Powers, 1 Wend. 451, Carpenter *v* Bailey, 53 N H. 590.

But this fact may be shown in mitigation of damages Farr *v.* Rasco, 9 Mich 353.

"It is actionable to repeat in good faith slanderous words concerning another, on an occasion not privileged, though at the same time a disbelief in their truth is expressed, and the purpose of the repetition be to obtain advice as to the propriety of informing the plaintiff of the charges * * * Every repetition of a slander is a wilful publication of it, rendering the speaker liable to an action. 'Tale bearers are as bad as tale makers.'" Branstetter *v.* Dorrough, 81 Ind. 531. See Clarkson *v* McCarty, 5 Blackf. 574, Cates *v* Kellog, 9 Ind. 506.

The repetition of slander is not to be justified by merely naming the person who first uttered it. "Such repetition extends the slander, and gives it additional credit. It is therefore unlawful unless believed to be true, and uttered on a justifiable occasion" Stevens *v.* Hartwell, 11 Metc. 550. See Jarnigan *v.* Fleming, 43 Miss. 711; 5 Am. Rep. 514, Miller *v* Kerr, 2 McCord, 285; 13 Am Dec. 722; Skinner *v.* Powers, 1

what he has heard. Libel may consist in a fair report of statements which were actually made, and on an occasion which then and there justified the original speaker in making them (z); slander in the repetition of a rumour merely as a rumour, and without expressing any belief in its truth (a) "A man may wrongfully and maliciously repeat that which another person may have uttered upon a justifiable occasion," and "as great an injury may accrue from the wrongful repetition as from the first publication of slander; the first utterer may have been a person insane or of bad character. The person who repeats it gives greater weight

(z) *Purcell v. Sowler* (1877), 2 C. P. Div. 215, 46 L. J. C. P. 308.

(a) *Watkin v. Hall* (1868), L. R. 3 Q. B. 396, 37 L. J. Q. B. 125.

Wend. 451, Fowler v. Chichester, 26 Ohio St. 9, Sans v. Joerris, 14 Wis. 663, Haines v. Welling, 7 Ohio St. 253, Sexton v. Todd, Wright, 317, Larkins v. Tartar, 3 Sneed (Tenn.), 681, Clarkson v. McCarty, 5 Blatchf. 571, Carter v. Kellogg, 9 Ind. 506.

To the contrary it was held in Johnson v. St. Louis etc. Co. (65 Mo. 539), that he who repeats a slander may shield himself, if at the time of the repetition he gives the plaintiff an action against the original author. See Treat v. Browning, 4 Conn. 408, 10 Am. Dec. 156, Titlow v. Jacket, 1 Harr. (Del.) 333, 26 Am. Dec. 399, Johnson v. Brown, 57 Barb. 118, Inman v. Foster, 8 Wend. 602, Tribue v. Mays, 3 Dana, 138, Dole v. Lyon, 10 Johns. 447, 6 Am. Dec. 346; Johnston v. Lance, 7 Ired. 448.

In the late case of Hardin v. Harshfield (Ky. App.-12 S. W. Rep. 779), it was held to be sufficient if the slanderous words were brought to the knowledge of the person influenced by them, by others, either with or without the authority of the defendant who spoke them. See Evans v. Smith, 5 T. B. Mon. 363, Kenney v. McLaughlin, 5 Gray, 3, Cole v. Perry, 8 Cow. 214, Root v. King, 7 Id. 613, Hastings v. Stetson, 126 Mass. 329, Shurtleff v. Parker, 130 Mass. 293, Cates v. Kellogg, 9 Ind. 506, Maples v. Weeks, 4 Wend. 659, Sheahan v. Collins, 20 Ill. 325, Freeman v. Price, 2 Bailey, 115, Dame v. Kenny, 25 N. H. 318; Walcott v. Hall, 6 Mass. 514, Johnson v. Stebbins, 5 Port. 364; Layton v. Harris, 3 Harr. (Del.) 406, Alderman v. French, 1 Pick. 1; Bodwell v. Swan, 3 Id. 376, Fowler v. Chichester, 26 Ohio St. 9; Sans v. Joerris, 14 Wis. 663, Fitzgerald v. Stewart, 53 Pa. St. 343. But see Terwilliger v. Wands, 17 N. Y. 61, Burt v. Advertiser Newsp. Co., 154 Mass. 238, 28 N. E. Rep. 1.

If the defendant only repeats a report which originated from the plaintiff's carelessness, the plaintiff cannot recover. Fitzgerald v. Stewart, 53 Pa. St. 343.

to the slander." (b) Circumstances of this kind may count for much in assessing damages, but they count for nothing towards determining whether the defendant is liable at all.

From this principle it follows, as regards spoken words, that if A. speak of Z. words actionable only with special damage, and B. repeat them, and special damage ensue from the repetition only, Z. shall have an action against B., but not against A. (c). As to the defendant's belief in the truth of the matter published or republished by him, that may affect the damages but cannot affect the liability. Good faith occurs as a material legal element only when we come to the exceptions from the general law that a man utters defamatory matter at his own peril.

3.—*Exceptions.*

Exceptions: fair comment. We now have to mention the conditions which exclude, if present, liability for words apparently injurious to reputation.

Nothing is a libel which is a fair comment on a subject

(b) Littledale J., *McPherson v. Daniels* (1829), 10 B. & C. 263, 273, adopted by Blackburn J., L. R. 3 Q. B. 409. The latter part of the 4th Resolution reported in the *Earl of Northampton's case*, 12 Co. Rep. 134, is not law. See per Parke J., 10 B. & C. at p. 275.

(c) See *Parkins v. Scott* (1862) 1 H. & C. 153, 31 L. J. Ex. 331, p. 392, above.

Fair comment. In accord with the text it may be said that by fair comment, or "fair criticism," is meant the truthful statement of facts with such reasonable opinions thereon of the speaker or writer as are expressed with good motives and for justifiable ends. Public men, public affairs and all subjects fairly open for public discussion may be criticised, with good faith and for the public benefit.

Freedom of speech and the liberty of the press are guaranteed by the constitution, are esteemed as the most sacred of the rights inherent in the individual, and recognized as the palladium of civil liberty. The right to publicly discuss public things, either orally or by writing belongs to every person and may be indulged without restraint so long as it is not *abused*. See Snyder v. Tutten, 34 Md. 128, 6 Am. Rep. 314; Press Co. v. Stewart, 119 Pa. St. 584.

"There is an important distinction to be noticed between the so-called privilege of fair criticism upon matters of public interest, and the privi-

fairly open to public discussion. This is a rule of common right, not of allowance to persons in any particular situa-

lege existing in the case, for instance, of the answers to inquiries about the character of servant. In the latter case, a *bona fide* statement not in excess of the occasion is privileged, although it turns out to be false. In the former what is privileged, if that is the proper term, is criticism, not statement, and however it might be if a person merely quoted or referred to a statement as made by others, and gave it no new sanction, if he takes upon himself in his own person to allege facts otherwise libellous, he will not be privileged if those facts are not true. The reason for the distinction lies in the different nature and degree of the exigency and of the damages of the two cases. * * * But what the interest of private citizens in public matters requires is freedom of discussion rather than statement. * * * The above distinction has been brought out more clearly in English decisions than it has in those of the United States." Following Scheckell v. Jackson, 10 Cush 25, Burt v Advertiser Newsp Co., 154 Mass. 212.

Liberty of the press. By liberty of the press is meant "the right to print and publish the truth, from good motives and justifiable ends." 3 Johns Cas. 394. The freedom of the press is permitted by law for the public good, inasmuch as the press, properly conducted, is conceded to be the most potential means for detecting crime, exposing fraud, revealing malign influences and purifying and protecting public affairs. The right to print and publish a newspaper containing fair comment is identical with the right of the individual to liberty of speech.

"It is a right which in every free country belongs to the citizen, and the exercise of it, within lawful and proper limits, affords some protection at least against official abuse and corruption. But there is a broad distinction between fair and legitimate discussion in regard to the conduct of a public man, and the imputation of corrupt motives, by which that conduct was supposed to be governed. And if one goes out of his way to asperse the personal character of a public man, and to ascribe to him base and corrupt motives, he must do so at his peril; and must either prove the truth of what he says, or answer in damages to the party injured. The fact that one is the proprietor of a newspaper, entitles him to no privilege in this respect, not possessed by the community in general." Negley v Farrow, 60 Md 176. See Hamilton v Eno, 81 N Y. 126, Kingston v. Palmer, 18 Ia. 327, Pratt v Pioneer Press Co , 30 Minn 44, Bronson v. Bruce, 59 Mich. 467, Perret v. N O Times Newspaper, 25 La. An 177, Detroit Daily Post Co v McArthur, 16 Mich. 451, Bathrick v The Detroit Post and Tribune Co , 50 Id 629, Barnes v Campbell (Pa), 14 At. Rep 129, Mallory v Pioneer Press Co , 34 Minn. 523, Commonwealth v Blanding, 3 Pick 304; 2 Kent. 17; Root v King, 1 Cow 928, s c King v Root, 4 Wend. 113; Loutham v Commonwealth, 79 Va 196

tion (d), and it is not correct to speak of utterances protected by it as being privileged. A man is no more *privileged* to make fair comments in public on the public conduct of others than to compete fairly with them in trade, or to build on his own land so as to darken their newly-made windows. There is not a cause of action with an excuse, but no cause of action at all. "The question is not whether the article is privileged, but whether it is a libel" (e). This is settled by the leading case of *Campell* v. *Spottiswoode* (f), confirmed by the Court of Appeal in *Merivale* v. *Carson* (g). On the other hand, the honesty of the critic's belief or motive is no defence. The right is to publish such comment as in the opinion of impartial bystanders, as represented by the jury, may fairly arise out of the matter in hand. Whatever goes beyond this, even if well meant, is libellous. The courts have, perhaps purposely, not fixed any standard of "fair criticism" (h). One test very commonly applicable is the distinction between action and motive; public acts and performances may be freely censured as to their merits or probable consequences, but wicked or dishonest motives must not be imputed upon mere surmise. Such imputations, even if honestly made, are wrongful, unless there is in fact good cause for them. "Where a person has done or published anything which may fairly be said to have invited comment . . . . every one has a right to make a fair and proper comment; and as long as he keeps within that limit, what he writes is not a libel; but that is not a privilege at all. . . . Honest belief may frequently be an element which the jury may take into consideration in considering whether or not an alleged

(d) See per Bowen L. J., *Merivale* v. *Carson* (1887), 20 Q. B. Div. at p. 282, 58 L. J. Q. B. 548.

(e) Lord Esher M. R., 20 Q. B. Div. at p. 280.

(f) 3 B. & S. 769, 32 L. J. Q. B. 185 (1863).

(g) (1887) 20 Q. B. Div. 275. This must be taken to overrule whatever was said to the contrary in *Henwood* v. *Harrison* (1872), L. R. 7 C. P. 606, 626, 41 L. J. C. P. 206.

(h) Bowen L. J., 20 Q. B. Div. at p. 283.

libel was in excess of a fair comment, but it cannot in itself prevent the matter being libellous" (*i*)

The case of a criticism fair in itself being proved to be due to unfair motives in the person making it is not known to have arisen, nor is it likely to arise, and it need not be here discussed (*j*). On principle it seems that the motive is immaterial; for if the criticism be in itself justifiable, there is nothing to complain of, unless it can be said that comment proceeding from an indirect and dishonest intention to injure the plaintiff is not criticism at all (*k*). Evidence tending to show the presence of improper motives might well also tend to show that the comment was not fair in itself, and thus be material on either view; as on the other hand to say of some kinds of criticism that there is no evidence of malice is practically equivalent to saying there is no evidence of the comment being otherwise than fair (*l*).

What is open to comment, matter of law. What acts and conduct are open to public comment is a question for the Court, but one of judicial common sense rather than of

---

(*i*) Blackburn J., *Campbell* v. *Spottiswoode*, 32 L. J. Q. B. at p. 202, cp. Bowen L. J., 20 Q. B. Div. at p. 281.

(*j*) See however *Wason* v. *Walter* (1868), L. R. 4 Q. B. at p. 96, 38 L. J. Q. B. 34, and *Stevens* v. *Sampson* (1879), 5 Ex. Div. 53, 19 L. J. Q. B. 120, and per Lord Esher M. R. 20 Q. B. Div. at p. 281.

(*k*) Lord Esher M. R., *Merivale* v. *Carson*, 20 Q. B. Div. 275, 281.

(*l*) On this ground the actual decision in *Henwood* v. *Harrison*, note (*g*), last page, may have been right, see however the dissenting judgment of Grove J.

What is open to Comment, matter of law. "It is a matter of law for the court to determine whether the occasion of writing that which would otherwise be actionable repels the inference of malice, and thus constitutes it a privileged communication." Neeb v. Hope, 111 Pa. St. 145. See Hagan v. Hendry, 68 Md. 191, Briggs v. Garrett, 111 Pa. St. 414, Locke v. Bradstreet, 22 Fed. Rep. 772, Montgomery v. Knox, 20 Fla. 380, Stewart v. Hall, 83 Ky. 382, Wharton v. Wright, 30 Ill. App. 343.

There are times when a private individual places himself in a position to invite public criticism as by publishing a book, or a musical composition, or an economic theory or an industrial enterprise, when such

technical definition. Subject-matter of this kind may be broadly classed under two types.

The matter may be in itself of interest to the common weal, as the conduct of persons in public offices, or affairs (*m*),

(*m*) Including the conduct at a public meeting of persons who attend it as private citizens. *Davis v Duncan* (1874) L R 9 C P 396, 43 L J C P 185 A clergyman is a public officer, or at any rate the conduct of public worship and whatever is incidental thereto is matter of public interest *Kelly v Tinling* (1865) L R 1 Q B 699, 35 L J Q B 310, cp *Kelly v Sherlock* (1866) L R 1 Q B at p 689, 35 L J Q B 209.

productions are subject to correct public discussion and fair comment, but only after publication

"To say that he is an author, editor or reviewer, is but saying that he is engaged in a profession which has been and may be eminently useful to mankind, and which would therefore seem to call for peculiar protection and encouragement. That the law should allow his productions to be criticised with great freedom, is not denied. If he has made himself ridiculous by his writings, he may be ridiculed; if they show him to be vicious his reviewer may say so. But the latter has no right, therefore, to violate the truth in either respect." *Cooper v Stone*, 24 Wend. 434.

So, when one becomes a candidate for public office he thereby deliberately places his conduct, character, and utterances before the public for their discussion and consideration, and they may be criticised according to the taste of the writer or speaker, who will be protected in so doing, if in their statement of or reference to the facts they observe an honest regard for the truth. *Belknap v Ball*, 83 Mich. 583, 47 N. W. Rep 674; *Walker v Tribune Co*, 29 Fed. Rep. 827; *McAllister v. Free Press Co*, 76 Mich 356; *Bailey v Publishing Co*, 40 Id. 257; *Crane v Waters*, 10 Fed Rep 619; *Express Printing Co v Copeland*, 64 Tex 354; *Upton v Hume* (Oreg.), 33 Pac. Rep. 810.

" Let his talents, his virtues, and such vices as are likely to affect his public character be freely discussed, but no falsehoods be propagated " *Brewer v Weakley*, 2 Overt 99.

"His talents and qualifications, mentally and physically for the office he asks at the hands of the people, may freely be commented on in publications in a newspaper, and, though such comment be harsh and unjust, no malice will be implied, for these are matters of opinion of which the voters are the only judges, but no one has a right by a publication to impute to such candidate falsely crimes, or allegations affecting his character, falsely " *Sweeney v Baker*, 13 W Va. 184. See *Renrick v. Wilcox*, 81 Ill 77; *Smith v. Burns*, 106 Mo 94; *Commonwealth v Clapp*, 4 Miss 163; *Wheaton v Beecher*, 79 Mich 443, 33 N W Rep 503; *Harwood v Keech*, 4 Hun, 389; *Burke v Muscarich*, 81 Cal 302; *Lewis v Few*, 5 Johns 1; *Bays v Hunt*, 60 Ia 251; *Mott v Dawson*, 46 Ia 533.

of those in authority, whether imperial or local (n), in the administration of the law, or the managers of public institutions in the affairs of those institutions, and the like.

Or it may be laid open to the public by the voluntary act of the person concerned. The writer of a book offered for sale, the composer of music publicly performed, the author of a work of art publicly exhibited, the manager of a public entertainment, and all who appear as performers therein, the propounder of an invention or discovery publicly described with his consent, are all deemed to submit their work to public opinion, and must take the risks of fair criticism, which criticism, being itself a public act, is in like manner open to reply within commensurate limits.

Whether comment is fair, matter of fact (if libellous construction possible). What is actually fair criticism is a question of fact, provided the words are capable of being understood in a sense beyond the fair (that is honest) expression of an unfavourable opinion, however strong, on that which the plaintiff has submitted to the public: this is only an application of the wider principle above stated as to the construction of a supposed libel (o).

In literary and artistic usage criticism is hardly allowed to be fair which does not show competent intelligence of

(n) *Purcell v. Sowler*, 2 C. P. Div. 215, 46 L. J. C. P. 308.

(o) *Merivale v. Carson* (1887), 20 Q. B. Div. 275, 58 L. J. Q. B. 518; *Jenner v. A'Beckett* (1871), L. R. 7 Q. B. 11, 41 L. J. Q. B. 14. Qu. whether the dissenting judgment of Lush J. was not right.

Whether comment is fair, for the jury to determine. After the jury have been instructed by the court that a matter submitted to them is a proper subject for public comment, or that the occasion was privileged, it is their duty to determine whether the comment made by the defendant is fair in fact. See *Hyde v. McCabe*, 100 Mo. 413, 13 S. W. Rep. 875; *Bacon v. Mich. Cent. R. R. Co.*, 66 Mich. 172; *Howland Blake v. Mfg Co.*, 156 Mass. 343, 31 N. E. Rep. 656; *Lally v. Emery*, 59 Hun, 237. And see, *ante*, p. 320.

the subject-matter. Courts of justice have not the means of applying so fine a test: and a right of criticism limited to experts would be no longer a common right but a privilege.

The right of fair criticism will, of course, not cover untrue statements concerning alleged specific acts of misconduct (*p*), or purporting to describe the actual contents of the work being criticised (*q*).

Justification on ground of truth. Defamation is not actionable if the defendant shows that the defamatory matter was true, and if it was so, the purpose or motive with

---

(*p*) Dairy v. Shepstone (1886), L. C. 11 App. Ca. P. 55 L. J. P. C. 51.

(*q*) Merivale v. Carson (1887), 20 Q. B. Div. 275.

Justification on ground of truth. Agreeing with the text is the rule in America that the truth of the charge, when specially pleaded and proved at the trial, is a complete defense in all civil actions of libel or slander. Nandy v. Wight, 26 Kan. 177, citing Castle v. Houston, 19 Id. 417. See Root v. King, 4 Wend. 114, 21 Am Dec. 102, Eveston v. Cramer, 54 Wis 220, Moore v. Mauk, 3 Ill App 114; Scott v Fleming, 17 Id. 564; Wonderly v Nokes, 8 Blackf 590, Mielenz v Quasdorf, 68 Ia 726. Riley v Norton, 65 Id 306, Forshee v Abrams, 2 Id 571, Gillis v Peck, 20 Conn 228, Brown v. Massachusetts Title Ins Co, 16 Mass 127, 23 N E Rep 733, Cameron v Tribune Assn, 7 N Y. S Rep. 737, McBee v Fulton, 47 Md 403, Parkhurst v Ketchum, 6 Id. 406, Watson v Moore, 2 Cush 133, Snow v Witcher, 9 Ired 346, Payne v Taylor, 14 La. An 407; Tunnell v. Furguson, 17 Ill App 76, Patterson v State, 12 Tex App 458, Welch v. Jugenheimer, 56 Ia. 11, Delaware S F. & M Ins Co v Croasdale, 6 Houst. 181; Wheaton v Beecher, 79 Mich 413, 44 N W Rep 927; Holmes v. Jones, 121 N Y. 461, 24 N. E Rep. 201, Morgan v Rice, 35 Mo App 591, McLean v Warring (Miss.), 13 So. Rep 230, Davis v Lyon, 91 N C 447 But proof of the truth of the charge cannot be introduced in justification under a general plea of not guilty. The plaintiff is entitled to have notice of the kind of defense which will be made at the trial and would of course be unprepared to meet proof of facts foreign to the pleadings Sweeney v Baker, 13 W. Va 205. See Foss v Hildredth, 10 Allen, 76, Snyder v Andrews, 6 Barb 56, Jarnigan v Fleming, 43 Miss. 227, Curtis v. Perkins, 66 Barb. 610, Donaghue v Gaffy, 53 Conn. 43, Hogan v Hendry, 68 Md 177, Barrows v Carpenter, 1 Cliff 204, Frederitze v Odenwalder, 2 Yeates, 243, Powers v Presgroves, 38 Miss. 227; Bourland v Edison, 8 Gratt. 27;

which it was published is irrelevant. For although in the current phrase the statement of matter "true in substance and in fact" is said to be justified, this is not because any merit is attached by the law to the disclosure of all truth

Shealton v. Collins, 20 Ill. 325, 71 Am Dec 74, Hutchinson v. Wheeler, 35 Vt 330, Padgett v. Sweeting, 65 Md 404, David v. Davey, 32 Ohio St 604, Thompson v. Bower, 1 Dougl 91, Porter v. Botkins, 59 Pa St 484, Thomas v. Dunaway, 30 Ill 373, Johnson v. Stebbins, 5 Ind 364, George v. Lemon, 19 Tex 150, Thill v. Smiles, 9 Cal 529, v. Hamilton, 19 Johns 349, Fidler v. Delavan, 20 Wend 57, Van Derveer v. Sutphin, 5 Ohio St 295, Holton v. Muzzy, 30 Vt 365, Hathorn v. Congress Spring Co, 44 Hun, 608, Jones v. Townsend, 21 Fla 440, Tallmadge v. Press Pub Co, 7 N Y S Rep 895, Ball v. Evenin Post Co, 3 Hun, 11, Blickenstaff v. Pium, 9 Ind 527, Petrie v. Rose, 5 Watts & S 364, Warner v. Holdbrunner, 7 Gill, 296, Douge v. Pierce, 13 Ala 127

It is the established English doctrine that where truth is pleaded in justification of the defamation, the defendant will not be allowed to prove palliating circumstances in mitigation, and this doctrine has been followed in a few American decisions See Alderman v. French, 1 Pick 18, Shelton v. Simmons, 12 Ala 466 But the prevailing rule in this country is to the contrary West v. Walker, 2 Swan, 32, Hawkins v. Globe Printing Co, 10 Mo App 174, Landis v. Shanklin, 1 Ind 92, Morehead v. Jones, 2 B Mon 210, Pallet v. Sargent, 36 N H 496, Snyder v. Andrews, 6 Barb 57, Purple v. Horton, 13 Id 9, Cooper v. Barber 24 Id 105

If a defendant maliciously and for the purpose of spreading and perpetuating the slander, pleads the truth of the words in justification and fails to prove it, it may be regarded as evidence proving or tending to prove malice in speaking the words originally, and may tend indirectly to increase the damages for speaking the slanderous words charged in the declaration by showing the degree of malice in speaking them See Klewin v. Bauman, 53 Wis 215, Henderson v. Fox, 83 Ga 233, 9 S. E Rep 869, Bennett v. Mathews, 64 Barb 411, Fero v. Ruscoe, 4 N Y 162, Beasley v. Meggs, 16 Ill 139, Spencer v. McMasters, 16 Ill 405, Robinson v. Drummond, 24 Ala 174, Doss v. Jones, 5 How (Miss) 158, Updegrove v. Zimmerman, 13 Pa St 619, Pool v. Devers, 30 Ala. 672, Richardson v. Roberts, 23 Ga 215, Lea v. Robertson, 1 Stew 138, Sweeney v. Baker, 13 W Va 207 Gilman v. Lowell, 8 Wend 575, Marks v. Baker, 28 Minn 162, Sloan v. Petrie, 15 Ill 425, Aird v. Fireman's Journal Co, 10 Daly, 254, Murphy v. Stout, 1 Ind 372, Soulty v. Miller, Ib Id 544, Decker v. Gaylord, 35 Hun, 584, Ransome v. Christian, 49 Ga 491, Cavanaugh v. Austin, 42 Vt 576, Pallet v. Sargent, 36 N H 496, Rayner v. Kinney, 14 Ohio (N S), 283, Thomas v. Dunaway 30 Ill 373

in season and out of season (indeed it may be a criminal offence), but because of the demerit attaching to the plaintiff if the imputation is true, whereby he is deemed to have no ground of complaint for the fact being communicated to his neighbours. It is not that uttering truth always carries its own justification, but that the law bars the other party of redress which he does not deserve. Thus the old rule is explained, that where truth is relied on for justification, it must be specially pleaded; the cause of action was confessed, but the special matter avoided the plaintiff's right (r). "The law will not permit a man to recover damages in respect of an injury to a character which he either does not or ought not to possess" (s). This defence, as authority and experience show, is not a favoured one. To adopt it is to forego the usual advantages of the defending party, and commit oneself to a counter-attack in which only complete success will be profitable, and failure will be disastrous.

Must be substantially complete. What the defendant has to prove is truth in substance, that is, he must show that the imputation made or repeated by him was true as

(r) Compare the similar doctrine in trespass, which has peculiar consequences. But of this in its place.

(s) Littledale J., 10 B. & C. at p. 272.

Must be substantially complete. The doctrine of the text is supported by the American authorities. Thus, in the case of Hay v. Reid (85 Mich. 296, 18 N. W. Rep. 507), the court held, that "Where an article contained several distinct libelous charges, a justification as to part of the charges, and not the whole, goes only in mitigation of damages, and does not warrant a verdict for the defendant." See Atkinson v. Detroit Free Press, 46 Mich. 348; McBee v. Fulton, 47 Md. 403; Scott v. McKinnish, 15 Ala. 662; Jones v. Greeley, 25 Fla. 629, 6 So. Rep. 448.

Upon the question of the *quantum* of proof required to support a plea of justification, see Fowler v. Wallace, 131 Ind. 347, 31 N. E. Rep. 53; Bell v. McGinnis, 40 Ohio St. 204, 48 Am. Rep. 673; Kane v. Hibernia Ins. Co., 10 Vroom, 697; Behrens v. Ins. Co., 58 Id. 26; Blazer v. Insurance Co., 7 Wis. 31; Thayer v. Boyle, 30 Me. 475; Elliott v. Van Buren,

a whole and in every material part thereof. He cannot justify part of a statement, and admit liability for part, without distinctly severing that which he justifies from that which he does not (*t*). What parts of a statement are material, in the sense that their accuracy or inaccuracy makes a sensible difference in the effect of the whole, is a question of fact (*u*).

There may be a further question whether the matter alleged as justification is sufficient, if proved, to cover the whole cause of action arising on the words complained of, and this appears to be a question of law, save so far as it depends on the fixing of that sense, out of two or more possible ones, which those words actually conveyed. It is a rule of law that one may not justify calling the editor of a journal a "felon editor" by showing that he was once convicted of felony. For a felon is one who has actually committed felony, and who has not ceased to be a felon by full endurance of the sentence of the law, or by a pardon; not a man erroneously convicted, or one who has been convicted and duly discharged. But it may be for a jury to say whether calling a man a "convicted felon" imputed the quality of felony generally, or only conveyed

(*t*) *Fleming v. Dollar* (1889), 2 Q. B. D. 188, 65 L. J. Q. B. 46.

(*u*) *Alexander v. North Eastern R. Co.* (1865), 6 B. & S. 340, 34 L. J. Q. B. 152.

33 Mich. 51, Gordan v. Parmelee, 15 Gray, 416, Folsom v. Brown, 25 N. H. 114, Bradish v. Bliss, 35 Vt. 326, Currie v. Richardson, 63 Vt. 617, 22 Atl. Rep. 625, Stallings v. Whittaker, 55 Ark. 494, 18 S. W. Rep. 329, Ellis v. Buzzell, 60 Me. 209, 11 Am. Rep. 204.

In all such cases the burden of proof is on the defendant. Edwards v. Knapp, 97 Mo. 432, Stewart v. Minnesota Tribune Co., 40 Minn. 101, 42 N. W. Rep. 787, McIntyre v. Bransford (Ky.), 17 S. W. Rep. 359, Tull v. David, 27 Ind. 377, Sons v. Gilbert, 12 Bush, 51, 23 Am. Rep. 508, Barfield v. Britt, 2 Jones L. 41, 62 Am. Dec. 190, Kidd v. Gleck, 17 Wis. 443, Bradley v. Kennedy, 2 Greene (Ia.), 231, Snyder v. Andrews, 6 Barb. 43, Fountain v. West, 23 Ia. 9, 92 Am. Dec. 406, Byrket v. Monahon, 7 Blackf. 83, 41 Am. Dec. 212, Burckhalter v. Coward, 16 S. C. 435, Ellis v. Lindly, 38 Ia. 461, Tucker v. Call, 45 Ind. 31, Williams v. Gunnels, 66 Ga. 521.

the fact that at some time he was convicted (*x*). Where the libel charges a criminal offence with circumstances of moral aggravation, it is not a sufficient justification to aver the committing of the offence without those circumstances, though in law they may be irrelevant, or relevant only as evidence of some element or condition of the offence (*y*). The limits of the authority which the court will exercise over juries in handling questions of "mixed fact and law" must be admitted to be hard to define in this and other branches of the law of defamation.

Defendant's belief immaterial. Apparently it would make no difference in law that the defendant had made a defamatory statement without any belief in its truth, if it turned out afterwards to have been true when made: as, conversely, it is certain that the most honest and even reasonable belief is of itself no justification. Costs, however, are now in the discretion of the Court.

Immunity of members of Parliament and judges. In order that public duties may be discharged without fear, unqualified protection is given to language used in the

---

(*x*) *Leyman v Latimer* (1878), 3 Ex. Div 352, 47 L J Ex 470

(*y*) *Helsham v Blackwood* (1851), 11 C B 125, 20 L J C P 187, a very curious case.

Defendant's belief immaterial Agreeing with the text, *vide* Foss *v* Hildreth, 10 Allen, 76, Blacker *v* Schoff (Ia), 48 N. W. Rep 1079, Fountain *v* West, 23 Ia 11, Watson *v* Moore, 2 Cush. 134, Wozelka *v* Hettrick, 93 N. C. 10, Beardsley *v* Bridgman, 17 Ia 290, Grimes *v* Coyle, 6 B Mon. 301, Woodruff *v* Richardson, 20 Conn 238, Powers *v*. Cary, 64 Me 9.

Immunity of members of parliament, judges and others The immunity of the communications mentioned in this paragraph is absolute.

Legislators A member of the legislature has immunity from an action for slander for words spoken in the discharge of his official duties, even though spoken maliciously and against the declared will of the house. These privileges are thus secured, not with the intention of

exercise of parliamentary and judicial functions. A member of Parliament cannot be lawfully molested outside Parliament by civil action, or otherwise, on account of anything

protecting the members for their own benefit, but to support the rights of the people, by enabling their representatives to execute the functions of their office without fear of prosecution. Coffin v. Coffin, 1 Mass 1. See Dunham v. Powers, 42 Vt. 1; Hastings v. Lusk, 22 Wend. 410; Wood v. Wiman, 47 Hun, 364; Perkins v. Mitchell, 31 Barb. 467.

Judicial proceedings. The rule is well settled by the authorities that anything pertinent to the issue, said in the regular course of judicial proceedings, though it impute crime and import malice, is not actionable. Hoar v. Wood, 3 Metc. 197. Whether the imputation be spoken or written, and made by a party to the proceedings, the judge, counsel, witness or juryman, if pertinent, it is privileged, and consequently lays no foundation for a private action or public prosecution. Hollis v. Meux, 69 Cal. 629; Prescott v. Tousey, 53 N. Y. Super. Ct. 56; Vinas v. Merchants' Mut. Ins. Co., 33 La. An. 1265; Allen v. Crofoot, 2 Wend. 516; Rainbow v. Benson, 71 Ia. 301; York v. Pease, 2 Gray, 282; Nissen v. Cramer, 104 N. C. 579, 10 S. L. Rep. 676; Hawks v. Evans, 76 Ia. 593; Randall v. Brigham, 7 Wall. 523; Rector v. Smith, 11 Ia. 302; Wyatt v. Buell, 47 Cal. 624; Lawson v. Hicks, 38 Ala. 279; Aylesworth v. St. Johns, 25 Hun, 156; Budgley v. Hedges, 2 N. J. L. 233; Bartlett v. Christhilf, 69 Md. 219; Spaids v. Barrett, 57 Ill. 289; Gardemal v. McWilliams, 43 La An. 154, 9 So. Rep. 106; Whitney v. Allen, 62 Ill. 472; Strauss v. Meyer, 48 Ill. 385; Bailey v. Dean, 5 Barb. 297; Gari v. Selden, 4 Comst. 91; Warner v. Paine, 2 Sandf. 195; Hart v. Baxter, 47 Mich. 198; McMillan v. Birch, 1 Binn. 178; Fish v. Sonlat, 33 La. An. 1400.

So, all pleadings, affidavits, and other documents necessary to the conduct of the cause are privileged. Gilbert v. People, 1 Denio, 41; Hartsock v. Reddick, 6 Blackf. 255; Warner v. Payne, 48 Ill. 386; Bailey v. Dean, 5 Barb. 297; Stewart v. Hall, 83 Ky. 375; Lanning v. Christie, 30 Ohio St. 115, 27 Am. Rep. 431; Vausse v. Lee, 1 Hill (S. C.), 197, 26 Am. Dec. 168; Lea v. White, 4 Sneed (Tenn.), 111.

Libellous charges made before a court not legally competent to investigate them, are actionable. Milam v. Burnsides, 1 Brev. 295.

"It seems to be well settled by the English authorities that judges, counsel, parties and witnesses are absolutely exempted from liability to an action for defamatory words published in the course of judicial proceedings. * * * The same doctrine is generally held in the American courts, with the qualification, as to parties, counsel and witnesses, that in order to be privileged, their statements made in the course of an action must be pertinent and material to the case." Rice v. Coolidge, 121 Mass. 393. See Barnes v. McCrate, 32 Me. 442; Kidder v. Parkhurst, 3 Allen, 393; Kean v. McLaughlin, 2 Serg. & R. 469; Ruohs v. Backer, 6

and by him in his place in either House (z). An action will not lie against a judge for any words used by him in his judicial capacity in a court of justice (a). It is not

---

t 1 Hen VIII c 5 (Pro Ricardo Strode), Bill of Rights, 1 Wm & M sess 2 "That the freedome of speech and debate or proceedings in Parlya ment ought not to be impeached or questioned in any court or place out of Parlyament"

(a) Scott v Stansfield (1868), L R 3

Exch 95, McLaughlin v Cowley, 127 Mass 316, Burlingame v Burlingame, 8 Cow 141, Post Pub Co v Moloney (Ohio), 33 N L Rep 921.

In determining what is pertinent much latitude must be allowed Hoar v Wood, 3 Metc 197

In Maulsby v Reifsnider (69 Md 162) the court with much reason said, in substance, that the words "relevant" and "pertinent" are not the best words that could be used

It is sufficient if the matter has reference or relation or any connection with the point in issue See State v Walt, 41 Kan 310, 21 Pac Rep 351

In Vermont it is held that if the party spoke the words *bona fide,* believing them to be pertinent no action of slander will lie. Mower v. Watson, 11 Vt 512 Torrey v Field, 10 Id 353

Parties Marsh v Ellsworth, 50 N Y 312, Morgan v Booth, 13 Bush 480 Rice v Coolidge, 121 Mass 393 Ring v Wheeler, 7 Cow. ; Hollis v Meux, 69 Cal 625, 58 Am. Rep 574, 11 Pac Rep 218, Lester v Thurmond, 51 Ga 118, Dada v Piper, 41 Hun, 254, Mower v. Watson 11 Vt 536, Maulsby v Reifsnider, 69 Md 161

In Hoar v Wood (3 Metc 193), Shaw, C J, said "Still this privilege must be restrained by some limit, and we consider that limit to be this, that a party or counsel shall not avail himself of his situation, to gratify private malice by uttering slanderous expressions, either against a party, witnesses or third persons, cause or subject-matter of the inquiry " And in Hastings v Lusk, the absolute and unqualified privilege laid down in several English cases is rejected See Scheffer v. Gooding, 2 Jones L 175, Stackpole v. Hennen, 6 Mart (N S) 481

Witnesses Calkins v. Sumner 13 Wis 193, White v. Carroll, 42 N. Y 161, 1 Am Rep 504, Liles v Gaster, 42 Ohio St 631, Burke v. Ryan, 36 La An 951, Spooner v Keeler, 51 N Y 527, Shadden v McElwee, 86 Tenn 146, Hunckell v. Vonhiff, 69 Md 179, McLaughlin v Charles, 11 N Y S Rep 608, Preston v Frey, 91 Cal 107, 27 Pac. Rep 533, Grove v Brandenburg, 7 Blackf 234, Bailey v Dean, 5 Barb 297, Terry v Fellows, 21 La An 375, Hutchinson v Lewis, 75 Ind 55, Steinecke v. Marx, 10 Mo App 580, Story v Wallace, 60 Ill 51, Cooper v Phipps (Oreg), 33 Pac Rep 985

Naval, Military, and other Public Affairs The *bona fide* exercise of naval, military, or other public authority is privileged See White v Nichols, How 266

open to discussion whether the words were or were not in the nature of fair comment on the matter in hand, or otherwise relevant or proper, or whether or not they were used in good faith.

Other persons in judicial proceedings. Parties, advocates, and witnesses in a court of justice are under the like protection. They are subject to the authority of the Court itself, but whatever they say in the course of the proceedings and with reference to the matter in hand is exempt from question elsewhere. It is not slander for a prisoner's counsel to make insinuations against the prosecutor, which might, if true, explain some of the facts proved, however gross and unfounded those insinuations may be (*b*); nor for a witness after his cross-examination to volunteer a statement of opinion by way of vindicating his credit, which involves a criminal accusation against a person wholly unconnected with the case (*c*). The only limitation is that the words must in some way have reference to the inquiry the Court is engaged in. A duly constituted military court of inquiry is for this purpose on the same footing as an ordinary court of justice (*d*). So is a select committee of the House of Commons (*e*). Statements coming within this rule are said to be "absolutely privileged." The reason for precluding all discussion of their reasonableness or good faith before another tribunal is one of public policy, laid down to the same effect in all the authorities. The law does not seek to protect a dishonest witness or a reck-

Ex. 220, 37 L. J. Ex. 155, the protection extends to judicial acts, see the chapter of General Exceptions above pp. 104—106, and further illustrations *ap.* Blake Odgers, 188.

(*b*) *Munster* v. *Lamb* (1883), 11 Q. B. Div. 588, where authorities are collected.

(*c*) *Seaman* v. *Netherclift* (1876), 2 C. P. Div. 53, 46 L. J. C. P. 128.

(*d*) *Dawkins* v. *Lord Rokeby* (1873-5),

Ex. Ch. and H. L., L. R. 8 Q. B. 255, 7 H. L. 744, 45 L. J. Q. B. 8, see opinion of judges 7 H. L. at p. 752, *Dawkins* v. *Prince Edward of Saxe Weimar* (1876), 1 Q. B. D. 499, 45 L. J. Q. B. 567.

(*e*) *Goffin* v. *Donnelly* (1881), 6 Q. B. D. 307, 50 L. J. Q. B. 303. A licensing meeting of a County Council is not a Court for this purpose: *Royal Aquarium Society* v. *Parkinson*, '92, 1 Q. B. 431, C. A.

less advocate, but deems this a less evil than exposing honest witnesses and advocates to vexatious actions.

Reports of officers, etc. As to reports made in the course of naval or military duty, but not with reference to any pending judicial proceeding, it is doubtful whether they come under this head or that of "qualified privilege." A majority of the Court of Queen's Bench has held (against a strong dissent), not exactly that they are "absolutely privileged," but that an ordinary court of law will not determine questions of naval or military discipline and duty. But the decision is not received as conclusive (*f*).

Qualified immunity of "privileged communications." There is an important class of cases in which a middle course is taken between the common rule of unqualified re-

---

(*f*) *Dawkins v. Lord Paulet* (1869), L. R. 5 Q. B. 94, 39 L. J. Q. B. 53, see the dissenting judgment of Cockburn C. J., and the notes of Mr. Justice Stephen, Dig. Cr. L. art 276, and Mr. Blake Odgers, *op cit.* 195. The reference of the Judicial Committee to the case in *Hart v. Gumpach* (1872), L. R. 4 P. C. 439, 464, 12 L. J. P. C. 25, is quite neutral. They declined to presume that such an "absolute privilege" existed by the law and customs of China as to official reports to the Chinese Government.

Qualified immunity of "privileged communications." As stated in the text, communications like those above mentioned, by members of legislative or judicial bodies, are absolutely privileged. There are certain occasions which permit communications not otherwise privileged, and, therefore, such communications may be said to be conditionally or qualifiedly privileged.

In Hastings v. Lusk (22 Wend. 414), the court said: "In one class of cases the law protects the defendant so far as not to impute malice to him from the mere fact of his having spoken words of the plaintiff which are in themselves actionable, though he may not be able to prove the truth of his allegations. But the plaintiff will be able to sustain his action for slander, if he can satisfy the jury, by other proof, that there was *actual malice* on the part of the defendant, and that he uttered the words for the mere purpose of defaming the plaintiff. In the other class of cases the privilege is an effectual shield to the defendant, so that no action of slander can be sustained against him, whatever his motive may have been in using slanderous words." See Bacon v. Mich. Cent. R. Co., 66 Mich. 172, Briggs v. Garrett, 111 Pa. St. 414, Moore v. Manufacturer's

sponsibility for one's statements, and the exceptional rules which give, as we have just seen, absolute protection to the kinds of statements covered by them. In many relations of life the law deems it politic and necessary to protect the honest expression of opinion concerning the character and merits of persons, to the extent appropriate to the nature of the occasion, but not necessary to prevent the person affected from showing, if he can, that an unfavourable opinion expressed concerning him is not honest. Occasions of this kind are said to be privileged, and communications made in pursuance of the duty or right incident to them are said to be privileged by the occasion. The term "qualified privilege" is often used to mark the requirement of good faith in such cases, in contrast to the cases of "absolute privilege" above mentioned. Fair reports of judicial and parliamentary proceedings are put by the latest authorities in the same category. Such reports must be fair and substantially correct in fact to begin with, and also must not be published from motives of personal ill-will; and this although the matter reported was "absolutely privileged" as to the original utterance of it.

Conditions of the privilege. The conditions of immunity may be thus summed up.—

The occasion must be privileged; and if the defendant establishes this, he will not be liable unless the plaintiff can prove (g) that the communication was not honestly made for the purpose of discharging a legal, moral or social duty, or with a view to the just protection of some private

---

(g) The burden of proof is not on the defendant to show his good faith. *Jenoure v. Delmege*, '91, A. C. 73, 60 L. J. P. C. 11, J. C.

Nat. Bank, 122 N. Y. 420, 25 N. E. Rep. 1048, King v. Patterson, 49 N. J. L. 420, Marks v. Baker, 28 Minn. 162, Nix v. Caldwell, 81 Ky. 295, Rubelman v. Larchman, 14 Mo. App. 601, Lowry v. Vedder, 40 Minn. 475, Smith v. Smith, 3 L. R. A. 52, 11 N. W. Rep. 499, Palmer v. Concord, 48 N. H. 211, Warden v. Whalen, 8 Pa. Co. Ct. Rep. 660, Metzler v. Romine, 9 Id. 171.

interest or of the public good by giving information appearing proper to be given, but from some improper motive and without due regard to truth.

Such proof may exist either in external evidence of personal ill-feeling or disregard of the truth of the matter, or in the manner or terms of the communication, or acts accompanying and giving point to it, being unreasonable and improper, "in excess of the occasion," as we say

"Express malice." The rule formerly was, and still sometimes is, expressed in an artificial manner derived from the style of pleading at common law.

The law, it is said, presumes or implies malice in all

"Express malice." Express malice must be specifically proved, that is, it must be shown that outside of the language itself there existed an intent to injure the individual defamed. Pollasky v. Minchener, 81 Mich. 280, 46 N. W. Rep. 5; Vickers v. Stoneman, 73 Mich. 419; Jno. W. Lovell Co. v. Houghton, 54 N. Y. Superior Ct. 60; Palmer v. Concord, 48 N. H. 211; Miner v. Detroit, etc., Co., 49 Mich. 358; Jellison v. Goodwin, 43 Me. 288.

Whatever tends to show the motive which prompted the utterance of the words is competent, under the general issue, as tending to prove presence or absence of malice. Cameron v. Tribune Assoc., 4 N. Y. S. Rep. 789; Steinecke v. Marx, 10 Mo. App. 580; Hotchkiss v. Porter, 30 Conn. 414; Gribble v. Pioneer Press Co., 34 Minn. 193; Hastings v. Stetson, 130 Mass. 76; York v. Pease, 2 Gray, 282; Goot v. Pulsifer, 122 Mass. 235; Dixon v. Allen, 69 Cal. 527; Lewis v. Chapman, 16 N. Y. 372; Wilson v. Noonan, 35 Wis. 321.) As, for example, in the Illinois case of Hintz v. Graupner (37 Ill. App. 510; 27 N. E. Rep. 935), it was held, that when defendant was asked why he made charges against plaintiff, and he said that he had a grudge against her father, it is competent to prove malice. Distinguishing Stowell v. Beagle, 57 Ill. 97. See Ward v. Beane, 57 Hun, 585; Grace v. McArthur, 76 Wis. 641; Freeman v. Sanderson, 123 Ind. 264; Wabash Print. & Pub. Co. v. Crumrine, 123 Ind. 89; Beneway v. Thorp, 77 Mich. 181. And in the case of Harris v. Zanone (93 Cal. 59, 28 Pac. Rep. 845), it was held that in an action for slander, in uttering defamatory words concerning plaintiff, evidence of the other utterance of words of similar import is admissible to show malice.

Express malice must be proven in privileged communications to entitle the plaintiff to recover. Remington v. Congdon, 2 Pick. 310, 13 Am. Dec. 431; King v. Root, 4 Wend. 113, 21 Am. Dec. 102; Fahr v. Hayes,

cases of defamatory words, this presumption may be rebutted by showing that the words were uttered on a privileged occasion; but after this the plaintiff may allege and prove express or actual malice, that is, wrong motive. He need not prove malice in the first instance, because the law presumes it; when the presumption is removed, the field is still open to proof. But the "malice in law" which was said to be presumed is not the same as the "express malice" which is matter of proof. To have a lawful occasion and abuse it may be as bad as doing harm without any lawful occasion, or worse; but it is a different thing in substance. It is better to say that where there is

---

50 N. J. L. 275, 13 At. Rep. 261; Conroy v. Pittsburgh Times, 139 Pa. St. 339, 21 At. Rep. 154, 27 W. N. C. 239; Schuyler v. Busbey, 68 Hun, 474, 23 N. Y. S. Rep. 102.

A repetition of the defamation may be shown to prove malice. Reiten v. Goedel, 33 Minn. 151; Ward v. Dick, 47 Conn. 300; Noeninger v. Vogt, 88 Mo. 589; Welch v. Tribune Pub. Co., 83 Mich. 661, 47 N. W. Rep. 562.

So, a failure to publish a retraction promptly is evidence of malice. Hermann v. Bradstreet Co., 19 Mo. App. 227. *Contra*, Bradley v. Cramer, 66 Wis. 297.

If the publication is ambiguous, express malice may be shown in order to enhance the damages. Huson v. Dale, 19 Mich. 29; Thompson v. Powning, 15 Nev. 195; Bush v. Brosser, 11 N. Y. 347.

Express malice may be shown in aggravation of damages. True v. Plumley, 36 Me. 481; Fowler v. Gilbert, 38 Mich. 292; Delaney v. Kaetel, 81 Wis. 353, 51 N. W. Rep. 559; Walker v. Wickens, 49 Kan. 42, 30 Pac. Rep. 181.

So circumstances which disprove malice, may be given in evidence in mitigation of damages. Gilman v. Lowell, 8 Wend. 575; Commonwealth v. Snelling, 15 Pick. 340; Sick v. Owen, 47 Cal. 252.

Where malice is not inferred by law from the defamatory matter itself it is a proper question for the jury to pass upon and determine. Lawson v. Hicks, 38 Ala. 287, 81 Am. Dec. 49; Nott v. Stoddard, 38 Vt. 32; Weaver v. Hendrick, 30 Mo. 506; Nebb v. Hope, 111 Pa. St. 145; Bacon v. Mich. Cent. R. Co., 66 Mich. 166, 31 Am. & Eng. R. Cas. 357; Coleman v. Playsted, 36 Barb. 26; Klinck v. Colby, 46 N. Y. 427; Hamilton v. Eno, 81 N. Y. 116; Adcocks v. Marsh, 8 Ired. 361; Alliger v. Brooklyn Daily Eagle, 6 N. Y. S. Rep. 110; Locke v. Bradstreet Co., 22 Fed. Rep. 772; Fowles v. Bowen, 30 N. Y. 20; Gassett v. Gilbert, 6 Gray, 94; Liddle v. Hodges, 2 Bosw. 537; Erwin v. Sumrow, 1 Hawks, 472.

a duty, though of imperfect obligation, or a right, though not answering to any legal duty, to communicate matter of a certain kind, a person acting on that occasion in discharge of the duty or exercise of the right incurs no liability, and the burden of proof is on those who allege that he was not so acting (*h*).

What are privileged occasions. The occasions giving rise to privileged communications may be in matters of legal or social duty, as where a confidential report is made to an official superior, or in the common case of giving a character to a servant; or they may be in the way of self-defence, or the defence of an interest common to those between whom the words or writing pass; or they may be addressed to persons in public authority with a view to the exercise of their authority for the public good; they may also be matter published in the ordinary sense of the word for purposes of general information.

Moral or social duty. As to occasions of private duty; the result of the authorities appears to be that any state of facts making it right in the interests of society for one

---

(*h*) See per Lord Blackburn, 7 App. Ca. 787.

Moral or social duty. There are communications which through public policy and for the good of society are recognized by law as privileged. But such communications must be made *bona fide* upon a subject-matter in which the party communicating has an interest, or in reference to which he has a duty, and to a person having a corresponding interest or duty.

Among communications belonging to this class are those of solicitor to client, relative to relative, master to servant, partner to partner, etc.

1. *Relatives.* Pertinent communications among relatives in the interest of each other, or from a stranger upon invitation, are privileged. Rude v. Nass, 79 Wis. 321, 48 N. W. Rep. 555. But the mere bonds of friendship are not sufficient to render defamatory communications in regard to another privileged. Byam v. Collins, 111 N. Y. 143; Joannes v. Bennett, 5 Allen, 169.

2. *Mercantile agencies confidential inquiries.* The reports of mercantile agencies made in strict confidence, to those of their subscribers who

person to communicate to another what he believes or has heard regarding any person's conduct or character will constitute a privileged occasion (*t*).

(*t*) See per Blackburn J. in *Davies v. ——* (1870), L. R. 5 Q. B. at p. 611.

have an interest in the matter reported, are privileged. In the case of Sunderlin v. Bradstreet (46 N. Y. 188), Mr. Justice Allen, in delivering the opinion of the court, said: "A communication is privileged within the rule when made in good faith, in answer to one having an interest in the information sought; and it will be privileged if volunteered, when the party to whom the communication is made has an interest in it, and the party to whom it is made stands in such relation to him as to make it a reasonable duty, or at least proper that he should give the information. . . . In those cases in which the publication has been held privileged the courts have held that there was a reasonable occasion or exigency, which for the common convenience and welfare of society, fairly warranted the communication is made. But neither the welfare nor convenience of society will be promoted by bringing a publication of matters, false in fact, injurious affecting the credit and finances of merchants and traders, broadcast over the land, within the protection of privileged communications."

In King v. Patterson (49 N. J. L. 14), the court said: "The publication of defamatory matter for personal gain, can be tolerated only on grounds of public convenience. . . . The rights of individuals ought not to yield to the exigencies of such a business more than the public interests require." See Taylor v. Church, 8 N. Y. 452, State v. Lansing, 18 Wis. 518, Ormsby v. Douglass, 37 N. Y. 477, Kingsbury v. Bradstreet, 35 Hun, 212, Lowry v. Vedder, 40 Minn. 475, 42 N. W. Rep. 542, Trussell v. Scarlett, 18 Fed. Rep. 214, Johnson v. The Bradstreet Co., 77 Ga. 172, Pollasky v. Minchener, 81 Mich. 280, 46 N. W. Rep. 5.

A pertinent answer to a confidential inquiry, though it communicates a defamatory charge, is privileged. But the sending and delivery of the answer must be done with proper caution and accuracy. Hubbard v. Rutledge, 57 Miss. 7, Allen v. Railroad Co., 100 N. C. 397, Beals v. Thompson, 149 Mass. 405, Klinck v. Colby, 46 N. Y. 427, Robinett v. Ruby, 13 Md. 95.

Also, where statements are volunteered but "where the relations of the parties are such as to afford reasonable ground for supposing innocent motives for giving the information," the communication is privileged. Bradstreet v. Gill, 72 Tex. 115, 9 S. W. Rep. 753, Park v. Detroit Free Press Co., 72 Mich. 560, 40 N. W. Rep. 731, Harper v. Harper, 10 Bush. 447, Parker v. McQueen, 8 B. Mon. 16, Erber v. Dunn, 12 Fed. Rep. 526, Alpin v. Morton, 21 Ohio St. 536, Perkins v. Mitchell 31 Barb. 461, Mott v. Dawson, 46 Ia. 533.

3. *Master and servant.* Any communication honestly made, relative

Answers to confidential inquiries, or to any inquiries made in the course of affairs for a reasonable purpose, are clearly privileged. So are communications made by a person to one to whom it is his especial duty to give information by virtue of a standing relation between them, as by a solicitor to his client about the soundness of a security, by a father to his daughter of full age about the character and standing of a suitor, and the like. Statements made without request and apart from any special relation of confidence may or may not be privileged according to the circumstances; but it cannot be prudently assumed that they will be (*j*). The nature of the interest for the sake of which the communication is made (as whether it be public or private, whether it is one touching the preservation of life, honour, or morals, or only matters of ordinary business), the apparent importance and urgency of the occasion, and other such points of discretion for which no general rule can be laid down, will all have their weight; how far any of them will outweigh the general presumption against officious interference must always be more or less doubtful (*k*).

Self-protection. Examples of privileged communications in self-protection, or the protection of a common interest, are a warning given by a master to his servants

---

(*j*) Cases of this kind have been very troublesome. See Blake Odgers 217—221.
(*k*) See *Coxhead v. Richards* (1846), 2 C. B. 569, 15 L. J. C. P. 278, where the Court was equally divided, rather as to the reasonably apparent urgency of the particular occasion than on any definable principle.

---

to the character of a former employee in reply to an inquiry from one to whom such servant has applied for employment is privileged. Terwilliger v. Wands, 17 N. Y. 54; Kennedy v. Gifford, 19 Wend. 298; Van Tassell v. Capron, 1 Denio, 250; Gassett v. Gilbert, 6 Gray, 94.

Self protection. Communications are privileged when made in self-defense, for example, if a man is attacked by a newspaper he may reply, but his reply must not be unnecessarily defamatory of his assailant and must be honestly made in self-defense. Chaffin v. Lynch, 83 Va. 106.

So, where the statement is invited by the plaintiff, as " where a mem-

not to associate with a former fellow-servant whom he has discharged on the ground of dishonesty (*l*); a letter from a creditor of a firm in liquidation to another of the creditors, conveying information and warning as to the conduct of a member of the debtor firm in its affairs (*m*). The holder of a public office, when an attack is publicly made on his official conduct, may defend himself with the like publicity (*n*).

Information for public good. Communications addressed in good faith to persons in a public position for the purpose of giving them information to be used for the redress

---

(*l*) Somerville v. Hawkins (1850), 10 C. B., 201, 1 C. L. R.

(*m*) Spill v. Maule 1869, L. R. Ch. R. 4 H. L. 232; 38 L. J. Ex. 138.

(*n*) Laughton v. Bishop of Sodor and Man (1872), L. R. 4 P. C. 495; 42 L. J. P. C. 11.

---

ber of a church had consented that the church should investigate any complaint which might be preferred against him in writing by a person not a member, it was held, that an action for a libel could not be sustained against such person making such complaint, without showing express malice." Remington v. Congdon, 2 Pick. 310. See Kirkpatrick v. Eagle Lodge, 26 Kan. 384; Fonville v. Nease, Dudley (S. C.), 303.

So, where there is any interest arising from the joint exercise of any legal right, privilege or duty, as that of two customers of the same bank or two creditors of the same debtor. Klinck v. Colby, 46 N. Y. 427; Gassett v. Gilbert, 6 Gray, 94; Shurtleff v. Stevens, 51 Vt. 501, 31 Am. Rep. 698; Shurtleff v. Parker, 130 Mass. 293, 39 Am. Rep. 454; Jarvis v. Hatheway, 3 Johns. 180; Combs v. Rose, 8 Blackf. 155; Rothholz v. Dunkle, 53 N. J. L. 438, 22 At. Rep. 193.

Information for public good. Petitions, memorials and all other proper communications of misconduct on the part of a public officer, to the authority having supervision of such office, are privileged communications.

In Gray v. Pentland (2 Serg. & R. 23, 4 Id. 10), it was held, that "Accusations preferred to the Governor against a person in office, are so far of the nature of judicial proceedings, that the accuser is not held to prove the truth of them." See Vanderzee v. McGregor, 12 Wend. 545, 27 Am. Dec. 156; Hay v. Reid, 85 Mich. 296; Kent v. Bongartz, 15 R. I. 72; Kimball v. Fernandez, 41 Wis. 329; Harris v. Harrington, 2 Tyler, 129; Elmer v. Fessenden, 151 Mass. 359, 22 N. E. Rep. 635; Wright v. Lathrop, 149 Mass. 385; Greenwood v. Cobbey, 26 Neb. 449, 42 N. W.

of grievances, the punishment of crime, or the security of public morals, are in like manner privileged, provided the subject-matter is at least reasonably believed to be within the competence of the person addressed (o). The communication to an incumbent of reports affecting the character of his curate is privileged, at all events if made by a neighbour or parishioner; so are consultations between the clergy of the immediate neighbourhood arising out of the same matter (p).

Rep. 119; Reid v. Delorme, 2 Brev. 76; Howard v. Thompson, 21 Wend. 319, 1 Am. Dec. 238; Bradley v. Heath, 12 Pick. 163, 22 Am. Dec. 418; Bodwell v. Osgood, 3 Pick. 379; Larkin v. Noonan, 19 Wis. 82.

But where a man exercises the citizen's right to denounce the action of a public officer, it is unlawful for him to make a false and malicious charge of crime or misdemeanor in office. Rowland v. DeCamp, 96 Pa. St. 493.

"Persons vested with the control of public institutions created by law, and having *quasi* judicial duties to discharge in respect to the public, are, while acting within the limits of their functions, *prima facie* exempt from liability for publications which would otherwise be defamatory," — trustees of a school. Following Howard v. Sexton, 4 N. Y. 159; Halstead v. Nelson, 36 Hun, 155. Same ruling applied to a medical society. McKnight v. Hasbrouck, 17 R. I. 70, 20 At. Rep. 95.

And to a secret society. Streety v. Wood, 15 Barb. 105. See Broughton v. McGrew, 39 Fed. Rep. 672. So with ecclesiastical matters, "If words actionable in themselves, be spoken between members of the same church, in the course of their religious discipline and without malice, no action will lie." Jarvis v. Hatheway, 3 Johns. 178, Am. Dec. 473; Lucas v. Case, 9 Bush, 297; Servatious v. Pichel, 34 Wis. 292; O'Donaghue v. McGovern, 23 Wend. 26; Chapman v. Calder, 14 Pa. St. 365; Farnsworth v. Storrs, 5 Cush. 412.

Fair reports. Fair reports (as distinguished from comment) are a distinct class of publications enjoying the protection of a "qualified privilege" to the extent to be mentioned. The fact that imputations have been made on a privileged occasion will, of course, not exempt from liability a person who repeats them on an occasion not privileged. Even if the original statement be made with circumstances of publicity, and be of the kind known as "absolutely privileged," it cannot be stated as a general rule that republication is justifiable. Certain specific immunities have been ordained by modern decisions and statutes. They rest on particular grounds, and are not to be extended (*q*). Matter not coming under any of them must stand on its own merits, if it can, as a fair comment on a subject of public interest.

Parliamentary papers. By statute (3 & 4 Vict. c. 9, A. D. 1840) the publication of any reports, papers, votes, or proceedings of either House of Parliament by the order or under the authority of that House is absolutely protected, and so is the republication in full. Extracts and abstracts are protected if in the opinion of the jury they were published *bona fide*, and without malice (*r*).

Parliamentary debates and judicial proceedings. Fair reports of parliamentary and public judicial proceedings are treated as privileged communications. It has long been settled (*s*) that fair and substantially accurate reports of proceedings in courts of justice are on this footing. As late as 1868 it was decided (*t*) that the same measure of

---

(*q*) See *Davis v. Shipstone* (1886), J. C. 11 App. Ca. 187, 55 L. J. P. C. 51.

(*r*) See Blake Odgers, *op. cit.* 185–6. The words of the Act, in their literal construction, appear to throw the burden of proving good faith on the publisher, which probably was not intended.

(*s*) Per cur. in *Wason v. Walter*, L. R. 4 Q. B. at p. 87.

(*t*) *Wason v. Walter* L. R. 4 Q. B. 73, 38 L. J. Q. B. 34. And editorial comments on a debate published by the same newspaper which publishes the report are entitled to the benefit of the general rule as to fair comment on public affairs *ib.* Cp. the German Federal Constitution, arts. 22, 30.

immunity extends to reports of parliamentary debates, notwithstanding that proceedings in Parliament are technically not public, and, still later, that it extends to fair reports of the quasi-judicial proceedings of a body established for public purposes, and invested with quasi-judicial authority for effecting those purposes (*u*). In the case of judicial proceedings it is immaterial whether they are preliminary or final, and, according to the prevailing modern opinion, whether contested or *ex parte*, and also whether the Court actually has jurisdiction or not, provided that it is acting in an apparently regular manner (*v*). The report need not be a report of the whole proceedings, provided it gives a fair and substantially complete account of the case, but whether it does give such an account has been thought to be a pure question of fact, even if the part which is separately reported be a judgment purporting to state the facts (*y*). The report must not in any case be partial to the extent of misrepresenting the judgment (*z*). It may be libellous to publish even a correct extract from a register of judgments in such a way as to suggest that a judgment is outstanding when it is in fact satisfied (*a*), but a correct copy of a document open to the public is not libellous without some such further defamatory addition (*aa*). By statute "a fair and accurate report in any newspaper of proceedings publicly heard before any court exercising judicial authority" is, "if published contemporaneously with such proceedings," privileged: which seems to mean

Allbutt v. General Council of Medical Education (1889), 23 Q. B. Div. 400, 58 L. J. Q. B. 606.

(*v*) *Usill v. Hales* (1878), 3 C. P. D. 319, 47 L. J. C. P. 323, where the proceeding reported was an application to a police magistrate, who, after hearing the facts stated, declined to act on the ground of want of jurisdiction. *Lewis v. Levy* (1858), 1 B. & El. 537, 27 L. J. Q. B. 282.

(*y*) *Macdougall v. Knight* (1889), 14 App. Ca. 194, 58 L. J. Q. B. 537. But in *Macdougall v. Knight* (1890), 25 Q. B. Div. 1, 59 L. J. Q. B. 517, the C. A. adhered to their previous view (17 Q. B. Div. 636, action between same parties) that a correct report of a judgment is privileged.

( ) *Haywood & Co. v. Haywood & Son* (1886), 34 Ch. D. 198, 56 L. J. Ch. 287.

(*a*) *Williams v. Smith* (1888), 22 Q. B. D. 134, 58 L. J. Q. B. 21.

(*aa*) *Searles v. Scarlett*, '92, 2 Q. B. 56, C. A., where the publication was expressly guarded: *qu.* as to *Williams v. Smith*, see it pp. 62, 63, 64.

absolutely privileged, as otherwise the statute would not add to the protection already given by the common law (*b*). The rule does not extend to justify the reproduction of matter in itself obscene, or otherwise unfit for general publication (*c*), or of proceedings of which the publication is forbidden by the Court in which they took place.

Volunteered reports. An ordinary newspaper report furnished by a regular reporter is all but conclusively presumed, if in fact fair and substantially correct, to have

---

(*b*) 51 & 52 Vict. c. 64, s. 4. The earlier cases are still material to show what is a fair and accurate report.

(*c*) Steele v. Brannan (1872), L. R. 7 C. P. 261 (a criminal case); 51 & 52 Vict. c. 64, s. 3.

Volunteered reports of public proceedings. It seems that a much larger liberty is exercised in this country than in England in the publication and criticism of the proceedings before public and judicial bodies. "So many municipal, parochial and other public corporations, so many large voluntary associations formed for almost every lawful purpose of benevolence, business or interest, are constantly holding meetings, in their nature public, and so usual is it that their proceedings are published for general use and information, that the law, to adapt itself to this necessary condition of society, must necessarily admit of these public proceedings and a just and proper publication of them, as far as it can be done consistently with private rights. * * * The general rule is, that any statement of wrongs and grievances, made by a party alleging himself injured thereby, though they affect the reputation and credit of another, if made to a tribunal or body having jurisdiction of the subject-matter, to inquire into the proceedings, and redress the grievance complained of, if found to exist, are not libelous, and that a fair statement of these proceedings when they have been acted upon and decided, made with an honest view of giving useful information and where the publication will not tend to obstruct the course of justice and interfere with a fair trial, is not libelous." Barrows v. Bell, 7 Gray, 312. See Story v. Wallace, 60 Ill. 51.

From what has been just said it may be reasonably concluded that fair reports of judicial proceedings are privileged. And this rule is true, as is clearly expressed in a brief quotation from the opinion of the court delivered in the case of Cincinnati Gazette Co. v. Timberlake (10 Ohio St. 552), as follows: "There is no doubt that a full, fair, and impartial report of a judicial trial, had in open court, where the parties interested have an opportunity of asserting and vindicating their rights, may be published with impunity. Such reports,

been published in good faith; but an outsider who sends to a public print even a fair report of judicial proceedings containing personal imputations invites the question whether he sent it honestly for purposes of information, or from a motive of personal hostility; if the latter is found to be the fact, he is liable to an action (*d*).

Newspaper reports of public meetings and of meetings of vestries, town councils, and other local authorities, and of their committees, of royal or parliamentary commissions, and of select committees, are privileged under the Law of Libel Amendment Act, 1888 (*e*). A public meeting is for this purpose "any meeting *bona fide* and lawfully held for a lawful purpose, and for the furtherance or discussion of any matter of public concern, whether the admission thereto be general or restricted." The defendant must not have refused on request to insert in the same newspaper a reasonable contradiction or explanation. Moreover "the publication of any matter not of public concern, and the publication of which is not for the public benefit," is not protected (*f*).

(*d*) Stevens v. Sampson (1879), 5 Ex. Div. 53, 44 L. J. Q. B. 120

(*e*) 51 & 52 Vict. c. 64, s. 1. The ill-drawn enactment of 1881 for the same purpose, 44 & 45 Vict. c. 61 s. 2, is repealed by sect. 2 of this Act. As to boards of guardians, see *Pittard* v. *Oliver*, '91, 1 Q. B. 474, 60 L. J. Q. B. 219, C. A.

(*f*) 51 & 52 Vict. c. 64, s. 4. In a civil action on whom is the burden of

---

unaccompanied by malicious and defamatory comment, have always been held privileged." But such reports must be confined to the actual proceedings, and must contain no defamatory headings or comments. Cowley *v* Pulsifer, 137 Mass. 392, Cone *v* Godshalk, 15 Phila Rep 575, Barker *v.* St Louis Dispatch Co., 3 Mo. App. 377, Scripps *v* Reilly, 35 Mich. 371, Pittock *v* O'Niell, 63 Pa St 253, 3 Am. Rep 544, Bissell *v* Press Pub Co., 62 Hun, 351, Johns *v* Press Pub Co., 19 N Y S Rep 3, Boehmer *v* Detroit Free Press Co., 94 Mich. 7, 53 N W Rep 822.

If such proceedings are *ex parte* merely, or indecent or blasphemous the privilege of reporting them is denied by law. See Terry *v* Fellows, 21 La An. 375, Torrey *v.* Field, 10 Vt 353, Saunders *v.* Baxter, 6 Heisk, 369, Sanford *v.* Bennett, 24 N Y. 20, McDermott *v.* The Evening Journal, 43 N J L 488.

Excess of privilege. In the case of privileged communications of a confidential kind, the failure to use ordinary means of ensuring privacy — as if the matter is sent on a post card instead of a sealed letter, or telegraphed without evident necessity — will destroy the privilege, either as evidence of malice, or because it constitutes a publication to persons in respect of whom there was not any privilege at all. The latter view seems on principle the better one (*g*). But the privilege of a person making a statement as matter of public duty at a meeting of a public body is not affected by unprivileged persons being present who are not there at his individual request or desire, or in any way under his individual control, though they may not have any strict right to be there, newspaper reporters for example (*h*). It would also seem that if a communication intended to be made on a privileged occasion is by the sender's negligence (as by putting letters in wrong envelopes) delivered to a person who is a stranger to that occasion, the sender has not any benefit of privilege. The contrary has been decided by a Divisional Court (*i*), but there is reason to think that the decision is by no means universally accepted in the profession as good law.

Honest belief is not necessarily reasonable belief. Where the existence of a privileged occasion is established, we have seen that the plaintiff must give affirmative proof of malice, that is, dishonest or reckless ill-will (*j*), in

proof as to this? See Blake Odgers 181-3, on the repealed section of 1881, where however this qualification was by way of condition and not by way of proviso.

(*g*) *Williamson* v. *Freer* (1874), L. R. 9 C. P. 39, 43 L. J. C. P. 161.

(*h*) *Pittard* v. *Oliver*, '91, 1 Q. B. 474, 60 L. J. Q. B. 219, C. A.

(*i*) *Tompson* v. *Dashwood* (1883), 11 Q. B. D. 43, 52 L. J. Q. B. 425.

(*j*) A statement made recklessly under the influence of e.g. gross prejudice against the plaintiff's occupation in general, though without any personal hostility towards him, may be malicious. *Royal Aquarium Society* v. *Parkinson*, '92, 1 Q. B. 431, C. A.

Excess of privilege. The doctrine stated in the text is sustained by the American authorities, for references to which, see *ante*, p. 333, note.

order to succeed. It is not for the defendant to prove that his belief was founded on reasonable grounds, and there is no difference in this respect between different kinds of privileged communication (*k*). To constitute malice there must be something more than the absence of reasonable ground for belief in the matter communicated. That may be evidence of reckless disregard of truth, but is not always even such evidence. A man may be honest and yet unreasonably credulous, or it may be proper for him to communicate reports or suspicions which he himself does not believe. In either case he is within the protection of the rule (*l*). It has been found difficult to impress this distinction upon juries, and the involved language of the authorities about "implied" and "express" malice has, no doubt, added to the difficulty. The result is that the power of the court to withhold a case from the jury on the ground of a total want of evidence has on this point been carried very far (*m*). In theory, however, the relation of the court to the jury is the same as in other questions of "mixed fact and law." Similar difficulties have been felt in the law of Negligence, as we shall see under that head.

Power of jury in assessing damages. In assessing damages the jury "are entitled to look at the whole conduct of the defendant from the time the libel was p

---

(*k*) *Jenoure v. Delmege*, '91, A. C. 73, 60 L. J. P. C. (J. C.)

(*l*) *Clark v. Molyneux* (1877), 3 Q. B. Div. 237, 47 L. J. Q. B. 230, per Bramwell L. J. at p. 244, per Brett L. J. at pp. 247 S., per Cotton L. J. at p. 249.

(*m*) *Laughton v. Bishop of Sodor and Man* (1872), L. R. 4 P. C. 495, 11 L. J. P. C. 11, and authorities there cited, *Spill v. Maule* (1869), Lx. Ch. L. R. 4 Lx. 232, 38 L. J. Ex. 138.

Power of jury in assessing damages. Supporting the text, *vide* Humphreys v. Parker, 52 Me. 502, Clarkson v. McCarty, 5 Blackf. 574, Broughton v. McGrew, 39 Fed. Rep. 672, Marks v. Jacobs, 76 Ind. 216, Henderson v. Fox, 83 Ga. 233, 9 S. E. Rep. 839, Lewis v. Chapman, 19 Barb. 252, Jones v. Greeley, 25 Fla. 629, 6 So. Rep. 448, Rogers v. Henry, 32 Wis. 627, Lowe v. Herald Co., 6 Utah, 175, 21 Pac. Rep. 991,

lished down to the time they gave their verdict. They may consider what his conduct has been before action, after action, and in court during the trial." And the verdict will not be set aside on the ground of the damages being excessive, unless the Court thinks the amount such as no twelve men could reasonably have given (n).

Special procedure in actions for newspaper libels. Lord Campbell's Act (6 & 7 Vict. c. 96, ss. 1, 2), contains special provisions as to proving the offer of an apology in mitigation of damages in actions for defamation, and payment into court together with apology in actions for libel in a public print (o).

Limits of interrogatories in action for libel. Where money has been paid into court in an action for libel, the plaintiff is not entitled to interrogate the defendant as to the sources of his information or the means used to verify it (p).

Bad reputation of plaintiff. A plaintiff's general bad repute cannot be pleaded as part of the defence to an

---

(n) *Praed v. Graham* (1889), 24 Q. B. Div. 53, 55.

(o) The Rules of Court of 1875 had the effect of enlarging and so far superseding the latter provision, but see now Order XXII. r. 1, and "The Annual Practice" thereon. See also 51 & 52 Vict. c. 64, s. 6.

(p) *Parnell v. Walter* (1890), 24 Q. B. D. 441.

Wimer v Allbaugh, 78 Ia 79, 42 N. W. Rep. 587, Kennedy v Woodrow, 6 Houst 46, Rutherford v Morning Journal Assoc., 47 Fed. Rep. 487 The verdict will not be interfered with unless grossly excessive Stafford v. Morning Journal Assoc., 68 Hun, 467, 22 N. Y. S. Rep. 1008, Rhodes v. Nagle, 66 Cal. 677, Wilson v Fitch, 41 Cal. 386, Holmes v. Jones, 69 Hun, 346, 23 N. Y. S. Rep. 631, Turner v. Stevens, 8 Utah, 75, 30 Pac Rep 24, Smith v Sun Pub. Co., 50 Fed. Rep. 399, Nunnally v Taliaferro, 82 Tex 286, 19 S. W. Rep. 149; Grace v. McArthur (Wis.), 45 N. W. Rep. 518.

action for defamation, for it is not directly material to the issue, but can be proved only in mitigation of damages(*q*)

Injunctions We have already seen (*r*) that an injunction may be granted to restrain the publication of defamatory matter, but, on an interlocutory application, only in a clear case (*r*), and not where the libel complained of is on the face of it too gross and absurd to do the plaintiff any material harm (*s*). Cases of this last kind may be more fitly dealt with by criminal proceedings

(*q*) *Wood* v *Durham* (1888), 21 Q B D 01, 57 L J Q B 547 [Walters v Smoot, 11 Ired 315, Burton v March, 6 Jones L 401, Bryan v Gurr, 27 Ga 578, Parkhurst v Ketchum, 6 Allen, 406, Powers v Presgroves, 38 Minn 227, Morey v Morning Journal Assoc , 123 N Y 207, 25 N E Rep 161]

(*r*) *Bonnard* v *Perryman*, '91, 2 Ch 269, 60 L J Ch 617, C A p 178, above, for a later example of injunction granted, see *Collard* v *Marshall*, '92, 1 Ch 571

(*s*) *Salomons* v *Knight*, '91, 2 Ch 294, 60 L J Ch 743, C A

Injunctions Contrary to the doctrine stated in the text, it is well settled in America that an injunction will not be granted to restrain libel or slander of title or reputation "Not that it is not a wrong, not that the wrong might not be irreparable, but simply because courts of chancery, in the exercise of the extraordinary powers lodged in them, have uniformly refused to act in such a case, leaving parties to their remedy at law * * * Equity, it must be remembered, will not enjoin every wrong There are injuries done by one man to another which no law will remedy. Telling lies, unless those of a peculiar character, is one of such injuries. * * * Libel and slander, however illegal and outrageous, will not be enjoined." The Singer, etc., Co *v* The Domestic, etc , Co , 49 Ga 73, 15 Am. Rep. 674

The exercise of this power by a court of equity would be repugnant to the provision of the constitution (Art. 1, § 8) which declares that every citizen may freely speak, write and publish his sentiments on all subjects, being responsible for the *abuse* of the right; and that no law shall be passed to restrain or abridge the liberty of speech or of the press. Guardian Soc *v* Roosevelt, 7 Daly, 191. See Maugher *v* Dick, 55 How Pr 132, Wetmore *v.* Scovell, 3 Edw. Ch. 515, Life Assoc *v* Boogher, 3 Mo App. 179, **Brandreth** *v.* **Lance**, 8 Paige, 23, 34 Am. Dec. 368. See *ante*, p 221

CHAPTER VIII.

WRONGS OF FRAUD AND MALICE.

I.— *Deceit.*

Nature of the wrong. In the foregoing chapters we dealt with wrongs affecting the so-called primary rights to security for a man's person, to the enjoyment of the society and obedience of his family, and to his reputation and good name. In these cases, exceptional conditions excepted, the knowledge or state of mind of the person violating the right is not material for determining his legal responsibility. This is so even in the law of defamation, as we have just seen, the artificial use of the word "malice" notwithstanding. We now come to a kind of wrongs in which either a positive wrongful intention, or such ignorance or indifference as amounts to guilty recklessness (in Roman terms either *dolus* or *culpa lata*) is a necessary element; so that liability is founded not in an absolute right of the plaintiff, but in the unrighteousness of the defendant.

Concurrent jurisdiction of common law and equity. The wrong called Deceit consists in leading a man into damage by wilfully or recklessly causing him to believe

---

Concurrent jurisdiction of common law and equity. In actions for deceit, in general, courts of law and courts of equity have concurrent jurisdiction. "It is admitted that in equity an actual design to mislead is not necessary if a party is actually misled by another in a bargain. * * * There is no reason for a difference in action in such cases between courts of law and courts of equity. Where an equitable

and act on a falsehood. It is a cause of action by the common law (the action being an action on the case founded on the ancient writ of deceit (a), which had a much narrower scope): and it has likewise been dealt with by courts of equity under the general jurisdiction of the Chancery in matters of fraud. The principles worked out in the two jurisdictions are believed to be identical (b), though there may be a theoretical difference as to the character of the remedy, which in the Court of Chancery did not purport to be damages but restitution (c). Since 1875, therefore, we have in this case a real and perfect fusion of rules of common law and equity which formerly were distinct, though parallel and similar.

Difficulties of the subject. complication with contract. The subject has been one of considerable difficulty for several reasons.

First, the law of tort is here much complicated with the

(a) F. N. B. 95 E sqq
(b) See per Lord Chelmsford, L. R. 6 H. L. at p 390
(c) See p. 227, above.

---

cause of grievance exists, it in no way differs from a legal one unless a different remedy is needed. A court of law cannot cancel a contract, and for such a purpose the equitable remedy must be sought. But where the relief desired is compensation for the wrong, the equitable remedy is much less appropriate, and an action in equity for mere damages will generally be denied, but denied only because the legal remedy is better. If there could be no legal remedy, there can be no doubt that equity would act. If the fraud is such that it creates a right of action anywhere, an action must lie on the case where a money judgment is needed." Holcomb v. Noble, 69 Mich. 397; 37 N. W. Rep. 497 See Matlock v Reppy, 47 Ark. 148, 14 S W Rep. 546; Smith v McIver, 9 Wheat. 532, Tomlin v. Cox, 4 Harr. (N. J) 76, Skine v. Simmons, 11 Ga. 401, Gilbert v. Borgatt, 10 Johns. 457.

There are, however, variances from this rule, but the authorities assuming to point out the distinction separating cases of law and of equity are not uniform Hazard v. Irwin, 18 Pick. 95; Burrows v. Alter, 7 Mo. 424, Higgs v. Smith, 3 A K. Marsh 338; Rogers v. Colt, 1 Zab. 713.

Dece*t* in connection with contract. In the execution of contracts good faith on the part of all the parties is required by law. "The con-

law of contract. A false statement may be the inducement to a contract, or may be part of a contract, and in those capacities may give rise to a claim for the rescission

---

tracting parties are bound to deal honestly and act in good faith with each other. There should be a reciprocity of candor and fairness. Both shall have equal knowledge concerning the subject matter of the contract; especially ought all the facts and circumstances which are likely to influence their action to be made known. If they have not mutually this knowledge, nor the same means of obtaining it, it is then a duty incumbent on the one having the superior information to disclose it to the other. In making the disclosure, he is bound to act in good faith and with regard to truth If he makes false representations regarding material facts, or intentionally conceals or suppresses them he acts fraudulently, and renders himself responsible for the consequences which may result." Mitchell v McDougall, 62 Ill. 501

And it is also true, that " The misrepresentation in order to affect the validity of the contract must relate to some matter of inducement to the making of the contract, in which from the relative position of the parties and their means of information, the one must necessarily be presumed to contract upon the faith and trust which he reposes in the representations of the other, on account of his superior information and knowledge in regard to the subject of the contract; for if the means of information are alike accessible to both, so that with ordinary prudence or vigilance the parties might rely upon their own judgment they must be presumed to have done so; or if they have not so informed themselves, must abide the consequences of their own inattention and carelessness. Such representations, therefore, to amount to fraud must have a decided and reliable character, holding out inducements to make the contract, calculated to mislead the purchaser and induce him to buy on the faith and confidence of the representations, and in the absence of such means of information to be derived from his own observation and inspection, and from which he could draw conclusions to guide him in making the contract independent of the representations of the vendor " Mr. Justice Walker in Yeates v Pryor, 11 Ark 58 See Mooney v. Miller, 102 Mass. 220; Morse v Dearborne, 109 Mass 593, Melville v. Gary, 76 Md 221, 24 A. Rep 604, Dargan v Ellis, 81 Tex. 194, Wimer v Smith, 22 Oreg. 469, 30 Pac. Rep 416, Davidson v Wheeler, 17 R. I. 433; 22 At. Rep. 1022, 2 Kent's Com 482, Hobbs v. Parker, 81 Me. 143, Stanhope v Swafford, 80 Ia 45, 45 N W. Rep. 403, Phelps v James, 79 Ia 262, 47 N. W Rep. 543

By the civil law the seller, by the very nature of the contract of sale, became bound in an implied warranty that the thing sold was exempt from defects, without any reference to his knowledge of them. But the common law of sales is different. "Here there is no implied warranty

of the contract obtained by its means, or for compensation for breach of the contract or of a collateral warranty. A false statement unconnected with any contract may like-

---

against defects unless there be fraud by some false representation or undue concealment." McAdams v Cates, 24 Mo. 224. "If a seller of goods deceives the buyer as to their quality, the buyer cannot avail himself of the deceit in defence against an action for their price, or reduction of damages therein, if the quality was open to his own observation and with ordinary diligence and prudence he could have ascertained it Brown v. Leach, 107 Mass. 364. On the other hand, "It is the duty of a vendor to disclose any defect in the article which he is vending, unless it is palpable to the purchaser." Singleton v Kennedy, 9 B. Mon 225. See Lobdell v Baker, 1 Metc 193. The fraudulent concealment by the vendor of a secret defect in an article sold by him, wholly unknown to the vendee, may be the foundation of an action for damages by him against the vendor, and perhaps authorize the vendee to rescind the contract on discovery of the fraud; because the law implies a warranty that the goods or articles sold are of a merchantable quality." Cross v. Peters, 1 Mo 393, Hazard v. Irwin, 18 Pick. 105. See Tyre v Causey, 4 Harr. (Del) 425, Fisher v Mellen, 103 Mass. 503, Rice v. Barrett, 116 Ill. 312, Hillman v Wilcox, 30 Mo. 170; McGregor v. Penn, 9 Yerg. 74, Tewkesbury v. Bennett, 31 Ia. 83; Iron Works v Moore, 78 Ill. 65, Stone v Covell, 29 Mich 359, Hawkins v. Pemberton, 51 N Y. 198, Morrill v Wallace, 9 N. H. 111; Chapman v Murch, 19 Johns. 290, Hubbell v Meigs, 50 N. Y. 491; Lomerson v. Johnston, 47 N. J. Eq. 312, 20 At. Rep. 675

"In the case of sale of property, the law presumes that the purchaser reposes confidence in the vendor, as to all such defects as are not within the reach of ordinary observation and therefore it imposes the duty on the vendor to disclose fully and fairly his knowledge of all such defects. But in ordinary cases, the vendor reposes no such confidence in the purchaser. The former does not look to the latter for information in regard to the qualities or condition of the thing sold, and is not deceived or misled by any information the latter may have in regard to it. And hence it has been held, that a purchaser may use any information he may have in regard to property, for his own advantage, without disclosing it, provided he does nothing to mislead or deceive." Likewise, it is true that the vendee is not, in general, bound to communicate to the vendor, intelligence of extrinsic circumstances, exclusively within the knowledge of the vendee, which may affect the price of the goods transferred Laidlaw v Organ, 2 Wheat. 178. See Kintzing v McElrath, 5 Pa St 467.

It is a rule of law no doubt as long established as the existence of fraud itself that fraudulent representation of material facts relating to subject of a contract render it invalid. Bond v. Ramsey, 89 Ill 29; Durkin

who create, by way of estoppel, an obligation analogous to contract. And a statement capable of being regarded in one or more of these ways may at the same time afford a cause of action in tort for deceit. "If, when a man thinks it highly probable that a thing exists, he chooses to say he knows the thing exists, that is really asserting what is false: it is positive fraud. That has been repeatedly laid down. . . . If you choose to say, and say without inquiry, 'I warrant that,' that is a contract. If you say, 'I know it,' and if you say that in order to save the trouble of inquiry, that is a false representation — you are saying what is false to induce them to act upon it" (d).

The grounds and results of those forms of liability are largely similar, but cannot be assumed to be identical. The authorities establishing what is a cause of action for deceit are to a large extent convertible with those which define the right to rescind a contract for fraud or misrepresentation, and the two classes of cases used to be cited without any express discrimination. We shall see however that discrimination is needful.

(d) Lord Blackburn, *Brownlie v. Campbell* (1880), 5 App. Ca. (Sc.) at p. 593.

---

v. Cobleigh, 156 Mass. 108, 30 N. E Rep. 474, High v Berrett, 148 Pa. St 261, 23 At. Rep 1004, 30 W. N C 31, Winter v. Bandel, 30 Ark 372 But fraudulent representations, relating not to the subject-matter of the contract, but to mere matters of collateral inducement, will not justify the setting aside of a contract or conveyance. Hill v. Bush, 19 Ark. 322

It has been held that misrepresentations in insurance cases, made by the insured, innocently, will not avoid the policy. "In order to defeat the contract the representations or answers to questions must be known to be false by the insured" Mut Ben Life Ins. Co. v. Robertson, 59 Ill 123. But the general rule seems to be to the contrary. Aetna Life Ins. Co. v. France, 91 U. S 510, Vose v. Eagle Life Ins. Co., 6 Cush. 42, Mut. Ben Life Ins Co. v. Cannon, 48 Ind. 264 "Thus, the answers contained in the application being in the nature of representations only, the question is of their substantial and not their literal truth. To defeat the policy they must be shown to be materially untrue, or untrue in some particular material to the risk." Campbell v N. E. Mut. Life Ins. Co, 98 Mass 395.

Questions of fraudulent intent Secondly, there are difficulties as to the amount of actual fraudulent intention that must be proved against a defendant. A man may be,

---

Fraudulent intent In general it may be said that fraudulent intent is essential to sustain an action of deceit. "Fraudulent intent is the gist of the action" Kootz v. Kaufman, 31 Mo App. 420. Such intent may be proved by evidence. This, however, is often difficult, or presumed by law. "In order to sustain an action for deceit, the fraudulent intent must be established, but it may be inferred from the fact that the false statements are made with knowledge of their falsity. And where a party who may be presumed to know, or who is in a position to know, the truth, deliberately makes unqualified representations in respect to a material matter, in such manner as to import knowledge by him of their truth, for the purpose of inducing another to act upon them, a similar inference may arise and, in such case, if a party has acted in reliance on such representations, he is entitled to maintain an action for the injury sustained thereby." Haven v. Neal, 43 Minn. 316. See Hubbard v. Weare, 79 Ia. 678, 44 N W. Rep. 915, First Nat Bank v. North (S. Dak), 51 N. W. Rep. 96; McIntyre v. Buell, 132 N Y. 192, 30 N. E. Rep. 896, Marshall v. Hubbard, 117 U S. 415, Barnett v Stanton, 2 Ala. 187; Edick v. Crim, 10 Barb. (N Y.), 445

On the other hand, where one innocently makes a representation to another which results in that other's deception and injury it is obviously unfortunate for both and the damage done cannot be adjusted without working a hardship on one or both of them, but as the policy of the law is to make persons responsible for their acts and utterances the majority of the decisions are to the effect that such injuries must be compensated. "A misrepresentation of a material fact, innocently made, but which acts as an inducement to the act of another, who is thereby injured, is a fraud which can be relieved in equity." Davis v. Heard, 44 Miss 477 "The doctrine is settled here by a long line of cases, that if there was in fact a misrepresentation, though made innocently, and its deceptive influence was effective, the consequences to the plaintiff being as serious as though it had proceeded from a vicious purpose, he would have a right of action for the damage caused thereby either at law or in equity." Holcomb v Noble, 69 Mich. 396, 37 N. W. Rep. 497, citing Baughman v Gould, 45 Mich. 483; 8 S. W. Rep 73, Converse v. Blumrich, 14 Mich 109, Steinback v. Hill, 25 Id 78, Webster v Baily, 31 Id. 36, Starkweather v Benjamin, 32 Id 305, and followed in Totten v Burhans, 91 Mich. 495, 51 N W Rep. 1119. So in Missouri. Ring v. Vogel Paint & Glass Co , 44 Mo App 111, but see Dunaley v. Rogers, 64 Mo. 203. So in Wisconsin Burke v Milwaukee etc. Ry. Co., 83 Wis 410, 53 N W. Rep 692

The question of fraudulent intent is usually one for the jury. Meyer

to all practical intents, deceived and led into loss by relying on words or conduct of another which did not proceed from any set purpose to deceive, but perhaps from an unfounded expectation that what he stated or suggested would be justified by the event. In such a case it seems hard that the party misled should not have a remedy, and yet there is something harsh in saying that the other is guilty of fraud or deceit. An over-sanguine and careless man may do as much harm as a deliberately fraudulent one, but the moral blame is not equal. Again, the jurisdiction of courts of equity in these matters has always been said to be founded on fraud. Equity judges, therefore, were unable to frame a terminology which should clearly distinguish fraud from culpable misrepresentation not amounting to fraud, but having similar consequences in law; and on the contrary they were driven, in order to maintain and extend a righteous and beneficial jurisdiction, to such vague and confusing phrases as "constructive fraud," or "conduct fraudulent in the eyes of this Court." Thus they obtained in a cumbrous fashion the results of the bolder Roman maxim *culpa lata dolo aequiparatur*. The results were good, but, being so obtained, entailed the cost of much laxity in terms and some laxity of thought. Of late years there has been a reaction against this habit, wholesome in the main, but not free from some danger of excess. "Legal fraud" is an objectionable term, but it does not follow that it has no real meaning (e). One might as well say that the "common counts" for money had and received, and the like, which before the Judicature Acts were annexed to most declarations in contract, disclosed no real cause of action, because the "contract implied in law"

(e) See per Lord Bramwell, *Weir v Bell,* 3 Ex D at p 243, *Derry v Peek,* 14 App Ca. at p 346

v Amidon, 23 Hun, 533, Hazard v Irwin, 18 Pick 95, Salisbury v. Howe, 27 N. Y. 128, Page v. Bent, 2 Metc. 371, Cowley v. Smith, 46 N J. L. 280; Humphrey v. Merriam, 32 Minn. 197; 20 N. W. Rep. 138.

which they supposed was not founded on any actual request or promise.

Fraud of agents. Thirdly, special difficulties of the same kind have arisen with regard to false statements made by an agent in the course of his business and for his principal's purposes, but without express authority to make such statements. Under these conditions it has been thought harsh to hold the principal answerable; and there is a further aggravation of difficulty in that class of cases (perhaps the most important) where the principal is a corporation, for a corporation has been supposed not to be capable of a fraudulent intention. We have already touched on this point (*f*); and the other difficulties appear to have been surmounted, or to be in the way of being surmounted by our modern authorities.

General conditions of the right of action. Having indicated the kind of problems to be met with, we proceed to the substance of the law.

To create a right of action for deceit there must be a statement made by the defendant, or for which he is answerable as principal, and with regard to that statement all the following conditions must concur:

(a) It is untrue in fact.
(b) The person making the statement, or the person responsible for it, either knows it to be untrue, or is culpably ignorant (that is, recklessly and consciously ignorant) (*g*) whether it be true or not.
(c) It is made to the intent that the plaintiff shall act upon it, or in a manner apparently fitted to induce him to act upon it (*h*).

(*f*) P 66, above. The difficulties may be said to have culminated in *Udell* v *Atherton* (1861), 7 H & N. 172, 30 L J. Ex. 337, where the Court was equally divided.

(*g*) Lord Herschell, *Derry* v. *Peek* (1889), 14 App Ca at p 371.
(*h*) See *Polhill* v. *Walter*, 3 B. & Ad. 114, 123.

(d) The plaintiff does act in reliance on the statement in the manner contemplated or manifestly probable, and thereby suffers damage (*i*).

There is no cause of action without both fraud (*j*) and actual damage, or the damage is the gist of the action (*k*).

And according to the general principles of civil liability, the damage must be the natural and probable consequence of the plaintiff's action on the faith of the defendant's statement.

(e) The statement must be in writing and signed in one class of cases, namely where it amounts to a guaranty. but this requirement is statutory, and as it did not apply to the Court of Chancery, does not seem to apply to the High Court of Justice in its equitable jurisdiction.

Of these heads in order.

Falsehood in fact. (a) A statement can be untrue in fact only if it purports to state matter of fact. A promise is distinct from a statement of fact, and breach of contract,

---

(*i*) Cp for the general rules Lord Hatherley (Page Wood V C), *Barry* v *Croskey* (1861), 2 J & H at pp 22-3, ap proved by Lord Cairns in *Peek* v. *Gurney*, L R 6 H L at p 413, Bowen L J, *Edgington* v *Fitzmaurice* (1885), 29 Ch Div at pp 481-2, and Lindley L J,

Smith v *Chadwick* (1882), 20 Ch. Div. at p 75

(*j*) *Derry* v *Peek* (1889), 14 App Ca 337, 374, 58 L J. Ch 864

(*k*) Lord Blackburn, *Smith* v *Chadwick* (1884), 9 App Ca at p 196

Falsehood in fact Promises and other representations made as to facts that will probably transpire in the future are mere expressions of opinion and when false cannot be made the ground of actions for deceit Gallagher *v* Brunel, 6 Cow. 347; Markel *v.* Mondy, 11 Neb 213, Pedrick *v* Porter, 5 Allen, 324, Saunders *v* McClintock, 46 Mo App 216, Farrar *v.* Bridges, 3 Humph 566, Murray *v.* Beckwith, 48 Ill. 891; Lexow *v.* Julian, 21 Hun, 577, Burt *v.* Bowles, 69 Ind. 1; Sieveking *v.* Litzle, 31 Id. 13, Long *v.* Woodman, 58 Me. 49 These representations of facts to come into existence in the future are such as are based upon general knowledge, information, and judgment, as distinguished from representations which, from knowledge peculiarly a party's own, for he may certainly know whether they are true or false. Sawyer *v.* Prickett, 19 Wall. 146. For a specific promise that a certain thing will or will not be

whether from want of power or of will to perform one's promise, is a different thing from deceit. Again a mere

done in the future, when made fraudulently, may be the means of effecting a cheat, and is actionable if injury results. Wilson v Eggleston, 27 Mich 257, Laing v. McKee, 13 Mich. 124, Goodwin v. Horne, 60 N. H. 485 Richardson v. Adams, 10 Yerg. 273; Gross v. McKee, 53 Miss. 536, Dowd v. Tucker, 41 Conn 197; Kimball v. Insurance Co., 9 Allen, 540, Morrill v. Blackman, 42 Conn 324, Rawdon v Blatchford, 1 Sandf. 344; Schufeldt v. Schlutzier, 21 Hun, 462; Johnson v. Monell, 2 Keyes, 663, Buckley v. Artcher, 21 Barb 585, Eaton v. Avery, 83 N. Y. 31.

A mere false assertion as a matter of opinion, which does not imply knowledge, is not generally deceit in law One reposes at his peril in the opinions of others when he has equal opportunity to form and exercise his own judgment

An expression of judgment or opinion does not amount to a warranty. Saunders v. Hatterman, 2 Ired. 32, McBeth v Craddock, 28 Mo. App 392, Medbury v Watson, 6 Metc 246, Ellis v. Andrews, 56 N. Y 83, Marshall v. Peck, 1 Dana, 611; Morrill v. Wallace, 9 N. H. 111; Dungan v. Coreton, 1 Ark 41, Frenzee v Miller, 37 Ind. 1, Fulton v. Hood, 34 Pa St 365, Roobins v Barton, 50 Kan. 120, 30 Pac. Rep. 686, Bristol v Braidwood, 28 Mich 191; Lehman v Shackelford, 50 Ala. 437, Payne v. Smith, 20 Ga 654, Sieveking v Litzlei, 31 Ind. 13, Mahurin v. Harding, 28 N H 32, Rowell v. Chase, 61 N. H 135, Darlin v. Stewart, 63 Vt. 575, 22 At Rep. 634; Nash v. Minnesota T. G. Co. (Mass.), 34 N. E. Rep. 625. But it might be otherwise if in connection with the expression of opinion there were false assertions of fact, calculated, if true, to give a basis for the opinion. McAleer v Horsey, 35 Md 439, Dargan v. Ellis, 81 Tex. 194, 16 S W Rep 789.

In the New York case of Chrysler v Canaday (90 N. Y 272), Miller J, in delivering the opinion of the court, said· "The rule is well settled that a naked assertion by a vendor of the value of the property offered for sale, even although untrue of itself and known to be such by him, unless there is a want of knowledge by the vendee, and the sale is made in entire reliance upon the representations made, or unless some artifice is employed to prevent inquiry or the obtaining of knowledge by the vendee, will not render the vendor responsible to the vendee for damages sustained by him." Therefore, for a vendor to assert that the lands he is negotiating to sell are of a particular value, greatly above their real worth, or to exaggerate their fertility or other good qualities, is no fraud. Holton v. Noble, 83 Cal 7; 23 Pac. Rep. 58, Sherwood v Salmon, 2 Day, 128; King v Mills, 10 Allen, 548, Barnett v Stanton, 2 Ala. 187; Mooney v. Miller, 102 Mass. 217, Manning v. Albee, 11 Allen, 520; Schumaker v. Mather, 133 N Y 590, 30 N. E 755, Gordan v Parmalle, 35 Ill App. 212; Credle v Swindle, 63 N. C 305; Simon v Canaday, 53 N Y. 298; 13 Am. Rep. 523, Holbrook v. Connor,

statement of opinion or inference, the facts on which it purports to be founded being notorious or equally known

60 Me. 578; Wilkinson v. Clauson, 29 Minn. 91; Hartman v. Flaherty, 80 Ind 472; Shade v. Creviston, 96 Ind. 491, Griel v Lomax, 86 Ala. 132; 5 So. Rep. 325; 6 La. Rep 741; Schumaker v. Mather, 133 N Y. 590; 30 N. E. Rep. 755 It is held by some courts that statements of value with intent to deceive are actionable. Cruess v Fessler, 89 Cal. 836; Gifford v. Carvell, 29 Cal. 589; Davis v. Jackson, 22 Ind. 283, Van Epps v. Harrison, 5 Hill, 63, Bradley v. Bosley, 1 Barb. 125, McAleer v. Horsey, 35 Md. 430; McFadden v. Robinson, 35 Ind. 24, Morehead v Eades, 3 Bush, 121; *Compare* Tuck v Downing, 76 Ill. 71, Hemner v Cooper, 8 Allen, 334, Cooper v. Lovering, 106 Mass 77.

A vendee of lands has a right to rely upon the positive statements of the vendor, as to the *quantity* of land bought. Hill v Brower, 76 N. C. 124, Cullum v. Branch Bank, 4 Ala 21, Sangster v. Prather, 34 Ind 504, Boon v Atwell, 46 N H 510, Whitney v. Allaire, 1 N. Y 305; Beardsley v. Duntley, 69 N. Y. 577; Starkweather v Benjamin, 32 Mich 305, Duncan v. Cobly, 139 Mass. 398; 1 N. E. 474 So, also, in respect to boundaries of land. Sanford v. Handy, 23 Wend 260, Weatherford v. Fishoack, 4 Ill. 170, Clark v. Baird, 9 N Y 183.

But there are exceptions to the general rule as above announced, as where there exist between the parties such relations of confidence that one would rely upon the opinion of the other in sincerity. Fisher v Budlong, 10 R. I 525; Tolman v. Smith, 43 Ill App. 562. Or where the party making the representations, makes them as the opinion of an expert and the party to whom the representations are made has not equal means of knowledge and relies upon the statement made to him Kost v Bender, 25 Mich 515, McGar v Williams, 26 Ala 467. Thus the purchaser of goods, the value of which can only be known to experts, may rely upon the vendor, who is a dealer in such goods, to speak the truth concerning them. Stewart v. Sterns, 63 N. H. 99; Collins v Jackson, 54 Id. 186; Pickard v. McCormick, 11 Id. 68, Pike v Fay, 101 Mass 134; Bradbury v Haines, 60 N. H 123; Hanger v. Evins, 38 Ark. 384; Weidner v Phillips, 39 Hun, 1; Grim v. Byrd, 32 Gratt 293; Loewer v Harris, 57 Fed. Rep. 368. The purchaser of a mill, who is ignorant of the business, but relies upon the positive statements of the owner as to its capacity and profitableness, has a remedy for deceit if the assertions are false Wise v Fuller, 29 J. J Eq 257. See Chase v. Broughton, 93 Mich. 285, 54 N. W Rep. 44 The same rule applies to sales of patents by dealers therein. Allen v Hart, 72 Ill. 104, Pefley v. Noland, 80 Ind 1 64, McKee v. Eaton, 26 Kan 226. See Long v Woodman, 58 Me. 49, Holbrook v. Connor, 60 Id 578; Banta v Palmer, 47 Ill 599; Hunter v McLaughlin, 43 Ind. 38; Dillman v Nadlehoffer, 119 Ill. 567; Bishop v Small, 63 Me. 12 False representation by one selling out his business, whether innocently or fraudulently made, that certain accounts

to both parties, is different from a statement importing that certain matters of fact are within the particular knowledge of the speaker. A man cannot hold me to account because he has lost money by following me in an opinion which turned out to be erroneous. In particular cases, however, it may be hard to draw the line between a mere expression of opinion and an assertion of specific fact (*k*). And a man's intention or purpose at a given time is in itself a matter of fact, and capable (though the proof be seldom easy) of being found as a fact. "The state of a man's mind is as much a fact as the state of his digestion" (*l*). It is settled that the vendor of goods can rescind the contract on the ground of fraud if he discovers within due time that the buyer intended not to pay the price (*m*).

When a prospectus is issued to shareholders in a company or the like to invite subscriptions to a loan, a statement of the purposes for which the money is wanted — in

---

(*k*) Compare *Pasley* v. *Freeman* (1789), 3 T. R 51, 1 R R. 634, with *Haycraft* v *Creasy* (1801), 2 East, 92, 6 R R 180, where Lord Kenyon's dissenting judgment may be more acceptable to the latter day reader than those of the majority

(*l*) Bowen L. J , 29 Ch Div 483

(*m*) *Clough* v *L and N W R Co* (1871), Ex. Ch L. R. 7 Ex 26, 41 L J Ex 17, op. per Mellish L J , *Ex parte Whittaker* (1875), 10 Ch at p 449 Whether in such case an action of deceit would lie is a merely speculative question, as if rescission is impracticable, and if the fraudulent buyer is worth suing, the obviously better course is to sue on the contract for the price See however *Williamson* v *Allison* (1802), 2 East, 146

---

included in the sale of his interest were collectible, entitle the purchaser to damages Totten *v.* Burhans, 91 Mich 495, 51 N W. 1119 See Crane *v* Elder, 48 Kan. 259, 29 Pac. Rep. 151.

One making false statements relative to the value of shares of stock in an incorporated company which he is selling, or exaggerated statements of the profits and prospects of the company, is not liable to an action for deceit. Ellis *v.* Andrews, 56 N. Y. 83; 15 Am. Rep. 379, Crook *v.* Cole, 10 Ind 485, Walker *v.* Mobile, etc. R. Co , 34 Miss 245, Markel *v.* Moody, 11 Neb. 213, Robinson *v.* Parks, 76 Md 118; 24 At Rep. 411 But "A false and fraudulent representation made with intent to deceive, as to material facts which necessarily affect the value of shares of stock in a corporation, constitutes a cause of action against the person making it, where by means thereof he has induced another to purchase such shares " Schwenk *v.* Naylor, 102 N. Y 683. See Gibson *v* Cunningham, 92 Mo 131, 5 S. W. Rep 12; Miller *v.* Curtis, 13 N. Y. S Rep. 604

other words, of the borrower's intention as to its application — is a material statement of fact, and if untrue may be ground for an action of deceit (*n*). The same principle would seem to apply to a man's statement of the reasons for his conduct, if intended or calculated to influence the conduct of those with whom he is dealing (*o*); as if an agent employed to buy falsely names, not merely as the highest price he is willing to give, but as the actual limit of his authority, a sum lower than that which he is really empowered to deal for.

Misrepresentations of law. A representation concerning a man's private rights, though it may involve matters of law, is as a whole deemed to be a statement of fact.

(*n*) *Edgington* v *Fitzmaurice* (1884), 29 Ch Div 459, 55 L J Ch 650

(*o*) It is submitted that the contrary opinion given in *Vernon* v. *Keys* (1810), Ex Ch 4 Taunt. 488, can no longer be considered law

---

Misrepresentations of law. The American authorities are in harmony with the text. For example, in Upton *v* Tribilcock (91 U S. 45), where an agent procuring subscriptions for stock of a corporation, represented that the subscribers would be liable for a certain percentage of the stock but the law made them responsible for the whole amount of the shares; it was held that a subscriber cannot defend on the ground of fraud. "There was here no error, mistake, or misrepresentation of any fact The defendant made the subscription he intended to make, and received the certificate he had stipulated for, * * * But in law the defendant incurred a larger liability than he anticipated." S. P, Ogilvie *v*. Knox Ins Co, 22 How. 380. See Steamboat Belfast *v.* Boon & Co 41 Ala. 50, Jagar *v.* Winslow, 30 Minn. 263; Townsend *v.* Cowles, 31 Ala. 428, Cowles *v.* Townsend, 37 Id. 77; Clem *v.* Newcastle, etc. R Co., 9 Ind. 488; Insurance Co. *v* Reed, 33 Ohio St. 283, Lexow *v.* Julian, 21 Hun, 577; Russell *v* Branham, 8 Blackf. 277, People *v.* Supervisors of San Francisco, 27 Cal. 655, Gormeley *v.* Gym. Assoc , 55 Wis. 350; Rogers *v* Place, 29 Ind 577.

But the rule does not apply to a case where there is an inseparable connection between false statements of law and fact. As where the holder of a note, the remedy upon which is barred by the statute, goes to the administrator of one of the two makers, and by representing it to be unpaid, and valid, and in full force in the law, procures a bond for the judgment of one-half thereof. Brown *v.* Rice's Admr , 26 Gratt. 467. So, a party can obtain redress when he has been induced to execute

Where officers of a company incorporated by a private Act of Parliament accept a bill in the name of the company, this is a representation that they have power so to do under the Act of Parliament, and the existence or non-existence of such power is a matter of fact. "Suppose I were to say I have a private Act of Parliament which gives me power to do so and so. Is not that an assertion that I have such an Act of Parliament? It appears to me to be as much a representation of a matter of fact as if I had said I have a particular bound copy of Johnson's Dictionary" (*p*). A statement about the existence or actual text of a public Act of Parliament, or a reported decision, would seem to be no less a statement of fact. With regard to statements of matters of general law made only by implication, or statements of pure propositions of the law, the rule may perhaps be this, that in dealings between parties who have equal means of ascertaining the law, the one will not be presumed to rely upon a statement of matter of law made by the other (*q*). It has never been decided whether

---

(*p*) *West London Commercial Bank* v. *Kitson* (1884), 13 Q B Div 360, per Bowen L. J at p 363, 53 L J Q B 345 Cp *Firbank's Executors* v *Humphreys* (1886), 18 Q B. Div 54, 56 L. J Q B. 57 (director's assertion of subsisting authority to issue debentures)

(*q*) This appears to be the real ground of *Rashdall* v *Ford* (1866), 2 Eq 750, 35 L J Ch. 769

---

bill of exchange, supposing it be an ordinary promissory note, from misrepresentations made by the other party Ross v. Drinkard, 35 Ala. 434, and in this case the following quotation from Townsend v. Cowles, (31 Ala 428) is approved· "If the defendant was in fact ignorant of the law, and the other party knowing him to be so and knowing the law, took advantage of such ignorance to mislead him by a false statement of the law, it would constitute a fraud."

In negotiations between parties holding confidential relations, false statements of the law may be actionable for deceit practiced. Cooke v Nathan, 16 Barb. 342; State v. Holloway, 8 Blackf. 45; Sims v. Ferrill, 45 Ga 585, Porter v. Wright, 6 Ind 183. As where an immigrant went to a certain country and there met an old friend, who professed to know all about the lands and titles thereto, and who sold him lands and asserted that the title was perfect, but which proved incorrect *Held*, that the buyer had redress for the deceit. Moreland v. Atchison, 19 Tex. 303.

proof of such reliance is admissible; it is submitted that if the case arose it could be received, though with caution. Of course a man will not in any event be liable to an action of deceit for misleading another by a statement of law, however erroneous, which at the time he really believed to be correct. That case would fall into the general category of honest though mistaken expressions of opinion. If there be any ground of liability, it is not fraud but negligence, and it must be shown that the duty of giving competent advice had been assumed or accepted.

Falsehood by garbled statements. It remains to be noted that a statement of which every part is literally true may be false as a whole, if by reason of the omission of material facts it is as a whole calculated to mislead a person ignorant of those facts into an inference contrary to the truth (*r*). "A suppression of the truth may amount to a suggestion of falsehood" (*s*).

Knowledge or belief of defendant. (b) As to the knowledge and belief of the person making the statement. He may believe it to be true (*t*). In that case he incurs

---

(*r*) "There must, in my opinion, be some active misstatement of fact, or at all events such a partial and fragmentary statement of fact as that the withholding of that which is not stated makes that which is stated absolutely false." Lord Cairns, L R 6 H L 403

(*s*) *Stewart* v. *Wyoming Ranche Co* (1888), 128 U S 383, 388

(*t*) *Collins* v *Evans* (1844), Ex Ch 5 Q. B 820, 13 L. J Q B 180. Good and probable reason as well as good faith was pleaded and proved

---

Falsehood by garbled statements. To tell half the truth to conceal the other half, amounts to a false statement, and differs in no respect from the case of false representations. Rhode v. Alley, 27 Tex 443

"Fraud may consist as well in a *suppressio veri* as in a *suggestio falsi*, for in either case, it may op rate to the injury of the innocent party" Mitchell v. McDougall, 62 Ill. 501. See Williams v. Spurr, 24 Mich 335, Fish v Cleland, 33 Ill. 238, Cleland v. Fish, 43 Ill. 282.

Knowledge or belief of defendant. The statement of the text is sustained by the American authorities. Thus in Hicks v. Stevens (21 Ill 186, 11 N E. Rep 244), the court said "To maintain an action at

no liability, nor is he bound to show that his belief was founded on such grounds as would produce the same belief in a prudent and competent man (*u*), except so far as the absence of reasonable cause may tend to the inference that there was not any real belief. An honest though dull man cannot be held guilty of fraud any more than of "express malice," although there is a point beyond which courts will not believe in honest stupidity. "If an untrue statement is made," said Lord Chelmsford, "founded upon a belief which is destitute of all reasonable grounds, or which the least inquiry would immediately correct, I do not see that it is not fairly and correctly characterized as misrepresentation and deceit" (*x*). Lord Cranworth preferred to say that such circumstances might be strong evidence, but only evidence, that the statement was not really believed to be true, and any liability of the parties "would be the consequence not of their having stated as true what they had not reasonable ground to believe to be true, but of their having stated as true what they did not believe to be true" (*y*). Lord Cranworth's opinion has been declared by the House of Lords (*z*), reversing the

(*u*) *Taylor* v *Ashton* (1843), 11 M & W 401, 12 L J Ex. 363, but the actual decision is not consistent with the doctrine of the modern cases on the duty of directors of companies See per Lord Herschell, 14 App Ca at p 375

(*x*) *Western Bank of Scotland* v. *Addie* (1867), L R 1 Sc at p 162
(*y*) *Ib*. at p 168
(*z*) *Derry* v. *Peek* (1889), 14 App Ca 337, 58 L J. Ch 864

---

law for fraud and deceit arising from false representations of a material matter connected with the transaction, it is necessary to show that the party making it knew it to be false, or occupied such a position as that the law would impute to him knowledge of the fact" See McDonald *v.* Trafton, 15 Me. 225; Case *v.* Voughton, 11 Wend. 106, King *v.* Eagle, 10 Allen, 548, Stimpson *v.* Helps, 9 Col. 33; 10 Pac. Rep. 290, Morse *v.* Dearborn, 109 Mass. 593; Smith *v* Richards, 13 Pet. 26, Cabbot *v.* Cristie, 42 Vt 121; Twitchell *v.* Bridge, 42 Vt. 68, Burnett *v* Stanton, 2 Ala 187, Bankhead *v.* Alloway, 6 Coldw. 56; Bristol *v.* Braidwood, 28 Mich. 191, Thompson *v.* Lee, 31 Ala. 292, Foard *v.* McComb, 12 Bush. 723; Elder *v.* Allison, 45 Ga. 13; Wilcox *v.* Iowa Wes Univ., 32 Ia. 367, Morgan *v.* Skiddy, 62 N. Y. 319, Davis *v.* Heard, 44 Miss. 50.

judgment of the Court of Appeal (a), to be the correct one. "The ground upon which an alleged belief was founded" is allowed to be "a most important test of its reality" (b); but if it can be found as a fact that a belief was really and honestly held, whether on reasonable grounds or not, a statement embodying that belief cannot render its maker liable in an action for deceit (c).

I have given reasons elsewhere (d) for thinking this decision of the House of Lords an unfortunate one. It would be out of place to repeat those reasons here. But it may be pointed out that the reversed opinion of the Court of Appeal coincides with that which has for many years prevailed in the leading American Courts (e), and has lately been thus expressed in Massachusetts:—

"It is well settled in this Commonwealth that the charge of fraudulent intent, in an action for deceit, may be maintained by proof of a statement made, as of the party's own knowledge, which is false, provided the thing stated is not merely a matter of opinion, estimate, or judgment, but is susceptible of actual knowledge; and in such case it is not necessary to make any further proof of an actual intent to deceive. The fraud consists in stating that the party knows the thing to exist, when he does not know it to exist; and if he does not know it to exist, he must ordinarily be deemed to know that he does not" (f).

Perhaps it would have been better on principle to hold the duty in these cases to be *quasi ex contractu*, and evade the barren controversy about "legal fraud." One who makes a statement as of fact to another, intending him to act thereon, might well be held to request him to act upon it; and it might also have been held to be an implied

---

(a) *Peck* v *Derry* (1887), 37 Ch Div 541, 57 L J Ch 347.

(b) Lord Herschell, 14 App Ca. at p. 375.

(c) *Acc Glasier* v *Rolls* (1889), 42 Ch Div 436, 58 L J Ch 820; *Low* v *Bouverie*, '91, 3 Ch 82, 60 L J Ch 594, C A

(d) L Q R v 410, for a different view, see Sir William Anson, *ib* vi 72

(e) Cooley on Torts, 501. The tendency appears as early as 1842, *Stone* v *Denny*, 4 Met (Mass) 151, 158

(f) *Chatham Furnace Co* v *Moffatt* (1888), 147 Mass 403

term or warranty in every such request that the party making it has some reasonable ground for believing what he affirms; not necessarily sufficient ground, but such as might then and there have seemed sufficient to a man of ordinary understanding. This would not have been more artificial than holding, as the Exchequer Chamber was once prepared to hold, that the highest *bona fide* bidder at an auction, advertised to be without reserve, can sue the auctioneer as on a contract that the sale is really without reserve, or that he has authority to sell without reserve (*g*).

And such a development would have been quite parallel to others which have taken place in the modern history of the law No one now regards an express warranty on a sale otherwise than as a matter of contract; yet until the latter part of the eighteenth century the common practice was to declare on such warranties in tort (*h*). But it seems now too late, at all events in this country, to follow such a line of speculation.

It has been suggested that it would be highly inconvenient to admit " inquiry into the reasonableness of a belief admitted to be honestly entertained " (*i*). I cannot see that the inquiry is more difficult or inconvenient than that which constantly takes place in questions of negligence, or that it is so difficult as those which are necessary in cases of malicious prosecution and abuse of privileged communications.

Representations subsequently discovered to be untrue. If, having honestly made a representation, a man discovers that it is not true before the other party has acted upon it, what is his position? It seems on principle that, as the

---

(*g*) *Warlow* v *Harrison* (1859), 1 E & E 309, 29 L J Q B 14

(*h*) *Williamson* v *Allison* (1802), 2 East. 446, 451 We need not remind the learned reader that the action of assumpsit itself was originally an action on the case for deceit in breaking a promise to the promisee's damage J B. Ames in Harvard Law Rev ii 1, 53.

(*i*) Sir W Anson, L. Q R. vi. 74.

offer of a contract is deemed to continue till revocation or acceptance, here the representation must be taken to be continuously made until it is acted upon, so that from the moment the party making it discovers that it is false and, having the means of communicating the truth to the other party, omits to do so, he is in point of law making a false representation with knowledge of its untruth. And such has been declared to be the rule of the Court of Chancery for the purpose of setting aside a deed. " The case is not at all varied by the circumstance that the untrue representation, or any of the untrue representations, may in the first instance have been the result of innocent error. If, after the error has been discovered, the party who has innocently made the incorrect representation suffers the other party to continue in error and act on the belief that no mistake has been made, this from the time of the discovery becomes, in the contemplation of this Court, a fraudulent misrepresentation, even though it was not so originally " (*j*). We do not know of any authority against this being the true doctrine of common law as well as of equity, or as applicable to an action for deceit as to the setting aside of a contract or conveyance. Analogy seems in its favour (*k*). Since the Judicature Acts, however, it is sufficient for English purposes to accept the doctrine from equity. The same rule holds if the representation was true when first made, but ceases to be true by reason of some event within the knowledge of the party making it and not within the knowledge of the party to whom it is made (*l*).

(*j*) *Reynell* v. *Sprye* (1852), 1 D M G. 660, 709, Lord Cranworth cp Jessel M. R , *Redgrave* v *Hurd* (1881), 20 Ch Div 12, 13, 51 L J Ch 113

(*k*) Compare the doctrine of continuous taking in trespass *de bonis asportatis*, which is carried out to the graver consequences in the criminal law Jessel M. R. assumed the common law rule to be in some way narrower than that of equity (20 Ch Div 13), but this was an extra judicial dictum, and see per Bowen L J , 34 Ch Div at p 594, declining to accept it.

(*l*) *Traill* v. *Baring* (1864), 4 D J S. 318; the difficulty of making out how there was any representation of fact in that case as distinguished from a promise or condition of a contract is not material to the present purpose.

Assertions made in reckless ignorance. On the other hand if a man states as fact what he does not believe to be fact, he speaks at his peril; and this whether he knows the contrary to be true or has no knowledge of the matter at all, for the pretence of having certain information which he has not is itself a deceit. "He takes upon himself to warrant his own belief of the truth of that which he so asserts" (m). "If persons take upon themselves to make assertions as to which they are ignorant whether they are true or untrue, they must, in a civil point of view, be held as responsible as if they had asserted that which they know to be untrue" (n). These dicta, one of an eminent common law judge, the other of an eminent chancellor, are

---

(m) Maule J, *Evans* v *Edmonds* (1853), 13 C B 777, 786, 22 L. J. C P 211

(n) Lord Cairns, *Reese River Silver Mining Co* v *Smith* (1869), L R 4 H L 64, 79, 39 L J Ch 849 See per Sir J Hannen in *Peek* v *Derry*, 37 Ch. Div at p. 581. Even Lord Bramwell allows Lord Cairns' dictum (14 App. Ca. at p. 351)

Assertions made in reckless ignorance. Agreeing with the text it was held by the court in McBeth v. Craddock (28 Mo. App 892), that the g'st of the action is the fraudulent representations of the defendant to plaintiff's damage. There must be fraud as distinguished from mere mistake. "It is not, however, always absolutely necessary that an actual falsehood should be uttered to render a party liable in an action of deceit. If he states material facts as of his knowledge, and not as a mere opinion or general assertion, about a matter of which he has no knowledge whatever, this distinct, wilful statement, in ignorance of the truth, is the same as the statement of a known falsehood, and will constitute a *scienter*. * * * All the authorities are agreed, that deceit may be committed not only with the careful intention of one who knows what he asserts to be true or false, but also with the reckless intention of one who does not know what he represents to be true or false, but who, for one reason or another is willing that his reckless representations should be believed." Stimson v. Helps, 9 Colo 33, 10 Pac. Rep. 291; Dunn v. Oldham, 63 Mo. 181; Caldwell v Henry, 76 Id. 254; Dulaney v Rogers, 64 Id. 204; Cummings v Cass, 53 N J. L. 77; 18 At. Rep. 972; Nauman v. Oberle, 90 Mo. 669; Kenny v. Railroad, 80 Id. 572, Koontz v. Kaufmann, 31 Mo. App. 418, Lahay v. City Nat. Bank, 15 Colo. 339; 25 Pac. Rep. 204; Busterud v. Farrington, 36 Minn 320, 31 N. W. Rep 360, citing numerous cases, Miner v. Medbury, 6 Wis 295, Smith v. Richards, 13 Pet. 26, The Montreal River Lumber Co. v Mihills, 80 Wis. 540; 50 N. W. Rep. 507.

now both classical; their direct application was to the repudiation of contracts obtained by fraud or misrepresentation, but they state a principle which is well understood to include liability in an action for deceit (*o*). The ignorance referred to is conscious ignorance, the state of mind of a man who asserts his belief in a fact " when he is conscious that he knows not whether it be true or false, and when he has therefore no such belief" (*p*).

Breach of a special duty to give correct information. With regard to transactions in which a more or less stringent duty of giving full and correct information (not

---

(*o*) *Taylor* v *Ashton* (1843), 11 M. & W. 401, 12 L J Ex 363, *Edgington* v *Fitzmaurice* (1885), 29 Ch Div 459, 479, 481, 55 L J Ch 650, cp. *Smith* v. *Chadwick*
(1881), 9 App Ca at p 190, per Lord Selborne
(*p*) Lord Herschell, *Derry* v *Peek*, 14 App Ca at p 371

Breach of special duty to give correct information. One who dissuades another from inquiry and deceives him to his prejudice is responsible. "If, in a contract of sale, the vendor knowingly allows the vendee to be deceived as to the thing sold in a material matter, his silence is grossly fraudulent in a moral point of view and may be safely treated accordingly in the law tribunals of the country. Although he is not required to give the purchaser all the information he possesses himself, he cannot be permitted to be silent when his silence operates virtually as a fraud. If he fails to disclose an intrinsic circumstance that is vital to the contract, knowing that the other party is acting upon the presumption that no such fact exists, it would seem to be quite as much a fraud as if he had expressly denied it, or asserted the reverse, or used any artifice to conceal it, or to call off the buyer's attention from it Common honesty, in such a case, requires a man to speak out." McAdams v. Cates, 24 Mo. 223. "The principle may be generalized, in other words, by saying that, to constitute fraud, in cases of mere silence, there must be the suppression of some material fact which honesty and good faith require to be disclosed under the facts in the particular case. There can usually be no fraud in silence, without intentional concealment, for it may be purely accidental. * * * Whether the duty to disclose exists in a given case, depends upon the fiduciary or other relation of the parties, the nature of the contract, the degree of trust reposed, whether expressly or impliedly, the value or nature of the particular fact, the relative knowledge of the contracting parties, and other circumstances of the case Griel v Lomax, 89 Ala 427. See Croswell v. Jack-

SPECIAL DUTY TO GIVE CORRECT INFORMATION.

merely of abstaining from falsehood or concealment equivalent to falsehood) is imposed on one of the parties, it may be doubted whether an obligation of this kind annexed

---

son, 53 N. J. L 656, 23 At. Rep. 426; Van Arsdale v. Howard, 5 Ala. 596; Jazan v. Foulmin, 9 Id. 662, 44 Am. Dec 418; Jordan v Pickett, 78 Ala 331, Moses v. Katzenberger, 84 Ala. 95; Hughes v. Robertson, 15 Am. Rep 104; Nicholson v. Janeway, 16 N. J. Eq. 585, Brown v. Montgomery, 20 N Y 287, Paddock v Strobridge, 29 Vt. 470, Sides v. Hilleary, 6 Harr & J. 86, Mitchell v. McDougall, 62 Ill. 498, Trigg v. Read, 5 Humph. 529; Smith v Insurance Co, 49 N Y. 211; Mintz v. Morrison, 17 Tex. 372, Belden v. Henriques, 8 Cal. 87, Junkins v. Simpson, 14 Mo 364; Dickinson v. Davis, 2 Leigh, 401, Ryan v. Ashton, 42 Ia. 365, Bank v. Albright, 21 Pa St, 228; Smith v. Osborn, 33 Mich. 410; Booth v. Storrs, 75 Ill. 438, Bank v. Cooper, 36 Mo 179; Blosson v. Barrett, 37 N Y. 434, Burns v Dockray, 156 Mass. 135; 30 N E. Rep. 551; Starkweather v. Benjamin, 32 Mich 306.

Mere passive concealment, unconnected with active misconduct which misleads the complainant, is not deception in the legal sense, and will not support an action of deceit. Williams v. Spurr, 24 Mich 335, Laidlow v Organ, 2 Wheat. 178; Law v. Grant, 37 Wis. 548; Hadley v. Importing Co, 13 Ohio St 502; Kintzing v McElrath, 5 Pa. St. 467, Atwood v. Chapman, 68 Me. 38. But when silence, of itself, amounts to an affirmation that a state of things exists which does not, as absolute a deception may be accomplished as could have resulted from positive assertion. For instance, one who sells goods on a credit has a right to suppose his vendee intends, at the time of purchase, to pay for them, and if the vendee on account of hopeless insolvency or other cause, which he concealed, intended not to pay for the goods as contracted, the concealment of this intention is a fraud, and the title to the goods will not pass. Oswego Starch Factory v Lendrum, 57 Ia 573, Houghtaling v. Hills, 59 Id 287; Donaldson v Farwell, 93 U. S 631, Nichols v Michael, 23 N. Y 189, Shipman v. Seymour, 40 Mich. 274, Bishop v Small, 63 N.C 12, Wright v Brown, 67 N Y. 1; Denoe v. Brandt, 53 Id. 462, Thompson v Rose, 16 Conn 71, Childs v. Merrill, 63 Vt 463, 22 At. Rep 626; Stewart v Emerson, 52 N. H. 301; Ayres v French, 41 Conn. 142; Smith v. Click, 1 Humph. 186, Dow v. Sanborn, 3 Allen, 181, Kitson v People (Ill), 23 N E Rep 1024, Rose v. Miner, 67 Mich 410, 35 N. W Rep 60, Newell v. Randall, 32 Minn 171

Contra, Bell v. Ellis, 33 Cal. 620, 630; Backentos v. Speicher, 81 Pa. St. 324, Smith v. Smith, 21 Id 367; Rodman v. Thalheimer, 75 Id. 232. There must be a preconceived intention to never pay for the goods. Burrill v Stevens, 73 Me 395. Not a mere absence of purpose to pay for them Catlin v Warren, 16 Ill App. 418; Flower v Farwell, 18 Id 254.

It is a fraud to give a check on a bank where the drawer has no funds

by law to particular classes of contracts can ever be treated as independent of contract. If a misrepresentation by a vendor of real property, for example, is wilfully or recklessly false, it comes within the general description of deceit. But there are errors of mere inadvertence which constantly suffice to avoid contracts of those kinds, and in such cases I do not think an action for deceit (or the analogous suit in equity) is known to have been main-

---

or none reasonably expected Misur v Russell, 29 Mich. 229, True v Thomas, 16 Mo 36; Harner v. Fisher, 58 Pa St. 453.

In the sale of meats and provisions to consumers there is an implied warranty that they are fit for consumption as such. And a sale of such articles which are unfit for consumption as food, without disclosing that fact, is fraudulent and actionable. Osgood v Lewis, 2 Harr & J. 495, Van Brocklin v. Fonda, 12 Johns 468; Devine v. McCormack, 50 Barb. 116, French v Vinning, 102 Mass 132; 3 Am. Rep. 140; Peckham v. Holman, 11 Pick. 484

Under the rule that such sale must be to a *consumer* has arisen the distinction between a sale by a wholesale dealer and a sale by a retail dealer. It has always been held that wholesale dealers do not impliedly warrant their provisions which they sell to retail dealers. Ryder v. Neitge, 21 Minn 70, Emerson v. Brigham, 10 Mass. 196, Hart v Wright, 17 Wend. 267, Goldrich v. Ryan, 3 E D Smith, 324; Moses v. Mead, 1 Denio, 378; Hyland v. Sherman, 2 E. D. Smith, 234, Rinschler v Jeliffe, 9 Daly, 469, Hargous v Stone, 5 N Y. 73, Best v Flint, 58 Vt. 543 On the other hand, it is a rule that there is an implied warranty in a sale of provisions by retail dealers to consumers. Moses v Mead, 1 Denio, 378, Bishop v. Weber, 139 Mass. 411; Hoe v. Sanborn, 21 N. Y. 552. A warranty is implied whether the vendor is a dealer or not, if he knows the article is purchased for immediate consumption. Hoover v Peters, 18 Mich. 51. See Goad v. Johnson, 6 Heisk, 340. But where the food is sold for other than human use the rule does not apply. Lukens v. Freiund, 27 Kan 664 It has been held that the sale of animals which the sellers know, but the purchaser does not, have a contagious disease, should be regarded as a fraud when the fact of the disease is not disclosed Jeffrey v. Bigelow, 12 Wend. 518, Grigsby v. Stapleton (Mo.), 7 S W. Rep. 421, Miss , etc. Ry. Co. v. Finley, 38 Kan 550; 16 Pac. Rep 951, Fultz v Wycoff, 25 Ind 321.

Infecting a pasture by one in possession as a mere licensee, and allowing the owner to turn in his cattle without informing him of the fact of the infection, is a fraud. Eaton v. Winnie, 20 Mich 156. See Kemmish v Ball, 30 Fed. Rep. 759 But unless the owner knows his cattle are diseased, he is not liable for their infecting cattle on a common range. Bradford v Floyd, 80 Mo. 207 See Hawks v Locke, 139 Mass. 205

tained. Since *Derry* v. *Peck* it seems clear that it could not be. As regards those kinds of contracts, therefore — but, it is submitted, those only — the right of action for misrepresentation as a wrong is not co-extensive with the right of rescission. In some cases compensation may be recovered as an exclusive or alternative remedy, but on different grounds, and subject to the special character and terms of the contract.

Estoppel. Burrowes v. Lock: former supposed rule of equity. In the absence of a positive duty to give correct information or full and correct answers to inquiry, and in the absence of fraud, there is still a limited class of cases in which a man may be held to make good his statement on the ground of estoppel. Until quite lately it was supposed to be a distinct rule of equity that a man who has misrepresented, in a matter of business, facts which were specially within his knowledge, cannot be heard to say that at the time of making his statement he forgot those facts. But since *Derry* v. *Peek* (*q*) this is not the rule of English courts. If there is no contract and no breach of specific duty, nothing short of fraud or estoppel will suffice. And we have to remember that estoppel does not give a cause of action but only supplies a kind of artificial evidence (*r*). One of the cases hitherto relied on for the supposed rule (*s*) can be supported on the ground of estoppel, but on that ground only; a later and apparently not less considered and authoritative one (*t*) cannot be supported at all.

(*q*) 14 App. Ca. 337, 58 L. J. Ch. 864
(*r*) *Low* v *Bouverie*, '91, 3 Ch. 82, C. A., see per Bowen L. J., at p. 105
(*s*) *Burrowes* v *Lock* (1805), 10 Ves. 470, see per Lindley L. J., '91, 3 Ch. at p. 101

(*t*) *Slim* v *Croucher* (1860), 1 D. F. J. 518, *Low* v *Bouverie*, above, per Lindley, L. J., '91, 3 Ch. at p. 102

Estoppel "An acceptance of land concerning which fraudulent representations were made, after knowledge of their falsity, produces neither a waiver nor an estoppel." Matlock *v* Reppy, 47 Ark. 148; 14 S. W. Rep. 546.

In short the decision of the House of Lords in *Derry* v *Peek* is that even the grossest carelessness in stating material facts is not equivalent to fraud; and the substance of the decision is not altered by the results turning out to be of wider scope, and to have more effect on other doctrines supposed to be settled, than at the time was apprehended by a tribunal of whose acting members not one had any working acquaintance with courts of equity.

Intention of the statement. (c) It is not a necessary condition of liability that the misrepresentation complained of should have been made directly to the plaintiff, or that the defendant should have intended or desired any harm to come to him. It is enough that the representation was intended for him to act upon, and that he has acted in the manner contemplated, and suffered damage which was a natural and probable consequence. If the seller of a gun asserts that it is the work of a well-known maker and safe to use, that, as between him and the buyer, is a warranty, and the buyer has a complete remedy in contract if the assertion is found untrue; and this will generally be his better remedy, as he need not then allege or prove anything about the defendant's knowledge; but he may none the less treat the warranty, if it be fraudulent, as a substantive ground of action in tort. If the buyer wants the gun, not for his own use, but for the use of a son to whom he means to give it, and the seller knows this, the seller's assertion is a representation on which he intends or expects the buyer's son to act. And if the seller has wilfully or recklessly asserted that which is false, and the gun, being in fact of inferior and unsafe manufacture, bursts in the hands of the purchaser's son and wounds him, the seller is liable to that son, not on his warranty (for there is no contract between them, and no consideration for any), but for a deceit (*u*). He

---

(*u*) *Langridge* v *Levy* (1837), 2 M. & W. 519, affirmed (very briefly) in Ex Ch. 4 M. & W. 338.

meant no other wrong than obtaining a better price than the gun was worth; probably he hoped it would be good enough not to burst, though not so good as he said it was; but he has put another in danger of life and limb by his falsehood, and he must abide the risk. We have to follow the authorities yet farther.

Representations to a class of persons: Polhill v. Walter. A statement circulated or published in order to be acted on by a certain class of persons, or at the pleasure of any one to whose hands it may come, is deemed to be made to that person who acts upon it, though he may be wholly unknown to the issuer of the statement. A bill is presented for acceptance at a merchant's office. He is not there, but a friend, not his partner or agent, who does his own business at the same place, is on the spot, and, assuming without inquiry that the bill is drawn and presented in the regular course of business, takes upon himself to accept the bill as agent for the drawee. Thereby he represents to every one who may become a holder of the bill in due course that he has authority to accept; and if he has in fact no authority, and his acceptance is not ratified by the nominal principal, he is liable to an action for deceit, though he may have thought his conduct was for the benefit of all parties, and expected that the acceptance would be ratified (x)

Denton v. G. N. R. Co. Again the current time-table of a railway company is a representation to persons meaning to travel by the company's trains that the company will use reasonable diligence to despatch trains at or about the stated times for the stated places. If a train which has been taken off is announced as still running, this is a false representation, and (belief in its truth on the part of the

(x) *Polhill* v *Walter* (1832), 3 B. & Ad 114 The more recent doctrine of implied warranty was then unknown [*Lindsey* v *Lindsey*, 34 Miss 432]

company's servants being out of the question) a person who by relying on it has missed an appointment and incurred loss may have an action for deceit against the company (*y*). Here there is no fraudulent intention. The default is really a negligent omission; a page of the tables should have been cancelled, or an erratum-slip added. And the negligence could hardly be called gross, but for the manifest importance to the public of accuracy in those announcements.

Peek v. Gurney. Again the prospectus of a new company, so far forth as it alleges matters of fact concerning the position and prospects of the undertaking, is a representation addressed to all persons who may apply for shares in the company; but it is not deemed to be addressed to persons who after the establishment of the company become purchasers of shares at one or more removes from the original holders (*z*), for the office of the prospectus is exhausted when once the shares are allotted. As regards those to whom it is addressed it matters not whether the promoters wilfully use misleading language or not, or do or do not expect that the undertaking will ultimately be successful. The material question is, " Was there or was there not misrepresentation in point of fact?" (*a*). Innocent or benevolent motives do not justify an unlawful intention in law, though they are too often allowed to do so in popular morality.

(*y*) So held unanimously in *Denton* v. *G N R. Co.* (1856), 5 E & B 860, 25 L. J. Q B 129 Lord Campbell C. J, and Wightman J, held (*dubit* Crompton J.) that there was also a cause of action in contract. The difficulty often felt about maintaining an action for deceit against a corporation does not seem to have occurred to any member of the Court. It is of course open to argument that this case is overruled by *Derry* v. *Peek*, 14 App. Ca. 337, 58 L J. Ch 864; and now *Low* v *Bouverie*, '01, 3 Ch 82, 60 L. J Ch 594, seems to point in the same direction

(*z*) *Peek* v *Gurney* (1873), L. R. 6 H. L. 377, 400, 411, 43 L J. Ch. 19

(*a*) Lord Cairns, L. R 6 H L. at p. 409 Cp per Lord Blackburn, *Smith* v. *Chadwick*, 9 App. Ca. at p. 201, Lord Herschell, *Derry* v. *Peek*, 14 App. Ca. at pp. 365, 871

DECEIT: RELIANCE ON REPRESENTATION. 375

Reliance on the representation. (d) As to the plaintiff's action on the faith of the defendant's representation.

A. by words or acts represents to B. that a certain state of things exists, in order to induce B. to act in a certain

---

Reliance on representation. To sustain an action for deceit it must be proved by evidence that the plaintiff in doing that which resulted to his injury acted upon the false representation of the defendant and not independently, to his injury. It is essential that such misrepresentation be the promoting and proximate cause of the injury, otherwise the deception has not accomplished its purpose and an action will not lie. Addington v Allen, 11 Wend. 374; Fishback v Miller, 15 Nev. 428, Lebby v. Ahrens, 26 S. C. 275; 2 S E. Rep 387; Winter v. Bandel, 30 Ark. 362, Black v. Black, 110 N. C. 399, 14 S. E Rep 971, Lewis v. Jewell, 151 Mass. 345; 24 N. E. Rep. 51; Ming v. Woolfolk, 116 U. S. 599; Ledbetter v. Davis, 121 Ind. 119, Roseman v Canovan, 43 Cal. 110, Webster v Bailey, 31 Mich. 36, Parmlee v. Adolph, 28 Ohio St. 10; Wakeman v Dalley, 51 N. Y. 27, Rish v. Von Lillenthal, 34 Wis. 250, Ladsley v Johns, 120 Ill 469; 12 N. E. Rep. 247, Fowler v. McCann (Wis), 56 N. W. Rep. 1085, Fulton v. Hood, 34 Pa St. 365; Pratt v. Philbrook, 41 Me. 132

Where a purchaser decides not to rely upon the statements of the vendor, but seeks independent means of investigation of his own, there is no deception, though he fails to discover an important fact, provided the vendor interposes no obstacles to a full and free investigation, and does nothing to mislead the purchaser Halls v. Thompson, 1 Smed. & M. 443. So, if the complainant did not rely upon the representations of the defendant because he did not believe them, or because he chose to act on his own judgement, he has no ground for relief. Nye v. Merriman, 35 Vt. 438, Hagee v. Grossman, 31 Ind. 223, Proctor v. McCold, 60 Ia 153, Doran v Eaton, 40 Minn 35. See Alden v. Wright, 47 Minn. 225; 49 N. W. Rep. 767; Nye v. Merriam, 35 Vt. 438; Veerol v Veerol, 63 N. Y 45, Fulton v. McDaniel, 23 Ga. 354, Byard v. Holmes, 34 N J L. 296, Redding v Goodwin, 44 Minn 355, 46 N. W. Rep 563; Hanson v. Edgerly, 29 N H. 343, Abbey v Dewey, 25 Pa. St. 413, Fuller v Hodgden, 25 Me. 243, Boyce v Watson, 20 Ga 517, Garrow v Davis, 15 How. 272, Ely v Stewart, 2 Md. 408, Ming v. Woolfolk, 116 U S 599, Runger v Brown, 29 Neb. 116; 37 N W. Rep 660; Anderson v Burnett, 6 Miss. 165, Taylor v. Guest, 58 N Y. 266; Rutherford v Williams, 42 Mo. 24, Shackelford v. Hendley, 1 A K Marsh. 496; Duncan v. Hogue, 24 Miss. 671; Slidel v Rightor, 3 La An. 199, Central Bank v. Copeland, 18 Md. 305; Bowman v Corithens, 40 Ind 90.

The false statement must relate and be material to the subject of the transaction and be a "substantial inducement" thereto to constitute a deceit, but it is not necessary that they be the *sole* inducements that led

way. The simplest case is where B., relying wholly on A.'s statement, and having no other source of information, acts in the manner contemplated. This needs no further comment. The case of B. disbelieving and rejecting A.'s assertion is equally simple.

---

to the close of the transaction. Ingraham v. Jordan, 55 Ga. 356, Selma v. Railroad Co., 51 Miss. 829; Hill v. Cailey, 8 Hun, 636; Hull v. Fields, 76 Va. 591; Winter v. Bandell, 30 Ark. 362; Safford v. Grant, 120 Mass. 20; James v. Hodsden, 47 Vt. 127; Mathews v. Bliss, 22 Pick. 48; Whiting v. Hill, 23 Mich. 399, 405.

"The maxim *caveat emptor*, is a rule of the common law, applicable to contracts of purchase of both real and personal property, and is adhered to, both in courts of law and courts of equity, where there is no cases of positive fraud a different rule applies. The law presumes that men will act honestly in their business transactions, and the maxim of *vigilantibus, non dormientibus jura subveniunt* only requires persons to use reasonable diligence to guard against fraud, such diligence as prudent men generally exercise under similar circumstances. * * * But the rules of law do not require a prudent man to deal with every one as rascal, and demand covenants to guard against the falsehood of every representation, which may be made as to facts which constitute material inducements to the contract. There must be a reasonable reliance upon the integrity of men, or the transactions of business, trade and commerce could not be conducted with that facility and confidence which are essential to successful enterprise and the advancement of individual and national wealth and prosperity. * * * If representations are made by one party to a trade which may be reasonably relied upon by the other party, and they constitute a material inducement to the contract — and such representations are false within the knowledge of the party making them — and they cause loss and damage to the party relying on them, and he has acted with ordinary prudence in the matter, he is entitled to relief in any court of justice." Walsh v. Hall, 66 N. C. 237. See Oswald v. McGehee, 28 Miss. 340; Fields v. Rouse, 3 Jones L. 72.

"It is as much an actionable fraud wilfully to deceive a credulous person with an improbable falsehood as it is to deceive a cautious, sagacious person with a plausible one. The law draws no line between the two falsehoods." Barndt v. Frederick, 78 Wis. 1, 47 N. W. Rep. 9. So, it has been said: "The law takes note of the ignorant, the credulous, and the unwary, and will make their ignorance and want of cunning their innocence, and protect them." Pearl v. Walter, 80 Mich. 322, citing McNamara v. Gargett, 68 Mich. 454; Davis v. Seeley, 71 Id. 209; followed in Leland v. Goodfellow, 84 Mich. 357; 47 N. W. Rep. 591. See Ingalls v. Miller, 121 Ind. 188; 22 N. E. Rep. 995.

Another case is that A.'s representation is never communicated to B. Here, though A. may have intended to deceive B., it is plain that he has not deceived him; and an unsuccessful attempt to deceive, however unrighteous it may be, does not cause damage, and is not an actionable wrong. A fraudulent seller of defective goods who patches up a flaw for the purpose of deceiving an inspection cannot be said to have thereby deceived a buyer who omits to make any inspection at all. We should say this was an obvious proposition, if it had not been judicially doubted (*b*). The buyer may be protected by a condition or warranty, express or implied by law from the nature of the particular transaction; but he cannot complain of a merely potential fraud directed against precautions which he did not use. A false witness who is in readiness but is not called is a bad man, but he does not commit perjury.

Means of knowledge immaterial without actual independent inquiry. Yet another case is that the plaintiff has at hand the means of testing the defendant's statement,

---

(*b*) *Horsfall* v. *Thomas* (1862), 1 H & C 90, 31 L J Ex 322, a case of contract, so that *a fortiori* an action for deceit would not lie, dissented from by Cock burn C J, L R. 6 Q B. at p 605. The case was a peculiar one, but could not have been otherwise decided

---

Means of knowledge immaterial without actual inquiry. "The proposition has now become very widely accepted at law as well as in equity, at least as a general doctrine, that a man may act upon a positive representation of fact notwithstanding the fact that the means of knowledge were specially open to him. * * * If the representations were of a character to induce action, and did induce it that is enough." Cottrell v. Crum, 100 Mo 397, 13 S W. Rep. 753 In the New York case of Mead v Bunn (32 N. Y 279), the court speaking through Porter J went so far as to say· "every contracting party has an absolute right to rely on the express statement of an existing fact, the truth of which is known to the opposite party, and unknown to him, as the basis of a mutual engagement; and he is under no obligation to investigate and verify statements, to the truth of which the other party to the contract, with full means of knowledge, has deliberately pledged his faith " See

indicated by the defendant himself, or otherwise within the plaintiff's power, and either does not use them or uses them in a partial and imperfect manner. Here it seems plausible at first sight to contend that a man who does not use obvious means of verifying the representations made to him does not deserve to be compensated for any loss he may incur by relying on them without inquiry. But the ground of this kind of redress is not the merit of the plaintiff, but the demerit of the defendant: and it is now settled law that one who chooses to make positive assertions without warrant shall not excuse himself by saying that the other party need not have relied upon them. He must show that his representation was not in fact relied upon. In the same spirit it is now understood (as we shall see in due place) that the defence of contributory negligence does not mean that the plaintiff is to be punished for his want of caution, but that an act or default of his own, and not the negligence of the defendant, was the proximate cause

---

Eaton *v* Winnie, 20 Mich 156, Dunn *v* White, 63 Mo 181, Duff *v.* Williams, 85 Pa St 490, Litchfield *v.* Hutchinson, 117 Mass. 195, Bird *v.* Kleiner, 41 Wis 134; Catzhausen *v* Simon, 47 Wis 103, Wheelden *v.* Lowell, 50 Me. 499, Lockridge *v* Foster, 5 Ill. 56; Parham *v* Randolph, 4 How. (Miss.) 435, Wharf *v.* Roberts, 88 Ill 426, Taylor *v.* Lith, 26 Ohio St 428, Pennsylvania R. Co *v.* Ogier, 35 Pa. St. 72; Ernst *v.* Hudson River R. Co , 35 N Y. 28; Gordon *v.* Grand St R. Co., 40 Barb. 550, Olson *v* Orton, 28 Minn. 36, Caldwell *v* Henry, 76 Mo. 254, Stewart *v.* Stearns, 63 N H. 99, McGibbons *v.* Wilder, 78 Ia 531.

"In an action for fraudulent misrepresentations in the sale to plaintiff of certain shares of corporate stock, a written agreement of the parties was put in evidence, reciting that 50 per cent. of the par value had been paid in cash, and 25 per cent. by a declaration of dividend out of net profits, and setting out the illegal financial condition of the company, and providing that the trade was to be conditional upon the representations as to the condition of the business and stock of said company, which might be verified by an expert book keeper of plaintiff's selection and at his expense. *Held*, That plaintiff's right to recover upon such representations, as fraudulent, is not concluded by his failure to avail himself of the right to make such examination through an expert."

Blacknall *v.* Rowland, 108 N. C 554, 13 S. E Rep. 191 See Taylor *v.* Saurman, 110 Pa. St. 8, 1 At Rep 40

of his damage. If the seller of a business fraudulently over-states the amount of the business and returns, and thereby obtains an excessive price, he is liable to an action for deceit at the suit of the buyer, although the books were accessible to the buyer before the sale was concluded (c).

Perfunctory inquiry will not do. And the same principle applies as long as the party substantially puts his trust in the representation made to him, even if he does use some observation of his own.

A cursory view of a house asserted by the vendor to be in good repair does not preclude the purchaser from complaining of substantial defects in repair which he afterwards discovers. "The purchaser is induced to make a less accurate examination by the representation, which he had a right to believe" (d). The buyer of a business is not deprived of redress for misrepresentation of the amount of profits, because he has seen or held in his hand a bundle of papers alleged to contain the entries showing those profits (e). An original shareholder in a company who was induced to apply for his shares by exaggerated and untrue statements in the prospectus is not less entitled to relief because facts negativing those statements are disclosed by documents referred to in the prospectus, which he might have seen by applying at the company's office (f).

In short, nothing will excuse a culpable misrepresentation short of proof that it was not relied on, either because the other party knew the truth, or because he relied wholly

---

(c) *Dobell* v *Stevens* (1825), 3 B. & C. 623

(d) *Dyer* v *Hargrave* (1805), 10 Ves. at p. 510 (cross suits for specific performance and compensation).

(e) *Redgrave* v *Hurd* (1881), 20 Ch. Div. 1, 51 L. J. Ch. 113 (action for specific performance, counter claim for rescission and damages)

(f) *Central R. Co. of Venezuela* v. *Kisch* (1867), L. R. 2 H. L. 99, 120, 36 L. J. Ch. 849, per Lord Chelmsford. A case of this kind alone would not prove the rule as a general one, promoters of a company being under a special duty of full disclosure

on his own investigation, or because the alleged fact did not influence his action at all. And the burden of this proof is on the person who has been proved guilty of material misrepresentation (*g*). He may prove any of these things if he can. It is not an absolute proposition of law that one who, having a certain allegation before him, acts as belief in that allegation would naturally induce a man to act, is deemed to have acted on the faith of that allegation. It is an inference of fact, and may be excluded by contrary proof. But the inference is often irresistible (*h*)

Ambiguous statements. Difficulties may arise on the construction of the statement alleged to be deceitful. Of course a man is responsible for the obvious meaning of his assertions; but where the meaning is obscure, it is for the party complaining to show that he relied upon the words in a sense in which they were false and misleading, and of which they were fairly capable (*i*) As most persons take the first construction of obscure words which happens to strike them for the obviously right and only reasonable construction, there must always be room for perplexity in questions of this kind. Even judicial minds will differ widely upon such points, after full discussion and consideration of the various constructions proposed (*k*)

Lord Tenterden's Act. (e) It has already been observed in general that a false representation may at the same time be a promise or term of a contract. In particular it may be such as to amount to, or to be in the nature

---

(*g*) See especially per Jessel M R, 20 Ch Div 21

(*h*) See per Lord Blackburn, *Smith* v *Chadwick*, 9 App Ca at p 196.

(*i*) *Smith* v *Chadwick* (1884), 9 App Ca 187, 53 L J Ch 873, especially Lord Blackburn's opinion

(*k*) In the case last cited (1881-2) (Fry J, and C. A 20 Ch. Div 27), Fry J and Lord Bramwell decidedly adopted one construction of a particular statement, Lindley L J the same, though less decidedly, and Cotton L. J another, while Jessel M R., Lord Selborne, Lord Blackburn, and Lord Watson thought it ambiguous

of, a guaranty. Now by the Statute of Frauds a guaranty cannot be sued on as a promise unless it is in writing and signed by the party to be charged or his agent. If an oral guaranty could be sued on in tort by treating it as a fraudulent affirmation instead of a promise, the statute might be largely evaded. Such actions, in fact, were a novelty a century and a quarter after the statute had been passed (*l*), much less were they foreseen at the time. It was pointed out, after the modern action for deceit was established, that the jurisdiction thus created was of dangerous latitude (*m*); and, at a time when the parties could not be witnesses in a court of common law, the objection had much force. By Lord Tenterden's Act, as it is commonly called (*n*), the following provision was made:—

"No action shall be brought whereby to charge any person upon or by reason of any representation or assur-

(*l*) See the dissenting judgment of Grose J. in *Pasley* v. *Freeman* (1789), 3 T R 51, 1 R R 634, 636, and 2 Sm L C
(*m*) By Lord Eldon in *Evans* v. *Bicknell* (1801), 6 Ves. 174, 182, 186, 5 R. R 245, 251, 255
(*n*) 9 Geo IV c. 14, s 6

Recommendation of credit "The doctrine is well established that in order to subject a defendant to damages for false recommendation as to the credit of a third person, the representation must not only be false, but fraudulent with intent to deceive, and, where a petition does not allege such intent to deceive and contains only a general allegation of fraud, it fails to state a cause of action for deceit" Redpath v. Lawrence, 42 Mo. App 101. "Where goods are sold upon credit to A , upon the fraudulent representation of B , and loss ensues, B is liable in an action on the case, although other inducements besides the representations made may have operated in the giving of the credit, it is enough if the vendor be moved by such representations, so that without it the goods would not have been parted with" Addington v Allen, 11 Wend. 375. See Hess v Culver, 77 Mich 598, 43 N W Rep 994, Daniel v Robinson, 33 N W. Rep 497. "Where a third person knowingly made a false statement to one, with intent to deceive and mislead him, and induce him to loan money to another, and the person to whom the statements were made had reasonable ground to rely upon them and did rely upon them, and was deceived by them into making the loan, he is entitled to recover from the person making the false statements such loss as he may have sustained by reason of their having been made" Bank of North America v York, 87 Mo 369

ance made or given concerning or relating to the character, conduct, credit, ability, trade, or dealings of any other person, to the intent or purpose that such other person may obtain credit, money, or goods upon (*o*), unless such representation or assurance be made in writing, signed by the party to be charged therewith."

This is something more stringent than the Statute of Frauds, for nothing is said, as in that statute, about the signature of a person "thereunto lawfully authorized," and it has been decided that signature by an agent will not do (*p*). Some doubt exists whether the word "ability" does or does not extend the enactment to cases where the representation is not in the nature of a guaranty at all, but an affirmation about some specific circumstance in a person's affairs. The better opinion seems to be that only statements really going to an assurance of personal credit are within the statute (*q*). Such a statement is not the less within it, however, because it includes the allegation of a specific collateral circumstance as a reason (*r*).

Quaere as to the law under the Judicature Acts. A more serious doubt is whether the enactment be now practically operative in England. The word "action" of course did not include a suit in equity at the date of the Act, and the High Court has succeeded to all (and in some points more than all) the equitable jurisdiction and powers of the Court of Chancery. But that Court would not in a case of fraud, however undoubted its jurisdiction, act on the plaintiff's oath against the defendant's, without the

---

(*o*) Sic. It is believed that the word "credit" was accidentally transposed, so that the true reading would be "obtain money or goods upon credit": see *Lyde* v. *Barnard* (1836), 1 M. & W. 101, per Parke B. Other conjectural emendations are suggested in his judgment and that of Lord Abinger.

(*p*) *Swift* v. *Jewsbury* (1874), Ex. Ch. L. R. 9 Q. B. 301, 43 L. J. Q. B. 56.

(*q*) Parke and Alderson BB. in *Lyde* v. *Barnard* (1836), note (*o*). contra Lord Abinger C. B. and Gurney B. And see *Bishop* v. *Balkis Consolidated Co.* (1890), 25 Q. B. Div. 512, 59 L. J. Q. B. 565.

(*r*) *Swann* v. *Phillips* (1838), 8 A. & E. 457.

corroboration of documents or other material facts, and it would seem that in every case of this kind where the Court of Chancery had concurrent jurisdiction with the courts of common law (and it is difficult to assign any where it had not), Lord Tenterden's Act is now superseded by this rule of evidence or judicial prudence.

Misrepresentations made by agents. There still remain the questions which arise in the case of a false representation made by an agent on account of his principal. Bear-

---

Misrepresentations made by agents. In America the rule is established that a principal is liable civilly for the neglect, fraud, deceit, or other wrongful act of his general agent, although personally innocent of the fraud Wright v Calhoun, 19 Tex. 420, Robinson v Walton, 58 Mo 380, Kennedy v. McKay, 14 Vroom (N. J), 288, Bank v. Campbell, 4 Humph 394. Johnson v. Barber, 5 Gilm. 425, Morton v. Scull, 23 Ark. 289, Jewett v Carter, 132 Mass. 335; Fitzsimmons v. Joslin, 21 Vt 129, Thompson v Brush Co., 31 Fed. Rep. 533, Witherwax v Riddle, 121 Ill. 140, 13 N. E. Rep 545, Upton v. Tribilcock, 91 U S. 45, Chester v. Dickerson, 52 Barb. 349, Bank v. Gray, 14 N H 331, The Mad. and Ind. R. Co v. The Norwich Sav. Society, 24 Md 457, DeVosse v City of Richmond, 18 Gratt 338, Reed v. Peterson, 91 Ill. 288, Busch v Wilcox, 82 Mich. 315, 46 N. W Rep. 940

But this rule does not apply to the acts of a *special* agent where such agent did not have and was not held out as having full authority to do that which he undertook to do, and where one dealing with him was informed or should have informed himself, of the limitations of his authority See Haskell v. Starbird, 152 Mass 112, Locke v Stearns, 1 Metc. 560, White v. Sawyer, 16 Gray, 586, 589 A *special* agent's acts bind his principal, unless the manner of doing the particular business be specified. If he makes false representations on the subject of dealing to influence the other party to close the transaction, the principal is responsible for the deceit. Sanford v. Handy, 23 Wend. 260; Putman v. Sullivan, 4 Mass 45.

"Although the representation might be false in fact, if innocently made by the agent, believing in the truth of what he asserted, it would afford no ground of action To constitute the fraud and deceit, the representation must be false and knowingly made." Lamm v Port, Deposit Homestead Assoc etc , 49 Md. 240 But "the existence of knowledge in the agent, however acquired, when acting for the principal is knowledge to the principal and the fraudulent representation or concealment of material facts by the agent when engaged in the principal

ing in mind that reckless ignorance is equivalent to guilty knowledge, we may state the alternatives to be considered as follows: —

The principal knows the representation to be false and authorizes the making of it. Here the principal is clearly liable; the agent is or is not liable according as he does not or does himself believe the representation to be true.

The principal knows the contrary of the representation

---

constructively through the agent." Tagg v. The Tenn. Nat Bank, 65 Tenn. 479.

It is not only a rule of law that the acts of an agent within the scope of his authority bind the principal, but it is also true that where one makes an unauthorized false representation for another and that the other knowingly accepts the benefit thereof he becomes liable therefor. "No one can hold an interest obtained through the fraud of another, any more than if the fraud were committed by himself. By receiving and retaining the benefit he incurs the obligation." Bowers v Johnson, 10 Sneed & M. 173. See Mundorff v. Wickersham, 63 Pa. St 87, Lane v Black, 21 W. Va. 617; Nat. Ins. Co. v. Minch, 53 N. Y. 144, Smith v. Tracy, 36 N. Y 79. "If a vendor of land knows *when he effects the sale*, that the purchaser has been induced to buy by the false and fraudulent representations of a third person, he is responsible for the fraud, though such third person *was not his agent.*" Law v Grant, 37 Wis 448 There are times when an agent may become *personally* liable in an action of deceit, as where he assumes to act in respect to a transaction over which he has no authority and with false representations mislead a person to his or her damages Johnson v Smith, 21 Conn. 627, White v Madison, 26 N Y. 117, Moise v Dearborn, 109 Mass 593 But see Newman v Sylvester, 42 Ind. 112 So for an independent fraud by an agent, not within the scope of his agency, the principal is not responsible Fellows v. Oneida, 36 Barb 655, Kelly v. Insurance Co, 3 Wis 254, Kennedy v Parke, 2 C E Green, 415

The fraud of an authorized agent will invalidate a contract, entered into by him on behalf of his principal, though in perpetrating the fraud. the agent acted without the knowledge or consent of the principal, Henderson v. Railroad Co, 17 Tex. 575 See American Insurance Co v Kuhlman, 6 Mo App 523, Ogilvie v Insurance Co., 22 How 380, Veagie v Williams, 8 Id 134

One partner is liable for the deceit of another partner in the firm business Lark v Stearns, 1 Metc 560; Durant v Rogers, 87 Ill 508, Linton v Harley, 14 Gray, 191, Castle v Ballard, 23 How. 172. See, *ante,* pp. 84, 103, 112

to be true, and it is made by the agent in the general course of his employment but without specific authority.

Here, if the agent does not believe his representation to be true, he commits a fraud in the course of his employment and for the principal's purposes, and, according to the general rule of liability for the acts and defaults of an agent, the principal is liable (s).

If the agent does believe the representation to be true, there is a difficulty; for the agent has not done any wrong and the principal has not authorized any. Yet the other party's damage is the same. That he may rescind the contract, if he has been misled into a contract, may now be taken as settled law (t). But what if there was not any contract, or rescission has become impossible? Has he a distinct ground of action, and if so, how? Shall we say that the agent had apparent authority to pledge the belief of his principal, and therefore the principal is liable? in other words, that the principal holds out the agent as having not only authority but sufficient information to enable third persons to deal with the agent as they would with the principal? Or shall we say, less artificially, that it is gross negligence to withhold from the agent information so material that for want of it he is likely to mislead third persons dealing with the principal through him, and such negligence is justly deemed equivalent to fraud? Such a thing may certainly be done with fraudulent purpose, in the hope that the agent will, by a statement imperfect or erroneous in that very particular, though not so to his knowledge, deceive the other party. Now this would beyond question be actual fraud in the principal, with the ordinary consequences (u). If the same thing

---

(s) Parke B., 6 M. & W. 373.

(t) See Principles of Contract, 552. In *Cornfoot* v. *Fowke*, 6 M. & W. 358, it is difficult to suppose that as a matter of fact the agent's assertion can have been otherwise than reckless, what was actually decided was that it was a direction to tell the jury without qualification "that the representation made by the agent must have the same effect as if made by the plaintiff himself," the defendant's plea averring fraud without qualification

(u) Admitted by all the Barons in

happens by inadvertence, it seems inconvenient to treat such inadvertence as venial, or exempt it from the like consequences. We think, therefore, that an action lies against the principal; whether properly to be described, under common law forms of pleading, as an action for deceit, or as an analogous but special action on the case, there is no occasion to consider (x).

On the other hand an honest and prudent agent may say, "To the best of my own belief such and such is the case," adding in express terms or by other clear indication — "but I have no information from my principal." Here there is no ground for complaint, the other party being fairly put on inquiry.

Liability of corporations herein. If the principal does not expressly authorize the representation, and does not know the contrary to be true, but the agent does, the representation being in a matter within the general scope of his authority, the principal is liable as he would be for any other wrongful act of an agent about his business. And as this liability is not founded on any personal default in the principal, it equally holds when the principal is a corpora-

---

Cornfoot v *Fowke*, Parke, 6 M & W. at pp 362, 374, Rolfe at p 370, Alderson at p 372. The broader view of Lord Abinger's dissenting judgment of course includes this

(x) The decision of the House of Lords in *Derry* v *Peek* (1889), 14 App Ca 337, 58 L J Ch 864, tends however to make this opinion less probable

---

Liability of corporations. "Natural persons are liable for the wrongful acts and neglect of their servants or agents, done in the course of their employment, and private corporations upon the same grounds of public policy are amenable to the same extent." Lamm v. Port, Deposit Homestead Ass'n, 49 Md. 241. In England the rule is that if the person has been induced to purchase shares of a corporation by the misrepresentations of its Directors and is damaged thereby he must bring an action of deceit against such directors individually; while in the United States it seems to be the rule that a corporation may be sued in such cases. Fogg v Griffin, 2 Allen, 1; Foster v. Essex Bank, 17 Mass. 479; Peebles v. Pataps Co., 77 N. C 233; Railroad Co. v. Schuyler, 34 N.Y. See, *ante*, pp. 66, 67, 68

tion (y). It has been suggested, but never decided, that it is limited to the amount by which the principal has profited through the agent's fraud. The Judicial Committee have held a principal liable who got no profit at all (z).

But it seems to be still arguable that the proposed limitation holds in the case of the defendant being a corporation (a), though it has been disregarded in at least one comparatively early decision of an English superior court the bearing of which on this point has apparently been overlooked (b). Ulpian, on the other hand, may be cited in its favour (c).

Reason of apparently hard law. The hardest case that can be put for the principal, and by no means an impossible one, is that the principal authorizes a specific statement which he believes to be true, and which at the time of giving the authority is true; before the agent has executed his authority the facts are materially changed to the knowledge of the agent, but unknown to the principal; the agent conceals this from the principal, and makes the statement as originally authorized. But the case is no harder than that of a manufacturer or carrier who finds himself exposed to heavy damages at the suit of an utter

---

(y) *Barwick* v *English Joint Stock Bank* (1867), Ex Ch L R 2 Ex 259, 36 L J Ex 147, *Mackay* v *Commercial Bank of New Brunswick* (1874), L R 5 P. C 394, 43 L. J P C. 31, *Swire* v *Francis* (1877), 3 App Ca 106, 47 L J P C 18 (J C), *Houldsworth* v *City of Glasgow Bank* (1880), Sc. 5 App Ca 317 See pp 85, 86, above

(z) *Swire* v. *Francis*, last note.

(a) Lord Cranworth in *Western Bank of Scotland* v *Addie* (1867), L R 1 Sc & D at pp. 166, 167 Lord Chelmsford's language is more guarded.

(b) *Denton* v *G. N. R Co.* (1856), p 269 above No case could be stronger, for (1) the defendant was a corporation, (2) there was no active or intentional falsehood, but the mere negligent continuance of an announcement no longer true, (3) the corporation derived no profit The point, however, was not discussed.

(c) D 4. 3, de dolo malo, 15 § 1 Sed an in municipes de dolo detur actio, dubitatur Et puto ex suo quidem dolo non posse dari, quid enim municipes dolo facere possunt? Sed si quid ad eos pervenit ex dolo eorum qui res eorum administrant, puto dandam The Roman lawyers adhered more closely to the original conception of moral fraud as the ground of action than our courts have done The *actio de dolo* was *famosa*, and was never an alternative remedy, but lay only when there was no other (si de his rebus alia actio non erit), D. *h. t* 1

stranger by reason of the negligence of a servant, although he has used all diligence in choosing his servants and providing for the careful direction of their work. The necessary and sufficient condition of the master's responsibility is that the act or default of the servant or agent belonged to the class of acts which he was put in the master's place to do, and was committed for the master's purposes. And "no sensible distinction can be drawn between the case of fraud and the case of any other wrong." The authority of *Barwick* v. *English Joint Stock Bank* (d) is believed, notwithstanding the doubts still sometimes expressed, to be conclusive.

II.— *Slander of Title.*

Slander of title. The wrong called Slander of Title is in truth a special variety of deceit, which differs from the ordinary type in that third persons, not the plaintiff him-

---

(d) L. R. 2 Ex. 259, 265.

Slander of title. An action for slander of title will lie against one who falsely and maliciously disparages the title of another to property, real or personal, and thereby causes him some special pecuniary loss or damage; and in order to maintain the action, it is necessary to establish each of these facts. Words spoken disparagingly of property, however false or malicious, are not in themselves actionable, unless special pecuniary damage has resulted therefrom as the direct and natural result of the utterance of the words. Burkett v Griffith, 90 Cal. 532, 27 Pac Rep 527. See Marsh v Billings, 7 Cush 322, Chesebro v Powers, 78 Mich 472; 44 N W Rep 290; Duncan v. Griswood, 18 S W. Rep. 354. To sustain an action for slander of title, malice, either express or implied, must be shown. Dodge v. Colby, 37 Hun, 515, Walden v Peters, 2 Rob (La) 331, Weakley v. Bostwick, 49 Mich. 374, Andrews v Deshler, 45 N J. L 167 Also, special damages to the plaintiff must be proven Swan v. Tappan, 5 Cush. 111, Tobias v. Harland, 4 Wend. 537; Gott v Pulsifer, 122 Mass. 235; 23 Am. Rep 322. In an action for slander of goods it must be shown that the defendant has injured the plaintiff by his false representations. The mere averment that the plaintiff was compelled to go out of business is not sufficient to sustain the action. Dudley v Briggs, 141 Mass 582.

self, are induced by the defendant's falsehood to act in a manner causing damage to the plaintiff. Notwithstanding the current name, an action for this cause is not like an action for ordinary defamation; it is "an action on the case for special damage sustained by reason of the speaking or publication of the slander of the plaintiff's title" (c). Also the wrong is a malicious one in the only proper sense of the word, that is, absence of good faith is an essential condition of liability (f); or actual malice, no less than special damage, is of the gist of the action.

Recent extensions of the principle. This kind of action is not frequent. Formerly it appears to have been applied only to statements in disparagement of the plaintiff's title to real property. It is now understood that the same reason applies to the protection of title to chattels, and of exclusive interests analogous to property, though not property in the strict sense, like patent rights and copyright. But an assertion of title made by way of self-defence or warning in any of these matters is not actionable, though the claim be mistaken, if it is made in good faith (g). In America the law has been extended to the protection of inchoate interests under an agreement. If A. has agreed to sell certain chattels to B., and C. by sending to A. a false telegram in the name of B., or by other wilfully false representation, induces A. to believe that B. does not want the goods, and to sell to C. instead, B. has an action against C. for the resulting loss to him, and it is held to make no difference that the original agree-

---

(c) Tindal C J, *Malachy* v. *Soper* (1836), 3 Bing N C. 371, Bigelow L C. 42, 52

(f) *Halsey* v *Brotherhood* (1881), 19 Ch Div 386, 51 L J Ch. 233, confirming previous authorities

(g) *Wren* v *Weild* (1869), L. R. 4 Q B 730, 38 L J Q B 127, *Halsey* v *Brotherhood, supra* (patent, in *Wren* v *Weild* the action is said to be of a new kind, but sustainable with proof of malice), *Steward* v *Young* (1870), L R. 5 C. P 122, 39 L J C P 85 (title to goods), *Dicks* v *Brooks* (1880), 15 Ch D. 22, 49 L J Ch 812 (copyright in design), see 19 Ch D. 391

ment was not enforceable for want of satisfying the Statute of Frauds (h).

A disparaging statement concerning a man's title to use an invention, design, or trade name, or his conduct in the matter of a contract, may amount to a libel or slander on him in the way of his business; in other words the special wrong of slander of title may be included in defamation, but it is evidently better for the plaintiff to rely on the general law of defamation if he can, as thus he escapes the troublesome burden of proving malice (i).

It has been held in Massachusetts that if A. has exclusive privileges under a contract with B., and X. by purposely misleading statements or signs induces the public to believe that X. has the same rights, and thereby diverts custom from A., X. is liable to an action at the suit of A. (k). In that case the defendants, who were coach owners, used the name of a hotel on their coaches and the drivers' caps, so as to suggest that they were authorized and employed by the hotel-keeper to ply between the hotel and the railway station; and there was some evidence of express statements by the defendants' servants that their coach was "the regular coach." The plaintiffs were the coach owners in fact authorized and employed by the hotel. The Court said that the defendants were free to compete with the plaintiffs for the carriage of passengers and goods to that hotel, and to advertise their intention of so doing in any honest way; but they must not falsely hold themselves out as having the patronage of the hotel, and there was evidence on which a jury might well find such holding out as a fact. The case forms, by the nature of its facts, a somewhat curious link between the general law of false representation and the special rules as to the infringement

(h) *Benton* v. *Pratt* (1829), 2 Wend. 385; *Rice* v. *Manley* (1876), 66 N. Y. (21 Sickels) 82.

(i) See *Thorley's Cattle Food Co.* v. *Massam* (1879), 14 Ch. Div. 763, *Dicks* v. *Brooks*, last note but one.

(k) *Marsh* v. *Billings* (1851), 7 Cush. 322, and Bigelow L. C. 59.

of rights to a trade mark or trade name (*l*). No English case much like it has been met with: its peculiarity is that no title to any property or to a defined legal right was in question. The hotelkeeper could not give a monopoly, but only a sort of preferential comity. But this is practically a valuable privilege in the nature of goodwill, and equally capable of being legally recognized and protected against fraudulent infringement. Goodwill in the accustomed sense does not need the same kind of protection, since it exists by virtue of some express contract which affords a more convenient remedy. Some years ago an attempt was made, by way of analogy to slander of title, to set up an exclusive right to the name of a house on behalf of the owner as against an adjacent owner. Such a right is not known to the law (*m*).

Trade marks and trade names. The protection of trade marks and trade names was originally undertaken by the courts on the ground of preventing fraud (*n*). But the right to a trade mark, after being more and more assimilated to proprietary rights (*o*), has become a statutory

---

(*l*) The instructions given at the trial (Bigelow L C at p 63) were held to have drawn too sharp a distinction, and to have laid down too narrow a measure of damages, and a new trial was ordered It was also said that actual damage need not be proved, *sed qu*

(*m*) *Day v Brownrigg* (1878) (reversing Malins V C), 10 Ch Div 294, 48 L J Ch 173

(*n*) See per Lord Blackburn, 6 App Ca at p 29, Lord Westbury, I R 5 H L at p 522, Mellish L J, 2 Ch D at p 153

(*o*) *Singer Manufacturing Co v Wilson* (1876), 2 Ch D 434, per Jessel M R at pp 411-2, James L J at p 451, Mellish L J at p 454

Trade marks and patent rights An action for slander of title to letters-patent may be maintained. Meyrose *v* Adams, 12 Mo. Ap 329, Andrews *v* Deshler, 45 N J. L. 167. In order to make out a case of deceit based on a trade-mark it must appear (1) that the defendant knew of the existence of the plaintiff's mark when he committed the alleged wrong, (2) that defendant intended to palm off these goods as the goods of the plaintiff, or to represent that the business which he was carrying on was the plaintiff's or the business of which the plaintiff had a special patronage; (3) that the public were deceived thereby Bigelow on Torts, 36

franchise analogous to patent rights and copyright (*p*); and in the case of a trade name, although the use of a similar name cannot be complained of unless it is shown to have a tendency to deceive customers, yet the tendency is enough, the plaintiff is not bound to prove any fraudulent intention or even negligence against the defendant (*q*). The wrong to be redressed is conceived no longer as a species of fraud, but as being to an incorporeal franchise what trespass is to the possession, or right to possession, of the corporeal subjects of property. We therefore do not pursue the topic here.

III.—*Malicious Prosecution and Abuse of Process.*

Malicious prosecution. We have here one of the few cases in which proof of evil motive is required to complete an actionable wrong. "In an action for malicious prosecution the plaintiff has to prove, first, that he was innocent

---

(*p*) Patents, Designs, and Trade Marks Act, 1883, 46 & 47 Vict. c. 57.
(*q*) *Hendriks* v. *Montagu* (1881), 17 Ch. Div. 638, 50 L. J. Ch. 456; *Singer Manufacturing Co.* v. *Loog* (1882), 8 App. Ca. 15.

Malicious prosecution. The numerous American authorities upon this subject agree with the text, *vide*, Shaul *v* Brown, 28 Iowa, 42; 4 Am Rep 151, Ball *v* Rawles, 93 Cal. 228, 28 Pac. Rep. 937, Tucker *v.* Cannon, 28 Neb 196, 44 N W Rep. 440, Peterson *v* Toner, 80 Mich 350, 45 N W. Rep. 346, Cooper *v.* Langway, 76 Tex 121, 13 S. W Rep 179; Pace *v.* Aubrey, 13 La An 1052, 10 So Rep. 381, Bennett *v* Aubrey, Id ; Shannon *v* Jones, 76 Tex 141, 13 S W. Rep 477, Taylor *v* Dominick, 36 S. C 308, 15 S E. Rep 591, Jones *v* Jenkins, 3 Wash St. 17; 27 Pac Rep 1022, McCormack *v* Perry, 47 Hun, 71; Rosenberg *v* Hart, 36 Ill App 262, Heyne *v* Blair, 62 N Y 19; *Ex parte* Wilson, 114 U S. 417, Bartlett *v* Brown, 6 R. I. 37, Pierce *v* Thompson, 6 Pick. 192, Cook *v.* Walker, 30 Ga 519, Ray *v* Law, 1 Pet. 207; Stocking *v* Howard, 73 Mo 25, Whitson *v.* May, 71 Ind 105; Green *v* Cochran, 43 Ia 544, Everett *v* Henderson, 146 Mass 93, Girot *v* Graham, 41 La An 511, 6 So Rep. 815; Jones *v* Jones, 71 Cal 89; 11 Pac Rep. 817, Bidwell *v* Osgood, 3 Pick 379, 15 Am Dec. 228, Bixby *v* Brundage, 2 Gray, 129, 61 Am Dec 443; Marshall *v* Betner, 17 Ala 832, Whiting *v.* Johnson, 6 Gray, 246, Stancliff *v* Palmeter 18 Ind 324, Bailey *v.* Dodge,

and that his innocence was pronounced by the tribunal before which the accusation was made; secondly, that there

28 Kan. 72, Collins v Love, 7 Blackf. 116; Smith v Deaver, 4 Jones L. 513, Hayes v Younglove, 7 B Mon. 445, Morris v Scott, 21 Wend 281, 34 Am Dec. 236, followed in Dennis v Ryan, 65 N Y 389, 1 Am. Lead Cas 254, Brelet v Mullen, 44 La. An. 194, 10 So Rep 865, Drayfus v. Aul, 29 Neb 191, 45 N W Rep. 282, Fugate v. Millar, 109 Mo. 281, 19 S. W Rep. 71

(1) *Malice.* To maintain an action for malicious prosecution malice on the part of the prosecutor, either express or implied, must be proved Malice may be presumed from a total want of probable cause for the prosecution. Forbes v. Hagman, 75 Va. 168, Joiner v. The Ocean Steamship Co, 86 Ga 238, 12 S E Rep. 361, Schlletz v Lauflitt, 63 Pa. St. 234, Murphy v Hobbs, 8 Colo. 17, Johnson v. Ebberts, 6 Sawyer, 538, Fhickinger v. Wagner, 46 Md. 580, Miller v. Williges, 18 Barb. 30, Ames v Scheider, 69 Ill 376, Smith v Austin, 49 Mich 286; Emerson v Cochran, 111 Pa St. 619, Stewart v. Sonneborn, 98 U S. 187, Wagstaff v. Schippel, 27 Kan. 450, Carson v. Edgeworth, 43 Mich 241, Bobson v. Kingsbury, 138 Mass 538, Harkrader v Moore, 44 Cal. 144, Ewing v. Sanford, 19 Ala. 605, Cooper v Utterback, 37 Md 282, Gulliford v Windel, 108 Pa St 142, Pangburn v. Bull, 1 Wend. 345, Merriam v Mitchell, 13 Me. 559, Gee v Culver, 13 Oreg 600, 11 Pac Rep 302, Brewer v Jacobs, 22 Fed Rep 217. But the mere discontinuance of a criminal prosecution, or the acquittal of the accused, will establish neither malice nor want of probable cause. Johns v Marsh, 52 Md 323, Spear v Illies, 67 Wis. 350, Hamilton v Smith, 39 Mich 222, Yocum v. Polly, 1 B Mon 358, Skidmore v Bricker, 77 Ill. 104, Bitting v Ten Eyck, 82 Md 421 The burden of proving that the prosecution was malicious is upon the plaintiff McKnown v Hunter, 30 N Y 625, Flickinger v Wagner, 46 Md 581 And the jury are the exclusive judges of malice. Stone v Stevens, 12 Conn 219, Center v Spring, 2 Clarke (Ia.), 393, Vinal v Core, 18 W Va 1.

(2) *Want of probable cause* In order that an action for malicious prosecution may be maintained, the plaintiff must show that the defendant had no probable cause for the commencement or the continuation of the proceeding complained of. "The *gravamen* of the action is that the defendant instituted the proceedings without probable cause, that is, without having at the time such knowledge or information of the circumstances as would superinduce in the mind of an ingenious and unprejudiced person of ordinary capacity a reasonable belief that the plaintiff was guilty of the charge. The defense must be that *he did believe* and *had reasonable grounds to believe at the time* that the accusation he made was well founded" Harkrader v Moore, 44 Cal 149; Brounstein v Wile, 65 Hun, 623, 20 N Y. S Rep 204, Pomeroy v Villavossa, 31 Id 590, Casto v De Uriarte, 16 Fed Rep 94, Walker v Camp, 63 Ia. 627;

was a want of reasonable and probable cause for the prosecution, or, as it may be otherwise stated, that the cir-

---

Wheeler v Nesbitt, 24 How 544; Landa v Obert, 45 Tex 539, Ames v Snider, 69 Ill. 376, Shaver v. Loucks, 58 Barb 426, Munns v Dupont, 3 Wash C. Ct 31, Glasgow v. Owen, 69 Tex 167, Sharpe v Johnson, 76 Mo 660; McGurn v Brackett, 33 Me 331, Bauer v Clay, 8 Kan. 580, Dwain v. Discalo, 66 Cal 415, Wilwarth v Mountford, 1 Wash. C Ct. 79, Boyd v Cross, 35 Md. 197, Bacon v Towne, 4 Cush. 217, Ulmer v Leland, 1 Greenl. 135, 10 Am. Dec. 48, Hampton v. Jones, 58 Ia 317, Carl v Ayers, 53 N Y 15, Brown v Willoughby, 5 Colo 1, Dale v Wisher, 72 Ill. 162; Casey v Sevatson, 30 Minn 516, Cole v Curtis, 16 Id. 182; Paddock v. Watts, 116 Ind 146, Jordan v G. S R. Co v Kriske, 30 Neb. 315, 16 N W Rep. 520, Cheever v Sweet, 151 Mass 186, 23 N W Rep 831, Sears v Hathaway, 12 Cal 277, Stansell v. Cleveland, 64 Tex. 660, Brennan v Tracy, 2 Mo App. 510 Neither is the defendant justified if he knew the facts constituting a probable cause but did not believe them Woodworth v. Mills, 61 Wis 44, Plummer v. Johnson (Wis), 33 N. W Rep. 331; Josselyon v. McAllister, 95 Mich 45

The expressions "reasonable cause" and "probable cause" have essentially the same meaning Stacy v Emery, 97 U S 642 "Just or proper cause" distinguished Van De Wiele v Callahan, 7 Daly, 386

It has been held that the question of probable cause is entirely independent of the plaintiff's actual guilt or innocence of the crime for which he was prosecuted Lyton v Baird, 95 Ind 349 See Woodworth v. Mills, 61 Wis. 44, Baldwin v. Weed, 17 Wend 224, Thompson v Lamley, 50 How Pr 105, Moore v. Sanborn, 42 Mo. 490, Callaway v Burr, 32 Mich 332, King v. Calvin, 11 R I 582, Miller v Milligan, 48 Barb. 30, French v. Smith, 4 Vt 363. But mere *belief* of a person making a criminal complaint, that it is true, does not alone justify a prosecution thereunder, it must rest on reasonable grounds and on such facts as would lead a person of ordinary caution to honestly suspect the accused of guilt. Spalding v Lowe, 56 Mich 366, Ross v. Langworthy, 13 Neb. 492, Ramsey v Arrott, 64 Tex 320, Hall v Suydam, 6 Barb. 83, Collins v Hayte, 50 Ill 353, Winebiddle v Porterfield, 9 Pa St. 137, Mowry v Whipple, 8 R I. 340, McClafferty v Philp, 151 Pa. St 86, 24 At. Rep 1042, 30 W. N C. 539

(3) *Termination of former action* No action for malicious prosecution can be maintained until the proceeding complained of has been legally terminated in favor of the defendant therein. "In a case of malicious prosecution the right of action accrues whenever the criminal proceeding is disposed of in such a manner that it cannot be revived, and the prosecutor if he proceeds further, will be put to a new one "

cumstances of the case were such as to be in the eyes of the judge inconsistent with the existence of reasonable and

---

Dreyfus v Aul, 29 Neb. 191; 45 N W Rep 282, citing Casebeer v Drahoble, 13 Neb. 465; 14 N. W. Rep. 597; Same v Rice, 18 Neb. 203, 94 N W. Rep 693 See Cardival v Smith, 109 Mass 158, 12 Am Rep 682, Leever v Hamil, 57 Ind 423; Hatch v. Cohen, 84 N C. 602, Lowe v Waterman, 17 N J. L 413, Swensgaird v Davis, 33 Minn. 368; Brown v. Randall, 36 Conn 56, O'Brien v Barry, 106 Mass 300, 8 Am Rep 329, Stone v. Crocker, 24 Pick. 87; Sales v Briggs, 4 Metc. 421, Bacon v Waters, 2 Allen, 400, Gillespie v. Hudson, 11 Kan. 163, Hamilburgh v. Shepard, 119 Mass 30; Spring v Besore, 12 B Mon. 551, West v Hayes, 104 Ind 251, Gorrell v. Snow, 31 Ind. 215, Steel v Williams, 18 Ind. 161, Robbins v Robbins, 133 N. Y. 597, 30 N E Rep 973; Sutton v McConnell, 46 Wis 270, 50 N. W Rep 414, Gallagher v Stoddard, 17 Hun, 101, Apgar v Woolston, 43 N J. L 57, Darnell v. Sallee ('Ind. App), 34 N E. Rep 1020

If the action has been appealed the appeal must have been determined Reynolds v. DeGreer, 13 Ill App 113, Nebenzahl v Townsend, 61 How Pr. 353; Howell v Edwards, 8 Ired 516.

The general rule as above laid down, however, does not prevail where the proceedings have been ex parte for the reason that the defendant in such cases has had no opportunity to disprove the charges preferred against him Bump v Betts, 19 Wend. 421, Fortman v. Rattler, 6 Ohio St. 548, Hyde v Greuch, 62 Md 577; Olson v. Neal, 63 Ia. 214, Seaill v McCrackin, 16 How . Pr 262.

A defendant who has been discharged on a preliminary hearing before a magistrate on charge of a crime, may sue his prosecutor therefor. Sayles v Briggs, 4 Metc 421, Burkett v Lavata, 15 La. An 337; Cardival v Smith, 109 Mass 158, Coffey v Myers, 84 Ind 105. So, if discharged on habeas corpus. Zebley v. Storey, 117 Pa. St 478, 12 At Rep 569.

Advice of counsel. It may be stated as a general rule that where a plaintiff who, after consulting counsel in good standing and fully and fairly disclosing the facts of his case within his knowledge, acts upon the advice of such counsel, is not liable in a suit for malicious prosecution Jackson v. Linnington, 47 Kan 396, 28 Pac. Rep 173, Miller v. C , M St P Ry Co., 41 Fed Rep 898, Rives v. Wood (Ky.), 15 S. W. Rep 131, Soule v Winslow, 66 Me. 447, Donnelly v Daggett, 145 Mass. 314, Walker v Camp, 69 Ia, 741, Eastman, v. Keasor, 44 N. H. 519, Hill v Palm, 38 Mo 13; Decoux v Lieux, 33 La An 392; Burnis v North, 64 Me 426, Fisher v Forrester, 33 Pa. St 501; Potter v Seale, 8 Cal 217; Rickord v. Cent. Pac R Co , 15 Nev 167, White v Carr, 71 Me 555, 36 Am Rep 353, Moore v. Mo Pac R Co , 37 Minn. 147; Gilbertson v. Fuller, 40 Minn. 413, Anderson v. Friend, 71 Ill. 475; Smith v. Astin, 49 Mich 286, Newton v. Weaver, 18 R I 616, Blunt v Little, 3 Mason, 102, Wilder v. Holden, 24 Pick 8, Roy v. Goings, 112

probable cause (r), and, lastly, that the proceedings of which he complains were initiated in a malicious spirit, that is, from an indirect and improper motive, and not in furtherance of justice" (s). And the plaintiff's case fails

(r) The facts have to be found by the jury, but the inference that on those facts there was or was not reasonable and probable cause is not for the jury but for the Court (p the authorities on false imprisonment, pp 259—266, above

(s) Bowen L J, *Abrath v N E R Co* (1883), 11 Q B Div 440, 455, 52 L J. Q B 620 the decision of the Court of Appeal was affirmed in H L (1886), 11 App. Ca 217, 55 L J Q B 457 A plaintiff who, being indicted on the prosecution complained of, has been found not guilty on a defect in the indictment (not now a probable event) is sufficiently innocent for this purpose *Hicks v. Fentham* (1791), 4 T R 247, 2 R R 374

Ill 656, Hurlbut v. Bonz (Tex Civ. App), 23 S W Rep 116, Stanton v Hart, 27 Mich 539, McCullough v Rice, 59 Ind 580, 15 Am. Rep. 358, Brobst v. Ruff, 100 Pa. St. 91; 45 Am Rep. 358, Sutton v McConnell, 46 Wis 270, 50 N W Rep. 411; Burgett v. Burgett, 43 Ind. 78; Beal v Robeson, 8 Ired, 276, Stone v Swift, 4 Pick 389, Smith v King, 62 Conn 515, 26 At Rep 1059, Rigdon v. Jordan, 81 Ga 668, Sweeney v Perney, 40 Kan. 102, Breitmesser v Steir, 13 Phila. Rep. 80, Williams v. Van Meter, 8 Mo 339; Straus v. Young, 37 Md 282

The reason of the rule is that such conduct by a person who feels aggrieved disproves malice and shows probable cause. "The fact that the defendant sought, received and acted upon the advice of counsel affords strong evidence that there was probable cause and that the prosecution was entered into in good faith and without malice" Spidmore v Bricker, 77 Ill 164 See Ames v. Snider, 69 Ill. 376, Wicker v Hotchkiss, 62 Ill 107; 14 Am Rep. 75, St. Johnsbury & Co v Hunt, 59 Vt. 294; Jones v Jones, 71 Cal. 89, Allen v. Codman, 139 Mass 136, Walter v Sample, 25 Pa. St. 275; Olmstead v Partridge, 16 Gray, 381, Hall v Suydam, 6 Barb 83, Cole v Curtis, 16 Min 182; Ash v. Marlow, 20 Ohio, 119; Wills v. Noyes, 12 Pick 324, Logan v. Maytag, 57 Ia 107; Norrel v Vogel, 39 Minn. 107; Prough v Emtriken, 11 Pa St 81, Schmidt v Wedman, 63 Pa St 173, Griffin v Chubb, 7 Tex 603, 58 Am. Dec. 85; Kimbal v Bates, 50 Me. 308, Chapman v. Dodd, 10 Minn 350; Davie v Wisher, 72 Ill 662; Cuthbert v. Galloway, 35 Fed. Rep. 466.

All the material facts known to the defendant, or which he could have ascertained by reasonable diligence, relative to the case, must have been stated Donnelly v. Daggett, 145 Mass. 314; Paddock v Watts, 116 Ind. 146; 18 N. E Rep 518; Motes v Bates, 80 Ala 382; Smith v Austin, 49 Mich 286, Forbes v Hagman, 75 Va 168; Sappington v. Watson, 50 Mo. 83, Cooper v Utterbact, 37 Md 282

Malicious prosecution by corporations, see, *ante*, p. 68.

Malicious prosecution and false imprisonment distinguished, see, *ante*, p 265, n 266

if his proof fails at any one of these points. So the law has been defined by a recent judgment of the Court of Appeal, confirmed by the House of Lords. It seems needless for the purposes of this work to add illustrations from earlier authorities.

It is no excuse for the defendant that he instituted the prosecution under the order of a Court, if the Court was moved by the defendant's false evidence (though not at his request) to give that order, and if the proceedings in the prosecution involved the repetition of the same falsehood. For otherwise the defendant would be allowed to take advantage of his own fraud upon the Court which ordered the prosecution (*t*).

As in the case of deceit, and for similar reasons, it has been doubted whether an action for malicious prosecution will lie against a corporation. It seems, on principle, that such an action will lie if the wrongful act was done by a servant of the corporation in the course of his employment and in the company's supposed interest, and it has been so held (*u*); but there are dicta to the contrary (*x*), and in particular a recent emphatic opinion of Lord Bramwell's(*y*), which, however, as pointed out by some of his colleagues at the time (*z*), was extra-judicial.

Malicious civil proceedings. Generally speaking, it is not an actionable wrong to institute civil proceedings without reasonable and probable cause, even if malice be proved.

(*t*) *Fitzjohn* v *Mackinder* (Ex Ch 1861), 9 C B N S 505, 30 L J C P 257 (diss Blackburn and Wightman JJ)

(*u*) *Edwards* v *Midland Rail Co* (1880), 6 Q B D 287, 50 L J Q B 281, Fry J

(*x*) See the judgment in the case last cited

(*y*) 11 App Ca at p 250

(*z*) Lord Fitzgerald, 11 App Ca at p 244, Lord Selborne at p 256

Malicious civil proceedings Agreeing with the text, in this country "the policy of the law has always been to guaranty immunity to suitors who, in good faith, adopt and pursue the due forms of the law, although they may ultimately fail to establish their claims" McFadden *v* Whitney, 51 N J 391, 18 At. Rep 63, citing Bitts *v* Meyer, 11 Vroom, 252; 29

For in contemplation of law the defendant who is unreasonably sued is sufficiently indemnified by a judgment in

---

Am. Rep. 233 See Mitchell v S. W. R. Co., 75 Ga 398; Potts v Imlay, 4 N J L 330, Parker v. Frambes, 2 Id. 156, Stimer v. Bryant, 81 Mich 166; 17 N. W. Rep. 1099. Mr. Justice Sharwood, in the case of Mayer v. Walter (64 Pa. St. 285), said: "If the person be not arrested, or his property seized, it is unimportant how futile and unfounded the action may be, as the plaintiff, in consideration of law, is punished by the payment of costs." Followed in Muldoon v. Rickey, 103 Pa. St. 113. See Eberly v. Rupp, 90 Pa. St. 259; Kramer v Stock, 10 Watts, 115, Westmore v Mellinger, 64 In. 741, 52 Am. Rep 465, Smith v Hintrager, 67 In. 109, McNamee v Minko, 49 Md, 122.

But in the United States there are, however, many decisions holding a contrary view and the recent cases undoubtedly established the rule that one who unsuccessfully proceeds civilly against another, with malice and without probable cause, is liable in damages to that other, although his person was not molested or his property seized. In the case of Smith v Burrus, 106 Mo. 91, 16 S W. Rep. 881, Sherwood, C J., in delivering the opinion of the court, said "The authorities are in conflict as to whether a petition states a cause of action which merely alleges that a civil action, brought and prosecuted maliciously and without probable cause, has been terminated in favor of the defendant, many of the authorities maintaining that no cause of action exists unless such civil process be accompanied by arrest of the person or seizure of the property, and that the plaintiff in such original action, in contemplation of law is sufficiently punished by the payment to costs. * * * But there are numerous and able decisions in opposition to this view, and it is difficult to combat the force of the reasoning they employ It is difficult to see why the right of the plaintiff, who, as defendant has been sued in a civil action maliciously and without probable cause, and who has been put to great expense in consequence thereof, should be altered or at all affected by the incident of his property having been attached or his person seized, for, in either case, the damage, the expense, and the cost of defending a suit, whether instituted by *ca sa.* or attachment, or by civil summons, would be the same, and it is clear that the recovery of costs would not, under our practice, reimburse him for the attorney's fees, something which and other incidental expenses he does recover under the English practice. * * * The better doctrine is that which allows an action to be maintained as well where property, etc. has not been seized as where it has."

See Duncan v Griswold (Ky. App), 18 S. W. Rep 354, Lindsay v. Larned, 17 Mass. 190; Autcliff v June, 81 Mich 477; 45 N. W. Rep. 1019, Kemp v. Brown, 43 Fed. Rep 391, Whipple v Fuller, 11 Conn 582, Closson v Staples, 42 Vt 209, McCardle v McGinley, 86 Ind. 538, 44 Am Rep. 343; Lockenour v Sides, 57 Ind. 360, 26 Am. Rep.

his favour which gives him his costs against the plaintiff (*a*). And special damage beyond the expense to which he

(*a*) It is common knowledge that the costs allowed in an action are hardly ever a real indemnity. The true reason is that litigation must end somewhere. If A may sue B for bringing a vexatious action, then, if A. fails to persuade the Court that B.'s original suit was vexatious, B may again sue A for bringing this latter action, and so *ad infinitum*.

58, White *v* Dingley, 4 Mass. 433, Brown *v*. Cape Girardeau, 90 Mo. 377; Woods *v*. Finnell, 13 Bush, 628, Payne *v* Donegan, 9 Ill. App. 566, O'Neill *v*. Johnson (Minn), 55 N W. Rep. 601. It is the universal doctrine in both the United States and England that if one maliciously and without probable cause, sue out a civil process and cause another to be arrested or his property attached, such one is liable for damages sustained thereby Moody *v* Deutsch, 85 Mo 212; Watkins *v*. Baird, 6 Mass 511, Krug *v*. Ward, 77 Ill. 603, Tomlinson *v* Warner, 9 Ohio, 104, Hayden *v*. Shed, 11 Mass. 500, Wood *v*. Weir, 5 B Mon. 544, Nelson *v*. Danielson, 82 Ill. 545; Pierce *v*. Thompson, 6 Pick 193, Walser *v*. Thies, 56 Mo 89. But see Witascheck *v*. Glass, 46 Mo. App 215, Stewart *v*. Sonneborn, 98 U S. 187, Newark Coal Co. *v*. Upson, 40 Ohio St. 17, Hoyt *v*. Macon, 2 Colo. 113, Butchers etc. Co. *v*. Crescent City etc. Co , 37 La. An 878, Noonan *v* Orton, 30 Wis. 356.

Abuse of process In the case of Wood *v*. Graves (144 Mass. 366), the court very concisely and clearly states the law of this action, as follows —

"There is no doubt that an action lies for the malicious abuse of lawful process, civil or criminal. It is to be assumed in such a case, that the process was lawfully issued for a just cause, and is valid in form, and that an arrest or other proceeding upon the process was justifiable and proper in its inception. But the grievances to be redressed arise in consequence of subsequent proceedings For example, if after the arrest, upon civil or criminal process, the person arrested is subjected to unwarrantable insults and indignities, is treated cruelly, is deprived of proper food or is otherwise treated with oppression and undue hardship he has a remedy by an action against the officer, and against others who unite with the officer in doing the wrong." See Johnson *v* Reed, 136 Mass 423, citing Page *v*. Cushing, 38 Me. 523. See Peters *v* Tunell, 43 Minn 459, 45 N W. Rep. 866; Casey *v* Hanrick, 69 Tex 44; 6 S. W. Rep 405, Wood *v*. Bailey (Mass.), 11 N E. Rep 573; Emery *v* Ginnan, 24 Ill App 65, Cuhady *v* Powell, 35 Id. 29, Barnett *v* Reed, 51 Pa. St. 190, Savage *v* Brewer, 16 Pick 453

"There is a distinction between a malicious use and a malicious abuse of legal process. An abuse is where the party employs it for some unlawful object, not the purpose it is intended by law to effect, in other words perversion of it. * * * On the other hand, legal process, civil or criminal, may be maliciously used so as to give rise to a cause of

has been put cannot well be so connected with the suit as a natural and probable consequence that the unrighteous plaintiff, on the ordinary principles of liability for indirect consequences, will be answerable for them (*b*). "In the present day, and according to our present law, the bringing of an ordinary action, however maliciously, and however great the want of reasonable and probable cause, will not support a subsequent action for malicious prosecution" (*c*).

But there are proceedings which, though civil, are not ordinary actions, and fall within the reason of the law which allows an action to lie for the malicious prosecution of a criminal charge. That reason is that prosecution on a charge "involving either scandal to reputation, or the possible loss of liberty to the person" (*d*), necessarily and manifestly imports damage. Now the commencement of proceedings in bankruptcy against a trader, or the analogous process of a petition to wind up a company, is in itself a blow struck at the credit of the person or company whose affairs are thus brought in question. Therefore such a proceeding, if instituted without reasonable and probable cause and with malice, is an actionable wrong (*e*). Other similar exceptional cases were possible so long as there

---

(*b*) See the full exposition in the Court of Appeal in *Quartz Hill Gold Mining Co* v *Eyre* (1883), 11 Q B Div 674, 52 L J. Q B 488, especially the judgment of Bowen L. J

(*c*) Bowen L J , 11 Q B D at p 690 There has been a contrary decision in Vermont *Glosson* v *Staples* (1869), 42 Vt 209, 1 Am Rep 316 We do not think it is generally accepted in other jurisdictions, it is certainly in accordance with the opinion expressed by Butler in his notes to Co Lit 161 *a*, but Butler does not attend to the distinction by which the authorities he relies on are explained

(*d*) 11 Q B Div 691

(*e*) *Quartz Hill Gold Mining Co* v *Eyre* (1883), note (*b*) The contrary opinions expressed in *Johnson* v *Emerson* (1871), L R 6 Ex 329, 40 L. J Ex 201, with reference to proceedings under the Bankruptcy Act of 1869, are disapproved under the old bankruptcy law it was well settled that an action might be brought for malicious proceedings

---

action where no object is contemplated to be gained by it other than its proper effect and execution." Mayer *v* Walter, 64 Pa. St 285, followed in Eberly *v* Rupp, 90 Id 259 See Juchter *v*. Boehm, 67 Ga 538, Crusselle *v* Pugh, 71 Id 717, Emerson *v* Cochran, 111 Pa. St 619, Smith *v*. Weeks, 60 Wis. 94

were forms of civil process commencing with personal attachment; but such procedure has not now any place in our system; and the rule that in an ordinary way a fresh action does not lie for suing a civil action without cause has been settled and accepted for a much longer time (*f*). In common law jurisdictions where a suit can be commenced by arrest of the defendant or attachment of his property, the old authorities and distinctions may still be material (*g*). The principles are the same as in actions for malicious prosecution, *mutatis mutandis*: thus an action for maliciously procuring the plaintiff to be adjudicated a bankrupt will not lie unless and until the adjudication has been set aside (*h*).

Probably an action will lie for bringing and prosecuting an action in the name of a third person maliciously (which must mean from ill-will to the defendant in the action, and without an honest belief that the proceedings are or will be authorized by the nominal plaintiff), and without reasonable or probable cause, whereby the party against whom that action is brought sustains damage; but certainly such an action does not lie without actual damage (*i*).

IV.— *Other Malicious Wrongs.*

Conspiracy. The modern action for malicious prosecution has taken the place of the old writ of conspiracy and the action on the case grounded thereon (*k*), out of which it

(*f*) *Savile* or *Savill* v. *Roberts* (1698), 1 Ld Raym 374, 379, 12 Mod 208, 210, and also in 5 Mod , Salkeld, and Carthew

(*g*) See Cooley on Torts, 187 As to British India, see *Raj Chunder* v *Roy Shama Soondari Debi*, I L R 4 Cal 583

(*h*) *Metropolitan Bank* v *Pooley* (1885), 10 App Ca 210, 54 L J. Q B 449

(*i*) *Cotterell* v *Jones* (1851), 11 C B 713, 21 L J C P 2

(*k*) F N B 114 D *sqq*

Conspiracy Criminal conspiracy is an indictable offence and must be prosecuted in the name of the State as other crimes. It is different in both character and effect from conspiracy in connection with a civil action By conspiracy in connection with a civil action, is meant the confederating and combining of two or more persons to jointly do

seems to have developed. Whether conspiracy is known to the law as a substantive wrong, or in other words whether two

---

something, for which either of them, doing the same thing alone, would be civilly responsible to any person injured thereby. That is, a conspiracy cannot be made the subject of a civil action unless something is done, which, without the conspiracy, would give a right of action. In the opinion of the court delivered in the late case of Van Horn v. Van Horn (52 N. J L. 286), is a very learned exposition of the history and present meaning of conspiracy, as follows " It is not necessary to consider the office of the ancient writ of conspiracy, and the process by which, in time, it was superseded by the later and more efficacious action on the case for conspiracy, and the still more modern action for malicious prosecution Nor will it now be advantageous to show how long and difficult it was to separate the idea of a criminal conspiracy at common law, where the agreement or conspiracy was the *gravamen* of the offence, from the real complaint in a civil action, that the combination of two or more persons has enabled them to inflict a great wrong on plaintiff The combination or conspiracy in the latter case was, therefore, a matter of aggravation and inducement only, of which one or all might be found guilty, while in the former, it was essential to show that two or more had joined in an agreement to do an unlawful act, or to do a lawful act in an unlawful manner. The distinction is now well established, that in civil actions the conspiracy is not the *gravamen* of the charge, but may be both pleaded and proved in aggravation of the wrong of which the plaintiff complains, and enabling him to recover against all as joint tortfeasors If he fails in the proof of a conspiracy or concerted design, he may still recover damages against such as are shown to be guilty of the tort without such agreement " It is therefore apparent that the damage done is the gist of the action, not the conspiracy When the mischief contemplated is accomplished, the conspiracy becomes important, as it may affect the means and measure of redress. The party wronged may look beyond the actual participants in committing the injury, and join with them as defendants all who conspired to accomplish it, and the fact of conspiracy may aggravate the wrong, but the simple act of conspiracy does not furnish a substantive ground of action " Robertson v Parks, 76 Md 118, 24 At Rep 413 See Booker v Puryear, 27 Neb. 34, 43 N W Rep 133 A simple conspiracy, however atrocious, unless it resulted in actual damage to the party, is not the subject of a civil action, something injurious may be *actually done* Hutchins v Hutchins, 7 Hill, 907, Stevens v Rowe, 59 N. H 579, Laverty v Vanarsdale, 3 Cush. 145, McHenry v Sneer 56 Ia 619, Percival v. Harres, 142 Pa. St 369, 21 At Rep 876, Russell v. Post, 138 U. S 125, People v. Flack, 125 N Y 374, 26 N. E. Rep 267, Allen v Kirk, 81 Ia 658 47 N W Rep 107, Hablichtel v. Yambert, 75 Ia, 539; People v Sheldon, 66 Hun, 590 21 N Y S Rep 590, Morley v.

or more persons can ever be joint wrong-doers, and liable to an action as such, by doing in execution of a previous agreement something it would not have been unlawful for them to do without such agreement, is a question of mixed history and speculation not wholly free from doubt. It seems however to be now settled for practical purposes that the conspiracy or "confederation" is only matter of inducement or evidence (*l*). "As a rule it is the damage

(*l*) *Mogul Steamship Company* v *McGregor*, '92, A C 25, in H L

Elsbree (Pa), 17 At Rep 212, Delz v Winfree, 80 Tex 400; 16 S. W Rep. 111, Beeler v. Webb, 113 Ill 436, Findlay v. McAllister, 113 U S. 104, Sheple v Page, 12 Vt. 519, Adler v Fenton, 21 How 107; Douglass v Winslow, 52 N. Y Superior Ct 139; Burton v. Fulton, 49 Pa St 151, Wildee v. McKee, 111 Pa. St 335 "It is well settled that the acts and declarations of one of several conspirators in pursuance of the original concerted plan, are, in contemplation of law, the acts and declarations of them all, and may be shown in evidence against each of them * * * Where the declarations are not acts in themselves, nor part of the *res gesta*, but a mere relation or narrative of some part of the transaction, or as to the share which other persons have had in the execution of a common design, they are not within the rule stated. * * * Declarations made after the common enterprise is at an end, whether by accomplishment or advancement, or which are not in furtherance of its object, are not within the rule and will be excluded excepting as against the one who made them." Taylor County v Standley, 79 Ia. 666; 44 N W Rep 913, reviewing the cases on this point. See Moore v Shields, 121 Ind. 267, N. E. Rep. 89, Lee v Lamprey, 43 N H 13, Page v Parker, 40 N H 62, Toledo, etc Ry. Co. v. Pennsylvania Co., 54 Fed. Rep 730, Soloman v. Kirkwood, 55 Mich 256, Am Fur. Co. v United States, 27 U S 358, Phœnix Ins Co. v Moog, 78 Ala. 284, Williams v. Dickenson, 28 Fla. 90, 9 So. Rep 847; Turner v State (Ala), 12 So. Rep 54 But such declarations are not admissible until after the conspiracy has been established by *prima facie* evidence Holiday v Jackson 30 Mo App 263 S. P., Rutherford v Schattman, 111 N. Y 605, 23 N I Rep 440

A conspiracy to defraud may be inferred from the circumstances under which the parties are found to have acted, without direct evidence of conspiracy Redding v Wright, 49 Minn 322, 51 N. W. Rep 1056.

Corporations An action may now be maintained against a corporation for damages caused by or resulting from a conspiracy in which it joined through its agents acting in the course of their employment See the cases cited, *ante*, p 67.

wrongfully done, and not the conspiracy, that is the gist of actions on the case for conspiracy" (*m*). "In all such cases it will be found that there existed either an ultimate object of malice or wrong, or wrongful means of execution involving elements of injury to the public, or at least disguising the pursuit of a lawful object" (*n*). Either the wrongful acts by which the plaintiff has suffered were such as one person could not commit alone (*o*), say a riot, or they were wrongful because malicious, and the malice is proved by showing that they were done in execution of a concerted design. In the singular case of *Gregory* v. *Duke of Brunswick* (*p*) the action was in effect for hissing the plaintiff off the stage of a theatre in pursuance of a malicious conspiracy between the defendants. The Court were of opinion that in point of law the conspiracy was material only as evidence of malice, but that in point of fact there was no other such evidence, and therefore the jury were rightly directed that without proof of it the plaintiff's case must fail.

"It may be true, in point of law, that, on the declaration as framed, one defendant might be convicted though the other were acquitted; but whether, as a matter of fact, the plaintiff could entitle himself to a verdict against one alone, is a very different question. It is to be borne in mind that the act of hissing in a public theatre is, *prima facie*, a lawful act; and even if it should be conceded that such an act, though done without concert with others, if done from a malicious motive, might furnish a ground of action, yet it would be very difficult to infer such a motive from the insulated acts of one person unconnected with others. Whether, on the facts capable of proof, such a case of malice could be made out against one of the defendants,

(*m*) Bowen L. J. in S. C. in C. A. (1889), 23 Q. B. Div. at p. 616.
(*n*) Lord Field, '92, A. C. at p. 52.
(*o*) "There are some forms of injury which can only be effected by the combination of many [persons]" Lord Hannen, '92, A. C. at p. 60.
(*p*) 6 Man. & Gr. 205, 953 (1844). The defendants justified in a plea which has the merit of being amusing.

as, apart from any combination between the two, would warrant the expectation of a verdict against the one alone, was for the consideration of the plaintiff's counsel; and, when he thought proper to rest his case wholly on proof of conspiracy, we think the judge was well warranted in treating the case as one in which, unless the conspiracy were established, there was no ground for saying that the plaintiff was entitled to a verdict; and it would have been unfair towards the defendants to submit it to the jury as a case against one of the defendants to the exclusion of the other, when the attention of their counsel had never been called to that view of the case, nor had any opportunity [been?] given them to advert to or to answer it. The case proved was, in fact, a case of conspiracy, or it was no case at all on which the jury could properly find a verdict for the plaintiff" (q).

Soon after this case was dealt with by the Court of Common Pleas in England, the Supreme Court of New York laid it down (not without examination of the earlier authorities) that conspiracy is not in itself a cause of action (r).

In 1889 the question was raised in a curious and important case in this country. The material facts may, perhaps, be fairly summarized, for the present purpose, as follows:—A., B., and C. were the only persons engaged in a certain foreign trade, and desired to keep the trade in their own hands. Q. threatened, and in fact commenced, to compete with them. A., B., and C. thereupon agreed to offer specially favourable terms to all customers who would agree to deal with themselves to the exclusion of Q. and all other competitors outside the combination. This action had the effect of driving Q. out of the market in question, as it was intended to do. It was held by the majority of the

---

(q) Per Coltman J., 6 Man. & Gr. at 104, and Bigelow L. C. 207. See Mr. p. 959 Bigelow's note thereon.
(r) *Hutchins* v. *Hutchins* (1845), 7 Hill.

Court of Appeal, and unanimously by the House of Lords, that A., B., and C. had done nothing which would have been unlawful if done by a single trader in his own sole interest, and that their action did not become unlawful by reason of being undertaken in concert by several persons for a common interest. The agreement was in restraint of trade, and could not have been enforced by any of the parties if the others had refused to execute it, but that did not make it punishable or wrongful (s).

It is possible, however, that an agreement of this kind might in some cases be held to amount to an indictable conspiracy on the ground of obvious and excessive public inconvenience (t). At the same time, even if this be admitted, it would not be easy for a court to say beforehand how far any particular trade combination was likely to have permanently mischievous results (u).

Malicious interference with one's occupation. There may be other malicious injuries not capable of more specific definition "where a violent or malicious act is done to a

---

(s) *Mogul Steamship Company* v. *McGregor* (1889), 23 Q. B. Div. 598, 58 L. J. Q. B. 465 (diss. Lord Esher M. R.), in H. L. '92, A. C. 25, 61 L. J. Q. B. 295. Lord Esher was apparently prepared to hold that whenever A and B make an agreement which, as between themselves, is void as in restraint of trade, and C suffers damage as a proximate consequence, A and B are wrongdoers as against C. This is clearly negatived by the decision of the House of Lords, see the opinions of Lord Halsbury L. C., Lord Watson, Lord Bramwell, and Lord Hannen.

(t) Bowen L. J., 23 Q. B. Div. at p. 618.
(u) Fry L. J., 23 Q. B. Div. at p. 628.

Malicious interference with one's occupation. To maliciously interfere with the business of a person engaged in a lawful occupation, with injurious results, constitutes a ground of action of trespass on the case. Such interference may be by a single individual or by a number of individuals conspiring together, and in the latter case the existence of the conspiracy should be considered as aggravating the wrong and enhancing the damages. To maintain a suit for the malicious interference with one's occupation it is necessary to prove "(1) Intentional and wilful acts (2) calculated to cause damage to the plaintiffs in their lawful business (3) done with the unlawful purpose to cause such damage and loss, without right or justifiable cause on the part of the defendant, (which constitutes malice,) and (4) actual damages and loss resulting."

man's occupation, profession, or way of getting a livelihood;" as where the plaintiff is owner of a decoy for catching wild fowl, and the defendant, without entering

---

Walker v. Cronin, 107 Mass. 562. While this is true, neither law nor reason will protect a person from the effects of honest competition. If disturbance or loss come as a result of competition, or the exercise of like rights by others, it is *damnum absque injuria*, unless some superior rights by contract or otherwise are interfered with.

"Freedom is the policy of this country. But freedom does not imply a right in one person, either alone or in combination with others, to disturb or annoy another, either directly or indirectly, in his lawful business or occupation or to threaten him with annoyance or injury, for the sake of compelling him to buy peace." Carew v. Rutherford, 106 Mass. 15. See Wilder v. McKee, 111 Pa. St. 335, Walker v. Cronin, 107 Mass. 561, *supra*. And in the same case the court further said "One of the aims of the common law has always been to protect every person against the wrongful acts of every other person, whether committed alone or in combination with others, and it has provided an action for injuries done by disturbing a person in the enjoyment of any right or privilege which he has. Many illustrations of this doctrine are given in Bac. Ab. Actions on the Case, F., among which are the following 'If A being a mason, and using to sell stones, is possessed of a certain stone-pit, and B intending to discredit it and deprive him of the profits of the said mine, imposes so great threats upon his workmen, and disturbs all comers, threatening to maim and vex them with suits if they buy any stones, so that some desist from working and others from buying, A shall have an action upon the case against B, from the profit of his mine thereby injured' So if a man menaces my tenants at will of life and member, *per quod* they depart from their tenures, an action upon the case lies against him. 'If a man discharges guns near my decoy-pond with design to damnify me by frightening away the wild fowl resorting thereto and the wild fowl are thereby frightened away and I am damnified, an action on the case lies against him' 'We have no doubt that a conspiracy against a mechanic who is under a necessity of employing workmen in order to carry on his business to obtain a sum of money from him, which he is under no legal liability to pay, by inducing his workmen to leave him and by deterring others from entering into his employment, or by threatening to do this, so that he is induced to pay the money demanded under a reasonable apprehension that he cannot carry on his business without yielding to the illegal demand, is an illegal, if not a criminal conspiracy, that the acts done under it are illegal, and that the money thus obtained may be recovered back, and, if the parties succeed in injuring his business, they are liable to pay all the damage thus done him'" Id 1 Followed in Snow v. Wheeler, 113 Mass. 186. See Sherry v Perkins, 147 Id 212, 17 N E Rep 307

on the plaintiff's land, wilfully fires off guns near to the decoy, and frightens wild fowl away from it (x). Not many examples of the kind are to be found, and this is natural, for they have to be sought in a kind of obscure middle region where the acts complained of are neither wrongful in themselves as amounting to trespass against the plaintiff or some third person (y), nuisance (z), or breach of an absolute specific duty, nor yet exempt from search into their motives as being done in the exercise of common right in the pursuit of a man's lawful occupation or the ordinary use of his property (a). Mere competition carried on for the purpose of gain, not out of actual malice, and not by unlawful means, such as molestation or intimidation, is not actionable, even though it be intended to drive a rival trader out of the field, and produce that result (b). "The policy of our law, as at present declared by the legislature, is against all fetters on combination and competition unaccompanied by violence or fraud or other like injurious acts" (c). Beyond generally forbidding the use of means unlawful in themselves, the law does not impose any restriction upon competition by one trader with another with the sole view of benefiting himself. A different question would arise if there were evidence of an intention on the defendant's part to injure the plaintiff without benefiting himself. "Thus, if several persons agree not to deal at all with a particular individual, as this could not, under ordinary circumstances, benefit the persons so agreeing" (d). Driving a public performer off the stage by

---

(x) *Carrington* v. *Taylor* (1809), 11 East, 571, following *Keeble* v. *Hickeringill* (1705), ib. 573 in notes, where see Holt's judgment. And see Lord Field's opinion in *Mogul Steamship Company* v. *McGregor*, '92, A. C. 25, 51.

(y) *Tarleton* v. *McGawley*, Peake, 270, 3 R. R. 689 the defendant's act in firing at negroes to prevent them from trading with the plaintiff's ship was of course unlawful *per se*.

(z) Cp. *Ibbotson* v. *Peat* (1865), 3 H. & C. 644, 34 L. J. Ex. 118.

(a) See p. 182, above.

(b) *Mogul Steamship Company* v. *McGregor*, above.

(c) Fry L. J., 23 Q. B. Div. at p. 628.

(d) Lord Hannen in *Mogul Steamship Company* v. *McGregor*, above.

marks of disapprobation which proceed not from an honest opinion of the demerits of his performance or person, but from private enmity, is, as we have just seen, a possible but doubtful instance of this sort of wrong (e). Holt put the case of a schoolmaster frightening away children from attendance at a rival school (f).

Contract. It is really on the same principle that an action has been held to lie for maliciously (that is, with the design of injuring the plaintiff or gaining some advan-

---

(e) *Gregory* v. *Duke of Brunswick,* supra, p. 404. (f) *Keeble* v. *Hickeringill,* note (x) last page.

Malicious interference with one's contract. It is not a legal wrong to peaceably persuade one not to enter the employment of another, but to maliciously interfere with a contract of service whereby any of the parties thereto are damnified is actionable. "On the other hand it has been decided that a mere conspiracy to break a contract for the delivery of property cannot constitute a tort, even though the contract be broken in pursuance of it, the ground of it being that the party to the contract might of his own violation have broken his promise without being liable as for a wrong, and ' that an act which, if done by one alone, constitutes no ground of an action of the case, cannot be made the ground of such action by alleging it to have been done by and through a conspiracy of several. The quality of the act, and the nature of the injury inflicted by it, must determine the question whether the action will lie.' It is difficult to understand, however, why a conspiracy to deprive one of labor contracted for can be any different in nature or damaging quality from a conspiracy to deprive him of property bargained for or of anything else of value. There is no peculiar sacredness to the right to service over any other right, and no good reason can be suggested for protecting it differently." Cooley on Torts, p 330. See *Wellington* v. *Small,* 3 Cush 145, *Van Horn* v *Van Horn,* 52 N J L 287, *Webber* v *Barry,* 66 Mich 127, 33 N W Rep 289, *Rogers* v *Evarts,* 17 N Y S Rep 264.

Trades unions. Where the object of labor unions, or organizations of workmen, is to discuss and agree upon their time of service, place of employment, price of wages, and other provisions for their mutual protection and benefit, they are lawful. But when they secretly combine and conspire to intimidate by threats and coerce others to abandon their employment or desist from seeking employment where they would otherwise be employed, and thus maliciously interfere with the business and with the contracts of employés, they are jointly and severally liable for the injury done by them "The labor and skill of the workmen, be it

tage at his expense) procuring a third person to break his contract with the plaintiff, and thereby causing damage to the plaintiff (g). The precise extent and bearing of the doctrine are discussed in the final chapter of this book with reference to the difficulties that have been felt about it, and expressed in dissenting judgments and elsewhere. Those difficulties (I submit and shall in that place endeavour to prove) either disappear or are greatly reduced when the cause of action is considered as belonging to the class in which malice, in the sense of actual ill-will, is a necessary element

Or franchise Generally speaking, every wilful interference with the exercise of a franchise is actionable without regard to the defendant's act being done in good faith, by reason of a mistaken notion of duty or claim of right, or being consciously wrongful. "If a man hath a franchise

---

(g) *Lumley* v *Gye* (1853), 2 E. & B 216, 22 L J Q B 463, *Bowen* v *Hall* (1881), 6 Q B Div 33, 50 L J Q B 305.

---

of high or low degree, the plant of the manufacturer, the equipment of the farmer, the investment of the commerce are in equal sense property." If men by acts of violence destroy either, they are guilty of crime. The anathemas of a secret organization of men combined for the purpose of controlling the industry of others by a species of intimidation that works upon the mind rather than the body, are quite as dangerous, and generally altogether more effective, than acts of actual violence And while such conspiracies may give to the individual directly affected by them a private right of action for damages, they at the same time lay the basis for an indictment on the ground that the State itself is directly concerned in the promotion of all legitimate industries and the development of all of its resources, and owes the duty of protection to its citizens engaged in the exercise of the callings State v. Stewart, 59 Vt 289 See the Master Stevedores' Assoc. v Walsh, 2 Daly, 1, State v Donaldson, 32 N. J. L 151, The People v Fisher, 14 Wend. 1, State v. Burnham, 15 N H. 404; Commonwealth v. Hunt, 4 Metc. 111; Sweeny v. Torrence, 11 Pa. Co. Ct R 497, Mayer v Association, 47 N. J. Eq 519, 20 At. Rep 492, Casey v Cincinnati Typo Union, 45 Fed. Rep 135. But one not injured in his business by a combination of dealers cannot complain of the combination as unlawful. Fairbank v. Newton, 50 Wis. 628.

and is hindered in the enjoyment thereof, an action doth he, which is an action upon the case" (*h*). But persons may as public officers be in a quasi-judicial position in which they will not be liable for an honest though mistaken exercise of discretion in rejecting a vote or the like, but will be liable for a wilful and conscious, and in that sense malicious, denial of right (*i*). In such cases the wrong, if any, belongs to the class we have just been considering.

Maintenance. The wrong of maintenance, or aiding a party in litigation without either interest in the suit, or lawful cause of kindred, affection, or charity for aiding him, is akin to malicious prosecution and other abuses of legal process; but the ground of it is not so much an independent wrong as particular damage resulting from "a wrong founded upon a prohibition by statute" — a series of early statutes said to be in affirmation of the common law — "which makes it a criminal act and a misdemeanor" (*k*). Hence it seems that a corporation cannot be guilty of maintenance (*k*). Actions for maintenance are in modern times rare though possible (*l*), and the decision of the Court of Appeal that mere charity, with or without reasonable ground, is an excuse for maintaining the suit of a stranger (*m*), does not tend to encourage them.

(*h*) Holt C. J. in *Ashby* v *White* at p. 13 of the special report first printed in 1837. The action was on the case merely because trespass would not lie for the infringement of an incorporeal right of that kind.

(*i*) *Tozer* v. *Child* (1857), Ex. Ch. 7 E. & B. 377, 26 L J Q B 151.

(*k*) Lord Selborne, *Metrop. Bank* v *Pooley* (1885), 10 App Ca 210, 218, 54 L J Q B 449.

(*l*) *Bradlaugh* v *Newdegate* (1883), 11 Q. B. D 1, 52 L J Q B 454.

(*m*) *Harris* v *Brisco* (1886), 17 Q B Div. 504, 55 L J Q B. 423.

CHAPTER IX.

WRONGS TO POSSESSION AND PROPERTY.

I.— Duties regarding Property generally.

Absolute duty to respect others' property Every kind of intermeddling with anything which is the subject of property is a wrong unless it is either authorized by some person entitled to deal with the thing in that particular way, or justified by authority of law, or (in some cases but by no means generally) excusable on the ground that it is done under a reasonable though mistaken supposition of lawful title or authority. Broadly speaking, we touch the property of others at our peril, and honest mistake in

---

Absolute duty to respect others' property The general proposition is affirmed in Amick v O'Hara, 6 Blackf 258, Cate v Cate, 14 N H 211, Bruch v Carter, 32 N J L 554, Dexter v Cole, 6 Wis 319, Magee v. Tappan, 23 Cal 306, Hobart v Haggett, 12 Me. 67, Luttrell v Hazen, 3 Sneed (Tenn.), 20, Brown v. Stackhouse, 155 Pa St 582, 26 At Rep 669, 32 W N C. 407

Thus, trespass lies against one who cuts or removes timber without lawful authority from the owner, though the trespasser believed he had proper authority from the actual owner Higginson v York, 5 Mass 341; Allison v Little, 85 Ala 512, Loevenberg v Rosenthal, 18 Oreg 178, 22 Pac Rep 601 An action lies for a trespass committed over a boundary line by mistake Blaen Avon Coal Co v. McCulloch, 59 Md. 403 Although the plaintiff's mistake had led the defendant to commit the trespass. Pearson v. Inlow. Advice of counsel will not justify a trespass on land Watson v State, 63 Ala 19 Nor will the desire of destroying an animal *feræ naturæ* Glenn v Kays, 1 Ill. App. 479.

A person who aids a grantee in a bill of sale in the removal of the property is liable where it turns out that the bill of sale was in fact a mortgage. Wallard v Wortham, 84 Ill. 446 See Flanders v Colby, 28 N H 34

There is room for distinction, however, where not only the result of

acting for our own interest (a), or even an honest intention to act for the benefit of the true owner (b), will avail us nothing if we transgress.

Title, justification, excuse. A man may be entitled in divers ways to deal with property moveable or immoveable, and within a wider or narrower range. He may be an owner in possession, with indefinite rights of use and dominion, free to give or to sell, nay to waste lands or destroy chattels if such be his pleasure. He may be a possessor with rights either determined as to length of time, or undetermined though determinable, and of an extent which may vary from being hardly distinguishable from full dominion to being strictly limited to a specific purpose. It belongs to the law of property to tell us what are the rights of owners and possessors, and by what acts in the law they may be created, transferred, or destroyed. Again, a man may have the right of using property to a limited extent, and either to the exclusion of all other persons besides the owner or possessor, or concurrently with other persons, without himself being either owner or possessor. The definition of such rights belongs to that part of the law of property which deals with easements and profits. Again, he may be authorized by law, for the execution of justice or for purposes of public safety and convenience, or under exceptional conditions for the true owner's benefit, to interfere with property to which he has no title and does not make any claim. We have seen some-

---

(a) *Hollins v. Fowler* (1875), L. R. 7 H. L. 757, 44 L. J. Q. B. 169.
(b) In trespass, *Kirk v. Gregory* (1876), 1 Ex. D. 55, 45 L. J. Ex. 186; in trover, *Hiort v. Bott* (1874), L. R. 9 Ex. 86, 43 L. J. Ex. 81.

the act, but, also the act itself was not intended. Thus, a person driving cattle along the highway is not liable for the conversion of cattle joining his drove without his notice. Young v. Vaughan, 1 Houst. 331; Brooks v. Olmstead, 17 Pa. St. 24. Nor is such person liable where cattle escape from the drove into plaintiff's property. Rightmire v. Shephard, 59 Hun, 620. But see Guille v. Swan, 19 Johns. 381, *supra*, 59.

what of this in the chapter of "General Exceptions." Again, he may be justified by a consent of the owner or possessor which does not give him any interest in the property, but merely excuses an act, or a series of acts, that otherwise would be wrongful. Such consent is known as a licence.

Title dependent on contract. Title to property, and authority to deal with property in specified ways, are commonly conferred by contract or in pursuance of some contract. Thus it oftentimes depends on the existence or on the true construction of a contract whether a right of property exists, or what is the extent of rights admitted to exist. A man obtains goods by fraud and sells them to another purchaser who buys in good faith, reasonably supposing that he is dealing with the true owner. The fraudulent re-seller may have made a contract which the original seller could have set aside, as against him,

---

Title dependent on contract. Goods feloniously obtained may be recovered from a *bona fide* purchaser Robinson v. Dauchy, 3 Barb 20, Robinson v. Skipworth, 23 Ind 311; Basset v Green, 2 Duv 560, Browning v Magill, 2 Har & J. 308 But this rule does not apply where the goods are obtained by a felony of statutory creation as distinguished from common law felonies Benedict v Williams, 48 Hun, 123

Where A hires a horse by giving a worthless check and then sells him to B, B cannot retain the horse. Dodd v Arnold, 28 Tex. 97

The doctrine of market overt as known in England is not recognized in this country Hardy v Metzgar, 2 Yeates, 347, Leckey v. McDermott, 8 Serg. & R. 580; Hosack v Weaver, 1 Yeates, 478, Rowland v Gundy, 1 Ohio, 263, Wheelwright v. DePeyster, 1 Johns. 471; Dame v. Baldwin, 8 Mass 518; Griffith v Fowler, 18 Vt 390

One acquiring property through fraud derives no title as against the injured party Wheaton v. Baker, 14 Barb 594, Mowey v Walsh, 8 Cow 238. But mere fraud in a sale gives no right to prevent an innocent vendee from taking away the property after delivery. McCarty v Vickery, 12 Johns. 318 However, where there is an entire absence of title in the seller, good faith will not protect the purchaser. Church v Mellville, 17 Oreg. 413, 21 Pac Rep 387 See *ante*, p 376.

Taking possession of goods under a contract which the taker of the goods never intended to carry out is as much a trespass as a forcible seizure Butler v. Collins, 12 Cal 457

on the ground of fraud. If so, he acquires property in the goods, though a defeasible property, and the ultimate purchaser in good faith has a good title. But the circumstances of the fraud may have been such that there was no true consent on the part of the first owner, no contract at all, and no right of property whatever, not so much as lawful possession, acquired by the apparent purchaser. If so, the defrauder has not any lawful interest which he can transfer even to a person acting in good faith and reasonably, and the ultimate purchaser acquires no manner of title, and notwithstanding his innocence is liable as a wrong-doer (c). Principles essentially similar, but affected in their application, and not unfrequently disguised, by the complexity of our law of real property, hold good of dealings with land (d).

Exceptional protection of certain dealings in good faith. Acts of persons dealing in good faith with an apparent owner may be, and have been, protected in various ways and to a varying extent by different systems of law. The purchaser from an apparent owner may acquire, as under the common-law rule of sales in market overt, a better title than his vendor had; or, by an extension in the same line, the dealings of apparently authorized agents in the way of sale or pledge may, for the security of commerce, have a special validity conferred on them, as under our Factors Act (e); or one who has innocently dealt with goods which he is now unable to produce or restore specifically may be held personally excused, saving the true owner's liberty to retake the goods if he can find them, and subject to the remedies over, if any, which may be available under a contract of sale or a warranty for the person dispossessed by the true owner. Excuse of this kind is

(c) *Hollins* v. *Fowler* (1875), L. R. 7 H. L. 757, 44 L. J. Q. B. 169; *Cundy* v. *Lindsay* (1878), 3 App. Ca. 459, 47 L. J. Q. B. 481.

(d) See *Pilcher* v. *Rawlins* (1871), L. R. 7 Ch. 259, 41 L. J. Ch. 485.

(e) Consolidated by the Factors Act, 1889, 52 & 53 Vict. c. 45.

however rarely admitted, though much the same result may sometimes be arrived at on special technical grounds.

The rights and remedies known to the common law are possessory. It would seem that, apart from doubtful questions of title (which no system of law can wholly avoid), there ought not to be great difficulty in determining what amounts to a wrong to property, and who is the person wronged. But in fact the common law does present great difficulties, and this because its remedies were bound, until a recent date, to medieval forms, and limited by medieval conceptions. The forms of action brought not Ownership but Possession to the front in accordance with a habit of thought which, strange as it may now seem to us, found the utmost difficulty in conceiving rights of property as having full existence or being capable of transfer and succession unless in close connexion with the physical control of something which could be passed from hand to hand, or at least a part of it delivered in the name of the whole (*f*). An owner in possession was protected against disturbance, but the rights of an owner out of possession were obscure and weak. To this day it continues so with regard to chattels. For many purposes the "true owner" of goods is the person, and only the person, entitled to immediate possession. The term is a short and convenient one, and may be used without scruple, but on condition of being rightly understood. Regularly the common law protects ownership only through possessory rights and remedies. The reversion or reversionary interest of the freeholder or general owner out of possession is indeed well known to our authorities, and by conveyancers it is regarded as a present estate or interest. But when it has to be defended in a court of com-

(*f*) See Mr. F. W. Maitland's articles on "The Seisin of Chattels" and "The Mystery of Seisin," L. Q. R. i. 324, ii. 481, where divers profitable comparisons of the rules concerning real and personal property will be found.

mon law, the forms of action treat it rather as the shadow cast before by a right to possess at a time still to come. It has been said that there is no doctrine of possession in our law. The reason of this appearance, an appearance capable of deceiving even learned persons, is that possession has all but swallowed up ownership, and the rights of a possessor, or one entitled to possess, have all but monopolized the very name of property. There is a common phrase in our books that possession is *prima facie* evidence of title. It would be less intelligible at first sight, but not less correct, to say that in the developed system of common law pleading and procedure, as it existed down to the middle of this century, proof of title was material only as evidence of a right to possess. And it must be remembered that although forms of action are no longer with us, causes of action are what they were, and cases may still occur where it is needful to go back to the vanished form as the witness and measure of subsisting rights. The sweeping protection given to rights of property at this day is made up by a number of theoretically distinct causes of action. The disturbed possessor had his action of trespass (in some special cases replevin); if at the time of the wrong done the person entitled to possess was not in actual legal possession, his remedy was detinue, or, in the developed system, trover. An owner who had neither possession nor the immediate right to possession could redress himself by a special action on the case, which did not acquire any technical name.

Possession and detention. Notwithstanding first appearances, then, the common law has a theory of possession, and a highly elaborated one. To discuss it fully would not be apppropriate here (*g*); but we have to bear in mind that it must be known who is in legal possession of any given

---

(*g*) See 'An Essay on Possession in the Common Law,' by Mr. (now Justice) R. S. Wright and the present writer (Oxford: Clarendon Press, 1888).

subject of property, and who is entitled to possess it, before we can tell what wrongs are capable of being committed, and against whom, by the person having physical control over it, or by others. Legal possession does not necessarily coincide either with actual physical control or the present power thereof (the "detention" of Continental terminology), or with the right to possess (constantly called "property" in our books); and it need not have a rightful origin. The separation of detention, possession in the strict sense, and the right to possess, is both possible and frequent. A. lends a book to B., gratuitously and not for any fixed time, and B gives the book to his servant to carry home. Here B.'s servant has physical possession, better named custody or detention, but neither legal possession (h) nor the right to possess. B has legal and rightful possession, and the right to possess as against every one but A; while A. has not possession, but has a right to possess which he can make absolute at any moment by determining the bailment to B., and which the law regards for many purposes as if it were already absolute. As to an actual legal possession (besides and beyond mere detention) being acquired by wrong, the wrongful change of possession was the very substance of disseisin as to land, and is still the very substance of trespass by taking and carrying away (*de bonis asportatis*), and as such it was and is a necessary goods condition of the offence of larceny at common law.

The common law, when it must choose between denying legal possession to the person apparently in possession, and attributing it to a wrong-doer, generally prefers the latter course. In Roman law there is no such general tendency, though the results are often similar (*i*).

(*h*) Yet it is not certain that he could not maintain trespass against a stranger, see *Moore* v *Robinson*, 2 B & Ad 817 The law about the custody of servants and persons in a like position has vacillated from time to time, and has never been defined as a whole

(*i*) Cp Holland, "Elements of Jurisprudence," 5th ed. pp 166–171

Trespass and conversion. Trespass is the wrongful disturbance of another person's possession of land (j) or goods. Therefore it cannot be committed by a person who is himself in possession, though in certain exceptional cases a dispunishable or even a rightful possessor of goods may by his own act, during a continuous physical control, make himself a mere trespasser. But a possessor may do wrong in other ways. He may commit waste as to the land he holds, or he may become liable to an action of ejectment by holding over after his title or interest is determined. As to goods he may detain them without right after it has become his duty to return them, or he may convert them to his own use, a phrase of which the scope has been greatly extended in the modern law. Thus we have two kinds of duty, namely to refrain from meddling with what is lawfully possessed by another, and to refrain from abusing possession which we have lawfully gotten under a limited title; and the breach of these produces distinct kinds of wrong, having, in the old system of the common law, their distinct and appropriate remedies. But a strict observance of these distinctions in practice would have led to intolerable results, and a working margin was given by beneficent fictions which (like most indirect and gradual reforms) extended the usefulness of the law at the cost of making it intricate and difficult to understand. On the one hand the remedies of an actual possessor were freely accorded to persons who had only the right to possess (k); on the other hand the person wronged was constantly allowed at his option to proceed against a mere

---

(j) Formerly it was said that trespass to land was a disturbance not amounting to disseisin, though it might be "vicina disseisinae," which is explained by "si ad commodum uti non possit" Bracton, fo 217 a. I do not think this distinction was regarded in any later period, or was ever attempted as to goods

(k) See *Smith v Milles*, 1 T R 480, and note that "constructive possession," as used in our books, includes (i) possession exercised through a servant or licensee, (ii) possession conferred by law, in certain cases, e g on an executor, independently of any physical apprehension or transfer, (iii) an immediate right to possess, which is distinct from actual possession.

trespasser as if the trespasser had only abused a lawful or at any rate excusable possession.

Alternative remedies. In the later history of common law pleading trespass and conversion became largely though not wholly interchangeable. Detinue, the older form of action for the recovery of chattels, was not abolished, but it was generally preferable to treat the detention as a conversion and sue in trover (*l*), so that trover practically superseded detinue, as the writ of right and the various assizes, the older and once the only proper remedies whereby

(*l*) Blackst. III. 152.

Alternative remedies. The gist of the action of detinue is the continuing nature of the act of detainer, whereas, trespass and trover are torts founded on an act which becomes complete by a single performance. Wittick v. Traun, 27 Ala. 562, 570; Harris v. Hillman, 26 Ala. 38; Charles v. Elliott, 1 Dev. & B. 465; Jennings v. Gibson, 1 Miss. 231; Haley v. Rowan, 5 Yerg. 301.

Thus, detinue cannot be maintained after the destruction of the chattel in dispute. Lindsey v. Perry, 1 Ala. 203; Caldwell v. Fenwick, 2 Dana, 232. Nor has plaintiff in detinue the right to elect to take damages instead of the specific property when tendered by defendant. Robinson v. Richards, 15 Ala. 354.

That the distinction between trespass and trover is sometimes of practical importance even under the codes, is shown in Grafton v. Carmichael, (48 Wis. 660.) This case is an action arising out of the seizure of certain goods of the plaintiff by the sheriff under the direction of the defendant. The petition charged the defendant with the *taking* of certain property of the plaintiff wrongfully and converting the same to his own use. The original *taking* under the attachment writ by the sheriff was valid but the sale thereunder was invalid by reason of certain omissions. The plaintiff's right to recover hinged upon whether his action was in trespass or trover — if the former, recovery was barred, as the original taking by the defendant was under a valid writ — if the latter, the plaintiff was entitled to recover for the actual conversion suffered under the defendant's illegal sale.

In the United States the action of replevin, called claim and delivery in some of the code States, has come to be the general remedy to determine the right of possession to specific chattels, its practical use in this respect in England being limited to cases of distress for rent or for cattle taken *damage feasant*.

a freeholder could recover possession of the land, were superseded by ejectment, a remedy at first introduced merely for the protection of leasehold interests. With all their artificial extensions these forms of action did not completely suffice. There might still be circumstances in which a special action on the case was required. And these complications cannot be said to be even now wholly obsolete. For exceptional circumstances may still occur in which it is doubtful whether an action lies without proof of actual damage, or, assuming that the plaintiff is entitled to judgment, whether that judgment shall be for the value of the goods wrongfully dealt with or only for his actual damage, which may be a nominal sum. Under such conditions we have to go back to the old forms and see what the appropriate action would have been. This is not a desirable state of the law (*m*), but while it exists we must take account of it.

II — *Trespass.*

What shall be said a trespass. Trespass may be committed by various kinds of acts, of which the most obvious are entry on another's land (trespass *quare clausum fregit*), and taking another's goods (trespass *de bonis asportatis*) (*n*). Notwithstanding that trespasses punishable in the king's court were said to be *vi et armis*, and were supposed to be punishable as a breach of the king's peace, neither the use of force, nor the breaking of an inclosure or transgression of a visible boundary, nor even an unlawful intention, is necessary to constitute an actionable trespass. It is likewise immaterial, in strictness of law, whether there be any actual damage or not. "Every invasion of private property, be it ever so minute, is a

---

(*m*) See per Thesiger L. J., 4 Ex. Div. 199.

(*n*) The exact parallel to trespass *de bonis asportatis* is of course not trespass *qu. cl. fr.* simply, but trespass amounting to a disseisin of the freeholder or ouster of the tenant for years or other interest not freehold.

trespass" (o). There is no doubt that if one walks across a stubble field without lawful authority or the occupier's leave, one is technically a trespasser, and it may be doubted whether persons who roam about common lands, not being in exercise of some particular right, are in a better position. It may be that, where the public enjoyment of such lands for sporting or other recreation is notorious, for example on Dartmoor (p), a licence (as to which more presently) would be implied. Oftentimes warnings or requests are addressed to the public to abstain from going on some specified part of open land or private ways, or from doing injurious acts. In such cases there seems to be a general licence to use the land or ways in conformity with the owner's will thus expressed. But even so, persons using the land are no more than "bare licensees," and their right is of the slenderest.

(o) *Lathi* v. *Carrington*, 19 St. Tr. 1066. "Property" here, as constantly in our books, really means possession or a right to possession.

(p) As a matter of fact, the Dartmoor hunt has an express licence from the Duchy of Cornwall.

What shall be said a trespass. Any unlawful interference with the possession of the property of others, whether with or without force, is a trespass. Dexter v Cole, 6 Wis 319, Norvell v Gray, 1 Swan, 96; Brown v Perkins, 1 Allen, 89, Hitch v Donnell, 74 Mo 163, Newkirk v. Sabler, 9 Barb 652, Mairs v Real Estate Assoc., 89 N Y. 498, Alexander v. Hard, 64 N Y 228, Halligan v Chicago & R I. R Co, 15 Ill 558; Gunsolus v Lormer, 54 Wis 630; 12 N. W. Rep 62, Moore v Perry, 61 Mo 174, Bascom v. Dempsey, 143 Mass. 409, Chandler v. Walker, 21 N. H. 282.

Trespass lies though the only damage be the treading down of turf. Dougherty v Stepp, 1 Dev & B 371. Or, even if no grass or herbage be in existence on the close. Nensorn v. Anderson, 2 Ired 42. See, *ante*, pp 9, 10.

Mere words do not constitute a trespass. Wheeler v Moore, Wright, 408. But one who stops on the sidewalk in front of a house to abuse its occupant is a trespasser Adams v Rivers, 11 Barb 390.

Sign painting on a wall of a house though with the tenant's consent is an interference with the owner's possession. Devlin v Snellenberg, 132 Pa St. 186, 18 At Rep 1119. But the mere use of gas after notice of arrears is no trespass Alexander Mining Co v Painter, 28 N E Rep. 113.

Quaere concerning balloons. It has been doubted whether it is a trespass to pass over land without touching the soil, as one may in a balloon, or to cause a material object, as shot fired from a gun, to pass over it. Lord Ellenborough thought it was not in itself a trespass "to interfere with the column of air superincumbent on the close," and that the remedy would be by action on the case for any actual damage: though he had no difficulty in holding that a man is a trespasser who fires a gun on his own land so that the shot fall on his neighbour's land (*q*). Fifty years later Lord Blackburn inclined to think differently (*r*), and his opinion seems the better. Clearly there can be a wrongful entry on land below the surface, as by mining, and in fact this kind of trespass is rather prominent in our modern books. It does not seem possible on the principles of the common law to assign any reason why an entry at any height above the surface should not also be a trespass. The improbability of actual damage may be an excellent practical reason for not suing a man who sails over one's land in a balloon; but this appears irrelevant to the pure legal theory. Trespasses clearly devoid of legal excuse are committed every day on the surface itself, and yet are of so harmless a kind that no reasonable occupier would or does take any notice

---

(*q*) *Pickering* v. *Rudd* (1815), 4 Camp. 219, 221.

(*r*) *Kenyon* v. *Hart* (1865), 6 B. & S. 249, 252, 34 L. J. M. C. 87, and see per Fry L. J. in *Wandsworth Board of Works* v. *United Telephone Co.* (1884), 13 Q. B. Div. 904, 927, 53 L. J. Q. B. 449. It may be otherwise, as in that case, where statutory interests in land are conferred for special purposes.

Quaere concerning balloons. *Vide* Guille v. Swan, 19 Johns. 381, *supra*, 39.

In Hunter v. Farren (127 Mass. 481), plaintiff had been driven from his house and land by defendant blasting on the highway, thereby causing rocks to fly over plaintiff's land. Plaintiff settled with defendant for the actual damage caused to his property by rocks striking it, but it was held, that the settlement was no bar to the trespass of the rocks which flew over his land and the damage resulting from loss of business.

of them. Then one can hardly doubt that it might be a nuisance, apart from any definite damage, to keep a balloon hovering over another man's land: but if it is not a trespass in law to have the balloon there at all, one does not see how a continuing trespass is to be committed by keeping it there. Again, it would be strange if we could object to shots being fired across our land only in the event of actual injury being caused, and the passage of the foreign body in the air above our soil being thus a mere incident in a distinct trespass to person or property. The doctrine suggested by Lord Ellenborough's dictum, if generally accepted and acted on, would so far be for the benefit of the public service that the existence of a right of "innocent passage" for projectiles over the heads and lands of the Queen's subjects would increase the somewhat limited facilities of the land forces for musketry and artillery practice at long ranges. But we are not aware that such a right has in fact been claimed or exercised.

Trespass by a man's cattle is dealt with exactly like trespass by himself; but in the modern view of the law this is only part of a more general rule or body of rules imposing an exceptionally strict and unqualified duty of safe custody on grounds of public expediency. In that connexion we shall accordingly return to the subject (s).

Trespass to goods. Trespass to goods may be committed by taking possession of them, or by any other act "in itself immediately injurious" to the goods in respect of the pos-

(s) Chap XII below

Trespass to goods. Following what has just been said under WHAT SHALL BE SAID A TRESPASS, it is a rule that a trespass to personal property is an injury to the right of possession. And the fact that the right was infringed without wrongful intent, or by accident or mistake, is no excuse. Dexter v Cole, 6 Wis 320, Lunt v Brown, 13 Me 236, Staples v. Smith, 48 Me 470, Ely v. Ehle, 3 N Y 507, Billingsly v. White, 59 Pa St. 469, Haythorn v Rushforth, 19 N. J. L. 160, Mugridge v. Eveleth, 9

sessor's interest (*t*), as by killing (*u*), beating (*x*), or chasing (*y*) animals, or defacing a work of art. Where the possession is changed the trespass is an *asportation* (from the old form of pleading, *cepit et asportavit* for inanimate chattels, *abduxit* for animals), and may amount to the offence of theft. Other trespasses to goods may be criminal offences under the head of malicious injury to property. The current but doubtful doctrine of the civil trespass being "merged in the felony" when the trespass is felonious has been considered in an earlier chapter (*z*). Authority, so far as known to the present writer, does not clearly show whether it is in strictness a trespass merely to lay hands on another's chattel without either dispossession (*a*) or actual damage. By the analogy of trespass to land it seems that it must be so. There is no doubt that the least actual damage would be enough (*b*). And cases are conceivable in which the power of treating a mere unauthorized touching as a trespass might be salutary and necessary, as where valuable objects are exhibited in places either public or open to a large class of persons. In the old precedents trespass to goods hardly occurs except in conjunction with trespass to land (*c*).

(*t*) Blackst. iii. 153.

(*u*) *Wright* v. *Ramscot*, 1 Saund. 83, 1 Wms. Saund. 108 (trespass for killing a mastiff).

(*x*) *Dand* v. *Sexton*, 3 T. R. 37 (trespass *vi et armis* for beating the plaintiff's dog).

(*y*) A form of writ is given for chasing the plaintiff's sheep with dogs, F. N. B. 90 L, so for shearing the plaintiff's sheep, *ib.* 87 G.

(*z*) P. 233, above.

(*a*) See *Gaylard* v. *Morris* (1849), 3 Ex. 695, 18 L. J. Ex. 297.

(*b*) "Scratching the panel of a carriage would be a trespass," Alderson B. in *Fouldes* v. *Willoughby*, 8 M. & W. 549.

(*c*) See F. N. B. 86–88, *passim*.

Metc. 233, *Stanley v. Gaylord*, 1 Cush. 536. *White v. Brantley*, 37 Ala. 430; *Hobart v. Hagget*, 12 Me. 67; *Gilman v. Emery*, 54 Me. 460; *Bruch v. Carter*, 32 N. J. L. 554; *Dufour v. Anderson*, 95 Ind. 302; *Burgess v. Graffam*, 18 Fed. Rep. 251; *Welsh v. Bell*, 32 Pa. St. 12.

III.—*Injuries to Reversion*

Wrongs to an owner not in possession. A person in possession of property may do wrong by refusing to deliver possession to a person entitled, or by otherwise assuming to deal with the property as owner or adversely to the true owner, or by dealing with it under colour of his real possessory title but in excess of his rights, or, where the nature of the object admits of it, by acts amounting to destruction or total change of character, such as breaking up land by opening mines, burning wood, grinding corn, or spinning cotton into yarn, which acts however are only the extreme exercise of assumed dominion. The law started from entirely distinct conceptions of the mere detaining of property from the person entitled, and the spoiling or altering it to the prejudice of one in reversion or remainder, or a general owner (*d*). For the former case the common law provided its most ancient remedies— the writ of right (and later the various assizes and the writ of entry) for land, and the parallel writ of detinue (parallel as being merely a variation of the writ of debt, which was precisely similar in form to the writ of right) for goods; to this must be added, in special, but once frequent and important cases, replevin (*e*). For the latter the writ of waste (as extended by the Statutes of Marlbridge and Gloucester) was available as to land; later this was supplanted by an action on the case (*f*) "in the

---

(*d*) As to the term "reversionary interest" applied to goods, *cp.* Dicey on Parties, 345. In one way "reversioner" would be more correct than "owner" or "general owner," for the person entitled to sue in trover or prosecute for theft is not necessarily *dominus*, and the *dominus* of the chattel may be disqualified from so suing or prosecuting.

(*e*) It seems useless to say more of replevin here. The curious reader may consult *Mennie* v. *Blake* (1856), 6 E. & B. 842, 25 L. J. Q. B. 399. For the earliest form of writ of entry see Close Rolls, vol. i. p. 52. Blackstone is wrong in stating it to have been older than the assizes.

(*f*) Under certain conditions waste might amount to trespass, Litt. s. 71, see more in sect. vii. of the present chapter.

Wrongs to an owner not in possession. See American notes under MODERN LAW OF WASTE, *post*, p. 429.

nature of waste," and in modern times the power and remedies of courts of equity have been found still more effectual (g). The process of devising a practical remedy for owners of chattels was more circuitous; they were helped by an action on the case which became a distinct species under the name of trover, derived from the usual though not necessary form of pleading, which alleged that the defendant found the plaintiff's goods and converted them to his own use (h). The original notion of *conversion* in personal chattels answers closely to that of *waste* in tenements; but it was soon extended so as to cover the whole ground of detinue (i), and largely overlap trespass, a mere trespasser whose acts would have amounted to conversion if done by a lawful possessor not being allowed to take exception to the true owner "waiving the trespass," and professing to assume in the defendant's favour that his possession had a lawful origin.

IV.—*Waste.*

Waste. Waste is any unauthorized act of a tenant for a freehold estate not of inheritance, or for any lesser interest, which tends to the destruction of the tenement, or otherwise to the injury of the inheritance. Such injury need not consist in loss of market value; an alteration not otherwise mischievous may be waste in that it throws doubt on the identification of the property, and thereby impairs

---

(g) For the history and old law, see Co Litt 53, 54, Blackst ii 281, iii. 225, notes to *Greene* v *Cole*, 2 Wms Saund 644, and *Woodhouse* v *Walker* (1880), 5 Q B D 404 The action of waste proper could be brought only " by him that hath the immediate estate of inheritance," Co Litt 53a

(h) Blackst iii 152, cf the judgment of Martin B in *Burroughes* v. *Bayne* (1860), 5 H & N 296, 29 L J Ex 185, 188, and as to the forms of pleading, Bro Ab Accion sur le Case, 103, 109, 113, and see Littleton's remark in 33 H VI, 27, pl 12, an action of detinue where a finding by the defendant was alleged, that "this declaration *per inventionem* is a new found Halliday", the case is translated by Mr R S. Wright in Pollock and Wright on Possession, 174

(i) Martin B, l c, whose phrase "in very ancient times" is a little misleading, for trover, as a settled common form, seems to date only from the 16th century, Reeves Hist Eng L iv 526

the evidence of title. It is said that every conversion of land from one species to another — as ploughing up woodland, or turning arable into pasture land — is waste, and it has even been said that building a new house is waste (*k*). But modern authority does not bear this out; "in order to prove waste you must prove an injury to the inheritance" either "in the sense of value" or "in the sense of destroying identity" (*l*). And in the United States, especially the Western States, many acts are held to be only in a natural and reasonable way of using and improving the land — clearing wild woods for example — which in England, or even in the Eastern States, would be manifest waste (*m*). As to permissive waste, *i. e.*, suffering the tenement to lose its value or go to ruin for want of necessary repair, a tenant for life or years is liable therefor if an express duty to repair is imposed upon him by the instrument creating his estate; otherwise he is not (*n*). It seems that it can in no case be waste to use a tenement in an apparently reasonable and proper manner, "having regard to its character and to the purposes for which it was intended to be used" (*o*), whatever the actual consequences of such user may be. Where a particular course of user has been carried on for a considerable course of time, with the apparent knowledge and assent of the owner of the inheritance, the Court will make all reasonable presumptions in favour of referring acts so done to a lawful origin (*p*). Destructive waste by a tenant at will may amount to trespass, in the strict sense, against the lessor.

(*k*) "If the tenant build a new house, it is waste, and if he suffer it to be wasted, it is a new waste" Co Litt 53 *a*

(*l*) *Jones* v *Chappell* (1875), 20 Eq 539, 540—2 (Jessel M R), *Mews* v *Cobley*, '92, 2 Ch 253

(*m*) Cooley on Torts, 333

(*n*) *Re Cartwright, Avis* v *Newman* (1889), 41 Ch D 532, 58 L J Ch 590 An equitable tenant for life is not liable for permissive waste *Powys* v *Blagrave* (1854), 4 D M G 448 *Re Hotchkys, Freke* v *Calmady* (1886), 32 Ch D 408, 55 L J Ch 546

(*o*) *Manchester Bonded Warehouse Co* v *Carr* (1880), 5 C P D 507, 512, 49 L J C P 809, following *Saner* v *Bilton* (1878), 7 Ch D 815, 821, 47 L J Ch 267, cp *Job* v *Potton* (1875), 20 Eq 84, 44 L J Ch 262

(*p*) *Elias* v *Snowdon Slate Quarries Co.* (1879), 4 App Ca 454, 465, 48 L J Ch 811

The reason will be more conveniently explained hereafter (q)

Modern law of waste: tenants for life. In modern practice, questions of waste arise either between a tenant for life (r) and those in remainder, or between landlord

---

(q) See below in sect. vii. of this chapter.

(r) In the United States where tenancy in dower is still common, there are many modern decisions on questions of waste arising out of such tenancies. See Cooley on Torts, 313, or Scribner on Dower (2nd ed 1883), i 212–214, ii 795 sqq.

Modern law of waste. What constitutes waste in England might not be considered waste in the United States, or vice versa. And this is because the material conditions of the two countries are different. See Kidd v. Dennison, 6 Barb. 19, Keller v. Eastman, 11 Vt 293, Findley v. Smith, 6 Munf 134.

In some parts of the United States standing timber is not regarded as valuable and its removal is the first step towards cultivation. Whether the removal of timber is waste depends on the circumstances, good husbandry being the test, and the question is for the jury. Alexander v Fisher, 7 Ala 514, Drown v. Smith, 52 Me 141, Gardner v Deering, 1 Page, 574, Wilkinson v Wilkinson, 59 Wis 557, Keeler v Eastman, 11 Vt. 293, McGregor v Brown, 10 N Y. 114, Chase v Hazelton, 7 N H 171, King v. Miller, 99 N C 583, 6 S E Rep 660, Clemence v Steere, 1 R I 222.

It is not waste to cut timber for necessary fences though timber is scarce Calvert v Rice, 91 Ky. 533, 16 S W Rep 351. Nor to cut fuel for a furnace from land which is attached to the furnace Den v Kinney, 5 N J L 552.

That the value of land is not diminished, or even increased, is no defence to actual waste Rossman v Adams, 91 Mich. 69, 51 N W. Rep. 685, Moses v Johnson, 88 Ala 517, 7 So. Rep 146.

When the chief inducement to cut timber is the profit from its sale, waste is committed Kidd v Dennison, 6 Barb. 19, Davis v. Gillian, 5 Ired Eq 308.

Selling hay off a farm is not waste, but aliter is to digging bog-grass Sarles v. Sarles, 3 Sandf Ch 601. So, taking clay from the soil for the manufacture of bricks is waste. University v Tucker, 31 W. Va 621, 8 S E Rep 410, Livingston v Reynolds, 2 Hill (Ky), 157. Also, letting hogs injure the character of meadow land is waste. Bellows v McGinnis, 17 Ind. 64.

Mere ill-husbandry is not waste Richards v Torbett, 3 Houst 172. Yet, it has been held that neglect to observe the proper rotation of crops was waste. Wilds v. Layton, 1 Del Ch. 226. And that the

and tenant. In the former case, the unauthorized cutting of timber is the most usual ground of complaint; in the latter, the forms of misuse or neglect are as various as the uses, agricultural, commercial, or manufacturing, for which the tenement may be let and occupied. With regard to timber, it is to be observed that there are "timber estates" on which wood is grown for the purpose of periodical cutting and sale, so that "cutting the timber is the mode of cultivation" (s). On such land cutting the timber is equivalent to taking a crop

---

(s) As to the general law concerning timber, and its possible variation by local custom, see the judgment of Jessel M. R., *Honywood* v. *Honywood* (1874), 18 Eq. 306, 309, 43 L. J. Ch. 652.

---

exhaustion of the soil by constant tillage was waste. Sales v. Sales, 3 Sandf. 601.

The tearing down of a house is waste though a better one replace it. Dooley v. Stringham, 4 Utah, 107, 7 Pac. Rep. 405.

It is permissive waste to allow land to be sold for taxes. Cannon v. Barry, 59 Miss. 289. Or to suffer a gin-house to be dismantled. Id. Or to suffer a pasture to be overrun with weeds. Clemence v. Steere, 1 R. I. 272. But it is not waste to allow buildings used for housing slaves before the emancipation to remain unrepaired thereafter unless their utility in some other direction be apparent. Sherrill v. Connor, 107 N. C. 630, 12 S. E. Rep. 588.

An action is maintainable for injury to a reversionary right. Webb v. Portland Mfg. Co., 3 Summ. 190. While a life tenant shall not open new or discontinued mines, (Gaines v. Greene, etc. Co., 32 N. J. Eq. 86, Franklin Coal Co. v. McMullen, 49 Md. 549), he may exhaust mines and quarries open at the commencement of the estate. Sayers v. Haskinson, 110 Pa. St. 473, 1 Atl. Rep. 508, McCord v. Oakland Quicksilver Co., 64 Cal. 134, 27 Pac. Rep. 863, Russell v. Merchants' Bank, 47 Minn. 286, 50 N. W. Rep. 228.

An injunction will issue upon threats to commit waste. White Water Valley Canal Co. v. Comeggs, 2 Ind. 469; Loundan v. Warfield, 3 J. J. Marsh 196. But not unless the injury would be irreparable and impossible to compensate by damages. Atkins v. Chilson, 7 Metc. 398, Poindexter v. Henderson, 1 Miss. 176. Where the title is in dispute no injunction will issue. McBride v. Board of Commrs., 44 Fed. Rep. 17, Nevitt v. Gillespie, 2 Miss. 108. But a majority of the late cases are to the contrary. Kinsler v. Clarke, 2 Hill Eq. 617, Snyder v. Hopkins, 31 Kan. 557, Duvall v. Waters, 1 Bland, 569; Lamier v. Allison, 31 Fed. Rep. 100. See cases cited, *ante*, p. 225.

off arable land, and if done in the usual course is not waste. A tenant for life whose estate is expressed to be without impeachment of waste may freely take timber and minerals for use, but, unless with further specific authority, he must not remove timber planted for ornament (save so far as the cutting of part is required for the preservation of the rest) (*t*), open a mine in a garden or pleasure-ground, or do like acts destructive to the individual character and amenity of the dwelling-place (*u*). The commission of such waste may be restrained by injunction, without regard to pecuniary damage to the inheritance: but, when it is once committed, the normal measure of damages can only be the actual loss of value (*v*). Further details on the subject would not be appropriate here. They belong rather to the law of Real Property.

Landlord and tenant. As between landlord and tenant the real matter in dispute, in a case of alleged waste, is commonly the extent of the tenant's obligation, under his express or implied covenants, to keep the property demised in safe condition or repair. Yet the wrong of waste is none the less committed (and under the old procedure was no less remediable by the appropriate action on the case) because it is also a breach of the tenant's contract (*x*). Since the Judicature Acts it is impossible to say whether an action alleging misuse of the tenement by a lessee is brought on the contract or as for a tort (*y*): doubtless it would be treated as an action of contract if it became necessary for any purpose to assign it to one or the other class.

(*t*) See *Baker v. Sebright* (1879), 13 Ch. D. 179, 49 L. J. Ch. 65, but it seems that a remainderman coming in time would be entitled to the supervision of the Court in such case, *ib.* 188

(*u*) Waste of this kind was known as "equitable waste," the commission of it by a tenant unimpeachable for waste not being treated as wrongful at common law, see now 36 & 37 Vict. c. 66 (the Supreme Court of Judicature Act, 1873), s. 25, sub-s. 3

(*v*) *Bubb v. Yelverton* (1870), 10 Eq. 465 Here the tenant for life had acted in good faith under the belief that he was improving the property Wanton acts of destruction would be very differently treated

(*x*) 2 Wms Saund 646

(*y*) *Eq Tucker v. Linger* (1882), 21 Ch Div 18, 51 L J Ch 713

V - Conversion.

Conversion: relation of trover to trespass. Conversion, according to recent authority, may be described as the wrong done by " an unauthorized act which deprives another of his property permanently or for an indefinite time " (*). Such an act may or may not include a trespass; whether it does or not is immaterial as regards the

---

(*) Bramwell B., adopting the expression of Bosanquet, *arg.*, *Hiort v. Bott* (1874), L. R. 9 Ex. 86, 89, 44 L. J. Ex. 81. All, or nearly all, the learning on the subject down to 1871 is collected (in a somewhat formless manner it must be allowed) in the notes to *Wilbraham v. Snow*, 2 Wm. Saund. 87.

Relation of trover to trespass. *Vide* Grafton *v.* Carmichael, 48 Wis. 660, *supra*, p. 420.

In order to maintain trover a general or special property in the plaintiff is required. Kemp *v.* Thompson, 17 Ala. 9, Glaze *v.* McMillion, 7 Port. 279, Taylor *v.* Howell, 4 Blackf. 317, Burton *v.* Dunning, 6 Id. 209. A mere equitable title without legal possession will not support the action. Fulton *v.* Fulton, 48 Barb. 581, Lespeyre *v.* McFarland, 2 Iowa 187, Northern R. R. Co *v.* Paine, 119 U. S. 561, Street *v.* Nelson, 80 Ala. 230. Nor will an executory contract for goods. Wood *v.* Atkinson, 2 Murph. 87, Jones *v.* Morris, 4 Ired. 370, Deeley *v.* Dwight, 132 N. Y. 59, 30 N. E. Rep. 258, Tuthill *v.* Wheeler, 6 Barb. 362, Whitcomb *v.* Hungerford, 12 Barb. 177.

A vendor reserving title till payment by vendee may bring trover. Bryant *v.* Clifford, 13 Metc. 138, Rhodes *v.* Dickinson, 79 Ga. 724, 4 S. E. Rep. 164. But see Newhall *v.* Kingsbury, 131 Mass. 445. But one who consigns goods to be paid for as sold cannot maintain trover. Hardy *v.* Munroe, 127 Mass. 64. Nor can a pledgor who parts with possession. Colby *v.* Cressy, 5 N. H. 237.

A creditor who holds his debtor's property under an agreement to sell and apply the proceeds on the debt may sue in trover. Fish *v.* Clifford, 54 Vt. 344. But a mortgagee cannot until default. Heflin *v.* Slay, 78 Ala. 180. *Contra*, Gibbs *v.* Weston, 110 Pa. St. 312, 1 Atl. Rep. 921. Nor can the general owner where there has been a lease of chattels. Fort *v.* Pursley, 82 Ill. 152, Owens *v.* Weedman, Id. 409. Nor can the reversioner of a life tenant of chattels bring trover during the life tenancy. Lewis *v.* Mobley, 4 Dev. & B. 323. But see Logan *v.* Hartford Coal Co., 9 Heisk. 689.

Possession, or the right of immediate possession, entitles one to maintain trespass against a wrong-doer. Staples *v.* Smith, 48 Me. 471, Becker *v.* Smith, 59 Pa. St. 475, Durfour *v.* Anderson, 95 Ind. 302, Muggridge *v.* Eveleth, 9 Metc. 233.

right of the plaintiff in a civil action, for even under the old forms he might "waive the trespass"; though as regards the possibility of the wrong-doer being criminally liable it may still be a vital question, trespass by taking and carrying away the goods being a necessary element in the offence of larceny at common law. But the definition of theft (in the first instance narrow but strictly consistent, afterwards complicated by some judicial refinements and by numerous unsystematic statutory additions) does not concern us here. The "property" of which the plaintiff is deprived — the subject-matter of the right which is violated — must be something which he has the immediate right to possess; only on this condition could one maintain the action of trover under the old forms. Thus, where goods had been sold and remained in the vendor's possession subject to the vendor's lien for unpaid purchase-money, the purchaser could not bring an action of trover against a stranger who removed the goods, at all events without payment or tender of the unpaid balance (*a*).

But an owner not entitled to immediate possession might have a special action on the case, not being trover, for any permanent injury to his interest, though the wrongful act might also be a trespass, conversion, or breach of contract as against the immediate possessor (*b*). As under the Judicature Acts the difference of form between trover and a special action which is not trover does not exist, there seems to be no good reason why the idea and the name of conversion should not be extended to cover these last-mentioned cases.

What amounts to conversion. On the other hand, the name has been thought altogether objectionable by con-

(*a*) *Lord* v. *Price* (1874), L R 9 Ex 54, 43 L J Ex 49

(*b*) *Mears* v. *L & S W R Co* (1862), 11 C P N S 850, 31 L J C P 220 This appears to have been overlooked in the reasoning if not in the decision of the Court in *Coupé Co* v *Maddick*, '91, 2 Q B 413, 60 L J Q B 676, which assumes that a bailor for a term has no remedy against a stranger who injures the chattel

siderable authorities (c) and certainly the natural meaning of converting property to one's own use has long been left behind. It came to be seen that the actual diversion of the benefit arising from use and possession was only one aspect of the wrong, and not a constant one. It did not

(c) See 2 Wms Saund 108, and per Bramwell L J, 4 Ex D 194

What amounts to conversion Any act of dominion wrongfully exercised over property in denial of the owner's right, or inconsistent with it, is a conversion McPheters v. Page, 83 Me 234, 22 At. Rep 101, Baker v. Beers, 64 N H. 102, 6 At Rep 35, Frome v Dennis, 45 N. J. L 515, Gordon v Stockdale, 89 Ind 240. See Robertson v Hunt, 77 Tex 321, 11 S W Rep 68, Rhodes v Dickinson, 79 Ga 724, 4 S. E Rep 14, Rodney Hunt Mach Co v Stewart, 57 Hun, 515, 11 N. Y S Rep 448, Lewis v Ocean Nav & Pier Co , 125 N. Y 341, 26 N E Rep 301, Olds v Chicago etc , 33 Ill App 445, Thomson v. Gortner, 73 Md 471, 21 At Rep 371, Balling v Kirley, 90 Ala 215, 7 So Rep 914, Omaha A & S Co v Rogers, 35 Neb 61, 52 N W. Rep 826, Smith v Wood, 63 Vt 534, 22 At Rep. 575, Johnson v Farr, 60 N H 426, Miller v Thompson, 60 Me 322, Peeve v. Fox, 40 Ill App 127, Loeffel v Pohlman, 47 Mo App 574, Petrie v. Williams, 68 Hun, 589, 23 N Y S Rep 237, Williams v Smith, 153 Pa St 462, 25 At. Rep 1122, Sanborn v Hamilton, 18 Vt 590, Alexander v Swackhamer, 105 Ind 81; 4 N. E. Rep. 433, Hewes v Platts, 12 Gray, 443

To maintain trover, there must be either, (1) a taking from the owner without his consent, (2) an assumption of ownership, (3) an illegal use or abuse of it, or (4), proof of demand and refusal. Kennett v Robinson, 2 J J. Marsh 84. See Parker v. First Nat Bank (N D), 54 N. W. Rep 313, Lopp v Pinover, 27 Ill. App. 169 Hence, it is held, that manual taking of property is not necessary to constitute conversion, if there is actual attempt at disposal. Webber v Davis, 44 Me 147, Dickey v Franklin Bank, 32 Me 572

The adulteration of liquor by a common carrier thereof is a conversion Dench v. Walker, 14 Mass 500, Young v Mason, 8 Pick 551 But a mere delay in transportation is no conversion Briggs v New York, etc , R Co 28 Barb. 515

A bank mingling a special deposit with general funds is guilty of conversion Monmouth Bank v Dunbar, 19 Ill 558 So is a carrier delivering goods to officers under an illegal attachment. Gibbons v Farwell, 58 Mich 233, 29 N W Rep 855.

One selling chattels not his own is liable for conversion though he believed he was selling his property Morrill v Moulton, 40 Vt 242, Johnson v Powers, Id 611 It is a rule that the innocent motive of a party converting property is no defence, but may be proved to reduce

matter to the plaintiff whether it was the defendant, or a third person taking delivery from the defendant, who used his goods, or whether they were used at all; the essence of the injury was that the use and possession were dealt with in a manner adverse to the plaintiff and inconsistent with his right of dominion

The grievance is the unauthorized assumption of the powers of the true owner. Actually dealing with another's goods as owner for however short a time and however limited a purpose (d) is therefore conversion, so is an act which in fact enables a third person to deal with them as owner, and which would make such dealing lawful only if done by the person really entitled to possess the goods (e) It makes no difference that such acts were done under a mistaken but honest and even reasonable supposition of being lawfully entitled (d), or even with the intention of benefiting the true owner (e), nor is a servant, or other merely ministerial agent, excused for assuming the dominion of goods on his master's or principal's behalf, though he " acted under an unavoidable ignorance and for

(d) *Hollins v Fowler* (1875), L R 7 H L 757, 44 L J Q B 169

(e) *Hiort v Bott*, L R 9 Ex 86, 43 L J Ex 81

---

exemplary damages. *Waverly T & I Co v St Louis Cooperage Co*, 112 Mo 383, 20 S. W. Rep 566, *Baltimore & O R Co v. O'Donnell*, 49 Ohio St 489, 32 N E. Rep 476, *Benton v Beattie*, 63 Vt 186, 22 Atl Rep 422, *Lahner v Hertzog*, 23 Ill App 308, *Williams v Deen* (Tex Civ App), 24 S W Rep. 536, *Kenney v Ranney* (Mich), 55 N. W Rep 982

In general, an agent making demand for his principal must give a fair proof of authority or the refusal will not sustain trover *Robertson v Crane*, 27 Miss 362, *Watt v Porter*, 2 Mass. 77

If a refusal is the result of a reasonable doubt in a doubtful matter trover will not lie *Robinson v Burleigh*, 5 N H 225, *Zachray v Pace*, 9 Ark 212, *Carroll v Mix*, 51 Barb. 212 But the refusal must be distinctly put on that ground *Ingalls v Bulkley*, 15 Ill 224

A qualified refusal is not conversion *per se* *Thomas v Sixpenny Bank*, 5 Bosw 293, *Ward v. Moffitt*, 38 Mo App 395.

Recovery in trover bars plaintiff's title to the property *Kenyon v Woodruff*, 33 Mich 310 But not if the judgement is unsatisfied. *Atwater*

his master's benefit" (*f*). It is common learning that a refusal to deliver possession to the true owner on demand is evidence of a conversion, but evidence only (*g*), that is, one natural inference if I hold a thing and will not deliver it to the owner is that I repudiate his ownership and mean to exercise dominion in spite of his title either on my own behalf or on some other claimant's. "If the refusal is in disregard of the plaintiff's title, and for the purpose of claiming the goods either for the defendant or for a third person, it is a conversion" (*h*). But this is not the only possible inference and may not be the right one. The refusal may be a qualified and provisional one: the possessor may say, "I am willing to do right, but that I may be sure I am doing right, give me reasonable proof that you are the true owner" and such a possessor, even if over-cautious in the amount of satisfaction he requires, can hardly be said to repudiate the true owner's claim (*i*). Or a servant having the mere custody of goods under the possession of his master as bailee — say the servant of a warehouseman having the key of the warehouse — may reasonably and justifiably say to the bailor demanding his goods "I cannot deliver them without my master's order"; and this is no conversion. "An unqualified refusal is almost always conclusive evidence of a conversion, but if there be a qualification annexed to it, the question

---

(*f*) *Stephens v Elwall* (1815), 4 M & S 259, admitted to be good law in *Hollins v Fowler*, L R 7 H L at pp 766, 795, and followed in *Barker v Furlong*, '91, 2 Ch 172, 60 L J Ch 368 Cp *Fine Art Society v Union Bank of London* (1886), 17 Q B Div 705, 56 L J Q B 70

(*g*) *Balme v Hutton*, Ex Ch (1833) 9 Bing 471, 479

(*h*) Opinion of Blackburn J in *Hollins v Fowler*, L R 7 H L at p 766

(*i*) See *Burroughes v Bayne* (1860), 5 H & N 296, 29 L J Ex 185, 188, *supra*, p 427

v Tupper, 43 Conn. 114; Singer Mfg. Co. *v* Skillman, 52 N J L 263, 19 At. Rep 260, Pryor *v* Portsmouth Cattle Co., (N M) 27 Pac Rep. 327 If the property is returned the damages are nominal Barrelet *v* Bellyard, 71 Ill 280. But a return may be refused Kelly *v* McDowall, 39 Ark. 387 A judgment for a conversion of chattels will bar a judgment for the recovery of any chattels covered by that act of conversion McCaffrey *v* Carter, 125 Mass 330.

then is whether it be a reasonable one" (k). Again there may be a wrongful dealing with goods, not under an adverse claim, but to avoid having anything to do with them or with their owner. Where a dispute arises between the master of a ferryboat and a passenger, and the master refuses to carry the passenger and puts his goods on shore, this may be a trespass, but it is not of itself a conversion (l). This seems of little importance in modern practice, but we shall see that it might still affect the measure of damages.

In many cases the refusal to deliver on demand not only proves but constitutes the conversion. When this is so, the Statute of Limitation runs from the date of the refusal, without regard to any prior act of conversion by a third person (m)

By a conversion the true owner is, in contemplation of law, totally deprived of his goods; therefore, except in a few very special cases (n), the measure of damages in an action of trover was the full value of the goods, and by a satisfied judgment (o) for the plaintiff the property in the goods, if they still existed *in specie*, was transferred to the defendant

Acts not amounting to conversion The mere assertion of a pretended right to deal with goods or threatening to prevent the owner from dealing with them is not conversion, though it may perhaps be a cause of action, if special damage can be shown (p), indeed it is doubtful

---

(k) *Alexander v Southey* (1821), 5 B & A 247, per Best J at p 250

(l) *Fouldes v Willoughby*, 8 M & W 540, cp *Hudson v McLaughlin* (1871), 107 Mass 587

(m) *Miller v Dell*, 91, 1 Q B 468, 60 L J Q B 404, C A.

(n) See per Bramwell L J, 3 Q B D 490, *Hiort v L & N W R Co* (1879), 4 Ex Div 188, 48 L J Ex 545, where however Bramwell L J was the only member of the Court who was clear that there was any conversion at all

(o) Not by judgment without satisfaction, *Ex parte Drake* (1877), 5 Ch Div 866, 46 L J Bk 29, following *Brinsmead v Harrison* (1871), L R 6 C P 584, 40 L J C P 281

(p) *England v Cowley* (1873), L R 8 Ex 126, see per Kelly C B. at p. 132, 42 L J Ex 80

whether a person not already in possession can commit the wrong of conversion by any act of interference limited to a special purpose and falling short of a total assumption of dominion against the true owner (*q*). An attempted sale of goods which does not affect the property, the seller having no title and the sale not being in market overt, nor yet the possession, there being no delivery, is not a conversion. If undertaken in good faith, it would seem not to be actionable at all; otherwise it might come within the analogy of slander of title. But if a wrongful sale is followed up by delivery, both the seller (*r*) and the buyer (*s*) are guilty of a conversion. Again, a mere collateral breach

---

(*q*) See per Bramwell B. and Kelly C. B. ib. 131, 132.

(*r*) *Lancashire Waggon Co.* v. *Fitzhugh* (1861), 6 H. & N. 502, 30 L. J. Ex. 231 (action by bailor against sheriff for selling the goods absolutely as goods of the bailee under a *fi. fa.*, the decision is on the pleadings only).

(*s*) *Cooper* v. *Willomatt* (1845), 1 C. B. 672, 14 L. J. C. P. 219.

Acts not amounting to conversion. Contrary to the initial statement of the text, it seems that there are cases where the mere claim of a right is as effectual a conversion as any physical act of authority or control. Thus in University of North Carolina *v.* State National Bank (96 N. C. 280, 3 S. E. Rep. 359), it was held that a mere claim by the bank of the right to apply bonds deposited as collateral by A. to secure a personal debt toward the payment of a debt owed to it by a corporation, was a conversion.

The mere purchase of goods from one who does not own them, does not constitute conversion. Valentine *v.* Duff (Ind. App.), 34 N. E. Rep. 453.

A sale on credit by an agent, authorized to sell for cash only, is not a conversion. Loveless *v.* Fowler, 79 Ga. 134, 4 S. E. Rep. 103; Moore *v.* McKibbin, 33 Barb. 246; Sargeant *v.* Blunt, 16 Johns. 74. But otherwise, where the agent exchanges instead of sells. Ainsworth *v.* Partello, 13 Ala. 160.

The accidental loss or destruction of an article by one lawfully in its possession, is not a conversion. Salt Springs Nat. Bank *v.* Wheeler, 48 N. Y. 492.

Merely moving timber from the highway where it is an illegal obstruction is not conversion. Plummer *v.* Brown, 8 Metc. 578.

For other cases illustrating the proposition, see Dozier *v.* Pillot, 79 Tex. 224, 14 S. W. Rep. 1027; Traylor *v.* Hughes, 88 Ala. 617; 7 So. Rep. 159, Lehigh etc. Co *v.* New Jersey etc. Co. (N. Y.), 26 At. Rep. 920 Freeman *v.* Grant, 132 N. Y. 22, 30 N. E. Rep. 247, Clegg *v.* Boston etc. Co., 149 Mass. 454, 21 N. E. Rep. 877.

of contract in dealing with goods entrusted to one is not a
conversion; as where the master of a ship would not sign a
bill of lading except with special terms which he had no
right to require, but took the cargo to the proper port and
was willing to deliver it, on payment of freight, to the
proper consignee (*t*).

Dealings under authority of apparent owner A
merely ministerial dealing with goods, at the request of an
apparent owner having the actual control of them, appears
not to be conversion (*u*), but the extent of this limitation
or exception is not precisely defined. The point is handled
in the opinion delivered to the House of Lords in *Hollins*

(*t*) *Jones v. Hough* (1879), 5 Ex Div
115, 41 L J Ex 211, cp *Heald v Carey*
(next note)

(*u*) *Heald v Carey* (1852) 11 C B
977, 21 L J C P 97, but this is really a
case of the class last mentioned, for the
defendant received the goods on behalf
of the true owner, and was held to have
done nothing with them that he might
not properly do

Dealings under authority of apparent owner Mere possession will
not justify a person in presuming title to be in the possessor. The purchaser from a thief in actual possession of goods acquires no title as
against the owner. Good faith and ignorance are no defense. Spraights
v Hawley, 39 N. Y. 441, Lee v McKay, 3 Ired 29, Omaha etc. Co v.
Tabor, 13 Colo 41, 21 Pac. Rep. 925, United States v Kelley, 3 Wash
Ter 421, 17 Pac Rep 878, Norris v. Hall, 41 Ala 510, Harris v Saunders, 2 Strobh. Eq 370, Cooper v Newman, 45 N H. 339, Gilmore v
Newton, 9 Allen, 171, Pease v. Smith, 61 N Y 477.

One innocently selling chattels under authority of the apparent owner
is liable in case he is mistaken. Spraights v Hawley, 39 N Y 441,
Kimball v Billings, 55 Me. 147, Briggs v. Haycock, 63 Cal 344, Scofield
v Kreiser, 3 N Y. S. Rep. 803.

Thus, an auctioneer innocently selling stolen property is liable in conversion Everett v Coffin, 6 Wend. 603, Milliken v Hathway, 148 Mass
69, 19 N E. Rep. 16, Hoffman v Carow, 22 Wend. 285, Robinson v
Bird, 158 Mass 357; 33 N E Rep. 391. But see Rogers v. Huse, 2 Cal
571 A commission merchant who sells goods ignorant of a title adverse to that of his principal, was held not liable in Abernathy v
Wheeler (Ky.), 17 S W Rep. 858. But see Taylor v Pope, 5 Coldw 413

A person who sends goods to a dealer for exhibition may bring trover
against a person who innocently purchases them from the dealer. Smith
v Clewes, 33 Hun, 501.

v. *Fowler* (v) by Lord Blackburn, then a Justice of the Queen's Bench, an opinion which gives in a relatively small compass a lucid and instructive view of the whole theory of the action of trover. It is there said that "on principle, one who deals with goods at the request of the person who has the actual custody of them, in the *bona fide* belief that the custodian is the true owner, or has the authority of the true owner, should be excused for what he does if the act is of such a nature as would be excused if done by the authority of the person in possession (x), if he was a finder of the goods, or intrusted with their custody." This excludes from protection, and was intended to exclude, such acts as those of the defendants in the case then at bar: they had bought cotton, innocently and without negligence, from a holder who had obtained it by fraud, and had no title, and they had immediately resold it to a firm for whom they habitually acted as cotton brokers, not making any profit beyond a broker's commission. Still it appeared to the majority of the judges and to the House of Lords that the transaction was not a purchase on account of a certain customer as principal, but a purchase with a mere expectation of that customer (or some other customer) taking the goods; the defendants therefore exercised a real and effective though transitory dominion; and having thus assumed to dispose of the goods, they were liable to the

(v) L. R. 7 H. L. at pp. 766—768.
(x) Observe that this means physical possession; in some of the cases proposed it would be accompanied by legal possession, in others not.

One innocently purchasing from a vendee with the title remaining in the vendor till payment is liable in trover. Carter v. Kingman, 103 Mass. 517.

One who purchases from a wife property belonging to her husband, is liable to the husband for conversion. Rice v. Yocum, 155 Pa. St. 538, 26 At. Rep. 698, 32 W. N. C. 356. See Mead v. Jack, 12 Daly, 65.

A teamster who hauls goods from an unlocked room at the instance of the house-owner is not liable therefor, though the property belongs to the person who hires the room. Garley v. Armistead, 148 Mass. 267, 19 N. E. Rep. 389.

true owner (*y*). So would the ultimate purchasers have been (though they bought and used the cotton in good faith), had the plaintiffs thought fit to sue them (*z*).

Acts of servants. But what of the servants of those purchasers, who handled the cotton under their authority and apparent title, and by making it into twist wholly changed its form? Assuredly this was conversion enough in fact and in the common sense of the word; but was it a conversion in law? Could any one of the factory hands have been made the nominal defendant and liable for the whole value of the cotton? Or if a thief brings corn to a miller, and the miller, honestly taking him to be the true owner, grinds the corn into meal and delivers the meal to him without notice of his want of title, is the miller, or are his servants, liable to the true owner for the value of the corn (*z*)? Lord Blackburn thought these questions open and doubtful. There appears to be nothing in the authorities to prevent it from being excusable to deal with goods merely as the servant or agent of an apparent owner in actual possession, or under a contract with such owner, according to the apparent owner's direction, neither the act done, nor the contract (if any), purporting to involve a transfer of the supposed property in the goods, and the ostensible owner's direction being one which he could law-

---

(*y*) See per Lord Cairns, 7 H. L. at p. 797. This principle applies to sale and delivery by an auctioneer without notice of the apparent owner's want of title. *Consolidated Co.* v. *Curtis*, '92, 1 Q. B. 495.
(*z*) Blackburn J., 7 H. L. 764, 768.

Acts of servants. An agent or servant in possession of property of another is liable for his dealings therewith adversely to the rights of the real owner. Lafayette County Bank *v.* Metcalf, 40 Mo. App. 494, Galbreath *v.* Epperson (Tenn.), 1 S. W. Rep. 157, Barnhart *v.* Ford, 37 Kan. 520, 15 Pac. Rep. 42.

Thus, an agent who, under orders from his principal, refuses delivery of goods is liable in trover. Singer Mfg. Co. *v.* King, 14 R. I. 511.

So, a broker selling cotton for a lessee with constructive notice of a landlord's lien for rent on the cotton, is liable to the landlord for conversion. Merchants' & P. Bank *v.* Meyer, 56 At. R. 499, 20 S. W. Rep. 406.

fully give if he were really entitled to his apparent interest, and being obeyed in the honest (a) belief that he is so entitled. It might or might not be convenient to hold a person excused who in good faith assumes to dispose of goods as the servant and under the authority and for the benefit of a person apparently entitled to possession but not already in possession. But this could not be done without overruling accepted authorities (b).

Redelivery by bailees. A bailee is *prima facie* estopped as between himself and the bailor from disputing the bailor's title (c). Hence, as he cannot be liable to two adverse claimants at once, he is also justified in redelivering to the bailor in pursuance of his employment, so long as he has not notice (or rather is not under the effective pressure) (d) of any paramount claim: it is only when he is in danger of such a claim that he is not bound to redeliver to the bailor (e). When there are really conflicting claims, the

---

(a) Should we say "honest and reasonable"? It seems not, a person doing a ministerial act of this kind honestly but not reasonably ought to be liable for negligence to the extent of the actual damage imputable to his negligence, not in trover for the full value of the goods, and even apart from the technical effect of conversion, negligence would be the substantial and rational ground of liability Behaviour grossly inconsistent with the common prudence of an honest man might here, as elsewhere, be evidence of bad faith

(b) See *Stephens* v *Elwall*, 4 M & S.

259, *Barker* v. *Furlong*, '91, 2 Ch 172, 60 L J Ch 368, p 430, above

(c) 7 Hen VII 22, pl 3, per Martin. Common learning in modern books.

(d) *Biddle* v *Bond* (1865), 6 B & S 225, 34 L J Q B 137, where it is said that there must be something equivalent to eviction by title paramount

(e) See *Sheridan* v *New Quay Co* (1858), 4 C B N S 618, 28 L J C P 58, *European and Australian Royal Mail Co* v *Royal Mail Steam Packet Co* (1861) 30 L J C P 247, Jessel M R in *Ex parte Davies* (1881), 19 Ch Div. 86, 90

Redilivery by bailees. A bailee who, under the bailor's orders, refuses delivery to one entitled thereto, as against the bailor, is liable for conversion. McAnnelly *v.* Chapman, 18 Tex 198; Smith *v.* Bell, 9 Mo. 873.

A sale of the bailed goods by the bailee terminates the bailment and renders the bailee liable for the conversion. Lovejoy *v.* Jones, 30 N. H 164; Hagood *v.* Elson, 21 Tex. 506, Follett *v.* Edwards, 30 Ill. App. 386. But when a factor sells his principal's goods with intent to embezzle the proceeds, conversion does not lie   Herron *v.* Hughes, 25 Cal. 555. But see White *v.* Wall, 40 Me. 574, Solomon *v.* Waas, 2 Hilt. 179.

contract of bailment does not prevent a bailee from taking
interpleader proceedings (*f*). This case evidently falls
within the principle suggested by Lord Blackburn; but the
rules depend on the special character of a bailee's contract.

Abuse of limited interest. Where a bailee has an
interest of his own in the goods (as in the common cases
of hiring and pledge) and under colour of that interest
deals with the goods in excess of his right, questions of
another kind arise. Any excess whatever by the possessor
of his rights under his contract with the owner will of
course be a breach of contract, and it may be a wrong.

(*f*) *Rogers v Lambert*, 91, 1 Q B 318, 60 L J Q B 187, following *Biddle v Bond*

Abuse of limited interest. One who misuses bailed goods or applies them to a purpose at variance with the bailment is liable for conversion. Ripley *v* Dolbier, 18 Me. 382, Forbes *v* Boston & L R Co , 148 Mass. 154, Crocker *v* Gulliver, 44 Me. 491, Erie Dispatch *v* Johnson, 3 Pick. (Tenn.) 490; 11 S. W. Rep. 441; Louisville & N. R. Co *v* Lawson, 88 Ky 496, 11 S. W. Rep. 511. But not where the property is destroyed. Harvey *v.* Epes, 12 Gratt. 153.

An illustration of frequent occurrence in the cases, is where a person drives a hired horse a greater distance or a different route from the one agreed on. Wheelock *v* Wheelwright, 5 Mass. 104; Homer *v.* Thwing, 3 Pick. 492, Lucas *v.* Trumbull, 15 Gray, 306, Woodman *v.* Hubbard, 25 N H 67; Fish *v.* Ferris, 5 Duer, 49; Freeman *v.* Boland, 14 R. I. 39, Disbrow *v* Tenbroeck, 4 E. D Smith, 397; Hart *v* Skinner, 16 Vt 138, Perham *v.* Coney, 117 Mass. 102. But not if the diversion is the result of error Spooner *v* Manchester, 133 Mass. 270; 43 Am. Rep. 14. See Harvey *v.* Epes, 12 Gratt 153; Johnson *v.* Weedman, 5 Ill. 495. A person hiring a horse to A. and return without stopping was not held guilty for conversion by stopping. Evans *v.* Mason, 64 N. Y. 98; 5 At Rep 766

An attempt to sell or mortgage a hired carriage amounts to conversion. Follett *v* Edwards, 30 Ill. App. 386.

An agister of a horse was held not liable for the horse's death, in Johnson *v.* Weedman, 5 Ill. 495.

A general hirer of a slave who sub-hires without consent of the bailor is liable for conversion. Bell *v.* Cummings, 3 Sneed (Tenn.), 275 So a carrier who employs a slave. Johnson *v.* The Arabia, 24 Mo. 86; Scruggs *v.* Davis, 5 Sneed (Tenn), 261.

A factor who ships by water instead of rail, as his principal directs, is liable for conversion Graves *v.* Smith, 14 Wis. 5

But it will not be the wrong of conversion unless the possessor's dealing is "wholly inconsistent with the contract under which he had the limited interest," as if a hirer for example destroys or sells the goods (*g*). That is a conversion, for it is deemed to be a repudiation of the contract, so that the owner who has parted with possession for a limited purpose is by the wrongful act itself restored to the immediate right of possession, and becomes the effectual "true owner" capable of suing for the goods or their value. But a merely irregular exercise of power, as a sub-pledge (*h*) or a premature sale (*i*), is not a conversion; it is at most a wrong done to the reversionary interest of an owner out of possession, and that owner must show that he is really damnified (*j*).

The technical distinction between an action of detinue or trover and a special action on the case here corresponds to the substantial and permanent difference between a wrongful act for which the defendant's rightful possession is merely the opportunity, and a more or less plausible abuse of the right itself.

The case of a common law lien, which gives no power of disposal at all, is different; there the holder's only right is to keep possession until his claim is satisfied. If he parts with possession, his right is gone, and his attempted disposal merely wrongful, and therefore he is liable for the full value (*k*). But a seller remaining in possession who re-sells before the buyer is in default is liable to the buyer

---

(*g*) Blackburn J., L. R. 1 Q. B. 614, *Cooper* v. *Willomatt*, 1 C. B. 672, 14 L. J. C. P. 219. It can be a trespass only if the bailment is at will.

(*h*) *Donald* v. *Suckling* (1866), L. R. 1 Q. B. 585, 35 L. J. Q. B. 232.

(*i*) *Halliday* v. *Holgate* (1868), Ex Ch L. R. 3 Ex. 299, see at p. 302, 37 L. J. Ex. 174.

(*j*) In *Johnson* v. *Stear* (1863), 15 C. B. N. S. 330, 33 L. J. C. P. 130, nominal damages were given, but it is doubtful whether, on the reasoning adopted by the majority of the Court, there should not have been judgment for the defendant see 2 Wms. Saund. 114, Blackburn J., L. R. 1 Q. B. 617, Bramwell L. J., 3 Q. B. D. 490.

(*k*) *Mulliner* v. *Florence* (1878), 3 Q. B. Div. 484, 47 L. J. Q. B. 700, where an innkeeper sold a guest's goods. A statutory power of sale was given to innkeepers very shortly after this decision (41 & 42 Vict. c. 38), but the principle may still be applicable in other cases.

only for the damage really sustained, that is, the amount (if any) by which the market price of the goods, at the time when the seller ought to have delivered them, exceeds the contract price (*l*). The seller cannot sue the buyer for the price of the goods, and if the buyer could recover the full value from the seller he would get it without any consideration: the real substance of the cause of action is the breach of contract, which is to be compensated according to the actual damage (*m*). A mortgagor having the possession and use of goods under covenants entitling him thereto for a certain time, determinable by default after notice, is virtually a bailee for a term, and, like bailees in general, may be guilty of conversion by an absolute disposal of the goods; and so may assignees claiming through him with no better title than his own; the point being, as in the other cases, that the act is entirely inconsistent with the terms of the bailment (*n*). One may be allowed to doubt, with Lord Blackburn, whether these fine distinc-

---

(*l*) *Chinery* v *Viall* (1860), 5 H & N 288, 29 L J Ex. 180. This rule cannot be applied in favour of a sub vendor sued for conversion by the ultimate purchaser, there being no privity between them *Johnson* v *Lancs and Yorkshire R Co* (1878), 3 C P. D 499

(*m*) "A man cannot merely by changing his form of action vary the amount of damage so as to recover more than the amount to which he is in law really entitled according to the true facts of the case and the real nature of the transaction" per Cur 29 L. J Ex 184

(*n*) *Fenn* v *Bittleston* (1851), 7 Ex 152, 21 L J Ex 41, where see the distinctions as to trespass and larceny carefully noted in the judgment delivered by Parke B *Conversion as between Co-owners — General and Special Property* — The normal rights of co owners as to possession and use may be modified by contract One of them may thus have the exclusive right to possess the chattel, and the other may have temporary possession or custody, as his bailee or servant, without the power of conferring any possessory right on a third person even as to his own share In *Nyberg* v *Handelaar*, '92, 2 Q B 202, A had sold a half share of a valuable chattel to B. on the terms that A. should retain possession until the chattel (a gold enamel box) could be sold for their common benefit Afterwards A let B have the box to take it to an auction room Then B, thus having manual possession of the box, delivered it to Z by way of pledge for a debt of his own The Court of Appeal held that Z had no defence to an action by A to recover the value of his half share The judgments proceed on the assumption that B, while remaining owner in common as to half the *property*, held the *possession* only as bailee for a special purpose, and his wrongful dealing with it determined the bailment, and revested A's right to immediate possession see *Fenn* v *Bittleston*, 7 Ex 152, and similar cases cited in text Qu whether, on the facts, B. were even a bailee, or were not rather in the position of a servant having bare custody

tions have done much good, and to wish "it had been originally determined that even in such cases the owner should bring a special action on the case and recover the damage which he actually sustained" (o). Certainly the law would have been simpler, perhaps it would have been juster. It may not be beyond the power of the House of Lords or the Court of Appeal to simplify it even now; but our business is to take account of the authorities as they stand. And, as they stand, we have to distinguish between —

(i.) Ordinary cases of conversion where the full value can be recovered:

(ii.) Cases where there is a conversion but only the plaintiff's actual damage can be recovered:

(iii.) Cases where there is a conversion but only nominal damages can be recovered; but such cases are anomalous, and depend on the substantial cause of action being the breach of a contract between the parties; it seems doubtful whether they ought ever to have been admitted:

(iv.) Cases where there is not a conversion, but an action (formerly a special or innominate action on the case) lies to recover the actual damage.

Conversion by estoppel. A man may be liable by estoppel as for the conversion of goods which he has represented to be in his possession or control, although in fact they were not so at any time when the plaintiff was entitled to possession (p). And he may be liable for conversion by refusal to deliver, when he has had possession and has wrongfully delivered the goods to a person having no title. He cannot deliver to the person entitled when the demand is made, but, having disabled himself by his own wrong, he

---

(o) L R 1 Q. B at p 614

(p) *Seton v Lafone* (1887), 19 Q B Div 68, 56 L J Q B 415

is in the same position as if he still had the goods and refused to deliver (*q*).

VI.— *Injuries between Tenants in Common.*

Trespasses between tenants in common. As between tenants in common of either land or chattels there cannot be trespass unless the act amounts to an actual ouster, *i. e.* dispossession. Short of that " trespass will not lie by the one against the other so far as the land is concerned " (*r*).

(*q*) *Bristol and W. of England Bank* v. *Midland R Co*, '01, 2 Q B 653, 65 L. T. 234, C A

(*r*) Lord Hatherley, *Jacobs* v. *Seward* (1872), L R 5 H L. 464, 472, 41 L. J. C. P. 221

Trespasses between tenants in common. Trespass lies for an actual ouster of one co-tenant by another. Erwin v. Olmstead, 7 Cow. 229; Filbert v Hoff, 42 Pa. St 97, McClure v. Thorpe, 68 Mich. 33; 35 N W. Rep. 829, Byam v. Bickford, 140 Mass. 31, 2 N E. Rep 687.

As to a tenant in common, acts which if committed by another would be ouster are not so unless capable of no other construction. Parker v. Locks & Canal, 3 Metc. 91.

There must be an actual hostile adverse possession coupled with notice thereof to the co-tenant. Chandler v Ricker, 49 Vt. 128; Ball v. Palmers, 81 Ill. 370; Culver v. Rhodes, 87 N. Y. 348; Noble v. McFarland, 52 Ill. 226.

Thus, the purchase of an outstanding title is not ouster, for the purchase inures to the benefit of the common title, by implication of law. Jones v. Stanton, 11 Mo. 433; Van Horne v. Stunda, 5 Johns Ch. 838; Weaver v Wible, 25 Pa. St 270; Tisdale v. Tisdale, 2 Sneed (Tenn), 596, Coleman v Coleman, 3 Dana, 228, Bracken v. Cooper, 80 Ill. 221; Page v Branch 97 N. C 97; 1 S. E Rep. 625. *Contra*, Peck v. Lockridge, 97 Mo. 549, 11 S. W. Rep 246; Clark v Cregs, 47 Barb 599. But a conveyance to a stranger adversely to the estate is ouster. Odom v. Weathersbee, 26 S. C. 244; 1 S. E Rep. 390; Cook v. Clinton, 64 Mich. 309, 31 N. W. Rep 317.

A mere formal demand of possession by one co-tenant met by a refusal is not ouster. Carpenter v Menderhall, 28 Cal. 484. Nor is a mere denial of the co-tenant's title. Campau v. Campau, 45 Mich. 367.

But *aliter* where the denial is incorporated in an answer to a suit. Greer v. Tripp, 56 Cal. 209. A denial of title coupled with possession professed to be adverse is evidence tending to show ouster. Carpenter v Gardiner, 29 Cal 160; Jefcoat v. Knott, 13 Rich. 50; Marcy v. Diverson, 8 Metc 544; Mayes v Manning, 73 Tex 43, 11 S. W Rep. 136;

In the same way acts of legitimate use of the common property cannot become a conversion through subsequent misappropriation, though the form in which the property exists may be wholly converted, in a wider sense, into other forms. There is no wrong to the co-tenant's right of property until there is an act inconsistent with the enjoyment of the property by both. For every tenant or owner in common is equally entitled to the occupation and use of the tenement or property (s); he can therefore become a trespasser only by the manifest assumption of an exclusive and hostile possession. It was for some time doubted whether even an actual expulsion of one tenant in common by another were a trespass, but the law was settled, in the latest period of the old forms of pleading, that

---

(s) Litt s 323

Bigelow v. Jones, 10 Pick. 161, Cummings v. Wyman, 10 Mass 464 The mere pernancy of profits is not ouster. Higbee v Rice, 5 Mass 350, Caldwell v. Neely, 81 N. C 114; Jones v Cohen, 82 N. C. 75; McGhee v Hall, 26 S C. 179, 1 S. E. Rep 711; Rodney v. McLaughlin, 97 Mo 426; 9 S. W. Rep 726; Hampton v. Wheeler, 99 N C 222, 6 S. E. Rep. 236, Sontag v Bigelow, 142 Ill 143; 31 N E Rep 674

Possession though exclusive will not be an ouster unless there is notice to the tenant of its adverse character. English v. Powell, 119 Ind 93; 21 N. E. Rep. 458. But any long continued series of acts indicating an attempt to exclude will amount to ouster Lebavour v. Howan, 3 Allen, 354 And where the possession is not severable, as of a wharf, the exclusive possession of one co-tenant is ouster. Annelly v. De Saussure, 26 S. C. 497, 2 S. E. Rep 490. So, as to a right of way exercised by a railroad over a farm held by it as tenant in common Childs v Kansas City R Co. (Mo), 17 S W. Rep 954. So, as to flooding joint property. Hutchinson v. Chase, 39 Me 508; Great Falls Co. v. Worcester, 15 N H. 412. So, as to moving furniture from house Keay v Goodwin, 16 Mass 1. See 33 Cent. L. J 297

A tenant may maintain trover against his co-tenant for conversion of chattels. Potter v Neal, 62 Hun, 158; Flint v. Franzman, 5 N. Y. S. Rep. 523, Le Barron v. Babcock, 46 Hun, 598, Id. v House, 122 N. Y. 153; 25 N. E. Rep 253, Weld v. Oliver, 21 Pick 559; Lobdell v Stowell, 51 N Y. 70; Wheeler v Wheeler, 88 Me. 347; Lewis v. Clark, 59 Vt 36', 8 At Rep. 158; White v Phelps, 12 N. H 382; Browning v. Cover, 108 Pa. St. 595 Replevin is not maintainable Busch v Nestee (Mich.), 35 N. W. Rep. 458.

it is (*t*). At first sight this seems an exception to the rule that a person who is lawfully in possession cannot commit trespass: but it is not so, for a tenant in common has legal possession only of his own share. Acts which involve the destruction of the property held in common, such as digging up and carrying away the soil, are deemed to include ouster (*u*); unless, of course, the very nature of the property (a coal-mine for example) be such that the working out of it is the natural and necessary course of use and enjoyment, in which case the working is treated as rightfully undertaken for the benefit of all entitled, and there is no question of trespass to property, but only, if dispute arises, of accounting for the proceeds (*v*).

VII.— *Extended Protection of Possession.*

Rights of de facto possessor against strangers. An important extension of legal protection and remedies has yet to be noticed. Trespass and other violations of possessory rights can be committed not only against the

(*t*) *Murray* v *Hall* (1849), 7 C. B 441, 18 L J C P 161, and Bigelow L C. 343
(*u*) *Wilkinson* v *Haygarth* (1846), 12 Q B 837, 16 L. J. Q B 103, Co Litt. 200
(*v*) *Job* v. *Potton* (1875), 20 Eq 84, 44 L J. Ch 262

Rights of de facto possessor against strangers In any action for the violation of possessory rights, the plaintiff's possession is sufficient against a stranger to the title. Carson v. Prater, 6 Coldw. 565, People v Sherwin, 2 Thomp. & C. 528; Sickles v. Gould, 51 How. Pr 22; Hebert v Lege, 29 So. An. 311; Aristland v. Potterfield, 9 W. Va. 438; Stratton v Lyons, 53 Vt. 641, Duncan v. Yordy, 27 Kan 848; Hunt v. Rich, 38 Me. 195, Johnson v. McIlvain, 1 Rice, 368, McCanon v. O'Connell, 7 Cal. 152, Barnstable v. Thatcher, 3 Metc. 239, Rogan v. Perry, 6 Wis. 194; Rollins v. Clay, 33 Me. 132. The leading American case on this subject is Gulf, C. & S F Ry Co. v. Johnson (54 Fed Rep. 474), in which the plaintiff while occupying land under a lease which was void by legal construction, suffered damages to his crops and other combustibles by reason of the escape of sparks from the defendant's passing engines Caldwell, J., in delivering the opinion of the court, said· "As against a wrong doer, possession is title. The presumption of the law is that the person who has possession has the property, and the law will not permit

person who is lawfully in possession, but against any person who has legal possession, whether rightful in its origin or not, so long as the intruder cannot justify his act under a better title. A mere stranger cannot be heard to say that one whose possession he has violated was not entitled to possess. Unless and until a superior title or justification is shown, existing legal possession is not only presumptive but conclusive evidence of the right to possess. Sometimes mere detention may be sufficient; but on principle it seems more correct to say that physical control or occupation is *prima facie* evidence that the owner is in exercise (on his own behalf or on that of another) of an actual legal possession, and then, if the contrary does not appear, the incidents of legal possession follow. The practical result is that an outstanding claim of a third party (*jus tertii*, as it is called) cannot be set up to excuse

---

that presumption to be rebutted by evidence that the property was in a third person, when offered as a defense by one who claims no title, and was a wrong-doer. One who goes through the country negligently or wilfully setting fire to people's pastures, haystacks, and houses will not, when called upon to pay for wrongful act, be heard to say that the legal title to the property destroyed was in a third person, and not in the person who had the actual possession. * * * It was found impossible for all persons to be constantly in possession of their property, and society devised other evidences of title In most controversies between rival claimants to property, these artificial or legal evidences of title are paramount and the best evidence, and must be produced; but, as against a wrong-doer claiming no right or title to the property, possession is as potent as it was before any other evidence of title to property was devised or recognized One cannot burn down another's house over his head, and, when called upon to pay for his wrongful act, reply that the logs out of which the house was built were cut upon the public lands of the United States, and therefore not the plaintiff's property; or put the plaintiff to the proof of his title to the land upon which the house stood, in the manner that would be necessary in an action of ejectment to recover the land from one in possession " Citing Northern P. R. Co. *v.* Lewis, 51 Fed Rep. 658; 2 C. C. A 446; 7 U. S. App. 254; and the text. See Wheeler *v* Lawson, 103 N. Y 40; 8 N. E. Rep. 360; Krewson *v.* Purdom, 13 Oreg. 563, 11 Pac. Rep. 281, Sherman *v.* Commercial Ptg. Co., 29 Mo App. 31; Leoncini *v.* Post, 13 N Y. S. Rep. 825. But see Rexroth *v.* Coon, 15 R. I. 35, 23 At Rep. 37.

either trespass or conversion: "against a wrong-doer, possession is a title": "any possession is a legal possession against a wrong-doer": or, as the Roman maxim runs, "adversus extraneos vitiosa possessio prodesse solet" (x). As regards real property, a possession commencing by trespass can be defended against a stranger not only by the first wrongful occupier, but by those claiming through him; in fact it is a good root of title as against every one except the person really entitled (y); and ultimately, by the operation of the Statutes of Limitation, it may become so as against him also.

The authorities do not clearly decide, but seem to imply, that it would make no difference if the *de facto* possession violated by the defendant were not only without title, but obviously wrongful. But the rule is in aid of *de facto* possession only. It will not help a claimant who has been in possession but has been dispossessed in a lawful manner and has not any right to possess (z).

This rule in favour of possessors is fundamental in both civil and criminal jurisdiction. It is indifferent for most practical purposes whether we deem the reason of the law to be that the existing possession is *prima facie* evidence of ownership or of the right to possess — "the presumption of law is that the person who has possession has the property" (a) — or, that for the sake of public peace and

---

(x) *Graham v. Peat* (1801), 1 East, 244, 246, 6 R. R. 268, *Jeffries v. G. W. R. Co.*, (1856), 5 E. & B. 802, 25 L. J. Q. B. 107, *Bourne v. Fosbrooke* (1865), 18 C. B. N. S. 515, 34 L. J. C. P. 164, extending the principle of *Armory v. Delamirie* (1722), 1 Str. 504 [505], and in 1 Sm. L. C., D. 41. 3, de poss 53, cf. Paulus Sent Rec v. 11 §2 "sufficit ad probationem si rem corporaliter teneam" And such use and enjoyment as the nature of the subject-matter admits of is good evidence of possession See *Harper v. Charlesworth* (1825), 4 B. & C. 574, and other authorities collected in Pollock and Wright on Possession, 31-35

(y) *Asher v. Whitlock* (1865), L. R. 1 Q. B. 1, 35 L. J. Q. B. 17, cp *Cutts v. Spring* (1818), 15 Mass. 135, and Bigelow L. C. 341, and *Rosenberg v. Cook*, (1881), 8 Q. B. Div 62, 51 L. J. Q. B. 170, and see further Pollock and Wright, *op cit* 95-99.

(z) *Buckley v. Gross* (1863), 3 B. & S. 566, 32 L. J. Q. B. 129

(a) Lord Campbell C. J. in *Jeffries v. G. W. R. Co* (1856), 5 E. & B. at p 806, 25 L J Q. B. 107; but this does not seem consistent with the protection of even a manifestly wrongful possessor against a new extraneous wrong doer. In Roman law a thief has the interdicts though not the *actio furti*, which requires a lawful

security, and as "an extension of that protection which the law throws around the person" (b), the existing possession is protected, without regard to its origin, against all men who cannot make out a better right: — or say (c) that the law protects possession for the sake of true owners, and to relieve them from the vexatious burden of continual proof of title, but cannot do this effectually without protecting wrongful possessors also. Such considerations may be guides and aids in the future development of the law, but none of them will adequately explain how or why it came to be what it is.

Rights of owner entitled to resume possession. Again, as *de facto* possession is thus protected, so *de jure* possession — if by that term we may designate an immediate right to possess when separated from actual legal possession — was even under the old system of pleading invested with the benefit of strictly possessory remedies; that is, an owner who had parted with possession, but was entitled to resume it at will, could sue in trespass for a disturbance by a stranger. Such is the case of a landlord where the tenancy is at will (d), or of a bailor where the bailment is revocable at will, or on a condition that can be

interest in the plaintiff, in the common law it seems that he can maintain trespass

(b) Lord Denman C J in *Rogers v Spence* (1841), 13 M & W. at p. 581 This is precisely Savigny's theory, which however is not now generally accepted by students of Roman Law In some respects it fits the common law better Mr Justice Holmes in "The Common Law" takes a view *ejusdem generis*, but distinct.

(c) With Ihering (Grund des Besitzesschutzes, 2d ed 1869) Cp the same author's "Der Besitzwille," 1889.

(d) Bro Ab Trespas, pl 131, 19 Hen VI 15, pl 94, where it is pointed out that the trespasser's act is one, but the causes of action are "diversis respectibus," as where a servant is beaten and the master has an action for loss of service

---

Rights of owner entitled to resume possession. Supporting the text, *vide*, Lunt *v*. Brown, 13 Me. 236, Staples *v*. Smith, 48 Me. 471, Mason *v*. Lewis, 1 Greene (Ia), 494, Pool *v* Mitchell, 1 Hill (S. C.), 404; Snyder *v*. Myers, 3 W A 195, and authorities cited, *ante*, p. 412 *et seq.*

A landlord may maintain trespass although the tenant is in possession. Fitch *v*. Gosser, 54 Mo. 267. *Contra*, Wentworth *v*. Portsmouth & D. R

satisfied at will, which last case includes that of a trustee of chattels remaining in the control and enjoyment of the *cestui que trust*, for the relation is that of bailment at will as regards the legal interest (e). In this way the same act may be a trespass both against the actual possessor and against the person entitled to resume possession. "He who has the property may have a writ of trespass, and he who has the custody another writ of trespass" (f). "If I let my land at will, and a stranger enters and digs in the land, the tenant may bring trespass for his loss, and I may bring trespass for the loss and destruction of my land" (d). And a lessor or bailor at will might have an action of trespass *vi et armis* against the lessee or bailee himself where the latter had abused the subject-matter in a manner so inconsistent with his contract as to amount to a determination of the letting or bailment. "If tenant at will commit voluntary waste, as in pulling down of houses, or in felling of trees, it is said that the lessor shall have an action of trespass for this against the lessee. As if I lend to one my sheep to tathe his land, or my oxen to plow the land, and he killeth my cattle, I may well have an action of trespass against him nothwithstanding the lending" (g).

An exclusive right of appropriating things in which property is acquired only by capture is on the same footing in respect of remedies as actual possession (h).

Rights of derivative possessors. Derivative possession is equally protected, through whatever number of removes

(e) See *Barker v. Furlong*, '91, 2 Ch. 172, 60 L J Ch 368.

(f) 48 Ed III 20, pl 8

(g) Litt. s 71 If any doubt be implied in Littleton's "it is said," Coke's commentary removes it Such an act "concerneth so much the freehold and inheritance, as it doth amount in law to a determination of his will."

(h) *Holford v. Bailey* (1849), 13 Q. B 426, 18 L. J. Q B. 109, Ex. Ch.

Co., 55 N H. 540, Lindenbower v. Bentley, 86 Mo 515, Delaney v. Erickson, 10 Neb. 492. The landlord of a tenant at will may maintain trespass. O'Brien v Cavanaugh, 61 Mich. 368, 28 N. W Rep. 127

it may have to be traced from the owner in possession, who (by modern lawyers at any rate) is assumed as the normal root of title. It may happen that a bailee delivers lawful possession to a third person, to hold as under-bailee from himself, or else as immediate bailee from the true owner: nay more, he may re-deliver possession to the bailor for a limited purpose, so that the bailor has possession and is entitled to possess, not in his original right, but in a subordinate right derived from his own bailee (*i*). Such a right, while it exists, is as fully protected as the primary right of the owner would have been, or the secondary right of the bailee would be.

Possession derived through trespasser. Troublesome questions were raised under the old law by the position of a person who had got possession of goods through delivery made by a mere trespasser or by an originally lawful possessor acting in excess of his right. One who receives from a trespasser, even with full knowledge, does not himself become a trespasser against the true owner, as he has not violated an existing lawful possession (*j*). The best proof that such is the law is the existence of the offence of receiving stolen goods as distinct from theft; if receiving from a trespasser made one a trespasser, the receipt of stolen goods with the intention of depriving the true owner of them would have been larceny at common law. Simi-

---

(*i*) *Roberts* v. *Wyatt* (1810), 2 Taunt. 268

(*j*) *Wilson* v *Barber* (1833), 4 B. & Ad 614

Possession derived through trespassers. The true owner of goods may recover them from the assignee of one who obtains them by fraud. Artman *v.* Walton, 12 Phila. Rep 442 Though there can be but one satisfaction trover lies against successive conversioners of the same property Mathews *v.* Menadger, 2 McLean, 145 And against *bona fide* purchasers from the original trespassers. Riley *v.* Boston Water Power Co., 11 Cush. 11; Champney *v.* Smith, 15 Gray, 512, Everett *v* Coffin, 6 Wend. 603; Hoffman *v.* Carow, 22 Wend 285; Spraights *v.* Hawley, 39 N Y 441, Garard *v* Pittsburgh etc. R Co, 29 Pa St 154.

larly where a bailee wrongfully delivers the goods over to a stranger; though the bailee's mere assent will not prevent a wrongful taking by the stranger from being a trespass (*k*).

The old law of real property was even more favourable to persons claiming through a disseisor; but it would be useless to give details here. At the present day the old forms of action are almost everywhere abolished, and it is quite certain that the possessor under a wrongful title, even if he is himself acting in good faith, is by the common law liable in some form to the true owner (*l*), and in the case of goods must submit to recapture if the owner can and will retake them (*m*). In the theoretically possible case of a series of changes of possession by independent trespasses, it would seem that every successive wrong-doer is a trespasser only as against his immediate predecessor, whose *de facto* possession he disturbed: though as regards land exceptions to this principle, the extent of which is not free from doubt, were introduced by the doctrine of "entry by relation" and the practice as to recovery of mesne profits. But this too is now, as regards civil liability, a matter of mere curiosity (*n*).

(*k*) 27 Hen VII 39, pl 49, cp 16 Hen VII 2, pl 7, *Mennie* v. *Blake* (1856), 6 E & B 842, 25 L J Q B 399

(*l*) 12 Edw IV 13, pl 9, but this was probably an innovation at the time, for Brian dissented The action appears to have been on the case for spoiling the goods

(*m*) See *Blades* v *Higgs* (1865), 11 H L. C 621, 34 L J C P. 286, where this was assumed without discussion, only the question of property being argued But probably that case goes too far in allowing recapture by force, except perhaps on fresh pursuit· see p. 470, below.

(*n*) The common law might conceivably have held that there was a kind of privity of wrongful estate between an original trespasser and persons claiming through him, and thus applied the doctrine of continuing trespass to such persons, and this would perhaps have been the more logical course But the natural dislike of the judges to multiplying capital felonies, operating on the intimate connexion between trespass and larceny, has in several directions prevented the law of trespass from being logical For the law of trespass to land as affected by relation, see *Barnett* v *Guildford* (1855), 11 Ex 19, 24 L J Ex 260, *Anderson* v. *Radcliffe* (1860), Ex Ch , E. B & E 819, 29 L. J. Q. B 128, and Bigelow L C. 361—370

VIII.— *Wrongs to Easements, etc.*

Violation of incorporeal rights. Easements and other incorporeal rights in property, "rather a fringe to property than property itself" as they have been ingeniously called (*o*), are not capable in an exact sense of being possessed. The enjoyment which may in time ripen into an easement is not possession, and gives no possessory right before the due time is fulfilled: "a man who has used a way ten years without title cannot sue even a stranger for stopping it" (*p*). The only possession that can come in question is the possession of the dominant tenement itself, the texture of legal rights and powers to which the "fringe" is incident. Nevertheless disturbance of easements and the like, as completely existing rights of use and enjoyment, is a wrong in the nature of trespass, and remediable by action without any allegation or proof of specific damage (*q*); the action was on the case under the old forms of pleading, since trespass was technically im-

(*o*) Mr Gibbons, Preface to the fifth edition of Gale on Easements, 1876
(*p*) Holmes, The Common Law, 240, 382
(*q*) 1 Wms. Saund. 626, *Harrop v Hirst* (1868), L R. 4 Ex. 43, 46, 38 L. J. Ex. 1

Violation of incorporeal rights. Possession for less than the prescriptive period will not raise the presumption of an easement by grant, and the possession must be continuous. Sargent *v.* Ballard, 9 Pick. 251, Gloucester *v.* Beach, 2 Id 60, n, Medford *v.* Pratt, 4 Id. 222; Gayetty *v.* Bethune, 14 Mass. 49, 55; Parker *v.* Foote, 19 Wend. 309; Luce *v.* Carley, 24 Id 451; Kirschmer *v* Western & A. R Co., 67 Ga. 760, Claflin *v.* Boston & A. R Co, 157 Mass. 489; 32 N. E. Rep. 659, Texas & W. R Co. *v.* Wilson (Tex), 18 S W. Rep. 352

An action of trespass cannot be brought for the interference with a right to carry water over a grantor's land. Baer *v.* Martin, 8 Blackf. 317. But in Massachusetts a few similar rights are made real property by statute and such action can be maintained. Jackson *v.* Rounseville, 5 Metc. 127. Generally, trespass lies for the disturbance of rights in incorporeal hereditaments, though practically these interferences are usually continuous in nature and best remedies in equity. See Tranger *v* Sassaman, 14 Pa. St 514

possible, though the act of disturbance might happen to include a distinct trespass of some kind, for which trespass would lie at the plaintiff's option.

To consider what amounts to the disturbance of rights *in re aliena* is in effect to consider the nature and extent of the rights themselves (*r*), and this does not enter into our plan, save so far as such matters come under the head of Nuisance, to which a separate chapter is given.

Franchises and incorporeal rights of the like nature, as patent and copyrights, present something more akin to possession, for their essence is exclusiveness; and indeed trespass was the proper remedy for the disturbance of a strictly exclusive right. "Trespass lies for breaking and entering a several fishery, though no fish are taken." And so it has always been held of a free warren (*s*). But the same remark applies; in almost every disputed case the question is of defining the right itself, or the conditions of the right (*r*); and *de facto* enjoyment does not even provisionally create any substantive right, but is material only as an incident in the proof of title.

IX.— *Grounds of Justification and Excuse.*

Licence Acts of interference with land or goods may be justified by the consent of the occupier or owner; or they may be justified or excused (sometimes excused rather than justified, as we shall see) by the authority of the law. That consent which, without passing any interest in the

---

(*r*) Thus *Hopkins* v *G N R Co* (1877), 2 Q B Div 224, 46 L. J Q B 265, sets bounds to the exclusive right conferred by the franchise of a ferry, and *Dalton* v *Angus* (1881), 6 App Ca. 740, 50 L J Q B 689, discusses with the utmost fulness the nature and extent of the right to lateral support for buildings. Both decisions were given in form, on a claim for damages from alleged wrongful acts Yet it is clear that a work on Torts is not the place to consider the many and diverse opinions expressed in *Dalton* v *Angus*, or to define the franchise of a ferry or market Again the later case of *Attorney General* v. *Horner* (1885),11 App Ca 66, 55 L J. Q. B 193, interprets the grant of a market *in alvo juxta quodam loco*, on an information alleging encroachment on public ways by the lessee of the market, and claiming an injunction

(*s*) *Holford* v *Bailey*, Ex Ch. (1848-9), 13 Q B. 426, 18 L J Q B. 109 See the authorities collected in argument, S C in court below, 8 Q B i t p 1010

property to which it relates, merely prevents the acts for which consent is given from being wrongful, is called a licence. There may be licences not affecting the use of property at all, and on the other hand a licence may be so connected with the transfer of property as to be in fact inseparable from it.

"A dispensation or licence properly passeth no interest, nor alters or transfers property in anything, but only makes an action lawful, which without it had been unlawful. As a licence to go beyond the seas, to hunt in a man's park, to come into his house, are only actions which without licence had been unlawful. But a licence to hunt in a man's park and carry away the deer killed to his own use, to cut down a tree in a man's ground, and to carry it away the next day after to his own use, are licences as to the acts of hunting and cutting down the tree, but as to the carrying away of the deer killed and tree cut down they are grants. So to licence a man to eat my meat, or to fire the wood in my chimney to warm him by; as to the actions of eating, firing my wood and warming him, they are licences: but it is consequent necessarily to those actions that my property be destroyed in the meat eaten, and in the wood burnt. So as in some cases by consequent and not directly, and as its effect, a dispensation or licence may destroy and alter property" (*u*)

(*u*) Vaughan C J, *Thomas* v *Sorrell*, Vaughan, 351

License License is permission or authority. It is a defense to trespass. With reference to real estate "A license is an authority or power to make use of land in some specific way, or to do certain acts or series of acts upon the land of another." Tiedeman's Real Property, § 651, citing Cook *v*. Stearns, 11 Mass 533, Mumford *v*. Whitney, 15 Wend 380, Blaisdell *v* Railroad, 51 N. H 485. See Lawrence *v*. Springer, 49 N J. Eq. 289, 24 At. Rep 933, Cahoon *v* Bayard, 123 N. Y. 298; 25 N. E. Rep. 376; Silby *v* Trotter, 29 N. J. Eq 228; Pursell *v*. Stover, 100 Pa St. 43; 20 At. Rep. 403; Baker *v*. Boston, 12 Pick. 184, Driscoll *v*. Marshall, 15 Gray, 62, Van Deusen *v*. Young, 29 N. Y. 9, Chynoweth *v*. Tenney, 10 Wis. 397

Revocation of licence: distinction when coupled with interest. Generally speaking, a licence is a mere voluntary suspension of the licensor's right to treat certain acts as wrongful, comes to an end by any transfer of the property with respect to which the licence is given (*v*), and is revoked by signifying to the licensee that it is no longer the licensor's will to allow the acts permitted by the licence. The revocation of a licence is in itself no less effectual though it may be a breach of contract. If the owner of land or a building admits people thereto on payment, as spectators of an entertainment or the like, it may be a breach of contract to require a person who has duly paid his money and entered to go out, but a person so required has no title to stay, and if he persists in staying

(*v*) *Wallis* v. *Harrison* (1838), 4 M. & W. 538, 8 L. J. Ex. 44.

Revocation of license. distinction when coupled with interest. Ordinarily a license is revokable at will. Houston v. Laffe, 46 N. H. 505, Carleton v. Redington, 21 N. H. 291, Hetfield v. Central R. Co., 29 N. J. L 571, Kimble v. Yates, 14 Ill 464; Jameson v. Millman, 3 Duer, 255, Dulneen v. Rich, 22 Wis. 550; White v Manhattan Ry. Co., 63 Hun, 634; 18 N. Y. S. Rep. 396, Giles v. Simonds, 15 Gray, 441, Burton t Scherff, 1 Allen, 133; Allen v Fiske, 42 Vt. 462, Eckerson v Crippen, 110 N. Y. 585, 18 N. E. Rep 443, Owen v. Field, 12 Allen, 457, Kremer v. Chicago, etc., Ry. Co., 51 Minn. 15; 52 N W Rep. 977; Cronkhite v. Cronkhite, 94 N. Y. 323; Fargis v. Walton, 107 N. Y 899, 14 N. E Rep. 303, Totel v Bonnefoy, 123 Ill. 653; 14 N. E Rep. 687, How v Searing, 6 Bosw 354, Lake Erie & W Ry. Co. v. Kennedy, 132 Ind. 274; 31 N. E. Rep. 943, Rayner v. Nugent, 60 Md 515; Parish v. Kaspare, 109 Ind. 586.

But if the license amounts to a legal grant it is irrevocable. Bracken v. Rushville, etc., R Co., 27 Ind. 346, Collins Co. v. Marcy, 25 Conn. 239, Rogers v. Cox, 96 Ind 157; Bingham v. Salene, 15 Oreg. 208; Nettleton v Sikes, 8 Metc. 34; Claflin v. Carpenter, 4 Metc. 580; Hetfield v. Central R. Co., 29 N. J. L. 571, Lewis v. McNatt, 65 N. C. 63; White v. Elwell, 48 Me. 360; Goff v. Obertenffer, 3 Phila. Rep. 71; Douglas v. Shumway, 13 Gray, 498. Thus, in Johnson v. Skillman (29 Minn. 97, 12 N W. Rep. 149), the court said: "In some cases where the license is connected with a valid grant, as of chattels or fixtures, upon the land of the licensor, susceptible of being removed, it is subsidiary to the right of the property, and irrevocable to the extent necessary to protect the licensee, and saves to him the right of entry — the right of possession following the right of property."

he is a trespasser. His only right is to sue on the contract (*x*): when, indeed, he may get an injunction, and so be indirectly restored to the enjoyment of the licence (*y*). But if a licence is part of a transaction whereby a lawful interest in some property, besides that which is the immediate subject of the licence, is conferred on the licensee, and the licence is necessary to his enjoyment of that interest, the licence is said to be "coupled with an interest" and cannot be revoked until its purpose is fulfilled: nay more, where the grant obviously cannot be enjoyed without an incidental licence, the law will annex the necessary licence to the grant. "A mere licence is revocable; but that which is called a licence is often something more than a licence; it often comprises or is connected with a grant, and then the party who has given it cannot in general revoke it so as to defeat his grant to which it was incident" (*z*). Thus the sale of a standing crop or of growing trees imports a licence to the buyer to enter on the land so far and so often as reasonably necessary for cutting and carrying off the crop or the trees, and the licence cannot be revoked until the agreed time, if any, or otherwise a reasonable time for that purpose has elapsed (*a*). The diversity to be noted between licence and grant is of respectable antiquity. In 1460 the defendant in an action of trespass set up a right of common; the plaintiff said an excessive number of beasts were put in; the defendant said this was by licence of the plaintiff, to which the plaintiff said the licence was revoked before the trespass complained of: Billing, then king's

---

(*x*) *Wood* v *Leadbitter* (1845), 13 M & W 838, 14 L J Ex 161, *Hyde* v *Graham* (1862), 1 H & C. 593, 32 L J Ex 27 A contract to carry passengers does not constitute or include a licence so as to let in this doctrine, though part or the whole of the journey may be on land belonging to the railway company or other carrier *Butler* v. *M S & L R Co* (1888), 21 Q. B Div 207, 57 L. J Q B 564. The reasoning is perhaps open to criticism see L Q R. v 99

(*y*) See *Frogley* v *Earl of Lovelace* (1859), Joh 333, where, however, the agreement was treated as an agreement to execute a legal grant.

(*z*) *Wood* v. *Leadbitter*, 13 M & W 838, 844, 14 L J Ex 161

(*a*) See further 2 Wms Saund 363-365, or Cooley on Torts, 51

serjeant, afterwards Chief Justice of the King's Bench under Edward IV., argued that a licence may be revoked at will even if expressed to be for a term, and this seems to have so much impressed the Court that the defendant, rather than take the risk of demurring, alleged a grant: the reporter's note shows that he thought the point new and interesting (b). But a licensee who has entered or placed goods on land under a revocable licence is entitled to have notice of revocation and a reasonable time to quit or remove his goods (c).

Executed licences. Again, if the acts licensed be such as have permanent results, as in altering the condition of land belonging to the licensee in a manner which, but for the licence, would be a nuisance to adjacent land of the licensor; there the licensor cannot, by merely revoking the licence, cast upon the licensee the burden of restoring the former state of things. A licence is in its nature revocable (d), but the revocation will not make it a trespass to leave things as the execution of the licence has made them. In this sense it is said that "a licence executed is not countermandable" (e). When a licence to do a particular thing once for all has been executed, there is nothing left to revoke.

(b) 39 Hen VI. 7 pl 12.
(c) *Cornish* v. *Stubbs* (1870), L. R. 5 C. P 334, 39 L J.C P 202, *Mellor* v. *Watkins* (1874), L R 9 Q B 400.
(d) *Wood* v *Leadbitter*, note (x), last page

(e) *Winter* v *Brockwell* (1807), 8 East, 308. This class of cases is expressly recognized and distinguished in *Wood* v. *Leadbitter*, 13 M & W at p 835

Executed licenses. In the United States the authorities are not uniform upon the question as to the right of a licensor to exercise the power of revocation where the licensee in pursuance of the license has expended money and incurred binding obligations.

Each case necessarily depends upon its own circumstances. It is established that for a sufficient cause a revocation may be enjoined by a court of equity See School District v. Lindsay, 47 Mo. App. 134, Harlan v. Logansport Nat. Gas Co., 133 Ind. 323; 52 N. E. Rep. 930; White v.

Whether and how far the licensor can get rid of the consequences if he mislikes them afterwards is another and distinct inquiry, which can be dealt with only by considering what those consequences are. He may doubtless get rid of them at his own charges if he lawfully can; but he cannot call on the licensee to take any active steps unless under some right expressly created or reserved.

For this purpose, therefore, there is a material difference between "a licence to do acts which consist in repetition, as to walk in a park, to use a carriage-way, to fish in the waters of another, or the like," which may be countermanded without putting the licensee in any worse position than before the licence was granted, and "a licence to construct a work which is attended with expense to the party using the licence, so that, after the same is countermanded, the party to whom it was granted may sustain a

---

Manhattan Ry. Co., 139 N. Y. 19, 34 N. E Rep. 887; Brauns v Glesige, 130 Ind 167; 29 N. E. Rep. 1061; Saucer v. Keller, 129 Ind. 475, 28 N. E. Rep 1117, Crousdale v. Lanigan, 59 Hun, 620, 13 N. Y. S Rep. 31, Grimshaw v Belcher, 88 Cal. 217, 26 Pac Rep. 84; Flickinger v Shaw, 87 Cal 126, 25 Pac. Rep. 268, Barnes v Barnes, 6 Vt 388, Ashman v Williams, 8 Pick 402, Williams v Flood, 63 Mich 487; Nowlin v. Whipple, 79 Ind. 481, Campbell v Indianapolis etc. R Co., 110 Ind 490; Morse v. Copeland, 2 Gray, 302; Baker v. Chicago etc, R Co , 57 Mo. 265; Southwestern R. Co v Mitchell, 69 Ga. 114, Morse v Copeland, 2 Gray, 302, Huff v McCauley, 53 Pa. St. 206; Rhodes v Otis, 33 Ala. 578; Fuhr v. Dean, 26 Mo. 116.

Equity will enforce the future enjoyment of a license executed in part where money has been expended and fixtures erected on its faith. Snowden v. Wilas, 19 Ind. 10, Stephen v. Brown, 19 Ind 367; Cook v Pridgen, 45 Ga. 331; Lee v. McLead, 17 Nev 280; Gibson v St. Louis A. & M Assoc, 33 Mo App 165; Grimshaw v. Belcher, 88 Cal. 217, 26 Pac. Rep 84, Wilson v. Chalfant, 15 Ohio, 248, Rerick v Kern, 14 Serg. & R. 267, Risien v. Brown, 73 Tex. 135, Lane v. Miller, 27 Ind. 534.

But in other well-considered cases the power of revocation is held to be absolute. Jackson & Sharp Co. v. Philadelphia etc. R. Co , 4 Del. Ch. 180; Lake Erie & W. Co. v Michener, 117 Ind 465; 20 N. E. Rep. 254; Kevitt v. McKeithan, 90 N. C 106; St. Louis Stock Yards v Wiggins Ferry Co , 112 Ill. 384; Williams v. Morrison, 32 Fed. Rep. 177; Ketchum v. Newman, 4 Daly, 57; 22 N. E. Rep. 1052 See cases cited, *ante,* p. 459.

heavy loss " (*f*). And this rule is as binding on a licensor's successors in title as on himself (*g*). But it is not applicable (in this country at any rate) to the extent of creating in or over land of the licensor an easement or other interest capable of being created only by deed (*h*).

In these cases, however, the licensee is not necessarily without remedy, for the facts may be such as to confer on him an interest which can be made good by way of equitable estoppel (*i*). This form of remedy has been extensively applied in the United States to meet the hardship caused by untimely revocation of parol licences to erect dams, divert water-courses, and the like (*j*).

The case of a contract to grant an easement or other interest in land must be carefully distinguished when it occurs (*k*).

Expression of licensor's will. The grant or revocation of a licence may be either by express words or by any act

(*f*) *Liggins* v. *Inge* (1831), 7 Bing. 682, 694, per cur

(*g*) *Ibid*

(*h*) *Wood* v *Leadbitter*, p 460, above; *Raffey* v *Henderson* (1851), 17 Q B 574, 21 L J Q B 49, *Hewitt* v *Isham* (1851), 7 Ex 77, 21 L. J Ex 35 (showing that conversely what purports to be a reservation in a parol demise may operate as a licence)

(*i*) See *Plimmer* v. *Mayor of Wellington, N Z* (1884), 9 App Ca 699, 53 L J P C 104, where the two principles do not appear to be sufficiently distinguished Cp *McManus* v. *Cooke* (1887), 35 Ch D. 681, 696, per Kay J , 56 L J Ch. 662

(*j*) Cooley on Torts, 307-310 It seems to have sometimes been thought in America that the only difficulty arises from the Statute of Frauds, which is of course a mistake *Wood* v *Leadbitter*, p. 831, above. The limits of the doctrine are in this country fixed by *Ramsden* v. *Dyson* (1868), L. R. 1 H L 129.

(*k*) See *Smart* v *Jones* (1864), 33 L J C. P 154

Expression of licensor's will. Agreeing with the text, *vide*, Kay v. Penn. R Co., 65 Pa. St. 273, Martin v. Houghton, 45 Barb 60, Adams v. Truman, 12 Johns. 408; Sterling v. Warden, 51 N. H. 231, Lakin v Ames, 10 Cush. 198, Cutler v. Smith, 57 Ill. 252, Fletcher v. Evans, 140 Mass. 241, Harmon v Harmon, 61 Me. 222.

The mere use of land by the licensor in a manner incompatible with the license terminates the license without notice. Simpson v Wright, 21 Ill. App. 67; Wilson v. St. Paul etc. R Co , 41 Minn. 56; 42 N. W. Rep 600. It is also terminated by the transfer of the property. Drake v. Wells, 11 Allen, 141, Prince v. Case, 10 Conn 382, Jenkins v. Lykes, 19 Fla. 146; Maxwell v. Bay City etc. Co., 41 Mich 453;

sufficiently signifying the licensor's will; if a man has leave and licence to pass through a certain gate, the licence is as effectually revoked by locking the gate as by a formal notice (*l*). In the common intercourse of life between friends and neighbours tacit licences are constantly given and acted upon.

Distinction from grant as regards strangers. We shall have something to say in another connexion (*m*) of the rights — or rather want of rights — of a "bare licensee." Here we may add that a licence, being only a personal right — or rather a waiver of the licensor's rights — is not assignable, and confers no right against any third person. If a so-called licence does operate to confer an exclusive right capable of being protected against a stranger, it must be that there is more than a licence, namely the grant of an interest or easement. And the question of grant or licence may further depend on the question whether the specified mode of use or enjoyment is known to the law as a substantive right or interest (*n*): a question that may be difficult. But it is submitted that

(*l*) See *Hyde* v. *Graham*, note (*x*), p. 460.
(*m*) Chap. XII. below, *ad fin.*
(*n*) Compare *Nuttall* v. *Bracewell* (1866), L R 2 Ex 1, 36 L. J Ex 1, with *Ormerod* v *Todmorden Mill Co* (1883), 11 Q B Div 155, 52 L. J. Q B 445, and see Gale on Easements, 5th ed 315 Contra the learned editors of Smith's Leading Cases, in the notes to *Armory* v *Delamirie*.

Giles *v* Simonds, 15 Gray, 441; Dark *v* Johnson, 55 Pa St. 164, Whitaker *v* Cauthorne, 3 Dev. L 389; Houx *v* Seat, 26 Mo. 178. Or, by the death of the licensor. Putney *v.* Day, 26 N H 430, Eggleston *v.* New York & C. R Co , 35 Barb 162; Carter *v.* Harlan, 6 Md 20, Jenkins *v.* Lykes, 19 Fla 148; 45 Am. Rep. 19.

Distinction from grant as regards strangers. A license is personal as between the parties and cannot be transferred by the licensee. Gronondyke *v.* Cramer, 2 Ind 382; Carleton *v.* Redington, 21 N. H. 291; Ruggles *v.* Lesure, 24 Pick 187; Harris *v* Gillingham, 6 N. H. 9; Paine *v.* Northern P. R. Co., 14 Fed. Rep 407; Reinmiller *v.* Skidmore, 7 Lans 161; Jackson *v* Batcock, 4 Johns. 418, Mendenhall *v.* Klinck, 51 N Y. 246, De Haro *v.* U. S , 5 Wall 599; Webb *v.* Walker, 31 Pa. St. 46; Blaisdell *v.* Railroad, 51 N H 485

on principle the distinction is clear. I call at my friend's house; a contractor who is doing some work on adjacent land has encumbered my friend's drive with rubbish; can it be said that this is a wrong to me without special damage? With such damage, indeed, it is (o), but only because a stranger cannot justify that which the occupier himself could not have justified. The license is material only as showing that I was not a wrong-doer myself; the complaint is founded on actual and specific injury, not on a *quasi* trespass. Our law of trespass is not so eminently reasonable that one need be anxious to extend to licensees the very large rights which it gives to owners and occupiers.

Justification by law. As to justification by authority of the law, this is of two kinds:

1. In favour of a true owner against a wrongful possessor: under this head come re-entry on land and retaking of goods.

2. In favour of a paramount right conferred by law against the rightful possessor; which may be in the execution of legal process, in the assertion or defence of private right, or in some cases by reason of necessity.

Re-entry: herein of forcible entry. A person entitled to the possession of lands or tenements does no wrong to the person wrongfully in possession by entering upon him; and it is said that by the old common law he might have entered by force. But forcible entry is an offence under the statute of 5 Ric. II. (A. D. 1381), which provided that "none from henceforth make any entry into any lands and tenements, but in case where entry is given by the law, and in such case not with strong hand nor with multitude of people, but only in peaceable and easy [the true reading of the Parliament Roll appears to be 'lisible, aisee, & peisible']

(o) *Corby* v. *Hill* (1858), 4 C B N S 556, 27 L. J C. P 318 See more in Chap. XII below

manner." This statute is still in force here, and "has been re-enacted in the several American States, or recognized as a part of the common law" (p). The offence is equally committed whether the person who enters by force is entitled to possession or not: but opinions have differed as to the effect of the statute in a court of civil jurisdiction. It has been held that a rightful owner who enters by force is not a trespasser, as regards the entry itself, but is liable for any independent act done by him in the course of his entry which is on the face of it wrongful, and could be justified only by a lawful possession (q); and, it should seem, for any other consequential damage, within the general limit of natural and probable consequence, distinguishable from the very act of eviction. This is a rather subtle result, and is further complicated by the rule of law which attaches legal possession to physical control, acquired even for a very short time, so it be " definite and appreciable " (r) by the rightful owner. A., being entitled to immediate possession (say as a mortgagee having the legal estate) effects an actual entry by taking off a lock, without having given any notice to quit to B. the precarious occupier; thus, " in a very

(p) Cooley on Torts, 323. For the remedial powers given to justices of the peace by later statutes, see Lambarde's Eirenarcha, cap 4, 15 Ric II c 2, is still nominally in force. As to what amounts to forcible entry, Jones v Foley, '91, 1 Q. B. 730, 60 L. J Q B 464

(q) Beddall v. Maitland (1881), 17 Ch D 174, 50 L. J Ch 401, Edwick v. Hawkes (1881), 18 Ch. D. 199, 50 L J Ch. 577, and authorities there discussed.
(r) Lord Cairns in Lows v. Telford (1876), 1 App Ca. at p 421

Re-entry herein of forcible entry. In general, under the statutes of forcible entry and detainer in the various States, the bare question of possession, irrespective of title, is presented. It is an accepted rule in America that where a person has the title and a right of present possession a peaceable entry will not make him a trespasser. Henderson v. Grewell, 8 Cal. 581; Tribble v. Frame, 7 J J. Marsh. 599, 617, Culver v. Smart, 1 Ind 65; Yeates v. Allin, 2 Dana, 134; Walton v File, 1 Dev. & B 567, Ostataga v Taylor, 44 Ill. App. 469, Brooke v. O'Boyle, 27 Ill App. 384, Illinois &c R. Co v. Cobb, 94 Ill. 55. Upon the question whether a person with title and the right to immediate possession may employ force, if necessary, in effecting an entry, see Hyatt v. Wood, 13 Johns. 150; Ives v. Ives, Id. 235, Johnson v. Hanahan, 1 Strobh 313.

rough and uncourteous way," that is, peaceably but only just peaceably, he gets possession: once gotten, however, his possession is both legal and rightful. If therefore B. turns him out again by force, there is reasonable and probable cause to indict B. for a forcible entry. So the House of Lords has decided (s). Nevertheless, according to later judgments, delivered indeed in a court of first instance, but one of them after consideration, and both learned and careful, A. commits a trespass if, being in possession by a forcible entry, he turns out B. (t). Moreover, the old authorities say that a forcible turning out of the person in present possession is itself a forcible entry, though the actual ingress were without violence. "He that entereth in a peaceable show (as the door being either open or but closed with a latch only), and yet when he is come in useth violence, and throweth out such as he findeth in the place, he (I say) shall not be excused: because his entry is not consummate by the only putting of his foot over the threshold, but by the action and demeanour that he offereth when he is come into the house" (u). And under the old statutes and practice, "if A. shall disseise B. of his land, and B. do enter again, and put out A. with force, A. shall be restored to his possession by the help of the justices of the peace, although his first entry were utterly wrongful: and (notwithstanding the same restitution is made) yet B. may well have an assize against A., or may enter peaceably upon him again" (x).

But old authorities also distinctly say that no action is given by the statute to a tenant who is put out with force by the person really entitled, "because that that entry is not any disseisin of him" (y). There is nothing in them to countenance the notion of the personal expulsion being

---

(s) *Lows* v *Telford* (1876), 1 App. Ca 414, 45 L J Ex. 613

(t) See the judgment of Fry J in *Beddall* v. *Maitland*, and *Edwick* v. *Hawkes*, note (q).

(u) Lambarde's Eirenarcha, cap. 4, p. 142, ed 1610

(x) Ib 148

(y) F. N B 248 H , Bro. Ab Forcible Entry, 29

a distinct wrong. The opinion of Parke and Alderson was in accordance with this (z), and the decision from which they dissented is reconcileable with the old books only by the ingenious distinction — certainly not made by the majority (a) — of collateral wrongs from the forcible eviction itself. The correct view seems to be that the possession of a rightful owner gained by forcible entry is lawful as between the parties, but he shall be punished for the breach of the peace by losing it, besides making a fine to the king. If the latest decisions are correct, the dispossessed intruder might nevertheless have had a civil remedy in some form (by special action on the case, it would seem) for incidental injuries to person or goods. This refinement does not appear to have occurred to any of the old pleaders.

Fresh re-entry on trespasser. A trespasser may in any case be turned off land before he has gained possession, and he does not gain possession until there has been something like acquiescence in the physical fact of his occupation on the part of the rightful owner. His condition is quite different from that of a rightful owner out of possession, who can recover legal possession by any kind of effective interruption of the intruder's actual and exclusive control. A person who had been dismissed from the office of schoolmaster and had given up possession of a room occupied by him in virtue of his

---

(z) *Newton* v *Harland* (1840), 1 M & G 644, 1 Scott N R. 474, in *Harvey* v. *Brydges* (1845), 14 M & W at pp 442-3, they declared themselves unconverted

(a) Tindal C J. said that possession gained by forcible entry was *illegal* 1 M & G. 658.

Fresh re-entry on trespasser. Mere occasional entries and trespasses do not confer any of the rights of a possessor in law upon the trespasser. Hughes *v.* Stevens, 36 Pa St 320, Ozark Land Co. *v.* Leonard, 20 Fed. Rep. 881; Ware *v.* Johnson, 55 Me 500; Illinois Coal Co. *v.* Cobb, 82 Ill. 183, Pettit *v.* Cowherd, 83 Va 20; 1 S. E. Rep. 393; Storrs *v.* Feick, 24 W. Va. 606, Gulledge *v* White, 73 Tex 498; 11 S. W. Rep. 527.

office, but had afterwards re-entered and occupied for eleven days, was held not entitled to sue in trespass for an expulsion by the trustees at the end of that time. "A mere trespasser cannot, by the very act of trespass, immediately and without acquiescence, give himself what the law understands by possession against the person whom he ejects, and drive him to produce his title, if he can without delay reinstate himself in his former possession" (*b*). There must be not only occupation, but effective occupation, for the acquisition of possessory rights. "In determining whether a sufficient possession was taken, much more unequivocal acts must be proved when the person who is said to have taken possession is a mere wrong-doer than when he has a right under his contract to take possession" (*c*). And unless and until possession has been acquired, the very continuance of the state of things which constitutes the trespass is a new trespass at every moment (*d*). We shall see that this has material consequences as regards the determination of a cause of excuse.

Recaption of goods. As regards goods which have been wrongfully taken, the taker is a trespasser all the time that

---

(*b*) *Browne* v *Dawson* (1840), 12 A. & E. 624, 629, 10 L J Q B. 7 If a new tresp isser entered in this state of things, could the trespasser in inchoate occupation sue him, or the last possessor? Possibly both

(*c*) Mellish L. J, *Ex parte Fletcher* (1877), 5 Ch Div 809, 812.

(*d*) *Holmes* v *Wilson* (1839), 10 A. & E 503, *Bowyer* v *Cook* (1847), 4 C B 236, 16 L J C. P 177, and see 2 Wms Saund 496

Recaption of goods A peaceable entry by an owner to retake goods from another's land or possession is not a trespass. Allen *v.* Feland, 10 B Mon. 306; Wheelden *v.* Lowell, 50 Me. 499, Chambers *v* Bedell, 2 Watts & S. 225; Richardson *v.* Anthony, 12 Vt 273; Harding *v.* Sandy, 43 Ill. App. 442. *Contra*, Jackson *v* Walsh, 14 Johns. 406; Morgan *v.* Varick, 8 Wand. 587; Newkirk *v.* Sabler, 9 Barb. 652, Heermance *v.* Vernoy, 6 Johns. 5; Roach *v.* Damon, 2 Humph. 425.

But in such case the use of force is not permissible. Salisbury *v.* Green, 17 R. I. 758, 24 At Rep 787. *Compare*, Mills *v.* Wooten, 59 Ill. 234.

his wrongful possession continues, so much so that "the removal of goods, wrongfully taken at first, from one place to another, is held to be a several trespass at each place" (e), and a supervening *animus furandi* at any moment of the continuing trespassory possession will complete the offence of larceny and make the trespasser a thief (f). Accordingly the true owner may retake the goods if he can, even from an innocent third person into whose hands they have come; and, as there is nothing in this case answering to the statutes of forcible entry, he may use (it is said) whatever force is reasonably necessary for the recaption (g). He may also enter on the first taker's land for the purpose of recapture if the taker has put the goods there (h); for they came there by the occupier's own wrong (i); but he cannot enter on a third person's land unless, it is said, the original taking was felonious (k), or perhaps, as it has been suggested, after the goods have been claimed and the occupier of the land has refused to deliver them (l). Possession is much more easily changed in the case of goods than in the case of land, a transitory and almost instantaneous control has often, in criminal courts, been held to amount to asportation. The difference may have been sharpened by the rules of criminal justice, but in a general way it lies rather in the nature of the facts than in any arbitrary divergence of legal principles in dealing with immoveable and moveable property.

(e) 1 Wms Saund 20

(f) *Reg* v *Riley* (1857), Dears 149, 22 L J M. C. 48

(g) *Blades* v. *Higgs* (1861), 10 C B N S 713, but the reasons given at page 720 seem wrong, and the decision itself is contrary to the common law as understood in the thirteenth century One who retook his own goods by force (save, perhaps, on fresh pursuit) was a trespasser and lost the goods It was even thought needful to state that he was not a felon See Britton, ed Nicholls, 1 57, 116. At all events maim or wounding is not justified for this cause but violence used in defence of a wrongful possession is a new assault, and commensurate resistance to it in personal self defence is justifiable

(h) *Patrick* v *Colerick* (1838), 3 M & W 483, explaining Blackst Comm iii 4.

(i) Per Littleton J , 9 Edw IV. 35, pl 10

(k) Blackstone, l c , *Anthony* v. *Haney* (1832), 8 Bing 187, and Bigelow L C 374

(l) Tindal C. J. in *Anthony* v *Haney* but this seems doubtful.

Process of law: breaking doors. One of the most important heads of justification under a paramount right is the execution of legal process. The mere taking and dealing with that which the law commands to be so taken and dealt with, be it the possession of land or goods, or both possession and property of goods, is of course no wrong, and in particular if possession of a house cannot be delivered in obedience to a writ without breaking the house open, broken it must be (*m*). It is equally settled on the other hand that "the sheriff must at his peril seize the goods of the party against whom the writ issues," and not any other goods which are wrongly supposed to be his; even unavoidable mistake is no excuse (*n*). More special rules have been laid down as to the extent to which private property which is not itself the immediate object of the

---

(*m*) *Semayne's Ca* (1604-5) 5 Co Rep 91 *b*, and in 1 Sm L C 693 As to the protection of subordinate officers acting in good faith, see in the Chapter of General Exceptions, p 130, above

(*n*) *Glasspoole* v *Young* (1829), 9 B & C. 696, *Garland* v. *Carlisle* (1837), 4 Cl & F.

Process of law. breaking doors. It is not legal to break into a dwelling house to serve civil process on the owner, or occupant, or his goods Oystead v. Shed, 13 Mass. 520; Ilsley v. Nichols, 12 Pick. 270; Calvert v. Stone, 10 B. Mon. 152; People v. Hubbard, 24 Wend. 369; State v. Claudius, 1 Mo. App. 551. Raising a latch is sufficient to make the entry illegal. Curtis v. Hubbard, 1 Hill, 336.

But where an officer is allowed to set foot in the house without force he may keep his possession. State v. Beckner (Ind.), 16 N. E. Rep. 553 If the door is open the officer may enter and break open inner doors, if property is concealed, and use such force as is necessary to serve the process. Prettyman v. Dean, 2 Harr. (Del.) 494; State v. Thackland, 1 Bay, 358; Hager v. Danforth, 20 Barb. 116.

A store occupied as a dwelling may not be entered by the dwelling door, but if there is a door common to both there may be a lawful entry. Stearns v. Vincent, 50 Mich. 209; 45 Am Rep. 37.

An officer may upon demand and refusal, break open a door to levy on goods of a person other than the occupant of the house. De Graffenried v Mitchell, 3 McCord, 506, Burton v. Wilkinson, 18 Vt. 186, Platt v Brown, 16 Pick. 553.

Contrary to the rule in England, it is held in the United States, that when process is executed illegally by breaking into a dwelling, the execution is void. Ilsley v. Nichols, 12 Pick. 270.

process may be invaded in executing the command of the law. The broad distinction is that outer doors may not be broken in execution of process at the suit of a private person; but at the suit of the Crown, or in execution of process for contempt of a House of Parliament (o), or of a Superior Court, they may, and must; and this, in the latter case, though the contempt consist in disobedience to an order made in a private suit (p). The authorities referred to will guide the reader, if desired, to further details.

Constables, revenue officers, and other public servants, and in some cases private persons, are authorized by divers statutes to enter on lands and into houses for divers purposes, with a view to the discovery or prevention of crime, or of frauds upon the public revenue. We shall not atempt to collect these provisions.

Distress. The right of distress, where it exists, justifies the taking of goods from the true owner: it seems that the distrainor, unlike a sheriff taking goods in execution, does not acquire possession, the goods being " in the custody of the law" (q). Most of the practical importance of the subject is in connexion with the law of landlord and tenant, and we shall not enter here on the learning of distress for rent and other charges on land (r)

(o) *Burdett* v *Abbott* (1811), 14 East, 1, a classical case

(p) And it is contempt in the sheriff himself not to execute such process by breaking in if necessary *Harvey* v. *Harvey* (1884), 26 Ch D. 644 Otherwise where attachment is, or was, merely a formal incident in ordinary civil process

(q) See *West* v *Nibbs* (1847), 4 C B 172, 17 L J. C P 150.

(r) As to distress in general, Blackst Comm book III c 1

Distress. Illustrating the common law right of a landlord to distrain the goods and chattels of his tenant for the payment of rent, see, Bailey v. Wright, 3 McCord, 484; Russel v. Doty, 4 Cow. 576; Slocum v Clark, 2 Hill, 475. Dumes v. McLoskey, 5 Ala 259; Richardson v. Vice, 4 Blackf. 13, Allen v. Agnew, 24 N. J. L. 443; Hartshorne v. Kiernan, 2 Halst. 29; Harrison v. Guill, 46 Ga. 427, Bukup v. Valentine, 19 Wend. 554; First Nat. Bank v Adam, 138 Ill 483; 28 N. E. Rep 955.

Distress has been either abolished or restricted in nearly all of the states of the United States.

Damage feasant. Distress damage feasant is the taking by an occupier of land of chattels (commonly but not necessarily animals) (s) found encumbering or doing damage on the land. The right given by the law is therefore a right of self-protection against the continuance of a trespass already commenced. It must be a manifest trespass; distress damage feasant is not allowed against a party having any colour of right, e. g., one commoner cannot distrain upon another commoner for surcharging (t). And where a man is lawfully driving cattle along a highway and some of them stray from it into ground not fenced off from the way, he is entitled to a reasonable time for driving them out before the occupier may distrain, and is excused for following them on the land for that purpose. What is reasonable time is a question of fact, to be determined with reference to all the circumstances of the transaction (u). And where cattle stray by reason of the defect of fences which the occupier is bound to repair, there is no actionable trespass and no right to distrain until the owner of the cattle has notice (x). In one respect distress damage

(s) "All chattels whatever are distrainable damage feasant," Gilbert on Distress and Replevin (4th ed 1823), 49. A locomotive has been distrained damage feasant, *Ambergate &c R. Co* v. *Midland R Co* (1853), 2 E & B 793, it was not actually straying, but had been put on the Midland Company's line without the statutable approval of that company

(t) *Cape* v *Scott* (1874), L. R. 9 Q B 269, 43 L J Q B 65

(u) *Goodwin* v *Cheveley* (1859), 4 H. & N 631, 28 L J Ex 298

(x) 2 Wms Saund. 671.

Damage feasant. In most of the states of the United States this subject is regulated by statute. Generally, the common law rule as to trespass by animals on uninclosed land has been declared inapplicable to the physical condition of this country, especially in the new and sparsely settled communities. See Sprague v. Fremont etc. R. Co., 6 Dak. 86, 50 N. W. Rep 617; Frazier v. Nortimus, 34 Ia 82; Oll v. Rowley, 69 Ill. 469, Ruyster v. Foy, 46 Ia. 132; Northcote v. Smith, 4 Ohio Cir. Ct Rep. 565, Little Rock etc. R. Co v. Finley, 37 Ark. 562.

The adoption of the stock laws is held to repeal the common law, in Eastman v. Rice, 14 Me. 419, Croker v. Mann, 3 Mo 472; Mooney v. Maynard, 1 Vt. 470. *Contra*, Stewart v. Benninger, 138 Pa. St. 437; 21 Am. Rep 159, Bulpit v Mathews, 42 Ill. App. 561.

feasant is more favoured than distress for rent. "For a rent or service the lord cannot distreine in the night, but in the day time: and so it is of a rent charge. But for damage feasant one may distreine in the night, otherwise it may be the beasts will be gone before he can take them" (*y*). But in other respects " damage feasant is the strictest distress that is, for the thing distrained must be taken in the very act," and held only as a pledge for its own individual trespass, and other requirements observed (*z*).

The right of distress damage feasant does not exclude the right to chase out trespassing beasts at one's election (*a*), or to remove inanimate chattels and replace them on the owner's land (*b*).

Entry of distrainor. Entry to take a distress must be peaceable and without breaking in; it is not lawful to open a window, though not fastened, and enter thereby (*c*). Distrainors for rent have been largely holpen by statute, but the common law has not forgotten its ancient strictness where express statutory provision is wanting.

In connexion with distress the Acts for the prevention of cruelty to animals have introduced special justifications: any one may enter a pound to supply necessary food and water to animals impounded, and there is an eventual power of sale, on certain conditions, to satisfy the cost thereof (*d*).

(*y*) Co Litt 142 *a*
(*z*) *Vaspor v. Edwards* (1701), 12 Mod 660, where the incidents of damage feasant generally are expounded
(*a*) *Tyrringham's Ca* , 4 Co. Rep 38 *b*
(*b*) *Rea* v *Sheward* (1839), 2 M & W 424.
(*c*) *Nash* v *Lucas* (1867), L R 2 Q B 590 Otherwise where the window is already partly open *Crabtree* v. *Robinson* (1885), 15 Q B D 312, 54 L J. Q B 514
(*d*) 12 & 13 Vict. c 92, s 6, 17 & 18 Vict c 60, s 1, superseding an earlier Act of William IV to the same effect. See Fisher's Digest, DISTRESS, s t "Pound and Poundage."

Entry of distrainor Agreeing with the text, *vide*, Williams *v* Spencer, 5 Johns. 353; State *v* Thackara, 1 Bay, 358.

A statute which authorizes a humane society to kill another's horse

Trespasses justified by necessity. Finally there are cases in which entry on land without consent is excused by the necessity of self-preservation, or the defence of the realm (c), or an act of charity preserving the occupier from irremediable loss, or sometimes by the public safety or convenience, as in putting out fires, or as where a highway is impassable, and passing over the land on either side is justified; but in this last-mentioned case it is perhaps rather a matter of positive common right than of excuse (f). Justifications of this kind are discussed in a case of the early sixteenth century, where a parson sued for

---

(c) See p 199, above.

(f) The justification or right, whichever it be, does not apply where there is only a limited dedication of a way, subject to the right of the owner of the soil to do acts, such as ploughing, which make it impassable or inconvenient at certain times *Arnold* v *Holbrook* (1873), L. R 8 Q B 96, 42 L. J. Q B. 80

---

summarily, without notice, is unconstitutional. Brill *v.* Ohio Humane Soc, 1 Ohio Cir Ct. Rep. 358

Trespasses justified by necessity. Certain necessities excuse acts otherwise wrongful. In the case of American Print Works *v.* Lawrence, (23 N J L. 604), the learning on this subject is collated and the court said: "The common law doctrine of necessity is one that is now too firmly established to be drawn in question, and yet, perhaps, necessarily from its character, it seems somewhat undefined as to its application and extent. It may, by the way, be remarked, that it is not less unquestionable as an established doctrine, because its origin so far as regards a justification at the common law, is only to be found in the illustrative arguments of the older authorities, and not in any direct adjudication. Its exercise must depend upon the nature and degree of necessity that calls the right into action, and which cannot be determined until the necessity is made to appear. The necessity must be immediate, imperative and in some cases extreme and overwhelming. Mere expediency or utility will not suffice." In this case the distinction is drawn between the limited rule that a person may protect himself or property when attacked, but not a stranger, and the broader rule, based on public good, that a person may protect the property of a stranger by destroying that of another where general destruction is impending, as a fire in a city. See Burton *v.* McClellan, 2 Ill. 434.

An entry on the land of another to save a boat from destruction was held to be not a trespass, in Proctor *v.* Adams, 113 Mass. 376.

A traveler on an obstructed highway may lawfully pass around the

trespass in carrying away his corn, and the defendant justified on the ground that the corn had been set out for tithes and was in danger of being spoilt, wherefor he took it and carried it to the plaintiff's barn to save it: to which the plaintiff demurred. Kingsmill J. said that a taking without consent must be justified either by public necessity, or "by reason of a condition in law"; neither of which grounds is present here; taking for the true owner's benefit is justifiable only if the danger be such that he will lose his goods without remedy if they are not taken. As examples of public necessity, he gives pulling down some houses to save others (in case of fire, presumably) (*g*), and entering in war time to make fortifications. "The defendant's intention," said Rede C. J., "is material in felony but not in trespass; and here it is not enough that he acted for the plaintiff's good." A stranger's beasts might have spoilt the corn, but the plaintiff would have had his remedy against their owner. "So where my beasts are doing damage in another man's land, I may not enter to drive them out, and yet it would be a good deed to drive them out so that they do no more damage; but it is otherwise if another man drive my horses into a stranger's land where they do damage, there I may justify entry to drive them out, because their wrong-doing took its beginning in

---

(*g*) Cp Littleton J in Y B 9 Ed IV. 35, "If a man *by negligence* suffer his house to burn, I who am his neighbour may break down the house to avoid the danger to me, for if I let the house stand, it may burn so that I cannot quench the fire afterwards"

---

obstruction over the land of another. Campbell *v.* Race, 7 Cush. 408; Morey *v* Fitzgerald, 56 Vt 487; Carey *v.* Rae, 58 Cal 159.

A person driving cattle along the highway commits no trespass by going on another's land to drive off escaping ones. Rightmore *v.* Shephard, 59 Hun, 620; 12 N Y. S. Rep. 800; Hartford *v.* Brady, 114 Mass. 466, Coal *v.* Crommet, 13 Me 250, Tonawanda R. Co. *v.* Munger, 5 Denio, 255

Upon the right of a city council to destroy liquor in the city for the purpose of preventing a possible riot, see Jones *v.* Richmond, 18 Gratt. 517.

a stranger's wrong. But here, because the party might have his remedy if the coin were anywise destroyed, the taking was not lawful. And it is not like the case where things are in danger of being lost by water, fire, or such like, for there the destruction is without remedy against any man. And so this plea is not good" (h). Fisher J. concurred. There is little or nothing to be added to the statement of the law, though it may be doubted whether it is now likely ever to be strictly applied. Excuse of this kind is always more readily allowed if the possessor of the land has created or contributed to the necessity by his own fault, as where the grantor of a private right of way has obstructed it so that the way cannot be used except by deviation on his adjacent land (i).

Foxhunting not privileged. At one time it was supposed that the law justified entering on land in fresh pursuit of a fox, because the destruction of noxious animals is to be encouraged; but this is not the law now. If it ever was, the reason for it has long ceased to exist (j). Practically foxhunters do well enough (in this part of the United Kingdom) with licence express or tacit.

Trespass ab initio. There is a curious and rather subtle distinction between justification by consent and justification or excuse under authority of law. A possessor by consent,

(h) 21 Hen VII 27, pl 5 (but the case seems really to belong to Hilary term of the next year, see S. C, Kellw 88 a, Frowike was still Chief Justice of Common Pleas in Trinity term 21 Hen VII, ib 86 b, pl 19, he died in the following vacation, and Rede was appointed in his stead, ib 85 b, where for Mich 22 Hen VII we should obviously read 21), cp. 37 Hen VI. 37, pl 26, 6 Ed. IV 8, pl 18, which seems to extend the justification to entry to retake goods which have come on another's land by inevitable accident, see Story, Bailments, § 83 a, note.

(i) Selby v Nettlefold (1873), 9 Ch 111, 43 L. J Ch 359

(j) Paul v Summerhayes (1878), 4 Q B D 9, 48 L J M C 33.

Hunting not privileged. The right to commit a trespass in pursuit of animals *feræ naturæ* does not exist Glenn v. Kays, 1 Ill. App. 479. See Sterling v Jackson, 69 Mich. 488, 37 N. W. Rep. 845.

or a licensee, may commit a wrong by abusing his power, but (subject to the peculiar exception in the case of letting or bailment at will mentioned above) (*k*) he is not a trespasser. If I lend you a horse to ride to York, and you ride to Carlisle, I shall not have (under the old forms of pleading) a general action of trespass, but an action on the case. So if a lessee for years holds over, he is not a trespasser, because his entry was authorized by the lessor (*l*). But " when entry, authority, or licence is given to any one by the law, and he doth abuse it, he shall be a trespasser, *ab initio*," that is, the authority or justification is not only determined, but treated as if it had never existed. " The law gives authority to enter into a common inn or tavern (*m*); so to the lord to distrain; to the owner of the ground to distrain damage feasant; to him in reversion to see if waste be done; to the commoner to enter upon the land to see his cattle; and such like . . . . But if he who enters into the inn or tavern doth a trespass, as if he carries away anything, or if the lord who distrains for rent (*n*), or the owner for damage feasant, works or kills the distress; or if he who enters to see waste breaks the house or stays there all night; or if the commoner cuts down a tree; in these and the like cases the law adjudges that he entered for that purpose, and because the act which

---

(*k*) P 443, above
(*l*) 21 Ed IV 76 b, pl. 9
(*m*) This is in respect of the public character of the innkeeper's employment.
(*n*) The liability of a distrainor for rent justly due, in respect of any subsequent irregularity, was reduced to the real amount of damage by 11 Geo II. c. 19, s 19 but this does not apply to a case where the distress was wholly un lawful Attack v *Bramwell* (1863), 3 B & S 520, 32 L J Q B. 146 Distrainors for damage feasant are still under the common law.

Trespass ab initio. Where one enters by public license or authority of law and thereafter does unlawful acts he becomes a trespasser *ab initio* and liable for the entire trespass, but one entering under contract or by consent of a private person is liable only for the injury consequent to the unwarrantable acts. Ballard *v.* Noakes, 2 Ark 45; Adams *v* Rivers, 11 Barb 390; Narehood *v.* Wilhelm, 69 Pa St 64 Faulkner *v.* Anderson, Gilmer, 221, Malcolm *v.* Spoor, 12 Metc 279, Brock *v* Stim-

demonstrates it is a trespass, he shall be a trespasser *ab initio*" (o). Or to state it less artificially, the effect of an authority given by law without the owner's consent is to protect the person exercising that authority from being dealt with as a trespasser so long — but so long only — as the authority is not abused. He is never doing a fully lawful act: he is rather an excusable trespasser, and becomes a trespasser without excuse if he exceeds his authority (p): "it shall be adjudged against the peace" (q). This doctrine has been applied in modern times to the lord of a manor taking an estray (r), and to a sheriff remaining in a house in possession of goods taken in execution for an unreasonably long time (s). It is applicable only when there has been some kind of active wrong-doing; not when there has been a mere refusal to do something one ought to do — as to pay for one's drink at an inn (t), or deliver up a distress upon a proper tender of the rent due (u). "If I distrain for rent, and afterwards the termor offers me the rent and the arrears, and I withhold the distress from him, yet he shall not have an action of trespass against me, but detinue, because it was lawful at the beginning, when I took the distress; but if I kill them or work them in my own plow, he shall have an action of trespass" (x). But it is to be observed that retaining legal possession after the expiration of authority has been held equivalent to a new

(o) The *Six Carpenters' Case*, 8 Co. Rep 146 a, b
(p) Cp Pollock and Wright on Possession, 144, 201
(q) 11 Hen IV 75, pl 16
(r) *Oxley* v. *Watts* (1785), 1 T. R. 12, 1 R R. 133
(s) *Ash* v *Dawnay* (1852), 8 Ex 237, 22 L. J. Ex 59, sed qu. if according to the old authorities, see Pollock and Wright on Possession, 82
(t) *Six Carpenters' Case*, note (o)
(u) *West* v *Nibbs* (1847), 4 C B 172, 17 L. J C P 150
(x) Littleton in 33 Hen VI 27, pl 12

son, 108 Mass. 520, Allen v. Crofoot, 5 Wend 506; Dingley v. Buffum, 57 Me 379, Esty v. Wilmot, 15 Gray, 168, Jewell v. Mahood, 44 N H. 474, Smith v. Pierce, 110 Mass 85; Mussey v. Cummings, 34 Me. 74; Burton v Calaway, 20 Ind. 469, Gardner v. Campbell, 15 Johns. 401; Edelman v Yeakel, 27 Pa. St. 26, Stone v. Knapp, 29 Vt 501; Cushing v Adams, 18 Pick 110.

taking, and therefore a positive act: hence (it seems) the distinction between the liability of a sheriff, who takes possession of the execution debtor's goods, and of a distrainor; the latter only takes the goods into "the custody of the law," and "the goods being in the custody of the law, the distrainor is under no legal obligation actively to re-deliver them" (*y*). Formerly these refinements were important as determining the proper form of action. Under the Judicature Acts they seem to be obsolete for most purposes of civil liability, though it is still possible that a question of the measure of damages may involve the point of trespass *ab initio*. Thus in the case of the distrainor refusing to give up the goods, there was no doubt that trover or detinue would lie (*z*): so that under the present practice there would be nothing to discuss.

X.—*Remedies.*

Taking or retaking goods. The only peculiar remedy available for this class of wrongs is distress damage feasant, which, though an imperfect remedy, is so far a remedy that it suspends the right of action for the trespass. The distrainor "has an adequate satisfaction for his damage till he lose it without default in himself;" in which case he may still have his action (*a*). It does not seem that the re-taking of goods taken by trespass extinguishes the true owner's right of action, though it would of course affect the amount of damages.

Costs where damages nominal. Actions for merely trifling trespasses were formerly discouraged by statutes providing that when less than 40s. were recovered no more

---

(*y*) *West* v. *Nibbs*, 4 C. B. at p. 184, per Wilde C. J.
(*z*) Wilde C. J. *l. c.*, Littleton *ubi sup.*
(*a*) *Vaspor* v. *Edwards*, 12 Mod. 660, per Holt C. J.

Taking or retaking of goods. See cases cited under DISTRESS and DAMAGE FEASANT, *ante*, pp. 472, 475.

costs than damages should be allowed except on the judge's certificate that the action was brought to try a right, or that the trespass was "wilful and malicious:" yet a trespass after notice not to trespass on the plaintiff's lands was held to be "wilful and malicious," and special communication of such notice to the defendant was not required (*b*). But these and many other statutes as to costs were superseded by the general provisions of the Judicature Acts, and the rule that a plaintiff recovering less than 10*l.* damages in an action "founded on tort" gets no costs in a Superior Court unless by special certificate or order (*c*); and they are now expressly repealed (*d*).

The Court is therefore not bound by any fixed rule; but it might possibly refer to the old practice for the purpose of informing its discretion. It seems likely that the common practice of putting up notice boards with these or the like words: "Trespassers will be prosecuted according to law"—words which are "if strictly construed, a wooden falsehood" (*e*), simple trespass not being punishable in courts of criminal jurisdiction—was originally intended to secure the benefit of these same statutes in the matter of costs. At this day it may be a question whether the Court would not be disposed to regard the threat of an impossible criminal prosecution as a fraud upon the public, and rather a cause for depriving the occupier of costs than for awarding them (*f*). Several better and safer forms of notice are available; a common American one, "no trespassing," is as good as any.

"Nothing on earth," said Sir Walter Scott, "would in-

(*b*) See *Bowyer* v *Cook* (1847), 4 C. B. 236, 16 L. J. C. P. 177, *Reynolds* v *Edwards* (1794), 6 T. R. 11, even where the defendant had intended and endeavoured to avoid trespassing, but this was doubted by Pollock C B in *Swinfen* v. *Bacon* (1860), 6 H. & N 184, 188, 30 L. J. Ex 33, 36.

(*c*) County Courts Act, 1888, s 116 (substituted for like provision of the repealed Act of 1867), and 45 & 46 Vict. c 57, s 4, see "The Annual Practice," 1892, pp 169, 172

(*d*) 42 & 43 Vict c 59

(*e*) F W Maitland, "Justice and Police," p 13

(*f*) At all events the threat of spring guns, still not quite unknown, can do the occupier no good, for to set spring guns is itself an offence

duce me to put up boards threatening prosecution, or cautioning one's fellow-creatures to beware of man-traps and spring-guns. I hold that all such things are not only in the highest degree offensive and hurtful to the feelings of people whom it is every way important to conciliate, but that they are also quite inefficient" (g). It must be remembered that Scott never ceased to be a lawyer as well as a man of letters. It was partly the legal knowledge and tastes displayed in the Waverly Novels that identified him in the eyes of the best critics as the author.

Injunctions. An injunction can be granted to restrain a continuing trespass, such as the laying and keeping of waterpipes under a man's ground without either his consent or justification by authority of law; and the plaintiff need not prove substantial damage to entitle himself to this form of relief (h). On the other hand the right to an injunction does not extend beyond the old common-law

---

(g) Lockhart's Life of Scott, vii 317, ed 1839, ex relatione Basil Hall.

(h) Goodson v. Richardson (1874), 9 Ch 221, 43 L J Ch. 790

Injunctions An injunction will issue as a matter of right in aid of the action of trespass where there is probability of irreparable injury, or inadequate pecuniary compensation, or a multiplicity of suits which cannot be otherwise prevented. See Stetson v Stevens, 64 Vt. 649; 25 At Rep 429; Ellis v. Wren, 84 Ky 254, 1 S. W Rep 440, Wood v. Braxton, 54 Fed Rep 1005, Natoma Co. v. Clarkin, 14 Cal 544; Tainter v. Mayor, 19 N J. Eq. 46, Sullivan v Rabb, 86 Ala 433; 5 So. Rep 746; Clendening v Ohl, 118 Ind. 46, 20 N E Rep 639, Clark v Jeffersonville R Co., 44 Ind 248, Murphy v. Lincoln, 63 Vt 278, 22 At Rep 418, Ohio River R Co. v Ward, 35 W Va 481, 14 S. E Rep 142; Richards v Dower, 64 Cal 62, 28 Pac Rep. 113, Miller v. Lynch, 149 Pa. St 460, 24 At Rep. 0, Gilchrist v VanDyke, 63 Vt. 75; 21 At Rep. 1099, Yates v. Town of West Grafton, 33 W Va 507, 11 S E. Rep 8, Lembeck v. Nye, 47 Ohio, 336, 24 N E. Rep. 686, Thompson v. Engle, 4 N J. Eq. 271, Parker v. Winnipescogee Co., 2 Black, 545; Saratoga Co v Deyoe, 77 N Y. 219

But in the absence of one or more of the above grounds and when an adequate remedy at law is available an injunction will not be granted. Thomas v James, 32 Ala. 723, Crown v Leonard, 32 Ga 241, New York P. & D. Establishment v Fitch, 1 Paige, 97; Hatcher v. Hampton, 7 Ga.

right to sue for damages: a reversioner cannot have an injunction without showing permanent injury to the reversion (*i*).

Of course it may be a substantial injury, though without any direct damage, to do acts on another man's land for one's own profit without his leave; for he is entitled to make one pay for the right to do them, and his power of withholding leave is worth to him precisely what it is worth to the other party to have it (*k*).

Effect of changes in procedure. Before the Common Law Procedure Acts an owner, tenant, or reversioner who had suffered undoubted injury might be defeated by bringing his action in the wrong form, as where he brought trespass and failed to show that he was in present possession at the time of the wrong done (*l*). But such cases can hardly occur now.

(*i*) *Cooper* v. *Crabtree* (1882), 20 Ch. Div 589, 51 L J. Ch. 585. In *Allen* v. *Martin* (1875), 20 Eq 462, the plaintiffs were in possession of part of the land affected

(*k*) See 9 Ch. 224, 20 Ch Div 592.
(*l*) *Brown* v *Notley* (1848), 3 Ex 221, 18 L. J Ex 39, *Pilgrim* v *Southampton &c. R Co* (1849), 8 C B 25, 18 L J. C P 330

49, James v. Dixon, 20 Mo 79; Smith v. Pettengill, 15 Vt 82; Robeling v First Nat. Bank, 30 Fed Rep. 744; Ewing v. Rourke, 14 Oreg. 514, 13 Pac. Rep. 483; Miller v. Burkett, 132 Ind 469; 32 N. E. Rep. 309, Heaney v Butte & M C. Co, 10 Mont. 590; 27 Pac. Rep. 379; Latham v Northern P R Co., 45 Fed. Rep. 721, McCullough v. City of Denver, 39 Fed Rep. 307, German v. Clark, 71 N. C. 417; West Point Iron Co. v. Reymert, 45 N. Y. 703, Burnley v Cook, 13 Tex. 586, 65 Am. Dec 79; Thornton v. Roll, 118 Ill. 350. See this subject discussed, *post*, p. 520.

CHAPTER X.

NUISANCE

Nuisance: public or private. Nuisance is the wrong done to a man by unlawfully disturbing him in the enjoyment of his property or, in some cases, in the exercise of a common right. The wrong is in some respects analogous to trespass, and the two may coincide, some kinds of nuisance being also continuing trespasses. The scope of nuisance, however, is wider. A nuisance may be public or private.

Public or common nuisances affect the Queen's subjects at large, or some considerable portion of them, such as the inhabitants of a town; and the person therein offending is liable to criminal prosecution (*a*). A public nuisance does not necessarily create a civil cause of action for any person; but it may do so under certain conditions. A

(*a*) There was formerly a mandatory writ for the abatement of public nuisances in cities and corporate towns and boroughs See the curious precedent in F N B 185 D Apparently the Queen's Bench Division still has in theory jurisdiction to grant such writs (as distinct from the common judgment on an indictment), see Russell on Crimes, 1 440.

Nuisance defined. "Anything constructed on a person's premises, which of itself, or by its intended use, directly injures a neighbor in the proper use and enjoyment of his property, is a nuisance." Grady *v* Wolsner, 46 Ala 382, see Stone *v.* Bumpus, 40 Cal 428

In the case of Hart *v.* Mayor etc. of Albany (9 Wend. 571), a floating storehouse is held to constitute a public nuisance See Pilcher *v.* Hart, 1 Humph. 524, Woodman *v* Kilbourn Mfg Co , 1 Abb. U S. 158, Gibson *v.* Black (Ky), 9 S W Rep 379

Public or common nuisances, defined The American cases define public nuisance substantially as the text, *vide* State *v.* Mayor etc. of Mo-

private nuisance affects only one person or a determinate number of persons, and is the ground of civil proceedings only. Generally it affects the control, use, or enjoyment

---

bile, 5 Port 279, Dierks v. Comm'r's of Highways, 142 Ill 197, 31 N E. Rep. 496, Town of Kirkwood v Cairnes, 11 Mo App. 88, State v Board of Health of Newark, 54 N. J. L. 825, 23 At Rep. 919; Commonwealth v. Ruddle, 142 Pa St. 111, 21 At Rep 811, 28 W. N C 227, Hussner v. Brooklyn City R. Co , 114 N. Y 433; 21 N. E Rep. 1002, Commonwealth v. Wilkesbarre & K. S Ry. Co., 127 Pa. St 278, 17 At Rep 996, 24 W. N. C 280; Seacord v. People, 121 Ill 623; 13 N. E Rep 191; People v Crounse, 51 Hun, 189, 4 N Y. S. Rep. 226, 7 N Y Crim. Rep. 11; State v. Laura Toole, 106 N. C. 736, 11 S. E. Rep. 168; Coffer v. Territory, 1 Wash St 325, 25 Pac Rep 632; Kuehn v City of Milwaukee, 83 Wis. 583, 53 N. W. Rep 912

"It may be observed generally that every nuisance is annoying to only a few of the citizens of a particular place They are the public of that locality. It is a public nuisance if it annoy such part of the people as necessarily come in contact with it" Hackney v. State, 8 Ind. 495. See Lansing v Smith, 14 Wend 10; Commonwealth v. Webb, 6 Rand 726, Commonwealth v Farris, 5 Rand. 691, State v. Baldwin, 1 Dev. & B 197, Ellis v State, 7 Blackf. 534, Green v Nunnemacher, 38 Wis. 50; Commonwealth v Perry, 139 Mass 198; Allen v State, 34 Tex. 230, Howard v See, 3 Sandf. 281, Beatty v. Gilmore, 16 Pa. St. 436, Monk v. Packard, 71 Me 309; Robinson v Baugh, 31 Mich 291, King v. Morris, etc R Co., 18 N. J. Eq 397.

But whether a thing is or is not a nuisance does not depend on the notions of people living in a designated locality. Owen v. Phillips, 73 Ind 284 See Prince v. Grantz, 118 Pa St. 402

"A public nuisance cannot exist in acts which are warranted by law or authorized by legislative sanction, even though the act complained of might, independent of the statute, be a nuisance " Darcantel v. People's Slaughter-house Refrigerator Co , 44 La 632; 11 So Rep 243. To illustrate, it has been held that a fire engine house in a city is not a nuisance. Van De Vere v. Kansas City, 107 Mo 83, 17 S W. Rep. 695 The authority of the legislature should doubtless be expressed and relate to matters of public utility in which the people have an interest and a right of control Baltimore & P R. Co. v. Fifth Baptist Church, 108 U S 317. See Cogswell v. N. Y., N H & H R. Co., 103 N Y. 10. But this rule is subject to the following qualification "In such cases the person is shielded from liability for damages that ensue, unless he is chargeable with negligence for the manner in which the act is done." Bohan v P J G L. Co., 122 N. Y 34, 25 N E Rep 246, citing Conklin v N Y , O & W. R Co , 102 N Y. 107, Beseman v Pennsylvania R Co., 50 N J L 235, Ottenot v N. Y , L & W R Co., 28 N. Y S Rep 483.

of immoveable property; but this is not a necessary element according to the modern view of the law. Certainly the owner or master of a ship lying in harbour, for example, might be entitled to complain of a nuisance created by an occupier on the wharf or shore which made the ship uninhabitable.

See Hinchman v. Patterson, etc. R Co., 17 N. J. Eq 75; People v. Sands, 1 Johns. 78, Edmondson v. City of Moberly, 98 Mo. 523; 11 S. W Rep 900; Masterson v. Short, 7 Robt. 290, Quinn v. Lowell Electric Light Corp , 110 Mass 106

See, *ante*, pp. 69, 70, 71, 154.

Public nuisance and private nuisance distinguished "A common or public nuisance is that which affects the people and as a violation of the public right either by direct encroachment upon public property or by doing some act which tends to a common injury or by omitting of that which the common good requires, and which it is the duty of the person to do. Public nuisances are founded upon wrongs that arise from unreasonable, unwarrantable and unlawful use of property, or from improper, indecent or unlawful conduct working an obstruction or injury to the public and producing material annoyance, inconvenience, and discomfort. Founded upon a wrong it is indictable and punishable as for a misdemeanor It is the duty of individuals to observe the rights of the public and to refrain from the doing of that which materially injures and annoys or inconveniences the people, and this extends even to business which would otherwise be lawful, for the public health, safety, convenience, comfort or morals, is of paramount importance, and that which affects or impairs it must give way for the general good In such case the question of negligence is not involved, for its injurious effect upon the public makes it a wrong which it is the duty of the court to punish rather than to protect. But a private nuisance rests upon a different principle. It is not necessarily founded upon a wrong, consequently cannot be indicted and punished as for an offense It is founded upon injuries that result from the violation of private rights and produce damages to but one or a few persons Injury and damage are essential elements, and yet they may both exist and still the act or thing producing them not be a nuisance. Every person has a right to a reasonable enjoyment of his own property, and so long as the use to which he devotes it violates no rights of another however much damage others may sustain therefrom, his use is lawful and it is *damnum absque injuria.*" Bohan v P. J G. L. Co., 122 N. Y. 32; 25 N E Rep. 246, citing Thurston v. Hancock, 12 Mass. 222, Campbell v Seaman, 63 N. Y. 568. See Page v Mille Lacs L. Co. (Minn.), 55 N. W. Rep. 608.

Private right of action for public nuisance. We shall first consider in what cases a common nuisance exposes the person answerable for it to civil as well as criminal process, in other words, is actionable as well as indictable.

"A common nuisance is an unlawful act or omission to discharge a legal duty, which act or omission endangers the lives, safety, health, property, or comfort of the public, or by which the public are obstructed in the exercise or enjoyment of any right common to all her Majesty's subjects" (*b*). Omission to repair a highway, or the placing of obstructions in a highway or public navigable river, is a familiar example.

(*b*) Criminal Code (Indictable Offences) Bill, 1879 (as amended in Committee), s 150, cp Stephen, Digest of Criminal Law, art. 176, and illustrations thereto, and the Indian Penal Code, s 268

Private right of action for public nuisance Private persons are not permitted to maintain suits to abate a public nuisance, as such a rule would inevitably lead to a multiplicity of suits involving the same question "Therefore, the courts very wisely and unswervingly adhere to the rule that an individual, in order to be entitled to a recovery for injuries sustained from a public nuisance must make out a clear case of special damages to himself, apart from the rest of the people, and of a different character, so that it cannot be fairly said to be a part of common injury resulting therefrom. It is not enough that he sustained more damage than another, it must be of a different character, special and apart from that which the public in general sustain, and not such as is common to every person who exercises the right that is injured" Snyder *v* Viola Mining and Smelting Co., 2 Idaho, 771; 26 Pac. Rep 124 See Lansing *v* Smith, 14 Wend. 10; Commonwealth *v.* Webb, 6 Rand. 729

That a public nuisance is indictable and may be abated after a verdict of guilty upon the indictment, is a proposition which is undoubted and has been sustained by numerous authorities. See Respublica *v.* Nowell, 3 Yeates, 417, 2 Am. Dec. 381; State *v.* King, 3 Ired. 411, Simpson *v* State, 10 Yerg 525; Boyer *v.* State, 16 Ind. 451; Palatka etc R Co. *v.* State, 23 Fla. 546; Marine Ins. Co *v.* St. L. I M. & S Ry Co., 41 Fed. Rep. 650; Flynn *v* Taylor, 53 Hun, 167; 6 N. Y. S. Rep. 96; Cohen *v* Mayer etc of New York, 113 N. Y. 535; Allen *v.* Lyon, 2 Root, 213; Dimmett *v.* Esridge, 6 Munf. 308, Columbus *v.* Jaques, 30 Ga. 506, Gerrish *v.* Brown, 51 Me. 256; Morton *v* Moore, 15 Gray, 573; Barnum *v.* Minnesota Transfer Ry. Co , 30 Minn. 365.

In order to sustain an indictment for nuisance it is enough to show that the exercise of a common right of the Queen's subjects has been sensibly interfered with. It is no answer to say that the state of things causing the obstruction is in some other way a public convenience. Thus it is an indictable nuisance at common law to lay down a tramway in a public street to the obstruction of the ordinary traffic, although the people who use the cars and save money and time by them may be greater in number than those who are obstructed in their use of the highway in the manner formerly accustomed (c).

It is also not material whether the obstruction interferes with the actual exercise of the right as it is for the time being exercised. The public are entitled, for example, to have the whole width of a public road kept free for passing and repassing, and an obstruction is not the less a nuisance because it is on a part of the highway not commonly used, or otherwise leaves room enough for the ordinary amount of traffic (d).

Further discussion and illustration of what amounts to an indictable nuisance must be sought in works on the criminal law.

Special damage must be shown. A private action can be maintained in respect of a public nuisance by a person who suffers thereby some particular loss or damage be-

---

(c) *R.* v. *Train* (1862), 2 B & S 640, 31 L. J M C 169 The tramways now in operation in many cities and towns have been made under statutory authority.

(d) *Turner* v *Ringwood Highway Board* (1870), 9 Eq 418. Compare the similar doctrine as to obstruction of lights, *infra*.

Special damages must be shown. As said in the text and in the last preceding note, a private action against a public nuisance can only be maintained by one who suffers some particular injury different in kind from that suffered by the public. See Cranford *v* Terrell, 128 N. Y. 343, 28 N. E. Rep. 514; Sparhawk *v* Union, etc R Co., 54 Pa. St. 401, School District *v*. Neil, 86 Kan. 617; 14 Pac. Rep. 253, Little Rock, etc R. Co. *v.* Brooks, 39 Ark 403, Kingsbury *v.* Flowers, 65 Ala 479; 39 Am Rep. 14; Nottingham *v* Baltimore & Potomac R. Co., 3 McArthur, 517; Payne *v.*

yond what is suffered by him in common with all other persons affected by the nuisance. Interference with a common right is not of itself a cause of action for the individual citizen. Particular damage (c) consequent on the interference is. If a man digs a trench across a highway, I cannot sue him simply because the trench prevents me from passing along the highway as I am entitled to do; for that is an inconvenience inflicted equally on all men who use the road. But if, while I am lawfully passing along after dark, I fall into this trench so that I break a limb, or goods which I am carrying are spoiled, I shall have my action; for this is a particular damage to myself resulting from the common nuisance, and distinct from the mere obstruction of the common right of passage which constitutes that nuisance (*f*). If a trader is conveying his goods in barges along a navigable river, and by reason of the navigation being unlawfully obstructed has to unload his merchandise and carry it overland at an increased expense, this is a particular damage which gives him a right of action (*g*). Though it is a sort of consequence likely to ensue in many individual cases, yet in every case it is a distinct and specific one.

(*c*) "Particular damage" and "special damage" are used indifferently in the authorities, the former seems preferable, for "special damage," as we have seen, has another technical meaning in the law of defamation

(*f*) Y. B 27 Hen VIII 27, pl 10 Action for stopping a highway, whereby it seems the plaintiff was deprived of the use of his own private way abutting thereon (the statement is rather obscure) per Fitzherbert, a man shall have his action for a public nuisance if he is more incommoded than others "If one make a ditch across the high road, and I come riding along the road at night, and I and my horse are thrown in the ditch so that I have thereby great damage and annoyance, I shall have my action against him who made this ditch, because I am more damaged than any other man" Held that sufficient particular damage was laid

(*g*) *Rose* v *Miles* (1815), 4 M & S. 101, and in Bigelow L. C 460

McKinley, 54 Cal 532; Parrott *v* Floyd, Id. 534, Coburn *v.* Ames, 52 Id. 385; Gordon *v* Baxter, 74 N. C. 470; Dudley *v.* Kennedy, 63 Me. 465; Blanc *v* Klumpke, 29 Cal. 159; Hartshorn *v.* Inhabitants of South Reading, 3 Allen, 501; Ofstie *v.* Kelly, 33 Minn. 440; De Laney *v* Blizzard, 7 Hun, 7

Where this test fails, there can be no particular damage in a legal sense. If the same man is at divers times delayed by the same obstruction, and incurs expense in removing it, this is not of itself sufficient particular damage; the damage, though real, is "common to all who might wish, by removing the obstruction, to raise the question of the right of the public to use the way" (*h*). The diversion of traffic or custom from a man's door by an obstruction of a highway, whereby his business is interrupted and his profits diminished, seems to be too remote a damage to give him a right of private action (*i*), unless indeed the obstruction is such as materially to impede the immediate access to the plaintiff's place of business more than other men's, and amounts to something like blocking up his doorway (*k*). Whether a given case falls under the rule or the exception must depend on the facts of that case: and what is the true principle, and what the extent of the exception, is open to some question (*l*). If horses and waggons are kept standing for an unreasonable time in the highway opposite a man's house, so that the access of customers is obstructed, the house is darkened, and the

---

(*h*) *Winterbottom* v *Lord Derby* (1867), L R 2 Ex 316, 322, 36 L J Ex 194

(*i*) *Ricket* v *Metrop R Co* (1867), L R 2 H L at pp 188, 199. See the comments of Willes J in *Beckett* v *Midland R Co*, L R 3 C P at p 100, where *Wilkes* v. *Hungerford Market Co* (1835), 2 Bing N. C 281, is treated as overruled by the remarks of Lord Chelmsford and Lord Cranworth Probably this would not be accepted in other jurisdictions where the common law is received. In Massachusetts, at least, *Wilkes* v. *Hungerford Market Co* was adopted by the Supreme Court in a very full and careful judgment *Stetson* v *Faxon* (1837), 19 Pick 147

(*k*) *Fritz* v *Hobson* (1880), 14 Ch. D. 542, 49 L J. Ch. 321

(*l*) In *Fritz* v *Hobson* (last note) Fry J. did not lay down any general proposition How far the principle of *Lyon* v *Fishmongers' Company* (1876), 1 App Ca. 662, 46 L J Ch 68, is really consistent with *Ricket* v *Metrop R Co* is a problem that can be finally solved only by the House of Lords itself According to *Lyon* v. *Fishmongers' Company* it should seem that blocking the access to a street is (if not justified) a violation of the distinct private right of every occupier in the street and such rights are not the less private and distinct because they may be many, see *Harrop* v *Hirst* (1868), L R 4 Ex 43, 38 L J Ex 1 In this view it is difficult to see that loss of custom is otherwise than a natural and probable consequence of the wrong And cp the case in 27 Hen VIII cited above, p 354 In *Ricket's ca.* Lord Westbury strongly dissented from the majority of the Lords present, L. R. 2 H L. at p 200

people in it are annoyed by bad smells, this damage is sufficiently "particular, direct, and substantial" to entitle the occupier to maintain an action (*m*).

Private nuisance, what. The conception of private nuisance was formerly limited to injuries done to a man's freehold by a neighbour's acts, of which stopping or narrowing rights of way and flooding land by the diversion of watercourses appear to have been the chief species (*n*). In the modern authorities it includes all injuries to an owner or occupier in the enjoyment of the property of

---

(*m*) *Benjamin* v *Storr* (1874), L R. 9 C P 400, 43 L J C. P 162. Compare further, as to damage from unreasonable user of a highway, *Harris* v *Mobbs* (1878), 3 Ex. D 268, *Wilkins* v. *Day* (1883), 12 Q B. D 1 0

(*n*) F N. B "Writ of Assize of Nuisance," 183 I *sqq*.

Private nuisance. If a person make an unreasonable, unwarrantable or unlawful use of his property, "so as to produce material annoyance, inconvenience, discomfort or hurt to his neighbor, he will be guilty of a nuisance to his neighbor And the law will hold him responsible for the consequent damages As to what is an unreasonable use of one's property cannot be defined by any certain general rules, but must depend upon the circumstances of each case The use of property in one locality and under some circumstances may be lawful and reasonable, which, under other circumstances, would be unlawful, unreasonable and a nuisance To constitute a nuisance, the use must be such as to produce a tangible and appreciable injury to neighboring property, or such as to render its enjoyment specially uncomfortable or inconvenient." Campbell *v.* Seaman, 63 N. Y 577, 26 Am Rep 562.

Accordingly in the case Cranford *v* Terrill (128 N Y. 344; 28 N. E Rep. 514) it was said by the court "If the use of the property is one which renders a neighbor's occupation and enjoyment physically uncomfortable, or which may be hurtful to the health, as where trades are conducted which are offensive by reason of odors, noises, or other injuries or annoying features, the private nuisance is deemed to be established. against which the protection of a court of equity power may be invoked." Cranford *v* Terrill, 128 N. Y. 344, 28 N. E. Rep. 514. See Chivery *v* Streeper, 24 Fla. 103; Porterfield *v* Bond, 38 Fed Rep. 391, Bohan *v* P. J G. L. Co , 45 Hun, 257; Freudenstein *v* Heine, 6 Mo. App. 287, Guille *v.* Swan, 19 Johns 381; Vandenburgh *v* Truax, 4 Denio, 464; 47 Am. Dec 268, Olmsted *v* Rich, 6 N Y. S Rep. 826; Bonnell *v.* Smith, 53 Ia. 281; Powell *v* Bentley & Gerwig Furniture Co , 34 W. Va 804, 12 S. E. Rep. 1086.

which he is in possession, without regard to the quality of the tenure (o). Blackstone's phrase is "anything done to the hurt or annoyance of the land, tenements or hereditaments of another" (p) — that is, so done without any lawful ground of justification or excuse. The ways in which this may happen are indefinite in number, but fall for practical purposes into certain well recognized classes.

Kinds of nuisance affecting — 1. Ownership Some acts are nuisances, according to the old authorities and the course of procedure on which they were founded, which

---

(o) See per Jessel M R. in *Jones v Chappell* (1875), 20 Eq at p 543

(p) Comm III 216

Ownership. Trees or overhanging branches, in so far as they are on or over the adjoining land, belong to the owner of such land and may be cut or trimmed by him at his pleasure. The fact that the owner of the land on which the trees were planted used them and converted the overhanging branches to his own use has no effect in rendering them a nuisance. Grandona v. Lovdal, 78 Cal. 611, 26 Pac Rep. 366. See Tissot v. Great Southern Tel. etc. Co., 39 La. An 996; Countryman v. Lighthill, 24 Hun, 405

In Meyer v. Metzler (51 Cal 142) the court said "It is found as a fact that the projection of the defendant's west wall prevents the plaintiff from raising and repairing his own building, which improvement it is also found that he is desirous of making," and it was held, that this amounted to an obstruction of the free use of the plaintiff's property, and was therefore a nuisance See Commonwealth v. Blaisdell, 107 Mass. 234, Wilmarth v Woodcock, 58 Mich. 402, 66 Mich. 331; 33 N. W. Rep. 400, Miles v. Worcester, 154 Mass 511; 28 N. E Rep 676

So, with reference to water-courses "It is a principle of the common law, that the erection of anything in the upper part of a stream of water, which poisons, corrupts, or renders it offensive and unwholesome, is actionable" Howell v. McCoy, 3 Rawle, 268. See Gladfelter v Walker, 40 Md. 1, Merrifield v. Lombard, 13 Allen, 16, Woodyear v. Schaefer, 57 Md 1, Jackman v Arlington Mills, 137 Mass 277; Holsman v. Boiling Spring Bleaching Co., 14 N J Eq. 335; Richmond Mfg. Co. v. Atlantic Delaine Co , 10 R I. 106, Lockwood etc. Co. v. Lawrence, 77 Me 297, Snow v. Parsons, 28 Vt. 459; Silver Spring, etc Co. v Wanskuck Co., 13 R I. 611; Merrifield v Worcester, 110 Mass 216; 14 Am. Rep. 592, Penn Coal Co. v. Sanderson, 113 Pa St. 126, Hauck v Tide Water Pipe Line Co., 153 Pa St 366, 26 At Rep. 644, 32 W. H C 45

With regard to lateral support of land it may be said, that a person

involve such direct interference with the rights of a possessor as to be also trespasses, or hardly distinguishable from trespasses. "A man shall have an assize of nuisance for building a house higher than his house, and so near his, that the rain which falleth upon that house falleth upon the plaintiff's house" (*q*). And it is stated to be a nuisance if a tree growing on my land overhangs the public road or my neighbour's land (*r*). In this class of cases nuisance means nothing more than encroachment on the legal powers and control of the public or of one's neighbour. It is generally, though not necessarily (*s*), a continuing trespass, for which however, in the days when forms of action were strict and a mistake in seeking the proper remedy was fatal, there was a greater variety and choice of remedies than for ordinary trespasses. Therefore it is in such a case needless to inquire, except for the assessment of damages, whether there is anything like nuisance in the popular sense. Still there is a real distinction between trespass and nuisance even when they are combined: the cause of action in trespass is interference with the right of a possessor in itself, while in nuisance it is the incommodity which is proved in fact to be the consequence, or is presumed by the law to be the natural

(*q*) F. N. B. 184 D., *Penruddock's ca.*, 5 Co. Rep. 100 b, *Fay v. Prentice* (1845), 1 C. B. 829, 14 L. J. C. P. 298.
(*r*) Best J. in *Earl of Lonsdale v. Nelson* (1823), 2 B. & C. 302, 311.

(*s*) *Fay v. Prentice*, note (*q*), where the Court was astute to support the declaration after verdict.

may for a lawful purpose dig into his own soil so near to the land of another, as to unsettle the foundation of a building thereon, and be answerable *only* for the natural and necessary consequences of his act in its effect upon the adjoining soil, and not for the value of the house of his neighbor put upon or near the line. Cahil v. Eastman, 18 Minn. 339; 10 Am. Rep. 184, Radcliff v Mayor etc. of Brooklyn, 4 N. Y. 196; Foley v. Wyeth, 2 Allen, 131, Patton v. Holland, 17 Johns. 92, La Sala v. Holbrook, 4 Paige, 169, Farrand v. Marshall, 21 Barb 409, Quincy v Jones, 76 Ill 231, Thurston v. Vermont Cent R Co., 25 Vt. 465; Tunstall v Christian, 80 Va 1; McMillan v Watt, 27 Ohio St 306.

and necessary consequence, of such interference: thus an overhanging roof or cornice is a nuisance to the land it overhangs because of the necessary tendency to discharge rain-water upon it (*t*).

2. Iura in re aliena. Another kind of nuisance consists in obstructions of rights of way and other rights over the property of others. "The parishioners may pull down a wall which is set up to their nuisance in their way to the church" (*u*). In modern times the most frequent and important examples of this class are cases of interference with rights to light. Here the right itself is a right not of dominion, but of use; and therefore no wrong is done (*v*) unless and until there is a sensible interference with its enjoyment, as we shall see hereafter. But it need not be proved that the interference causes any immediate harm or loss. It is enough that a legal right of use and enjoyment is interfered with by conduct which, if persisted in without protest, would furnish evidence in derogation of the right itself (*w*).

3. Convenience and enjoyment. A third kind, and that which is most commonly spoken of by the technical name, is the continuous doing of something which interferes

---

(*t*) *Baten's ca.*, 9 Co. Rep. 53 *b*
(*u*) F. N. B. 185 B.
(*v*) Otherwise as to public ways, see

Turner v. *Ringwood Highway Board* (1870), 9 Eq. 418.
(*u*) *Harrop* v. *Hirst* (1868), L. R. 4 Ex. 43, 38 L. J. Ex. 1.

Iura in re aliena. "It is clear that, when any public way is unnecessarily obstructed, any individual who wants to use it in a lawful way may remove the obstruction." Arundel *v.* McCulloch, 10 Mass. 70. See Burnham *v.* Hotchkiss, 14 Conn. 310; Low *v.* Knowlton, 26 Me. 128, 45 Am. Dec. 100. See *post*, p. 513. With reference to interference with lights, see, *post*, pp. 508 *et seq.*

Convenience and enjoyment. Much that has been already said indicates that the *continuity* of the cause of complaint is necessary before it can be adjudged a nuisance, and this is true. No single act or occurrence however violent or offensive, unhealthful or injurious in its consequences

with another's health or comfort in the occupation of his property, such as carrying on a noisy or offensive trade.

---

can constitute a nuisance, for it is essential that there be continuous repetition of the alleged wrong. Omaha etc R. Co. v. Standen, 22 Neb. 343, 35 N. W. Rep. 183; Turner v. Holtzman, 54 Md. 148, 39 Am Rep. 361, Baldwin v. Oskaloosa Gas Light Co , 57 Ia. 51, Brown v. Carolina Central Ry. Co , 83 N C. 128, Baugh v. State, 14 Ind. 29; Wroe v. State, 8 Md 416, State v Hull, 21 Me 84. While it is not essential that the injury should be strictly continuous, it must not be only occasional or accidental Rouse v. Martin, 75 Ala. 570, English v. Progress etc. Co., 95 Ala. 259, 10 So Rep 135. Thus trifling or occasional noises incident to the ordinary use of property, or in pursuance of a trade or calling do not, ordinarily, constitute a nuisance, though those in the neighborhood are disturbed. Rogers v. Elliott, 116 Mass 849. But where noises are continuous and disturb the neighborhood they have frequently been declared to be a nuisance, as in Davis v. Sawyer (133 Mass. 289, 43 Am. Rep. 519), the ringing of a heavy factory bell early in the morning was adjudged a nuisance And in McKeon v. Lee (51 N Y 300, 10 Am. Rep. 659), sawing of marble, accompanied by a jar which shook the plaintiff's building, was held to be a nuisance which should be enjoined. In a number of other cases noises of diverse kinds have been held to constitute nuisances See State v. Powell, 70 N. C. 67; Commonwealth v. Oakes, 113 Mass. 8; Commonwealth v Harris, 101 Id. 29, Parker v Union Woolen Works, 42 Conn. 399; Night v Goodyear, etc. Mfg Co , 38 Id. 438, 9 Am Rep 406, Brill v Flager, 23 Wend 354; Tanner v Village of Albion, 5 Hill, 123, Wallace v. Auer, 10 Phila. Rep. 356, Bishop v Banks, 33 Conn. 121; 87 Am. Dec 197, Dargan v. Waddill, 9 Ired. 244 , 49 Am. Dec. 421. See *noises, post*, p 504.

"No principle is better settled than that where a trade or business is carried on in such a manner as to interfere with a reasonable and comfortable enjoyment by another of his property, or which occasions material injury to the property itself, a wrong is done to the neighboring owner, for which an action will lie. And this, too, is without regard to the locality where such business is carried on; and this too, although the business may be a lawful business and one useful to the public, and although the best and most approved appliances and methods may be used in the conduct and management of the business." Susquehanna Fertilizer Co. v. Malone, 73 Md. 276. "If one carried on a lawful trade or business in such a manner as to prove a nuisance to his neighbor he must answer in damages, and it is not necessary to a right of action that the owner should be driven from his dwelling, it is enough that the enjoyment of life and property be rendered uncomfortable." Bohan v. P J G L. Co , 122 N Y. 23; 25 N. E Rep. 246, Ballentine v. Webb, 84 Mich 38, 47 N W Rep 485; Gilbert v Showerman, 23 Mich 448; Cleveland v Gas Light Co., 20 N J Eq 205.

Continuity is a material factor: merely temporary inconvenience caused to a neighbour by "the execution of lawful works in the ordinary user of land" is not a nuisance (*x*).

Measure of nuisance. What amount of annoyance or inconvenience will amount to a nuisance in point of law cannot, by the nature of the question, be defined in precise terms (*y*). Attempts have been made to set more or less arbitrary limits to the jurisdiction of the Court, especially in cases of miscellaneous nuisance, as we may call them, but they have failed in every direction.

Injury to health need not be shown (*a*) It is not necessary to constitute a private nuisance that the acts or state of things complained of should be noxious in the sense of being injurious to health. It is enough that there is a material interference with the ordinary comfort and convenience of life—"the physical comfort of human existence"—by an ordinary and reasonable standard (*z*),

(*x*) *Harrison* v *Southwark & Vauxhall Water Co*, '91, 2 Ch 409, 60 L J Ch 630
(*y*) As to the construction of "nuisance" in a covenant, which it seems need not be confined to tortious nuisance, see *Tod Heatly* v *Benham* (1888), 40 Ch Div 80, 58 L J Ch 83
(*z*) *Walter* v *Selfe*, 4 De G & Sm 315 321, 322, 20 L J Ch 433 (Knight Bruce V-C 1851), *Crump* v *Lambert* (1867), 3 Eq 409

Injury to health need not be shown Agreeing with the text, *vide* Croker v Birge, 9 Ga. 428, Cleveland *v*. Gaslight Co., 20 N J. Eq. 205, *supra*.

In Hazard Powder Co *v* Volger, 58 Fed Rep. 156, Justice Caldwell, delivering the opinion, said "The maintenance by the defendant of a powder magazine containing a large quantity of powder, within the city limits, in violation of the city ordinance, was a nuisance which rendered the defendant liable for the injury resulting to the plaintiff from its explosion It is no defense to such an action that the magazine was properly constructed and the powder carefully stored therein, and that the explosion was due to no personal negligence of the defendant or its agents. It is liable for the injuries resulting from its explosion from any cause, because its location under the ordinance made it a nuisance. Powder Co *v* Tearney, 131 Ill. 322, 23 N. E Rep. 389; Cheatham *v* Shearon, 1 Swan, 213, 1 Dill Mun Corp, sec 374, note, p 449"

there must be something more than mere loss of amenity (a), but there need not be positive hurt or disease.

Plaintiff not disentitled by having come to the nuisance. (b) In ascertaining whether the property of the plaintiff is in fact injured, or his comfort or convenience in

---

(a) *Salvin v. North Brancepath Coal Co* (1874), 9 Ch. 705, 44 L. J. Ch 149, see judgment of James L. J at pp. 709, 710

Plaintiff not disentitled by having come to the nuisance. It is a general rule that the fact that the plaintiff "came to a nuisance," constitutes no defense to this action. Hazard Powder Co. v Volger, 58 Fed. Rep 152, *citing* Marine Ins. Co. *v.* St Louis, I. M. & S. R. Co., 41 Fed. Rep 643, 652, 653; Railroad Co. *v* English, 98 Ga. 366.

With the contrary rule the material development of the country would often be hindered and public improvements sometimes prohibited In the building of cities the extension of residence additions frequently necessitates the removal of offensive trades and industries into less populous districts But in the adjustment of the equities between the parties in such cases regard should be had for all the circumstances, including the kind and degree of the annoyance, the time established, the difficulty of removal, and the value of the property or business complained of It was said by Justice Sharswood in Weir's Appeal (74 Pa St 230) "There is a very marked distinction to be observed in reason and equity between the cases of a business long established in a particular locality, which has become a nuisance from the growth of population and the erection of dwellings in proximity to it and that of a new erection threatened in such vicinity. Carrying on an offensive trade for any number of years, in a place remote from buildings and public roads, does not entitle the owner to continue it in the same place after the houses have been built and roads laid out in the neighborhood, to the occupants of which and the travellers upon which, it is a nuisance As the city extends, such nuisances should be removed to the vacant grounds beyond the immediate neighborhood of the residences of the citizens * * * It certainly ought to be a much clearer case, however, to justify a court of equity in stretching forth the strong arm of injunctions to compel a man to remove an establishment in which he has invested his capital and been carrying on a business for a long period of time, than in the case of one who comes into a neighborhood proposing to establish such a business for the first time, and who is met at the threshold of his enterprise by a remonstrance and notice that if he persists in his purpose application will be made to the court of equity to prevent him " We may supplement these well considered remarks by saying that they apply with especial force to a case where the property

fact materially interfered with, by an alleged nuisance, regard is had to the character of the neighbourhood and the pre-existing circumstances (b). But the fact that the plaintiff was already exposed to some inconvenience of the same kind will not of itself deprive him of his remedy. Even if there was already a nuisance, that is not a reason why the defendant should set up an additional nuisance (c). The fact that other persons are wrong-doers in the like sort is no excuse for a wrong-doer. If it is said "This is but one nuisance among many," the answer is that, if the others were away, this one remaining would clearly be a wrong, but a man cannot be made a wrong-doer by the lawful acts of third persons, and if it is not a wrong now, a prescriptive right to continue it in all events might be acquired under cover of the other nuisances; therefore it must be wrongful from the first (d). Neither does it make any difference that the very nuisance complained of existed before the plaintiff became owner or occupier. It was at one time held that if a man came to the nuisance, as was said, he had no remedy (e); but this has long ceased to be law as regards both the remedy by damages (f) and the remedy by injunction (g). The defendant may in some cases justify by prescription, or the plaintiff be barred of

---

(b) *St Helen's Smelting Co v Tipping* (1865), 11 H L C 642, 35 L J Q B 66, *Sturges* v *Bridgman* (1879), 11 Ch Div. at p 865

(c) *Walter* v *Selfe*, note (z)

(d) *Crossley* v *Lightowler* (1867), 2 Ch. 478, 36 L J Ch 584 The same point was (among others) decided many years earlier (1849), in *Wood* v *Waud*, 3 Ex 748, 18 L J Ex 305

(e) Blackstone ii 403

(f) E g *St Helen's Smelting Co* v *Tipping* (1865), 11 H. L C 642, 35 L J. Q B. 66

(g) *Tipping* v *St Helen's Smelting Co*. (1865), 1 Ch 66, a suit for injunction on the same facts, *Fleming* v *Hislop* (1886), 11 App Ca (Sc) 686, 688, 697

---

alleged to be a nuisance cannot be removed, and a decree to abate it means its destruction, in such cases a court of equity should move slowly and decline to act upon conflicting evidence. Appeal of McClain (Pa), 18 At. Rep 1066 See People v. White Lead Works, 82 Mich. 477; 46 N W Rep. 735, Commonwealth v Upton, 6 Gray, 472; Susquehanna Fertilizing Co v Malone, 73 Md 281, 20 At Rep 900.

the most effectual remedies by acquiescence. But these are distinct and special grounds of defence, and if relied on must be fully made out by appropriate proof

Further, the wrong and the right of action begin only when the nuisance begins. Therefore if Peter has for many years carried on a noisy business on his own land, and his neighbour John makes a new building on his own adjoining land, in the occupation whereof he finds the noise, vibration, or the like, caused by Peter's business to be a nuisance, Peter cannot justify continuing his operations as against John by showing that before John's building was occupied, John or his predecessors in title made no complaint (*h*).

Innocent or necessary character per se of offensive occupation is no answer. (c) Again a nuisance is not justified by showing that the trade or occupation causing

(*h*) Sturges v. Bridgman (1879), 11 Ch. Div. 852, 18 L. J. Ch. 875.

Innocent or necessary character per se of offensive occupation is no answer. It has been concisely said: "The best intentions cannot prevent an act from being a nuisance where it otherwise is such, and the worst intentions cannot make an act a nuisance where it otherwise is not. The intention might, to be sure, be a proper subject of inquiry upon the question of exemplary damages." Bonnell v. Smith, 53 Ia. 282. While it is a general rule that the court will not justify a positive nuisance for the reason that it is a public necessity yet public benefits and advantages are properly considered in determining such questions, and if the individual injury be trifling and the public benefit great that which is complained of will be usually not interfered with by law. Justice Harlan in delivering the opinion of the court in the case of New Orleans Gas Light Co. v. Louisiana Light Co. (115 U. S. 650–669), said: "The manufacture of gas and its distribution for public and private use by means of pipes laid, under legislative authority, in the streets and ways of the city, is not an ordinary business in which every one may engage, but is a franchise belonging to the government, to be granted for the accomplishment for public objects to whomsoever and upon what terms it pleases. It is a business of the public nature and makes a public necessity for which the State may make provision. It is one which so far from affecting the public injuriously as to become one of the most important agencies of civilization for the promoting of the public convenience and public

the annoyance is, apart from that annoyance, an innocent or laudable one. "The building of a lime-kiln is good and profitable; but if it be built so near a house that when it burns the smoke thereof enters into the house, so that none can dwell there, an action lies for it" (*i*). "A tan-house is necessary, for all men wear shoes; and nevertheless it may be pulled down if it be erected to the nuisance of another. In like manner of a glass-house, and they ought to be erected in places convenient for them" (*j*). So it is an actionable nuisance to keep a pigstye so near my neighbour's house as to make it unwholesome and unfit for habitation, though the keeping of swine may be needful for the sustenance of man (*k*). Learned and charitable foundations are commended in sundry places of our books; but the fact that a new building is being erected by a college for purposes of good education and the advancement of learning will not make it the less a wrong if the sawing of stone by the builders drives a neighbouring inhabitant out of his house.

(*i*) *Aldred's ca.*, 9 Co Rep. 59 *a*.
(*j*) *Jones* v *Powell*, Palm 539, approved and explained by Ex. Ch. in *Bamford* v *Turnley* (1862), 3 B. & S 66, 31 L J Q B 286. As to "convenient" see next paragraph.

(*k*) *Aldred's ca* note (*i*). Cp *Broder* v *Saillard* (1876), 2 Ch D 692, 701 (Jessel M R), 45 L J Ch 414, followed and perhaps extended in *Reinhardt* v *Mentasti* (1889), 42 Ch D 685, 58 L. J. Ch 787

---

safety." It is stated, further, in this case, that such a business should, however, be carried on in such a manner as to not unnecessarily affect and injure others Improper places for the establishment of a business may be selected or the business may be conducted without the proper skill, and in either case it becomes a nuisance. See City of Fresno *v.* Fresno etc Co (Cal), 32 Pac Rep. 943

In the case of Pilcher *v* Hart (1 Humphries, 524) where a wharfboat had been erected in a navigable stream it was held, that if the navigation be not impeded by the erection, or if the public advantage greatly overbalances the inconvenience produced it would not be a nuisance. See Radcliff *v.* Mayor etc. Brooklyn, 4 N. Y. 195, Works *v.* Junction R. Co. 5 McLean, 425; Carroll *v.* Wisconsin Cent. R. Co., 40 Minn 168; 41 N. W. Rep. 661.

Convenience of place per se no answer. (d) Where the nuisance complained of consists wholly or chiefly in damage to property, such damage must be proved as is of appreciable magnitude and apparent to persons of common intelligence, not merely something discoverable only by scientific tests (l). And acts in themselves lawful and innoxious do not become a nuisance merely because they make a neighbouring house or room less fit for carrying on some particular industry, without interfering with the

---

(l) Salvin v. North Brancepeth Coal Co (1874), 9 Ch 705, 44 L J Ch 149

Convenience of place per se is no answer. In accord with the text, in the case of the Susquehanna Fertilizer Co v Malone (73 Md 280, 20 At. Rep 900), the court said "We cannot agree with the appellant that the court ought to have directed the jury to find whether the place where the factory was located was a *convenient and proper place* for the carrying on of the appellant's business, and whether such a use of his property was a reasonable use, and if they should so find the verdict must be for the defendant It may be convenient to the defendant, and it may be convenient to the public, but, in the eye of the law, no place can be convenient for the carrying on of a business which is a nuisance, and which causes substantial injury to the property of another Nor can any use of one's own land be said to be a reasonable use, which deprives an adjoining owner of the lawful use and enjoyment of his property. * * * So we take the law to be well settled that, in actions of this kind, the question whether the place where the trade or business is carried on, is a proper and convenient place for the purpose, or whether the use by the defendant of his own land is, under circumstances, a reasonable use, are questions which ought now to be submitted to the finding of the jury We fully agree that, in actions of this kind, the law does not regard trifling inconveniences, that everything must be looked at from a reasonable point of view, that in determining the question of nuisance in such cases, the locality and all the surrounding circumstances should be taken into consideration, and that where expensive works have been erected and carried on, which are useful and needful to the public, persons cannot stand on extreme rights, and bring actions in respect to every trifling annoyance, otherwise, business should not be carried on in such places But still if the result of the trade or business thus carried on is such as to interfere with the physical comfort, by another, of his property or such as to occasion substantial injury to the property itself, there is wrong to the neighboring owner for which an action will lie"

ordinary enjoyment of life (m). But where material damage in this sense is proved, or material discomfort according to a sober and reasonable standard of comfort, it is no answer to say that the offending work or manufacture is carried on at a place in itself proper and convenient for the purpose. A right to do something that otherwise would be a nuisance may be established by prescription, but nothing less will serve. Or in other words a place is not in the sense of the law convenient for me to burn bricks in, or smelt copper, or carry on chemical works, if that use of the place is convenient to myself but creates a nuisance to my neighbour (n)

Modes of annoyance. (o) No particular combination of sources of annoyance is necessary to constitute a nuisance, nor are the possible sources of annoyance exhaustively

---

(m) *Robinson v Kilvert* (1889), 41 Ch Div 88, 58 L J Ch 392 The ordinary enjoyment of life, however, seems to include the maintenance of a due temperature in one's wine cellar *Reinhardt v Mentasti*, note (k) above

(n) *St Helen's Smelting Co v Tipping* (1865), 11 H L C 642, 35 L J Q B 66,

Bigelow L C 454, *Bamford v Turnley* (1862), Ex Ch 3 B & S 66, 31 L J Q B 286, *Carey v Ledbitter* (1862-3), 13 C B N S 470, 32 L J C P 104. These authorities overrule *Hole v Barlow* (1858), 4 C B N S 334, 27 L J C P 207, see *Shotts Iron Co. v Inglis* (1882), 7 App Ca Sc at p 528

Modes annoyance The decided cases show the character and extent of wrongs constituting nuisances, and illustrate the application of the very general rules that have been formulated in law for determining what are and what are not nuisances It may be said here that it is always essential that the injury be substantial and apparent, and that it be the natural consequential result of that which is charged to create the nuisance Norcross v. Thoms, 51 Me 504. For the reason that nearly every material thing may, by its unlawful nature or unlawful use or condition, become a nuisance, the cases deciding the various questions are so numerous that it is found to be impracticable to even digest them here and the following statement of classified citations to them has been arranged.

Blasting. Blasting rock, to the danger of the neighborhood, is ordinarily a nuisance. Rogers v. Hanfield, 14 Daly, 339, Hunter v. Farren, 127 Mass. 481, 34 Am Dec 423, Hay v Cohoes Co , 2 N. Y 159, 51 Am. Dec. 179; Tremain v Cohoes Co., 2 N Y. 163, 51 Am. Dec. 284, Scott v. Bay, 3 Md 431.

Cemetery A cemetery or tomb may by reason of its location or con-

defined by any rule of law. "Smoke, unaccompanied with noise or noxious vapour, noise alone, offensive vapours alone,

---

dition become a nuisance. Barnes v Hathorn, 54 Me 124, Kingbury v Flowers, 65 Ala 479; 39 Am. Rep 14; Begein v Anderson, 28 Ind. 79, Monk v Packard, 71 Me. 309, 36 Am Rep 315; Dunn v. Austin (Tex.), 11 S W. Rep. 1125, Musgrove v. St Louis Church, 10 La. An. 118; Jung v Neraz, 71 Tex 396.

Diseased beasts. The owner of domestic animals, having an infectious or contagious disease, who sells them to one who is not informed of their condition or allows them to run at large, may thus create a nuisance and become responsible therefor. Jeffrey v Bigelow, 13 Wend 518, Fisher v Clark, 41 Barb 329, Kemmish v Ball, 30 Fed Rep 759, Hawks v Locke, 139 Mass 205

Explosive and inflammable substances. Explosive and inflammable substances, when so kept as to specially endanger lives or property of people living in the neighborhood, are a nuisance. Cuff v. Newark, etc R Co, 3 N J L. 17, 10 Am Rep 205; McAndrews v. Collerd, 42 Id. 189, 36 Am Rep 508, Cook v Anderson, 85 Ala 99, Boston, etc R Co. v Carney, 107 Mass. 568, Cutter v Towne, 98 Mass 567, Meyers v. Malcolm, 6 Hill, 292, 41 Am Dec 744, People v Sands, 1 Johns 78; 3 Am Dec 296; Heeg v Licht, 80 N Y. 579, 36 Am Rep. 654, Comminge v Stevenson, 76 Tex. 642, Cheatham v Shearon, 1 Swan, 213, Laflin-Rand Powder Co v Tearney, 131 Ill. 322, 23 N E Rep 389, Conklin v. Thompson, 29 Barb 218, Cole v Fisher, 11 Mass 137; Hazard Powder Co v Volger, 58 Fed. Rep. 152, 158

Fire-arms. The continuous use of fire-arms to the danger of persons in the vicinity is a nuisance. Conradt v. Clauve, 93 Ind. 476, Jenne v. Sutton, 43 N J. L. 257, Welch v Durand, 36 Conn 182, Bullock v. Babcock, 3 Wend 391, Chataigne v. Bergeron, 10 La An. 699, Sutton v. Bonnett, 114 Ind 243, 16 N. E Rep 180

Fires. Inasmuch as fire is a dangerous element care in using it is required of every one, otherwise it may become a nuisance. Scott v. Hale, 16 Me 326, Sweeney v. Merrill, 38 Kan. 218, 16 Pac. Rep. 454, Hewey v Nourse, 54 Me. 256, Barnard v Poor, 21 Pick 378, Bachelder v Heagan, 18 Me 30, Fahn v Reichart, 8 Wis 225, Mich. Cent. R Co v Anderson, 20 Mich 244, Tourtellot v Rosebrook, 11 Metc. 462, Miller v Martin, 16 Mo. 508, Averitt v Murrell, 4 Jones L 322; Gagg v Vetter, 41 Ind. 228, Teall v Barton, 40 Barb. 137; Calkins v Barger, 44 Id 424, Catron v Nichols, 81 Mo 80, Higgins v Dewey, 107 Mass 494; 9 Am Rep 63, Garrett v. Freeman, 5 Jones L. 78, Jacobs v. Andrew, 4 Ia 506, Johnston v. Barber, 10 Ill. 125, Armstrong v. Cooley, Id. 509, Wilson v. Peverly, 2 N H 548; Ayer v. Starkey, 30 Conn 304; Finley v Langston, 12 Mo 120, Burton v McClellan, 3 Ill. 434; Cook v Johnston, 58 Mich 437

Fires communicated by machinery. Those using machinery, which is

although not injurious to health, may severally constitute a nuisance to the owner of adjoining or neighbouring

likely to cause or scatter fire are required by law to use the best approved appliances for the prevention of danger, and to exercise due care in the operation of the machinery. Teal v Barton, 40 Barb. 137; Sheldon v. Hud. Riv. R. Co , 29 Id 226, Jefferis v. Phila etc. R Co., 3 Houst. 117, Huyett v Phila. etc R Co , 23 Pa St 373, McCready v. So. Car. R Co , 2 Strobh 356, Hull v Sac Val R. Co , 14 Cal 387; Mobile, etc R Co v. Gray, 62 Miss 383, Hoff v West Jersey R. Co , 45 N. J. L 201; Ill. Cent. R. Co v. McCleland, 42 Ill 355; Frankford, etc. Co. v Phila. etc. R Co , 54 Pa. St. 345, Anderson v Cape Fear Steamboat Co., 64 N. C. 399, Chicago, etc. R Co. v McCahill, 54 Ill. 28, Toledo etc. R. Co. v Corn, 71 Ill. 493, Penn. R. Co. v. Hope, 80 Pa. St. 373, Lehigh etc. R Co v. McKeen, 90 Id 122, Brushberg v. Milw etc Ry Co , 55 Wis 106; Erd v. Chicago, etc R Co , 30 Id. 110; Ellis v. Portsmouth, etc. R. Co , 2 Ired 138, Ruffner v. Railroad Co , 34 Ohio St. 96, Chapman v Atlantic, etc R Co , 37 Me. 92; Pratt v Same, 42 Id. 579, Rowell v. Railroad Co , 57 N. H. 132, Simmonds v New York, etc R Co., 52 Conn. 264, Webb v. Rome, etc. R. Co , 49 N. Y. 420; Gibbons v. Wisconsin, etc. Ry. Co., 66 Wis. 161, Flynn v. San Francisco, etc Ry Co , 40 Cal 14.

Noises. Offensive noises may constitute a nuisance Ordinarily, trifling or occasional noises incident to the accustomed use of property, or pursuance of a trade, do not . The time, locality, and character of the noise are often important in determining the question of nuisance or no nuisance. See *ante*, p 495 See Brill v. Flager, 23 Wend 354, Bloomhuff v State, 8 Blackf 205, People v. Sergeant, 8 Cow. 139, Snyder v Cabel, 29 W. Va 48, 1 S E Rep. 241; Dargan v Waddill, 9 Ired 244; Hurlbut v McKone, 55 Conn 31, 10 A. Rep. 164, Davidson v Isham, 9 N J. Eq 186, Balt etc. R. Co. v. Fifth Bapt Church, 108 U S. 317, Green v Lake, 54 Miss 540, Rhodes v Dunbar, 57 Pa St 274, Duncan v. Hayes, 22 N. J. Eq. 25. Whitney v. Bartholomew, 21 Conn 213, Pach v Geoffroy, 67 Hun, 401, 22 N Y. S. Rep. 275

Offensive odors In determining whether or not certain odors and stenches constitute a nuisance, all the circumstances of the case must be considered Thus, the kind of business, trade or occupation producing the cause of complaint, its location and lawful or unlawful character are all elements to be considered The odors must be sensibly offensive or produce such actual physical discomfort as to interfere materially with comfort, but it is not necessary that they be positively hurtful or unwholesome Norcross v. Thoms, 51 Me. 503; Davidson v Isham, 9 N J. Eq 186, State v Board of Health, 16 Mo App. 8, Cleveland v. Citizens' Gas Light Co , 20 N. J Eq. 201; Wolcott v. Melick, 11 Id. 204; 66 Am Dec 790, Commonwealth v Brown, 13 Metc. 365, Kirkman v. Handy, 11 Humph 406, 54 Am Dec 45, Pickard v Collins, 23 Barb 444, Story v Hammond, 4 Ohio, 376, Peck v Elder, 3 Sandf. 126, Cropsey v. Murphy,

property" (o). The persistent ringing and tolling of large bells (p), the loud music, shouting, and other noises

(o) Romilly M. R. *Crump* v *Lambert* (1867), 3 Eq at p 412
(p) *Soltau* v *De Held* (1851), 2 Sim N S 133 The bells belonged to a Roman Catholic church, the judgment points out (at p 160) that such a building is not a church in the eye of the law, and can not claim the same privileges as a parish church in respect of bell ringing

---

1 Hilt 126; Shaw v Cummiskey, 7 Pick. 76; Miller v Tinehart, 4 Leigh, 569, Green v Savannah, 6 Ga 1, Beach v. People, 11 Mich 106, Neal v. Henry, Meigs, 17, Rhodes v. Whitehead, 27 Tex. 304; 84 Am. Dec. 631, Commonwealth v. Reed, 34 Pa. St. 275; 75 Am Dec. 661, Commonwealth v Brown, 13 Metc. 365; Warwick v. Wah Lee, 10 Phila Rep. 160; Ahle v. Reinbach, 76 Ill. 322, Jarvis v. St. Louis, etc. R. Co , 26 Mo. App 253; Ellis v Kansas City R. Co., 63 Mo. 131, 21 Am Rep. 436, Beckley v. Skrob, 19 Mo. App. 75, State v. Moore, 31 Conn. 479; 83 Am. Dec. 159; Francis v Schollkoff, 53 N. Y 152, Smith v McConathy, 11 Mo. 517, Stowe v Miles, 39 Conn. 426, Manhattan Mfg Co. v Van Keuren, 23 N J Eq. 251; Eames v New Eng. Worsted Co., 11 Metc. 570; City of Rochester v. Simpson, 134 N Y. 414, 31 N E. Rep 871.

The balance of the cases on this subject have been arranged in the following subdivisions —

Boiling establishment. Blunt v. Hay, 4 Sandf. Ch 362; Howard v Lee, 3 Id. 281, Smith v. Cummings, 2 Pars. Eq Cas. 92, State v Neidt (N. J.) 19 At. Rep. 318, Winslow v. Bloomington, 24 Ill. App 647, Peck v Elder, 3 Sandf. 126, Dana v. Valentine, 5 Met 8, Dubois v Budlong, 15 Abb. Pr. 445, Meigs. v. Lister, 23 N J. Eq. 320, 25 Id. 489, Czarnicki's Appeal (Pa), 11 At Rep 660.

Cesspools Ball v Nye, 99 Mass. 582, 97 Am Dec. 56, Wahle v. Reinbach, 76 Ill. 322, Marshall v. Cohen, 44 Ga. 489, 9 Am. Rep 170; Perrine v Taylor, 43 N J. Eq. 128; Haugh's Appeal, 102 Pa St. 42, 48 Am Rep. 193.

Gas works. Pottstown Gas Co. v Murphy, 39 Pa. St 257; Hunt v Lowell Gas Light Co , 8 Allen, 69, Wragg v Commercial Gas Co , 33 Gas. Jour 119, Cleveland v. Citizens Gas Light Co , 20 N. J. Eq. 201, Columbus Gas Light, etc Co. v Freeland, 12 Ohio St. 392, Pensacola Gas Co. v Pebley, 25 Fla. 381, Brown v. Illius, 27 Conn 84, 71 Am. Dec. 49, Ottawa Gas Light Co. v Thompson, 39 Ill 598, Same v. Graham, 28 Id. 73, 81 Am Dec. 263

Livery stables, cattle yards, etc. Rounsaville v Kohlheim, 68 Ga. 668; 45 Am Rep 505, Filson v. Crawford, 5 N. Y S Rep 882, Keiser v. Lovett, 85 Md. 240, 44 Am. Rep 10, St. James Church v. Arrington, 36 Ma 548, Hastings v Aiken, 1 Gray, 163, Flint v Russell, 5 Dill 151; ... Olinger, 50 Ia. 571, 33 Am. Rep 138, Kirkman v. Handy, 11 ... 406, 54 Am Dec. 45, Burditt v Swenson, 17 Tex 489, 67 Am. ... Aldrich v Howard, 8 R I 246, 86 Am Dec 615, Coker v.

attending the performances of a circus (q), the collection of a crowd of disorderly people by a noisy entertainment

(q) Inchbald v Barrington (1869) 4 Ch. 388 the circus was eighty five yards from the plaintiff's house, and "throughout the performance there was music, including a trombone and other wind instruments and a violoncello, and great noise, with shouting and cracking of whips"

Blige, 10 Ga 336, Dargan v Waddill, 9 Ired 244, 49 Am. Dec. 421, Norwood v. Dickey, 18 Ga. 537, Gifford v. Hulett, 62 Vt 342, 19 At. Rep. 230, Curtis v Winslow, 38 Vt 690, State v Payson, 37 Me 361, Baker v Bohannan, 69 Ia. 60, Trulock v. Merte, 72 Ia. 510, State v. Kaster, 35 Ia. 221, Sutterloh v Mayor, etc of Cedar Keys, 15 Fla 306, Ill Cent. R. Co v. Grabill, 50 Ill 241, Ohio, etc R Co v. Simon, 40 Md 278, Philips v. City of Denver (Colo), 34 Pac. Rep 902

Slaughter houses Commonwealth v. Upton, 6 Gray, 176, Fay v Whitman, 100 Mass. 76, Allen v State, 34 Tex. 230, Dennis v State, 91 Ind 73, Peck v Elder, 3 Sandf 126, Shively v. Cedar Rapids, etc Ry Co, (Iowa), 36 N W Rep 133, Dubois v Budlong, 15 Abb Pr. 445, Selfried v Hays, 81 Ky. 377, Babcock v New Jersey Stock Yard Co., 20 N. J. Eq 296, Somerville v O'Neil, 114 Mass 353, Watertown v Sawyer, 109 Id 320, State v Wilson, 43 N. H 415, 82 Am. Dec 463, State v Shelbyville, 4 Sneed (Tenn.), 176, Reichert v. Geers, 98 Md 73, 49 Am Rep 736, Phillips v. State, 7 Baxt 151, Smith v. McConathy, 11 Mo 517, Bishop v. Banks, 33 Conn 121, 87 Am Dec. 197, Pruner v. Pendleton, 75 Va. 516, 40 Am Rep 738, Minke v Hopeman, 87 Ill 450, State v. Wolf (N. C), 17 S E. Rep 528

Tanneries Thomas v Blackney, 17 Barb 654, State v Street Commissioners, 36 N J L 283, Francis v Schoellkopf, 53 N Y 152, Pennoyer v Allen, 56 Wis 502, Fisher v Clark, 41 Barb 332, Weil v. Ricord, 24 N J Eq 169, Kennedy v. Phelps, 10 La An 227.

Smoke, vapors, etc Where one pollutes the air on the premises of another with smoke, vapors and noxious gases, thus producing injury to property, health or comfort, the wrong has in many cases been held to constitute a nuisance. Catlin v Valentine, 9 Paige, 575, 38 Am Dec 567, Smith v McConathy, 11 Mo 517, Ross v Butler, 19 N J Eq 294, 97 Am. Dec. 654, Rhodes v. Dunbar, 57 Pa St 274, 98 Am Dec 221; Hyatt v Myers, 71 N. C 271, Hutchins v. Smith, 63 Barb. 252; Duncan v Hayes, 22 N J. Eq 26, Wesson v Washburn Iron Co, 13 Allen, 95, 90 Am. Dec 181, Daniels v. Keokuk Water Works, 61 Ia. 549, Richard's Appeal, 57 Pa St. 105, 98 Am Dec. 202; Thebaut v. Canova, 11 Fla. 143; Norcross v. Thoms, 51 Me. 503, 81 Am. Dec. 588, Hurlburt v McKone, 55 Conn. 31, Carhart v Auburn Gas Light Co., 22 Barb. 297, Adams v Michael, 38 Md. 123; 17 Am. Rep 515; Fuscher v Spalding, 2 La. An 778, Cogswell v. New York, etc R. Co., 103 N Y. 10, 59 Am Rep 751; Beir v. Cooke, 37 Hun, 38, Campbell v. Seaman, 63 N Y 368, 20 Am. Rep. 567, Sellers v. Parvis & Williams Co, 30 Fed Rep 164. Fogarty v Junction City etc. Co, 50 Kan 476, 31 Pac Rep 1052

of music and fireworks (r), to the grave annoyance of dwellers in the neighbourhood, have all been held to be nuisances and restrained by the authority of the Court. The use of a dwelling-house in a street of dwelling-houses, in an ordinary and accustomed manner, is not a nuisance though it may produce more or less noise and inconvenience to a neighbour. But the conversion of part of a house to an unusual purpose, or the simple maintenance of an arrangement which offends neighbours by noise or otherwise to an unusual and excessive extent, may be an actionable nuisance. Many houses have stables attached to them, but the man who turns the whole ground floor of a London house into a stable, or otherwise keeps a stable so near a neighbour's living rooms that the inhabitants are disturbed all night (even though he has done nothing beyond using the arrangements of the house as he found them), does so at his own risk (s).

"In making out a case of nuisance of this character, there are always two things to be considered, the right of the plaintiff, and the right of the defendant. If the houses adjoining each other are so built that from the commencement of their existence it is manifest that each adjoining inhabitant was intended to enjoy his own property for the ordinary purposes for which it and all the different parts of it were constructed, then so long as the house is so used there is nothing that can be regarded in law as a nuisance which the other party has a right to prevent. But, on the other hand, if either party turns his house, or any portion of it, to unusual purposes in such a manner as to produce a substantial injury to his neighbour, it appears to me that that is not according to principle or authority a reasonable use of his own property; and

---

(r) *Walker* v *Brewster* (1867), 5 Eq 24, 37 L J Ch 33 It was not decided whether the noise would alone have been a nuisance, but *Wickens* V C strongly inclined to think it would, see at p 34

(s) *Ball* v *Ray* (1873), 8 Ch 467 *Broder* v *Saillard* (1876), 2 Ch. D 692, 15 L J Ch 414

his neighbour, showing substantial injury, is entitled to protection" (*t*).

Injury common to the plaintiff with others (*f*) Where a distinct private right is infringed, though it be only a right enjoyed in common with other persons, it is immaterial that the plaintiff suffered no specific injury beyond those other persons, or no specific injury at all. Thus any one commoner can sue a stranger who lets his cattle depasture the common (*u*); and any one of a number of inhabitants entitled by local custom to a particular water supply can sue a neighbour who obstructs that supply (*v*). It should seem from the *ratio decidendi* of the House of Lords in *Lyon* v. *Fishmongers' Company* (*x*), that the rights of access to a highway or a navigable river incident to the occupation of tenements thereto adjacent are private rights within the meaning of this rule (*y*).

Injury caused by independent acts of different persons. (*g*) A cause of action for nuisance may be created by independent acts of different persons, though the acts of any one of those persons would not amount to a nuisance. "Suppose one person leaves a wheelbarrow standing on a way, that may cause no appreciable inconvenience, but if a hundred do so, that may cause a serious inconvenience, which a person entitled to the use of the way has a right to prevent; and it is no defence to any one person among the hundred to say that what he does causes of itself no damage to the complainant" (*z*).

Obstruction of lights. A species of nuisance which has become prominent in modern law, by reason of the increased

---

(*t*) Lord Selborne L C, 8 Ch at p 460
(*u*) Notes to *Mellor* v *Spateman*, 1 Wms Saund 626
(*v*) *Harrop* v *Hirst* (1868), L. R. 4 Ex 43, 37 L J Ex 1

(*x*) 1 App. Ca. 662.
(*y*) *Fritz* v. *Hobson* (1880), 14 Ch. D. 542 49 L. J. Ch. 321, *supra*, p 356.
(*z*) *Thorpe* v. *Brumfitt* (1873), 8 Ch. 650, 656, per James L J

closeness and height of buildings in towns, is the obstruction of light: often the phrase "light and air" is used, but the addition is useless if not misleading, inasmuch as a specific right to the access of air over a neighbour's land is not known to the law (a).

It seems proper (though at the risk of digressing from the law of Torts into the law of Easements) to state here the rules on this head as settled by the decisions of the last twenty years or thereabouts.

Nature of the right. The right to light, to begin with, is not a natural right incident to the ownership of windows, but an easement to which title must be shown by grant (b),

---

(a) *City of London Brewery Co v. Tennant* (1873), 9 Ch at p 221, *Webb v. Bird* (1862), 1 x Ch 13 C B N S 841, 31 L J C P Rep., *Bryant v Lefever* (1879), 4 C P. Div 172, especially per Cotton L J at p 180, 18 L. J Ch 380, *Harris v De Pinna* (1886), 33 Ch Div 238, per Chitty J at p 250, and Cotton L. J at p 259

(b) Notwithstanding the doubts expressed by Littledale J in *Moore v Rawson* (1824), 3 B & C at p 340 see per Lord Selborne, *Dalton v. Angus* (1881), 6 App. Ca at p 794, and Lord Blackburn, ib 823, and the judgments and opinions in that case *passim* as to the peculiar character of negative easements

---

Obstruction of lights. Ordinarily darkening another's windows "or depriving him of a prospect, by building on one's own land, invades no legal right" Pickard *v.* Collins, 23 Barb 458 But otherwise, when done for the purpose of gratifying spite and malice Burke *v* Smith, 69 Mich 389, 37 N. W. Rep 838 See Kirkwood *v* Finegan (Mich), 55 N W Rep 157

In the United States the easement of light cannot be acquired by prescription. In Tunstall *v* Christian (80 Va 4), the court said "But the English doctrine of 'ancient lights' has been repudiated by the American courts as irreconcilable with principle, and not adapted to the rapid physical development of the country, especially in cities and towns" See Parker *v* Foote, 19 Wend 309, Ward *v*. Neal, 37 Ala. 500, Craig *v* Dee, 14 Gray, 583, Cherry *v* Stein, 11 Md. 1, Myers *v*. Gemmel, 10 Barb. 537, Haverstick *v* Sipe, 33 Pa. St 368, Hubbard *v*. Town, 33 Vt. 295, Morrison *v* Marquardt, 4 Ia 35, Mullen *v* Stricker, 19 Ohio St 135, Powell *v*. Sims, 5 W Va 1, Turner *v*. Thompson, 49 Ga. 19, Stein *v* Hauck, 56 Ia 65, Keats *v* Hugo, 115 Mass. 207; Kelper *v*. Klein, 51 Ind. 316, Lapere *v* Lucky, 23 Kan 534. *Contra*, Ray *v* Sweeney, 14 Burk, 1, Robinson *v*. Maxwell, 2 N J Eq 57, McCready *v*. Thompson, Dudley Eq 30, Pond *v*. Metropolitan E R. Co, 42 Hun, 567, Mahan *v* Brown, 13 Wend 263

express or implied, or by prescription at common law, or under the Prescription Act. The Prescription Act has not altered the nature or extent of the right, but has only provided a new mode of acquiring and claiming it (c), without taking away any mode which existed at common law (d). The right can be claimed only in respect of a building; the use of an open piece of ground for a purpose requiring light will not create an easement against an adjacent owner (e).

Any substantial diminution is a wrong. Assuming the right to be established, there is a wrongful disturbance if the building in respect of which it exists is so far deprived of access of light as to render it materially less fit for comfortable or beneficial use or enjoyment in its existing condition; if a dwelling-house, for ordinary habitation; if a warehouse or shop, for the conduct of business (f).

This does not mean that an obstruction is not wrongful if it leaves sufficient light for the conduct of the business or occupation carried on in the dominant tenement for the time being. The question is not what is the least amount of light the plaintiff can live or work with, but whether the light, as his tenement was entitled to it and enjoyed it, has been substantially diminished. Even if a subdued or reflected light is better for the plaintiff's business than a direct one, he is not the less entitled to regulate his light for himself (g).

(c) *Kelk* v *Pearson* (1871), 6 Ch at pp 811, 813, cf 9 Ch 219.

(d) *Aynsley* v *Glover* (1875), 10 Ch 283, 44 L J. Ch 523. Since the Prescription Act, however, the formerly accustomed method of claiming under the fiction of a lost grant appears to be obsolete.

(e) See *Potts* v *Smith* (1868), 6 Eq 311, 315, 38 L J Ch 58.

(f) *Kelk* v *Pearson* (1871), 6 Ch 809, 811, *City of London Brewery Co* v *Tennant* (1873), 9 Ch at p 216, 43 L J Ch 457.

(g) *Yates* v *Jack* (1866), 1 Ch 295. *Lanfranchi* v *Mackenzie*, 4 Eq 421, 36 L J Ch 518 (1867, before Malins V C) seems to have been decided, on the whole, on the ground that there was not any material diminution. So far as it suggests that there is a distinction in law between ordinary and extraordinary amounts of light, or that a plaintiff claiming what is called an extraordinary amount ought to show that the defendant had notice of the nature of his business, it cannot be accepted as authority

Supposed rule or presumption as to angle of 45°. For some years it was supposed, by analogy to a regulation in one of the Metropolitan Local Management Acts as to the proportion between the height of new buildings and the width of streets (*h*), that a building did not constitute a material obstruction in the eye of the law or at least was presumed not to be such, if its elevation subtended an angle not exceeding 45° at the base of the light alleged to be obstructed, or, as it was sometimes put, left 45° of light to the plaintiff. But it has been conclusively declared by the Court of Appeal that there is no such rule (*i*). Every case must be dealt with on its own facts. The statutory regulation is framed on considerations of general public convenience, irrespective of private titles. Where an individual is entitled to more light than the statute would secure for him, there is no warrant in the statute, or in anything that can be thence inferred, for depriving him of it.

Enlargement or alteration of lights. An existing right to light is not lost by enlarging, rebuilding, or altering (*j*), the windows for which access of light is claimed. So long as the ancient lights, or a substantial part thereof (*k*), remain substantially capable of continuous enjoyment (*l*), so

---

(*h*) 25 & 26 Vict. c. 102, s. 85.

(*i*) *Parker* v. *First Avenue Hotel Co.* (1883), 24 Ch. Div. 282; *Ecclesiastical Commissioners* v. *Kino* (1880), 14 Ch. Div. 213, 49 L. J. Ch. 529.

(*j*) *Tapling* v. *Jones* (1865), 11 H. L. C. 290, 34 L. J. C. P. 342; *Aynsley* v. *Glover* (1874-5), 18 Eq. 544, 43 L. J. Ch. 777, 10 Ch. 283, 44 L. J. Ch. 523; *Ecclesiastical Commissioners* v. *Kino*, 14 Ch. Div. 213; *Greenwood* v. *Hornsey* (1886), 33 Ch. D. 471, 55 L. J. Ch. 917.

(*k*) *Newson* v. *Pender* (1884), 27 Ch. Div. 43, 61. It is not necessary that the "structural identity" of the old windows should be preserved, the right is to light as measured by the ancient apertures, but not merely as incident to certain defined apertures in a certain place. *Scott* v. *Pape* (1886), 31 Ch. Div. 554, 55 L. J. Ch. 426; *National Provincial Plate Glass Insurance Co.* v. *Prudential Assurance Co.* (1877), 6 Ch. D. 757, 46 L. J. Ch. 871. But there must at all events be a definite mode of access, *Harris* v. *De Pinna* (1886), 33 Ch. Div. 238, 56 L. J. Ch. 344.

(*l*) The alteration or rebuilding must be continuous enough to show that the right is not abandoned, see *Moore* v. *Rawson* (1824), 3 B. & C. 322. All the local circumstances will be considered, *Bullers* v. *Dickinson* (1885), 29 Ch. D. 155, 54 L. J. Ch. 776. There must be some specific identification of the old light as coincident with the new. *Pendarves* v. *Monro*, '92, 1 Ch. 611.

long the existing right continues and is protected by the same remedies (*m*). And an existing right to light is not lost by interruption which is not continuous in time and quantity, but temporary and of fluctuating amount (*n*).

It makes no difference that the owner of a servient tenement may, by the situation and arrangement of the buildings, be unable to prevent a right being acquired in respect of the new light otherwise than by obstructing the old light also (*o*). For there is no such thing as a specific right to obstruct new lights. A man may build on his own land, and he may build so as to darken any light which is not ancient (as on the other hand it is undoubted law that his neighbor may open lights overlooking his land), but he must do it so as not to interfere with lights in respect of which a right has been acquired

"Nuisance" to market or ferry. Disturbing the private franchise of a market or a ferry is commonly reckoned a species of nuisance in our books (*p*). But this classification seems rather to depend on accidents of procedure than on any substantial resemblance between interference with peculiar rights of this kind and such injuries to the enjoyment of common rights of property as we have been considering. The quasi-proprietary right to a market or a ferry is of such a nature that the kind of disturbance called "nuisance" in the old books is the only way in which it can be violated at all. If disturbing a market is a nuisance, an infringement of copyright must be a nuisance, too, unless the term is to be conventionally restricted to the violation of rights not depending on any statute.

Remedies for nuisance. The remedies for nuisance are threefold: abatement, damages, and injunction: of which

(*m*) *Staight* v *Burn* (1869), 5 Ch. per Giffard L J at p 167

(*n*) *Fresland* v *Bingham* (1889), 41 Ch Div 268

(*o*) *Tapling* v *Jones* (1865), 11 H. L. C 290, 34 L. J C P 342

(*p*) Blackst Comm iii 218

the first is by the act of the party aggrieved, the others by process of law. Damages are recoverable in all cases where nuisance is proved, but in many cases are not an adequate remedy. The more stringent remedy by injunction is available in such cases, and often takes the place of abatement where that would be too hazardous a proceeding.

Abatement. The abatement of obstructions to highways, and the like, is still of importance as a means of asserting public rights. Private rights which tend to the benefit of the public, or a considerable class of persons, such as rights of common, have within recent times been successfully maintained in the same manner, though not without the addition of judicial proceedings (*q*). It is decided that not only walls, fences, and such like encroachments which obstruct rights of common may be removed, but a house wrongfully built on a common may be pulled down by a commoner if it is not removed after notice (*r*) within a reasonable time (*s*).

If another man's tree overhangs my land, I may lawfully cut the overhanging branches (*t*), and in these cases where

---

(*q*) Smith v. Earl Brownlow (1869), 9 Eq. 241 (the case of Berkhamstead Common), Williams on Rights of Common, 1 s.

(*r*) Pulling down the house without notice while there are people in it is a trespass. *Perry* v. *Fitzhoue* (1845), 8 Q. B. 757, 15 L. J. Q. B. 239; *Jones* v. *Jones* (69) 1 H. & C. 1, 31 L. J. Ex. 506, following *Perry* v. *Fitzhoue* with some doubt. The case of a man pulling down buildings wrongfully erected on his own land is different, *ib*.; *Burling* v. *Read* (1850), 11 Q. B. 904, 19 L. J. Q. B. 291.

(*s*) *Davies* v. *Williams* (1851), 16 Q. B. 546, 20 L. J. Q. B. 330.

(*t*) *Norris* v. *Baker*, 1 Rolle's Rep. 393, per Croke; *Lonsdale* v. *Nelson*, 2 B. & C. 311, per Best.

Abatement. The term "abatement" as applied to nuisance is defined, as "The removal, prostration, or destruction of that which causes a nuisance, whether by breaking or pulling it down, or otherwise removing, disintegrating or effacing it. The remedy which the law allows a party injured by a nuisance of destroying or removing it by his own act, so as he commits no riot in doing it, nor occasions (in the case of a private nuisance) any damage beyond what the removal of the inconvenience necessarily required." Black's Law Dic., p. 5. See this subject further, *post*, p. 515. As to overhanging branches, see, *ante*, p. 492.

the nuisance is in the nature of a trespass, and can be abated without entering on another's land, it does not appear that the wrong-doer is entitled to notice. But if the nuisance is on the wrong-doer's own tenement, he ought first to be warned and required to abate it himself (u) After notice and refusal, entry on the land to abate the nuisance may be justified; but it is a hazardous course at best for a man thus to take the law into his own hands, and in modern times it can seldom, if ever, be advisable.

Notice to wrong-doer. In the case of abating nuisances to a right of common, notice is not strictly necessary unless the encroachment is a dwelling-house in actual occupation; but if there is a question of right to be tried, the more reasonable course is to give notice (x). The same

---

(u) This has always been understood to be the law, and seems to follow a fortiori from the doctrine of *Perry v. Fitzhowe*, n (r), last page

(x) Per James L J, *Commissioners of Sewers v Glasse* (1872), 7 Ch at p 464

Notice to wrong doer. Ordinarily a person responsible for the existence of a nuisance is entitled to a reasonable notice to remove and abate it before an action can be maintained against him therefor But it seems that where the acts constituting the nuisance are in themselves unlawful, or where there is danger of irreparable injury, no notice is required. United States Illuminating Co. v. Grant, 55 Hun, 235, 7 N Y. S Rep. 788, Dunsbach v. Hollister, 2 N. Y. S. Rep 94, McGowan v Mo. Pac Ry. Co, 23 Mo. App. 203, Groff v. Akenbrandt, 19 Ill App. 148, Verder v Ellsworth, 59 Vt 354, 10 At Rep 89, George v The Wabash Western Ry Co, 40 Mo App. 444, Harvey v Dewoody, 18 Ark 252, Swett v Sprague, 55 Me. 190, Haggerty v Thompson, 45 Hun, 398 Thus, in Matthews v. Mo Pac. Ry. Co (26 Mo. App. 75), it was held, that he who continues a nuisance which obstructs a public highway is responsible for injuries resulting from such obstruction, without proof of notice to him of its existence

The above general rule is subject, however, to the qualification as announced by the court in the case of Grigsby v Clear Lake Water Co (40 Cal 407), as follows "The rule seems too well established that a party who is not the original creator of a nuisance is entitled to notice that it is a nuisance, and a request must be made, that it may be abated before an action will lie for that purpose, unless it appear that he had knowledge of the hurtful character of the erection" See West v. Louisville, C & L R Co , 8 Bush, 408.

rule seems on principle to be applicable to the obstruction of a right of way. As to the extent of the right, "where a fence has been erected upon a common, inclosing and separating parts of that common from the residue, and thereby interfering with the rights of the commoners, the latter are not by law restrained in the exercise of those rights to pulling down so much of that fence as it may be necessary for them to remove for the purpose of enabling their cattle to enter and feed upon the residue of the common, but they are entitled to consider the whole of that fence so erected upon the common a nuisance, and to remove it accordingly" (*y*).

Nuisances of omission. It is doubtful whether there is any private right to abate a nuisance consisting only in omission except where the person aggrieved can do it with-

---

(*y*) Bayley J. in *Arlett* v. *Ellis* (1827), 7 B. & C. 346, 362, and earlier authorities there cited. The first is 15 Hen. VII. 10, pl. 18. There is a diversity where the fence preventing access to the common is not on the common itself *ibid.*

Nuisances of omission. *Notice* To maintain an action against one responsible for a nuisance of omission it is essential that he should have been given reasonable notice to remove and abate the nuisance.

Abatement "The true theory of abatement of nuisance is that an individual citizen may abate a private nuisance injurious to him when he could bring an action, and, also when a common nuisance obstructs his individual right, he may remove it to enable him to enjoy that right, and he cannot be called in question for so doing. As in the case of obstruction across a public highway and an unauthorized bridge over a navigable water-course, if he has occasion to use it, he may remove it, by way of abatement But this would not justify strangers being inhabitants of other parts of the commonwealth, having no occasion to use it, to do the same. Some of the earlier cases, perhaps, in laying down the general proposition that private subjects may abate a common nuisance, do not expressly mark this distinction, but we think upon authority of modern cases, where the distinctions are more accurately made, and upon principle, this is the true rule of law." Brown *v.* Perkins, 12 Gray, 89, Meeker *v* Van Renselaer, 15 Wend 397; Wood on Nuisances, 2nd Ed., §§ 735, *et seq.*, Day *v* Day, 4 Md. 262, Renwick *v* Morris, 7 Hill, 575; Brown *v.* DeGroff, 50 N J. L. 409; 14 At. Rep. 219; Whetmore *v.* Tracy, 14 Wend 250, 28 Am. Dec 559, Clark *v.* Lake St. Clair, etc. Ice Com-

out leaving his own tenement in respect of which he suffers, and perhaps except in cases of urgency such as to make the act necessary for the immediate safety of life or property. "Nuisances by an act of commission are committed in defiance of those whom such nuisances injure, and the injured party may abate them without notice to the person who committed them; but there is no decided case which sanctions the abatement by an individual of nuisances from omission, except that of cutting the branches of trees which overhang a public road, or the private property of the person who cuts them. . . . The security of lives and

---

pany, 21 Mich. 508, Gray v. Ayres, 7 Dana, 375; School District v. Neil, 36 Kan. 617, City of McGregor v. Boyle, 34 Iowa 268, Welch v. Stowell, 2 Dougl 332, State v Keran, 5 R. I 497, Crosland v. Pottsville Borough, 126 Pa St 522, 21 W N C 321, Hickey v. Michigan C R. Co (Mich.), 55 N. W. Rep 989

Thus, applying the principle to the case of ferocious dogs, "If a dog is so ferocious that he will bite men in the street and is at large he is a nuisance, and may be killed by any one" Dunlap v Snyder, 17 Barb 561. See Brown v Carpenter, 26 Va. 638, Stump v. McNairy, 5 Humph 363; Oliver v Loftin, 4 Ala. 240 But see Harrower v Ritson, 37 Barb 301, Griffith v. McCollum, 46 Id. 561, Peckham v Henderson, 27 Id. 267.

One who undertakes to abate a private nuisance without recourse to law acts at his peril, and if his conduct should afterwards be adjudged unwarranted or if he go beyond what is necessary to protect his right he is liable for his illegal conduct in the first instance, or for the excess of abatement in the second instance "A party by erecting a nuisance does not put himself, or his property, beyond the protection of the law. If an individual or member of a community can with reasonable care, notwithstanding the act complained of, enjoy the right or franchise belonging to him he is not at liberty to destroy or interfere with the property of the wrong-doer" Harrower v Ritson, 37 Barb 310. Thus, in Brightman v Bristol (65 Me. 443), the court said "When it is the use of the building which constitutes a nuisance, the abatement consists in putting a stop to such. The law allows its officers, in execution of its sentence, only to do what is necessary to abate the nuisance, and nothing more, *a fortiori* it will not sanction destruction without limit by individuals It would be absurd to hold that a manufactory lawful in itself, but producing 'offensive smells' is at the mercy of every passer-by whose olfactory nerves are disagreeably affected by its necessary processes" See Ely v Supervisors of Niagara County, 4 Barb 659, Earp v. Lee, 71 Ind. 193

property may sometimes require so speedy a remedy as not to allow time to call on the person on whose property the mischief has arisen to remedy it. In such cases an individual would be justified in abating a nuisance from omission without notice. In all other cases of such nuisances persons should not take the law into their own hands, but follow the advice of Lord Hale and appeal to a court of justice" (z)

In every case the party taking on himself to abate a nuisance must avoid doing any unnecessary damage, as is shown by the old form of pleading in justification. Thus it is lawful to remove a gate or barrier which obstructs a right of way, but not to break or deface it beyond what is necessary for the purpose of removing it. And where a structure, say a dam or weir across a stream, is in part lawful and in part unlawful, a party abating that which is unlawful cannot justify interference with the rest. He must distinguish them at his peril (a). But this does not mean that the wrong-doer is always entitled to have a nuisance abated in the manner most convenient to himself. The convenience of innocent third persons or of the public may also be in question. And the abator cannot justify doing harm to innocent persons which he might have avoided In such a case, therefore, it may be necessary and proper "to abate the nuisance in a manner more onerous to the wrong-doer" (b) Practically the remedy of abatement is now in use only as to rights of common (as we have already hinted), rights of way, and sometimes rights of water; and even in those cases it ought never to be used without good advisement.

Old writs. Formerly there were processes of judicial abatement available for freeholders under the writ *Quod*

(z) Best, J in *Earl of Lonsdale v Nelson* (1823) 2 B. & C. at p 311
(a) *Greenslade v Halliday* (1830), 6 Bing. 73
(b) *Roberts v. Rose* (1865), Ex. Ch. L. R. 1 Ex 82, 89

permittat and the assize of nuisance (c). But these were cumbrous and tedious remedies, and, like the other forms of real action, were obsolete in practice long before they were finally abolished (d), the remedies by action on the case at law and by injunction in the Court of Chancery having superseded them.

Damages There is not much to be said of the remedy in damages as applicable to this particular class of wrongs. Persistence in a proved nuisance is stated to be a just cause

---

(c) F N B 121 H, 183 I, *Baten's ca* 9 Co Rep 55 a, Blackst Comm III 221
(d) See note (3) to *Penruddock's ca*,
5 Co Rep 100 b, in ed Thomas & Fraser, 1826

Old writs The common law remedies were "(1) *Quod permittat prosternere* This was in the nature of a writ of right, therefore subject to great delays. It commanded the defendant to permit the plaintiff to abate the nuisance, or show cause against the same; and plaintiff could have a judgment to abate the nuisance and for damages against the defendant. (2) An assize of nuisance, in which the sheriff was commanded to summon a jury to view the premises, and, if they found for the plaintiff, he had judgment to have the nuisance abated, and for damages." Powell v. Bentley & Gerwig Furniture Co, 34 W Va 803, 12 S. E Rep. 1086 Both of these writs have been abolished in England by statute and in the United States they are obsolete. Hutchins v Smith, 63 Barb 251, Clark v Peckham, 9 R I. 455, Klutz v McNeal, 1 Denio, 436, Livezly v Gorgas, 1 Binn 251, Barnet v Ihrie, 17 Serg & R 174

Damages One injured by a nuisance may recover of another responsible therefor to the amount of actual damages sustained Where the plaintiff proves that a legal right of his has been infringed by the nuisance he is entitled to a recovery of nominal damages even though he fail to prove actual damage, or even though the property has been actually benefited by the nuisance. Ripka v Sergeant, 7 Watts & S. 9, 42 Am. Dec. 214, Pastorius v Fisher, 1 Rawle, 27, Frank v New Orleans etc R. Co., 20 La. An 25, Tootle v Clifton, 22 Ohio St. 247, Hatch v Dwight, 17 Mass. 289, 9 Am Dec 145, McKnight v Ratchliff, 44 Pa St. 156, Chipman v. Hibberd, 6 Cal 162, Thayer v. Brooks, 17 Ohio, 489; 49 Am Dec. 474, Luther v Winnisimmet, 9 Cush 171, Taber v Hutson, 5 Ind. 322; 61 Am. Dec 96, Howes v. Ashfield, 99 Mass. 540, Stowell v. Lincoln, 11 Gray, 434; Cooper v. Randall, 55 Ill. 23; Marcy v Fries, 18 K in. 345, Kimel v Kimel, 4 Jones L 121, Wesson v Washburg Iron Co., 13 Allen, 95, 90 Am Dec 181.

The rules that prevail in general in the awarding of damages for other

for giving exemplary damages (c). There is a place for nominal damages in cases where the nuisance consists merely in the obstruction of a right of legal enjoyment,

(c) Blackst Comm III 220

---

torts apply to nuisances, therefore, exemplary damages are not recoverable in the absence of proof of malice or wanton recklessness, but malice may be inferred from the circumstances, as where the nuisance is continued after a verdict or judgment against it. Morford v. Woodworth 7 Ind. 83, McFadden v. Rausch, 119 Pa St. 507; Silver v. Creek Navigation Co v. Mangum, 64 Miss. 682; Parrott v. Housatonic R Co., 47 Conn 575, Hayes v Askew, 7 Jones L 272, Pickett v. Crook, 20 Wis. 58, Windham v Rhame, 11 Rich. L 283, 73 Am. Dec. 116, Jefcoat v Knotts, Id 619, Long v. Trexler (Pa) 8 At Rep 620, New Orleans etc R Co v Statham, 42 Miss. 607; 97 Am. Dec. 418; Keay v. New Orleans Canal Co , 7 La. An 259, Dorsey v. Manlove, 14 Cal 553

"The authorities sustain the proposition that in actions to recover damages resulting from a permanent or continuing nuisance, and the damages are necessarily continuous, the recovery can be had for such damages only as had been sustained prior to bringing the suit. Wood Nuis , §§ 869, 870, 873, Field Dam., §§ 748, 749; Pinney v. Berry, 61 Mo. 359 But, when the action is brought not only to recover damages, but to abate the nuisance, as in this case, we think it more in accord with the long established policy of our laws to prevent, as far as possible, a multiplicity of suits, to hold that the recovery may be had for all damages sustained down to the trial, rather than put the plaintiff to another action, after the nuisance has been abated, to recover for damages sustained between the institution of the suit and the time of the trial." Comminge v. Stevenson, 76 Tex. 645, 13 S W. Rep. 558. See Bizer v. The Ottumwa Hydraulic Power Co , 70 Ia 147, citing Powers v. City of Council Bluffs, 45 Id 652, Van Orsdal v. Railroad Co , 56 Id 470. And see Illinois C R Co. v Graball, 50 Ill 241, 248, Finley v. Hershey, 41 Iowa 389, Duryea v. New York, 26 Hun, 120; Troy v Cheshire R Co , 23 N. H 83, 55 Am Dec 177; Hopkins v Western Pac. R Co., 50 Cal 190, Shaw v Etterbridge, 3 Jones L. 300, Hargreaves v. Kimberly, 26 W. Va. 787, 53 Am. Rep 121, Barrick v. Schifferdicker, 1 N. Y S. Rep 21.

In fixing the amount of damages the recovery should, ordinarily, be limited to the actual damages sustained. For permanent injuries to realty, the measure of damages is the difference between what the property would have sold for before and after the injury. Seely v. Alden, 61 Pa. St 302; McGuire v. Grant, 25 N J. L. 356, 64 Am. Dec. 49, Ferguson v Firmenich Mfg. Co., 77 Ia. 576; Schuylkill Nav. Co. v. Farr, 4 Watts & S 362. But where the injury is only temporary, affecting the enjoyment and occupancy of realty, the measure of damages is

such as a right of common, which does not cause any specific harm or loss to the plaintiff. At common law damages could not be awarded for any injury received from the continuance of a nuisance since the commencement of the action; for this was a new cause of action for which damages might be separately recovered. But under the present procedure damages in respect of any continuing cause of action are assessed down to the date of the assessment (*f*)

Injunctions. The most efficient and flexible remedy is that of injunction. Under this form the Court can prevent that from being done which, if done, would cause a nui-

---

(*f*) Rules of the Supreme Court, 1883, Ord XXXVI r 58 (no 182). The like power had already been exercised by the Court (see *Fritz* v *Hobson* (1880), 14 Ch D. 542, 557), when damages were given in addition to or in substitution for an injunction under Lord Cairns' Act, 21 & 22 Vict c 27 This Act is now repealed by the Statute Law Revision and Civil Procedure Act, 1883, 46 & 47 Vict. c 49, but the power conferred by it still exists, and is applicable in such actions as formerly would have been Chancery suits for an injunction, and the result may be to dispense with statutory requirements as to notice of action, etc, which would not have applied to such suits *Chapman* v *Auckland Union* (1889), 23 Q B. Div. 294, 299, 300, 58 L J Q B 504 The Act did not confer any power to give damages where no actionable wrong had been done, *e g*, in a case of merely threatened injury *Dreyfus* v *Peruvian Guano Co* (1889), 43 Ch Div. 316, 333, 342

---

generally the loss of rents or the depreciation in rental value. Givens *v.* Van Studdiford, 4 Mo App. 503, Chipman *v* Palmer, 9 Hun, 517; Chicago *v* Huenerbein, 85 Ill 594, 28 Am Rep. 626, Colrick *v* Swinburne, 105 N Y 503; Crawford *v.* Parsons, 63 N H. 438; Michel *v.* Monroe Co, 39 Hun, 47; Randolf *v* Town of Bloomfield, 77 Ia 50, Murray *v.* Archer, 5 N Y. S Rep 326, Carll *v* Union Depot, etc Co., 32 Minn. 101, South Bend *v* Paxon, 67 Ind. 228.

Injunctions. Where there is impending danger of an irreparable injury or extraordinary continuing annoyance to the complainant, a court of equity will generally grant a preliminary injunction restraining the nuisance.

This protection is extended to the complainant by the court, at its discretion, for three reasons: "*First*, that he has no adequate remedy at law; *second*, to prevent a multiplicity of actions, *third*, to prevent irreparable injury by the continuance of the nuisance itself" Knox *v* Mayor etc of New York, 55 Barb 407.

In the case of Dittman *v* Repp, (50 Md 517), the court in substance

sance; it can command the destruction of buildings (g) or the cessation of works (h) which violate a neighbour's rights, where there is a disputed question of right between

(g) *I q Kelk v Pearson* (1871), 6 Ch. 809

(h) The form of order does not go to prohibit the carrying on of such and such operations absolutely, but "so as to cause a nuisance to the plaintiff," or like words see *Linqwood v. Stowmarket Co* (1865), 1 Eq 77, 336, and other precedents in Seton, Pt II. ch. 5, s 5, cp *Fleming v. Hislop* (1886), 11 App. Ca (Sc) 686

said, that the criterion for determining whether a court of equity will interfere and restrain by an injunction an existing and threatening nuisance to a party's dwelling is, whether the nuisance complained of will or does produce such a condition of things as, in the judgment of reasonable men, is naturally productive of actual physical discomfort to persons of ordinary sensibilities, and of ordinary tastes and habits, and is, in view of the circumstances of the case, is unreasonable and in derogation of the rights of the complainant In another case it is said by the court " A private person or a corporation has no right to an injunction merely to restrain another from committing some apprehended violation of law Nor has such private person or corporation any right to an injunction to restrain another from doing any particular act unless performance of the act would result to the injury of the party seeking the relief, and even in order to entitle the party seeking the relief to the relief sought, the contemplated injury must be substantial and not merely nominal, and must be special and particular as to the party seeking the relief, and different in kind from that which will affect the public in general " Water Supply Co *v* City of Potwin, 43 Kan 414; 23 P Rep. 578 See Pfingst *v.* Senn (Ky), 23 S. W. Rep 358, Powell *v.* Macon & I S R. Co (Ga), 17 S. E Rep 1027

"The foundation of this jurisdiction of equity, in assuming to restrain nuisances, rests in the imperative necessity of preventing irreparable injury and a multiplicity of suits at law * * * It is the exercise of an extraordinary power, which, as was long ago said by this court, should be 'cautiously and sparingly exercised ' * * * And the injunction, therefore, of a private nuisance, will generally be granted only where there is a strong and mischievous case of pressing necessity and not because of a trifling discomfort or inconvenience suffered by the party complaining. * * * The rule has long been recognized as quite different where the thing sought to be prohibited is *per se* a nuisance, and where it is not unavoidably noxious in itself, but *may* prove so according to circumstances, or otherwise. In the first class of cases an injunction will ordinarily be granted without waiting for the result of a trial at law In the second class the court will generally refuse to interfere until the matter has been tried at law " Rouse *v.* Martin, 75 Ala. 510; 51

the parties, it can suspend the operations complained of until that question is finally decided (*i*); and its orders may be either absolute or conditional upon the fulfilment

(*i*) Even a mandatory injunction may be granted, in an extreme case, at an interlocutory stage where, after notice of motion and before the hearing, the defendant had rapidly run up the wall complained of, he was ordered to pull it down without regard to the general merits Daniel v Ferguson, '01, 2 Ch 27, C A

Am Rep 168, citing State v. Mayor etc of Mobile, 5 Port 279, Ray v Lynes, 10 Ala 63, St James Church v Arrington, 36 Ala 546, Powell v. Bentley & Gerwig Furniture Co , 31 W. Va 804; 12 S E Rep. 1087, Carlisle v. Cooper, 21 N. J Eq. 579, Commonwealth v. Croushore, 145 Pa St. 162, 22 At Rep. 807, Voice v. Page, 28 Neb. 294, 44 N W Rep 452, Indianapolis Water Co v American Strawboard Co , 53 Fed. Rep 970; Hennessey v Carmony (N J Eq), 25 At Rep. 374, Smith v McDowell (Ill), 35 N E. Rep. 141, City of Grand Rapids v Weiden (Mich.), 56 N. W. Rep 233

In cases where invasions of a party's legal rights are of frequent occurrence, the right to an injunction is said to be almost a matter of positive right.

"And courts of equity will more readily interpose in such instances where the damages recovered are merely nominal, and, therefore, inadequate to prevent a repetition of the injury." Paddock v. Somes, 102 Mo 238, 14 N. W. Rep 746. See Gardner v Stroever, 89 Cal 26, 26 Pac Rep 618; Learned v Castle, 78 Cal. 454, 21 Pac Rep 11; Farrell v Cook, 16 Neb. 483, 19 Am Rep 721, New York etc. R. Co. v City of Rochester, 127 N Y. 591, 28 N. E. Rep. 416, Ballentine v. Webb, 48 Mich 38, 47 N W. Rep 485, Penrose v. Nixon, 140 Pa. St. 45, 21 At. Rep. 364; Straus v Barnett, 140 Pa St 111, 71 At. Rep. 253, Newark Aqueduct Board v City of Passaic, 46 N J. Eq. 552, 20 At Rep. 54, 22 At Rep 55; Born v Loflin & Rand Powder Co , 84 Ga 217, 10 S E Rep. 738, Rogers v Hatfield, 44 Daly, 339, Hacke's App., 101 Pa St 249, Morris & E. R Co v Prudden, 20 N. J. Eq. 530.

The injunction should be confined in its application to the specific injury; thus in the case of McMenomy v Band (87 Cal 134; 26 Pac. Rep 795) it was held, that where the injurious effects complained of as resulting from the running of a foundry and machinery may be prevented without entirely abating or enjoining the works or the operations thereof, only the cause of the specific injurious effects proved should be enjoined, leaving the defendant at liberty to operate his works, if he can, and elect to do so, in such manner as to remove the cause and prevent the injury

"Courts of equity will not enjoin an act which would otherwise be lawful but which is made unlawful by an ordinance or by-law of a city or

by either or both of the parties of such undertakings as appear just in the particular case (*i*).

It is a matter of common learning and practice that an injunction is not, like damages, a remedy (as it is said) *ex debito justitiæ*. Whether it shall be granted or not in a given case is in the judicial discretion of the Court, now guided by principles which have become pretty well settled. In order to obtain an injunction it must be shown that the injury complained of as present or impending is such as by reason of its gravity, or its permanent character, or both, cannot be adequately compensated in damages (*j*). The injury must be either irreparable or continuous (*k*) This remedy is therefore not appropriate for damage which is in its nature temporary and intermittent (*l*), or is accidental and occasional (*m*), or for an interference with legal rights which is trifling in amount and effect (*n*).

Apprehension of future mischief from something in itself lawful and capable of being done without creating a nuisance is no ground for an injunction (*o*) "There must, if no

---

(*i*) Thus where the complaint was of special damage or danger from something alleged to be a public nuisance, an interlocutory injunction has been granted on the terms of the plaintiff bringing an indictment, *Hepburn* v *Lordan* (1865), 2 H & M 345, 352, 34 L J Ch 293

(*j*) *Cooke* v *Forbes*, 5 Eq 166, 173 (Page Wood V C 1867), *A G* v. *Sheffield &c Co* (next note but one)

(*k*) Page Wood L J , 4 Ch at p 81

(*l*) *A G* v *Sheffield Gas Consumers' Co* (1853), 3 D M G 304, 22 L J Ch 811 (breaking up streets to lay gas pipes),

followed by *A G* v *Cambridge Consumers' Gas Co* (1868), 4 Ch 71, 38 L J Ch 94

(*m*) *Cooke* v *Forbes* (1867), 5 Eq 166 (escape of fumes from works where the precautions used were shown to be as a rule sufficient)

(*n*) *Gaunt* v *Finney* (1872), 8 Ch 8, 42 L. J Ch 122 (case of nuisance from noise broke down, slight obstruction to ancient light held no ground for injunction)

(*o*) See the cases reviewed by Pearson J , *Fletcher* v *Bealey* (1885), 28 Ch D. 688, 54 L J Ch 424

---

town, unless the act is shown to be a nuisance *per se*." Warren *v* Cavanaugh, 33 Mo. App 102, citing Phillips *v*. Allen, 41 Pa. St. 481, Schuster *v* Board of Health, 49 Barb. 451, President *v* Moore, 34 Wis. 450, Smith *v* Lockwood, 13 Barb. 209, Village of St John *v*. McFarlan, 33 Mich 72 See Burwell *v* Comm'rs, 93 N. C. 73, 53 Am. Rep 454, Babcock *v* N J. Stock Yard Co , 20 N. J. Eq 296

See INJUNCTIONS, *ante*, p. 224

actual damage is proved, be proof of imminent danger, and there must also be proof that the apprehended damage will, if it comes, be very substantial" (p). But where a nuisance is shown to exist, all the probable consequences are taken into account in determining whether the injury is serious within the meaning of the rule on which the Court acts (q). But there must be substantial injury in view to begin with. The following passages from a judgment of the late Lord Justice James will be found instructive on this point:—

"In this case the Master of the Rolls has dismissed with costs the bill of the plaintiff.

"The bill, in substance, sought by a mandatory injunction to prevent the defendants, who are a great colliery company, from erecting or working any coke ovens or other ovens to the nuisance of the plaintiff, the nuisance alleged being from smoke and deleterious vapours.

"The Master of the Rolls thought it right to lay down what he conceived to be the principle of law applicable to a case of this kind, which principle he found expressed in the case of *St. Helen's Smelting Company* v. *Tipping* (r), in which Mr. Justice Mellor gave a very elaborate charge to the jury, which was afterwards the subject of a very elaborate discussion and consideration in the House of Lords. The Master of the Rolls derived from that case this principle; that in any case of this kind, where the plaintiff was seeking to interfere with a great work carried on, so far as the work itself is concerned, in the normal and useful manner, the plaintiff must show substantial, or, as the Master of the Rolls expressed it, 'visible' damage. The term 'visible' was very much quarrelled with before us, as not being accurate in point of law. It was stated

---

(p) 28 Ch D at p 698 A premature action of this kind may be dismissed without prejudice to future proceedings in the event of actual and imminent danger ib 701

(q) *Goldsmid* v *Tunbridge Wells Improvement Commrs* (1866), 1 Ch 349, 354, 35 L J Ch 382

(r) 11 H. L. C 642 (1865)

that the word used in the judgment of the Lord Chancellor was 'sensible.' I do not think that there is much difference between the two expressions. When the Master of the Rolls said that the damage must be visible, it appears to me that he was quite right; and as I understand the proposition, it amounts to this, that, although when you once establish the fact of actual substantial damage, it is quite right and legitimate to have recourse to scientific evidence as to the causes of that damage, still, if you are obliged to start with scientific evidence, such as the microscope of the naturalist, or the tests of the chemist, for the purpose of establishing the damage itself, that evidence will not suffice. The damage must be such as can be shown by plain witness to a plain common juryman.

"The damage must also be substantial, and it must be, in my view, actual, that is to say, the Court has, in dealing with questions of this kind, no right to take into account contingent, prospective, or remote damage. I would illustrate this by analogy. The law does not take notice of the imperceptible accretions to a river bank, or to the sea-shore, although after the lapse of years they become perfectly measurable and ascertainable; and if in the course of nature the thing itself is so imperceptible, so slow, and so gradual as to require a great lapse of time before the results are made palpable to the ordinary senses of mankind, the law disregards that kind of imperceptible operation. So, if it were made out that every minute a millionth of a grain of poison were absorbed by a tree, or a millionth of a grain of dust deposited upon a tree, that would not afford a ground for interfering, although after the lapse of a million minutes the grains of poison or the grains of dust could be easily detected.

"It would have been wrong, as it seems to me, for this Court in the reign of Henry VI. to have interfered with the further use of sea coal in London, because it had been ascertained to their satisfaction, or predicted to their satisfaction, that by the reign of Queen Victoria both white and red roses would have ceased to bloom in the Temple Gardens. If some picturesque haven opens its arms to invite the commerce of the world, it is not for this Court to forbid the embrace, although the fruit of it should be the sights, and sounds, and smells of a common seaport and shipbuilding town, which would drive the Dryads and their masters from their ancient solitudes.

"With respect to this particular property before us, I observe that the defendants have established themselves on a peninsula which extends far into the heart of the ornamental and picturesque grounds of the plaintiff. If, instead of erecting coke ovens at that spot, they had been minded, as apparently some persons in the neighborhood on the other side have done, to import ironstone, and to erect smelting furnaces, forges, and mills, and had filled the whole of the peninsula with a mining and manufacturing village, with beer-shops, and pig-styes, and dog-kennels, which would have utterly destroyed the beauty and the amenity of the plaintiff's ground, this Court could not, in my judgment, have interfered. A man to whom Providence has given an estate, under which there are veins of coal worth perhaps hundreds or thousands of pounds per acre, must take the gift with the consequences and concomitants of the mineral wealth in which he is a participant" (s).

It is not a necessary condition of obtaining an injunction to show material specific damage. Continuous interference with a legal right in a manner capable of producing material damage is enough (t).

Difficulty or expense of abatement no answer The difficulty or expense which the party liable for a nuisance

---

(s) James L. J., *Salvin* v *North Brancepeth Coal Co* (1874), 9 Ch. 705, at p. 708.

(t) *Clowes* v *Staffordshire Potteries Waterworks Co* (1872), 8 Ch. 125, 142, 42 L. J. Ch. 107, cp. *Pennington* v *Brinsop Hall Coal Co* (1877), 5 Ch. D. 769, 46 L. J. Ch. 773.

may have to incur in removing it makes no difference to his liability, any more than a debtor's being unable to pay makes default in payment the less a breach of contract. And this principle applies not only to the right in itself, but to the remedy by injunction. The Court will use a discretion in granting reasonable time for the execution of its orders, or extending that time afterwards on cause shown. But where an injunction is the only adequate remedy for the plaintiff, the trouble and expense to which the defendant may be put in obeying the order of the Court are in themselves no reason for withholding it (*u*).

Parties entitled to sue for nuisance. As to the person entitled to sue for a nuisance, as regards interference with the actual enjoyment of property, only the

(*u*) *A. G. v. Colney Hatch Lunatic Asylum* (1868), 4 Ch. 146.

Difficulty or expense of abatement no answer. It is a general rule that where a nuisance is judicially declared to exist its abatement or removal will be required even though the expense be large and the difficulty great. In the case of Baltimore & Y. T. R. v. State (63 Md. 571), it was held to be no answer to an indictment against the company for permitting its turn-pike to fall into such a ruinous and defective condition for want of due repair, as to amount to a public nuisance, that the company was pecuniarily unable to abate it.

Parties entitled to sue for nuisance. If the estate is affected by the nuisance and the injury be permanent the owner is the proper person to bring an action therefor, but the person in lawful possession of the premises should sue for injuries to the enjoyment and occupancy of the premises. Lockett v. Fort Worth & R. G. Ry. Co., 78 Tex. 211, 14 S. W. Rep. 564. In the case of Bier v. Cooke (37 Hun, 38), where the plaintiff, the lessee for a term of three years of a dwelling-house, brought an action to restrain the defendant from so conducting the business of manufacturing sashes, blinds and boxes in the adjoining premises as to allow the steam, smoke, soot, cinders and partly burning shavings issuing therefrom to come upon and into the plaintiff's premises to her annoyance, it was held that she was entitled to an injunction.

As has heretofore been said, every individual who receives *actual* damage from nuisance may maintain a private suit for his own injury, so in Kavanaugh v. Barber (59 Hun, 60, 12 N. Y. S. Rep. 603), it is held

tenant in possession can sue; but the landlord or reversioner can sue if the injury is of such a nature as to affect his estate, say by permanent depreciation of the property, or by setting up an adverse claim of right (x). A lessee who has underlet cannot sue alone in respect of a temporary nuisance, though he may properly sue as co-plaintiff with the actual occupier (y). A nuisance caused by the improper use of a highway, such as keeping carts and vans standing an unreasonable time, is not one for which a reversioner can sue; for he suffers no present damage, and, inasmuch as no length of time will justify a public nuisance, he is in no danger of an adverse right being established (z).

The reversioner cannot sue in respect of a nuisance in its

(x) See Dicey on Parties, 40
(y) Jones v. Chappell (1875), 20 Eq 539, 44 L J Ch 658, which also discredits the supposition that a weekly tenant cannot sue
(z) Mott v Shoelbred (1875), 20 Eq 22, 44 L J Ch 380

that a married man, residing with his children and wife in a house owned by the latter, may maintain an action to recover damages resulting from a nuisance in the vicinity thereof, where it inflicts a particular injury upon him. In this case the court said "It is certain that the individual action, is not by any means confined to cases which affect the realty."

If the action is at law, those having distinct interests affected by the same nuisance must bring separate actions. Hellams v Switzer, 24 S C 39, Great Falls Co. v. Worster, 15 N H 412. But a contrary rule prevails in equity, where several different persons whose injuries from the same nuisance vary only in degree may join, as in Rowbotham v Jones (47 N J. Eq 337, 20 At Rep 731), it was held that several owners of distinct tenements may join in a suit to restrain a nuisance, or other grievance, which is common to all of them, affecting each in a similar way, but may not so join when the object of the suit is to restrain that which does a distinct special injury to each of their properties. See Fogg v N C O Ry, 20 Nev 441, 23 Pac Rep 840, Marselis v Bunking Co, 1 N J Eq 31, Hinchman v Railroad Co, 17 Id 75, Grant v Schmidt, 22 Minn 1, Davidson v Isham, 9 N. J. Eq 186, Seifried v Hays, 81 Ky 377, 50 Am Rep 167; Reid v Gifford, Hopk Ch. 419, Murray v Hay, 1 Barb 59, 43 Am Dec 773, Town of Sullivan v Phillips, 110 Ind 320. Contra, Hinchman v Patterson etc R. Co, 17 N J. Eq 75, Morris etc R Co v Prudden, 20 Id 530, Demarest v Hardham, 34 Id 469, Snyder v Cabell, 29 W Va 48

nature temporary, such as noise and smoke, even if the nuisance drives away his tenants (*a*), or by reason thereof he can get only a reduced rent on the renewal of the tenancy (*b*). "Since, in order to give a reversioner an action of this kind, there must be some injury done to the inheritance, the necessity is involved of the injury being of a permanent character" (*c*). But as a matter of pleading it is sufficient for the reversioner to allege a state of things which is capable of being permanently injurious (*d*).

Parties liable. As to liability: The person primarily liable for a nuisance is he who actually creates it, whether on his own land or not (*e*). The owner or occupier of land

---

(*a*) *Simpson v. Savage* (1856), 1 C. B.
N. S. 347, 26 L. J. C. P. 50.
(*b*) *Mayfield v. Oxford &c. R. Co.*
(1860) 1 H. & N. 742, 27 L. J. N. 265.
(*c*) Per cur. 1 C. B. N. S. at p. 361.

(*d*) *Metropolitan Association v. Petch* (1858), 5 C. B. N. S. 504, 27 L. J. C. P. 330.
(*e*) See *Thompson v. Gibson* (1841), 7 M. & W. 456.

Parties liable. Agreeing with the text that he who creates a nuisance or continues a nuisance created by another is liable therefor. See Cobb v. Smith, 38 Wis. 33, citing Staple v. Spring, 10 Mass. 72, Hodges v. Hodges, 5 Metc., 205, Conhocton Stone Co. v. Buffalo, etc. Ry., 52 Barb. 390, Smith v. Elliott, 9 Pa. St. 345. See Whitenack v. Philadelphia & R. R. Co., 57 Fed. Rep. 901.

Also, "A person, who contributes to the production of a nuisance, may be chargeable therewith in a separate action, although many others contributed thereto, and his act alone would not constitute a nuisance, if the combined effect is to create an actionable injury. So if several persons drain their premises in the same ditch, the waters from which are discharged near the premises of another, and produce an injury to his person or his comfortable enjoyment, each of the persons so using the drain is liable, *in separate actions* for the damages occasioned him * * * But in such case the defendant is chargeable only to the extent of the injury done by himself. Chipman v. Palmer, 77 N. Y. 51. See Keys v. Gold Co., 53 Cal. 724, Martinowsky v. City of Hannibal, 35 Mo. App. 77, Harley v. Merrill Brick Co. (Ia.), 48 N. W. Rep. 1000, Chenango v. Lewis Bridge Co., 63 Barb. 111, Chipman v. Palmer, 9 Hun, 517, 77 N. Y. 51, 33 Am. Rep. 566. Or they may be sued jointly at the option of the plaintiff. Rogers v. Stewart, 5 Vt. 215, 26 Am. Dec. 296, Anderson v. Dickie, 26 How. Pr. 105, Grogan v. Pope Iron etc. Co., 87 Mo. 323, Buddington v. Shearer, 20 Pick. 477.

If one permits the establishment of a public nuisance upon property under *his control*, though incidental to a work otherwise lawful, he will

on which a nuisance is created, though not by himself or by his servants, may also be liable in certain conditions. If a man lets a house or land with a nuisance on it, he as well as the lessee is answerable for the continuance thereof (*f*),

(*f*) *Todd v. Flight* (1860), 9 C. B. N. S. 377, 30 L. J. C. P. 21. The extension of this in *Gandy v. Jubber* (1864), 5 B. & S. 78, 33 L. J. Q. B. 151, by treating the landlord's passive continuance of a yearly tenancy as equivalent to a reletting, so as to make him liable for a nuisance created since the original demise, is inconsistent with the later authorities cited below, and in that case a judgment reversing the decision was actually prepared for delivery in the Ex. Ch., but the plaintiff meanwhile agreed to a *stet processus* on the recommendation of the Court: see 5 B. & S. 485, and the text of the undelivered judgment in 9 B. & S. 15. The decision of the Q. B. has however been held to apply to a weekly tenancy, on the ground that its continuance from week to week is mere matter of contract: *Sandford v. Clarke* (1888), 21 Q. B. D. 398, 57 L. J. Q. B. 507.

be liable. Davie *v.* Levy, 39 La. An. 551, 2 So. Rep. 395. See Pierce *v.* German L.w & Loan Soc., 72 Cal. 180, 13 Pac. Rep. 478.

Where one who has erected a nuisance on his land conveys the land to a purchaser who continues the nuisance, the vendor remains liable, and the purchaser is also liable if after notice he does not remove it. Thus in Brady *v.* Weeks (3 Barb. 161), the court said: "Whenever the erector of a nuisance owns the premises on which the nuisance is erected, and lets the premises to another, an action on the case will lie against him, for the injury the nuisance occasions while the premises are in the occupation of his lessee. The demise in such case affirms the continuance of the nuisance, and it may be said to be a continuation of the nuisance by the lessor." See Waggoner *v.* Jermaine, 3 Denio, 310; Plumer *v.* Harper, 3 N. H. 88; Staple *v.* Spring, 10 Mass. 74; Sloggy *v.* Dilworth (Minn.), 36 N. W. Rep. 451; Alexander *v.* Kerr, 2 Rawle, 83; Blunt *v.* Aiken, 15 Wend. 522; Rouse *v.* Chicago etc. R. Co., 42 Ill. App. 421; Lohmiller *v.* The Indian Fork Water Power Co., 51 Wis. 683; Walter *v.* Commissioners, 35 Md. 385; Steinke *v.* Bentley (Ind. App.), 34 N. E. Rep. 97. In the case of Slight *v.* Gutzlaff (35 Wis. 675), it was held that where a lessee or grantee *continues* a nuisance, of a nature not essentially unlawful, erected by his lessor or grantor, he is liable to an action for it only *after notice* to reform and abate it. But in Dickson *v.* Chicago, etc. R. Co. (71 Mo. 575) it was held to be sufficient if he knew of the existence of the nuisance. See Morris etc. Co *v.* Ryerson, 27 N. J. L. 457. It is an undisputed proposition that the tenant is liable for a nuisance produced only by his own act. Tale *v.* Missouri etc. R. Co., 64 Mo. 149; Wasner *v.* Delaware etc. Co., 80 N. Y. 212; Tow *v.* Roberts, 108 Pa. St. 489; Knauss *v.* Brua, 107 Pa. St. 85; Samuelson *v.* Cleveland etc., 40 Mich. 164; Owings *v.* Jones, 9 Md. 108; Norton *v.* Wiswall, 26 Barb. 618; Helmstreet *v.* Howland, 5 Denio, 68; St. Louis *v.* Kaine, 2 Mo. App. 66; Felton *v.* Deall, 22 Vt. 170; Mahoney *v.* Atlantic etc. R. Co., 63 Me. 68; Schmidt *v.* Cook, 25 N. Y. S. Rep. 799, 30 Abb. N. C. 285, 4 Misc. Rep. 85.

Private corporations are liable for nuisances like individuals and so

if it is caused by the omission of repairs which as between himself and the tenant he is bound to do (*f*), but not otherwise (*g*). If the landlord has not agreed to repair, he is not liable for defects of repair happening during the tenancy, even if he habitually looks to the repairs in fact (*h*). It seems the better opinion that where the tenant is bound to repair, the lessor's knowledge, at the time of letting, of the state of the property demised makes no difference and that only something amounting to an authority to continue the nuisance will make him liable (*i*).

Again an occupier who by licence (not parting with the possession) authorizes the doing on his land of something whereby a nuisance is created is liable (*k*). But a lessor is not liable merely because he has demised to a tenant something capable of being so used as to create a nuisance, and the tenant has so used it (*l*). Nor is the owner not in possession bound to take any active steps to remove a nuisance which has been created on his land without his authority and against his will (*m*).

If one who has erected a nuisance on his land conveys the land to a purchaser who continues the nuisance, the vendor remains liable (*n*), and the purchaser is also liable if on request he does not remove it (*o*).

(*g*) *Pretty* v. *Bickmore* (1873), L. R. 8 C. P. 401. *Gwinnell* v. *Eamer* (1875), L. R. 10 C. P. 658.

(*h*) *Nelson* v. *Liverpool Brewery Co.* (1877), 2 C. P. D. 311, 46 L. J. C. P. 675. *Rich* v. *Basterfield* (1847), 4 C. B. 783, 16 L. J. C. P. 273.

(*o*) *Pretty* v. *Bickmore* (1873), L. R. 8 C. P. 401. *Gwinnell* v. *Eamer* (1875), L. R. 10 C. P. 658.

(*k*) *White* v. *Jameson* (1874), 18 Eq. 303.

(*l*) *Rich* v. *Basterfield* (1847), 4 C. B. 783, 16 L. J. C. P. 273.

(*m*) *Saxby* v. *Manchester & Sheffield R. Co.* (1869), L. R. 4 C. P. 198, 38 L. J. C. P. 153, where the defendants had given the plaintiff licence to abate the nuisance himself so far as they were concerned.

(*n*) *Roswell* v. *Prior* (1701), 12 Mod. 635.

(*o*) *Penruddock's ca.*, 5 Co. Rep. 101 a.

---

it municipal corporations except when shielded by special laws Mehrhof etc. Co. v. Delaware, etc. R Co., 51 N. J. L. 56, 16 At. Rep. 12; Taylor v. Mayor, etc. of Cumberland, 64 Md. 78, 20 At. Rep. 1027, Lostutter v. The City of Aurora, 126 Ind. 436, 26 N. E. Rep. 184, Mootry v. Town of Danbury, 45 Conn. 550, Hubbell v. City of Viroqua, 67 Wis. 343, 30 N. W. Rep. 847, Attwood v. City of Bangor, 83 Me. 582, 22 At. Rep. 466, Bacon v. City of Boston, 154 Mass. 100, 28 N. E. Rep. 9. See corporation cases cited generally under MOORS OF ANNOYANCE, *ante*, p. 502.

CHAPTER XI.

NEGLIGENCE (a).

I. — *The General Conception.*

Omission contrasted with action as ground of liability For acts and their results (within the limits expressed by the term "natural and probable consequences," and discussed in a foregoing chapter, and subject to the grounds of justification and excuse which have also been discussed) the actor is, generally speaking, held answerable by law. For mere omission a man is not, generally speaking, held answerable. Not that the consequences or the moral gravity of an omission are necessarily less. One who refrains from stirring to help another may be, according to the circumstances, a man of common though no more than common good will and courage, a fool, a churl, a coward, or little better than a murderer. But, unless he is under some specific duty of action, his omission will not in any case be either an offence or a civil wrong. The law does not and cannot undertake to make men render active service to their neighbours at all times when a good or a brave man would do so (b). Some already existing relation of duty must be established, which relation will be found in most cases, though not in all, to depend on a foregoing voluntary act of the party held liable. He was

---

(a) Those who seek fuller information on the subject of this chapter may find it in Mr Thomas Beven's exhaustive and scholarly monograph ("Principles of the Law of Negligence," London, 1889).

(b) See Note M. to the Indian Penal Code as originally framed by the Commissioners Yet attempts of this kind have been made in one or two recent Continental proposals for the improvement of criminal law

not in the first instance bound to do anything at all; but by some independent motion of his own he has given hostages, so to speak, to the law. Thus I am not compelled to be a parent; but if I am one, I must maintain my children. I am not compelled to employ servants; but if I do, I must answer for their conduct in the course of their employment. The widest rule of this kind is that which is developed in the law of Negligence. One who enters on the doing of anything attended with risk to the persons or property of others is held answerable for the use of a certain measure of caution to guard against that risk. To name one of the commonest applications, "those who go personally or bring property where they know that they or it may come into collision with the persons or property of others have by law a duty cast upon them to use reasonable care and skill to avoid such a collision" (c). The caution that is required is in proportion to the magnitude and the apparent imminence of the risk: and we shall see that for certain cases the policy of the law has been to lay down exceptionally strict and definite rules. While some acts and occupations are more obviously dangerous than others, there is hardly any kind of human action that may not, under some circumstances, be a source of some danger.

General duty of caution in acts. Thus we arrive at the general rule that every one is bound to exercise due care towards his neighbours in his acts and conduct, or rather

(c) Lord Blackburn, 3 App. Ca. at p. 1206.

General duty of caution in acts. Every person is bound to exercise that degree of care, with reference to others, which is dictated by common prudence. Also, the care exercised must, in each instance, be commensurate with the apparent avoidable danger. "A careful man is guided by a reasonable estimate of possibilities. His precaution is measured by that which appears likely in the usual course of things. The rule does not require him to use every possible precaution to avoid injury to others. He is only required to use such reasonable precautions to prevent accidents as would ordinarily be

omits or falls short of it at his peril; the peril, namely, of being liable to make good whatever harm may be a proved consequence of the default (d)

Overlapping of contract and tort. In some cases this ground of liability may co-exist with a liability on contract towards the same person, and arising (as regards the

(d) Cp per Brett M. R., *Heaven v. Pender* (1883), 11 Q B Div at p 507

---

adopted by careful, prudent persons under like circumstances" Baker v Savage, 45 N Y 191, followed in Schmidt v S & H P Ry Co, 132 N Y 566, 30 N E Rep 389 See Indianapolis Union Ry Co v Boettcher, 131 Ind 82, 22 N. E Rep. 551, Presby v Grand Trunk Ry (N H), 22 At Rep 554, Albee v The Chappaqua Shoe Mfg Co, 62 Hun, 223, 16 N Y S Rep 687, G C & S F Ry. Co v Box, 81 Tex 670, 17 S W. Rep 375, S W Tel. & Telephone Co v Robinson, 50 Fed. Rep 810, 1 C C A 681, Schubert v Clark Co, 49 Minn. 331, Heizer v Kingsland etc. Co, 110 Mo 605, 19 S W Rep 630, McNally v Colwell, 91 Mich. 527; 52 N. W Rep. 70, Cowley v Colwell, 91 Mich 537, 52 N. W Rep 73, Dehring v Comstock, 78 Mich 153, 43 N. W. Rep 1019, Unger v. Forty-second etc. R. Co., 51 N Y 501, Maker v. Slater Mill Power Co., 15 R I. 112, Kalbus v. Abbott, 77 Wis. 627, 46 N. W Rep. 810, Shelly v City of Austin, 74 Tex. 608, 12 S. W Rep. 753

Thus, "The law imposes upon all persons using a highway, whether upon land or water, the obligation to exercise ordinary care to avoid inflicting injury upon others" Kelsey v. Barney, 12 N Y. 429, City of Austin v Ritz, 72 Tex 392, 9 S W Rep. 884, Middlestadt v Morrison (Wis), 44 N W Rep 1103, Potter v Moran, 61 Mich 60, 27 N W. Rep 854; Stringer v Frost, 116 Ind. 477, 19 N E Rep. 331, Wendell v. N Y Cent. etc R R. Co, 91 N. Y. 420, Williams v. Grealy, 112 Mass 79, Harris v Simon (N. C.), 10 S E Rep 1076, Hudson v Houser, 123 Ind 309, 24 N E Rep 243, Riley v Farnum, 62 N H. 42, Alexander v Humber, 86 Ky 565, Murphy v Orr, 96 N Y 114.

Overlapping of contract and tort Where there exists between the parties relations of *duty* as defined above and they have been disregarded, the right of action in favor of the injured party against the negligent party is not prohibited by the fact that the *duty* itself arose out of a contract The foundation of an action may be a contract, and the *gravamen* of it the breach of the contract. Unless the contract creates a relation, out of which relation springs a duty, independent of the mere contract obligation, though there may be a breach of the contract, there is no tort, since there is no duty to be violated. "It may be granted that an omission to perform a contract is never a tort, unless

breach) out of the same facts. Where a man interferes gratuitously, he is bound to act in a reasonable and prudent manner according to the circumstances and opportunities of the case. And this duty is not affected by the fact, if so it be, that he is acting for reward, in other words, under a contract, and may be liable on the contract (e). The two duties are distinct, except so far as the same party cannot be compensated twice over for the

(e) This appears to be the substance of the rule intended to be laid down by Brett M. R. in *Heaven v. Pender* (1883), 11 Q. B. D. at pp. 507-510, his judgment was however understood by the other members of the Court (Cotton and Bowen L. JJ.) as formulating some wider rule to which they could not assent. The case itself comes under the special rules defining the duty of occupiers (see Chap. XII below). And, so far as the judgment of Brett M. R. purported to exhibit those rules as a simple deduction from the general rule as to negligence, it is submitted that the dissent of the Lords Justices was well founded. And see Cooley on Negligence, 63.

the omission is also an omission of a legal duty, yet, such legal duty may arise, not merely out of certain relations of trust and confidence, inherent in the nature of the contract itself, but may spring from extraneous circumstances, not constituting elements of the contract as such, although connected with and dependent upon it and born of that wider range of legal duty which is due from every man to his fellow, * * * The whole doctrine is accurately and concisely stated in 1 Chit. Pl. 135 that 'if a common-law duty results to be sued in tort from any negligence or misfeasance in the execution of the contract.'" Rich v. New York Cent. etc. R. Co., 87 N. Y. 389, 11 Am. and Eng. R. Cas. 534, citing Kerwhacker v. C. C. & C. R. Co., 3 Ohio St. 188, Benton v. Pratt, 2 Wend. 385, Bebinger v. Sweet, 1 Abb. N. C. 263. See Robinson v. Threadgill, 13 Ired. 39, Champlain v. Rowley, 13 Wend. 261; Dean v. McLean, 48 Vt. 412, 21 Am. Rep. 130, Bell v. Cummings, 3 Sneed (Tenn.), 149, Vanleer v. Fain, 6 Humph. 104. Horsely v. Branch, 1 Id. 198, Lane v. Cameron, 38 Wis. 603.

"The principle running through all the cases seem to be that where the action is maintainable for the tort simply, without reference to any contract between the parties, the action is one of tort purely, although the existence of a contract may have been the occasion or furnished the opportunity for committing the tort. But where the action is not maintainable without proving and pleading the contract, where the gist of the action is the breach of the contract, either by malfeasance or nonfeasance, it is, in substance, whatever may be the form of the pleading, an action on the contract, and hence all persons jointly liable must be sued." Whittaker v. Collins, 34 Minn. 299. See Weld v. Saratoga & S. R. Co., 19 Wend. 533.

same facts, once for the breach of contract and again for the wrong. Historically the liability in tort is older; and indeed it was by a special development of this view that the action of assumpsit, afterwards the common mode of enforcing simple contracts, was brought into use (*f*). "If a smith prick my horse with a nail, etc., I shall have my action upon the case against him, *without any warranty by the smith to do it well.* . . . For it is the duty of every artificer to exercise his art rightly and truly as he ought" (*g*). This overlapping of the regions of Contract and Tort gives rise to troublesome questions which we are not yet ready to discuss. They are dealt with in the concluding chapter of this book. Meanwhile we shall have to use for authority and illustration many cases where there was a co-existing duty *ex contractu*, or even where the duty actually enforced was of that kind. For the obligation of many contracts is, by usage and the nature of the case, not to perform something absolutely, but to use all reasonable skill and care to perform it. Putting aside the responsibilities of common carriers and innkeepers, which are peculiar, we have this state of things in most agreements for custody or conveyance, a railway company's contract with a passenger for one. In such cases a total refusal or failure to perform the contract is rare. The kind of breach commonly complained of is want of due care in the course of performance. Now the same facts may admit of being also regarded as a wrong apart from the contract, or they may not. But in either case the questions, what was the measure of due care as between the defendant and the plaintiff, and whether such care was used, have to be dealt with on the same principles. In other words, negligence in performing a contract and

---

(*f*) Cp. the present writer's "Principles of Contract," p. 141, 5th ed., and Prof. Ames's articles, "The History of Assumpsit," in Harv. Law Rev. ii. 1, 53.

(*g*) F. N. B. 94 D. As to the assumption of special skill being a material element cp. *Shiells* v. *Blackburne* (1789), 2 H. Bl. 158, 2 R. R. 750; where "gross negligence" appears to mean merely actionable negligence.

negligence independent of contract create liability in different ways: but the authorities that determine for us what is meant by negligence are in the main applicable to both.

Definition of negligence. The general rule was thus stated by Baron Alderson: "Negligence is the omission to do something which a reasonable man, guided upon those

---

Definition of negligence. The American cases defining negligence are in harmony with the text, *vide* Great Western R. Co. v. Haworth, 39 Ill 353; Chicago, etc. R. Co. v. Johnson, 103 Ill 521, citing Towanda R Co. v. Munger, 5 Denio, 267, Gardner v Heartt, 3 Id. 236, Railroad Co. v. Jones, 95 U. S. 439, Great Western R. Co. v. Haworth, 39 Ill. 353. See Hammond v. Town of Mukwa, 40 Wis. 35; Wilson v. New York, etc. R Co., 11 Gill. & J. 58; Kansas City etc. R. Co. v Stone, 49 Fed Rep 209, 4 U. S. App. 109; 1 C. C. A. 231; Doyle v Chicago, St. P. & K C Ry Co., 77 Ia. 607; 42 N. W. Rep. 555; Kasparl v. Marsh, 74 Wis. 566, 43 N. W. Rep. 368; Rosenfield v. Arwe, 44 Minn. 395, 46 N. W. Rep 768, Simmons v. Everson, 125 N. Y 319; 26 N. E. Rep. 911, Tucker v. Illinois C. R. Co., 42 La. An. 114; 7 So Rep. 124, Smothurst v. Barton Square Church, 148 Mass. 265; 19 N. E. Rep. 387; City of Anderson v. East, 117 Ind. 126; 19 N. E. Rep. 726, Holmes v Drew, 151 Mass 578; 25 N. E. Rep 22; Galloway v. Chicago, etc Ry. Co. (Ia.), 54 N. W. Rep. 447, Holmes v. Atchison, etc. R Co, 48 Mo. App. 79; Texas & P. Ry. Co. v. Gorman (Tex. Civ. App) 21 S. W. Rep. 158.

One may act in perfect good faith and still be guilty of gross negligence. Negligence and willfulness are the opposite of each other. They indicate radically different mental states. Lincoln v. Buckmaster, 32 Vt. 642; Sharp v. Bonner, 36 Ga 418; Grand Trunk Ry. Co. v. Ives, 144 U. S. 47; 12 S. Ct. Rep. 679, Blaen Avon Coal Co. v. McCulloh, 59 Md. 403, Wallard v. Wortham, 84 Ill. 446, Noyes v. Shepherd, 30 Me. 173; McLelland v Louisville, etc. R. Co., 94 Md. 276, Morgan v. Curley, 142 Mass. 107, Smith v. Goodman, 75 Ga. 198; West v. Forrest, 114 Mass. 519, Jefferson, etc. R. Co. v. Riley, 89 Ind. 568; Carter v. Louisville etc. R Co., 98 Ind. 555; 8 Am & Eng. R. Cas. 347, 22 Am. & Eng. R. Cas. 360, Brown v. Chicago, etc. R. Co., 54 Wis. 342, 3 Am. & Eng. R. Cas. 444, Columbus etc. R. Co v. Bridges, 86 Ala. 448, Peoria Bridge Assn. v Loomis, 20 Ill. 235, 71 Am. Dec 263; Toledo etc. R. Co. v. Bryan, 107 Ind. 51; Cleveland etc. R Co. v. Asbury, 120 Ind. 289; Louisville etc. R. Co. v. Filbern, 6 Bush, 574; 99 Am. Dec. 690; Lexington v. Lewis, 10 Bush, 677; Paducah etc. R Co. v. Letcher (Ky.), 12 Am. & Eng. R. Cas. 61; Moody v. McDonald, 4 Cal. 297, Norfolk etc. R. Co. v. Ormsby, 27 Gratt. 455.

The questions which arise upon what constitutes negligence, usually

considerations which ordinarily regulate the conduct of human affairs, would do, or doing something which a prudent and reasonable man would not do" (*h*). It was not necessary for him to state, but we have always to remember, that negligence will not be a ground of legal liability unless the party whose conduct is in question is already in a situation that brings him under the duty of taking care. This, it will be observed, says nothing of the party's state of mind, and rightly. Jurisprudence is not psychology,

---

(*h*) *Blyth* v. *Birmingham Waterworks Co* (1856), 11 Ex. at p 781, 25 L. J. Ex. at p. 213, adopted by Brett J in *Smith* v *L & S W. R Co* (1870), L. R 5 C. P. at p 102.

---

relate not to the meaning of the word, but the question of fact "Negligence, in one sense is a quality attaching to acts dependent upon and arising out of the duties and relations of the parties concerned, and is as much a fact to be found by the jury as the alleged acts to which it attaches, by virtue of such duties and relations" Texas & P. Ry. Co. v. Murphy, 46 Tex 366, followed in Rowland v. Murphy, 66 Id. 536; 1 S. W. Rep. 658. See Kerwhacker v. C. C. & C. R. Co., 3 Ohio St. 186; Carter v. Columbia & G R. Co., 19 S. C. 24, Salmon v Railroad Co., 38 N. J. L. 11; Sunney v. Holt, 15 Fed. Rep. 880, Backus v. Hart, 18 Id. 691, Parrott v. Wells, 15 Wall. 534, Crandall v. Goodrich Transp. Co., 16 Fed. Rep. 75; Baltimore, etc R. Co v Jones, 95 U S. 439.

From the definitions it may be concluded that the term negligence, in its legal acceptation, includes acts of omission as well as of commission, while diligence implies action as well as forbearance to act. Grant v. Moseley, 29 Ala 302.

The Roman jurists maintained that there were but two grades of negligence, *culpa*, gross negligence, and *culpa levis*, ordinary negligence. But the common law recognizes a triple classification: ordinary negligence, slight negligence and gross negligence See Louisville etc. R. Co. v. McCoy (Ky.), 15 Am. & Eng R. Cas. 277; Fowler v. Baltimore etc. R.Co., 18 W. Va 579; 8 Am. & Eng. R. Cas. 480; Wabash etc. R. Co. v. Locke, 112 Ind. 404, Milwaukee etc. R. Co. v. Arms, 91 U. S. 494; Simpkins v. Columbia etc R Co., 20 S. C. 258; 19 Am. & Eng. R Cas 467; Richmond etc. R. Co v. Howard, 79 Ga. 44, Wormell v. Maine Cent. R. Co., 79 Me. 397; Am. & Eng. R. Cas. 272; Norfolk etc. R. Co v. Budge, 85 Va. 68; Meredith v. Reed, 26 Ind. 334; Pratt v. Wells, Fargo etc., 15 Wall. 524; Petrie v. Columbia & G. R Co., 29 S. C. 303; 7 S. E. Rep. 515; Cayzer v. Taylor, 10 Gray, 274; Cunningham v. Hall, 4 Allen, 268; Central R. R. Co. v. Moore, 24 N J. L. 624; Penn. R. Co v. Ogler, 35 Pa St. 60.

and law disregards many psychological distinctions not because lawyers are ignorant of their existence, but because for legal purposes it is impracticable or useless to regard them. Even if the terms were used by lawyers in a peculiar sense, there would be no need for apology; but the legal sense is the natural one. Negligence is the contrary of diligence, and no one describes diligence as a state of mind. The question for judges and juries is not what a man was thinking or not thinking about, expecting or not expecting, but whether his behaviour was or was not such as we demand of a prudent man under the given circumstances. Facts which were known to him, or by the use of appropriate diligence would have been known to a prudent man in his place, come into account as part of the circumstances. Even as to these the point of actual knowledge is a subordinate one as regards the theoretical foundation of liability. The question is not so much what a man of whom diligence was required actually thought of or perceived, as what would have been perceived by a man of ordinary sense who did think (*i*). A man's responsibility may be increased by his happening to be in possession of some material information beyond what he might be expected to have. But this is a rare case.

As matter of evidence and practice, proof of actual knowledge may be of great importance. If danger of a well understood kind has in fact been expressly brought to the defendant's notice as the result of his conduct, and the express warning has been disregarded or rejected (*j*), it is both easier and more convincing to prove this than to show in a general way what a prudent man in the defendant's place ought to have known. In an extreme case reckless omission to use care, after notice of the risk, may be held, as matter of fact, to prove a mischievous inten-

---

(*i*) Brett M. R., 11 Q. B. Div 508.
(*j*) As in *Vaughan* v *Menlove* (1887), 3 Bing. N C 468, where the defendant after being warned that his haystack was likely to take fire, said he would chance it (pp. 471, 477).

tion; or, in the terms of Roman law, *culpa lata* may be equivalent to *dolus*. For purposes of civil liability it is seldom (if ever) necessary to decide this point.

The standard of duty does not vary with individual ability. We have assumed that the standard of duty is not the foresight and caution which this or that particular man is capable of, but the foresight and caution of a prudent man — the average prudent man, or, as our books rather affect to say, a reasonable man — standing in this or that man's shoes (*k*). This idea so pervades the mass of

---

(*l*) Compare the Aristotelian use of ὁ φρόνιμος or ὁ σπουδαῖος in determining the standard of moral duty

---

The standard of duty does not vary with individual ability. To establish a rule that the standard of duty varies with either the physical or mental ability of each individual would not only be unreasonable but impracticable, since, it would then become necessary to inquire into the capacity for diligence and caution in each particular case and determine whether the degree of care exercised was or was not commensurate with the ability of the individual, without reference to precedent or the established rules of law. Accordingly in the case of Worthington v. Mencer (Ala.), 11 So. Rep. 78, the court said: "If he was merely a person of dull mind, who could labor for his own livelihood, and there was no apparent necessity of putting him under the protection of a guardian to keep him out of harm's way, he is chargeable with the same degree of care for his personal safety as one of brighter intellect, as any attempt to fraud and adopt varying rules of responsibility to varying degrees of intelligence would necessarily involve confusion and uncertainty in the law." See Berg v. City of Milwaukee, 83 Wis. 599, 53 N. W Rep 890.

In America where women have triumphantly entered the forum, the pulpit and the political arena, and where in a few of the States the ancient principles of the common law have been overthrown and females invested with the statutory right to vote and hold office, it is natural that there should have arisen the question whether sex affected this standard of duty. In the case of Hessenyer v. Michigan Cent R. (48 Mich 205; 42 Am. Rep. 470), it is said by the court that, "Sex is certainly no excuse for negligence. * * * And if we judge of ordinary care by the standard of what is commonly looked for and expected, we should probably agree that a woman would be more prudent, careful and particular in many positions and in the performance of many duties than a man would." Citing Fox v Glastenberg, 29 Conn. 204.

our authorities that it can be appreciated only by some familiarity with them. In the year 1837 it was formally and decisively enounced by the Court of Common Pleas (*l*). The action was against an occupier who had built a rick of hay on the verge of his own land, in such a state that there was evident danger of fire, and left it there after repeated warning. The hayrick did heat, broke into flame, and set fire to buildings which in turn communicated the fire to the plaintiff's cottages, and the cottages were destroyed. At the trial the jury were directed " that the question for them to consider was whether the fire had been occasioned by gross negligence on the part of the defendant," and " that he was bound to proceed with such reasonable caution as a prudent man would have exercised under such circumstances." A rule for a new trial was obtained " on the ground that the jury should have been directed to consider, not whether the defendant had been guilty of gross negligence with reference to the standard of ordinary prudence, a standard too uncertain to afford any criterion; but whether he had acted *bona fide* to the best of his judgment; if he had, he ought not to be responsible for the misfortune of not possessing the highest (*m*) order of negligence." The Court unanimously declined to accede to this view. They declared that the care of a prudent man was the accustomed and the proper measure of duty. It had always been so laid down, and the alleged uncertainty of the rule had been found no obstacle to its application by juries. It is not for the Court to define a prudent man, but for the jury to say whether the defendant behaved like one. " Instead of saying that the liability for negligence should be coextensive with the judgment of each individual — which would be as variable as the length of the foot of each

(*l*) *Vaughan* v *Menlove* (1837), 3 Bing N. C. 468

(*m*) This misrepresents the rule of law not the highest intelligence, but intelligence not below the average prudent man's, being required

individual — we ought rather to adhere to the rule which requires in all cases a regard to caution such as a man of ordinary prudence would observe" (n). Quite lately the same principle has been enforced in the Supreme Court of Massachusetts. "If a man's conduct is such as would be reckless in a man of ordinary prudence, it is reckless in him. Unless he can bring himself within some broadly defined exception to general rules, the law deliberately leaves his personal equation or idiosyncracies out of account, and peremptorily assumes that he has as much capacity to judge and to foresee consequences as a man of ordinary prudence would have in the same situation" (o).

Diligence includes competence. It will be remembered that the general duty of diligence includes the particular duty of competence in cases where the matter taken in hand is of a sort requiring more than the knowledge or ability which any prudent man may be expected to have. The test is whether the defendant has done "all that any skilful person could reasonably be required to do in such a case" (p). This is not an exception or extension, but a necessary application of the general rule. For a reasonable man will know the bounds of his competence, and will not intermeddle (save in extraordinary emergency) where he is not competent.

(n) Tindal C J, 3 Bing N. C. at p. 475
(o) *Commonwealth* v *Pierce* (1884), 138 Mass 165, 52 Am Rep 264, per Holmes J See too per Bayley J in *Jones* v. *Bird* (1822), 5 B & A. at pp 845-6
(p) Bayley J , 5 B. & A at p. 846.

Diligence includes competence This subject is fully discussed in preceding pages (26, 27). For additional authorities, *vide* Davis *v.* Chapman, 83 Va 67; 1 S E Rep. 472; Union P. Ry. Co *v* Estes, 37 Kan 715; Alexander *v* Louisville etc. R Co., 83 Ky 589; 2 Am. & Eng. R Cas. 458; Squire *v.* Wright, 1 Mo App 172, Nelson *v.* Chicago etc. Ry Co., 60 Wis. 320, 22 Am. & Eng. R. Cas. 391; The New World *v* King, 16 How. 469, Page *v* Wells, 37 Mich. 415; Cunningham *v* Hall, 4 Allen, 276

II — *Evidence of Negligence.*

Negligence a question of mixed fact and law. Due care and caution, as we have seen, is the diligence of a reasonable man, and includes reasonable competence in cases where special competence is needful to ensure safety. Whether due care and caution have been used in a given case is, by the nature of things, a question of fact. But it is not a pure question of fact in the sense of being open as a matter of course and without limit. Not every one who suffers harm which he thinks can be set down to his neighbour's default is thereby entitled to the chance of a jury giving him damages. The field of inquiry has limits defined, or capable of definition, by legal principle and judicial discussion. Before the Court or the jury can proceed to pass upon the facts alleged by the plaintiff, the Court must be satisfied that those facts, if proved, are in law capable of supporting the inference that the defendant has failed in

---

Negligence a question of mixed fact and law. It may be said that the law determines the duty and the evidence shows whether the duty was performed. When there is no evidence of negligence, or where the facts in the case are undisputed and conclusively established, and there is no reasonable chance for drawing different conclusions from them, the question is one of law for the court, otherwise it is for the jury. "The court is required to charge the law, and the jury to find the facts. The law, however, does not state what facts proved will show the absence of ordinary care. It could not do so as applicable to every case which arises. The cases involving this question are so different in their facts, so various, so complicated, and arising under so many different circumstances, that it would be utterly impossible to lay down any general principle of law by which every special case could be measured and tested as to the fact of negligence, and which would enable the judge to say to the jury, as matter of law, such and such facts show absence or presence of ordinary care " Bridger v. Railroad Co., 25 N. C. 30. See Carrico v. West Virginia C. & P. Ry. Co., 35 W. Va. 397; 14 S. E. Rep. 12; Nolan v. New York, etc. R. Co., 53 Conn. 471, Needham v. Louisville & N. R. Co , 85 Ky. 423, 3 S. W. Rep. 797; Pittsburg, etc. R Co. v. Evans, 53 Pa. St 250; Eagan v Fitchburg R. Co., 101 Mass. 315, Maloy v. New York Cent. R. Co., 58 Barb. 182, Gagg v. Vetter, 41 Ind. 254, Pennsylvania Canal Co

what the law requires at his hands. In the current forensic phrase, there must be evidence of negligence. The peculiar relation of the judge to the jury in our common law system has given occasion for frequent and minute discussion on the propriety of leaving or not leaving for the decision of the jury the facts alleged by a plaintiff as proof of negligence. Such discussions are not carried on in the manner best fitted to promote the clear statement of principles; it is difficult to sum up their results, and not always easy to reconcile them.

The tendency of modern rulings of Courts of Appeal has

---

v. Bentley, 66 Pa. St. 30; Emery v. Railroad, 102 N. C 280; 9 S. E. Rep. 189, Chicago City Ry. Co. v Robinson, 127 Ill. 1; Pike v. Grand Trunk Ry. Co., 39 Fed. Rep 258; Scheffer v. Railroad Co., 105 U. S. 249, Purvis v. Coleman, 1 Bosw. 321, Catawissa etc R. Co. v. Armstrong, 52 Pa. St. 282; Baltimore etc. R. Co. v. State, 86 Md. 366; Detroit etc. R. Co. v. Van Steinburg, 17 Mich 118; Philadelphia, etc R v. Frank, 67 Md. 839, Sutton v. New York, etc. R. Co., 66 N. Y. 243; Chicago etc. R. Co. v. McLanlen, 84 Ill 109, Tarwater v Hannibal R Co., 42 Mo. 193, Coppins v. New York, etc. R. Co , 43 Hun, 26, Simms v. South Carolina R. Co , 27 S.C 268, 30 Am. & Eng. R Cas. 571, Ohio etc. R. Co. v. Collarn, 73 Ind. 261; 5 Am. & Eng. R. Cas 554; Lincoln v. Gillilan, 18 Neb 114; Johnson v. Missouri Pac R. Co., 18 Neb. 690, Hathaway v. East Tennessee, etc. R. Co , 29 Fed. Rep 489; Hoyt v. Hudson, 41 Wis. 105, Philadelphia, etc R Co. v Schertle, 97 Pa St. 450; 2 Am. & Eng. R Cas 168; Boland v Missouri R Co , 36 Mo 484; Brower v. Edson, 47 Mich. 91; Barton v St Louis, etc , R. Co. 52 Mo. 253; New York, etc. R. Co v. Skinner, 19 Pa St 298, New Jersey Express Co. v. Nichols, 33 N. J. L. 434; Pennsylvania R Co. v. Righter, 42 Id. 180; 2 Am. & Eng. R. Cas. 220; Sullivan v Chrysolyte Mining Co., 21 Fed Rep. 892; Pleasants v. Fant, 22 Wall. 116, Filer v. New York Cent. R. Co., 49 N. Y. 47, Beaulieu v Portland Co., 48 Me 291, Cagger v. Lansing, 64 N. Y. 417; Bagley v. Cleveland Rolling Mill, 21 Fed. Rep. 159; Barton v. St. Louis & I. M. R. Co , 52 Mo. 253, Atkinson v. The Illinois Milk Co., 44 Mo. App 153, Chaffie v. Old Colony R. Co , 17 R. I. 658; 24 At Rep. 141; Woolwine v. C. & O. R. Co., 36 W. Va 329, 15 S. E Rep 85, Sexton v. Zett, 44 N. Y. 430; Woolfolk v. Macon & A. R. Co , 56 Ga. 457; Mississippi Cent. R. Co. v. Mason, 51 Miss. 234; Gonzolas v. New York etc. R. Co., 38 N. Y. 442; Goodlett v Louisville & N R. R. Co., 122 U. S. 391; Crowley v Strouse (Cal), 33 Pac. Rep. 456; State v Lauer (N. J.), 26 At. Rep. 180; Chicago, B. & Q. R. Co. v. Landauer (Neb.), 54 N. W. Rep. 976.

been, if not to enlarge the province of the jury, to arrest the process of curtailing it. Some distinct boundaries, however, are established.

Burden of proof. Where there is no contract between the parties, the burden of proof is on him who complains of negligence. He must not only show that he suffered

---

Burden of proof. Agreeing with the text that the burden of proof is on the plaintiff are numerous American cases. The plaintiff is not bound to prove more than enough to raise a fair presumption of negligence, on the part of the defendant, to plaintiff's injury. Rosenfield v. Ariol, 14 Minn. 395, 44 N. W Rep. 768. See Halbrook v. Utica etc. R. Co., 12 N. Y. 236; 64 Am. Dec. 502; Searles v. Manhattan R. Co., 101 N Y 661; 25 Am & Eng. R. Cas. 358; Seybold v. New York, etc R. Co., 95 N Y 562; 47 Am. Rep. 75; 18 Am. & Eng. R. Cas. 162, Hayes v. Mich. Cent. R Co., 111 U. S 228; 15 Am. & Eng. R. Cas. 394, Philadelphia etc. R. Co. v. Stibbing, 62 Md. 504; 19 Am. & Eng R. Cas. 3., Caldwell v. New Jersey Steamboat Co, 47 N. Y. 291, Stratton v Central City H. R. Co., 95 Ill 25; 1 Am. & Eng. R. Cas 115; Kane v. Hibernia Ins. Co., 39 N. J. L. 697, 23 Am. Rep. 239; Welch v. Jugenheimer, 56 Ia. 11, 41 Am. Rep 77, overruling Barton v. Thompson, 46 Ia. 80; 26 Am. Rep. 181; Hershberger v. Lynch (Pa.), 11 At. Rep. 642, Haskins v. Utah Northern Ry Co. (Idaho), 13 Pac Rep. 343; Seybolt v. New York etc. R. Co, 95 N. Y 562, 47 Am. Rep. 75, Gliddon v. McKintry, 25 Ala. 408, Chicago, B & Q. R. Co. v. Harwood, 90 Ill. 425; Allen v. Willard, 57 Pa St. 374; Hobson v New Mexico & A. R. Co. (Ariz), 11 Pac. Rep. 545, Dowell v. Guthrie, 99 Mo. 653, 12 S. W. Rep. 900, Thompson v. Duncan, 76 Ala. 339.

Where the rights and duties are equal and one is injured by another it is incumbent upon him to prove that the other was negligent before he can recover therefor. Thus, "foot passengers have equal rights in the streets with those mounted on horseback or driving in carriages. Neither have a priority of right over the other. Both are bound to use reasonable care to avoid collision." Stringer v Frost, 116 Ind. 477, 19 N. E Rep. 431, citing Belton v. Baxter, 54 N. Y. 245. So, where two persons collide in the street and one is injured it cannot be inferred that the other was negligent. See Hazel v Peoples' Pass. Ry. Co., 132 Pa St. 96; 18 At. Rep. 1116, 25 W N. C. 345; Piollet v. Simmers, 106 Pa. St 95; Pittsb. etc. Ry. Co v. Taylor, 104 Id. 306; North Side Street Ry. Co. v. Tippins (Tex. App) 14 S. W Rep. 1067; Broschart v. Tuttle, 59 Conn. 1; 21 At. Rep 925.

In England it is a general rule that it is not incumbent upon the plaintiff to prove that he was free from negligence or was using ordinary care While this doctrine has been followed in America by a number of cases,

harm in such a manner that it might be caused by the defendant's negligence; he must show that it was so caused, and to do this he must prove facts inconsistent with due diligence on the part of the defendant. "Where the evidence given is equally consistent with the existence or non-existence of negligence, it is not competent to the judge to leave the matter to the jury" (r).

(r) Williams J. in *Hammack* v *White* (1862), 11 C. B. N. S 588, 31 L. J. C P. 129, *Cotton* v. *Wood* (1860), 8 C. B. N. S 568, 29 L. J. C P 333, *Wakelin* v. *L & S W. R Co.* (1886), 12 App Ca 41.

---

the majority of the cases are to the contrary In the opinion of the court in the case of Owens v Railroad Co (88 N C. 506), the authorities are reviewed and this subject discussed. See Railroad Co. v. Gladman, 15 Wall 401, Indianapolis etc R Co. v Horst, 93 U S. 291. The rule is stated by the court in Hickley v. Railroad Co (120 Mass 262), as follows· "While, however, the plaintiff is to show that he was in the exercise of due care, and that no negligence of his contributed to the injury, this may be shown by proving the facts and circumstances from which it may fairly be inferred, and if all the circumstances under which an accident took place are put in evidence, and upon an examination of them nothing is found in the conduct of the plaintiff to which negligence can be fairly imputed, the mere absence of fault may justify the jury in finding due care on his part. See Mayo v. Boston & Maine Railroad, 104 Mass. 137. But, if there is only a partial disclosure of the facts, and no evidence is offered showing the conduct of the party injured in regard to matters specially requiring care on his part, the data for such an instance is not sufficient. It can only be warranted when circumstances are shown which fairly indicate care or exclude the idea of negligence on his part. Crafts v. Boston, 109 Mass. 519" Followed in Texas & N. O R. Co. v. Crowder, 63 Tex. 504. See Barber v Essex, 27 Vt. 62; Ribble v Starrat, 83 Mich. 140, 47 N W. Rep. 244; Strand v Chicago & W. M. Ry. Co., 67 Mich. 380; 34 N W. Rep 712, Lesaw v Maine Cent. R. Co , 77 Me. 85; Haws v Burlington, etc Ry Co., 64 Ia 315, Murphy v. Deane, 101 Mass. 455, Benson v. Titcomb, 72 Me. 31; McCully v Clarke, 40 Pa St. 399; Burns v Chicago etc. R. Co., 69 Ia. 450; 28 Am. & Eng. R. Cas. 409; 59 Am. Rep. 227; Hart v Hudson River Bridge Co., 80 N. Y. 622, Smith v Boston Gas Co., 129 Mass. 313; Street Ry. Co. v. Nothenius, 40 Ohio St. 376; 19 Am & Eng. R Cas. 191, Johnson v. Hudson R. R. Co., 20 N.Y. 65; 75 Am. Dec. 375; Tolman v. Syracuse etc. R. Co., 98 N. Y. 198; 23 Am. & Eng R. Cas 313; 50 Am. Rep. 649; Adams v. Young, 44 Ohio St. 80; 58 Am Rep. 789; Lee v. Troy Cit. Gas Co , 98 N. Y 115, Cassidy v Angel, 12 R. I. 447; 34 Am Rep 790, Pennsylvania R Co. v. Weber, 76

Nothing can be inferred, for example, from the bare fact that a foot-passenger is knocked down by a carriage in a place where they have an equal right to be, or by a train at a level crossing (s). Those who pass and repass in frequented roads are bound to use due care, be it on foot or on horseback, or with carriages: and before one can complain of another, he must show wherein care was wanting. "When the balance is even as to which party is in fault, the one who relies upon the negligence of the other is bound to turn the scale" (t). It cannot be assumed, in the absence of all explanation, that a train ran over a man more than the man ran against the train (u). If the carriage was being driven furiously, or on the wrong side of the road, that is another matter. But the addition of an ambiguous circumstance will not do.

Thus in *Cotton* v. *Wood* (v), the plaintiff's wife, having safely crossed in front of an omnibus, was startled by some other carriage, and ran back; the driver had seen her pass, and then turned round to speak to the conductor, so that he did not see her return in time to pull up and avoid mischief. The omnibus was on its right side and going at a moderate pace. Here there was no evidence of negligence on the part of the defendant, the owner of the omnibus (x). His servants, on the plaintiff's own showing, had not done anything inconsistent with due care. There was no proof that the driver turned round to speak to the conductor otherwise than for a lawful or necessary purpose, or had any reason to apprehend that somebody would run

(s) *Wakelin* v *L & S. W R Co*, last note.
(t) Erle C J, *Cotton* v. *Wood*, note (r).
(u) Lord Halsbury, 12 App. Ca. at p.
(v) See note (r) above
(x) It would be convenient if one could in these running-down cases on land personify the vehicle, like a ship.

Pa St. 157; 18 Am. Rep. 407; Schum v. Pennsylvania R. Co., 107 Pa. St. 8, 52 Am. Rep. 468; Stepp v. Chicago etc. R. Co., 85 Mo. 225; Ruffner v. Cincinnati etc. R. Co., 34 Ohio St. 96; Hinckley v. Cape Cod R. Co., 120 Mass. 257.

under the horses' feet at that particular moment. Again if a horse being ridden (*y*) or driven (*z*) in an ordinary manner runs away without apparent cause, and in spite of the rider's or driver's efforts trespasses on the footway and there does damage, this is not evidence of negligence. The plaintiff ought to show positively want of care, or want of skill, or that the owner or person in charge of the horse knew it to be unmanageable. " To hold that the mere fact of a horse bolting is *per se* evidence of negligence would be mere reckless guesswork " (*a*).

Sometimes it is said that the burden of proof is on the plaintiff to show that he was himself using due care, and it has been attempted to make this supposed principle a guide to the result to be arrived at in cases where the defence of contributory negligence is set up. This view seems to be rather prevalent in America (*b*), but in the present writer's opinion it is unsound. The current of English authority is against it, and it has been distinctly rejected in the House of Lords (*c*). What we consider to be the true view of contributory negligence will be presently explained.

Where there is contract or undertaking. This general principle has to be modified where there is a relation of contract between the parties, and (it should seem) when

---

(*y*) *Hammack* v. *White* (1862), 11 C. B. N S 588, 31 L J C P 129

(*z*) *Manzoni* v. *Douglas* (1880), 6 Q B. D 145, 50 L J Q B 289, where it was unsuccessfully attempted to shake the authority of *Hammack* v *White* The cases relied on for that purpose belong to a special class

(*a*) Lindley J., 6 Q B. D. at p. 158.
(*b*) *E. g Murphy* v. *Deane*, 101 Mass. 455
(*c*) *Wakelin* v *L & S W R. Co.* (1886), 12 App. Ca. 41, 47, 51, 56 L. J Q B 229, per Lord Watson and Lord Fitzgerald

---

Where there is contract or undertaking In *Chapman v. New Haven Railroad Co.* (19 N. Y. 341), it appears that there was a collision between the trains of two railroad companies, by which the plaintiff, a passenger in one of them, was injured. It was held, that the passenger by the railroad was not so identified with the proprietors of the train conveying him, or with their servants, as to be responsible for the negligence, and

there is a personal undertaking without a contract. A coach runs against a cart; the cart is damaged, the coach is upset, and a passenger in the coach is hurt. The owner of the cart must prove that the driver of the coach was in fault. But the passenger in the coach can say to the owner: "You promised for gain and reward to bring me safely to my journey's end, so far as reasonable care and skill could attain it. Here am I thrown out on the road with a broken head. Your contract is not performed; it is for you to show that the misadventure is due to a cause for which you are not answerable" (d).

When a railway train runs off the line, or runs into another train, both permanent way and carriages, or both trains (as the case may be) being under the same company's control, these facts, if unexplained, are as between the company and a passenger evidence of negligence (e).

(d) In other words (to anticipate part of a special discussion) the obligation does not become greater if we regard the liability as *ex delicto* instead of *ex contractu*, but neither does it become less.

(e) *Carpue* v *London & Brighton R. Co.* (1844), 5 Q B 747, 751, 13 L J Q B 138, *Skinner* v *L B & S C R. Co* (1850), 5 Ex 787

---

that he might recover against the proprietors of another train for injuries sustained for the collision through the negligence although there was such negligence in the management of the train conveying him as would have defeated an action by its owners. See Dyer v. Erie Ry Co., 71 N. Y. 228, Kansas City R etc. Co. v Stoner, 49 Fed. Rep. 209, 4 U S. App. 109, 1C C A. 231, Transfer Co. v Kelly, 36 Ohio St. 86, Wabash, St L & P Ry Co. v. Shacklet, 105 Ill. 364; Danville etc. Co. v. Stewart, 2 Metc. (Ky.) 119; Louisville etc R. Co. v. Case, 9 Bush, 728, Cuddy v Horn, 46 Mich. 596; State v Boston & M. R. Co., 80 Me 430, 15 At. Rep. 36; Holzab v. Railroad Co, 38 La. An. 185; 58 Am. Rep. 177

"There is no distinction in principle whether the passenger be on a public conveyance like a railroad train or an omnibus, or be on a hack hired from a public stand in the street for a drive. Those on a hack do not become responsible for the negligence of the driver if they exercised no control over him further than to indicate the route they wish to travel or the places to which they wish to go" Little v. Hackett, 116 U. S 379 See New York etc R Co. v. Steinbrenner, 47 N J. L. 161

In like manner if a man has undertaken, whether for reward or not, to do something requiring special skill, he may fairly be called on, if things go wrong, to prove his competence: though if he is a competent man, the mere fact of a mishap (being of a kind that even a competent person is exposed to) would of itself be no evidence of negligence. We shall see later that, where special duties of safe keeping or repair are imposed by the policy of the law, the fact of an accident happening is held, in the same manner, to cast the burden of proving diligence on the person who is answerable for it, or in other words raises a presumption of negligence. This is said without prejudice to the yet stricter rule of liability that holds in certain cases.

Things within defendant's control. Again there is a presumption of negligence when the cause of the mischief was apparently under the control of the defendant or his servants. The rule was declared by the Exchequer Chamber in 1865 (*f*), in these terms: —

"There must be reasonable evidence of negligence.

"But where the thing is shown to be under the management of the defendant or his servants, and the accident is such as in the ordinary course of things does not happen

---

(*f*) *Scott* v *London Dock Co*, 3 H & C 596, 34 L J Ex 220

Things within defendant's control The limited number of American cases on this subject support the statement of the text. Thus, in Treadwell *v.* Whittier (80 Cal 574, 19 N E. Rep. 331), it was held, that a plaintiff injured through the fall of a hydraulic elevator operated by the defendants, in which he was carried as a passenger, need only prove that he sustained injury by the breaking of the machinery by which he was carried, and that such machinery was under the control and management of the defendants, in order to make a case raising a presumption of negligence on the part of the defendants. See Dehring *v.* Comstock, 78 Mich. 153; Gardner *v.* Bennett, 38 N. Y. 197; Blake *v.* Ferris, 5 N Y. 48; Kelly *v* Mayor, 11 Id. 432; Vincent *v.* Cook, 4 Hun, 318, Robinson *v* N Y Cent. etc. R. Co., 65 Barb. 155.

if those who have the management use proper care, it affords reasonable evidence, in the absence of explanation by the defendants, that the accident arose from want of care."

Therefore if I am lawfully and as of right (*g*) passing in a place where people are handling heavy goods, and goods being lowered by a crane fall upon me and knock me down, this is evidence of negligence against the employer of the men who were working the crane (*h*).

Common course of affairs judicially noticed. The court will take judicial notice of what happens in the ordinary course of things, at all events to the extent of using their knowledge of the common affairs of life to complete or correct what is stated by witnesses. Judges do not affect, for example, to be ignorant that the slipping of one passenger out of several thousand in hurrying up the stairs of a railway station is not an event so much out of the run of pure accidents as to throw suspicion on the safety of the staircase (*i*).

On evidence sufficient in law, question is for jury. When we have once got something more than an ambiguously balanced state of facts; when the evidence, if

---

(*g*) That is not merely by the defendant's licence, as will be explained later.
(*h*) 3 H & C 596, Crompton, Byles, Blackburn, Keating, JJ., *diss.* Erle C. J. and Mellor J., but no dissenting judgment was delivered, nor does the precise ground of dissent appear.
(*i*) *Crafter* v *Metrop R Co* (1866), L. R. 1 C. P. 300, 35 L J C. P. 132

Common course of affairs judicially noticed. In the case of Harris v Cameron (81 Wis 239, 51 N. W. Rep. 437), where the facts, in substance, were that a father had purchased for his eleven year old son, an air gun, intended and commonly used as a toy and play-thing but by the careless use of which by another boy, to whom the son had loaned it, the eye of a third boy was destroyed. The court said "This court can take judicial knowledge of the nature and use of this air gun as it can of 'beer' (Briffitt v. State, 58 Wis. 39; 16 N. W. Rep. 39), or of 'gas' (Shepherd v. Gas-Light Co., 6 Wis. 539); or of an express or freight 'car' (Nichols v State, 68 Wis. 416; 32 N W. Rep. 543)."

believed, is less consistent with diligence than with negligence on the defendant's part, or shows the non-performance of a specific positive duty laid on him by statute,

---

On evidence sufficient in law, question for the jury. The rule stated in the text is recognized in America. See Cumberland R. Co v. Maugans, 61 Md 53; Lasky v. Canadian P. Ry Co., 83 Me 461, 22 At. Rep. 368; C B U. P. R Co. v. Hotham, 22 Kan 41. The classification of the cases within the province of the jury announced by editors Russell and Minor (16 Am. & Eng. Enc of Law, 406), is "1 When the facts which, if true, would constitute evidence of negligence, are controverted. 2. When such facts are not disputed, but there may be a fair difference of opinion as to whether the inference of negligence should be drawn. 3. When the facts are in dispute and the inferences to be drawn therefrom are doubtful" See Pittsburg etc R R Co. v. Andrews, 39 Md 444; Brahm v. Schwartz (Pa.), 18 At Rep. 643; Maher v. Manhattan Ry. Co., 53 Hun, 510; 6 N. Y. S. Rep 809; Richard v Schleusner, 41 Minn 49, 42 N. W. Rep. 599, Richmond & D R. Co v Howard, 79 Ga. 44; Fiske v Forsyth Dyeing Co., 57 Conn 118, G C & S. F. Ry. Co. v. Greenlee, 70 Tex 533; Needham v. L & N. R. Co , 85 Ky. 423, Ilwaco Ry. & Nav. Co v Hedrick, 1 Wash. St. 446; 25 Pac Rep 335, Quirk v Holt, 99 Mass. 164; Johnson v Bruner, 61 Pa St. 58, Balt. & O. R Co. v. Boteler, 38 Md. 568; Kansas P Ry. Co v. Richardson, 25 Kan. 391; McCready v South Car. R. R. Co , 2 Strobh. 356; Augusta & K R. Co v. Killian, 79 Ga. 234, 4 S E Rep. 165, Nugent v Boston, C. & M. R. Corp , 80 Me. 62, 12 At Rep. 797, Louisville & N R. Co. v. Mitchel, 87 Ky. 327 , 8 S. W. Rep. 706; Chautauqua Lake Ice Co. v. McLuckey (Pa.), 11 At. Rep. 616, Branham v. Central Railroad, 78 Ga 35; 1 S E. Rep 274; New York and C. M. S. & Co. v. Rogers, 11 Colo 6, 16 Pac. 719, Abel v. President, etc Co , 103 N Y. 581; 57 Am Rep. 773, Morse v. Belfast, 77 Me. 44, Lesaw v. Maine Cent R. Co , Id. 85; Dexter v. McCready, 54 Conn. 171; Stoker v. City of Minneapolis, 32 Minn. 478, Colorado Cent. R. Co. v Martin, 7 Colo. 592; Fassett v. Roxbury, 55 Vt. 552; Ruland v. South Newmarket, 59 N H. 291, Village of Jefferson v Chapman, 127 Ill 437; 20 N. E. Rep. 33; Ravencraft v Missouri Pac Ry. Co., 27 Mo. App. 617; Dealey v. Muller, 149 Mass 432; 21 N E. Rep. 763; City of Champaign v Jones, 132 Ill 304; 23 N. E Rep 1125, Frankord & B. T. Co. v. Phila. & T R Co., 54 Pa St. 345; Texas & P. Ry. Co. v. Murphy, 46 Tex. 356; Sloan v. Central Iowa R. Co., 62 Ia. 728; 11 Am. & Eng. R. Cas 145; Griffin v Auburn, 58 N. H. 121; Texas etc. R. Co v. Levi, 59 Tex. 674, 13 Am. & Eng. R Cas. 464; White v. Missouri Pac. R. Co., 31 Kan. 280; 13 Am. & Eng. R. Cas. 473, Hathaway v. East Tennessee, etc. R. Co., 29 Fed. Rep 489; Orange etc. R Co. v Ward, 47 N. J. L. 560; Tyler v. New York etc. R Co , 137 Mass. 238, 19 Am. & Eng. R. Cas. 296; Grabel v Wapello Coal Co , 30 W. Va 228; Ferry v. Manhattan P. Co., 54 N. Y Superior Ct. 325 Drevis v. Woods, 71 Wis. 329; Baldwin v. St.

contract, or otherwise; then the judgment whether the plaintiff has suffered by the defendant's negligence is a judgment of fact, and on a trial by jury must be left as such in the hands of the jury (*k*). It is true that the rules as to remoteness of damage set some bounds to the connexion of the defendant's negligence with the plaintiff's loss (*l*). But even in this respect considerable latitude has been allowed (*m*). Railway accidents have for the last thirty years or more been the most frequent occasions of defining, or attempting to define, the frontier between the province of the jury and that of the Court.

Recent railway cases on level crossings and "invitation to alight." Two considerable and well marked groups of cases stand out from the rest. One set may be broadly described as level crossing cases, and culminated in *North Eastern Railway Company* v. *Wanless*, decided by the House of Lords in 1874 (*n*); the other may still more roughly (but in a manner which readers familiar with the reports will at once understand) be called "invitation to alight" cases. These are now governed by *Bridges* v. *North London Railway Company* (*o*), another decision of the House of Lords which followed closely on *Wanless's* case. In neither of these cases did the House of Lords intend to lay down any new rule, nor any exceptional rule as regards railway companies; yet it was found needful a few years later to restate the general principle which had been supposed to be impugned. This was done in *Metropolitan Railway Company* v. *Jackson* (*p*).

(*k*) This is well put in the judgment in *M'Cully* v *Clark* (Pennsylvania, 1861). Bigelow L C 559

(*l*) *Metrop R Co* v *Jackson* (1877), 3 App Ca 193, 47 L J C P. 303.

(*m*) See *Williams* v *G W R Co* (1874), L R 9 Ex. 157, 43 L J Ex 105, *supra*, p.

38 Op per Lord Halsbury, 12 App Ca at p 43.

(*n*) L. R. 7 H L, 12, 43 L J Q B 185.

(*o*) L. R. 7 H L. 213, 43 L J Q B. 151 (1873-4)

(*p*) 3 App. Ca. 193, 47 L. J. C. P 303 (1877)

Louis etc R. Co., 72 In 45, Faris v Hoberg (Ind), 33 N. E Rep. 1028, Cincinnati etc Ry Co. v. Grames (Ind App), 34 N E. Rep. 613

Explanation in Metr. R. Co. v. Jackson. "The judge has a certain duty to discharge, and the jurors have another and a different duty. The judge has to say whether any facts have been established by evidence from which negligence *may be* reasonably inferred; the jurors have to say whether, from those facts, when submitted to them, negligence *ought to be* inferred. It is, in my opinion, of the greatest importance in the administration of justice that these separate functions should be maintained, and should be maintained distinct. It would be a serious inroad on the province of the jury, if, in a case where there are facts from which negligence may reasonably be inferred, the judge were to withdraw the case from the jury upon the ground that, in his opinion, negligence ought not to be inferred; and it would, on the other hand, place in the hands of the jurors a power which might be exercised in the most arbitrary manner, if they were at liberty to hold that negligence might be inferred from any state of facts whatever (*q*).

"On a trial by jury it is, I conceive, undoubted that the facts are for the jury, and the law for the judge. It is not, however, in many cases practicable completely to sever the law from the facts.

"But I think it has always been considered a question of law to be determined by the judge, subject, of course, to review, whether there is evidence which, if it is believed, and the counter evidence, if any, not believed, would establish the facts in controversy. It is for the jury to say whether, and how far, the evidence is to be believed. And if the facts as to which evidence is given are such that from them a farther inference of fact may legitimately be drawn, it is for the jury to say whether that inference is to be drawn or not. But it is for the judge to determine, subject to review, as a matter of law, whether from those facts that farther inference may legitimately be drawn" (*r*).

(*q*) Lord Cairns, at p. 197. (*r*) Lord Blackburn at p. 207.

The case itself was decided on the ground that the hurt suffered by the plaintiff was not the proximate consequence of any proved negligence of the defendants; not that there was no proof of the defendants having been negligent at all, for there was evidence which, if believed, showed mismanagement, and would have been quite enough to fix on the defendant company liability to make good any damage distinctly attributable to such mismanagement as its "natural and probable" consequence (*s*). As between the plaintiff and the defendant, however, evidence of negligence which cannot be reasonably deemed the cause of his injury is plainly the same thing as a total want of evidence. Any one can see that a man whose complaint is that his thumb was crushed in the door of a railway carriage would waste his trouble in proving (for example) that the train had not a head-light. The House of Lords determined, after no small difference of learned opinions below, that it availed him nothing to prove overcrowding and scrambling for seats. The irrelevance is more obvious in the one case than in the other, but it is only a matter of degree (*ss*).

The "level crossing" type of cases. In the "level crossing" group of cases we have some one crossing a railway at a place made and provided by the company for that

---

Ryder v *Wombwell* (1868), in Ex Ch., L R 4 Ex. 32, 38 L. J. Ex 8, which Lord Blackburn goes on to cite with approval.

(*s*) See pp 32, 36, above

(*ss*) Cp. *Pounder* v. *N. E R. Co.*, '92, 1 Q. B 385 (plaintiff assaulted by persons who had crowded in).

Railroad crossings "It is doubtless a rule of law that a person approaching a railroad crossing is bound, in so doing, to exercise such care, caution and circumspection to foresee danger and avoid injury as ordinary prudence would require, having in view all the known dangers of the situation; but precisely what such requirements would be must manifestly differ with the ever-varying circumstances under which such approach may be made. Ordinarily, of course, the diligent use of the senses of sight and hearing is the most obvious and practicable means of avoiding injury in such cases, but occasions may, and often do, arise

purpose, and where the company is under the statutory duty of observing certain precautions. The party assumes that the line is clear; his assumption is erroneous, and he

---

where the use of the senses would be unavailable, or where their non-use may be excused. The view may be obstructed by intervening objects, or by the darkness of the night. Other and louder noises, as is often the case in a city, may confuse the sense of hearing, and render its use impracticable

The railway company, by its flagman or other agent or agency, may put the person off his guard and induce him to cross the track without resorting to the usual precautions.

The duty may be more or less varied by the age, degree of intelligence, and mental capacity of the party and by a variety of other circumstances by which he might be surrounded " Terre Haute & I. R Co. v. Voelker, 129 Ill. 540, 22 N. E. Rep. 28. See Smedis v Brooklyn etc. R. Co, 88 N. Y. 13, 8 Am. & Eng R. Cas. 445, Guggenheim v. Lake Shore etc. R Co, 57 Mich 488, 22 Am & Eng. R. Cas. 546; Geveke v. Grand Rapids etc R Co., 57 Mich. 589, 22 Am & Eng. R Cas. 551, Louisville etc. R. Co. v Schmidt, 81 Ind. 264, 8 Am & Eng. R. Cas. 248, Pittsburg etc R. Co. v Martin, 82 Ind. 476; 8 Am. & Eng. R. Cas. 253; Kelley v. St Paul etc. R. Co., 29 Minn. 1; 6 Am. & Eng. R. Cas. 93; O'Mara v. Hudson River R. Co., 38 N Y 445, Baltimore etc. R. Co. v. Fitzpatrick, 35 Ind. 32; Pennsylvania R. Co. v. Killips, 88 Pa St. 413; Reading etc. R Co. v. Richtle, 102 Pa. St. 425, 19 Am & Eng. R. Cas. 267; Marcott v. Marquette etc. R Co., 29 N Y 315; Salter v. Utica etc. R Co., 88 N. Y 42, 8 Am. & Eng. R. Cas. 437, Continental Imp Co v Stead, 95 U. S. 161; Frick v. St. Louis etc. R. Co., 75 Mo. 595, 8 Am. & Eng. R. Cas. 280, 288, St Louis etc. R Co v Mathias, 50 Ind. 65; East Tennessee R Co. v White, 5 Lea, 540, 8 Am. & Eng. R. Cas. 65; Norton v Eastern R. Co , 113 Mass. 366, Sanborn v Detroit, etc. R Co , 91 Mich. 538; 50 Am & Eng. R. Cas. 114; Pollock v Eastern R. Co , 124 Mass 158; Parvis v. Phila. W. & B R. Co. (Del.), 17 At. Rep 705.

"Again, failure to look and listen for an approaching train, though such failure may contribute to the injury, can not, under all circumstances, be regarded as negligence. * * * When, therefore, a person about to cross a railroad track under a given state of circumstances, exercises that degree and amount of care which prudent persons usually exercise under like circumstances, he is without fault. In other words, when the circumstances are such that prudent persons would not ordinarily look or listen for an approaching train, there is no negligence in omitting to look or listen

If this be correct, it is plain, as a general rule, that whether contributory negligence existed or not, is a mixed question of law and facts, that is to say, a fact for the jury to find from such testimony as the law

is run down by a passing train. Here the company has not entered into any contract with him; and he must prove either that the company did something which would lead a reasonable man to assume that the line was clear for crossing (*t*), or that there was something in their arrangements which made it impracticable or unreasonably difficult to ascertain whether the line was clear or not. Proof of negligence in the air, so to speak, will not do. "Mere allegation or proof that the company were guilty of negligence is altogether irrelevant; they might be guilty of many negligent acts or omissions, which might possibly have occasioned injury to somebody, but had no connexion whatever with the injury for which redress is sought, and therefore the plaintiff must allege and prove, not merely that they were negligent, but that their negligence caused or materially contributed to the injury" (*u*). What may reasonably be held to amount to such proof cannot be laid down in general terms. "You

---

(*t*) As in *Wanless's* case, L. R. 7 H. L. 12, 43 L J Q B 185, where the gates (intended primarily for the protection of carriage traffic) were left open when they ought not to have been, so that the plaintiff was thrown off his guard.

(*u*) Lord Watson, *Wakelin v L. & S W R Co* (1886), 12 App. Ca 41, 47, 56 L J Q B 229

---

regards competent to prove it, and to be found in accordance with such rules as the court may give to the jury for their guidance."

Cleveland etc R Co. *v.* Crawford, 24 Ohio St. 631, 15 Am. Rep. 633. See Cincinnati, etc. R. Co *v.* Howard, 124 Ind 280, Schofield *v.* Railroad Co, 114 U S. 615; 19 Am. & Eng. P. Cas. 353, Stackus *v.* N. Y. Cent. etc R. Co, 79 N. Y. 464; Petty *v.* Hannibal etc. R Co., 88 Mo 306; 28 Am & Eng R Cas 618, Beisiegel *v.* N Y etc. R. Co., 34 N. Y. 622, Greavy *v* Long Island R. Co, 101 N. Y. 419, 24 Am. & Eng. R. Cas. 473; Funston *v* Chicago etc R Co, 61 Ia. 452, 14 Am & Eng R Cas 640; Nehrbas *v* Central Pac R. Co, 62 Cal. 320, 14 Am & Eng. R. Cas. 670, Pennsylvania R Co. *v.* Garvey, 108 Pa. St. 369; Drain *v* St Louis etc. R. Co, 86 Mo 574, Loucks *v.* Chicago etc. R Co, 31 Minn 526; 19 Am & Eng. R. Cas. 305, Johnson *v.* Missouri Pac R. Co., 56 Mich 1, Scott *v.* Wilmington etc R Co, 96 N. C. 428, 2 S. E Rep 151; Ferguson *v.* Wisconsin, etc. R Co, 63 Wis. 145, 19 Am & Eng R Cas. 285, Orange etc. H. R. Co. *v* Ward, 47 N. J L 560, Copley *v.* New Haven R Co., 136 Mass. 6; 19 Am. & Eng. R Cas 572, Leavitt *v* Chicago etc R. Co, 64 Wis 228

must look at each case, and all the facts of the case, before you make up your mind what the railway company ought to do" (x). But unless the plaintiff's own evidence shows that the accident was due to his own want of ordinary care (as where in broad daylight he did not look out at all) (y), the tendency of modern authority is to leave the matter very much at large for the jury. In *Dublin, Wicklow and Wexford Railway Co.* v. *Slattery* (z), the only point of negligence made against the railway company was that the train which ran over and killed the plaintiff's husband did not whistle before running through the station where he was crossing the line. It was night at the time, but not a thick night. Ten witnesses distinctly and positively testified that the engine did whistle. Three swore

---

(x) Bowen L J, *Darcy* v *L & S. W R. Co* (1883), 12 Q B Div at p 76

(y) *Darcy* v *L & S W R Co* (1883), 12 Q B. Div 70, 53 L J Q B 58 a case which perhaps belongs properly to the head of contributory negligence, of which more presently. Only the circumstance of daylight seems to distinguish this from *Slattery's* case (next note).

(z) 3 App Ca. 1155. Nearly all the modern cases on "evidence of negligence" were cited in the argument (p 1161). Observe that the question of the verdict being against the weight of evidence was not open (p 1162)

Invitation to alight It is a general rule that where a train overshoots or stops short of the platform at a station, the railroad company is bound to either back the train to the usual place of alighting, or warn the passengers of the special dangers incident to the unusual place, and assist the passenger to alight. See Memphis etc. R. Co. v. Whitfield, 44 Miss 460, 7 Am Rep 699, Pennsylvania R. Co. v. Aspell, 23 Pa. St. 149, Hartwig v Chicago & N W Ry. Co., 49 Wis. 358; 1 Am. & Eng. R. Cas. 65; Columbus etc R Co v. Farrell, 81 Ind. 408; McDonald v Chicago & N. W R. Co., 26 Ia 124, Delamatyr v. Railroad Co, 59 N. Y. 351.

Thus, in Foss v. Boston & M R. Co, 47 Am. & Eng R. Cas 566, it was held that a passenger who has been carried beyond the station platform, has a right to rely on the assistance offered by the conductor and brakeman, to aid her in getting off the train, and if, by reason of the flustered state of her mind and the fear of being carried beyond her destination, she does not notice the distance of the car-step from the ground, and they fail to assist her from the car without injury, it is the fault of the carrier. The English cases seem to not carry the doctrine to this extreme and many of the American cases impose greater duties upon the passenger. See St. Louis, etc. R. Co v. Cantrell, 37 Ark. 519; 40 Am. Rep. 105; Commonwealth v. Boston & M. R. Co., 129 Mass. 500; 37 Am. Rep. 382

that they did not hear it. A jury having found for the plaintiff, it was held by the majority of the House of Lords that the Court could not enter a verdict for the defendants, although they did not conceal their opinion that the actual verdict was a perverse one (a).

The "invitation to alight" group. In the other group, which we have called "invitation to alight" cases, the nature of the facts is, if anything, less favourable to the defendant. A train stopping at a station overshoots the platform so that the front carriages stop at a place more or less inconvenient, or it may be dangerous, for persons of ordinary bodily ability to alight. A passenger bound for that station, or otherwise minded to alight, is unaware (as by reason of darkness, or the like, he well may be) of the inconvenience of the place (b), or else is aware of it, but takes the attendant risk rather than be carried beyond his destination. In either case he gets out as best he can, and, whether through false security, or in spite of such caution as he can use, has a fall or is otherwise hurt. Here the passenger is entitled by his contract with the company to reasonable accommodation, and they ought to give him facilities for alighting in a reasonably convenient manner. Overshooting the platform is not of itself negligence, for that can be set right by backing the train (c). It is a question of fact whether under the particular circumstances the company's servants were reasonably diligent for the accommodation of the passengers (d), and whether the passenger, if he alighted knowing the nature

---

(a) The majority consisted of Lord Cairns (who thought the verdict could not have stood if the accident had happened by daylight), Lord Penzance, Lord O'Hagan, Lord Selborne, and Lord Gordon, the minority of Lord Hatherley, Lord Coleridge, and Lord Blackburn *Flhs* v. *G W R Co* (Ex Ch 1874), L R 9 C P 551, 43 L. J C P 304, does not seem consistent with this decision, there was difference of opinion in that case also.

(b) *Cockle* v. *S E R C*, (1872), Ex. Ch L R 7 C P. 321, 41 L. J. C. P 140

(c) *Siner* v. *G. W R Co* (1869), Ex. Ch. L. R. 4 Ex 117, 38 L J Ex 67

(d) *Bridges* v *N London R Co*, p. 395, above

of the place, did so under a reasonable apprehension that he must alight there or not at all (e)

Complications with contributory negligence, etc. All these cases are apt to be complicated with issues of contributory negligence and other similar though not identical questions. We shall advert to these presently. It will be convenient now to take a case outside these particular types, and free from their complications, in which the difficulty of deciding what is "evidence of negligence" is illustrated.

Other illustrations of "evidence of negligence": Smith v. L. & S. W. R. Co. Such an one is *Smith* v. *London and South Western Railway Company* (f). The facts are, in this country and climate, of an exceptional kind, but the case is interesting because, though distinctly within the line at which the freedom of the jury ceases, that line is shown by the tone and language of the judgments in both the Common Pleas and the Exchequer Chamber to be nearly approached. The action was in respect of property burnt

---

(e) *Robson* v. *N. E. R. Co.*, 2 Q B Div 85, 46 L J. Q B 50, *Rose* v *N E R Co*, 2 Ex. Div. 218, 46 L J Ex 374 (both in 1876)

(f) L R 5 C P 98, 39 L. J C P 68, in F\ Ch 6 C P. 14, 40 L J C. P 21 (1870) The accident took place in the extraordinarily warm and dry summer of 1868

Evidence of negligence. In the case of Larkin v. O'Neill (119 N Y 225), the facts were that an action was brought to recover damages for injuries alleged to have been caused by defendant's negligence, where it appeared that the plaintiff, a woman thirty-five years old, had been in the habit for ten years, of making purchases at defendant's dry-goods store, and that she fell while descending a broad carpeted staircase in the store It was held that the defendant was not liable and the court said. "The line must be drawn in this case between suggestions and possible precautions, and evidence of actual negligence, such as ought reasonably and properly be left to a jury. It is difficult, in some cases, to determine where the line is to be drawn, but here I have no hesitation in saying that there was no evidence of negligence which could be properly left to the jury."

by fire, communicated from sparks which had escaped from the defendant company's locomotives. The material elements of fact were the following.

Hot dry weather had prevailed for some time, and at the time of the accident a strong S. E. wind was blowing.

About a fortnight earlier grass had been cut by the defendants' servants on the banks adjoining the line, and the boundary hedge trimmed, and the cuttings and trimmings had, on the morning of the fire (g), been raked into heaps, and lay along the bank inside the hedge. These cuttings and trimmings were, by reason of the state of the weather, very dry and inflammable.

Next the hedge there was a stubble field; beyond that a road; on the other side of the road a cottage belonging to the plaintiff, 200 yards in all distant from the railway.

Two trains passed, and immediately or shortly afterwards the strip of grass between the railroad and the hedge was seen to be on fire. Notwithstanding all efforts

---

(g) See statement of the facts in the report in Ex Ch L R. 6 C P. at p. 15

Carrying fire in locomotives. The doctrine is now well settled in the United States and in England, that when the legislature has authorized the use of fire in locomotives, and every reasonable precaution is observed to prevent injury, the company will not be liable for damage by fire unless guilty of negligence. By the current of authorities it is the duty of railroad companies to use none but locomotive engines of the safest modern construction, supplied with all the best approved appliances to prevent the escape of sparks therefrom endangering the property of others, and operated with due care. Smith v New York etc. R Co, 19 N. Y 127, Field v. New York Cent. R. Co., 32 N. Y. 346, Bedell v Long Island R R. Co, 44 N. Y. 369, Flinn v. New York etc. R. Co, 67 Hun, 361, 22 N. Y. S. Rep. 473; Edrington v. Louisville, etc. Ry. Co, 41 La. An. 96, 6 So. Rep. 19; Hagan v. Chicago, etc. Co, 86 Mich. 615, 49 N W. Rep. 509, Hockstedler v. Dubuque & S. C Ry. Co. (Ia.), 55 N. W Rep 74; Smith v. Chicago, etc. Ry. Co. (S D), 55 N. W. Rep. 717, Loudy v. Clarke, 45 Minn. 477; 48 N. W Rep. 22, Jacksonville, etc. Ry. Co. v. Peninsular Land etc Co., 27 Fla 157; 9 So. Rep. 661, Rost v. Missouri P. Ry. Co., 76 Tex. 168; 12 S W. Rep. 1131; Missouri P. Ry. Co v Platzer, 73 Tex 117, 11 S. W Rep. 160; Bullis v. Chicago, etc. Ry. Co., 76 Ia 680, Eddy v Lafayette, 49 Fed Rep 807, 4 U. S. App. 247;

made to subdue it, the fire burnt through the hedge, spread over the stubble field, crossed the road, and consumed the plaintiff's cottage.

There was no evidence that the railway engines were improperly constructed or worked with reference to the escape of sparks, and no direct evidence that the fire came from one of them.

The jury found for the plaintiff, and it was held (though with some difficulty) (*h*) that they were warranted in so finding on the ground that the defendants were negligent, having regard to the prevailing weather, in leaving the dry trimmings in such a place and for so long a time. The risk, though unusual, was apparent, and the company was bound to be careful in proportion. "The more likely

(*h*) Brett J dissented in the Common Pleas, and Blackburn J. expressed some doubt in the Ex. Ch on the ground that the particular damage in question could not have reasonably been anticipated.

---

1 C. C. A. 441; Kelsey *v.* Chicago & N. W. Ry. Co (S. D), 45 N W Rep. 204; Burroughs *v* Housatonic R. Co , 15 Conn. 124; Huyett *v.* Phila , etc R Co , 23 Pa St 373; Diamond *v* Northern Pac. R. Co., 6 Mont. 580, 29 Am & Eng. R Cas. 117; Texas etc R Co *v.* Medaris, 64 Tex 92; 29 Am & Eng. R. Cas 159, Burlington etc R Co. *v* Westover, 4 Neb 268, Texas, etc. R. Co. *v.* Levi, 59 Tex. 674; 13 Am. & Eng. R. Cas. 464, Brown *v.* Atlanta, etc. R. Co , 19 S C. 39, 13 Am. & Eng. R Cas. 479, Hoff *v* West Jersey R. Co., 45 N. J L. 201, 13 Am. & Eng. R Cas. 476, Anderson *v* Cape Fear Steamboat Co., 64 N. C. 399; Case *v.* North Cent. R. Co , 54 Barb. 644; Chicago, etc., R. Co *v* Quaintance, 58 Ill. 389, White *v* Chicago, M. & St. P. Ry. Co (S D), 47 N W. Rep. 146; Jackson *v* Chicago & N W. R Co , 31 Ia. 176, 7 Am Rep 120; Small *v.* Chicago etc. R Co., 50 Ia 338, Webb *v* Rome, etc. R. Co., 49 N Y. 420; Leavenworth, etc R. Co. *v.* Cook, 18 Kan. 261, Home Ins. Co. *v* Pennsylvania R Co , 11 Hun, 182, Phila etc R Co *v.* Yerger, 73 Pa. St. 121, 2 Am. & Eng R. Cas. 271; Indianapolis etc. R. Co *v* Paramore, 31 Ind. 143; Morris, etc , R Co *v* State, 36 N. J 553, McHugh *v.* Chicago, etc , R. Co., 41 Wis 78; Woodson *v.* Milwaukee, etc., R. Co., 21 Minn 60; Atchison, etc., R. Co. *v.* Riggs, 31 Kan. 622; Kansas, etc. R Co *v.* Butts, 7 Kan. 308; Rood *v.* N Y & E R Co , 18 Barb. 80, Reading R. Co. *v.* Yeiser, 8 Pa. St 366, Sheldon *v.* Hudson River R Co., 14 N. Y. 218; Balt., etc., R Co *v* Woodruff, 4 Md. 242, Flynn *v* Railroad Co., 40 Cal. 14; Jefferis *v* Phila etc , R Co , 3 Houst. 447

the hedge was to take fire, the more incumbent it was upon the company to take care that no inflammable material remained near to it" (*i*). Thus there was evidence enough (though it seems only just enough) to be left for the jury to decide upon. Special danger was apparent, and it would have been easy to use appropriate caution. On the other hand the happening of an accident in extraordinary circumstances, from a cause not apparent, and in a manner that could not have been prevented by any ordinary measures of precaution, is not of itself any evidence of negligence (*k*). And a staircase which has been used by many thousand persons without accident cannot be pronounced dangerous and defective merely because the plaintiff has slipped on it, and somebody can be found to suggest improvements (*l*).

No precise general rule can be given. Illustrations might be largely multiplied, and may be found in abundance in Mr. Horace Smith's, Mr. Campbell's, or Mr. Beven's monograph, or by means of the citations and discussions in the leading cases themselves. Enough has been said to show that by the nature of the problem no general formula can be laid down except in some such purposely vague terms as were used in *Scott* v. *London Dock Co.* (*m*).

Due care varies as apparent risk: application of this to accidents through personal infirmity. We have said that the amount of caution required of a citizen in his

(*i*) Lush J in Ex Ch L. R. 6 C P. at p 23

(*k*) *Blyth* v *Birmingham Waterworks Co* (1856), 11 Ex 781, 25 L J Ex. 212, *supra*, p 12

(*l*) *Crafter* v *Metrop R Co* (1868), L R 1 C P 300, 35 L J C P. 132 the plaintiff slipped on the brass "nosing" of the steps (this being the material in common use, whereof the Court took judicial notice " with the common experience which every one has," per Willes J at p 303), and it was suggested that lead would have been a safer material

(*m*) P. 550, above

Degree of care commensurate with apparent risk While ordinary prudence is required of every one with respect to the safety of others

conduct is proportioned to the amount of apparent danger. In estimating the probability of danger to others, we are entitled to assume, in the absence of anything to show the contrary, that they have the full use of common faculties, and are capable of exercising ordinary caution. If a workman throws down a heavy object from a roof or scaffolding "in a country village, where few passengers are," he is free from criminal liability at all events, provided " he calls out to all people to have a care" (n). Now some passer-by may be deaf, and may suffer by not hearing the warning. That will be his misfortune, and may be unaccompanied by any imprudence on his part; but it cannot be set down to the fault of the workman. If the workman had no particular reason to suppose that the next passer-by would be deaf, he was bound only to such caution as suffices for those who have ears to hear. The same rule must hold if a deaf man is

---

(n) Blackst Comm iv 192 D 9 2, ad leg Aquil 31 In a civil action it would probably be left to the jury whether, on the whole, the work was being done with reasonable care

---

and their property, at all times, there may be occasions when more than ordinary prudence is demanded by the apparent risk. The acknowledged indiscretion of children and the infirmity of persons whose disability is apparent is notice to all persons whose duty it is to show them care that a higher degree of care should be exercised towards them than towards persons apparently discreet and sound In the case of Spokane Truck & Dray Co v Hoefer (2 Wash. 45, 25 Pac. Rep 1072) it was held, that a person who undertakes to hoist a heavy safe from a court, through which people are accustomed to pass back and forth, into an upper story of the building, is bound to use such care as the nature of the employment, and the situation and the circumstances surrounding the same, require of a prudent person, experienced and skilled in such or similar work. See St. Louis, etc. Ry. Co v Freeman, 36 Ark. 41, Clements v Louisiana Electric Light Co., 44 La. 692, 11 So Rep. 51, Brickett v. Knickerbocker Ice Co., 110 N Y. 504; Standard Oil Co. v. Tierney (Ky. App.), 17 S W Rep 1025, Calvin v. Peabody, 155 Mass 104; N. E. Rep 59, Henry v Klopfer, 147 Pa. St. 178; 23 At. Rep. 331; 29 W. N. C. 331, Id 23 At. Rep. 338; 29 W. N. C 331; Barnum v. Terpenning, 75 Mich. 557; 42 N. W. Rep. 967; Phillips v. Dewald, 79 Ga 732; Bennett v. New York etc. R. Co., 57 Conn. 426.

run over for want of hearing a shout or a whistle (o), or a blind man for want of seeing a light, or if a colour-blind man, being unable to make out a red danger flag, gets in the line of fire of rifle or artillery practice; or if in any of those circumstances a child of tender years, or an idiot, suffers through mere ignorance of the meaning which the warning sight or sound conveys to a grown man with his wits about him. And this is not because there is any fault in the person harmed, for there may well be no fault at all. Whatever we think, or a jury might think, of a blind man walking alone, it can hardly be deemed inconsistent with common prudence for a deaf man to do so; and it is known that colour-blind people, and those with whom they live, often remain ignorant of their failing until it is disclosed by exact observation or by some accident. It is not that the law censures a deaf man for not hearing, or a colour-blind one for not perceiving a red flag. The normal measure of the caution required from a lawful man must be fixed with regard to other men's normal powers of taking care of themselves, and abnormal infirmity can make a difference only when it is shown that in the particular case it was apparent.

Distinction where the person acting has notice of special danger to an infirm or helpless person. On the other hand it seems clear that greater care is required of us when it does appear that we are dealing with persons of less than ordinary faculty. Thus if a man driving sees that a blind man, an aged man, or a cripple is crossing the

---

(o) Cp *Skelton* v. *L. & N. W. R Co.* (1867), L. R. 2 C. P 631, 36 L J C P 249, decided however on the ground that the accident was wholly due to the man's own want of care.

Where the person acting has notice of special danger to an infirm person. Supporting the text, *vide* I. & G. N. Ry. Co. *v.* Smith, 62 Tex. 254; Louisville etc R Co. *v.* Sullivan, 81 Ky. 624; 50 Am. Rep. 186; Maloy *v.* Wabash, etc Ry Co, 84 Mo 270

road ahead, he must govern his course and speed accordingly. He will not discharge himself, in the event of a mishap, merely by showing that a young and active man with good sight would have come to no harm. In like manner if one sees a child, or other person manifestly incapable of normal discretion, exposed to risk from one's action, it seems that proportionate care is required; and it further seems on principle immaterial that the child would not be there but for the carelessness of some parent or guardian or his servant. These propositions are not supported by any distinct authority in our law that I am aware of (p). But they seem to follow from admitted principles, and to throw some light on questions which arise under the head of contributory negligence.

III — *Contributory Negligence.*

Actionable negligence must be proximate cause of harm; where plaintiff's own negligence is immediate cause, no remedy. In order that a man's negligence may entitle another to a remedy against him, that other must have suffered harm whereof this negligence is a proximate cause. Now I may be negligent, and my negligence may be the occasion of some one suffering harm, and yet the

---

(p) In the United States there is some see Wharton, §§ 307, 310, Cooley on Torts, 683, Beven on Negligence, 8.

Contributory negligence A learned author has announced the following definition. "Contributory negligence, in its legal signification, is such an act or omission on the part of a plaintiff, amounting to a want of ordinary care, as, concurring or co-operating with the negligent act of the defendant, is a proximate cause or occasion of the injury complained of. To constitute contributory negligence there must be a want of ordinary care on the part of the plaintiff, and a proximate connection between that and the injury."—Beach on Contrib Neg. 7.

"The whole doctrine of contributory negligence is bottomed on the maxim, *In jure non remota causa, sed proxima,* spectatur" L. R etc Ry. *v.* Haynes, 47 Ark 502, 1 S. W. Rep. 774. A few cases are Americus,

immediate cause of the damage may be not my want of care but his own. Had I been careful to begin with, he would not have been in danger; but had he, being so put

etc R v. Luckie (Ga), 13 S E. Rep 105, Pfister v. Gerwig, 122 Ind 302, 23 N E. Rep. 1011, Howard v Kansas City, etc. R. Co, 41 Kan 407; 21 Pac. Rep 267; Andrews v Mason City & Ft D. Ry Co., 77 Ia. 669, 42 N W Rep. 513; Ridings v Hannibal & St. Jo. Ry. Co., 33 Mo. App. 535; Inland & Seaboard Coasting Co v. Folson, 139 U S 558; 11 S Ct. Rep 653; Cornell v Electric Ry Co, 82 Mich. 495; 46 N. W. Rep. 791; Moore v Norfolk & W R. Co, 87 Va. 489; 12 S. E Rep 969; LaRiviere v. Pemberton, 46 Minn. 5, 18 N. W. Rep. 406; Hinz v. Starn, 46 Hun, 526, Parker v Georgia P Ry. Co, 83 Ga. 589, Dun v Seaboard & R R Co, 78 Va. 645, Richmond & D Ry. Co. v. Yeamans, 86 Va 866, 12 S E Rep. 916, McKellei v. Township of Moultor, 78 Mich. 485, 14 N. W. Rep 412, Kentucky Cent. R Co v. Thomas, 79 Ky 160, 1 Am. & Eng. R Cas 79, 80; 42 Am. Rep. 208, Richmond etc. R Co v. Anderson, 31 Gratt 812; Paducah, etc. R. Co v Hoehl, 12 Bush, 41; Colorado, etc. R Co. v. Holmes, 5 Colo 197, 8 Am & Eng R. Cas. 410; Woods v. Jones, 34 La An. 1086, 15 Am. Rep. 555, Spencer v. Balt & O R Co, 4 Mackey, 138, 54 Am. Rep 269, 272, Scheffer v Railroad Co., 105 U. S 249; 8 Am. & Eng. R. Cas. 61, Iron R. Co v. Mowery, 86 Ohio St 418, 3 Am. & Eng. R Cas. 361; Stevenson v. Chicago etc R. Co, 18 Fed Rep 493, Linnehan v. Sampson, 126 Mass 506, 30 Am. Rep. 692, Indianapolis etc R Co. v. Stout, 53 Ind. 143; Mobile, etc. R. Co. v Ashcroft, 48 Ala. 15; Turner v. Buchanan, 82 Ind. 147, 42 Am. Rep 485; Wilson v Northern Pac. R Co, 26 Minn. 278; 37 Am. Rep. 410, Pittsburg, etc R. Co. v. Rohrman (Pa), 12 Am. & Eng. R. Cas. 176; Patterson's Ry. Acc. Law, 62 et seq.

Unless the defendant has been negligent, there can be no contributory negligence on the part of the plaintiff. So, no matter how negligent the plaintiff may be, he is not guilty of contributory negligence if purposely injured by the defendant. Ruter v. Foy, 46 Ia. 132; Carter v. Louisville, etc. R Co., 98 Ind 552, 22 Am & Eng. R. Cas. 360, Steinmitz v. Kelly, 72 Ind. 442, 37 Am. Rep. 170; Patterson's Ry. Acc. Law, § 50, p. 49, Harris v. Minneapolis etc. R. Co., 37 Minn. 47; 33 N. W. Rep 12 It may, therefore, be concluded that if the injured person had no actual knowledge of the danger that threatened him, and would in the exercise of ordinary care have apprehended it, he cannot be charged with contributory negligence. Bennett v. Railroad Co, 102 U. S 577; 1 Am. & Eng. R Cas. 71, Hayward v Merrill, 94 Ill. 349, 34 Am. Rep 229, Jeffrey v. Keokuk, etc R. Co., 56 Ia 546; 5 Am. & Eng R Cas 568; Langman v. St. Louis etc. R. Co, 72 Mo. 392, 8 Am. & Eng. R Cas. 355; Murray v. McShane, 52 Md 217; 36 Am. Rep. 86; Dush v. Fitzhugh, 2 Lea, 807; McGary v. Loomis, 63 N. Y. 104, 20 A. M. Rep 510; Gray v. Scott, 66 Pa.

in danger, used reasonable care for his own safety or that of his property, the damage would still not have happened. Thus my original negligence is a comparatively remote

---

Co. 115, Washington v Balt. & O. R. Co., 17 W Va. 190, 10 Am. & Eng. Cas. 740; Varney v. Manchester, 58 N H. 430, 42 Am. Rep. 592

The converse of the rule last above announced may be found in the doctrine, that, if defendant knew, or had reason to apprehend, special dangers from his acts or omissions, or had greater capacity for understanding the harmful results likely to follow from his conduct than the injured person had, he will be liable, notwithstanding acts or omissions on the part of the injured person, that with equal knowledge of the danger, or capacity to apprehend it, would have been contributory negligence. Jones v Florence Mining Co., Sioux City etc. Ry Co., 2 Dill. 294, Railroad v. Stout, 17 Wall. 657; Keff v. Milwaukee etc. R. Co, 21 Minn. 207; 18 Am Rep 393, Philadelphia etc R. Co v Spearen, 47 Pa. St. 300; Bransom v. Labrot, 81 Ky. 638; 50 Am. Rep 193; Holden v. Fitchburg R. Co., 129 Mass. 268, 2 Am. & Eng R. Cas 94, 37 Am. Rep. 343, Baltimore etc. R Co. v. Rowan, 104 Md 88, 23 Am. & Eng. R. Cas. 390; Louisville etc. R Co. v. Frowley, 110 Md. 18, 22; 28 Am & Eng. R. Cas. 308, Whirley v. Whiteman, 1 Head, 611; Smith v Car Works (Mich.), 12 Am & Eng Corp. Cas 269; Brush Electric Lighting Co v. Kelly, 126 Ind. 222, 25 N. E. Rep. 812 Where one incurs danger in an attempt to save the life of another or in the discharge of a duty his conduct cannot be charged against him as contributory negligence. Donahoe v Wabash, etc R. Co., 83 Mo. 560, 53 Am. Rep. 594, Eckert v. L. I. R Co., 57 Barb. 555; 43 N. Y. 503, 3 Am. Rep 721; Evansville etc. R. Co. v. Hiatt, 17 Ind 102; Pennsylvania Co. v. Roney, 89 Ind 453, 12 Am & Eng. R. Cas. 323, 46 Am. Rep. 173, Central R. Co. v Crosby, 74 Ga 737; 58 Am. Rep. 463, Atlanta etc. R. Co v Ray, 70 Ga 674; 22 Am. & Eng R. Cas. 281, Cottrill v. Chicago, M. & St P. R. Co., 47 Wis 634, 32 Am Rep. 796; Central R Co. v. Sears, 61 Ga. 279

As said on a preceding page (391) the question whether the burden of proving contributory negligence rests on the defendant who pleads it, or its absence on the plaintiff who alleges its non-existence, is very much mooted, and a discussion of the perplexing rulings of the courts could not be undertaken here with either propriety or hope of solution. Among the cases holding that the burden is on the plaintiff are the following Greenleaf v. Ill etc R. Co, 29 Ia 14, 4 Am. Rep. 181; Slossen v Burlington, etc R. Co, 55 Ia 294, 7 Am & Eng. R. Cas 509; Mount Vernon v Dusonchett, 2 Ind 586, 54 Am. Dec. 467, Cincinnati etc. R Co. v Butler, 103 Ind 31, 23 Am. & Eng. R Cas. 262; State v. Maine Cent R Co., 76 M 357; 19 Am & Eng R. Cas. 312; 49 Am. Rep. 662; Kennard v Burton, 25 Me 39, 43 Am Dec. 249, Detroit & Milwaukee R. Co. v. Van Steinburg, 17 Mich 99, Teifel v Hilsendegin, 44 Mich. 461; Doggett v. Richmond etc R Co, 78 N. C 305, Indiana etc R. Co. v.

cause of the harm, and as things turn out the proximate cause is the sufferer's own fault, or rather (since a man is under no positive duty to be careful in his own interest) he cannot ascribe it to the fault of another. In a state of facts answering this general description the person harmed is by the rule of the common law not entitled to any remedy. He is said to be "guilty of contributory negligence;" a phrase well established in our forensic usage, though not free from objection. It rather suggests, as the ground of the doctrine, that a man who does not take ordinary care for his own safety is to be in a manner punished for his carelessness by disability to sue any one else whose carelessness was concerned in producing the damage. But this view is neither a reasonable one, nor supported by modern authority, and it is already distinctly rejected by writers of no small weight (*q*). And it stands ill with the common practice of our courts, founded on

---

(*q*) See Campbell, 180, Horace Smith, 226, and Wharton, §§ 300 *sqq*, who gives the same conclusions in a more elaborate form. The use of such phrases as *in pari delicto*, though not without authority, is likewise confusing and objectionable.

Greene, 106 Ind 279, 25 Am & Eng. R Cas. 322; 55 Am. Rep. 736; Chase v Maine etc R Co., 77 Me 62; 19 Am. & Eng. R. Cas. 356. *Contra*, O'Brien v. Tatum, 84 Ala. 186, 4 So. Rep 159; Buesching v. St. Louis Gaslight Co, 73 Mo. 229; 39 Am Rep. 503, Rapp v St. J. & I R. Co, 106 Mo 423, 17 S. W. Rep 487, Watson v. Oxanna Land Co. 92 Ala. 320; 8 So Rep. 772, Georgia Pac. Ry. v. Davis, 92 Ala. 300; 9 So. Rep 252, Denver & R. G R. Co. v Ryan, 17 Colo. 98; 28 Pac. Rep. 78, Hough v Railroad Co., 100 U S. 213; Railroad Co. v Gladman, 15 Wall. 401; Indianapolis etc R. Co. v Horst, 93 U.S 291; Dallas etc. R. Co. v Spicker, 61 Tex. 427; 21 Am. & Eng. R. Cas 160, 48 Am. Rep 297; Prideaux v. Mineral Point, 43 Wis 513, 28 Am. Rep 558, Fowler v. Baltimore etc. R Co., 18 W. Va. 579; 8 Am. & Eng. R. Cas. 480; McDougall v. Cent. R. Co., 63 Cal. 431; 12 Am. & Eng. R. Cas. 143; May v. Hanson, 5 Cal. 360, 63 Am. Dec. 135; Louisville etc R Co v. Goetz, 79 Ky. 442, 14 Am & Eng. R Cas. 627, 42 Am. Rep. 227; Hocum v. Weltherick, 22 Minn 152; Sanderson v. Frazier, 8 Colo. 79, 54 Am. Rep. 544, Sheff v. Huntington, 16 W. Va. 307, Bromley v. Birmingham M. R. Co. (Ala.), 11 So. Rep. 841, Washington & G R. Co. v. Fobriner, 147 U S. 571; 13 S. Ct. Rep. 557.

constant experience of the way in which this question presents itself in real life. "The received and usual way of directing a jury . . . is to say that if the plaintiff could, by the exercise of such care and skill as he was bound to exercise, have avoided the consequence of the defendant's negligence, he cannot recover" (r). That is to say, he is not to lose his remedy merely because he has been negligent at some stage of the business, though without that negligence the subsequent events might not or could not have happened; but only if he has been negligent in the final stage and at the decisive point of the event, so that the mischief, as and when it happens, is immediately due to his own want of care and not to the defendant's. Again the penal theory of contributory negligence fails to account for the accepted qualification of the rule, "namely, that though the plaintiff may have been guilty of negligence, and although that negligence may in fact have contributed to the accident, yet if the defendant could in the result, by the exercise of ordinary care and diligence, have avoided the mischief which happened, the plaintiff's negligence will not excuse him" (s). And in a recent leading case, of which there will be more to say, the criterion of what was the proximate cause of the injury is adopted throughout (t).

The element of truth which the penal theory, as I have called it, presents in a distorted form, is that the rule is not merely a logical deduction, but is founded in public utility. "The ultimate justification of the rule is in reasons of policy, viz. the desire to prevent accidents by inducing each member of the community to act up to the standard of due care set by the law. If he does not, he is deprived of the assistance of the law" (u).

(r) Lord Blackburn, 3 App. Ca at p 1207
(s) Lord Penzance, *Radley* v. *L. & N. W. R. Co.* (1876), 1 App Ca at p 759
(t) *The Bernina* (1887), 12 P D 36, 56 L. J P. 38, affd nom. *Mills* v *Armstrong* (1888), 13 App Ca 1, 57 L. J. P 65, see especially the judgment of Lindley L J, and cp. *Little* v. *Hackett* (1886), 116 U. S 366, 371.
(u) W. Schofield in Harv. Law Rev. iii 270.

Tuff v. Warman. The leading case which settled the doctrine in its modern form is *Tuff* v. *Warman* (x). The action was against the pilot of a steamer in the Thames for running down the plaintiff's barge; the plaintiff's own evidence showed that there was no look-out on the barge; as to the conduct of the steamer the evidence was conflicting, but according to the plaintiff's witnesses she might easily have cleared the barge. Willes J. left it to the jury to say whether the want of a look-out was negligence on the part of the plaintiff, and if so, whether it "directly contributed to the accident." This was objected to as too favourable to the plaintiff, but was upheld both in the full Court of Common Pleas and in the Exchequer Chamber. In the considered judgment on appeal (y) it is said that the proper question for the jury is "whether the damage was occasioned entirely by the negligence or improper conduct of the defendant, or whether the plaintiff himself so far contributed to the misfortune by his own negligence or want of ordinary and common care and caution that, but for such negligence or want of ordinary care and caution on his part, the misfortune would not have happened." But negligence will not disentitle the plaintiff to recover, unless it be such that without it the harm complained of would (z) not have happened; "nor if the defendant might by the exercise of care on his part have avoided the consequences of the neglect or carelessness of the plaintiff."

Radley v. L. & N. W. R. Co. In *Radley v. London and North Western Railway Co.* (a), this doctrine received a striking confirmation.

The defendant railway company was in the habit of taking full trucks from the siding of the plaintiffs, colliery

---

(x) 2 C B N S 740, 5 C. B. N. S. 573, 27 L J C P 322 (1857-8).

(y) 5 C B N S at p 585.

(z) Not "could" see Beven on Negligence, 132

(a) 1 App. Ca. 754, 46 L J. Ex 573, reversing the judgment of the Exchequer Chamber, L R. 10 Ex 100, and restoring that of the Court of the Exchequer, L. R. 9 Ex 71 (1874-6)

owners, and returning the empty trucks there. Over this siding was a bridge eight feet high from the ground. On a Saturday afternoon, when all the colliery men had left work, the servants of the railway ran some trucks on the siding and left them there. One of the plaintiffs' men knew this, but nothing was done to remove the trucks. The first of these trucks contained another broken-down truck, and their joint height amounted to eleven feet. On the Sunday evening the railway servants brought on the siding a line of empty trucks, and pushed on in front of them all those previously left on the siding. Some resistance was felt, and the power of the engine pushing the trucks was increased. The two trucks at the head of the line, not being able to pass under the bridge, struck it and broke it down. An action was brought to recover damages for the injury. The defence was contributory negligence, on the ground that the plaintiffs' servants ought to have moved the first set of trucks to a safe place, or at any rate not have left the piled-up truck in a dangerous position. The judge at the trial told the jury that the plaintiffs must satisfy them that the accident "happened by the negligence of the defendant's servants, and without any contributory negligence of their own; in other words, that it was solely by the negligence of the defendant's servants."

On these facts and under this direction the jury found that there was contributory negligence on the part of the plaintiffs, and a verdict was entered for the defendants. The Court of Exchequer (b) held that there was no evidence of contributory negligence, chiefly on the ground that the plaintiffs were not bound to expect or provide against the negligence of the defendants. The Exchequer Chamber (c) held that there was evidence of the plaintiffs having omitted to use reasonable precaution, and that the direction given to the jury was sufficient. In the House of

---

(b) Bramwell and Amphlett BB

(c) Blackburn, Mellor, Lush, Grove, Brett, Archibald JJ, diss. Denman J.

Lords it was held (d) that there was a question of fact for the jury, but the law had not been sufficiently stated to them. They had not been clearly informed, as they should have been, that not every negligence on the part of the plaintiff which in any degree contributes to the mischief will bar him of his remedy, but only such negligence that the defendant could not by the exercise of ordinary care have avoided the result.

"It is true that in part of his summing-up, the learned judge pointed attention to the conduct of the engine-driver, in determining to force his way through the obstruction, as fit to be considered by the jury on the question of negligence; but he failed to add that if they thought the engine-driver might at this stage of the matter by ordinary care have avoided all accident, any previous negligence of the plaintiffs would not preclude them from recovering.

"In point of fact the evidence was strong to show that this was the immediate cause of the accident, and the jury might well think that ordinary care and diligence on the part of the engine-driver would, notwithstanding any previous negligence of the plaintiffs in leaving the loaded-up truck on the line, have made the accident impossible. The substantial defect of the learned judge's charge is that that question was never put to the jury" (e).

"Proximate" or "decisive" cause? This leaves no doubt that the true ground of contributory negligence being a bar to recovery is that it is the proximate cause of

---

(d) By Lord Penzance, Lord Cairns, Lord Blackburn (thus retracting his opinion in the Ex Ch), and Lord Gordon

(e) Lord Penzance, 1 App Ca at p. 760

Proximate cause. Proximate means direct or immediate. In the case of Montgomery Gas Light Co. v. Montgomery & E. Ry. Co. (86 Ala. 381, 580, 5 Rep 765) the court said: "It is objected, that the circuit court in defining the phrase *contributory negligence* embraced in it the idea, that

the mischief; and negligence on the plaintiff's part which is only part of the inducing causes (*f*) will not disable him. I say "the proximate cause," considering the term as now established by usage and authority. But I would still suggest, as I did in the first edition, that "decisive" might convey the meaning more exactly. For if the defendant's original negligence were so far remote from the plaintiff's damage as not to be part at least of its "proximate cause" within the more general meaning of that term,

---

(*f*) Or, as Mr Wharton puts it, not a cause but a condition

---

it must have been of a character to have 'essentially contributed' to the injury set out in the complaint. It is often said, that no negligence on the part of the plaintiff, which remotely contributes to produce an injury, will debar him from a recovery, and it is variously stated, that no negligence is contributory and proximate, in the order of cause and effect, unless it 'substantially' or 'essentially,' or 'directly' tends to produce such injury, or is an 'efficient cause' or 'actual and efficient' cause in producing it These terms of description are often used indifferently to distinguish the direct and immediate or judicial cause of the injury, from a remote cause or mere condition of such injury, and they cannot be said to be either erroneous or misleading." Government St. R. Co. v. Hanlon, 53 Ala 70, approved. See Hoag v Railroad, 85 Pa. St 292; Beach on Contrib. Neg. 25 and 28, Jung v. City of Stevens Point, 74 Wis. 554. "The act or omission on the part of a plaintiff claimed to have contributed to the injury must have direct relation to the act or omission charged to be negligence on the part of the defendant" McQuilken v Central P R Co , 64 Cal 463, 16 Am. & Eng R. Cas 353. See Trow v. Vermont C. R. Co., 24 Vt. 487, 58 Am Dec. 191, Fowler v. Balt & O. R. Co., 48 W. Va. 579, 8 Am & Eng. R. Cas 480, Meeks v. Southern P R. Co., 56 Cal. 513, 8 Am. & Eng R Cas 214; Zemp v. Wilmington etc. R. Co., 9 Rich. 84, 64 Am Dec. 763, Alexander v. Town of New Castle, 115 Ind 51; 17 N. E. Rep. 200, Pastime v Adams, 49 Cal. 87, Railway Co v Kellogg, 94 U S. 474; Thompson v. Louisville & N R Co , 91 Ala. 496; 8 So Rep. 408, Blaine v. C. & O. R , 9 W. Va. 267, Williams v Edmunds, 75 Mich 97, Smith v. French, 83 Me. 108; 21 At Rep. 739, Cline v Crescent City R R Co., 43 La. An 333; 9 So. Rep. 122; St. Louis etc., Ry Co. v McKinsey, 78 Tex. 298, 14 S. W. Rep 645, Mars v. Del & H. Canal Co., 54 Hun, 631; 8 N Y. S. Rep. 107, Banks v. Wabash Western Ry Co., 40 Mo. App 464; Nagel v Railroad, 75 Mo. 661, Steamboat Farmer v. McCraw, 26 Ala 189; Grant v Moseley, 29 Id. 304; Beers v. Housatonic R. Co., 19 Conn. 566, Marcott v Railroad Co., 47 Mich. 1; 49 Id 99; 4 Am & Eng R. Cas 548, James v James (Ark) 23 S. W. Rep 1099.

the plaintiff would not have any case at all, and the question of contributory negligence could not arise. We shall immediately see, moreover, that independent negligent acts of A. and B. may both be proximate in respect of harm suffered by Z., though either of them, if committed by Z. himself, would have prevented him from having any remedy for the other. Thus it appears that the term "proximate" is not used in precisely the same sense in fixing a negligent defendant's liability and a negligent plaintiff's disability.

The plaintiff's negligence, if it is to disable him, has to be somehow more proximate than the defendant's. It seems dangerously ambiguous to use "proximate" in a special emphatic sense without further or otherwise marking the difference. If we said "decisive" we should at any rate avoid this danger.

Self-created disability to avoid consequences of another's negligence. It would seem that a person who has by his own act or default deprived himself of ordinary ability to avoid the consequences of another's negligence can be in no better position than if, having such ability, he had failed to avoid them; unless, indeed, the other has notice of his

---

Self-created disability to avoid consequences of another's negligence. The rule that where a person by either act or omission deprives himself of ordinary ability to avoid the consequences of another's negligence forfeits his right to complain of injury received therefrom is recognized and established in America, although it seems that in a majority of the cases intoxication was the cause of the disability. "Intoxication on the part of the deceased will not, as a matter of law, establish the charge of contributory negligence set up in the answer, but it is a fact from which contributory negligence may be inferred. The weight of such evidence depends much upon the degree of intoxication, not drunkenness to any degree as a fact which should be considered on the question of contributory negligence." Buddenberg v. Chouteau Transp Co., 108 Mo 394; 18 S. W Rep 971, citing Beach Contrib. Neg, Sec 66, Fitzgerald v Town of Weston, 52 Wis 355; 9 N. W. Rep. 13; Bishop on Non-Contract Law, Sec 513; East Tennessee etc. R. Co. v.

inability in time to use care appropriate to the emergency; in which case the failure to use that care is the decisive negligence. A. and B. are driving in opposite directions on the same road on a dark night. B. is driving at a dangerous speed, and A. is asleep, but B. cannot see that he is asleep. Suppose that A., had he been awake, might have avoided a collision by ordinary care notwithstanding B.'s negligence. Can A. be heard to say that there is no contributory negligence on his part because he was asleep? It seems not. Suppose, on the other hand, that the same thing takes place by daylight or on a fine moonlight night, so that B. would with common care and attention perceive A.'s condition. Here B. would be bound, it seems, to use special caution no less than if A. had been disabled, say by a sudden paralytic stroke, without default of his own. So if a man meets a runaway horse, he cannot tell whether it is loose by negligence or by inevitable accident, nor can this make any difference to what a prudent man could or would do, nor, therefore, to the legal measure of the diligence required (*g*).

Earlier illustrations: Davies v. Mann. Cases earlier than *Tuff* v. *Warman* (*h*) are now material only as illustrations. A celebrated one is the "donkey case," *Davies* v *Mann* (*i*). There the plaintiff had turned his ass loose in a highway with his forefeet fettered, and it was run over by the defendant's waggon, going at "a smartish pace." It was held a proper direction to the jury that, whatever

(*g*) Cp Mr W. Schofield's article in Harv Law Rev. iii 263
(*h*) 5 C B N. S 573, 27 L J C P 322
(*i*) 10 M & W 546, 12 L. J Ex 10 (1842)

Winters, 85 Tenn 246; Monk *v* New Utrecht, 104 N. Y. 552; Alger *v.* Lowell, 3 Allen, 402, Barbee *v.* Reese, 60 Miss. 906, Reed *v.* Harper, 25 Ia. 87; McKee *v.* Ingall, 5 Ill. 30; Illinois Cent. R. Co *v* Cragin, 71 Ill. 177, Hubbard *v.* Mason City, 60 Ia. 400; Weltoy *v.* Indianapolis, etc R Co., 105 Ind 55; Anderson *v* The E. B Ward, Jr., 38 Fed. Rep. 44. See *Drunkenness*, *ante*, p 59.

they thought of the plaintiff's conduct, he was still entitled to his remedy if the accident might have been avoided by the exercise of ordinary care on the part of the driver. Otherwise " a man might justify the driving over goods left on a public highway, or even over a man lying asleep there, or the purposely running against a carriage going on the wrong side of the road " (*j*). With this may be compared the not much later case of *Mayor of Colchester* v. *Brooke* (*k*), where it was laid down (among many other matters) that if a ship runs on a bed of oysters in a river, and could with due care and skill have passed clear of them, the fact of the oyster-bed being a nuisance to the navigation does not afford an excuse. The facts of *Davies* v. *Mann* suggest many speculative variations, and the decision has been much and not always wisely discussed in America, though uniformly followed in this country (*l*).

Butterfield v Forrester. *Butterfield* v. *Forrester* (*m*) is a good example of obvious fault on both sides, where the plaintiff's damage was immediately due to his own want of care. The defendant had put up a pole across a public thoroughfare in Derby, which he had no right to do. The plaintiff was riding that way at eight o'clock in the evening in August, when dusk was coming on, but the obstruction was still visible a hundred yards off: he was riding violently, came against the pole, and fell with his horse. It was left to the jury whether the plaintiff, riding with reasonable and ordinary care, could have seen and avoided the obstruction; if they thought he could, they were to find for the defendant; and they did so. The judge's direction was affirmed on motion for a new trial. "One person being in fault will not dispense with another's using ordinary care for himself." Here it can hardly be said that the position of

(*j*) Parke B., 10 M. & W. at p. 549, cp. his judgment in *Bridge* v *Grand Junction R Co* (1838), 3 M. & W. at p. 248.

(*k*) 7 Q. B 339, 376, 15 L. J. Q B 59
(*l*) See Harv Law Rev. iii 272, 276
(*m*) 11 East, 60 (1809)

the pole across the road was not a *proximate* cause of the fall. But it was not the whole proximate cause. The other and *decisive* cause which concurred was the plaintiff's failure to see and avoid the pole in his way.

On the whole, then, if the plaintiff's "fault, whether of omission or of commission, has been the proximate cause of the injury, he is without remedy against one also in the wrong" (*n*). On the other hand, if the defendant's fault has been the proximate cause he is not excused merely by showing that the plaintiff's fault at some earlier stage created the opportunity for the fault which was that cause (*o*). If it is not possible to say whether the plaintiff's or the defendant's negligence were the proximate (or decisive) cause of the damage, it may be said that the plaintiff cannot succeed because he has failed to prove that he has been injured by the defendant's negligence (*p*). On the other hand it might be suggested that, since contributory negligence is a matter of defence of which the burden of proof is on the defendant (*q*), the defendant would in such a case have failed to make out his defence, and the plaintiff, having proved that the defendant's negligence was a proximate cause if not the whole proximate cause of his damage, would still be entitled to succeed. The defendant must allege and prove not merely that the plaintiff was negligent, but that the plaintiff could by the exercise of ordinary care have avoided the consequences of the defendant's negligence (*r*). It is a question, either way, whether the plaintiff shall recover his whole damages or nothing, for the common law, whether reasonably or not (*s*), has made no provision for apportioning damages in such cases. A learned writer (whose preference for being anonymous I

(*n*) *Little v. Hackett* (1886), 116 U S 366, 371, *Butterfield v Forrester*, above

(*o*) *Radley v L & N W R Co*; *Davies v Mann*

(*p*) Per Lindley L. J., *The Bernina*, 12 P. D 58, 89

(*q*) Lord Watson (Lord Blackburn agreeing), *Wakelin v L & S W. R Co* (1886), 12 App Ca at pp 47–49

(*r*) *Bridge v Grand Junction R Co* (1838), 3 M & W. 248

(*s*) See per Lindley, L J , 12 P. D 89.

respect but regret) has suggested that "hardly sufficient attention has been paid herein to the distinction between cases where the negligent acts are *simultaneous* and those where they are *successive*. In regard to the former class, such as *Dublin, Wicklow & Wexford Ry. Co.* v. *Slattery* (*t*), or the case of two persons colliding at a street corner, the rule is, that *if the plaintiff could by the exercise of ordinary care have avoided the accident he cannot recover*. In regard to the latter class of cases, such as *Davies* v. *Mann* (*u*) and *Radley* v. *L. & N. W. Ry. Co.* (*x*), the rule may be stated thus: that *he who last has an opportunity of avoiding the accident, notwithstanding the negligence of the other, is solely responsible*. And the ground of both rules is the same: that the law looks to the *proximate cause*, or in other words, will not measure out responsibility in halves or other fractions, but holds that person liable who was *in the main* the cause of the injury" (*y*).

Another kind of question arises where a person is injured without any fault of his own, but by the combined effects of the negligence of two persons, of whom the one is not responsible for the other. It has been supposed that A. could avail himself, as against Z. who has been injured without any want of due care on his own part, of the so-called contributory negligence of a third person B. "It is true you were injured by my negligence, but it would not have happened if B. had not been negligent also, therefore you cannot sue me, or at all events not apart from B." Recent authority is decidedly against allowing such a defence, and in one particular class of cases it has been emphatically disallowed. It must, however, be open to A. to answer to Z.: "You were not injured by my negligence at all, but only and wholly by B.'s." It seems to be a question of fact rather than of law what respective degrees of connexion, in kind and degree

(*t*) 3 App Ca 1155
(*u*) 12 M & W. 546
(*x*) 1 App Ca 754, 46 L J. Ex. 573.
(*y*) L Q R v. 87.

between the damage suffered by Z. and the independent negligent conduct of A. and B. will make it proper to say that Z. was injured by the negligence of A. alone, or of B. alone, or of both A. and B. But if this last conclusion be arrived at, it is now quite clear that Z. can sue both A. and B. (*z*).

The exploded doctrine of "identification." In a case now overruled, a different doctrine was set up which, although never willingly received and seldom acted on, remained of more or less authority for nearly forty years. The supposed rule was that if A. is travelling in a vehicle, whether carriage or ship, which belongs to B. and is under the control of B.'s servants, and A. is injured in a collision with another vehicle belonging to Z., and under the control of Z.'s servants, which collision is caused partly by the negligence of B.'s servants and partly by that of Z.'s servants, A. cannot recover against Z. The passenger, it was said, must be considered as having in some sense "identified himself" with the vehicle in which he has chosen to travel, so that for the purpose of complaining of any outsider's negligence he is not in any better position than the person who has the actual control (*a*). It is very difficult to see what this supposed "identification" really meant. With regard to any actual facts or intentions of parties, it is plainly a figment. No passenger carried for hire intends or expects to be answerable for the negligence of the driver, guard, conductor, master, or whoever the person in charge may be. He naturally intends and justly expects, on the contrary, to hold every such person and his superiors answerable to himself. Why that right should exclude a concurrent right against other persons who have also been negligent in the same transaction was never really

---

(*z*) *Little* v. *Hackett* (1886), 116 U. S. 366, *Mills* v *Armstrong* (1888), 13 App Ca 1, overruling *Thorogood* v *Bryan* (1849), 8 C. B. 115, 18 L. J. C. P. 336.

(*a*) Judgments in *Thorogood* v *Bryan*, see 12 P D. at pp 64–67, 13 App Ca. at pp 6, 7, 17

explained. Yet the eminent judges (b) who invented "identification" must have meant something. They would seem to have assumed, rather than concluded, that the plaintiff was bound to show, even in a case where no negligence of his own was alleged, that the defendant's negligence was not only a cause of the damage sustained, but the whole of the cause. But this is not so. The strict analysis of the proximate or immediate cause of the event, the inquiry who could last have prevented the mischief by the exercise of due care, is relevant only where the defendant says that the plaintiff suffered by his own negligence. Where negligent acts of two or more independent persons have between them caused damage to a third, the sufferer is not driven to apply any such analysis to find out whom he can sue. He is entitled — of course within the limits set by the general rules as to remoteness of damage — to sue all or any of the negligent persons. It is no concern of his whether there is any duty of contribution or indemnity as between those persons, though in any case he plainly cannot recover in the whole more than his whole damage.

The phrase "contributory negligence of a third person," which has sometimes been used, must therefore be rejected as misleading. Peter, being sued by Andrew for causing him harm by negligence, may prove if he can that not his negligence, but wholly and only John's, harmed Andrew. It is useless for him to show that John's negligence was "contributory" to the harm, except so far as evidence which proved this, though failing to prove more, might practically tend to reduce the damages.

It is impossible to lay down rules for determining whether harm has been caused by A.'s and B.'s negligence together, or by A.'s or B.'s alone. The question is essentially one of fact. There is no reason, however, why joint negligence should not be successive as well as simultaneous,

---

(b) Coltman, Maule, Cresswell, and Vaughan Williams JJ.

and there is some authority to show that it may be. A wrongful or negligent voluntary act of Peter may create a state of things giving an opportunity for another wrongful or negligent act of John, as well as for pure accidents. If harm is then caused by John's act, which act is of a kind that Peter might have reasonably foreseen, Peter and John may both be liable, and this whether John's act be wilful or not, for many kinds of negligent and wilfully wrongful acts are unhappily common, and a prudent man cannot shut his eyes to the probability that somebody will commit them if temptation is put in the way. One is not entitled to make obvious occasions for negligence. A. leaves the flap of a cellar in an insecure position on a highway where all manner of persons, adult and infant, wise and foolish, are accustomed to pass. B. in carelessly passing, or playing with the flap, brings it down on himself, or on C. In the former case B. has suffered from his own negligence and cannot sue A. In the latter, B. is liable to C., but it may well be that a prudent man in A.'s place would have foreseen and guarded against the risk of a thing so left exposed in a public place being meddled with by some careless person, and if a jury is of that opinion A. may also be liable to C. (c) Where A. placed a dangerous obstruction in a road, and it was removed by some unexplained act of an unknown third person to another part of the same road where Z., a person lawfully using the road, came against it in the dark and was injured, A. was held liable to Z., though there was nothing to show whether the third person's act was or was not lawful or done for a lawful purpose (d).

Accidents to children in custody of adult. Another special class of cases requires consideration. If A. is a

---

(c) *Hughes* v *Macfie* (1863), 2 H & C 744, 33 L J Ex 177, and see *Clark* v *Chambers* (1878), 3 Q B D at pp 330–336,
p 48, above, *Dixon* v *Bell*, 5 M & S 198, p 146, below
(d) *Clark* v *Chambers* last note

child of tender years (or other person incapable of taking ordinary care of himself), but in the custody of M., an adult, and one or both of them suffer harm under circumstances tending to prove negligence on the part of Z., and also contributory negligence on the part of M (*c*), Z. will not be liable to A. if M.'s negligence alone was the proximate cause of the mischief. Therefore if M. could, by

---

(*c*) Waite v N L R Co (1859), Ex Ch 1 B & L 719, 27 L J Q B. 417, 28 L J Q B 258 This case is expressly left untouched by *Mills v Armstrong*, 13 App Ca 1 (see at pp 10, 19), 57 L J P 65

Accidents to children in custody of adult It may be stated as a general rule, that where a child of tender years, while in the custody of an adult, is injured by the negligence of another, and it is proved that the negligence of the adult so contributed to the injury that under the same circumstances except that, if the adult had been alone and so injured, his contributory negligence would have barred his right of action, then the right of action for the child's injury is barred for the same reason The negligence of the adult is imputed to the child In deciding cases of this class the difficulties that have been met are to determine (1) Whether the child is wholly incapable of exercising care, (2) what amounts to custody. These are questions of fact and properly go to the jury It may be said that, in general, it is incumbent upon the adult to show himself free from contributory negligence. See Ratte v Dawson, 50 Minn. 450, 52 N W. Rep. 965; Texas & P. Ry Co. v Morin, 66 Tex 133, 18 S W Rep 315 But see Shippy v. Village of Au Sable, 85 Mich 280, 48 N W Rep. 587, Battishill v. Humphreys, 64 Mich. 503, 31 N. W Rep 894.

"Some authorities seem to make a distinction between cases where the contributory negligence of the parent occurs while he has the child under his immediate control, and other cases which occur when the child is away from the parent" Norfolk & W R Co. *v* Groseclose's Admr., 88 Va 267, 13 S E Rep. 455. See Mayor, etc. of Vicksburg *v.* McLain, (Miss.), 6 So. Rep. 774, Jeffersonville, etc R. Co *v.* Bowen, 40 Md 545, Pittsburg, A & M. Ry. Co *v* Pearson, 72 Pa. St 169, Smith *v* Hestonville, etc Ry. Co , 92 Pa. St. 450; 37 Am Rep 705, Cauley *v* Pitts , etc. Ry. Co , 95 Pa. St 398, Wright *v* Malden & M. R R Co , 4 Allen, 283, Holly *v* Boston Gas Light Co., 8 Gray, 123, Gibbons *v* Williams, 135 Mass , 333, Griffin *v.* Lawrence, Id 363, Payne *v.* Humeston & S. Ry Co , 70 Ia. 584; 31 N. W. Rep 886; Cartarso *v* The Burgundia, 29 Fed. Rep 464, Gunderson *v* Northwestern Elevator Co , 47 Minn 161, 49 N. W. Rep. 694 But see Erie Pass Ry Co. *v* Schuster, 11 Pa St. 412; 57 Am. Rep. 471.

such reasonable diligence as is commonly expected of persons having the care of young children, have avoided the consequences of Z.'s negligence, A. is not entitled to sue Z. and this not because M.'s negligence is imputed by a fiction of law to A., who by the hypothesis is incapable of either diligence or negligence, but because the needful foundation of liability is wanting, namely, that Z.'s negligence, and not something else for which Z. is not answerable and which Z. had no reason to anticipate, should be the proximate cause.

Children, etc., unattended. Now take the case of a child not old enough to use ordinary care for its own safety, which by the carelessness of the person in charge of it is allowed to go alone in a place where it is exposed to danger. If the child comes to harm, does the antecedent negligence of the custodian

---

Children unattended. It is an accepted rule that the law does not exact from an infant the same degree of care and prudence in the presence of danger as is exacted from adults. An infant is bound only to exercise that care which can reasonably be expected of one of its age. In the case of Cleveland Rolling Mill v. Corrigan (46 Ohio, 283, 20 N. E Rep 469), the court said: "We think it a sound rule, therefore, that, in the application of the doctrine of contributory negligence to children, in actions by them, or in their behalf, for injuries occasioned by the negligence of others, their conduct should not be judged by the same rule which governs that of adults, and, while it is their duty to exercise ordinary care to avoid the injuries of which they complain, ordinary care for them is that degree of care which children of the same age, of ordinary care and prudence, are accustomed to exercise under similar circumstances" See Railroad Co. v Stout, 17 Wall 660; Wright v Detroit, etc. Ry Co , 77 Mich 123; 43 N. W 765; Hassenger v. Railroad Co., 48 Mich 205; 12 N W. Rep. 155, Snow v Provincetown, 120 Mass; 580; Kay v Railroad Co , 65 Pa St 269, Lynch v. Smith, 104 Mass. 52, Plumley v Birge, 124 Mass 57, 26 Am. Rep. 645, Balt. City Ry v. McDonnell, 43 Md 534, Government St. R Co. v Hanlon, 53 Ala. 70, Morrissey v. Eastern R. Co , 126 Mass. 377, Jones v Utica & B. R. R Co., 36 Hun, 115; Matley v Whittier Machine Co , 140 Mass 337, Byrne v. New York Cent etc. R. Co , 83 N Y 621, Wiswell v Doyle (Mass), 35 N. E. Rep. 107, Chicago etc R Co v Grablin, 56 N. W. Rep. 796, Sheridan v. Brooklyn & N R Co. 36 N Y 42, Rockford etc. Co. v

make any difference to the legal result? On principle surely not, unless a case can be conceived in which that negligence is the proximate cause. The defendant's duty

---

Delaney, 82 Ill. 198; Vickers v. Atlanta & W. P. R. Co., 64 Ga. 306; St. Louis & S. F. Ry. Co. v. Valirius, 56 Md. 512, McMillan v. B. & M. R. Co., 16 Ia. 231.

There have been cases holding that an infant under seven years of age is conclusively presumed to be without discretion and incapable of negligence, and that between seven and fourteen years of age an infant is, prima facie, incapable of exercising judgement and discretion Norfolk & P. R. Co. v. Ormsby, 27 Gratt. 155, O'Conner v. Illinois Cent. R. Co., 44 La. An. 339, 10 So. Rep. 678, Iron Co. v. Brawley (Ala.), 9 So. Rep. 555, Eswin v. St. Louis etc. Ry. Co., 96 Mo. 290, 9 S. W. Rep. 577; Pennsylvania Co. v. James, 81 Pa. St. 194, Kreig v. Wells, 1 E. D. Smith (N. Y.), 76, Hartfield v. Roper, 21 Wend. 615, 34 Am. Dec. 273, Callahan v. Bean, 9 Allen, 401, Mascheck v. St. Louis etc. R. Co., 3 Mo. App. 600; 71 Mo. 276, 2 Am. & Eng. R. Cas. 38, Mackey v. City, 64 Miss. 774, 2 So. Rep. 178, Houston & T. C. Ry. Co. v. Simpson, 60 Tex. 103.

Yet, it seems that all the cases agree that testimony is admissible to show on the contrary, that infants may become responsible for negligence at an earlier age. It may, therefore, be said "The law fixes no arbitrary period when the immunity of children ceases and the responsibilities of life begin It would be irrational to hold that a man was responsible for his negligence at twenty-one years of age, and not responsible a day or week prior thereto." Nagle v. Allegheny Valley R. Co., 88 Pa. St. 35 See McGovern v. New York etc. R. Co., 67 N. Y. 417, Wendell v. Id., 91 Id. 420, Stone v. Dry Dock R. Co., 115 Id. 104, Westerfield v. Levi Bros., 43 La. An. 63, 9 So. Rep. 52, Tucker v. New York etc. R. Co., 124 N. Y. 318, 26 N. E. Rep. 916, Westerbrook v. Mobile etc. R. Co., 66 Miss. 560, 6 So. Rep. 321, Western & A. R. Co. v. Young, 81 Ga. 397, 7 S. E. Rep. 91, Kansas P. Ry. Co. v. Whipple, 39 Kan. 531, 18 Pac. Rep. 730, Baker v. Railroad Co., 68 Mich. 90; 35 N. W. Rep. 836, Powers v. Harlow, 53 Mich. 507; 19 N. W. Rep. 257, Cassida v. Navigation Co., 14 Oreg. 551; 13 Pac. Rep. 438, Huff v. Ames, 16 Neb. 139; 19 N. W. Rep. 623.

The late cases hold, almost without exception, that the proprietors of turn-tables, and other dangerous machinery, which is likely to excite the curiosity of children or afford them amusement, are liable for injuries to them, through failure to observe a corresponding degree of care. Schmidt v. Kansas City Distilling Co., 90 Mo. 293; 1 S. W. Rep. 865, Rosenberg v. Durfee, 87 Cal. 545; 26 Pac. Rep. 793, Daniels v. New York etc. R., 154 Mass. 351; 28 N. E. Rep. 283, citing numerous cases; Ft. Worth & D. C. Ry. Co. v. Robertson (Tex.), 16 S W. Rep. 1093; Barrett v. Southern P. Co., 91 Cal. 296. 27 Pac. Rep. 666, O'Malley v. St. Paul, M. & M. Ry. Co., 43 Minn. 289, 45 N. W. Rep. 440 Ilwaco Ry. & Nav. Co. v.

can be measured by his notice of special risk and his means of avoiding it; there is no reason for making it vary with the diligence or negligence of a third person in giving occasion for the risk to exist. If the defendant is so negligent that an adult in the plaintiff's position could not have saved himself by reasonable care, he is liable. If he is aware of the plaintiff's helplessness, and fails to use such special precaution as is reasonably possible, then also, we submit, he is liable. If he did not know, and could not with ordinary diligence have known, the plaintiff to be incapable of taking care of himself (*f*), and has used such diligence as would be sufficient towards an adult; or if, being aware of the danger, he did use such additional caution as he reasonably could; or if the facts were such that no additional caution was practicable, and there is no evidence of negligence according to the ordinary standard (*g*), then the defendant is not liable.

No English decision has been met with that goes the length of depriving a child of redress on the ground that a third person negligently allowed it to go alone (*h*). In America there have been such decisions in Massachusetts (*i*), New York, and elsewhere: "but there are as many decisions to the contrary" (*j*); and it is submitted

---

(*f*) This might happen in various ways, by reason of darkness or otherwise.

(*g*) *Singleton* v. *E. C. R. Co.* (1889), 7 C. B. N. S. 287, is a case of this kind, as it was decided not on the fiction of imputing a third person's negligence to a child, but on the ground (whether rightly taken or not) that there was no evidence of negligence at all.

(*h*) *Mangan* v. *Atterton* (1886), L. R. 1 Ex. 239, 35 L. J. Ex. 161, comes near it.

But that case went partly on the ground of the damage being too remote, and since *Clark* v. *Chambers* (1878), 3 Q. B. D. 327, 47 L. J. Q. B. 427, *supra*, p. 46, it is of doubtful authority. For our own part we think it is not law.

(*i*) Holmes, The Common Law, 128.

(*j*) Bigelow L. C. 729, and see Horace Smith, 211. In Vermont (*Robinson* v. *Cone*, 22 Vt. 213, 224, *ap.* Cooley on Torts, 681), the view maintained in the text is distinctly taken. "We are satisfied that

Hedrick, 1 Wash St 446, 25 Pac Rep 335, Gavin v. Chicago, 97 Ill. 66; Bay Shore R. Co v. Harris, 67 Ala. 6, McGreary v. Eastern R. Co., 135 Mass 363, 15 Am & Eng. R. Cas. 407; Fisk v Missouri Furnace Co., 10 Mo App 62

that both on principle and according to the latest authority of the highest tribunals in both countries they are right.

Child v. Hearn. In one peculiar case (k) the now exploded doctrine of "identification" (l) was brought in, gratuitously as it would seem. The plaintiff was a platelayer working on a railway; the railway company was by statute bound to maintain a fence to prevent animals (m) from straying off the adjoining land; the defendant was an adjacent owner who kept pigs. The fence was insufficient to keep out pigs (n). Some pigs of the defendant's found their way on to the line, it did not appear how, and upset a trolly worked by hand on which the plaintiff and others were riding back from their work. The plaintiff's case appears to be bad on one or both of two grounds; there was no proof of actual negligence on the defendant's part, and even if his common-law duty to fence was not altogether superseded, as regards that boundary, by the Act casting the duty on the railway company, he was entitled to assume that the company would perform their duty; and also the damage was too remote (o). But the ground actually taken was "that the servant can be in no better position than the master when he is using the master's property for the master's purposes," or "the plaintiff is identified with the land which he was using for

---

although a child or idiot or lunatic may to some extent have escaped into the highway, through the fault or negligence of his keeper, and so be improperly there, yet if he is hurt by the negligence of the defendant, he is not precluded from his redress If one know that such a person is on the highway, or on a railway, he is bound to a proportionate degree of watchfulness, and what would be but ordinary neglect in regard to one whom the defendant supposed a person of full age and capacity, would be gross neglect as to a child, or one known to be incapable of escaping danger." So, too, Bigelow 730

(k) *Child v. Hearn.* (1871), L R 9 Ex 176, 13 L J Ex 100

(l) P 580, above

(m) "Cattle," held by the court to include pigs

(n) That is, pigs of average vigour and obstinacy, see per Bramwell B , whose judgment (pp 181, 182), is almost a caricature of the general idea of the "reasonable man" It was alleged, but not found as a fact, that the defendant had previously been warned by some one of his pigs being out he line.

(o) Note in Addison on Torts, 5th ed.

27

his own convenience." This ground would now clearly be untenable.

Admiralty rule of dividing loss. The common law rule of contributory negligence is unknown to the maritime law administered in courts of Admiralty jurisdiction. Under a rough working rule commonly called *judicium rusticum*, and apparently derived from early medieval codes or customs, with none of which, however, it coincides in its modern application (*p*), the loss is equally divided in cases of collision where both ships are found to have been in fault. "The ancient rule applied only where there was no fault in either ship" (*q*); as adopted in England, it seems more than doubtful whether the rule made any distinction, until quite late in the eighteenth century, between cases of negligence and of pure accident. However that may be, it dates from a time when any more refined working out of principles was impossible (*r*). As a rule of thumb, which frankly renounces the pretence of being anything more, it is not amiss, and it appears to be generally accepted by those whom it concerns, although, as Mr. Marsden's researches have shown, for about a century it has been applied for a wholly different purpose from that for which it was introduced in the older maritime law, and in a wholly different class of cases. By the Judicature Act, 1873 (*r*), the *judicium rusticum* is expressly preserved in the Admiralty Division.

(*p*) Marsden on Collisions at Sea, ch 6 (3d ed.), and see an article by the same writer in L. Q. R. ii. 357

(*q*) Op. cit. 130

(*r*) Writers on maritime law state the rule of the common law to be that when both ships are in fault neither can recover anything. This may have been practically so in the first half of the century, but it is neither a complete nor a correct version of the law laid down in *Tuff* v. *Warman*, 5 C. B. N. S. 573, 27 L. J. C. P. 322. As long ago as 1838 it was distinctly pointed out that "there may have been negligence in both parties, and yet the plaintiff may be entitled to recover." Parke B. in *Bridge* v. *Grand Junction R. Co.* (1838), 3 M. & W. 244, 248

(*r*) S. 25, sub s. 9. The first intention of the framers of the Act was otherwise. See Marsden, p. 134, 3d ed.

IV.—*Auxiliary Rules and Presumptions.*

Action under difficulty caused by another's negligence. There are certain conditions under which the normal standard of a reasonable man's prudence is peculiarly difficult to apply, by reason of one party's choice of alternatives, or opportunities of judgment, being affected by the conduct of the other. Such difficulties occur mostly in questions of contributory negligence. In the first place, a man who by another's want of care finds himself in a position of imminent danger cannot be held guilty of negligence merely because in that emergency he does not act in the best way to avoid the danger. That which appears the best way to a court examining the matter afterwards at leisure and with full knowledge is not necessarily obvious even to a prudent and skilful man on

---

Action under difficulty caused by another's negligence. Agreeing with the text, *vide* Wesley Coal Co *v.* Healer, 84 Ill. 126, followed in Silver Cord C M Co *v.* McDonald, 14 Colo. 191, 23 Pac. Rep. 346 Collins *v.* Davidson, 19 Fed Rep. 83. In the leading case of Brookhaven Lumber Co. *v.* Illinois Central R Co. (68 Miss 432; 10 So. Rep. 66) where the facts were, that by the wrongful act of some unknown person, a switch leading upon a side track was left open, and, beyond this on the side track another switch was misplaced. At night the engineer of a passenger train, running on a down grade thirty-five miles an hour, at a distance of 800 feet, saw that the first switch was open and promptly applied the air brakes but the train rushed upon the side track, and was derailed at the second switch and ran into a mill shed, which would not have been struck but for that switch, that the engineer did not see.

In a case against the company by the owner of the property destroyed by fire communicated in the collision the court said: "the engineer was only required to act in view of what he then saw, situated as he was, and that suddenly and unexpectedly confronted with a complicated difficulty impossible to have been foreseen, he is not to be held accountable for failure to exercise that cool and unembarrassed and unerring judgment which we, freed from sudden surprise and danger, could now form and execute. He appears to have done the best he could, situated as he was, and nothing more could reasonably be required of him."

See Lawrence *v.* Green, 71 Cal. 421; Dutzi *v.* Geisel, 23 Mo. App. 676, Karr *v* Parks, 40 Cal. 188; Culyer *v.* Decker, 20 Hun, 174; Lowery *v.*

a sudden alarm. Still less can the party whose fault brought on the risk be heard to complain of the other's error of judgment. This rule has been chiefly applied in maritime cases, where a ship placed in peril by another's improper navigation has at the last moment taken a wrong course (*s*): but there is authority for it elsewhere. A person who finds the gates of a level railway crossing open, and is thereby misled into thinking the line safe for crossing, is not bound to minute circumspection, and if he is run over by a train the company may be liable to him although "he did not use his faculties so clearly as he might have done under other circumstances" (*t*). "One should not be held too strictly for a hasty attempt to avert a suddenly impending danger, even though his effort is ill-judged" (*u*).

(*s*) *The Bywell Castle* (1879), 4 P. Div. 219, *The Tasmania* (1890), 15 App. Ca. 223, 225, per Lord Herschell, and see other examples collected in Marsden on Collisions at Sea, pp 4, 5, 3d ed

(*t*) *N. E. R. Co.* v. *Wanless* (1874), L. R. 7 H. L. at p 16, cp. *Slattery's ca.* (1878), 3 App Ca at p 1193

(*u*) *Briggs* v. *Union Street Ry* (1888), 148 Mass 72, 76

Manhattan Ry Co., 99 N. Y. 158, 52 Am. Rep. 12, Marks v. St. Paul, etc. Ry Co., 30 Minn. 493, Moore v. Edison, etc. Co., 43 La. An. 792, 9 So Rep. 433, Lincoln Rapid Transit Co. v. Nichols (Neb.), 55 N. W. Rep. 872, Gibbons v. Wilkesbarre etc. St. Ry. Co., 155 Pa. St. 279; 26 At. Rep. 117

The master is not liable for an error of judgment of the servant in extricating an injured person from a perilous situation. "A right of action under such circumstances, can arise only where the injury was inflicted or increased because of the doing or the omission to do some act or acts the doing of which or the omission to do which was other than the result of an error of judgment as to the means to be used in extricating the plaintiff. Any other rule would, where there were various steps in the happening of an action culminating in the injuries suffered, authorize a division of liability as to those various steps, which contribute to the happening of the whole accident." Rhing v. B'way & S A. R. Co., 53 Hun, 323, 6 N. Y. S. Rep. 641

But "if one acts unreasonably rashly, or becomes frightened at a trivial occurrence, not calculated to alarm a reasonably prudent man, and thereby brings injury upon himself, there is no liability." South Covington etc. Ry. Co. v. Ware, 84 Ky. 271, 1 S. W. Rep. 493 See McLean v. Schuyler Steam Tow-Boat Line, 52 Hun, 43, 4 N. Y. S. Rep. 790.

No duty to anticipate negligence of others. One might generalize the r[ule] in some such form as this: not only a man cannot with impunity harm others by his negligence, but his negligence cannot put them in a worse position with regard to the estimation of default. You shall not drive a man into a situation where there is loss or

---

No duty to anticipate negligence of others "Any citizen in the possession of his own business may everywhere act upon the assumption that no other citizen will by misfeasance, or nonfeasance, cause him an injury, unless there is something in the circumstances of the case which casts upon him the duty of actual vigilance for his own safety. "New York etc. R. Co. v A. R Co, 129 N Y. 602; 29 N. E. Rep. 829. "'It is a sound rule of law that it is not contributory negligence not to look out for danger when there is no reason to apprehend any' Beach Contrib Neg 41, and cases cited. The authorities cited by the learned commentator go much further than the text, and state the rule to be that every one has a right to presume that others, owing a special duty to guard against danger, will perform that duty." Engel v. Smith, 82 Mich 1, 46 N. W Rep 22. "It cannot, therefore, be said as a matter of law, that one is guilty of negligence who does not anticipate, and take special precaution against, injury from the reckless and improper conduct of others in riding or driving at an unusual and dangerous rate of speed" Stringer v Frost, 116 Md 480, 19 N E Rep 331 Again, in Brosnan v Sweetzer (127 Ind. 1, 26 N E Rep 555), where the defendant had in their store a trap-door in the floor in front of the counter. Plaintiff, a customer, walked over this floor while closed, and when attempting to walk back while it was open, though she did not see it, she fell through and was injured. The court said "She had the right to rely upon the floor being in good, safe condition She had no reason to suspect danger"

See Frank v City of St. Louis, 110 Mo. 516, 19 S. W. Rep 938; Bowen v Flanagan, 84 Va 313, Hannem v. Pence, 40 Minn. 127, 41 N. W Rep. 659, Dickson v Hollister, 123 Pa St. 430, 23 W. N. C 128, Galvin v. Mayor, etc of New York, 112 N. Y 228, 19 N. E. Rep. 675, Perry v. Smith, 156 Mass 340, 51 N. E Rep. 9, Kennayde v Pacific R. Co, 45 Mo 255; White v. Cincinnati, etc Ry Co, 89 Ky 478, 12 S W. Rep. 136, Jacksonville, T & K Ry. Co. v Peninsular Land etc Co, 27 Fla 157, 9 So Rep 675, Fisk v Wait, 104 Mass. 71, Moulton v Aldrich, 28 Kan 300, Fox v. Sackett, 10 Allen, 533, Damour v Lyons, 44 Ia. 276; Harpel v Curtis, 1 E D Smith, 78; Brown v Lynn, 31 Pa St. 510; Barton v. Syracuse, 37 Barb 292; Morrisey v. Wiggins Ferry Co, 47 N. W 521; Thomp Car. of Pass. 243; Robinson v. Railroad Co., 48 Cal 409

risk every way, and then say that he suffered by his own imprudence. Neither shall you complain that he did not foresee and provide against your negligence. We are entitled to count on the ordinary prudence of our fellow-men until we have specific warning to the contrary. The driver of a carriage assumes that other vehicles will observe the rule of the road, the master of a vessel that other ships will obey the statutory and other rules of navigation, and the like. And generally no man is bound (either for the establishment of his own claims, or to avoid claims of third persons against him) to use special precaution against merely possible want of care or skill on the part of other persons who are not his servants or under his authority or control (*x*).

It is not, as a matter of law, negligent in a passenger on a railway to put his hand on the door or the window-rod, though it might occur to a very prudent man to try first whether it was properly fastened; for it is the company's business to have the door properly fastened (*y*). On the other hand if something goes wrong which does not cause any pressing danger or inconvenience, and the passenger comes to harm in endeavouring to set it right himself, he cannot hold the company liable (*z*).

Choice of risks under stress of another's negligence. We have a somewhat different case when a person, having an apparent dilemma of evils or risks put before him by

(*x*) See *Daniel* v *Metrop R Co* (1871), L R 5 H L 45, 40 L J C P 121

(*y*) *Gee* v *Metrop R Co* (1873), Ex Ch L R 8 Q B 161, 42 L J Q B 105. There was some difference of opinion how far the question of contributory negligence in fact was fit to be put to the jury

(*z*) This is the principle applied in *Adams* v *L & Y R Co* (1869), L R 4 C P 739, 38 L J C P 277, though (it seems) not rightly in the particular case, see in *Gee* v *Metrop R Co.*, L R 8 Q B at pp. 161, 173, 176.

Choice of risks under stress of another's negligence. "One may, without fault of his own, be in a situation where he must choose a perilous alternative. The degree of danger, the stress of circumstances, the

another's default, makes an active choice between them. The principle applied is not dissimilar: it is not necessarily and of itself contributory negligence to do something which, apart from the state of things due to the defendant's negligence, would be imprudent.

Clayards v. Dethick. The earliest case where this point is distinctly raised and treated by a full Court is *Clayards v. Dethick* (a). The plaintiff was a cab-owner. The defendants, for the purpose of making a drain, had opened a trench along the passage which afforded the only outlet from the stables occupied by the plaintiff to the street. The opening was not fenced, and the earth and gravel excavated from the trench were thrown up in a bank on that side of it where the free space was wider, thus increasing the obstruction. In this state of things the plaintiff attempted to get two of his horses out of the mews. One he succeeded in leading out over the gravel, by the advice of one of the defendants then present. With the other he failed, the rubbish giving way and letting the horse down into the trench. Neither defendant was present at that time (b). The jury were directed "that it could not be

---

(a) 12 Q. B. 439 (1848). The rule was laid down by Lord Ellenborough at nisi prius as early as 1816, *Jones v. Boyce*, 1 Stark. 493, cited by Montague Smith J., L. R. 10 C. P. at p. 743. The plaintiff was an outside passenger on a coach, and jumped off to avoid what seemed an imminent upset, the coach was however not upset. It was left to the jury whether by the defendant's fault he "was placed in such a situation as to render what he did a prudent precaution for the purpose of self preservation."

(b) Evidence was given by the defendants, but apparently not believed by the jury, that their men expressly warned the plaintiff against the course he took.

---

expectation or hope that others will fully perform the duties resting on them, may all have to be considered." *Miner v. Conn. River R. Co.*, 153 Mass. 398, 26 N. E. Rep. 995. Thus, a woman being obliged to throw herself on a railroad platform to escape being struck by a piece of timber projecting from a car in motion, had her health impaired by the fright thus occasioned. It was held that she was entitled to recover damages for such impairment of her health. *Buchanan v. West Jersey R. Co.*, 52 N. J. 265, 19 Atl. Rep. 254. See *Austin & N. W. Ry. Co. v. Beatty*, 73 Tex. 593, 11 S. W. Rep. 858.

the plaintiff's duty to refrain altogether from coming out of the mews merely because the defendants had made the passage in some degree dangerous: that the defendants were not entitled to keep the occupiers of the mews in a state of siege till the passage was declared safe, first creating a nuisance and then excusing themselves by giving notice that there was some danger: though if the plaintiff had persisted in running upon a great and obvious danger, his action could not be maintained." This direction was approved. Whether the plaintiff had suffered by the defendants' negligence, or by his own rash action, was a matter of fact and of degree properly left to the jury: "the whole question was whether the danger was so obvious that the plaintiff could not with common prudence make the attempt." The decision has been adversely criticised by Lord Bramwell, but principle and authority seem on the whole to support it (*c*).

One or two of the railway cases grouped for practical purposes under the catch-word "invitation to alight" have been decided, in part at least, on the principle that, where a passenger is under reasonable apprehension that if he does not alight at the place where he is (though an unsafe or unfit one) he will not have time to alight at all, he may be justified in taking the risk of alighting as best he can at that place (*d*); notwithstanding that he might, by declining that risk and letting himself be carried on to the next station, have entitled himself to recover damages for the loss of time and resulting expense (*e*).

Doctrine of New York Courts. There has been a line of cases of this class in the State of New York, where a

---

(*c*) See Appendix B to Smith on Negligence, 2d ed. I agree with Mr. Smith's observations *ad fin.*, p. 279.

(*d*) *Robson* v *N E R Co* (1875-6), L R 10 Q P 271, 274, 44 L J Q B 112 (in 2 Q B Div 85, 46 L J Q B 50), *Rose* v *N E R Co* (1876), 2 Ex Div 248, 46 L J Ex 374.

(*e*) Contra Bramwell L J in *Lax* v *Corporation of Darlington* (1879), 5 Ex D at p 35, but the last mentioned cases had not been cited.

view is taken less favourable to the plaintiff than the rule of *Clayards* v. *Dethick*. If a train fails to stop, and only slackens speed, at a station where it is timed to stop, and a passenger alights from it while in motion at the invitation of the company's servants (*f*), the matter is for the jury; so if a train does not stop a reasonable time for passengers to alight, and starts while one is alighting (*g*). Otherwise it is held that the passenger alights at his own risk. If he wants to hold the company liable he must go on to the next station and sue for the resulting damage (*h*).

On the other hand, where the defendant's negligence has put the plaintiff in a situation of imminent peril, the plaintiff may hold the defendant liable for the natural consequences of action taken on the first alarm, though such action may turn out to have been unnecessary (*i*). It is also held that the running of even an obvious and great risk in order to save human life may be justified, as against those by whose default that life is put in peril (*k*). And this seems just, for a contrary doctrine would have the effect of making it safer for the wrong-doer to create a great risk than a small one. Or we may put it thus; that the law does not think so meanly of mankind as to hold it otherwise than a natural and probable consequence of a helpless person being put in danger that some ablebodied person should expose himself to the same danger to effect a rescue.

Separation of law and fact in United States. American jurisprudence is exceedingly rich in illustrations of the

---

(*f*) *Filer* v *N Y Central R R Co* (1872) 49 N Y (4 Sickels) 47

(*g*) 63 N Y at p 559

(*h*) *Burrows* v *Erie R Co* (1876), 63 N Y (18 Sickels) 556

(*i*) *Coulter* v *Express Co* (1874), 56 N Y (11 Sickels) 585, *Twomley* v *Central Park R R Co* (1878), 69 N Y (24 Sickels) 158. Cp *Jones* v. *Boyce*, 1 Starr 493

(*k*) *Eckert* v *Long Island R R Co* (1871), 43 N Y 502, 3 Am Rep 721 (action by representative of a man killed in getting a child off the railway track in front of a train which was being negligently driven)

Separation of law and fact in United States See NEGLIGENCE A QUESTION OF MIXED FACT AND LAW, *ante*, p 543, and BURDEN OF PROOF, *ante*, p 545

questions discussed in this chapter, and American cases are constantly, and sometimes very freely, cited and even judicially reviewed (*l*) in our courts. It may therefore be useful to call attention to the peculiar turn given by legislation in many of the States to the treatment of points of "mixed law and fact." I refer to those States where the judge is forbidden by statute (in some cases by the Constitution of the State) (*m*) to charge the jury as to matter of fact. Under such a rule the summing-up becomes a categorical enumeration of all the specific inferences of fact which it is open to the jury to find, and which in the opinion of the Court would have different legal consequences, together with a statement of those legal consequences as leading to a verdict for the plaintiff or the defendant. And it is the habit of counsel to frame elaborate statements of the propositions of law for which they contend as limiting the admissible findings of fact, or as applicable to the facts which may be found, and to tender them to the Court as the proper instructions to be given to the jury. Hence there is an amount of minute discussion beyond what we are accustomed to in this country, and it is a matter of great importance, where an appeal is contemplated, to get as little as possible left at large as matter of fact. Thus attempts are frequently made to persuade a Court to lay down as matter of law that particular acts are or are not contributory negligence (*n*). Probably the common American doctrine that the plaintiff has to prove, as a sort of preliminary issue, that he was in the exercise of due care, has its origin in this practice. It is not necessary or proper for an English lawyer to criticize the convenience of

---

(*l*) *E. g.* Lord Esher's judgment in *The Bernina*, 12 P. Div. at pp. 77-82. Cp. per Lord Herschell in *Mills* v. *Armstrong*, 13 App. Ca. at p. 10.

(*m*) Stimson American Statute Law, p. 132, § 605.

(*n*) For a strong example see *Kane* v. *N. Central R. Co.*, 128 U. S. 91. In *Washington &c. R. R. Co.* v. *McDade* (1889), 135 U. S. 554, 561, "counsel for the defendant asked the Court to grant twenty separate prayers for instructions to the jury."

a rigid statutory definition of the provinces of judge and jury. But English practitioners consulting the American reports must bear its prevalence in mind, or they may find many things hardly intelligible, and perhaps even suppose the substantive differences between English and American opinion upon points of pure law to be greater than they really are.

CHAPTER XII.

DUTIES OF INSURING SAFETY.

Exceptions to general limits of duties of caution. In general, those who in person go about an undertaking attended with risk to their neighbours, or set it in motion by the hand of a servant, are answerable for the conduct of that undertaking with diligence proportioned to the apparent risk. To this rule the policy of the law makes exceptions on both sides. As we have seen in the chapter of General Exceptions, men are free to seek their own advantage in the ordinary pursuit of business or uses of property, though a probable or even intended result may be to diminish the profit or convenience of others. We now have to consider the cases where a stricter duty has been imposed. As a matter of history, such cases cannot easily be referred to any definite principle. But the ground on which a rule of strict obligation has been maintained and consolidated by modern authorities is the magnitude of the danger, coupled with the difficulty of

---

Exceptions to general limits of duties of caution. In the case of Morgan v Cox (22 Mo. 376), the court said "Every person, however, who is performing an act, is bound to take some care in what he is doing. He cannot exercise his own indisputable rights without observing proper precaution not to cause others more damage than can be deemed fairly incident to such exercise. '*Sic utero tuo ut alienum non laedas*' And therefore, although the mere exercise of a right is not a wrong in any case, any negligence in the exercise of it, that causes a loss to another, is an injury conferring upon him a right of action It is correctly said, that generally between persons standing in no particular relation to each other, that alone is reasonable care, which, in the judgment of men in general, is proportionate to the probability of injury to others, and consequently, he who does what is more than ordinarily dangerous, is bound to use more than ordinary care." See Todd v. Cochell, 17 Cal 98

proving negligence as the specific cause in the event of the danger having ripened into actual harm. The law might have been content with applying the general standard of reasonable care, in the sense that a reasonable man dealing with a dangerous thing — fire, flood-water, poison, deadly weapons, weights projecting or suspended over a thoroughfare, or whatsoever else it be — will exercise a keener foresight and use more anxious precaution than if it were an object unlikely to cause harm, such as a faggot, or a loaf of bread. A prudent man does not handle a loaded gun or a sharp sword in the same fashion as a stick or a shovel. But the course adopted in England has been to preclude questions of detail by making the duty absolute; or, if we prefer to put it in that form, to consolidate the judgment of fact into an unbending rule of law. The law takes notice that certain things are a source of extraordinary risk, and a man who exposes his neighbour to such risk is held, although his act is not of itself wrongful, to insure his neighbour against any consequent harm not due to some cause beyond human foresight and control

Rylands v. Fletcher. Various particular rules of this kind (now to be regarded as applications of a more general one) are recognized in our law from early times. The generalization was effected as late as 1868, by the leading case of *Rylands* v. *Fletcher*, where the judgment of the Exchequer Chamber delivered by Blackburn J. was adopted in terms by the House of Lords.

The nature of the facts in *Fletcher* v. *Rylands*, and the question of law raised by them, are for our purpose best shown by the judgment itself (*a*): —

Judgment of Ex. Ch "It appears from the statement in the case, that the plaintiff was damaged by his property

---

(*a*) L. R. 1 Ex at p 278, per Willes, Blackburn, Keating, Mellor, Montague Smith, and Lush JJ. For the statements of fact referred to, see at pp. 267-269.

being flooded by water, which, without any fault on his part, broke out of a reservoir, constructed on the defendants' land by the defendants' orders, and maintained by the defendants

"It appears from the statement in the case, that the coal under the defendants' land had at some remote period been worked out; but this was unknown at the time when the defendants gave directions to erect the reservoir, and the water in the reservoir would not have escaped from the defendants' land, and no mischief would have been done to the plaintiff, but for this latent defect in the defendants' subsoil. And it further appears that the defendants selected competent engineers and contractors to make their reservoir, and themselves personally continued in total ignorance of what we have called the latent defect in the subsoil; but that these persons employed by them in the course of the work became aware of the existence of the ancient shafts filled up with soil, though they did not know or suspect that they were shafts communicating with old workings.

"It is found that the defendants personally were free from all blame, but that in fact proper care and skill was not used by the persons employed by them, to provide for the sufficiency of the reservoir with reference to these shafts. The consequence was that the reservoir when filled with water burst into the shafts, the water flowed down through them into the old workings, and thence into the plaintiff's mine, and there did the mischief.

"The plaintiff, though free from all blame on his part, must bear the loss unless he can establish that it was the consequence of some default for which the defendants are responsible. The question of law therefore arises, what is the obligation which the law casts on a person who, like the defendants, lawfully brings on his land something which, though harmless whilst it remains there, will naturally do mischief if it escape out of his land. It is agreed on all hands that he must take care to keep in that which he has brought on the land and keeps there, in order that it may not escape and damage his neighbours; but the question arises whether the duty which the law casts upon him, under such circumstances, is an absolute duty to keep it in at his peril, or is, as the majority of the Court of Exchequer have thought, merely a duty to take all reasonable and prudent precautions in order to keep it in, but no more. If the first be the law, the person who has brought on his land and kept there something dangerous, and failed to keep it in, is responsible for all the natural consequences of its escape. If the second be the limit of his duty, he would not be answerable except on proof of negligence, and consequently would not be answerable for escape arising from any latent defect which ordinary prudence and skill could not detect. . . . .

"We think that the true rule of law is, that the person who for his own purposes brings on his lands, and collects and keeps there, anything likely to do mischief if it escapes, must keep it in at his peril, and, if it does not do so, is *prima facie* answerable for all the damage which is the natural consequence of its escape. He can excuse himself by showing that the escape was owing to the plaintiff's default; or perhaps that the escape was the consequence of *vis major*, or the act of God; but as nothing of this sort exists here, it is unnecessary to inquire what excuse would be sufficient. The general rule, as above stated, seems on principle just. The person whose grass or corn is eaten down by the escaping cattle of his neighbour, or whose mine is flooded by the water from his neighbour's reservoir, or whose cellar is invaded by the filth of his neighbour's privy, or whose habitation is made unhealthy by the fumes and noisome vapours of his neighbour's alkali works, is damnified without any fault of his own; and it seems but reasonable and just that the neighbour who has brought something on his own property which was not naturally there, harmless to others so long as it is confined to his own property, but which he knows to be mischievous if it gets on his neighbour's, should be obliged to make good the damage which ensues if he does not succeed in confining it to his own property. But for his act in bringing it there, no mischief could have accrued, and it seems but just that he should at his peril keep it there so that no mischief may accrue, or answer for the natural and anticipated consequences. And upon authority, this we think is established to be the law, whether the things so brought be beasts, or water, or filth, or stenches."

Affirmation thereof by H L Not only was this decision affirmed in the House of Lords (b), but the reasons given for it were fully confirmed. "If a person brings or accumulates on his land anything which, if it should escape, may cause damage to his neighbours, he does so at his peril. If it does escape and cause damage, he is responsible, however careful he may have been, and whatever precautions he may have taken to prevent the damage" (c). It was not overlooked that a line had to be drawn between this rule and the general immunity given to landowners for acts done in the "natural user" of their land, or "exercise of ordinary rights"—an immunity which extends, as had already been settled by the House of Lords itself (d), even to obviously probable consequences. Here Lord Cairns pointed out that the defendants had for their own purposes made "a non-natural use" of their land, by collecting water "in quantities and in a manner not the result of any work or operation on or under the land."

The detailed illustration of the rule in *Rylands* v. *Fletcher*, as governing the mutual claims and duties of

---

(b) *Rylands* v *Fletcher* (1868), L R 3 H L 330, 37 L J Ex 161

(c) Lord Cranworth, at p 340

(d) *Chasemore* v *Richards* (1859), 7 H L C 349, 29 L. J. Ex 81

adjacent landowners, belongs to the law of property rather than to the subject of this work (e). We shall return presently to the special classes of cases (more or less discussed in the judgment of the Exchequer Chamber) for which a similar rule of strict responsibility had been established earlier. As laying down a positive rule of law, the decision in *Rylands* v. *Fletcher* is not open to criticism in this country (f). But in the judgment of the Exchequer Chamber itself the possibility of exceptions is suggested, and we shall see that the tendency of later decisions has been rather to encourage the discovery of exceptions than otherwise. A rule casting the responsibility of an insurer on innocent persons is a hard rule, though it may be a just one; and it needs to be maintained by very strong evidence (g) or on very clear grounds of policy. Now the judgment in *Fletcher* v. *Rylands* (h), carefully prepared as it evidently was, hardly seems to make such grounds clear enough for universal acceptance. The liability seems to be rested only in part on the evidently hazardous character of the state of things artificially maintained by the defendants on their land. In part the case is assimilated to that of a nuisance (i), and in part, also, traces are apparent of the formerly prevalent theory that a man's voluntary acts, even when lawful and free from negligence, are *prima facie* done at his peril (k), a theory which modern authorities have explicitly rejected

(e) See *Fletcher* v *Smith* (1877), 2 App Ca 781, 47 L J Ex. 4, *Humphries* v *Cousins* (1877), 2 C P D 239, 46 L. J C P 48, *Hurdman* v *North Eastern R Co.* (1878), 3 C P Div 168, 47 L J C P 368, and for the distinction as to "natural course of user," *Wilson* v *Waddell*, H L (Sc), 2 App Ca 95

(f) Judicial opinions still differ in the United States See Bigelow L C 497-500 The case has been cited with approval in Massachusetts (*Shipley* v *Fifty Associates*, 106 Mass 194, *Gorham* v *Gross*, 125 Mass 232, *Mears* v *Dole*, 135 Mass 508), but distinctly disallowed in New York *Losee* v *Buchanan*, 51 N Y (6 Sickels) 476.

(g) See *Reg.* v *Commissioners of Sewers for Essex* (1885), 14 Q B Div 561

(h) L R. 1 Ex 277 *sqq*

(i) See especially at pp 285-6 But can an isolated accident, however mischievous in its results, be a nuisance? though its consequences may, as where a branch lopped or blown down from a tree is left lying across a highway

(k) L R 1 Ex 286-7, 3 H. L. 341

in America, and do not encourage in England, except so far as *Rylands* v. *Fletcher* may itself be capable of being used for that purpose (*l*). Putting that question aside, one does not see why the policy of the law might not have been satisfied by requiring the defendant to insure diligence in proportion to the manifest risk (not merely the diligence of himself and his servants, but the actual use of due care in the matter, whether by servants, contractors, or others), and throwing the burden of proof on him in cases where the matter is peculiarly within his knowledge. This indeed is what the law has done as regards duties of safe repair, as we shall presently see. Doubtless it is possible to consider *Rylands* v. *Fletcher* as having only fixed a special rule about adjacent landowners (*m*): but it was certainly intended to enunciate something much wider.

Character of later cases. Yet no case has been found, not being closely similar in its facts, or within some previously recognized category, in which the unqualified rule of liability without proof of negligence has been enforced. We have cases where damages have been recovered for the loss of animals by the escape, if so it may be called, of poisonous vegetation or other matters from a neighbour's land. Thus the owner of yew trees, whose branches project over his boundary, so that his neighbour's horse eats of them and is thereby poisoned, is held liable (*n*); and the same rule has been applied where a fence of wire rope was in bad repair, so that pieces of rusted iron wire fell from it into a close adjoining that of the occupier, who was bound to maintain the fence, and were swallowed by cattle

---

(*l*) See *The Nitro-glycerine Case* (1872), 15 Wall. 524, *Brown* v. *Kendall* (1850), 6 Cush. 292, *Holmes* v. *Mather* (1875) L. R. 10 Ex. 261, 44 L. J. Ex. 176, *Stanley* v. *Powell*, '91, 1 Q. B. 86, 60 L. J. Q. B. 52.

(*m*) Martin B., L. R. 6 Ex. at p. 223.

(*n*) *Crowhurst* v. *Amersham Burial Board* (1878), 4 Ex. D. 5, 48 L. J. Ex. 109.

Wilson v. *Newberry* (1871), L. R. 7 Q. B. 31, 41 L. J. Q. B. 31, is not inconsistent, for there it was only averred that clippings from the defendants' yew trees were on the plaintiff's land, and the clipping might, for all that appeared, have been the act of a stranger.

which died thereof (o). In these cases, however, it was not contended, nor was it possible to contend, that the defendants had used any care at all. The arguments for the defence went either on the acts complained of being within the "natural user" of the land, or on the damage not being such as could have been reasonably anticipated (p). We may add that having a tree, noxious or not, permanently projecting over a neighbour's land is of itself a nuisance, and letting decayed pieces of a fence, or anything else, fall upon a neighbour's land for want of due repair is of itself a trespass. Then in *Ballard* v. *Tomlinson* (q) the sewage collected by the defendant in his disused well was an absolutely noxious thing, and his case was, not that he had done his best to prevent it from poisoning the water which supplied the plaintiff's well, but that he was not bound to do anything.

Exception of act of God. On the other hand, the rule in *Rylands* v. *Fletcher* has been decided by the Court of Appeal not to apply to damage of which the immediate cause is the act of God (r). And the act of God does not

(o) *Firth v. Bowling Iron Co* (1878), 3 C P D 254, 47 L J C P. 358

(p) The former ground was chiefly relied on in *Crowhurst's case*, the latter in *Firth's*.

(q) 29 Ch Div 115 (1885), 54 L J Ch 454

(r) Act of God = vis major = θεοῦ βία. see D 19 2 locati conducti, 25, § 6 The classical signification of "vis major" is however wider for some purposes, *Nugent* v *Smith*, 1 C P. Div. 423, 429, per Cockburn C J

Exception of act of God. The doctrine stated in the text is sustained by numerous American authorities, vide Long v Penn R Co , 174 Pa St. 343 2> At Rep 459; 29 W N C 375, Blythe v. Denver & R G Ry Co , 15 Colo 333, 25 Pac. Rep. 702, Black v. Chicago, B & Q R. Co., 30 Neb. 197, 46 N W Rep 428, Southern Ex Co v Glenn, 16 Lea, 472, 1 S. W. Rep 102, Elliott v Russell, 10 Johns 1; Pittsburg, etc., R Co. v. Gilliland, 56 Pa St 445, International, etc , R Co. v. Halloren, 53 Tex. 16; 3 Am & Eng R. Cas 343, Baltimore, etc , R Co v Sulphur Springs, etc., Dist , 96 Pa St 65, 2 Am & Eng R. Cas. 166, Phila etc. R Co. v Anderson, 94 Pa. St 351, 6 Am & Eng. R. Cas 407, Nashville, etc , R. Co v Davis, 6 Heisk 261, Gates v. Southern Minn. R. Co. 28 Minn 110, 2 Am & Eng R Cas. 237, Sheldon v Sherman, 42 N. Y 484, Campbell v Bear River Co., 35 Cal 679, Chidester v Consolidated D Co., 59 Cal

necessarily mean an operation of natural forces so violent and unexpected that no human foresight or skill could possibly have prevented its effects. It is enough that the accident should be such as human foresight could not be reasonably expected to anticipate; and whether it comes within this description is a question of fact (s). The only

(s) *Nichols v. Marsland* (1875-6), L. R. 10 Ex. 255, 2 Ex. D. 1, 46 L. J. Ex. 174. Note that Lord Bramwell, who in *Rylands v. Fletcher* took the view that ultimately prevailed, was also a party to this decision. The defendant was an owner of artificial pools, formed by damming a natural stream, into which the water was finally let off by a system of weirs. The rainfall accompanying an extremely violent thunderstorm broke the embankments, and the rush of water down the stream carried away four county bridges, in respect of which damage the action was brought.

179, Richardson v. Kier, 34 Cal. 63, Tenny v. Miners' Ditch Co., 7 Cal. 335, Wolf v St Louis, etc., Co., 10 Cal. 541; Lapham v. Curtis, 5 Vt. 371, Reed v Spaulding, 30 N. Y. 630, Wallace v Clayton, 42 Ga 448, Bell v McClintock, 9 Watts, 119, Nashville, etc., R Co v King, 6 Heisk 269, Ballentine v North Mo R Co, 40 Mo. 491; Bowman v Teal, 23 Wend. 306, Parsons v Hardy, 14 Wend 215, Engster v West, 35 La. An 119, 48 Am Rep 232, McGraw v. Baltimore, etc R. Co, 18 W. Va. 361; 9 Am. & Eng R. Cas 188, Allen v Mercantile M Ins. Co, 44 N Y. 437, 4 Am. Rep 700, Wing v N. Y etc. R Co, 1 Hilt 700, Harris v Rand, 4 N. H 259, 17 Am. Dec 421, Lowe v Moss, 12 Ill 477, West v. Berlin, 3 Ia 532, Worth v Edmunds, 52 Barb. 40, Vail v Pacific R. Co., 63 Mo 230, Ward v. Vance, 93 Pa St. 499, Gillott v. Ellis, 11 Ill 579; Allegheny v Zimmerman, 95 Pa St 287, 40 Am Rep. 649, Colt v. McMeehen, 6 Johns 159, 5 Am Dec 200, Friend v. Wood, 6 Gratt. 195; Railroad Co v Reeves, 10 Wall 176, Steele v McTyer, 31 Ala 667, 70 Am Dec 516, McArthur v Sears, 21 Wend 190; Hays v Kennedy, 41 Pa St 378, Chicago R. Co. v Shea, 66 Ill 471.

It seems necessary to emphasize only the rule that the cause must be free from the intervention of any human agency Michaels v. N Y etc., R Co, 30 N Y 564, Steele v. McTyer, 31 Ala. 667, 70 Am Dec. 516, Campbell v Moore, Harp. 468, Polock v Pioche, 35 Cal. 416, Chicago etc., R Co. v Sawyer, 69 Ill 285, 18 Am Rep. 613; Garrison v Memphis Ins Co, 19 How 315, Hill v Railroad Cos, 13 Wall. 372, Chevallier v Straham, 2 Tex 115, Parker v Flagg, 26 Me. 219, Merchants' Des. Co. v Smith, 76 Ill 542, Hollister v Nowlen, 19 Wend. 234, Lyon v. Mells, 6 How 419, McCall v Brock, 5 Strobh 119, Pennsylvania R Co. v. Fries, 87 Pa St 234, Hill v Sturgeon, 28 Mo 323; McPadden v Railroad Co. 44 N Y. 478, Bowman v Teall, 23 Wend 306, Heazle v Railroad Co, 76 Ill 501; Crosby v. Fitch, 12 Conn. 410; Sherman v. Wells, 28 Barb. 403, Richards v Gilbert, 5 Day 415.

material element of fact which distinguished the case referred to from *Rylands* v. *Fletcher* was that the overflow which burst the defendant's embankment, and set the stored-up water in destructive motion, was due to an extraordinary storm. Now it is not because due diligence has been used that an accident which nevertheless happens is attributable to the act of God. And experience of danger previously unknown may doubtless raise the standard of due diligence for after-time (*t*). But the accidents that happen in spite of actual prudence, and yet might have been prevented by some reasonably conceivable prudence, are not numerous, nor are juries, even if able to appreciate so fine a distinction, likely to be much disposed to apply it (*u*). The authority of *Rylands* v. *Fletcher* is unquestioned, but *Nichols* v. *Marsland* has practically empowered juries to mitigate the rule whenever its operation seems too harsh.

Act of stranger, &c. Again the principal rule does not apply where the immediate cause of damage is the act of a stranger (*x*), nor where the artificial work which is the source of danger is maintained for the common benefit of the plaintiff and the defendant (*y*); and there is some ground for also making an exception where the immediate cause of the harm, though in itself trivial, is of a kind outside reasonable expectation (*z*).

(*t*) See *Reg.* v. *Commissioners of Sewers* &c., as to assess in judgment of Q. B. D., 1881, L. R. at p. 94.

(*u*) Whenever the world grows wiser it convicts those that came before of negligence: Bramwell B., L. R. 6 Ex. at p. 222. But juries do not, unless a defendant is a railway company.

(*x*) *Box* v. *Jubb* (1879) 4 Ex. D. 76. *Is* L. J. Ex. 417. *Wilson* v. *Newberry* (1871), L. R. 7 Q. B. 31. J. Q. B. 31 is really a decision on the same point.

(*y*) *Carstairs* v. *Taylor* (1871), L. R. 6 Ex. 21, 21 L. J. Ex. 2), *ep. Madras R. Co.* v. *Zemindar of Carvatenagaram*, L. R. 1 Ind. Ap. p. 364.

(*z*) *Carstairs* v. *Taylor*, last note, but the other ground seems the principal one. The plaintiff was the defendant's tenant; the defendant occupied the upper part of the house. A rat gnawed a hole in a rain-water box maintained by the defendant, and water escaped through it and damaged the plaintiff's goods on the ground floor. Questions as to the relation of particular kinds of damage to conventional exceptions in contracts for safe carriage or custody are of course on a different footing. See as to rats in a ship *Hamilton* v. *Pandorf* (1887), 12 App. Ca. 518.

Works required or authorized by law. There is yet another exception in favour of persons acting in the performance of a legal duty, or in the exercise of powers specially conferred by law. Where a zamindar maintained, and was by custom bound to maintain, an ancient tank for the general benefit of agriculture in the district, the Judicial Committee agreed with the High Court of Madras in holding that he was not liable for the consequences of an overflow caused by extraordinary rainfall, no negligence being shown (a). In the climate of India the storing of water in artificial tanks is not only a natural but a necessary mode of using land (b). In like manner the owners of a canal constructed under the authority of an Act of Parliament are not bound at their peril to keep the water from escaping into a mine worked under the canal (c). On the same principle a railway company authorized by Parliament to use locomotive engines on its line is bound to take all reasonable measures of precaution to prevent the escape of fire from its engines, but is not bound to more. If, notwithstanding the best practicable care and caution, sparks do escape and set fire to the property of adjacent owners, the company is not liable (d). The burden of proof appears to be on the company to show that due care was used (e), but there is some doubt as to this (f).

(a) *Madras R. Co. v. Zemindar of Carvatenagaram*, L R 1 Ind App 364, S C, 14 Ben L R 209

(b) See per Holloway J. in the Court below, 6 Mad H C at p 184

(c) *Dunn v. Birmingham Canal Co* (1872), L R Ch L R 8 Q B 42, 42 L J Q B 34 The principle was hardly disputed, the point which caused some difficulty being whether the defendants were bound to exercise for the plaintiff's benefit certain optional powers given by the same statute

(d) *Vaughan v Taff Vale R Co.* (1860), Ex Ch 5 H & N 679, 29 L J Ex 247, cp L R 4 H L 201, 202, *Fremantle v L & N W R Co* (1861), 10 C P N S 89, 31 L J C P 12

(e) The escape of sparks has been held to be *prima facie* evidence of negligence, *Piggott v L C R Co* (1846), 3 C B 229, 15 L J C P 235, cp per Blackburn J in *Vaughan v Taff Vale R Co*

(f) *Smith v L & S W R Co* (1870) Ex Ch L R 6 C P 14, seems to imply the contrary view, but *Piggott v E C R*

Works required or authorized by law. See this subject and cases cited, *ante*, pp 152–160 502.

G. W. R. Co. of Canada v. Braid. Some years before the decision of *Rylands* v. *Fletcher*, the duty of a railway company as to the safe maintenance of its works was considered by the Judicial Committee on appeal from Upper Canada (g). The persons whose rights against the company were in question were passengers in a train which fell into a gap in an embankment, the earth having given way by reason of a heavy rain-storm. It was held that "the railway company ought to have constructed their works in such a manner as to be capable of resisting all the violence of weather which in the climate of Canada might be expected, though perhaps rarely, to occur." And the manner in which the evidence was dealt with amounts to holding that the failure of works of this kind under any violence of weather, not beyond reasonable prevision, is of itself evidence of negligence. Thus the duty affirmed is a strict duty of diligence, but not a duty of insurance. Let us suppose now (what is likely enough as matter of fact) that in an accident of this kind the collapse of the embankment throws water, or earth, or both, upon a neighbour's land so as to do damage there. The result of applying the rule in *Rylands* v. *Fletcher*, will be that the duty of the railway company as landowner to the adjacent landowner is higher than its duty as carrier to persons whom it has contracted to carry safely; or property is more highly regarded than life and limb, and a general duty than a special one.

If the embankment was constructed under statutory authority (as in most cases it would be) that would bring the case within one of the recognized exceptions to *Rylands*

(o) was not cited. It may be that in the course of a generation the presumption of negligence has been found no longer tenable, experience having shown the occasional escape of sparks to be consistent with all practicable care. Such a reaction would hardly have found favour, however, with the Court which decided *Fletcher* v. *Rylands* in the Exchequer Chamber.

(g) *G. W. R. Co. of Canada* v. *Braid* (1863), 1 Moo. P. C. N. S. 101. There were some minor points on the evidence (whether one of the sufferers was not travelling at his own risk &c.), which were overruled or regarded as not open, and are therefore not noticed in the text.

v. *Fletcher*. But a difficulty which may vanish in practice is not therefore inconsiderable in principle.

Other cases of Insurance liability. We shall now shortly notice the authorities, antecedent to or independent of *Rylands* v. *Fletcher*, which establish the rule of absolute or all but absolute responsibility for certain special risks.

Duty of keeping in cattle. Cattle trespass is an old and well settled head, perhaps the oldest. It is the nature of cattle and other live stock to stray if not kept in, and to do damage if they stray; and the owner is bound to keep them from straying on the land of others at his peril,

---

Duty of keeping in cattle. In America the common-law rule, as announced by the text, has obtained in some of the States, but in others it has been modified or abrogated by statute, as not suited to condition of new and sparsely settled countries. Sprague v Fremont, etc. R Co., 6 Dak 86, 50 N. W. Rep 617, Macon, etc. R Co v Lester, 30 Ga 914; Hannibal, etc. R. Co. v. Kenney, 41 Mo. 271, McPheeters v Hannibal, etc. R Co., 45 Mo 22, McKay v Woodle, 6 Ired 352, State v Lamb, 8 Ired 229, Jones v Witherspoon, 7 Jones L 555, Kerwhacker v. Cleveland, etc. R. Co., 3 Ohio St 172, Cincinnati, etc. R Co v. Watterson, 4 Ohio St 424, Cleveland, etc R Co v Elliott, 4 Ohio St 474, Marietta, etc. R Co. v. Stephenson, 24 Ohio St 48, Cranston v. Cincinnati, etc. R Co, 1 Handy, 193, Phelps v Cousins, 29 Ohio St 135, Campbell v. Bridwell, 5 Oreg. 311, Little Rock, etc. R Co v Finley, 37 Ark 562, Waters v. Moss, 12 Cal 535, Logan v Gedney, 38 Cal 579; Comerford v. Dupuy, 17 Cal 308, Doherty v. Thayer, 31 Cal. 141, Richmond v Sacramento, etc. R Co, 18 Cal. 351, Morris v Fraker, 5 Colo. 425; Willard v Mathesus, 7 Colo 66, Studwell v Ritch, 14 Conn. 292, Wright v Wright, 21 Conn. 329, Barnum v Van Dusen, 16 Conn 200, Hine v Wooding, 37 Conn 123, Bissel v Southworth, 1 Root, 269; Macon, etc. R Co v Lester, 30 Ga. 914; Georgia R Co v Neely, 56 Ga 540; Central, etc. R Co v Davis, 19 Ga. 437, Seeley v Peters, 10 Ill 130, Westgate v Carr, 43 Ill 450, Headen v. Rust, 39 Ill. 186, Stoner v Shugart, 45 Ill. 76, Chicago, etc. R. Co v. Patchin, 16 Ill 201; Alton, etc. R. Co v Baugh, 14 Ill 211, Misner v Lighthall, 13 Ill 609, Ozburn v Adams, 70 Ill. 291, D'Arcy v. Miller, 86 Ill. 102, Montgomery v Handy, 62 Miss. 16, Vicksburg, etc. R Co v. Patton, 31 Miss 156, New Orleans, etc R. Co v. Field, 46 Miss 573, Gorman v Pacific R. Co., 26

though liable only for natural and probable consequences, not for an unexpected event, such as a horse not previously known to be vicious kicking a human being (h). So strict is the rule that if any part of an animal which the owner is bound to keep in is over the boundary, this constitutes a trespass. The owner of a stallion has been held liable on this ground for damage done by the horse kicking and bit-

---

(h) Cox v. Burbidge (1863), 13 C. B. N. S. 430, 32 L. J. C. P. 89

Mo 111, Ealy v Fleming 16 Mo 154; Tarwater v Hannibal, etc. R. Co. 42 Mo 193, Cameron v Crenshaw, 24 Mo 199; Chase v. Chase, 15 Nev 259, Laws v North Carolina R. Co., 7 Jones L. 468, Nelson v Stewart, 2 Murph 298, Murray v South Carolina R Co., 10 Rich. 227, Danner v. South Carolina R. Co., 4 Rich. 329, s. c. 55 Am Dec 678, Wilson v Wilmington, etc R Co., 10 Rich 52, Blaine v. Chesapeak, etc R. Co., 9 W. Va 252, Baylor v Baltimore, etc. R. Co., 9 W. Va 270, Delaney v Erickson, 11 Neb. 533, Mobile, etc. R. Co. v. Williams, 53 Ala. 595, Kerr v Sandiford, 39 Ala 317, Polk v Lane, 4 Yerg 36, State v Council, 1 Tenn. 305, Bowers v Horan, 98 Mich. 420, 53 N. W. Rep 535, Tenhopen v. Walker (Mich.), 55 N. W. Rep. 657, O'Riley v Diss, 11 Mo App 184, Stewart v. Benninger, 138 Pa St 437, 27 W. N. C 381, Hardenburgh v Lockwood, 25 Barb 9, Cowles v Balzer, 47 Barb. 562, Ryan v. Rochester R Co., 9 How Pr 153, Marsh v N. Y. etc R Co., 14 Barb 364; Heath v Coltenbach, 5 Ia 190; Wagner v Bissell, 3 Ia. 396, Alger v. Mississippi etc R. Co., 10 Ia. 268; Whitbeck v. Dubuque, etc., R Co., 21 Ia., 103, Duffus Judd, v 48 Ia 256, Frazier v Nortimus, 34 Ia. 82, Broadwell v. Wilcox, 22 Ia 568; Hallock v. Hughes, 42 Ia 516; Little v. Maguire, 38 Ia 560, Little v Lathrop, 5 Me. 356, Knox v. Tucker, 48 Me. 373, Bradbury v. Gilford, 53 Me. 99, Heath v. Ricker, 2 Me 408, Cool v. Crommet, 13 Me 250, Gooch v. Stephenson, 13 Me. 371, Eastman v Rice, 14 Me 419, Lord v Wormwood, 29 Me 282, 50 Am Dec 589, Webber v Closson, 35 Me. 26, Sturtevant v Merrill, 34 Me 62, N. Y etc R. Co. v. Skinner, 19 Pa St 298, Gregg v Gregg, 55 Pa St 227, Milligan v Wehinger, 68 Pa St 235, Knight v. Albert, 6 Pa. St. 172, 47 Am. Dec. 478, Rangler v McCreight, 27 Pa St 95, Mitchell v Wolf, 46 Pa St. 147; Fleming v. Ramsey, 46 Pa St 252; Stephens v. Shriver, 25 Pa St 78; Jackson v Rutland, etc., R Co., 25 Vt 150, 60 Am. Dec. 246, Hurd v. Rutland, etc. R Co., 25 Vt 116; Keenan v Kavanaugh, 44 Vt 268, Trow v. Vermont, etc., R Co., 24 Vt 488, 58 Am Dec 191; Sorenberger v Houghton, 40 Vt 150, Clark v. Adams, 18 Vt 425, 46 Am. Dec. 161; Holden v Shattuck, 34 Vt 336, Wilder v. Wilder, 38 Vt. 678; Saxton v. Bacon, 31 Vt 540, McCall v Chamberlain, 13 Wis. 640.

ing the plaintiff's mare through a wire fence which separated their closes (*i*). The result of the authorities is stated to be "that in the case of animals trespassing on land, the mere act of the animal belonging to a man, which he could not foresee, or which he took all reasonable means of preventing, may be a trespass, inasmuch as the same act if done by himself would have been a trespass" (*k*).

Blackstone (*l*) says that "a man is answerable for not only his own trespass, but that of his cattle also:" but in the same breath he speaks of "negligent keeping" as the ground of liability, so that it seems doubtful whether the law was then clearly understood to be as it was laid down a century later in *Cox* v. *Burbidge* (*m*). Observe that the only reason given in the earlier books (as indeed it still prevails in quite recent cases) is the archaic one that trespass by a man's cattle is equivalent to trespass by himself.

The rule does not apply to damage done by cattle straying off a highway on which they are being lawfully driven; in such case the owner is liable only on proof of negligence (*n*); and the law is the same for a town street as for a country road (*o*). Also a man may be bound by prescription to maintain a fence against his neighbour's cattle (*p*).

"Whether the owner of a dog is answerable in trespass for every unauthorized entry of the animal into the land of another, as is the case with an ox," is an undecided

---

(*i*) *Ellis* v *Loftus Iron Co* (1874), L. R. 10 C. P. 10, 44 L. J. C. P. 24, a stronger case than *Lee* v *Riley* (1865), 18 C. B. N. S. 722, 34 L. J. C. P. 212, there cited and followed.

(*k*) Brett J., L. R. 10 C. P. at p. 13, cp. the remarks on the general law in *Smith* v. *Cook* (1875), 1 Q. B. D. 79, 45 L. J. Q. B. 122 (itself a case of contract).

(*l*) Comm. iii. 211.

(*m*) 13 C. B. N. S. 430, 32 L. J. C. P. 8).

(*n*) *Goodwin* v. *Cheveley* (1859), 4 H. & N. 631, 28 L. J. Ex. 298. A contrary opinion was expressed by Littleton, 20 Edw. IV. 11, pl. 10, cited in *Read* v *Edwards*, 17 C. B. N. S. 245, 34 L. J. C. P. at p. 32.

(*o*) *Tillett* v. *Ward* (1882), 10 Q. B. D. 17, 52 L. J. Q. B. 61, where an ox being driven through a town strayed into a shop.

(*p*) So held as early as 1441-2 Y. B. 19 H. VI. 33, pl. 68.

point. The better opinion seems to favour a negative answer (q).

Dangerous or vicious animals. Closely connected with this doctrine is the responsibility of owners of dangerous animals. "A person keeping a mischievous animal with knowledge of its propensities is bound to keep it secure at his peril." If it escapes and does mischief, he is liable without proof of negligence, neither is proof required that he knew the animal to be mischievous, if it is of a notoriously fierce or mischievous species (r). If the animal is of a tame and domestic kind, the owner is liable only on

---

(q) Read v. Edwards (1864), 17 C. B. N. S. 245, 34 L. J. C. P. 31, and see Millen v. Fawdry, Latch, 119.

(r) As to monkeys, May v. Burdett (1846), 9 Q. B. 101, and 1 Hale, P. C. 430, there cited. An elephant is a dangerous animal in England. Filburn v. Aquarium Co. (1890), 25 Q. B. Div. 258, 59 L. J. Q. B. 471.

Dangerous or vicious animals. Of one keeping wild animals a very high degree of care is demanded. Scribner v. Kelley, 38 Barb. 14, Vredenburg v. Behan, 33 La. An. 627, Van Leuven v. Lyke, 1 N. Y. 516; 49 Am. Dec. 346, Earl v. Van Alstyne, 8 Barb. 630.

With reference to domestic animals, in the case of Losee v. Buchanan (51 N. Y. 476), the court said, "the owner is not responsible for such injuries as they are not accustomed to do, by the exercise of vicious propensities which they do not usually have, unless it can be shown that he has knowledge of the vicious habit and propensity. As to all animals, the owner can usually restrain and keep them under control, and if he will keep them he must do so. If he does not, he is responsible for any damage which their well-known disposition leads them to commit. I believe the liability to be based upon the fault which the law attributes to him, and no further actual negligence need be proved than the fact that they are at large unrestrained."

In the case of Klenberg v. Russell (125 Ind. 531; 25 N. E. Rep. 596), the foregoing is approved and Fletcher v. Rylands cited. "The gist of the action is not the keeping of animals, but the keeping with knowledge of the mischievous propensity, whether proceeding from a savage disposition or not." Evans v. McDermott, 49 N. J. L. 163; 6 At. Rep. 653, 60 Am. Rep. 605. See Sylvester v. Maag, 155 Pa. St. 227, 26 At. Rep. 880. Nehr v. State, 35 Neb. 638; 53 N. W. Rep. 589, Robinson v. Marino, 3 Wash. St. 434, 28 Pac. Rep. 752, Fake v. Addicks, 45 Minn. 38, 47 N.

proof that he knew the particular animal to be "accustomed to bite mankind," as the common form of pleading ran in the case of dogs, or otherwise vicious; but when such proof is supplied, the duty is absolute as in the former case. It is enough to show that the animal has on foregoing occasions manifested a savage disposition, whether with the actual result of doing mischief on any of those occasions or not (s). But the necessity of proving the *scienter*, as it used to be called from the language of pleadings, is often a greater burden on the plaintiff than that of proving negligence would be, and as regards injury to cattle or sheep it has been done away with by statute.

(s) *Worth v. Gilling* (1866), 1 R. 2 C. P. 1. As to what is sufficient notice to the defendant through his servants, *Baldwin v. Casella* (1872), L. R. 7 Ex. 325, 41 L. J. Ex. 167, *Applebee v. Percy* (1874), L. R. 9 C. P. 647, 43 L. J. C. P. 365.

W. Rep. 50, Vrooman v. Lawyer, 13 Johns. 339, Durham v. Musselman, 2 Blackf. 96, Smith v. Causey, 22 Ala. 568, Wormley v. Gregg, 65 Ill. 251, Deuther v. Baker, 22 Wis. 73, Mann v. Welland, 81 Pa. St. 243, Coggswell v. Baldwin, 15 Vt. 404, Partlow v. Haggarty, 35 Ind. 178, Williams v. Moray, 74 Ind. 25, Wolf v. Chalker, 31 Conn. 121, Oakes v. Spaulding, 40 Vt. 347, Kittredge v. Elliott, 16 N. H. 77, Rider v. White, 65 N. H. 54, Lyons v. Merrick, 105 Mass. 71, Linnehan v. Simpson, 126 Mass. 510, Coggswell v. Baldwin, 15 Vt. 404, Marble v. Ross, 124 Mass. 44, Miller v. Curry, 122 Ind. 403, 24 N. E. Rep. 216, State v. McDermott, 49 N. J. L. 163, 6 At. Rep. 656, McGuire v. Ringrose, 41 La. An. 1029, 6 So. Rep. 895, Shaw v. Craft, 37 Fed. 317, Staetter v. McArthur, 33 Mo. App. 218, Laherty v. Hogan, 13 Daly, 533, Bell v. Leslie, 24 Mo. App. 661, Kin mouth v. McDougall, 64 Hun, 636, Hammond v. Melton, 42 Ill. App. 186, Gurison v. Barnes, Id. 21.

In several of the United States, statutes have been passed holding the owners of dogs to a greater responsibility than at common law. See Smith v. Montgomery, 52 Me. 178, Orne v. Roberts, 51 N. H. 110; Jones v. Sherwood, 37 Conn. 466; Smith v. Skut, 31 Barb. 333, Oslncup v. Nichols, 49 Barb. 145, Auchmuty v. Ham, 1 Denio, 195, Fairchild v. Bentley, 30 Barb. 147, Paff v. Slack, 7 Pa. St. 254, Campbell v. Brown 19 Pa. St. 359, Kerr v. O'Connor, 63 Pa. St. 341, Mitchell v. Clapp, 12 Cush. 278, Pressey v. Wirth, 3 Allen, 191, Brewer v. Crosby, 11 Gray, 29, Smith v. Causey, 22 Ala. 568, Swift v. Applebone, 23 Mich. 252, Elliott v. Herz, 29 Mich. 202, Chunot v. Larson, 43 Wis. 536, 28 Am. Rep. 567, Job v. Harlan, 13 Ohio St. 485, Gries v. Zeck, 24 Ohio St. 329, Mercale v. Down, 64 Wis. 323.

And the occupier of the place where a dog is kept is presumed for this purpose to be the owner of the dog (*t*).

The word "cattle" includes horses (*u*) and perhaps pigs (*v*).

Fire, firearms, etc. The risk incident to dealing with fire, firearms, explosive or highly inflammable matters, corrosive or otherwise dangerous or noxious fluids, and (it is apprehended) poisons, is accounted by the common law among those which subject the actor to strict responsibility. Sometimes the term "consummate care" is used to describe the amount of caution required: but it is

---

(*t*) 28 & 29 Vict. c. 60 (A.D. 1865). There is a similar Act for Scotland, 26 & 27 Vict. c. 100. See Campbell on Negligence 2nd ed. pp. 54-55. Further protection against mischievous or masterless dogs is given by 34 & 35 Vict. c. 56, a

statute of public police regulations outside the scope of this work.

(*u*) *Wright* v. *Pearson* (1869), L. R. 4 Q. B. 582.

(*v*) *Child* v. *Hearn* (1874), L. R. 9 Ex. 176, 43 L. J. Ex. 100 (on a different Act).

Fire, fire-arms, etc. In the Vermont case of Hadley v. Cross (31 Vt. 586) it was held, that one using explosive machinery and substances involving the personal safety and lives of others is required to exercise nothing less than the most watchful care and the most active diligence. See Wellington v. Downer Kerosine Oil Co., 104 Mass. 68; Furth v. Foster, 7 Robt. 154; Losee v. Buchanan, 51 N. Y. 476; Marshall v. Wellwood, 38 N. J. L. 339; Spencer v. Campbell, 9 Watts & S. 32; McAndrews v. Collerd, 42 N. J. L. 189, 36 Am. Rep. 508; Devlin v. Gallagher, 6 Daly, 494; Koster v. Noonan, 8 Id. 231; Beauchamp v. Saginaw Mining Co., 50 Mich. 163, 15 Am. Rep. 30; Hay v. The Cohoes Co., 2 N. Y. 159; Colton v. Onderdonk, 69 Cal. 155; Allison v. Western, etc. R. Co., 64 N. C. 383.

One who sells gun-powder to an inexperienced child is liable for injuries to him from its explosion. Carter v. Towne, 98 Mass. 567. So as to a toy pistol. Binford v. Johnson, 82 Ind. 426, 42 Am. Rep. 508. For the unlawful or negligent discharge of fire-works, resulting in injury, one is liable. Colvin v. Peabody, 155 Mass. 104; Conklin v. Thompson, 29 Barb. 218; McDade v. City of Chester (Pa.), 20 Am. & Eng. Corp. Cas. 110; Bradley v. Andrews, 51 Vt. 530; Fisk v. Wait, 104 Mass. 71; Jenne v. Sutton, 43 N. J. L. 257, 39 Am. Rep. 578.

In Cullum v. Wacne (40 Mo. 131) one exposing liquid poison resembling water in jars on his premises is liable for the death of a laborer who by mistake drank the poison. See Henry v. Dennis, 95 Ind. 452, 47 Am. Rep. 378; Bishop v. Weber, 139 Mass. 411, 1 N. E. Rep. 154.

doubtful whether even this be strong enough. At least, we do not know of any English case of this kind (not falling under some recognized head of exception) where unsuccessful diligence on the defendant's part was held to exonerate him.

Duty of keeping in fire. As to fire, we find it in the fifteenth century stated to be the custom of the realm (which is the same thing as the common law) that every man must safely keep his own fire so that no damage in any wise happen to his neighbour (*x*). In declaring on this custom, however, the averment was "*ignem suum tam negligenter custodivit*," and it does not appear whether the allegation of negligence was traversable or not (*y*). We shall see that later authorities have adopted the stricter view.

The common law rule applied to a fire made out of doors (for burning weeds or the like) as well as to fire in a dwelling-house (*z*). Here too it looks as if negligence was the gist of the action, which is described (in Lord Raymond's report) as "case grounded upon the common custom of the realm for negligently keeping his fire." *Semble*, if the fire were carried by sudden tempest it would

---

(*x*) Y B 2 Hen IV 18, pl 5. This may be founded on ancient Germanic custom cp Ll Langob cc 147, 148 (A D. 643), where a man who carries fire more than nine feet from the hearth is said to do so at his peril

(*y*) Blackstone (1 431) seems to assume negligence as a condition of liability

(*z*) *Tuberil* or *Tuberville* v *Stamp*, 1 Salk. 13, s c 1 Ld Raym 264

Duty of keeping in fire In the United States the right of a person to kindle a fire on his own land, using reasonable care and diligence to prevent its spreading and doing injury to the lands of others, is recognized. But "a man who negligently sets fire on his own land, and keeps it negligently, is liable to an action at common law for any injury done by the spreading or communication of the fire directly from his own land to the property of another, whether through the air or along the ground, and whether he might or might not have reasonably anticipated the particular manner and direction in which it is actually communicated." Higgins v. Dewey, 107 Mass 494 See Tourtellot v Rosebrook, 11 Metc 460,

be excusable as the act of God. Liability for domestic fires has been dealt with by statute, and a man is not now answerable for damage done by a fire which began in his house or on his land by accident and without negligence (a).

The use of fire for non-domestic purposes, if we may coin the phrase, remains a ground of the strictest responsibility.

Carrying fire in locomotives. Decisions of our own time have settled that one who brings fire into dangerous proximity to his neighbour's property, in such ways as by running locomotive engines on a railway without express statutory authority for their use (b), or bringing a traction engine on a highway (c), does so at his peril. And a company authorized by statute to run a steam-engine on a

---

(a) 14 Geo. III. c. 78, s. 86, as interpreted in *Filliter v. Phippard* (1847), 11 Q. B. 47, 17 L. J. Q. B. 89. There was an earlier statute of Anne to a like effect, 1 Blackst. Comm. 431, and see per Cur. in *Filliter v. Phippard*. It would seem that even at common law the defendant would not be liable unless he knowingly lighted or kept some fire to begin with, for otherwise how could it be described as *ignis suus*?

(b) *Jones v. Festiniog R. Co.* (1868), L. R. 3 Q. B. 733, 37 L. J. Q. B. 214. Here diligence was proved, but the company held nevertheless liable. The rule was expressly stated to be an application of the wider principle of *Rylands v. Fletcher*, see per Blackburn J. at p. 736.

(c) *Powell v. Fall* (1880), 5 Q. B. Div. 597, 49 L. J. Q. B. 428. The use of traction engines on highways is regulated by statute, but not authorized in the sense of diminishing the owner's liability for nuisance or otherwise, see the sections of the Locomotive Acts, 1861 and 1865, in the judgment of Mellor J. at p. 598. The dictum of Bramwell L. J. at p. 601, that *Vaughan v. Taff Vale R. Co.* (1860), 5 N. Ch. 5 H. & N. 679, 29 L. J. Ex. 247, p. 439, above, was wrongly decided, is extra judicial. That case was not only itself decided by a Court of co-ordinate authority, but has been approved in the House of Lords, *Hammersmith R. Co. v. Brand* (1869), L. R. 4 H. L. at p. 202, and see the opinion of Blackburn J. at p. 197.

Bernard v. Poor, 21 Pick. 380, Powers v. Craig, 22 Neb. 621, 35 N. W. Rep. 888, Sweeny v. Merrill, 38 Kan. 216, 16 Pac. Rep. 454, Richards v. Schleusner, 41 Minn. 49, 42 N. W. Rep. 599, John Mouat Lumber Co. v. Wilmore, 15 Colo. 136; 25 Pac. Rep. 556, Delaware, etc. R. Co. v. Salmon, 39 N. J. L. 299, disapproving 35 N. Y. 210, and 62 Pa. St. 353. But see McGibbon v. Baxter, 51 Hun, 587, 4 N. Y. S. Rep. 382, Louisville, etc., Ry. Co. v. Hart, 119 Ind. 273, 21 N. E. Rep. 753, Clark v. Foot, 8 Johns. 421, Stewart v. Hawley, 22 Barb. 619.

highway still does so at its peril as regards the safe condition of the way (d).

It seems permissible to entertain some doubt as to the historical foundation of this doctrine, and in the modern practice of the United States it has not found acceptance (e). In New York it has, after careful discussion, been expressly disallowed (f).

Fire-arms. Dixon v. Bell. Loaded fire-arms are regarded as highly dangerous things, and persons dealing with them are answerable for damage done by their explosion, even if they have used apparently sufficient precaution. A man sent his maiden servant to fetch a flint-lock gun which was kept loaded, with a message to the master of the house to take out the priming first. This was done, and the gun delivered to the girl; she loitered on her errand, and (thinking, presumably, that the gun would not go off) pointed it in sport at a child, and drew the trigger. The gun went off and the child was seriously wounded. The owner was held liable, although he had used care, perhaps as much care as would commonly be thought enough.

(d) *Sadler v. South Staffordshire, &c. Tramways Co.* (1889) 23 Q. B. Div. 17, 58 L. J. Q. B. 421 (car ran off line through a defect in the points; the line did not belong to the defendant company, who had running powers over it).

(e) It appears to be held everywhere that unless the original act is in itself unlawful, the gist of the action is negligence; see Cooley on Torts 589—594.

(f) *Losee v. Buchanan* (1873), 51 N. Y.

476, the owner of a steam boiler was held not liable, independently of negligence, for an explosion which threw it into the plaintiff's buildings. For the previous authorities as to fire, it formerly being that in order to succeed the plaintiff must prove negligence, see it pp. 487 s. *Rylands v. Fletcher* is disapproved as being in conflict with the current of American authority.

Fire-arms. In the case of *Morgan v. Cox* (22 Mo. 373), *Dixon v. Bell*, *supra*, is cited, and upon this subject the court said, that one handling a fire-arm is liable for injuries resulting from its accidental discharge, unless the injury was inevitable, and utterly without the fault of the alleged wrong-doer. See *Chataigne v. Bergeron*, 10 La. An. 699, *Chiles v. Drake*, 2 Metc. (Ky.) 146, *Moody v. Ward*, 13 Mass. 299, *Castle v. Duryee*, 2 Keyes, 169, *Rhodes v. Roberts*, 1 Stew. 145, *Cale v. Fisher*, 11 Miss. 137.

"It was incumbent on him who, by charging the gun, had made it capable of doing mischief, to render it safe and innoxious. This might have been done by the discharge or drawing of the contents. The gun ought to have been so left as to be out of all reach of doing harm" (g). This amounts to saying that in dealing with a dangerous instrument of this kind the only caution that will be held adequate in point of law is to abolish its dangerous character altogether. Observe that the intervening negligence of the servant (which could hardly by any ingenuity have been imputed to her master as being in the course of her employment) was no defence. Experience unhappily shows that if loaded fire-arms are left within the reach of children or fools, no consequence is more natural or probable than that some such person will discharge them to the injury of himself or others.

Explosives and other dangerous goods. On a like principle it is held that people sending goods of an explosive or dangerous nature to be carried are bound to give reasonable notice of their nature, and, if they do not, are liable for resulting damage. So it was held when nitric acid was sent to a carrier without warning, and the carrier's servant, handling it as he would handle a vessel of any harmless fluid, was injured by its escape (h). The same rule has been applied in British India to the case of an explosive mixture being sent for carriage by railway without warning of its character, and exploding in the railway

(g) Dixon v. Bell (1816), 5 M. & S. 198, and in Bigelow L. C. 68. It might have been said that sending an incompetent person to fetch a loaded gun was evidence of negligence (see the first count of the declaration), but that is not the ground taken by the Court (Lord Ellenborough C. J. and Bayley J.).

(h) Farrant v. Barnes (1862), 11 C. B. N. S. 553, 31 L. J. C. P. 137. The duty seems to be antecedent, not incident, to the contract of carriage.

Explosives and other dangerous goods. Sustaining the text, vid. The Nitro-Glycerine Case, 15 Wall. 524, Barney v. Burstenbinder, 7 Lans. 210, Sothfld v. Sommers, 9 Ben. 526.

company's office, where it was being handled along with other goods (i); and it has been held in a similar case in Massachusetts that the consignor's liability is none the less because the danger of the transport, and the damage actually resulting, have been increased by another consignor independently sending other dangerous goods by the same conveyance (k).

Gas escapes. Gas (the ordinary illuminating coal-gas) is not of itself, perhaps, a dangerous thing, but with atmospheric air forms a highly dangerous explosive mixture, and also makes the mixed atmosphere incapable of supporting life (l). Persons undertaking to deal with it are therefore bound, at all events, to use all reasonable diligence to prevent an escape which may have such results. A gas-fitter left an imperfectly connected tube in the place where

(i) *Lyell v. Ganga Dai*, I. L. R. 1 All. 60.

(k) *Boston & Albany R. R. Co. v. Shanly* (1871), 107 Mass. 568, ("duabn," a nitroglycerine compound, and exploders, had been ordered by one customer of two separate makers, and by them separately consigned to the railway company without notice of their character: held on demurrer that both manufacturers were rightly sued in one action by the company).

(l) See *Smith v. Boston Gas Light Co.*, 129 Mass. 318.

Gas escapes. The American authorities agree with the statement of the text. In the case of *Chisholm v Atlanta Gas Light Co* (57 Ga 29), the court said: "The principle applicable to the defendant in this, that in the conduct of its business as a gas producer and furnisher thereof to its customers, it is bound to use such ordinary skill and diligence as is proportioned to the delicacy, difficulty and nature of that particular business." See *Powers v Boston Gas-Light Co.*, 158 Mass 257, 33 N. E Rep. 523, *Holly v Boston Gas-Light Co*, 8 Gray, 134, *Lanigan v New York Gas-Light Co.*, 71 N. Y. 29, *Oil City Gas Co v. Robinson*, 99 Pa St. 1, *Bartlett v Boston Gas-Light Co.*, 117 Mass 534, 20 Am & Eng Corp Cas 380, *Schmeer v Gas-Light Co*, 65 Hun, 378, 20 N Y S. Rep 168, *Lowell Gas-Light Co*, 3 Allen, 410, *Hutchinson v Boston Gas-Light Co*, 122 Mass 219, *Schermerhorn v The Metropolitan Gas-Light Co*, 5 Daly, 144, *Louisville Gas Co v. Gutenkuntz*, 82 Ky 432, *Lannen v. The Albany Gas-Light Co.*, 44 N. Y. 459; 46 Barb 264, *Butcher v Providence G Co*, 12 R I 149, *Dillon v Washington G Co*, 1 McArthur, 626, *Koelsch v Philadelphia Co*, 152 Pa St 355, 25 At Rep 522 31 W N C 341

he was working under a contract with the occupier; a third person, a servant of that occupier, entering the room with a light in fulfilment of his ordinary duties, was hurt by an explosion due to the escape of gas from the tube so left; the gas-fitter was held liable as for a "misfeasance independent of contract." (*m*)

Poisonous drugs Thomas v Winchester. Poisons can do as much mischief as loaded fire-arms or explosives, though the danger and the appropriate precautions are different

A wholesale druggist in New York purported to sell extract of dandelion to a retail druggist. The thing delivered was in truth extract of belladonna, which by the negligence of the wholesale dealer's assistant had been wrongly labelled By the retail druggist this extract was sold to a country practitioner, and by him to a customer, who took it as and for extract of dandelion, and thereby

---

(*n* *Parry v Smith* (1879), 4 C. P. D. 325, 48 L. J. C. P. 731 (Lopes J.) Negligence was found as a fact

---

Poisonous drugs In Davidson *v* Nichols (11 Allen, 514), Thomas *v* Winchester, *supra*, is limited, in its application, to deadly poisons dangerous to human life, and it is held that the sale of an article in itself harmless, and which becomes dangerous only by being used in combination with some other article, without any knowledge by the vendor that it is to be used in such combination, does not render him liable to an action by one who purchases the article from the original vendee, and who is injured by using it in dangerous combination with another article, although by mistake the article actually sold is different from that which is intended to be sold

If an apothecary negligently sells a deadly poison as and for a harmless medicine, to A., who buys it to administer to B., a dose of it, as a medicine from which he dies in a few hours, a right of action in tort against the apothecary survives to B's administrator. Norton *v* Sewall, 106 Mass 143, 8 Am Rep 298, Brunswig *v* White, 70 Tex. 504, 8 S. W Rep 85, Davis *v* Guarnieri, 45 Ohio St 470, 15 N. E. Rep 350, Walton *v* Booth, 34 La. An. 913 But see Ray *v* Burbank, 61 Ga. 505, 54 Am Rep. 103 Gould *v* Slater Woolen Co, 147 Mass 315, Wohlbohrt *v.* Beckert, 92 N Y 490, 12 Abb. N Cas. 478, 44 Am Rep. 406.

was made seriously ill. The Court of Appeals held the wholesale dealer liable to the consumer. "The defendant was a dealer in poisonous drugs .... The death or great bodily harm of some person was the natural and almost inevitable consequence of the sale of belladonna by means of the false label." And the existence of a contract between the defendant and the immediate purchaser from him could make no difference, as its non-existence would have made none. "The plaintiff's injury and their remedy would have stood on the same principle, if the defendant had given the belladonna to Dr. Foord" (the country practitioner) "without price, or if he had put it in his shop without his knowledge, under circumstances which would probably have led to its sale" — or administration without sale — "on the faith of the label" (*n*). This case has been thought in England to go too far, but it is hard to see in what respect it goes farther than *Dixon* v. *Bell*. So far as the cases are dissimilar, the damage would seem to be not more but less remote. If one sends belladonna into the world labelled as dandelion (the two extracts being otherwise distinguishable only by minute examination), it is a more than probable consequence that some one will take it as and for dandelion and be the worse for it and this without any action on the part of others necessarily involving want of due care (*o*).

It can hardly be said that a wrongly labelled poison, whose true character is not discoverable by any ordinary examination such as a careful purchaser could or would make, is in itself less dangerous than a loaded gun. The event, indeed, shows the contrary.

Difficulties felt in England· George v. Skivington Nevertheless difficulties are felt in England about admitting

---

(*n*) *Thomas* v *Winchester* (1852), 6 N. Y 397, Bigelow L C 602

(*o*) The jury found that there was not any negligence on the part of the intermediate dealers, the Court, however, were of opinion that this was immaterial

this application of a principle which in other directions is both more widely and more strictly applied in this country than in the United States (p). In 1869 the Court of Exchequer made a rather hesitating step towards it, putting their judgment partly on the ground that the dispenser of the mischievous drug (in this case a hair wash) knew that it was intended to be used by the very person whom it in fact injured (q). The cause of action seems to have been treated as in the nature of deceit, and *Thomas* v. *Winchester* does not seem to have been known either to counsel or to the Court. In the line actually taken one sees the tendency to assume that the ground of liability, if any, must be either warranty or fraud. But this is erroneous, as the judgment in *Thomas* v. *Winchester* carefully and clearly shows. Whether that case was well decided appears to be a perfectly open question for our courts (r). In the present writer's opinion it is good law, and ought to be followed. Certainly it comes within the language of Parke B. in *Longmeid* v. *Holliday* (s), which does not deny legal responsibility "when any one delivers to another without notice an instrument in its nature dangerous under particular circumstances, as a loaded gun which he himself has loaded, and that other person to whom it is delivered is injured thereby; or if he places it in a situation easily accessible to a third person who sustains damage from it." In that case the defendant had sold a dangerous thing, namely an ill-made lamp, which exploded in use, but it was found as a fact that he sold it in good faith, and it was not

(p) See per Brett M. R., *Heaven* v. *Pender* (1883), 11 Q. B. Div. at p. 511, in a judgment which itself endeavours to lay down a much wider rule.

(r) *George* v. *Skivington* (1869), L. R. 5 Ex. 1, 39 L. J. Ex. 8.

(q) *Dixon* v. *Bell* (1816), 5 M. & S. 198, *Bigelow* L. C. 568 (supra, p. 446), has never been disapproved that we know of, but it has not been so actively followed that the Court of Appeal need be precluded from free discussion of the principle involved. In *Langridge* v. *Levy* (1837), 2 M. & W. at p. 530, the Court was somewhat astute to avoid discussing that principle, and declined to commit itself. *Dixon* v. *Bell* is cited by Parke B. as a strong case and apparently with hesitating acceptance, in *Longmeid* v. *Holliday* (1851), 6 Ex. 761, 20 L. J. Ex. 430.

(s) 20 L. J. Ex. at p. 433.

found that there was any negligence on his part. As lamps are not in their nature explosive, it was quite rightly held that on those facts the defendant could be liable only ex contractu, and therefore not to any person who could not sue on his contract or on a warranty therein expressed or implied.

Duties of occupiers of buildings, &c., in respect of safe repair. We now come to the duties imposed by law on the occupiers of buildings, or persons having the control of other structures intended for human use and occupation, in respect of the safe condition of the building or structure Under this head there are distinctions to be noted both as to the extent of the duty, and as to the persons to whom it is owed

Extent of the duty. The duty is founded not on ownership, but on possession, in other words, on the structure being maintained under the control and for the purposes of the person held answerable. It goes beyond the common doctrine of responsibility for servants, for the occupier cannot discharge himself by employing an independent contractor for the maintenance and repair of the structure, however careful he may be in the choice of that

---

Extent of the duty. Concurring with the statement of the text, the American cases hold that a lessor occupying a building is *prima facie* liable to third persons for damages accruing to them from defects therein. O'Connor v. Andrews, 81 Tex. 28, 16 S W Rep. 628, Readman v Conway, 126 Mass. 374; Mellen v. Morrill, 126 Mass 545, Khron v Brock, 144 Mass 516, Sinton v. Butler, 40 Ohio St. 158, Kalis v Shattuck, 69 Cal. 593, 58 Am Rep 568; Cleveland Co-operative Stove Co v Wheeler, 14 Ill App 112, Baird v Shipman, 13 Ill. 16, 23 N E Rep 584, Odell v. Solomon, 99 N W 637, Moore v Ocean Steam Nav Co, 24 Fed Rep. 237, Onderdonk v. Smith, 21 Fed Rep 588, Pennsylvania R Co v Atha, 22 Fed Rep 921.

But there are cases where the owner and not the occupant of the property may be liable See Marshall v Heard, 59 Tex. 267, citing Staple v Spring, 10 Mass 72, Durant v. Palmer, 29 N. J. L. 544; Irvine v. Wood, 51 N Y 228

contractor. Thus the duty is described as being impersonal rather than personal. Personal diligence on the part of the occupier and his servants is immaterial. The structure has to be in a reasonably safe condition, so far as the exercise of reasonable care and skill can make it so (*t*). To that extent there is a limited duty of insurance, as one may call it, though not a strict duty of insurance such as exists in the classes of cases governed by *Rylands* v. *Fletcher*.

Modern date of the settled rule: Indermaur v. Dames. The separation of this rule from the ordinary law of negligence, which is inadequate to account for it, has been the work of quite recent times. As lately as 1864 (*u*) the Lord Chief Baron Pigot (of Ireland), in a very careful judgment, confessed the difficulty of discovering any general rule at all. Two years later a judgment of the Court of Common Pleas, delivered by Willes J., and confirmed by the Exchequer Chamber, gave us an exposition which has since been regarded on both sides of the Atlantic as a leading authority (*x*). The plaintiff was a journeyman gas-fitter, employed to examine and test some new burners which had been supplied by his employer for use in the defendant's sugar-refinery. While on an upper floor of the building, he fell through an unfenced shaft which was used in working hours for raising and lowering sugar. It was found as a fact that there was no want of reasonable care on the plaintiff's part, which amounts to saying that even to a careful person not already acquainted with the building the danger was an unexpected and concealed one. The Court held that on the admitted facts

---

(*t*) Per Montague Smith J. in Ex. Ch., *Francis* v. *Cockrell* (1870), Ex. Ch. L. R. 5 Q. B. 501, 515, 39 L. J. Q. B. 291. Other cases well showing this point are *Pickard* v. *Smith*, 10 C. B. N. S. 470, *John* v. *Bacon* (1870), L. R. 5 C. P. 437, 39 L. J. C. P. 365.

(*u*) *Sullivan* v. *Waters*, 14 Ir. C. L. R. 460. See, however, *Quarman* v. *Burnett* (1840), 6 M. & W. at p. 510, where there is a suggestion of the modern rule.

(*x*) *Indermaur* v. *Dames* (1866), L. R. 1 C. P. 274, 35 L. J. C. P. 184, 2 C. P. 311, 36 L. J. C. P. 181, constantly cited in later cases, and reprinted in Bigelow L. C.

the plaintiff was in the building as "a person on lawful business, in the course of fulfilling a contract in which both the plaintiff and the defendant had an interest, and not upon bare permission." They therefore had to deal with the general question of law "as to the duty of the occupier of a building with reference to persons resorting thereto in the course of business, upon his invitation express or implied. The common case is that of a customer in a shop, but it is obvious that this is only one of a class.

"The class to which the customer belongs includes persons who go not as mere volunteers, or licensees, or guests, or servants, or persons whose employment is such that danger may be considered as bargained for, but who go upon business which concerns the occupier, and upon his invitation, express or implied.

"And, with respect to such a visitor at least, we consider it settled law, that he, using reasonable care on his part for his own safety, is entitled to expect that the occupier shall on his part use reasonable care to prevent damage from unusual danger, which he knows or ought to know; and that, where there is evidence of neglect, the question whether such reasonable care has been taken, by notice, lighting, guarding or otherwise, and whether there was contributory negligence in the sufferer, must be determined by a jury as a matter of fact" (y).

The Court goes on to admit that "there was no absolute duty to prevent danger, but only a duty to make the place as little dangerous as such a place would reasonably be, having regard to the contrivances necessarily used in carrying on the business." On the facts they held that "there was evidence for the jury that the plaintiff was in the place by the tacit invitation of the defendant, upon business in which he was concerned; that there was by reason of the shaft unusual danger, known to the defendant; and that

(y) L. R. 1 C. P. at p. 288.

the plaintiff sustained damage by reason of that danger, and of the neglect of the defendant and his servants to use reasonably sufficient means to avert or warn him of it." The judgment in the Exchequer Chamber (*o*) is little more than a simple affirmation of this.

Persons entitled to safety. It is hardly needful to add that a customer, or other person entitled to the like measure of care, is protected not only while he is actually doing his business, but while he is entering and leaving (*a*). And the amount of care required is so carefully indicated by Willes J. that little remains to be said on that score. The recent cases are important chiefly as showing in respect of

---

Persons entitled to safety A concise statement of the law of this subject is that of Mr. Justice Gray in delivering the opinion of the court in Carleton v. Franconia Iron Co (99 Mass. 216), as follows:—

"The owner or occupier of land is liable in damages to those coming to it, using due care at his invitation or inducement, express or implied, on any business to be transacted or permitted by him, for an injury occasioned by the unsafe condition of the land or of the access to it, which is known to him and not to them, and which he has negligently suffered to exist, and has given them no notice of it." See Currier v. Boston Music Hall, 135 Mass. 414, Pastene v. Adams, 49 Cal. 87, Foster v. Phipps, 52 N. Y. 354, City of Anderson v. East, 117 Ind. 126, 19 N. E. Rep 726, Convers v. Walker, 30 Hun, 596, Camp v. Wood, 76 N. Y. 92, Henkel v. Murr, 31 Hun, 28, Edwards v. New York etc R Co., 23 Id. 634, Lamparter v. Wallbaum, 45 Ill. 444, Welch v. McAllister, 15 Mo. App. 492, Donnelly v. Hufschmidt, 79 Cal. 74, Evansville etc R Co. v. Griffin, 100 Ind. 221, 50 Am. Rep. 783, Powers v. Harlow, 53 Mich. 507, 51 Am. Rep. 157, Texas etc R Co. v. Best, 66 Tex 116, Houston v. Texas etc. R Co., 64 Tex 251, 53 Am. Rep. 756, 21 Am. & Eng. R Cas 336, McKone v. Michigan, etc. R Co., 51 Mich. 601, 47 Am. Rep. 596, 13 Am. & Eng. R Cas 29, Conradt v. Clauve, 93 Ind. 476, 47 Am. Rep. 388, Davis v. Central Congregational Soc., 129 Mass. 367, 37 Am. Rep. 368, Campbell v. Portland Sugar Co., 62 Me. 552, 16 Am. Rep. 503, Harris v. Perry, 89 N. Y. 308, reversing s. c. 23 Hun (N. Y.) 244, Benson v. Suarez, 19 Abb. Pr. 61, 43 Barb. 408, Davenport v. Buckman, 10 Bosw. 20, 16 Abb. Pr. 341, Anderson v. Dickie, 26 How.

what kinds of property the duty exists, and what persons have the same rights as a customer. In both directions the law seems to have become, on the whole, more stringent in the present generation. With regard to the person, one acquires this right to safety by being upon the spot, or engaged in work on or about the property whose condition is in question, in the course of any business in which the occupier has an interest. It is not necessary that there should be any direct or apparent benefit to the occupier from the particular transaction (*b*). Where gangways for access to ships in a dock were provided by the dock company, the company has been held answerable for their safe condition to a person having lawful business on board one of the ships; for the providing of access for all such persons is part of a dock-owner's business; they are paid for it by the owners of the ships on behalf of all who use it (*c*). A workman was employed under contract with a ship-owner to paint his ship lying in a dry dock, and the dock-owner provided a staging for the workmen's use; a rope by which the staging was supported, not being of proper strength, broke and let down the staging, and the man fell into the dock and was hurt; the dock-owner was held liable to him (*d*). It was contended that the staging had been delivered into the control of the ship-

---

(*b*) See *Holmes v. N. J. R. Co.* (1869-71), L. R. 4 Ex. 254, in Ex. Ch. L. R. 6 Ex. 123, 40 L. J. Ex. 121, *White v. France* (1877), 2 C. P. D. 308, 46 L. J. C. P. 823.

(*c*) *Smith v. London & St. Katharine Docks Co.* (1868), L. R. 3 C. P. 326, 37 L. J. C. P. 217 (Bovill C. J. and Byles J., dub. Keating J.)

(*d*) *Heaven v. Pender* (1883), 11 Q. B. Div. 503, 52 L. J. Q. B. 702.

Pr. 105, *Cannavan v. Concklin*, 1 Abb. Pr. (N. S.) 271. To illustrate, in the case of *Latham v. Roach* (72 Ill. 179), it was held that, individuals who hold a fair and erect structures for the use of their patrons, are liable for injury such patrons may receive by the breaking down or falling of such structures, if caused by the negligent or unskillful manner of their construction.

So, a dry-dock company were held liable for splitting the sound and strong keel of a vessel, by using a hydraulic dock without employing the usual precautions. *The Sappho*, 44 Fed. Rep. 359.

owner, and became as it were part of the ship, but this was held no reason for discharging the dock-owner from responsibility for the condition of the staging as it was delivered. Persons doing work on ships in the dock "must be considered as invited by the dock-owner to use the dock and all appliances provided by the dock-owner as incident to the use of the dock." (e)

Duty in respect of carriages, ships, &c. The possession of any structure to which human beings are intended to commit themselves or their property, animate or inanimate, entails this duty on the occupier, or rather controller.

(e) Per Cotton and Bowen L. JJ. at p. 35. The judgment of Brett M. R. attempts to lay down a wider principle with which the Lords Justices did not agree. See p. 34 above. It must be taken as a fact, though it is not clearly stated, that the defective condition of the rope might have been discovered by reasonably careful examination when the staging was put up.

Duty in respect of carriages, ships, etc. Carriers are required to use ordinary and reasonable care. T. & St. L. R. v. Suggs, 62 Tex. 323, 21 Am. & Eng. R. Cas. 175, Robinson v. N. Y. etc. R., 9 Fed. Rep. 877; 20 Blatchf. 338, P., P. & J. R. v. Reynolds, 88 Ill. 418, O'Donnell v. A. V. R., 59 Pa. St. 259, C. C., C. & J. R. v. Newell, 75 Ind. 542, 8 Am. & Eng. R. Cas. 377, George v. St. Louis etc. R., 34 Ark. 613, 1 Am. & Eng. R. Cas. 291, Texas & P. R. v. Hardin, 62 Tex. 267, 21 Am. & Eng. R. Cas. 160, B. S. O. & B. R. v. Rainbolt, 99 Ind. 551, 21 Am. & Eng. R. Cas. 160, D. & W. R. v. Spicher, 61 Tex. 427, 21 Am. & Eng. R. Cas. 160; I. & G. N. R. v. Halloren, 53 Tex. 46, 3 Am. & Eng. R. Cas. 313; P. & R. I. R. Lane, 83 Ill. 449, Pennsylvania Co. v. Roy, 102 U. S. 451, 1 Am. & Eng. R. Cas. 225, G. R. & I. R. v. Boyd, 65 Ind. 525, T. W. & W. R. v. Beggs, 85 Ill. 80.

Thus, a railroad company owes a duty to persons lawfully on their premises, and in making the access to their stations safe. Tobin v. P. S. & P. R. R. Co., 59 Me. 183. In Wendell v. Baxter (12 Gray, 494), it is held, that the owners of a private wharf owe a duty to one employed to carry the mail from a steamboat to the proprietors of which the owners of the wharf had left a part of it, and they not on the ground of any contract between them and the plaintiff, but because of the duty which the law imposed upon them to make and keep their wharf safe for all who were on it for a lawful business purpose, so long as they should permit it to be open and used. See Stratton v. Staples, 59 Me. 94, Low v. Grand Trunk Ry. Co., 72 Me. 318, Cook v. New York etc. Co., 1 Hilt. 436.

Vessels are liable for improper stowage. The Rebecca, 1 Ware, 188,

It extends to gangways or staging in a dock, as we have just seen; to a temporary stand put up for seeing a race or the like (*f*); to carriages travelling on a railway or road (*g*), or in which goods are despatched (*h*); to ships (*i*); to wharves, in respect of the safety of the frontage for ships moored at or approaching the wharf (*j*); and to market-places (*k*).

In the case of a wharfinger he is bound to use reasonable care to ascertain whether the bed of the harbour or river adjacent is in a safe condition to be used by a vessel coming to discharge at his wharf at reasonable times, having regard to the conditions of tide, the ship's draught of water and the like. But this duty exists only so far as the river bed is in the wharfinger's possession or control (*l*). For although the state of the ground be not within his

---

(*f*) *Francis* v *Cockrell* (1870), Ex Ch. L. R. 5 Q B 184, 501, 39 L. J. Q B 113, 291. The plaintiff had paid money for admission, therefore there was a duty *ex contractu*, but the judgments in the Ex. Ch., see especially per Martin B, also affirm a duty independent of contract. This is one of the most explicit authorities showing that the duty extends to the acts of contractors as well as servants

(*g*) *Foulkes* v *Metrop District R. Co.* (1880), 5 C P Div 157, 49 L. J. C. P. 361; *Moffatt* v. *Bateman* (1869), L. R. 3 P. C. 115.

(*h*) *Elliott* v. *Hall* (1885), 15 Q B. D. 315, 54 L J Q B. 518 The seller of coals sent them to the buyer in a truck with a dangerously loose trap-door in it, and the buyer's servant in the course of unloading the truck fell through and was hurt.

(*i*) *Hayn* v. *Culliford* (1879), 4 C. P. Div 182, 48 L. J. C. P. 372

(*j*) *The Moorcock* (1889), 14 P. Div. 64, 58 L. J. P. 73.

(*k*) *Lax* v *Corporation of Darlington* (1879), 5 Ex Div. 28, 49 L J. Ex. 105.

(*l*) *The Calliope* '91, A C 11, 60 L. J. P. 28, reversing the decision of the C. A., 14 P Div 138, 58 L. J. P. 76, on a different view of the facts. The reasons given in *The Moorcock*, note (*j*) above, seem to be to some extent qualified by this, though the decision itself is approved by Lord Watson, '91, A. C. at p. 22.

Warring v. Morse, 7 Ala. 343; Joliet S. S. Co. v. Yeaton, 29 Fed. Rep. 331, Mephams v. Biessel, 9 Wall. 320, The Excellent, 16 Fed Rep. 148. And for unseaworthiness. Tennessee v. Fardos, 7 La. An. 28; Hackhouse v. Sneed, 1 Murph. 173; Bowling v. Theband, 42 Fed Rep. 787; Bell v. Reed, 4 Binn. 127; 5 Am. Dec. 398; The Rover, 33 Fed. Rep. 515; West v. The Berlin, 3 Ia. 532. And for other negligence. The Barracouta, 40 Fed. Rep. 498; The Dan, 40 Fed Rep. 691; Taylor v. Mexican G. R. Co., 2 La. An. 654; The Gloaming, 46 Fed. Rep. 671; The H. G. Johnson, 48 Fed Rep. 696.

control, it is a matter more ascertainable by him than by the shipowner.

A railway passenger using one company's train with a ticket issued by another company under an arrangement made between the companies for their common benefit is entitled, whether or not he can be said to have contracted with the first-mentioned company, to reasonably safe provision for his conveyance, not only as regards the construction of the carriage itself, but as regards its fitness and safety in relation to other appliances (as the platform of a station) in connexion with which it is intended to be used (*m*). Where goods are lawfully shipped with the shipowner's consent, it is the shipowner's duty (even if he is not bound to the owner by any contract) not to let other cargo which will damage them be stowed in contact with them (*n*). Owners of a cattle-market are bound to leave the market-place in a reasonably safe condition for the cattle of persons who come to the market and pay toll for its use (*o*).

Limits of the duty. In the various applications we have mentioned, the duty does not extend to defects incapable of being discovered by the exercise of reasonable care, such

---

(*m*) *Foulkes* v. *Metrop. District R. Co.* (1880), 5 C. P. Div 157, 49 L. J C P. 361.

(*n*) *Hayn* v. *Culliford* (1879), 4 C. P. Div 182, 48 L. J. C P 372.

(*o*) *Lax* v. *Corporation of Darlington* (1879), 5 Ex Div. 28, 49 L. J. Ex. 105 (the plaintiff's cow was killed by a spiked fence round a statue in the market place). A good summary of the law, as far as it goes, is given in the argument of Cave J (then Q. C) for the plaintiff at p. 81 The question of the danger being obvious was considered not open on the appeal; if it had been, *qu.* as to the result, per Bramwell L J. It has been held in Minnesota (1889), that the owner of a building frequented by the public is bound not to allow a man of known dangerous temper to be employed about the building. *Dean* v. *St Paul Union Depot Co.*, 29 Am. Law Reg 22

Limits of the duty. Supporting the text, *vide* Schubert v. J. R. Clark Co. (Minn), 51 N. W. Rep 1103, Richmond & D. R. Co. v. Elliott, 149 U. S 266; 13 S. Ct. Rep. 837; Lindley v. Hunt, 22 Fed. Rep. 52; Bartlett v. Hoppock, 34 N. Y. 118; 88 Am. Dec. 428; Poland v. Miller, 95 Ind 387; 48 Am. Rep. 780; Rodgers v. Niles, 11 Ohio St. 48; 78 Am Dec. 290; Robinson Machine Works v. Chandler, 56 Ind 575; Curtis & Co.

as latent flaws in metal (*p*); though it does extend to all such as care and skill (not merely care and skill on the part of the defendant) can guard against (*q*).

Again, when the builder of a ship or carriage, or the maker of a machine, has delivered it out of his own possession and control to a purchaser, he is under no duty to persons using it as to its safe condition, unless the thing was in itself of a noxious or dangerous kind, or (it seems) unless he had actual knowledge of its being in such a state as would amount to a concealed danger to persons using it in an ordinary manner and with ordinary care (*r*).

Volenti non fit iniuria. Liability under the rule in *Indermaur* v. *Dames* (*s*) may be avoided not only by showing contributory negligence in the plaintiff, but by

---

(*p*) *Readhead* v *Midland R Co.* (1869), Ex. Ch. L. R. 4 Q B. 379, a case of contract between carrier and passenger, but the principle is the same, and indeed the duty may be put on either ground, see *Hyman* v *Nye* (1881), 6 Q B. D 685, 689, per Lindley J This does not however qualify the law as to the seller's implied warranty on the sale of a chattel for a specific purpose, there the warranty is absolute that the chattel is reasonably fit for that purpose, and there is no exception of latent defects: *Randall* v. *Newson* (1877), 2 Q. B. Div. 102, 46 L J Q B. 257

(*q*) *Hyman* v *Nye* (1881), 6 Q. B. D. at p 687.

(*r*) *Winterbottom* v *Wright*, 10 M. & W 109, *Collis* v *Selden* (1868), L. R. 3 C P. 495, 37 L. J. C P. 233, *Losee* v. *Clute*, 51 N. Y 494

(*s*) P 625, above

Mfg. Co. v Williams, 48 Ark. 325; Woodle v. Whitney, 23 Wis. 55, 99 Am. Dec. 102, Olrich v. Stohrer, 12 Phila. Rep. 199; Hoe v. Sanborn, 21 N Y. 552; 28 Am. Dec. 163; Getty v. Rountree, 2 Pinney, 379; 2 Chand. 28, 54 Am. Dec. 130; Shatto v. Abernethy, 35 Minn. 538; Kellogg Bridge Co. v. Hamilton, 110 U. S. 108; Gerst v. Jones, 32 Gratt 518; 34 Am. Rep. 773; Hight v. Bacon, 126 Mass 10; Dearborn v. Downing, 77 Me 457, Pease v. Sabin, 38 Vt. 432, 91 Am Dec. 364, Byers v. Chaplin, 28 Ohio St. 306; Dayton v. Hoogland, 39 Id 682, Leopold v. Van Kirk, 27 Wis. 152; Bragg v. Morrill, 24 Am Rep. 106; Bagley v. Cleveland Rolling Mill Co., 21 Fed. Rep. 159; Eagan v. Call, 34 Pa. St. 236, 75 Am. Dec 653; French v. Vining, 102 Mass. 132; Dickinson v. Gay, 7 Allen, 29: 83 Am. Dec. 656, Dounce v. Dow, 64 N. Y. 411.

Volenti non fit iniuria. In the United States many of the authorities go further than the rule stated in the text and hold that the safety of one is not insured where risks are assumed which are either known or are so patent that by the use of observation and ordinary prudence they

showing that the risk was as well known to him as to the defendant, and that with such knowledge he voluntarily exposed himself to it (*t*); but this will not excuse the breach of a positive statutory duty (*u*).

Duty towards passers-by. Occupiers of fixed property are under a like duty towards persons passing or being on

(*t*) *Thomas* v. *Quartermaine*, 18 Q. B. Div. 685, 56 L. J. Q. B. 340

(*u*) Dicta of L JJ *ibid.*, and *Baddeley* v. *Earl Granville* (1887), 19 Q. B D. 423, 56 L. J. Q B 501. See further *Yarmouth* v. *France*, *ib* 647, and p. 105, above. *Smith* v. *Baker*, '91, A C. 325, 60 L. J. Q. B. 683, was a case not of this class, but (as the facts were found) of negligence in conducting a specific operation.

---

could have been seen and avoided. See Hoosier Stone Co. v. McCain, 133 Ind 231, 31 N E. Rep. 956; Chism v. Martin, 57 Ark. 83; 20 S. W. Rep 808; Gulf C. & S. F. Ry. Co. v. Montgomery, 85 Tex. 64, 19 S. W. Rep. 1015; St Louis & S. F. Ry. Co. v. Traweek, 84 Tex. 65; 19 S. W. Rep 370; Rogers v. Leyden, 127 Ind. 50, 26 N. E. Rep. 210; Diehl v. Lehigh Iron Co , 140 Pa. St 487; 21 At. Rep. 430; 27 W. N. C. 552; Missouri P. Ry. Co. v. Somers, 78 Tex. 439; Anderson v. Minnesota & N. W. R Co., 39 Minn. 523, 41 N. W. Rep. 104, Mansfield, etc., Coal Co. v. McEnery, 91 Pa St. 185, 33 Am. Rep. 662; Goldstein v. Chicago, etc. R. Co., 46 Wis. 404; Pittsburg, etc. R. Co. v. Collins, 87 Pa. St. 405, 30 Am. Rep. 371, Mohan v Syracuse, etc., R. Co., 73 N. Y. 585; Baltimore, etc., R. Co. v. Depew, 40 Ohio St. 121; 12 Am. & Eng R. Cas. 64; Erie v. Magill, 101 Pa. St. 616; 47 Am. Rep. 739, Collett v. Leavenworth, 27 Kan. 673.

But it should be remembered that, "The fact that a person voluntarily takes some risk, is not conclusive evidence, under all circumstances, that he is not using due care" Lawless v. Conn. R. Co., 136 Mass. 1; 18 Am & Eng. R. Cas. 96. See Harris v. Township of Clinton, 64 Mich. 447, 7 West Rep 666, Dewire v. Bailey, 131 Mass. 196; 45 Am. Rep 219; Looney v. McLean, 129 Mass. 33; 37 Am. Rep. 295; Filer v. N. Y Cent R. Co., 49 N Y. 47; 10 Am. Rep 327; Albion v. Hetrick, 90 Ind. 545, 46 Am Rep. 230; Wassner v. Delaware, etc. Co., 80 N. Y. 212; 1 Am. & Eng. R. Cas. 122; 36 Am Rep. 608; Baldwin v. St. Louis, etc., R. Co., 63 Ia 210; 15 Am. & Eng R. Cas. 166.

Duty towards passers-by. As stated in the text, persons lawfully traveling by the property of others are entitled to that reasonable protection which their safety requires. In the case of Hannem v. Pence (40 Minn. 130, 41 N. W. Rep. 657), the court said: "A man has no right to construct his roof so as to discharge upon his neighbor's land, water, ice or snow which would not naturally fall there, and the persons of those

adjacent land by their invitation in the sense above mentioned, or in the exercise of an independent right.

In *Barnes* v. *Ward* (x), the defendant, a builder, had left the area of an unfinished house open and unfenced. A person lawfully walking after dark along the public path on which the house abutted fell into the area and was killed. An action was brought under Lord Campbell's Act, and the case was twice argued; the main point for the defence being that the defendant had only dug a hole in his own land, as he lawfully might, and was not under any duty to fence or guard it, as it did not interfere with the use of the right of way. The Court held there was a good cause of action, the excavation being so close to the public way as to make it unsafe to persons using it with ordinary

(x) 9 C. B. 392, 19 L. J. C. P. 195 (1850), cp D 9, 2, ad leg Aquil 28.

---

who are lawfully traveling a street are certainly as much entitled to protection as the property of an adjoining owner." Citing Cahill v. Eastman, 18 Minn 292, and other cases.

In Dehring v. Comstock (78 Mich. 153; 43 N. W. Rep. 1049) it was held to be negligence to throw bales of hay, weighing 140 pounds, from a barn-loft down into a public side-walk, without first looking into the street to see if any one is near by, and giving sufficient warning to prevent approach before casting them down.

Again, in Corrigan v. Union Sugar Refinery (98 Mass. 577), it was held that, one whose servant carelessly throws a keg out of a window so that it injures a person in a passage-way below is liable for such injury, even if his title in the way is such as not to render him responsible for any defect therein, and that he may at any time revoke the permission by which the person injured is passing over it. See Hunt v. Hoyt, 20 Ill. 544; Brezee v. Powers, 80 Mich. 172, 45 N. W. Rep 130, Davis v. Michigan B. T. Co., 61 Mich. 307; 28 N W Rep. 108, St. Louis, I. M. & S Ry. Co v. Hopkins, 54 Ark. 209; 15 S W. Rep. 610; McIntire v. Roberts, 149 Mass. 450; 22 N E Rep. 13; Ster v Tuety, 45 Hun, 49, McGuire v Spence, 91 N. Y 303, 42 Am. Rep 601, note; Dixon v. Pluns (Cal), 31 Pac. Rep. 931; Mullen v. St John, 57 N. Y. 567

In order to be a traveler, in this sense, it is not necessary that one should be constantly moving, stops of reasonable duration and of business of social character may be made. Smethurst v Proprietors Ind. Cong. Church, 148 Mass 261, 19 N. E. Rep. 387, citing O'Linda v. Lathrop, 21 Pick 292, Judd v Fargo, 107 Mass. 264.

care. The making of such an excavation amounts to a public nuisance "even though the danger consists in the risk of accidentally deviating from the road." Lately it has been held that one who by lawful authority diverts a public path is bound to provide reasonable means to warn and protect travellers against going astray at the point of diversion (*y*).

In *Corby* v. *Hill* (*z*) the plaintiff was a person using a private way with the consent of the owners and occupiers. The defendant had the like consent, as he alleged, to put slates and other materials on the road. No light or other safeguard or warning was provided. The plaintiff's horse, being driven on the road after dark, ran into the heap of materials and was injured. It was held immaterial whether the defendant was acting under licence from the owners or not. If not, he was a mere trespasser; but the owners themselves could not have justified putting a concealed and dangerous obstruction in the way of persons to whom they had held out the road as a means of access (*a*).

Here the plaintiff was (it seems) (*b*) only a licensee, but while the licence was in force he was entitled not to have the condition of the way so altered as to set a trap for him. The case, therefore, marks exactly the point in which a licensee's condition is better than a trespasser's.

Presumption of negligence (res ipsa loquitur). Where damage is done by the falling of objects into a highway from a building, the modern rule is that the accident, in

---

(*y*) *Hurst* v *Taylor* (1885), 14 Q. B. D. 918, 54 L J Q B 310, defendants, railway contractors, had (within the statutory powers) diverted a footpath to make the line, but did not fence off the old direction of the path, plaintiff walking after dark, followed the old direction, got on the railway and fell over a bridge

(*z*) 4 C. B N. S 556, 27 L. J C. P 318 (1858)

(*a*) Cp. *Sweeney* v *Old Colony & Newport R R Co* (1865), 10 Allen (Mass.). 368, and Bigelow L C. 660.

(*b*) The language of the judgments leaves it not quite clear whether the continued permission to use the road for access to a public building (the Hanwell Lunatic Asylum) did not amount to an "invitation" in the special sense of this class of cases

the absence of explanation, is of itself evidence of negligence. In other words, the burden of proof is on the occupier of the building. If he cannot show that the accident was due to some cause consistent with the due repair and careful management of the structure, he is liable. The authorities, though not numerous, are sufficient to establish the rule, one of them being the decision of a Court of appeal. In *Byrne* v. *Boadle* (c) a barrel of flour fell from a window in defendant's warehouse in Liverpool, and knocked down the plaintiff, who was lawfully passing in the public street. There was no evidence to show how or by whom the barrel was being handled. The Court said this was enough to raise against the defendant a presumption of negligence which it was for him to rebut. "It is the duty of persons who keep barrels in a warehouse to take care that they do not roll out. . . . A barrel could not roll out of a warehouse without some negligence, and to

---

(c) 2 H. & C. 722, 33 L J Ex. 13, and in Bigelow L C 578 (1863)

Presumption of negligence As a rule negligence is not presumed But there are cases where negligence is not to be presumed from the fact of damage, yet the circumstances under which the injury occurred may be such as to create the presumption. This is the application of the phrase *res ipsa loquitur*. Thus, where a railroad accident, caused by the cars leaving the track, occurs, the presumption of negligence arises by virtue of this maxim. Seybolt *v* New York, etc. R. Co., 95 N. Y. 562, 18 Am. & Eng. R Cas. 162

So, in the case of Holbrook *v.* The Utica, etc. R Co (12 N. Y. 263; 64 Am. Dec. 562, note) the court said: "For example a passenger's leg is broken while on his passage in a railroad car. This mere fact is no evidence of negligence on the part of the carrier until something further is shown. If the witness who swears to the injury, testifies also that it was caused by a crash in a collision with another train belonging to the same carriers, the presumption of negligence immediately arises; not however from the fact that the leg was broken, but from the circumstances attending the fact * * * The presumption arises from the cause of the injury or from other circumstances attending it, and not from the injury itself. See Lowery *v.* Manhattan R. Co., 99 N. Y. 158, Wiedmer *v.* New York Elevated R. Co., 41 Hun, 284; Mulcairns *v* Janesville, 67 Wis. 24; Dougherty *v* Missouri R Co., 81 Mo. 325, 21 Am & Eng. R Cas. 497; 51 Am. Rep 239, Rose *v* Stephens, etc., Co., 20 Blatchf.

say that a plaintiff who is injured by it must call witnesses from the warehouse to prove negligence seems to me preposterous. So in the building or repairing a house, or putting pots on the chimneys, if a person passing along the road is injured by something falling upon him, I think the accident alone would be *prima facie* evidence of negligence" (*d*). This was followed, perhaps extended, in *Kearney* v. *London, Brighton and South Coast Railway Co.* (*e*). There as the plaintiff was passing along a highway spanned by a railway bridge, a brick fell out of one of the piers of the bridge and struck and injured him. A train had passed immediately before. There was not any evidence as to the condition of the bridge and brickwork, except that after the accident other bricks were found to have fallen out. The Court held the maxim " res ipsa

---

(*d*) Per Pollock C B Op *Scott* v. *London Dock Co* (1865), 3 H. & C 596, 34 L. J. 1 x 220, p 550, above

(*e*) Ex. Ch. L J. R. 6 Q. B. 759, 40 L. J. Q. B. 285 (1871).

411; 11 Fed. Rep. 438; The Reliance, 4 Woods, 420; 2 Fed. Rep. 249, Posey *v.* Scoville, 10 Fed. Rep. 140; Robinson *v.* New York Cent. etc , R. Co., 20 Blatchf. 338; White *v.* Boston, etc. R. Co., 144 Mass. 104; 30 Am. & Eng. R. Cas. 615; Cummins *v.* National Furnace Co., 60 Wis. 603; Bedford etc. R. Co. *v.* Rainbolt, 99 Ind. 551; 21 Am. & Eng. R. Cas. 466; Texas, etc. Co. *v.* Suggs, 62 Tex. 323; Laing *v* Colder, 8 Pa. St. 479; Meier *v.* Penn. R. Co , 64 Pa. St. 225; Sullivan *v.* Phila. etc., R. Co., 30 Pa. St. 234, Louisville etc., Ry. Co *v.* Jones, 108 Ind. 551; Eagle Packing Co. *v.* Defries, 94 Ill. 598, Pres., etc , Balt. etc. Road *v.* Leonhardt, 66 Md. 70; Memphis, etc., Co. *v* McCool, 83 Ind. 392, Smith *v.* St. Paul, etc., Co , 32 Minn. 1, Moore *v.* Des Moines, etc., Co , 69 Ia 491; Iron etc. R Co. *v* Mowery, 36 Ohio St. 418; Centr. Pass , etc., Co *v.* Kuhn, 86 Ky 578; 6 S. W. Rep 441; Welch *v.* Durand, 36 Conn. 182; Chataigne *v* Bergeron, 10 La. An 699; Morgan *v.* Cox, 22 Mo. 373, Buck *v.* Penn. R. Co , 150 Pa. St. 170; 24 At Rep. 678; 30 W N C. 400; Kirst *v.* M , L. S. & W. R. Co , 46 Wis 489.

It is a general rule that the employer is not liable for the negligence of his contractor. Wood *v.* The Ind. School Dist , 44 Ia. 27; Reed *v.* Allegheny City, 79 Pa. St. 300, City of Rochester *v.* Montgomery, 72 N Y. 65, Roemer *v.* Striker (Super. N. Y.), 21 N Y S. Rep. 1090, 2 Misc Rep 573; Samyn *v.* McClosky, 2 Ohio St. 536; Kepperly *v* Ramsden, 83 Ill 354 See, *ante*, pp. 121, *et seq.*

loquitur" to be applicable. "The defendants were under the common law liability to keep the bridge in safe condition for the public using the highway to pass under it;" and when "a brick fell out of the pier of the bridge without any assignable cause except the slight vibration caused by a passing train," it was for the defendants to show, if they could, that the event was consistent with due diligence having been used to keep the bridge in safe repair (*f*). This decision has been followed, in the stronger case of a whole building falling into the street, in the State of New York. "Buildings properly constructed do not fall without adequate cause" (*g*).

In a later case (*h*) the occupier of a house from which a lamp projected over the street was held liable for damage done by its fall, though he had employed a competent person (not his servant) to put the lamp in repair: the fall was in fact due to the decayed condition of the attachment of the lamp to its bracket, which had escaped notice. "It was the defendant's duty to make the lamp reasonably safe, the contractor failed to do that . . . . therefore the defendant has not done his duty, and he is liable to the plaintiff for the consequences" (*i*). In this case negligence on the contractor's part was found as a fact.

Combining the principles affirmed in these authorities, we see that the owner of property abutting on a highway is under a positive duty to keep his property from being a cause of danger to the public by reason of any defect either in structure, repair, or use and management, which reasonable care and skill can guard against.

Distinctions. But where an accident happens in the course of doing on fixed property work which is proper of itself, and not usually done by servants, and there is no

---

(*f*) Per Cur. L. R. 6 Q. B. at pp 761, 762

(*g*) *Mullen* v *St. John,* 57 N Y 567, 569

(*h*) *Tarry* v. *Ashton* (1876), 1 Q B. D. 314, 45 L J Q B 260

(*i*) Per Blackburn J at p 319.

proof either that the work was under the occupier's control or that the accident was due to any defective condition of the structure itself with reference to its ordinary purposes, the occupier is not liable (*k*). In other words, he does not answer for the care or skill of an independent and apparently competent contractor in the doing of that which, though connected with the repair of a structure for whose condition the occupier does answer, is in itself merely incident to the contractor's business and under his order and control.

There are cases involving principles and considerations very similar to these, but concerning the special duties of adjacent landowners or occupiers to one another rather than any general duty to the public or to a class of persons. We must be content here to indicate their existence though in practice the distinction is not always easy to maintain (*l*).

Position of licensees. Thus far we have spoken of the duties owed to persons who are brought within these risks of unsafe condition or repair by the occupier's invitation

---

(*k*) *Welfare* v *London & Brighton R. Co* (1869), L. R 4 Q B 693, 38 L J Q B. 241, a decision on peculiar facts, where perhaps a very little more evidence might have turned the scale in favour of the plaintiff

(*l*) See *Bower* v *Peate* (1876), 1 Q B. D 321, 45 L. J Q. B 446, *Hughes* v. *Percival* (1883), 8 App Ca 443, 52 L J Q B 719, and cp *Gorham* v *Gross*, 125 Mass. 232

Position of licensees. As stated in the text the licensee must assume the ordinary risks of the place where the license is to be enjoyed. Vanderbeck *v.* Hendry, 34 N. J L. 467; Metcalfe *v.* Cunard Steamship Co, 117 Mass 66. At the same time the licensee is liable for damages resulting from his negligence in the performance of the act or excessive use of the privilege Selden *v.* Del. & H. Canal Co., 29 N. Y. 634; McKnight *v* Ratcliff, 44 Pa. St. 159; Dean *v* McLean, 48 Vt 412; Eaton *v* Wenn, 20 Mich 156; Norton *v.* Craig, 68 Me 275; Smith *v* Amer. Institute, 9 Daly, 526, Gardner *v.* Rowland, 2 Ired. 247, Dempsey *v* Kipp, 62 Barb 311, Luford *v* Putnam, 35 N. H 563; Murray *v* Gibson, 21 Ill. App 488; Cook *v* Stearns, 11 Mass 533, Breitenbach *v* Trowbridge, 64 Mich 393; 31 N W Rep 402; Fletcher *v.* Evans, 140 Mass. 241, Cushing *v.*

on a matter of common interest, or are there in the exercise of a right. We have still to note the plight of him who comes on or near another's property as a "bare licensee." Such an one appears to be (with the possible exception of a mortgagee in possession) about the least favoured in the law of men who are not actual wrong-doers. He must take the property as he finds it, and is entitled only not to be led into danger by "something like fraud" (m).

Persons who by the mere gratuitous permission of owners or occupiers take a short cut across a waste piece of land (n), or pass over private bridges (o), or have the run of a building (p), cannot expect to find the land free from holes or ditches, or the bridges to be in safe repair, or the passages and stairs to be commodious and free from dangerous places. If the occupier, while the permission continues, does something that creates a concealed danger to people availing themselves of it, he may well be liable (q). And he would of course be liable, not for failure in a special duty, but for wilful wrong, if he purposely made his property dangerous to persons using ordinary care, and then held out his permission as an inducement to come on it. Apart from this improbable case, the licensee's rights are measured, at best, by the actual state of the property at the time of the licence.

"If I dedicate a way to the public which is full of ruts and holes, the public must take it as it is. If I dig a pit

(m) Willes J., *Gautret* v. *Egerton* (1867), L. R. 2 C. P. at p 375
(n) *Hounsell* v. *Smyth* (1860), 7 C B. N. S 731, 29 L. J C. P 203
(o) *Gautret* v. *Egerton* (1867), L. R 2 C. P 371, 36 L. J C P. 191
(p) *Sullivan* v *Waters* (1864), 14 Ir. C. L. R 460
(q) *Corby* v *Hill* (1858), 4 C. B N. S. 556, 27 L. J C P 318, p 635, above.

Adams, 18 Pick. 110; Ferrin *v.* Symonds, 11 N. H. 368; Van Brunt *v.* Schenck, 13 Johns. 414, Edelman *v.* Yeakel, 27 Pa. St 26; Faulkner *v.* Anderson, Gilmer, 221; Jewell *v* Mahood, 44 N H. 874, Ballard *v.* Noaks, 2 Ark. 45.

in it, I may be liable for the consequences: but, if I do nothing, I am not " (r).

The occupier of a yard in which machinery was in motion allowed certain workmen (not employed in his own business) to use, for their own convenience, a path crossing it. This did not make it his duty to fence the machinery at all, or if he did so to fence it sufficiently; though he might have been liable if he had put up an insecure guard which by the false appearance of security acted as a trap (s). The plaintiff, by having permission to use the path, had not the right to find it in any particular state of safety or convenience.

"Permission involves leave and licence, but it gives no *right*. If I avail myself of permission to cross a man's land I do so by virtue of a licence, not of a right. It is an abuse of language to call it a right: it is an excuse or licence, so that the party cannot be treated as a trespasser" (t). In the language of Continental jurisprudence, there is no question of *culpa* between a gratuitous licensee and the licensor, as regards the safe condition of the property to which the licence applies. Nothing short of *dolus* will make the licensor liable (u).

Host and guest. Invitation is a word applied in common speech to the relation of host and guest. But a guest (that is, a visitor who does not pay for his entertainment)

(r) Willes J., L. R. 2 C. P. at p. 373.

(s) *Bolch* v. *Smith* (1862), 7 H. & N. 736, 31 L. J. Ex. 201

(t) Martin B., 7 H. & N. at p. 745. *Batchelor* v. *Fortescue* (1883), 11 Q. B. Div. 474, 478, seems rather to stand upon the ground that the plaintiff had gone out of his way to create the risk for himself. As between himself and the defendant, he had no title at all to be where he was. Cp. D. 9. 2 ad leg. Aquil. 31 *ad fin.* " culpa ab eo exigenda non est, cum divinare non potuerit an per eum locum aliquis transiturus sit. " In *Ivay*

v. *Hedges* (1882), 9 Q. B. D. 80, the question was more of the terms of the contract between landlord and tenant than of a duty imposed by law. Quaere, whether in that case the danger to which the tenant was exposed might not have well been held to be in the nature of a trap. The defect was a non-apparent one, and the landlord knew of it.

(u) Cp *Blackmore* v. *Bristol and Exeter R. Co.* (1858), 8 E. & B. 1035, 27 L. J. Q. B. 167, where it seems that the plaintiff's intestate was not even a licensee, but see 11 Q. B. D 516

has not the benefit of the legal doctrine of invitation in the sense now before us. He is in point of law nothing but a licensee. The reason given is that he cannot have higher rights than a member of the household of which he has for the time being become, as it were, a part (x). All he is entitled to is not to be led into danger known to his host, and not known or reasonably apparent to himself.

On the same principle, a man who offers another a seat in his carriage is not answerable for an accident due to any defect in the carriage of which he was not aware (y).

Liability of licensor for "ordinary negligence." It may probably be assumed that a licensor is answerable to the licensee for ordinary negligence (z), in the sense that his own act or omission will make him liable if it is such that it would create liability as between two persons having an equal right to be there: for example, if J. S. allows me to use his private road, it will hardly be said that, without express warning, I am to take the risk of J. S. driving furiously thereon. But the whole subject of a licensee's rights and risks is still by no means free from difficulty.

(x) *Southcote* v. *Stanley* (1856), 1 H & N. 247, 25 L J. Ex 339 But *quaere* if this explanation be not *obscurum per obscurius*. Cp *Abraham* v *Reynolds*, 5 H & N at p. 148, where the same line of thought appears.

(y) *Moffatt* v. *Bateman* (1869), L. R. 3 P. C 115.

(z) Horace Smith, 38 Campbell, 119.

Host and guest. A traveler who pays for being entertained is entitled to the protection of his property afforded by the common law. Curtis v. Murphy, 63 Wis 4; 53 Am. Rep. 242; Russell v Fagan (Del.), 8 At Rep. 258; Walling v. Potter, 35 Conn. 183, Manning v Wells, 9 Humph. 746, 51 Am. Dec. 688, Clute v. Wiggins, 14 Johns 175; 7 Am. Dec. 451; Horner v. Harvey, 3 N. M. 197; 5 Pac. Rep. 329.

A "boarder" is a resident who is entertained at a special rate and for an agreed time. To him the keeper's obligation is near to that of a bailee. Chamberlain v. Masterson, 26 Ala 371; Vance v. Throckmorton, 5 Bush, 41; Neal v. Wilcox, 4 Jones L. 46; 67 Am. Dec 266; Shoecraft v. Bailey, 25 Ia. 553, Hancock v. Rand, 94 N. Y 1; 46 Am Rep. 112.

A "visitor" is one entertained temporarily and without charge. Gastenhoffer v Clair, 10 Daly, 265; Kopper v. Willis, 9 Id. 460, Carter v. Hobbs, 12 Mich. 52; 83 Am Dec. 762; Fitch v. Custer, 17 Hun, 126.

Liability of owner not in occupation? It does not appear to have been ever decided how far, if at all, an owner of property not in possession can be subject to the kind of duties we have been considering. We have seen that in certain conditions he may be liable for nuisance (a). But, since the ground of these special duties regarding safe condition and repair is the relation created by the occupier's express or tacit "invitation," it may be doubted whether the person injured can sue the owner in the first instance, even if the defect or default by which he suffered is, as between owner and occupier, a breach of the owner's obligation.

(a) See p. 531, above. Campbell, pp. 26, 27. [Tucker v Illinois Cent R Co, 42 La An. 114, 7 So. Rep. 124, Wilkinson v Detroit Steel & Spring Works, 73 Mich. 405, 41 N W Rep. 490, O'Connor v Andrews, 81 Tex. 28, 16 S. W. Rep. 628.]

CHAPTER XIII.

SPECIAL RELATIONS OF CONTRACT AND TORT.

Original theory of forms of action. The original theory of the common law seems to have been that there were a certain number of definite and mutually exclusive causes of action, expressed in appropriate forms. The test for ascertaining the existence or non-existence of a legal remedy in a given case was to see whether the facts could be brought under one of these forms. Not only this, but the party seeking legal redress had to discover and use the right form at his peril. So had the defendant if he relied on any special ground of defence as opposed to the *general issue*. If this theory had been strictly carried out, confusion between forms or causes of action would not have been possible. But strict adherence to the requirements of such a theory could be kept up only at the price of intolerable inconvenience. Hence, not only new remedies were introduced, but relaxations of the older definitions were allowed. The number of cases in which there was a substantial grievance without remedy was greatly diminished, but the old sharply drawn lines of definition were overstepped at various points, and became obscured. Thus different forms and causes of action overlapped. In many cases the new form, having been introduced for greater practical convenience, simply took the place of the older, as an alternative which in practice was always or almost always preferred: but in other cases one or another remedy might be better according to the circumstances. Hence, different remedies for similar or identical causes of action remained in use after the freedom of choice had been established with more or less difficulty.

On the debatable ground thus created between those states of fact which clearly give rise to only one kind of action and those which clearly offered an alternative, there arose a new kind of question, more refined and indeterminate than those of the earlier system, because less reducible to the test of fixed forms

Actions on the case. The great instrument of transformation was the introduction of actions on the case by the Statute of Westminster (*a*). Certain types of action on the case became in effect new and well recognized forms of action. But it was never admitted that the virtue of the statute had been exhausted, and it was probably rather the timidity of pleaders than the unwillingness of the judges that prevented the development from being even greater than it was. It may be asked in this connexion why some form of action on the case was not devised to compete with the jurisdiction of the Court of Chancery in enforcing trusts. An action on the case analogous to the action of account, if not the action of account itself, might well have been held to lie against a feoffee to uses at the suit of *cestui que use* Probably the reason is to be sought in the inadequacy of the common law remedies, which no expansion of pleading could have got over. The theory of a system of equitable rights wholly outside the common law and its process, and inhabiting a region of mysteries unlawful for a common lawyer to meddle with, was not the cause but the consequence of the Court of Chancery's final triumph.

The history of the Roman *legis actiones* may in a general way be compared with that of common law pleading in its earlier stages; and it may be found that the praetorian

(*a*) 12 Edw I, c 24

actions have not less in common with our actions on the case than with the remedies peculiar to courts of equity, which our text-writers have habitually likened to them.

Causes of action: modern classification of them as founded on contract or tort. Forms of action are now abolished in England. But the forms of action were only the marks and appointed trappings of causes of action; and to maintain an action there must still be some cause of action known to the law. Where there is an apparent alternative, we are no longer bound to choose at our peril, and at the very outset, on which ground we will proceed, but we must have at least one definite ground. The question, therefore, whether any cause of action is raised by given facts is as important as ever it was. The question whether there be more than one is not as a rule material in questions between the same parties. But it may be (and has been) material under exceptional conditions: and where the suggested distinct causes of action affect different parties it may still be of capital importance.

In modern English practice, personal (*b*) causes of action cognizable by the superior courts of common law (and now by the High Court in the jurisdiction derived from them) have been regarded as arising either out of contract or out of wrongs independent of contract. This division was no doubt convenient for the working lawyer's ordinary uses, and it received the high sanction of the framers of the Common Law Procedure Act, besides other statutes dealing with procedure. But it does not rest on any historical authority, nor can it be successfully defended as a scientific dichotomy. In fact the historical causes above mentioned have led to intersection of the two regions, with considerable perplexity for the consequence.

We have causes of action nominally in contract which

(*b*) I do not think it was ever attempted to bring the real actions under this classification

are not founded on the breach of any agreement, and we have torts which are not in any natural sense independent of contract.

This border-land between the law of tort and the law of contract will be the subject of examination in this chapter.

Classes of questions arising. The questions to be dealt with may be distributed under the following heads:—
1. Alternative forms of remedy on the same cause of action.
2. Concurrent or alternative causes of action.
3. Causes of action in tort dependent on a contract not between the same parties.
4. Measure of damages and other incidents of the remedy.

I.— *Alternative Forms of Remedy on the same Cause of Action.*

One cause of action and alternative remedies. It may be hard to decide whether particular cases fall under this head or under the second, that is, whether there is one cause of action which the pleader has or had the choice of describing in two ways, or two distinct causes of action which may possibly confer rights on and against different parties. In fact the most difficult questions we shall meet with are of this kind.

The common law doctrine of misfeasance. Misfeasance in doing an act in itself not unlawful is ground for an action on the case (c). It is immaterial that the act was not one which the defendant was bound to do at all (d).

(c) And strictly, not for an action of trespass, but there are classes of facts which may be regarded as constituting either wrongs of misfeasance (case), or acts which might be justified under some common or particular claim of right, but not being duly done fail of such justification and are merely wrongful (trespass)

(d) *Gladwell* v *Steggal* (1839), 5 Bing

If a man will set about actions attended with risk to others, the law casts on him the duty of care and competence. It is equally immaterial that the defendant may have bound himself to do the act, or to do it competently. The undertaking, if undertaking there was in that sense, is but the occasion and inducement of the wrong. From this root we have, as a direct growth, the whole modern doctrine of negligence. We also have, by a more artificial process, the modern method of enforcing simple contracts, through the specialized form of this kind of action called *assumpsit* (e): the obligation being extended, by a bold and strictly illogical step, to cases of pure non-feasance (f), and guarded by the requirement of consideration. Gradually assumpsit came to be thought of as founded on a duty *ex contractu*; so much so that it might not be joined with another cause of action on the case, such as conversion. From a variety of action on the

N C 7 13, 5 Scott 60, 8 L J C P 361; action by an infant for incompetence in surgical treatment In such an action the plaintiff's consent is material only because without it the defendant would be a mere trespasser, and the incompetence would not be the gist of the action, but matter for aggravation of damages To the same effect is *Pippin v Sheppard* (1822), 11 Price, 400, holding that a declaration against a surgeon for improper treatment was not bad for not showing by whom the surgeon was retained or to be paid As to the assumption of special skill being material, see *Shiells* v *Blackburne* (1789), 1 H Bl. 158, 2 R R. 750

(e) O W Holmes, The Common Law, pp 274 sqq , J B Ames in Harv. Law Rev 11. 1, 53.

(f) An analogy to this in the Roman theory of *culpa*, under the Lex Aquilia, can hardly be sustained See the passages in D. 9 2 collected and discussed in Dr Grueber's treatise, at pp 87, 202. On the other hand the decision in *Slade's case*, 4 Co Rep 91 a, that the existence of a cause of action in debt did not exclude assumpsit, was in full accordance with the original conception

Misfeasance. Defined as in the text, *vide* Black's Law Dic 779; Anderson's Dic of Law, 450; Colte v. Lynes, 33 Conn 109, Roberts v. State, 7 Coldw 359; Horner v Lawrence, 37 N. J L 46; Berghoff v. McDonald, 87 Ind. 549; Bell v. Josselyn, 3 Gray, 309, Harriman v Stowe, 57 Mo. 93; Elmore v. Brooks, 6 Heisk. 45; Bliss v Schaub, 48 Barb 339, Richardson v. Kimball, 28 Me. 464; Erwin v. Davenport, 9 Heisk 44, Clark v. Lovering, 37 Minn. 120; 33 N W Rep 776; Delaney v. Rochereau, 34 La An. 1123; 44 Am. Rep 456; Crane v. Onderdonk, 67 Barb 47; Bennett v. Ives, 30 Conn 329; Hedden v Griffin, 136 Mass. 229; 49 Am. Rep. 25; Reed v. Petterson, 91 Ill 288, 297

case it had become a perfect species, and in common use its origin was forgotten. But the old root was there still, and had life in it at need. Thus it might happen that facts or pleadings which, in the current modern view showed an imperfect cause of action in assumpsit would yet suffice to give the plaintiff judgment on the more ancient ground of misfeasance in a duty imposed by law. In the latest period of common law pleading the House of Lords upheld in this manner a declaration for negligence in the execution of an employment, which averred an undertaking of the employment, but not any promise to the plaintiff, nor, in terms, any consideration (*g*). And it was said that a breach of duty in the course of employment under a contract would give rise to an action either in contract or in tort at the plaintiff's election (*h*). This, it will be seen, is confined to an active misdoing; notwithstanding the verbal laxity of one or two passages, the House of Lords did not authorize parties to treat the mere non-performance of a promise as a substantive tort (*i*). Until the beginning of this century it was the common practice to sue in tort for the breach of an express warranty, though it was needless to allege or prove the defendant's knowledge of the assertion being false (*j*).

On the other hand, it was held for a considerable time (*k*) that an action against a common carrier for loss of goods, even when framed in tort, "sounded in contract" so much that it could not be distinguished from assumpsit, and a count so framed could not be properly joined with other

---

(*g*) *Brown* v. *Boorman* (1844), 11 Cl. & F. 1. The defendant's pleader appears to have been unable to refer the declaration to any certain species; to make sure of having it somewhere he pleaded — (1) not guilty, (2) *non assumpsit*; (3) a traverse of the alleged employment.

(*h*) Per Lord Campbell.

(*i*) *Courtenay* v. *Earle* (1850), 10 C. B. 73, 20 L. J. C. P. 7. See especially the dicta of Maule J. in the course of the argument. In that case it was attempted to join counts, which were in substance for the non-payment of a bill of exchange, with a count in trover.

(*j*) *Williamson* v. *Allison* (1802), 2 East, 446.

(*k*) From 1695, *Dalston* v. *Janson*, 5 Mod. 89, 1 Ld. Raym. 58, till 1766, when the last mentioned case and others to the same effect were overruled in *Dickon* v. *Clifton*, 2 Wils. 319.

forms of case, such as trover. At a later time it was held, for the purpose of a plea in abatement, that the declaration against a carrier on the custom of the realm was in substance *ex contractu* (*l*).

There are certain kinds of employment, namely those of a carrier and an innkeeper, which are deemed public in a special sense. If a man holds himself out as exercising one of these, the law casts on him the duty of not refusing the benefit thereof, so far forth as his means extend, to any person who properly applies for it. The innkeeper must not without a reasonable cause refuse to entertain a traveller, or the carrier to convey goods. Thus we have a duty attached to the mere profession of the employment, and antecedent to the formation of any contract; and if the duty is broken, there is not a breach of contract but a tort, for which the remedy under the common law forms of pleading is an action on the case. In effect refusing to enter into the appropriate contract is of itself a tort. Duties of the same class may be created by statute, expressly or by necessary implication; they are imposed for the benefit of the public, and generally by way of return for privileges conferred by the same statutes, or by others *in pari materia*, on the persons or corporations who may be concerned.

Special duty of carriers and inn-keepers by "custom of the realm." Here the duty is imposed by the general law, though by a peculiar and somewhat anomalous rule;

(*l*) *Buddle* v *Wilson* (1795), 6 T R 369, 3 R R 202, see Mr Campbell's note at p. 206

Special duty of carriers and innkeepers. *Carriers.* One engaged in the business of common carriage derives certain benefits from the uniform patronage of the public in consideration of which every proper individual may demand of him corresponding uniformity in service. The very definition of a common carrier excludes the right to grant monopolies or give preference and implies an equal readiness to serve all who may apply in the order of their application. New England Exp. Co. v

and it gives rise to an obligation upon a simple non-feasance, unless we say that the profession of a "public employment" in this sense is itself a continuing act, in

---

Maine Cent. R., 57 Me. 188, Chicago & A. R. Co. v. Suffern, 129 Ill. 274; 21 N. E. Rep. 824; Land v. Wilmington & W. R. Co., 104 N. C 48; 10 S. E. Rep. 80, Avinger v. Railway Co., 29 S C 265; Houston, etc., R. v. Smith, 63 Tex. 322, 22 Am. & Eng. R. Cas. 421; Kenney v. Grand Trunk, etc. R, 59 Barb. 104; 47 N. Y. 525; Chicago, etc. R v People, 67 Ill 11, 16 Am Rep. 599, Messenger v. Pennsylvania R., 37 N. J. L 531; 19 Am. Rep 457, Wheeler v San Francisco, etc. R., 31 Cal. 46; McDuffee v. Railroad, 52 N H 730, Pearson v. Duane, 71 U. S. 605: 18 L. Ed. 447.

By the "Interstate Commerce Law" (24 U. S. St. at Large, p. 382), undue preference and discriminations in commerce between the States are prohibited. See Little Rock & M. R. Co. v East Tenn. etc. R. Co, 17 Fed Rep. 771; Interstate Commerce Commission v. Balt. & C. R. Co., 145 U S. 263, 12 S. Ct. Rep 844, New York & N. E. R. Co., 50 Fed. Rep. 867.

Innkeepers. By the common law the innkeeper is regarded as a servant of the public and as such he is bound to lodge and entertain, to the extent of his accommodations, all suitable persons who may apply, or render himself liable to the applicant in damages. Hancock v. Rand, 94 N Y 1; 46 Am. Rep. 112, Atwater v. Sawer, 76 Me. 539; Mowers v. Fethers, 61 N Y 34, 19 Am. Rep. 244, Halett v. Swift, 35 N Y. 577, Grinnell v Cook, 3 Hill, 485; 38 Am. Dec. 668, Ingalsbee v. Wood, 36 Barb. 455, 33 N. Y 577; Civil Rights Bill, 1 Hughes (U S), 541, Pinkerton v. Woodward, 33 Cal. 557; Dickerson v. Rogers, 4 Humph 179, Southwood v. Myers, 3 Bush, 681; Watson v. Cross, 2 Duv. 147, McCarthy v. Niskern, 22 Minn. 80; Willis v McMahan, 89 Cal 156, 26 Pac Rep 649. In Beale v. Posey (72 Ala. 823), the court said "There was (at common law), as little discretion left to him (an innkeeper), in the choice of his guests as there was to the common carrier in the selection of the persons for whom he would perform his duties. Each is engaged in public employment, bound, in the absence of reasonable grounds for refusal, to serve all having a necessity for their services "

But an innkeeper has sufficient grounds for exclusion where the person refused admission was at the time drunk, disorderly, irresponsible or disreputable. McKee v Owen, 15 Mich. 115, Markham v Brown, 8 N. H. 523, 31 Am Dec 209, Commonwealth v Power, 7 Metc. 596; Curtis v Murphy, 63 Wis. 4; 53 Am. Rep. 242.

The common law regulations of carriers and innkeepers prevail in the United States subject to a few well defined limitations. In 1875 Congress enacted, "That all persons within the jurisdiction of the United States shall be entitled to the full and equal enjoyment of the accommo-

relation to which the refusal to exercise that employment on due demand is a misfeasance. But on this latter view there would be no reason why the public profession of any trade or calling whatever should not have the like consequences; and such an extension of the law has never been proposed.

The term "custom of the realm" has been appropriated to the description of this kind of duties by the current usage of lawyers, derived apparently from the old current form of declaration. It seems however that in strictness "custom of the realm" has no meaning except as a synonym of the common law, so that express averment of it was superfluous (*l*).

Even where the breach of duty is subsequent to a complete contract in any employment of this kind, it was long the prevailing opinion that the obligation was still founded on the custom of the realm, and that the plaintiff might escape objections which (under the old forms of procedure) would have been fatal in an action on a contract (*m*).

Alternative of form does not affect substance of duty or liability. In all other cases under this head there are not two distinct causes of action even in the alternative,

---

(*l*) *Pozzi* v *Shipton* (1839), 8 A & E 963, 975, 8 L J Q B 1. Cp *Tattan* v *G*. *W R Co*. (1860), 2 E. & E 844, 29 L. J Q B 184, Y B 2 Hen IV 18, pl. 5
(*m*) *Pozzi* v *Shipton*, last note

---

dations, advantages, facilities and priviliges of inns, public conveyances, on land and water, theaters and other places of public amusement, subject only to the condition and limitations established by law, and applicable alike to citizens of every race and color, regardless of any previous condition of servitude" Laws, 1875, Ch. 114 The Supreme Court of the United States very wisely held these provisions unconstitutional as applied to the several States. Civil Rights Cases (1883), 109 U S 3.

Since that time the legislatures of many of the States have passed laws regulating these subjects and the object and effect of these laws are to make the legal duties of carriers, innkeepers, etc., more consistent with the requirements of our heterogeneous population and unequal social condition. See, *ante*, p. 642.

nor distinct remedies, but one cause of action with, at most, one remedy in alternative forms. And it was an established rule, as long as the forms of action were in use, that the rights and liabilities of the parties were not to be altered by varying the form. Where there is an undertaking without a contract, there is a duty incident to the undertaking (*n*), and if it is broken there is a tort, and nothing else. The rule that if there is a specific contract, the more general duty is superseded by it, does not prevent the general duty from being relied on where there is no contract at all (*o*). Even where there is a contract, our authorities do not say that the more general duty ceases to exist, or that a tort cannot be committed; but they say that the duty is "founded on contract." The contract, with its incidents either express or attached by law, becomes the only measure of the duties between the parties. There might be a choice, therefore, between forms of pleading, but the plaintiff could not by any device of form get more than was contained in the defendant's obligation under the contract.

Thus an infant could not be made chargeable for what was in substance a breach of contract by suing him in an action on the case; and the rule appears to have been first laid down for this special purpose. All the infants in England would be ruined, it was said, if such actions were allowed (*p*). So a purchaser of goods on credit, if the vendor resold the goods before default in payment, could treat this as a conversion and sue in trover; but as against the seller he could recover no more than his actual damage, in other words the substance of the right was governed wholly by the contract (*q*).

(*n*) *Gladwell v Steggall* (1839), 5 Bing N C 733, 8 Scott, 60, 8 L. J C P 361

(*o*) *Austin v G W. R Co* (1867), L. R 2 Q B 442, where the judgment of Blackburn J gives the true reason See further below

(*p*) *Jennings v Rundall* (1799), 8 T R 335, 4 R R 680, p 50, above.

(*q*) *Chinery v Viall* (1860), 5 H. & N 288, 29 L. J Ex 180; p. 445, above

Yet the converse of this rule does not hold without qualification. There are cases in which the remedy on a contract partakes of the restrictions usually incident to the remedy for a tort; but there are also cases in which not only an actual contract, but the fiction of a contract, can be made to afford a better remedy than the more obvious manner of regarding the facts.

Moreover it was held, for the benefit of plaintiffs, that where a man had a substantial cause of action on a contract he should not lose its incidents, such as the right to a verdict for nominal damages in default of proving special damage, by framing his action on the case (r).

In modern view the obligation is wholly in contract. Now that forms of pleading are generally abolished or greatly simplified, it seems better to say that wherever there is a contract to do something, the obligation of the contract is the only obligation, between the parties with regard to the performance, and any action for failure or negligence therein is an action on the contract; and this whether there was a duty antecedent to the contract or not. So much, in effect, has been laid down by the Court of Appeal as regards the statutory distinction of actions by the County Courts Act, 1867, for certain purposes of costs, as being "founded on contract" or "founded on tort" (s).

From this point of view the permanent result of the older theory has been to provide a definite measure for duties of voluntary diligence, whether undertaken by contract or gratuitously, and to add implied warranties of exceptional stringency to the contracts of carriers, innkeepers, and those others (if any) whose employments fall

---

(r) *Marzetti* v *Williams* (1830), 1 B. & Ad 415, action by customer against banker for dishonouring cheque

(s) *Fleming* v *Manchester, Sheffield & Lincolnshire R. Co.* (1878), 4 Q. B. D 81

It is impossible to reconcile the grounds of this decision with those of *Poss* v *Shipton* (1839), 8 A. & E. 963, 8 L. J. Q. B. 1, p 652, above.

under the special rule attributed to the "custom of the realm" (*t*).

Limits of the rule. All these rules and restrictions, however, must be taken with regard to their appropriate subject-matter. They do not exclude the possibility of cases occurring in which there is more than an alternative of form.

If John has contracted with Peter, Peter cannot make John liable beyond his contract; that is, where the facts are such that a cause of action would remain if some necessary element of contract, consideration for example, were subtracted, Peter can, so to speak, waive John's promise if he think fit, and treat him in point of form as having committed a wrong; but in point of substance he cannot thereby make John's position worse. In saying this, however, we are still far from saying that there can in no case be a relation between Peter and John which includes the facts of a contract (and to that extent is determined by the obligation of the contract), but in some way extends beyond those facts, and may produce duties really independent of contract. Much less have we said that the existence of such a relation is not to be taken into account in ascertaining what may be John's duties and liabilities to William or Andrew, who has not any contract with John. In pursuing such questions we come upon real difficulties of principle. This class of cases will furnish our next head.

(*t*) It has been suggested that a ship owner may be under this responsibility, not because he is a common carrier, but by reason of a distinct though similar custom extending to shipowners who carry goods for hire without being common carriers, *Nugent* v. *Smith* (1876), 1 C P D 14, 45 L. J C P. 19, but the decision was reversed on appeal, 1 C. P. D 423, 45 L. J. C P. 697, and the propositions of the Court below specifically controverted by Cockburn C J., see 1 C. P D at pp 426 *sqq* I am not aware of any other kind of employment to which the "custom of the realm" has been held to apply.

II.— *Concurrent Causes of Action.*

Concurrent causes of action. Herein we have to consider —

(a) Cases where it is doubtful whether a contract has been formed or there is a contract "implied in law" without any real agreement in fact, and the same act which is a breach of the contract, if any, is at all events a tort;

(b) Cases where A. can sue B. for a tort though the same facts may give him a cause of action against M. for breach of contract;

(c) Cases where A. can sue B. for a tort though B.'s misfeasance may be a breach of a contract made not with A. but with M.

Cases of tort, whether contract or no contract between same parties. (a) There are two modern railway cases in which the majority of the Court held the defendants liable on a contract, but it was also said that even if there was no contract there was an independent cause of action. In *Denton* v. *Great Northern Railway Company* (u), an intending passenger was held to have a remedy for damage sustained by acting on an erroneous

---

(u) 5 E & B 860, 25 L. J. Q B 129 (1856), see p. 373 above, and Principles of Contract, 5th ed 15, 16. The case is perhaps open to the remark that a doubtful tort and the breach of a doubtful contract were allowed to save one another from adequate criticism.

Cases of tort regardless of contract. Supporting the text, vide Frink v. Potter, 17 Ill 406, Havens v. Hartford etc. R Co , 28 Conn. 69, Hammond v N E R Co , 6 S C. 130; Heim v. McCaughan, 32 Miss. 17; New Orleans, etc. R. Co. v Hurst, 36 Miss. 660; Cregin v. Brooklyn & C. R. Co , 75 N. Y 192, Ames v. Union R. Co , 117 Mass. 541, Pennsylvania Co. v. Hoagland, 78 Ind. 203 Railroads are certainly liable in an action on contract for damages resulting to patrons from errors in their published time tables Gordon v Manchester, etc R Co., 52 N. H. 596, Sears v Eastern R. Co , 14 Allen, 433, Weed v. Panama R Co , 17 N. Y. 362.

announcement in the company's current time-table, probably on the footing of the time-table being the proposal of a contract, but certainly on the ground of its being a false representation. In *Austin* v. *Great Western Railway Company* (v), an action for harm suffered in some accident of which the nature and particulars are not reported, the plaintiff was a young child just above the age up to which children were entitled to pass free. The plaintiff's mother, who had charge of him, took a ticket for herself only. It was held that the company was liable either on an entire contract to carry the mother and the child (enuring, it seems, for the benefit of both, so that the action was properly brought by the child) (w), or independently of contract, because the child was accepted as a passenger, and this cast a duty on the company to carry him safely (x). Such a passenger is, in the absence of fraud, in the position of using the railway company's property by invitation, and is entitled to the protection given to persons in that position by a class of authorities now well established (y). Whether the company is under quite the same duty towards him, in respect of the amount of diligence required, as towards a passenger with whom there is an actual contract, is not so clear on principle (z). The point is not discussed in any of the cases now under review.

Again if a servant travelling with his master on a railway loses his luggage by the negligence of the company's servants, it is immaterial that his ticket was paid for by his master, and he can sue in his own name for the loss. Even if the payment is not regarded as made by the master as the servant's agent, as between themselves and the company (a), the company has accepted the servant

(v) L. R. 2 Q. B. 442 (1867).
(w) Per Lush J. at p. 447.
(x) Per Blackburn J. at p. 445, and see per Grove J. in *Foulkes* v. *Metrop. District R. Co.* (1880), 4 C. P. D. at p. 279, 45 L. J. C. P. 555.

(y) See Chap. XII p. 598 above.
(z) See *Moffatt* v. *Bateman* (1869), L. R. 3 P. C. 115.
(a) Suppose the master by accident had left his money at home, and the servant had paid both fares out of his

and his goods to be carried, and is answerable upon the general duty thus arising, a duty which would still exist if the passenger and his goods were lawfully in the train without any contract at all (*b*). Evidently the plaintiff in a case of this kind must make his choice of remedies, and cannot have a double compensation for the same matter, first as a breach of contract and then as a tort; at the same time the rule that the defendant's liability must not be increased by varying the form of the claim is not here applicable, since the plaintiff may rely on the tort notwithstanding the existence of doubt whether there be any contract, or, if there be, whether the plaintiff can sue on it.

Contract "implied in law" and waiver of tort. On the other hand we have cases in which an obvious tort is turned into a much less obvious breach of contract with

---

own money could it be argued that the master had no contract with the company?

(*b*) *Marshall v. York, Newcastle & Berwick R Co* (1851), 11 C. B. 655, 21 L. J. C. P. 34; approved by Blackburn J in *Austin v G W. R Co*, note (*c*), p. 657.

Contract "implied in law" and waiver of tort. Numerous decisions in the United States hold that assumpsit cannot be maintained unless the property of which the plaintiff was deprived has been converted into money. Noyes *v*. Loring, 55 Me. 408; Miller *v*. King, 67 Ala 575, Jones *v*. Hoar, 5 Pick. 285, Sanders *v*. Hamilton, 3 Dana, 550, Barlow *v* Stalworth, 27 Ga 117, Willett *v*. Willett, 3 Watts, 277; Mann *v* Locke, 11 N. H 246; Smith *v*. Jernigan, 83 Ala. 256; 3 So. Rep. 515; Saville *v* Welch, 58 Vt 683; Miller *v*. King, 67 Ala 575; Morrison *v* Rogers, 3 Ill 317, Emerson *v*. McNamara, 41 Mo 565, O'Reer *v*. Strong, 13 Ill 688, Wagner *v*. Peterson, 83 Pa. St 238, Pearsoll *v* Chapin, 44 Pa St 9, Township of Buckeye *v* Clark, 90 Mich 432, 51 N W Rep 528, Elliott *v* Jackson, 3 Wis 649; Bethlehem *v* Perseverance Fire Co., 81 Pa. St. 445, Pike *v*. Bright, 29 Ala. 332; Hawk *v*. Thorn, 54 Barb. 164, Stearns *v* Dillingham, 22 Vt 624; Carleton *v* Haywood, 49 N. H 314; Isaacs *v* Herman, 49 Miss 449, Guthrie *v* Wickliffe, 1 A K Marsh 83

But other cases hold that if the defendant has in any manner converted the property to his use, suit on an implied contract may be maintained. Evans *v* Miller, 58 Miss 120; Budd *v* Hiler, 27 N. J 43; Welch *v* Bagg, 12 Mich. 42, Norden *v* Jones, 33 Wis. 600, Baker *v* Cory, 15 Ohio, 9, Labeaume *v* Hill, 1 Mo 42, Hill *v* Davis, 3 N H 384, Bowen *v*. School

the undisguised purpose of giving a better and more convenient remedy. Thus it is an actionable wrong to retain money paid by mistake, or on a consideration which has failed, and the like; but in the eighteenth century the fiction of a promise "implied in law" to repay the money so held was introduced, and afforded "a very extensive and beneficial remedy, applicable to almost every case where the defendant has received money which *ex aequo et bono* he ought to refund" (c), and even to cases where goods taken or retained by wrong had been converted into money. The plaintiff was said to "waive the tort" for the purpose of suing in assumpsit on the fictitious contract. Hence the late Mr Adolphus wrote in his idyllic poem "The Circuiteers":

"Thoughts much too deep for tears subdue the Court
When I *assumpsit* bring and godlike waive a tort" (d)

This kind of action was much fostered by Lord Mansfield, whose exposition confessed the fiction of the form while it justified the utility of the substance (e).

Implied warranty of agent's authority (Collen v. Wright). Within still recent memory an essentially similar fiction of law has been introduced in the case of an

(c) Blackst. iii 163
(d) I Q R i 233
(e) *Moses v MacFerlan*, 2 Burr 1005, cp Leake on Contracts, 1st ed 39, 48

Distr., Mich 149, Webster v Drinkwater, 5 Me 319; Floyd v Wiley, 1 Mo 643, Fiquint v Allison, 12 Mich. 328, Ford v. Caldwell, 3 Hill, 248; Tightmeyer v Mongold, 20 Kan. 90, Fuller v. Duren, 36 Ala. 73.

Implied warranty of agent's authority In the case of Jefts v. York (10 Cush 395, 50 Am. Dec. 791) the court said. "If one falsely represents that he has authority, by which another, relying on the representation, is misled, he is liable, and by acting as agent for another, when he is not, though he thinks he is, he tacitly and impliedly represents himself authorized without knowing the fact to be true, it is in the nature of a false warranty, and he is liable. But in both cases his liability is founded on the ground of deceit, and the remedy is by action a tort"

ostensible agent obtaining a contract in the name of a principle whose authority he misrepresents. A person so acting is liable for deceit; but that liability, being purely in tort, does not extend to his executors, neither can he be held personally liable on a contract which he purported to make in the name of an existing principal. To meet this difficulty it was held in *Collen* v. *Wright* (*f*) that when a man purports to contract as agent there is an implied warranty that he is really authorized by the person named as principal, on which warranty he or his estate will be answerable *ex contractu*. Just as in the case of the old "common counts," the fact that the action lies against executors shows that there is not merely one cause of action capable of being expressed, under the old system of pleading, in different ways, but two distinct though concurrent causes of action, with a remedy upon either at the plaintiff's election.

We pass from these to the more troublesome cases where the causes of action in contract and in tort are not between the same parties.

Concurrent causes of action against different parties in contract and in tort. (b) There may be two causes of action with a common plaintiff, or the same facts may give

(*f*) Ex Ch (1857), 8 E & B 647, 27 L. J Q B 215

See Duncan v Niles, 32 Ill 532, Taylor v Shelton, 30 Conn. 122; Long v Colburn, 11 Mass 97; 6 Am. Dec. 160; Draper v. Massachusetts, etc., Co., 5 Allen, 339, Patterson v. Lippincott, 47 N J L. 457, 1 At. Rep. 506; 54 Am. Rep. 178; Ballou v. Talbot, 16 Mass. 461, 8 Am. Dec. 146, Trowbridge v. Scudder, 11 Cush 83, Sherman v Fitch, 98 Mass. 63, Bartlett v. Tucker, 104 Mass 340; 6 Am. Rep. 240, Tucker Mfg. Co v Fairbanks, 98 Mass. 105, Johnson v. Smith, 21 Conn 627, Noyes v Loring, 55 Me 408; McCurdy v. Rogers, 21 Wis. 197; 91 Am. Dec 468, Warren v. Banning, 67 Hun, 649; 21 N. Y. S. Rep. 883; Porter v. Day, 44 Ill. App 256, Neufeld v. Beidler, 37 Id. 34; Cole v O'Brien, 84 Neb. 63, 51 N W. Rep 316, Farmers' Co-Op. Trust Co. v. Floyd, 47 Ohio St. 525; 26 N. E. Rep. 110.

Z. a remedy in contract against A., and also a remedy in tort against B.

Dalyell v. Tyrer. The lessee of a steam ferry at Liverpool, having to meet an unusual press of traffic, hired a vessel with its crew from other shipowners to help in the work of the ferry for a day. The plaintiff held a season-ticket for the ferry, and therefore had a contract with the lessee to be carried across with due skill and care. He crossed on this day in the hired vessel; by the negligence of some of the crew there was an accident in mooring the vessel on her arrival at the farther shore, and the plaintiff was hurt. He sued not the lessee of the ferry but the owners of the hired vessel; and it was held that he was entitled to do so. The persons managing the vessel were still the servants of the defendants, her owners, though working her under a contract of hiring for the purposes of the ferry; and the defendants would be answerable for their negligence to a mere stranger lawfully on board the vessel or standing on the pier at which she was brought up. The plaintiff was lawfully on their vessel with their consent, and they were not the less responsible to him because he was there in exercise of a right acquired by contract upon a consideration paid to some one else (*g*).

Foulkes v. Met. Dist. R. Co. The latest and most authoritative decision on facts of this kind was given by the Court of Appeal in 1880 (*h*).

(*g*) *Dalyell v. Tyrer* (1858), E B & E 899, 28 L. J Q B 52
(*h*) *Foulkes v. Metrop Dist R Co.*, 5 C P Div. 157, 49 L. J C P. 361   Cp *Berringer v G E. R. Co* (1879), 4 C P. D 163, 48 L. J C. P 400

Concurrent causes of action against different parties in contract and in tort Sustaining the proposition (b) stated in the text it was held in Kennedy *v.* McKay (43 N. J. L 290; 39 Am Rep 581) that an innocent vendor cannot be sued in tort for the fraud of his agent in effecting a sale. "In such a juncture the aggrieved vendee has, at law, two and only two remedies; the first being a rescission of the contract of sale and a reclamation of the money paid by him from the vendors, or a suit against the agent, founded on the deceit."

The plaintiff, a railway passenger with a return ticket alighting at his destination at the end of the return journey, was hurt by reason of the carriages being unsuitable to the height of the platform at that station. This station and platform belonged to one company (the South Western), by whose clerk the plaintiff's ticket had been issued: the train belonged to another company (the District) who used the station and adjoining line under running powers. There was an agreement between the two companies whereby the profits of the traffic were divided. The plaintiff sued the District Company, and it was held that they were liable to him even if his contract was with the South Western Company alone. The District Company received him as a passenger in their train, and were bound to provide carriages not only safe and sound in themselves, but safe with reference to the permanent way and appliances of the line. In breach of this duty they provided, according to the facts as determined by the jury, a train so ordered that "in truth the combined arrangements were a trap or snare," and would have given the plaintiff a cause of action though he had been carried gratuitously (*i*). He had been actually received by the defendants as a passenger, and thereby they undertook the duty of not exposing him to unreasonable peril in any matter incident to the journey.

Causes of action in contract and tort at suit of different plaintiffs. (*c*) There may be two causes of action with a common defendant, or the same act or event which

---

(*i*) Bramwell L J, 5 C. P Div at p. 159. See the judgment of Thesiger L J, for a fuller statement of the nature of the duty Comparison of these two judgments leaves it capable of doubt whether the defendants would have been liable for a mere non feasance.

Causes of action in contract and tort at suit of different plaintiffs. In Ames *v.* Union Railway Company (117 Mass. 541), under the rule *quod servitum amisit*, the right of a master to recover for a personal injury to his apprentice was sustained See Woodward *v.* Washburn, 3 Denio, 369, Kennedy *v.* Shea, 110 Mass. 147.

makes A. liable for a breach of contract to B. may make him liable for a tort to Z.

The case already mentioned of the servant travelling by railway with his master would be an example of this if it were determined on any particular state of facts that the railway company contracted only with the master. They would not be less under a duty to the servant and liable for a breach thereof because they might also be liable to the master for other consequences on the ground of a breach of their contract with him (*k*).

Again, an officer in Her Majesty's service and his baggage were carried under a contract made with the carriers on behalf of the Government of India; this did not prevent the carriers from being liable to the officer if his goods were destroyed in the course of the journey by the negligence of their servants. "The contract is no concern of the plaintiff's; the act was none the less a wrong to him" (*l*). He could not charge the defendants with a breach of contract, but they remained answerable for "an affirmative act injurious to the plaintiff's property" (*m*).

Alton v. Midland R. Co., qu. whether good law. The decision of the Court of Common Pleas in *Alton* v. *Midland Railway Co.* (*n*) is difficult to reconcile with the foregoing authorities. A servant travelling by railway on his master's business (having paid his own fare) received hurt, as was alleged, by the negligence of the railway company's servants, and the master sued the company for loss of ser-

---

(*k*) *Marshall's ca.* (1851), 11 C. B. 655, 21 L. J. C. P. 34, *supra*, p. 638.

(*l*) *Martin* v *G I P R Co* (1867), L. R. 3 Ex 9, per Bramwell B at p 14, 37 L. J. Ex 27

(*m*) Channell B *ibid*, Kelly C B and Pigott B doubted The later case of *Becker* v *G E R Co* (1870), L R. 5 Q B 241, 39 L J Q B. 122, is distinguishable all it decides is that if A delivers B's goods to a railway company as A's own ordinary luggage, and the company receives them to be carried as such, B cannot sue the company for the loss of the goods Martin's case, however, was not cited

(*n*) 19 C B N. S. 213, 34 L J C. P 292 (1865) This case was not cited either in *Martin* v *G. I. P R. Co.* or *Foulkes* v. *Met Dist. R Co*

vice consequent on this injury. It was held that the action would not lie, the supposed cause of action arising, in the opinion of the Court, wholly out of the company's contract of carriage, which contract being made with the servant, no third person could found any right upon it. "The rights founded on contract belong to the person who has stipulated for them" (o); and it is denied that there was any duty independent of contract (p). But it is not explained in any of the judgments how this view is consistent with the authorities relied on for the plaintiff, and in particular with *Marshall's* case, a former decision of the same Court. The test question, whether the reception of the plaintiff's servant as a passenger would not have created a duty to carry him safely if there had not been any contract with him, is not directly, or, it is submitted, adequately dealt with. The case, though expressly treated by the Court as of general importance, has been but little cited, or relied on during the twenty-five years that have now passed; and the correctness of the decision was disputed (extra-judicially, it is true) by Sir E. V. Williams (q). A directly contrary decision has also been given in the State of Massachusetts (r). *Alton's* case, moreover, seems to be virtually overruled by *Foulkes's* case, which proceeds on the existence of a duty not only in form but in substance independent of contract. The only way of maintaining the authority of both decisions would be to say that in *Alton's* case the master could not recover because the servant had a contract with the defendant railway company, but that he might have been entitled to recover if the servant had

(o) Willes J., 19 C. B. N. S. at p. 240
(p) Montague Smith J. at p. 245
(q) "The Court decided this case on the principle that one who is no party to a contract cannot sue in respect of the breach of a duty arising out of the contract. But it may be doubted whether this was correct, for the duty, as appears by the series of cases cited in the earlier part of this note, does not exclusively arise out of the contract, but out of the common law obligation of the defendants as carriers." 1 Wms. Saund. 474, Sir E. V. Williams was a member of the Court which decided *Marshall's* case, *supra*, p. 658.

(r) *Ames v. Union R. Co.* (1875), 117 Mass. 541, expressly following *Marshall's* ca. (1851), 11 C. B. 655, 21 L. J. C. P. 34, *supra*, p. 658

been travelling with a free pass, or with a ticket taken and paid for by a stranger, or issued by another company, or had suffered from a fault in the permanent way or the structure of a station. But such a distinction does not appear reasonable.

It might perhaps have been argued that at all events such negligence must be shown as would make a carrier of passengers liable to a person being carried gratuitously; it might also be open to argument whether the person injured (apparently a commercial traveller) was really the servant of the plaintiff in such a sense that an action could be maintained for the loss of his service. Doubtless the action for wrong to a servant *per quod servitium amisit* is of an archaic character and not favoured in our modern law, and this may have unconsciously influenced the Court. Neither of these points, however, was discussed, nor indeed were they open to discussion upon the issues of law raised by the pleadings, on which alone the case was argued and decided. The questions what degree of negligence must be shown, whether a mere non-feasance would be enough, or the like, could have been properly raised only when the evidence came out (*s*).

The most ingenious reason for the judgment of the Court is that of Willes J., who said that to allow such an action would be to allow a stranger to exercise and determine the election (of suing in contract or tort) which the law gives only to the person actually injured. But it is submitted that the latter is (or was) required to elect between the two causes of action as a matter of remedy, not of right, and because he is to be compensated once and once only for the same damage; and that such election neither affects nor is affected by the position of a third person. Moreover the master does not sue as a person claiming through the servant, but in a distinct right.

(*s*) Compare Mr. Henry T Terry's criticism in "Leading Principles of Anglo American Law," Philadelphia, 1884, pp 485-4&3.

The cause of action and the measure of damages are different (*t*). On the whole the weight of principle and authority seems to be so strong against *Alton's* case that, notwithstanding the respect due to the Court before which it came, and which included one of the greatest masters of the common law at any time, the only legitimate conclusion is that it was wrongly decided.

It must be admitted that the Court of Appeal itself has spoken with a somewhat ambiguous voice (*u*). We should be bound, however, to prefer the latter and more considered decision even if it did not appear to be more in harmony with the general current of authorities.

Winterbottom v. Wright, &c. It appears, then, that there is a certain tendency to hold that facts which constitute a contract cannot have any other legal effect. We think we have shown that such is not really the law, and we may add that the authorities commonly relied on for this proposition really prove something different and much more rational, namely, that if A. breaks his contract with B. (which may happen without any personal default in A. or A.'s servants), that is not of itself sufficient to make A. liable to C., a stranger to the contract for consequential damage. This, and only this, is the substance of the perfectly correct decisions of the Court of Exchequer in *Winterbottom* v. *Wright* (*x*) and *Longmeid* v. *Holliday* (*y*). In each case the defendant delivered, under a contract of sale or hiring, a chattel which was in fact unsafe to use, but in the one case was not alleged, in the other was alleged but not proved, to have been so to his knowledge. In each case a stranger to the contract, using the chattel — a coach in the one case, a lamp in the other — in the

---

(*t*) See p. 272 above
(*u*) The actual decision of *Fleming's* case (p. 654 above) is on a minute point of statutory procedure, but its grounds are not easy to reconcile with those of *Foulkes's* case.
(*x*) 10 M. & W. 109, 11 L J Ex. 415 1842)
(*y*) 6 Ex 761, 20 L J. Ex 430 (1851).

ordinary way, came to harm through its dangerous condition, and was held not to have any cause of action against the purveyor. Not in contract, for there was no contract between these parties; not in tort, for no bad faith or negligence on the defendant's part was proved. If bad faith (*z*) or misfeasance by want of ordinary care (*a*) had been shown, or, it may be, if the chattels in question had been of the class of eminently dangerous things which a man deals with at his peril (*b*), the result would have been different. With regard to the last-mentioned class of things the policy of the law has created a stringent and peculiar duty, to which the ordinary rule that the plaintiff must make out either wilful wrong-doing or negligence does not apply. There remain over some few miscellaneous cases currently cited on these topics, of which we have purposely said nothing because they are little or nothing more than warnings to pleaders (*c*).

Concurrence of breach of contract with delict in Roman law. If, after this examination of the authorities, we cannot get rid of the notion that the concurrence of distinct causes of action *ex delicto* and *ex contractu* is a mere accident of common law procedure, we have only to turn to the Roman system and find the same thing occurring there. A freeborn *filius familias*, being an apprentice, is immoderately beaten by his master for clumsiness about his work. The apprentice's father may have an action against

---

(*z*) *Langridge* v. *Levy* (1837), 2 M. & W. 519.

(*a*) *George* v *Skivington* (1869), L. R. 5 Ex. 1, 38 L J Ex 8

(*b*) See *Thomas* v *Winchester* (1852), 6 N Y 397, Bigelow L. C 602, p. 622 above.

(*c*) Such is *Collis* v. *Selden* (1868), L. R 3 C P 495, 37 L J C P 233, where the declaration attempted to make a man liable for creating a dangerous state of things, without any allegation that he knew of the danger, or had any control over the thing he worked upon or the place where it was, or that the plaintiff was anything more than a "bare licensee" *Tollit* v. *Sherstone*, 5 M & W. 283, is another study in bad pleading which adds nothing to the substance of the law. So *Howard* v *Shepherd* (1850), 9 C. B 296, exhibits an attempt to disguise a manifestly defective cause of action in assumpsit by declaring in the general form of case.

the master either on the contract of hiring (*ex locato*) (*d*), or at his option an action under the *lex Aquilia*, since the excess in an act of correction which within reasonable bounds would have been lawful amounts to *culpa* (*e*). It is like the English cases we have cited where there was held to be a clear cause of action independent of contract, so that it was not necessary for the plaintiff to make out a breach of contract as between the defendant and himself.

III.— *Causes of Action in Tort dependent on a Contract not between the same Parties.*

Causes of action dependent on collateral contract. What did Lumley v. Gye decide? (*a*) When a binding promise is made, an obligation is created which remains in force until extinguished by the performance or discharge of the contract. Does the duty thus owed to the promisee constitute the object of a kind of real right which a stranger to the contract can infringe, and thereby render himself answerable *ex delicto?* In other words, does a man's title to the performance of a promise contain an element analogous to ownership or possession? The general principles of the law (notwithstanding forms of speech once in use, and warranted by considerable authority) (*f*) seem to call for a negative answer. It would confuse every accustomed boundary between real and personal rights, dominion and obligation, to hold that one who without any ill-will to Peter prevents Andrew from performing his contract with Peter may be a kind of trespasser against Peter (*g*). For Peter has his

---

(*d*) D 19, 2 *locati conducti*, 13, § 4

(*e*) D 9, 2 5, § 3, Grueber on the Lex Aquilia, p. 14 the translation there given is not altogether correct, but the inaccuracies do not affect the law of the passage And see D h t 27, §§ 11, 33, Grueber, p 230

(*f*) Blackstone, II 442, speaks of a contract to pay a sum of money as transferring a property in that sum, but he forthwith adds that this property is "not in possession but in action merely," *i. e.* it is not property in a strict sense there is a *res* but not a *dominus*, *Vermögen* but not *Eigenthum*

(*g*) We have no right to say that a

remedy against Andrew, and never looked to having any other; and Andrew's motives for breaking his contract are not material. Yet there is some show of authority for affirming the proposition thus condemned. It was decided by the Court of Queen's Bench in *Lumley* v. *Gye* (1853) (*h*), and by the Court of Appeal in *Bowen* v. *Hall* (1881) (*i*), that an action lies, under certain conditions, for procuring a third person to break his contract with the plaintiff. We must, therefore, examine what the conditions of these cases were, and how far the rule laid down by them really extends.

Special damage and malice are of the gist of the action. First, it is admitted that actual damage must be alleged and proved (*j*). This at once shows that the right violated is not an absolute and independent one like a right of property, for the possibility of a judgment for nominal damages is in our law the touchstone of such rights. Where specific damage is necessary to support an action, the right which has been infringed cannot be a right of property, though in some cases it may be incident to property.

Next, the defendant's act must be malicious, in the sense of being aimed at obtaining some advantage for himself at the plaintiff's expense, or at any rate at causing loss or damage to the plaintiff. In the decided cases the defendant's object was to withdraw from a rival in business, and procure for himself, the services of a peculiarly skilled person — in the earlier case an operatic singer, in the later a craftsman to whom, in common with only a few others, a

---

system of law is not conceivable where such a doctrine would be natural or even necessary. But that system, if it did exist, would be not at all like the Roman law and not much like the common law

(*h*) 2 E & B 216, 22 L J Q B. 463, by Crompton, Erle, and Wightman JJ *diss* Coleridge J

(*i*) 6 Q. B. Div 333, 50 L. J. Q B. 305; by Lord Selborne L. C. and Brett L. J., *diss* Lord Coleridge C J.

(*j*) See the declaration in *Lumley* v *Gye* In *Bowen* v. *Hall* it does not appear how the claim for damages was framed, but in the opinion of the majority of the Court there was evidence of special damage, see 6 Q B D 337

particular process of manufacture was known. Various cases may be put of a man advising a friend, in all honesty and without ill-will to the other contracting party, to abide the risks of breaking an onerous or mischievous contract rather than those of performing it (*k*). And it would be unreasonable in such cases to treat the giving of such advice, if it be acted on, as a wrong. Lucilia has imprudently accepted an offer of marriage from Titius, her inferior in birth, station, and breeding: Lucilia's brother Marcus, knowing Titius to be a man of bad character, persuades Lucilia to break off the match: shall any law founded in reason say that Marcus is liable to an action at the suit of Titius? Assuredly not: and there is no decision that authorizes any such proposition even by way of plausible extension. There must be a wrongful intent to do harm to the plaintiff before the right of action for procuring a breach of contract can be established. Mere knowledge that there is a subsisting contract will not do. The breach of contract is in truth material only because it excludes the defence that the act complained of, though harmful and intended to do harm, was done in the exercise of a common right.

Question of remoteness of damage. In this view the real point of difficulty is reduced to this, that the damage may be deemed too remote to found the action upon. For if A. persuades B. to break his contract with Z. the proximate cause of Z.'s damage, in one sense, is not the conduct of A. but the voluntary act or default of B. We do not think it can be denied that there was a period in the history of the law when this objection would have been held conclusive. Certainly Lord Ellenborough laid it down as a general rule of law that a man is answerable only for "legal and natural consequence," not for "an illegal con-

---

(*k*) See the dissenting judgment of Sir John Coleridge in *Lumley* v. *Gye*.

sequence," that is, a wrongful act of a third person (*l*). But this opinion is now disapproved (*m*).

The tendency of our later authorities is to measure responsibility for the consequences of an act by that which appeared or should have appeared to the actor as natural and probable, and not to lay down fixed rules which may run counter to the obvious facts. Here the consequence is not only natural and probable — if A.'s action has any consequence at all — but is designed by A.: it would, therefore, be contrary to the facts to hold that the interposition of B.'s voluntary agency necessarily breaks the chain of proximate cause and probable consequence. A proximate cause need not be an immediate cause.

Liability for negligence, as we have seen (*n*), is not always or even generally excluded by what is called "contributory negligence of a third person." In any case it would be strange if it lay in a man's mouth to say that the consequence which he deliberately planned and procured is too remote for the law to treat as a consequence. The iniquity of such a defence is obvious in the grosser examples of the criminal law. Commanding, procuring, or inciting to a murder cannot have any "legal consequence," the act of compliance or obedience being a crime; but no one has suggested on this ground any doubt that the procurement is also a crime.

Motive as an ingredient in the wrong. It may likewise be said that the general habit of the law is not to regard motive as distinguished from intent, and that the decision in *Lumley* v. *Gye*, as here understood and limited, is therefore anomalous at best. Now the general habit is as stated, but there are well established exceptions to it, of which the action for malicious prosecution is the most conspicuous:

(*l*) *Vicars* v. *Wilcocks* (1807), 8 East, 1, and in 2 Sm. L. C.

(*m*) See *Lynch* v. *Knight* (1861), 9 H. L. C. 577, and notes to *Vicars* v. *Wilcocks* in Sm. L. C.

(*n*) Pp. 577–582, above.

there it is clear law that indirect and improper motive must be added to the other conditions to complete the cause of action. The malicious procuring of a breach of contract, or of certain kinds of contracts, forms one more exception. It may be that the special damage which is the ground of the action must be such as cannot be redressed in an action for the breach of contract itself; in other words, that the contract must be for personal services, or otherwise of such a kind that an action against the contracting party would not afford an adequate remedy. But then the remedy against the wrong-doer will not be adequate either; so that there does not appear to be much rational ground for this limitation. The obvious historical connexion with the action for enticing away a servant will not help to fix the modern principle. Coleridge J. rightly saw that there was no choice between facing the broader issues now indicated and refusing altogether to allow that any cause of action appeared

American doctrine. In America the decision in *Lumley v. Gye* has been followed in Massachusetts (*o*) and elsewhere, and is generally accepted, with some such limitation as here maintained. The rule "does not apply to a case of interference by way of friendly advice, honestly given; nor is it in denial of the right of free expression of opinion" (*p*).

(*o*) *Walker v Cronin* (1871), 107 Mass 555, a case very like *Bowen v Hall*

(*p*) 107 Mass 566 I owe the following additional references to State reports

American doctrine. Vide Upton v Vail, 6 Johns 181, Gallagher v Brunel, 6 Cow. 346; Carew v. Rutherford, 106 Mass. 1. Advice rashly or indiscreetly given, but without any fraudulent intention, is not sufficient to support the action. Young v. Covell, 8 Johns. 23, Addington v. Allen, 11 Wend. 374. But the intention need not be to defraud the plaintiff in particular. Williams v Wood, 14 Wend. 126, Stafford v. Newsom, 9 Ired. 507. Fraud will be presumed from the falsity. Clapton v. Cozart, 13 Smed. & M 363 See American notes under MORAL OR SOCIAL DUTY, *ante*, p. 335

Wilful interference with contract without persuasion. It is, perhaps, needless to consider specially the case of a man wilfully preventing the performance of a contract by means other than persuasion; for in almost every such case the means employed must include an act in itself unlawful (as disabling one of the contracting parties by personal violence, or destroying or spoiling a specific thing contracted for); and, if so, the question comes round again to the general principles of remoteness of damage (*q*).

Damage to stranger by breach of contract. (b) Procuring a breach of contract, then, may be actionable if maliciously done, or a contracting party may indirectly through the contract, though not upon it, have an action against a stranger. Can he become liable to a stranger? We have already seen that a misfeasance by a contracting party in the performance of his contract may be an independent wrong as against a stranger to the contract, and as such may give that stranger a right of action (*r*). On the other hand, a breach of contract, as such, will generally not be a cause of action for a stranger (*s*). And on this principle it is held by our courts that where a message is incorrectly transmitted by the servants of a telegraph company, and the person to whom it is delivered thereby sustains damage, that person has not any remedy against the company. For the duty to transmit and deliver the message arises wholly out of the contract with the sender, and there is no duty towards the receiver. Wilful alteration of a message might be the ground of an action for deceit against the person who altered it, as he would have

---

to the kindness of an American friend — *Rice* v *Manley*, 66 N Y (21 Sickels) 82, *Benton* v *Pratt*, 2 Wend. 385 (see p 390 above), *Jones* v *Blocker*, 43 Ga. 331, *Haskin* v. *Royster*, 70 N C 601, *Jones* v *Starly*, 70 N C 355, *Dickson* v *Dickson*, 13 Ia An 1261, *Burger* v *Carpenter*, 2 S C 7.

(*q*) See Mr William Schofield on "The principle of *Lumley* v *Gye* and its application," Harv. Law Rev ii. 19

(*r*) P 662 above.

(*s*) The exceptions to this rule are much wider in America than in England.

knowingly made a false statement as to the contents of the message which passed through his hands. But a mere mistake in reading off or transmitting a letter or figure, though it may materially affect the sense of the despatch, cannot be treated as a deceit (*t*).

Position of receiver of erroneous telegram: different views in England and U. S. "In America, on the other hand, one who receives a telegram which, owing to the negligence of the telegraph company, is altered or in other

---

(*t*) *Dickson* v *Reuter's Telegram Co.* (1877), 3 C. P. Div 1, 47 L. J. C. P. 1, confirming *Playford* v. *U. K Electric Telegraph Co.* (1869), L. R. 4 Q B. 706, 38 L. J. Q. B. 249.

Position of receiver of erroneous telegram—American doctrine. "The right of the receiver of a telegram which, owing to the negligence of the telegraph company, is altered or in other respects untrue, to maintain an action against the telegraph company for the loss which he sustains through acting upon that telegram, is conclusively settled in America." Gray on Communications by Telegraph, 374.

This right of action has been rested on the following grounds: (1) A telegraph company is in the exercise of a public occupation and owes a duty to every one beneficially interested in the message. (2) The person addressed is the beneficiary of a contract. Considering these grounds separately: (1) A telegraph company is in the exercise of a public calling. Being thus bound to serve all those who wish to employ it and usually relied upon to correctly communicate messages of great importance, from public necessity rather than from precedent has evolved the right of a receiver or addressee of a message to be protected from the injurious effects of misleading statements. N. Y. & W. P. T. Co, *v.* Dryburg, 35 Pa. St. 298; Aiken *v.* W. U. T. Co., 5 S. C. 358, 370; Elwood *v.* W. U. T Co , 45 N. Y 549; Bank of California *v.* W. U. T. Co, 52 Cal. 280; 5 Cent. L. J. 265; Elsey *v.* Postal T. Co., 8 N. Y. S. Rep. 117; W. U T. Co. *v.* Adams, 75 Tex. 531; 6 Law Rep. An. 844; 12 S. W Rep 857; De La Grange *v.* S. W. T. Co , 25 La. An 383, Tyler *v.* W. U. T. Co., 60 Ill. 421; 74 Ill. 168; W. U. T. Co *v.* Blanchard, 68 Ga 299; Leonard *v.* N. Y. A & B T Co , 41 N. Y. 544, Lowery *v.* W. U. T Co., N. Y. 193, W. U T. Co. *v.* Neill, 57 Tex. 283; Rose *v.* U. S. T. Co., 3 Abb. Pr. (N.S.) 408 (2) Contrary to the rule in England and in a few States of the United States, in a majority of the States it is held that one who was not a party to a contract can sue for its breach where that contract was made expressly for his benefit. But it seems reasonable that the right of the addressee, who is not a party to a contract to communicate

respects untrue, is invariably permitted to maintain an action against the telegraph company for the loss that he sustains through acting upon that telegram:" the latest commentator on the American authorities, however, finds the reasoning of the English courts difficult to answer (*u*).

(*u*) Gray on Communication by Telegraph (Boston, 1885), §§ 71-73, where authorities are collected And see Wharton on Contracts, §§ 791, 1056, who defends the American rule on somewhat novel speculative grounds Perhaps the common law ought to have a theory of *culpa in contrahendo*, but the lamented author's ingenuity will not persuade many common lawyers that it has And if it had, I fail to see how that could affect the position of parties between whom there is not even the offer of a contract.

---

the message, to sue as beneficiary for a breach thereof, should be restricted to those cases where the message was dispatched for his special benefit. Hendrick *v.* Lindsay, 93 U. S. 143; Kaufman *v.* United States Nat. Bank (Neb.), 48 N W. Rep. 738, G., C., & S F. Ry. Co. *v* Levy, 59 Tex 563, Garnsay *v* Rogers, 47 N. Y. 233, Coleman *v* Whitney, 62 Vt. 123, 20 At Rep. 322; So Rolle *v.* W U T. Co , 55 Tex. 308; Martin *v* W U T. Co., 1 Tex Civ. App 143, 20 S. W. Rep. 860, W U.T. Co. *v* Berlinger, 84 Tex. 38. The settled rule in America is that telegraph companies are liable for all damage occasioned the addressee by delaying delivery of the message. "It seems reasonable, that for all purposes of liability, the telegraph company shall be considered as much the agent of him who receives as of him who sends the message." New York, etc , Tel Co. *v* Dryburg, 35 Pa. St. 303, 78 Am. Dec. 338. See W. U. Tel Co *v.* Newhouse (Ind App.) 33 N. E. Rep. 800; W. U. T. Co. *v.* Lindley, 89 Ga. 484; 155 S. E Rep 636, W. U. T. Co. *v.* Jones (Tex.), 16 S. W Rep 1006. And see 24 Wkly. Law Bul. 147; 33 Cent Law J. 147.

"It may be assumed that an entire stranger, who does not sustain towards either the sender or addressee the relation of principal to his agent cannot maintain the action, because there is neither any privity of contract as to him, nor is he in the contemplation of both parties to the transaction which takes place when the dispatch is sent." Thompson on Electricity, citing Deslottes *v* Baltimore, etc Tel. Co., 40 La. An. 183; 21 Am & Eng. Corp. Cas. 158, 3 So. Rep. 566, 3 Rail. & Corp. L. J 342.

Where the person addressed was the original employer of the telegraph company, the company becomes responsible to the addressee on the contract. Durkee *v.* Vt. C. Rd. Co., 29 Vt. 127.

Where the addressee does not sustain towards the sender the relation of a principal to his agent, he cannot sue on contract but his remedy is in tort The theory of such an action is misfeasance. W. U. T Co. *v.* Dubois, 128 Ill. 248; 21 N E Rep. 4, 15 Am. St Rep. 109.

As to liability for mental condition resulting from delinquent delivery of telegraphic message, see *ante*, p. 55.

And the American decisions appear to rest more on a strong sense of public expediency than on any one definite legal theory. The suggestion that there is something like a bailment of the message may be at once dismissed. Having regard to the extension of the action for deceit in certain English cases (*x*), there is perhaps more to be said for the theory of misrepresentation than our courts have admitted; but this too is precarious ground. The real question of principle is whether a general duty of using adequate care can be made out. I am not bound to undertake telegraphic business at all; but if I do, am I not bound to know that errors in the transmission of messages may naturally and probably damnify the receivers? and am I not therefore bound, whether I am forwarding the messages under any contract or not, to use reasonable care to ensure correctness? I cannot warrant the authenticity or the material truth of the despatch, but shall I not be diligent in that which lies within my power, namely the delivery to the receiver of those words or figures which the sender intended him to receive? If the affirmative answer be right, the receiver who is misled may have a cause of action, namely for negligence in the execution of a voluntary undertaking attended with obvious risk. But a negative answer is given by our own courts, on the ground that the ordinary law of negligence has never been held to extend to negligence in the statement of facts (if it did, there would be no need of special rules as to deceit); and that the delivery of a message, whether by telegraph or otherwise, is nothing but a statement that certain words have been communicated by the sender to the messenger for the purpose of being by him communicated to the receiver. It may perhaps be said against this that the nature of telegraph business creates a special duty of diligence in correct statement, so that an action as for deceit will lie

(*x*) See especially *Denton* v. *G. N. R. Co* (1856), 5 E. & B. 860, 25 L. J. Q. B. 129, p. 373 above.

without actual fraud. But since the recent cases following *Derry* v. *Peek* (y) this could hardly be argued in England. Perhaps it would be better to say that the systematic undertaking to deliver messages in a certain way (much more the existence of a corporation for that special purpose) puts the case in a category of its own apart from representations of fact made in the common intercourse of life, or the repetition of any such representation. Thus we should come back to the old ground of the action on the case for misfeasance. The telegraph company would be in the same plight as the smith who pricks a horse with a nail, or the unskilful surgeon, and liable without any question of contract or warranty. Such liability would not necessarily be towards the receiver only, though damages incurred by any other person would in most cases be too remote. The Court of Appeal has for the present disposed of the matter for this country, and inland communication by telegraph is now in the hands of the Postmaster-General, who could not be sued even if the American doctrine were adopted. With regard to foreign telegrams, however, the rule is still of importance, and until the House of Lords has spoken it is still open to discussion.

The conflict considered on principle. In the present writer's opinion the American decisions, though not all the reasons given for them, are on principle correct. The undertaking to transmit a sequence of letters or figures (which may compose significant words and sentences, but also may be, and often are, mere unintelligible symbols to the transmitter) is a wholly different thing from the statement of an alleged fact or the expression of a professed opinion in one's own language. Generally speaking, there is no such thing as liability for negligence

(y) See p. 372 above.

in word as distinguished from act; and this difference is founded in the nature of the thing (z). If a man asserts as true that which he does not believe to be true, that is deceit; and this includes, as we have seen, making assertions as of his own knowledge about things of which he is consciously ignorant. If he only speaks, and purports to speak, according to his information and belief, then he speaks for his own part both honestly and truly, though his information and belief may be in themselves erroneous, and though if he had taken ordinary pains his information might have been better. If he expresses an opinion, that is his opinion for what it is worth, and others must estimate its worth for themselves. In either case, in the absence of a special duty to give correct information or a competent opinion, there is no question of wrong doing. If the speaker has not come under any such duty, he was not bound to have any information or to frame any opinion. But where a particular duty has been assumed, it makes no difference that the speaking or writing of a form of words is an incident in the performance. If a medical practitioner miscopies a formula from a pharmacopœia or medical treatise, and his patient is poisoned by the druggist making it up as so copied, surely that is actionable negligence, and actionable apart from any contract. Yet his intention was only to repeat what he found in the book. It is true that the prescription, even if he states it to be taken out of the book, is his prescription, and he is answerable for its being a fit one; if it be exactly copied from a current book of good repute which states it to be applicable to such cases as the one in hand, that will be evidence, but only evidence, that the advice was competent.

Again the negligent misreading of an ancient record by

(z) The law of defamation stands apart but it is no exception to the proposition in the text, for it is not a law requiring care and caution in greater or less degree, but a law of absolute responsibility qualified by absolute exceptions, and where malice has to be proved, the grossest negligence is only evidence of malice

a professed palæographist might well be a direct and natural cause of damage; if such a person, being employed under a contract with a solicitor, made a negligent mistake to the prejudice of the ultimate client, is it clear that the client might not have an action against him? If not, he may with impunity be negligent to the verge of fraud; for the solicitor, not being damnified, would have no cause of action, or at most a right to nominal damages on the contract. The telegraph clerk's case is more like one of these (we do not say they are precisely analogous) than the mere reporting or repetition of supposed facts. There remains, no doubt, the argument that liability must not be indefinitely extended. But no one has proposed to abolish the general rule as to remoteness of damage, of which the importance, it is submitted, is apt to be obscured by contriving hard and fast rules in order to limit the possible combinations of the elements of liability. Thus it seems that even on the American view damages could not be recovered for loss arising out of an error in a ciphered telegram, for the telegraph company would have no notice of what the natural and probable consequences of error would be (a).

Uncertainty still remaining in English doctrine. Taking together all the matters hitherto discussed in this chapter, it appears that different views and tendencies have on different occasions prevailed even in the same court, and that we are not yet in possession of a complete and consistent doctrine. *Fleming's* case (b) is reconcilable, but only just reconcilable, with *Foulkes's* case (c) and *Dickson* v. *Reuter's Telegram Co.* (d), though not directly opposed to *Bowen* v. *Hall* (e), is certainly not conceived in the same spirit.

(a) Cp *Sanders* v. *Stuart* (1876), 1 C. P. D. 326, 45 L. J. C. P. 682.
(b) 4 Q B Div 81
(c) 5 C P Div 157, 49 L J C. P. 361
(d) 3 C. P. Div. 1, 47 L J C. P 1
(e) 6 Q B Div 333, 50 L J Q B 305

Character of morally innocent acts affected by extraneous contract. (e) There are likewise cases where an innocent and even a prudent person will find himself within his right, or a wrong-doer, according as there has or has not been a contract between other parties under which the property or lawful possession of goods has been transferred. If a man fraudulently acquires property in goods, or gets delivery of possession with the consent of the true owner, he has a real though a defeasible title, and at any time before the contract is avoided (be it of sale or any form of bailment) he can give an indefeasible title by delivery over to a buyer or lender for valuable consideration given in good faith (*f*). On the other hand a man may obtain the actual control and apparent dominion of goods not only without having acquired the property, but without any rightful transfer of possession. He may obtain possession by a mere trick, for example by pretend-

---

(*f*) See the principle explained, and worked out in relation to complicated facts, in *Pease v Gloahec*, L. R. 1 P. C. 219, 35 L. J. P. C. 66

Character of morally innocent acts affected by extraneous contract. The rule that a *bona fide* purchaser for a valuable consideration, from a seller who has obtained goods through fraud, is protected, is followed in numerous decisions in the United States. The equity of this rule rests in the fact that the original seller has invested his buyer with the possession and apparent ownership of the goods and must suffer from his misplaced confidence rather than the subsequent and misled innocent purchaser Barnard *v* Campbell, 65 Barb 286, 55 N. Y. 456; 58 N. Y. 73, Jones *v* Christian, 86 Va 1017; Carme *v*. Rauh, 100 Md. 247, Frey *v* Harrison, 29 Ill App 300, Globe Milling Co. *v* Minneapolis Elevator Co., 44 Minn. 153, Saltus *v*. Everett, 20 Wend. 279, 32 Am. Dec. 541; Benedict *v*. Williams, 48 Hun, 123, Dows *v*. Rush, 28 Barb. 157, Hall *v* Hinks, 21 Md 417, Cockran *v* Stewart, 21 Minn 435, Root *v*. French, 13 Wend 570, 28 Am Dec. 428, William *v* Russell, 39 Conn 406; First Nat. Bank *v*. Cook Carriage Co., 70 Miss. 587, 12 So. Rep. 598, Rowley *v* Bigelow, 12 Pick. 307, 23 Am. Dec. 607, A. H. Whitney Co *v*. Burnham, 48 Mo. App. 340, Sword *v* Young, 89 Tenn. 126; 14 S. W Rep 481; Id. 604, Traywick *v*. Keeble, 93 Ala 498, 8 So. Rep. 573; Robinson *v* Pogue, 86 Ala 275, 5 So. Rep 685, Frey *v*. Harrison, 29 Ill. App 300, Neff *v* Landis, 110 Pa St. 204, 1 At Rep 177

ing to be another person with whom the other party really intends to deal (g), or the agent of that person (h). In such a case a third person, even if he has no means of knowing the actual possessor's want of title, cannot acquire a good title from him unless the sale is in market overt, or the transaction is within some special statutory protection, as that of the Factors Acts. He deals, however innocently, at his peril. In these cases there may be hardship, but there is nothing anomalous. It is not really a contract between other parties that determines whether a legal wrong has been committed or not, but the existence or non-existence of rights of property and possession — rights available against all the world — which in their turn exist or not according as there has been a contract, though perhaps vitiated by fraud as between the original parties, or a fraudulent obtaining of possession (i) without any contract. The question is purely of the distribution of real rights as affording occasion for their infringement, it may be an unconscious infringement. A man cannot be liable to A for meddling with A.'s goods while there is an unsettled question whether the goods are A's or B's. But it cannot be a proposition in the law of torts that the goods are A.'s or B's, and it can be said to be, in a qualified sense, a proposition in the law of contract only because in the common law property and the right to possession can on the one hand be transferred by contract without delivery or any other overt act, and on the other hand the legal effect of a manual delivery or consignment may depend on the presence or absence of a true consent to the apparent purpose and effect of the act. The contract, or the absence

(g) *Cundy* v *Lindsay*, 3 App Ca 459, 47 L J Q B 481

(h) *Hardman* v *Booth*, 1 H & C 803, 32 L J Ex 105

(i) It will be remembered that the essence of trespass *de bonis asportatis* is depriving the true owner of possession a thief has possession in law, though a wrongful possession, and the lawful possessor of goods cannot at common law steal them, except in the cases of "breaking bulk" and the like, where it is held that the fraudulent dealing determines the bailment

of a contract, is only part of the incidents determining the legal situation on which the alleged tortious act operates. There are two questions, always conceivably and often practically distinct: Were the goods in question the goods of the plaintiff? Did the act complained of amount to a trespass or conversion? Both must be distinctly answered in the affirmative to make out the plaintiff's claim, and they depend on quite different principles (*k*). There is therefore no complication of contract and tort in these cases, but only — if we may so call it — a dramatic juxtaposition.

IV — *Measure of Damages and other Incidents of the Remedy.*

Measure of damages, &c With regard to the measure of damages, the same principles are to a great extent applicable to cases of contract and of tort, and even rules which are generally peculiar to one branch of the law may be applied to the other in exceptional classes of cases.

The liability of a wrong-doer for his act is determined, as we have seen, by the extent to which the harm suffered by the plaintiff was a natural and probable consequence of the act. This appears to be also the true measure of liability for breach of contract; "the rule with regard to

---

(*k*) See *passim* in the opinions delivered in *Hollins* v *Fowler*, L. R. 7 H. L. 757, 44 L J Q B 169

Measure of damages. Upon this subject the American decisions seem to substantially agree with the English rule. "The value of property constitutes the measure or the element of damages, in a great variety of cases, both of tort and of contract; and where there are no such aggravations as call for or justify exemplary damages, in actions in which such damages are recoverable, the value is ascertained and adopted as the measure of compensation for being deprived of the property, the same in actions of tort and in actions upon contract. In both cases, the value is the legal and fixed measure of damages, and not discretionary with the jury " 1 Sutherland on Dam. (1st ed.) 178.

The cases illustrating the application of this rule are numerous and only a few are here cited. Brewster *v* Landview, 119 Ill. 554; Bank of Montgomery *v*. Reese, 26 Pa St. 143; Bailey *v*. M & St. P. Ry. Co. (S.

remoteness of damage is precisely the same whether the damages are claimed in actions of contract or of tort" (*l*); the judgment of what is natural and probable being taken as it would have been formed by a reasonable man in the defendant's place at the date of the wrongful act, or the conclusion of the contract, as the case may be. No doubt there have been in the law of contract quite recent opinions of considerable authority casting doubt on the rule of *Hadley* v. *Baxendale* (*m*), and tending to show that a contracting party can be held answerable for special consequences of a breach of his contract only if there has been something amounting to an undertaking on his part to bear such consequences; on this view even express notice of the probable consequences — if they be not in themselves of a common and obvious kind, such as the plaintiff's loss of a difference between the contract and the market price of marketable goods which the defendant fails to deliver — would not of itself suffice (*n*).

(*l*) Brett M R, *The Notting Hill* (1884), 9 P Div 104, 113, 53 L J P 56
(*m*) 9 Ex 341, 23 L. J Ex 179 (1854)
(*n*) *Horne* v. *Midland R Co* (1873), Ex Ch , L. R 8 C. P. 131, 42 L J C P 59

D), 54 N W. Rep. 596, Coulson v. Panhandle Nat Bank, 54 Fed Rep 855, Bates v Diamond Crystal Salt Co (Neb), 55 N W. Rep. 258, Corbett v. Anderson (Wis), 54 N. W. Rep. 727; Goodell v Bluff City Lbr Co., 57 Ark. 203; 21 S W Rep 104, Adams Ex. Co v. Egbert, 36 Pa St 360, White v McNett, 33 N. Y. 371, Rand v. White Mts. R. Co., 10 N H. 424, Pinkerston v. Manchester R. Co., 42 N H. 424, Enders v Board Public Works, 1 Gratt 364, Dana v. Fielder, 12 N. Y. 48; Clement. v Hawks Man Co , 117 Mass. 363; Danforth v. Walker, 37 Vt 239, Ganson v Madigan, 13 Wis 67, Hale v. Front, 35 Cal. 229, Springer v. Berry, 47 Me 330, Dustin v McAndrews, 44 N. Y 72, Marshall v. Piles, 3 Bush, 249, Camp v. Hamlin, 55 Ga. 259, Kennedy v. Whitewell, 4 Pick. 466, Gregg v Fitzhugh, 36 Tex. 127; Bush v. Holmes, 53 Me. 417, Baseman v Rose, 10 Ala. 212, Suydam v Jenkins, 3 Sandf. 641, Grand Towner Co. v Phillips, 23 Wall 471, Rider v Kelly, 32 Vt 268, Hutchins v Ladd, 16 Mich. 491, Underhill v Goff, 48 Ill. 198, Scott v. Rogers, 31 N. Y. 676, Bicknell v. Waterman, 5 R. I 43, West v. Pritchard, 19 Conn. 212; Parsons v. Martin, 11 Gray, 111, Rider v. Kelly, 32 Vt 268; Whitesell v Forehand, 79 N. C 230, Hancock v. Gomez, 50 N Y. 669, Bello v. Cunningham, 3 Pet 59, Heinnemann v. Heard, 50 N. Y. 27

Rule as to consequential damage, how far alike in contract and tort. But the Court of Appeal has more lately disapproved this view, pointing out that a contracting party's liability to pay damages for a breach is not created by his agreement to be liable, but is imposed by law. "A person contemplates the performance and not the breach of his contract, he does not enter into a kind of second contract to pay damages, but he is liable to make good those injuries which he is aware that his default may occasion to the contractee" (o).

The general principle, therefore, is still the same in contract as in tort, whatever difficulty may be found in working it out in a wholly satisfactory manner in relation to the various combinations of fact occurring in practice (p).

One point may be suggested as needful to be borne in mind to give a consistent doctrine. Strictly speaking, it

---

(o) *Hydraulic Engineering Co. v. McHaffie* (1878), 4 Q. B. Div. 670, per Bramwell L. J. at p. 674; Brett and Cotton L. JJ. are no less explicit. The time to be looked to is that of entering into the contract *ib*. In *McMahon v. Field* (1881), 7 Q. B. Div. 591, 50 L. J. Q. B. 552, the supposed necessity of a special undertaking is not put forward at all. Mr. J. D. Mayne, though he still (4th ed. 1884) holds by *Horne v. Midland R. Co.*, very pertinently asks where is the consideration for such an undertaking.

(p) As to the treatment of consequential damage where a false statement is made which may be treated either as a deceit or as a broken warranty, see *Smith v. Green* (1875), 1 C. P. D. 92, 45 L. J. C. P. 28.

Rule as to consequential damages. One breaking a contract is liable for only such consequences as were a direct result of the breach, and contemplated by the construction of the contract. One committing a tort, without malice, is liable for all the natural consequences of the wrongful acts. As it may be presumed that the contracting parties contemplated the usual and natural consequences of a breach when the contract was made, the difficulty of establishing any practical distinction between the results of breach of contract and of tort, is apparent. Warwick v. Hutchinson, 43 N. J. L. 61; Stewart v. Lanier House Co., 75 Ga. 582; Frohreich v. Gammon, 28 Minn. 476; Booth v. Spuyten Duy. R. M. Co., 60 N. Y. 492; Miller v. Mariners Church, 7 Greenl. 55; Lawrence v. Wardell, 6 Barb. 423; Winne v. Kelly, 34 Ia. 339; Blagen v. Thompson (Oreg.), 31 Pac. Rep. 647; Chicago & A. R. Co. v. Fisher, 38 Ill. App. 33; Ward v. Hudson River Bldg. Co., 125 N. Y. 230, 26 N. E. Rep. 256. See also authorities cited in the last preceding American note.

is not notice of apprehended consequences that is material, but notice of the existing facts by reason whereof those consequences will naturally and probably ensue upon a breach of the contract (*q*).

Vindictive character of action for breach of promise of marriage. Exemplary or vindictive damages, as a rule, cannot be recovered in an action on a contract, and it makes no difference that the breach of contract is a misfeasance capable of being treated as a wrong. Actions for breach of promise of marriage are an exception, perhaps in law, certainly in fact: it is impossible to analyse the estimate formed by a jury in such a case, or to prevent them from giving, if so minded, damages which in truth are, and are intended to be, exemplary (*r*). Strictly the

---

(*q*) According to Alderson B. in *Hadley v. Baxendale*, it is the knowledge of "special circumstances under which the contract was actually made" that has to be looked to, *i. e.* the probability of the consequence is only matter of inference.

(*r*) See *Berry v. Da Costa* (1866), L. R. 1 C. P. 331, 35 L. J. C. P. 191.

Vindictive character of action for breach of promise of marriage. In numerous American decisions it has been held that, in actions for breach of contract, the right of recovery is wholly independent of the motive which induced the wrongful act or omission. Grand Tower Co. v. Phillips, 23 Wall 171, Duche v. Wilson, 37 Hun, 519, Toledo, etc. R. Co v. Roberts, 71 Ill 540; Walsh v Chicago, etc. R. Co., 42 Wis 23, Krom v. Schoonmaker, 3 Barb. 647, Sheik v Hobson, 64 Ia 146; Drohn v Brewer, 77 Ill 280; Raynor v. Nims, 37 Mich. 34, 26 Am. Rep. 493, Philadelphia etc R Co v Hoeflich, 62 Md. 301; 50 Am. Rep. 223, Cady v Case, 45 Kan. 733, 26 Pac. Rep. 448; Arzaga v Villalba, 85 Cal. 191

Vindictive or exemplary damages are usually awarded in breach of promise suits. The amount is estimated according to plaintiff's loss of reputation, wealth, social position, and prospects in life, as well as the endurance of mortification, pain and disgrace Fiddler v McKinney, 21 Ill 308 Malone v. Ryan 14 R I. 614, McKinsey v. Squires, 32 W Va. 41, 9 S. E. Rep 55, Chellis v Chapman, 7 N Y. S. Rep 78, 26 N. E. Rep. 308, Coryell v. Colbaugh, 1 N J. L 77, White v Thomas, 12 Ohio St 313, Giese v. Schultz, 53 Wis 462, Smith v Sherman, 4 Cush 408; Wells v Padgett, 8 Barb. 323, Wilber v Johnson, 58 Mo. 600; Tobin v. Shaw, 45 Me 331, Collins v. Mack, 31 Ark 684, Vanderpool v. Richardson, 52 Mich 336, Bennett v. Beam, 42 Mich 349

damages are by way of compensation, but they are "almost always considered by the jury somewhat *in poenam*" (s). Like results might conceivably follow in the case of other breaches of contract accompanied with circumstances of wanton injury or contumely.

Contracts on which executors cannot sue. In another respect breach of promise of marriage is like a tort: executors cannot sue for it without proof of special damage to their testator's personal estate; nor does the action lie against executors without special damage (t). "Executors and administrators are the representatives of the temporal property, that is, the debts and goods of the deceased, but not of their wrongs, except where those wrongs operate to the temporal injury of their personal estate. But in that case the special damage ought to be stated on the record; otherwise the Court cannot intend it" (u). The same rule appears to hold as concerning injuries to the person caused by unskilful medical treatment, negligence of carriers of passengers or their servants, and the like, although the duty to be performed was under a contract (x). Positive authority, however, has not been found on the extent of this analogy. The language used by the Court of King's Bench is at any rate not convincing, for although certainly a wrong is not property, the right to recover damages for a wrong is a chose in action; neither can the distinction

---

(s) Le Blanc J in *Chamberlain v Williamson* (1814), 2 M & S 408, 414

(t) *Finlay v Chirney* (1888), 20 Q. B. Div 494, 57 L J Q B 247

(u) *Chamberlain v Williamson*, 2 M & S at p 115

(x) *Chamberlain v Williamson*, last note, Willes J in *Alton v Midland R Co.*, 19 C B N S at p 242, 34 L J C P at p 298, cp *Beckham v Drake* (1841), 8 M & W at p 854, 1 Wms Saund 242, and see more in Williams on Executors, pt. 2, bk. 3, ch 1, § 1, and *Raymond v Fitch* (1835), 2 C M & R 588

Contracts on which executors cannot sue The right to sue upon the breach of a promise of marriage does not survive against a party's representatives unless there has been special damage. Smith *v.* Sherman, 4 Cush. 408, Shuler *v* Millsape, 71 N C. 297, Kelley *v* Riley, 106 Mass. 330, Wade *v* Kalbfleisch, 50 N Y 282, Grubb *v* Sult, 32 Gratt 203.

between liquidated and unliquidated damages afford a test, for that would exclude causes of action on which executors have always been able to sue. We have considered in an earlier chapter the exceptional converse cases in which by statute or otherwise a cause of action for a tort which a person might have sued on in his lifetime survives to his personal representatives.

Where there was one cause of action with an option to sue in tort or in contract, the incidents of the remedy generally were determined once for all, under the old common law practice, by the plaintiff's election of his form of action. But this has long ceased to be of practical importance in England, and, it is believed, in most jurisdictions.

TABLE OF CASES CITED.

The References are to Pages.

A.

Abbey v. Dewey, 375
Abbott v. Abbott, 64
Abbott v. Booth, 264
Abbott v. Kansas City etc. R Co., 185.
Abel v. President, etc. Co., 552
Abend v. Terre Haute & I. R. Co., 120, 192.
Abernathy v. Wheeler, 430
Abraham v. Reynolds, 612
Abrahams v. Deakin, 109
Abrahams v. Kidney, 278
Abrath v. N F R Co, 308.
Abt v. Burgheim, 204
Acheson v. Miller, 231
Achton v. Piper, 286, 291.
Ackers v. Howard, 149
Acton v. Blundell, 178, 179, 183
Adams v. Cole, 112.
Adams v. Cost, 100
Adams v. Iron Cliffs Co, 120
Adams v. Lawson, 287, 306
Adams v. L & Y R Co., 592.
Adams v. Main, 271
Adams v. Marshall, 24
Adams v. Michael, 506
Adams v. Rankin, 295
Adams v. Rivers, 422, 178
Adams v. Stone, 297
Adams v. Truman, 163
Adams v. Wagoner, 186
Adams v. Young, 13, 546
Adams I N Co v. Egbert, 683
Adamson v. Jarvis, 232
Adcock v. Marsh, 131
Addie v. Western Bank of Scotland, 113
Addington v. Allen, 375, 381, 672
Adkin v. Newell, 267
Adler v. Fenton, 463
Aetna Ins Co v. Boone, 29
Aetna Life Ins Co v. France, 352
Aetna Life Ins Co v. Paul, 67
Acton v. Cooper, 142
A G v. Cambridge Consumers' Gas Co, 5
A G v. Colney Hatch Lunatic Asylum, 527
A G v. Sheffield Gas Consumers' Co, 23
A G v. Tomline, 175.
Agincourt, The, 152
Ahern v. Collins, 260
Ahle v. Reinbach, 505.
Aiken v. W U T Co, 674
Ainsworth v. Partello, 438.
Aird v. Fireman's Journal Co, 324
Akerly v. Haines, 281
Alabama etc. R Co v. Waller, 125

Alabama, G S R Co v Arnold, 220
Alabama, G S R Co v. Chapman, 13
Alabama, G S R Co v Frazier, 220
Alabama, G S R Co v Sellors, 220
Albro v. The Chappaqua Shoe Mfg Co, 534
Albion v. Hetrick, 633
Albro v Jaquith, 81
Alden v. Wright, 375
Alder v Buckley, 27
Alderman v French, 816, 824.
Alderson v Walstoll, 162
Aldred's Case, 500.
Aldrich v Brown, 312
Aldrich v Gorham, 43
Aldrich v. Howard, 505
Aldrich v. Parnell, 230
Aldrich v Press Printing Co, 66
Aldrich v. Wright, 263, 206
Alexander v Alexander, 294
Alexander v Big Rapids, 70
Alexander v Dyer, 213
Alexander v Fisher, 429
Alexander v. Hard, 422
Alexander v Humber, 534
Alexander v Jenkins, 303
Alexander v. Kerr, 540
Alexander v. Louisville etc. R Co, 542
Alexander v Moise, 225
Alexander v Town of New Castle, 371
Alexander v North Eastern R Co, 326
Alexander v. Southey, 417
Alexander v Swackhamer, 434
Alexander Mining Co v Painter, 422
Alger v Lowell, 576
Alger v Mississippi etc R Co, 611
Allaire v Whitney, 214
Allbutt v General Council etc, 146, 341
Allegheny v Zimmerman, 50, 606
Allen v Codman, 396.
Allen v. Crofoot, 328, 479
Allen v Feland, 469.
Allen v Fiske, 459
Allen v Gray, 138
Allen v Hallet, 151
Allen v Hart, 858.
Allen v Hillman, 800.
Allen v Kirk, 402
Allen v Lonard, 263
Allen v L & S. W R Co, 109.
Allen v Lyon, 487
Allen v Martin, 483
Allen v McCullough, 64
Allen v. Mercantile M Ins Co, 606
Allen v News Pub Co, 289.
Allen v Railroad Co, 336
Allen v State, 506, 485
Allen v Truesdell, 37
Allen v Willard, 545

TABLE OF CASES CITED.

The References are to Pages.

Allen v. Wortham, 310.
Allentown v. Kramer, 69
Alliger v. Brooklyn Daily Eagle, 334.
Allison v. Little, 0, 412
Allison v. Rheem, 262
Allison Mfg Co v McCormick, 164.
Allred v Bray, 81.
Allsop v Allsop, 294
Almy v. Harris, 228
Alpin v. Morton, 880
Althen v. Kelley, 225.
Althorf v Wolfe, 81
Alton v. Hope, 70
Alton v. Midland Railway Co, 663, 664, 666, 685.
Alton, etc R Co v Baugh, 619
Ambler v Church, 139
Ambergate etc R Co v Midland R Co, 173
American Express Co v Patterson, 68
American Fur Co v United States, 403
American Insurance Co v Kuhlman, 384
American M T Co v Middleton, 238
American Print Works v Lawrence, 199, 173
Americus, etc R v Luckie, 666
Ames v Snider, 194 195, 196.
Ames v Union R. Co, 271, 276, 676, 662, 664
Amick v O'Hara 9, 10 112
Amoskeag Mfg Co v Trainer, 181
Amott v Standard Assn, 312
Amy v Watertown, 245.
Anderson v Beck, 260
Anderson v Burnett, 375
Anderson v Cape Fear Steamboat Co, 561, 562
Anderson v Dickie, 529, 627
Anderson, City of, v East, 647, 627
Anderson v Friend, 395
Anderson v Hill, 64
Anderson v Line, 63
Anderson v Milwaukee, etc Ry, 233
Anderson v Minnesota & N W R Co, 643.
Anderson v Radcliffe, 155
Anderson v Ryan, 278
Anderson v Smith, 204
Anderson v State, 119
Anderson v The I R Ward, Jr, 576
Andover v Gould, 228.
Anderson v Ogden 123.
Andrews v Bodecker, 91
Andrews v Deshler, '58, 391
Andrews v Green, 110
Andrews v Hoppenheafer 294
Andrews v Mason City & Ft D Ry Co, 567
Andrews v Murray, 231
Andrews v Orabee, 63
Andrews v Wells, 110
Andrews v Woodmansee, 312
Angel v Eureka Club, 87
Anheuser Busch Brewing Assn v Clarke, 225
Annas v Milwaukee, etc, R. Co, 82
Annelly v De Saussure, 418
Annen v Willard, 92
Anthony v Haney 470
Anthony v Sliad 10
Apgar v Woolston, 195
Applebee v Percy, 614

Aristland v Potterfield, 149
Arlette v Killin, 516
Armentrout v Moranda, 287, 289
Armory v Delamirie, 461, 464
Armstrong v Cooley, 87, 112, 501,
Armstrong Co. v Clarion Co., 232
Ara v Knauss, 70
Arnold v Holbrook, 475
Arp v State, 151
Arthur v Case, 225
Artman v. Walton, 454.
Arundel v McCulloch, 464
Arzaga v Villalba, 220, 685
Ash v. Dawnay, 170.
Ash v Marlow, 390
Ashby v White, 118, 149, 215, 411.
Asher v Whitlock, 451
Ashley v Port Huron, 70
Ashmun v Williams, 162
Ashworth v Stannix, 127
Aston v Nolan, 92
Athens Mfg Co v Rucker, 214
Atchison v Goodrich Transp Co, 4°
Atchison v Twine, 82
Atchison etc R Co v Gallins, 98
Atchison etc R Co v McKee, 194
Atchison etc R Co v Moore, 123
Atchison, etc R Co v Randall, 110
Atchison, etc, R Co v Riggs, 563,
Atchison, etc, R Co v Stafford, 41.
Atchison, etc, R Co v Thul, 101.
Atkins v Chilson, 130
Atkins v Johnson, 231, 310
Atkins v Newell, 265
Atkinson v Atkinson, 142
Atkinson v Detroit Free Press, 325
Atkinson v Gatcher 112
Atkinson v Newcastle Waterworks, 15, 229
Atkinson v The Illinois Milk Co, 511
Atlanta, etc, R Co v Ayres, 8
Atlanta etc R Co v Ray 568
Atlanta etc R Co v Kimberly, 92
Attack v Bramwell, 478
Attaway v Cartersville, 110
Attorney General v Horner, 457
Atwood v City of Bangor, 531
Atwater v Sawer, 60
Atwater v Tupper, 415, 416
Atwood v Chapman, 369
Auburn, etc, R Co v Douglass, 33, 182 224
Auchmuty v Ham, 611
Auditor v Atchison etc R Co, 145
Augusta & K R Co v Killian, 562
Aucrett v Thompson, 142
Aulzy v Birkhead, 281
Austin v Bacon, 63
Austin v Burrows, 10
Austin v Carswell, 234
Austin v Dowling, 266, 267
Austin v G W R Co, 653, 657, 658,
Austin, City of, v Ritz, 554
Austin & N W Ry Co v Beatty, 591
Autcliffe v June, 398
Averett v Thompson, 142
Averitt v Merrell, 503
Avery v Meikle, 22,
Avinger v Railway Co, 651
Avis v Newman, 428.
Averigg v New York, etc, R Co, 100.
Ayer v Ashmead, 230
Ayer v Stuckey 503
Aylesworth v St Johns, 398.

TABLE OF CASES CITED. 691

The References are to Pages.

Aynsley v. Glover, 510, 511
Ayres v. French, 369.
Ayres v. Grider, 200

B.

Babcock v. New Jersey Stock Yard Co., 500, 524
Bachelder v. Heagan, 501
Bachentoss v. Speicher, 369
Backus v. Hart, 518
Bacon v. City of Boston, 511
Bacon v. Mich. Cent. R. Co., 67, 131, 334
Bacon v. Towne, 191
Bacon v. Waters, 395
Backhouse v. Bonomi, 216, 244
Baddeley v. Earl Granville, 643
Badgley v. Decker, 281
Badgley v. Hedges, 328
Baer v. Martin, 156
Bagby v. Harris, 214
Bagley v. Cleveland Rolling Mill, 544, 612
Bailey v. Dean, 294, 328, 329
Bailey v. Dodge, 392
Bailey v. Glover, 216
Bailey v. M. & St. P. Ry. Co., 652
Bailey v. Publishing Co., 324
Bailey v. Reed, 213
Bailey v. Tipton, 112
Bailey v. Troy & B. R. Co., 92
Bailey v. Wiggins, 204
Bailey v. Wright, 472
Bain v. Merrick, 40
Baird v. Householder, 265
Baird v. Shipman, 624
Baird v. Wells, 117
Baker v. Beers, 134
Baker v. Bohannan, 506
Baker v. Boston, 158
Baker v. Braham, 246
Baker v. Chicago, etc., R. Co., 162
Baker v. Cory, 638
Baker v. Furlong, 142, 153
Baker v. Kinsey, 100, 108
Baker v. Railroad Co., 585
Baker v. Savage, 198, 531
Baker v. Schright, 131
Baker v. Stone, 60
Baker v. Young, 63, 64
Baldwin v. Casella, 614
Baldwin v. Elphinston, 308
Baldwin v. Hayden, 201, 207
Baldwin v. Oskaloosa Gas Light Co., 495
Baldwin v. St. Louis, etc., R. Co., 123, 552, 565
Baldwin v. Weed, 91
Ball v. Breckenridge, 114
Ball, Ex parte, 26
Ball v. Bennett, 63, 64
Ball v. Bruce, 278
Ball v. Evening Post Co., 324
Ball v. Nye, 501
Ball v. Palmer, 447
Ball v. Rawles, 52
Ball v. Ray, 507
Ballworkish Mining Co. v. Harrison, 177
Ballantine v. Golding, 241
Ballard v. Noakes, 478, 610
Ballard v. Tomlinson, 179
Ballentine v. North Mo. R. Co., 606
Ballentine v. Webb, 495, 522
Balling v. Kirley, 411
Ballou v. Chicago, etc. R. Co., 193
Ballou v. Talbot, 630
Ballow v. Farnum, 91
Balme v. Hutton, 143, 436
Baltimore City Ry. v. McDonnell, 584
Baltimore & O. R. Co. v. Andrews, 120
Baltimore & O. R. Co. v. Baugh, 120
Baltimore & O. R. Co. v. Boteler, 552
Baltimore & O. R. Co. v. O'Donnell, 145
Baltimore & P. R. Co. v. Reaney, 29
Baltimore & Y. T. R. v. State, 527
Baltimore, etc., R. Co. v. Boone, 10
Baltimore, etc., R. Co. v. Depew, 63
Baltimore, etc. R. Co. v. Fifth Bapt. Church, 485, 504
Baltimore, etc. R. Co. v. Fitzpatrick, 530
Baltimore, etc. R. Co. v. Jones, 539
Baltimore, etc. R. Co. v. Kempt, 57
Baltimore, etc. R. Co. v. McKenzie, 193
Baltimore, etc. R. Co. v. Rowan, 564
Baltimore, etc. R. Co. v. State, 544
Baltimore, etc., R. Co. v. Sulphur Springs, etc. Dist., 605
Baltimore, etc. R. Co. v. Woodruff, 562
Baltimore R. Co. v. Richie, 81
Bamford v. Turnley, 500, 502
Bangor, etc., R. R. v. Smith, 31
Bangs v. Little, 154
Banister v. Pennsylvania Co., 99
Banks v. Albright, 369
Bank v. Campbell, 383
Bank v. Cooper, 369
Bank v. Gray, 383
Bankhead v. Alloway, 363
Bank of California v. W. U. T. Co., 674
Bank of Montgomery v. Reese, 682
Bank of New South Wales v. Ouston, 109
Bank of North America v. York, 381
Banks v. Wabash Western Ry. Co., 574
Banner v. Clay, 261
Bapta v. Palmer, 358
Barbeo v. Armistead, 271
Barbee v. Reese, 250, 576
Barber v. Essex, 510
Barbour v. Stephenson, 277, 281
Bard v. John, 100
Barden v. Felch, 87
Barden v. Fitch, 230
Barfield v. Britt, 626
Barham v. Turbeville, 61
Barholt v. Wright, 254
Barhydt v. Valk, 264
Barkdoo v. Randall, 138
Barker v. Braham, 87
Barker v. Furlong, 436
Barker v. St. Louis Dispatch Co., 343
Barley v. Bessing, 231
Barlow v. Stalworth, 658
Barnard v. Campbell, 680
Barnard v. Poor, 503, 617
Barnard v. Press Pub. Co., 311
Barnards v. State, 201
Barndt v. Frederick, 376
Barnes v. Allen, 271, 273
Barnes v. Barnes, 462
Barnes v. Campbell, 348
Barnes v. Harris, 63
Barnes v. Hathorn, 503
Barnes v. Martin, 25
Barnes v. McCrate, 328
Barnes v. Means, 27
Barnes v. Trundy, 294

TABLE OF CASES CITED.

The References are to Pages.

Barnes v. Ward, 206, 634
Barnet v. Ihrie, 518.
Barnett v. Guilford, 455.
Barnett v. Reed, 399
Barnett v. Stanton, 353, 357.
Barnett v Ward, 205.
Barney v. Burstenbinder, 610
Barney v Pinkham, 27.
Barnstable v. Thatcher, 449
Barnum v. Minnesota Transfer Ry. Co., 487
Barnum v. Terpening, 564.
Barnum v. Van Dusen, 610
Barracouta, The, 630
Barrelet v Bellyard, 130
Barrett v Southern P. Co., 585.
Barrick v. Schifferdicker, 510
Barlow v Pave, 143.
Barrows v Bell, 312
Barrows v. Carpenter, 623.
Barry v Croskey, 350.
Barstow v Old Colony R. Co., 120
Bartlett v Brown, 392
Bartlett v Christhilf, 328
Bartlett v. Happock, 631.
Bartlett v Tucker, 660
Bartlett, etc., Co. v. Roach, 21
Bartley v Richtmeyer, 277, 278
Barton v Dunning, 432.
Barton v Pepin Co Ag Soc., 15.
Barton v St. Louis, etc. R Co., 544
Barton v Syracuse, 591.
Barton v. Taylor, 115
Barton v. Thompson, 545
Barton's Hill Coal Co v Reid, 90.
Barwick v English Joint Stock Bank, 88, 112, 113, 187
Bascom v Dempsey, 122
Basore v Henkel, 225
Bass v Chicago & N. W. Ry Co., 87
Bassett v Green, 414
Bassett v Salisbury, 213
Bassett v Salisbury Mfg Co., 211
Basil v Limore, 291
Baseman v Rose, 683
Batchelor v Fortesque, 641
Bates's Case, 194
Bates v Diamond Crystal Salt Co., 683
Batchrich v The Detroit Post and Tribune Co., 318
Battishill v Humphreys, 583
Bauer v Clay, 394
Baughman v Gould, 353
Baum v Mullen, 64
Baumann v Grubbs, 213
Baxter v Bush, 64.
Baxter v Chicago, etc., R. Co., 101
Baxter v Doe, 21
Baxter v Roberts, 192.
Baxter v Warner, 91
Bayley v Manchester, Sheffield and Lincolnshire R Co., 105, 106
Baylis v Schwalbach Cycle Co., 110
Baylor v Baltimore, etc R Co, 611
Bay Shore R Co v Harris, 586
Bays v Hunt, 297, 321
Beach v. Fulton Bank, 67
Beach v Hancock, 250
Beach v People, 505
Beach v Ranny, 293
Beach v Trudgain, 199.
Beal v Robeson, 396.
Beal v. Posey, 651.

Beals v. Thompson, 336
Bean v. Hubbard, 112, 172
Beardslee v Richardson, 27
Beardsley v Bridgman, 415, 627.
Beardsley v Duntler, 358
Beasley v Meigs, 324
Beasley v Roney, 65
Beatty v Gilmore, 185
Beatty v. Perkins, 111.
Beatty v Tillman, 91
Beauchamp v Saginaw Mining Co., 37, 615
Beaulieu v Portland Co., 110, 514.
Beaumont v. Greathead, 215
Bebinger v. Sweet, 583
Becher v G. B. R. Co., 603
Beck v Stitzel, 300.
Becker v Janinski, 27, 213
Becker v Smith, 182
Beckett v. Midland R Co., 499.
Beckley v Newcomb, 61.
Beckley v Skrob, 505
Beckwith v Oatman, 26
Beddall v Maitland, 466, 467
Beddow v Beddow, 226
Bedell v Long Island R R Co, 501
Bedford etc R Co v Rainbolt, 637.
Beeler v Turnpike Co., 223
Beeler v. Webb, 403
Beers v Arkansas, 186
Beers v. Housatonic, 574
Begeln v Anderson, 503
Behrens v Ins Co., 325
Behrens v McKinzie, 59
Beir v Cooke, 596
Beisiegel v N Y. etc R Co, 557
Bolden v. Henriques 49
Belding v Black Hills & Ft P R Co., 81
Belfast Steamboat v Boon & Co., 360.
Belknap v. Ball, 321
Bell v Cummings, 443, 535
Bell v Ellis, 369
Bell v Fernold, 291
Bell v Hansley, 186, 253
Bell v. Josselyn, 648
Bell v Leslie, 614
Bell v Loomis, 230
Bell v McClintock, 606
Bell v McGinnis, 323
Bell v Midland R Co, 222
Bell v Norfolk S R Co, 157
Bell v Reed, 660
Belle v Cunningham, 683
Bellman v Indianapolis, etc., R. Co, 37
Bellons v McGinnis, 64, 129
Belton v Baxter, 545
Benedict v. Williams, 414, 680
Beneway v Thorp 311
Bangston v Chicago etc R Co, 192
Benjamin v Storr, 191
Benley v Wiggins, 118
Benn v Null, 116
Bennett v Beam, 685
Bennett v Bennett, 272
Bennett v Drain Commissioner, 228.
Bennett v Fulmer, 145
Bennett v Ives, 618
Bennett v Joes, 81
Bennett v Mathews, 324
Bennett v New York etc R. Co., 584.
Bennett v. Railroad Co, 567
Bennett v Smith, 272
Bennett v Truebody, 91.
Benson v Cent Pac Ry. Co., 45

TABLE OF CASES CITED.

693

The References are to Pages.

Benson v. Remington, 278.
Benson v. Suarez, 627
Benson v. Titcomb, 516
Benton v. Beattie, 435
Benton v. Pratt, 9 100, 585, 673
Benzing v. Steinway, 117
Berdan v. Davis, 209
Berea Stone Co v. Kraft, 124
Berg v. City of Milwaukee, 510
Berghoff v. McDonald, 618
Bergin v. Hayward, 262
Bergman v. Jones, 287, 295, 305
Bergquist v. City of Minneapolis, 120
Burston v. Staples, 120
Berranger v. Hartman Steel Co, 91
Berringer v. G E R Co, 661
Berry v. DaCosta, 222, 685.
Berts v. Vreeland, 211.
Berson v. Ewing, 244
Beseman v. Pennsylvania R Co, 157, 185
Bessi v. Chesapeake & O Ry Co, 110
Bessey v. Olliott, 1 Raym, 170
Best v. Flint, 170
Bethlehem v. Perseverance Fire Co, 608
Betts v. Gibbins, 232
Beyard v. Hoffman, 138, 148
Bicknell v. Waterman, 683
Biddle v. Bond, 142, 143
Bidwell v. Osgood, 192
Bier v. Cooke, 627
Biere v. Jeffersonville M & I R Co 120
Bigenstaff v. Paulet, 271
Bigelow v. Jones, 443
Bigelow v. Walker, 20
Billings v. Lafferty, 115
Billings v. Russell, 112
Billingsly v. White, 124
Billings v. Wink, 294
Binford v. Johnson, 37, 615
Binford v. Young, 312
Bingham v. Salene, 159
Birch v. Benton, 294
Bird v. Holbrook, 191, 206
Bird v. Jones, 261
Bird v. Kleiner, 378
Birmingham v. Lewis, 70
Birmingham, City of v. McCreary 61
Birmingham Water Works Co v. Hubbard, 110
Biscoe v. G F R Co, 158
Bishop v. Bekins Consolidated Co, 382
Bishop v. Banks, 495, 506
Bishop v. Kinney, 250
Bishop v. Smith, 358, 369
Bishop v. Weber, 27, 370, 615
Bissell v. Cornell, 295
Bissell v. Larned, 228
Bissell v. Press Pub Co 343
Bissell v. Southworth 610
Bitting v. Ten Eyck, 593
Butts v. Meyer, 397
Bixby v. Brundage, 192
Bixby v. Dunlap, 275
Bizer v. The Ottumwa Hydraulic Power Co, 519
Bizzell v. Brooker, 152
Black v. Black, 375
Black v. Chicago, B & Q R Co, 605
Blacker v. Schoff 427
Blacknall v. Rowland, 378
Blad v. Bamfield 238, 240
Blades v. Higgs, 45, 170

Black Avon Coal Co. v. McCulloch, 412, 547
Blagen v. Thompson, 684.
Blagge v. Ilsley, 278
Blaine v. C & O R, 574, 611.
Blair v. Bromley, 111.
Blair v. Chicago & A. Ry. Co, 271.
Blaisdell v. Railroad, 458, 464.
Blake v. Barnard, 251
Blake v. Ferris, 92, 550.
Blake v. Maine Cent R Co, 125
Blake v. Midland R Co., 77, 79
Blakeman v. Blakeman, 311.
Blakemore v. Bristol & Exeter R Co., 641.
Blamires v. Lane and Yorkshire R Co, 230
Blanc v. Klumpke, 489
Blanchard v. Ilsley, 270
Blassinigame v. Glaves, 234
Blazer v. Insurance Co, 325.
Blazinski v. Perkins, 120
Blenzau v. Mason City, 70
Blickenstaff v. Perrin, 311.
Blickenstaff v. Prim, 321
Bliss v. Greeley, 178
Bliss v. Johnson, 201, 204
Bliss v. Schaub, 618
Bissett v. Daniel, 147.
Blodgett v. Stone, 9
Blood v. Sayre, 138.
Bloodgood v. Ayres, 178
Bloodworth v. Gray, 300
Bloom v. Bloom, 312
Bloomhuff v. State, 504
Bloomington v. Mulvin, 70
Bloss v. Tobey, 299
Blossom v. Barrett 369
Bloyd v. St Louis & S F Ry Co, 123
Blumhardt v. Rohr, 294
Blunt v. Aiken, 530
Blunt v. Hay, 505
Blunt v. Little 395
Blyth v. Birmingham Waterworks Co, 45, 50, 51, 538, 563, 605
Blythe v. Denver & R G Ry Co, 605
Boatwright v. Northeastern R Co, 123
Bonz v. Tate, 267
Bobo v. Browner, 63
Bobson v. Kingsbury, 593
Bodwell v. Osgood, 306, 239
Bodwell v. Swan, 316
Boescher v. Lutz, 202.
Boeger v. Langberg 267
Boehmer v. Detroit Free Press Co, 343
Boetcher v. Staples 235
Bogers v. Wilson 267
Bohan v. P J G L Co, 485, 486, 491, 495
Bohnd v. Missouri R Co, 544
Bolch v. Smith, 641
Bolingbroke v. Swindon Local Board, 109
Bolman v. Overall, 271.
Bolton v. Miller, 278
Bond v. Hilton 214
Bond v. Ramsey, 351
Bondurant v. Lane, 214
Bonesteel v. Bonesteel, 260
Bonifaco v. Relyea, 94
Bonnard v. Perryman, 226, 347
Bonnell v. Dunn, 230
Bonnell v. Smith, 491, 499
Bonner v. Bryant, 101
Bonner v. State 250
Bonnet v. Whitcomb, 125

TABLE OF CASES CITED.

The References are to Pages.

Boogher v. Life Assn, 66, 68.
Booker v Puryear, 402.
Boon v. Atwell, 358
Boot v Pratt, 24
Booth v. Spuyten Duy. R M Co, 684.
Booth v. Storrs, 309
Borden v. Fitch, 138
Borgman v Omaha & St L R Co, 123.
Born v Loflin & Rand Powder Co, 532.
Borrows v Ellison, 244
Boston & Albany R R Co v Shanly, 620.
Boston, etc, R. Co. v Carney, 503.
Boston W P Co v Boston etc Co, 224
Boston & W R Co v Dana, 234
Boswell v. Laird, 92.
Bostwick v Nickelson, 291.
Boulard v Calhoun, 109
Boullamet v Phillips, 305
Bouland v Edison, 323
Bourne v. Fasbrooke, 451.
Bourieslan v Detroit, 312
Boutilier v Milwaukee, 51
Bowden v. Grey, 271
Bowditch v Boston, 199
Bowen v. Flanagan, 591.
Bowen v Hall, 410 669, 670
Bowen v School Distr, 658.
Bower v Peate, 639
Bowers v. Horan, 611
Bowers v Johnson, 881
Bowes v City of Boston, 30
Bowker v Evans, 72
Bowman v Corithers, 375.
Bowman v. Tallman, 27
Bowman v. Teal, 606
Bowring v Theband, 630.
Bowyer v Cook, 181
Box v. Jubb, 607.
Boyce v Aubuchon, 313
Boyce v Railroad Co, 239.
Boyce v Watson, 875.
Boyd v Byrd, 277
Boyd v Cross, 391
Boyer v Bolender, 231.
Boyer v Cook, 469
Boyer v State, 487.
Boyle v Case, 248
Boyle v State, 311.
Boynton v Remington, 310
Boynton v Shaw Stocking Co, 304
Brabbitts v Chicago, etc R Co, 194
Brace v Brink, 297
Bracken v Cooper, 447
Bracken v Rushville, etc, R. Co, 459
Brackett v Lubke, 91
Bracy v Kibbe, 278
Bradbury v Gilford, 611
Bradbury v. Haines, 358.
Bradford v Floyd, 370
Bradish v Bliss, 326
Bradlaugh v Gassett, 145
Bradlaugh v Newdigate, 411
Bradley v Andrews, 615
Bradley v Bosley, 358
Bradley v Cramer, 295, 334
Bradley v Fisher, 138
Bradley v Heath, 339
Bradley v Kennedy, 326
Bradshaw v Lancashire and Yorkshire R Co, 77
Bradstreet v. Gill, 336.
Bradt v Towsley, 298
Brady v Weeks, 530
Bragg v Morrill, 632

Brahm v. Schwartz, 552
Brainard v Dunning, 87
Brandreth v Lance, 447
Branham v. Central Railroad, 522.
Branner v Stormont, 27.
Branson v Labrot, 568
Branstetter v Dorrough, 115
Brantley v Wolf, 60
Brauns v George, 462
Brazil v. Moran, 61
Brazil v Peterson, 99
Breckenridge Co v Hicks, 194
Breckwoldt v. Morris, 111
Breitenbach v Trowbridge, 250, 639
Brelot v Mullen, 303
Brennan v. Gordon, 125
Brennon v Tracy, 391
Brent v. Davis, 111
Brewer v Boston etc R Co, 157
Brewer v Crosby, 614
Brewer v Jacobs, 395
Brewer v. Weakley, 301, 321
Brewster v Sandwich, 682
Brewster v Van Liew, 217
Brezee v Powers, 634
Brick v Rochester, etc, R Co, 124, 191
Bricker v Lightner, 245
Bricker v Potts, 296
Brickett v Knickerbocker Ice Co, 581
Bridge v Grand Junction R Co, 577, 578, 588
Bridger v Railroad Co, 513
Bridges v New London R Co, 552, 559,
Brifitt v. State, 551
Briggs v Evans, 278
Briggs v. Garrett, 320, 331.
Briggs v. Haycock, 489
Briggs v. New York, etc R Co., 434.
Briggs v Taylor, 27
Briggs v Union Street Ry, 590.
Brightman v. Bristol, 516
Brill v Flager, 495, 501
Brill v Ohio Humane Soc, 475
Brinsmead v. Harrison, 231 437
Bristol v Braidwood, 357, 363.
Bristol etc Bank v Midland R. Co., 417
British Mutual Banking Co v Charnwood Forest R Co, 112, 113,
Broadwell v Kansas, 69
Broadwell v. Wilcox, 611
Brobst v Ruff, 396
Brock v. Stimpson, 260, 478.
Broder v. Saillard, 507.
Brodie v Rutledge, 138
Brodley v Davis, 142
Brokaw v. N J R etc, Co, 67, 112.
Brokaw v Railroad Co, 67
Bromley v Birmingham M R, Co., 569
Bronson v Bruce, 318
Brooke v Tradesman's Nat Bank, 30.
Brooke v O'Boyle, 466
Brooker v Coffin, 295, 297, 298
Brookhaven Lumber Co v. Ill Cent R Co, 589.
Brooks v Hoyt, 223
Brooks v Mangan, 261.
Brooks v Norcross 225
Brooks v Olmstead, 413
Brooks v. Schuyerin, 271.
Brophy v Bartlett, 94
Bro-chart v Tuttle, 545
Brosman v Sweetzer, 591.
Brothers v. Morris, 204
Broughton v Jackson, 268

TABLE OF CASES CITED.

The References are to Pages.

Broughton v. McGrow, 305, 319, 317
Broughton v Smart, 278.
Brower v. Edson, 514.
Brown v. Atlantic, etc R Co 502
Brown v. Boom Co, 104
Brown v Boorman, 619.
Brown v. Cape Girardeau, 399
Brown v. Carolina Central Ry Co, 493
Brown v Carpenter, 516.
Brown v. Cayuga etc R Co, 157
Brown v Chadsey, 205.
Brown v. Chicago, etc, R. Co, 37, 537
Brown v Collins, 101
Brown v DeGroff, 513
Brown v Eastern and Midlands R Co, 57
Brown v Emerson, 217
Brown v. Howard, 114, 151
Brown v Howard Ins Co, 20
Brown v Howe, 59.
Brown v Illus, 505
Brown v Kendall, 162, 169, 173, 604
Brown v Kingsley, 276
Brown v Lamberton, 312
Brown v Leach, 351
Brown v Lent 84
Brown v Lynn, 591
Brown v Massachusetts Title Ins Co, 5..
Brown v Mins 100
Brown v Montgomery, 109
Brown v Natles, 483
Brown v Perkins, 422 515
Brown v Purvance, 100
Brown v Randall, 395
Brown v Rice's Admr, 360
Brown v Schnett, 123
Brown v Smith, 91
Brown v Stackhouse, 412
Brown v. Swineford, 235
Brown v Vannaman, 300
Brown v Willoughby, 391
Browne v. Dawson, 469
Brownell v Carnley, 142.
Browner v Sterdevant, 81
Browning v Cover 448
Browning v Magill, 414.
Brownlie v Campbell, 352
Brownstein v Wiles, 393
Bruce v Soule, 299.
Bruch v Carter, 425
Bruck v Carter, 412
Brueshaber v Hertling, 305
Brunsden v Humphrey, 224
Brunsing v White, 621
Brushaber v Stegeman, 259
Brushberg v Milw etc Ry Co, 504
Brush Electric Lighting Co v Kelly, 568
Bryan v Bates, 262
Bryan v Gurr, 347
Bryant v Clifford, 432
Bryant v Herbert, 16
Bryant v Lefever, 509
B S O & B R v Rainbolt, 629
Bubb v Yelverton, 431
Buchanan v Howland, 225
Buchanan v West Jersey R Co, 593
Buck v Hersey 300, 301
Buck v Penn R Co, 637
Buckley v Artcher, 357
Buckley v Gross, 451
Buckley v. Knapp, 309
Buckstaff v Vinll, 287, 311
Budd v Hiler, 658

Buddenberg v. Chouteau Transp Co., 575.
Buddington v. Shearer, 529
Buddington v Smith, 151.
Buddle v. Wilson, 650
Buenching v St Louis Gaslight Co., 69
Buffalo Lubricating Oil Co v Standard Oil Co, 66, 67.
Bukup v Valentine, 473
Bullard v Saratoga Victory Mfg Co, 153
Bullers v Dickinson, 611.
Bullis v Chicago, etc Ry Co, 561
Bullock v Babcock, 59, 503.
Bullock v. Koon, 311
Bulmer v. Bulmer, 78
Bulpit v Mathews, 473.
Bump v. Betts, 395
Bunnell v Greathead, 274
Burckhalter v Coward, 826
Burch v Carter, 9, 10
Burchy v Town of Lake, 157
Burdett v Abbott, 473.
Burditt v Swenson, 505
Burford v Wible, 291, 295.
Burger v Carpenter, 673
Burgess v Burgess, 185
Burgess v Graham, 425.
Burgett v Burgett, 398
Burke v Mascarich, 301, 321
Burke v Milwaukee, etc, Ry Co, 353
Burke v Norwich R. Co, 95
Burke v. Shaw, 108
Burke v Smith, 33, 509
Burke v Ryan, 329.
Burkett v Griffith, 388.
Burkett v Lanata, 217, 395
Burling v Read, 513
Burlingame v Burlingame, 294, 329
Burlinghand v Wylee, 265
Burlington R Co v Westover, 44, 562
Burmis v North, 395
Burnard v Haggis, 62
Burnett v Stanton, 368
Burnham v Hotchkiss, 404
Burnham v Stevens, 138
Burnley v. Cook, 483.
Burns v Chicago etc R. Co., 546
Burns v Dockray, 369
Burns v Erben, 263
Burns v Grand Rapids, etc, Co., 82
Burns v Hill, 60.
Burns v Poulsom, 101.
Burns v. State, 253
Burnside v Matthews, 59
Burrill v. Stevens, 169
Burroughs v Housatonic R Co, 153, 562
Burroughs v Saterlee, 178
Burrous v Alter, 319
Burrowes v Lock 227 371
Burrowes v. Lock, 227, 371
Burrows v Erie R Co, 595
Burt v Advertiser Newsp Co, 316, 318
Burt v Bowles, 556
Burt v McBruin, 306
Burtch v. Nickerson, 302
Burton v Calloway, 142, 479
Burton v Davis, 164.
Burton v Fulton, 403
Burton v Galveston & H R Co., 91
Burton v March, 317.
Burton v McClellan, 199, 475, 503
Burton v Scherff, 459
Burton v Wilkinson, 471
Buzzell v. Manufacturing Co, 117

TABLE OF CASES CITED.

The References are to Pages.

Busch v. Wentee, 418
Busch v. Wilcox, 383
Bush v. Bronner, 331
Bush v. Holmes, 683
Bush v. Stahman, 94
Busteed v. Parsons, 138
Busterrud v. Farrington, 167
Butcher v. Providence G. Co., 620
Butcher v. Nack V. etc., R. Co., 44
Butchers etc. Co. v. Crescent City etc. Co., 399
Butchers' Ice, etc., Coal Co. v. City of Philadelphia, 69
Butler v. Collins, 114
Butler v. Kent, 148
Butler v. McLellan, 151
Butler v. M. S. & L. R. Co., 160
Butler v. Townsend, 120
Butler Co. v. McCann, 279
Butterfield v. Ashley, 275
Butterfield v. Buffum, 112
Butterfield v. Forrester, 577, 578
Byam v. Bickford, 117
Byam v. Collins, 335
Byard v. Holmes, 175
Byers v. Chapin, 632
Byne v. Hatcher, 87
Byrket v. Monahan, 305, 826
Byrne v. Bondie, 636
Byrne v. New York Cent. etc. R. Co., 584
Byrnes v. New York, etc., R. Co., 120

C.

Cabbot v. Cristie, 363
Cade v. Redditt, 202, 315
Cady v. Case, 220, 689
Cagger v. Lansing, 514
Cahill v. Eastman, 193, 634
Cahills v. Layton, 164
Cahoon v. Bayard, 168
Cairo etc. R. Co. v. Warsley, 157
Calder v. Halket, 139
Caldwell v. Arnold, 112
Caldwell v. Brown, 117
Caldwell v. Farrell, 9, 186
Caldwell v. Fenwick, 429
Caldwell v. Henry, 367
Caldwell v. Neely, 148
Caldwell v. New Jersey Steamboat Co., 515
Cole v. Fisher, 618
Caledonian R. Co. v. Walker's Trustees, 155
California Fig Syrup Co. v. Improved Fig Syrup Co., 225
Calkins v. Barger, 503
Calkins v. Sumner, 329
Calkins v. Wheaton, 312
Callahan v. Bean, 585
Callahan v. Burlington R. Co., 92
Callahan v. Warne, 615
Callins v. Hayte, 391
Calliope, The, 630
Callis v. Selden, 632
Galloway v. Burr, 394
Calvert v. Rice, 429
Calvert v. Stone, 471
Calvin v. Holbrook, 112
Calvin v. Peabody, 561
Cameron v. Tribune Ass'n, 323, 333
Camp v. Ganley, 142

Camp v. Hamlin, 683
Camp v. Martin, 801
Camp v. Mosley, 141
Camp v. Wood, 627
Campau v. Campau, 447
Campbell v. Bannister, 296
Campbell v. Bear River Co., 665
Campbell v. Bridwell, 610
Campbell v. Brown, 611
Campbell v. Campbell, 296, 311
Campbell v. Carter, 272
Campbell v. Cooper, 276
Campbell v. Indianapolis, etc., R. Co., 462
Campbell v. Moore, 606
Campbell v. N. E. Mut. Life Ins. Co., 25
Campbell v. Northern Pac. R. Co., 103
Campbell v. Perkins, 61
Campbell v. Phelps, 231
Campbell v. Portland Sugar Co., 627
Campbell v. Pullman Palace Car Co., 105
Campbell v. Race, 670
Campbell v. Seaman, 500, 489, 491
Campbell v. Spottiswoode, 319
Campbell v. Stairt, 116
Campbell v. Stokes, 62
Campbell v. Stillwater, 29, 42
Campbell etc. Co. v. Manhattan etc. Ry. Co., 225
Camp Point Mfg. Co. v. Ballon, 193
C. & A. R. R. Co. v. Pennell, 45
Candee v. Deere, 184
C. & J. R. v. Newell, 629
Candy v. Lindsay, 415
Canefox v. Crenshaw, 611
Cannavan v. Conklin, 628
Canning v. Williamston, 55
Cannon v. Bart, 410
Cannon v. Windsor, 59
Cape v. Scott, 173
Capital and Counties Bank v. Henty, 313
Carder v. Forehand, 281
Cardiff v. Louisville etc., R. Co., 107
Cordival v. Smith, 395
Cardwell v. American Bridge Co., 156
Carew v. Rutherford, 258, 275, 407, 672
Cary v. Berkshire R. Co., 60
Carey v. Ledbetter, 502
Carey v. Rae, 476
Cargill v. Slate, 261
Carl v. Ayers, 394
Carle v. Bangor, etc., R. Co., 117
Carleton v. Akron Sewer Pipe Co., 261
Carleton v. Franconia Iron Co., 627
Carleton v. Haywood, 63, 64, 65s
Carleton v. Redington, 459, 464
Carlett v. Leavenworth, 633
Carll v. Union Depot, etc. Co., 520
Carlisle v. Cooper, 522
Carlsbad, City of v. Tibbetts, 225
Carme v. Rauh, 680
Carmichael v. Dolen, 252
Carmichael v. Shiel, 295
Cornelius v. Hambey, 274
Carney v. Hadley, 225
Carona v. Galveston, etc., R. Co., 120
Carpenter v. Bailey, 315
Carpenter v. Carpenter, 60
Carpenter v. Gardiner, 447
Carpenter v. Mendenhall, 447
Carpenter v. Mexican Nat R. Co., 122
Carpue v. London & Brighton R. Co., 542
Carr v. Easton, 271
Carr v. North River Const Co., 120

TABLE OF CASES CITED.

The References are to Pages.

Carr v State, 248
Carrico v West Virginia C & P. Ry Co., 541
Carrigan v Union Sugar Refinery, 634
Carrington v Taylor, 405
Carroll v Mix, 115.
Carroll v Mo Pac R. Co., 81
Carroll v White, 295, 301
Carroll v Wisconsin Cent R Co., 600
Carsluke v Mapledoram, 100
Carson v Edgeworth, 393
Carson v Prater, 419
Carstairs v. Taylor, 607
Cartarso v The Burgundia, 583
Carter v Andrews, 295, 296
Carter v Columbia & G R Co., 538
Carter v Dow, 148
Carter v Good, 234
Carter v Hobbs, 612
Carter v Howe Machine Co., 63
Carter v Jackson, 64
Carter v Kingman, 410.
Carter v Louisville, etc., Ry Co., 104, 55, 567
Carter v Towne, 503
Cartwright R, 128
Cary v Allen, 288
Case v Buckley, 294
Case v North Cent R Co., 562
Case v Shepherd, 138
Case v Youghton, 363
Casebeert v Drahable, 395
Casey v Cincinnati Type Union, 410
Casey v Hanrick, 399
Casey v Severson, 394
Cass v Anderson, 295
Casselman v Winship, 297
Cassidy v Navigation Co., 585.
Cassidy v Angel, 546
Cassin v Delaney, 64
Castle v Ballard, 384
Castle v Duryee, 167, 618
Castle v Houston, 123
Castleberg v Kelley, 81
Casto v De Uriarte, 393.
Catawissa etc R Co v. Armstrong, 544
Cate v Cate, 9, 40, 112
Cates v Kellog, 315, 316
Catlin v Valentine, 606
Catlin v Warren, 369
Catron v Nichols, 503
Cattle v Harold, 225
Catzhausen v Simon, 378
Caughey v Smith, 276
Caules v Pitts, etc. Ry Co., 583
Caulfield v Bullock, 148
Cavanaugh v Austin, 324
Cavanaugh v Dinsmore, 95, 100
Caverly v McOwen, 27
Cawles v State, 248
Cawthorn v Deas, 109
Cazzer v Taylor, 538
C B C P R. Co v Hotham, 552
Center v Spring, 193
Central Bank v Copeland, 375
Central, etc R Co v Davis, 610
Central Pass, etc., Co v Kuhn, 637
Central L Co v Crosby, 568
Central R Co v Moore, 538
Central R Co v Peacock, 110
Central R Co v Sears, 568
Central R Co of Venezuela v Kisch, 79
Central Trust Co v Wabash, St L & P R Co., 121

Certwell v Hoyt, 218
Chaddock v Briggs, 299, 301.
Chaffee v Pease, 9
Chaffie v. Old Colony R. Co., 544
Chaffin v. Lynch, 337.
Chamber v. State, 251.
Chamberlain v Boyd, 293
Chamberlain v. Hazlewood, 275.
Chamberlain v. Masterson, 642
Chamberlain v Ward, 90
Chamberlain v. Williamson, 73, 486
Chambers v Bedell, 469
Champaign, City of, v Jones, 552
Champion v Vincent, 213
Champlain v Rowley, 535
Champney v. Smith, 454.
Chandler v. Ricker, 147.
Chandler v Walker, 422
Chanviere v. Filage, 64
Chapman v. Atlantic, etc R Co., 504
Chapman v Auckland Union, 520
Chapman v. Bostwick, 114
Chapman v Calder, 319
Chapman v Dodd, 396
Chapman v Dyett, 265
Chapman v Morgan, 238
Chapman v Mutch, 454
Chapman v New Haven Railroad Co., 518
Chapman v New York, etc, R Co., 104.
Chapman v. Rothwell, 627
Chapman v State, 218
Chapman v. W U Tel Co., 55, 56
Charlebois v. Gogebic & M R. Co., 92
Charles v. Elliott, 420
Charles v Taylor, 121.
Charless v Rankin, 216.
Charlock v Freed, 92
Chase v Broughton, 358.
Chase v Chase, 611.
Chase v Fish, 262.
Chase v Hazleton, 420.
Chase v Maine etc R Co., 569
Chasemore v Richards, 178, 179, 182
Chase v Silverton, 178
Chase v. W U Tel Co., 56
Chasemore v Richards, 602.
Chataigne v Bergeron, 503, 618, 617
Chatfield v Wilson, 153, 178, 182
Chatham Furnace Co v Moffatt, 364
Chautauqua Lake Ice Co v. McLuckey, 552
Cheatham v Shearon, 498, 503
Cheeney v Nebraska etc., Stone Co., 40
Cheever v Ladd, 70
Cheever v Sweet, 394
Chellis v Chapman, 222, 685
Chenango v Lewis Bridge Co., 529
Cherokee Nation v State of Georgia, 133
Cherry v Stein, 509.
Chesapeake, etc., R. Co v. Higgins, 211
Chesebro v Powers, 388
Chester v Dickinson, 114, 383
Chevalier v Strahan, 606
Chicago v Anderson Pressed Brick Co., 125.
Chicago v Dermody, 69.
Chicago v Elzeman, 218
Chicago v Hessing, 82
Chicago v Huenerbein, 520.
Chicago v Jones, 69
Chicago v Martin, 235
Chicago v Mayor, 81
Chicago v Robbins, 93.

TABLE OF CASES CITED.

The References are to Pages.

Chicago v. Starr, 42
Chicago & A. R. Co v Fisher, 684
Chicago & A. R. Co. v. Murphy, 116
Chicago & A. R. Co v Suffern, 601
Chicago & E. I. R. v Henry, 122
Chicago & E. R. Co v Flexman, 105
Chicago & G. W. R. Co v Travis, 104
Chicago, K. & W. R. Co v Willochy, 240
Chicago, M. & S. R. Co v Ross, 129
Chicago, M. & St. P. R. Co v West, 101, 104
Chicago & N. W. Ry Co v Tulto, 240
Chicago, B. & Q. R. Co v Casey, 100
Chicago, B. & Q. R. Co v Harwood, 540
Chicago, B. & Q. R. Co v Landauer, 544
Chicago, B. & S. R. Co v Epperson, 108
Chicago, City of, v Babcock, 240
Chicago City R Co v Hennessey, 92
Chicago City Ry Co v. Robinson, 544
Chicago, D. & D. Co v. McMahon, 123
Chicago, etc. Co v Schroeder, 82
Chicago etc R Co v Doyle, 125
Chicago, etc., R. Co. v Flagg, 224
Chicago etc R Co v Grablin, 584
Chicago, etc. R Co v Johnson, 517
Chicago etc R Co v Landstrom, 124
Chicago etc R Co v Mahoney, 193
Chicago, etc R Co v. McCahill, 504
Chicago, etc., R Co v McKean, 223
Chicago etc R Co v McLanien, 544
Chicago etc R Co v. Moranda, 124
Chicago etc, R Co v Morris, 82
Chicago, etc., R Co v Patchin, 610
Chicago, etc R v. People, 654
Chicago etc R Co v Quaintance, 662
Chicago etc R Co v Ross, 123
Chicago, etc R Co v Sawyer, 606
Chicago, etc., R Co. v. Swett, 82
Chicago etc R Co v West, 126
Chicago, etc., R Co v Wilson, 218
Chicago etc Ry Co v. Becker, 164
Chicago R Co. v Shea, 608
Chicago R Co v Volk, 91
Chicago, R I & P R Co v Conklin, 101
Chicago, St L & P R Co. v Williams, 43
Chidester v Consolidated D. Co., 605
Chifferell v Watson, 219
Child v Hearn, 587, 615.
Childress v Yourie, 37.
Childrey v Huntington, 45
Childs v Kansas City R. Co , 448
Childs v Merrill, 369.
Chiles v Drake, 220, 618.
Chinery v Viall, 445, 653
Chipman v Hibberd, 518
Chipman v Palmer, 520, 529
Chisholm v Atlanta Gas Light Co , 620.
Chisholm v Georgia, 136
Chism v Martin, 613
Chivery v Strecker, 491
Chope v Eureka, 70
Chrisman v Carney, 261, 264.
Christal v Craig, 297
Christopherson v Bare, 255.
Chrysler v Canaday, 357
Chunot v. Larson, 614
Church v Mansfield, 108.
Church v Mellville, 414
Church v Sparrow, 114
Churchhill v Holt, 232
Churchill v. Hulbert, 206
Chynoweth v Tenney, 158.
Cincinnati v. Stone, 91.

Cincinnati etc R Co, v. Butler, 694
Cincinnati, etc R Co v Howard, 557
Cincinnati, etc, R Co v Mealor, 140
Cincinnati, etc., R. Co v Smith, 64
Cincinnati, etc R Co v Watterson, 640
Cincinnati Gazette Co v Timberlake, 41
Cincinnati, H & D R Co v McMullen, 124
Citizens Loan F & S Assn v Friendly, 26
Citizens Natural Gas Co v Shenango Natural Gas Co , 224
Claflin v Boston & A R Co, 46
Claflin v Carpenter, 159
Clapp v Kemp, 91
Clarissy v Metropolitan Fire Dept , 69
Clark v Adams, 611
Clark v Baird, 158
Clark v Bayer, 64
Clark v. Bond, 112
Clark v Chambers, 48, 49, 53, 54, 502, 504
Clark v. Cregg, 147
Clark v Downing, 251
Clark v Epworth, 70
Clark v Fitch, 91, 278, 311
Clark v Foote, 617
Clark v Fry, 87
Clark v Holmes, 118
Clark v Kelliher, 202
Clark v Lake St Clair, etc Ice Company, 515
Clark v Lovering, 618
Clark v Molyneux, 139, 345
Clark v. Munsell, 315
Clark v Peckham, 518
Clark v Trail, 213
Clark v Woods, 111
Clarke v Vermont & J R Co , 92
Clarkson v McCarty, 292, 315, 316, 315
Clay v. Caperton, 262
Clay v State, 309
Clayards v Dethick, 593
Cleather v Twisten, 111
Clegg v Boston etc, Co , 438.
Cleghorn v N Y Cent etc , R Co , 67
Cleland v Fish, 162
Clem v Holmes, 251
Clem v Newcastle, etc , R Co , 360
Clemence v Auburn, 70
Clemence v Steere, 429, 430
Clement v Hawks Man Co , 683
Clement v Wafer, 64
Clements v Louisiana Electric Co , 564
Clendening v Ohl, 482
Cleveland v Citizens Gas Light Co , 504, 505
Cleveland v Gas Light Co , 495, 496
Cleveland v Rogers, 262
Cleveland Co operative Stove Co v Wheeler, 624
Cleveland etc R Co v Asbury, 557
Cleveland etc R Co v Crawford 557
Cleveland, etc R Co v Elliott, 610
Cleveland Rolling Mill v Corrigan, 584
Clews v Traer, 215
Clifton v Grayson, 264, 265
Cline v Crescent City R R Co , 674
Clinton v Nelson, 262
Claton v York, 277
Close v Cooper, 201, 256
Closson v Staples, 398
Clough v L and N W R Co , 339
Clouser v Clapper, 274

TABLE OF CASES CITED 699

The References are to Pages.

Clowes v. Staffordshire Potteries Water works Co., 520
Clute v. Wiggins, 612
Coal Grommet, 148
Coal Creek M Co. v Davis, 120
Cobb v. Columbia & G R Co., 100
Cobb v. Smith, 529
Coburn v. Harwood, 29
Coburn v. Kennedy, 189
Cochran v. Ammon, 281
Cochran v. Tobey, 260, 263
Cockly v. S I R Co., 559
Cocking v. Butterfield, 410
Codran v. Stewart, 680
Coe v. Schultz, 193
Coffeen v. Brunton, 225
Coffee v. Territory, 485
Coffey v. Myers, 49
Coggin v. Collin, 23
Cogborn v. Spence, 112
Cogswell v. Baldwin, 611
Cogswell v. New York, etc R Co., 185, 46
Cohen v. Dry Dock, etc, R Co., 110
Cohen v. Mayor etc of New York, 187
Coit v. Wallace, 222
Coit v. Lyne, 648
Coker v. Birge, 50
Coker v. Crozier, 81
Colby v. Reynolds, 288
Cole v. City of Muscatine, 228
Cole v. Curtis, 391, 399
Cole v. Fisher, 503
Cole v. McGlathry?
Cole v. O'Brien, 660
Cole v. Turner, 247, 254
Cole v. Perry, 316
Colegrove v. New York, etc R Co., 230
Coleman v. Chadwick, 216
Coleman v. Coleman, 147
Coleman v. New York, etc, R Co., 105
Coleman v. Playstead, 295, 334
Collen v. Wright, 74, 660
Collins v. Davidson, 589
Collins v. Evans, 362
Collins v. Jackson, 58
Collins v. Love, 373
Collins v. White, 273
Coleman v. Wilmington, C & A R Co., 123
Cole S M Co v Virginia etc Co., 225
Collard v. Marshall, 226
Collard v. Marshall, 47
Collins v. Lyins, 232
Collins v. Mick, 222, 685
Collins Co v Marcy, 459
Colls v. Selden, 667
Colly v. Cressy, 432
Colorado Cent R Co v Martin, 552
Colorado etc R Co v Holmes, 567
Colorado M R Co v O'Brien, 123, 194
Colorado M R Co v Naylon, 124
Colrick v. Swinburne, 244, 520
Colt v. McMechen, 606
Colton v. Onderdonk, 615
Columbus etc R Co v. Bridges, 537
Columbus etc R Co v Farrell, 558
Columbus v. Jaques, 487
Columbus & I R Co v O'Brien, 121
Columbus Gas Light, etc. Co v Freeland, 505
Colvin v. Peabody, 99
Combs v. Rose, 58
Come v. Knowles, 250

Comer v. Knowles, 267
Comer v Taylor, 270
Comerford v Dufruy, 610
Commings v Stevenson, 503, 519
Commissioners v Bank, 228
Commissioners v Duckett, 24
Commissioners of Sewers v Glasse, 514
Commonwealth v. Blabsdell, 192
Commonwealth v Blanding, 107, 314
Commonwealth v. Bonner, 10
Commonwealth v. Boston & M R Co, 558
Commonwealth v Brown, 504, 508
Commonwealth v Calley, 149
Commonwealth v. Chapu, 321
Commonwealth v Coilberg, 187
Commonwealth v. Croushore, 523
Commonwealth v Deacon, 263
Commonwealth v Elkner, 201
Commonwealth v. Farris, 485
Commonwealth v Harris, 195
Commonwealth v Hunt, 410
Commonwealth v. Hurley, 250
Commonwealth v Kennard, 256
Commonwealth v Kneeland, 313
Commonwealth v Malone, 257
Commonwealth v Mann, 258
Commonwealth v McAfee, 150
Commonwealth v McLaughlin, 251
Commonwealth v Morgan, 310
Commonwealth v Oakes, 195
Commonwealth v Parker, 185
Commonwealth v Perry, 485
Commonwealth v Pierce, 2 5, 542
Commonwealth v. Power, 651
Commonwealth v Reed, 505
Commonwealth v Ruddle, 485
Commonwealth v Snelling, 105, 134
Commonwealth v Stratton, 248
Commonwealth v Upton, 498, 506
Commonwealth v Webb, 485, 487
Commonwealth v White, 250, 256
Commonwealth v. Wilkesbarre & L S Ry Co, 485
Concord Bank v Gregg, 112
Cone v Godshalk, 313
Congreve v. Morgan, 87
Conhocton Stone Co. v Buffalo, etc Ry, 529
Conklin v N. Y., O & W R Co, 485
Conklin v Thompson, 61, 503, 615
Conkling v Pacific Imp. Co, 225
Conley v Portland, 122
Conlon v Eastern R Co, 98
Conlon v Oregon, etc R Co, 193
Connecticut Ins Co v New York, etc, R Co, 30
Connecticut Mut. Life Ins Co v New York & N H R Co, 80
Connell v W U Tel. Co, 56
Connelly v Wood, 138
Conner v Pioneer Fire proof Const Co, 218
Conradt v Clanve, 503, 627
Conroy v Pittsburgh Times, 334
Conroy v Vulcan Iron Works, 194
Consolidated Coal Co v Bonner, 125
Consolidated Coal Co v. Wombacker, 123
Consolidated Ice M Co v Keifer, 97
Continental Imp Co v Stead, 556
Converse v Blumrich, 353
Convers v Walker, 627
Conway v Reed, 61

TABLE OF CASES CITED.

The References are to Pages.

Conway v. Russell, 9.
Cook v. Anderson, 503.
Cook v. Chicago etc. Ry Co, 215
Cook v. Clinton, 417.
Cook v. Cool, 291
Cook v. Flin, 235.
Cook v. Hopper, 230
Cook v. Johnston, 503
Cook v. New York etc. R. Co., 629
Cook v. Pridgeon, 162
Cook v. Stearns, 158, 639
Cook v. St. Paul, etc R Co., 192
Cook v. Walker, 302.
Cook v. Wood, 271
Cook v. Forbes, 523
Cooke v. Nathan, 361
Cool v. Crommet, 611.
Coolidge v. Alcock, 245.
Coolidge v. Neat, 222
Combs v. Purington, 109
Coomes v. Houghton, 87
Coons v. Robinson, 296
Cooper v. Barber, 321
Cooper v. Crabtree, 183
Cooper v. Langway, 302
Cooper v. Lovering, 358
Cooper v. McJunkin, 110
Cooper v. McKenna, 218
Coon v. Mafflit, 277
Cooper v. Mullins, 116, 124.
Cooper v. Newman, 139
Cooper v. Phipps, 239
Cooper v. Randall, 518
Cooper v. State, 250
Cooper v. Stone, 321
Cooper v. Utterback, 193, 196
Cooper v. Willomatt, 113, 114
Copen v. Foster, 148
Copley v. G & B Sewing Machine Co, 68
Copley v. New Haven R Co, 557
Copper v. Lee, 215
Copping v. New York & H R R Co, 125
Coplins v. New York, etc R Co, 514
Corby v. Hill, 465, 635, 640
Corbett v. Anderson, 683
Cornelius v. Van Slyke, 312
Cornell v. Electric Ry Co, 567
Cornell v. State, 150
Corner v. Mackintosh 87
Cornfoot v. Fowke, 385 386
Corning v. Troy, I & N Factory, 221
Cornish v. Accident Insurance Co, 197
Cornish v. Stubbs, 461
Corwin v. Walter, 255.
Cory v. Silcox, 213
Coryell v. Colbaugh, 222, 685.
Cotterell v. Jones, 401
Cotton v. Wood, 546, 547
Cotrell v. Crum, 377
Cottrill v. Chicago, M & St. P R Co, 568.
Couch v. Steele, 229
Coulson v. Panhandle Nat Bank, 683
Coulter v. Express Co, 595
Coulter v. Lower, 265.
Counties Bank v. Henty, 306.
Countryman v. Lighthill, 192
County of Nelson v. Northcot, 11
Coupal v. Ward, 262
Coupé Co v. Maddick, 433
Courtenay v. Earle, 649
Courtney v. Baker, 97
Coves v. Hannibal, etc R Co, 19.

Covington St. Ry Co v. Packer, 56.
Cowan v. Chicago etc R. Co, 125.
Coward v. Baddely, 264.
Cowles v. Balzer, 611
Cowlen v. Richmond, etc R Co., 124
Cowles v. Townsend, 360.
Cowley v. Colwell, 554
Cowley v. Davidson, 214
Cowley v. Pulsifer, 313.
Cowley v. Smith, 354
Cox v. Burbidge, 19, 610, 612.
Cox v. Douglass, 224
Cox v. Kenhey, 110
Cox v. Sullivan, 26.
Cox v. Syenite Granite Co., 123
Cox v. Whitfield, 271
Coxhead v. Richards, 337
Crafter v. Metrop R Co, 551, 563.
Crabtree v. Robinson, 471
Cracker v. Chicago, etc., R. Co., 218.
Crafts v. Boston, 516
Cragie v. Hadley, 67.
Craig v. Brown, 300
Craig v. Dee, 609
Craig v. Sedalia, 70
Craker v. Chicago & N W R Co, 67, 87.
Crandall v. Goodrich Transp Co, 538.
Crane v. Elder, 559
Crane v. Onderdonk, 618
Crane v. Waters, 321
Cranford v. Terrell, 188, 191
Crans v. Hunte, 112
Cranston v. Cincinnati etc R Co., 610
Crawford v. Doggett, 64
Crawford v. Parsons, 520
Crawford v. Wilson, 294
Crawson v. W U Tel Co., 56.
Credle v. Swindle, 157
Cressey v. Parks, 218
Croker v. Chicago & N W R Co., 100
Cronsdale v. Bright, 309, 310
Crocker v. Gulliver, 111
Crocker v. New London, etc., R. Co., 103.
Crockett v. Calvert, 94
Cracknell v. Corporation of Thetford, 156
Croft v. Alison, 99
Croker v. Birge, 196.
Croker v. Mann, 473
Chance v. Angell, 206
Crankhite v. Crankhite, 153.
Crook v. Cole, 349
Cropsey v. Murphy, 501
Crosby v. Fitch, 606
Crosland v. Pottsville Borough, 516.
Cross v. Everts, 63
Cross v. Guthery, 81
Cross v. Kent, 59
Cross v. Peters, 551
Crossley v. Lightowler, 498.
Croswell v. Jackson, 368
Crousdale v. Lanigan, 462
Crow v. State, 250
Crowell v. Gleason, 260
Crowhurst's Case, 605
Crowhurst v. Amersham Burial Board, 604
Crowley v. Strouse, 544
Crown v. Leonard, 482
Cruess v. Fessler, 558
Cruikshank v. Gordon, 301
Crumble v. Wallsend Local Board, 214.
Crump v. Lambert, 490, 505
Crusselle v. Pugh, 100

TABLE OF CASES CITED.

The References are to Pages.

Crystal v. Craig, 314
Cubitt v. O'Dell, 40
Cuddy v. Horn, 549
Cuervo v. Jacob Henkel Co., 225
Culf v. Newark, etc., R. Co., 593
Cuhady v. Powell, 389
Cubban v. Norton, 123
Cullen v. Thompson's Trustees and Kerr, 5
Cullum v. Branch Bank, 358
Culp v. Culp, 213
Calver v. Chicago etc. Ry Co., 211
Culver v. Rhodes, 147
Culver v. Smart, 160
Culver v. Decker, 580
Cumber and v. Wilson, 69
Cumberland R. Co. v. Mangans, 552
Cummings v. Cass, 367
Cummins v. National Furnace Co., 637
Cummings v. Wyman, 418
Cumpston v. Lambert, 231
Cundy v. Lindsay, 641
Cunningham v. Hall, 538, 542
Cunningham v. Union Pac R Co., 124
Currie v. Richardson, 326
Currier v. Boston Music Hall, 627
Currier v. Brown, 230
Curry v. Collins, 207
Curry v. Pringle, 201
Curtin v. Patton, 60
Curtis v. Carson, 256
Curtis v. Hubbard, 471
Curtis v. Murphy, 612, 651
Curtis v. Mussey, 395, 810
Curtis v. Perkins, 323
Curtis v. Winslow, 506
Curtis & Co Mfg Co v. Williams, 631
Cushing v. Adams, 479, 639
Cushman v. Ryan, 151
Custard v. Burdett, 213
Cuthbert v. Galloway, 396
Cutler v. Smith, 463
Cutts v. Spring, 151
Czarnicchi's Appeal, 505

D.

Dan, The, 639
D & W R v. Spicker, 629
Dahl v. Piper, 329
Dade Coal Co v. Haslett, 59
Daring v. State, 262
Daggett v. Wallace, 222
Daley v. Houston, 63, 64
Dain v. Wyckoff, 277
Dale v. Grant, 29
Dallas etc R Co v. Spicker, 569
Dalston v. Janson, 649
Dalton v. Angus, 157, 509
Dalton v. S E R Co., 79
Dalvell v. Tyrer, 95, 661
Dame v. Baldwin, 411
Dame v. Kenny, 116
Damon v. Moore, 278
Damont v. Lyons, 591
Dan v. Fielder, 684
Dan v. Valentine, 505
Dand v. Sexton, 425
Danenhoter v. State, 149
Danforth v. Walker, 683
Daniel v. Chesapeake & O R Co., 121
Daniel v. Ferguson, 522
Daniel v. Metrop. R. Co., 592
Daniel v. Swearengen, 270
Daniel v. Town of Princeton (Ky.), 225
Danila v. Clegg, 108
Daniels v. Keokuk Water Works, 590
Daniels v. New York etc. R., 585
Daniels v. Union P R Co., 121
Danner v. South Carolina R Co., 611
Danville etc. Co. v. Stewart, 549
Darcautel v. People's Slaughter house Ref Co, 485
D'Arcy v. Miller, 610
Dargan v. Ellis, 350, 357
Dargan v. Waddill, 405, 504
Darle v. Briggs, 243
Dark v. Johnson, 464
Darley Main Colliery Co v. Mitchell, 214
Darlin v. Stewart, 357
Darmstaetter v. Moynahan, 91
Darnell v. Sallee, 395
Douglass v. Winslow, 401
Daunce v. Daw, 632
Davenport v. Buckman, 627
Davey v. L & S W R. Co, 598
Davidson v. Abbott, 278, 279, 281
Davidson v. Goodall, 218
Davidson v. Isham, 504, 528
Davidson v. Nichols, 26, 621
Davidson v. Smith, 64
Davidson v. Southern P Co, 193
Davidson v. Wheeler, 350
Davidson v. Young, 60
Davie v. Levy, 536
Davie v. Wisher, 394, 396
Davies, Ex parte, 412
Davies v. Griffith, 125
Davies v. Johnston, 311
Davies v. Mann, 576, 577, 578, 579
Davies v. Marshall, 190
Davies v. Snead, 336
Davies v. Solomon, 293
Davies v. Williams, 513
Davis v. Brown, 291
Davis v. Carey, 297
Davis v. Central Congregational Soc., 627
Davis v. Chapman, 512
Davis v. Davis, 300
Davis v. Detroit, etc R. Co, 193
Davis v. Duncan, 321
Davis v. Gardiner, 293
Davis v. Gilliam, 429
Davis v. Graham, 194
Davis v. Guarnieri, 621
Davis v. Heard, 353, 363
Davis v. Jackson, 358
Davis v. Lyon, 323
Davis v. New York, etc. Co., 82
Davis v. Michigan B T Co, 631
Davis v. Saunders, 172
Davis v. Sawyer, 495
Davis v. Seeley, 376
Davis v. Shepstone, 323, 310
Davis v. Sladden, 291
Davis v. Webster, 142
Davis v. Werden, 306
Davis v. Whitridge, 201
Davis v. Wilson, 262
Dawkins v. Antrobus, 147
Dawkins v. Gulf C & S F R. Co, 100
Dawkins v. Lord Paulet, 331
Dawkins v. Lord Rokeby, 140, 330
Dawning v. McFadden, 145

TABLE OF CASES CITED.

The References are to Pages.

Dawkins v Prince Edward of Saxe Weimar, 140, 340.
Dawson v Holt, 250
Day v Brownrigg, 185, 391.
Day v. Day, 615
Dayharsh v. Hannibal & St. J R Co., 121.
Dayton v. Hoogland, 633
Dayton v Wilkes, 310.
Deal v Harris, 118
Dealey v. Muller, 552
Dean v Ann Arbor St Ry Co., 156
Dean v McLean, 635, 639.
Dean v Peel, 280
Dean v St Paul Union Depot Co, 634.
Deane v. Bennett, 117, 118
Deane v Clayton, 204
Deane v Randolph, 60
Dearborn v Dearborn, 26
Dearborn v Downing, 632
Dearth v Baker, 614
DeBawn v Bean, 154
Decker v Gaylord, 421
Decker v Shepherd, 400
DeCourcy v Cox, 264.
Decaux v. Lieux, 395
Deday v. Lowell, 312
Dee v Hyland, 241
Deeley v Dwight, 132
Deford v State, 92
De Francis v Spencer, 164
Degg v Midland R Co, 126
DeGraff v New York, etc R Co, 193
DeGraffenried v Mitchell, 171
DeHaro v U. S, 464
Dehring v. Comstock, 534, 550, 634
Diehl v Ottenville, 110.
De La Grang v S W T Co, 674
DeLimatyr v Railroad Co, 558
DeLaney v Blizzard, 189
Delancy v Erickson, 453, 611
Delaney v Knetel, 313, 334
Delaney v Rochereau, 645
Del & H C Co v Clark, 184
Delaware & H C Co v Torrey, 213
Delaware etc Ins Co. v Croasdale, 106, 323
Delaware, etc R Co v Salmon, 41, 647
Dells v Stollenwerk, 100, 108
Delphi v Lowery, 211.
Delvec v Boardman, 276
Delz v. Winfree, 103
DeMarentile v Oliver, 251
Demarest v Hudham, 528.
Demarest v Haring, 294
Demarest v Little, 82
Democrat Pub Co v Jones, 291
Dempsey v Chambers, 87
Dempsey v Kipp 639
Den v Kinney, 429
Dench v Walker, 454
Denis v Leclerc, 224
Dennick v Railroad Co, 82
Dennis v Ryan, 294
Dennis v State 506
Denoe v Brandt, 369
Dent v King, 231
Denton v G N R Co, 373, 374, 387, 656, 676
Denver v Dunsmore, 70
Denver v Rhodes, 69
Denver & R G R v Harris, 67, 68
Denver & R G R Co v Ryan, 564
Denver, S P & P R Co v Conway, 99

Derry v. Peek, 354, 355, 356, 363, 366, 371, 373, 374, 376, 677.
Deskins v Gose, 149
Deslottes v Baltimore, etc, Tel. Co., 673.
Desmond v. Brown, 300
Detroit & Milwaukee R Co v Van Steinburg, 568
Detroit, City of, v. Beckman, 70,
Detroit Daily Post Co. v. McArthur, 313
Detroit etc R Co v Van Steinburg, 644
Devendorf v Wert, 213, 214.
Devine v McCormack, 370.
Devlin v. Gallagher, 615
Devlin v Smith, 92
Devlin v Snellenburg, 122
DeVosse v City of Richmond, 381
DeWahl v. Braune 60
Dewitt v Bailey, 643.
Dexter v Cole, 9, 40, 412, 422, 424
Dexter v McCready, 652
Dexter v Spear, 284, 288
Dexter v Faber 290.
Dial v Halter, 291
Diamond v Northern Pac R Co, 563.
Dibble v Jones, 60
Dicken v Shepherd, 313
Dickerson v Dickson, 284
Dickerson v Rogers, 654
Dickeson v Watson, 170
Dickey v Andros, 206
Dickey v Franklin Bank, 134
Dickinson v Barber, 59
Dickinson v Davis, 369
Dickinson v Gay, 632
Dickinson v N E R Co, 77
Dickson v Clifton, 649
Dicks v Brooks, 389, 390.
Dickson v Chicago, etc R Co., 530
Dickson v Dickson, 208, 673
Dickson v Hollister, 15, 591
Dickson v. Phillips, 296
Dickson v Reuter's Telegram Co., 674, 679.
Diehl v Lehigh Iron Co, 633
Dierks v Comm'rs of Highways, 485.
Dietrichs v Schaw, 264
Dillingham v Anthony, 110
Dillman v Nadlehoffer 358
Dillon v Washington G Co, 620
Dimmitt v Esridge, 187
Dingley v Buffum, 479
Disbrow v Tenbroeck, 443.
Dislie v Walther, 294
Ditcham v Bond, 275
Dittman v Repp, 520
Dixon v. Allen, 305 353
Dixon v Baker, 70
Dixon v Bell, 168, 582, 618, 619.
Dixon v Chicago & A R Co, 121.
Dixon v Clow, 9, 213
Dixon v Pluns, 634
Dobell v Napier, 210
Dobell v. Stevens 50
Dodd v Arnold, 414
Dodds v Henry, 101
Dodge v Colby, 188
Dodge v Essex Co, 157
Doggett v Adams, 214
Doggett v Richmond etc R Co., 42, 568
Doherty v Thayer 610
Dole v Erskine, 186, 201, 256
Dole v Lyon, 316
Dole v Van Rensselaer 301
Donaghue v Gaffy, 323

TABLE OF CASES CITED.

The References are to Pages.

Donahoe v. Richards, 143
Donahoe v. Wabash, etc. R Co, 509.
Donald v. Suckling, 414
Donaldson v. Farwell, 309
Donaldson v. Miss & Mo R Co, 97.
Donnelly v. Daggett, 305, 306
Donnelly v. Hufschmidt, 627.
Donovan v. Gay, 211.
Dooley v. Stringham, 410
Dooley v. Sullivan, 70
Dooley Block v. Salt Lake Rapid Transit Co, 155
Dorin v. Eaton, 375
Doran v. Smith, 61
Doro v. Milwaukee, 70
Doremus v. McCormick, 114
Dorland v. Patterson, 295 311, 312.
Dorrah v. Railroad Co, 55
Dorsey v. Manlove, 519
Dorsey v. Whipps, 297
Doss v. Jones, 324
Doss v. Secretary of State for India in Council, 134
Dottoyer v. Bushey, 298
Douce v. Pierce, 324
Daugherty v. Missouri R Co, 636
Daugherty v. Stepp 422
Dwight v. Penobscot Log Driving Co, 1"
Douglass v. Shumway, 159
Douglass v. Stephens, 91
Doulson v. Matthews, 240
Dow v. Julian, 224
Dow v. Sanborn, 969
Dowd v. Tucker 357
Dowell v. Guthrie, 545
Bowlen v. State, 140
Dowling v. Allen, 124
Downing v. Wilson, 294
Downs v. Allen, 213
Dows v. Rush, 650
Doyle v. Chicago, St. P & K C Ry Co, 567
Doyle v. Doyle, 260
Doyle v. Jessup 275
Doxley v. Roberts, 303
Dozier v. Pillot, 488
Drafus v. Aul 313,
Drain v. St Louis etc R Co, 557
Drake, Ex parte 437
Drake v. Wells 463
Draper v. Massachusetts, etc, Co, 680
Dresser v. Woods 552
Drew v. Comstock, 196
Drew v. Peer, 9
Dreyfus v. Aul 395
Dreyfus v. Peruvian Guano Co, 218, 521.
Drinkhorn v. Dubel 257
Driscoll v. Marshall, 438
Drish v. Davenport 281
Drohn v. Brewer, 40, 220, 683.
Drown v. Smith 429
Drum v. Harrison, 213
Drummond v. City of Eau Claire, 69
Drummond v. Leslie 311
Dube v. City of Lewiston, 122
Dublin, Wicklow and Wexford Ry Co v. Slattery 568 579
Dubois v. Allen, 276
Dubois v. Budlong, 505, 506
Du Boulay v. Du Boulay, 185
Dubuque Wood etc, Assn v. Dubuque 34
Duche v. Wilson 84

Duckworth v. Johnson, 70
Dudley v. Briggs, 388
Dudley v. Mayhew, 24
Duff v. Williams, 378
Duffies v. Duffies, 273
Duffus v. Judd, 611
Duffy v. Oliver, 122
Dufour v. Anderson, 425.
Duggins v. Watson, 110
Duincen v. Rick, 43
Duke of Brunswick v. Harmer, 308
Duke of Brunswick v. King of Hanover, 136
Dulaney v. Rogers, 367.
Dames v. McCloskey, 172
Dun v. Bank, 336
Dun v. Seaboard & R R Co, 567
Dunnley v. Rogers, 153
Duncan v. Cobby, 358
Duncan v. Commonwealth, 253
Duncan v. Godfrey, 504
Duncan v. Hayes, 508
Duncan v. Hogue 375
Duncan v. Niles, 660
Duncan v. Yordy, 449
Dungan v. Coreton, 337
Dunham v. Powers 328
Dunlap v. Snyder 516
Dunlap v. Wagner, 29
Dunn v. Austin, 503
Dunn v. Birmingham Canal Co, 606.
Dunn v. Gilman, 141
Dunn v. Hall, 310
Dunn v. Oldham, 367
Dunn v. White 379
Dunnell v. Fiske, 112
Dunning v. Bird, 202
Dunsbach v. Hollister, 514
Dunston v. Peter-on, 143
DuPratt v. Lick 92
Durand v. Borough of Ansonia, 157
Durand v. Hollins, 133
Durango, City of, v. Luttrells, 157.
Durant v. Palmer, 624
Durant v. Rogers, 184
Durfour v. Anderson, 432
Durham v. Musselman 614
Durkee v. Vt C Rd Co, 675
Durkin v. Cobleigh, 834
Duryea v. New York 519
Dus v. Fitzhugh, 567
Dustin v. McAndrews, 683
Dusy v. Helm, 205
Dutzi v. Geisel 589
Duval v. Davey, 324
Duvall v. Waters, 450
Dwain v. Discols, 394
Dwyer v. Hickler, 120
Dwyer v. St Louis, etc R Co, 194.
Dyer v. Erie Ry Co, 549
Dyer v. Hargrave, 379
Dyer v. St Louis & S F R Co, 211.

E

Fagan v. Call, 632
Eigan v. Fitchburg R. Co, 543
Fagin v. Murray, 276
Eager v. Grimwood, 280
Eagle Packing Co v. Defries 637
Eames v. New Eng Worsted Co, 505.

TABLE OF CASES CITED.

The References are to Pages.

Earl v Van Alstyne, 617.
Earle v. Hall, 91
Earl of Lonsdale v Nelson, 517, 493
Early v Fleming, 611
Earp v. Lee, 518
Eason v State, 262.
Eason v S. & E. T. Ry Co, 120
Easterbrook v. Erie R Co, 217
Eastman v Keasan, 395
Eastman v Rice, 473, 611.
East St L Packing Co v. Hightower, 193
East Tennessee R Co. v White, 556
East Tennessee etc R Co v Gurley, 125
Eaton v Avery, 357
Eaton v European R. Co, 91
Eaton v Hill, 62.
Eaton v. Lyman, 218
Eaton v Wenn, 619
Eaton v Winnie, 370, 378
Eberly v Rupp, 398, 400
Ecclesiastical Comm'rs v Kino, 511
Eckerson v Crippen, 459
Eckert v L. I. R Co, 508, 595
Eddy v Lafayette, 561
Edelman v Yenkel, 479, 610
Edgerly v Swain, 298
Edgington v Fitzmaurice, 356, 360, 368.
Edick v Crim, 851
Edmondson v City of Moberly, 489
Edmundson v Pittsburg, etc R Co, 92
Edrington v Louisville etc Ry Co, 561
Edwards v Ferguson, 145
Edwards v Knapp, 326
Edwards v L & N W R Co, 109
Edwards v Leavitt, 235
Edwards v Midland Rail Co, 197
Edwards v New York etc R Co., 627.
Edwards v San Jose 311
Edwick v. Hawkes, 466, 467
Eggleston v Lykes, 461
Ellenberger v Prot Mut F Ins Co, 112
Elam v Badger, 312
Elder v Allison, 361
Elder v Bemis, 87
Elder v Morrison, 111
Electro Silicon Co v Levy, 225
Elgin v Kimball, 69
Elias v Snowdon Slate Quarries Co, 428
Ellegard v Ackland, 99
Ellington v Ellington, 277, 278
Elliott, Ex parte, 237
Elliott v Brown, 201
Elliott v Hall, 630
Elliott v Herz, 614.
Elliott v Jackson, 658
Elliott v Russell, 605
Elliott v Van Buren, 325
Ellis v Andrews, 157, 359.
Ellis v Buzzell, 326
Ellis v Cleveland, 261
Ellis v Duncan, 178
Ellis v G W R Co, 558, 559
Ellis v Iowa City, 157
Ellis v Kansas City R Co, 50.
Ellis v Lindly, 326
Ellis v Loftus Iron Co, 49, 612.
Ellis v Portsmouth, etc R Co, 504
Ellis v Sheffield Gas Consumers Co, 86
Ellis v State, 485
Ellis v Wren, 482
Ellithorpe v Reidessell, 213
Ellsworth v Hayes, 291
Elmer v Fessenden, 158

Elmore v Brooks, 648.
Elsoy v Postal T Co, 674.
Elsmore v Longfellow, 142
Elster v City of Springfield, 176.
Elwell v. Martin, 91.
Elwood v W. U T. Co, 674
Ely v Ehle, 424.
Ely v Stewart 375.
Ely v Supervisors of Niagara County, 510
Ely v. Thomson, 118
Emblen v. Myers, 221
Emerson v Brigham, 370.
Emerson v. Cochran, 393, 400.
Emerson v McNamara, 658
Emory v Ginnan, 399.
Emery v. Gowen, 277
Emory v Hapgood, 265
Emery v Miller, 813
Emery v. Railroad, 644
Emmons v Pottle, 309
Enders v Beck, 61.
Enders v Board Public Works, 637.
Endsley v. Johns, 375
Engel v Smith, 594
England v Cowley, 437
Englehardt v State, 250.
English v. Powell, 418
English v Progress etc Co, 66.
Entick v Carrington, 10, 135, 491
Erber v Dunn, 348
Erd v Chicago, etc R. Co., 504.
Erie v Magill, 633
Erie Dispatch v Johnson, 443
Erie Pass Ry Co v Schuster, 583.
Erskine v Hohnback, 262
Erston v. Cramer, 306
Ernst v Hudson River R Co., 378.
Erwin v Davenport, 649
Erwin v. Olmstead, 447
Erwin v. Sumrow, 111
Escanaba v Chicago 156
Estahan v Card, 312.
Estes v Antrobus, 307
Estes v Worthington, 225
Estopinal v Peyroux, 138.
Esty v Wilmot, 179
Eswin v St Louis, etc Ry Co, 665.
Evans v American Iron & Tube Co., 17.
Evans v Bicknell, 381
Evans v Carbon Hill Coal Co., 193.
Evans v Davidson, 110.
Evans v Edmonds, 367
Evans v Lippincott 120
Evans v Mason, 443
Evans v McDermott, 613.
Evans v Miller, 658
Evans v Smith, 316
Evans v Waite, 186
Evans v Walton, 278.
Evans v Watrous, 26
Evansville, etc, R Co v Baum, 84, 168
Evansville, etc R Co. v Griffin, 67
Evansville & R R Co v Madux, 193.
Evening Journal Assn v McDermott, 67
Everett v Coffin, 439, 454
Everett v Henderson, 892.
Eveston v. Cramer, 323.
European etc Co v Royal Mail Co., 442
Ewing v Pittsburgh etc, Ry Co., 69.
Ewing v Rourke, 483
Ewing v Sanford, 393

TABLE OF CASES CITED.

The References are to Pages.

Excellent The, 630
Express Printing Co. v. Copeland, 251
Eyre, Ex parte, 111

F.

Faber v. Eiler, 391
Facundes v. Central P. R. Co., 120
Fahn v. Reichart, 182, 503
Fahr v. Hayes, 111
Fairbank v. Newton, 410
Fairchild v. Bentley, 611
Fairhurst v. Liverpool Adelphi Loan Ass'n, 45
Falk v. Carpenter, 81
Fales v. Addicks, 611
Falsom v. Brown, 158
Falvey v. Stanford, 212
Faly v. Mo. Pac. R. Co., 110
Farbh v. Bradford, 225
Farewell v. Boston & W. R. Co., 121
Farles v. Walton, 459
Farmers Co. Opr. Trust Co. v. Floyd 110
Farnam v. Brooks, 45
Farn v. Collr. States 146,
Farr v. Rusco 41,
Farrand v. Marshall 216, 19.
Farrant v. Barne, 619
Farrar v. Bridges, 56
Farrell v. Calwell 218
Farrell v. Cook 522
Farwell v. Becker 232
Farwell v. Boston, etc., Corporation 89-90, 113
Fa-- v. Roxbury, 652
Faucett v. Courtney, 251
Faulkes v. Metrop. District R. Co., 630
Faulkner v. Anderson, 478, 610
Fauster v. Parsons, 148.
Fay v. Davidson, 91
Fay v. Prentice, 193.
Fay v. Strawn 26
Fay v. Whitman, 506,
Fearn v. Shiley, 213
Fetch v. Allen 117
Felkner v. Scarlet 279
Fellows v. Oneida, 181
Felthum v. England, 124
Felton v. Deall 530
Fenville v. Condest, 26
Fenn v. Hitcheson 113
Fenton v. Toledo etc. Co. 44
Fenton v. Wilson S. M. Co., 68
Fergison v. Bobo, 60
Ferguson v. Brooks, 63
Ferguson v. Collins 65, 64
Ferguson v. Ermenich Mfg. Co. 519
Ferguson v. Wisconsin etc. R. Co., 557
Fernshee v. Meyer 279
Feroy v. Ruston 424
Ferrell v. Loskin 276
Ferrin v. Symonds 640
Ferris v. Welborn, 225
Ferry v. Manhattan P. Co., 542
Fertich v. Michermer, 149
Fevells v. Collins, 243
Fiddler v. McKinney 685
Field v. Delavan, 324
Field v. Colson, 401
Field v. New York Cent. R. Co., 561
Fields v. Rowse, 1,6
Filber v. Dantermann, 291, 512

Filber v. Hobb, 117
Filburn v. Aquarium, 811
Filer v. New York Cent. R. Co., 514, 595, 633
Filkbrown v. Hoar, 220
Filliter v. Phippard, 617.
Filson v. Crawford, 505
Finch v. Riverside & A. Ry. Co., 16
Findlay v. McAllister, 403
Fine Art Society v. Union Bank of London, 136
Fink v. Des Moines Ice Co. 123
Fink v. Missouri Furnace Co., 92
Finlay v. Chirney, 71, 680
Finley v. Hershey, 619
Finley v. Langston 504
Findley v. Smith, 129
Finley v. St. Louis Refrigerator Co., 265
Fiquant v. Allison, 659
Firbanks Executors v. Humphreys, 564
Fire Ass'n v. Fleming, 263
Firestone v. Rice, 267
First Cong. Ch. v. Muscatine, 67
First Nat. Bank, In re 81
First Nat. Bank v. Adam, 172
First Nat. Bank v. Cook Carriage Co., 680
First Nat. Bank v. North, 301
First Nat. Bank of Meadville v. Fourth Nat. Bank of N. Y. 26
Firth v. Bowling Iron Co., 605
Fischer v. Niccolls, 27
Fish v. Cleland 82
Fish v. Clifford, 142
Fish v. Ferris, 62, 144
Fish v. Soniat, 128
Fishback v. Miller 175
Fish Bros. Wagon Co. v. La Belle Wagon Co., 181
Fishel v. Lueckel, 224
Fisher v. Ludlong, 358
Fisher v. Clark, 503, 506
Fisher v. Forrester, 89
Fisher v. Jackson, 148
Fisher v. Keane, 147
Fisher v. Langbein, 264
Fisher v. McGirr, 199
Fisher v. Mellen, 351
Fisher v. Oregon etc. R. Co., 125
Fishkill Saving Inst. v. Bostwick 47
Fisk v. Missouri Furnace Co., 586
Fisk v. Walt, 591, 615
Fiske v. Forsyth Dyeing Co., 552
Fitch v. Custer, 642
Fitch v. Gosser, 452
Fitz v. Hall, 60
Fitzgerald v. Cavin, 190
Fitzgerald v. Fitzgerald, 248
Fitzgerald v. Honkomp, 117
Fitzgerald v. Redfield, 500
Fitzgerald v. Stewart, 116
Fitzgerald v. Town of Weston, 577
Fitzgerald v. Vulvin, 253
Fitzjohn v. Mackinder, 266, 397
Fitzpatrick v. Boston & M. R. R., 214
Fitzsimmons v. Joslin, 383
Flavin v. Nicholls, 208
Flanders v. Colby, 412
Flanders v. Norwood, 70
Flatow v. Van Bramsen, 291, 502
Flect v. Hollenkemp 26
Fleischmann v. Starkes, 184
Fleming's case, 666, 679

TABLE OF CASES CITED.

The References are to Pages.

Fleming v. Dollar, 320.
Fleming v Hislop, 408, 521.
Fleming v. Manchester, Sheffield & Lincolnshire R. Co., 654.
Fleming v. Ramsey, 611.
Fletcher, Ex parte, 469
Fletcher v. Bealey, 523.
Fletcher v. Cole, 206
Fletcher v Evans, 639
Fletcher v. Evenns, 463.
Fletcher v. Ingram, 114.
Fletcher v People, 140
Fletcher v. Rylands, 599, 603, 609, 613
Fletcher v. Smith, 601
Flewster v Royle, 267.
Flickinger v Shaw, 402.
Flickinger v. Wagner, 393.
Flike v Boston & A R. Co., 125.
Flinn v. New York etc. R. Co., 561.
Flint v. Franzman, 44 .
Flint v Russell, 505.
Flint etc R Co. v Detroit etc. R Co., 163
Flora v Maney, 70.
Flower v Farwell, 360
Flower v Pennsylvania R Co., 126
Floyd v State, 257, 259, 262
Floyd v Wiley, 659
Fluker v Georgia Railroad & Banking Co., 271.
Flynn v Railroad Co., 562
Flynn v Solem, 122
Flynn v San Francisco, etc Ry Co., 91
Flynn v Taylor, 187
Foard v McComb, 363
Fogarty v Junction City etc Co., 506
Fogg v. Boston & L. R. Co., 66, 68
Fogg v Griffin, 366
Fogg v. N C O Ry, 528
Foley v Jersey City etc Co., 192.
Foley v Wyeth, 216, 493
Follett v Edwards, 442, 443
Folcom v Marsh, 224
Fonville v McNease, 287
Fonville v Nease, 138
Foot v Brown, 300
Foral v Hellett, 312
Forbes v Boston & L R Co., 443
Forbes v Hagman, 393, 396
Ford v Caldwell, 659.
Ford v Johnson, 297.
Ford v Monroe, 81
Ford v Taggart, 202.
Fordyce v Stone, 214.
Fornwalt v Hylton, 9
Forsdike v Stone, 221
Forshee v Abrams, 323.
Forsythe v Hooper, 91
Fort v Pursley, 432
Fort Wayne v Coombs, 70.
Fortman v Rattler, 395
Fortune v Jones, 204
Fortune v Trainor, 106
Forward v Adams, 301
Foss v Boston & M R. Co., 558
Foss v Hildredth, 323, 327.
Foss v Stewart, 142
Foster v Essex Bank, 108, 386
Foster v Scripps 301
Foster v Small, 301.
Fotheringham v Adams Express Co, 260
Fouldes v Willoughby, 425, 437
Foulger v Newcomb, 303

Foulkes v. Metrop. District R. Co., 601, 603, 604.
Fountain v. West, 326, 327.
Foval v. Hallett, 312.
Fowler v. Baltimore etc. R. Co., 568, 569, 574.
Fowler v. Chichester, 63, 316.
Fowler v. Gilbert, 544.
Fowler v Jenkins, 33
Fowler v. McCann, 375.
Fowler v. Sergeant, 26, 27.
Fowler v. Wallace, 315.
Fowles v Bowen, 301, 302, 307, 334.
Fox v. Baltimore R Co., 154
Fox v. Glastenbury, 540.
Fox v. Jones, 26.
Fox v. Sackett, 591.
Fox v. Stevens, 281.
Frace v New York, L E & W R Co., 43,
Fraker v. St. Paul etc R. Co., 122.
Francalse v. Schultz, 184.
Francis v. Cockrell, 625
Francis v. Schoellkopf, 214, 505, 506.
Francisco v. State, 260
Frank v City of St Louis, 591.
Frank v. New Orleans, etc. R Co., 518.
Frankford, etc., Co. v. Phila. etc., R. Co., 561.
Frankfort Bank v Johnson, 112
Franklin v McCarkle, 278, 281
Franklin v. S. E R Co, 79,
Franklin Coal Co. v. McMullen 430
Frankord & B T. Co v Phila. & T R Co., 552.
Fraser v Freeman, 110
Fraser v. Red River Lbr Co., 120
Fray v Blackburn, 140,
Frazier v Brown, 178
Frazier v Norrimus 473, 611.
Frazier v Turner, 261, 264.
Fredestize v Odenwalder, 323.
Frederickson v Singer Mfg Co., 248.
Freeman v Boland, 62, 443
Freeman v Cornwall, 145.
Freeman v. Grant, 438.
Freeman v Price, 316
Freeman v. Saunderson, 298, 333.
Freeman v Sayre, 216
Freke v Calmady, 428
Fremantle v L & N W. R Co., 606.
French v Bancroft, 260
French v. Creswell, 110
French v. Smith, 554
French v Vining, 370, 632.
Frenzee v Miller, 357
Freudenstein v Heine, 491
Fresno, City of, v Fresno, etc. Co., 500
Frey v Harrison, 680.
Frick v St Louis, etc R Co., 556
Fritz v Hobson, 490, 508, 520
Friend v Wood, 606.
Frink v Potter, 656.
Frogley v Earl of Lovelace, 460, 461
Frohrelch v Gammon, 684
Frolich v McKiernan, 206
Fronio v Dennis, 434
Frost v. Domestic, etc., Co., 68
Frost v Grand Trunk R. Co., 164
Frowbridge v Ballard, 141
Fry v Bennett, 305, 306,
Fry v Derstler, 274
Fry v. Leslie, 61, 281
Ft Worth & D. C Ry Co v Robertson, 585

TABLE OF CASES CITED.

The References are to Pages.

Fugate v Millar, 303
Fuhr v Dean, 462
Fulgham v State, 150
Fullam v Stearns, 211
Fuller v Bowker, 260
Fuller v Daniels, 225
Fuller v Duren, 65
Fuller v Hodgden, 375
Fulton v Fulton, 412
Fulton v Hood, 157, 375
Fulton v McDaniel, 175
Fulton v Stalls, 263
Fulton County S R Co v McConnell, 92
Fultz v Wycoff, 370
Funston v Chicago etc R Co, 557
Furman v Van Sise, 277
Furth v Foster, 61
Fuscher v Spalding, 506

G.

Gabe v McGinnis, 312
Gage v Shelton, 234
Gass v Vetter 193, 501, 513
Gaines v Greene etc Co, 430
Gainesville etc R Co v Hall, 154
Galbraith v Epperson, 111
Gale v McDaniel, 211
Gale v Parrott, 276
Galena R Co v Rae, 112
Galesburg v Higley, 69
Gallagher v Brunel 356, 672
Gallagher v Dodge, 182
Gallagher v Piper, 125
Gallagher v State, 267
Gallagher v Stoddard, 395
Galligan v Manufacturing Co, 24
Galloway v Chicago, etc Ry Co, 537
Galow v Stewart, 191
Galveston etc R Co v Farmer, 122
Galvin v Mayor etc of New York, 594
Gambich v Wurst, 24
Gandy v Jubber, 530
Ganson v Madigan, 683
Garrard v Pittsburg etc R Co, 454
Garland v McWilliams, 328
Gardner v Alering, 429
Gardner v Bennett, 550
Gardner v Campbell, 479
Gardner v Hewitt, 537
Gardner v Rowland, 639
Gardner v Stroever 522
Garfield v Douglass, 138
Garley v Armistead, 440
Garnett v Bradley, 215
Garnsey v Rogers, 675
Garr v Selden, 300, 328
Garrett v Taylor, 284
Garrett v Bickler, 344
Garrett v Dickerson 295, 311
Garrett v Freeman, 503
Garretzen v Duenckel, 101, 110
Garrison v Birnes, 614
Garrison v Burden, 274
Garrison v Memphis Ins Co, 606
Garrow v Davis, 375
Garvey v Dung, 110
Gaskins v Atlanta, 70
Gaslight and Coke Co v Vestry of St Mary Abbotts, 159
Gassett v Gilbert, 334, 337, 338
Gastenhoffer v Claire, 642

Gately v Kniss, 92
Gates v Fleischer, 27
Gates v Lonsburg, 119
Gates v Southern Minn. R Co, 605
Gault v Fleming, 305
Gault v Humes, 164
Gaunt v Finney, 523
Gautret v Egerton, 610
Gavin v Chicago, 580
Gayetty v Bethune, 156
Gaylord v Morris, 125
G C. & S F Ry Co v Box, 534
G C. & S F. Ry Co v Greenlee, 552
G C. & S F Ry Co. v Levy, 674
Gibbs v. Guild, 215
Geddis v Proprietors of Bann Reservoir, 155
Gee v Culver, 394
Geer v Metropolitan R Co, 109, 592
Geer v Darrow, 92, 96
Geise v Schultz, 281
Geisler v Brown, 293
Gelzenlechter v Nehmeyer, 264, 265
Gennenzo v De Forest, 61
George v Haverhill, 218
George v Lemon, 324
George v Skivington, 622, 667
George v St Louis etc R, 629
George v The Wabash Western Ry Co, 544
George v Van Horn, 279
Georgetown etc R Co v Doyle, 157
Georgia v Kilford, 286
Georgia R Co v Neely, 610
Georgia R Co v Pittman, 81
Georgia Pac Ry v Davis, 569
Georgia Pac Ry Co v Fullerton, 218
Geraty v Stern, 110
Germain v Clark, 183
Germania Ins Co v The Lady Pike, 96
Gerrish v Brown, 487
Gerst v Jones, 632
Getchell v Hill, 27
Getchell v Lindley, 27
Gettins v Scudder, 26
Getty v Rountree, 632
Getzler v Witzel, 206
Geveke v Grand Rapids etc R Co, 556
G H & S A Ry Co v Donaho, 109
Gheen v Johnson, 28
Gholston v Gholston, 150
Gibbons v Farwell, 431
Gibbons v Pepper, 172
Gibbons v Wilkesbarre etc St Ry Co, 590
Gibbons v. Williams, 583
Gibbons v Wisconsin, etc, Ry Co, 504
Gibbs v Belcher, 81
Gibbs v Chase, 9
Gibbs v Dewey, 294
Gibbs v Randlett, 261
Gibbs v Weston, 452
Gibson v Black, 184
Gibson v Cincinnati Inquirer, 312
Gibson v Cunningham, 359
Gibson v Evans, 311
Gibson v Gibson, 64, 295
Gibson v Spear, 60
Gibson v St Louis A & M Assoc, 462
Gibson v Williams, 295
Giddens v Mirk, 294
Giese v Shultz, 685
Gifford v Hulet, 506
Gifford v Weber, 213

The References are to Pages.

Gilbert v. Beach, 92
Gilbert v. Borgatt, 349
Gilbert v. Emmons, 265.
Gilbert v. Palmer, 305
Gilbert v. People, 328
Gilbert v. Showerman, 195
Gilbertson v. Fuller, 305
Gilchrist v. Van Dyke, 182
Giles v. Simonds, 159, 464
Gillespie v. Hudson, 305
Gillespie v. McGowan, 21
Gilliam v. South & N. A. R. Co., 108
Gilliford v. Windell, 99.
Gillingham v. Ohio River R. Co., 264
Gillison v. Charleston, 71
Gillott v. Ellis, 606
Gilman v. Emery, 425
Gilman v. Hunnewell, 184, 22.
Gilman v. Lowell, 296 324, 344
Gilmartin v. New York, 97
Gilmore v. Driscoll, 216
Gilmore v. Newton, 139
Gilson v. Collins, 26
Ginot v. Graham, 392
Givens v. Van Studdiford, 520
Gladfelter v. Walker, 192
Gladwell v. Steggall, 27, 617, 604
Glasgow v. Owen, 491
Glaster v. Rolls, 364
Glasspoole v. Young H., 171
Glaze v. McMillion, 432.
Glenson v. Clark, 26
Glendon Iron Co v. Uhler, 15 182, 184
Glenn v. Hays, 199, H., 177
Gliddon v. McKinley, 545
Gloaming, The, 630
Globe Milling Co v. Minneapolis Elevator Co., 680
Glossom v. Staples, 400
Gloucester v. Beach, 156.
Glover v. L. & S W Rail Co., 11
G. N. R. v. Halloren, 629
Goad v. Johnson, 370.
Goddard v. Grand Trunk R., 67, 105
Godillot v. Harris, 225
Goetchens v. Mathewson, 148
Goetz v. Ambs, 223.
Goff v. G N R Co, 107
Goff v. Obertenffer, 159
Goffin v. Donnelly, 330
Gold v. Bissell, 260, 264
Golden v. Newbrand, 107.
Golderman v. Stearns, 299
Goldrich v. Ryan, 370
Goldsmid v. Tunbridge Wells Improvement Commrs., 524
Goldsmith v. Joy, 253
Goldstein v. Chicago, etc., R. Co., 633
Gongolas v. New York etc R Co., 544
Gooch v. Stephenson, 611
Goodale v. Tuttle, 178
Goodale v. Shurman, 211
Goodell v. Bluff City Ice Co., 663
Goodiett v. Louisville & N R R Co., 514
Goodrich v. Hooper, 286
Goodrich v. Woolcott, 312
Goodson v. Richardson, 182
Goodspeed v. East Haddam Bank, 67, 68
Goodwin v. Chevley, 173, 612
Goodwin v. Horne, 357
Goodyear v. Day 225
Goodyear v. Phelps, 67
Goot v. Pulsifer, 338

Gordan v. Parmalle, 357.
Gordon v. Farrar, 118
Gordon v. Grand St R Co., 778.
Gordon v. Manchester, etc. R Co., 676
Gordon v. Parmelee, 120.
Gordon v. Stockdale, 111
Gorham v. Gross, 664, 639
Gorham v. Ives, 201 205
Gorman v. Pacific R. Co., 619
Gorman v. State, 119.
Gormley v. Gym Assoc, 360
Gormly v. Vulcan Iron Works, 121
Gorrell v. Snow, 305
Gorris v. Scott, 25, 230
Gorton v. Frizzell, 204
Gosden v. Elphich, 267
Goshen Turnpike Co v. Sears, 42.
Gott v. Pulsifer, 301, 305, 388
Gottchnet v. Hubacheck, 312
Gough v. Goldsmith, 307
Gould v. Gould, 230
Gould v. Hammond, 145
Gould v. Slater Woolen Co., 164, 621
Gourdier v. Cormack, 92
Government St R Co v. Hanlon, 574, 534
Grabel v. Wapello Coal Co., 552
Grable v. Margrave, 281
Grace v. McArthur, 135, 346.
Grace v. Teague, 264
Grady v. Wolsner, 184
Grafton v. Carmichael, 112 120, 432
Graham v. Dahlonega G. M. Co., 225
Graham v. Gautier, 27
Graham v. Pacific R Co., 211
Graham v. Peat, 451
Graham v. Roder, 220
Graham v. Smith, 279
Grainger v. Hill, 259
Gramm v. Boener 27
Grandona v. Lovdal, 492
G R & I R v. Boyd, 629
Grand Rapids, City of, v. Welden, 52
Grand Tower Co v. Phillips, 683, 685
Grand Trunk Ry Co v. Ives, 557
Grand Trunk R Co v. Latham 84
Grand Trunk R of Canada v. Jennings, 79
Grant v. Moseley, 568, 574
Grant v. Power Co., 21
Grant v. Schmidt, 528
Grant v. Slater, 228
Grant v. Union Pac Ry. Co., 164
Grant v. Willey, 222
Gravelle v. Minneapolis & St L. R. Co., 124
Graves v. Smith, 413
Gray v. Ayres, 206, 516
Gray v. Boston Gas light Co., 232
Gray v. Durland, 279
Gray v. Kimball, 111
Gray v. Pentland, 338
Gray v. Pullen, 85
Gray v. Scott, 567
Great Falls Co v. Worcester, 448, 589
Great Western R Co v. Haworth, 537
Greavy v. Long Island R. Co., 557
Green v. Bantz, 125
Green v. Boston, etc., R. Co., 218.
Green v. Cochran, 392
Green v. Hudson River R Co., 81
Green v. Lake, 501
Green v. Nunnemacher, 485
Green v. Pennsylvania R Co., 220.
Green v. Ramsey, 264

TABLE OF CASES CITED

The References are to Pages.

Green v Savannah, 505
Green v Sperry, 61, 62
Green v Telfair, 311
Green v Bishop, 224
Green v Cole, 427
Greenfield Bank v Leavit, 223
Greenland v Chaplin, 15
Greenleaf v Dubuque R. Co., 104
Greenleaf v Francis, 178
Greenleaf v Illinois etc R Co, 104, 568
Greenlade v Halliday, 517
Greenwood v Cobbey, 119
Greenwood v Greenwood, 278
Greenwood v Hornsey, 511
Greer v Tripp, 417
Gregg v Fitzhugh, 683
Gregg v Gregg, 611
Gregory v Atkins, 111
Gregory v Brooks, 116
Gregory v Duke of Brunswick, 401
Gregory v Piper, 98
Gregory's Admr v Ohio River R Co, 97
Gribble v Pioneer Press Co, 300, 353
Grier v Lomax, 168
Gries v Zeck, 614
Griffin v Auburn, 552
Griffin v Chubb, 316
Griffin v Coleman, 264
Griffin v Lawrence, 583
Griffin v Ohio & M Ry Co, 153
Griffin v Rising, 118
Griffin v Shreveport & A R Co, 157
Griffith v Fowler, 111
Griffith v McCallum, 516
Griffiths v London & St Katherine Docks Co, 125
Griffiths v Woltrum 54
Grifford v Carvell, 358
Grigsby v Clear Lake Water Co, 514
Grigsby v Stapleton, 570
Grill v Lomax, 358
Grim v Byrd, 58
Grimes v Coyle, 327
Grimsby v Hudnell, 243
Grimshaw v Belcher, 162
Grinham v Willey, 266
Grinnell v Cook, 651
Grinnell v Wells, 281
Groff v Akenbrandt, 544
Grogan v Pope Iron etc Co, 529
Gromendyke v Cramer, 464
Gross v McKee, 357
Gross v Pennsylvania P & B. R Co, 121
Grotton v Glidden, 186
Grove v Brandenburg, 329
Grover v Van Duyn, 138
Groves v Rochester, 70
Grubb v Suit, 686
Grumon v Raymond 264
Grumond v Raymond, 264
Grund v Van Vleck, 87
Grunell v Wells 280
Guard v Risk, 295, 311
Guardian Soc v Roosevelt, 347
Gudger v Penland, 296
Gudger v Western etc R. Co, 157
Guernsey v Lowell, 263
Guest v Reynolds, 24, 216
Guggenheim v Lake Shore etc R Co, 556
Guille v Swan, 9, 39, 413, 423, 491
Gulf, C & S F Ry Co v Johnson, 449
Gulf C & S F Ry Co v Montgomery, 63

Gulf, C & S. F. Tel. Co v. Richardson, 55
Gulf & S F R. Co v Kirkland, 104
Gulledge v White, 468
Gully v Smith, 25
Gumsby v Hankins, 120
Gunderson v North Western Elevator Co, 583
Gunsalus v Tormoi, 422
Guthrie v Wickliffe, 658
Gwinell v Eamer, 541
G W R Co of Canada v Baird, 609
Gwynn v Duffield, 20
Gyre v Culver, 201

H.

Haack v Fearing, 110
Hablichtel v Yambert, 402
Hacke's Appeal, 522
Hacket v Lawrence, 263
Hacket v. King, 265
Hackney v State, 485
Hadlek v. Heywood, 273
Hadley v Baxendale, 31, 683, 685
Hadley v Cross, 615
Hadley v Importing Co., 369
Hagan v Chicago, etc Ry Co, 561
Hagan v Hendry, 305, 320
Hagee v. Grossman, 375
Hager v Darforth, 171
Haggerty v Thompson, 511
Hagood v Elson, 443
Haight v Badgeley, 275
Haight v Cornell, 312
Hailes v Marks, 208
Haines v Campbell, 312, 313
Haines v. Welling, 316
Haire v Reese, 27
Hake v Bromes, 288
Halbrook v Utica etc R Co, 545
Haldeman v Bruckhart, 178
Hale v Front, 683
Hale v Johnson, 92
Hale v Lawrence, 199
Halett v Swift, 651
Haley v Kelm, 119
Haley v. Mobile & O R Co, 81
Haley v Rowan, 420
Haley v State, 305
Hall v Corcoran, 62
Hall v Fearnley, 172
Hall v Fond du Lac, 218
Hall v. Galveston, etc, R. Co, 121
Hall v Hinks, 680
Hall v Hollander, 281
Hall v Railroad Cos, 606
Hall v Suydam, 394, 396
Hall v Younts, 114
Halley, The, 97, 237, 240
Halley v Gregg, 294
Halliday v Holgate, 444
Halligan v Chicago & R I R Co, 422
Hallock v Hughes, 611
Halloran v Bray, 228
Halls v Thompson, 375
Halsey v Brotherhood 389
Halstead v Nelson, 339
Hambly v Trott, 82, 83
Hamford v Kansas City, 70
Hamilburgh v. Shephard, 395
Hamilton v Fno, 318

TABLE OF CASES CITED.

The References are to Pages.

Hamilton v Ens, 334
Hamilton v Lomax, 278.
Hamilton v Pandorf, 607
Hamilton v Smith, 393
Hamilton v. Texas etc R Co, 627
Hamilton v Third Ave R Co, 229
Hamilton v Vicksburg etc R Co, 146
Hamilton v Ward, 211
Hamilton v Williams, 133
Hammersmith R Co v Brand, 175, 617
Hammock v White, 28, 510, 518
Hammond v Melton, 611
Hammond v Mukwa, 218
Hammond v N E R Co, 656
Hammond v Town of Mukwa, 537
Hampton v Taylor, 13
Hampton v Jones, 301
Hampton v Wheeler, 118
Hancock v Gomez, 683
Hancock v Rand, 642, 651
Hancock v Stephens, 512
Handy v Brookline, 70
Handy v Foley, 64
Hanger v Evins, 58
Hankins v New York, etc, R Co, 120
Hanna v Grand Trunk Ry Co, 259
Hannan v Gross 248
Hannem v Pence, 601, 603
Hannem v Fales, 216
Hannibal etc R Co v Fox, 125
Hannibal etc R Co v Kennes, 610
Hannon v Guzzard, 118
Hans v Louisiana, 156
Hansford v Payne, 26
Hanson v Edgerly, 175
Hanson v McCue, 178
Harbach v Des Moines & K C Ry Co, 214
Harcourt v Harrison, 591
Hardenburgh v Lockwood, 611
Harden v Harshfield, 316
Harding v Larned, 59
Harding v Sands, 169
Harding v Weld, 59
Hardman v Booth, 681
Hardy v Metzger, 411
Hardy v Munroe, 132
Hargan v Purdy, 301
Hargous v Stone, 370
Hargreaves v Kimberly, 519
Harkrader v Moore, 363
Harlan v Logansport Nat Gas Co, 161
Harley v Merrill Brick Co, 529
Harman v Johnson, 114
Harmon v Harmon, 463
Harner v Fisher, 370
Haroketh v Bar, 281
Harpel v Curtis, 591
Harper v Charlesworth, 451
Harper v Harper, 536
Harper v Indianapolis & St L R Co, 125
Harper v Tuffkin, 279
Harriman v Railway Co 110
Harriman v Stowe, 26, 54, 648
Harrington v Commissioners, 115
Harris v Bailey, 300
Harris v Briscoe, 411
Harris v Cameron, 551
Harris v DePinna, 509, 511
Harris v Gillingham, 464
Harris v Hillman, 420
Harris v Harrington, 388
Harris v Harris, 243

Harris v. McNamar, 92
Harris v Minneapolis etc R Co, 567
Harris v Mobbs, 10, 191
Harris v Nicholas, 108
Harris v Perry, 627
Harris v Rand, 606
Harris v Ross, 513
Harris v Saunders, 139
Harris v Simon, 631
Harris v Terry, 291
Harris v Township of Clinton, 611
Harris v Zanone, 305, 533
Harrison v Berkley, 12
Harrison v Bush, 119
Harrison v Collins, 92
Harrison v. Denver etc Ry Co, 191
Harrison v Finley, 311
Harrison v. Guill, 171
Harrison v Harrison, 236
Harrison v Marshall, 18
Harrison v Mitchell, 87
Harrison v Mosley, 81
Harrison v Southwark & Vauxhall Water Co, Ld, 103
Hanlon v Wisdom, 191
Harrop v Hirst, 110, 169, 111, 508
Harrower v Ritson, 516
Hart v Baxter, 178
Hart v Evening News Assoc, 287
Hart v Gumpach, 331
Hart v Hudson River Bridge Co, 516
Hart v Mayor etc of Albany, 481
Hart v New York R D C Co, 122
Hart v Red Cedar, 64
Hart v Ryan, 92
Hart v Skinner, 115
Hart v Wall, 313
Hart v Wright, 670
Hartfield v Roper, 61, 585
Hartford v Brady, 176
Hartley v Cummings, 145
Hartman v Flaherty, 68
Hartshorn v Chaddock 247
Hartshorn v Inhabitants of South Read ing, 189
Hartshorne v Kiernan, 472
Hartsock v Reddick, 184
Hartwig v Bay State S & L Co 91
Hartwig v Chicago & N W R Co, 508
Harvey v Bridges, 468
Harvard v Delaware & H C Co, 121
Harvey v Dewoody, 514
Harvey v Dunlap, 167
Harvey v Epes, 443
Harvey v Harvey, 472
Harwood v Keech, 321
Harwood v Siphers, 264 265
Harwood v Tompkins, 33
Haskell v Shurson, 224
Haskell v Starbird, 353
Haskins v Lumsden, 315
Haskins v N N & H R R Co, 116
Haskins v Royster, 216, 673
Haskins v Stewart, 161
Haskins v Utah Northern Ry Co, 365
Hass v Philadelphia, etc, Steamship Co, 92
Hassenger v Railroad Co, 584
Hastings v Aiken, 503
Hastings v Livermore, 9
Hastings v Lusk, 325, 729, 731
Hastings v Stetson, 292, 316, 333
Hasty v Sears, 117
Hatch v Cohen, 395

TABLE OF CASES CITED.

The References are to Pages.

Hatch v. Donnell, 10, 214, 422
Hatch v. Dwight, 518
Hatch v. Fuller, 581
Hatch v. Patten, 306
Hatch v. Pendergast, 93
Hatch v. Potter 195
Hatch v. Vermont Cent. R Co., 157
Hauchard v. Mege, 70
Hatcher v. Hampton, 483
Hatfield v. Towsley, 138
Hathaway v. East Tennessee, etc. R Co., 514, 554
Hathaway v. Rice, 119
Hathorn v. Congress Spring Co., 134
Hathorn v. Richmond 27
Hatt v. Tub Water Pipe Line Co., 132
Hauck's Appeal 105
Hauser v. State, 24
Haussy v. Kohler 464
Havens v. Neal 554
Havens v. Hartford, etc. R Co., 656
Haverlock v. Sipe 70
Haw v. Ridgway 260
Hawes v. Knowles 53
Hawk v. Harman 64
Hawks v. Inman 64
Hawley v. Globe Printing Co., 124
Hawkins v. Pemberton, 351
Hawley v. State 40
Hawks v. Evans 25
Hawks v. Locke, 370 503
Hawksworth v. Thompson, 84
Hawley v. Cowles, 22
Hawn v. Banghart 276 281
Haws v. Burlington, etc. Ry Co., 516
Hawyer v. Whalen 87
Hay v. Cohoes Co. 502, 615
Hy v. Reid 525, 58
Haycraft v. Creasy 350
Hayden v. Manufacturing Co., 117
Hayden v. Shed 591
Hayes v. Askew, 519
Hayes v. Island 345
Hayes v. Michigan Cent R Co., 21, 47, 545
Hayes v. Mitchell 260
Hayes v. Parker 60
Hayes v. Younglove, 393
Haymen v. Governors of Rugby School, 118
Hayn v. Culliford, 650
Hayner v. Cowden 301
Haynes v. Nowlen 272.
Haynes v. State, 256
Hays v. Borders 273
Hays v. Bricrly, 313
Hays v. Creary 264
Hays v. Gainesville St R. Co., 99
Hays v. Hays 311
Hays v. Kennedy, 606
Hays v. Miller, 89
Hays v. Mitchell, 295
Hays v. Sinclair 281
Hathorn v. Rushforth, 124
Hayward v. Merrill, 567
Haywood & Co. v. Haywood & Son, 341
Hazard v. Irwin, 349, 351, 354
Hazard Powder Co. v. Volger, 496, 497, 503
Hazel v. Clark, 201, 256
Hazel v. Peoples' Pass Ry Co., 545
Hazelton v. Week, 9
Hazen v. Boston etc Co., 157
Headen v. Rust, 610

Heald v. Carey, 119
Healey v. Gregg, 299
Heaney v. Butte & M C Co., 483
Heath v. Cottenbach, 611
Heath v. Ricker, 611
Heaven v. Pender, 544, 545, 624, 628
Hazle v. Railroad Co., 606
Hebert v. Lege, 119
Heckle v. Larvey, 64
Hedden v. Griffin, 648
Hedges v. Tagg, 480
Hedley v. Pinkney and Sons' S S Co., 125
Heeg v. Licht, 603
Heeney v. Sprague, 24
Heinrich v. Pullman, etc., Co., 101
Hermance v. Vernoy, 169
Hefferen v. Northern P R Co., 117
Hefferman v. Benkard, 94
Heflin v. Slay, 432
Heft v. Glanding 223
Helm v. McCaughan, 114, 656
Helmstreet v. Howland 530
Heme v. Chicago & N W R Co., 122
Heineman v. Heard, 26, 683
Hendricks v. Kerchner, 279
Helzer v. Kingsland etc Co., 64
Helkams v. Switzer, 528
Heller v. City of Alvarado 254
Helsham v. Blackwood, 327
Hemmer v. Cooper, 358
Hempstead v. Cargill, 244
Henchman v. Patterson etc R Co., 78
Hendershott v. Ottumwa 70
Henderson v. Fox, 24, 315
Henderson v. Grewell, 406
Henderson v. Railroad Co., 116 199, 81
Henderson v. Sullivan 298
Hendrick v. Lindsay 675
Hendricks v. Montagu 192
Hendrickson v. Kingsbury 245
Hendrickson v. Sullivan, 294
Henkel v. Muri, 627
Henley v. Robb, 243
Hennessey v. Clemons, 522
Henning v. Bull, 154
Henry v. Dennis, 23, 615
Henry v. Klopfer, 564
Henry v. Southern Pacific R Co., 42
Henwood v. Harrison 349
Hepburn v. Jordan 523
Herdic v. Young, 248
Heritage v. Dodge, 149
Hermann v. Bradstreet Co., 295, 334
Herman v. Cundiff, 296
Hermann Lorg v. Beam, 226
Herrick v. Lapham, 294
Herrick v. Winn, 239
Herring v. State, 260
Herron v. Hughes, 442
Hershberger v. Lynch, 545
Herzog v. Graham, 262
Hess v. Culver, 384
Hess v. Fockler 314
Hess v. Johnson, 144
Hess v. Sparks 296
Hesse v. Knippel 27
Hessmyer v. Michigan Cent R., 540
Hotfield v. Central R Co., 459
Hetherington v. N E R Co., 79
Hewes v. Platts 434
Hewe v. Nourse, 503
Hewitt v. Mason, 299
Hewitt v. Isham, 463

TABLE OF CASES CITED.

The References are to Pages.

Howitt v. Newburger, 205.
Howitt v. Pioneer Press Co., 67
Howitt v. Prime, 278
Howitt v. Smith, 87.
Howitt v. Swift, 84
Hoxamer v. Weber, 92
Haygood v. The State, 91.
Hoyne v. Blair, 392
Heywood v. Tilison, 83, 153
Hibbard v. W U Tel Co., 211
Hickey v. Merchants & M T Co., 91
Hickey v. Michigan C R Co., 516
Hickey v. Grosjean, 112
Hickman v. Hickman, 245
Hickman v. Mackey, 125
Hicks v. Dorn, 141
Hicks v. Stevens, 362
Higbee v. Rice, 118
Higginbotham v. State, 250
Higgins v. Dewey, 604, 616
Higgins v. Glens Falls, 70
Higgins v. McCabe, 27
Higgins v. Minaghan, 204
Higgins v. Watervliet Turnpike Co., 104, 105
Higinson v. York, 9, 112
Higgs v. Smith, 649
High v. Berrett, 542
Hight v. Bacon, 632
Hildebrand v. McCrum, 269.
Hill v. Bigge, 115
Hill v. Brown, 308
Hill v. Bush, 352
Hill v. Carley, 576.
Hill v. Davis, 658
Hill v. Haynes, 262
Hill v. New River Co., 16, 51
Hill v. Palm, 395
Hill v. Rogers, 204
Hill v. Sturgeon, 606
Hill v. Taylor, 266, 267
Hill v. Windsor, 37, 42
Hillhouse v. Dunning, 257
Hillhouse v. Peck, 294
Hillard v. Richardson, 92, 94
Hillman v. Wilcox, 351
Hilts v. Chicago & G T R Co., 125
Hinchman v. Patterson, etc R Co., 486.
Hinchman v. Railroad Co., 528
Hinckley v. Cape Cod R Co., 517
Hinckley v. Emerson, 202
Hinds v. Ducmacker, 84
Hinds v. Harbon, 34.
Hinds v. Jones, 64
Hine v. Cushing, 218.
Hine v. Wooding, 610
Hinkle v. Davenport, 315.
Hinkle v. State, 149
Hintz v. Grupner, 333
Hinz v. Starn, 567
Hiort v. Bott, 113, 432, 435
Hiort v. L & N W R Co., 437.
Hitchcock v. Burgett, 27
Hitchins v. Frostburg, 69
Hitte v. Republican Valley R Co., 92
Hoadley v. Nor Transp Co., 51
Hoadley v. Watson, 235.
Hoag v. Hatch, 291
Hoag v. Railroad, 29, 42, 50, 574
Hoar v. Merritt, 120
Hoar v. Wood, 328, 329
Hobart v. Haggett, 112, 425
Hobbs v. Parker, 350
Hobbs v. Ray, 265

Hobson v. Fullerton, 279.
Hobson v. New Mexico & A R Co., 121, 675
Hockstedler v. Dubuque & C Ry Co., 564.
Horum v. Weltherick, 569
Hodges v. Hodges, 529
Hoit v. Sanborn, 370, 631.
Holt v. West Jersey R Co., 504, 562
Hoffman v. Carew, 149, 454
Hoffman v. New York, etc., P Co., 104, 105
Hoffman v. Kemerer, 281
Hofnagle v. New York C & H R R Co., 122.
Hogan v. Cregan, 281
Hogan v. Hendry, 383
Hogan v. Wolf, 241
Hogg v. Dorrah, 302
Hogg v. Ward, 261
Huggott v. Bigley, 115
Hogue v. Penn, 141
Holbrook v. Connor, 157, 158
Holbrook v. The Utica, etc R Co., 630.
Holcomb v. Noble, 349, 453
Holden v. Fitchburg R Co., 119, 568
Holden v. Shattuck, 641
Hole v. Barlow, 502
Holford v. Bailes, 154, 157
Holiday v. Jackson, 403
Holley v. Mix, 263
Holliday v. Kennard, 26
Hollingsworth v. Shaw, 294
Hollins v. Fowler, 10, 111, 135, 136, 139, 140, 682
Hollis v. Mons, 328, 329
Hollis v. Wells, 271
Hollister v. Nowlen, 666
Hollock v. Dominey, 265
Holly v. Boston Gas Light Co., 583, 620
Holmes v. Atchison, etc., R Co., 537
Holmes v. Drew, 547
Holmes v. Harrington, 37
Holmes v. Holmes, etc Co., 184
Holmes v. Jones, 12, 316
Holmes v. Mather, 28, 161, 172, 192, 198, 604
Holmes v. N F R Co., 628
Holmes v. Wakefield, 104
Holmes v. Wilson, 469
Holsman v. Boiling Spring Bleaching Co., 492
Holson v. Perry, 202
Holt v. Turpin, 296
Holton v. Muzzy, 324
Holton v. Noble, 157
Holtzman v. Hoy, 27
Holzab v. Railroad Co., 519
Home Ins Co. v. Pennsylvania R Co., 562
Homer v. Illinois, etc., R Co., 117
Homer v. Thriving, 62, 413
Honsee v. Hammond, 213
Honywood v. Honywood, 430
Hood v. N Y & N H R Co., 67
Hooker v. Miller, 206
Hooper v. Smith, 141
Hoosier Stone Co. v. McCain, 192
Hoover v. Peters, 570
Hope v. Evered, 266
Hopkins v. G N R Co., 497
Hopkins v. Mathias, 276
Hopkins v. Western Pac R Co., 519
Hopner v. McDowan 261
Horback v. Elder, 232

TABLE OF CASES CITED.

The References are to Pages.

Horne v. Midland, 683, 684.
Horner v. Pudil, 110.
Horner v. Harvey, 64.
Horner v. Lawrence, 618
Hosketh v. Barr, 278
Horsely v. Branch, 545
Horsfall v. Thomas, 477
Horton v. Payne, 64
Hoxack v. Weaver, 111
Hoomer v. DeYoung, 110
Hotchkiss v. Oliphant, 295
Hotchkiss v. Porter, 65
Hotchkys, Re, 428
Hoth v. Peters, 122
Hough v. Railroad Co., 117, 124, 194, 569
Houghtaling v. Hills, 49
Houlder v. Smith, 639
Houlsworth v. City of Glasgow Bank, 113, 587
House v. House, 297
Houser v. Chicago, etc. R. Co., 194
Houston v. Laffe, 159
Houston & T. C. Ry. Co. v. Simpson, 155
Houston, etc., R. Co. v. Boehm, 218
Houston, etc., R. Co. v. Burke, 218
Houston, etc., R. Co. v. Cowser, 82
Houston, etc., R. Co. v. Fowler, 194
Houston, etc., R. Co. v. Marcellos, 124
Houston, etc., R. Co. v. Meyers, 19
Houston, etc., R. v. Smith, 61
Houston, etc., R. Co. v. Terry, 24
Houston Water Work. Co. v. Kennedy, 211
Hoxie v. Scut, 464
Hover v. Burkhoff, 24
Hoyseradish Co. v. McCain, 663
How v. Sculin, 147
Howard v. Grover, 26
Howard v. Kansas City, etc. R. Co., 567
Howard v. Lee, 185, 305
Howard v. Sexton, 339
Howard v. Shepherd, 667
Howard v. Thompson, 41
Howard Oil Co. v. Davis, 218
Howe Machine Co. v. Sowder, 67
Howe v. Newmarch, 99
Howell v. Edwards, 295
Howell v. McCoy, 492
Howes v. Ashfield, 518
Howk v. Minnick, 231
Howland v. Day, 201, 256
Howland Chair v. Mfg Co., 322
Howlett v. Tuttles, 234
Hoyt v. Hudson, 544
Hoyt v. Jeffers, 44, 153
Hoyt v. Macon, 599
Hubbard v. Lord, 112
Hubbard v. Mason City, 576
Hubbard v. Rutledge, 536.
Hubbard v. Town, 509
Hubbard v. Weare, 454
Hubbell v. City of Viroqua, 531
Hubbell v. Meiggs, 351
Hubble v. Forgarth, 63
Huber v. Steiner, 211
Huchting v. Engel, 64
Huckle v. Money, 220
Hudkins v. Haskins, 277
Hudson v. Garner, 305, 311
Hudson v. Houser, 531
Hudson v. State, 275
Huff v. Ames, 585
Huff v. Lord, 91
Hull v. McCauley, 462

Hull v. Watkins, 275
Huffman v. Chicago, etc. R. Co., 125
Hugh v. New Orleans, etc., R. Co., 81
Hughes v. Engin, 120
Hughes v. Macfie, 542
Hughes v. Percival, 659
Hughes v. Robertson, 309
Hughes v. Stevens, 168
Huling v. Huling, 272
Hull v. Fields, 350
Hull v. Sac. Val. R. Co., 504
Hulihan v. Green Bay etc. R. Co., 125
Hulme v. Shreve, 22.
Humphrey v. Douglass, 61
Humphrey v. Merriam, 354
Humphries v. Cousins, 603
Humphreys v. Parker, 305, 345
Hunckell v. Youhill, 329
Hunt v. Hoyt, 631
Hunt v. Lowell Gas Light Co., 56,
Hunt v. Rich, 149
Hunt v. Somonds, 182
Hunter v. Farren, 124, 502.
Hunter v. Mathis, 115
Hunter v. McLaughlin, 58.
Huntoon v. Hazleton, 270
Hurd v. Rutland, etc. R. Co., 611
Hurdman v. N. E. R. Co., 179, 603.
Hulburt v. McKone, 508
Hulbut v. Boax, 146
Hurlbut v. McCone, 504
Hurst v. Taylor, 635
Huse v. Inter Ocean Co., 287
Huson v. Dale, 345, 344
Hussey v. Coger, 42
Hussey v. Klug, 67
Hussey v. Norfolk, So. R. Co., 68
Hussner v. Brooklyn City R. Co., 485
Hutcheson v. Peck, 274
Hutching v. Laplet, 64
Hutchins v. Hutchins, 402, 405
Hutchins v. Judd, 683
Hutchins v. Smith, 506, 578
Hutchinson v. Boston Gas Light Co., 620
Hutchinson v. Chase, 118
Hutchinson v. Lewis, 329
Hutchinson v. Olympia, 70
Hutchinson v. Wheeler, 324
Huyett v. Phila. etc. R. Co., 504, 562.
Hyams v. Webster, 85
Hyatt v. Adams, 81
Hyatt v. Myers, 506
Hyatt v. Wood, 466
Hyde v. Graham, 460, 464
Hyde v. Grench, 395
Hyde v. McCabe, 322
Hydraulic Engineering Co., 684
Hyland v. Sherman, 370
Hyman v. Nye, 632.

I.

I. & G. N. Ry. Co. v. Smith, 565
Ibbotson v. Peat, 408.
Illinois Cent. R. Co. v. Allen, 185
Illinois Coal Co. v. Cobb, 468.
Illinois Cent. R. Co. v. Graball, 506, 519
Illinois Cent. R. Co. v. McClelland, 504
Illinois Cent. R. Co. v. Pendergrass, 81
Illinois Cent. R. Co. v. Ross, 97
Illinois Cent. R. Co. v. Sheehan, 105
Illinois Cent. R. Co. v. Smith, 105

TABLE OF CASES CITED.

The References are to Pages.

Illinois Cent. R Co v Sutton, 55
Illinois, etc R Co v Cobo, 166
Illinois, etc R Co v Cox, 117
Illinois Central, etc Co v Cragin, 82, 670
Illinois Cent etc, Co v Crudup, 82
Illinois R Co v Grabbe, 64
Holt v Wilkes, 101
Hoen v City of Springfield, 70
Hoy v Nichol, 171
Hurico Ry & Nav Co v Hedrick, 562, 683
Incbbald v Burlington, 600
Indermanr v Dames 624, 652
Inderwick v Snell, 147
Indiana etc R Co v Greene, 68
Indiana Mfg. Co v Millican, 125
Indianapolis v Emmelmann, 69
Indianapolis etc R Co v Flanigan, 192
Indianapolis etc R Co v Horst, 516, 654
Indianapolis etc, R Cas. Co v Morgenstern, 149
Indianapolis etc R Co v Paramore, 662
Indianapolis, etc R Co v Stables, 51
Indianapolis etc R Co v Stout, 65
Indianapolis, etc P Co v Fox, 194
Indianapolis Journal Nwp Co v Pugh, 278
Indianapolis Nat Gas Co v Kibby, 224
Indianapolis San etc Horrelly, 40
Indianapolis Union Ry Co v Boettcher, 534
Indianapolis Water Co v Am Strawboard Co, 72
Ingalls v Buckley 139
Ingalls v Miller, 376
Ingalsbee v Wood, 651
Ingersoll v Jones 27 281
Inland & Seaboard Coasting Co v Tolson, 567
Ingraham v Jordan, 576
Inman v Foster, 316
Innes v Wylie, 201
Insurance Co v Brame, 81
Insurance Co v Peed, 464
International & G N R Co v Ryan 120
International, etc, R Co v Holloren, 605
Interstate Commerce Commission v Balt & C R Co, 654
Iron Age Pub Co v Crudup, 294 295
Iron Co v Brawley, 633
Iron Mountain Bank v Mercantile Bank, 68
Iron Mountain R Co v Bingham, 157
Iron R Co v Mowery 567, 657
Iron Works v Moore, 561
Irons v Fields, 240
Irwin v Dearman, 281
Irwin v Scribner 230
Irvine v Wood, 624
Isaacs v Herman, 658.
Isackson v New York, etc, R Co, 104
Ivy v Hedges, 641.
Ives v Ives, 466

J.

Jackman v Arlington Mills, 192
Jackson v Adams, 297
Jackson v Babcock, 464

Jackson v Chicago & N W, R Co, 65
Jackson v Kirby, 64
Jackson v Huntington, 315
Jackson v Hoopesville, 450
Jackson v Rutland, etc R Co, 604
Jackson v St Louis etc R Co, 78
Jackson v Walsh, 169
Jackson v Wood, 112
Jackson & Sharp Co v Philadelphia etc, R Co, 562
Jacksonville Journal Co v Beymer, 9
Jacksonville T & K W Ry Co, Penin sular Land, etc, Co, 3, 57, 564, 571
Jacobs v Andrew, 104
Jacobs v Pollard, 211
Jacobs v Seward, 147
Jacques v Great Falls Mfg Co, 149
Jagar v Winslow, 380
James v Campbell, 171
James v Dixon, 184
James v Emmet Mining Co, 129
James v Hodsden, 370
James v James, 574
Jamison v Milliman, 149
Jamison v Moyetc, 230
Jordan v Wells, 129
Judine v Cornell 105
Jurnigan v Fleming 31, 421
Jarrett v Gwathney, 112
Jarvis v Hathaway 158, 79
Jarvis v St Louis etc R Co, 505
Josselyn v McAllster, 34
Jay v Almy, 134
Jean v Toulmin 309
Jean v Sandiford, 611
Jeffa etc v Knott, 117, 519
Jefferies v Hargus 9
Jeffries v Phila etc, R Co, 304, 562
Jefferson v Chapman 69
Jeffersonville, etc R Co v Bowen, 583
Jeffersonville, etc, R Co v Hendricks, 82
Jeffersonville, etc, R Co v Riley 17, 537
Jeffersonville R Co v Rogers, 104
Jeffrey v Bigelow, 370, 40
Jeffrey v Keokuk, etc R Co, 567
Jeffries v Ankeny, 148
Jeffries v G W R Co, 151
Jefts v York, 650
Jellison v Goodwin 333
Jenkins v Fowler, 33
Jenkins v Lykes, 405
Jenkins v Mahopac Iron Ore Co, 129
Jenkins v Waldron, 148
Jenks v Williams 33
Jenne v Sutton, 503, 615
Jenner v A'Beckett, 322
Jennings v Gibson, 120
Jennings v Randall, 64 653
Jenoure v Delmege, 332, 345
Jewell v Colby, 59
Jewell v Mahood 179, 640
Jewett v Carter, 383
Jewett v Whitney, 214
Jex v Straus, 30
Joannes v Bennett, 335
Joannes v Burt, 290
Job v Harlam, 614
Job v Potton, 428, 449
Joel v Morison, 101
John v Bacon, 825.
John Manat Lumber Co v Wilmore, 617
Johns v Marsh, 303
Johns v Press Pub Co, 343

The References are to Pages.

Johnson, The H. O., 610.
Johnson v. Ashland Water Works Co., 18.
Johnson v. Barber, 84, 110, 112, 383, 504.
Johnson v. Benton, 53, 265.
Johnson v. Brown, 316.
Johnson v. Bruner, 542.
Johnson v. Chicago, etc., R. Co., 34.
Johnson v. City of Boston, 121.
Johnson v. Dist. of Columbia, 11.
Johnson v. Ebberts, 893.
Johnson v. Emerson, 400.
Johnson v. Farr, 431.
Johnson v. Hannahan, 166.
Johnson v. Hudson R. R. Co., 548.
Johnson v. Lane and Yorkshire R. Co., 34.
Johnson v. Lindsay, 96, 136.
Johnson v. McConnell, 252.
Johnson v. McGruder, 419.
Johnson v. Missouri, etc. R. Co., 514, 57.
Johnson v. Moss, 0, 37.
Johnson v. Morrow, 291.
Johnson v. Netherland S. S. Co., 122.
Johnson v. Patterson, 202.
Johnson v. Perry, 204.
Johnson v. The H. O., 66.
Johnson v. Power, 434.
Johnson v. Reed, 17.
Johnson v. Robertson, 6.
Johnson v. Roe, 24.
Johnson v. Shields, 85, 206.
Johnson v. Simonton, 404.
Johnson v. Skillman, 149.
Johnson v. Smith, 484, 660.
Johnson v. State, 248, 249, 250, 258.
Johnson v. Stear, 441.
Johnson v. Stubbles, 319, 424.
Johnson v. St. Louis Dispatch Co., 67, 11.
Johnson v. The Arabia, 413.
Johnson v. The Bradstreet Co., 536.
Johnson v. Thompson, 20.
Johnson v. Torpy, 231.
Johnson v. Von Kettler, 264.
Johnson v. Woodman, 143.
Johnston v. Disbrow, 273, 291.
Johnston v. Lance, 316.
Johnston v. Louisville, 228.
Johnston v. Sutton, 144.
Johner v. Ocean Steamship Co., 262, 393.
Jolley v. Harwood, 69.
Joliet, City of, v. Conway, 218.
Joliet S. S. Co. v. Yeaton, 630.
Jones v. Angell, 27.
Jones v. Bird, 542.
Jones v. Boucher, 673.
Jones v. Boyce, 593, 595.
Jones v. Brown, 115.
Jones v. Chipman, 315.
Jones v. Chappell, 4 8, 492, 528.
Jones v. Christian, 680.
Jones v. Cohen, 448.
Jones v. Corporation of Liverpool, 95.
Jones v. Dixer, 491.
Jones v. Erie & W. V. R. Co., 156.
Jones v. Festiniog R. Co., 617.
Jones v. Foley, 116.
Jones v. Gib. Ins. 204, 206.
Jones v. Godwin, 227.
Jones v. Greeley, 625, 315.
Jones v. Houtos.
Jones v. Hough, 19.
Jones v. Jenkins, 782.

Jones v. Jennings, 211.
Jones v. Jones, 34, 392, 393.
Jones v. Lake Shore, etc. R. Co., 191.
Jones v. Morris, 112.
Jones v. Powell, 500.
Jones v. Richmond, 178.
Jones v. Sherwood, 644.
Jones v. Stanton, 447.
Jones v. Starly, 67.
Jones v. St. Louis etc. Ry. Co., 157.
Jones v. St. Louis N. & P. Packet Co., 97.
Jones v. Townsend, 134.
Jones v. Utica & B. R. R. Co., 584.
Jones v. Van Doren, 9.
Jones v. Witherspoon, 640.
Jordan v. Alabama etc. R. Co., 67.
Jordan v. G. S. & Co. v. Fisher, 391.
Jordan v. Puckett, 569.
Jordan v. Wyatt, 9.
Jordan v. Crump, 204.
Joslin v. Grand Rapids Ice Co., 94.
Josselyn v. McAllister, 263.
Juchter v. Boehm, 100.
Judd v. Largo, 641.
Julbes S. S. Co. v. Merchant, 120.
Jung v. City of Stevens Point, 571.
Jung v. Nenz, 503.
Junkins v. Simpson, 69.

K.

K —— v. H ——, 307.
Kahl v. Love, 30.
Kalbus v. Abbott, 534.
Kalis v. Shattuck, 624.
Kendall v. Bassett, 144.
Kamerick v. Castleman, 9.
Kankakee v. Linden, 70.
Kane v. Hibernia Ins. Co., 125, 54.
Kane v. N. Central R. Co.
Kankakee v. Kankakee etc. R. Co., 225.
Kansas City, etc., R. Co. v. Cook, 217.
Kansas City, etc., R. Co. v. Kelley, 104, 105.
Kansas City, etc. R. Co. v. St. Joseph Terminal R. Co., 146.
Kansas City M. & B. R. Co. v. Burton, 123.
Kansas City R. etc. Co. v. Stoner, 537, 549.
Kansas, etc. R. Co. v. Butts, 62.
Kansas N. & D. Ry. Co. v. Mahler, 156.
Kansas, Pac. R. Co. v. Cutter, 82.
Kansas Pac. R. Co. v. Richardson, 552.
Kansas Pac. R. Co. v. Whipple, 585.
Karr v. Parks, 589.
Kaspari v. Marsh, 537.
Kauch v. Blinn, 299.
Kaufmann v. United States Nat. Bank, 675.
Kavanaugh v. Barber, 527.
Kavanaugh v. Janesville, 271.
Kay v. Railroad Co. 463, 584.
Keane v. McLaughlin, 328.
Kearney v. Boston & W. R. Corp., 80.
Kearney v. London, Brighton & South Coast Railway Co., 637.
Keating v. Cincinnati, 70.
Keats v. Hugo, 509.
Keay v. Goodwin, 148.
Keay v. New Orleans Canal Co., 50.
Kedrolivansky v. Niebaum, 286.
Keeble v. Hickeringill, 181, 285, 404.
Keedy v. Howe, 110.

TABLE OF CASES CITED.

The References are to Pages.

Kooler v Eastman, 129
Koen v Coleman, 63,
Keen v Hartman, 63,
Keenan v Cook, 118
Keenan v Kavanaugh, 611
Keene v Kimball, 221
Keep v Quallman, 250
Kell v Milwaukee etc R Co, 564
Kehoe v Allen, 120
Keighly v Bell, 111
Keller v Lesaford, 293.
Kelm v Ruff, 308
Kelper v Klein, 509,
Kekert v Lovett, 505
Kell v Penrson, 510, 521.
Keller v Eastman, 129
Kelley v Riley 686.
Kelly v Ryus 123
Kelloy v Silver Spring Bleaching Co, 193
Kelley v St Paul, etc R Co, 566
Kellogg Bridge Co v Hamilton 132
K Hogg v Janesville, 70
Kellogg v Payne, 92
Kelly v Donnelly, 278
Kelly v Erie Tel & P Co, 121, 1..
Kelly v Flaherty, 298
Kelly v Huffington, 291
Kelly v Insurance Co, 181
Kelly v Mayor, 550
Kelly v McDonald 211, 436.
Kelly v Sherlock, 211, 421
Kelly v Timlin, 321
Kelsey v Barney, 54
Kelsey v Chicago & N. W. Ry. Co 562
Kelsey v Jewett, 81
Kemlie v Sass, 287
Kemmish v Ball, 170, 503
Kemmitt v Adamson, 220
Kemp v Brown, 98.
Kemp v Neville, 139
Kemp v Thompson 112
Kendall v Brown, 27
Kendrish v McCrary, 276, 281
Keniston v Little, 362
Kennard v Burton 568
Kennayde v Pacific R Co, 591
Kennedy v Tanor, 262
Kennedy v Gifford, 312, 337
Kennedy v McVoy, 68, 383, 661
Kennedy v Parke, 351
Kennedy v Phelps, 506
Kennedy v Shea, 277, 662
Kennedy v Whitewell, 683
Kennedy v Woodrow, 316
Kennett v Robinson, 434
Kenney v Grand Trunk etc R, 651
Kenney v McLaughlin, 316
Kenney v Ranney, 435
Kenny v Cunard S S Co, 122
Kenny v Railroad, 367
Kent v Bougartz, 305 338
Kentucky Cent R Co v Thomas, 567
Kenyon v Hart, 423
Kenyon v Woodruff, 135.
Kepperly v Ramsden, 637
Kerlin v Chicago, etc, R Co, 120
Kersey v Kansas City etc R Co, 125
Kerr v Mount, 112
Kerr v O'Connor, 614
Kerwhacker v Cleveland etc R Co 535, 535, 610
Kessler v Smith, 82
Kester v W U Tel Co, 50

Ketcham v Cohn, 87,
Ketcham v Newman, 462
Kevitt v McKithen, 462
Keyer v Chicago etc R Co, 21
Keyser v Minneapolis & St P Ry Co, 85
Keys v Gold Co, 529.
Keystone Bridge Co v Newberry, 132
Khron v Brock 624
Kidd v Denniman, 129
Kidd v Gleck, 426.
Kidder v Parkhurst, 428
Klebs v Oliver, 291
Kile v Youmans, 153, 293
Kilgore v Jordan, 60
Kilpatrick v Frost, 141
Kilroy v Delaware & H C Co 120
Kimball v Bates, 106
Kimball v Billings, 149
Kimball v Fernandez 418
Kimball v Holmes 215
Kimball v Insurance Co, 157
Kimble v Yates, 150
Kimbrough v Mitchell, 61
Kimel v Kimel, 518
Kimple v State, 203
King v Calvin, 394
King v Engle, 923
King v London Improved Cab Co 6
King v Miller, 129
King v Mills, 357
King v Morris, 485
King v Patterson 312, 116
King v Root, 305 318, 353
Kingsbury v Bradstreet 136
Kingsbury v Flowers 188, 503
Kingston v Palmer, 318
Kinmouth v McDougall, 611
Kinner v Grant, 300
Kinney v Carbin, 122
Kinney v Hosen, 291
Kinney v Laughtenour, 278
Kinney v Nash, 301
Kinney v Tekamah, 70
Kinsler v Clarke, 130
Kintz v McNeal 618
Kintzing v McElrath, 151, 169
Kirk v Atlanta & C A R Co, 122, 124.
Kirk v Gregory, 113.
Kirk v Todd, 83
Kirkland v State, 248 251
Kirkman v Handy, 504, 505
Kirkpatrick v Hall, 61
Kirkpatrick v Eagle Lodge, 338
Kirkwood v Finegan, 509
Kirkwood, Town of, v Cairnes, 485
Kirschner v Western & A R Co, 456.
Kirst v M L S & W R. Co, 637.
Kitson v People, 369
Kittredge v Elliott, 614
Klauder v McGrath, 230
Kleuberg v Russell 613
Klewin v Bauman, 295, 298, 324
Klinck v Colby, 334, 336, 338
Kline v C P R Co, 104
Klupp v United Ice L'nes, 164
Knathla v Oregon, etc R. Co, 120
Knauss v Brua, 530
Knickerbocker v Colver, 230
Knickerbocker Ins Co v Ecclesine, 66
Knight v Albert, 611
Knight v Blackford, 301
Knight v Cooper, 192
Knight v Foster, 292, 311
Knight v Nelson, 87

TABLE OF CASES CITED.

The References are to Pages.

Knight v Railroad Co, 82, 249
Knight v Wilcox, 271, 278
Knisley v Stein, 241
Knox v Mayor etc of New York, 520
Knox v Tucker, 611
Kobs v Minneapolis, 69
Koehler v Philadelphia Co, 620
Kohn v Lovett, 164
Kolb v O'Brien, 223
Kooster v Kaufmann, &c, 367
Kopper v Willis, 642
Korah v Ottawa, 96
Kosminsky v Goldberg, 61
Kraft v Bender, 358
Koster v Noonan, 615
Kowing v Manley, 64
Kramer v Market Street R Co, 81
Kramer v Witt, 193
Kranz v Baltimore, 70
Krebs v Thomas, 267
Kreig v Wells, 55
Kremer v Chicago, etc, Ry Co, 459
Kress v etc, 18
Krewson v Purdon, 150
Krippner v Jacob, 14
Krom v Schoonmaker, 59, 68
Knox v Chicago etc R Co, 491
Krug v Borough of Mary, 157
Kuh v West, 39
Knight v Eastern R Co, 67, 68

L.

Lachet v Lutz, 19
Lafayette County Bank v Metcalf, 411
Lahiff v New Orleans & L R Co, 108
Lain v Willard, 214
Laflin Rand Powder Co v Tenney, 503
Laing v Mart in, 396
Lagron v Mobile & O R Co, 122
Lahay v City Nat Bank, 367
Liberty v Hogan, 644
Laidlaw v Organ, 541, 369
Laing v Colder, 647
Laing v McKee, 57
Lake Erie & W R Co v Christison, 213
Lake Erie & W Ry Co v Kennedy, 459
Lake Erie & W Co v Michener, 462
Lake Shore etc R Co v Hutchins, 137
Lalor v Ames, 163
Lilly v Emery, 522
Libby v Chicago etc, R Co, 116
Lamb v Stone, 24
Lamb v Taylor, 275
Lambert v Bessey, P Raym 170
Lamm Lot Deposit Homestead Assoc etc v etc, 86
Lamporter v Wilbram, 627
Lancaster v Lane, 18
Lancaster Bank v Moore, 59
Land v Wilmington & W R Co, 651
Lander v Court, 394
Lander v Miles, 265
Lander v Seaver, 110
Lindley v Shanklin, 324
L A N W R Co v Bradley, 158
Landon v Humphrey, 27
Landreth v Landreth, 184
Landt v Hilts, 262
Lane v Atlantic Works, 12
Lane v Black, 84
Lane v Cameron, 55

Lane v Miller, 462
Lanfranchi v Mackenzie, 510
Langer v Benedict, 143, 260
Langford v Poston & V R Co, 264
Langman v St Louis etc R Co, 567
Langridge v Levy, 372, 623, 667
Lanier v Allison, 22, 410
Lanigan v New York Gas Light Co, 620
Lannen v The Albany Gas Light Co, 620
Lansing v Christie, 328
Lanar v North Carolina R Co, 611
Lansing v Carpenter, 287, 101
Lansing v Smith, 485, 487
Lansing v Stone, 164
Lansing v Toolan, 69
Lapere v Lucky, 509
Lapham v Curtis, 606
Lapham v Noble, 300
Lard v Carbon Iron Mfg Co, 153
LaRiviere v Pemberton, 567
Lark v Stearns, 154
Larkin v Noonan, 350
Larkins v Tartar, 316
Larmore v Crown Paint Iron Co, 133
Larned v Wheeler, 118
Larock v Ogdensburg & L C R Co, 91
Larow v Chute, 92
Larson v Metropolitan S R Co, 91
Lasala v Holbrook, 216, 493
Lascy v Chute, 642
Lasky v Canadian P R Co, 120, 52
Latham v Northern P R Co, 183
Lathem v Roach, 628
Lathrop v Arnold, 142
Laughlin v Bascom, 512
Laughlin v State, 122
Laughton v Bishop of Sodor and Man, 358, 115
Lavery v Crooke, 278, 251
Laverty v Vanarsdale, 162
Lavinia v State, 260
Law v Grant, 369, 384
Lawler v Androscoggin R Co, 122
Lawless v Conn R Co, 633
Lawrence v Green, 589
Lawrence v Springer, 158
Lawrence v Wardell, 684
Lawson v Hicks, 328, 334
Lawson v State, 248, 250
Lawyer v Fritcher, 271
Lax v Corporation of Darlington, 191, 594, 630
Layton v Harris, 287, 316
Lee v Charrington, 266
Lea v Robertson, 324
Lea v White, 328
Leame v Bray, 171
Lem v Burbank, 91
Learned v Castle, 522
Leary v Boston, etc R Co, 193
Leavenworth, etc R Co v Cook, 562
Leavenworth, etc Ry Co v Curtin, 157
Leavenworth, etc Ry Co v Forbes, 99
Lewitt v Chicago etc R Co, 557
Lewitt v Sizer, 112
LeBarron v Babcock, 448
Lebavour v Howl, 118
Libby v Ahrens, 375
Lehmune v Hill, 658
Leber v Minneapolis & N W R Co, 87
Leckey v Bloser, 281
Leckey v McDermott, 411

TABLE OF CASES CITED.

The References are to Pages.

Le Clah v. First Div. St. P. & R. R. Co., 111.
Ledbetter v. Davis, 175
Lee v. City of Minneapolis, 70
Lee v. Hodges, 278
Lee v. Lamprey, 103
Lee v. McKay, 449
Lee v. McLeod, 162
Lee v. Riley, 40, 612
Lee v. Troy Cit. Gas Co., 516
Lee v. West, 275
Leed v. Richmond, 70
Leeson v. Gen. El Counc'l etc., 116
Leever v. Hamil, 395
Legg v. Dunleavy, 287.
Legott v. G. N. R Co., 77
Lehigh etc R Co v New Jersey Co, 158
Lehigh, etc R Co v McKeen, 504
Lehigh Valley Co v Jones, 122
Lehman v Shackelford, 357
Lehn v. San Francisco, 69
Leighton v Sargent, 26
Leland v Goodnow, 376
Lembeck v Nye, 182
Lemon v Newton, 69
Lemons v Wells, 296
Lempriere v Lange, 61
Leonard v Columbia S. N. Co, 82, 249
Leonard v N Y N & R I Co, 671
Leoncini v Post, 110
Leopold v Van Kirk, 642
Lesaw v Maine Cent R Co, 516, 722
Lespero v McFarland, 157
Lester v Thurmond, 129
Letzker v Huntington, 265
Levenworth v Cases, 70
Leverick v Meigs, 26
Levines v Post, 101
Levy v Salt Lake City, 69
Lewis v Avery, 261
Lewis v Chapman, 105, 111, 113
Lewis v Clark, 118
Lewis v Few, 521
Lewis v Flint & P M Ry Co, 164
Lewis v Hawley, 102
Lewis v Hudson, 295
Lewis v Jewell, 375
Lewis v Levy, 111
Lewis v Littlefield, 61
Lewis v McDaniel, 291
Lewis v McNott, 459
Lewis v Mobley, 42
Lewis v Ocean Nav & Pier Co, 434
Lexington v Lewis, 547
Lexow v Julian, 356, 360
Leyman v Latimer, 299, 327
Libby v Berry, 61
Lick v Owen, 305
Liddle v Hodges, 334
Life Assoc v Boogher, 317
Liggins v Inge, 463
Lilis v Guster, 303, 329
Lilienthal v Campbell, 145
Lilly v Boyd, 24
Limekiller v Hannibal, etc Co, 82
Limly v Illinois Cent R Co, 67
Limpus v London General Omnibus Co 111
Lincoln v Buckmaster, 537
Lincoln v Cross, 112
Lincoln v Gillilan, 544
Lincoln v Hapgood, 148
Lincoln v Walker, 69
Lincoln Coal M. Co v McNally, 122

Lincoln Rapid Transit Co. v Nichols, 660
Lindenblower v Bentley, 155
Lindley v. Hunt, 641
Lindsay v. Griffin, 116
Lindsay v Larned, 398
Lindsey v. Lindsey, 273
Lindsey v Perry, 429
Lindvall v. Woods, 123
Lingwood v Stowmarket Co, 521
Lining v. Bentham, 118
Linnehan v. Rollins, 91
Linnehan v Simpson, 597, 614
Linney v Maton, 298
Linton v. Harley, 381
Lipo v Blackwelder, 202
Lipe v. Eisenlerd, 91, 274
Lister v Perryman, 268
Litchfield v Hutchinson, 378
Little v Downing, 211
Little v Hackett, 95, 619, 679, 678, 680.
Little v Lathrop, 611
Little v. Mugahi, 611
Little v Moore, 118
Little v Stanback, 213
Littlefield v Norwich, 70
Little Miami R Co v Wetmore, 108
Little Rock & M R Co v East Tenn. etc R Co, 674
Little Rock, etc. R Co v Brooks, 488.
Little Rock, etc R Co v Duffy, 192, 191
Little Rock etc R Co v Hulse, 175, 610
Little Rock, etc R Co v Townsend, 175
Little Schuylkill etc Co v Richards, 59
Livermore v Blatchelder, 202
Lively v Gorgas, 518
Livingston v Cox, 60, 62
Livingston v Jefferson, 239
Livingston v Livingston, 224
Livingston v Moongem Coal Co, 218.
Livingston v Reynolds, 421
Livingstone v Burroughs, 267
Lobdell v Baker, 61
Lobdell v Stowell, 418
Lobauchere v Wharncliffe, 147
Lock v Ashton, 267
Locke v. Bradstreet, 320, 314
Locke v Stearns, 112, 183
Lockenour v Sides, 398
Lockett v Fort Worth & R. G. Ry. Co. 627.
Lockridge v Foster, 378
Lockwood v Bartlett, 111
Lockwood v Linsford, 225
Lockwood, etc Co v Lawrence, 492.
Loeifel v Pohlman, 111
Loevenberg v Rosenthal, 412
Loewer v Harris, 358
Lofrano v New York, etc Co, 193
Logan v Austin, 185
Logan v Gedney, 610
Logan v Hartford Coal Co, 432
Logan v Logan, 272
Logan v Murray, 279
Logansport v Dick, 69
Lohmiller v The Indian Fort Water Power Co, 530
Lohner v Hertzog, 135
Lomerson v Johnston, 351
London and Brighton R Co v Truman, 159, 160
London Brewery Co, City of, v Tennant, 507, 510
Long v Chicago, etc, R Co., 108
Long v Colburn, 660
Long v Hitchcock, 81

TABLE OF CASES CITED.

The References are to Pages.

Long v. Long, 118
Long v. Moon, 92
Long v. Morrison, 26, 27
Long v. Penn R Co, 605
Long v. State, 256
Long v. Tressler, 519
Long v. Woodman, 358, 359
Longmeid v. Holliday, 624
Longwood Valley R Co v Baker, 224
Lonsdale v. Nelson, 519
Loomis v. Terry, 206
Looney v. McLean, 653
Loper v. W U Tel Co, 55
Lopp v. Ployer, 431
Lord v. Price, 433
Lord v. Wormwood, 611
Loser v. Buchanan, 152, 603, 613, 615, 618
Losdalter v. The City of Aurora, 531
Lotto v. Davenport, 500
Louch v. Chicago etc R Co, 557
Loudy v. Clarke, 564
Louland v. Pride, 184
Louisiana Mut Ins Co v Tweed, 37
Louisville & N R Co v Kelsey, 15
Louisville & N R Co v Lawson, 113
Louisville & N R Co v Martin, 122
Louisville & N R Co v Mitchell 72
Louisville & N R Co v Sheets, 121
Louisville etc R Co v Case, 514
Louisville, etc R Co v Douglas 106
Louisville etc R Co v Filbern, 557
Louisville etc R Co v Fowley 568
Louisville etc R Co v Goetz, 50
Louisville etc R Co v Graham, 123
Louisville, etc, R Co v Guthrie, 12
Louisville, etc R Co v Krinning, 57
Louisville etc R Co v McCoy, 538
Louisville, etc R Co v Orr, 193
Louisville etc R Co v Schmidt, 556
Louisville etc R Co v Sullivan, 569
Louisville, etc, Ry Co v Hart, 617
Louisville etc Ry Co v Jones, 657
Louisville Gas Co v Gutenkuntz, 629
Loundin v Warfield, 130
Louther v Earl of Radnor, 139
Loutham v Commonwealth, 318
Love v Masoner, 281
Love v Moynehan 206
Lovell Co, The Jno W. v. Houghton, 35
Lovejoy v Jones, 412
Loveless v Fowler, 438
Lovell v Howell 118
Lovett v Salem & S D R Co, 104
Low v Bouverie, 364, 371, 374
Low v Grand Trunk Ry Co 629
Low v Knowlton, 494
Low v Fox, 65
Lower Herald Co, 315
Lower Moss, 606
Lower Waterman, 395
Lowell v Boston & L R Co, 91, 232
Lowell Gas Light Co, 629
Lowenburg v Rosenthal, 9
Lowery v Manhattan R Co, 37, 589, 640
Lowery v W U T Co, 674
Lowis v Vedder, 132, 336
Lows v Telford, 466, 467
Lowther v Earl of Radnor 159
L E etc Ry v Haynes, 566
Luby v Woodhouse 135
Lucas v Case, 117, 339
Lucas v Flinn 25
Lucas v Trumbull, 443

Luce v. Carley, 450
Luce v Chicago, etc, R Co., 110
Luck v. Ripon, 218
Ludington v Peek, 144, 265
Luecker v Steffen, 281
Luford v Putnam, 639
Luke v. Calhoun Co, 82
Lukehart v Beverly, 204
Lukens v Ireland, 370
Lumley v Caswell, 194
Lumley v. Gye, 74, 271, 275, 410, 668, 669, 670, 671, 672, 673
Lund v Hersey F'b'r Co, 123
Lunt v Brown, 424, 459
Luther v Winnisimmet, 178, 519
Luttrell v Hazen, 99, 412
Lyde's Appeal, 179
Lyde v Barnard, 382
Lyell v. Ganga Dai, 166, 620
Lyle v Clason, 307
Lynch v Knight, 291, 293, 671
Lynch v Mercantile Trust Co, 112
Lynch v. Metropolitan Elevated R Co, 68, 107
Lynch v Nurdin, 18
Lynch v Smith, 584
Lynde v Johnston, 301
Lyon v Cambridge, 70
Lyon v Fishmongers' Company, 490, 508
Lyon v Meils, 606
Lyons v Merrick, 611
Lyton v Baird, 394
Little v Chicago & W M R Co, 129, 194

M.

Mabin v Webster, 223
Macy v Childress, 152
Macfadzen v Olivant, 274
Machine Co v Haven, 213
Mackay v Commercial Bank of New Brunswick, 113, 387
Mackey v City, 585
Macon, etc R Co v Lester, 610
Mail and Ind R Co, The, v The Norwich & N Society, 383
Maddison v. Alderson, 115
Madras R. Co v Zemindar of Carvatenagaram, 607, 608
Magee v Tappan, 412
Maginnay v Sandck, 278
Maguire v Hughes, 18
Mahan v Brown, 33, 509
Maher v Manhattan Ry Co, 552
Mahoney v Atlantic etc R Co, 40
Mahoney v Dore, 193
Mahurin v Harding, 357
Maline v. City of Rich Hill, 271
Mains v Whiting, 300
Mairs v Real Estate Assoc, 422
Maises v Thornton, 301
Maker v Slater Mill Power Co, 534
Malachy v Soper, 439
Malcolm v Fuller, 123
Malcolm v Spoon, 478
Malcohnson v Scott, 262
Mall v Lord, 107
Mallineumi v Gronland, 265
Mallack v Ridley, 107
Mallory v Pioneer Press Co, 318
Malloy v Bennett, 291
Malone v Hanley, 192

TABLE OF CASES CITED.

The References are to Pages.

Malone v. Hathaway, 119
Malone v. Pittsburgh & L. E. R. Co., 30
Malone v. Ryan, 222, 685
Maloney v. Donne, 260
Maloy v. New York Cent. R. Co., 541
Maloy v. Wabash, etc. Ry. Co., 565
Manchester Bonded Warehouse Co. v. Carr, 128
Manchester South Jn. Co. v. Fullerton, 67
Mandeville v. Guernsey, 263
Maner v. State, 260
Mangan v. Atterton, 580
Manhattan Mfg. Co. v. Van Keuren, 505
Manley v. Field, 280
Mann v. Locke, 658
Mann v. Welland, 614
Manner v. Simpson, 288
Manning v. Albee, 157
Manning v. Mitchell, 260
Manning v. State of Nicaragua, 116
Manning v. Wells, 612
Mansville Co. v. Worcester, 239
Mansfield, etc. Coal Co. v. McEnery, 633
Manzant v. Douglas, 518
Maples v. Weeks, 317, 319
Marble v. Ross, 611
Marble v. Worcester, 29
March v. Davison, 101
Marcott v. Marquette etc. R. Co., 76
Marcott v. Railroad Co., 571
Marey v. Davison, 117
Marcy v. Tiles, 518
Marietta, etc. R. Co. v. Stephenson, 610
Marin v. Sattefield, 220
Marine Ins. Co. v. St. Louis, I. M. & S. R. Co., 157, 497
Marion v. Chicago etc. R. Co., 108, 110
Marion v. C. R. I. & P. R. Co., 67
Markel v. Moody, 356
Markel v. Moody, 359
Marker v. Dunn, 292
Markey v. Rand, 112
Markham v. Brown, 651
Markley v. Whitman, 218
Marks v. Baker, 321, 352
Marks v. Jacobs, 345
Marks v. St. Paul, etc. Ry. Co., 590
Mars v. Del. & H. Canal Co., 574
Marsellis v. Banking Co., 528
Marsh v. Billings, 188, 390
Marsh v. Bristol, 257
Marsh v. Ellsworth, 329
Marsh v. Keating, 2 d., 257
Marsh v. N. Y. etc. R. Co., 611
Marshall's Case, 663, 664
Marshall v. Betner, 392
Marshall v. Blackshire, 204
Marshall v. Cohen, 505
Marshall v. Heard, 624
Marshall v. Heller, 260
Marshall v. Herman, 120
Marshall v. Hubbard, 353
Marshall v. Oakes, 64
Marshall v. Peck, 357
Marshall v. Pilies, 683
Marshall v. St. Louis, K. C. & N. Ry. Co., 104
Marshall v. Turnbull, 225
Marshall v. Wellwood, 645
Marshall v. Wing, 61
Marshall v. York, Newcastle & Berwick R. Co., 658
Marshalsea, The, 143

Marth, Township of, 217
Martin v. Chicago, etc., 157
Martin v. G. T. P. R. Co., 664
Martin v. Houghton, 163
Martin v. Payne, 278, 280
Martin v. Richards, 90
Martin v. Tribune Assn., 92
Martin v. Van Schaick, 319
Martin v. W. U. T. Co., 875
Matthowsky v. City of Hannibal, 529
Marks v. State, 255
Marvin v. Chicago, M. & St. P. Ry. Co., 43
Maschek v. St. Louis etc. R. Co., 589
Mason v. Lewis, 152
Mason v. Mason, 115
Mason v. Vance, 111
Massey v. Brown, 268
Massuere v. Dickens, 295, 305
Masterson v. Short, 186
Master Stevedore's Assoc. v. Walsh, 410
Matthews v. Bliss, 76
Matthews v. Torry, 151
Matthews v. Menedger, 151
Matley v. Whittier Machine Co., 584
Matlock v. Reppy, 140, 374
Matsell v. Flannagan, 221
Matthes v. Kerrigan, 92
Matthews v. Peach, 312
Matthews v. Case, 122
Matthews v. Cowan, 61
Matthews v. Flestel, 61
Matthews v. Fuller, 26
Matthews v. Missouri P. Ry. Co., 211, 514
Mattice v. Wilcox, 100
Maugher v. Dick, 317
Maulsby v. Reifsneider, 329
Maund v. Monmouthshire Canal Co., 68
Maxwell v. Bay City etc. Co., 46
May v. Burdett, 613
May v. Hanson, 569
Maybee v. Fisk, 312
Mayer v. Association, 110
Mayer v. Schleichter, 293
Mayer v. Walter, 409
Mayer v. Manning, 147
Maynard v. Fireman's Fund Ins Co., 66, 112
Mayo v. Boston & Maine Railroad, 548
Mayor of Colchester v. Brooke, 577
Mayor of London v. Cox, 143
Mayor of Manchester v. Williams, 13, 297
Mayor of Nashville v. Nichol, 70
Mayor of Rome v. Dodd, 70
Mayor of Savannah v. Waldner, 69
Mayor etc. v. Ferry Co., 67
Mayor etc. of Vicksburg v. McLain, 358
Mayrant v. Richardson, 302
Mayson v. Sheppard, 296
Mayton v. T. & P. Ry. Co., 126
McAdams v. Cates, 351, 368
McAleer v. Horsey, 357, 358
McAllister v. Albany, 70
McAllister v. Free Press Co., 321
McAndrews v. Collerd, 503, 615
McAnnelly v. Chapman, 442
McArthur v. Sears, 606
McBee v. Fulton, 323, 325
McBeth v. Craddock, 357, 367
McBride v. Board of Commrs, 439
McBride v. Indianapolis Frog & Switch Co., 549
McBride v. Union P. R. Co., 122
McCabe v. Jones, 310

TABLE OF CASES CITED. 721

The References are to Pages.

McCaffrey v. Carter, 436
McCaffrey v. Twenty-third St. R. Co., 164
McCaleb v. Smith, 296
McCall v. Brock, 600
McCall v. Chamberlain, 611
McCampbell v. Cunard S. S. Co., 194
McCandless v. McWha, 26
McCann v. Kings Co. L. R. Co., 92
McCann v. Tillinghast, 110
McCannon v. O'Connell, 419
McCardle v. McGinley, 348
McCarrahan v. Lavers, 265
McCarthy v. Boston, 108
McCarthy v. DeArmit, 262
McCarthy v. Niskern, 651
McCarthy v. Second Parish, 92
McCarty v. Bauer, 27
McCarty v. Fremont, 201, 203
McCarty v. Vickey, 414
McCauley v. Logan, 164
McClafferty v. Philp, 394
McClain, Appeal of, 408
McClellen v. Adams, 186
McClinathan v. Oswego, etc., R. Co., 84
McClary v. Sioux City, etc., R. Co., 29, 42
McCleary v. Kent, 92
McClelland v. Hurdle, 178
McClelland v. Louisville, etc., Ry. Co., 50
McClenaghan v. Brock, 108
McClung v. Dearborne, 87
McClure v. Miller, 81
McClure v. Thorpe, 117
McCombs v. Tuttle, 307
McCoon v. Smith, 61
McCord v. Oakland Quicksilver Co., 49
McCormick v. Perry, 392
McCoull v. Manchester, 70
McCoy v. Empire Warehouse Co., 120
McCoy v. McKowen, 108
McCready v. So. Car. R. Co., 504
McCready v. Thompson, 509
McCubbin v. Hastings, 26
McCullough v. City of Denver, 183
McCullough v. Rice, 96
McCullough v. Shoneman, 87
McCullough v. St. Paul, M. & M. Ry. Co., 17
McCullough v. Walton, 220
McCully v. Clarke, 516
McCurdy v. Rogers, 660
McDade v. City of Chester, 615
McDaniel v. Needham, 217
McDaniel v. Tebbetts, 115
McDermott v. Evening Journal, 54
McDermott v. Pacific R. Co., 116
McDonald, In re, 296
McDonald v. Ashland, 70
McDonald v. Chicago & N. W. R. Co., 85
McDonald v. Eagle & Phenix Mf. Co., 122
McDonald v. Hazeltine, 117
McDonald v. New York, etc., R. Co., 120
McDonald v. Press Pub. Co., 295
McDonald v. Redburg, 109
McDonald v. Snelling, 29, 42
McDonald v. Trafton, 563
McDonald v. Walker, 211
McDonnell v. Cambridge R. Co., 213
McDonnell v. Rifle Broom Co., 92
McDonough v. Virginia City, 70
McDougald v. Bellamy, 112
McDougall v. Cent. R. Co., 569
McDuffie v. Kilroad, 651
McElligott v. Randolph, 123

McFadden v. Rausch, 519
McFadden v. Robinson, 358
McFadden v. Whitney, 397
McGar v. Williams, 68
McGary v. Loomis, 567
McGhee v. Hall, 118
McGibbon v. Baxter, 617
McGibbons v. Wilder, 578
McGinty v. Athol Reservoir Co., 122
McGlynn v. Brodie, 192
McGovern v. New York etc. R. Co., 585
McGowan v. Mo. Pac. Ry. Co., 514
McGraw v. Baltimore, etc. R. Co., 600
McGready v. South Car. R. Co., 552
McGreary v. Eastern R. Co., 580
McGregor v. Brown, 439
McGregor v. Penn, 851
McGregor, City of, v. Boyle, 516
McGrew v. Stone, 29, 42
McGuire v. Blair, 301
McGuire v. Cartersville, 69
McGuire v. Galligan, 142
McGuire v. Grant, 510
McGuire v. Ringrose, 614
McGuire v. Spence, 634
McGurn v. Brackett, 494
McHenry v. Sneer, 402
McHugh v. Chicago, etc. R. Co., 562
McHugh v. Pundt, 141
McIlvoy v. Cockran, 201, 256
McIntire v. Plaisted, 204
McIntire v. Roberts, 64
McIntire R. Co. v. Bolton, 98
McIntyre v. Bransford, 326
McIntyre v. Buell, 353
McIntyre v. Sholty, 59
McKay v. Irvine, 110, 112
McKay v. Northern P. R. Co., 120
McKay v. State, 248
McKay v. Woodle, 610
McKee v. Eaton, 578
McKee v. Ingalls, 60, 296, 305, 576
McKee v. Owen, 651
McKee v. Wilson, 286, 300
McKeller v. Township of Monitor, 567
McKennon v. Greer, 96
McKenzie v. Des Moines Pub. Co., 300
McKeon v. Lee
McKeown v. Lee, 64
McKinley v. C. Ry. Co., 104
McKinley v. L., 311
McKinney v. Lovetts, 295
McKinson v. Squires, 685
McKnight v. Hasbrouck, 39
McKnight v. Ratcliff, 518, 639
McKnown v. Hunter, 343
McKone v. Michigan, etc. R. Co., 627
McLaughlin v. Bascom, 311
McLaughlin v. Charles, 320
McLaughlin v. Cowley, 329
McLaughlin v. Pryor, 95
McLean v. Blue Point Min. G. Co., 122
McLean v. Cook, 141
McLean v. Jackson, 243
McLean v. Schuyler Steam Tow-Boat Line, 590
McLean v. Warring, 323
McLelland v. Louisville, etc. R. Co., 537
McLennon v. Richards, 262
McLeod v. R. Broad Co., 229
McMahon v. Field, 484
McManus v. Cooke, 463
McManus v. Crickett, 111
McManus v. Lee, 230

TABLE OF CASES CITED.

The References are to Pages.

McMasters v. Illinois Central R Co, 120
McMenomy v Bund, 622
McMillan v B & M R Co, 585
McMillan v Watt, 194
McMillan v Birch 301, 328
McNab v Tolot, 69
McNally v Colwell, 511
McNamara v Gargett, 376
McNamee v Minke, 408
McNay v Stratton, 260
McNeilus v Lowe, 27
McNulta v Palston, 157
McPadden v Railroad Co, 606
McPheters v Hannibal, etc. R Co, 610
McPherson v Daniels, 306, 127
McPherson v State, 257
McPheters v Pa Co, 411
McQueen v Fulgham, 64, 192, 208
McQueen v Beck, 261
McQuilken v Central P R Co, 574
McVeigh v United States, 69
McWhorter v Batten, 271
McWilliams v Fraggs, 220
Mead v Bunn, 177
Meade v Jack, 110
Meadow v Wise, 142
Means v Dole, 66
Mears v L & S W R Co, 413
Medbury v Watson, 157
Medford v Pratt, 156
Mechen v Van Rensselaer, 115
Meeks v Southern P R Co, 574
Meeker v Fond du Lac, 271
Mohan v Syracuse, etc, R Co, 6
Mehrhof etc Co v Delaware, etc R Co, 631
Meddle v Anthis, 235
Meder v Penn R Co, 637
Meigs v Lister, 505
Mele v Delaware & H C Co, 120
Mellon v Morrill, 624
Mellor v Spateman, 508
Mellor v Watkins, 44
Melville v Gary, 350
Melvin v Weiant, 294, 297
Membery v G W R Co, 194, 195
Memphis etc R Co v McCool 647
Memphis etc R Co v Hicks 157
Memphis R Co v Thomas, 117
Memphis etc R Co v Whitfield, 558
Mendenhall v Klinck, 464
Meneely v Meneely, 184
Mennie v Blake, 126, 435
Mentser v Armour, 125
Mephams v Bressel, 630
Mercato v Down, 644
Mercer v Corbin, 218, 252
Mercer v Whimsley, 278
Merchants & P Bank v Meyer, 411
Merchants' Dis Co v Smith, 606
Merchants' Nat Bank v State Nat Bank, 67
Meredith v Reed, 538
Merest v Harvey, 20
Merivale v Carson, 319
Merriam v Cunningham, 60
Merriam v Mitchell, 93
Merrifield v Lombard, 492
Merrifield v Worcester, 492
Merrick v Claremont, 11
Merrills v Tariff etc Co, 67
Merryweather v Nixan, 232
Mersey Docks Trustees v Gibbs, 74, 114, 155

Messenger v Pennsylvania R
Metcalf v Cunard Steamship Co, 619
Metropolitan Association v Petch, 529
Metropolitan Asylum District v Hill, 139
Metropolitan Bank v Pooley, 101
Metropolitan Ry Co v Wright, 212
Metropolitan Ry Co v Jackson, 40, 543, 554
Metzler v Romine, 382
Meux v Cobley, 128
Meyer v Amidon, 353
Meyer v Metzler, 492
Meyer v Second Ave R Co, 195
Meyrose v Adams, 391
Mich Cent R Co v Anderson, 503
Michael v Stanton 91
Michaels v N Y etc R Co, 600
Michaelson v Dennison, 151
Mehan v Wyatt, 213
Michel v Dunkle, 271
Michel v Monroe Co, 520
Mechill v Mill Co etc, 36
Michigan v Coleman, 242
Michoud v Girod, 215
Middlestadt v Morrison, 534
Midland Insurance Co v Smith, 230
Mielenz v Quasdorf, 304, 312, 314
Milkchill v Bates, 100
Milam v Burnsides, 328
Milburn v Gilman, 141
Milburn v Byrne, 275
Miles v Worcester, 192
Millen v Fawdry, 613
Miller v Adams, 265
Miller v Baker, 9
Miller v Burkett, 183
Miller v Burlington & O R, 67
Miller v Butler, 295, 307
Miller v C M St P Ry Co, 395
Miller v Craig, 199
Miller v Curry, 614
Miller v Curtis, 359
Miller v Dell, 241, 402, 437
Miller v Fenton, 231
Miller v Grace, 267
Miller v Keokuk etc, Ry Co, 244
Miller v Kerr, 315
Miller v King, 658
Miller v Lynch, 482
Miller v Mariners Church, 684
Miller v Martin, 503
Miller v Milligan, 394
Miller v. Missouri P R Co, 121
Miller v State, 255
Miller v Southern P R Co, 120
Miller v Switzer, 64
Miller v Thompson, 434
Miller v Truehart, 505
Miller v Umbehower, 81
Miller v Union P R Co, 124
Miller v Willigen, 393
Miller v Woodhead, 24
Milligan v Wehinger, 611
Milliken v Hathway, 439
Millison v Hoch, 220
Mills v Armstrong, 570, 580, 583, 594
Mills v United States, 156
Mills v Wooten, 464
Milwaukee Bank v City Bank, 26
Milwaukee & M R R Co v Finney, 87
Milwaukee & St P Ry Co v Kellogg, 34
Milwaukee etc R Co v Arms 538
Miner v Conn River R Co, 593
Miner v Medbury, 367

TABLE OF CASES CITED.

The References are to Pages.

Minge v. Woolfolk, 9, 875.
Minks v. Hopeman, 508.
Minning v. Mitchell, 201.
Mintz v. Morrison, 409.
Misner v. Lighthall, 610.
Misner v. Russell, 370.
Mississippi Cent R Co v. Mason, 511.
Mississippi etc Ry Co, v. Finly, 370.
Missouri Furnace Co v. Abend, 102.
Missouri Pac Ry Co v. Lewis, 82.
Missouri Pac Ry Co v. Peregoy, 123.
Missouri Pac Ry Co v. Pintzer, 561.
Missouri Pac Ry Co v. Sasse, 123.
Missouri Pac Ry Co v. Somers, 193, 633.
Missouri Pac Ry Co, v. Williams, 123.
Mitchell v. Allen, 230.
Mitchell v. Bradstreet Co, 302.
Mitchell v. Clapp, 611.
Mitchell v. Crassweller, 99, 102, 111.
Mitchell v. Dudley Main Colliery Co., 216.
Mitchell v. Harmony, 84, 111.
Mitchell v. Malone, 207.
Mitchell v. Mayor of Rome etc. 211, 216.
Mitchell v. McDonald Co., '62, 69.
Mitchell v. Mitchell, 230.
Mitchell v. Robinson, 121.
Mitchell v. State, 234.
Mitchell v. S W R Co., 58.
Mitchell v. Woll, 611.
Mix v. McCoy, 60.
Mix v. Woodward, 312.
Moberly v. Preston, 290, 296, 315.
Mobile & M Ry Co v. Smith, 99.
Mobile, etc P Co v. Ashcroft, 567.
Mobile, etc P Co v. Gray, 504.
Mobile, etc R Co v. Williams, 611.
Moe v. Smiley, 51.
Moffatt v. Bateman, 630, 612, 657.
Mogul Steamship Co v. McGregor, 177, 182, 227, 285, 403, 406.
Mohry v. Hoffman, 278.
Moir v. Hopkins, 112.
Molloy v. New York, etc, R Co, 101.
Money v. Lower Vein Coal Co, 193.
Monk v. New Utrecht, 576.
Monk v. Packard, 189, 503.
Monmouth Park v. Dunbar, 434.
Monongahela City v. Fischer, 70.
Montgomery v. Dooley, 295.
Montgomery v. Dooley, 291.
Montgomery v. Handy, 610.
Montgomery v. Knox, 320.
Montgomery v. Thompson, 185.
Montgomery Gas Light Co v. Montgomery & I Ry Co, 573.
Montreal River Lumber Co v. Mihills, 367.
Monroe v. Stickney, 214.
Monument Bank v. Globe Works, 67.
Moody v. Baker, 29.
Moody v. Deutsch, 39.
Moody v. McDonald, 537.
Moody v. Ward, 618.
Mooney v. Coolidge, 225.
Mooney v. Maynard 473.
Mooney v. Miller Co, 357.
Moorcock, The, 630.
Moore v. Ames, 138.
Moore v. Appleton, 230, 231.
Moore v. City of Waco, 213.
Moore v. Columbia & G R Co, 97.
Moore v. Des Moines, etc, Co, 637.
Moore v. Durgin, 262.

Moore v. Eastman, 61.
Moore v. Floyd, 211.
Moore v. Manufacturers Nat Bank, 531.
Moore v. Manssini, 22.
Moore v. Mauk, 323.
Moore v. McKibbin, 18.
Moore v. Metrop R Co, 107.
Moore v. Mo Pac R Co, 555.
Moore v. Norfolk & W R Co, 567.
Moore v. Ocean Steam Nav Co, 624.
Moore v. Perry, 122.
Moore v. Rawson, 509, 511.
Moore v. Robinson, 118.
Moore v. Sanborn, 304.
Moore v. Shields, 103.
Moore v. Stevenson, 291.
Moore v. Thompson, 260.
Moore v. Wallis, 213.
Moore v. White, 224.
Moody v. Town of Danbury, 31.
Moran v. Devlin, 69.
Moran v. Miami County, 68.
Morasse v. Brochu, 291, 400.
Morehead v. Eades, 18.
Morehead v. Gilmore, 111.
Morehead v. Jones, 124.
Moreland v. Atchison, 361.
Morey v. Fitzgerald, 176.
Morey v. Morning Journal Assoc., 317.
Morford v. Woodworth, 519.
Morgan v. Bliss, 11.
Morgan v. Booth, 329.
Morgan v. Bowman, 91.
Morgan v. Cox, 598, 618, 637.
Morgan v. Curley, 637.
Morgan v. Dawks, 278.
Morgan v. Dudley, 148.
Morgan v. Rise, 173.
Morgan v. Rose, 281.
Morgan v. Schwachofer, 225.
Morgan v. Skiddy, 303.
Morgan v. Smith, 26.
Morgan v. State, 250.
Morgan v. Vale of Neath R Co, 119.
Morgan v. Varick, 9, 469.
Morier v. Minneapolis, etc, R Co, 108.
Moritz v. Ganhart, 278.
Morley v. Chase, 263.
Morley v. Elsbree, 402.
Morrell v. Phelnfrank, 91.
Morrill v. Aden, 61.
Morrill v. Blackman, 357.
Morrill v. Moulton, 434.
Morrill v. Wallace, 351, 357.
Morris v. Casel, 256.
Morris v. Chicago, 239.
Morris v. Fraker, 610.
Morris v. Platt, 164, 167, 201, 204.
Morris v. Scott, 33, 393.
Morris v. Shaw, 220.
Morris & E R Co v. Prudden, 22, 528.
Morris etc Co v. Ryerson, 130.
Morris etc R Co v. State, 562.
Morris v. Wiggins Ferry Co, 501.
Morrison v. Davis, 51.
Morrison v. Marquardt, 509.
Morrison v. Phillips etc Cons Co, 193.
Morrison v. Rogers, 608.
Morrissey v. Eastern R Co, 584.
Morrow v. Wood, 10.
Morse v. Belfast, 572.
Morse v. Copeland, 162.
Morse v. Crawford, 59.
Morse v. Dearborne, 360, 363.

The References are to Pages.

Morae v. Duncan, 220
Morse v Worcester, 69.
Mortimer v Thomas, 263
Morton v Detroit etc R Co., 121.
Morton v. Met. Life Ins. Co., 67, 68
Morton v. Moore, 487.
Morton v Scull, 383
Moses v. Dubois, 250
Moses v. Johnson, 429.
Moses v. Katzen Verger, 800
Moses v. MacFerlan, 669
Moses v. Manhattan R. Co., 151
Moses v. Mead, 370
Mosier v. Stoll, 311.
Moslcott v. McFido, 272.
Mosley v. Chamberlain, 117
Moss v. Pacific R Co, 125
Mostyn v Fabrigas, 185, 230.
Motes v. Bates, 300.
Mott v Comstock, 302.
Mott v. Consumer's Ice Co, 110
Mott v. Dawson, 321, 338
Mott v Shoolbred, 528
Moulton v. Aldrich, 501.
Mount Vernon v Dusenbett, 588.
Mouse's case, 200.
Mower v Stickney, 142
Mower v Watson, 620
Mowers v. Fethers, 651
Mowey v Walsh, 414.
Mowrey v. Wood, 220.
Mowry v. Chase, 260.
Mowry v Whipple, 801
Moxham, The M, 237, 238 239.
Moynihan v. Hills Co., 124
Mugridge v Eveleth, 421, 432
Mulcairns v. Janesville, 69, 636.
Muldoon v Rickey, 108
Mullan v Phila & S M S S Co, 123
Mullan v Steamship Co, 91
Mullen v. St John, 634, 638
Mullen v Stricker, 509.
Mulligan v Cole, 313
Mulligan v New York & R B R Co, 100
Mulliner v Florence, 444
Mulvehall v. Millward, 278
Mulvey v Rhode Island Locomotive Works, 124.
Mumby v Bowden, 91
Mumford v Oxford etc R. Co, 529
Mumford v. Whitney, 458
Mundorff v Wickersham, 112, 384
Mundy v Wight, 323.
Munger v. Hess, 61
Munns v Dupont, 594
Munster v Lamb, 330.
Murdock v. Boston & A R R Co, 68
Murphy v. Boston & A R Co, 124
Murphy v Central Park R Co, 110
Murphy v Chicago, etc. R Co, 241.
Murphy v. Deane, 546, 548.
Murphy v. Hobbs, 234, 393.
Murphy v Lincoln, 482.
Murphy v Lowell, 69
Murphy v. Martin, 266.
Murphy v. Orr, 534
Murphy v. Ramsey, 148
Murphy v. Stout, 324
Murphy v. Wilson, 230.
Murray v. Archer, 520.
Murray v Baker, 243.
Murray v. Beckwith, 356.
Murray v Boyne, 201
Murray v Currie, 93, 95.

Murray v Gibson, 639.
Murray v Hall, 449
Murray v. Hay, 528.
Murray v McShane, 507
Murray v South Carolina R. Co, 116, 611
Murry v McAllister, 284
Muso v. Stern, 91
Musgrave v. Chung Tecong Toy, 136.
Musgrove v St Louis Church, 563.
Musselman v Marquis, 225
Mussey v Cummings, 142, 479
Mut. Ben Life Ins Co. v. Cannon, 352.
Mut. Ben. Life Ins. Co. v. Robertson, 352
Myers v. Gemmel, 509
Myers v Gilbert, 114.
Myles v. Myles, 26.

N.

Nagel v. Alleghany Valley R. Co, 585
Nagel v Railroad, 571.
Nall v. Louisville etc R Co., 123
Narehood v Wilhelm, 478
Nash v. Lucas, 474
Nash v Minnesota T G Co, 357
Nashville & C. R. Co. v. Starnes, 87, 108
Nashville etc R Co. v. Carroll, 121
Nashville etc. R Co v Davis, 605
Nashville etc R. Co v Elliott, 193
Nashville etc R. Co v Jones, 121
Nashville, etc, R. Co v. King, 606.
Nat Bank v Graham, 67, 68.
Nat Bk of Metropolis v Sprague, 271.
National Copper Co. v. The Minnesota Mining Co, 153.
Nat Ins Co. v. Minch, 381
Natoma etc. Co v. Clarkin, 235, 482
Nat. Provincial Plate Glass Ins Co v Prudential Assurance Co., 611
Nat Reserve Fund Life Assn v Spectatur Co., 66
Nanman v Oberle, 367
Neal v Gillett, 61
Neal v Hart, 267
Neal v Henry, 605
Neal v. Joyner 262.
Neal v State, 149
Near v Wilcox, 612.
Nebb v Hope, 334.
Nebenzahl v Townsend, 395
Nelb v Hope, 287, 324
Needham v Grand Tr R Co, 51, 52
Needham v Louisville & N R. Co., 543, 552
Neff v. Landis, 680
Negley v Farra, 310, 318.
Nehr v State, 613
Nehrbas v Central Pac R Co, 537
Nelson v Barchentus, 313
Nelson v Chicago, etc, Ry Co, 45, 164, 542.
Nelson v. Danielson, 299
Nelson v Liverpool Brewery Co, 531
Nelson v Musgroove, 287.
Nelson v Stewart, 611.
Nemitz v Conrad, 261
Nento v Denman, 146
N E R. Co. v Wanless, 590.
Nesbet v Sawyer, 224
Ness v. Hamilton, 324.
Neth v. Crofat, 262
Nettleton v Sikes, 459

TABLE OF CASES CITED.

The References are to Pages.

Nauert v. Boston, 69
Newfeld v Boldion, 660
Nevitt v Gillespie, 140
New Albany etc R Co. v. Peterson, 178
Newark Aqueduct Board v City of Passaic, 522.
Newark Coal Co. v Upson, 399
Nesbury v Munnhower, 262.
Newell v Cowan, 231.
Newell v Randall, 369
New England Dredging Co. v Rockport Granite Co, 87.
New England Exp Co v. Maine Cent R, 650
New Jersey etc R Co v. Young, 194
New Jersey Express Co v. Nichols, 544
Newhall v. Kingsbury, 432.
Newkirk v Sabler, 10, 201, 122, 460
Newman v Alvord, 184
Newman v Richardson, 111
Newman v. Sylvester, 481
Newmeister v Dubuque, 271
New Orleans & N. E. R. Co. v Reese, 92.
New Orleans, etc. R Co v Field, 610
New Orleans, etc., R Co v Hanning, 103
New Orleans etc. R Co v. Hughes, 125.
New Orleans etc v R Co v Hurst, 656
New Orleans, etc, R R Co v Norwood, 91
New Orleans etc. R Co v Statham 519.
New Orleans Gas Light Co. v. Louisiana Light Co, 199
Newport News & M V R. Co v Old Colony R Co, 123
Newsom v Anderson, 422.
Newsom v Jackson, 81.
Newton v Harland, 468
Newton v. Locklin, 262.
Newton v Weaver, 395
New World v King, 542
New York and C M S & Co v. Rogers, 552
New York & N Ry. Co v New York & N E R Co, 651
New York B & P. Co. v Gutta Percha & R Mfg Co, 225
New York etc R Co v A R Co, 591
New York etc R Co v Bell, 124
New York etc R Co v City of Rochester, 522
New York, etc R Co v. Lyons, 193
New York etc, R. Co v Schuyler, 67, 225
New York, etc R Co v Skinner, 544
New York, etc, R Co v Steinbreuner, 94, 519
New York, L E & H R Co v. Harring, 105
New York P. & D Establishment, 482
Niantic C & M Co v Leonhard, 120.
Nichols v City of Duluth, 157
Nicholson v Janeway, 369
Nichols v Jones, 223
Nichols v Marsland, 161, 606, 607
Nichols v Michael, 369
Nichols v Nowling, 232
Nichols v State, 551
Nicholson v. New York etc, R Co, 211
Nickleson v Stryker, 277.
Nidover v Hall, 298
Night v Goodyear, etc Mfg Co, 495
Niles v How, 238.

Nipp v. Wischeart, 248
Nimon v. Jamon, 328
Nitro glycerine Case, 164, 174.
Nitro glycerine Case, The, 604, 610
Nix v. Caldwell, 112
Nix v. Texas & P. R. Co., 123
Noble v McFarland, 417
Noblesville, etc, Co v Gause, 109
Noeninger v Vogt, 331.
Nolte v. Brown, 275
Nolan v Jones, 61.
Nolan v. New York, etc. R. Co., 513.
Nolan v. Traber, 64
Noonan v Albany, 71.
Noonan v New York, etc., R Co, 421
Noonan v Orton, 899.
Norcross v. Nunan, 141
Norcross v Thoms, 503, 504, 506
Norden v. Jones, 658.
Norfolk & P. R. Co v Ormsby, 585
Norfolk & W. R. Co v. Groseclose's Admr, 583
Norfolk & W. R Co. v. Jackson, 193.
Norfolk & W. R Co v. Lipscomb, 223.
Norfolk etc R. Co. v. Rudge, 538
Norfolk etc. R Co v Ormsby, 537.
Norrel v Vogel, 396
Norris v. Baker, 513.
Norris v Hall, 439.
Norris v. Vance, 60
North American D & I Co v. The River Mersey, 90
North Carolina v Temple, 136
North Chicago R M. Co v Johnson, 121.
Northcote v Smith, 473.
North Eastern R Co v. Wanless, 553
Northern Cent R. Co v Canton Co, 312.
Northern Pac R Co v Herbert, 88, 99, 124
Northern P. R Co v Lewis, 450
Northern P R Co v. O B en, 121
Northern R R Co. v. Paine, 432
North Side Street Ry Co v Tippins, 545.
North Vernon v Voegler, 69
Northwestern R Co. v. Hack, 101
Norton, The E M, 96
Norton v Craig, 639
Norton v Eastern R Co, 556
Norton v. Sewall, 621
Norton v Wiswall, 530
Norvell v. Gray, 422
Norwood v. Dickey, 506
Norwood v Gonzales County, 243
Nott v. Stoddard, 334
Nottingham v. Baltimore & Potomac R Co, 488.
Notting Hill, The, 683.
Nowell v Tripp, 262
Nowlin v. Whipple, 462
Noyes v Hall, 295
Noyes v Loring, 658, 660
Noyes v. Shepherd, 537
Nugent v Boston, C & M R Corp, 552
Nugent v. Smith, 605, 655.
Nunnally v Taliaferro, 346
Nuttall v Bracewell, 464
N. Y. & W. P. T. Co. v Dryburg, 674, 675
Nyberg v Handelaar, 445
Nye v Merriman, 375
N Y etc R Co. v Skinner, 611.

O.

Oakey v Dalton, 76.
Oakland City A & I Soc. v Bingham, 103
O'Brien v Barry, 395
O'Brien v. Cavanaugh, 453.
O'Brien v St. Paul, 69
O'Connell v Baltimore etc R Co, 144
O'Conner v. O'Connor, 511
O'Connor v Andrews, 624.
Ocean Co v Sprague etc Co, 152
Ocean Steamship Co v Cheyney, 120
Ochsenhein v Shapley, 103, 104
Odell v. Salomon, 624.
Oden v. Weathersbee, 417
O'Donagh et v McGovern, 339.
O'Donnell v A V R, 620
Ofallo v Keely, 189
Ogden v Claycomb, 200, 250
Ogden v Riley, 298
O'Hanlon v Myers, 701
Ogilvie v. Knox, 860
Ohio etc R Co v Collarn, 514
Ohio River R Co v Ward, 492
Oil v Rowley, 173
Oil City Gas Co v Robinson, 620.
Oil Creek, etc R Co v. Keighron, 90
Oldham v Sparks, 20
Olds v. Chicago etc, 434
Oliver v Berry, 213.
Oliver v LaValle, 55
Oliver v. Loftin, 516.
Oliver v McLellan, 61
Oliver v Perkins, 230.
Oliver v White, 112
Olmstead v Doland, 267.
Olmsted v Miller, 203
Olmsted v. Rich, 401.
Olrich v Stohrer, 632.
Olson v Clyde, 122.
Olson v Neal, 395
Olson v Orton, 378
Omaha v. Jensen, 69.
Omaha A & S. Co v Rogers, 434
Omaha & R V Co v Brown, 244
Omaha etc R Co v Janecek, 154
Omaha etc. R Co v Standen, 495
Omaha etc Co v Tabor, 439
O'Malley v St Paul, M & M Ry. Co, 555
O'Mara v Hudson River R Co, 556.
Onderdonk v Smith, 624.
O'Neil v Johnson, 399
Orange etc H R. Co. v Ward, 552, 557
O'Reer v Strong, 658.
O'Riley v. Diss 611
Ormerod v Todmorden Mill Co, 434
Ornsby v Douglass, 336
Orne v Roberts, 614.
O'Rourke v Hart, 92
Orr v Home Mutual Ins Co, 182
Orr v Littlefield, 225
Ortman v Greenman, 741
Osborn v. Gillett, 71, 75, 273
Osborn v McMaster, 99.
Osborn v. Morgan, 84.
Osgood v Lewis, 370
O'Shaughnessy v Baxter, 142
Ostrom v Calkins, 300
Ostatago v Taylor, 465
Oswald v McGehee, 376
Oswego Starch Factory v. Lendrum, 369
Ottenot v N Y, L & W. R Co, 455

Owen v. Field, 456,
Owen v. O'Reilly, 213.
Owen v. Phillips, 485.
Owens v. Railroad Co, 646.
Owens v Snodgrass, 93.
Owsley v. Montgomery, etc R R. Co, 68
Oxford v Patel, 110.
Oxley v. Watts, 179
Ozark Land Co v Leonard, 468

P.

Pace v. Aubrey, 312
Pach v Godfroy, 504.
Pacific Ins Co v Conard, 223.
Paddock v Somes, 523
Paddock v Strobridge, 369
Paddock v Watts, 191, 306.
Philgott v. Swolting, 321
Padmore v Pletz, 161
Paducah, etc R Co v. Hoehl, 567
Paducah etc R Co v Letcher, 537
Paff v Slack, 611.
Page v Bent, 354
Page v Branch, 447
Page v Cushing, 390
Page v Du Puy, 112
Page v. Freeman, 230.
Page v Mills Mfg Co, 486.
Page v. Parker, 403.
Page v Wells, 512
Paine v. Chandler, 182
Paine v Farr, 223
Paine v. Northern P R Co, 464
Painter v Ives, 265
Paland v. Chicago, etc R Co, 192
Palatka etc. R Co v State, 487
Pallet v. Sargent, 124
Palmer v Chicago etc R Co, 252.
Palmer v Concord, 332, 333
Palmer v. Denver, etc R Co, 102.
Palmer v Gallup, 214.
Palmer v Harris, 308
Palmer v London, 93
Palmer v. Manhattan R Co, 166
Palmer v Mich. Cent. R. Co, 125
Palmer v Thorpe, 298
P. & R. v Reynolds, 629
P. & R J R v. Lane, 629
Pangburn v Bull, 893
Pantzar v Tilly Foster Mn. Co, 117
Papot v Trowell, 243
Pappa v Rose, 140
Pardo v Bingham, 243
Parham v Randolph 378
Parish v Kaspare, 454
Park v Detroit Free Press Co, 336
Park v Hopkins, 64
Park v City of Seattle, 157.
Parker v. Elliott, 279
Parker v First Avenue Hotel Co, 511
Parker v. First Nat Bank, 434
Parker v Flagg, 606
Parker v. Foote, 456, 509
Parker v Frambes 394
Parker v. Georgia P Ry. Co., 567
Parker v Lanier, 220
Parker v Lewis, 204, 305
Parker v. Lack & Canal, 447
Parker v McQueen, 336.
Parker v. Meek, 279
Parker v. Misc, 9

TABLE OF CASES CITED.

The References are to Pages.

Parker v Union Woolen Works, 495
Parker v. Winnipeseogee Co., 452.
Parker v Prescott, 816.
Parkham v Decatur, 199.
Parkhurst v Ketchum 323, 317.
Parkins v Scott, 202, 317
Parlement Belge, The, 137
Parmer v Anderson, 297
Parmlee v Leonard, 112
Parmlee v Adolph, 975
Parnell v Walter, 319
Parrish v. Pensacola & A R Co., 120
Parrott v Floyd, 189
Parrott v. Hartsfield, 302
Parrott v. Housatonic R. Co , 519
Parrott v Wells 538.
Parry v Smith, 621
Parsons v. Brown, 204
Parsons v Hardy, 608
Parsons v Martin, 683
Parsons v Winchell, 100
Partlow v Hargarts, 611
Partridge v General Council etc 116
Parvis v Phila W & B R Co , 556
Pasley v Freeman, 351, 381
Pastine v Adams, 627
Pastime v Adams 574
Pastorius v Fisher, 518
Patch v The Tribune Assoc., 311
Patrick v Colerick, 170
Patten v Marden, 225
Patten v Wiggins, 26
Patterson v D'Auterive, 148
Patterson v Detroit, etc , R Co , 24
Patterson v Frazer, 63.
Patterson v Hayden, 281
Patterson v Lippincott, 660.
Patterson v Nuller, 150
Patterson v Pittsburgh, etc R Co , 194
Patterson v Shaw, 107.
Patterson v South & N A R Co., 220
Patterson v State, 323
Patterson v Thompson, 278
Patterson v Westervelt, 214
Patton v Holland, 493
Patton v People, 255, 257.
Patzack v Von Gerichten, 138.
Paul v Halferty, 804
Paul v Slason, 214
Paul v Summerhayes, 477
Paulmier v Erie R Co., 82.
Paw v. Beckner, 262
Paxton v Bayer, 153.
Payne v Allen, 151
Payne v Donegan, 399.
Payne v Green, 141.
Payne v Humeston & S. Ry Co , 583
Payne v McKinley, 488, 489
Payne v. Smith, 357
Payne v. Taylor, 323.
Payson v Macomber, 260.
P C & St L R Co v Sponier, 211.
Pearl v Walter, 376
Pearson v Duane, 651
Pearson v Inlow, 412.
Pearsol v Chapin, 658.
Pease v Glo hec, 680.
Pease v Sabin, 632
Pease v Smith, 439
Peck v Bank of America, 245
Peck v Cooper, 67, 84.
Peck v Derry, 364, 367
Peck v Elder, 504, 505, 506
Peck v Gerney, 84

Peck v Lockridge, 117.
Peck v. Martin, 27.
Peck v. Rooke, 204
Peckham v Henderson, 516.
Peckham v. Holman, 370
Pedrech v Porter, 350.
Peek v. Derry, 227
Peek v Gurney, 227, 356, 374.
Pefley v. Noland, 159
Peigne v Sutcliffe, 61.
Pells v Snell, 211
Pence v Dozier, 278
Pendarves v Monro, 611.
Pendleburgh v. Greenhalgh, 91
Pendergrast v. Foley, 215
Penn. Co. v Lynch, 121
Penn Coal Co v Sanderson, 153, 210, 492.
Pennington v Brinsop Hall Coal Co , 526
Pennington v Yell, 26
Pennoyer v Allen, 506.
Penn R Co. v Hope, 501
Penn R Co v Ogler, 538.
Pennsylvania Canal Co v Bentley, 513, 644
Pennsylvania Co. v Lynch, 192
Pennsylvania Co. v. Ray, 620
Pennsylvania Co v Roney, 568
Pennsylvania Co etc v Pennsylvania S V. R Co , 155
Pennsylvania R Co v. Aspell, 555
Pennsylvania R. Co v Atha, 624
Pennsylvania R Co v Fries, 606
Pennsylvania R. Co. v. Garvey, 557
Pennsylvania R Co v. Hoagland, 450
Pennsylvania R Co. v. Hope, 12
Pennsylvania Co v James, 585.
Pennsylvania R Co v. Kerr, 29, 42, 44
Pennsylvania R. Co. v. Killips, 556.
Pennsylvania R. Co v Ogler, 378
Pennsylvania R. Co. v. Righter, 541
Pennsylvania R. Co. v Toomey, 105
Pennsylvania R Co v Vandiver, 105
Pennsylvania S V. R. Co v. Walsh, 157
Pennsylvania R. Co. v. Weber, 546
Penrice v Wallace, 199.
Penrose v Curren, 62
Penrose v Nixon, 522
Penruddocks Ca , 493, 521.
Pensacola Gas Co v Pebley, 505
People v Albany, etc , R Co , 67.
People v Cooper, 149.
People v Craunse, 485.
People v Dann, 255.
People v Flack, 402
People v. Hubbard, 471
People v Lennon, 256
People v Lilley, 252, 253
People v Pearl, 257
People v. Richards, 308
People v Rockwell 45
People v Sands, 456, 503
People v Sergeant, 504
People v Sheldon, 402
People v Sherwin, 449
People v Supervisors of San Francisco, 360
People v Talmage, 136.
People v. White Lead Works, 498
People v Islas, 258.
Peoples v Smith, 264
Peoples Gas Co v Tyner, 178
People, The, v Fisher, 410
Peoria Bridge Assn v Loomis, 537.
Peoria, etc., Ins Co. v. Frost, 81

TABLE OF CASES CITED.

The References are to Pages.

Percival v. Harron, 102
Percy v. Clavy, 212
Perdue v. Burnett, 290
Perham v. Coney, 447.
Perkins v. Mitchell, 328, 330.
Perkins v. Rorer, 284.
Perley v. Eastern R Co , 41
Perret v. N. O. Times Newspaper, 110, 818
Perrin v. Wells, 217
Perrin v Taylor, 505.
Perry v. Fitzhowe, 513, 514.
Perry v. Lovejoy, 272.
Perry v. Mann, 312.
Perry v. Smith, 591.
Perryman v Lister, 268.
Peschel v. Chicago etc. R. Co., 122
Peter v Blocker, 275.
Peters v. Lake, 273, 274, 281
Peters v. Peters, 61.
Peters v. Turell, 399.
Peterson v. Haffner, 35, 61, 180, 218
Peterson v Sentman, 313
Peterson v Toner, 392.
Peterson v Whitebreast C & M Co , 122.
Petrie v Columbia & G. R. Co , 538
Petrie v. Rose, 24
Petrie v Williams, 414
Pettibone v Simpson, 293
Pettigrew v Evansville, 225.
Pettit v Cowlerd, 468
Petty v. Hannibal etc. R. Co., 557.
Pfingst v Senn, 521
Pfister v. Gerwig, 567.
Pholin v Kenderline, 281.
Phelps v. Cousins, 610.
Phelps v James, 360
Phelps v. Lill, 158.
Phelps v Nowlen, 153.
Phelps v Waite, 84
Philadelphia & R R Co v. Derby, 110.
Philadelphia etc , R Co. v. Anderson, 605
Philadelphia, etc R. Co. v Lrank, 544.
Philadelphia etc R. Co v Hoeflich, 220
Philadelphia, etc R Co v Schertle, 544
Philadelphia etc. R Co v. Spearen, 568.
Philadelphia etc R Co v Stibbing, 545.
Philadelphia etc R Co v Yerger, 562
Philadelphia, W & B R Co v Philadelphia, etc., Towboat Co , 99
Philadelphia, W & B R. Co. v Quigley, 67, 220
Philbrick v Foster, 201, 256
Philippi v Wolf, 271, 274
Philips v City of Denver, 506
Phil'ips v Fadden, 262.
Phillips v Allen, 523
Phillips v Ayre, 135
Phillips v. Barnet, 65.
Phillips v Bordman, 216
Phillips v Dewald, 564
Phillips v Dickerson, 30, 42
Phillips v Eyre, 238, 239, 240
Phillips v Homfray 83
Phillips v Hoyle, 281
Phillips v. Kelley, 208, 235
Phillips v L & S W R. Co., 212, 219
Phillips v Phillips, 64.
Phillips v Richardson, 64
Phillips v. State, 506
Phœnix Ins Co. v Moog, 403
Pickard v Collins, 504, 509
Pickard v McCormack, 358

Pickard v. Smith, 625
Pickens v Decker, 69.
Pickering v James, 149
Pickering v Rudd, 421
Pickett v. Crooke, 619
Pierce v German Law & Loan Soc., 530,
Pierce v. Guilford, 225.
Pierce v Hubbard, 264.
Pierce v. Thompson, 392, 509.
Pierce v. Wood, 114.
Pierson v. Glalo, 205
Piggott v. E C R Co., 608
Pike v. Bright, 658
Pike v. Chicago & A. R Co , 121
Pike v Fay, 858
Pike v. Grand Trunk Ry. Co , 514.
Pike v. Hanson, 260
Pike v Megoun, 145.
Pike v. Van Wormer, 200
Pilcher v. Hart, 484, 500
Pilcher v. Rawlins, 415
Pilgrim v Southampton etc. R. Co., 483.
Pink v Catnlek, 295.
Pinkerton v Manchester R. Co., 683.
Pinkerton v. Woodward, 851.
Pinney v Berry, 519.
Piollot v. Simmers, 515
Piper v Hoard, 215
Piper v Pearson, 138
Pippin v Sheppard, 648
Pitford v Armstrong, 201, 257
Pittard v. Oliver, 343, 344
Pittock v O'Nicll, 813, 843
Pitts v Hale, 81.
Pittsburg, A & M Ry Co. v Pearson, 633.
Pittsburg etc R R Co. v Andrews, 632
Pittsburgh, etc. R Co v Collins, 611,
Pittsburgh, etc R Co v Evans, 543
Pittsburg, etc . R. Co v Gilliland, 603
Pittsburg etc R Co. v Hine, 228
Pittsburg, etc , R Co. v Kirk, 104.
Pittsburg etc R Co , v. Martin, 656.
Pittsburg, etc , R Co v Noel, 44, 197
Pittsburg, etc , R. Co. v Rohrman, 567.
Pittsburg, etc , R Co v Shields, 110
Pittsburg etc R Co. v. Taylor, 37, 543.
Planters' Rice Mill Co. v' Olmstead, 68.
Platt v Brown, 171
Pleasants v. Fant, 544
Pledger v Hathcock, 298.
Plimmer v. Mayor of Wellington, 463.
Plumer v Harper, 530.
Plumley v Birge, 584
Plummer v Brown, 438.
Plummer v Herbut, 223
Plummer v Johnson, 394
Plummer v. Webb, 275.
Poeppers v M K & P. Ry Co., 44.
Poindexter v Henderson, 430
Poland v Earhart, 45.
Poland v Miller, 631
Polhill v Walter, 855, 878
Polk v Lane, 611
Pollard v Baldwin, 143
Pollard v Lyon, 289, 293
Polirsky v Minchener, 333, 336
Pollock v Eastern R Co , 556
Polock v. Ploche, 606
Pomeroy v Villavossa, 893
Pond v Metropolitan E R Co , 509.
Pond v People, 256
Pontifex v Bignold, 216
Ponton v Wilmington, etc., R. Co., 117.
Pool v Devers, 324

TABLE OF CASES CITED.

The References are to Pages.

Pool v. Mitchell, 152
Pool v. Southern P R Co, 121
Porterfield v Bond, 191
Porter v Botkins, 521
Porter v Day, 660
Porter v Dunn, 271
Porter v Hannibal R Co, 191
Porter v. Silver Creek & M O Co, 25
Porter v The O. R. J. & P R Co, 107
Porter v Thomas, 81
Porter v. Wright, 361
Posey v Scoville, 637.
Post Pub Co v Maloney, 205, 329
Potter v. Brown, 241
Potter v Faulkner, 126, 168.
Potter v Moran, 534.
Potter v. Muller, 226.
Potter v Neal, 418.
Potter v Scaife, 395.
Potter v. Warner, 27
Potts v Hines, 213
Potts v. Imboy, 398
Potts v Smith, 510
Potts v W. U. Tel Co, 55
Pottstown Gas Co v Murphy, 505
Poulk v Slocum, 285
Poulton v L & S W R Co, 108
Pounder v N E R Co, 555
Powder Co v Tearney, 496.
Powell v Bentley & Gerwig Furniture Co, 191, 518, 52?
Powell v Deveney, 40, 110
Powell v Fall, 617.
Powell v Macon & I S R. Co, 521.
Powell v Sims, 509.
Powers, In re, 262
Powers v Boston Gas Light Co, 620
Powers v Cary, 327
Powers v City of Council Bluffs, 519
Powers v Craig, 617.
Powers v Harlow, 585, 627
Powers v Lewis, 70
Powers v Pine, 311
Powers v Presgroves, 323, 317
Powys v Blagrave, 128
Pozzi v Shipton, 652, 654
Praed v. Graham, 346
Pratt v Lull, 252.
Pratt v Atlantic etc R Co, 504
Pratt v Gardner, 138
Pratt v. Philbrook, 375
Pratt v Pioneer Press Co, 318
Pratt v Wells, Fargo etc, 538
Prentice v Village, 192
Presby v Grand Trunk Ry, 534
Prescott v Fonsey, 807
Prescott v Norris, 61.
Prescott v Tansey, 328
Pres, etc, Bult, etc, Road v Leonhardt, 637.
President v Moore, 523
Presland v Bingham, 512
Press Co v Stewart, 317.
Presser v State, 206
Pressey v Wirth, 614
Preston v Fre, 329
Pretty v Bickmore, 531
Prettyman v Dean, 471
Prewitt v State, 150
Prideaux v Mineral Point, 569
Priestley v Fowler, 115
Prince v Case, 463.
Prince v Grintz, 455
Printup v Patton, 230

Printup v. Smith, 241
Proctor v Adams, 199, 175.
Proctor v. McCord, 375
Proctor v Owens, 295.
Proctor v Webster, 840
Propson v Leathem, 125.
Prosser v Callis, 201.
Prough v. Entrikon, 396
Pruner v Pendleton, 506
Pryor v Portsmouth Cattle Co, 116
Pugh v. McCarty, 312
Pulling v G E R Co, 77.
Pullman v Hill & Co, 308, 309
Purcell v Lawler, 310, 322
Purple v Horton, 324
Purcell v Horne, 249
Pursell v Stover, 168
Purvis v Coleman, 514
Putman v. Sullivan, 383.
Putnam v Valentine, 224
Putney v. Day, 464.
Pym v. G N. R. Co, 79

Q.

Quarman v Burnett, 95, 625
Quartz Hill etc Co v Beall, 226
Quartz Hill Gold Mining Co v Eyre, 400.
Quick v Miller, 61.
Quigley v Central Pac. Ry Co, 55
Quigley v McKee, 205
Quilty v Battie, 63
Quimby v. Blackey, 245
Quincy v Jones, 493
Quinn v Complete Electric Co, 91
Quinn v. Donovan, 27
Quinn v. Heisel, 262
Quinn v Lowell Electric Light Corp, 486.
Quinn v. O'Gara, 291
Quinn v Power, 99, 101
Quirk v Holt, 552

R.

R. v. Oatesworth, 249
R v Duckworth, 251
R v James, 251
R v Latimer, 171.
R v St George, 251
R v Train, 488
Radcliff v Mayor etc of Brooklyn, 193, 500
Radley v L. & N. W R. Co., 570, 571, 578, 579
Rafferty v. People, 142, 264.
Raffey v Henderson, 463
Ragsdale v Barnes, 243
Ragsdale v Northern P R Co, 121
Rail v Potts, 148
Railroad Co. v Barron, 82
Railroad Co v English, 497
Railroad Co v Gladman, 546, 569
Railroad Co v Guthrie, 45
Railroad Co v. Jones, 537
Railroad Co v Reeves, 606
Railroad Co. v Schuyler, 386.
Railroad Co v Schwindling, 24
Railroad Co v Stout, 568, 584
Railway Co v Kellogg, 574
Rainbow v Benson, 328

TABLE OF CASES CITED.

The References are to Pages.

Rains v. St L. etc R Co, 193
Raj Chunder v Ray Shema Boondari Debi, 101.
Rajmohun Bose v East India R. Co, 159
Rammell v. Otis, 100
Ramsden v Boston & A R Co., 67, 110
Ramsden v Dyson, 164.
Ramsey v. Ariott, 301.
Ramsey v. Gould, 182
Rand v White Mts R. Co., 683
Randall v Brigham, 138, 324
Randall v Eastern R Co, 70
Randall v. Evening News Assoc, 313
Randall v. Hazelton, 14.
Randall v Newson, 632
Randlette v Judkins, 24
Randolf v Town of Bloomfield, 520.
Randolph v Hannibal & St J R Co, 105
Ranger v Goodrich, 294, 295, 298
Rangler v McCreight, 611.
Rankin v Merchants & M T Co, 91
Rankine v. Elliott, 311.
Ransom v. Citizens' Ry Co, 156
Ransome v. Christian, 324
Rapp v St J & I R. Co, 509
Rashdall v Ford, 361
Rathburn v Emigh, 302
Ratto v. Dawson, 683
Ravencraft v Missouri Pac Ry. Co., 552.
Rawdon v Blatchford, 357.
Ray v Burbank, 26, 621
Ray v. Law, 392
Ray v. Lynes, 522
Ray v Sweeney, 509
Ray v Tubbs, 62
Raymond v Fitch, 683
Rayner v. Kinney, 324
Rayner v Mitchell, 102
Rayner v Nugent, 459
Rayner v. Nims, 40, 220, 685
Rea v Harrington, 295
Rea v. Saeward, 474
Rea v Tucker, 281
Read v. Coker, 252.
Read v Edwards, 612, 613
Read v G E. R Co, 80
Readhead v Midland R Co, 632
Reading etc R Co v Ritchie, 556
Reading R Co v Telser, 562.
Readman v. Conway, 624
Rearick v Wilcox, 321
Rector v Smith, 328
Reddall v Bryan, 224.
Redding v Goodwin, 375
Reading v Wright, 403
Redgrove v. Hurd, 366, 379
Redpath v. Lawrence, 381
Redway v. Gray, 295
Reece v. Taylor, 257
Reed v Allegheny City, 637
Reed v Harper, 60, 576
Reed v. Home Savings Bank, 67, 68
Reed v Nutt, 258
Reed v Peterson, 383, 648
Reed v Spaulding, 606
Reed v Williams, 276
Reeder v Purdy, 272
Reenholts v Becker, 291
Reese v Biddle, 122
Reese v W U. Tel Co, 55
Reese River Silver Mining Co v Smith, 367
Reeve v Fox, 431.
Reeves v. Bowden, 311

Reg . Comrs. of h. for E., 603, 607.
Reg. v. Coney, 187, 188
Reg. v Jackson, 150
Reg. v. Looley, 241
Reg. v Lewis, 187
Reg v Orton, 189
Reg v Riley, 470
Reg v. Williams, 71.
Rehhert v. Gerts, 500
Reid v. Clark, 222.
Reid v. De Lorme, 339
Reid v Gifford, 528.
Reilley v Cavanaugh, 26
Reinhardt v. Mentasti, 500, 502
Reinmiller v Skidmore, 461
Reiper v Nichols, 45
Reiton v Goode, 431.
Rehance, The, 637
Remington v Coughdon, 333, 338.
Renck v McGregor, 263
Rend v. Chicago, etc Ry Co, 231
Renfro v Chicago, etc R Co, 110
Renner v Canfield, 30, 55
Rentz v. Etna Ins Co, 109
Renwick v Morris, 515
Repler v Ponts, 262
Republican v Sparhawk, 199
Republican Pub Co v Miner, 257
Rerick v Keru, 16?
Respublica v. DeLongchamps, 248.
Respublica v Newell, 487
Rex v Pease, 156.
Rexroth v Coon, 450
Reynell v Sprye, 366
Reynold v Robinson, 271
Reynolds v. De Greer, 305
Reynolds v Edwards, 481
Reynolds v. Franklin, 217
Reynolds v. Graves, 27
Reynolds v Hanrahan, 81
Reynolds v. Hennessy, 215
Reynolds v Hindman, 24
Reynolds v Shuler, 9
Reynolds v Witte, 112
Rhine v. B'way & S A R Co, 590
Rhoda v Annis, 112
Rhode v Alley, 362
Rhodes v. Dickinson, 432, 434
Rhodes v Dunbar, 504, 506
Rhodes v Farish, 244.
Rhodes v Nagle, 316
Rhodes v Otis, 462
Rhodes v Roberts, 618
Rhodes v Rogers, 235
Rhodes v Whitehead, 505
Ribble v Starrat, 546
Rice v Barrett, 351
Rice v Boyer, 60
Rice v Coolidge, 24, 328, 329
Rice v Evansville, 70
Rice v Manley, 390, 673
Rice v Yocum, 440
Rich v. Basterfield, 531.
Rich v Bell, 214
Rich v New York Cent etc. R. Co, 83
Richard s Appeal, 506
Richard v. Schleusner, 552
Richards v Dorver, 225, 482.
Richards v. Gilbert, 606
Richards v. Rough, 164.
Richards v Schleusener, 617
Richards v Tarbot, 429
Richardson v Adams, 837
Richardson v Anthony, 469

TABLE OF CASES CITED.

The References are to Pages.

Richardson v. Kier, 606
Richardson v Kimball, 91, 618
Richardson v Roberts, 324
Richardson v. Van Ness, 91
Richardson v. Vermont etc R. Co., 157
Richardson v. Vico, 172
Richels v State, 252
Richmond v. Lake, 250
Richmond v. Sacramento, etc R. Co., 610
Richmond & D R Co v. Elliott, 321
Richmond & D R Co. v Jones, 122
Richmond & D Ry Co v Yeamans, 567
Richmond etc R Co v Anderson 567
Richmond etc R Co v. Howard, 538, 542
Richmond Mfg. Co v. Atlantic Delaine Co., 192
Rickir v Freeman, 37, 248 252
Ricket v McLeon R Co, 490
Ricond v Cent Pac. R Co, 63, 595
Riddle v McGinnis, 278
Riddle v Proprietors, 67
Rider v Kelly, 683
Rider v White, 611
Riding v Smith, 292 301
Ridings v Hannib I & St Jo Ry Co, 567
Rigoon v Jordan, 306
Riggs v Denniston, 100
Richtmire v Shephard 413, 476
Riley v. Boston Water Power Co, 454
Riley v Farnum, 534
Riley v Norton, 323
Riley v State Line Steamship Co, 91
Ring v Vogel Paint & Glass Co, 353
Ring v Wheeler, 329
Rinschler v Jolliffe, 370
Ripka v Sergeant, 518
Ripley v Dobler, 413
Rippey v Miller, 223
Rish v Von Lilienthal, 375
Risien v Brown, 462
Rist v Faux, 280
Ritchey v West, 27
Rives v Wood, 395
Roach v Caldbeck, 235
Roach v. Damon, 469
Roath v Driscoll, 178
Robbins v Barton, 857
Robbins v Chicago, 93
Robbins v Robbins, 395
Robling v First Nat Bank, 483
Robert Marys' Case, 273
Robert v Lisenbee, 81
Roberts v Connelly, 278
Roberts v Ramsey 296
Roberts v Roberts 293
Roberts v Rose, 517
Roberts v. State, 648
Roberts v Wyatt, 454
Robertson v Bennett, 310
Robertson v Crane, 435
Robertson v Hunt, 434
Robertson v Parks, 402
Robinett v. Ruby, 836
Robinson v Baugh 485
Robinson v. Bird, 439
Robinson v Burleigh, 435
Robinson v Cone, 586
Robinson v Dauchy, 414
Robinson v Drummond, 324
Robinson v. Hawkins, 201, 256
Robinson v Keyser, 295
Robinson v Klivert, 502
Robinson v Marino, 613
Robinson v. Maxwell, 509

Robinson v. Parks, 359
Robinson v. Pogue, 680
Robinson v Railroad Co, 550, 591, 620, 637
Robinson v. Richards, 420
Robinson v. Skipworth, 411
Robinson v Threadgill, 515
Robinson v. Walton, 353
Robinson v Webb, 88, 110
Robinson Machine Works v. Chandler, 631
Robson v N E R Co, 109, 560, 591
Roby v. Murphy, 297
Rochester, City of, v. Montgomery, 617
Rochester, City of, v Simpson, 595
Rock v. McClaren, 297
Rockford v Hildebrand, 60
Rockford v. Tripp, 30
Rockford, etc, R. Co., v Delaney, 82, 581
Rockingham Ins Co. v. Boscher, 80
Rocky Mountain Nat. Bank v McCaskill, 114
Rockwell v Third Av. R Co, 218
Rockwood v Wilson, 157
Rodgers v Kline, 301, 306
Rodgers v Lacey, 285, 298
Rodgers v Niles, 631
Rodman v. Thalheimer, 860
Rodney v McLaughlin, 418
Rodney Hunt Mach Co v Stewart, 431
Roe v Chitwood, 311
Roemer v. Striker, 637
Rogahn v Moore Mfg & F Co, 109
Rogan v Perry, 449
Rogers v Colt, 310
Rogers v Cox 459
Rogers v Elliott, 495
Rogers v. Evarts, 281, 409
Rogers v Hanfield, 502
Rogers v. Hatfield, 522
Rogers v Henry, 845
Rogers v Hine, 439
Rogers v Lacey, 311
Rogers v Lambert, 443
Rogers v. Leyden, 638
Rogers v Manufacturing Co, 117
Rogers v. Place, 360
Rogers v Rajendro Dutt, 180, 181, 182
Rogers v Spence, 221, 452
Rogers v. Stewart, 529
Rogers v Taintor, 184
Rogers L. & M. Works v Erie Ry Co, 224
Rogers L. & M Works v Hand, 122
Rohan v Sawin, 262
Rolland v Batchelder, 807
Rollins v. Chalmers, 281
Rollins v Clay, 449
Rome & D R Co. v Chasteen, 92
Romney Marsh, Bailiffs of, v Trinity House, 48
Romona Oölite Stone Co. v Johnson, 125
Rood v N Y. & E R Co, 562
Roope v D'Avigdor, 236
Root v French, 680
Root v King, 287, 316, 318
Root v Stevenson, 62
Roots v Stone, 26
Rose v Miles, 489
Rose v. Miner, 369
Rose v N E R Co, 560
Rose v Stephens, etc, Co, 636
Rose v U S T Co, 674
Rosen v. Stein, 267
Rosenberg v Cook, 451

The References are to Pages.

Rosenberg v. Durfee, 685.
Rosenberg v Hart, 902.
Rosenberry v Slade, 270.
Rosenfield v Arros, 537, 515.
Rosewater v Hoffman, 294.
Rosewell v. Prior, 531.
Ross v. Butler, 506
Ross v. City of Clinton, 71
Ross v Drinkard, 801
Ross v. Langworthy, 301.
Ross v Morrow, 213
Ross v. Rittenhouse, 198.
Ross v. Scott, 223
Rossman v Adams, 225, 429
Rossman v Canevan, 375
Rost v Missouri Pac Ry. Co, 561
Roth v Smith, 367.
Rothholz v. Dunkle, 338
Dunks v. Del L. & W. R Co., 103.
Rourke v White Moss Colliery Co, 96
Rounsaville v Kohlhelm, 505
Rouse v. Chicago etc R. Co, 530
Rouse v Martin, 405, 521.
Roux v. Blodgett & Davis Lbr Co, 120
Rower, The, 630
Rowbotham v Jones, 528
Rowe v Lent, 27
Rowell v Chase, 857.
Rowell v. Lailroad Co, 501
Rowell v Williams, 60.
Rowland v DeCamp, 839
Rowland v. Gundy, 414
Rowland v Murphy, 538
Rowley v Bigelow, 660.
Rown v Christopher & T R Co, 106
Roy v Goings, 395
Royal Aquarium Society v Parkinson, 330, 114.
Royal etc Co v. Sherrel, 181
Rozell v Anderson, 70
Runn v. Perry, 133
Rubelman v Larchman, 332
Rude v Nass, 135
Ruffner v Cincinnati etc R Co, 547
Ruffner v Railroad Co, 504.
Ruffner v Williams, 261
Ruggles v Lesure, 464.
Ruland v South Newmarket, 552
Rulbe v Hanna, 272
Rummell v Dilworth, 91
Rundell v Butler, 295
Runger v Brown, 375.
Ruohs v Backer, 328
Rush v Cavanaugh, 300.
Russell v Barrow, 201
Russell v Branham, 360
Russell v Burlington, 70
Russell v Chambers, 27
Russel v Doty, 472
Russell v Fagan, 642
Russell v Huthony, 361
Russell v Major, 199
Russell v Merchants' Bank, 436
Russell v Post, 402
Russell v Tillotson, 193
Rust v Victoria Graving Dock Co., 219.
Ruter v Foy, 567
Rutherford v Folger, 243
Rutherford v Morning Journal Assoc., 346
Rutherford v Schattman, 403
Rutherford v. Williams, 175
Ruyster v Foy, 473
Ryan v. Ashton, 369

Ryan v. Bagaley, 124
Ryan v. Chicago & N. W. R Co., 121.
Ryan v Fralick, 273
Ryan v. Miller, 21
Ryan v Porter Mfg. Co., 193
Ryan v. Rochester R Co, 611
Ryckman v Delaware, 319
Ryder v Neil, 370
Ryder v Wombwell, 555.
Rylands v Fletcher, 10, 171, 173, 192, 593, 602, 603, 604, 605, 606, 607, 609, 610, 617, 619

S.

S. v. S., 236
Sabine, etc., R Co. v. Jenchini, 218
Sadler v. Henlock, 93.
Sadler v South Staffordshire, etc, Tramways Co, 618.
Sadowski v. Michigan Car Co., 120.
Safford v. Grant, 376.
Sagers v. Nuckolls, 81.
Salem Bank v Gloucester Bank, 29
Sales v. Briggs, 395.
Sallsburg v. Green, 469
Sallsbury v Howe, 851
Salmon v Delaware, etc. R Co., 41
Salmon v. Railroad Co, 518
Salmons v. Knight, 226, 347
Salter v. Howard, 270
Salter v Utica etc. R Co, 656.
Salt Lake City v. Hollister, 67
Salt Springs Nat Bank v Wheeler, 433.
Saltus v Everett, 680,
Salvin v North Braucepeth Coal Co., 497, 501, 526
Sampson v Smith, 151.
Samuels v Evening Mail Assn, 67
Samuels v Richmond & D R Co, 230
Samuelson v Cleveland etc, 530
Samyn v McClosky, 637
Sanborn v Detroit etc. R Co., 656
Sanborn v. Hamilton, 484.
Sanders v. Hamilton, 653.
Sanders v Jacobs, 184.
Sanders v. Stuart, 679
Sanders v Caldwell, 311
Sanderson v Frazier, 560.
Sauer v. Bilton, 428
Sandford v Clarke, 530
Sanford v Bennett, 843.
Sanford v Eighth Ave R Co., 105
Sanford v Handy, 112, 338, 383.
Sanford v Standard Oil Co., 121
Sangster v Prather, 358
Sans v Joerris, 316.
Sapp v Roberts, 225.
Sappington v Watson, 376
Saratoga Co v Deyoe, 482.
Sargeant v Blunt, 438
Sargent v Ballard, 456
Sargent v Mathewson, 276
Sarles v Sarles, 429, 430
Sasser v Davis, 243
Satterly v Morgan, 125
Saucer v Keller, 462
Saulsbury v Ithica, 70
Saunderlin v Bradstreet, 312.
Saunders v Baxter, 843.
Saunders v Hatterman, 357
Saunders v. McClintock, 356.
Savacool v Boughton, 142, 262.
Savage v Brewer, 399

TABLE OF CASES CITED.

The References are to Pages.

Savage v. Lullin, 40.
Savannah v. Donnelly, 69
Savannah & W. R Co., v. Phillips, 94.
Savannah St. R. Co. v. Bryan, 105
Savile or Savill v. Roberts, 461.
Saville v Welch, 658
Savoie v Scanlan, 296.
Sawyer v. Elfert, 205.
Sawyer v. Martins, 89
Sawyer v Prickett, 358
Sawyer Spindle Co v. Turner, 225
Saxby v. Manchester & Sheffield R Co., 631.
Saxton v. Bacon, 611.
Sayers v. Haskinson, 480.
Sayles v Briggs, 395.
Sayward v Carlson, 122.
Scarborough v. Alabama Midland R Co., 92.
Schaefer v Osterbrink, 91, 101
Schaeffer v. Township of Jackson, 44
Schattner v. City of Kansas, 69
Scheckell v Jackson, 318
Scheffer v. Railroad Co., 80, 544, 567
Scheffer v Minneapolis, etc , Ry , 81
Schelter v Gooding, 529
Schelter v York, 151
Schenck v Schenck, 308
Schenk v. Strong, 92
Scherman v. Fitch, 660
Schermerhorn v. The Metropolitan Gas-Light Co , 620
Schilla e Legler, 313
Schlietz v Lanfitt, 343
Schmeer v. Gas Light Co , 620
Schmidt v Adams, 87, 110
Schmidt v Cook, 530
Schmidt v Dogan, 81
Schmidt v. Kansas City Distilling Co , 555
Schmidt v. S & H. P Ry Co , 534
Schmidt v Wedman, 396
Schmidt v Witherick, 296.
Schmitherner v Eisoman, 60
Schneider v McLane, 262
Schofield v Railroad Co., 557
School Dist v Bragdon, 61.
School District v Lindsay, 461
School District v Neil, 488, 516.
Schoonover v Brigh., 225.
Schorn v Berry, 274
Schreiber v Sharpless, 81.
Schroeder v Chicago & A R Co , 123
Schroeder v Michigan Car Co , 164
Schrubbe v Connell, 91
Schubert v Clarke Co , 534, 631.
Schufeldt v Schintzler, 357
Schular v Hudson River R Co , 92
Schultz v. Schultz, 64
Schulz v Third Ave R. Co , 105
Schum v Pennsylvania R Co , 517.
Schumacher v Railroad Co , 211
Schumaker v Mather, 357, 358
Schuster v Board of Health, 523
Schuyler v. Busbey, 334
Schuylkill Nav Co v Farr, 519
Schwartz v. Gilmore, 91
Schwenk t Naylor, 359.
Scidmore v. Smith, 275.
Scirolo v Neeves, 262
Scogland v Minneapolis St Ry Co , 271.
Scott v. Bay, 502
Scott v Fleming, 258, 323.
Scott v. Hale, 503

Scott v. Hunter, 29, 51.
Scofield v. Kreiser, 4 0
Scott v. London Dock Co., 550, 563, 637
Scott v. McKinnish, 825
Scott v Montgomery, 218
Scott v Rogers, 687
Scott v. Seymour, 238.
Scott v Shepherd, 31, 37, 170, 201
Scott v Stansfield, 139, 140, 329
Scott v. Swoope, 122.
Scott v Watson, 61.
Scott v. Wilmington etc R Co , 557.
Scott's Trustees v Moss, 10
Scribner v. Bench, 201, 256
Scribner v Kelley, 613
Scripps v Reilly, 500, 818
Scruggs v. Davis, 44 ?
Seacord v. People, 485
Seager v. Sligerland, 270.
Seale v. G. C. & S F Ry Co , 45
Seaman v Nethercliff, 330
Searles v. Manhattan R. Co., 545
Searles v. Scarlett, 341
Searll v McCrackin, 895
Sears v. Eastern R. Co., 658.
Sears v Hathaway, 301
Seat v Moreland, 214
Seaton v Oodray, 296.
Secor v Harris, 301
Secretary of State in Council of India v Kamachee Boye Sahaba, 1 F.
Sedalia Gaslight Co v Mercer, 157
Seeley v Peters, 810
Seely v. Alden, 519
Seely v Blair, 300, 301
Seifert v Brooklyn, 115
Seifried v Hays, 506, 528.
Selby v. Nettlefold, 477
Selden v Bank of Commerce, 114
Selden v. Del & Hud Canal Co , 639.
Sellers v Parvis & Williams Co , 506
Selma v. Railroad Co , 876.
Selser v Montgomery, 308
Selz v Unna, 232
Semayne's Co , 471
Semour v Greenwood, 106
Seneca Falls v Zalinski, 70
Seneca Road Co. v Auburn, etc R Co , 214
Seroka v Kattenburg, 66
Servations v Pichel, 339.
Seton v Lafone, 38, 416
Seward t The Vera Cruz, 78
Sewell v Catlin, 295, 302
Sexton v Todd, 316
Sexton v Zett, 544
Seybold v New York, etc. R Co , 545, 636.
Seymour v Greenwood, 111.
Shackelford v Hendley, 375
Shackett v Shackett, 150.
Shadden v. McElwee, 329
Shade v Creviston, 358
Shaefer v Sheppard, 271.
Shafer v Stull, 224
Shaldey v Wells, 262.
Shank v Northern etc. R. Co., 122.
Shannon v Jones, 392
Shapleigh v Wyman, 198
Sharp v Bonner, 537.
Sharp v Miller, 244
Sharp v Powell, 51, 53, 54.
Sharp v. Johnson, 394
Sharpe v Williams, 230.
Shatto v. Abernethy, 632

TABLE OF CASES CITED.

The References are to Pages.

Shattuc v. McArthur, 295.
Shattuck v. Allen, 412.
Shattuck v. Hammond, 281.
Shaul v Brown, 392.
Shaver v. Loucks, 394
Shaver v Shaver, 181
Shaw v. Coffin, 61
Shaw v Craft, 614
Shaw v Cummiskey, 565.
Shaw v. Davis, 141
Shaw v Etterbridge, 519.
Shaw v New York etc R Co, 157
Shaw v. Port Phillp Gold Mining Co, 112.
Shawneetown v Mason, 70
Shay v Thompson, 186
Shea v Sixth Ave R Co, 101
Sheehan v Collins 316, 324
Sheeut v. McDowell, 112
Sheehan v Sturgis, 149
Sheff v Huntington, 569
Shell v Van Deusen, 397.
Shelk v. Hobson, 220
Shelk v. Hobson, 645
Shelby v Sun Printing & Pub. Co Assoc, 295
Sheldon v. Hill 264
Sheldon v Hud Riv. R Co, 504, 502
Sheldon v Kalamazoo, 69
Sheldon v Kibbe, 210
Sheldon v Sherman, 605
Sheldon v Stryker, 142
Shelly v. City of Austin, 634
Shelton v. Nance, 288
Shelton v Simmons, 324
Shepheard v Whitaker, 303.
Shepherd v Gas Light Co., 551
Shople v Page, 401
Sheridan v. Brooklyn & N R Co, 584
Sheridan v Charlick, 95, 100, 108
Sheridan v New Quay Co, 442
Sherman v. Commercial Ptg. Co., 450
Sherman v Johnson, 81.
Sherman v Wells, 606.
Shorner v. Spear, 231
Sherrill v Connor, 450.
Sheery v Perkins, 407
Sherwood v Chace, 296.
Sherwood v Hall, 275
Sherwood v Salmon, 357.
Sherwood v Titman, 274
Shewalter v Borgman, 281.
Shields v. Blackburne, 536, 648.
Shipley v Fifty Associates, 603.
Shipman v Burrows, 291
Shipman v Seymour, 369
Shippy v Am. Sable, 70
Shippy v Village of Au Sable, 593
Shirns v Olinger, 505
Shirley v Waco Tap R Co, 220
Shively v Cedar Rapids, etc Ry Co, 506.
Shoe & Leather Bank v Thompson, 66
Shoecraft v Bailey, 642
Shoemaker v Nesbit, 145
Shorter v. People, 255
Shotts Iron Co v Inglis, 502
Shreckengast v. Ealey, 222
Shufoy v Bartley, 206.
Shuler v Millsape, 686
Shurtleff v. Parker, 292, 316, 338.
Shurtleff v Stevens, 338.
Sick v Owen, 334
Sickles v Gould, 449
Sidekum v Wabash, etc, Ry Co, 218
Sides v Hilleary, 369

Sidgreaves v. Myatt, 294.
Sievoking v. Litzler, 356, 357
Sikes v. Sheldon, 164
Sikes v. Thompson, 61
Silby v Trotter, 153
Sillars v Collier, 601.
Silva v Garcia, 225
Silver Cord C. M Co, v. McDonald, 570.
Silver Spring, etc. Co. v. Wanskuck Co, 402.
Simkin v L & N. W. R Co, 57.
Simmonds v. Holmes, 291.
Simmonds v New York, etc., R. Co., 41, 501.
Simmons v. Everson, 637
Simmons v Gaynor, 198
Simmons v. Holster, 310
Simmons v Morse, 311.
Simmons Medicine Co v. Mansfield Drug Co, 184
Simms v. South Carolina R Co, 544.
Simon v Canaday, 357.
Simonin v New York, etc, R Co., 101
Simons v Monier, 142
Simpkins v Columbia etc R. Co., 558.
Simpson v Grayson, 276, 277.
Simpson v Pettibone, 298.
Simpson v Savage, 529
Simpson v State, 250, 487
Simpson v. Wright, 463
Sims v Ferrill, 361
Sims v. Reed, 142
Siner v. G W R Co, 559
Singer, etc, Co v Domestic, etc., Co., 347
Singer Mfg Co. v. King, 441.
Singer Mfg. Co v Loog, 392
Singer Mfg Co v Rahn, 91, 99.
Singer Mfg Co v. Skillman, 436.
Singer Mfg Co. v. Wilson, 391.
Singleton v E C R Co, 686.
Singleton v Kennedy, 351.
Sinten v. Butler, 624
Sioux City, etc R Co. v. Finlayson, 124.
Sioux City & P R Co. v. Smith, 123.
Sisco v Cheeney, 64
Sisson v. Johnson, 225.
Six Carpenters' Case, 470
Skelton v L & N W R Co, 505.
Skidmore v Bricker, 363
Skine v. Simmons, 349
Skinner v Grant, 315
Skinner v L B & S C. R Co, 549.
Skinner v Powers 315
Skipp v. E. C R. Co, 126
Slade's case, 648
Slattern v Des Moines etc R. Co., 157
Slattery's case, 548
Sledge v Clopton, 243
Sleight v Levenworth, 260.
Sleight v. Ogle 267
Slidel v. Rightor, 375
Slight v Gutzlaff, 530.
Slim v Croucher, 227
Sloan v Central Iowa R Co, 552.
Sloan v New York Central R. Co., 271
Sloan v Petrie, 324
Slocum v. Clark, 472
Slocum v Dilworth, 530.
Slossem v Burlington, etc R. Co., 563.
Small v Chicago etc R Co, 562.
Small v Howard, 27.
Smalley v City of Appleton, 43.
Smart v Blanchard, 287, 95

The References are to Pages.

Smart v. Jones, 463.
Smedis v. Brooklyn etc. R Co, 550.
Smethurst v. Barton Square Church, 587.
Smith v. Adams, 178
Smith v. Alexandria, 71
Smith v. Amer. Institute, 630
Smith v. Ashley, 310
Smith v. Austin, 393, 395, 396
Smith v. Baker, 173, 195, 196, 197, 199, 633
Smith v. Bayright, 213.
Smith v. Bell, 142
Smith v. Boston Gas Light Co, 518, 620
Smith v. Brown, 77
Smith v. Burns, 321, 398
Smith v. Car Works, 508
Smith v. Causer, 611
Smith v. Chadwick, 356, 369, 380
Smith v. Chicago, etc Ry. Co., 501.
Smith v. Clews, 489
Smith v. Click, 369
Smith v. Cook, 612.
Smith v. Cummings, 505
Smith v. Denver, 893
Smith v. Earl Brownlow, 513
Smith v. Elliott, 520
Smith v. Enconbas, 213
Smith v. French, 671
Smith v. Gafford, 296
Smith v. Goodman, 31, 637.
Smith v. Green, 38 684
Smith v. Hestonville, etc Ry. Co., 583
Smith v. Hintrager, 398
Smith v. Insurance Co., 869.
Smith v. Jernigan, 658
Smith v. King, 396
Smith v. Kron, 61
Smith v. L S W R. Co, 538, 560, 608
Smith v. Lockwood, 523
Smith v. London & St Katharine Docks Co, 628
Smith v. Lyke, 272
Smith v. Martin, 279
Smith v. Mayor, 70
Smith v. McConathy, 505, 506
Smith v. McDowell, 522
Smith v. McIver, 319
Smith v. Milles, 419.
Smith v. Montgomery, 614
Smith v. New York, etc. R. Co., 561.
Smith v. Osborn, 369
Smith v. Oxford Iron Co, 124
Smith v. Pettengill, 483
Smith v. Pierce, 479
Smith v. Richards, 363, 367
Smith v. Roch, 235
Smith v. Rodecap, 305
Smith v. Sellers, 193
Smith v. Sandwick, 374.
Smith v. Sherman, 685, 686
Smith v. Silence 298
Smith v. Simmons, 92
Smith v. Simon, 186
Smith v. Skut, 614
Smith v. Slocum, 257
Smith v. Smith, 63, 294, 832, 369
Smith v. Spitz, 160
Smith v. State, 253, 260
Smith v. Stewart, 294
Smith v. St Paul, etc, Co, 637
Smith v. Sun Pub Co., 346.
Smith v. Sydney, 267
Smith v. Talbot, 245.
Smith v. Tracy, 384
Smith v. Tsenhour, 144

Smith v. Webster, 101.
Smith v. Weeks, 400.
Smith v. Whiting, 213, 214.
Smith v. Wood, 434.
Snediker v. Poorbaugh, 208.
Sneesby v L & Y Rail. Co, 98.
Snodgrass v. Bradley, 110
Snow v Grace 223
Snow v Judson, 801.
Snow v. Parsons, 492
Snow v. Provincetown, 584.
Snow v Wheeler, 407
Snow v. Witcher, 627
Snowden v. Idaho, Quartz Mining Co 193
Snowden v. State, 149
Snowden v Wilas, 462
Snyder v. Andrews, 307, 311, 312, 323, 324, 326.
Snyder v. Cabel, 501, 528.
Snyder v Hopkins, 430.
Snyder v Myers, 452
Snyder v Tutter, 317.
Snyder v Viola Mining & S Co, 120, 487
Snydam v Jenkins, 683.
Soan v Gilbert, 826.
Sofield v Sommers, 619
Soloman v. Kirkwood, 403.
Soloman v Waas, 63 412
Soloman R Co v Jones, 121
Soltan v. Delfeld, 565
Somerville v O'Neil, 506
Somethurst v Proprietors Ind Cong. Church, 634
Sommerville v Hawkins, 338
Sontag v Bigelow, 418.
Sorenberger v Houghton, 611
Soreson v Dundas 260
So Rallo v. W U. T Co, 675.
Sorrucco v Geary, 199.
Sosat v. State, 202
Soule v Winslow, 395
Soulty v. Miller, 324
South v Denniston, 278
Southard v Rexford, 222
South Bend v Paxon, 520
South Carolina R Co v Nix, 82
Southcote v Stanley, 642
South Covington etc, Ry Co v. Gest, 217, 245.
South Covington etc., Ry. Co v Ware, 590
Southern Express Co v Brown, 91
Southern Express Co v Fitzner, 100, 108
Southern Express Co v Glenn, 605
Southern P R Co v Dufour 178
Southern P R Co. v Lasch, 194
Southern R Co v Kendrick, 213
South Omaha v Cunningham, 70
South Royalton Bank v. Suffolk Bank, 83, 182
South Side, etc, Co v Frich, 45.
Southwestern R Co v Mitchell, 462
Southwick v Estes, 110
Southwood v Myers, 651.
Spaids v Barrett, 328
Spaits v Poundstone, 307
Spalding v Lowe, 394
Spalding v Oakes, 232
Sparhawk v Union etc. R Co, 488.
Spear v Illes, 393
Spear v Marquette, etc. R. Co, 197.
Speight v Oliviera, 279, 281.
Spelman v Portage, 70
Spencer v Balt & O R. Co, 567

TABLE OF CASES CITED.

The References are to Pages.

Spencer v. Campbell, 615
Spencer v Kelley, 90
Spencer v. McMasters, 295.
Spencer v. Ohio & M R Co, 120
Spencers v McMasters, 324.
Spicer v. Waters, 218
Spidmore v. Bricker, 390
Spiering v Andrews, 301.
Spisak v. Baltimore & O. R. Co., 91.
Spill v Paulo, 328.
Spill v Maule, 345
Spokane Truck & Dray Co. v Hoefer, 504
Spooner v. Keeler, 290, 820
Spooner v. Manchester, 443.
Sprague v. Fremont etc, R Co, 473, 610.
Spraights v Hawley, 430, 454.
Spring v. Besore, 385
Springer v Berry, 683.
Springfield v. LeClaire, 70
Springfield v. Scheerers, 69
Sproul v. Hemmingway, 91.
Sproul v. Pillsbury, 307.
Squire v Wright, 642.
Stackpole v. Hennen, 329
Stackus v N. Y. Cent. etc. R Co., 557.
Stacy v. Emory, 394
Stacy v Portland Pub Co, 815.
Staetter v. McArthur, 614
Stafford v Morning Journal Assoc, 346
Stafford v. Newsom, 672
Stallings v Whittaker, 295.
Stancliff v Palmeter, 392
Standard Oil Co v Tierney, 164, 564.
Standish v Naragansett S. S Co, 68.
Stanfield v Boyer, 298
Stanhope v. Swafford, 114, 350.
Stanley v. Gaylord, 425
Stanley v Powell, 173
Stanley v Webb, 312
Stansell v Cleveland, 394
Stanton v. Hart, 396
Stanton v Louisville & N R Co 44
Stanton Mfg Co v McFarland, 225
Staple v Spring, 529, 530, 624
Staples v Smith, 424, 432, 452
Starbird v Frankfort, 64
Starkweather v Benjamin, 353, 358, 369
State v. Abbot, 257
State v Alford, 149.
State v Baker, 250
State v. Baldwin, 485.
State v Beck, 185, 253
State v Beckner, 471
State v Blackwell, 251
State v Board of Health, 504
State v Board of Health of Newark, 485.
State v Boston & M R. Co., 549.
State v Briggs, 253.
State v Brooks, 256
State v Burke, 204
State v. Burnham, 410.
State v Burroughs, 294.
State v Burtman, 315.
State v. Burwell, 257.
State v Calhoun, 243.
State v. Cherry, 251
State v Chipman, 250.
State v Church, 250.
State v Claudius, 471.
State v Council, 611.
State v. Crow, 251
State v. Davis, 248, 250
State v Dixon, 256
State v. Donaldson, 410

State v. Epperson, 250.
State v Furlong, 248.
State v Gibson, 257.
State v. Gould, 312
State v. Greer, 257.
State v. Guest, 261.
State v. Hastings, 138, 145.
State v. Holloway, 301.
State v. Hull, 150.
State v Jeandell, 311
State v. Jones, 149
State v Kastner, 506.
State v Keran, 510.
State v. King, 487.
State v. Lamb, 610.
State v Lansing, 330
State v. Lanner, 544.
State v. Laura Toole, 485
State v Lunsford, 259.
State v. Maine Cent R. Co., 508.
State v Marsteller, 250
State v. Martin, 142, 250.
State v. Mayor etc. of Mobile, 484, 485, 522.
State v. McDermott, 614.
State v McDonald, 148.
State v McNally, 141
State v Middleham, 257.
State v. Mizner, 149.
State v. Mooney, 253.
State v Moore, 505.
State v. Morgan, 250.
State v Myersfield, 250.
State v. Myers, 250
State v. Nash, 256.
State v Neely, 250.
State v Neff, 150
State v Neldt, 505.
State v Oliver, 150
State v. Parker, 260
State v Payson, 506.
State v. Peacock, 257.
State v. Powell, 495
State v Rawles, 250
State v Rhodes, 150.
State v Schmidt, 301.
State v. Shelbyville, 506
State v Shepherd, 250
State v Sims, 251
State v. Smith, 248.
State v Spear, 295
State v. Stewart, 410.
State v. Stockton, 257
State v. Street Comm'ssioners, 506.
State v Taylor, 250
State v Thackara, 474
State v Tinchland, 471
State v Vanderbilt, 149
State v Vannoy, 250.
State v Wait, 529
State v. Walker, 84
State v. Weed, 142
State v Williams, 147
State v. Wilson, 506
State v Wolf, 506
State v Workman, 253
State v Wright, 248
Staub v Van Benthuysen, 809.
Staten v. State, 257
Stattings v Whittaker, 326.
Stauss v Meyer, 291
St Clair Nail Co v. Smith, 184
Steamboat Farmer v McCraw, 574.
Stearns v. City of Richmond, 157
Stearns v Dillingham, 658.

TABLE OF CASES CITED.

The References are to Pages.

Stearns v. Sampson, 83.
Stearns v. Vincent, 471.
Stool v. Williams, 395
Steele v. Brannan, 342
Steele v. McTyer, 606
Steele v. Smith, 110
Steele v. Southwick, 287
Steffen v. Chicago, etc. R. Co., 193.
Stelber v. Wensell, 311.
Stein v. Hauch 509.
Steinback v. Hill, 354.
Steincke v. Max, 329, 333.
Steinke v. Bentley, 530
Steinmetz v. Kelly, 256, 567.
Stekete v. Kinsm, 308
Stephen v. Brown, 462
Stephens v. Elwall, 436, 442
Stephens v. Myers 262
Stephens v. Shriver, 611
Stephens v. Wilkins, 142
Stepenson v. Duncan, 194.
Stephenson v. South Pac R Co, 100
Stepp v. Chicago etc R. Co, 547
Ster v. Tuely, 634
Sterling v. Jackson, 177
Sterling v. Juggenheimer, 205
Sterling v. Thomas, 69
Sterling v. Warden, 163.
Stetson v. Faxon, 490
Stetson v. Kempton, 81
Stetson v. Stevens, 225, 482.
Stevens v. Armstrong, 85
Stevens v. Hartwell, 305
Stevens v. Jeacocke, 229.
Stevens v. Kelley, 33
Stevens v. Rowe, 402
Stevens v. Sampson, 320, 343.
Stevens v. Walker, 26
Stevenson v. Chicago, etc R Co., 567.
Stevenson v. Wallace, 216.
Stevenson v. Watson, 110
Steward v. Young, 389
Stewart v. Benninger, 473, 611
Stewart v. Brooklyn etc R. Co., 105
Stewart v. Cooley, 138
Stewart v. Emerson, 369.
Stewart v. Hall, 320, 328
Stewart v. Hawley, 617
Stewart v. Lanier House Co, 684
Stewart v. Sonneborn, 893, 899
Stewart v. Stearns, 878
Stewart v. Sterns, 358
Stewart v. Wells, 230
Stewart v. Wyoming Ranch Co, 362
Stimer v. Bryant, 398
Stiles v. Tilford, 281
Stim v. Croucher, 371
Stimpson v. Helps, 863, 867
St James Church v. Arrington, 505, 522
St John v. Paine, 96
St Johnsburg & Co v. Hunt, 396
St J M & S R Co v Tonley 92
St Louis v. Kine, 530.
St. Louis, A & T R Co v Knott, 92
St Louis, A & T R Co. v McKinsey, 43
St Louis, A & T R Co v Welch, 120
St. Louis & S L Ry Co v Valirius, 585
St Louis & S F Ry Co v Traweek, 613
St Louis & S F Ry Co v Weaver, 121
St Louis, etc R Co v Cantrell, 558
St Louis etc R Co v. Harper, 124
St Louis etc R Co v Mathias, 656
St Louis etc R Co v Willis, 91
St. Louis etc. Ry Co v. Briggs, 244

St Louis, etc. Ry. Co. v. Freeman, 564.
St Louis etc. Py. Co. v. Kelton, 183
St Louis, etc. Ry. Co v. Lyman, 217
St. Louis etc. Ry. Co, v McKinsey 571
St. Louis, I M. & S. Ry. Co. v Hopkins, 634
St Louis Stock Yards v. Wiggins Ferry Co., 462
St Helen's Smelting Co. v. Tipping, 498, 502, 524
St Martin v Desnoyer, 294.
Stoddard v. Bird, 265
Stocking v. Howard, 392.
Stockmoyer v Reed, 123.
Stoeckman v Terre Haute, etc. R. Co., 239.
Stoker v. City of Minneapolis, 552
Stoker v St Louis, etc, R. Co, 82
Stone v Bampus, 184
Stone v Cheshire R Co, 93
Stone v. Codman, 111
Stone v Covell, 831
Stone v Crocker, 395.
Stone v. Denny, 364.
Stone v Dry Dock R Co., 585
Stone v. Hill, 95.
Stone v Knapp, 479.
Stone v. Stevins, 893
Stone v Swift, 890
Stoner v Western Transportation Co, 95
Stoneman v. Commonwealth, 201, 257
Stoner v Shugart, 610
Stoner v Texas & P Ry. Co, 217
Storey v Ashton, 102.
Storrs v Felch, 468
Story v Hammond, 504
Story v Wallace, 309, 329, 342
Staudt v. Shepherd, 277, 281
Stoughton v Mott, 142.
Stout v Wren, 185, 253
Stovel v Lawrence, 265
Stow v Converse, 288
Stowe v Heywood, 235, 271
Stowe v Miles, 505.
Stowell v Begle, 333
Stowell v Lincoln, 214, 518
Stoyel v Lawrence, 264
Straight v Burn, 512
Strand v Chicago & W. M Ry Co, 546.
Stratton v Central City H. R. Co., 545
Stratton v. Lyons, 449
Stratton v Staples, 629.
Straus v Barnett, 522
Strauss v Meyer, 328
Strauss v Young, 896
Street v Nelson, 432
Street v Union Bank etc, 185
Street Ry Co v Nothenius, 546.
Streety v Wood, 839
Strickler v Midland Ry Co, 244
Strikeman v Dawson, 61
Stringer v Frost, 534, 545, 591
Stringham v Hilton, 117
Stringham v Stewart, 120
Stroebel v Whitney, 205, 206
Strong v Ives, 261.
Strouse v Whittlesey, 164
Stuart v Minnesota Tribune Co, 326.
Stuart v W U Tel Co, 55
Stuber v McEntee, 125
Studwell v Ritch, 610
Studwell v Shafter, 61
Sturner v Pitchman, 295
Stump v McNairy, 516

TABLE OF CASES CITED

The References are to Pages.

Sturm v Hammond, 274
Sturbridge v Winslow, 202
Sturges v Bridgman, 498, 499.
Sturtevant v Merrill, 611
Sullens v. Chicago etc. Ry Co, 324
Sullivan v. Chrysolyte Mining Co, 544
Sullivan v. Farley, 143
Sullivan v Mississippi R Co, 117
Sullivan v Missouri P R Co, 121
Sullivan v Phila etc, R Co, 637
Sullivan v Rabb, 482
Sullivan v Spencer, 135.
Sullivan v Tioga R Co, 121.
Sullivan v Waters, 625 610
Sullivan, Town of, v Phillips, 523.
Summer v St Paul, 70
Summer v Utley, 101
Sunderlin v Bradstreet, 749
Sunney v Holt, 598
Susquehanna Depot v Simmons, 64
Susquehanna Fertilizer Co v Malone, 495, 498, 601
Sutterloh v Mayor, etc of Cedar Keys, 596.
Sutton v Bennett, 503
Sutton v McConnell, 305, 396
Sutton v New York, etc R Co, 123, 544
Sutton v Town of Wauwatosa, 208
Swann v Phillips 382
Swan v Tappan, 361, 388
Swanson v City of LaFayette, 192
Sweeney v Baker, 321, 323, 124.
Sweeney v Central Pac R Co, 193
Sweeney v Gulf R Co, 123
Sweeney v Merrill, 604, 617
Sweeney v. Old Colony & Newport R R Co, 635.
Sweeney v Perney, 396
Sweeney v Torrence, 410.
Sweeny v Murphy, 92
Swensgaard v Davis, 395
Swett v Cutts, 226
Swett v Sprague, 514
Swift v Loury, 15
Swift v Applebone, 614
Swift v Eastern Warehouse Co, 30
Swift v Jewsbury, 352
Swire v Francis, 157
Switzner v McCulloch, 225
Sword v Young, 680
S W Tel & Telephone Co. v. Robinson, 534
Sylvester v Mang, 613
Symoulds v. Carter, 295
Syndacker v Brosso, 265.

T.

Taafe v Kyne, 261
Taber v Hutson, 518
Taggs v Town Nat Bank, 112
Tainter v Mayor, 182
Tate v Missouri etc R Co, 510.
Tallmadge v Press Pub Co, 324
T & St L R v Suggs, 628.
Tandy v Westmoreland, 135.
Tanner v Village of Albion, 495
Tapling v Jones, 511, 512
Tarleton v McGawley, 284, 408
Tarry v Ashton, 648
Tarver v State, 250 251
Tarvis v Barger, 279

Tarwater v. Hannibal R Co, 544, 61).
Tasker v Stanley, 271
Tate v. Missouri R Co, 70
Tatlaw v. Jackot, 316
Tattan v. G W R Co, 652.
Tavor v State, 250
Taylor v. Alexander, 144
Taylor v Ashton, 363, 368.
Taylor v. Church, 346
Taylor v. Dominick, 392
Taylor v Evansville & T H R Co, 143
Taylor v Greenhalgh, 91
Taylor v Guest, D, 475.
Taylor v Howell, 142.
Taylor v Jones, 112.
Taylor v Knowland, 294.
Taylor v. Lith, 378
Taylor v Mayor, etc of Cumberland, 631
Taylor v. Mexican G R Co, 630
Taylor v Plymouth, 10)
Taylor v Pope, 449
Taylor v. Saurman, 879
Taylor v Shelkett, 281
Taylor v Shelton, 660
Taylor v Strong, 262
Taylor v. Trask, 265
Taylor County v Standley, 403
Taylor etc R Co, v Taylor, 103
Taylor's Admr v Penna Co, 82
Teal v. Barton, 593, 601
Tefft v Ashbaugh, 141
Tefft v. Wilcox, 27
Teifel v Hilsendegin, 508.
Telegraph Co v Rogers, 68.
Tenhopen v Walker, 611
Tennesco v Farden, 630
Tennessee C & R Co v Roddy, 21
Tenney v Harvey, 263
Tenny v Miners' Ditch Co, 600.
Terre Haute v. Hudnut, 70
Terre Haute & I R Co v Jackson, 103
Terre Haute & I R Co v Voelker, 339
Terre Haute & S R Co v Jackson, 110
Terre Haute, etc, R Co v Buck, 37
Terry v Fellows, 329, 343
Terry v Hutchinson, 280
Terwilliger v. Wands, 298, 316, 337
Tewksbury v. Bennett, 851
Texas & N O R. Co v Crowder, 544
Texas & P Ry. Co v Cox, 239
Texas & P Ry. v Doherty, 43
Texas & P Ry Co, v Gorman, 537.
Texas & P R v Hardin, 629
Texas & R Co v Harrington, 119, 121
Texas & P Ry. Co v Moody, 108
Texas & P Ry Co. v Morin, 583.
Texas & P Ry Co v Murphy, 538, 562
Texas & W R Co v Wilson, 436.
Texas, etc Co v Suggs, 637
Texas, etc, R Co v Best, 627
Texas etc R Co v Levi, 552, 562.
Texas etc R Co v Medaris, 562
Tex Mex Ry Co v Douglas, 55.
Thall v Sulley, 324
Thames Steamboat Co v Housatonic Co, 108
Tharsis Sulphur Co v Loftus, 140.
Thatcher v Phinney, 63
Thayer v Boyle, 325
Thayer v Brooks, 518.
Thayer v City of Boston, 92.
Thebant v Canova, 596
Thomas v Beasdale, 294
Thomas v Brackney, 508.

TABLE OF CASES CITED. 739

The References are to Pages.

Thomas v. Dunaway, 324.
Thomas v. James, 482
Thomas v. Quartermaine, 125, 194, 195, 197, 613
Thomas v Scher, 20
Thomas v. Sixpenny Bank, 445
Thomas v Sorrell, 158
Thomas v Williams, 225.
Thomas v Winchester, 621, 622, 667
Thomkins v Sands, 138
Thompson v Berry, 201, 256
Thompson v Bowers, 315, 321
Thompson v Brush Co , 381
Thompson v Chicago etc R. Co , 127
Thompson v Clendening, 281
Thompson v Dashwood, 309.
Thompson v Duncan, 545
Thompson v Engle, 482.
Thompson v Gibson, 529
Thompson v Gortner, 134.
Thompson v Grimes, 312
Thompson v Lumley, 391.
Thompson v Lee, 561
Thompson v Louisville & N R Co , 671
Thompson v Patterson, 278
Thompson v Powning, 311, 334
Thompson v Rose, 369
Thompson v Ross, 280.
Thompson v State, 257
Thompson v W U Tel Co , 55
Thorley's Cattle Food Co. v Massam, 126, 690
Thorn v Moses, 307
Thorn v Sweeney, 225.
Thorton v Roll, 483
Thorton v Thorton, 33.
Thorogood v Bryan, 580
Thorp v Minor, 100, 109
Thorpe v Brumfitt, 508
Thorpe v Missouri P. R. Co , 194
Thorpe v Wray, 265.
Thrall v Knapp, 253
Thrussell v Handyside, 195, 199
Thurton v Hancock, 480
Thurston v. Mustin, 225
Thurston v Prentiss, 228
Thurston v Vermont Cent R Co , 493
Thying v Fitchburg R Co , 120.
Tier v Hoffin, 310
Tiffin v McCormack, 92
Tifft v Tifft, 61
Tightmeyer v Mongold, 659
Tillett v Ward, 612
Tillotson v Cheetham, 281
Tillson v Robbins, 287, 283
Tilly v N Y, etc , R Co , 82
Timothy v Simpson, 264
Tipping v St Helen's Smelting Co , 498
Tisdale v Tisdale, 447
Tissot v Great Southern Tel etc Co , 492
Titcomb v Fitchburg R Co , 24.
Titus v Bradford, etc R Co , 192
Tobias v Harland, 291, 388.
Tobin v Deal, 9
Tobin v P S & P R. R. Co., 629.
Tobin v Shaw, 685
Todd v Kochell, 598.
Todd v Flight, 530
Todd v Rough, 294
Tod Heatly v Benham, 496
Toledo v Cone, 91
Toledo, etc. R Co v Arnold, 211
Toledo etc. R Co v Bryan, 537

Toledo, etc R Co v Corn, 504
Toledo, etc. Ry Co v Harman, 110
Toledo, etc R Co v Mutherabaugh, 42
Toledo, etc. Ry Co v Pennsylvania Co ,
Toledo, etc R Co v Roberts, 685
Tollit v. Sherstone, 667
Tolman v. Smith, 358.
Tolman v Syracuse etc R Co , 510.
Tomlin v Cox, 349
Tomlinson v Derby, 218
Tomlinson v Warner, 399
Tomkins v. Holliston, 215
Tompson v Dashwood, 344
Tonawanda R. Co., v Munger, 476, 537.
Tootle v. Clifton, 519.
Topeka v Tuttle, 87.
Torrance v. Hurst, 287
Torre v Summers, 281.
Torrey v Field, 320, 313
Totel v. Bonnefoy, 459
Totten v Burhans, 863, 359
Totten v. Phipps, 627
Touhey v Ring, 264.
Toung v Wiley, 63
Tourtellot v Rosebrook, 501, 616
Tow v. Roberts, 530
Townsend v Bell, 214
Townsend v. Cowles, 360, 361
Township of Buckeye v Clark, 653.
Township of West Mahoney v Watson, 42.
Tozern v. Child, 119, 411
Trabue v Mays, 290, 305, 312, 316
Tracy v. Williams, 138, 264
Traill v Baring, 366
Trammell v Russellville, 201, 262
Tranger v Sassaman, 156
Transfer Co v Kelly, 549
Travis v Pierson, 218
Traylor v Hughes, 438
Traywick v Keeble, 680
Tradwell v Whittier, 550
Treasurer v. Cleary, 136
Treat v Browning, 316
Tremain v Cohoes Co , 502
Trenton Ins Co v Perrine, 66
Tribble v Frame, 466.
Trigg v Read, 369
Trow v Vermont C R Co., 574, 611
Trowbridge v True, 224
Trowbridge v Scudder, 560.
Troy v Cheshire R Co , 519
Troy etc R Co v Boston etc R.Co , 224
True v Plumley, 305, 312, 334
True v Thomas, 370
Trulock v Merte, 506
Truman v Taylor, 295
Trussell v Scarlett, 336
Trustees etc v. Youmans, 178
Truth Pub Co v Reed, 301
Tryon v Whitmarsh, 9
Tuberville v. Savage, 252
Tuberville v Stampe, 90, 616
Tuck v Downing, 358.
Tucker v. Call 326
Tucker v Cannon, 392
Tucker v Cole, 114
Tucker v Illinois C. R Co , 537
Tucker v Jerris, 87
Tucker v Linger, 431
Tucker v Moreland, 60
Tucker v New York etc. R Co , 585
Tucker v Walters 257
Tucker Mfg. Co. v. Fairbanks, 660

TABLE OF CASES CITED.

The References are to Pages.

Tudor Iron Works v Weber, 121
Tuel v. Wenton, 99, 101
Tuff v Warman 571, 576, 598
Tull v David, 326
Fuller v. Voght, 110
Tullidge v Wade, 221, 275.
Tunnell v Ferguson, 324
Tunney v Midland R Co., 118
Tunstall v Christian, 403, 500
Turner v Buchanan, 507
Turner v Eaton, 271
Turner v Holtzman, 195
Turner v Ringwood Highway Board, 188, 191
Turner v State, 276, 403.
Turner v Stevens, 310
Turner v Thompson, 509
Turnpike Co v Champney, 148.
Turpen v. Booth, 145.
Turpin v Remy, 208
Turrill v Dolloway, 311.
Tutein v Harley, 42
Tuthill v. Wheeler, 183
Tuttle v. Bishop, 312.
Tuttle v Railway, 117
Tuttles v Chicago, R I etc. R Co, 274
T W & W R v Beggs, 629
Tweedy v State, 256
Twitchell v. Bridge, 363
Twornley v Central Park R R Co, 595.
Twycross v Grant, 73, 76.
Tyler v New York etc R Co, 572
Tyler v Ricamoro, 41
Tyler v W U Tel Co, 56, 671
Tyner v Cory, 202
Tyre v Causey, 351
Tyrringham's Co, 471
Tyson v South & N A R Co, 125

U

Udell v. Atherton, 355
Ulmer v Leland, 304
Umlack v. Lake Shore, etc. R Co, 193
Umbler v Whipple, 243
Underhill v Goff, 683
Underhill v Welton, 296
Underwood v Henson, 170.
Unger v Forty-second etc R Co, 531.
Union Ice Co v Crowell, 218
Union P Ry Co v Estes, 542
United States v Alden, 151
United States v Hand, 250
United States v Kelley, 439
United States v Kierman, 250
United States v Lunt, 251
United States v Memphis etc R Co, 87
United States v Ortega, 218
United States v Richardson, 250
United States v Small, 251
United States Illuminating Co v Grant, 514
United States Mortgage Co v Henderson, 26
University v Tucker, 429
University of North Carolina v State National Bank, 438
Updegrove v Zimmerman, 324
Upton v Hume, 321
Upton v Tribilcock, 112, 380, 383
Upton v Upton, 299.
Upton v. Vail, 9, 672.

Uransky v. Drydock, F B & B R Co, 274
Usher v Severance, 305.
Usill v Hales, 311
Uttley v Burns, 27

V.

Vail v Pacific R Co, 606
Valentine v. Duff, 658.
Vallance v Falle, 229
Van Aukin v Westfall, 294.
Van Arnum v. Ayres, 272.
Van Aredulo v Howard, 309
Van Atsdal v. Burlington etc., Ry. Co, 241
Vance v Erie R Co., 68, 112
Van Brocklin v Fonda, 370
Van Brunt v Schenck, 610
Vance v Throckmorton, 612
Vance v Vance, 243
Vandenburgh v Truax, 30, 252, 491
Van Den Heuvel v National Fursece Co, 119
Vanderbeck v Hendry, 633
Vanderheyden v Young, 118.
Vanderpool v Husson 92
Vanderpool v Richardson, 683
Vanderslip v Roe, 295, 312
Van Derveer v Sutphin, 121
Vanderzee v McGregor, 338
Van Densen v Young, 218, 458
Van De Vere v Kansas City, 485
Van De Wiele v Callahan, 394.
Vandiver v Pollak, 212
Van Epps v Harrison, 358
Van Horne v Stands, 447
Van Horn v Van Horn, 402, 400
Van Kowron v Switzer, '41
Vanleen v Fain, 635
Van Lenven v Lyke, 813
Van Ness v Hamilton, 294.
Van Orsdal v Railroad Co, 519.
Van Pelt v Davenport, 70
Van Steenbergh v Bigelow, 145
Van Tassell v Capron, 337
Van Vacter v McKillip, 273
Van Vactor v. Walkup, 311
Varney v Manchester, 568.
Varnum v Martin, 26
Varril v Heald, 223
Vasper v Edwards 174, 480
Vaughan v Taff Vale R Co, 156, 608, 611
Vaughn v. Menlove, 539, 541
Vauese v Lee, 328
Vawter v. Miss, etc, Co, 82
Veagle v Williams, 384
Veerol v. Veerol, 375
Veneman v Jones, 265
Venneman v Powers, 64.
Verder v Ellsworth, 514.
Verhalf v Van Houwenlengen, 274
Vermilya v Chicago, etc., R. Co., 218
Vernon v Keys, 360.
Vestry of St Pancras v Batterbury, 29
Vicars v Wilcocks, 291, 671.
Vickers v Atlanta & W P R Co, 55
Vickers v Stoneman, 294, 313, 330.
Vicksburg, etc R Co v Patton, 512
Victorian Railway Commissioners v Coultas, 56
Victory v Baker, 153

TABLE OF CASES CITED. 741

The References are to Pages.

Victory v Fitzpatrick, 228
Village of Jefferson v Chapman, 552
Village of St. John v McFarlan, 523
Villepique v Shuler, 279
Vinal v Core, 894
Vinas v. Merchants, etc, Ins Co, 67, 328
Vincennes Water Supply Co v White, 62
Vincent v Cook, 580
Voltz v. Blackman, 220
Von Kettler v Johnson, 204
Vore v Page, 522
Vosberg v Putney, 252
Vose v Eagle Life Ins Co, 152
Vossel v Cole, 278, 279
Vosseen v Daniel, 109
Vredenburg v. Behan, 613
Vredenburgh v Hendricks, 265
Vrooman v Lawyer, 614

W.

Wabash, etc, R Co v Farver, 92
Wabash, etc, R Co v Locke, 42, 101, 538
Wabash, etc, Co v Shacklett, 8', 519
Wabash Print & Pub Co v Crumrine, 83
Wabash R Co v Savage, 105
Wabash W Ry Co v Morgan, 218
Waddell v Simonson, 122
Wade v. Kalbfleisch, 686
Wade v Leroy, 218
Wadsworth v W U Tel. Co, 55
Wagamann v Ryers, 311
Waggoner v Jermaine, 530
Wagner v Bill, 64
Wagner v Bissell, 611
Wagner v Holdbrinner, 324
Wagner v Peterson, 658
Wagstaff v Schippel, 393
Wahle v Reinbach, 505
Walte v N E R Co, 583
Wakelin v. L. & S W. R. Co, 546, 547, 548, 557, 578
Wakely v Hart, 263
Wakeman v Dalley, 375
Wakeman v New York etc R Co, 224
Wakeman v Robinson, 172
Walcott v Hall, 316
Walden v Peters, 388
Waldron v Haverhill, 70
Waldron v Waldron, 272
Walker v Bolling, 117
Walker v Brewster, 507
Walker v Camp, 393, 395
Walker v Cronin, 275, 407, 672
Walker v Fitts, 185
Walker v Hallock, 138, 145
Walker v. Mobile, etc, R Co, 359
Walker v State, 245, 265
Walker v Tribune Co, 291, 321
Walker v Wickens, 334
Wall v State, 257
Wall v Trumbull, 145
Wallace v. Auer, 495
Wallace v Clark, 281
Wallace v Clayton, 606
Wallace v Finberg, 110
Wallard v Wortham, 412, 537
Waller v Fisher, 93
Walling v Potter, 642
Wallis v Harrison, 459

Walpole v Carlisle, 27
Walsh v. Chicago, etc R Co., 685
Walsh v Hall, 176
Walsh v Whiteley, 197
Walser v Thies, 890
Walter v Commissioners, 530
Walter v. Sample, 898
Walter v Selfe, 496, 498
Walters v. Moss, 610
Walters v. Smoot, 347
Walton v Booth, 20, 621
Walton v File, 466
Walton v. New York, etc, R Co, 108
Walton v Singleton, 295, 112
Wandell v Edwards, 281
Wandsworth Board of Works v. United Telephone Co, 423
Wanless's Case, 557
Wannamaker v Bowes, 228
Ward v. Beane, 813
Ward v Chamberlain, 96
Ward v Clark, 290
Ward v. Conatser, 59
Ward v. Dick, 331
Ward v Hobbs, 25
Ward v Hudson River Bldg. Co, 684
Ward v Lloyd, 237, 238
Ward v. Moffett, 135
Ward v Neal, 509
Ward v Vance, 606
Ward v Young, 88, 91
Warden v Whalen, 332
Ware v Clowney, 301
Ware v Johnson, 463
Warlow v Harrison, 365
Warmington v Atchison, etc, R Co, 120
Warner v Erie, etc R Co., 194
Warner v Payne, 325
Warner v Riddiford, 259
Warner v Shed, 141
Warner v Winters, 114
Warnock v Mitchell, 307
Warren v Banning, 660
Warren v Cavanaugh, 523
Warren v. State, 251
Warren v Warren, 272
Warring v. Morse, 630
Warwick v. Hutchinson, 684
Warwick v Wah Lee, 505
Washington etc R R Co. v McDade, 596
Washington v Balt & O R Co, 568
Washington & G R Co v Fobriner, 569
Wasner v Delaware etc Co, 530, 633
Wason v. Walter, 320, 340
Wasson v Mitchell, 145
Waterburg v Lockwood, 141
Water Supply Co. v City of Potwin, 521
Watertown v Sawyer, 506
Watkins v Baird, 399
Watkins v Hall, 316
Watson v. City of Kingston, 153
Watson v Cross, 651
Watson v. McCarthy, 299
Watson v. Moeller, 213
Watson v Moore, 323, 327
Watson v. Muirhead, 26
Watson v Oxanna Land Co, 569
Watson v State, 412
Watson v Trask, 304
Watson v Watson, 243
Watt v Porter, 485
Waugh v Shunk, 26

The References are to Pages.

Waugh v. Waugh, 812
Waverly T & I Co v St Louis Cooperage Co 436
Way v. Illinois, etc R Co, 104
Way v Powers, 100
Way v Townsend, 138
Weakley v. Bostwick, 388
Weathersbee v Farrar 63
Weatherford v Ishmael, 359
Weaver v Devendorf, 115.
Weaver v Hendrick, 311
Weaver v Ward, 161, 170
Weaver v Wible, 417
Webb v Beavan, 297.
Webb v Bird, 500
Webb v Denver & R G R Co, 222
Webb v Portland Mfg Co 9, 211, 440
Webb v Rome, etc R Co, 501, 502
Webb v Walker, 404
Webber v Barry, 405
Webber v Closson, 611
Webber v Davis, 431
Webber v Kenny 205
Webber v Piper, 117
Weber Wagon Co v Kehl, 191
Webster v Bally 353, 370
Webster v Drinkwater, 650
Webster v Whitworth
Weckerly v Geyer, 118
Wedgwood v Chicago, etc R Co, 178
Weed v Hibbins, 312
Weed v Panama R Co, 110, 650
Worms v Mathieson, 125.
Weldner v Phillips, 158
Weightman v Washington, 67.
Weigrette v Darr, 103.
Weir v Record, 506
Well v Schmidt 403.
Weir's Appeal, 497
Weir v Allen, 304
Weir v Bell, 354
Weis v Hoss, 313
Welch v Hugg, 058
Welch v Duran, 252, 503, 637
Welch v Jugenheimer, 323, 545
Welch v. McAllister, 627
Welch v Stowell, 516
Welch v Tribune Pub Co, 334
Weld v Oliver, 148
Weld v Saratoga & S R Co, 535.
Weldon v DeBathe 65
Weldon v Harlem R Co., 108
Weldon v Neal, 216
Weldon v Winslow, 65
Welfare v London & Brighton R Co, 639
Wellington v Downer Kerosin Oil Co, 615
Wellington v Small, 409
Wellock v Constantine, 236
Wells v Abrahams 236, 237
Wells v Padgett, 685
Welsh v Bell, 425.
Weltey v Indianapolis, etc R Co, 576
Wendell v. Baxter, 629
Wendell v. Mayor of Troy 70
Wendell v New York etc R Co, 534, 585
Wendell v Railway Co, 198
Wennan v Ash, 300
Wennhak v. Morgan, 221, 399
Wentworth v Portsmouth & D R Co, 452, 453
Wentworth v Sawyer, 142
Werges v St Louis etc Ry Co, 244
Wert v Strause, 278

Wesley Coal Co v. Henley, 507
Wesson v. Washburn Iron Co, 040, 041
West v Berlin, 608, 640
West v. Forrest, 93, 597.
West v Hanrahan, 205
West v Hayes, 805
West v Louisville, C & L R Co, 614
West v. Moore, 61
West v Nichols, 473, 479, 480
West v Pickard, 684
West v Smallwood, 260
West v Walker, 421
Westbrook v Mize, 230
Westerbrook v Mobile etc R Co, 665
Westenfeld v Levi Bros, 685
Western & A R Co v Young, 583
Western Bank of Scotland v Addie, "63, 387.
Western News Co v Dilmarth, 67
Western Ry v. Mutch, 15
West etc Co v Regnier, 225.
Westfield v. Mayo, 242
Westgate v Carr, 610
Westlake v Westlake, 272
West London Commercial Bank v Kitson, 301
Westmore v Mellinger, 309
West Orange v Field, 71
West Point Iron Co v Reymert, 483
Wetmore v Stovell, 317
Whalley v Lane and Yorkshire R. Co., 20.
Wharf v Roberts, 378
Wharfboat Assn v. Wood, 61
Wharton v Wright, 420
Whatman v Peterson 101
Wheatley v Baugh, 178.
Wheaton v Baker 414
Wheaton v Beecher, 310, 321, 323.
Wheelden v Lowell, 378, 460
Wheeler v. Boyce, 48.
Wheeler v Gavin, 201
Wheeler v. Lawson, 450
Wheeler v. Mason Manufacturing Co., 129
Wheeler v Moore 422
Wheeler v Nesbitt, 394
Wheeler v. Patterson, 148
Wheeler v San Francisco, etc. R., 652
Wheeler v Shields, 315
Wheeler v Wheeler, 448.
Wheeler v Worcester, 200.
Wheelock v Wheelwright, 443.
Wheelwright v DePeyster, 414
Whelan v New York, etc, R Co, 912
Wheless v Second Nat Bank, 62
Whetmore v Tracy, 515
Whipple v. Fuller, 498
Whirley v. Whiteman, 563
Whitaker v Cauthorne, 404
Whitaker v Forbes, 239
Whitbeck v Dubuque etc R. Co., 611
Whitcomb v Hungerford, 432.
White v Bank, 104
White v Boston, etc, R Co, 637
White v Brantley, 425.
White v Carr, 395
White v Carroll, 33, 329
White v Chicago, M & St Py Co, 52
White v Cincinnati etc Ry Co, 661
White v Dingley, 399.
White v Elwell, 459
White v France, 628
White v Jameson, 531

The References are to Pages.

White v. Lang, 209.
White v. Madison, 884
White v. Manhattan Ry Co, 459, 461
White v. McNett, 683
White v. Missouri Pac R Co, 552
White v. Murtland, 277, 278, 281.
White v. Nellis, 278
White v. Nichols, 284, 320
White v. Phelps 448
White v. Ross 271.
White v. Sawyer, 68, 383
White v. Spettigue, 234.
White v. State, 251
White v. Thomas, 685.
White v. Wall, 442.
White Water Valley Canal Co v Commegs 130
White Co, G G v Miller, 225
Whitenack v Philadelphia & R R Co,
Whitesell v Forehand, 683
Whitford v Panama R. Co., 61
Whitham v Kershaw, 219, 222, 227
Whiting v. Hill, 378
Whiting v Johnson, 302.
Whitney v Allaire, 58
Whitney v Allen 428
Whitney v Bartholomew, 501
Whitney Co, A H v Burnham, 680
Whitney v Elmer, 278
Whitney v Martin, 26
Whiton v Chicago, etc, R Co, 81
Whitson v May, 392
Whittaker, Ex parte, 359
Whittaker v Collins, 5.55
Wicker v Hotchkiss, 196
Wicks v Fenham, 196
Widrig v Oyer, 286, 294.
Wiedner v New York Elevated R Co, 636
Wiel v Israel, 287
Wiener v Hammel, 92
Wiggett v Fox, 126
Wigsell v School for Indigent Blind, 227
Wilber v Johnson, 685
Wilbraham v Snow, 432
Wilcox v Iowa Wes Univ, 363
Wilcox v Moon, 308.
Wilcox v Richmond & D. R. Co, 55
Wilcox v Wheeler, 225
Wild v Waygood, 95
Wildee v McKee, 403.
Wilder v Holden, 395.
Wilder v McKee, 407.
Wilder v Wilder, 611
Wilds v Bogan, 281
Wilds v Layton, 429
Wilkes v Hungerford Market Co., 490
Wilkins v Day, 491
Wilkins v Gilmore, 91
Wilkinson v. Clanson, 358.
Wilkinson v Detroit Steel and Spring Works, 643.
Wilkinson v Haygarth, 449
Wilkinson v Searcy, 223
Wilkinson v Wilkinson, 429.
Willard v Mathesus, 610.
Willett v Willett, 658
Willey v Carpenter 253.
Willey v Hunter, 218.
Williams v Carle
Williams v Davenport, 300.
Williams v Deen, 435
Williams v. Dickinson, 234, 403.

Williams v. Edmunds, 571
Williams v Flood, 162
Williams v. Gresley, 198, 531
Williams v Great Western Ry. Co, 47
Williams v Gunnels, 426
Williams v. G W. R. Co, 553
Williams v Higgins, 96.
Williams v. Hill, 291, 293
Williams v. Holdridge, 299
Williams v Jones, 164
Williams v Karnes, 280
Williams v Morr,, 614
Williams v Morrison, 462
Williams v Palace Car Co, 87, 98
Williams v. Planter's Ins Co, 68
Williams v Pomeroy Coal Co., 153
Williams v. Russell, 629
Williams v. Sheldon, 230
Williams v Smith, 311 131
Williams v. Spencer, 471
Williams v Spurr, 362, 369
Williams v. Van Meter, 396
Williams v Wood, 672
Williamson v Allison, 359, 365, 649
Williamson v Freer, 307, 311
Williamsport, etc, R Co v Commonwealth, 136
Willingham v. King, 59
Willis v. MacInchian, 139
Willis v McMahan, 651
Willis v Oregon R & N Co., 122
Wills v Noyes, 396
Willy v Mulledy, 24.
Wilmarth v. Burt, 262
Wilmarth v Woodcock, 492
Wilmot v Howard, 26.
Wilson, Ex parte, 392.
Wilson v Barber, 454
Wilson v Beighler, 295
Wilson v Chalfant, 462
Wilson v Cottman, 301, 302
Wilson v Dubois, 24
Wilson v Dumreath etc Co, 122
Wilson v. Eggleston 857.
Wilson v Fitch, 66, 346.
Wilson v. Franklin, 144
Wilson v Golt, 298
Wilson v Gunning, 40
Wilson v McCrory, 295
Wilson v McLaughlin, 437
Wilson v Merry, 117, 124
Wilson v Newberry, 604, 607
Wilson v New York etc R Co, 537.
Wilson v Noonan, 333
Wilson v. Northern Pac R. Co, 567
Wilson v People, 252.
Wilson v. Peverly, 112, 503
Wilson v Robinson, 264
Wilson v Rochester, etc, R Co, 24
Wilson v. Runyan, 291
Wilson v St Paul etc. R Co, 463
Wilson v. Tatum, 296
Wilson v The Mary, 151.
Wilson v Tumman, 86
Wilson v Vaughn, 235.
Wilson v Waddell, 603.
Wilson v. Wheeling, 70.
Wilson v. Wilmington, etc. R. Co, 611
Wilson v Wilson, 243.
Wilson v Woonan, 305
Wilste v State Board Bridge Co, 108.
Wilt v Welsh, 60, 62
Wilton Mfg Co v Butler, 142
Wilwarth v Mountford, 394

TABLE OF CASES CITED.

The References are to Pages.

Wimer v. Allbaugh, 346
Wimer v. Smith, 358.
Winbigler v City of Los Angeles, 69
Winchell v Argus Co, 287
Windham v Simms, 519
Windsor v Oliver, 500
Winebiddle v Porterfield, 801.
Wing v. N Y etc R. Co, 606
Winne v Kelly, 681
Winslow v Bloomington, 505
Winsmore v Greenbank, 276
Winter v Bandel, 375, 376.
Winter v. Brockwell, 161
Winter v Sunwalt, 207
Winterbottom v Lord Derby, 190.
Winterbottom v. Wright, 642, 660.
Wintringham v Lafoy, 9
Wintusha v Louisville & N R Co, 230
Wisconsin Cent R Co v Ross, 230
Wise t Fuller, 353
Wiswell v Doyle, 681
Witascheck v Glass, 399
Witcher v Brewer, 114
Witherspoon v Woods, 143
Witherwax v Riddle, 983.
Wittick v Traun, 420
Wohlbehrt v Bockort, 624
Wolcott v Mellck, 504
Wolf v Chalker, 9, 614
Wolf v Mills, 114.
Wolf v. St Louis, etc, Co, 606
Wolf v Wolf, 272
Wolfe v. Merseroau, 101.
Wolters v Schultz, 222
Wonderly v Nokes, 823
Wonson v Sayward, 286.
Wood v. Atkinson, 482
Wood v Bailey, 899
Wood v. Braxton, 482
Wood v Clapp, 26, 27.
Wood v Cobb, 95
Wood v. Detroit St Ry., 110.
Wood v Durham, 347
Wood v Graves, 260, 899.
Wood v. Leadbitter, 460, 463
Wood v Mathews, 271, 274
Wood v Ruland, 138
Wood v. The Ind School Dist, 637
Wood v Wand, 498
Wood v Weir, 591
Wood v Wiman, 328.
Wood v Wood, 147
Woodard v Washburn, 260
Woodbury v Thompson, 293, 298.
Worden v. Western, 239
Wooden v. Western etc R Co., 123
Woodhouse v Walker, 76, 427
Woodle v Whitney, 632
Woodley v. Metr Dist R Co, 191
Woolfolk v Macon & A R Co, 544
Woodman v Howell, 201, 204
Woodman v Hubbard, 62, 443
Woodman v Kilbourn Mfg Co., 484
Woodruff v Richardson, 327
Woodruff v Woodruff, 252.
Woods v Davis, 141
Woods v Finnell, 399.
Woods v Jones, 507
Woods v Lindrall, 123.
Woods v St Paul, etc, R Co, 193
Woods v Wiman, 307
Woodson v Milwaukee, etc R Co, 562
Woodward v Barnes, 63
Woodward v. Chicago, etc, R Co, 81

Woodward v Michigan, etc, R Co, 81, 82
Woodward v St Louis, etc, R. Co, 68
Woodward v Walton, 275
Woodward v Washburn, 86.
Woolwine v C. & O R Co, 514.
Woolworth v Mills, 894
Woodyear v. Schaefer, 192
Worheide v Missouri C & T Co, 101
Works v Junction R Co, 560.
Wornell v. Maine Cent. R Co, 618
Wormby v Gregg, 614
Worth v. Butler, 311
Worth v Edmunds, 606
Worth v. Gilling, 614.
Worthington v Mencer, 540
Wozelka v Hettrick, 305, 327.
Wragg v. Commercial Gas Co, 505
Wren v Weild, 889.
Wright v Brown, 369
Wright v Calhoun, 383
Wright v Clark, 161
Wright v. Crompton, 84
Wright v Detroit, etc. Ry. Co., 681
Wray t Evans, 94
Wright v Lathrop, 338.
Wright v Leonard, 66
Wright v. Malden & M R. R. Co., 583
Wright v. Paige, 291
Wright t Pearson, 615.
Wright v. Ramscot, 425.
Wright v Rouse, 188
Wright v Stowe, 213
Wright v. Syracuse etc R. Co, 214
Wright v West, 243
Wright v Wilcox, 81, 100, 110
Wright v Wright, 610
Wroe v State, 495.
W. U. T. Co v Adams, 674
W U T Co. v. Herdue, 65
W. U T Co v Beringer, 55, 675.
W U T Co v Blanchard, 674.
W U T Co v. Carter, 55, 56
W. U T Co v. Dubois, 675.
W U T Co v. Jones, 675
W U T Co v Lindley, 675.
W. U T Co v Neill, 674
W U T Co v Newhouse, 55, 675
W. U. T. Co. v Rosentreter, 55
W U T Co v. Simpson, 211.
W. U. T. Co. v. Stratemeier, 55
W U. T Co. v Stephens, 55
Wyandotte, City of, v. Agon, 271
Wyatt v. Buell, 828
Wyatt v Williams, 81.
Wyllie v Palmer, 95
Wyman v. Leavitt, 55.
Wynne v. Parsons, 305.

Y.

Yager v. Atlantic etc R Co, 122
Yarborough v Bank of England, 63
Yarmouth v France, 194, 195, 631.
Yates v Brown, 96.
Yates v. Jack, 510
Yates v. Lansing, 138.
Yates & McCullach Iron Co, 121
Yates v Squires, 108
Yates v Town of West Grafton, 42
Yeager v. Knight, 60

TABLE OF CASES CITED.

The References are to Pages.

Yeates v. Allin, 466.
Yeaton v. Pryor, 350.
Yeates v. Read, 306.
Yeaton v. Railroad Corp., 117.
Yerger v. Warren, 108.
Yoakum v. Dunn, 55.
Yocum v. Polly, 393.
Yopst v. Yopst, 271.
York v. Pease, 328, 331.
Young v. Clogg, 307.
Young v. Covell, 672.
Young v. Gentis, 217.
Young v. Herbert, 138.
Young v. Kansas City, 70.
Young v. Kuhn, 294.
Young v. Mason, 431.
Young v. Miller, 294.
Young v. New York R. Co., 95.

Young v. Tel. Co., 55.
Young v. Vaughan, 413.
Yundt v. Hartrunft, 273.

Z.

Zabriskie v. Cleveland &c. Co., 68.
Zebley v. Storey, 395.
Zackray v. Pace, 485.
Ziegler v. Day, 121.
Zollif v. Jennings, 295.
Zemp v. Wilmington, etc. R. Co., 574.
Zerbing v. Mourer, 270.
Zier v. Hoflin, 30.
Zintek v. Stimson Mill Co., 123.
Zuckerman v. Sonnenschein, 305.

INDEX.

The italic letters refer to foot-notes, thus 270 *s* means note *s* on page 270. The American notes are referred to thus (Ed n.).

The References are to Pages.

ABATEMENT,
    of nuisance, 210, 487, 513, 515 (Ed. n.)
    whether applicable to nuisance by omission, 515, 516
    unnecessary damage must be avoided in, 517
    ancient process for, 517.
    difficulty of, no excuse, 526, 527 (Ed. n.)

ABUSE OF PROCESS. See PROCESS

ACCIDENT,
    inevitable, damage caused by, 160
    inevitable, 160–174.
    American law as to, 162 *x*, 164–168.
    inevitable, English authorities as to, 168
    inevitable, cases of, distinguished from those of voluntary risk, 190
    liability for, in special cases, 595.
    non-liability for, in special cases, 607
    non liability for, in performance of duty, 608
    negligence when presumed from, 609.

ACT OF GOD,
    non-liability for, 50 (Ed. n.), 85, 605   See WIND.

ACT OF PARLIAMENT,
    remedy under, when exclusive, 228.
    damage must be within mischief of, 229.

ACTION,
    forms of, 2, 13, 14.
    causes of, in contract or tort, 3, 5
    on the case, 13, 14, 645.
    convicted felons and alien enemies cannot have, 60.
    by or against husband and wife, 63 (Ed n.), 64
    personal, effect of party's death on, 71.
    survival of cause of personal, exception in early English law, 72.
    for injury *per quod servitium amisit*, 74, 270, 278.
    for wrongs to property, when it survives for or against executors, 76.

The References are to Pages.

ACTION — *Continued.*
    cause of, under Lord Campbell's act, 77–79.
    effect of death of party after appeal, 81 (Ed. n.).
    against viceroy or colonial governor, 185.
    by State against another, 196 (Ed. n.)
    right of, for damage in execution of authorized works, 151, 158.
    where damage is gist of, 215.
    cause of, when it arises, 215, 216 (Ed. n.).
    single or severable, 223.
    for breach of statutory duty, 227.
    against joint wrong-doers, exhausted by judgment against any, 231
    when wrong amounts to felony, 238.
    local or transitory, 238.
    limitation of, 242.
    runs from what time, 244.
    exception of concealed fraud, 245.
    of deceit against corporations, 380 (Ed n.).
    malicious bringing of, whether it can be a tort, 397.
    changes in procedure, 483.
    history of forms of, 505.
    early theory of causes of, 644.
    on the case, development of, 645.
    causes of, their modern classification, 646.
    form of, duty not varied by, 652.
    concurrent causes of, in contract and tort, 656.
        against different parties, 660
    in contract and tort by different plaintiffs, 662.
    in tort dependent on a contract not between the same parties, 668.
    real, when abolished, 2.
        form of writ of right, 14.
        replaced by action of ejectment, 209 *a*. See REMEDIES

ACTS,
    voluntary, liability for accidental consequences of, 163, 167, 178.

ACTS OF STATE, 132. See EXCEPTIONS, FOREIGN POWERS, GOVERNOR, VICEROY.

ADMINISTRATOR,
    May be sued for death of intestate, when, 81 (Ed. n.), 82 (Ed. n.).

ADMIRALTY,
    Rule of, where both ships are in fault, 588.

ADVERTISEMENT,
    Effect of libellous, 310 (Ed. n).

ADVICE OF COUNSEL. See COUNSEL.

INDEX.

The References are to Pages.

AGENT,
Assumption of skill by, 26 (Ed. n.)
implied warranty of authority by, 74 *k*.
liability of principal for authorized or ratified acts of, 84.
fraud of, 112
when entitled to indemnity, 201.
liability of person assuming authority as, 373
misrepresentations by, 383.
false representations made by or through, 383, 384.
when personally liable, 384 (Ed. n).
how far corporation can be liable for deceit of, 386.
conversion by, 411, 413 (Ed n)
implied warranty of authority of,
659. See PRINCIPAL AND AGENT.

AGISTER,
not liable for animal's death, 143 (Ed. n.).

AGREEMENT,
unlawful, cause of action connected with, 208.

AIR,
no specific right to access of, 509

AIR GUN,
injury with, 551 (Ed. n.).

ALIEN ENEMY,
cannot sue, 59, 60 (Ed n.).

ALTERUM NON LAEDERE,
relation of law of torts to, 12

AMENDMENT,
of statement of claim to increase damages claimed, 218 *s*.

AMERICAN LAW,
as to contributory negligence, 13, 590*u*, 595
want of ordinary care, 49 *f*.
convicts, 59, 60 (Ed n).
alien enemy, 60 (Ed. n.).
liability of corporations, 68 *t*.
gives compensation for damage by death, 80
as to liability of master for acts of servant, 88.
doctrine of a common employment in, 118.
employers' liability in, 127.
as to judicial acts, corresponds with English, 141.
inevitable accident being no ground of liability, 160 *et seq*.
on accidents during Sunday traveling, 208.

The References are to Pages.

AMERICAN LAW — *Continued.*
    as to slander of title, 390.
        conspiracy not being cause of action, 402 (Ed. n.), 403.
        malicious wrongs, 406.
        waste, 427, 429 r.
        parol licences, 463.
        negligence, 540, 548 b, 566 p, 686.
    Lumley v. *Gye,* followed in, 672
    as to causing breach of contract, 673.
        rights of receiver of telegram, 674.

ANGLO-SAXON LAW,
    of torts, 22.

ANGUISH,
    no cause of action, 55 (Ed. n).

ANIMALS,
    killing of, in defence of property, 202.
    trespasses by, 202, 203.
    prevention of cruelty to, 474.
    mischievous, responsibility for, 613.

APOTHECARY,
    assumption of skill by, 26 (Ed. n)   See POISON.

APPEAL,
    effect of, upon death, 81 (Ed. n)

APPRENTICE,
    master may sue for injury to, 271 (Ed n)

ARBITRATION,
    how death of party before award affects cause of action, 71.

ARBITRATORS,
    not liable for errors in judgment, 140, 145 (Ed. n)

ARREST,
    authority of servant to make, 107.
    officer making, liable for mistakes, 142 (Ed n.), 143
    when justified, 260 (Ed. n), 261 (Ed. n), 262.
    who is answerable for, 264. See FALSE IMPRISONMENT, IMPRISONMENT.

ASPORTATION, 425.

ASSAULT,
    corporations liable for, 67 (Ed n)
    when not justified by consent, 186
    acts for benefit of persons who cannot consent, 199, 200

The References are to Pages.

ASSAULT — Continued.
self-defence, 201, 255.
what is, 219, 252.
what is not, 251 (Ed. n.), 252, 254.
words cannot be, 252 (Ed. n.), 254.
justification by consent, 253 (Ed. n.), 254.
menace distinguished from, 258.
when action barred by summary process, 258. See DEFENCE, SELF-DEFENCE.

ASSENT. See CONSENT.

ASSETS,
following property or its value into wrong-doer's, 81.

ASSUMPSIT,
action of, its relation to negligence, 534
development of, from general action on the case, 648.
implied, where tort waived, 658.

ASSUMPTION OF SKILL. See AGENT, APOTHECARY, ATTORNEY, CARRIER, ENGINEER, MASTER AND SERVANT, PHYSICIANS AND SURGEONS, SKILL

ATTORNEY,
assumption of skill by, 26 (Ed n.).
slander of, 300 (Ed. n.).
immunity of, 329 (Ed n), 300. See COUNSEL

AUTHORITIES OF NECESSITY,
exception of, 151

AUTHORIZED WORKS,
exception of, liability in, 152, 608.
care required in, 157.

AVERAGE,
general law of, 200.

BAILEE,
justification of, in re-delivery to bailor, 442.
interpleader by, 442, 443.
excessive acts of, when conversion, 442, 443.
liable to action of trespass for abusing subject-matter of bailment at will, 452.
bailment over by, 453
and bailor, concurrent right of suit in, 454

BALLOON,
trespass by, 40 n, 423.

The References are to Pages.

BANK,
    check fraudulently drawn, 369 (Ed. n.).
    conversion by, 484 (Ed. n.).

BANKRUPTCY,
    no duty to prosecute upon trustee in, 286
    debt discharged by, in American law, 241
    imputation of, to tradesman, actionable, 302 (Ed. n.), 303.
    malicious proceedings in, 400.

BARRISTER,
    revising, powers of, 139.
    slander of, 301 (Ed. n.), 303. And see ATTORNEY, COUNSEL.

BATTERY,
    corporation liable for, 67 (Ed. n.)
    what is, 247-249. See ASSAULT

BELLS,
    ringing of, when a nuisance, 495 (Ed. n.).

BICYCLE,
    riding over person with, 248 (Ed. n.).

BILL-POSTER,
    employer liable for wantonness of, 100 (Ed. n.).

BLASTING,
    may be a nuisance, 502 (Ed. n.)

BOARDER,
    defined, 642 (Ed. n.)

BOAT,
    liability of owner, 100 (Ed. n.) See SHIP.

BOILING ESTABLISHMENTS,
    may be a nuisance, 503 (Ed. n.).

BOXING-MATCHES,
    generally unlawful, 186 (Ed. n.)

BRANCHES,
    overhanging See TREE

BREACH OF PEACE,
    justifies arrest, 261 (Ed. n.), 262 (Ed. n.), 264 l.

BREACH OF PROMISE. See MARRIAGE.

BREAKING DOORS,
    when justified, 471

BROKER,
    liable for conversion, 441 (Ed. n.)

The References are to Pages.

BUILDINGS,
    duty of keeping in safe condition, 624, 627.
    occupiers of, duty of, to passers-by, 633, 638.
    falling into street, 635.

BURDEN OF PROOF. See PROOF.

BUSINESS,
    slander on, injunction to restrain, 224.
    slander of a man in the way of his, 300 et seq.
    words indirectly causing damage in, 308.
    malicious interference with, 406.

BY-STANDER,
    plight of, when injured, 167, 201.
    hearing slander, 312 (Ed n.)

CAIRNS'S ACT (LORD), 520 f.

CAMPBELL'S ACT (LORD), 6 & 7 Vict. c. 96,
    as to pleading apology, etc., in action for defamation, 346.

CAMPBELL'S ACT (LORD), 9 & 10 Vict. c. 93
    what relatives may recover under, 77 t.
    claim under, does not lie in Admiralty jurisdiction, 77 t.
    construction of, 78.
    what damages may be recovered under, 79.
    cause of action under, not cumulative, 80.

CANAL,
    escape of water from, 608.

CANDIDATE,
    fair comment upon, 321 (Ed n).

CAPACITY,
    personal, with respect to torts, 58 et seq

CARRIAGE,
    responsibilities of owner of, 629, 631, 642.

CARRIER,
    common, interfering with passengers by guards, 104
        conversion by, 434 (Ed. n.).
        duty of, 629, 650, 661.

CASE,
    action on the, development of, 645.

CASTLE See DWELLING

CATERER,
    assumption of skill by, 27 (Ed n)

CATTLE,
  infecting pasture with, 370 (Ed. n.).
  conversion of, 413 (Ed. n.).
  trespass by, 424, 610.
  damage feasant, 473, 478.
  liability for trespass by, 610.
  bitten by dog, no *scienter* need be proved, 614.
  right of owners of, to safe condition of market-place, 631. See STOCK.

CATTLE-YARD,
  may be a nuisance, 505 (Ed. n.).

CAUSE,
  immediate or proximate, 29, 30, 36, 37, 42.
  reasonable and probable, for imprisonment, 267
  proximate, in law of negligence, 565, 573, 578 And see PROXIMATE CAUSE.
  of action See ACTION.

CAUTION,
  consummate, required with dangerous instrument, 54. See NEGLIGENCE.

CAVEAT EMPTOR,
  rule of, 376 (Ed. n.)

CEMETERY,
  may be a nuisance, 502 (Ed. n.).

CESSPOOLS,
  may be a nuisance, 505 (Ed n)

CHILDREN,
  injury to, 47, 48.
  may be corrected by parent, 149
  service of, 282.
  degree of care towards, 564 (Ed. n.), 565.
  when deprived of remedy by contributory negligence of parent, etc., 582.

CHURCH COUNCIL,
  investigations by, when privileged, 146 (Ed n), 339 (Ed n).

CIVIL PROCEEDINGS,
  malicious bringing of, whether a tort, 397

CLERGYMAN,
  slander of, 301 (Ed n)
  complaint to, regarding curate, 339.

The References are to Pages.

CLERK,
    slander of, 800 (Ed. n.).

CLUB,
    quasi-judicial power of committee, 146.
    cases on expulsion from, 147 s, t.
    chance of being elected to, no subject of legal loss, 299.

COLLECTORS OF CUSTOMS,
    exception of liability, 145 (Ed. n).

COLLEGE,
    quasi-judicial powers of, 146.

COLLISION,
    between vehicles in street, 218 (Ed. n), 549 (Ed. n.).
        railroad trains, 518 (Ed. n), 549
        ships, 588
    See NEGLIGENCE, RAILWAY.

COLONIAL GOVERNMENT,
    liable for management of public harbour, 71

COLONIAL LEGISLATURE,
    control of, over its own members, 145 p

COLONY,
    governor of, liable in courts of colony for debt, 135.

COMMAND AND RATIFICATION, 87. And see MASTER AND SERVANT.

COMITY,
    rule of, as to suits affecting foreign sovereigns and states, 136

COMMENT,
    fair, not actionable, 317.
    what is open to, 320, 322. See CANDIDATE, MUSICAL COMPOSITION,
        WRITER.

COMMON,
    no distress by commoners *inter se*, 472.

"COMMON EMPLOYMENT,"
    the doctrine of, 118
    what is, 119.
    relative rank of servants immaterial, 121

COMMON RIGHTS,
    immunity in exercise of, 174.

COMMONER,
    any one can sue for injury, 508.
    may pull down house on common after notice, 514.
    may pull down fence without notice, 515.

The References are to Pages.

COMMUNICATION,
  what is privileged, 331, 335, 340. See IMMUNITY, PRIVILEGE.

COMPANY,
  fraud of directors, 113.
  remedy of shareholder against, for fraud, 113.
  removal of director, 147 a.
  false statements in prospectus of, 359, 374.
  representations in prospectus of, 370.
  malicious proceedings to wind up, 400.

COMPENSATION,
  statutory, for damage done by authorized works, 155.

COMPETENCE,
  what is, and when required, 27 (Ed. n), 542.

COMPETITION,
  in business or trade, no wrong, 174-177.
  as to malice in connection with, where acts lawful, 1822 z, a.
  combination in trade to exclusion of, may not be wrong, 405.

CONCEALMENT,
  when illegal, 368-370.

CONFIDENTIAL INQUIRIES,
  privileged, 337. See MERCANTILE AGENCIES, RELATIVES.

CONSENT,
  effect of, in justifying force, 185, 186, 190, 253 (Ed n), 254.
  when a bar to action for seduction, 279 (Ed n).

CONSEQUENCES,
  liability for, 29.
  near or remote, 30-35, 41, 54. See INTENTION.
  "natural and probable," 32, 35, 303, 304.
  liability of wilful wrong-doer for, 33, 52.
  natural in kind though not in circumstance, 54
  supposed limitation of liability to "legal and natural," 670. See CAUSE

CONSPIRACY,
  Corporations liable for, 67 (Ed n.), 403
  whether a substantive wrong, 401.
  how far trade combination to exclusion of other traders is a, 403, 409 (Ed. n.).

CONSTABLE,
  must produce warrant, 142, 143.
  is liable for mistake of fact, 142 (Ed.n.), 143.

CONSTABLE — *Continued.*
    statutory protection of, 143, 215
    protection of, by statute of limitation, 245
    powers of, to arrest on suspicion, 282.
    protection of, in cases of forcible entry, 471, 472.

CONSTRUCTIVE SERVICE. See SERVICE.

"CONSUMMATE CARE,"
    cannot always avoid accident, 160
    requirement of, 167.

CONTAGIOUS DISEASE,
    imputation of, 299

CONTEMPT OF COURT,
    corporations liable for, 67 (Ed. n.)

CONTINUITY,
    necessary to constitute nuisance, 494.

CONTRACT,
    actions of, as opposed to tort, 2, 5, 16.
    violation of duty arising out of, 29 (Ed. n.).
    right of action upon, not extended by changing form, 60.
    law of, complicated with that of tort in province of deceit, 349.
    malicious interference with, 409, 673
    effect of, on title to property, 350, 414.
    overlaps with tort in law of negligence, 534
    effect of, on negligence, 548.
    relations of, to tort, 644 *et seq.*
    negligence in performing, how far a tort, 649, 653
    breach of duty founded on, 652.
    rights arising from, not affected by suing in case, 654
    where action of tort lies notwithstanding existence of doubt as to, 656
    implied in law, as alternative of tort, 658.
    with one party, compatible with actionable breach of duty in same matter by another, 660.
    breach of, whether third party can sue for an act which is, 663
    with servant, effect of, on master's rights, 663
    stranger to, cannot sue for damage consequential on mere breach of, 666
    breach of, concurring with delict in Roman law, 667.
    causing breach of, under what conditions a tort, 668
    existence or non-existence of, as affecting position of third parties, 680
    measure of damages in, as compared with tort, 682.
    to marry, exceptional features of, 684, 686 (Ed. n). See DECEIT.

The References are to Pages.

CONTRACTOR,
when not a servant, 92 (Ed. n).
Independent, responsibility of occupier for acts and defaults of, 205.
duties extending to acts of 686 f, 687 (Ed. n.), 689. See INDEPENDENT CONTRACTOR.

CONTRIBUTION,
between wrong-doers, 231.

CONTRIBUTORY NEGLIGENCE,
not punishable as a positive wrong, 207.
plaintiff is not bound to negative, 518.
what it is, 566.
proper direction to jury, 567 (Ed. n.), 569, 570
rule of, founded in public utility, 570
true ground of "proximate" or "decisive" cause, 573, 577-580.
self-created disability to avoid consequences of another's negligence, 575.
intoxication is not, 575 (Ed. n.)
illustrations, 576.
as to damages in cases of, 578
of third persons, effect of, 579, 580, 671.
negligent acts simultaneous or successive, 579.
doctrine of "identification" now not law, 580, 587
accidents to children in custody of adult or unattended, 582, 583, (Ed. n.), 584.
unknown in Admiralty jurisdiction, 588.
separation of law and fact in the United States, 595. And see NEGLIGENCE.

CONTROL,
assumption of, 94, 96. See MASTER AND SERVANT

CONVERSION,
anomaly of, 13.
corporations liable for, 67 (Ed. n.).
right to follow property, 81.
exemplary damages recoverable in, 220 (Ed n)
what is, 419, 420 (Ed. n), 432, et seq
distinguished from injury to reversionary interest, 433.
meaning of, extended, 433, 434 (Ed n.)
by bank, 434 (Ed n.).
carrier, 434 (Ed. n.).
acts in good faith may be, 435, 439 (Ed n).
refusal as evidence, 436.
mere claim of title or collateral breach of contract is not, 437.
qu as to dealings under apparent authority, 439.

The References are to Pages.

CONVERSION — Continued.
    by auctioneer, 439 (Ed n.).
        agent or servant, 441, 443 (Ed. n.).
        bailees, 442.
        distinction between varieties of, and cases of injury without conversion, 446.
        estoppel, 446.
    of chattels by co-tenant, 448, (Ed. n.). See TRESPASS, TROVER.

CONVICT.
    cannot sue, 59, 60 (Ed. n.).

COPYRIGHT,
    injunction to restrain infringement of, 224 (Ed. n.)
    principle of slander of title extending to, 390. See TRADE MARKS.

CORPORAL PUNISHMENT, 149. See CHILDREN, HUSBAND AND WIFE, LUNATIC, SHIP.

CORPORATION,
    liability of, for wrongs, 66.
        assault and battery, 67 (Ed. n.).
        conspiracy, 67 (Ed. n.).
        contempt of court, 67 (Ed. n.)
        conversion, 67 (Ed. n)
        deceit, 67 (Ed n.).
        false imprisonment, 68 (Ed. n).
        malicious prosecution, 68 (Ed. n.), 397.
    liable for trespass, 68 t.
    responsibility for performance of public duties, 69.
    may be liable for fraud, etc , of its agents, 112 p. 113, 386.
    cannot commit maintenance, semble, 411.
    may be liable for a nuisance, 530 (Ed. n). See PROSPECTUS, STOCKS

COSTS,
    relation of, to damages, 213 l.
    present procedure as to, 215 l
    presumed to be indemnity to successful defendant, 397–399

COUNSEL,
    advice of, no excuse for false imprisonment, 263 (Ed. n)
    immunity of words spoken by, 328 (Ed. n.), 329 (Ed. n.), 330.
    advice of, excuse for malicious prosecution, 895 (Ed. n.). See ATTORNEY.

COUNTY COUNCIL,
    licensing sessions of, 330

COUNTY COURT,
    statutory distinction of actions in, 654.

The References are to Pages.

COUNTY COURT JUDGE,
    powers of, 135.

COURSE OF EMPLOYMENT,
    what is in, 97. See MASTER AND SERVANT

COURT,
    privilege of statements made, 330
    control of, over jury, 345.
    judicial notice by, 551. See IMMUNITY, JUDICIAL PROCEEDINGS.

COURT AND JURY,
    functions of, in cases of negligence, 513, 514.
    usual and proper direction as to contributory negligence, 566 *et seq*

COURT-MARTIAL,
    protection of members of, 140.
    whether action lies for bringing one before, without probable cause, 144.

CREDIT,
    intention to not pay for goods bought on, 369 (Ed. n.)
    recommendation of, 381 (Ed. n.)

CRIME,
    oral imputation of, when actionable, 294.

CRIMINAL CONVERSATION,
    former action of, 273.

CRIMINAL LAW,
    attempted personal offences, 34 *m*
    what is immediate cause of death in, 42
    individuals bound to enforce, 141, 237 *r*.
    forfeiture of deodand, 162.
    as to self-defence, 201.
    conversion necessary for larceny, 432.
    distinction of receiving from theft in, 454
    as to asportation, 470.
    prosecution for public nuisance, 484 *et seq*.

CRITICISM,
    limits of allowable, 317, 320. See COMMENT, REPORTS.

CROSSINGS,
    over railway, 198 (Ed. n.), 553.

CROWD,
    injuries by, 39, 40.

CULPA,
    defined, 18

The References are to Pages.

CULPA — Continued.
equivalence of *culpa lata* to *dolus*, 378, 509, 510
licensor not liable to gratuitous licensee for, 640.

CUSTODY,
distinguished from possession, 416, 417.

CUSTOM,
loss of, no right of action for, 176, 177, 181

CUSTOM OF THE REALM,
meaning of, 652, 654.

CUSTOMER,
right of, to safe condition of buildings, etc., 591 (Ed n), 626, 627.

DAMAGE,
relation of, to wrongful act, 20, 21.
for "nervous or mental shock," whether too remote, 54.
from authorized acts, 152, 154, 157 (Ed n)
unavoidable, no action for, 155.
effect of, as regards limitation, 244.
special, in law of slander, what, 290.
special, involves definite temporal loss, 292.
actual, unnecessary to constitute trespass, 421.
particular, in action for public nuisance, 487, 488.
not when private right infringed, 499.
irreparable, injunction will restrain, 520
special, procuring breach of contract actionable only with, 669.
remoteness of, 35, 41 *et seq.*, 670.

DAMAGE FEASANT, 473, 478.

DAMAGES,
measure of, 31, 211.
for nervous or mental shock, 54.
measure of, where death results, 81 (Ed. n.), 82 (Ed n.).
excessive award of, will be set aside, 211 (Ed n) 212.
nominal, ordinary, or exemplary, 212, 213 (Ed n).
carrying costs, 213 *l*, 214 *m*, 215 *n*
nominal, as test of absolute right, 214.
when damage gist of action, 215.
ordinary, measure of, 217.
in cases of personal injury, 218 (Ed. n.).
for special value of property injured, 218 (Ed n.).
exemplary, 219, 220 (Ed. n.).
for false imprisonment, 220.
mitigated, 222.
only once given for same cause of action, 223.

DAMAGES — *Continued.*
Injunction, distinguished, 224.
for false representation, 227.
measure of, in action for inducing plaintiff by false statements to take shares in company, 227 *s*.
in actions for seduction, 276.
mitigation of, by apology, in action for slander or libel, 316.
in action for trover, 487.
relation of costs to, 480.
for nuisance, 512, 518.
to what date assessed, 520.
in cases of contributory negligence, 578, 579.
measure of, in contract and tort, 682
for breach of promise of marriage, 222, 685 See EXEMPLARY DAMAGES, JURY, MITIGATION OF DAMAGES.

DAMNUM SINE INJURIA, 22, 175

DANGER,
going to, 190.
imminent, duty of person repelling, 201.
position of, one knowing, 206.
diligence proportioned to, 563.
concealed, to bare licensee, 639, 640
licensor, liable for, 640.

DANGEROUS THINGS,
strict responsibility in dealing with, 29, 169, 170, 598, 601, 613, 618, 622. See INSTRUMENT, DANGEROUS

DEATH,
of party, effect of, on rights of action, 55, 274 (Ed n)
of human being, said to be never cause of action at common law, 72
effect on license, 464 (Ed. n.). See ACTION.

DEBT,
right of retaining, 210.

DECEIT,
corporation liable for, 67 (Ed. n.).
action of, damage must be shown, 216
may give innocent agent claim for indemnity, 232, *f*.
what, 348.
complication with contract, 349
sale, 349, 357 (Ed. n.), 368 (Ed. n.), 370 (Ed. n.)
fraudulent intent in, 353.
conditions of right to sue for, 355.
no cause of action without both fraud and actual damage, 355.

INDEX. 763

The References are to Pages.

DECEIT — *Continued.*
    must include knowledge of untruth or culpable ignorance, 355.
        falsehood in fact, 356.
    mere opinion, not, 357 (Ed. n.)
    in relations of confidence, 358 (Ed. n.), 361 (Ed. n.)
    may include misstatement of law, 360
    by gambling, 362.
    statement believed by maker at the time is not, 362.
    ground of belief looked to as test of its reality, 362.
    American law as to, 364.
    effect of subsequent discovery of untruth, 365
    reckless assertion, 367.
    breach of special duty, 368
    intention as element of, 372.
    by public representations, 373.
    as regards prospectus of new company, 374. And see PROSPECTUS
    statement not relied on is not, 375
    rule of caveat emptor, 376 (Ed n)
    mere fraudulent intention, not, 377,
    effect of plaintiff's means of knowledge, 377
        perfunctory inquiry, 379.
    as to reliance on ambiguous statements, 380.
    effect of misrepresentation by or through agent, 383
    by agent of corporation, 386.
    action of, against falsifier of telegram, 674 *et seq.* See FRAUD, MISREPRESENTATION.

DEFAMATION,
    damages in action of, 215.
    special damage, 217, 290, 292.
    of female's reputation, 292 (Ed n).
    gross, damages for, 221.
    in general, 286, 304.
    spiritual, 298 *t*
    of one in his business, 300–304.
    in what sense "malicious," 305.
    "publication" of, 306
    construction of words as to defamatory meaning, 311.
    by repetition, 315.
    exception of fair comment, 317.
    justified by truth of matter, 323
    immunity of speech in Parliament, 327.
        in meetings of county council, 330
        words used by judges and others in judicial proceedings, 329.
        naval and military, judicial or official proceedings, 329 (Ed n.), 331
        privileged communications generally, 331.

The References are to Pages.

DEFAMATION — *Continued.*
 exception of "express malice," 333
 what are privileged occasions, 335
 privilege of fair reports, 340.
 newspaper reports of public meetings, 342 See IMMUNITY, INJUNCTION, LIBEL, LIBERTY OF THE PRESS, MEMORIALS, PETITIONS, REPORTS, SLANDER

DEFECT,
 latent, non-responsibility for, 631.
 in structure, responsibility of occupier for, 633–637.

DEFENCE See DWELLING, FAMILY, SELF-DEFENCE, SELF-HELP.

DELICTS.
 Roman law of, 17–19
  terminology of, Austin on, 19 s.

DEPARTMENTS,
 whether servants in different, are fellow-servants, 124 (Ed. n.).

DETENTION. See FALSE IMPRISONMENT, IMPRISONMENT, POSSESSION.

DETINUE, 14, 16.
 nature of writ of, 120 (Ed. n.), 426

DIGEST,
 of Justinian, *ad legem Aquiliam*, 17 And see LEX AQUILIA.

DILIGENCE,
 liability even when utmost used, 11–13
 amount of, required by law, 25, 26 See DUTY
 general standard of, 532, 540.
 includes competent skill where required, 539, 542, 550.
 due, varies as apparent risk, 563

DISABILITY,
 suspending statute of limitation, 243

DISCRETION,
 where given by legislature must be exercised with regard to other rights, 157.

DISEASED BEASTS,
 may be a nuisance, 503 (Ed. n.).

DISTRESS,
 in general, 472.
 damage feasant, 473, 478
  conditions of, 474, 475.
 for rent, 472, 478 n
 liability for, 479.

DISTRESS — *Continued.*
  excess in distress damage feasant, effect of, 180.

DOCKS,
  owner of, answerable for safety of appliances, 628.

DOG,
  may be killed, when, 516 (Ed. n.)
  whether owner liable for mere trespass of, 612.
  liability for vice or, 614.
  statutory protection against, 614 (Ed. n), 615 t.

DOGS,
  separation of fighting, resulting in accident, 166.

DOG-SPEARS,
  authorities on injuries by, 203 a.

DOLUS, 18, 71, 848.

DOMINUS PRO TEMPORE, 95.

DRIVER,
  relation of, to passengers, 94.
  course of employment of, 100 (Ed. n.)
  duty of, 198

DRIVERS,
  negligence of both, 580.

DRUNKEN MAN,
  liable for tort, 59 (Ed. n.).
  authorized restraint of, 151.
  may be exclud´ by innkeeper, 651 (Ed n). See CONTRIBUTORY
    NEGLIGENCE.

DUEL,
  always unlawful, 188.

DUTIES,
  absolute, imposed by policy of law, 7, 19
  relation of legal to moral, 9, 12
  to one's neighbor, expanded in law of torts, 12.
  of insuring safety, 598 *et seq*.

DUTY,
  absolute, 20, 85.
  limited, 20.
  of diligence, 20, 25.
  to one's neighbor, nowhere broadly stated, 23.
  specific legal acts in breach of, 24.
  of respecting property, 25.

The References are to Pages.

DUTY — Continued.
    arising out of contract, 20 (Ed. n.).
    of warning, knowledge of risk opposed to, 192.
    statutory, remedy for breach of, 228.
    to give correct information, 368
    of caution, 533. And see NEGLIGENCE
    omission of legal, 534 (Ed. n.).
    standard of, does not vary with individuals, 540.
    towards passers-by, 633
    breach of, in course of employment, action for, 619

DWELLING,
    defence of, 257 (Ed. n)

EASEMENT,
    disturbance of, analogous to trespass, 156.
    license cannot confer, 457, 463
    of light, 508, 509

EDITOR,
    admitting publication, not bound to disclose actual author, 311. See JOURNALIST.

ELECTION,
    liability of officers holding, 148, 149
    to sue in contract or tort for misfeasance, 647
    doctrine of, seems not applicable when duties are distinct in substance, 665.

ELEVATOR,
    injury by, 550 (Ed. n.).

EMBEZZLEMENT,
    when not consequence of collusion, 44 (Ed. n)

EMERGENCY,
    skill not required in action under, 27 (Ed. n.) See NECESSITY.

EMPLOYE,
    assumes risk of employment, 192-195. See SERVANT

EMPLOYER,
    when answerable as master, 90 et seq.
    not liable for negligence of his contractor, 637 (Ed. n). See INDEPENDENT CONTRACTOR, MASTER AND SERVANT

EMPLOYER'S LIABILITY ACT,
    as regards "volenti non fit injuria," 195

EMPLOYMENT,
    what is course of, 97 See MASTER AND SERVANT
    public, of carriers and innkeepers, 630

The References are to Pages.

ENGINEER,
    assumption of skill by, 27 (Ed. n.)

ENTRY,
    by relation, 465.
    when justified, 465 et seq.
    fresh, on trespasser, 468.
    to take distress, 474
    of necessity, 475

EQUITY,
    remedies formerly peculiar to, 209.
    former concurrent jurisdiction of, in cases of deceit, 321 See INJUNCTION.
    protects executed licenses, 462 (Ed. n.)

ERROR,
    clerical, responsibility for, 303, 679

ESTOPPEL,
    if no contract or breach of specific duty, statements to be made good only on ground of fraud or, 371
    conversion by, 446.

EVIDENCE,
    of malice, 345
    of conversion, 436.
    of negligence, 539, 543, 560, 595.
    question whether there is any for court inference from admitted evidence for jury, 551.
    of contributory negligence, 571.

EXCAVATIONS,
    by municipalities, 70 (Ed. n).
        neighbors, 216

EXCEPTIONS TO LIABILITY, 130 et seq. See ACTS OF STATE, AUTHORITIES OF NECESSITY, AUTHORIZED WORKS, EXECUTIVE ACTS, JUDICIAL ACTS, PARENT, QUASI-JUDICIAL ACTS.

EXCESS,
    master liable for servant's, 103.

EX CONTRACTU,
    effect of death of party on actions of, 71, 74

EX DELICTO,
    Roman system compared, 17, 18, 19
    effect of death of party on actions of, 71, 73

EXECUTION,
    of process, justification of trespass in, 471 See PROCESS
        specific orders, 98

The References are to Pages.

EXECUTIVE ACTS,
immunity of, 108 (Ed. n.), 111.

EXECUTORS,
cannot be sued for testator's torts, 71 *et seq.*
statutory rights of action by, for wrongs to testator's property, 75, 76.
liability of, for wrongs of testator, 76.
    to restore property or its value, 88.
whether not bound to prosecute for felony before bringing civil action, 236.
cannot sue for personal injuries to testator, even on a contract, 686.

EXEMPLARY DAMAGES,
when recoverable, 219, 220 (Ed. n.).
in seduction cases, 281 (Ed. n.) See DAMAGES.

EXPLOSIVES,
liability for improper dealing with, 164, 165, 615 (Ed. n.), 619.
may be a nuisance, 503 (Ed. n.).
liability for sending without notice, 619.

EXPRESS MALICE. See MALICE, MALICE IN FACT.

FACTORS ACTS,
validity of dealings under, 415.
good title acquired under, 681.

FACULTIES,
ordinary use of, presumed, 564.

FAIR COMMENT,
justifiable, 317. See COMMENT.

FALSEHOOD. See DECEIT, FRAUD, MISREPRESENTATION.

FALSE IMPRISONMENT,
corporation liable for, 68 (Ed. n.)
what is, 259–262.
prosecutor or officer answerable for, 264.
distinguished from malicious prosecution, 265 (Ed. n.), 266.
reasonable and probable cause, 267. See COUNSEL, IMPRISONMENT.

FAMILY,
relations, 214, 269.
defence of, 257 (Ed n.). See HUSBAND AND WIFE, PARENT.

FELLOW-SERVANTS,
may recover for other's negligence, 84 (Ed n.)
master not liable for injury by, 115, 116.
servants need not be about same kind of work, 118, 119.
rank of servants immaterial, 121.

The References are to Pages.

FELLOW-SERVANTS — *Continued*
    employed in different departments, 121 (Ed. n.)
    servants of sub-contractor not, with servants of principal contractor, 126.
    volunteer assistant becomes, 126.
    exception where master interferes, 127. See MASTER AND SERVANT.

FELONY,
    "merger" of trespass in, 233, 236.
    arrest for, justification of, 262, 263.
    imputation of, when libellous, 294, 299, 326.

FENCE,
    when trespass for defective, 473.
    falling in neighbour's land, 604.
    duty to maintain, 610.

FERRY,
    refusal to carry passengers by, 137.
    franchise of, 157 r.
    nuisance to, 517.

FINE,
    in trespass under old law, 3.

FIRE,
    causing horse to run away, 37 (Ed. n.).
    escape of, from railway engines, 43 (Ed. n.), 560, 561 (Ed. n.), 617.
    when proximate cause of injury, 43 (Ed. n.), 51 (Ed. n.)
        master is not liable for servant's, 107 (Ed. n.)
    negligence as to, 539.
    safe-keeping of, 616.
    responsibility for carrying, 617.

FIRE-ARMS,
    accidents with, 167.
    may be a nuisance, 503 (Ed. n.).
    consummate caution required in dealing with, 615, 618.

FIRM,
    co-partners liable for other's fraud, 114.

FOOTMAN,
    must use care in crossing street, 197 (Ed. n.), 198.

FORCIBLE ENTRY,
    statutes against, 465, 466 (Ed. n.)
    with good title, whether civilly wrongful, 468.

The References are to Pages.

FOREIGN LANGUAGE,
  publication of defamation in, 307 (Ed. n.), 308 (Ed. n.), 312 (Ed. n.).

FOREIGN POWERS,
  exception of acts of, 186.

FORNICATION,
  imputation of, may be slanderous under statute, 298 (Ed. n.)

FOX-HUNTING,
  trespass in, not justified, 477.

FRANCE (law of),
  Conseil d'Etat inquiries into "acts of state," 187.
  rule of, of five years' prescription, 241.

FRANCHISE,
  malicious interference with exercise of, 410.

FRAUD,
  of infant, 68
  of agent or servant, 112
  of partners, 114, 384 (Ed n.)
  compensation for, in equity, formerly by way of restitution, 227.
  concealed, effect of, on period of limitation, 245
  remedies for, 277.
  in sales, 349-357, 368 (Ed. n.), 370 (Ed n)
      insurance, 352 (Ed n).
  intent, 353. See INTENTION.
  equitable jurisdiction founded on, 353, 354.
  "constructive," 354.
  "legal," 354.
  of agents, 355
  by suppressing truth, 362, 368, 369 (Ed n).
  relation of, to infringement of trade-marks, etc , 391
  effect of, on transfer of property or possession, 414, 415 See
      BANK CHECK, DECEIT, MISREPRESENTATION, PASTURE.

FROST,
  damage brought about by extraordinary, 50.

GAS,
  escape of, 620.

GAS WELL,
  owner may explode, 178 (Ed. n).

GAS WORKS,
  may be a nuisance, 505 (Ed. n)

GERMANIC LAW,
  of torts, 22.
      self-help, 210.

The References are to Pages.

GOD,
    exception of act of, 605.

GOOD FAITH,
    no excuse for unlawful act, 9 (Ed. n.), 10, 484 (Ed. n), 587 (Ed n.). See Deceit, Fraud.

GOOD-WILL,
    protection of privileges analogous to, 891.

GOVERNOR,
    colonial, actions against, 135.

GRADING,
    by municipalities, 70 (Ed n.)

GRANT,
    distinguished from license, 459.
    but may be inseparably connected with license, 460
    distinction of licence from, as regards strangers, 464

GUARANTY,
    misrepresentations amounting to, 380, 381

GUEST,
    gratuitous, is mere licensee in law, 641, 642 (Ed n) See Innkeeper

GUNPOWDER. See Explosives

HARBOR,
    public management of, 71

HIGHWAY,
    defective or obstructed, when not cause of injury, 44 (Ed n), 577
    justification for deviating from, 475.
    nuisances by obstruction of, 488, 489, 490, 491
    cattle straying off, 612.
    traction or steam engine on, 617
    rights of persons using, to safe condition of adjacent property, 633, 636, 637.

HORSE,
    injuries caused by, 49.
    conversion of, 413 (Ed n).
    trespass by, 611, 612

HOST See Guest.

HUMANE SOCIETY,
    authority of, 474.

HUNTING,
    not privileged, 477. See Ed. n.

The References are to Pages.

HUSBAND AND WIFE,
    action by and against, 6d. See Action.
    action of personal tort between, does not lie, 65 (Ed n.), 65
    husband may not now beat wife, 150 a (Ed. n).
    action for taking or enticing away wife, 244, 269, 270, 271 (Ed n.),
        husband, 272 (Ed. n.).
        assault or *crim. con* , 2 ?.
        loss of consortium between, is special damage, 293.
    libel on husband by letter to wife, 309.

"INDENTIFICATION,"
    exploded doctrine of, in cases of negligence, 580, 588

IMMEDIATE CAUSE. See Cause, Proximate Cause.

IMMUNITY. See Church Council, Counsel, Court, Judges, Judicial Acts, Judicial Proceedings, Legislature, Military Officer, Naval Officer, Parliament, Parties, Pleadings, Privilege, Tax-Assessors, Witness.

IMPEACHMENT,
    proper remedy for wrongs by judges, 138 (Ed n.).

IMPLIED MALICE,
    in defamation, 305. See Malice.

IMPRISONMENT,
    does not affect period of limitation, 243 *p.*

IMPRISONMENT, FALSE,
    damages for, 220.
    justified by local act of indemnity, 238.
    definition of, 259–263.
    who is answerable for, 264.
    on mistaken charge, followed by remand, 267
    what is reasonable cause for, 267 See Counsel, False Imprisonment.

INCORPOREAL RIGHTS,
    of property, violation of, 456. See Easement, License.

INDEMNITY,
    claim to, of agent who has acted in good faith, 232
    colonial Act of, 238.

IMPRUDENCE,
    wrongs of, 11.

"INDEPENDENT CONTRACTOR," 87. See Ed n 91 (Ed n.), 93, 94, (Ed n.), 266

INDEX.

The References are to Pages.

INDIA, BRITISH,
dealings of East India Company with native States, 133, 134.
protection of executive and judicial officers in, 113 *l*, 114.

INDIAN NATIONS,
relation of, to United States, 183 (Ed. n).

INFANT,
cannot be made liable on contract by changing form of action, 60
liability of, for torts, 60.
liable for substantive wrong though occasioned by contract, 61
cannot take advantage of his own fraud, 63
whether liability limited to wrongs *contra pacem*, 66
not made liable on contract by suing in form of tort, 658.

INFIRM PERSON,
greater care in dealing with, 564 (Ed n), 565

INFLAMMABLE SUBSTANCES,
may be a nuisance, 503 (Ed. n)

INFORMATION,
duty to give correct, 368.

INJUNCTION,
jurisdiction to grant, 224.
to restrain waste, 225 (Ed. n.), 480 (Ed. n).
continuing trespass, 225 (Ed. n.), 482
interlocutory, 226, 227 *s*, 523 *i*.
to restrain defamation, 317.
to restrain nuisance, 512, 520.
mandatory, 522 *i*.
on what principles granted, 226, 523.
not refused on ground of difficulty of removing nuisance, 526
under C. L P Acts, 209 *b*.
See COPYRIGHTS, LIBEL, LIGHT, PATENT RIGHTS, TRADE-MARKS, TRESPASS, WATER.

INNKEEPER,
selling goods of guest, 444 *k*.
cannot dispute entry of guest, 478.
duty of, 650, 651 (Ed. n.). See GUEST.

INNS OF COURT,
quasi-judicial powers of, 145.

INNUENDO,
when defamatory, 265 (Ed. n.)
meaning and necessity of, 311, 313 (Ed n)

The References are to Pages.

INSTRUMENT, DANGEROUS,
  responsibility of person using, 53, 599, 628. See DANGEROUS THINGS.

INSURANCE,
  duty in nature of, 20, 603.
  construction of policy of, excepting obvious risk, 197
  effect of, on necessity of salvage work, 200 s
  fraud in, 352 (Ed. n.).

INTENTION,
  not material in trespass, 9, 18
  general relation of, to liability, 32, 33, 372
  inference or presumption of, 35
  when fraudulent, 359, 364, 372. See DECEIT, MOTIVE.

INTIMIDATION,
  of servants and tenants, 283
  when "picketing" becomes, 284 q. See FALSE IMPRISONMENT

INTOXICATION. See DRUNKEN MAN.

INVITATION,
  rights of persons coming on another's property by, 625 sqq

"INVITATION TO ALIGHT,"
  cases, 553, 558 (Ed n), 659

IRELAND,
  Lord-Lieutenant exempt from actions in, for official acts, 135

JOINT WRONG-DOERS,
  may be sued jointly or severally, 230, 231

JOURNALIST,
  liability of, 309, 310 (Ed. n). See EDITOR.

JUDGE,
  protection of, in exercise of office, 138
  of inferior court must show jurisdiction, 139.
  not liable for latent want of jurisdiction, 139
  allegation of malice will not support action against, 140
  must grant *habeas corpus* even in vacation, 140
  could not refuse to seal bill of exceptions, 140
  immunity of, 327
  See IMPEACHMENT, JUDICIAL ACTS, JUDICIAL PROCEEDINGS

JUDGMENT,
  against one of several wrong-doers, effect of, 231
  in trover, 435 (Ed n)

JUDICIAL ACTS,
  immunity of, 138, 327.

The References are to Pages.

JUDICIAL ACTS — *Continued*
 of persons not judges, immunity for, 140
 distinguished from ministerial, 148, 263, 264.
 protection of, 327. See ELECTION, QUASI-JUDICIAL ACTS.

JUDICIAL PROCEEDINGS,
 immunity of, 328 (Ed. n.).
 reports of, 328 (Ed. n.), 340, 342 (Ed. n.).

JUDICIAL REMEDIES. See REMEDIES.

JUDICUM RUSTICUM, 588

JURISDICTION,
 acts in excess of, 138 (Ed. n.), 139.
 to grant injunctions, 224
 local limits of, 238

JURORS,
 immunity of, 145 (Ed. n.)

JURY,
 duty of, to determine malice in defamation, 331 (Ed. n.)
 power of, to assess damages, 315
 question of negligence for, when, 551, 552 (Ed. n.)
 duty of, to determine fraudulent intent, 353 (Ed. n.) See COURT
  AND JURY, DAMAGES, VERDICT.

JUS TERTI
 cannot justify trespass or conversion, 150.

JUSTICE OF THE PEACE,
 limitation of actions against, 243
 memorial as to conduct of, 339 *o*

JUSTIFICATION AND EXCUSE,
 general grounds of, 130 *et seq.*
 of arrest and imprisonment, 262.
 of defamatory statement by truth, 323. And see TRUTH
 by license, 457
 by authority of law, 465
 for re-entry on land, 465, 468.
 for retaking goods, 469.
 under legal process, 471.
 for taking distress, 472
 determination of, 480. See PRIVILEGE

LABOR ORGANIZATION. See TRADES UNION

LABOURERS, STATUTE OF,
 action under, 276, 283

The References are to Pages.

LAND,
    acts done in natural user of, not wrongful, 177.
    artificial works on, 129 x.
    assertions as to quality of, 357 (Ed. n).
    acceptance as estoppel, 371 (Ed. n). See LATTERAL SUPPORT, TIMBER, WASTE.

LANDLORD AND TENANT,
    questions of waste between, 431.
    which liable for nuisances, 528. See BUILDINGS, TENANTS.

LANDOWNERS,
    adjacent, duties, 216, 492 (Ed. n.), 634
    entitled to resume possession, 449, 452.
    duty of, as to escape of dangerous or noxious things, 601, 604

LARCENY,
    when trespass becomes, 470.

LATTERAL SUPPORT,
    property owner entitled to, 216, 492 (Ed. n.).

LAW,
    misrepresentation of, 360.

LEAVE AND LICENSE,
    defence of, 185 *et seq*.
    as justification for assault, 252, 253 (Ed. n). And see LICENSE,

LEGISLATORS,
    immunity of, 327 (Ed. n.).

LESSEE,
    for years holding over, no trespasser, 478.

LETTER,
    publication of defamation by, 307 (Ed. n), 308, 309.

LEVY,
    officer liable for mistake in making, 142 (Ed n), 143

LEX AQUILIA,
    rules of liability under, compared with English law, 163 *a*.
    digest on, compared with English law, 224 *l*.
    Roman law of, liability under, 641 *t*, 668 *e*

LEX FORI,
    regard to, in American courts, 81 (Ed. n.), 82 (Ed. n.).
        English courts, 237, 238, 239 (Ed. n.)
    See ACTION, REMEDIES

LIBEL,
    damages for trespass on plaintiff's paper, where no libel for want of publication, 221.

The References are to Pages.

LIBEL — *Continued.*
    Injunction to restrain publication of, 224, 317
    defined, 286
    slander distinguished from, 286, 287 (Ed. n.).
    what is *prima facie* libellous, 290.
    what is publication, 306.
    by letter, 307 (Ed. n.), 308, 309.
    in foreign language, 307 (Ed. n.), 308 (Ed. n.), 312 (Ed. n.).
    assignee of newspaper liable for, 310 (Ed. n.).
    advertisement as, 310 (Ed. n.)
    construction of, 311.
    fair comment is not, 317.
    Law of Libel Amendment Acts, 1888, 343.
    And see DEFAMATION, SLANDER.

LIBERTY OF THE PRESS, 318 (Ed. n.)

LICENSE,
    to apply bodily force, 186, 253 (Ed. n.), 254.
    to do bodily harm, good only with just cause, 186.
    obtained by fraud, void, 190.
    what, 457, 458 (Ed. n.).
    revocable unless coupled with interest, 459.
    may be annexed by law to grant, 459 (Ed. n.), 460.
    revocation of executed, having permanent results, 461
    how given or revoked, 463, 464
    interest by way of equitable estoppel arising from, 463.
    not assignable, 464.
    does not confer rights *in rem*, 464, 465. See CONSENT.

LICENSEE,
    liable for infecting pasture, 370 (Ed. n.).
    rights of, in use of way, 635.
    what risks he must take, 639.

LICENSOR,
    liable for ordinary negligence, 642.

LIEN,
    distinguished from conversion, 444.

LIGHT,
    obstruction of, 508, 509 (Ed. n.).
    nature of the right to, 509.
    what amounts to disturbance of, 510, 511.
    the supposed rule as to angle of 45°, 511
    effect of altering or enlarging windows, 511, 512.

LIGHTS,
    management of, by municipalities, 70 (Ed. n.)

The References are to Pages.

LIMITATION,
    statute of, 58, 242
    effect of foreign law of, 240.
    exception of concealed fraud, 245
    where damage gist of action, 244.

LIVERY STABLES,
    may be a nuisance, 505 (Ed n)

LOCAL ACTION,
    distinguished from transitory, 239

LOCAL LAW,
    acts justified by, 237, 238

LUNATIC,
    liability of, for torts, 59 (Ed n)
    authorized restraint of, 150

MAINTENANCE,
    actions for, 411.

MALA PROHIBITA,
    no longer different in result from *mala in se*, 25

MALICE,
    need not be shown where there is wantonness, 39, 40 (Ed n)
    cases on, in connection with competition in business, 182 a, z
    ambiguity of the word, 182 z.
    effect of, in exercise of common right, 182
    not ingredient of assault with dangerous weapon, 251 (Ed n)
    "implied," meaning of, in defamation, 305
    express, in communication on privileged occasions, 331 (Ed n), 333
    evidence of, 333, 334, 345
    essential in slander of title, 389
    procuring breach of contract actionable only with, 670
    See ASSAULT, FALSE IMPRISONMENT, MALICIOUS PROSECUTION

"MALICE IN FACT," 69, 333, 345

MALICIOUS CIVIL PROCEEDINGS, 397

MALICIOUS HINDRANCE,
    by combination in trade, 405.

MALICIOUS INJURIES,
    by interference with lawful occupation, etc, 406.
        contract, 409.
        franchise, 410.

MALICIOUS PROSECUTION,
    corporation liable for, 68 (Ed n.), 397

The References are to Pages.

MALICIOUS PROSECUTION — *Continued*.
    distinguished from false imprisonment, 265 (Ed. n.), 266.
    action of, 392.
    malice in, 393 (Ed. n.).
    want of probable cause, 393 (Ed. n.)
    termination of former action, 394 (Ed. n.)
    action for, for prosecuting action in name of third person, 401. See PROCESS.

MANDAMUS, 209 *b*.

MARKET,
    franchise of, 157 *r*
    nuisance to, 512.

MARKET OVERT,
    not recognized in America, 411 (Ed. n.).
    title acquired in, 415, 681.

MARKET PLACE,
    duty of person controlling structures in, 630.

MARRIAGE,
    breach of promise of, 71, 222, 682, 685, 686

MARRIED WOMAN,
    damages and costs recovered against, how paid, c, 63, 64
    can now sue and be sued alone, 64
    whether liability at common law limited to wrongs *contra pacem*, 66. See HUSBAND AND WIFE.

MARRIED WOMEN'S PROPERTY ACT,
    effect of, 4.
    right of action under, how limited, 65.

MASTER See MASTER AND SERVANT, SHIP

MASTER AND SERVANT,
    master responsible for servant's negligence, 20
    whether master can have action for loss of service when servant is killed by the injury, 74.
    liability of master for acts and defaults of servants, 84 *et seq*
    command and ratification, 87.
    rule as to liability of master, 88.
        reason of, 89.
    temporary transfer of service, 95
    execution of specific orders, 98
    deviation from master's orders, 100
    liability of master for servant's excessive acts, 103 (Ed. n.), 104
        mistakes, 103, 590 (Ed. n.)

The References are to Pages.

MASTER AND SERVANT — *Continued*
    making arrest, 106.
    acts outside of authority, 107
    wilful wrongs, 109, 110 (Ed. n.).
    disobedient acts, 110 (Ed. n).
    fraud, 112.
    forgery, 112 c.
injuries to servant by fellow-servant, 115, 116 See FELLOW SERVANTS
master must furnish suitable materials, 124.
    choose proper servants, 125.
    provide safe place to work, 125 (Ed n)
defence of servant by master, 201 a
action for enticing away, 270.
    beating servant, 271 (Ed n), 272, 283
services of child, 282
doctrine of constructive service, 283
menacing servants, 283, 284 (Ed. n.)
master giving character, 335, 336 (Ed n)
warning by master to fellow-servants privileged, 337
as passengers by railway, 657
whether master can sue for loss of service by a breach of contract with servant, 663
See APPRENTICE, SEDUCTION, SERVANT, SERVICE

MAXIMS,
    honeste vivere, 12.
    alterum non laedere, 12 (Ed n), 13
    suum cuique tribuere, 12 (Ed n), 13
    damnum sine injuria, 23, 156 (Ed n), 175
    imperitia culpae adnumeratur, 28
    in jure non remota causa sed proxima spectatur, 30
    a man is presumed to intend the natural consequences of his acts, 35.
    actio personalis moritur cum persona, 71
    qui facit per alium facit per se, 89
    respondeat superior, 89
    sic utere tuo ut alienum non laedas, 131, 153, 598 (Ed n).
    nullus videtur dolo facere qui suo jure utitur, 153 c
    animus vicino nocendi, 183
    volenti non fit injuria, 185, 190, 195, 197, 632
    culpa lata dolo aequiparatur, 354.
    vigilantibus non dormientibus jura subveniunt, 376 (Ed n)
    adversus extraneos vitiosa possessio prodess solet, 451.
    res ipsa loquitur, 635, 636 (Ed n)

MEASURE OF DAMAGES See DAMAGES

The References are to Pages.

MEATS,
sale of, 370 (Ed. n.)

MEDICAL EDUCATION,
general council of, powers of, over registered medical practitioner, 146

MEETING,
public, newspaper reports of, 312.

MEMORIALS,
when privileged, 338 (Ed. n.)

MENACE,
when actionable, 258
to servant, 283

MENTAL OR NERVOUS SHOCK,
damages for, whether too remote, 54–57

MERCANTILE AGENCIES,
how far privileged, 335 (Ed. n.)

MILITARY COMPANY,
injury by, to spectator, 167

MILITARY COURT,
privilege of, 331

MILITARY OFFICER,
privilege of, 143, 145 (Ed. n.), 329 (Ed. n.), 331

MINES,
may be opened, when, 431

MINISTER,
of Baptist chapel, removal of, 147 t

MINISTERIAL ACTS,
distinguished from judicial, 148

MISFEASANCE,
common law doctrine of, 647.
defined, 648 (Ed. n.).

MISREPRESENTATION,
in insurance, 352 (Ed. n.).
of fact or law, 360
by omission, 362
knowledge or belief of defendant, 362.
by reckless assertion, 367.
by breach of special duty of disclosure, qu. whether deceit, 368
not deceit, in the absence of fraud or positive duty to disclose, 371.
reliance of plaintiff on defendant, 375

The References are to Pages.

MISREPRESENTATION — *Continued.*
    construction of ambiguous statement, 350.
    amounting to promise or guaranty, 356, 380, 381
    intention to harm by the, not necessary condition of liability, 871
    by or through agent, 383   See DECEIT, FRAUD.

MISTAKE,
    does not excuse interference with property, 9 (Ed. n.), 10
    master liable for servant's, 103.
    of prosecutor, 267
        sheriff, in taking goods, 142 (Ed. n.), 143, 171. See ARREST.

MITIGATION OF DAMAGES,
    rule of, 222, 223 (Ed. n.).
    effect of violent words, 253 (Ed. n.)
        advice of counsel, 263 (Ed. n.)
        negligence, 279
        current reports, 315
        partial justification, 325 (Ed. n.)
        disproof of malice, 334 (Ed. n.)
        apology, 346

MODES OF ANNOYANCE. See BELLS, BLASTING, BOILING ESTABLISHMENTS, CATTLE YARD, CEMETERY, CESSPOOLS, DISEASED BEASTS, EXPLOSIVES, GAS WORKS, INFLAMMABLE SUBSTANCES, FIRE, FILE ARMS, LIVERY STABLES, NOISES, OFFENSIVE ODORS, SLAUGHTER-HOUSES, SMOKE, TANNERIES, TREE, VAPORS

MORTGAGOR,
    may be guilty of conversion, 445
    forcible entry of, upon mortgagee in possession, 465, 466

MORAL BLAME, 4 (Ed. n.), 9 (Ed. n.), 10, 11, 680

MOTIVE,
    malicious, not cause of action, 33
    whether material in exercise of rights, 183
    considered in aggravation or reduction of damages, 222, 223
    when material part of cause of action, 671, 672 See INTENTION.

MUNICIPAL CORPORATION,
    acts of, 69 (Ed. n.) See CORPORATION.

MUSICAL COMPOSITION,
    fair comment upon, 320 (Ed. n.), 322.

NAME,
    no exclusive right to use of, 184.
    of house, no exclusive right to, 391, 392

INDEX. 783

The References are to Pages.

NATURAL JUSTICE,
 must be observed in exercise of quasi-judicial powers, 146.

"NATURAL USER,"
 of property, non-liability for, 602

NAVAL OFFICER,
 privilege of, 113, 115, 829 (Ed n), 831.

NAVIGATION,
 negligence in, 48, 588
 requirements of, as limiting statutory powers, 156.

NECESSITY,
 as excuse for unskilled person, 28
 as justification generally, 199.
 "compulsive," 201, 205
 destruction of property justified by, 200
 trespasses justified by, 175. See TRESPASS
 nuisance not justified by, 199

NEGLIGENCE,
 liability for, 11.
 equivalent to *culpa*, 18.
 liability for, depends on probability of consequence, 12–16
 in conduct of master's business, 98.
 accident is not, 160, 164
 contributory, 170 *t*.
 question of, excluded when a risk is voluntarily taken, 190
 knowledge of risk opposed to duty of warning, 192 *et seq*
 aggravated by recklessness, 221.
 as ground of action against servant for conversion, 142 *n*
 general notion of, 532.
 concurrence of liability *ex contractu* and *ex delicto*, 534 et seq
 defined, 537
 grades of, 538 (Ed n).
 failure in average prudence is, 540
 sex is no excuse for, 540 (Ed n)
 evidence of, 543, 560.
 burden of proof on plaintiff, 545, 548, 568
 how affected by contract, 548
 when presumed, 550, 551.
 duties of judge and jury, 551 (Ed n), 554   And see CONTRIBUTORY NEGLIGENCE
 principles illustrated by railway cases, 553   And see RAILWAY
 due care varies as apparent risk, 563.
 notice of special danger through personal infirmity, 565
 of independent persons may be joint wrong, 582

The References are to Pages.

NEGLIGENCE — *Continued*
    as to action under difficulty caused by another's negligence, 589.
    one is not bound to anticipate another's, 591.
    choice of risks caused by another's, 592
    presumption of, in cases of unexplained accident, 635, 635 (Ed. n.)
    liability of licensor for, 642
    liability for, concurrent with another party's liability on contract, 660.
    general doctrine of, not applicable to statements, 677. See AIR GUN, COLLISION, CROSSINGS, FIRE, INVITATION TO ALIGHT, RAILWAY, RISK, SHIP.

NERVOUS SHOCK. See MENTAL OR NERVOUS SHOCK

NEWSPAPER,
    proprietor of, responsible for every thing published, 309
    vendor of, not liable for libel, 309
    assignee of, liable for libel, 310 (Ed. n.)
    volunteered reports to, 342.
    Law of Libel Amendment Act, 1888, 343
    special procedure in action for libel, 346. See EDITOR, JOURNALIST, LIBERTY OF THE PRESS, REPORTS.

NEW TRIAL,
    for excessive or inadequate damages, 213. And see COURT AND JURY.

NOISES,
    railroad liable for, when, 154 (Ed. n.), 495 (Ed. n.).
    may be a nuisance, 495 (Ed. n.), 504 (Ed. n.), 505. See BELLS

NOTICE,
    licence may be ended without, 463.
    of nuisance, 514, 515 (Ed. n.).
    effect of, on liability for negligence, 539, 540
    judicial, of common facts, 551
    of special risks, 563, 565
    of special circumstances, as affecting measure of damages, 682.

NUISANCE,
    when justified by statutory authority, 157–160.
    public or private, 484, 486 (Ed. n.), 491
    defined, 484 (Ed. n.)
    particular damage from public, 487.
        private, 488.
    private, what, 491.
    affecting ownership, 492. And see TREE
        easements, 494
        comfort and enjoyment, 494.

The References are to Pages.

NUISANCE — *Continued*
    what amount of injury amounts to, 496.
    doctrine of "coming to nuisance" abrogated, 497
    acts in themselves useful and in convenient places may be, 499, 501.
    miscellaneous forms of, 502 *et seq.*
    by use of property for unusual purpose, 507
    by injury common to many persons, 508.
    by independent acts of different persons, 508.
    by obstruction of light, 508, 509 (Ed n). And see LIGHT.
    to market or ferry, 512.
    remedies for, 512
    abatement of, 513, 526, 527 (Ed. n.)
    notice before abatement, when required, 514, 515 (Ed n.)
    duties of person abating, 515.
    old writs, 517, 518 (Ed n)
    damages, 518
    injunction, 520. And see INJUNCTION
    parties entitled to sue for, 527, 528
        liable for, 529.
    liabilities of lessor and lessee for, 530 (Ed n), 531
    when vendor or purchaser liable, 531
    whether a single accident can be, 603 *i.*

OBLIGATION,
    ex delicto in Roman law, 17.
    quasi ex delicto, 18
    and ownership, 668

OCCUPATION,
    malicious interference with, 406

OFFENSIVE ODORS,
    may be a nuisance, 503, 504 (Ed n)

OFFICE,
    judicial or ministerial, 148

OFFICERS,
    public, acts of, 141.
    excess of authority by, 142.
    naval and military, acts of, 143
    subordinate, to what extent protected, 144.
    commanding, liability of, for accident, 167.
    liable for breach of duty to individual, 214 (Ed. n)
    liability of, for malicious misconduct, 411 See ELECTION, MILITARY OFFICER, NAVAL OFFICER, PUBLIC OFFICER

OMISSION,
    of legal duty, liability for, 11, 20, 24

The References are to Pages.

OPINION,
    expression of, not deceit, 357 (Ed n.)

ORDERS,
    execution of specific, 98. See MASTER AND SERVANT.

OUSTER,
    of one co-tenant by another, 417.

OWNERSHIP,
    relation of duty, 624, 648, 668

PAMPHLETS,
    distributing of, publishes their contents, 307 (Ed n.)

PARENT,
    authority of, 149 et seq. See CHILDREN, STEP-FATHER

PARLIAMENT,
    disciplinary orders of House of Commons not examinable, 114, 145.
    may give a governing body absolute powers, 115.
    position of presiding and returning officers at election for, 148
    protection of words spoken in, 327.
        proceedings of Committee, 330
        publication of papers and proceedings, 340
    fair reports of debates in, 341

PARTIES,
    privilege of, in court, 228 (Ed. n), 330.

PARTNER,
    liability of, for co-partner's fraud, 114, 384 (Ed. n)
        to servant of firm, 127
    expulsion of, 147

PASSENGER,
    rights of person accepted as, 104, 657, 661
    may be arrested to prevent mutiny, 152 See CROSSINGS, INVITATION TO ALIGHT, RAILWAY

PASSERS-BY,
    duty towards, 633

PASTURE,
    licensee of, liable for infecting, 370 (Ed n)
    waste of, 430 (Ed. n.).

PATENT RIGHTS,
    injunction restraining infringement of, 225 (Ed n)
    principle of slander of title extended to, 389.
    relation of, to possession, 457 See TRADE MARKS

INDEX.

The References are to Pages.

PERCOLATION,
    underground, no cause of action for, 177, *et seq*

PERSON,
    wrongs to the, 7. See ASSAULT

PERSONALTY. See PROPERTY

PERSONS AFFECTED BY TORTS, 58. See ALIEN ENEMY, CONVICT, DRUNKEN MAN, INFANT, LUNATIC, MARRIED WOMAN

PERSONAL ESTATE,
    damaged by personal injury, no cause of action, 76.

PERSONAL STATUS,
    immaterial, 58

PETITIONS,
    when privileged, 338

PHYSICIANS AND SURGEONS,
    assumption of skill by, 27 (Ed. n.).
    slander of, 301 (Ld. n.), 303

"PICKLING," 284 *g*

PIGS,
    may be cattle by statute, 587 *m*, 615 *v*
    average obstinacy of, 587 *n*

PLAINTIFF,
    a wrong-doer, may still recover, 205.

PLEADINGS,
    privilege of, 328 (Ed. n.).

PLEDGEE,
    abuse of authority by, when conversion, 443

POISON,
    responsibility of persons dealing with, 615 (Ed. n.), 621. See APOTHECARY.

POLICEMAN,
    has power of common law constable, 264

POSSESSION,
    wrongs to, 412 *et seq.*
    more regarded than ownership in the early law, 416
    right to, commonly called property, 418
    distinguished from custody, 418 *h*
    relation of trespass to, 419.
    constructive, 419 *k*
    right to immediate, plaintiff in trover must have, 432

The References are to Pages.

POSSESSION — *Continued*
    without title, protected against strangers, 419.
    why protected by law, 452
    derivative, 453.
    of receiver or taker from trespasser, 454
    restitution of, after forcible entry, 466
    taken by trespass, when complete, 468
    owner not in, how far liable, 648
    obtaining of, by trick, 680   See CONVERSION, REVERSION, TRESPASS.

POST-CARD,
    sending defamatory matter on, 311

POUND,
    feeding animals in, 475, 476

PRECEPTS,
    of Justinian, 12.

PREMATURE DELIVERY,
    resulting from shock, 30 (Ed n), 55 (Ed n)

PRESCRIPTION ACT,
    effect of, on right to light, 509 (Ed n), 510.

PRINCIPAL AND AGENT,
    when principal must indemnify agent, 232.
    liability of principal for fraud of agent, 383.
    where principal is a corporation, 386
    reason of liability, 387.
    liability of agent misrepresenting principal's authority, 659. See AGENT

PRINTING OF LIBEL,
    prima facie a publication, 308 *k*

PRISON,
    what is, 259.

PRIVATE DEFENCE. See SELF-DEFENCE

PRIVILEGE,
    "absolute," in law of defamation, 330
    judicial and parliamentary, in law of defamation, 331
    "qualified," 331, 340.
    conditions of, 332
    privileged occasions and excess, 335, 344
    of communications in interest of society or in self-protection, 335, 337.
    of information for public good, 338

The References are to Pages.

PRIVILEGE — *Continued*
    fair reports, 349. See FAIR COMMENT, IMMUNITY, MERCANTILE, AGENCIES, RELATIVES

PRIZE FIGHT,
    why unlawful, 186 (Ed. n.), 187–189
    presence at, 188

PROBABLE CONSEQUENCE. See CONSEQUENCE.

PROCESS,
    abuse of, 892, 899 (Ed. n.)
    service of, 471

PROMISES,
    effect of, 356.

PROOF,
    of negligence, 543, 545
        contributory negligence, 548, 568.

PROPERTY,
    wrongs to, 7, 10, 13, 16, 25
    right to follow, when converted, 81
    duty to respect, 412
    of goods, commonly means right to possess, 418, 432.
    transferred by satisfied judgment in trover, 437

PROSECUTION,
    whether necessary before offender can be civilly sued, 233 *et seq.* See CONVERSION.

PROSPECTUS,
    binds issuer, when, 83, 359, 371

PROXIMATE CAUSE,
    what, 29–32, 42–57. See CAUSE

PUBLIC OFFICER,
    slander of 301 (Ed. n.). See OFFICERS

PUBLIC WORKS,
    management of, 69 See EXCAVATIONS, GRADING, HARBOR, LIGHTS, SEWERS, SIDEWALKS, STREET GRADES AND GRADING, STREETS AND SIDEWALKS.

PUBLICATION,
    of libel, what, 306.
    vicarious, 309
    by agent, 309 See DEFAMATION, FOREIGN LANGUAGE, LETTERS.

PUNITIVE DAMAGES See EXEMPLARY DAMAGES

The References are to Pages.

PURCHASER,
  innocent, may be liable for conversion, 488, 489

QUASI-JUDICIAL ACTS, 115 et seq., 899 (Ed. n.)

RAILWAY,
  statutes as to fences and appliances, 24 (Ed. n.)
  unguarded crossing, responsibility of company for, 24, 47.
  remoteness of damage suffered on, 41, 49.
  overcrowded carriage in, 50.
  liability of company for mistaken acts of servants, 101
  not liable for acts of servants outside of authority, 107, 108 (Ed. n.)
  liable under statutes for noise, smoke and vibration, 154 (Ed. n.)
  immunity or liability of company for damage in execution of undertaking, 155, 156, 159
  effect of statement in company's time-tables, 378. See TIME TABLES.
  distraint of engine damage feasant, 478 s
  evidence of negligence in accidents on, 553
  level crossing cases, 553
  "Invitation to alight" cases, 426, 553, 558 (Ed. n.), 559
  escape of sparks, 560, 561 (Ed. n.).
  where train fails to stop, 595.
  liability of company for damage by escape of sparks, 560, 561, 609, 617
    breaking down of embankment, 609
  duty of company as to safety of carriages and platforms, 631.
    of structures, as regards passers-by, 634.
  liabilities of company from assumption of duty, independent of contract, 656, 662
  See CROSSINGS, COLLISION, CONTRIBUTORY NEGLIGENCE, NEGLIGENCE.

RATIFICATION,
  by master, makes him responsible, 89, 110 (Ed. n.)

RATS,
  damage by, 607 z

REASONABLE CAUSE,
  for imprisonment, 262

RECAPTION,
  of goods wrongfully taken, 469, 480. See REMEDIES.

RECKLESSNESS See WANTONNESS

RELATIVES,
  communications between, when privileged, 335 (Ed. n.), 337.

The References are to Pages.

REMEDIES,
    at common law in general, 209
    self-help, 210.
    judicial, 211
    damages, 211
    kinds of damages, 212
    measure of damages, 217
    Injunctions, 224
    damages or compensation for deceit, 227.
    for breach of statutory duty, 228
    for fraud, 227 et seq
        acts justified by law, 238, 239 (Ed n.).
    possessory, 416, 420
    distress damage feasant, 480
    for nuisance, 512
    alternative, on one cause of action, 647. See ACTION

REMORSE,
    damages for, not recoverable, 55 (Ed n). See CONSEQUENCES

REMOTENESS,
    of consequence or damage, 35, 49

RENT,
    distress for, 472, 478 n

REPETITION,
    See CONTINUITY, DEFAMATION, REPORTS, WORDS

REPLEVIN,
    417, 420 (Ed n.), 426

REPORTS,
    repetition of, may be libelous, 315
    of naval and military officers, how far privileged, 331.
    confidential, to official superiors, 385.
    fair, of public proceedings, 342
    newspaper, of public meetings, 344.

REPRESENTATION,
    compensation or damages for false, 227
    to a class of persons, 373. See DECEIT, MISREPRESENTATION.

RES JUDICATA, 231.

RETREAT,
    no duty to, when assaulted, 256 (Ed n)

REVENGE,
    unlawful, 257 (Ed. n)

The References are to Pages.

REVENUE OFFICERS,
    protection of, in case of forcible entry, 171

REVERSION,
    injury to, measure of damages, 218, 126, 130 (Ed. n).

REVOCATION,
    of license, 159, 164.

RIGHT,
    when violated, no damage need be shown, 9 (Ed. n.), 10.
    exercise of, not cause of action, 175 *t*, 176
    whether it can be made wrongful by malice in fact, 182.
    assertion of, distinguished from self-defence, 201
    absolute, at least nominal damages recoverable for violation of, 211

RISK,
    voluntary taking of, 170 *t*, 172, 173, 190, 195, 632. See VOLUNTARY
        TAKING OF RISK.
    due care varies with, 563
    notice of special, 565
    choice of, under stress of another's negligence, 592. See CONSENT,
        EMPLOYE, LICENSE, SERVANT.

ROMAN LAW,
    of obligations *ex delicto*, 8, 17
    the Twelve Tables, 20
    as to effect of death of party on rights of action, 71 *et seq*
    on the value of human life, 75 *m*
    noxal actions of, 162
    does not make a man liable for inevitable accidents, 163
    distinguishes right to personal security from that of property, 224.
    animus vicino nocendi, 183
    of possession, 419, 451 *a*, 452 *b*.
    legis actiones in, compared with common law forms of action, 645
    theory of *culpa* in, 648 *f*
    concurrent breach of contract with delict in, 667

RUNNING-DOWN CASES, 171, 172, 223.

RYLANDS *v* FLETCHER,
    the rule in, 599 *et seq*

SAFETY,
    duties of insuring, 598 *et seq*
    persons entitled to, 627

SALES See DECEIT, FRAUD

SCANDALUM MAGNATUM, 285 *b*

INDEX.

The References are to Pages.

SCHOOL COMMISSIONERS,
    exception of liability of, 115 (Ed. n.)

SCHOOL TEACHER,
    may reasonably punish pupil, 119 (Ed. n)

SCIENTER,
    doctrine of, as to damage by animals, 614

SCOTLAND (law of),
    as to trespass by parachute, 40 n.
    gives compensation for damage by death, 77 n, 80
    theory of "common employment" forced upon, 118.
    as to *aemulatio vicini*, 183
    as to protection against dangerous animals, 615 t

SECRET SOCIETY   See CHURCH COUNCIL, TRADE UNION.

SEDUCTION,
    action for, 276
    defined, 276 (Ed. n)
    what is service for this purpose, 276–280.
    who may sue for, 277 (Ed. n), 280
    consent to, may bar action, 279 (Ed. n)
    damages, 280, 281 (Ed. n.).

SELF-DEFENCE,
    right of, 201
    assertion of disputed right distinguished from, 203
    injuries to third person resulting from, 25, 210.
    against wrongful assault, 255.
    in defamation, 337   See ASSAULT, BATTERY, DEFENCE

SELF-HELP, 210   And see ABATEMENT, DISTRESS, RECAPTION.

SELF-PROTECTION,
    communication in, privileged, 337

SEPARATE PROPERTY,
    costs and damages payable out of, 63, 64
    trespasser on, 65
    whether husband can be indemnified from, 65.

SERVANT,
    liability of master for acts of, 84.
    who is, 90
    may change master *pro tempore*, 95.
    what is course of service, 97
    negligence of, in conduct of master's business, 98.
    execution of specific orders, 98
    departure from master's business, 100.

The References are to Pages.

SERVANT — *Continued.*
    mistake or excess of authority by, 103.
    interference with passengers by, 104
    arrest of supposed offender by, 106.
    acts of, outside his authority, 107.
    wilful wrongs of, for master's purposes, 109.
    fraud of, 11″
    injuries to, by fellow-servant, 115 *et seq*
    injury to, where master interferes in person, 127
    enticing away of, 270.
    master may sue for injury to, 271 (Ed. n.), 275.
    detention or haboring of, 276 (Ed. n).
    intimidation of, 283, 284 (Ed n.).
    custody of possession of, 418, h.
    conversion by, in master's interest, not excusable, 436
    but qu as to acts done under master's possession and apparent ownership, 439
    conversion by, 441. See MASTER AND SERVANT.

SERVICE,
    temporary transfer of, 95.
    loss of, ground of action, 271 (Ed n).
    proved or presumed in action for seduction, 276 *et seq*
    of young child, 282.
    constructive, 283 See CHILDREN, SEDUCTION

SEWERS,
    management of, by municipalities, 70 (Ed n)

SEX,
    no excuse for negligence, 540 (Ed. n).

SHERIFF,
    immunity or liability of, 143
    power and duty of, to break doors, etc , in execution of process, 471
    remaining unduly long in possession, 479.

SHIP,
    owner of, liable for officers' torts, 96.
    master's authority to use force, 151.
    right of shipowner to refuse services of particular tug, 180, 181
    owner's liability, how affected by neglect of statutory regulations, 229, 230
    master may complain of nuisance near by, 486
    contributory negligence of, 571, 588
    rule of Admiralty as to division of damage, 588.
    duty of owner as to safety of cargo, 629
    liability of owner as carrier, 655 t.

The References are to Pages.

SHIPPER,
   must mark dangerous goods, 164

SHOOTING,
   liability for accident in, 168 et seq. See MILITARY COMPANY.

SKILL,
   requirement of, in particular undertakings, 26, 27, 542, 550. See ASSUMPTION OF SKILL

SLANDER,
   injunction to restrain, 224.
   defined, 286
   libel distinguished, 286, 287 (Ed. n.).
   when actionable, 289
   special damage, 290
   temporal loss necessary to special damage, 292
   repetition of, 292
   imputation of crime, 294
      by allusion, 295 (Ed. n.)
      interrogation, 295 (Ed. n.)
      innuendo, 295 (Ed. n.)
   imputation of impossible crime, 296 (Ed. n.),
      fornication, 298 (Ed. n.).
      contagious disease, 299
   disparagement in office or business, 300.
   of title of invention, design, trade name, etc. See SLANDER OF TITLE
   indirect damage in business, 303
   of property used in business, 304 (Ed. n.)
   Slander of Women Act, 1891, 298.
   See ATTORNEY, CLERK, CLERGYMAN, PHYSICIAN AND SURGEON, PUBLIC OFFICER, TRADER

SLANDER OF TITLE, 177, 338
   relation of, to ordinary defamation, 388.

SLAUGHTER-HOUSES,
   may be a nuisance, 506 (Ed. n.).

SMOKE,
   railroad liable for, when, 154 (Ed. n.).
   may be a nuisance, 506 (Ed. n.)

SOCIETY,
   liable for violence in expulsion, 147 (Ed. n.).
   for prevention of cruelty, 474.

SOVEREIGN,
   foreign, cannot be sued in England for political acts, 186.

The References are to Pages.

SOVEREIGNTY,
    acts of, how far examinable, 136.

SPECIAL DAMAGE,
    involves definite temporal loss, 292. See DAMAGE.

SPORT,
    hurt received in lawful, 187, 188 o, 190, 255.

SPRING-GUNS,
    authorities on injuries by, 192 z, 206.
    threat of, useless, 481.

SQUIB CASE. See *Scott* v *Shepherd*, TABLE OF CASES

STAIRCASE,
    when not dangerous, 551, 563.

STAND,
    safety of, guaranteed by contractor, 630.

STATE,
    acts of, 132. See ACTS OF STATE.
    cannot be sued in court of another State, 136 (Ed. n.).

STATUTE,
    duties created by, breach of, 21, 25, 228
    authorizing suit for death, 77, 80, 81 (Ed. n.)
    acts authorized by, 157.
    caution required in exercise of powers conferred by, 157.
    remedies under, 228

STEP-FATHER,
    may correct child, 149 (Ed. n.).
        sue for seduction of step-daughter, 278 (Ed. n.)

STOCK,
    damage by, 473 See CATTLE

STOCKS,
    misrepresentation concerning, 359, 360 (Ed. n.), 378 (Ed. n.), 386.
      See CORPORATION, PROSPECTUS

STOWAGE,
    ship liable for improper, 629 (Ed. n.).

STRANGER,
    right of de facto possessor against, 449
    cannot acquire right of licensee, 164.
    exception of act of, 607
    has no cause of action on breach of contract, 673.

STREAM See WATER

INDEX.

The References are to Pages.

STREET,
 care in crossing, 197 (Ed n), 198

STREET GRADES AND GRADING,
 by municipalities, 70 (Ed. n)

STREETS AND SIDEWALKS,
 defective, 69 (Ed n)

SUICIDE,
 when not immediate consequence of personal injury, 30 (Ed. n.)

SUNDAY,
 statutes for observance of, in United States, 208.

SURGEON,
 action against, for misfeasance, 617 d See PHYSICIANS AND SURGEONS.

TANNERIES,
 may be a nuisance, 506 (Ed. n)

TAX-ASSESSORS,
 exception of liability, 145 (Ed. n.)

TELEGRAPH,
 delinquent delivery of message, 55 (Ed n.), 674
 sending defamatory matter by, 344.
 conflict between English and American authorities as to rights of receiver of message, 674, 675

TENANTS,
 intimidation of, 283, 284 h.
 in common trespass between, 447 See WASTE.

TENTERDEN'S ACT (LORD), 382
 qu how far now operative, 383

THIRD PERSON,
 intervention of, no excuse for negligence, 53 ?
 injuries resulting to, from self-defense, 34, 203, 204

THIEF,
 can convey no title to stolen goods, 439 (Ed n), 441

THREATS,
 justify use of force by officer, 263 (Ed. n.)
 by notice boards to trespassers, 481

TIMBER,
 cutting of, when trespass, 412 (Ed. n).
 waste by cutting, 429 (Ed n.), 430
 when licence to cut, is implied, 460

The References are to Pages.

TIME-TABLE,
    passenger entitled to rely upon, 371, 656 (Ed n.).

TITLE. See SLANDER OF TITLE.

TORT,
    what is, 1, 4, 19, 20.
    action of (as opposed to contract), 2
    wrongs which are not, 3, 4
    former criminal character of action for, an exclusively common law term, 3, 4.
    principles of, 5
    generic division of, 6-8
    wilful, negligent, or involuntary, 8.
    from ethical stand point, 12
    general characters of, 19, 20.
    law of, in three main heads, 23.
    persons affected by, 58 *et seq*
    exceptions to liability for, 130   See EXCEPTIONS
    dependent on contract, 414
    relations of, to contract, 641.
    case of, whether contract or no contract between same parties, 656.
    waiver of, for purpose of suing in contract, 658
    cause of action in, co-existing with contract, 660   See WRONGS

TRADE MARKS,
    protection of, 184 (Ed. n.), 391
        by injunction, 225 (Ed. n.)   See COPYRIGHT, NAME, PATENT RIGHTS

TRADE UNION,
    when unlawful, 409 (Ed. n).

TRADER,
    defamation of, 302 (Ed n.)   See COMPETITION.

TRAMWAY,
    nuisance by, 488.

TRANSFER OF SERVICE, 95.

TRANSITORY ACTION,
    distinguished from local, 239

TRAP,
    dangers in nature of, 635, 640, 641.
    set by railway company, 662.

TRAVELLER,
    may pass around obstructions, 475 (Ed. n)
    duty towards, 633, 634, 642 (Ed. n).   See CROSSINGS

INDEX.

The References are to Pages.

TREE,
    projecting over neighbor's land, 492 (Ed. n), 513, 604

TRESPASS,
    the least invasion of property is, 10
    anomaly of, 14.
    writ of, 14.
    law of, general, 16.
    liability for consequences of, 40, 41
    action of, dies with wrong-doer, 72
    inevitable accident as excuse for, 162 s, 163 et seq
    strict archaic theory of, 168.
    special justification, when proper, 171.
    immunity of public officer, 141 (Ed n)
    injuries to, when actionable or not, 191, 205, 206
    necessity as excuse for, 199, 175, (Ed n.).
    damages in action of, 212 et seq.
    actual damage not material in, 213
    wanton, 219
    aggravated, 220, 221
    injunction restraining, 225 (Ed n)
    "merged in felony," 233, 236
    to foreign land not actionable, 239.
    by taking away wife, etc , 270, 271 (Ed n)
    by taking away husband, 272 (Ed. n).
    or case, whether action for seduction in, 274 d, 275 f
    relation of, to larceny, 425, 432.
    to land or goods, what, 421, 422 (Ed n), 424
    relation of, to conversion, 419, 426
        detinue, 420 (Ed. n)
    to land, by what acts committed, 421, 476
    above or under ground, 423
    by cattle, 424, 476
    to goods, how committed, 424
    relation of, to trover, 432.
    between tenants in common, 447.
    owner entitled to immediate possession may sue for, 452
    justification or excuse for, 465 et seq
    continuing, 469, 470.
    by necessity, 475
    in fox-hunting, 477.
    ab initio, 477, 478 (Ed n.).
    ab initio cannot arise from nonfeasance, 478, 479
    costs in actions for, 480.
    continuing, restrainable by injunction, 482
    distinguished from nuisance, 484 et seq
    by cattle, 610 See CATTLE, CONVERSION, TIMBER

The References are to Pages.

TRESPASSER,
    not disqualified to sue, 205, 206 (Ed. n.)
    effect of delivery by, 451.
    notice-board warning to, 481.

TROVER,
    action of, 244, 427, 432, 434.
    relation of, to trespass, 432.
    effect of judgement, 435 (Ed n.).
    special action in some cases where trover does not lie, 411
    See CONVERSION.

TRUSTEE IN BANKRUPTCY,
    not bound to prosecute for felony before bringing civil action, 230

TRUTH,
    as justification, 318 (Ed. n.), 323
    maliciously pleaded, 324 (Ed. n.)
    must be substantially complete, 325.
    defendant's belief in, immaterial, 327.

TURN TABLES,
    liability of proprietors of, 585 (Ed n.).

UNAVOIDABLE DAMAGE,
    no action for, 50, 155, 156.

UNDERSELLING,
    no action maintainable for, 176

UNIVERSITY,
    quasi judicial powers of, 145

UNSEAWORTHINESS,
    ship liable for, 630 (Ed n.).

USER,
    reasonable presumption of, 429, 430

VAPORS,
    may be a nuisance, 506 (Ed n.)

VENDEE. See DECEIT

VEHICLE,
    safety of, how far guaranteed by builder, 632

VENEREAL DISEASE,
    false charge of, actionable, 299

VERDICT,
    excessive, will be set aside, 211 (Ed n.), 212
    in cases of reduction, 281 (Ed. n.)

VICARIOUS PUBLICATION See PUBLICATION.

The References are to Pages.

VICEROY,
local actions against, 185.

VI ET ARMIS,
what trespass is, 187.

VINDICTIVE DAMAGES. See EXEMPLARY DAMAGES.

VIS MAJOR. See ACT OF GOD

VISITOR,
defined, 642 (Ed. n.).

VOLUNTARY TAKING OF RISK,
continuing to do work under risk which is incident to the work itself is, 192.
whether plaintiff *nolens* or *volens* question of fact, 195
except where risk obvious, 196
relation of negligence of employer to, 196
consent to particular hazard necessary to constitute, 196
distinction where no negligence, 197. See CONSENT

VOLUNTEER,
skill not demanded of, 27 (Ed. n.).
in no better plight than servant, 126

WANTONNESS,
actual malice need not be shown, 39, 40, 100 (Ed. n), 105 (Ed. n).
See MALICE, WILFUL ACT

WARRANTY,
duties in nature of, 86.
expression of opinion is not, 357 (Ed. n)
obligation of, on sale for specific purpose, 632 p
implied, of agent's authority, 74 k, 660

WASTE,
injunction restraining, 225 (Ed n), 430 (Ed n).
remedies for, 426.
what is, 427, 429 (Ed n.).
reasonable user of tenement is not, 428.
by cutting timber, etc , 428, 429 (Ed n)
equitable, 431 u.
as between landlord and tenant, 431.

WATER,
under land, rights of using, 177, 178 (Ed. n).
rights to, protected by injunction, 225 (Ed n.)
responsibility of persons artificially collecting, 599, 600.
except where storage is a duty, 608

The References are to Pages.

WAY,
> limited right of, 475 f.

WELLS,
> digging into underground stream, 177, 178 (Ed n).

WHARFINGER,
> duties of, as regards river bed in his possession, 680.

WILFUL ACTS,
> liability for, 8, 33, 52, 109, 219 (Ed n). See WANTONNESS.

WIND,
> injury by, 29 (Ed n.), 50 (Ed. n.), 71 See ACT OF GOD.

WINDOWS,
> prospective, 179, 180
> alteration in, does not destroy claim to light, 511

WITNESS,
> immunity of words spoken by, 328 (Ed n), 329 (Ed n.), 330.

WORDS,
> cannot be assault, 252 (Ed n), 254.
> imprisonment by, 259 (Ed n)
> repetition of, 292, 308, 315
> cannot be trespass, 422 (Ed n) See DEFAMATION

WORKS OF NECESSITY, 199. See AUTHORIZED WORKS, NECESSITY

WRIT,
> of right, 14 l.
> of debt, 14.
> of detinue, 14–16.
> of deceit, 14 m
> of trespass, 14 m.
> of trespass on the case, 14, 24.
> quod permittat, 517

WRITER,
> fair comment on works of, privileged, 321 (Ed n), 322

WRONG-DOER,
> not necessarily disentitled to sue for wrong to himself, 205, 206.

WRONG-DOERS,
> do not forfeit rights of action, 205–208.
> joint liability of, 230
> contribution between, 231

The References are to Pages.

WRONGS,
    without moral blame, 4 (Ed n.), 9 (Ed n.), 10, 11.
    to the person, 7.
    to property, 7.
    to person and property, 7. See TORT.
    of imprudence and omission, 11, 20
    intended or not, 20
    compensation for. See DAMAGES.
    And see INTENTION, REMEDIES, WILFUL ACT.

CPSIA information can be obtained
at www.ICGtesting.com
Printed in the USA
BVHW012255030922
646237BV00011B/402